INSIGHTS to PRAYER
עיון תפלה

❦

AN EXPLANATION OF THE WEEKDAY PRAYERS
AND SELECTIONS ON THE PESACH HAGGADAH

❦

Rabbi Shimon Schwab
זצלל"ה

Rav Schwab

Published by
Mesorah Publications, ltd

on PRAYER

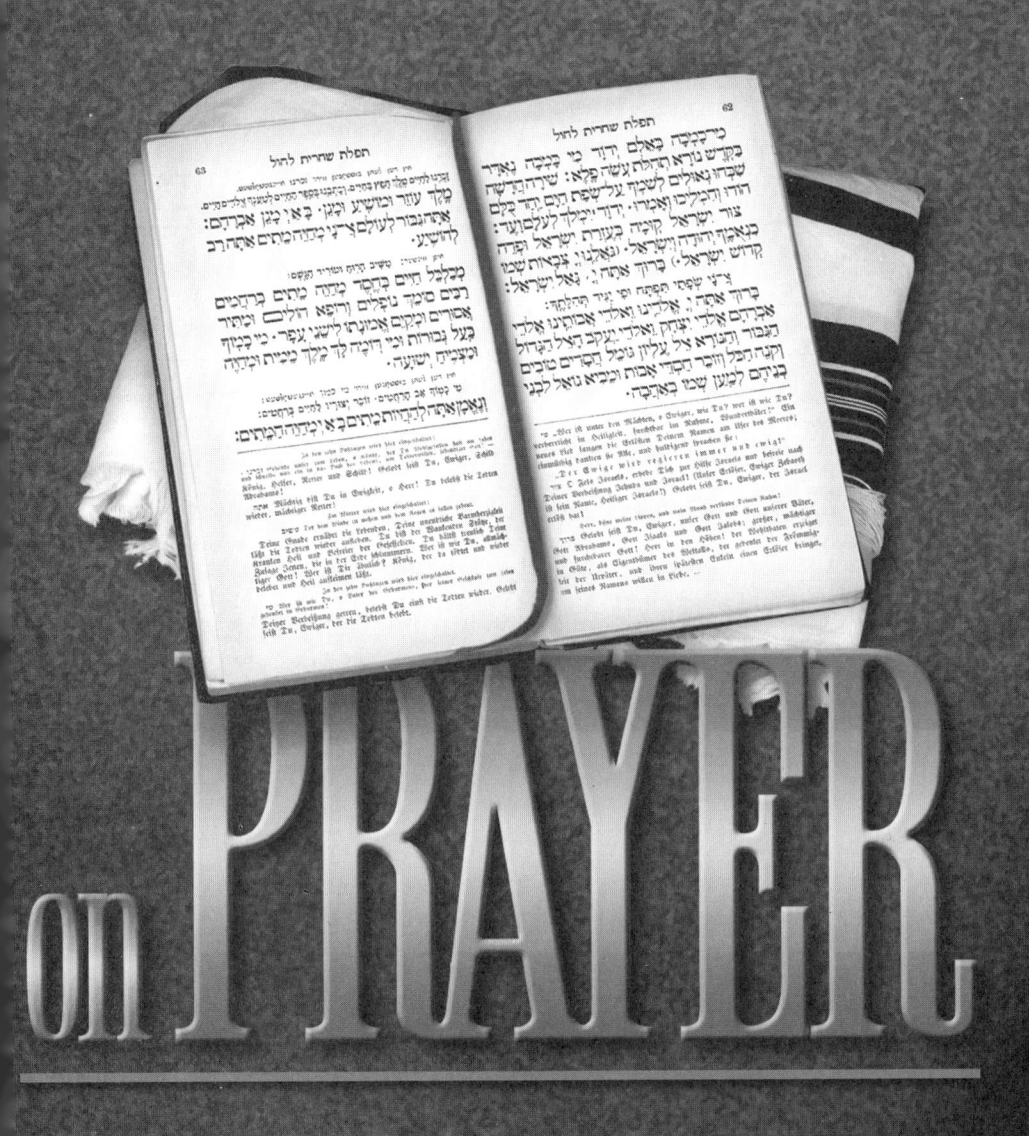

The teachings of
RABBI SHIMON SCHWAB זצ״ל
on the Siddur

FIRST EDITION
First Impression . . . February 2001
Second Impression . . . March 2001
Third Impression . . . June 2001

SECOND EDITION — REVISED AND EXPANDED
First Impression . . . January 2002
Second Impression . . . May 2003

Published and Distributed by
MESORAH PUBLICATIONS, Ltd.
4401 Second Avenue
Brooklyn, New York 11232

Distributed in Europe by
LEHMANNS
Unit E, Viking Industrial Park
Rolling Mill Road
Jarrow, Tyne & Wear NE32 3DP
England

Distributed in Australia & New Zealand by
GOLDS WORLD OF JUDAICA
3-13 William Street
Balaclava, Melbourne 3183
Victoria Australia

Distributed in Israel by
SIFRIATI / A. GITLER — BOOKS
6 Hayarkon Street
Bnei Brak 51127

Distributed in South Africa by
KOLLEL BOOKSHOP
Shop 8A Norwood Hypermarket
Norwood 2196, Johannesburg, South Africa

THE ARTSCROLL SERIES®
RAV SCHWAB ON PRAYER
© Copyright 2001, by MESORAH PUBLICATIONS, Ltd.
4401 Second Avenue / Brooklyn, N.Y. 11232 / (718) 921-9000 / www.artscroll.com

---

ALL RIGHTS RESERVED.

No part of this book may be reproduced
in any form — including photocopying and retrieval systems —
without **written** *permission from the copyright holder,*
except by a reviewer who wishes to quote brief passages in connection with a review
written for inclusion in magazines or newspapers.

THE RIGHTS OF THE COPYRIGHT HOLDER WILL BE STRICTLY ENFORCED.

ISBN
1-57819-512-8 (hard cover)
1-57819-513-6 (paperback)

Typography by Compuscribe at ArtScroll Studios, Ltd.

Printed in the United States of America by Noble Book Press
Bound by Sefercraft, Quality Bookbinders, Ltd. Brooklyn, N.Y.

IN MEMORIAM

This publication has been made possible
by the generosity of
Yitzchok and Barbara Lehman Siegel and Family
of Silver Spring, Maryland

In memory of dear parents

ר' יעקב בן צבי הלוי

וזוגתו שרה ראסא בת רפא־ל זלל״ה

Jacob and Rose Siegel

Members of Congregation Shearith Israel of Baltimore.
Their home was always open to the needy and the poor.
May the efforts of their children and grandchildren
on behalf of the dissemination of the thoughts
and teachings of Rav Shimon Schwab זצ״ל
remain an everlasting zechus for their *neshamos*.

תהא נפשותם צרורות בצרור החיים

ב"ה

Rav Zachariah Gelley
152 Bennett Avenue
New York, N.Y. 10040
Study (212) 927-4497
Home (212) 740-6706

זכרי׳ געללעי
רב ואב״ד ק״ק
קהל עדת ישרון
נוא יארק, נ.י.

    Our Chachomim tell us that *tefilla* — notwithstanding its elevated nature — is among the things which most people tend to treat lightly: "דברים העומדים ברומו של עולם ובני אדם מזלזלין בהן" (ברכות ו:). The *tefillos* are not apppreciated enough because most people do not understand their underlying meaning.

    Rav Schwab, זצ״ל, did a great service to our *Kehilla* and to *Klal Yisroel* by means of his regular Sunday morning lectures which he called "*Iyun Tefilla*", in which he systematically explained the deeper meaning of our daily *tefillos*. He had a special gift for explaining the most profound subjects in a manner by which they could be readily understood by the general public.

    We now owe a special debt of gratitude to his son, Mr. Moshe Schwab, and to those who helped him, for making the treasure of these *shiurim* available to the Torah world at large.

    It is especially gratifying that Yeshiva Rabbi Samson Raphael Hirsch will be the beneficiary of the profits produced by the sponsorship and sales of this *Sefer*. The Yeshiva was very dear to Rav Schwab's heart, and its support as a result of his *divrei torah* will be a great *zechus* for his *neshomo*.

    May the *zechus* of this great *tzadik* bring *brocho* to all those who share in this monumental work.

                                                           Rav Zachariah Gelley

Tamuz 5760

~§ Table of Contents

Biography of Rav S. Schwab ix
Editor's Foreword xxi
Introduction by the Author זצ״ל xxv

אדון עולם / Adon Olam 3
ברכת על נטילת ידים / Bircas Al Netilas Yadayim 12
ברכת אשר יצר / Bircas Asher Yatzar 18
ברכת אלהי נשמה / Bircas Elohai Neshamah 25
ברכת השחר / Birchos HaShachar 28
יהי רצון שתצילני / Yehi Ratzon She'tatzileini 46
רבון כל העולמים / Ribbon Kol HaOlamim 49
אתה הוא ה׳ אלהינו בשמים ובארץ /
 Atah Hu Hashem Eloheinu BaShamayim Uva'Aretz 67
ברכות התורה / Birchos HaTorah 74
ברכות כהנים / Bircas Kohanim 80
אלו דברים שאין להם שעור / Eilu Devarim She'ein Lahem Shiur 83
אלו דברים שאדם אוכל פרותיהם / Eilu Devarim She'adam O'cheil Peiroseihem 85
פרשת התמיד / Parashas HaTamid 91
איזהו מקומן / Eizehu Mekoman 104
ברייתא דרבי ישמעאל / Baraisa D'Rabbi Yishmael 106
עטיפת הטלית והנחת תפילין / Atifas HaTallis Vahanachas Tefillin 107
הקדמה לפסוקי דזמרה / Hakdamah L'Pesukei d'Zimrah 113
ברוך שאמר / Baruch She'amar 121
הודו / Hodu 131
מזמור לתודה / Mizmor L'Sodah 158
יהי כבוד / Yehi Chevod 163
אשרי / Ashrei 167
הללוי׳ הללי נפשי / Halleluyah Halleli Nafshi 183
הללוי׳ כי טוב זמרה אלהינו / Halleluyah Ki Tov Zamrah Eloheinu 191
הללוי׳ הללו את ה׳ מן השמים / Halleluyah Hallelu Es Hashem Min HaShamayim ... 198
הללוי׳ שירו לה׳ שיר חדש / Halleluyah Shiru Lashem Shir Chadash ... 201
הללוי׳ הללו אל בקדשו / Halleluyah Hallelu Eil B'Kadsho 209
ברוך ה׳ לעולם אמן ואמן / Baruch Hashem L'Olam Amen V'Amen 214
ויברך דוד / Vayevarech Dovid 216
אז ישיר / Az Yashir 233
ישתבח / Yishtabach 247

קדיש וברכו / Kaddish U'Barchu	251
ברכת יוצר אור / Bircas Yotzer Ohr	259
קדושה דישיבה / Kedushah D'Yeshivah	273
לאל ברוך נעימות יתנו / L'Eil Baruch Ne'imos Yiteinu	281
ברכת אהבה רבה / Bircas Ahavah Rabbah	289
קריאת שמע / Krias Shema	308
אמת ויציב / Emes V'Yatziv	378
עזרת אבותינו / Ezras Avoseinu	385
הקדמה לשמונה עשרה / Hakdamah L'Shemoneh Esrei	401
המקורות לשמונה עשרה / The Origin of Shemoneh Esrei	405
הסמליות של המספר שמונה עשרה בתפלה / The Symbolism of "Eighteen" in Tefillah	409
תפלת העמידה – שמונה עשרה / Tefillas HaAmidah — Shemoneh Esrei	412
אבות / Avos	413
גבורות / Gevuros	422
קדושת השם / Kedushas Hashem	431
קדושה דעמידה / Kedushah D'Amidah	434
בינה / Binah	440
תשובה / Teshuvah	445
סליחה / Selichah	450
גאולה / Geulah	451
רפואה / Refuah	454
ברכת השנים / Bircas HaShanim	461
קיבוץ גלויות / Kibbutz Galuyos	467
דין / Din	472
ברכת המינים / Bircas HaMinim	475
צדיקים / Tzaddikim	480
בנין ירושלים / Binyan Yerushalayim	485
מלכות בית דוד / Malchus Beis Dovid	493
שומע תפלה / Shome'a Tefillah	497
עבודה / Avodah	502
יעלה ויבא / Yaaleh VeYavo	507
הודאה / Hodaah	513
מודים דרבנן / Modim D'Rabbanan	521
ד"ת על פורים / A Torah Thought on Purim	526
ברכת כהנים – שלום / Bircas Kohanim — Shalom	528
אלהי נצור וגו׳ / Elohai Netzor	535
ביאורים על הגדה של פסח / Selections on the Pesach Haggadah	541

~§ Biography of Rav Shimon Schwab זצללה"ה

Rav Shimon Schwab was born in Frankfurt am Main, Germany, on the 7th of Teves, 5669, December 30, 1908, the eldest of the five sons of Leopold and Hanna Schwab (nee Erlanger). There were no daughters. The Schwab family had lived in Frankfurt since the early part of the 19th century, when Rav Schwab's great-grandfather, Loeb Schwab, moved to Frankfurt from Uhlfeld, Bavaria. Leopold Schwab was a highly respected member of the Frankfurt community, active in all aspects of *kehillah* life. Of the five sons, three became *rabbanim* and *roshei yeshivah,* and two became model *baalei battim* and lay leaders.

Rav Schwab received his early education at the famed "Hirsch-realschule" in Frankfurt — as had his father and grandfather before him — which was founded by Rav Samson Raphael Hirsch. Among his teachers was Rav Joseph Breuer, with whom he would later share the Rabbinate of K'hal Adath Jeshurun in New York. Rav Schwab's grandfather, Moses Loeb Schwab, was one of the early students of Rav Samson Raphael Hirsch in Frankfurt, and he would record his lectures in the then newly developed method called shorthand. Many of these notes were later used by Rav Hirsch in his compilation of his monumental work on *Chumash.*

At age 15, Shimon Schwab entered the Yeshivah of Frankfurt, headed by Rabbi Salamon Breuer, Rav of of K'hal Adath Jeshurun of Frankfurt, where he studied for two years.

In 1926, the young Shimon Schwab entered the Telshe Yeshivah, one of the first German *bachurim* to study in Lithuanian yeshivos. There he remained, absorbed in his learning under such great masters as Rav Joseph Leib Bloch and Rav Chaim Rabinowitz (Telzer) for approximately three years. Rav Schwab would refer to these years as the happiest of his youth.

During the summer months of 1929, Rav Schwab accepted his first educational position as an instructor at the Yeshivah "Eitz Chaim" in Montreux, Switzerland. It was during this period that he came into close daily contact with the great *Gaon* and *poseik hador,* HaRav Chaim Ozer Grodzenski זצ"ל, of Vilna, who was spending some time in Montreux. In his association with the great *poseik hador,* albeit for a short while, Shimon Schwab gained a great deal of practical wisdom in the application of Torah *and mitzvos* in keeping with the Talmudic dictum: גְּדוֹלָה שִׁמּוּשָׁהּ שֶׁל תּוֹרָה יוֹתֵר מִלִּמּוּדָהּ (*Berachos* 7b).

BIOGRAPHY ~ ix

The Rav entered the Mirrer Yeshivah in the fall of 1929 and studied under such great Torah luminaries as Rav Eliezer Yehudah Finkel, the *Rosh Yeshivah* and Rav Yerucham Levovitz, the famed Mirrer *Mashgiach,* whose *mussar* and wisdom he would often quote in his *shiurim* and lectures. While still a *bachur* in the Mirrer Yeshivah, the Rav would give *shiurim* for *baalei battim* in a local *beis hamidrash.* His personal papers show the text of a *derashah* which he delivered in the main *shul* of Mir on the occasion of the 42nd *yahrtzeit* of Rav Samson Raphael Hirsch, 27th of Teves, 1930.

The Rav remained in the Mirrer Yeshivah until 1931. During this period, he came into contact with many of the greatest *gedolim* of the day, including the *Chafetz Chaim,* of whom he would speak and lecture throughout his rabbinical career. In a postcard to his parents, bearing the postmark of Radin, dated 3/30/30, which he sent immediately after meeting this world-famous *gaon* and *tzaddik,* Rav Schwab described him as having the "radiance of the *Shechinah* on his face."

These *gedolim* were highly influential in the Rav's development, in which he synthesized the best of Eastern European Jewish Torah learning with the teachings of Rav Samson Raphael Hirsch and Rav Salamon Breuer.

Before leaving the Mirrer Yeshivah, the Rav received *semichah,* his rabbinical ordination, from the Mirrer *Rosh Yeshivah,* Rav Eliezer Yehudah Finkel, and from Rav Zvi Hirsch Kamai, the Rav of Mir, and an approbation from Rav Chaim Ozer Grodzenski. In May 1931, the young, newly ordained Rav took his first rabbinical position, that of *"Rabbinatsassessor"* (Rabbinical Assistant) to Rav Yonah Mertzbach, in Darmstadt, Germany. It would be some fifty years later that Rav Schwab would deliver a *hesped* for Rav Mertzbach — in Hebrew — when Rav Schwab chanced to be on a trip to Eretz Yisrael at the time of Rav Mertzbach's passing.

On the 11th of Cheshvan 5691, October 22, 1931, the Rav married Recha Froehlich of Gelsenkirchen, Germany, the daughter of Abraham and Gutel Froehlich (nee Seewald of Babenhausen).

The Rebbetzin was born on December 21, 1908, in Michelstadt, in Odenwald, Hessen, Germany, where her father was the "Jewish School" teacher, which position included the task of being the local *shochet* and *chazzan.* In 1914, the Froehlich family moved from Michelstadt to Gelsenkirchen, where Abraham Froehlich was an upstanding member of the Jewish community. He was regularly *kovei'a ittim l'Torah* by learning a daily private *shiur* with Rabbi Gans, a *talmid chacham* for whom he provided a livelihood and a beautiful apartment. The local *chassidishe shtiebel* also benefited from Mr. Froehlich's generosity. He provided the *shtiebel* with the use of a house at the rear of his property for a *minyan* and *mikveh* for men. Abraham Froehlich went out of his way to be friendly and helpful to the newcomers to the Jewish community in Gelsenkirchen.

Rebbetzin Schwab received her secular education at the Lyceum and Hohere Tochterschule in Gelsenkirchen. Her Jewish education was received from Rabbi Herman Klein of Gelsenkirchen, who later became a Rav in Berlin and Buenos Aires. The Rebbetzin also attended Pensionat Markus in Montreaux, Switzerland.

The young couple, Rav and Rebbetzin Schwab, lived in Darmstadt for two years, where the Rav received his early experience in the field of *kashrus* supervision, as part of his duties as Rabbinical Assistant. It was there that two of their five children were born: Moses L. in 1932, and Judith in 1933.

In September 1933, the Rav accepted his first full rabbinical position, that of *"Bezirksrabbiner,"* or District Rabbi, of Ichenhausen, Bavaria, which was an ancient *kehillah* in Southern Germany. This position included responsibility for the religious and educational needs not only of Ichenhausen, an old market town with a Jewish population of about 350, but also of several old, small *kehillos* in the hamlets and villages which dotted the countryside surrounding Ichenhausen. These communities were Nordlingen, Fischach, Krumbach, Buttenwiesen, Oettingen, Harburg, Wallerstein, and others, many of which no longer could maintain a regular *minyan.*

The young, energetic Rav, fresh from his own yeshivah experience, planned to start a yeshivah and dormitory for German *bachurim* in Ichenhausen, in conjunction with the Frankfurt Yeshivah. This would have been the first such institution in all of Bavaria. In fact, in the spring of 1934, after a year's planning and preparation — including gaining the permission of the Gestapo — the doors of the yeshivah opened but, sadly, stayed open for one day only! On the second morning, all the streets in town were plastered with anti-Semitic posters by the local "Hitler Youth" thugs against this new Jewish "provocation" in their midst, and urged violence against it. The local police chief, who was not a Nazi, warned Rav Schwab that the "Hitler Youth" were preparing a "pogrom" against the yeshivah and its students that very night. Despite the Bezirksrabbiner's personal plea to the Gestapo chief in Ichenhausen — who was seated between two snarling dogs — he was told that he had already notified his superiors in Munich that "he could not guarantee the safety" of the yeshivah students — unless they left town before nightfall, *that night.*

The Rav would sadly recall how, after his meeting with the Gestapo, he proceeded immediately to the *beis hamidrash,* which was vibrant with the *kol Torah* of his unsuspecting *talmidim,* and told them to close their Gemaras, pack their belongings, and head immediately for the train station to make the last train out that day. The Rav accompanied his *bachurim* down the hill to the train station — amid jeers and catcalls from the local thugs — paid all of their travel expenses, and saw them safely aboard the train. Other than suffering verbal abuse, none of the *bachurim,* nor the Rav, was injured in this incident. Rav Schwab could not risk the possibility of any harm coming to his *bachurim.*

Much later, the Rav would discover that the renowned Rav Yehudah HaChassid predicted in his will, written some 800 years earlier, that "a man in the Land of Schwaben (the area where Ichenhausen is located) would not be successful in educating young boys as yeshivah students." (See *Sefer Chassidim, Margaliyos* ed., last item of the צואה, §56.) The Rav was deeply moved by the holiness of this *tzaddik,* whose ancient will became a reality in the Rav's lifetime.

While the clouds of the forthcoming calamity were gathering, the Rav's heart was burning to reach out to German Jewry with a call to *teshuvah.* He wrote a series of articles on this subject which were printed in the German-Jewish publication, "Israelit," in Frankfurt. He later incorporated them into his literary masterpiece, *Heimkehr Ins Judentum,* which was published in Frankfurt in late 1934. This book became an immediate sensation and a springboard for discussion throughout Jewish Germany. The Rav records that about 850 copies of this book were purchased.

During the Ichenhausen period, in June, 1935, the third of the Rav and Rebbetzin's children, Joseph Chaim, was born. Now with a wife and three children, the Rav was actively seeking a rabbinical position outside of Germany. A month-long trip to Eretz Yisrael in the fall of 1935 for this purpose proved unsuccessful. Nevertheless, the constant taunts and threats by the local Nazi thugs kept emigration from Germany a primary consideration in the Rav's mind.

On Shushan Purim 1936, the Rav was the subject of a libelous accusation that he had, in one of his sermons, publicly maligned Hitler, *yemach shemo,* and was brought before the Gestapo to explain himself. Making direct eye contact with the Nazi official, he forcefully explained that this was an outright lie. He had used the German word *"vermittler"* in his disparagement of the sin of the Golden Calf, which a spy had misunderstood as "Hitler." After this explanation, he was told that his case would be reviewed and that he would be advised of the outcome.

Needless to say, the Rav feared for his life after that meeting. The Rav records in his diary that he was advised in the middle of Iyar that the matter had been dropped. During this period of some two months, the Rav slept only fitfully, with his clothes on, for fear that he would be arrested in the middle of the night, taken to jail, or out in the woods to be beaten and left to die — as had already occurred to several others. If this was to be his fate, he would face it with dignity — and with his clothes on — as would befit that of a Jewish leader. This incident speaks volumes of the Rav's concept of *kavod habriyos* — and especially that of members of the Rabbinate, whom he conceived of as *sheluchei d'Rachmana,* God's emissaries.

In the summer of 1936, the Rav met Rabbi Leo Jung, of New York, who was in Zurich for a visit with his wife's family. Rabbi Jung recommended a vacant rabbinical position in the German-oriented Congregation Shearith Israel in Baltimore, and told the Rav to contact Mr. Nathan Adler, a prominent board member, regarding this position, Unbeknown to the Rav, Mr. Adler happened to be a distant relative. After an exchange of letters, arrangements were made for a trial Shabbos in Baltimore, on *Parashas Ki Seitzei,* August 29, 1936. The language of the congregation was English, and the Rav, after a great deal of effort and preparation, delivered his first sermon in English at Shearith Israel on that Shabbos, and also gave *shiurim* in Yiddish for the older *baalei battim.* On the following Sunday evening, he addressed the congregation again in English. He was told that the board of directors would be meeting to decide on his candidacy right after Rosh Hashanah, and he would be advised of their decision immediately.

After a two-week stay in America, the Rav returned to Ichenhausen in time for the beginning of *Selichos,* as he had promised his congregants, and anxiously awaited the outcome of the board meeting. Mr. Nathan Adler strongly encouraged the board to elect Rabbi Schwab as their Rav. On the 8th of Tishrei, September 24, 1936, the Rav received a telegram from Mr. Samuel Rauneker, the acting president of the congregation, containing two words: "Unanimously Elected." The Rav's English was so rudimentary at that time, that while he knew what "elected" meant, he had no idea what "unanimously" meant. It was only after consulting his well-thumbed dictionary that he rejoiced and recited the *berachah* of *hatov v'hameitiv.* The Rav immediately began to make preparations for the family's departure for America, to begin the next chapter in their lives.

An entire book could be written about the events which occurred between the American congregation's acceptance of their new 27-year-old rabbi from Germany, whose English left much to be desired, and the actual arrival in New York of Rabbi and Mrs. Shimon Schwab, accompanied by their three small children, and a young "mother's helper," Gretel Spanier, on the 10th of Teves, December 24, 1936. Suffice it to say, this three-month period was full of events which can only be explained as outright miracles.

Congregation Shearith Israel was a venerable institution in Baltimore, and was a unique *shul,* with its ancient time-hallowed German *minhagim.* For five years the congregation had been without a rabbi. The Board of Directors, under the influence of Mr. Nathan Adler, had energetically kept the mission and purpose of the congregation in line with its original charter, that of uncompromising adherence to the *Shulchan Aruch,* despite strong pressure from many of its congregants, who were more "liberal minded." An old but as yet unwritten statute of the congregation limited membership to *shomrei Shabbos* — everyone else could be "seat holders" only, without voting rights — and this had become a great bone of contention within the congregation at the time of the Rav's arrival at Shearith Israel.

After much consultation with prominent *gedolei harabbanim* in America, Rav Schwab made the halachic decision to enforce this statute, and membership was refused to non-*shomrei Shabbos*. The Rav, in his halachic opinion letter, made it clear that — while this statute would have to be enforced — he nevertheless welcomed every one of the seat holders to all services and activities of the congregation, including full use of the afternoon "Hebrew School" of the congregation for their children. He had hoped thereby to attract them to become more committed to Judaism, and eventually to become *shomrei Torah u'mitzvos*. He was encouraged in his stand by the Agudas HaRabbanim of America, and especially by the *gadol* Rav Dov Aryeh Levinthal of Philadelphia. In their letters of encouragement, each invoked the *pasuk:* שְׁאֵרִית יִשְׂרָאֵל לֹא יַעֲשׂוּ עַוְלָה, *the remnant of Israel will not commit corruption* (Zephaniah 3:13). The great *gaon* Rav Elchonon Wasserman, זצ"ל-הי"ד, who was visiting America at that time, and spent a Shabbos at the Rav's home, also strongly applauded this *p'sak din*.

However, over one hundred of the congregants rebelled against this decision, and left Shearith Israel to form their own "Modern Orthodox" congregation, and purchased a building for this purpose a short distance away. The great influx of Orthodox Jews of the late 30's had not yet begun, and Shearith Israel was left with only a small fraction of its original congregants.

As an illustration of Rav Schwab's graciousness toward his opponents in this matter, the Rav and Rebbetzin would have, as a regular guest at their Shabbos table, the newly hired young rabbi of the "breakaway" congregation, who was as yet unmarried.

Nevertheless, this decision established the Rav as an uncompromising proponent of Torah-true Orthodoxy in America, and he was highly respected for his leadership and consistency even among those in Baltimore who opposed him in this regard. In those days there were very few *rabbanim* in America who were willing to lead their congregations, rather than be led by the whims of their congregants.

America at that time was still a veritable wasteland of Judaism, with a few oases in its midst. The city of Baltimore was fortunate in possessing a Hebrew day school, Talmudical Academy, and also a *yeshivah gedolah,* Ner Israel. Upon his arrival in Baltimore, Rav Schwab immediately became active on the Board of Education at Talmudical Academy, and as a daily instructor in the yeshivah — albeit unpaid — and enjoyed the close company of its *rosh yeshivah,* Rav Yaakov Yitzchak HaLevi Ruderman.

In 1937 and 1938 two more sons were born: Myer Jerucham, and Jacob Boruch. Fortunately, there was a Jewish day school for the boys, but there was no Jewish girls school in Baltimore at that time. Judith had to attend public school, including a public high school for girls. She received her elementary Jewish education from private teachers at home. She later attended the Beth Jacob High School in Williamsburg to complement her Jewish education. Recognizing this great void in Jewish education in Baltimore, the Rav and a group of dedicated *baalei battim* founded the Bais Yaakov School for Girls of Baltimore. This school today is the largest Jewish girls school in America, outside of New York.

In the ensuing years, swelled by the influx of many German refugees and others, congregation Shearith Israel, by then known as "Rabbi Schwab's Shul," became a vibrant center of Orthodox Jewish life. The Rav was deeply involved in *hatzalah* efforts both prior to and during the war years. With the help of several of his influential congregants, he was responsible for the issuing of many affidavits for refugees, who were fleeing Hitler's firestorm in Germany, to enable them to come to America. Many of these settled in Baltimore and joined Shearith Israel, where they felt comfortable with its familiar German *minhag Ashkenaz* and its Rav with whom they could converse in their native tongue. Interestingly, one of these affidavits was for the late Dr. Raphael Moller and his family in 1940. The Rav could not know that many years later, he would work closely with Dr. Moller at the helm of K'hal Adath Jeshurun in Washington Heights.

The home of the Rav and Rebbetzin became a center of *hachnassas orchim* and a place of warmth and encouragement for these many newly arrived, penniless refugees in a strange new land. If the dining-room table could talk, it would tell many fascinating tales and experiences of the varied and sundry guests, ranging from plain ordinary people, poor and downtrodden widows and orphans, to the many famous *gedolei Yisrael* who benefited from Rav and Rebbetzin Schwab's hospitality.

That simple dining-room table, with its extra "pull-out leaves" for guests, enriched by the *divrei Torah* and stories of *gedolim* and Jewish history so masterfully told by Rav Schwab during the Shabbos and Yom Tov meals which were so beautifully prepared by the Rebbetzin, was the center of the Torah *chinuch* of the Schwab children, and enhanced their sense of security in their Jewish practice and thought. By this time, Rav Schwab had already established himself as a forceful and gifted orator both in English and Yiddish, and as an outspoken spokesman for Torah-true Orthodoxy.

Agudath Israel of America was emerging as a vibrant force for Orthodoxy and *hatzalah* efforts in the United States during this period. In Baltimore in 1941 Rav Schwab organized the second annual Agudah Convention. This כְּנֵסִיָּה לְשֵׁם שָׁמַיִם, *assembly for God's sake,* attracted many *rabbanim* and *baalei battim*. Among the honored guests were the renowned *gaon,* Rav Aharon Kotler, and the fiery Agudah lay leader, *Moreinu* Yaakov Rosenheim, who had been one of the Rav's early mentors in Frankfurt. A group of young activists, including Moshe Sherer, a student at Yeshivas Ner Israel, helped both in organizing and managing this convention. The first "Agudah Convention" met in 1940 in Cincinnati, under the leadership of Rabbi Eliezer Silver.

In addition to his educational efforts in the day school, yeshivah, and Bais Yaakov school, the Rav instituted an exacting level of *kashrus* in town. In 1941, he also led members of his congregation and others in the organization of a strictly Orthodox *chevrah kaddisha,* as a part of the social welfare organization — which he named *Chevrah Ahavas Chessed* — founded by German Jewish refugees, who were not all necessarily very Orthodox. However, out of their high regard for Rav Schwab, he was readily recognized as their Rabbi, and they followed his *p'sak din* in all religious matters. Rav Schwab wrote a definitive set of *dinim* and *minhagim* for the *chevrah kaddisha,* which is still in use to this day.

By this time, the Rav had become quite proficient in English, and he delivered numerous adult lectures and classes. The participants at these classes benefited greatly from his unique ability to explain difficult subjects in simple language.

The Rav's pen was also busy during those early years. At the request of Rav Elchonon Wasserman, he authored the book, *Beis HaSho'evah,* which dealt with the coming of *Mashiach,* and it was published anonymously in 1941. In the summer of 1951, he published *Shemesh Marpei,* containing excerpts of the explanations of Rav Samson Raphael Hirsch on *sefer Bereishis.* During these years, he also published numerous articles which appeared in various periodicals.

In June 1945, the war was drawing to a close, and the new "United Nations" was in formation in San Francisco. The Rav was asked by Agudath Israel to partake in a delegation to present its official position on matters of worldwide vital Jewish interest, both here and in Eretz Yisrael. During that conference, the Rav met the world leaders of the day.

In the summer of 1951, Rav Schwab spearheaded a delegation of activists to Eretz Yisrael to study the problem of the thousands of newly arrived refugees from Yemen and North Africa, who were living in *maabarot* (transition camps), and were rapidly being absorbed into secular and even antireligious circles in Eretz Yisrael. These activists were members of the *P'eylim* organization and were deeply involved in intensive educational efforts to save these pious and innocent *Sefardim* from losing their ancient religious heritage. During this trip, the Rav came into contact with the great *gedolim* of Eretz Yisrael, including the Chazon Ish and the Brisker Rav. On his return to America, Rav Schwab created a great deal of enthusiasm for the cause of *P'eylim,* and much was accomplished in this respect, resulting in the rescue of countless Jewish souls in Eretz Yisrael.

During his twenty-one-year tenure in Baltimore, Rav Schwab left an indelible impression on the city, and contributed greatly toward its development as America's foremost Torah city outside of New York.

At age 50, in the prime of his life, three days after Lag BaOmer, May 11, 1958, Rav Schwab joined the Rabbinate of K'hal Adath Jeshurun of Washington Heights, New York City, together with Rav Dr. Joseph Breuer. A year later, Rav Breuer wrote in an essay he had prepared for posthumous publication: "Already in his first year . . . Rabbi Schwab proved to be the right leader for our *kehillah*. May Hashem continue to lend him His assistance."

Rav Schwab's tenure at K'hal Adath Jeshurun, first in association with Rav Breuer, then on his own, and subsequently with Rav Zachariah Gelley, *shlita*, was a most momentous one. K'hal Adath Jeshurun provided him with a platform from which he grew even greater in stature as he aged, and became recognized as a worldwide Torah spokesman, *poseik*, and leader. During the Rav's thirty-seven-year tenure at K'hal Adath Jeshurun, he maintained — and beautifully interpreted — its sacred traditions, with which he was so familiar from the Frankfurt of his youth, while at the same time winning the devoted allegiance to these time-hallowed *minhagim* of a new generation of American-born congregants.

Under Rav Schwab's leadership at KAJ, the use of English replaced German in the sermons, *shiurim, derashos,* and publications, to make the teaching of Torah, and especially the Hirschian philosophy, accessible to the younger members. In so doing, he also unequivocally clarified the meaning of *"Torah im Derech Eretz,"* which has so often been misunderstood. The changeover to English was gradual. In fact, in his early years at KAJ, Rav Schwab would deliver *shiurim* in impeccable German for the benefit of those members who were more comfortable with that language.

The Rav was always most interested in the educational activities of the *kehillah*. He was therefore at the forefront of the drive to vastly expand the yeshivah's educational focus. As dean of the yeshivah, he was instrumental, together with Rav Breuer, in the founding of such institutions as the Mesivta and Bais Yaakov, the Beis HaMidrash, Teachers' Seminary, and Kollel.

The Rav's devotion to his flock was legendary. He was a trusted confidant, and his ready smile, wise counsel, *berachos* and *tefillos* for the needy and sick, were sought from far and wide, in good times and difficult ones. While dispensing advice, he was especially outstanding in his unyielding devotion to *emes* (truth). Once he had arrived at a conclusion which he considered to be *emes*, he would not waver from it. His devotion to his children and grandchildren was well known. They would consult him on major and minor matters, and ask for his advice and *berachos*. He would say a special *tefillah* for each one of his expectant granddaughters.

He was scrupulously honest in financial matters; he detested deceit and pretension of any kind. He was a true *baal tzedakah,* very often helping those in need without their knowledge. His heart was especially warm to those who had personal family problems due to an inadequate income. He would scrupulously adhere to the laws of *maaser kesafim* — which he, personally, extended to the full *chomesh.* He would keep an exact record of his credits and debits in his *maaser* account, and on his birthday each year, he would clear the slate and forgive any credits due him. He once told a visitor, who had been having financial difficulties, that the secret of a good *parnassah* is the scrupulous adherence to *maaser.*

One could confide in him with complete confidence, in good times and bad. He answered *she'eilos* from anonymous callers, with uncanny precision. He would often say a *tefillah* that *Hakadosh Baruch Hu* grant him the wisdom to give the right answers. On one occasion, he gave what he later thought was an unclear answer, which could be misunderstood, but since the caller was anonymous, he *davened* that the caller would call again. Within minutes, the phone rang, and it was the same caller, providing the Rav with the opportunity to clarify his *p'sak.* The *siyata d'Shmaya* that he merited was obvious.

The Rav assisted many in their quest for employment and housing. In the area of *shidduchim,* the Rebbetzin was actively involved with him, and together they were instrumental in bringing about at least sixteen marriages. The Rebbetzin, שתחי׳, was also very active in all areas of *kehillah* life, especially the sisterhood and *chevrah kaddisha d'nashim.* Her *hachnassas orchim* and acts of kindness on behalf of the poor, aged, and infirm are well known, and deserve the utmost praise.

During his tenure at KAJ, the Rav was also very active in Jewish life outside the *kehillah.* He was particularly interested in the field of Torah *chinuch,* and gave encouragement and honor to those who chose this noble profession. Rav Schwab would often compare them to the *Leviim* of old, whose main function was to teach Torah to the nation (see *Maayan Beis HaSho'evah, Pinchas, Nimukim* 26:14). He was a champion of decent, realistic wages for all those working in this field, in order to attract the most capable people to this high calling. He was consulted on all major matters by Torah Umesorah, and headed their Rabbinical *Beis Din.* He addressed their annual conventions many times.

His skilled oratory was always eagerly anticipated at the annual conventions of Agudath Israel of America. To illustrate his point, he would often weave tales of his experiences with the *gedolim* of the prior generation, such as the Chafetz Chaim, into his addresses, in an effort to drive home his messages. These audiences were never disappointed.

Many other organizations and yeshivos benefited from his addresses. The *kehillos* of Zurich and Basel, Switzerland also invited Rav Schwab to address them on various occasions.

The *kinah* which Rav Schwab composed, at the suggestion of Rav Breuer, in memory of the six million *kedoshim*, is recited on Tishah B'Av not only at KAJ, but also in many *kehillos* throughout the world.

Many literary achievements filled the Rav's busy schedule while at KAJ. Besides his numerous articles in the "Mitteilungen," there were other literary pieces published in various magazines of Jewish interest, here and abroad. The booklet "These and Those" made a great impression on the world of Torah-true Jewish education, with its clear examination of Jewish educational goals.

The Rav and תבל"ח, the Rebbetzin, spent many summers at "Torah Institute," a camp for *baalei teshuvah* in Moodus, Connecticut, in the company of their daughter, Judy, and her husband, the late Rabbi Yaakov C. Rosenberg ל"צז. The camp and its parent yeshivah in Yerushalayim, Machon Shlomo, were founded by Rabbi Rosenberg, who was very successful in teaching mature newcomers to Judaism to live committed Torah lives. Rav Schwab was available at the camp to give *shiurim* and personal guidance to the tutors and many of the "campers," whom Rav Schwab would call *mevakshei Hashem*.

Many of the Rav's major addresses, articles, and lectures to the *kehillah*, and elsewhere, were incorporated into a "trilogy" of three books:

Selected Writings, published by the 1988 graduating class of Mesivta Rabbi Samson Raphael Hirsch on the occasion of the Rav's thirtieth anniversary with the *kehillah.*

Selected Speeches, published in 1991, which includes his in-depth study on Jewish Chronology, to which Rav Schwab devoted a great deal of effort and time.

Selected Essays, published in October, 1994, which includes selections from *These and Those,* and some translated sections of *Heimkehr Ins Judentum.*

In 1992 Rav Schwab encouraged — and financed — the publication by Rabbi Eliyahu Meir Klugman of a major collection of the Hebrew correspondence, *Sheilos U'Teshuvos,* and personal papers of Rav Samson Raphael Hirsch which had never before been available to the public. The Rav considered it a special *zechus* for the *neshamah* of Rav Hirsch to have these papers, replete with his Torah thought, disseminated to the Torah world at large. The Rav named the *sefer Shemesh Marpei,* which alludes to the name *Samson Raphael,* just as he had done to his own rendition of Rav Samson Raphael Hirsch's explanations on *Bereishis* in the *sefer* he had published many years earlier in Baltimore.

Unquestionably, the Rav's "Magnum Opus" was his *Maayan Beis HaSho'evah,* which is a veritable treasure trove of his most original and profound thoughts on *Chumash,* and on other topics. Excerpts, appropriate to *simchos* and other occasions, are often quoted from this enormously popular *sefer.*

At the age of 86, on *Purim Katan,* the 14th of Adar I, February 13, 1995, at approximately 7 p.m., surrounded by his children, Rav Shimon Schwab peacefully returned his pure *neshamah* to its Maker, amid the saying of *Vidui, Shema Yisrael,* and the *Shemos HaKedoshim,* of which he clearly was aware, until his *neshamah* departed from his body. The *levayah* was held the next day, at noon, from the *Beis Haknesses* of K'hal Adath Jeshurun, with brief words by Rav Gelley, and the recital of several chapters of *Tehillim,* all in accordance with his will that a *hesped* not be said at his *levayah.* The *aron* was carried up Bennett Avenue, accompanied by thousands of mourners in silent dignity, and he was brought to burial at the cemetery of K'hal Adath Jeshurun, in Clifton, New Jersey. At the conclusion of the *shivah,* an *azkarah* was held in *shul* to honor his memory.

These few pages are inadequate to fully describe the life of Rav Shimon Schwab, Rav and *Manhig b'Yisrael.* This would require an entire book, which is now in preparation. However, this article gives us a glimpse of a man who was an *eved Hashem,* who had utilized his life for that highest purpose. This was a man who achieved the fulfillment of the daily *tefillah,* לְמַעַן לֹא נִיגַע לָרִיק וְלֹא נֵלֵד לַבֶּהָלָה, *so that we do not struggle in vain nor produce for futility.*

יהי זכרו ברוך ותהא נשמתו צרורה בצרור החיים

Moshe Schwab

~§ Editor's Foreword

This work consists of an adaptation of a series of lectures by Rav Shimon Schwab *z"tl* at Congregation K'hal Adath Jeshurun. These were delivered in English on Sunday mornings, over a period of a year and a half, from חדש חשון תשנ"ב עד חדש ניסן תשנ"ג [October 1991 to March 1993].

The Rav named the series עִיּוּן תְּפִלָּה, *Iyun Tefillah,* as his purpose was to offer insights into our daily prayers by highlighting the meaning and explaining the background of the text chosen by *Chazal* for the *davening.* Although these lectures were not intended to include a line by line translation of the *tefillah* — nevertheless, the Rav, in his unique style of teaching, offers many translations and clarifications of words and phrases, which help the student to enhance his understanding of the meaning of the *tefillos.*

In these *shiurim* the Rav shares with his students the outcome of a lifetime of studying the *tefillos* as one would study any other part of Torah. His purpose in learning the *tefillos* was to elevate his own *tefillah* to that of true *avodah shebelev,* and to teach others to do so. And he was indeed successful in developing his personal *tefillah* into a lofty level of *avodas Hashem.* Whoever had the *zechus* to observe him during his *tefillah* could sense that his outwardly calm, yet intense, demeanor reflected his deep concentration on the words of the *tefillah* and his awareness that he was communicating directly with the *Ribbono Shel Olam.* His personal example influenced many people to improve and elevate their own *tefillah.*

The Rav was a true *baal tefillah* in every sense. Having mastered the art of the proper *dikduk* of *lashon hakodesh* as a young boy, he combined the correct pronunciation of the *tefillos* with a mature understanding of the thoughts expressed by them. This was the result of his thorough knowledge of their sources in *Tanach,* especially *Tehillim,* as well as those in the Talmud, Midrash, *halachah, Aggadah, Rishonim, Acharonim,* and the *poskim.*

Rav Schwab was blessed with a resonant tenor voice which enhanced his speech and *tefillos.* His beautiful rendition of *Lechah Dodi* is still used at K'hal Adath Jeshurun at *Kabbalas Shabbos,* and his various renditions of the *zemiros* for Shabbos and Yom Tov — and other occasions — are fondly remembered by our family, as well as by the numerous guests who were present at those *seudos.* The Rav served as the *shaliach tzibbur* for the *Ne'ilah* service for many years. His melodious and deeply thoughtful rendition of this *tefillah* of Yom Kippur was an uplifting experience never to be forgotten by anyone who merited to hear it.

The Rav exemplified adherence to the dictum of *shetikah yafah bish'as hatefillah*. Once he began his *tefillah* he would not interrupt until it was finished. He often wrote and lectured on the importance of this subject. He even encouraged his followers to sign a pledge not to talk during *davening*, and rewarded them with the special *Mi Shebeirach* blessing which was composed by the saintly Tosefos Yom Tov. This is still recited at K'hal Adath Jeshurun during the three Festivals of Pesach, Shavuos, and Succos during *"matnas yad."*

[The *minhag*, called *matnas yad*, occurs on the last day of the Festival, after the Torah reading. On that day a *Mi Shebeirach* blessing is recited by the Rav for all those who donate for the needs of the congregation. The expression is taken from the Torah reading of the day, אִישׁ כְּמַתְּנַת יָדוֹ, *every one according to what he can give* (*Devarim* 16:17).]

The text of the *tefillos* which the Rav used for these lectures, and for his own personal use, was that of *Sfas Emes*, which is known worldwide as the "Roedelheim *Siddur*." This *siddur* was first published as *Safah Berurah* about two hundred years ago in Germany by Wolf Heidenheim, who is referred to in the *Mishnah Berurah* as החכם רוו״ה. It was widely used in Germany and many parts of Western Europe until the destruction. It is now used in congregations which follow the *nusach Ashkenaz* as practiced in pre-World War II Germany. The most notable of these is K'hal Adath Jeshurun, where Rav Schwab graced the Rabbinate for over thirty-six years.

Rav Schwab's failing health made it impossible for him to continue these lectures, and they ended with the conclusion of the weekday *Shemoneh Esrei*. He had hoped to teach all of the *tefillos*, including those of Shabbos and Yom Tov. Unfortunately, this was not to be, truly a great loss. חֲבַל עַל דְּאָבְדִין וְלָא מִשְׁתַּכְּחִין.

Most of the references in this work were provided by Rabbi Dovid Margareten of Monsey, New York. These were taken from *Sefer Iyun Tefillah*, the Hebrew version of these lectures which he wrote, and its publication is currently in preparation. Rabbi Margareten was also actively involved in assisting the Rav in the writing of *Maayan Beis HaSho'evah*. We are deeply indebted to him for sharing with us his immense knowledge of the Talmud, *Poskim, Rishonim, Acharonim,* and responsa, the application of which greatly enhances the meaning of the Rav's thoughts.

We are deeply grateful to Rabbi Eliezer Gevirtz of Yeshivah Rabbi Samson Raphael Hirsch for his very valuable assistance in editing the entire English manuscript and for his constructive suggestions during the production of this work.

We are deeply grateful to our publishers, Artscroll/Mesorah, headed by Rabbis Meir Zlotowitz and Nosson Scherman, and their entire production staff, for each individual's participation in his or her own area of expertise, which resulted in this beautiful and aesthetically pleasing sefer, which is so obviously a labor of love. We are especially grateful to Mrs. Judi Dick for her critical review of the entire manuscript and for her very helpful and constructive suggestions.

A great debt of gratitude is due to Mr. Norbert Wartelsky who not only oversaw the professional taping of the Rav's *Iyun Tefillah* series on which this work is based, but also helped disseminate these *shiurim* by providing duplication and distribution services of the tapes for the benefit of Yeshiva Rabbi S. R. Hirsch. Also, our special thanks are due to Messrs. Chaim Aschkenasy and Ben Ettlinger who were very helpful in the recording process. We also extend our sincere gratitude to Mr. Pinchas Katzenstein who acted as our treasurer during the production of both the English and Hebrew versions of this project.

Regarding the style of this work, an attempt was made to convey the beauty and passion of the author's delivery. We have therefore preserved the Rav's practice of freely intermingling Hebrew and English phrases, as well as the use of some redundancy of words to impress a point. Furthermore, the student of this work will quickly discover that the Rav used these lectures not only to explain the *tefillos*, but also as an opportunity to teach and explain the basic tenets of Torah-true Judaism. And in so doing, the Rav sprinkled some of these *shiurim* with personal anecdotes to illustrate certain important points.

I wish to express my heartfelt deepest appreciation to my dear wife, and life's partner, Miriam שתחי׳, who provided me with an atmosphere of tranquility and peace of mind so that I could devote almost all of my free time and energy to concentrate on this project. She relinquished uncounted hours — days and nights — of my companionship to allow me the freedom to see this work through to completion. She therefore has an equal share in this undertaking. וּנְוַת בַּיִת תְּחַלֵּק שָׁלָל, *She who dwells within the house shares the rewards* (*Psalms* 68:13). For this, and for all of her other *gemillos chassadim* to me, our children, grandchildren, and to the many others who are the beneficiaries of her giving heart, may she be blessed with בִּרְכוֹת שָׁמַיִם מֵעַל for many healthy and happy years to come, לְאֹרֶךְ יָמִים טוֹבִים בָּזֶה וּבְבָא.

At this occasion I express my deepest gratitude to my late father-in-law, Mr. Morris Rokowsky ז״ל החבר ר׳ מאיר בן החי״ר יצחק, and שתבל״ח my dear mother-in-law, Mrs. Rachel Rokowsky שתחי׳, for all the love, warmth, and *gemillos chassadim* which they have shown to me and our family throughout the years, during good times and difficult ones. Mr. Rokowsky, while still living in Switzerland, on the brink of the great catastrophe which struck our people, was personally responsible for the rescue of about 2,000 Jews. The family which they raised, and their efforts in the fields of Jewish education, *tzedakah,* and *chessed* are well known, and have established the Rokowskys as one of the outstanding families in contemporary Jewish life. וּתְהִי מַשְׂכֻּרְתּוֹ שְׁלֵמָה מֵעִם ה' אֱלֹקֵי יִשְׂרָאֵל.

In closing, I wish to express my deepest appreciation to our friend, Mr. Yitzchok Siegel, of Silver Spring, Maryland (whom we fondly remember from our youth in Baltimore as "Pitzy"), who encouraged the publication of this English version of *"Iyun Tefillah."* Very fittingly, he and his wife, Barbara Lehman Siegel, have sponsored this *sefer* in memory of Mr. Siegel's parents, Mr. and Mrs. Jacob Siegel ע"ה, who were exemplary members of Congregation Shearith Israel of Baltimore, where Rav Schwab was the Rabbi from 1936 to 1958. May the Torah which is learned from this *sefer* be an everlasting *zechus* for their *neshamos.*

The profits generated by this book, and the forthcoming Hebrew version, will accrue to the benefit of Yeshivah Rabbi Samson Raphael Hirsch. The material as well as the spiritual welfare of the yeshivah, as an integral part of K'hal Adas Jeshurun, were very dear to Rav Schwab. Even as his strength was ebbing, in a great final expression of responsibility for the students and teachers of the yeshivah, Rav Schwab arranged for the liquidation of its then existing debt just weeks before he returned his pure *neshamah* to his Maker.

וִיהִי רָצוֹן מִלִּפְנֵי אָבִינוּ שֶׁבַּשָּׁמַיִם שֶׁיְּהֵא הַסֵּפֶר הַזֶּה זְכוּת וְעִלּוּי לְנִשְׁמָתוֹ הַטְּהוֹרָה וּתְהֵא נִשְׁמָתוֹ צְרוּרָה בִּצְרוֹר הַחַיִּים בְּגַן עֵדֶן וְיִזְכֶּה לִתְחִיַּת הַמֵּתִים עִם כָּל צַדִּיקֵי וַחֲסִידֵי יִשְׂרָאֵל, אָמֵן.

וּמִטַּעַם כָּל הַמִּשְׁפָּחָה אָנוּ מְשַׁגְּרִים בְּרָכָה מְיֻחֶדֶת לִכְבוֹד אִמֵּנוּ מוֹרָתֵנוּ, אֵשֶׁת חָבֵר כְּחָבֵר, בַּעֲלַת חֶסֶד נִפְלָאָה, עֵזֶר הָיְתָה לְבַעֲלָהּ בְּמֶשֶׁךְ שִׁשִּׁים וְשָׁלשׁ שָׁנָה, מָסְרָה נַפְשָׁהּ לְהַכְנָסַת אוֹרְחִים וְסַעַד לַחוֹלִים וְעִדּוּד לַעֲגוּמוֹת נֶפֶשׁ, הָאִשָּׁה הַחֲשׁוּבָה הָרַבָּנִית מָרַת רַייכֶל בַּת הֶחָבֵר ר' אַבְרָהָם (פְּרוֹיְלִיךְ) שֶׁתִּחְיֶה לְאֹרֶךְ יָמִים טוֹבִים.

Moshe Schwab

בלאאמו"ר שמעון בן החבר ר' יהודה, צללה"ה

Brooklyn, NY
שבט תשס"א / February 2001

~§ Introduction by the Author זצ״ל

This series of lectures is called עִיּוּן תְּפִלָּה (*Iyun Tefillah*). The word *iyun* is derived from עַיִן, *ayin,* the eye, and the meaning is to focus one's attention on *tefillah.* As we know, *Iyun Tefillah* is among those activities whose benefits are enjoyed in this world — we can learn so much from it here and now — but whose principal reward remains to be received in the world to come: אֵלּוּ דְבָרִים שֶׁאָדָם אוֹכֵל פֵּרוֹתֵיהֶם בָּעוֹלָם הַזֶּה וְהַקֶּרֶן קַיֶּמֶת לוֹ לָעוֹלָם הַבָּא, (*Talmud Bavli, Shabbos* 127a, and *Yerushalmi, Peah* (ירושלמי פאה פ״א) Ch. 1). There are many commentaries on the *siddur,* dating back to the early *Rishonim.* To name just a few, there is the commentary of Avudraham, who lived about 500 years ago; the *siddur* of Rav Hertz *Shaliach Tzibbur,* who was a Kabbalist; the famous *Derech HaChaim* by Rav Yaakov MiLisa; and the *Amudei HaShamayim* by Rav Yaakov Emden. We also certainly cannot overlook mentioning the commentary of Rav Samson Raphael Hirsch, whose opponents scoffingly referred to him as a *siddur lamdan,* as if it were belittling to occupy one's mind with explaining the *siddur.* Of course, they ignored the fact that Rav Hirsch was following in the footsteps of many *Rishonim* and *Acharonim* who had offered commentary on the prayers.

The purpose of *Iyun Tefillah* is to learn and know the meaning of the words, *before saying them* in *davening.* This follows the dictum of *Chovos HaLevavos* (*Shaar Ahavas Hashem* Ch. 6), שֶׁלֹּא יַקְדִּים בָּהּ [בַּתְּפִלָּה] לְשׁוֹנְךָ אֶת לִבְּךָ, that when one prays *he should not allow his mouth to precede his heart.* This means that one is to fully comprehend the words of the *tefillah before* they are expressed. The *Chovos HaLevavos* is chastising those who *do know* the meaning of the words, but concentrate on their meaning only *after* expressing the words. However, merely mouthing the words without *ever* knowing their meaning is פִּטְפּוּטֵי דְבָרִים בְּעָלְמָא, *mere lip service,* which is hardly considered *tefillah,* and which should cause an intelligent person to be ashamed.

It is the opinion of the Rambam, and those who follow his view, that *tefillah* is a *mitzvah min haTorah,* a Torah-based obligation, which is derived from וּלְעָבְדוֹ בְּכָל לְבַבְכֶם, *to serve Him with all your heart* (*Deuteronomy* 11:13). *Avodah shebelev,* service of the heart, refers to *tefillah* (*Taanis* 2a). Therefore, according to this view, when one *davens* he is fulfilling a commandment in the Torah. But, the details of prayer — the how, what, and when to *daven* — are not dictated by the Torah; before the Sages composed specific texts for our *tefillos,* each individual had the right to select his own prayers.

Our present-day specific text, which is called מַטְבֵּעַ שֶׁטָּבְעוּ חֲכָמִים [*matbei'a shetavu Chachamim*], a formula coined by the Sages, originated with *Anshei Knesses HaGedolah,* and is therefore of Rabbinic origin. This includes the *Seder Tefillah,* the order of the prayer; *Dinei VeNusach HaTefillah,* the laws and the text of the Prayer; *Kaddish; Barchu; Kedushah; Shemoneh Esrei; Tefillah B'Tzibbur,* the Communal Prayer; *Berachos,* Blessings; *Kiddush* and *Havdalah,* etc. (See *Berachos* 33a; *Megillah* 17b.)

The *Anshei Knesses HaGedolah* lived at the beginning of the Second Temple Era and consisted of one hundred and twenty Elders, among whom were many prophets. (See *Megillah* 17b.) We therefore have every reason to focus intently on our *tefillos,* which were composed by sages and prophets, and to delve deeply into their meaning, just as we do with *Tanach,* seeking the *p'shat* (meaning), *remez* (allusion), and *sod* (hidden meaning) of each word.

The reason the Sages instituted these specific prayers instead of leaving their texts to the prerogative of the individual may be as follows. The Gemara tells us that the *Anshei Knesses HaGedolah* eradicated the *yetzer hara* of idol worship through their *tefillos* (*Sanhedrin* 64a). The desire to worship idols had plagued our forefathers throughout the entire period of the *Tanach.* We find constant admonishments against idolatry in the Torah starting with the Ten Commandments, and continuing throughout. We find expressions such as הִשָּׁמְרוּ לָכֶם פֶּן יִפְתֶּה לְבַבְכֶם וְסַרְתֶּם וַעֲבַדְתֶּם אֱלֹהִים אֲחֵרִים, *Beware for yourselves, lest your heart be seduced and you turn astray and serve gods of others* (*Devarim* 11:16), and many, many additional references. Clearly, then, there must have been a terribly powerful and awesome *yetzer hara* for idol worship which is totally unknown to us.

When we see the statues of idols in museums today, we cannot understand how highly intelligent people like the Egyptians, who were advanced in the sciences and arts, could have worshiped these images. Despite their advances in astronomy — they had developed quite accurate calendars — they still worshipped the sun, moon, and stars; prayed to rain gods and fertility gods; and made images of them to which they prayed and bowed. All this is completely incomprehensible to us. This worship must have provided the people with a mystical experience which gave them a superb sense of bliss or supposed contact with other-worldly forces. (See *Ramban, Shemos* 20:3.) Whatever it may have been, we do not understand it, and it has not existed since the beginning of the Second Temple Era.

The Vilna Gaon (HaGra) frequently writes (see commentary on *Seder Olam* 29) that the *yetzer hara* of idolatry was related to the power of prophecy. Once the evil inclination for idol worship was eliminated, the power of prophecy ended as well. With the passing of the prophets, Chaggai, Zechariah, and Malachi, the era of prophecy ended, and with it the *Tanach* was completed. Although we find Talmudic statements regarding individuals who still heard a *bas kol,* and certainly the inspiration of *ruach hakodesh* never ceased to exist among great *tzaddikim,* nevertheless, actual prophecy, whereby *HaKadosh Baruch Hu* communicates directly with an individual, had ceased. The Gemara (*Megillah* 3a) says that even Daniel was not a prophet. However, Ezra, according to the opinion that he was identified with Malachi, was a prophet (*Megillah* 15a). Even *Megillas Esther* was not written with prophecy, but rather with *ruach hakodesh*. (See *Megillah* 7a.)

The Talmud (*Megillah* 14a) tells us that הַרְבֵּה נְבִיאִים עָמְדוּ לָהֶם לְיִשְׂרָאֵל כִּפְלַיִם כְּיוֹצְאֵי מִצְרָיִם, *Numerous prophets arose for Israel, twice as many as the number of people coming out of Egypt.* This means that there were 1,200,000 prophets, although we enumerate only forty-eight prophets and seven prophetesses (those whose prophecies were relevant to future generations). This is truly astonishing. If I may say so, this vast number means there was a widespread "chemistry" of *koach hanevuah,* power of prophecy, extant in the Jewish *neshamah* (soul). Our forefathers, who experienced so many wondrous miracles such as the Exodus, Splitting the Sea, *Matan Torah,* and many more, consequently became permeated with this power. Even generations as late as those of the Babylonian Exile, who were contemporaries of the great later prophets such as Yechezkel and Yirmiyahu, and subsequently Chaggai, Zechariah, and Malachi, continued to be closely associated with prophecy which had become part of the spiritual makeup of the nation.

It is no wonder then that, originally, the Sages left the implementation of the positive commandment of *tefillah* to the individual. People were able to compose their own prayers as a result of their inherent power of prophecy. Potentially everyone could become a prophet.

By the way, this does not mean that they did not possess the same *yetzer hara* for *kinah* (jealousy), *taavah* (lust), or *kavod* (honor) as we do. We know of the existence of the "false prophets." The Torah (*Deuteronomy* 13:2) states that there may arise among the Jewish people false prophets and "dreamers" who attempt to influence individuals — or entire groups — to worship idols, etc. They may even perform "signs and wonders" to convince the people of their validity.

Nevertheless, as long as the *koach hanevuah* existed in the Jewish *neshamah,* the people were able to formulate their own prayers. Being thus imbued, the words simply sprang from their hearts. Therefore, for example, we have the Torah commandment of וְאָכַלְתָּ וְשָׂבָעְתָּ וּבֵרַכְתָּ, *You shall eat, and be satisfied, and bless,* but the Torah left the exact wording of *Bircas HaMazon* unspecified. The Talmud (*Berachos* 48b) tells us that although Moshe instituted the first blessing (*Hazan*), Yehoshua instituted the second (*Ha'aretz*), and Dovid HaMelech instituted the blessing to rebuild Jerusalem, the exact wording of these blessings was still left to the individual to formulate.

INTRODUCTION ❧ xxvii

However, this was no longer possible after the cessation of the power of prophecy, and so the Sages had to formalize specific texts for all blessings and prayers.

It is significant that the *Anshei Knesses HaGedolah* formulated the basic text of the *tefillos* which we have today most probably *even before* prophecy disappeared. מֵאָה וְעֶשְׂרִים זְקֵנִים וּבָהֶם כַּמָּה נְבִיאִים תִּיקְּנוּ שְׁמוֹנֶה עֶשְׂרֵה בְּרָכוֹת עַל הַסֵּדֶר, *One hundred twenty elders — among them several prophets — instituted the order of the berachos in the Shemoneh Esrei* (Megillah 17b). They had prepared for the coming decline even while prophecy still existed.

We find in *Pirkei Avos* 1:1 the famous dicta of the *Anshei Knesses HaGedolah*: הֱווּ מְתוּנִים בַּדִּין וְהַעֲמִידוּ תַלְמִידִים הַרְבֵּה, וַעֲשׂוּ סְיָג לַתּוֹרָה, *Be deliberate in judgment; develop many disciples; and make a fence (laws of protection) for the Torah.* These three declarations were clearly intended for the ensuing period where the sages and leaders of the generation would no longer merit prophecy.

When judges had the insight of prophecy, they could discern immediately who was right or wrong. They did not need lengthy deliberations. However, once they no longer had the benefit of prophecy, they had to be very careful and deliberate before arriving at their *psak din*. So the word went out: הֱווּ מְתוּנִים בַּדִּין, *be deliberate in judgment.*

The *Anshei Knesses HaGedolah* further advised, הַעֲמִידוּ תַלְמִידִים הַרְבֵּה, *develop many disciples.* This was *not* previously the general practice regarding all Torah topics. The Mishnah (*Chagigah* 11b) tells us that there are certain areas of study which belong to the *sodos haTorah,* such as *Maaseh Bereishis* and *Maaseh Merkavah,* which are not suitable for general study, but were intended only for selected individuals who are well versed in the Kabbalistic wisdom which was handed down by the prophets. The entire story of *Maaseh Bereishis* which we find in the Torah conceals the underlying secrets of Creation which were left for Oral Torah, and is of such an esoteric nature as to be suitable only for the select few. In the case of *Maaseh Merkavah,* which deals with angels and the Throne of Glory, only highly qualified individuals are eligible for its study. So these areas of Torah were *not* to be taught to "many disciples." We find the term *bnei haneviim* used in connection with the prophet Eliyahu (*Melachim II* 2:3) and other prophets. These were the disciples, a few select individuals. However, once prophecy was eliminated, the dictum was issued: הַעֲמִידוּ תַלְמִידִים הַרְבֵּה, the more, the better. This was because, with the absence of prophecy, Torah scholarship was such that, רַק אֶחָד מֵאֶלֶף יוֹצֵא לְהוֹרָאָה, *only one out of a thousand students is suitable to become a* בַּעַל הוֹרָאָה (halachic decisor) (*Midrash Koheles* 7:28). So it was necessary to teach a great number of disciples, in the hope that a few would emerge as *poskim* and learned leaders.

Finally, עֲשׂוּ סְיָג לַתּוֹרָה, there arose the need to *make a fence for the Torah.*

During the era of prophecy there was no need for formalized *siyagim*, fences. As an example, the Torah says, וְשָׁמְרוּ בְנֵי יִשְׂרָאֵל אֶת הַשַּׁבָּת, which means, "watch the Shabbos." In addition to the thirty-nine *melachos* themselves, there is the requirement to watch and protect the laws of Shabbos from being violated. (See *Mechilta, Parashas Bo* 12:17.) This is the source of all the Rabbinic injunctions of Shabbos. For instance, doing business on Shabbos is prohibited Rabbinically because of the ruling: lest one write; to ride an animal is prohibited by the decree: lest one tears off a twig to use as a switch. During the time when prophecy permeated *Klal Yisrael*, these restrictions were self-understood. Shabbos was a day of rest for man and beast. Those of that era understood what Shabbos meant. Under special circumstances they might ride an animal on Shabbos. We find an example in the case of the Shunamite woman (*Melachim II* 4:22) where she asks her husband for a donkey so she can ride to the Man of God. Whereupon, her husband asks her, מַדּוּעַ אַתְּ הֹלֶכֶת אֵלָיו הַיּוֹם לֹא חֹדֶשׁ וְלֹא שַׁבָּת (ibid. v.23). Not knowing the urgency of the situation, he wondered why she would go to the *Ish HaElokim* on a day that was neither Shabbos nor Rosh Chodesh. Here we see clearly that they *would* ride on Shabbos under exceptional circumstances. In order to seek advice from an *Ish HaElokim* they would ride. While their instinctive *koach hanevuah* made them understand that it was against the spirit of Shabbos to ride an animal, it was not yet prohibited as a general *siyag*, and therefore, would have been permitted for extenuating circumstances.

However, with the elimination of *nevuah*, the *Anshei Knesses HaGedolah* found it necessary to make סְיָג לַתּוֹרָה, to erect barriers, and make definite decrees to replace the heretofore instinctive protection for the Torah. Now certain activities would be prohibited by *gezeirah* under all circumstances [with very limited exceptions].

In summary, the *Anshei Knesses HaGedolah* formulated the basic text of our prayers in anticipation of the cessation of prophecy, which had been inherent in the spiritual makeup of *klal Yisrael*, and would cease to exist concurrent with the elimination of the *yetzer hara* for idolatry.

In *Kovetz Igros* 1:209, the Chazon Ish states that the fact that we do not have the evil inclination for idolatry does not make us greater than our forefathers who did possess it. On the contrary, it makes us lesser individuals. We no longer have to struggle against the powerful desire to be idolatrous, so we are not able to fulfill the mitzvah of הִשָּׁמְרוּ לָכֶם פֶּן יִפְתֶּה לְבַבְכֶם וְסַרְתֶּם וַעֲבַדְתֶּם אֱלֹהִים אֲחֵרִים, *Beware for yourselves, lest your heart be seduced and you turn astray and serve gods of others* (*Devarim* 11:16). Although we do struggle against non belief and atheism which is wide spread in the world today, it still does not compare to the constant and overwhelming urge for idol worship which our ancestors faced.

We know that our daily prayers were established by the Sages to correspond to the daily *tamid* sacrifice (*Berachos* 26a). תְּפִלּוֹת כְּנֶגֶד תְּמִידִים תִּקְּנוּם, *The prayers were instituted corresponding to the tamid offerings.* Our *tefillah* makes it possible for a person to come close to Hashem just as a *korban* — which comes from the word *karov* — brings a person close to *HaKadosh Baruch Hu*. The Vilna Gaon (*Peirush* to *Shir HaShirim* 1:16) raises the obvious question: If *tefillah* can bring us close to Hashem, why do we need *korbanos*? We close our *tefillos* with the words: יְהִי רָצוֹן... שֶׁיִּבָּנֶה בֵּית הַמִּקְדָּשׁ בִּמְהֵרָה בְיָמֵינוּ... וְשָׁם נַעֲבָדְךָ בְּיִרְאָה כִּימֵי עוֹלָם וּכְשָׁנִים קַדְמוֹנִיּוֹת, *May it be Your will ... that the Holy Temple be rebuilt speedily in our days ... and may we serve You with reverence, as in days of old and in former years.* This means that for now we are using prayer as a means of coming close to *HaKadosh Baruch Hu,* but we pray that eventually we may be able to resume the *avodah* in the *Beis HaMikdash* (Holy Temple). What superior quality does the *korban* have that *tefillah* does not possess? The answer given by the Vilna Gaon is that while *tefillah* makes it possible for us to obtain *selichah* (forgiveness), *mechilah* (pardon), and *kapparah* (atonement), and we can indeed come very close to Hashem, nevertheless, the wrongs which we have done still exist. However, the *korban* causes the wrongdoing to disappear. This is what the Torah calls רֵיחַ נִיחוֹחַ לַה׳, *a pleasing aroma for Hashem*. This is why we yearn to bring *korbanos* in addition to our *tefillos*. There will then be no more *mechitzah* (separation) between the *neshamah* and *HaKadosh Baruch Hu*.

We are, therefore, not surprised to find that the order of the *tefillos* closely follows the architecture of the *Beis HaMikdash*. To begin with, the entrance of the *Beis HaMikdash* was through the *Ezras Nashim,* where people would assemble before the doors were opened. Thus, we find (*Psalms* 134:1): הִנֵּה בָּרְכוּ אֶת ה׳, כָּל עַבְדֵי ה׳ הָעֹמְדִים בְּבֵית ה׳ בַּלֵּילוֹת, *Behold, bless Hashem, all you servants of Hashem, who stand in the House of Hashem in the nights.* Now, we know there is no sacrificial service at night. The doors of the *Heichal* were not opened, and the *avodah* did not commence until the signal was given that the day had begun (*Tamid* 30a). These *avdei Hashem* were gathered in the *Ezras Nashim* in the early predawn hours in eager anticipation of the opening of the *Heichal* doors. While they were there, many would either be reciting *Psalms* or otherwise beseeching Hashem, while some might be learning Torah. This was the place where the king read from the Torah during *Hakheil,* as well as the place of *simchas beis hasho'evah*. In short, it was a place of general assembly.

This place of general gathering, the *Ezras Nashim,* corresponds to the part of our *siddur* which precedes the actual *Shacharis* service: אֲדוֹן עוֹלָם, בִּרְכַּת נְטִילַת יָדַיִם, אֲשֶׁר יָצַר, אֱלֹהַי נְשָׁמָה.

During this period before the *tefillah,* some people might also say *Psalms* or *techinos;* others may say *maamados*. All of these are similar to the activities which took place in the *Ezras Nashim* prior to the opening of the doors of the *Heichal*.

It is also striking that, corresponding to the fifteen steps which lead up from the *Ezras Nashim* to the Israelite Courtyard, we find the fifteen *Birchos HaShachar*, starting from *Who gave the heart understanding,* and ending with *Who bestows beneficent kindnesses on His people Yisrael.* This last blessing corresponds to our impending arrival at the Israelite Courtyard, access to which is limited to the Jewish people.

Now, as we proceed, we are facing the great entrance gates to the *Azarah,* called the Gates of Nikanor, leaving the entire non-Jewish world behind us. This area begins the camp of the *Shechinah* and is off limits to the rest of the world (see *Keilim* 1:8 with *Rash*). At this point in our prayers, we allude to this by continuing with: רִבּוֹן כָּל הָעוֹלָמִים ... הֲלֹא כָל הַגִּבּוֹרִים כְּאַיִן לְפָנֶיךָ וְאַנְשֵׁי הַשֵּׁם כְּלֹא הָיוּ ... אֲבָל אֲנַחְנוּ עַמְּךָ בְּנֵי בְרִיתֶךָ בְּנֵי אַבְרָהָם אֹהַבְךָ ... זֶרַע יִצְחָק יְחִידוֹ ... עֲדַת יַעֲקֹב בִּנְךָ בְּכוֹרֶךָ וכו׳, *Master of all worlds!* ... *Are not all the mighty like nothing before You, the famous as if they had never existed ... But we are Your people, members of Your covenant, children of Avraham, Your beloved ... the offspring of Yitzchak, his only son ... the community of Yaakov, Your firstborn son,* etc. We continue with שְׁמַע יִשְׂרָאֵל, *Shema,* and end with בָּרוּךְ אַתָּה ה׳ מְקַדֵּשׁ אֶת שִׁמְךָ בָּרַבִּים, *Blessed are You, Hashem, Who sanctifies Your Name among the multitudes,* which is a special *berachah* for *kiddush Hashem*.

We now find ourselves in the *Ezras Yisrael,* the Israelite Courtyard. This area, eleven *amos* deep, is the portion of the *Azarah* designated exclusively for *Bnei Yisrael.* It is to this area that we allude in our ongoing *tefillah* of: אַתָּה הוּא ה׳ אֱלֹהֵינוּ ... קַבֵּץ קוֹיֶךָ מֵאַרְבַּע כַּנְפוֹת הָאָרֶץ ... בָּעֵת הַהִיא אָבִיא אֶתְכֶם וגו׳, *It is You, Who are Hashem, our God ... Gather in those who yearn for You, from the four corners of the earth ... At that time I will bring you* etc. We pray that the time may come when we will again be together in this place.

Continuing forward, we reach the עֶזְרַת כֹּהֲנִים, the area reserved for *Kohanim* only, the beginning of which was delineated by a platform, called "*duchan,*" which consisted of three steps, where the threefold blessing, called *Bircas Kohanim,* was said (see *Middos* 2:46). At this point, we, correspondingly, say the threefold *birchos haTorah,* followed by the threefold *Bircas Kohanim* (*Bamidbar* 6:24-6:27). This is then followed by the Mishnah: אֵלּוּ דְבָרִים שֶׁאֵין לָהֶם שִׁעוּר, *These are the precepts that have no prescribed measure,* etc. (*Shabbos* 127a). In this manner we have followed the threefold blessing over the Torah with a threefold selection from its three parts: *Mikra,* Mishnah, and Gemara.

Direcly ahead lies the מִזְבֵּחַ, *the Altar.* Correspondingly, it is here that we say the פָּרָשַׁת הַתָּמִיד, the portion of the Torah regarding the daily *korban* offerings, and the Mishnaic chapter, אֵיזֶהוּ מְקוֹמָן, containing all the basic *halachos* of the *korbanos*.

Further on, beyond the *Mizbe'ach*, is an area called בֵּין הָאוּלָם וְלַמִּזְבֵּחַ, *between the Ulam Hall and the Mizbe'ach*, which has an even higher קְדֻשָּׁה (see *Keilim* Ch. 1, mishnah 9). Here there are twelve steps leading up to the *Ulam Hall*, the Antechamber (*Middos* 3:6), which, counting the floor, totals thirteen steps.

Therefore, very fittingly, it is at this point that we say the *baraisa*: רַבִּי יִשְׁמָעֵאל אוֹמֵר: בִּשְׁלֹשׁ עֶשְׂרֵה מִדּוֹת וכו', *Rabbi Yishmael says: Through thirteen rules*, etc. (Intro. to *Sifra*).

We are now at the *Ulam*, the Antechamber leading to the *Heichal*. In Zechariah 86:11-14, we find that the *Navi* was commanded to make two crowns of gold and silver, which were eventually to be used for the *Melech HaMashiach* and the *Kohen Gadol*. These crowns were placed in the windows in the ceiling of the *Heichal*. The Mishnah (*Middos* 3:8) tells us that the young *Kohanim*, "*Pirchei Kehunah*," would climb up the golden chains that hung from the ceiling of the *Ulam*, to see these crowns. These chains are alluded to by the words of the *Pesukei d'Zimrah*, which are linked and interconnected like a chain. (Ed. note: See comments on יְהִי כְבוֹד.)

We are introduced to the *Ulam* at בָּרוּךְ שֶׁאָמַר, *Baruch She'amar*, which corresponds to the *Pesach HaUlam*, its entrance, and continue on with the *Pesukei d'Zimrah*, corresponding to the *Ulam* itself. At the conclusion of *Pesukei d'Zimrah*, we symbolically leave the *Ulam* by saying יִשְׁתַּבַּח, *Yishtabach*. We then arrive, symbolically, at the *Pesach HaHeichal*, the entrance of the *Heichal*, which is very similar to the *Pesach HaUlam*. For this reason, the words of *Baruch She'amar* and *Yishtabach* are very similar.

We now enter the *Heichal*, the "Holy Palace." On our right we find the *Shulchan*, on the left the *Menorah*. These are represented by the two *berachos* of *Krias Shema*: first, יוֹצֵר אוֹר וּבוֹרֵא חֹשֶׁךְ, *Who forms light and creates darkness*, corresponding to the *Shulchan*, which represents the material revelation of *HaKadosh Baruch Hu* in our lives; second, אַהֲבָה רַבָּה, *with abundant love*, which asks for understanding of Torah, corresponding to the *Menorah*, which represents the spiritual revelation of *HaKadosh Baruch Hu* through Torah.

There are two ways in which to achieve the love and fear of Hashem. One way is the physical approach, as we find in *Rambam* (*Hilchos Yesodei HaTorah* 232). There he describes how, upon reflecting on the awesomeness of the entire physical world and the grandeur of the Creation, one is overcome with the desire to become close to the Creator. This approach is reflected in the *berachah* of *Yotzeir Ohr*, alluding to the *Shulchan*, which represents our physical life.

The other method is to find Him through *talmud Torah*, learning Torah, which is reflected in the *berachah* of *Ahavah Rabbah*, and this is symbolized by the *Menorah*.

We now reach the *Mizbach HaKetores,* the purpose of which is to produce רֵיחַ נִיחוֹחַ לַה׳, *a pleasant scent to Hashem,* symbolizing pure *ahavas Hashem v'yiraso.* While the Outer *Mizbe'ach* is where we approach *HaKadosh Baruch Hu* with our material-physical existence, including our food and joy, as expressed by *menachos* and *nesachim,* here at the *Mizbach HaKetores* we offer our *neshamah* to Hashem. At this point in our *tefillah* we say *Shema Yisrael,* in which we are commanded to give even our lives to *HaKadosh Baruch Hu,* when we say וְאָהַבְתָּ אֵת ה׳ אֱלֹהֶיךָ בְּכָל לְבָבְךָ וּבְכָל נַפְשְׁךָ וּבְכָל מְאֹדֶךָ, *You shall love Hashem, your God, with all your heart, with all your soul, and with all your resources (Devarim 6:5).*

We now advance to the great *Paroches* adjacent to the *Kodesh HaKadashim.* This is symbolized in our *tefillah* of *Geulah,* where we recognize the Hand of *HaKadosh Baruch Hu* in bringing us close to Him through *yetzias Mitzrayim,* and we pray for the future *geulah* (redemption). The *halachah* requires us to be *someich geulah l'tefillah,* to join the Redemption Blessing to Prayer, and to immediately begin *Shemoneh Esrei.* The Exodus from Egypt took place through the personal intervention of Hashem, as we read in the *Haggadah:* אֲנִי וְלֹא מַלְאָךְ אֲנִי וְלֹא שָׂרָף אֲנִי וְלֹא הַשָּׁלִיחַ אֲנִי הוּא וְלֹא אַחֵר, *Myself, and not an angel; Myself and not a seraph; Myself and not a messenger, I and none other.* At the redemption from Egypt, there was such a clear manifestation of the *yad Hashem,* Hand of God, that no other explanation for the *nissim* (miracles) of the *geulah* was possible. We, too, are to begin our *tefillah* with this same clarity of *emunah* (faith).

Finally, we are now symbolically in the *Kodesh HaKadashim* alone with the *Ribbono Shel Olam.* This is what is meant when *Chazal* say that during *Shemoneh Esrei* one should be מְכַוֵּן לִבּוֹ כְּנֶגֶד בֵּית קָדְשֵׁי הַקֳּדָשִׁים, *He should concentrate his thoughts towards the Holy of Holies.*

When the silent prayer is completed, we take three steps backwards: back to the *Heichal,* back to the *Ulam,* back to the *Azarah.* It is here that we repeat the *Shemoneh Esrei* in the place where the *tzibbur* gathered. Finally, as we continue to exit, we find ourselves back in the *Ezras Nashim,* where we say *techinos, selichos, krias haTorah, Kedushah d'sidra, mizmorei Tehillim* etc.

This, then, gives us an idea of the organization of our *tefillos* by our Sages and *Neviim* who used the architecture of the *Beis HaMikdash* as a blueprint for the order in which we are to be *mispallel.* This is why we call our prayer book *siddur,* which literally means "order," because the order of the *tefillah* is of the essence.

With this introduction, let us now start to explain our *tefillos.*

אֲדוֹן עוֹלָם / Adon Olam

The exact origin of this *tefillah* is unclear. According to some opinions, it was formulated by the *Geonim*, and according to others it was written by Rabbi Shlomo ibn Gabirol. Regardless of who actually wrote the text, the overriding question that must be addressed is why the *mesadrei hatefillah*, those who organized our *tefillah*, chose *Adon Olam* with which to begin our daily *tefillah* in the morning, and with which to end our bedtime *Krias Shema* at night. To do so, let us focus on the first word: אֲדוֹן, *Adon*.

The most important word in all of our *tefillos* is the Name of *HaKadosh Baruch Hu*. In place of the Ineffable Name, which is written י־ה־ו־ה, we use *Adonoi* (my Master), the first person of the word אֲדוֹן. This word is written with a *cholam*, which can be pronounced variously as: "OH" or "OI" or "AW," depending on individual *minhagim*. However, it certainly is not pronounced "EE." Consequently, the often mispronounced word "Ahdeenoy" is *not* the Name of *HaKadosh Baruch Hu* and is totally meaningless. The use of this word for *Shem HaKadosh* is a travesty, and those who pronounce it this way should be corrected. Since the word *Adonoi* is our substitute for the Ineffable Name, it must be used only for *tefillah*, or when learning Torah, which involves the use of God's Name.

The use of the plural form of *Adon* — namely, *Adonim*, which becomes *Adonoi* in the first person — even if it refers to a single master, is common in *lashon hakodesh*. Literally, it means a single individual, who is a master of many slaves. For instance, we find אֲדֹנֵי יוֹסֵף (*Bereishis* 39:20), which describes Joseph's master, an individual, who was also a master of many other slaves. Likewise, we find וְאִם אֲדוֹנִים אָנִי, *And if I am a Master* (*Malachi* 1:6).

So we use the plural *Adonoi* and also *Elohim* when referring to *HaKadosh Baruch Hu* in the "Majestic Plural" sense. We personalize this "Mastership" by using *Adonoi* meaning "my personal Master."

The Talmud (*Berachos* 7b) tells us that the first person to use the word *Adonoi* when referring to Hashem was Avraham Avinu: אָמַר ר׳ יוֹחָנָן מִשּׁוּם ר׳ שִׁמְעוֹן בֶּן יוֹחַאי: מִיּוֹם שֶׁבָּרָא הקב״ה אֶת הָעוֹלָם לֹא הָיָה אָדָם שֶׁקְּרָאוֹ להקב״ה אָדוֹן עַד שֶׁבָּא אַבְרָהָם וּקְרָאוֹ אָדוֹן שֶׁנֶּאֱמַר: וַיֹּאמַר אֲדֹנָי אֱלֹהִים בַּמָּה אֵדַע כִּי אִירָשֶׁנָּה, *R' Yochanan said in the name of R' Shimon ben Yochai: From the day the Holy One, Blessed is He, created the world, there was no person who called the Holy One, Blessed is He, "Lord," until Avraham came and called Him "Lord." As it is stated: "And he said: My Lord Hashem/Elohim: Whereby shall I know that I am to inherit it?"* (*Bereishis* 15:8).

The Gemara there continues:

אָמַר רַב: אַף דָּנִיֵּאל לֹא נַעֲנָה אֶלָּא בִּשְׁבִיל אַבְרָהָם, שֶׁנֶּאֱמַר: וְעַתָּה שְׁמַע אֱלֹהֵינוּ אֶל תְּפִלַּת עַבְדְּךָ וְאֶל תַּחֲנוּנָיו וְהָאֵר פָּנֶיךָ עַל מִקְדָּשְׁךָ הַשָּׁמֵם לְמַעַן אֲדֹנָי, *Rav said: Daniel too was answered only because of the merit of Avraham, for it is stated: "And now, pay heed, our God, to the prayer of Your servant and to his supplications, and let Your countenance shine upon Your desolate Temple for the sake of my Lord."*

This means that even Daniel's pleas were heard only when he referred to *HaKadosh Baruch Hu* as *Adonoi*, meaning: "Answer me in the *zechus* (merit) of Avraham, who first called You *Adon*." We quote this as part of our *techinos* (supplications) on Mondays and Thursdays in וְהוּא רַחוּם.

The world had to wait until Avraham Avinu discovered that *HaKadosh Baruch Hu* should be addressed as *Adonoi*. What did he discover, that none of his illustrious ancestors — Mesushelach, or Noach, or Shem — knew?

To understand this, we must analyze the true meaning of *Adon* (master). A master has a personal relationship with his servant. Whenever the servant performs his duties, he is directly serving his master. By way of contrast, a *melech* (king) has only a very general relationship with his subjects, because he has an entire nation to govern, and very few people know him personally. We refer to *HaKadosh Baruch Hu* as *Melech HaOlam* in all of our *berachos,* and a *berachah* is not complete without this reference. However, we preface this appellation with *Baruch Atah Adonoi,* meaning that we recognize *HaKadosh Baruch Hu* as our Master, before referring to Him as the King of the universe. So, when addressing *HaKadosh Baruch Hu,* we recognize first that He is "my personal Master," with whom I have a personal relationship — He knows me! Then we acknowledge that *my Master* is the King of the universe.

So while the earlier great *tzaddikim* recognized Hashem as *Melech HaOlam,* the Universal King, it was only Avraham Avinu who recognized that the *Adon* of the world is really *Adonoi,* each individual's personal Master. He taught that while *HaKadosh Baruch Hu* is the *Melech HaOlam,* nevertheless, he is aware of each individual, akin to the relationship of a servant to his master, and thus each individual has a personal relationship to *HaKadosh Baruch Hu.*

This personal relationship of *HaKadosh Baruch Hu* with His creatures applies not only to human beings, but also to the universe as a whole. We are aware that there are billions of stars in billions of galaxies in the cosmos, yet *HaKadosh Baruch Hu* has a personal relationship with each one of them, and He has a purpose for each one of them. This is the meaning of the words we repeat daily in *Pesukei d'Zimrah*: מוֹנֶה מִסְפָּר לַכּוֹכָבִים לְכֻלָּם שֵׁמוֹת יִקְרָא, *He counts the number of the stars, to all of them He assigns names (Psalms 147:4).* To Him all these billions of heavenly bodies are just מִסְפָּר, a small number, because He has a personal relationship with each one. "To all of them He assigns names" means each one has a purpose. So when a person stands before Hashem in *tefillah,* he should know that while *HaKadosh Baruch Hu* is truly the *Melech HaOlam,* the King of the universe, He nevertheless has a personal relationship with each individual; He is *Adonoi,* my Master.

I heard a story from Rav Yosef Breuer, which he told about his father, my Rebbe, Rav Shlomo Zalman (Solomon) Breuer. The elder Rav Breuer was a very good friend of Rav Shimon Sofer, the Rav of Cracow, a brother of the *Ksav Sofer,* and a son of the *Chasam Sofer.* Once when the two friends met, Rav Shimon Sofer asked Rav Breuer to tell him a short *"vort"* from his father-in-law, Rav Samson R. Hirsch. Upon which, Rav Breuer told him that Rav Hirsch would point out that while *Adon Olam* describes the unfathomable eternity and omnipotence of Hashem, it nevertheless makes reference to Him in a very personal way: וְהוּא אֵלִי, *He is My God.* Each person in his *tefillah* says: "I have a personal relationship with *HaKadosh Baruch Hu,* He is my personal God."

Therefore, whenever a person says the word *Adonoi,* my Master, no matter how small he thinks he is, he is in direct contact with God. This thought is the introduction to any individual's *iyun tefillah,* concentration on prayer. There is nothing mystical or supernatural about it. It should be the most natural thing in the world. Someone once asked me how one *davens* with *kavannah* (intent), for one simply cannot concentrate for so long. I advised him to simply start by saying *Baruch Atah Adonoi,* and to concentrate on its meaning. He should continue with this thought every time these words occur. If a person practices this often enough, his *kavannah* will eventually flow over to the rest of the *tefillos.*

We can now understand why our days start and end with *Adon Olam,* which expresses the most basic concept of our *tefillos,* that no matter how insignificant we may be, no matter how full of shortcomings we are, we still have the right to approach *HaKadosh Baruch Hu* directly. The אָדוֹן of all creation is אֵלִי, my personal God. We fall asleep each night with the words: בְּיָדוֹ אַפְקִיד רוּחִי בְּעֵת אִישָׁן וְאָעִירָה, *I entrust my spirit into His hand when I go to sleep and when I am awake.* Despite the fact that we live in a dangerous world, and do not know what the next minute may bring, nevertheless, when we are about to drift off to sleep, we entrust our lives to Hashem's hands. To quote a prosaic commercial slogan, "Relax and leave the driving to us." So too, we should also have this feeling that we are in good hands, and place our complete trust in our *personal Adon.* Therefore, we close our eyes at night and say: אֲדֹנָי לִי וְלֹא אִירָא, *Hashem is with me, I shall not fear.*

If *iyun tefillah* teaches nothing but what to think when we say *Baruch Atah Adonoi,* and to say it with meaning, the ensuing *tefillah* will result in אוֹכֵל

פֵּרוֹתֵיהֶם בָּעוֹלָם הַזֶּה וְהַקֶּרֶן קַיֶּמֶת לוֹ לָעוֹלָם הַבָּא, [these are the the precepts whose] *fruits a person enjoys in this world but whose principal remains intact for him in the World to Come.* Now let us examine this *shir* of *Adon Olam* in detail.

It immediately strikes us that the first three lines are based on the familiar words: ה׳ מֶלֶךְ, ה׳ מָלַךְ, ה׳ יִמְלֹךְ, *Hashem reigns, Hashem reigned, Hashem shall reign for all eternity.*

In the first line we have: אֲדוֹן עוֹלָם אֲשֶׁר מָלַךְ, *Master of the universe Who reigned;*

In the second: אֲזַי מֶלֶךְ שְׁמוֹ נִקְרָא, *[since] then as "King" is His Name proclaimed;*

And in the third: לְבַדּוֹ יִמְלוֹךְ נוֹרָא, *He, the Awesome One, will reign alone.*

So, at the very beginning of our *tefillah,* we affirm our *emunah* that HaKadosh Baruch Hu always did, and does now, and will always, reign over the universe. He is eternal and not limited by time or space.

However, the last part of the first line presents a problem: He reigned בְּטֶרֶם כָּל יְצִיר נִבְרָא, *before any form was created.* Over whom did He reign? How can there be a *Melech HaOlam,* a king without anything over which to reign?

By way of response, let us introduce a concept of which — although it is Kabbalistic — we should have, at least, some rudimentary knowledge. The *Chachmei HaKabbalah* explain that there are four distinct worlds.

The first is the *Olam Ha'asiyah,* which is our world, the known universe. The word *oseh* always connotes putting the finishing touches on something which has previously been made. Thus, וַיְכַל אֱלֹהִים ... אֲשֶׁר עָשָׂה, *God completed . . . which He had done* (Genesis 2:2).

On the next level, there is the *Olam Hayetzirah.* This is the world "in formation," where HaKadosh Baruch Hu structures and forms the things which will eventually exist in the *Olam Ha'asiyah.*

The third level is the *Olam Haberiyah.* This is the world of creation from nothing, the world of *yeish mei'ayin.* In physical terms, this is the beginning of existence.

We refer to *Olam Hayetzirah* and *Olam Haberiyah* in the words: אֲדוֹן עוֹלָם אֲשֶׁר מָלַךְ בְּטֶרֶם כָּל יְצִיר נִבְרָא, *Master of the universe, Who reigned before any form was created.* He reigned even before the existence of *Olam Hayetzirah* and *Olam Haberiyah.* This refers to His reign over the highest "world," as follows.

The fourth level, which is the highest world, and is something of which we have no understanding, is called the *Olam Ha'atzilus.* This is the world before Creation, the world which is *eitzel,* adjacent to, HaKadosh Baruch Hu. We find this in *Bamidbar* (11:17), וְאָצַלְתִּי מִן הָרוּחַ אֲשֶׁר עָלֶיךָ, which means that Hashem tells Moshe, "I will cause the Sanhedrin to share some of your *ruach hakodesh.*" Some understanding of this concept can be derived from a careful perusal of the *peirush* of Rav Samson Raphael Hirsch on the second word in the Torah, בָּרָא, *bara*. He explains that this word has the general meaning of bringing something from the inside to the outside, from nonexistence to existence. Rav Hirsch must be alluding here to this *Olam Ha'atzilus*, without specifically saying so. So the meaning of בְּרֵאשִׁית בָּרָא אֱלֹהִים, *In the beginning of God creating*, is that before *HaKadosh Baruch Hu* created anything, before *yeish mei'ayin*, He had what we would call, in human terms, "a plan" of what to create. This "plan" was then brought forth from His "mind." This is what the Torah calls *bara*, creating. This revelation (*bara*) is what brought the *Olam Ha'atzilus* into existence.

In Kabbalistic terms, this "plan," or first revelation of *HaKadosh Baruch Hu*, is called "*Chochmah*" (infinite wisdom). He revealed firstly that He exists; without this revelation His existence would be unknown. He also revealed what is called His "*Binah*" as well as a combination of "*Chochmah*" and "*Binah*" which is called "*Daas.*" Now, in order to bring something forth, or to reveal it, there must be something to which it can be revealed, a receptacle. It is this completely spiritual "receptacle" which is called *Olam Ha'atzilus*. These thoughts are so completely awe inspiring that it is very difficult to talk about them.

Therefore, the meaning of אֲדוֹן עוֹלָם אֲשֶׁר מָלַךְ בְּטֶרֶם כָּל יְצִיר נִבְרָא is that *HaKadosh Baruch Hu* reigned over the completely spiritual forces of *Olam Ha'atzilus*, to whom He revealed His existence and His "plans for Creation." He thus reigned before יְצִיר נִבְרָא, *any form was created*, before He brought anything into existence, *yeish mei'ayin*, *ex nihilo*, from the "inside" to the "outside."

The revelation by *HaKadosh Baruch Hu* of His plan for Creation to the spiritual forces of *Olam Ha'atzilus* is called "Torah" by *Chazal* in their veiled language, and it is this which is meant by the statement that "Torah was created before Creation of the world" (*Shabbos* 88b). Furthermore, we find in the Midrash that *HaKadosh Baruch Hu* looked into the Torah and created the world (*Bereishis Rabbah* Ch. 1). Here, too, *Chazal* are referring to the *blueprint of the world*, which is called Torah.

These plans were then implemented through the *asarah ma'amaros* (ten utterances) during the six days of Creation, and resulted in the world we know today (see *Pirkei Avos* 5:1).

❦ ❦ ❦

§⇨ לְעֵת נַעֲשָׂה בְחֶפְצוֹ כֹּל אֲזַי מֶלֶךְ שְׁמוֹ נִקְרָא — **Then, when everything was done according to His will**, when our world, the *Olam Ha'asiyah*, came into existence, **He could be called Melech,** "King", first by the *malachim* (angels), and then by human beings.

ADON OLAM   7

◆§ וְאַחֲרֵי כִּכְלוֹת הַכֹּל לְבַדּוֹ יִמְלוֹךְ נוֹרָא — **And after everything comes to an end, He will reign alone. Awesome!** Rav Samson R. Hirsch in his *Siddur* explains that this is truly a most frightening — awesome — thought: that at any moment, *HaKadosh Baruch Hu* could put an end to all existence, but He himself would remain the same as He was before.

The word יִמְלוֹךְ, *He will reign,* refers to the *Olam Hatechiyah,* the world of the future *techiyas hameisim* (Resurrection of the Dead) about which we know almost nothing. כָּל הַנְּבִיאִים כּוּלָן לֹא נִתְנַבְּאוּ אֶלָּא לִימוֹת הַמָּשִׁיחַ אֲבָל לָעוֹלָם הַבָּא עַיִן לֹא רָאָתָה אֱלֹהִים זוּלָתְךָ, *All the prophets prophesied only about the Messianic era; but as for the World to Come: No eye except yours, O God, has seen* (*Berachos* 34b). After this world ends, there will be a new world, for those who merit it, and we pray that we will be among them. It is over this future world, the *Olam Hatechiyah,* that לְבַדּוֹ יִמְלוֹךְ נוֹרָא, *He, alone, will reign.* Truly an awesome concept.

◆§ וְהוּא הָיָה וְהוּא הֹוֶה וְהוּא יִהְיֶה בְּתִפְאָרָה — **It is He Who was, He Who is, and He Who shall remain, in splendor.** The *Shulchan Aruch, Orach Chaim* (*Siman* 5; see *Mishnah Berurah* ibid. §2) says that while we are forbidden to pronounce י-ה-ו-ה, the Ineffable Name of *HaKadosh Baruch Hu,* and, instead, we use the word *Adonoi,* which means He is the Master of everything, nevertheless, we should still concentrate on the meaning of the Name as it is written: י-ה-ו-ה, which is that *HaKadosh Baruch Hu* is Eternal: He was; He is; and He will be. Some of the *Acharonim,* as summarized by the *Mishnah Berurah,* are of the opinion that we are required to concentrate on the Eternal aspect of the Name of *HaKadosh Baruch Hu* only while saying *Shema Yisrael.* Otherwise, when making *berachos* or saying *tefillos,* when we pronounce *Adonoi,* it is sufficient to think only of the meaning: He is my Master and I am His servant. However, in any circumstances, it is important to keep in mind that one is not to simply "blurt out" the words of a *berachah* — וְלֹא יִזְרוֹק בְּרָכָה מִפִּיו, *one should not throw a blessing from his mouth* (*Berachos* 47a). So, when making a *berachah,* one should be cognizant of the fundamentally important meaning of the words *Baruch Atah Adonoi.*

◆§ וְהוּא אֶחָד — **He is [One] alone.** After affirming our *emunah* in the eternity of *HaKadosh Baruch Hu,* we here affirm His absolute Oneness, which is called *Achdus Hapeshutah.* This concept is very difficult for the human mind to comprehend because, to our minds, any number can be subdivided, even the number one . . . the number one can be subdivided into smaller units. However, the Oneness of *HaKadosh Baruch Hu* is absolute; nothing comparable exists.

These two aspects of *HaKadosh Baruch Hu,* His Eternal Existence and His Oneness, always go together, as is evidenced in the first two commandments of the *Aseres HaDibros* : אָנֹכִי ה' אֱלֹהֶיךָ, *I, Hashem, am Your God,* and

לֹא יִהְיֶה לְךָ, *Do not recognize (the gods of others)*, which are included in the same paragraph.

◆§ וְאֵין שֵׁנִי לְהַמְשִׁיל לוֹ לְהַחְבִּירָה — **There is none other to compare to Him, to declare as His equal.** God is not definable. Nor does He have a colleague to share His Divinity. This is in contradistinction to Christian theology.

◆§ בְּלִי רֵאשִׁית בְּלִי תַכְלִית — **He has no beginning and no end.** He is Infinite. This concept is incomprehensible to the human mind, but *HaKadosh Baruch Hu* revealed this tenet of our *emunah* to us, through His Torah.

◆§ וְלוֹ הָעֹז וְהַמִּשְׂרָה — **To Him belong all Power and Supremacy.** To the human mind, infinity, something without a beginning or an end, by definition, is nothing. Yet, *HaKadosh Baruch Hu* is Infinite, and has Supreme Power over everything else. The human mind cannot comprehend infinity, and certainly not the coexistence of the Infinity of *HaKadosh Baruch Hu* and His creation. Yet, this is what *HaKadosh Baruch Hu* has revealed about Himself, to us, through His Torah. And despite the fact that His Creation includes the free choice of human beings to rebel against His Will, and they do so, nevertheless, He alone is the Supreme Ruler of the destiny of the world.

◆§ וְהוּא אֵלִי וְחַי גֹּאֲלִי — **He is my God, my living Redeemer.** *He* — this Infinite, Incomprehensible, Supremely Powerful Being, which defies our power of conception — *is my God!* He has a personal relationship with me. The word אל always infers *middas harachamim* (the attribute of mercy). The fact that my mother conceived me, that I was born, and that I am able to function as a viable human being, are all attributable to His mercy. And if the *middas hadin* (attribute of justice) strikes, He is my Living Redeemer — as in וַאֲנִי יָדַעְתִּי גֹּאֲלִי חָי, *But I know that my Redeemer lives* (*Job* 19:25).

Rav Samson R. Hirsch explains (*Exodus* 6:6) that the word *go'eil* is found in the Torah in connection with someone who is so deeply in debt that he is forced to sell his property, and his closest relative comes to "bail him out," to redeem his property for him: וּבָא גֹאֲלוֹ הַקָּרֹב אֵלָיו, *his redeemer who is closest to him shall come* (*Vayikra* 25:25). The *go'eil* of a person is his closest relative. So what we mean here is: If I am the recipient of *rachamim* (mercy) in my life, then He is its source. But, if His *gezeiras hadin* (decree of judgment) were to strike, then I can look to Him as חַי גֹּאֲלִי, my closest living relative, Who will redeem me. However, if, in His Infinite Wisdom, He decides not to redeem me, and I do not experience the *rachamim,* and I suffer ח״ו, then:

◆§ וְצוּר חֶבְלִי בְּעֵת צָרָה — **He is the Rock of my pain in time of distress.** He gives me the strength to be able to bear and accept my suffering.

וְהוּא נִסִּי וּמָנוֹס לִי — He is my banner and my refuge. I look to *HaKadosh Baruch Hu* as my "banner," as in a battle, where one looks at a banner or standard for encouragement to continue the battle. The reference here could be to physical battles against one's enemies, or spiritual struggles with weaknesses, doubts, or temptations to do *aveiros*. Moshe Rabbeinu gave the name *Hashem Nisi* to the *mizbe'ach* which he erected after the victory over Amalek (*Shemos* 17:15). This name is explained by Rashi to mean God is the One Who performed the miracle which made me win. So, if I win, He is the cause of my victory. However, if I lose the battle, He is מָנוֹס לִי, *my refuge*, my escape. I will run right back to Him; I will be *chozer b'teshuvah*.

מְנָת כּוֹסִי בְּיוֹם אֶקְרָא — He is the portion in my cup, on the day I call. What we refer to in English as *fate* does not exist. Judaism teaches, instead, a concept called *hashgachah pratis*, which means that *HaKadosh Baruch Hu* has an individual relationship with every one of His creatures. He apportions a destiny to each individual, analogous to one who holds up his cup to be filled. Sometimes the cup is filled with something sweet, sometimes with something bitter, or a mixture of both. Sometimes the cup overflows, sometimes it barely receives anything. Some people receive a "rough deal" in life; they never make it, either in terms of health, or finances, or any success in their lives. However, this phrase means that I know that whenever I call to Him, and I hold up my cup for His answer, He always responds. I know that *HaKadosh Baruch Hu* is *shomei'a tefillah*, He hears my prayers. He always gives me an answer: sometimes in a way I understand, which makes me very grateful, and sometimes in a way I do not, because my mind is limited. My personal relationship with *HaKadosh Baruch Hu* gives me the right to be *mispallel* (pray) to Him, and I have *emunah* that He hears me.

There is a difference between *emunah* and *bitachon*. The *Chazon Ish* in his *sefer Emunah U'Bitachon* (2:1) explains that *emunah* (faith) is the *halachah*, that which we are required to do, and *bitachon* (trust) is the *ma'aseh*, the carrying out in practice of this *emunah*.

Emunah means that we are convinced that *HaKadosh Baruch Hu* has a personal relationship with each one of His creatures, and that when we are *mispallel* to Him, He listens to us. Our happiness comes from Him, as does our unhappiness. He wants us to be in contact with Him. This is the *halachah*, the way it should be.

Bitachon, the practical carrying out of this *emunah*, means entrusting our entire existence to *HaKadosh Baruch Hu*, and this is the meaning of the next stanza:

בְּיָדוֹ אַפְקִיד רוּחִי בְּעֵת אִישַׁן וְאָעִירָה — I entrust my spirit into His hand when I go to sleep and when I am awake. My body and my soul are in His hands. As I fall asleep, and lose my conscious existence, I fully entrust my "soul," my conscious life, to Him, and when I am awake, I trust that He will keep me alive, as long as He sees fit. I have the knowledge that I am in His hands during every period of my life.

וְעִם רוּחִי גְוִיָּתִי ה' לִי וְלֹא אִירָא — **And with my spirit, my body. Hashem is with me, I shall not fear.** I ask *HaKadosh Baruch Hu* that my *bitachon* in Him, my personal relationship with Him, shall be so secure that I will not have any fears. The real proof of *bitachon* is that one is unafraid. One cannot talk of "having *bitachon*" if he is fearful in the face of danger.

In *Shemoneh Esrei,* in עַל הַצַּדִּיקִים, we say: וְתֵן שָׂכָר טוֹב לְכָל הַבּוֹטְחִים בְּשִׁמְךָ בֶּאֱמֶת, *and give goodly reward to all who trust in Your Name in truth.* We ask *HaKadosh Baruch Hu* to reward those who "trust in Your Name *in truth.*" "Truly" trusting in *HaKadosh Baruch Hu* means having absolute trust in Him — even in the face of danger. If one thinks he has trust in *HaKadosh Baruch Hu,* but is still afraid, he has fooled himself, for this is not *bitachon be'emes* (sincere trust).

In *Havdalah* on *motza'ei Shabbos* we say, הִנֵּה אֵל יְשׁוּעָתִי אֶבְטַח וְלֹא אֶפְחָד, *Behold, God is my salvation, I shall trust and not fear* (*Yeshayahu* 12:2), which means, when I place my trust in the God of my salvation, I will not have any fear. True *bitachon* obviates fear. Here, at the end of *Adon Olam,* we finally use the word *Adonoi* referring, for the first time, to *HaKadosh Baruch Hu* as my Master. After having defined His role in our lives, and our personal relationship with Him, and having placed our complete trust in Him, our *tefillah* is that ה' לִי וְלֹא אִירָא, *Hashem is with me, I shall not fear,* that our level of *bitachon* shall be such that we will have nothing to fear. If a person has the *zechus* of reaching this level of *bitachon,* he is indeed very fortunate. It is with this thought of complete *bitachon* in *HaKadosh Baruch Hu* that we introduce our daily *tefillos.*

בִּרְכַּת עַל נְטִילַת יָדַיִם / Bircas Al Netilas Yadayim

It is a *mitzvah d'Rabbanan* for every Jewish person to wash his or her hands upon arising in the morning, and to recite the *berachah* of *al netilas yadayim*. There are different opinions as to the reason for this *mitzvah*. According to the *Rosh*, the reason is that during sleep one may have touched parts of the body which are usually covered, thus rendering himself unfit for *berachos* or *tefillah*.

According to the *Rashba*, the reason for *netilas yadayim* is that each morning a person receives a new gift of life, and thus becomes "newly born." This is based on the *pasuk*: חֲדָשִׁים לַבְּקָרִים רַבָּה אֱמוּנָתֶךָ, *They are new every morning; great is Your faithfulness!* (*Eichah* 3:23). Each morning we receive new life. So every morning we rededicate our lives to serving *HaKadosh Baruch Hu*, just as the *Kohanim* in the *Beis HaMikdash* did each morning, prior to beginning the *avodah*. Following this opinion, *netilas yadayim* becomes obligatory only upon daybreak.

Consequently, if one arises before dawn, such as on the days when *Selichos* are recited, one must wash *netilas yadayim* after daybreak.

In practice, to avoid a *safeik berachah* (a doubt concerning the requirement of reciting a *berachah*), if one does arise before dawn, he should wash his hands without a *berachah*, and later, after daybreak, wash again and make the *berachah* of *al netilas yadayim*. For this reason, after the *Selichos* are completed, our *kehillah* has the *minhag* (custom) that the *chazzan* announces in a loud voice, "*Al netilas yadayim*," to remind the congregation to wash their hands again before the beginning of *tefillas Shacharis*.

Another practical difference between the two opinions would occur if one were to sleep with gloves on, or when fully dressed — such as during an airplane flight — and thus would not touch any covered part of his body, or if one does not sleep at all during the night. According to the *Rosh*, one would then not be required to wash his hands, because they would not be contaminated. But, according to the *Rashba*, one would still be required to wash his hands, since the dawning of a new day requires one to rededicate himself to *avodas Hashem*. In such cases, we would wash the hands without the *berachah*, following the rule of *safeik berachah lehakeil*, when in doubt do not say the *berachah*, to avoid the possibility of uttering the *Shem Shamayim l'vatalah*, the Heavenly Name in vain.

According to our *minhag*, the *berachah* of *al netilas yadayim* is recited during the *tefillah,* following *Adon Olam.* This is an exception to the general rule that *berachos* for *mitzvos* are to be recited עוֹבֵר לַעֲשִׂיָּתָן, *before* performing the *mitzvah.* The reason for this exception is because in the morning, when we are still in a state of impurity, we are unfit to make any *berachos.* Therefore, the *berachah* of *al netilas yadayim* can be made only *after* the washing. Now, since the rule of עוֹבֵר לַעֲשִׂיָּתָן does not apply to the *berachah* of *al netilas yadayim,* our *minhag* is to postpone it until one comes to the *beis haknesses,* where the *chazzan* says it aloud to remind everyone to make the *berachah.* The same exception applies upon immersing in a *mikveh,* in which case the *berachah* for *mikveh* immersion is made *after* the immersion. This is especially true in the case of *tevilas geirim,* as a part of the conversion process, when the individual is not obligated to perform *mitzvos* — such as reciting the *berachah* — until after the *tevilah.* However, regarding the *berachah* of *al netilas yadayim* in the morning, one certainly has the option of reciting it earlier, immediately after he has washed his hands properly, rather than waiting until he comes to *shul.*

At this point, before we go any further, I would like to explain the meaning of בָּרוּךְ אַתָּה ה׳, *Baruch Atah Adonoi,* with which we begin all of our *berachos.* The word *baruch* is usually translated to mean "blessed." The concept of "blessing *HaKadosh Baruch Hu"* must be understood. How can we, mere mortals, give our sanction to the *Borei Olam* (Creator of the world), as if we had the power to affect Him through our words of blessing? For this reason, some of the *mefarshei hatefillah* (cf. *Derech HaChaim* quoting *Avudraham*) explain *Baruch Atah* to mean, "You are the source of all blessings," etc. However, this still leaves unexplained certain usages, such as: אֲבָרְכָה אֶת ה׳, *I shall bless Hashem* (*Tehillim* 34:2), or וַאֲנַחְנוּ נְבָרֵךְ יָהּ, *But we will bless God* (ibid. 115:18). There are many more such examples.

We therefore think that the sense in which the word *baruch* is used in our *berachos* is that of *ribui,* meaning *to add, to increase.* For instance, וּבֵרַךְ אֶת לַחְמְךָ וְאֶת מֵימֶיךָ, *He will increase your bread and your water* (*Shemos* 23:25). It is in this sense that we say to *HaKadosh Baruch Hu* as an introduction to every *berachah*: It is our *tefillah* that You may be increasingly recognized in the world; by our own personal, enhanced *emunah,* and also by the world at large, so that more and more people will live their lives according to Your Will. This interpretation is supported by the words of the *Kaddish,* in which the *chazzan* recites: יִתְגַּדַּל וְיִתְקַדַּשׁ שְׁמֵהּ רַבָּא, *May His great Name be increasingly exalted and,* consequently, *be increasingly sanctified in the world.* To this, the congregation responds: יְהֵא שְׁמֵהּ רַבָּא מְבָרַךְ לְעָלַם, meaning that the congregation joins in this *tefillah* of יִתְגַּדַּל וְיִתְקַדַּשׁ, and affirms the wish that His great Name shall indeed be מְבָרַךְ, meaning that He shall be increasingly recognized, obeyed and sanctified in the world.

It is in this sense that *Chazal* tell us that when the *Kohen Gadol,* R' Yishmael, entered the *Kodesh HaKadashim* on Yom Kippur, he heard the Divine Voice asking to be blessed: To which R' Yishmael responded: יְהִי רָצוֹן וְיָגוֹלוּ רַחֲמֶיךָ עַל מִדּוֹתֶיךָ... (*Berachos* 7a). This *berachah* was a *tefillah* that more and more *rachamim* may come into the world. So when we human beings speak of "blessing" *HaKadosh Baruch Hu,* we mean that we pray that we, together with growing numbers of people, may abide by His Will, and thus increase the *kiddush Hashem* in the world.

❧ ❧ ❧

אַתָּה — **You.** This word, "You," is most revealing. We are speaking directly to *HaKadosh Baruch Hu.* Through *tefillah,* we come as close to Him as possible. Consequently, this word should be uttered in a quiet, reverential tone.

ה' אֱלֹהֵינוּ — **Hashem, our God.** We have previously offered some thoughts concerning the meaning of the Ineffable Name, which we pronounce *Adonoi* in our commentary on *Adon Olam.* Concerning אֱלֹהֵינוּ, *Eloheinu,* the *Shulchan Aruch, Orach Chaim* 5, explains that when saying this word, we should be aware of its meaning of: תַּקִּיף בַּעַל הַיְכוֹלֶת, וּבַעַל הַכֹּחוֹת כֻּלָּם, *He is Almighty with Infinite Ability, and the Sole Master of All Forces.* Rav Samson R. Hirsch explains that the root of אֱלֹהִים is אֵלֶה, *eileh* (these), meaning that He is the Supreme Power over *eileh,* "these," meaning everything that exists. As *Am Yisrael,* we have a special relationship with *HaKadosh Baruch Hu.* He has revealed Himself to us as אָנֹכִי ה' אֱלֹהֶיךָ, *I am Hashem, your God,* and consequently, we call him אֱלֹהֵינוּ, *Eloheinu, our God.*

מֶלֶךְ הָעוֹלָם — **The King of the universe.** The word *olam,* which is translated as world, has the underlying meaning, throughout the *Tanach,* of something hidden, נֶעְלָם. We speak of מִן הָעוֹלָם וְעַד הָעוֹלָם, from the mystery-shrouded beginning of the world until its unknown ending (*Tehillim* 106:48). We have been assigned by *HaKadosh Baruch Hu* to fulfill our role in this world between our hidden beginnings and our unknown departure from this world. Furthermore, even the physical world is in reality hidden from us. We see only the surface of any matter, which is composed of molecules, which are themselves composed of atoms, which are held together by electrons and neutrons. We do not understand how matter is held together. And on a metaphysical level, our world is only the exterior, visible manifestation of the spiritual world which controls it, similar to the hands of a clock which are controlled by a hidden mechanism. The spiritual world of *Kisei HaKavod* (Throne of Glory), *malachim* (angels), *Gan Eden* (Garden of Eden), and *Gehinnom* are completely *ne'elam* (hidden) from us. So we refer to *HaKadosh Baruch Hu* as the Supreme Ruler of the *olam,* the world of which we have no real understanding. And finally, the meaning of events which occur in this world is also *ne'elam,* hidden from us. We see a world of chaotic events, in which nature is seemingly uncontrolled. There are floods, earthquakes, volcanic eruptions, and storms, in which millions of people die. When Avraham Avinu discovered the existence of *HaKadosh Baruch Hu,* he understood that we, as humans, cannot fathom the Divine management of the world. The Midrash (*Bereishis Rabbah* 39:2) illustrates this as follows: מָשָׁל לְאֶחָד שֶׁהָיָה עוֹבֵר מִמָּקוֹם לְמָקוֹם וְרָאָה בִּירָה אַחַת דּוֹלֶקֶת אָמַר שֶׁמָּא תֹּאמַר שֶׁהַבִּירָה הַזּוֹ בְּלֹא מַנְהִיג, הֵצִיץ עָלָיו בַּעַל הַבִּירָה, אָמַר לוֹ אֲנִי הוּא בַּעַל הַבִּירָה, *This can be compared to a traveler who happened upon a palace which was being consumed by fire. He wondered how it was possible that such a magnificent structure could be left without an owner to protect it. Suddenly, the owner of the palace appeared and told him, "I am the owner of this palace."* It is my will that it burn.

So the universe is really a hidden entity of which we have very little understanding, and *HaKadosh Baruch Hu* is the *Melech HaOlam,* the King of the universe, which is hidden from our understanding.

אֲשֶׁר קִדְּשָׁנוּ בְּמִצְוֹתָיו וְצִוָּנוּ — **Who has sanctified us with His commandments and has commanded us.** We do not simply say *Baruch Atah . . . shetzivanu* — "Blessed are You . . . Who has commanded," but we add the words: *asher kideshanu b'mitzvosav,* "Who has sanctified us with His commandments." These words express a very profound element of our unique role as members of *Am Yisrael,* which is the fact that the *physical body* of a Jewish person has been sanctified by *HaKadosh Baruch Hu.* This *kedushah* originates from Avraham Avinu, from the time that he entered into the *bris milah.* To be sure, *any* human being, having been created in the *tzelem Elokim* (image of God), can attain a high level of *spiritual* sanctification, *kedushas hanefesh,* and can even reach such a level of *tzidkus* (righteousness) that he would merit the title *chasidei umos ha'olam.* נֹחַ אִישׁ צַדִּיק תָּמִים, *Noach was a righteous man, perfect . . .* and שֵׁם וָעֵבֶר, *Shem and Ever,* were certainly prime examples of this. Such people certainly receive their appropriate reward in *Olam Haba.* (See *Rambam, Hil. Melachim* end of Ch. 8.) We find *HaKadosh Baruch Hu* describing Iyov, a non-Jew, as עַבְדִּי אִיּוֹב, *My servant Iyov* (*Iyov* 1:8). We even find *Neviim* among the *umos ha'olam.* However, only *Am Yisrael* was given *kedushas haguf* — the sanctity of the body of a Jew — by *HaKadosh Baruch Hu.* [Ed. note: See *Maayan Beis HaSho'evah, Bo* 13:1 for a broader discussion on the concept of *kedushas haguf.*]

When Avraham Avinu went to the *Akeidah* with Yitzchak, they were accompanied by two "servants." We are told: וַיֹּאמֶר אַבְרָהָם אֶל נְעָרָיו שְׁבוּ לָכֶם פֹּה עִם הַחֲמוֹר וַאֲנִי וְהַנַּעַר נֵלְכָה עַד כֹּה, *And Avraham said to his young men, "Stay* here by yourselves with the donkey, while I and the lad will go yonder" (*Bereishis* 22:5). Avraham tells his servants to wait "with the donkey," while he and Yitzchak proceed toward the *Akeidah*. According to *Chazal* (*Targum Yonasan* ad loc.), these "servants" were two of the most highly accomplished people in the world. One was Eliezer, the great *chassid umos ha'olam,* and the other was Yishmael, who became the great *baal teshuvah* of the *umos ha'olam.*

Therefore, *Chazal's* comment on the words עִם הַחֲמוֹר, *with the donkey,* is seemingly disparaging: עַם הַדּוֹמֶה לַחֲמוֹר, *They are a nation compared to a donkey* (*Kesubos* 111a). However, upon deeper insight, we see in this expression an illustration of the glaring difference even between these two giants of the *umos ha'olam* and Avraham and Yitzchak. When the entourage reached the foot of *Har HaMoriyah,* Avraham Avinu told his servants: "No matter what heights of spirituality you have reached, since *HaKadosh Baruch Hu* has not given you *kedushas haguf,* you must wait here *with the donkey,* while my son and I proceed further. While it is true that you have attained great spiritual heights, you have not been given *kedushas haguf.*" This is illustrated by the *mitzvah* of *pidyon peter chamor,* the redemption of a firstborn male donkey, which is based strictly on its *kedushas damim,* in which the value of the object and not the object itself becomes sanctified, and therefore the object never attains *kedushas haguf.* Therefore, Avraham tells his "servants": What we are about to do, and I cannot reveal that yet, is based on our *kedushas haguf* (our physical sanctification), which *HaKadosh Baruch Hu* in His wisdom has given only to us. [See further on this subject in *Maayan Beis HaSho'evah,* Terumah 25:3.]

Therefore, before we do a *mitzvah* with our bodies, we recognize its inherent holiness, *kedushas haguf,* and say: אֲשֶׁר קִדְּשָׁנוּ בְּמִצְוֹתָיו, You, *HaKadosh Baruch Hu,* have sanctified our bodies through Your *mitzvos.* This is what is meant when we ask *HaKadosh Baruch Hu:* קַדְּשֵׁנוּ בְּמִצְוֹתֶיךָ, give us opportunities to sanctify our bodies by doing Your *mitzvos.* Since this is so, only those *mitzvos* which we perform with our body require a *birchas hamitzvah.* Therefore, we do not make a *berachah* on *mitzvos* which are done with the mind. As an example, *birchos haTorah* would not be required if one merely thinks of *divrei Torah* without pronouncing any words. Also, a *berachah* is not recited for *Krias Shema,* despite the fact that we are required to say the words, because its primary function is that of *kabbalas ol Malchus Shamayim,* which is a mental, not a physical, activity. The same applies to the *mitzvah* of *tefillah* which does not require a *berachah* because it, too, is primarily a mental activity.

Furthermore, this inherent *kedushas haguf* of a Yisrael is the reason that the body of a deceased Jewish person must be treated with great reverence, and be buried as soon as possible. A *ger tzedek* (righteous convert) once asked me to learn Torah with him. While we were discussing the subject of *meis mitzvah* as it applies to a *Kohen,* he asked me if a *Kohen* would be required to bury the unattended and abandoned body of a non-Jew and thus render himself ritually impure. I answered him that the reason *meis mitzvah* supersedes most other *mitzvos* is because the body of a Jewish person has been granted inherent sanctity by *HaKadosh Baruch Hu* and must therefore be buried. In the case of a non-Jew, even one whose spirituality may have attained great heights while he was alive, nevertheless, once the *tzelem Elokim* leaves him, his body has no special *kedushah,* and there is no *mitzvah* that it be buried. Therefore, a *Kohen* would not be permitted to become *tamei* to bury the body of a non-Jew. I went on to point out to him that despite the great spiritual heights he may have reached before his *geirus* (conversion), he, as part of *umos ha'olam,* did not possess this special *kedushas haguf* which *HaKadosh Baruch Hu* granted to *Am Yisrael* through His *mitzvos.* However, this very same body receives the *kedushas haguf* of a Jew through *bris milah, tevilah,* and his acceptance of the *mitzvos.*

עַל נְטִילַת יָדַיִם — **Regarding washing the hands.** The *mitzvah* is not to wash one's hands in the sense of cleaning them. This is presupposed. Rather, the meaning is "uplifting of the hands," as in וַיְנַטְּלֵם וַיְנַשְּׂאֵם כָּל יְמֵי עוֹלָם, *He lifted them and bore them all the days of the world* (*Yeshayahu* 63:9). *HaKadosh Baruch Hu* has lifted us up from a purely physical existence to a higher state. When one washes his hands and makes this *berachah,* he is elevating them to the service of *HaKadosh Baruch Hu.*

בִּרְכַּת אֲשֶׁר יָצַר / Bircas Asher Yatzar

The human being is comprised of both a spiritual and physical aspect. This *berachah*, אֲשֶׁר יָצַר, expresses our gratitude to *HaKadosh Baruch Hu* for the marvelous structure and functioning of the human body, and the *berachah* of אֱלֹהַי נְשָׁמָה, which follows, addresses the spiritual aspect of the human being.

אֲשֶׁר יָצַר אֶת הָאָדָם בְּחָכְמָה, *Who fashioned man with wisdom,* is a universal expression of *shevach v'hodaah* (praise and gratitude) on behalf of all human beings, not only Jews. We acknowledge in this *berachah* that the properly functioning, normal, healthy human body is a marvelous gift that *HaKadosh Baruch Hu* has given to man.

The famous 19th-century naturalist, Alexander von Humboldt, is said to have commented that he had reviewed the prayer books of many religions, and found no other prayer comparable to אֲשֶׁר יָצַר.

❧ ❧ ❧

אֲשֶׁר יָצַר אֶת הָאָדָם בְּחָכְמָה — **Who fashioned man with wisdom.** Here we praise *HaKadosh Baruch Hu* for His wisdom in the creation of the complex human body.

וּבָרָא בוֹ נְקָבִים נְקָבִים חֲלוּלִים חֲלוּלִים גָּלוּי וְיָדוּעַ לִפְנֵי כִסֵּא כְבוֹדֶךָ שֶׁאִם יִפָּתֵחַ אֶחָד מֵהֶם, אוֹ יִסָּתֵם אֶחָד מֵהֶם — **He created within him many openings and many cavities. It is openly known before Your Throne of Glory. That if one of the organs which is usually closed should open,** referring to the חֲלוּלִים, **or if one that should be open were to close,** referring to the נְקָבִים (*Rashi, Berachos* 60b), then:

אִי אֶפְשַׁר לְהִתְקַיֵּם וְלַעֲמוֹד לְפָנֶיךָ — **It would be impossible to exist and to stand before You.** The *Shulchan Aruch, Orach Chaim* 6:1, has the text of this *berachah* continuing with אֲפִילוּ שָׁעָה אֶחָת, meaning that it would be impossible, *for even one moment,* to exist and stand before *HaKadosh Baruch Hu* if these organs were not working properly. However, it is the consensus of most *Acharonim* that these words not be included in the *berachah,* because man *can* exist for a short while — albeit in a precarious condition — even in the event of a rupture or a closure of these organs. (See *Mishnah Berurah* ibid.).

בָּרוּךְ אַתָּה ה' רוֹפֵא כָל בָּשָׂר וּמַפְלִיא לַעֲשׂוֹת — **Blessed are You, Hashem, Who heals all flesh and acts wondrously.** We bless *HaKadosh Baruch Hu* Who heals all flesh and, in doing so, performs wondrous deeds. The greatest act of healing that a physician can perform is the prevention of disease and sickness. So here we thank *HaKadosh Baruch Hu*, the Great Healer, for the normal functioning of the healthy human body. כָּל הַמַּחֲלָה אֲשֶׁר שַׂמְתִּי בְמִצְרַיִם לֹא אָשִׂים עָלֶיךָ כִּי אֲנִי ה' רֹפְאֶךָ, *Any of the diseases that I placed upon Egypt, I will not bring upon you, for I am Hashem, your Healer* (*Shemos* 15:26). Here we have the prevention of disease being called "healing."

While this *berachah* was instituted by the Sages to be said after one's bodily functions have been attended to, it has become part of our *tefillas Shacharis* and, according to some opinions, should be said in the morning even if one did not have the need to utilize these functions, because it is a general *birchas hodaah* to Hashem for the wondrous creation of the normal, healthy human body. However, in practice, according to the opinion of the majority of *poskim*, it should be said only after actually utilizing these functions.

The *Mechaber* (*Shulchan Aruch, Orach Chaim* 7:3) is of the opinion that if one forgot to say אֲשֶׁר יָצַר, and then has to relieve himself again, he would have to say the *berachah* twice. However, this too is not the majority opinion. Therefore, in practice, one would not make the *berachah* twice, as this would be a case of *safeik berachah*. This practice of constantly expressing thanks for the normal functioning of the human body is incorporated in the *Shemoneh Esrei*, when we say: רְפָאֵנוּ ה' וְנֵרָפֵא הוֹשִׁיעֵנוּ וְנִוָּשֵׁעָה כִּי תְהִלָּתֵנוּ אָתָּה, *Heal us Hashem — then we will be healed; save us — then we will be saved, for You are our [constant source] of praise* (cf. *Yirmiyahu* 17:14). These words reflect the idea that we should constantly express our gratitude to *HaKadosh Baruch Hu* for the normal and healthy functioning of our bodies.

It behooves us to be aware of the miraculous endowment which *HaKadosh Baruch Hu* has granted us in the form of the human body. Medical science continues to discover more and more knowledge of the human body and its miraculous workings. What was modern medical practice 100 years ago is by and large obsolete today. If a famous surgeon — who lived in the late 19th century — were to perform an operation in one of today's modern operating rooms, utilizing the medical skills of yesteryear, he could be charged with gross malfeasance and endangerment of life. Similarly, modern medical practice of today will most probably be considered obsolete in the future in the wake of ongoing new scientific discoveries about the human body. Despite the enormous strides that medicine has made, and continues to make, a large part of the complex structure and functions of the human body remains unknown. It is truly a source of wonderment and amazement.

When we contemplate the miraculous workings of our various חֲלוּלִים, *cavities* — such as the trachea, esophagus, bladder, rectum, and the entire digestive system, respiratory system, and circulatory system — and realize that a sudden and unexpected rupture, or blockage, in any of these organs would pose a mortal danger, we are all the more amazed at the marvelous wonder which *HaKadosh Baruch Hu* has granted us in the form of the normal, healthy functioning of these organs.

Most people take the normal functioning of their bodies for granted. Unless one has pain, or is informed by a physician after an examination that *chas v'shalom* "all is not well," one tends to ignore the crucial life-sustaining systems of the body. It is therefore so important to utilize the *berachah* of אֲשֶׁר יָצַר to focus our recognition on the fact that it is only due to the *nissim* (miracles) regularly performed by *HaKadosh Baruch Hu* that our bodily organs function normally.

My Rebbe, the Mirrer *Mashgiach*, R' Yerucham Levovitz, would humorously illustrate this idea by saying that the students really ought to send a telegram to their parents after each use of their bodily functions, to tell them that, *baruch Hashem*, they are well.

We find an interesting reference to the wondrous workings of the normal, healthy body in *Tehillim* (35:10), which we also quote in the *Nishmas* prayer: כָּל עַצְמֹתַי תֹּאמַרְנָה ה' מִי כָמוֹךָ, מַצִּיל עָנִי מֵחָזָק מִמֶּנּוּ וְעָנִי וְאֶבְיוֹן מִגֹּזְלוֹ, *All my limbs will say, "Hashem, who is like You? Deliverer of the poor from one mightier than he, of the poor and the destitute from the one who robs him."* On the surface, there seems to be no connection between the first part of this *pasuk*, which refers to the body, and the second part, which refers to the protection of the poor.

However, upon reflection, we think that the second part of this sentence also refers to the body. And the meaning is: My body, with all its marvelous and wondrous complexity, exudes praise and fairly shouts to its Creator: ה' מִי כָמוֹךָ, *Hashem, who is like You.* And this awesome creation of Yours, this body, has a marvelous digestive system, which passes the nutrients — through the bloodstream — to its various parts. Furthermore, miraculously, it has inherent internal controls which protect the smaller organs from being overwhelmed by the demands of the larger ones, thus allowing the necessary nutrients to pass through even to the "poorest" and smallest of the organs: מַצִּיל עָנִי מֵחָזָק מִמֶּנּוּ וְעָנִי וְאֶבְיוֹן מִגֹּזְלוֹ.

We find: וּמִבְּשָׂרִי אֶחֱזֶה אֱלוֹהַּ, *I see [the judgment of] God from my flesh* (*Iyov* 19:26). Here Iyov is saying that when he contemplates the workings of the body, and all its marvelous systems, he becomes acutely aware of the fact that *HaKadosh Baruch Hu* has created it.

However, there are several difficulties with the wording of this *berachah*. As previously pointed out, the *berachos* were composed by our Sages and the *Anshei Knesses HaGedolah*, many of whom were *Neviim* or possessed *ruach hakodesh*. We should therefore carefully study the text, paying close attention to each word, much as one would study *Mishnah* or *Gemara*.

First, אֲשֶׁר יָצַר אֶת הָאָדָם בְּחָכְמָה begs the question: What is so unique about the bodily systems of the human being? Don't these systems exist in animals? Don't horses, dogs or chickens have similar systems? Don't even lesser creatures have miraculous bodily systems? Indeed the *berachah* ends: רוֹפֵא כָל בָּשָׂר, *He heals **all flesh.***

Second, what does the repetition נְקָבִים נְקָבִים חֲלוּלִים חֲלוּלִים mean? Third, we say גָּלוּי וְיָדוּעַ לִפְנֵי כִסֵּא כְבוֹדֶךָ, *it is openly known before Your Throne of Glory* etc. This means that the *malachim* and other spiritual creatures, which exist before Your Throne, who have been appointed by *HaKadosh Baruch Hu* to bring sickness to the world — including the *malach hamaves* (Angel of Death) — and are ready to carry out their grim duties if mandated by You, know very well what potential danger exists within the body. It is more than strange that the Sages chose the concept of the Throne of Glory when making this point. On the surface it would seem somewhat indelicate to utilize these words when praising *HaKadosh Baruch Hu* for our miraculous digestive system. We are accustomed to invoking this lofty concept at the highest levels of our *tefillos,* as, for instance, in the *Zichronos* portion of our Rosh Hashanah prayers, when we say אֵין שִׁכְחָה לִפְנֵי כִסֵּא כְבוֹדֶךָ, *There is no forgetfulness before Your Throne of Glory.* What connection is there between the Throne of Glory and our most basic bodily functions?

Finally, what is the meaning of אִי אֶפְשַׁר לְהִתְקַיֵּם וְלַעֲמוֹד לְפָנֶיךָ, *it would be impossible to exist and to stand before You.* What do we add by the words וְלַעֲמוֹד לְפָנֶיךָ, *to stand before You?*

The author of the *Shulchan Aruch,* obviously having been aware of these difficulties, entitled the section (*Orach Chaim* 6) dealing with this *berachah*: דִּין בִּרְכַּת אֲשֶׁר יָצַר וֵאלֹהַי נְשָׁמָה וּפֵירוּשָׁיו, *The Law of the Blessings Asher Yatzar and Elohai Neshamah and Their Interpretations.* This, despite the fact that generally he limits his work to codifying only the final *p'sak din* (decision) of each *halachah.* However, in the case of the *berachah* of *asher yatzar,* he goes to great lengths to explain and interpret the blessing in detail. He compares the human body, with its myriad tubular systems and openings, to a balloon filled with air. If the balloon is punctured, even with a tiny hole, the air escapes, and the balloon collapses. Similarly, he says, the fact that the *neshamah* (soul) a spiritual entity, stays within the *guf* (body) despite its many openings, is miraculous. He goes into even greater detail in his *sefer Beis Yosef* (see *Tur* ibid.). The *Rema,* in the same section, succinctly explains it as: שֶׁמַּפְלִיא לַעֲשׂוֹת בַּמֶּה שֶׁשּׁוֹמֵר רוּחַ הָאָדָם בְּקִרְבּוֹ וְקוֹשֵׁר דָּבָר רוּחָנִי בְּדָבָר גַּשְׁמִי, *It is a miraculous wonder that He keeps the soul of the person within him, attaching a spiritual entity to a physical one.*

Both the *Mechaber* and *Rema* are pointing out the incongruity of the human being. The "spiritual entity," the *neshamah,* comes from beneath the Throne of Glory, a concept which human beings cannot even comprehend.

When Moshe Rabbeinu asked *HaKadosh Baruch Hu*: הַרְאֵנִי נָא אֶת כְּבֹדֶךָ, *Show me Your glory* (*Shemos* 33:18), he was told: לֹא יִרְאַנִי הָאָדָם וָחָי, *No human being can see Me and live* (ibid. v. 20). Furthermore, even the angels who stand before the Throne of Glory do not fully comprehend *HaKadosh Baruch Hu*: מְשָׁרְתָיו שׁוֹאֲלִים זֶה לָזֶה אַיֵּה מְקוֹם כְּבוֹדוֹ, *His ministering angels ask one another, "Where is the place of His glory?"* And this sublime spiritual entity, the *neshamah hakedoshah* (holy soul) which is called חֵלֶק אֱלוֹהַּ מִמַּעַל, having originated from *HaKadosh Baruch Hu*, Who is incomprehensible, has been attached to a physical body which, in its most mundane function, expels decaying matter. What a contrast! So, מַפְלִיא לַעֲשׂוֹת, *He acts wondrously*, means that *HaKadosh Baruch Hu* has attached the highest form of *ruchniyus* (spirituality) to the lowest level of *gashmiyus* (physicality). This is indeed "wondrous."

The expression מַפְלִיא לַעֲשׂוֹת regarding the human body originates from *Tehillim* 139:13,14, where Dovid HaMelech describes the miracle of his existence with the words: תְּסֻכֵּנִי בְּבֶטֶן אִמִּי. אוֹדְךָ עַל כִּי נוֹרָאוֹת נִפְלֵיתִי, נִפְלָאִים מַעֲשֶׂיךָ וְנַפְשִׁי יֹדַעַת מְאֹד, *You have covered me in the womb of my mother. I acknowledge you, for I am awesomely, wondrously fashioned; wondrous are Your works, and my soul knows it (very) well.* This means that my soul is acutely aware that — from the moment of my conception, and throughout my existence, in which You have combined two disparate elements, the *guf* and the *neshamah*, which could separate at any moment, and yet they function together — נִפְלָאִים מַעֲשֶׂיךָ, *Your deeds are wondrous*.

So, אֲשֶׁר יָצַר אֶת הָאָדָם בְּחָכְמָה refers specifically to man, to this unique combination of two such very disparate elements: *guf* and *tzelem Elokim*, as described in *Bereishis* 1:27: וַיִּבְרָא אֱלֹהִים אֶת הָאָדָם בְּצַלְמוֹ בְּצֶלֶם אֱלֹהִים בָּרָא אֹתוֹ, *So God created man in His image, in the image of God He created him.*

Furthermore, this *berachah* refers to the *complete human being*. In Kabbalistic terms the human body is called אָדָם הָרוּחָנִי, "spiritual man," because the human body contains not only רמ"ח אֵבָרִים, 248 *organs*, and שס"ה גִידִים, 365 *sinews*, in the physical sense, but it also contains the same number of spiritual organs. We have many expressions for our spiritual and emotional functions which utilize parts of our body as metaphors. Some examples are: לֵב שֹׁמֵעַ, *an understanding heart*, meaning intelligence (*Melachim I* 3:9); לֵב נִשְׁבָּר, *a broken heart*, meaning humility (*Tehillim* 51:19); הָמוּ מֵעַי, *my intestines pain*, meaning feelings of sympathy (*Yirmiyahu* 31:19); כְּלָיוֹת יוֹעֲצוֹת, *the kidneys advise*, meaning intuition (*Berachos* 61a).

If a good and kind person were to receive a heart or kidney transplant from a vicious criminal, with evil propensities, it would not affect his noble qualities; or if his intestines were removed, he would still retain his sympathetic feelings.

So אֲשֶׁר יָצַר אֶת הָאָדָם means that man, and only man, was created with

נְקָבִים נְקָבִים and חֲלוּלִים חֲלוּלִים, a unique *"parallel system"* of organs. For each physical נֶקֶב there is a spiritual one, and for each physical חָלוּל there is a spiritual one. We therefore thank *HaKadosh Baruch Hu* for having created us to function as a dual being, utilizing our physical and spiritual aspects combined.

And, regarding both aspects, we say: שֶׁאִם יִפָּתֵחַ אֶחָד מֵהֶם אוֹ יִסָּתֵם אֶחָד מֵהֶם אִי אֶפְשָׁר לְהִתְקַיֵּם וְלַעֲמוֹד לְפָנֶיךָ, Every *one* of these physical organs — and its spiritual counterpart — has a vital role to play in our existence.

Finally, the meaning of the seemingly extra word in לְהִתְקַיֵּם וְלַעֲמוֹד לְפָנֶיךָ is that if one's body does not work properly, and he cannot control his excretory functions, he may be able to exist, לְהִתְקַיֵּם, but he cannot לַעֲמוֹד, stand before *HaKadosh Baruch Hu* in *tefillah,* or learn Torah, or perform certain *mitzvos* because of the restriction of וְהָיָה מַחֲנֶיךָ קָדוֹשׁ, which requires a clean body (see *Berachos* 25a). The ending of the *berachah* consists of two parts: רוֹפֵא כָל בָּשָׂר, *He heals all flesh,* meaning, we thank *HaKadosh Baruch Hu* for the normal, healthy workings of the bodily systems of all creatures; and וּמַפְלִיא לַעֲשׂוֹת, *He acts wondrously.* This refers specifically to *Adam,* the human being, within whose marvelous bodily systems *HaKadosh Baruch Hu* has implanted the *neshamah,* the חֵלֶק אֱלוֹהַּ מִמַּעַל, and keeps it alive. We are, indeed, awestruck by this living, functioning creation: the healthy human being. Even the sick body has been given the power by *HaKadosh Baruch Hu* to withstand the ravages of disease, and to survive as long as He deems it fit for the *neshamah* to stay with the *guf.*

A very strange event is recorded in *Shmuel I* (4:5 — 7:21), at the time of the death of Eli HaKohen. The Philistines had won a victory against the Jewish people, in which the *Aron HaKodesh* was captured and kept in the Philistines' possession for seven months. While the *Aron HaKodesh* was in their possession, *HaKadosh Baruch Hu* afflicted the Philistines with a plague of the swelling of the lower bowel, resulting in hemorrhoids protruding from their bodies, the tissue of which subsequently decayed. While they were asleep, mice would come and gnaw at the decaying matter (see *Radak* ibid.). The Philistines, recognizing that this widespread epidemic was the result of their having taken the *Aron HaKodesh,* decided to return it — together with an "appeasement offering" to *Elokei Yisrael.* This gift was so strange that, were it not in *Tanach,* it would be extremely distasteful to describe. It consisted of five golden molds of hemorrhoids, and five golden mice, corresponding to the five molds of hemorrhoids. These "offerings" were placed in an *argaz* (box) next to the *Aron HaKodesh* and returned to the *Bnei Yisrael.*

Astonishingly, these gifts were not only accepted by the *Bnei Yisrael* but were permanently placed next to the *Aron HaKadesh,* in the *Kodesh HaKadashim.* In fact, the Gemara (*Yoma* 52b) says that this box — containing its objects — will be returned *l'asid lavo* (in the future) together with the other Temple vessels. According to one opinion, the original *sefer Torah* written by Moshe Rabbeinu was placed on top of this box. (See *Bava Basra* 14a.)

So, our holiest object, the *sefer Torah,* dictated by *HaKadosh Baruch Hu* and written by Moshe Rabbeinu, the source of the entire Written Torah, which was kept in our holiest place, the *Kodesh HaKadashim,* rested on top of this box which contained these most base objects!

This unlikely combination of objects was permanently placed in the *Kodesh HaKadashim,* our holiest place, as an illustration of the makeup of the human being: a combination of pure *ruchniyus* — the *neshamah* — bound together with the mundane, turbid, physical body, which will eventually decay and rot.

So the *Kodesh HaKadashim,* the place on earth where man stands לִפְנֵי כִסֵּא כְבוֹדֶךָ, *before Your Throne of Glory,* contains this unusual combination of holy vessels as a representation of the disparate makeup of the human being. This unlikely makeup of the human being, with each part having its unique purpose, testifies that *HaKadosh Baruch Hu* is מַפְלִיא לַעֲשׂוֹת.

We have shown by our detailed explanations of this *berachah* that, if recited with the proper *kavannah* (intent), the *berachah* of *asher yatzar* can be a source of a great deal of *yiras Shamayim, emunah,* and *bitachon.*

בִּרְכַּת אֱלֹהַי נְשָׁמָה / Bircas Elohai Neshamah

There is a dispute among the *Rishonim* as to whether אֱלֹהַי נְשָׁמָה follows immediately after אֲשֶׁר יָצַר, or whether the *birchos haTorah* are interjected between them.

Our *minhag* (custom), based on the *Tur* (see *Orach Chaim* 6) and other *Rishonim* and *Acharonim,* including the Vilna Gaon, has אֱלֹהַי נְשָׁמָה following immediately after אֲשֶׁר יָצַר. This is so because אֱלֹהַי נְשָׁמָה does not start with the usual introductory words, *Baruch Atah Hashem,* and therefore should be recited *semuchah l'chavertah,* following a *berachah* which begins and ends *Baruch Atah Hashem,* in this case, the *berachah* of *asher yatzar.*

However, the other opinion — held by the *Mechaber* (see ibid.) and other *Rishonim* — is that אֱלֹהַי נְשָׁמָה, as a *birchas hodaah* (thanksgiving blessing), would not be bound by the rule requiring the opening words *Baruch Atah Hashem,* and thus would not have to be said following a *berachah* that begins this way. [See *Tosafos, Berachos* 46a, s.v. כל הברכות.]

The source for this opinion is found in *Talmud Yerushalmi, Berachos* 60a, which states that when one awakens in the morning, he should immediately say אֱלֹהַי נְשָׁמָה, without the necessity of preceding it with *Baruch Atah Hashem.* [In prevailing practice, this was replaced by *Modeh Ani,* and אֱלֹהַי נְשָׁמָה was inserted into the *tefillah.*]

In any event, one should follow the custom of his place in regard to the order of these *berachos.*

❧ ❧ ❧

אֱלֹהַי נְשָׁמָה שֶׁנָּתַתָּ בִּי — **My God, the soul You placed within me.** The wording of this *berachah,* in the first person singular, emphasizes the strictly personal nature of one's own *neshamah.* In utilizing the word אֱלֹהַי, *My God,* one expresses a most personal relationship to *HaKadosh Baruch Hu.* With the words נְשָׁמָה שֶׁנָּתַתָּ בִּי, *the soul You placed within me,* the individual is referring to his own personal and unique *neshamah,* which is unlike any other *neshamah.* The בִּי, *me,* is uniquely personal. *HaKadosh Baruch Hu* has breathed some of his uniqueness into every one of us. *Bereishis* 2:7 states: וַיִּפַּח בְּאַפָּיו נִשְׁמַת חַיִּים, *He blew into his nostrils a living soul. Zohar HaKadosh* to this verse comments: מַאן דְּנָפַח מִתּוֹכֵיהּ נָפַח, *If one blows into another, he breathes something of himself into him.* Therefore the *neshamah* which *HaKadosh Baruch Hu* has given me,

טְהוֹרָה הִיא — **is pure.** Since *HaKadosh Baruch Hu* is holy and pure, the *neshamah,* too, carries this characteristic. This *neshamah* remains pure despite the *aveiros* (sins) that its human personality may do.

Even the worst criminal in the world still retains a *neshamah tehorah.* The prevailing religion in the world for approximately the last 2,000 years has at its core the doctrine that man has a sinful soul, and is therefore condemned to Hell, unless he accepts certain theological beliefs. Judaism totally rejects this concept. The *neshamah,* coming from *HaKadosh Baruch Hu,* is pure — and remains pure.

In saying this *tefillah,* one should be aware of his own individual personality, having within him a *neshamah* that is totally unique. No two *neshamos* are exactly alike. Just as *HaKadosh Baruch Hu* is Echad, Yachid *U'Meyuchad,* singular and unique, לְהַמְשִׁיל לוֹ לְהַחְבִּירָה, nothing exists with which to compare Him, so too is one's own *neshamah.* No one in the world ever had — or will have — a *neshamah* exactly like mine. What I feel, no one in the world shares. The most astute psychoanalyst in the world cannot really understand the depth of "me"; only אֱלֹהַי, *my God,* with whom I have a personal relationship, truly knows "me."

The wording of the beginning of this *berachah* describes the *neshamah* in four ways, corresponding to the "four worlds of Creation," which we discussed in *Adon Olam:*

טְהוֹרָה הִיא, *it is pure.* This refers to the origin of the *neshamah* in the *Olam Ha'atzilus.* It is as pure as pure can be. It is *chelek Elokai mima'al,* of the Essence of *HaKadosh Baruch Hu.* Just as He is pure, so too is the *neshamah.* Similarly, we find, קְדוֹשִׁים תִּהְיוּ כִּי קָדוֹשׁ אֲנִי ה' אֱלֹהֵיכֶם, *You shall be holy because I, Hashem, your God, am holy* (*Vayikra* 19:2). The commandment to "be holy because God is holy" can be understood only if the human being has something "of the Essence of God" in his makeup. Otherwise, it would be similar to a commandment say, to "Be almighty, because God is Almighty." However, *kedushah* is possible for man, because *HaKadosh Baruch Hu* has given us "part of His Essence," in the form of the *neshamah tehorah.*

◆§ אַתָּה בְרָאתָהּ — **You have created it,** *yeish mei'ayin, from nothing.* The *neshamah* is not eternal; it did not always exist. This refers to the next descending level, that of *Olam Haberiyah.*

◆§ אַתָּה יְצַרְתָּהּ — **You have formed it.** You made my personal *neshamah* to fit "me." Only I have this *neshamah;* it is unique to me. This refers to the third level, that of *Olam Hayetzirah.*

◆§ אַתָּה נְפַחְתָּהּ בִּי — **You have breathed it into me.** You have given me life. This is the fourth, and final, stage of creation, the *Olam Ha'asiyah,* the world in which we live. As long as *HaKadosh Baruch Hu* allows me to have this *neshamah,* I am here.

ו**ְאַתָּה מְשַׁמְּרָהּ בְּקִרְבִּי** — **And You keep it within me.** The *neshamah* is very elusive; it could escape my body at any moment. Nevertheless, You keep me alive by allowing my *neshamah* to stay within me as long as You see fit.

וְאַתָּה עָתִיד לִטְּלָהּ מִמֶּנִּי — **You will, one day, take my [*neshamah*] from me.** Although we say this every day, referring to our eventual demise, and we know this to be true, it does not make us sad or afraid, because we also know that:

וּלְהַחֲזִירָהּ בִּי לֶעָתִיד לָבֹא — **You will return it to me at some future time,** whenever *HaKadosh Baruch Hu* sees fit to do so.

The meaning of בִּי is that despite the fact that my body will decay after my death, *HaKadosh Baruch Hu* will recreate it. My *neshamah* will return into my re-created body at the time of *techiyas hameisim*, the Resurrection of the Dead.

כָּל זְמַן שֶׁהַנְּשָׁמָה בְקִרְבִּי — **As long as the soul is within me.** Every moment of my existence in this world,

מוֹדֶה אֲנִי לְפָנֶיךָ ה׳ אֱלֹהַי וֵאלֹהֵי אֲבוֹתַי — **I gratefully thank You, Hashem, my God and the God of my forefathers.** The word מוֹדֶה here is used in the sense of its use in "*modeh b'shtar*" (*Kesubos* 19a) meaning admission or acknowledgment of a fact. (See R' S.R. Hirsch to *Vayikra* 5:5 and *Tehillim* 9:2.) As long as I am alive, and have my *neshamah* within me, I openly acknowledge that You are the —

רִבּוֹן כָּל הַמַּעֲשִׂים — **Master of everything in this world,** that of the *Olam Ha'asiyah,* the physical universe, from the largest to the smallest creature,

אֲדוֹן כָּל הַנְּשָׁמוֹת — the personal Master, the **Lord of every *neshamah*.**

בָּרוּךְ אַתָּה ה׳ הַמַּחֲזִיר נְשָׁמוֹת לִפְגָרִים מֵתִים — **Blessed are You, Hashem, Who restores souls to dead bodies.** We conclude this *berachah* by confirming our belief in *techiyas hameisim*. We say here that *HaKadosh Baruch Hu* returns souls to the dead bodies. In our daily cycle of sleeping and awakening, we experience something of the miracle of *techiyas hameisim*. While we are asleep, our consciousness leaves us and, upon our awakening, it returns. In fact, *Chazal* call sleep "one-sixtieth of death" (*Berachos* 57b). The very fact that we are alive is an act of *techiyas hameisim*. So to us, our daily awakening is a small taste of the actual *techiyas hameisim,* and we utilize it as a reminder and confirmation of one of the essentials of our *emunah,* namely *techiyas hameisim*.

If one forgot to say this *berachah,* and has already completed the *Shemoneh Esrei,* he need not say it later, because he has confirmed his *emunah* by saying בָּרוּךְ אַתָּה ה׳ מְחַיֵּה הַמֵּתִים. Hopefully, *b'ezras Hashem,* we will discuss this subject further when we reach the *Shemoneh Esrei*.

בִּרְכוֹת הַשַּׁחַר / Birchos HaShachar

The reciting of these fifteen *berachos* which we say each morning is based on two different sources. One is in *Berachos* 60b, which lists them according to the usual order of a person's wake-up and dressing procedure in the morning, as follows:

Upon awakening, one is to say אֱלֹהַי נְשָׁמָה. [According to the accepted *minhag*, however, we say מוֹדֶה אֲנִי instead. The reason for the change is not within the scope of this *shiur*.]

The Gemara continues: כִּי שָׁמַע קוֹל תַּרְנְגוֹלָא, When he hears the rooster crowing, he is to say בָּרוּךְ אֲשֶׁר נָתַן לַשֶּׂכְוִי בִינָה לְהַבְחִין בֵּין יוֹם וּבֵין לַיְלָה, *Blessed . . . Who gave the heart understanding to distinguish between day and night* (see further for another meaning of שֶׂכְוִי).

When he touches his eyes, בָּרוּךְ פּוֹקֵחַ עִוְרִים, *Blessed . . . Who gives sight to the blind;*

When he moves his limbs and sits up, בָּרוּךְ מַתִּיר אֲסוּרִים, *Blessed . . . Who releases the bound;*

When he gets dressed, בָּרוּךְ מַלְבִּישׁ עֲרֻמִּים, *Blessed . . . Who clothes the naked;*

When he stands up, בָּרוּךְ זוֹקֵף כְּפוּפִים, *Blessed . . . Who straightens the bent;*

When he feels the "terra firma" under his feet, בָּרוּךְ רוֹקַע הָאָרֶץ עַל הַמָּיִם, *Blessed . . . Who spreads out the earth upon the waters;*

When he takes a step, בָּרוּךְ הַמֵּכִין מִצְעֲדֵי גָבֶר, *Blessed . . . Who firms man's footsteps;*

When he ties his shoes, בָּרוּךְ שֶׁעָשָׂה לִי כָּל צָרְכִּי, *Blessed. . . Who has provided me my every need;*

When he puts on his belt, בָּרוּךְ אוֹזֵר יִשְׂרָאֵל בִּגְבוּרָה, *Blessed . . . Who girds Israel with strength;*

When he covers his head, בָּרוּךְ עוֹטֵר יִשְׂרָאֵל בְּתִפְאָרָה, *Blessed . . . Who crowns Israel with splendor.*

The *berachah* of הַנּוֹתֵן לַיָּעֵף כֹּחַ, *Who gives strength to the weary,* is not mentioned in the Gemara at all.

We find three additional *berachos* in *Menachos* 43b, not related to the "order of arising," as follows:

שֶׁלֹּא עָשַׂנִי גּוֹי, *for not having made me a gentile;*

שֶׁלֹּא עָשַׂנִי עָבֶד, *for not having made me a slave;*

שֶׁלֹּא עָשַׂנִי אִשָּׁה, *for not having made me a woman.*

We must explain why those who organized our *tefillah* saw fit to insert these three *berachos* after אֲשֶׁר נָתַן לַשֶּׂכְוִי בִינָה. It is noteworthy that the old *minhag Sefard* had them listed *after* the entire "order of arising" list, which would be more in accordances with both *Gemaras*. However, this was eventually changed to conform to the generally accepted *minhag* which we have today.

To understand the reason, let us start by explaining this first *berachah*. We will then proceed to explain the other *berachos*.

❦ ❦ ❦

אֲשֶׁר נָתַן לַשֶּׂכְוִי בִינָה — **Who gave the heart understanding.** This, and not הַנּוֹתֵן לַשֶּׂכְוִי בִינָה, is the text according to our *minhag Ashkenaz*, and is based on the *pasuk,* אוֹ מִי נָתַן לַשֶּׂכְוִי בִינָה, *Who imbued the heart with understanding* (*Iyov* 38:36), and follows the rule that אֵין לְשַׁנּוֹת מִלְּשׁוֹן הַכָּתוּב, It is improper to change the language of a written *pasuk*. [Similarly, we say הַנּוֹתֵן לַיָּעֵף כֹּחַ, in accordance with נֹתֵן לַיָּעֵף כֹּחַ, *He gives strength to the weary* (*Isaiah* 40:29).]

The meaning of שֶׂכְוִי, according to *Rashi* and *Tosafos*, is "rooster." In Arabic a rooster is called שֶׂכְוִי (*Rosh Hashanah* 26a). The word בִּינָה is derived from בֵּין, which means to distinguish between things. So the *berachah* means that *HaKadosh Baruch Hu,* at the time of Creation, gave the rooster the innate "understanding," meaning, the ability to discern, to make the fine distinction, לְהַבְחִין בֵּין, between the darkness of the night and that of the impending daybreak, which he announces by his crowing.

Therefore, upon awakening, the person marvels at, and gives thanks to, *HaKadosh Baruch Hu* for the miraculous creation of a rooster's brain, the size of a thimble, which nevertheless has the intelligence to recognize the first sign of the diminishing darkness which precedes the break of dawn. It should therefore follow that if one does not hear a rooster crow, as for instance in our urban society, one would not make this *berachah*. However, according to *Tosafos*, the *berachah* was intended to give thanks to *HaKadosh Baruch Hu* for the existence of this miraculous cognitive ability, even if one does not actually hear the rooster heralding a new day.

According to the students of *Rabbeinu Yonah*, and followed by the *Rosh*, the word שֶׂכְוִי has an additional meaning, that of "seeing," or "insight," from סָכָה, or שָׂכה (ס and שׂ are often interchanged), especially in connection with the insight of the heart, as in מַשְׂכִּיוֹת לֵבָב, *the heart's images* etc. (*Tehillim* 73:7). The *berachah* would then refer to the ability of the human heart to distinguish between day and night. So combining both meanings, this *berachah* gives thanks to *HaKadosh Baruch Hu* for the cognitive power of the rooster which, in turn, makes our heart aware of the impending break of dawn. We shall explain the significance of this.

It is noteworthy that this *berachah* is recited only in the morning, despite the fact that the degree of darkness in the evening before צֵאת הַכּוֹכָבִים, *the emergence of the stars,* is similar to that of the morning before עֲלוֹת הַשַּׁחַר, *the rise of dawn.* In the evening, the rooster is silent, and no special *berachah* is made. This may hold the clue for the meaning of the entire *berachah.*

The emotions evoked by the impending change are completely different in the morning and evening. In the early morning, as the day breaks, we have a wonderful feeling of anticipating the beginning of a new day. We look forward to it with happy expectancy. It is for this emotion — this pleasant, hopeful optimism, which the crowing of the rooster evokes in our hearts — that we give thanks. However, in the evening, when day is done, with impending nightfall, no such emotion is evoked. On the contrary, it could be somewhat depressing. So we wait, once again, for the opportunity to make a new *berachah* at the break of tomorrow's dawn.

Based on the foregoing, we can now understand the reason why the *berachah* of שֶׁלֹּא עָשַׂנִי גּוֹי is inserted at this point. Rabbi Samson R. Hirsch in his *peirush* on *tefillah* explains that just as the rooster has been given the ability by *HaKadosh Baruch Hu* to distinguish between day and night, while the difference is still hardly noticeable, and announces it to the world with his loud crowing, so too has *HaKadosh Baruch Hu* given the Jewish people the mandate to enlighten the world with the great truths taught by the Torah, even if the world is still "dark." We have been given this mandate as מַמְלֶכֶת כֹּהֲנִים וְגוֹי קָדוֹשׁ, *a kingdom of ministers and a holy nation,* to be *a light unto the nations* (Shemos 19:6). So we gratefully acknowledge our spiritual leadership, and say: בָּרוּךְ אַתָּה ה' אֱלֹהֵינוּ מֶלֶךְ הָעוֹלָם שֶׁלֹּא עָשַׂנִי גּוֹי.

◆§ שֶׁלֹּא עָשַׂנִי גּוֹי. שֶׁלֹּא עָשַׂנִי עָבֶד. שֶׁלֹּא עָשַׂנִי אִשָּׁה §◆ — **He has not made me a gentile. He has not made me a slave. He has not made me a woman.**

The Roedelheim *Siddur* has the text here as שֶׁלֹּא עָשַׂנִי נָכְרִי instead of the generally accepted שֶׁלֹּא עָשַׂנִי גּוֹי. However, this was a relatively recent innovation by Wolf Heidenheim and Dr. Baer of Bibrich and one other scholar. These authorities were of the opinion that גּוֹי would simply mean "nation," and would not convey the meaning "non-Jew." They therefore changed the heretofore accepted word גּוֹי to נָכְרִי. However, this was not widely accepted, because the word נָכְרִי only means "stranger," an estranged person, another group. But the word גּוֹי in the language of the Sages is definitely used to convey the meaning "non-Jew."

In the Gemara we often find the acronym עכו"ם for עוֹבֵד כּוֹכָבִים וּמַזָּלוֹת, *worshipers of stars and mazalos,* which was a refinement to satisfy the Christian censors. Although we do find in the Torah the Jewish people being called גּוֹי, as in גּוֹי קָדוֹשׁ (Shemos 19:6), nevertheless, our *berachos* utilize the *lashon hakodesh* used by the *Anshei Knesses HaGedolah* which is known as *lashon Chachamim* (the language of the Sages). In the language of the Sages, a member of the non-Jewish world is simply called *goy.* The different usages of Hebrew are expressed as לְעַצְמָה לְעַצְמָה חֲכָמִים וּלְשׁוֹן תּוֹרָה לְשׁוֹן, *the language of the Torah is distinct, and the language of the Sages is distinct* (*Avodah Zarah* 58b). There are numerous examples of these variations with regard to *berachos*.

There is another version of this *berachah* which I found in the old *siddur* of Rav Hertz *Shaliach Tzibbur*, with the words שֶׁעָשַׂנִי יִשְׂרָאֵל. This is also not in accord with our Gemara. So we will retain the generally accepted version: שֶׁלֹּא עָשַׂנִי גּוֹי.

It is important to understand why the Sages expressed the three *berachos* in the negative: שֶׁלֹּא עָשַׂנִי גּוֹי, שֶׁלֹּא עָשַׂנִי עָבֶד, שֶׁלֹּא עָשַׂנִי אִשָּׁה. Why not say: שֶׁעָשַׂנִי יִשְׂרָאֵל, שֶׁעָשַׂנִי בֶּן חוֹרִין, שֶׁעָשַׂנִי אִישׁ, just as the women actually do say שֶׁעָשַׂנִי כִּרְצוֹנוֹ, *for having made me according to His will*? The reason given by *Bach, Orach Chaim* 46, is based on *Eruvin* 13b, where there is a dispute which persisted for two and a half years between Beis Shammai and Beis Hillel as to whether נוֹחַ לוֹ לְאָדָם שֶׁלֹּא נִבְרָא יוֹתֵר מִשֶּׁנִּבְרָא. Since a person comes into the world and commits so many *aveiros*, wasting the precious *neshamah* which *HaKadosh Baruch Hu* has bestowed upon him, might it perhaps not be better, as far as *kiddush Hashem* is concerned, if he were not created at all?

Eventually, the matter was decided by a vote that it indeed would have been better (for most people — other than *tzaddikim*) if man had not been created. However, עַכְשָׁיו שֶׁנִּבְרָא, now that man *was* created, יְפַשְׁפֵּשׁ בְּמַעֲשָׂיו, he should make the best of it; he should examine his deeds and try to improve himself to the best of his ability. So we therefore do not express the *berachah* in the positive שֶׁעָשַׂנִי יִשְׂרָאֵל וכו׳. Instead, we say that, under the circumstances, we are thankful that שֶׁלֹּא עָשַׂנִי גּוֹי. [The question of whether a *ger* (convert) would actually say שֶׁעָשַׂנִי יִשְׂרָאֵל is discussed by the *poskim*.]

These three *berachos* have caused quite a stir and much criticism. It sounds as if we are arrogantly expressing our superiority that we are not non-Jews, slaves, or women. This applies especially to a woman, since it smacks of male chauvinism — especially in our time. However, upon deeper reflection, we get a much clearer picture of what this means.

Does שֶׁלֹּא עָשַׂנִי גּוֹי mean that Hashem did not make me:

- like Mesushelach, the *tzaddik* for whom the *mabul* (flood) was postponed seven days?
- or like Noach who is called *ish tzaddik*, in whose merit all present-day mankind exists?
- or like Shem and Ever, who were the teachers of Yitzchak and Yaakov?
- or like Yisro, in whose honor an entire *parashah* was added to the Torah?
- or like Iyov, who was called עַבְדִּי אִיּוֹב, *my servant Iyov*, and was almost as great as Avraham Avinu?

BIRCHOS HASHACHAR 31

Does שֶׁלֹּא עָשַׂנִי עָבֶד mean that Hashem did not make me like Eliezer the servant of Avraham, of whom it says, הַמֹּשֵׁל בְּכָל אֲשֶׁר לוֹ, which is explained by *Rashi* to mean הַמֹּשֵׁל בְּיִצְרוֹ כְּרַבּוֹ, he ruled over his *yetzer hara* just as his master Avraham did (*Bereishis Rabbah* 59:8)? Furthermore, Eliezer was known as Damesek Eliezer because דּוֹלֶה וּמַשְׁקֶה מִתּוֹרָתוֹ שֶׁל רַבּוֹ לַאֲחֵרִים, he *"watered" the world with the teachings of his master [Avraham]* (*Yoma* 28b). This *"eved"* was *zocheh* to *nissim* (miracles) in his search for a bride for Yitzchak.

Or does it mean that Hashem did not make me like Tovi the servant of Rabban Gamliel, whose master testified that he was a *talmid chacham* and was worthy of *semichah* (*Succah* 20b, *Yoma* 87b)? Would Rabban Gamliel call any one of us a *talmid chacham*?

Or does it mean that Hashem did not make me like אַמְתָא דְּבֵי רַבִּי, *the handmaiden of the house of R' Yehudah HaNasi,* to whom the Sages would come with their questions? (*Rosh Hashanah* 26b, *Moed Katan* 17a).

Does שֶׁלֹּא עָשַׂנִי אִשָּׁה mean that Hashem did not make me a woman:

- like one of the matriarchs, Sarah, Rivkah, Rachel, and Leah?
- like Devorah the Prophetess?
- like Queen Esther?

It is therefore clear that these *berachos* do not represent the "arrogant and eminent superiority" of a Jewish male over a non-Jew, a servant or a woman.

Rather, they express thanks to *HaKadosh Baruch Hu* for the special opportunities of *mitzvos* which a Jewish male was granted, more than those assigned to:

- a non-Jew, who has only the seven *mitzvos* of *bnei Noach,* even if *he is Noach,* a righteous person;
- a servant, who has *mitzvos* like a woman, even if *he is Eliezer,* the servant of Avraham;
- a woman, who has all *mitzvos except* the few מִצְוֹת עֲשֵׂה שֶׁהַזְּמַן גְּרָמָא, *time-bound mitzvos,* even if *she is Devorah* the Prophetess.

Even if these individuals voluntarily perform *mitzvos* from which they are exempt, their reward is much less than that of one who is *mandated* to perform them. *Chazal* call this גָּדוֹל הַמְצֻוֶּה וְעוֹשֶׂה מִמִּי שֶׁאֵינוֹ מְצֻוֶּה וְעוֹשֶׂה (*Avodah Zarah* 3a). *Tosafos* (ibid.) explains this based on the fact that the person who is mandated to perform a *mitzvah* has a constant struggle with the *yetzer hara.* Thus the greater the temptation to violate a *mitzvah,* the greater the reward for performing it.

This goes contrary to our simplistic notion that one should be entitled to a greater reward for "volunteering" to do a *mitzvah* than if he were commanded to do so. Our ego, our nature, prefers that we do things out of "the goodness of our heart," rather than because we are required to do so. However, as far as *mitzvos* are concerned, the opposite is true.

The *berachah* made by women is שֶׁעָשַׂנִי כִּרְצוֹנוֹ, which reflects the fact that women are exempt from certain *mitzvos*. The different natures of men and women require a difference in the *mitzvos* needed to elevate them and bring them closer to *HaKadosh Baruch Hu*.

As an example, if a man would fail to put on *tefillin*, he would be considered קַרְקַפְתָּא דְּלָא מַנַּח תְּפִילִין and would be a פּוֹשֵׁעַ יִשְׂרָאֵל בְּגוּפוֹ, i.e., one who is severely lacking *yiras Shamayim* (*Rosh Hashanah* 17a). However, a woman is not only exempt from this *mitzvah*, as a מִצְוָה עֲשֵׂה שֶׁהַזְּמַן גְּרָמָא, a time-bound commandment, but would be frowned upon for putting on *tefillin*. (See *Orach Chaim* 38:3-2, *Rema*.) A woman can have the same *yiras Shamayim* as a man without her putting on *tefillin*.

The purpose of the fulfillment of all *mitzvos* is to form a bond with *HaKadosh Baruch Hu*. The performance of *mitzvos* with love creates this bond. This is meant by *Devarim* 11:13: וְהָיָה אִם שָׁמֹעַ תִּשְׁמְעוּ אֶל מִצְוֹתַי אֲשֶׁר אָנֹכִי מְצַוֶּה אֶתְכֶם הַיּוֹם לְאַהֲבָה אֶת ה׳ אֱלֹהֵיכֶם וּלְעָבְדוֹ בְּכָל לְבַבְכֶם וּבְכָל נַפְשְׁכֶם, *If you obey My mitzvos which I am commanding you today, to love Hashem your God and to worship Him with all of your hearts and your being*. The *mitzvos* are a means of bringing a person close to God. If a man having been commanded by God to put on *tallis* and *tefillin* does not do so, or if he fails to perform any other *mitzvah* which he is obligated to do, he lacks the connection with *HaKadosh Baruch Hu* which these *mitzvos* would create. Men, by their nature, require more *mitzvos* to bring them close to God. However, women were created with an innate nature which is *more in accordance with the will of HaKadosh Baruch Hu than men*. They do not require the same "corrections" as men do to bring them close to God. שֶׁעָשַׂנִי כִּרְצוֹנוֹ means "He has made me in accordance with His will," which means that women do not require all the *mitzvos* which men do to achieve לְאַהֲבָה אֶת ה׳ אֱלֹהֵיכֶם וּלְעָבְדוֹ, the love and worship of Hashem.

[A similar thought is expressed by Rabbi Dr. Eli Munk in *The World of Prayer*.]

The same idea applies to *talmud Torah* (Torah study), from which women are exempt. To be sure, a woman must learn the laws of the *mitzvos* in order to do them properly, and it is therefore required that she say *birchos haTorah* in Shacharis. However, learning for the sake of learning, just to occupy one's mind with the intricacies of Torah, even if the practical application of the law is already known, is limited to men. A woman who learns Torah does not become greater in *yiras Shamayim* because of it. True, she may become very learned in Torah, but this is not the object of *talmud Torah*. A woman may become a great philosopher or scientist, but Torah is not philosophy or science. Torah is the way *HaKadosh Baruch Hu* communicates with us. If a man is a great *talmid chacham*, having learned the entire Talmud, and has not become a greater *yarei Shamayim*, this learning has not achieved its purpose. If a woman were to learn and know Gemara just as well as a man, it still would not make her one iota better than she is. It would have no influence on her relationship with *HaKadosh Baruch Hu*. שֶׁעָשַׂנִי כִּרְצוֹנוֹ means that a woman does not need *talmud Torah* to come close to *HaKadosh Baruch Hu*. A woman can even have prophecy — the closest possible relationship to *HaKadosh Baruch Hu* — without learning Torah.

According to the *minhag* of Frankfurt which was prevalent in all of Southern Germany, and is also our *minhag,* we say the *berachah* of מַלְבִּישׁ עֲרֻמִּים before פּוֹקֵחַ עִוְרִים. This is the reverse of the order found in the Gemara.

This change is supported by *Shulchan Aruch, Orach Chaim* 46:1: כְּשֶׁלּוֹבֵשׁ יְבָרֵךְ מַלְבִּישׁ עֲרֻמִּים, כְּשֶׁיַּנִּיחַ יָדוֹ עַל עֵינָיו יְבָרֵךְ פּוֹקֵחַ עִוְרִים. *Magen Avraham* (ibid.) comments on this that since one has not yet washed his hands at this point, he may touch his eyes only with the aid of a garment. This would then require putting on a garment first (מַלְבִּישׁ עֲרֻמִּים) and then — via the garment — touching the eyes and saying פּוֹקֵחַ עִוְרִים. However, according to the present prevailing order, whereby one washes his hands before making all these *berachos,* there would be no problem in touching the eyes first.

So while *minhag Frankfurt* follows the order of the *Shulchan Aruch,* the generally accepted *minhag* of saying פּוֹקֵחַ עִוְרִים followed by מַלְבִּישׁ עֲרֻמִּים reflects the reality of our present-day order of washing our hands before saying all the *berachos,* which would allow one to touch his eyes before dressing.

❦ מַלְבִּישׁ עֲרֻמִּים — **Who clothes the naked.** The simple meaning of this *berachah* is to thank *HaKadosh Baruch Hu* for giving us clothing as protection against the elements. More profoundly, though, it refers to the gift of garments by *HaKadosh Baruch Hu* to Adam and Chavah when they left *Gan Eden.* The human being was originally created naked. However, when he gave preeminence to the demands of his body and committed the sin of the *eitz hadaas* (Tree of Knowledge) in an animal-like fashion, it became necessary for *HaKadosh Baruch Hu* to clothe his body, which is similar to that of an animal, so that he be ever cognizant of his superiority over the animals. The human being is the only creature on earth that has free will. He has the ability to overcome his animalistic urges. Clothing, then, symbolically distinguishes men from animals. Thus, the concept of *tzenius* (modesty) was born. One covers those portions of the body which humans have in common with the animals. However, the face, which portrays man's superiority over animals, and the hands, with which we control the world, need not be clothed.

❦ פּוֹקֵחַ עִוְרִים — **Who gives sight to the blind.** This means that *HaKadosh Baruch Hu* makes the blind see. It would be good to close our eyes momentarily while making this *berachah* and imagine how our whole life would change if we could no longer open them. Then, when we open our eyes again, we come to appreciate the miracle of sight. How sweet it is, as expressed by the words: וּמָתוֹק הָאוֹר וְטוֹב לַעֵינָיִם, *Sweet is the light and it is good for the eyes* (*Koheles* 11:7).

מַתִּיר אֲסוּרִים — Who releases the bound. This *berachah* means literally that *HaKadosh Baruch Hu* unties those that are bound, that are tied up. Our ability to move is a gift from Him, not to be taken for granted. While we are asleep, we have no voluntary control over our movements, similar to one who is tied up or paralyzed *chas v'shalom.* Each morning when we awaken, we recognize this gift anew. Included in this *berachah* is our *hakaras hatov* to *HaKadosh Baruch Hu* for the power of speech and hearing. These abilities were also "tied up," not functioning, during sleep.

The next *berachah* is זוֹקֵף כְּפוּפִים. We have the strength and energy to get up out of bed! Even one who is too sick to get out of bed, or is deaf, dumb, or blind, *chas v'shalom*, would still make these *berachos,* because they were composed for those who have normal human functions, and they can be of help to those who, unfortunately, lack them.

רוֹקַע הָאָרֶץ עַל הַמָּיִם — Who spreads out the earth upon the waters. When we arise, we stand on firm ground. The crust of the earth covers an interior which is liquid, made up of water, and, at its center, molten metal. If *HaKadosh Baruch Hu* would not have solidified the surface of the earth, life, as we know it, would be impossible. I experienced two earthquakes in my life; one was in Germany, the other in Los Angeles. These occurrences made me so much more thankful to *HaKadosh Baruch Hu* for the secure feeling of standing on firm ground. Our Sages (*Tamid* 32a) tell us that even experienced sailors, who spend most of their life at sea, do not feel fully secure until they make landfall. The same feeling applies to air travel in our time. No matter how experienced the traveler, there is a certain sense of security when one steps out onto terra firma.

שֶׁעָשָׂה לִי כָּל צָרְכִּי — Who has provided me my every need. This *berachah* was originally intended to be said when the shoes are put on, as this is usually done upon finishing dressing. It is noteworthy that this is the only *berachah* in which the word לִי appears. The individual person stresses that *HaKadosh Baruch Hu* has given *me* all that *I* need. I have awakened, regained my senses, walked and gotten dressed. *I have everything;* I am happy with my lot. Regarding *others,* however, it would be highly inappropriate to say שֶׁעָשָׂה לָנוּ כָּל צָרְכֵּנוּ, "Who has provided *us* with all our needs." We are required to attempt to help others improve their lot in life with *gemilus chassadim* (acts of lovingkindness). [For further development of this ethical concept see *Maayan Beis HaSho'evah, Lech Lecha* 12:10.]

BIRCHOS HASHACHAR 35

◆§ אֲשֶׁר הֵכִין מִצְעֲדֵי גָבֶר — **Who firms man's footsteps.** Our *minhag* follows the opinion of the *Rosh* in regard to this text, instead of the generally used הַמֵּכִין. The simple meaning of this *berachah* is thanking *HaKadosh Baruch Hu* for our ability to walk. If a person cannot walk, he still says it because other people can walk and help him.

Up to this point in our *berachos* we have thanked *HaKadosh Baruch Hu* for what He has done for us, concluding with שֶׁעָשָׂה לִי כָּל צְרָכִי. However, beginning with this *berachah,* as we begin walking, we focus on which direction in life we have decided to take. We can choose to go "right" or "left," either to follow the paths of *HaKadosh Baruch Hu* — וְהָלַכְתָּ בִּדְרָכָיו — or not. Regardless of the path we choose, we will lead our lives in accordance with our free will. We have the ability to make our own decisions about life. If we choose the *derech hachaim,* the proper way of life, we can be assured that *HaKadosh Baruch Hu* will help us follow this path. Our *Chachamim* express this as בָּא לִיטַהֵר מְסַיְּיעִים אוֹתוֹ, *If one comes to purify himself, they help him* (Shabbos 104a), and if not, we will be held responsible.

◆§ אוֹזֵר יִשְׂרָאֵל בִּגְבוּרָה — **Who girds Israel with strength.** This *berachah* was originally intended to be said when we put on our belts (or close the top button of our pants). Up to this point we mention *chasdei Hashem* (God's kindness) which apply to all mankind. Now, however, we say that we, *Klal Yisrael,* have been given the special opportunity and strength, through Torah and *mitzvos,* to make our human aspect dominate the animal aspect of our body. This refers to the *halachah* that when one expresses words of Torah or *tefillah,* the upper part of the body, representing the "human" aspect, must be separated from the lower, or animal part, by means of a belt or other enclosure. This *halachah* is called: שֶׁלֹּא יְהֵא לִבּוֹ רוֹאֶה אֶת הָעֶרְוָה (cf. *Berachos* 25b). Notwithstanding the essential importance of the animal aspect of our lives, it must always be kept in check by our human side. This takes a great deal of effort. With this *berachah* we thank *HaKadosh Baruch Hu* for giving us the strength to control our animal instincts, so that they serve our human aspect, in accordance with the requirements of the Torah.

At every *bris milah,* we say the words צִוָּה לְהַצִּיל יְדִידוּת שְׁאֵרֵנוּ מִשַּׁחַת לְמַעַן בְּרִיתוֹ אֲשֶׁר שָׂם בִּבְשָׂרֵנוּ, *We pray that HaKadosh Baruch Hu will decree to save the friendship of our bodies from destruction for the sake of the covenant that He established in our flesh.* The *bris milah* creates a covenant, a "friendship," and an understanding that the human aspect is to dominate the animal aspect of our bodies. So we pray that this harmonious combination, forming the Jewish male, be preserved from destruction. This strength of dominance was given to *Klal Yisrael* through Torah and *mitzvos* and this is the גְּבוּרָה to which we refer in our *berachah.* The next *berachah,* which is also specifically for Israel, is:

◆§ עוֹטֵר יִשְׂרָאֵל בְּתִפְאָרָה — **Who crowns Israel with splendor.** The simple reference is — as mentioned in the Gemara — to covering the head upon dressing, which is then culminated by putting on the *tefillin shel rosh*. Therefore, according to the *minhag* of Frankfurt which we follow, we do not say this *berachah* at Shacharis on Tishah B'Av, but do so at Minchah when we put on our *tefillin*.

However, on a deeper level, the *berachah* refers to the fact that the *mitzvos* which a person performs are the *malachim*, (angels) which protect him. The Rambam says: אָמְרוּ חֲכָמִים הָרִאשׁוֹנִים: כָּל מִי שֶׁיֵּשׁ לוֹ תְּפִלִּין בְּרֹאשׁוֹ וּבִזְרוֹעוֹ וְצִיצִית בְּבִגְדוֹ וּמְזוּזָה בְּפִתְחוֹ מוּחְזָק הוּא שֶׁלֹּא יֶחֱטָא שֶׁהֲרֵי יֵשׁ לוֹ מַזְכִּירִים רַבִּים, וְהֵן הֵם הַמַּלְאָכִים שֶׁמַּצִּילִין אוֹתוֹ מִלַּחֲטוֹא, *Our Early Sages said: Everyone who has tefillin on his head and his arm, and tzitzis on his garment, and a mezuzah on his doorpost is assured that he will not sin. For he has many reminders, and they are the angels who save him from sinning* (Rambam, Hil. Mezuzah 87:13). When a person performs *mitzvos* he is actually surrounded by *malachim*: מִימִינִי מִיכָאֵל וּמִשְּׂמֹאלִי גַּבְרִיאֵל וּמִלְּפָנַי אוּרִיאֵל וּמֵאֲחוֹרַי רְפָאֵל וְעַל רֹאשִׁי שְׁכִינַת אֵל, *May Michael be at my right, Gavriel at my left, Uriel before me, Rephael behind me, and above my head the Presence of God* (Pirkei D'Rabbi Eliezer Ch. 4). If a person communicates with *HaKadosh Baruch Hu* and is surrounded by the *malachim* of his *mitzvos*, then the *Shechinah* is above his head. The word *Shechinah* comes from *shachein*, which means "close." *HaKadosh Baruch Hu* comes close to him. Thus, עוֹטֵר יִשְׂרָאֵל בְּתִפְאָרָה, He crowns Yisrael with the glory of His *Shechinah,* as a result of our *mitzvos*.

Just as we make a separation between the human and animal parts of the body, so do we separate our mind, our intelligence, from that of *HaKadosh Baruch Hu* by covering our head and, symbolically, our intelligence, as "*ervah*," "unrefined nakedness," compared to the *Daas Elyon,* the omniscience of *HaKadosh Baruch Hu*. I inferred this truly profound thought from a footnote in *Chorev* by R' Samson R. Hirsch (see *Chukim* 14-4). Women express this same idea through the *tzenius* of their clothing, and for married women this includes the covering of the hair.

◆§ הַנּוֹתֵן לַיָּעֵף כֹּחַ — **Who gives strength to the weary.** This *berachah* is not found in the Gemara at all. It originated with *Rabbanan Savorai* who edited the Gemara — and sometimes added some material — during the period between the *Amoraim* and the *Geonim*. The simple meaning of this *berachah* is that *HaKadosh Baruch Hu* replenishes a person's strength. He feels refreshed upon awakening, although he had gone to sleep feeling tired. On the surface, this *berachah* seems to be in the wrong place in this list. First, it does not refer specially to Yisrael, as do the previous two. Second, by this time in the order of the *berachos,* we are already wide awake. We have already acknowledged that we awoke, that we can see, that we can stand up, walk, and put on clothing. We are all ready to face our day. Now we seem to be starting all over again. This *berachah* belongs at the beginning of the order.

The answer is found in the meaning of יָעֵף. The source of this *berachah* is נֹתֵן לַיָּעֵף כֹּחַ וּלְאֵין אוֹנִים עָצְמָה יַרְבֶּה, *He gives strength to the weary, and grants abundant might to the powerless* (*Yeshayahu* 40:29).

According to the context there, the word יָעֵף means exhausted, worn out. All of the *mefarshim,* including *Targum* and *Radak,* explain that this *pasuk* refers to *Klal Yisrael,* who are completely exhausted from the *galus* (exile) which they have had to endure for so long. (Simple tiredness would be expressed as עָיֵף.)

The *Rabbanan Savorai* who authored this *berachah* foresaw that the coming of *Mashiach* was not imminent at that time, and that the *galus* would be prolonged. They therefore wanted the Jewish people to express the thought that while we must face a hostile world, seemingly with no end in sight, we thank *HaKadosh Baruch Hu* for giving us the strength to live with it and tolerate it as a nation. So, while the simple meaning of this *berachah* certainly does refer to the feeling of refreshment upon awakening, its deeper meaning is the acknowledgment that *HaKadosh Baruch Hu* has given us, the Jewish nation, the special strength to endure our long, and often bitter, *galus.* We thus understand why this *berachah* was placed together with the others which refer specifically to *Klal Yisrael.*

הַמַּעֲבִיר שֵׁנָה מֵעֵינָי וּתְנוּמָה מֵעַפְעַפָּי — **Who removes sleep from my eyes and slumber from my eyelids.** Slumber — or sleepiness — is the state of dozing, between actual sleep and complete wakefulness. This is called נִים וְלֹא נִים תִּיר וְלֹא תִּיר (*Pesachim* 120b). It is said to exist when the dozing person is alert enough to respond to his name being called, but he is not fully awake.

This *berachah* presents quite a few difficulties. First, it too seems to belong at the beginning of our list. We have long since awakened, dressed, walked, etc. Why do we wait until this point to thank *HaKadosh Baruch Hu* for removing the slumber and sleep from our eyes? Second, what connection does this *berachah* have with the previous three *berachos* which specifically refer to *Klal Yisrael*? This is further complicated by the fact that the ending *does* refer to the Jewish nation: הַגּוֹמֵל חֲסָדִים טוֹבִים לְעַמּוֹ יִשְׂרָאֵל, *Who bestows beneficent kindnesses upon His people Yisrael.*

This seems to contradict the general rule of *berachos* that the ending must be similar to the beginning. We start by thanking *HaKadosh Baruch Hu* for our having awakened, something which all people have in common, and end by expressing our gratitude for His special kindness to *Klal Yisrael.* The third difficulty is with the text, which starts with the personal: הַמַּעֲבִיר שֵׁנָה מֵעֵינָי וּתְנוּמָה מֵעַפְעַפָּי, and then continues in the plural, שֶׁתַּרְגִּילֵנוּ בְּתוֹרָתֶךְ וְדַבְּקֵנוּ,

בְּמִצְוֹתֶיךָ וְאַל תְּבִיאֵנוּ, and so on throughout, including the ending, which refers to all of Yisrael.

These questions serve to highlight the deeper meaning of this *berachah*. While the simple meaning of the words definitely refers to our having awakened again, however, in a broader sense, we are here giving thanks to *HaKadosh Baruch Hu* for our *special* awakening as members of *Klal Yisrael*. At the creation of Chavah, we find the words וַיַּפֵּל ה׳ אֱלֹהִים תַּרְדֵּמָה עַל הָאָדָם וַיִּישָׁן, *Hashem made a deep sleep fall upon Adam and he slept* (*Bereishis* 2:21). The Torah then continues to describe how Chavah was created: וַיִּקַּח אַחַת מִצַּלְעֹתָיו . . . וַיִּבֶן ה׳ אֱלֹהִים אֶת הַצֵּלָע . . . וַיְבִאֶהָ אֶל הָאָדָם (ibid. vs. 21,22). *HaKadosh Baruch Hu* formed the woman out of one side of Adam, who was originally created with two sides (*Eruvin* 18a). Whereupon, we find Adam happily exclaiming: זֹאת הַפַּעַם עֶצֶם מֵעֲצָמַי וּבָשָׂר מִבְּשָׂרִי לְזֹאת יִקָּרֵא אִשָּׁה, *This time it is bone of my bones and flesh of my flesh. This should be called woman* (*Bereishis* 2:23). However, it is noteworthy that after his deep sleep we do not find that Adam ever awoke! While he was in the original state of creation, before being divided into man and woman, this "dual" Adam HaRishon was able to perceive the *Shechinah,* and was cognizant of מְלֹא כָל הָאָרֶץ כְּבוֹדוֹ, *the entire world is filled with His glory*. Once the "anesthesia" of תַּרְדֵּמָה, *deep sleep,* fell upon him, Adam and his counterpart Chavah did not regain this state of superawareness of the presence of *HaKadosh Baruch Hu*. They, and all humanity which followed, remained in the same limited state of awareness in which we live today.

However, we, as *Bnei Yisrael,* did historically receive flashes of a clear perception of the presence of *HaKadosh Baruch Hu*. We had the experience of *yetzias Mitzrayim, krias Yam Suf, Matan Torah,* and all the *nissim geluyim* (open miracles) in the desert. We are able to exclaim, מַלְכוּתְךָ רָאוּ בָנֶיךָ, *Your children beheld Your majesty,* because we did, for short periods of time, come out of the תַּרְדֵּמָה of mankind.

My Rebbe, Rav Yerucham Levovitz, the Mirrer *Mashgiach,* illustrated this concept with a beautiful *mashal* (parable). There was once an institute for people who were blind from birth. They lived in this institute, married, worked, and led otherwise full lives. A famous professor of opthalmalogy visited the institute and asked for a volunteer for a new operation which he had developed. He claimed that with this procedure he could restore sight, but the vision would last only for about twenty-four hours.

One person did volunteer and underwent the operation. The result was as predicted: For the first time in his life this man saw the world: the faces of human beings, his wife, his child smiling at him; colors, flowers, trees, houses. During the day he saw the sun; at night, the moon and the stars. He saw the world! He then went to sleep as usual, but upon awakening he was as blind as ever. However, after this experience, he was elected the leader of this institute for the blind. He knew how the world really looked and could act as an adviser to his associates in the institute.

This, said Rav Yerucham, is the experience of *Klal Yisrael* in history. While mankind remained in a state of תַּרְדֵּמָה, we were privileged to see glimpses of *Malchus Shamayim,* the reign of God's kingdom, during our great historical experiences. When we heard אָנֹכִי ה׳ אֱלֹהֶיךָ at *Matan Torah,* we perceived the presence of *HaKadosh Baruch Hu* with such clarity that the Torah tells us אַתָּה הָרְאֵתָ לָדַעַת כִּי ה׳ הוּא הָאֱלֹהִים אֵין עוֹד מִלְבַדּוֹ, *You have been shown in order to know that Hashem is The God! there is none besides Him* (Devarim 4:35). Rashi (ibid.) comments on this: כְּשֶׁנָּתַן הקב״ה אֶת הַתּוֹרָה פָּתַח לָהֶם שִׁבְעָה רְקִיעִים וְרָאוּ שֶׁהוּא יְחִידִי, *When God gave the Torah He opened the seven Heavens for them . . . and they saw that He is the One and Only.* We were actually *shown,* and made to intellectualize, as much as is humanly possible, the presence of *HaKadosh Baruch Hu,* the One and Only Creator.

However, after our great historical experiences of revelations of *HaKadosh Baruch Hu,* we, too, slipped back into our תַּרְדֵּמָה state of ordinary life. But, after we were singularly privileged to have had these glimpses, we were appointed by *HaKadosh Baruch Hu* to be the מַמְלֶכֶת כֹּהֲנִים וְגוֹי קָדוֹשׁ, the spiritual teachers of the rest of mankind.

So this *berachah* of הַמַּעֲבִיר שֵׁנָה מֵעֵינַי וּתְנוּמָה מֵעַפְעַפָּי, in its broadest sense, thanks *HaKadosh Baruch Hu* for having "awakened" us, albeit for short periods of time, from mankind's slumber, and for allowing us to clearly witness the presence of *HaKadosh Baruch Hu* in this world. However, this *berachah* is only said in the first person, מֵעֵינַי . . . עַפְעַפָּי, because, unfortunately, many of us are still "blind" — as is the rest of the world. We therefore continue this *berachah* with the following *tefillah*:

◈— **And may it be Your will . . . that You accustom us to [study] Your Torah and attach us to Your commandments.** וִיהִי רָצוֹן מִלְּפָנֶיךָ . . . שֶׁתַּרְגִּילֵנוּ בְּתוֹרָתֶךָ וְדַבְּקֵנוּ בְּמִצְוֹתֶיךָ ◈— We ask that *HaKadosh Baruch Hu* help us become knowledgeable in Torah and attached to His *mitzvos,* so that we will become privileged to be among the "sighted" ones of the world, as is expressed in *Ahavah Rabbah —* וְהָאֵר עֵינֵינוּ בְּתוֹרָתֶךָ, *enlighten our eyes in Your Torah.* [The author further develops this thought in his comments on אַהֲבָה רַבָּה, see there.]

◈— **Do not let us come into the power of error, nor into the power of transgression and sin.** וְאַל תְּבִיאֵנוּ לֹא לִידֵי חֵטְא וְלֹא לִידֵי עֲבֵרָה וְעָוֹן ◈— Unfortunately, these words have been wrongly translated in the English version of the *siddur* of R' Samson R. Hirsch as "Do not lead us into sin." *This is absolute heresy! HaKadosh Baruch Hu* does not "lead" people into sin. The original German correctly uses the words "*lass uns nicht kommen,*" meaning, "do not let us come" (to sin). The correct meaning here is, as *Chazal* tell us,

הַבָּא לִיטַמֵּא פּוֹתְחִין לוֹ, **If a person decides to do an** *aveirah,* **in accordance with his free will, the "doors are open"** (*Shabbos* 104a). It is his choice. So we ask *HaKadosh Baruch Hu* to help us overcome our temptations, and not make it easy for us to do the sin. The word תְּבִיאֵנוּ means *to come back,* as in יָצָא וּבָא. Before a person reaches the level of תַּרְגִּילֵנוּ בְּתוֹרָתֶךָ, and becoming attached to the *mitzvos,* he has done many *aveiros* out of a lack of knowledge, or a lack of determination to overcome his temptations. We now ask *HaKadosh Baruch Hu* not to make it easy for us to "backslide," to come back to our old ways.

There is a difference between the three types of sin: חֵטְא, עֲבֵרָה, עָוֹן. חֵטְא definitely means a sin which is done *b'shogeig,* by mistake. An example would be if one did a forbidden *melachah* on Shabbos either because he did not know that it was forbidden, or because he did not know it was Shabbos. Now, since *aveirah goreres aveirah,* one sin begets another sin, the next level of sin is עֲבֵרָה, correctly translated as *transgression.* He has crossed the line of the permissible. At first, he mistakenly commits the sin, and then repeats it until it becomes habitual and normal conduct to him, which he now considers permissible. אָמַר רַב הוּנָא כֵּיוָן שֶׁעָבַר אָדָם עֲבֵרָה וְשָׁנָה בָּהּ נַעֲשֵׂית לוֹ הוּתְּרָה לוֹ, *Rav Huna said: When a person commits a sin and repeats it, it becomes, for him, "permissible"* (*Yoma* 86b).

So we ask *HaKadosh Baruch Hu* that if we have already done a חֵטְא by mistake, let it not develop further. The first level of escalation is עֲבֵרָה, habitual conduct. Eventually, this can grow into עָוֹן, a knowing and willful violation of the law. The person has lost the horror of the sin and he now knowingly does the *aveirah b'meizid,* intentionally.

וְלֹא לִידֵי נִסָּיוֹן — **Do not let us fall into the hands of** (be captured by) **temptation.** Although we have just finished asking for help and protection against the different forms of sin, we now ask *HaKadosh Baruch Hu* to give us the strength to overcome the daily tests in our lives. Every person struggles with many *nisyonos* (challenges) in his life. But each person is also given the potential strength to overcome the tests which he must face. We now ask *HaKadosh Baruch Hu* to give us the willpower and fortitude to implement the strength within us to overcome our tests. We also ask that we not be faced with those *nisyonos* that we do not have the power to overcome.

וְלֹא לִידֵי בִזָּיוֹן — **Do not let us become disgraced.** We are disgraced when we fail our *nisyonos,* knowing very well that others were faced with the same temptations and *did* overcome them. This refers not only to public *bizayon* (embarrassment) in this world, but also to shame in *Olam Haba.* When the time comes for us to offer a *din v'cheshbon* (accounting of our lives) after we leave this world, all of our deeds are clearly detailed before the Heavenly court. I once heard Rav Elyah Lopian say that the Heavenly Court consists of the *neshamos* of the *tzaddikim* who lived in our time, including the parents and *Rebbe'im* of the person who is being judged. They now sit and listen to all the details of the *aveiros* which he or she did. No matter how cleverly they were hidden during life, everything is now out in the open! These *neshamos* also faced the same *nisyonos* while they were alive, but they overcame them. This is the ultimate shame. So our *tefillah* is that we not succumb to the *nisyonos,* and to the inevitable result — shame in this world and in the World to Come.

וְאַל תַּשְׁלֶט בָּנוּ יֵצֶר הָרָע — **Let not the Evil Inclination dominate us.** We ask that *HaKadosh Baruch Hu* not allow the *yetzer hara* to become a ruler, a power, over us. The Gemara (*Succah* 52b) quotes, צוֹפֶה רָשָׁע לַצַּדִּיק וּמְבַקֵּשׁ לַהֲמִיתוֹ, *The wicked one watches for the righteous and seeks to kill him* (*Tehillim* 37:32), explaining that this refers to the person's constant struggle within himself. יִצְרוֹ שֶׁל אָדָם מִתְגַּבֵּר עָלָיו בְּכָל יוֹם . . . וְאִלְמָלֵא הקב״ה שֶׁעוֹזֵר לוֹ אֵינוֹ יָכוֹל לוֹ. This means that every day a person's *yetzer* attempts to overpower him and if it would not be for the help of *HaKadosh Baruch Hu,* the person could not overcome it.

We know that each person has two opposite forces within himself, the *yetzer hatov* and the *yetzer hara. Berachos* 61a quotes the *pasuk,* וַיִּיצֶר ה׳ אֱלֹהִים אֶת הָאָדָם, *And Hashem God formed the man* (*Bereishis* 2:7). The spelling of וַיִּיצֶר (with two *yudin*) is a reference to two "creations" within the person, the *yetzer hatov* and the *yetzer hara.* We have an inner drive, a fascination, with the *tov,* and a similar fascination with the *ra.* We are an enigma to ourselves. The very same person who has total *emunah* in *HaKadosh Baruch Hu* while saying *Shema Yisrael* at the end of *Ne'ilah* on Yom Kippur has, in other circumstances, a desire for *zenus* and *minus* (sexual sins and apostasy). The Torah tells us, וְלֹא תָתוּרוּ אַחֲרֵי לְבַבְכֶם וְאַחֲרֵי עֵינֵיכֶם, *and you shall not explore after your heart and after your eyes* (*Bamidbar* 15:39). The Gemara there explains this as follows: אַחֲרֵי לְבַבְכֶם זוֹ מִינוּת, וְאַחֲרֵי עֵינֵיכֶם זֶה הִרְהוּר עֲבֵירָה. The Torah here warns us to be wary of the two basic *yetzer hara* instincts. One is *minus* or *avodah zarah,* which today is atheism or agnosticism, and is indicated by לְבַבְכֶם; the other is called עֵינֵיכֶם, which arouses one to sin, to lustful thoughts, and leads to *zenus.* The *pasuk* continues, אֲשֶׁר אַתֶּם זֹנִים אַחֲרֵיהֶם, *after which you stray.* If you follow these thoughts you ipso facto become diverted from *HaKadosh Baruch Hu.* Although, normally, thinking about an *aveirah* does not become part of it (*Kiddushin* 40a), with regard to *zenus* and *avodah zarah,* the thought itself is the *aveirah.*

The Vilna Gaon (see *Oros HaGra, Shaar HaAvodah, B'Iyanei Tefillah,* end of Ch. 3) has a beautiful *peirush* on the mishnah in *Berachos* 30b which says: אֲפִילוּ נָחָשׁ כָּרוּךְ עַל עֲקֵבוֹ לֹא יַפְסִיק, *A person should not interrupt* (his *Shemoneh Esrei*) *even if a snake winds itself around his heel.* On which the Gemara comments (ibid. 33a), אֲבָל עַקְרָב פַּסִיק, *but if a scorpion (threatens him), he should interrupt* his *tefillah* and run away. This, explains the *Gra,* refers to our subject. The *yetzer hara* for *zenus* is called *"nachash"* (serpent). If thoughts of *zenus* enter one's mind during *Shemoneh Esrei,* he should just ignore them and keep on *davening*. But, if a thought of *kefirah* (apostasy) enters his mind, then he must be *mafsik,* he must stop his *tefillah.* The *yetzer hara* for apostasy is called *"akrav"* (scorpion). One cannot address *HaKadosh Baruch Hu* if he does not believe in Him.

So in this *tefillah,* which is of vital importance, we ask *HaKadosh Baruch Hu* to help us overcome the *yetzer hara* which is inherent in every person, and with which we have a lifelong struggle. It is so powerful that if *HaKadosh Baruch Hu* would not help us, we could not overcome it.

◆§ וְהַרְחִיקֵנוּ מֵאָדָם רָע וּמֵחָבֵר רָע §◆ — **Keep us far away from an evil person and an evil associate.** אָדָם רָע means an evil person who has lost his *tzelem Elokim.* The superiority which man has over animals, the מוֹתַר הָאָדָם מִן הַבְּהֵמָה, becomes אָיִן, *nothing,* without the *tzelem Elokim.* If the human being becomes impoverished of this most basic element, he becomes the poorest of the poor. This is alluded to by the phrase מֵאָדָם רָע which is an acronym for the Hebrew words for poor: מִסְכֵּן; אֶבְיוֹן; דָּל; מָךְ; רָשׁ; עָנִי. This does not mean that the poor person is *adam ra,* but *adam ra* describes the *poorest human being possible,* one who is devoid of the very quality that gave him his humanity, his *tzelem Elokim.*

חָבֵר רָע could be a friend or an associate, but is one who is a bad person. His influence could be detrimental, especially if he is a friend. He could be a boss, or co-worker with whom I associate in business. But he is an evil person. We pray that the circumstances of our lives not bring us into contact with such people.

◆§ וְדַבְּקֵנוּ בְּיֵצֶר הַטּוֹב וּבְמַעֲשִׂים טוֹבִים §◆ — **Attach us to the Good Inclination and to good deeds.** Everybody has an inborn *yetzer hatov* to do good deeds. Some people are inclined to give *tzedakah,* some to learn Torah, some to perform service to *Klal Yisrael,* to love *HaKadosh Baruch Hu,* and to keep His *mitzvos.* Everybody has these natural inclinations, but we do not always follow through on them. Our *tefillah* here is that we may be "attached to," or follow, our natural desire to do good on a regular, continuing basis.

◆§ וְכוֹף אֶת יִצְרֵנוּ לְהִשְׁתַּעְבֶּד לָךְ §◆ — **Force our *yetzer,*** our impulse, **to be subservient to You.** We are referring to ***our** yetzer,* as in יֵצֶר מַחְשְׁבוֹת לְבַב עַמֶּךָ, *inclination of the thoughts of your people's heart* (*Divrei HaYamim I* 29:18), which means the *yetzer hatov.* The *yetzer hatov* is an impulse like the *yetzer hara* except with the opposite motivation.

If we follow the *yetzer hatov,* uncontrolled by the rule of *halachah,* it too can lead us astray. This, for example, was the *sin* of Nadav and Avihu. They had an overwhelming desire to come close to *HaKadosh Baruch Hu* by bringing a voluntary *ketores* offering into the *Kodesh HaKodashim,* although they knew they were risking their lives by doing so. We cannot fathom the *yetzer hatov* of these *kedoshim,* but we do know that it was אֲשֶׁר לֹא צִוָּה אֹתָם, *that He had not commanded them* (*Vayikra* 10:1).

As another example, a person could become so angry at somebody doing an *aveirah* that he becomes a *kana'i,* a zealot, and shames the person publicly, or otherwise harms him in a way that does not accord with *halachah.* Such a person is driven by his untrammeled *yetzer hatov* but is not acting properly. We therefore ask *HaKadosh Baruch Hu* to make our *yetzer hatov,* which strives to do good, function only to serve Him.

§ וְתִנֵּנוּ הַיּוֹם וּבְכָל יוֹם לְחֵן וּלְחֶסֶד וּלְרַחֲמִים — **Grant us today and every day grace, kindness, and mercy.** Bestow upon us the blessing that we be accepted in the world with חֵן. This is commonly translated as "grace" or "favor," but it is not an accurate translation. (In the German-Jewish vernacular there is a word *bacheint,* which means something like a "nice person.") In any case, the word חֵן is definitely related to the word *chinom* which means "free" or "unearned." We find this sense of the word used in the *pasuk,* וְנֹחַ מָצָא חֵן בְּעֵינֵי ה', *But Noach found grace in the eyes of Hashem* (*Bereishis* 6:8). Even Noach could not rely on his own merits to be saved (*Sanhedrin* 108a). He was saved only because he found חֵן בְּעֵינֵי ה'. So we ask *HaKadosh Baruch Hu* that we find "favor" in His eyes, and in the eyes of all people with whom we associate.

רַחֲמִים, *rachamim,* is compassion for the deserving person. He has earned the mercy of *HaKadosh Baruch Hu.* חֶסֶד, *chessed,* is somewhere in between *chein* and *rachamim.* We say here that whether we deserve it or not, or are somewhere in between, we ask that *HaKadosh Baruch Hu* grant us kindness and mercy, purely because He loves us, as *Bnei Yisrael.* As the *pasuk* says, וְעַל כָּל פְּשָׁעִים תְּכַסֶּה אַהֲבָה, *but love covers all offenses* (*Proverbs* 10:12).

§ בְּעֵינֶיךָ וּבְעֵינֵי כָל רוֹאֵינוּ — **In Your eyes and in the eyes of all those who see us.** We know that everyone has the very normal desire to be liked by others. This is especially so among our close relatives, but is also true for all people. In addition, if one is well liked by people, he is usually well liked by *HaKadosh Baruch Hu* (*Pirkei Avos* 3:13). So we ask here that we find "favor" in the eyes of *HaKadosh Baruch Hu* which will be reflected by all those with whom we associate.

§ וְתִגְמְלֵנוּ חֲסָדִים טוֹבִים — **Bestow upon us beneficent kindnesses.** The word *gomeil* means, literally, to ripen. When a fruit ripens it is called *gomeil,* as in וַיִּגְמֹל שְׁקֵדִים, *and almonds ripened* (*Bamidbar* 17:23), so *gomeil* really means the fullest development of a particular object. It could also refer to punishment, which is the result of crimes, as in גְּמֻלְךָ יָשׁוּב בְּרֹאשֶׁךָ, *your requital shall return upon your head* (*Ovadiah* 1:15). So we ask *HaKadosh Baruch Hu,* וְתִגְמְלֵנוּ, to grant us חֲסָדִים, the full measure of His graciousness, which will also be טוֹבִים, meaning that they will lead also to the benefit of others. A *chessed tov* is something which is granted to me, with which I can also bestow favors upon others. This is the true, full measure, or ripened endowment for which we are *mispallel* here.

◆§ בָּרוּךְ אַתָּה ה׳ גּוֹמֵל חֲסָדִים טוֹבִים לְעַמּוֹ יִשְׂרָאֵל — **Blessed are You, Hashem, Who bestows beneficent kindnesses upon His people Israel.** He bestows upon us the full measure of His kindness, which we have called חֲסָדִים טוֹבִים. The full meaning of this *berachah* is now clear. It started with הַמַּעֲבִיר שֵׁנָה מֵעֵינַי וכו׳, which we explained as referring to *Klal Yisrael*. Since we have the Torah and *mitzvos*, and are attached to them, *HaKadosh Baruch Hu* has removed the "slumber from our eyes"; therefore, I, as a member of *Klal Yisrael,* can see the world clearly. We now conclude this *berachah* with the words גּוֹמֵל חֲסָדִים טוֹבִים לְעַמּוֹ יִשְׂרָאֵל. The fullest measure of all His *chassadim* is that He has "awakened us from our slumber," and opened our eyes, through our attachment to Torah and *mitzvos*. This is, therefore, חֲסָדִים טוֹבִים, because it will benefit us as well as the rest of the world.

‎יְהִי רָצוֹן שֶׁתַּצִּילֵנִי / Yehi Ratzon Shetatzileini

The previous יְהִי רָצוֹן, ending with גּוֹמֵל חֲסָדִים טוֹבִים לְעַמּוֹ יִשְׂרָאֵל, is written in the plural form — as a communal *tefillah* on behalf of the entire nation. However, the present *tefillah* is for the individual.

In *Berachos* 16b, we find a listing of various special *tefillos* with which some of the *Tannaim* and *Amoraim* concluded the *Shemoneh Esrei*. The *tefillah* אֱלֹהַי נְצוֹר, which we recite after *Shemoneh Esrei*, is based on that of Mar the son of Ravina who was the last of the *Amoraim*.

Rabbeinu HaKadosh (R' Yehudah HaNasi, also known as Rebbi), who was the last of the *Tannaim,* would conclude his *Shemoneh Esrei* with our יְהִי רָצוֹן שֶׁתַּצִּילֵנִי. According to some opinions, the ones who organized the *tefillos* — who were either the *Rabbanan Savorai* or the *Geonim* — placed this *tefillah* here, after the first eighteen *berachos* of the morning (עַל נְטִילַת יָדַיִם, אֲשֶׁר יָצַר, אֱלֹהַי נְשָׁמָה, followed by the fifteen בִּרְכוֹת הַשַּׁחַר), corresponding to that which Rebbi would say after his *tefillah* of eighteen *berachos,* the *Shemoneh Esrei*.

❧ ❧ ❧

‎⊰ יְהִי רָצוֹן מִלְּפָנֶיךָ ⊱ — The words יְהִי רָצוֹן מִלְּפָנֶיךָ are difficult to translate. This phrase is customarily rendered as "May it be Your will." However, this meaning is inaccurate, because it would then have to be expressed as יְהִי רְצוֹנְךָ. Literally, our phrase means, "May it be the will which comes from before You." This seemingly convoluted language requires an explanation.

There are two meanings for the word רָצוֹן. Basically, it has the meaning of *will,* or *want,* as we say in Hebrew: אֲנִי רוֹצֶה. However, it also has an additional meaning, that of *goodwill* or *well liked,* as in יְהִי רְצוּי אֶחָיו, *he shall be pleasing to his brothers* (*Devarim* 33:24). By these words, Moshe Rabbeinu is giving a *berachah* to Asher that he be well liked by his brothers.

We have many other examples of this meaning. Here are a few: יִהְיוּ לְרָצוֹן אִמְרֵי פִי, *May the expressions of my mouth please You* (*Tehillim* 19:15); כִּי רוֹצֶה ה' אֶת יְרֵאָיו, *Hashem is pleased with those who fear Him* (*Tehillim* 147:11); כִּי רוֹצֶה ה' בְּעַמּוֹ, *Hashem is pleased with His people* (*Tehillim* 149:4); כִּי בָם רָצָה לְהָנִיחַ לָהֶם, *He was pleased with them, to give them (a day of) rest* (*Maariv* for Shabbos).

In all these examples we find the concept of *HaKadosh Baruch Hu* having רָצוֹן, or *goodwill,* toward his people, especially toward those whom He loves, and who love Him. However, this goodwill is not visible on earth. It is known only לְפָנָיו, *before Him;* it is in Heaven. So the meaning here is that we ask *Ha-Kadosh Baruch Hu*: May Your רָצוֹן, Your *goodwill,* come forth מִלְּפָנֶיךָ, *from before You,* and may we experience this רָצוֹן by the fulfillment of our *tefillos*.

◈§ ה' אֱלֹהַי וֵאלֹהֵי אֲבוֹתַי שֶׁתַּצִילֵנִי — **That You, Hashem, my God, and the God of my forefathers, may save me** — today and every day. As previously mentioned, this *tefillah* is for each individual's protection.

In the previous יְהִי רָצוֹן we asked that we, as a nation, *b'zechus harabim* (in the communal merit of the Jewish nation), be kept *far away* from evil people — וְהַרְחִיקֵנוּ מֵאָדָם רָע וּמֵחָבֵר רָע. And, indeed, the *berachah* ends with גּוֹמֵל חֲסָדִים טוֹבִים לְעַמּוֹ יִשְׂרָאֵל. However, in this *tefillah*, the individual asks HaKadosh Baruch Hu for protection when he, personally, not having the *zechus harabim*, is threatened by *imminent* danger from אָדָם רָע וְחָבֵר רָע, who may already be posing a threat to his safety or well being. The category of שָׁכֵן רָע, a bad neighbor, is added in this *tefillah* because such a person poses an imminent threat to our well being. The individual therefore asks: ה' אֱלֹהַי וֵאלֹהֵי אֲבוֹתַי, *my personal God and the God of my forefathers,* שֶׁתַּצִילֵנִי — *save me, rescue me,* from such imminent danger.

◈§ הַיּוֹם וּבְכָל יוֹם — **Today and every day.** While our *tefillah* refers to this very day, we do not wish to sound as if this would exclude future days.
[Note: A source for the need of exactitude in the wording of our *tefillos* can be found in *Zohar HaKadosh* 1:169.]

◈§ מֵעַזֵּי פָנִים — **From brazen men,** from people who have the character flaw of עַז פָּנִים, a harsh face, the opposite of בּוֹשׁ פָּנִים, a soft face. Such people have *chutzpah;* they have no respect for the *tzelem Elokim* inherent in all human beings. They have no *kavod habriyos* (respect for mankind); they are shameless. In German there is a word, *"unverschamt,"* which aptly describes this. These types of people are a threat to us. We find these words in the mishnah: עַז פָּנִים לְגֵיהִנָּם וּבֹשֶׁת פָּנִים לְגַן עֵדֶן, *The brazen goes to Gehinnom, but the shamefaced goes to Gan Eden* (*Pirkei Avos* 5:24).

◈§ וּמֵעַזּוּת פָּנִים — **And from brazenness** — our own harshness of face. If we are forced to deal with others who are *azei panim,* and must respond to them in kind, we too can develop the bad *middah* of brazenness by our reactions, and we ourselves thus become an עַז פָּנִים. So we ask HaKadosh Baruch Hu to save us from both.

◈§ וּמִפֶּגַע רָע — **An evil mishap.** The word פֶּגַע means to meet someone or something unexpectedly. As in, חֵרֵשׁ שׁוֹטֶה וְקָטָן פְּגִיעָתָן רָעָה (*Bava Kamma* 87a), meaning if one has an unexpected confrontation with any of these — a deaf-mute, a deranged person or a minor — it is unfortunate, because he is responsible if he injures any of them or causes them damage, but these people have no legal liability toward him. The meaning here is similar. We ask that HaKadosh Baruch Hu protect us from unexpected or unforeseen mishaps. While these may be unforeseen by us, they are by no means "accidents." Our Sages tell us (*Chullin* 7b): אֵין אָדָם נוֹקֵף אֶצְבָּעוֹ מִלְּמַטָּה אֶלָּא אִם

כֵּן מַכְרִיזִין עָלָיו מִלְמַעְלָה, *A person does not even hurt his finger in this, the lower world, unless it has been preordained in the Heavenly Court that this should happen.*

◆§ וּמִשָּׂטָן הַמַּשְׁחִית ◆§ — **And from a destructive antagonist.** The simple meaning of the word שָׂטָן is antagonist. We find this in the verse, וַיָּקֶם ה' שָׂטָן לִשְׁלֹמֹה אֵת הֲדַד הָאֲדֹמִי, *Hashem stirred up an antagonist against Solomon, Hadad the Edomite* (*Melachim I* 11:14). When Shlomo HaMelech, at the end of his life, deviated somewhat from the proper path, *HaKadosh Baruch Hu* caused an antagonist to rise up against him, in the person of Hadad the Edomite. So שָׂטָן הַמַּשְׁחִית means a destructive antagonist, a criminal. Translated into our ordinary terms we might say, "May *HaKadosh Baruch Hu* protect us from accidents and criminal violence." This is especially meaningful in our times when violence is so prevalent. *Tur, Orach Chaim* 46, remarks that one is free, at this point, to add any of his own personal fears and concerns for his safety. He offers examples such as מִגַּנָּב, וְגַזְלָן, וְאָלָם, וְאַכְזָר, וכו׳. These extra requests can even be said in one's own vernacular, if he cannot do so in *lashon hakodesh*. However, with the proper *kavannah* (intent) these additional potential sources of danger are really included in פֶּגַע רָע and שָׂטָן הַמַּשְׁחִית.

◆§ מִדִּין קָשֶׁה ◆§ — **A harsh judgment.** This does not necessarily mean in *beis din* or in court; it can also refer to the way in which we are "judged" by people in our relationships and actions. We ask that we be judged by our fellow men, either by public opinion, or by our close associates, *l'chaf zechus,* in which they give us the benefit of their doubts about our actions. Indeed, *Chazal* in *Shevuos* 30a derive the *obligation* to give one's fellow Jew the benefit of the doubt from בְּצֶדֶק תִּשְׁפֹּט עֲמִיתֶךָ, *With righteousness shall you judge your fellow* (*Vayikra* 19:15). If we do not receive beneficial treatment, either judicially or by our fellow men, we are then said to suffer a דִּין קָשֶׁה, which we pray shall not happen.

◆§ וּמִבַּעַל דִּין קָשֶׁה ◆§ — **And a harsh opponent.** This refers to a plaintiff who may have a legitimate claim against another, and mercilessly presses his claim. An example would be a landlord who evicts a tenant for nonpayment of rent in the middle of the winter. It could also refer to arguments and differences of a nonjudicial nature among people. My opponent, who may have some kind of a legitimate complaint against me, may be unyielding and stubborn, and refuse to compromise and settle our differences. This could result in long-lasting animosity and destroy relationships. We therefore ask to be spared from any kind of בַּעַל דִּין קָשֶׁה, in matters judicial or interpersonal.

◆§ בֵּין שֶׁהוּא בֶן בְּרִית וּבֵין שֶׁאֵינוֹ בֶן בְּרִית ◆§ — **Whether he** [my opponent] **is Jewish or not Jewish.** Unfortunately, there are among our brethren some who could be called בַּעַל דִּין קָשֶׁה.

רִבּוֹן כָּל הָעוֹלָמִים לֹא עַל צִדְקוֹתֵינוּ
Ribbon Kol HaOlamim Lo Al Tzidkoseinu

The *Tur,* Siman 46, writes as follows: בְּסִדּוּרֵי אַשְׁכְּנַז כָּתוּב אַחֲרֵי יְהִי רָצוֹן רִבּוֹן כָּל הָעוֹלָמִים לֹא עַל צִדְקוֹתֵינוּ אֲנַחְנוּ מַפִּילִים תַּחֲנוּנֵינוּ לְפָנֶיךָ, וכו׳. This means that after we have finished asking *HaKadosh Baruch Hu* to save us from all the evil people mentioned previously, we now begin this *tefillah* by saying that it is not with a feeling of self-righteousness and superiority over the אָדָם רָע that we pray to You. We do not come before You as *tzaddikim,* but rather with humility we throw ourselves upon Your mercy.

The *Rema* (*Darchei Moshe* ibid.) comments on this: וְכֵן הַמִּנְהָג וְהַסֵּדֶר בַּסִּדּוּרִים שֶׁלָּנוּ, *This is the minhag and order in our siddurim.* However, continues *Rema,* this must be preceded by the words:

לְעוֹלָם יְהֵא אָדָם יְרֵא שָׁמַיִם בְּסֵתֶר וכו׳

The words of this *tefillah* are taken from a group of *Baraisos* known as *Tanna d'Vei Eliyahu.* We are not sure exactly who the author was. Some say there was a *Tanna* who had *gilui Eliyahu,* to whom Eliyahu HaNavi appeared, while others say there was a *Tanna* who was called *Abba* Eliyahu, and he composed these *Baraisos*. In any event, this *Baraisa* (see *Tanna d'Vei Eliyahu Rabbah,* end of Ch. 21) begins with the words לְעוֹלָם יְהֵא אָדָם יְרֵא שָׁמַיִם בְּסֵתֶר, *Always let a person be God fearing privately* etc., and is followed by the entire text of our *tefillah* ending with the words בְּשׁוּבִי אֶת שְׁבוּתֵיכֶם לְעֵינֵיכֶם אָמַר ה׳, *When I bring back your captivity before your own eyes, said Hashem.* It is interesting to understand why the *Rema* requires us to preface this *tefillah* with the actual beginning of the *Baraisa,* which are really words of *mussar* and not part of the *tefillah* which follows it. I saw an ingenious explanation of this in the *siddur* צְלוֹתָא דְאַבְרָהָם by R'Avraham M'Tchechinov, as follows. Since this *berachah* is not mentioned in the Gemara, there is a difference of *minhagim* between *Bnei Ashkenaz* and *Minhag Polin* as to whether to end this *tefillah* with the *berachah* בָּרוּךְ אַתָּה ה׳ מְקַדֵּשׁ אֶת שִׁמְךָ בָּרַבִּים [as we do] or to end it with בָּרוּךְ מְקַדֵּשׁ שְׁמוֹ בָּרַבִּים, without using the *Shem* (Name of Hashem). This difference of *minhagim* creates a situation of *safeik berachah,* a doubt concerning the requirement of reciting a *berachah.* Therefore, to avoid this problem, the *Rema* advises us to "learn" this *Baraisa* in its entirety, which then becomes *talmud Torah,* and, as such, every word may be said, including the *Shem.* A similar solution is given by the *Acharonim* for one who is in doubt if the time has passed for saying *kiddush levanah.* He should read the *nusach* (text) found in *Sanhedrin* 42a word for word, including the *berachah* at the end, so that it becomes *talmud Torah* with no problem of mentioning Hashem's Name in vain.

Now let us explain the meaning of לְעוֹלָם יְהֵא אָדָם יְרֵא שָׁמַיִם בְּסֵתֶר. The *Shibbolei HaLeket* (*Tefillah* 6) says that this declaration was said at the time of *gezeiras ha'shemad*, when Jews were forbidden to keep the Torah publicly, so we remind ourselves to be יְרֵא שָׁמַיִם בְּסֵתֶר, despite our exterior demeanor. This explains the ending, מְקַדֵּשׁ אֶת שִׁמְךָ בָּרַבִּים, which means we hope for the time when we can practice Torah and *mitzvos* publicly.

However, this *Baraisa* seems to have a broader application as well, because it uses the word לְעוֹלָם, which means this applies under *all circumstances*. Furthermore, we find the use of the word בְּסֵתֶר in *Tanna d'Vei Eliyahu* (Ch. 18) when it is obvious that it does not apply to a time of danger. For example, in אַשְׁרֵי מִי שֶׁהוּא יְרֵא שָׁמַיִם בְּסֵתֶר, *Praiseworthy is he who is God fearing privately,* the word אַשְׁרֵי indicates the *ideal* situation, and would not be used if the reference is to a time of danger. Second, we find there: מַעֲשֶׂה בְּכֹהֵן אֶחָד שֶׁהָיָה יְרֵא שָׁמַיִם בְּסֵתֶר בִּימֵי עֶזְרָא, *There was an event involving a certain Kohen who was God fearing privately in the days of Ezra.* There was no danger during the period of Ezra. So it is clear that while this certainly applies to dangerous times, it also applies when we do not have to hide our practice of Judaism.

The meaning of יִרְאַת שָׁמַיִם, *fear of Heaven*, does not only include fear of being punished for *aveiros*. It also has the meaning of *yiras haRomemus*, the feeling of awe at the thought of the "height" or Omnipresence of *HaKadosh Baruch Hu*. Rabbi Samson R. Hirsch explains that יִרְאָה, *yirah*, comes from ירא, which is related to קרא, the root of לִקְרַאת, *to meet*. So יִרְאָה, *fear,* means that a person should have the feeling that he is in the presence of — meeting with — *HaKadosh Baruch Hu*. This is what is to be understood by שִׁוִּיתִי ה׳ לְנֶגְדִּי תָמִיד, *I have set Hashem before me always* (*Tehillim* 16:8).

❧ ❧ ❧

ᴥ§ לְעוֹלָם יְהֵא אָדָם יְרֵא שָׁמַיִם בְּסֵתֶר — Always let a person be God fearing privately. We are taught here that we are not to flaunt our *yiras Shamayim* (fear of Heaven) publicly. This is a general rule לְעוֹלָם, applicable not only during *gezeiras ha'shemad*, but rather always. It is the meaning of the verse, הַצְנֵעַ לֶכֶת עִם אֱלֹהֶיךָ, *walk humbly with your God* (*Michah* 6:8). This refers not only to clothing in the narrow sense of *tzenius*, but it also refers to our relationship עִם ה׳ אֱלֹהֶיךָ, which is to be a very private one. The more *yiras Shamayim* a person has, the less he shows it in public. If a person brags about his *yiras Shamayim*, it is obviously flawed. This is analogous to a thermos bottle which is warm on the outside — a sure sign that it is broken on the inside. True *yiras Shamayim* is internal. The words used by Yaakov Avinu in his final address to his son, Yosef HaTzaddik are: וַתֵּשֶׁב בְּאֵיתָן קַשְׁתּוֹ, *His bow was firmly emplaced* (*Bereishis* 49:24). This is explained by the *Targum*: דְּקַיֵּם אוֹרַיְתָא בְּסִתְרָא, *He kept the Torah privately*. This is the essence of *yiras Shamayim*. It is a very private and personal relationship with *HaKadosh Baruch Hu*.

An illustration of this can be found in the description of the *Mishkan*. The Torah describes, at least three times, the intricate details of the *klei ha-Mishkan* (the vessels of the *Mishkan*), their composition of precious metals, the details of their construction, the gold-covered *kerashim* enveloped by the beautiful tapestry of *yerios* artistically woven with their *Keruvim* (cherubs). However, all this beauty was completely covered by the *yerios izim*, which were simple black covers made of goat hair. When one came to the *Mishkan*, all that was visible from the outside was a rectangular enclosure with a black goat hair cover. Furthermore, no one was even permitted to enter the *Kodesh* except Aaron and his sons. This was symbolic of the principle of הַצְנֵעַ לֶכֶת עִם אֱלֹהֶיךָ. The *kedushah* remains private and internal — בְּסֵתֶר. [Ed. note: See further on this subject in *Maayan Beis HaSho'evah*, *Haftarah* to *Parashas Balak*: וְהַצְנֵעַ לֶכֶת עִם אֱלֹהֶיךָ.]

◆§ וּמוֹדֶה עַל הָאֱמֶת — **Acknowledge the truth.** This has two meanings. First, it refers to our relationship with our fellow human beings. If, in a discussion or argument, one is shown to be wrong, he should admit it, and not try to justify his position. Second, it also refers to lifelong justification of opinions and ideas that are totally wrong. Some people go through life stubbornly holding on to false positions. *Tanna d'Vei Eliyahu* here teaches us to be honest with ourselves and admit our mistakes. An example of this can be seen by the behavior of Yosef's brothers. They were convinced that they were absolutely justified in selling him because, in their minds, he was a *rasha*, an evil person, and a threat to the stability of their family. However, twenty years later, while incarcerated and reviewing their lives, they realized they had made a terrible mistake. They cried out: אֲבָל אֲשֵׁמִים אֲנַחְנוּ עַל אָחִינוּ, *Indeed, we are guilty concerning our brother* (*Bereishis* 42:21). At this moment they were מוֹדֶה עַל הָאֱמֶת. They admitted that their long-held opinion was all wrong.

◆§ וְדוֹבֵר אֱמֶת בִּלְבָבוֹ — **Speak the truth within his heart** (from *Tehillim* 15:2). We must speak the truth in our heart, and examine our own behavior and attitudes. If we are wrong, we are wrong. We should admit it to ourselves. It is to be בִּלְבָבוֹ.

The Gemara (*Makkos* 24a) gives an additional application of these words: כְּגוֹן רַב סַפְרָא — This is explained by *Rashi* as referring to the time that a customer came to Rav Safra and offered him 80 "dollars" for some precious object which he had for sale. However, Rav Safra was in the midst of *davening* and did not reply. Thereupon, the customer, thinking his offer was too low, increased his bid to 100. When Rav Safra finished his *tefillah,* he sold the item to him for the original offer of 80, because he had accepted it in his mind during *davening.* He was practicing דּוֹבֵר אֱמֶת בִּלְבָבוֹ.

§ וַיַּשְׁכֵּם וַיֹּאמַר — **And arise early and proclaim.** One should get up early in the morning, and before any other *tefillah,* should say the following:

§ רִבּוֹן כָּל הָעוֹלָמִים — **Master of all time periods.** The word עוֹלָמִים presents difficulties. It is almost untranslatable. If עוֹלָם is used here in the sense of "world," then the plural would be עוֹלָמוֹת. We do, actually, use it in this sense later in this *tefillah*: אַתָּה הוּא בָּעוֹלָם הַזֶּה וְאַתָּה הוּא לָעוֹלָם הַבָּא. However, the usage עוֹלָמִים must be the plural of the other meaning of the word — that of eternity. It would therefore mean, "Master of all eternities," conveying the idea that He lives forever. Similarly, we speak of *HaKadosh Baruch Hu* as being (in בָּרוּךְ שֶׁאָמַר and יִשְׁתַּבַּח) חֵי הָעוֹלָמִים.

Rav Samson R. Hirsch explains the word עוֹלָם as coming from עלם, from which we get נֶעְלָם, hidden. In *Tehillim* (106:48) we find מִן הָעוֹלָם וְעַד הָעוֹלָם, meaning *HaKadosh Baruch Hu* is hidden from us from the beginning of time to the end of time. The origin of Creation is hidden. Even the words בְּרֵאשִׁית בָּרָא אֱלֹהִים veil the true secrets of *maaseh Bereishis*. Very few of our Sages were privy to understanding the real meaning of it. And the future is certainly hidden. Even the *Neviim* (Prophets) did not know about the details of the times of *Mashiach* and *techiyas hameisim* (Resurrection of the Dead).

This is expressed in, עַיִן לֹא רָאָתָה אֱלֹהִים זוּלָתְךָ, *No eye has ever perceived it, only Elohim* (Isaiah 64:3). Not only is the distant future hidden, but the immediate future, the next second of our lives, is also hidden from us. From one minute to the next there may be occurrences which could drastically change our whole lives. We are only familiar with the recorded past, and the present. Everything else is עוֹלָם, hidden, of which *HaKadosh Baruch Hu* is the Master, the רִבּוֹן. So the closest meaning would be, "He is the Master of all unknown time periods."

§ Not — לֹא עַל צִדְקוֹתֵינוּ אֲנַחְנוּ מַפִּילִים תַּחֲנוּנֵינוּ לְפָנֶיךָ כִּי עַל רַחֲמֶיךָ הָרַבִּים **because of our righteousness do we "throw" our pleas,** unworthy as we are, **before You, but rather because of Your great compassion** (Daniel 9:18). This is a familiar *pasuk,* which we repeat many times during *Selichos*. The word תַּחֲנוּנֵינוּ we know as coming from חִנָּם, which means free, or unearned. We ask *HaKadosh Baruch Hu* to have mercy on us, although we are unworthy and have not earned it. מַפִּילִים תַּחֲנוּנֵינוּ literally means we "throw down" our pleas. These words evoke the vision of an ordinary citizen coming before a king with a petition. Trembling with fear, he does not have the audacity to actually hand the petition to the king. Rather, he falls to his knees and bows in homage while placing it on the floor in front of the king's throne. His only hope is the king's mercy. כִּי עַל רַחֲמֶיךָ הָרַבִּים were the words Daniel used when he pleaded with *HaKadosh Baruch Hu* in his heart-rending *tefillah* for the rebuilding of *Yerushalayim*. This is the thought which should go through our mind when we ask *HaKadosh Baruch Hu* to be merciful with us, although we have not earned it.

מָה אֲנַחְנוּ מֶה חַיֵּינוּ מֶה חַסְדֵּנוּ מַה צִּדְקוֹתֵינוּ מַה יְשׁוּעָתֵנוּ מַה כֹּחֵנוּ מַה גְּבוּרָתֵנוּ — **What are we? What is our life? What is our kindness? What is our righteousness? What is our salvation? What is our strength? What is our might?** This is a moving, emotional *vidui* (confession) which we say on behalf of *all mankind*. These words have been incorporated into the *tefillah* of Yom Kippur with one slight variation. On Yom Kippur we say מַה יִּשְׁעֵנוּ instead of מַה יְשׁוּעָתֵנוּ. This conforms to לְדָוִד ה' אוֹרִי וְיִשְׁעִי, *By David, Hashem is my light and my salvation* (Tehillim 27:1), on which *Chazal* comment: אוֹרִי בְּרֹאשׁ הַשָּׁנָה וְיִשְׁעִי בְּיוֹם הַכִּפּוּרִים (*Midrash Shochar Tov* 27).

All of humankind, הָאָדָם, was created *b'tzelem Elokim, in the image of God,* and as such, man is expected to conform to certain basic standards of *derech eretz*, basic decent human behavior, which, our *Chachamim* tell us, came to mankind before Torah: דֶּרֶךְ אֶרֶץ קָדְמָה לְתוֹרָה (*Vayikra Rabbah* 9:3). As an example, we find Avraham Avinu saying to Avimelech: רַק אֵין יִרְאַת אֱלֹהִים בַּמָּקוֹם הַזֶּה, *There is no fear of Heaven in this place* (Bereishis 20:11). Such fear was to be expected from any decent society. Further, we find Lavan characterized as a *rasha* because he spoke out of turn, before his father (see Rashi on *Bereishis* 24:3). This, despite the fact that there is no *mitzvah* of *kibbud av v'eim* (respect for parents) for a Noahide. However, it is expected that any person created *b'tzelem Elokim* would have an inborn sense of honoring his father. We, *Klal Yisrael*, have been chosen by *HaKadosh Baruch Hu* to be His *am segulah*, His treasured nation (Shemos 19:5), and as his firstborn son בְּנִי בְכֹרִי יִשְׂרָאֵל (*Shemos* 4:22), a role model to teach the world of the existence of *HaKadosh Baruch Hu* and the moral laws that He demands of humankind. This is what we mean when we pray for the day when וְהָיָה ה' לְמֶלֶךְ עַל כָּל הָאָרֶץ — the whole world will finally recognize the existence of *HaKadosh Baruch Hu*. For the time being, though, we have failed in our mission to mankind; we are not yet a role model for the world. We therefore offer this *vidui* on behalf of all mankind.

What we mean here is that all the efforts by the decent people in the world to refine human life and uplift it to reflect the *tzelem Elokim* have not worked. Civilization, with all its accomplishments — including the great humanistic efforts, ethics, political and judicial systems, great philosophies, astounding scientific discoveries, beautiful art and esthetics, the harnessing of the forces of nature, and all the new inventions and innovations which make life more comfortable — did not succeed in uplifting mankind. We see this clearly today, more than at any other time in history.

מַה נֹּאמַר לְפָנֶיךָ ה׳ אֱלֹהֵינוּ וֵאלֹהֵי אֲבוֹתֵינוּ — **What can we say before You, Hashem, our God, and the God of our forefathers.** We who have been selected by You to enlighten the world so that they would recognize the *Ribbono Shel Olam*, have, unfortunately, failed in our mission. So we humbly say this *vidui* in our capacity as the children of Your chosen forefathers, on behalf of all mankind.

הֲלֹא כָּל הַגִּבּוֹרִים כְּאַיִן לְפָנֶיךָ וְאַנְשֵׁי הַשֵּׁם כְּלֹא הָיוּ וַחֲכָמִים כִּבְלִי מַדָּע וּנְבוֹנִים כִּבְלִי הַשְׂכֵּל — **All the powerful people are like nothing before You, the famous as if they had never existed, the wise as if devoid of wisdom and the perceptive as if devoid of intelligence.** While they lived, other nations trembled before their might. Now they are gone, relegated to the history books. The great philosophers and scientists of the past have been superseded, and much of their knowledge is now considered foolishness.

כִּי רֹב מַעֲשֵׂיהֶם תֹּהוּ — **For most of their deeds are desolate.** Most of their accomplishments have not resulted in the betterment of mankind. Their lives have been wasted. Today is the 10th of November (1991), the anniversary of the pogroms of *Kristallnacht* in 1938 in Germany, which was the precursor of the great *churban* in Europe. Imagine, this "nation of poets and thinkers" was, at its core, really nothing but a horde of highly organized wild animals. All their developments in medicine, science, art, music, and philosophy did not make them one iota more human. And so it was throughout most of history. Even in our great democracy here in America, freedom has led to the morality of the jungle and ethical anarchy.

וִימֵי חַיֵּיהֶם הֶבֶל לְפָנֶיךָ — **And the days of their lives are empty before You.** After all his worldly accomplishments, man has shown that he is nothing but an intelligent animal. Man has even developed the means to blow himself out of existence and destroy the planet Earth with him.

וּמוֹתַר הָאָדָם מִן הַבְּהֵמָה אָיִן כִּי הַכֹּל הָבֶל — **After all the many thousands of years of the development of civilization, man's superiority over animals is nothing, for all his efforts are for naught.** Never was this *tefillah* more appropriate in every detail than today. When I was young — and certainly when my parents were young — people believed that civilization had developed into a progressive state (*"Fortschritt"*) of better living. We see today that it was all a myth — הַכֹּל הָבֶל.

When we look at the construction of this *tefillah*, we recognize that it is based on the verse, הֲבֵל הֲבָלִים אָמַר קֹהֶלֶת הֲבֵל הֲבָלִים הַכֹּל הָבֶל, *Futility of* futilities! — said Koheles — futility of futilities! All is futile! (Koheles 1:2). There are a total of seven הֲבָלִים, as follows:

$$\begin{aligned}
\text{הֶבֶל} &= 1 \\
\text{הֲבָלִים} &= 2 \\
\text{הֶבֶל} &= 1 \\
\text{הֲבָלִים} &= 2 \\
\text{הָבֶל} &= 1 \\
\hline
&\ 7
\end{aligned}$$

This is explained by *Midrash Rabbah* (ibid.) as referring to the seven time periods of human life, from birth to old age. All of this is described by *Koheles* as הֶבֶל, *nothingness*.

Furthermore, the word מָה is used seven times in this *tefillah*, describing our pitiful weaknesses, our "what are we's"? This pattern continues with the seven phrases:

הֲלֹא כָּל הַגִּבּוֹרִים כְּאַיִן לְפָנֶיךָ
וְאַנְשֵׁי הַשֵּׁם כְּלֹא הָיוּ
וַחֲכָמִים כִּבְלִי מַדָּע
וּנְבוֹנִים כִּבְלִי הַשְׂכֵּל
כִּי רוֹב מַעֲשֵׂיהֶם תֹּהוּ
וִימֵי חַיֵּיהֶם הֶבֶל לְפָנֶיךָ
וּמוֹתַר הָאָדָם מִן הַבְּהֵמָה אָיִן

However, when the *tefillah* focuses on the joy of our role as עַמְּךָ בְּנֵי בְרִיתֶךָ, these seven הֲבָלִים are offset by seven laudatory expressions:

לְהוֹדוֹת לְךָ
וּלְשַׁבֵּחֲךָ
וּלְפָאֶרְךָ
וּלְבָרֵךְ
וּלְקַדֵּשׁ
וְלָתֵת שֶׁבַח
וְהוֹדָיָה לִשְׁמֶךָ

So we see that if we study the *tefillos* carefully, we can discover the secrets of their construction by our Prophets and Sages.

According to the order of our *tefillah,* corresponding to the architecture of the *Beis HaMikdash* which we outlined in our introduction, we are now leaving the entire non-Jewish world behind us. We have ascended the fifteen steps, and are proceeding through the great Gates of Nikanor into the *Ezras Yisrael,* taking a "leave of absence" from the rest of the world. The world of הַכֹּל הָבֶל is left behind, and we now focus on our role as יִשְׂרָאֵל and יְשֻׁרוּן. We therefore proudly declare:

RIBBON KOL HAOLAMIM 55

⇨ **אֲבָל אֲנַחְנוּ עַמְּךָ בְּנֵי בְרִיתֶךָ — But in truth we are Your nation, Your covenanted children.** The meaning of אֲבָל is *"in truth,"* as in אֲבָל אֲשֵׁמִים אֲנַחְנוּ, *Indeed, we are guilty* (*Bereishis* 42:21). We now announce — and we should really shout it from the rooftops of the world — that while we have failed in our mission to improve the world, we nevertheless are separate from the rest of mankind in that we are בְּנֵי בְרִיתֶךָ, the nation with whom You have made a covenant. And this is not due to our merit, but only because we are the children of Avraham, Yitzchak and Yaakov. We are the children of Your covenant, first, because we are:

⇨ **בְּנֵי אַבְרָהָם אֹהַבְךָ — the children of Your beloved Avraham,** as is expressed so powerfully in *Nechemiah* 9:6-8, and which we include in our daily *Pesukei d'Zimrah*: אַתָּה הוּא ה' לְבַדֶּךָ, אַתָּה עָשִׂיתָ אֶת הַשָּׁמַיִם, שְׁמֵי הַשָּׁמַיִם וְכָל צְבָאָם, הָאָרֶץ וְכָל אֲשֶׁר עָלֶיהָ, הַיַּמִּים וְכָל אֲשֶׁר בָּהֶם, וְאַתָּה מְחַיֶּה אֶת כֻּלָּם, וּצְבָא הַשָּׁמַיִם לְךָ מִשְׁתַּחֲוִים. אַתָּה הוּא ה' הָאֱלֹהִים אֲשֶׁר בָּחַרְתָּ בְּאַבְרָם וְהוֹצֵאתוֹ מֵאוּר כַּשְׂדִּים וְשַׂמְתָּ שְּׁמוֹ אַבְרָהָם. וּמָצָאתָ אֶת לְבָבוֹ נֶאֱמָן לְפָנֶיךָ וְכָרוֹת עִמּוֹ הַבְּרִית, *You alone are Hashem; You made the heavens, the most exalted heavens and all their legion, the earth and all that is upon it, the seas and all that is in them, and You give them all life; and the heavenly legion bows to You. You are Hashem the God, You selected Avram and brought him out of Ur Casdim, and changed his name to Avraham. You found his heart faithful before You, and You sealed the covenant with him.* Out of the vastness of the universe and all creation, physical and metaphysical, You, the Creator, selected one little child, who rediscovered Your existence, to be the father of Your future *am segulah*.

⇨ **שֶׁנִּשְׁבַּעְתָּ לוֹ בְּהַר הַמּוֹרִיָּה — To whom You made an oath at** the time of the *Akeidah* on **Har HaMoriyah:** בִּי נִשְׁבַּעְתִּי נְאֻם ה'. . . כִּי בָרֵךְ אֲבָרֶכְךָ וְהַרְבָּה אַרְבֶּה אֶת זַרְעֲךָ כְּכוֹכְבֵי הַשָּׁמַיִם וְכַחוֹל אֲשֶׁר עַל שְׂפַת הַיָּם וְיִרַשׁ זַרְעֲךָ אֵת שַׁעַר אֹיְבָיו וְהִתְבָּרְכוּ בְזַרְעֲךָ כֹּל גּוֹיֵי הָאָרֶץ, *By Myself, I swear — the wording of Hashem — that I should surely bless you and greatly increase your offspring like the stars of the heavens and like the sand on the seashore; and your offspring shall inherit the gate of its enemy. And all the nations of the earth shall bless themselves by your offspring* (*Bereishis* 22:16-18). God swore an oath to Avraham that his children would become great and world renowned. We express our gratitude here that *we* are those children. And, second, we are your covenanted children because we are:

⇨ **זֶרַע יִצְחָק יְחִידוֹ — the offspring of Yitzchak, the only one** of Avraham's eight children who followed in his footsteps: כִּי בְיִצְחָק יִקָּרֵא לְךָ זָרַע, *only Yitzchak's offspring will be considered yours* (*Bereishis* 21:12). Yitzchak was the only one who was like Avraham — God calls him יְחִידְךָ . . . בִּנְךָ (*Bereishis* 22:2), *your only son*. He even looked and acted like Avraham. (See *Rashi* to *Bereishis* 25:19.)

◦§ שֶׁנֶּעֱקַד עַל גַּב הַמִּזְבֵּחַ — **Who was bound atop the altar.** Yitzchak proved his *emunah*, his faith in Hashem, when he unhesitatingly allowed himself to be prepared as a *korban*. Yitzchak became the prototype for *mesiras nefesh*, wherein one offers body and soul up to *HaKadosh Baruch Hu* if the occasion requires it. For this reason, the *Selichos* which deal either with *Akeidas Yitzchak* or with persecutions of our people, where many gave their lives *al kiddush Hashem* (in sanctification of the Name), are called *Akeidah*.

◦§ Third, we are עֲדַת יַעֲקֹב בִּנְךָ בְּכוֹרֶךָ — **the congregation of Yaakov, Your firstborn son.** Despite the bitter protestations of Eisav to the contrary, You selected Yaakov as your firstborn son. He became the father of the twelve *shevatim* (tribes), which constituted the first עֵדָה, *congregation,* of the developing nation that was to become בְּנִי בְכוֹרִי יִשְׂרָאֵל. "I consider *Bnei Yisrael* to be My *bechor*" was the message which Moshe Rabbeinu brought to Pharaoh in the Name of *HaKadosh Baruch Hu*. Rabbi Samson R. Hirsch explains that just as the *bechor* is to be the role model for the other children, so is *Am Yisrael* to be a role model for the rest of the world, to save the whole world.

◦§ מֵאַהֲבָתְךָ שֶׁאָהַבְתָּ אוֹתוֹ וּמִשִּׂמְחָתְךָ שֶׁשָּׂמַחְתָּ בּוֹ קָרָאתָ אֶת שְׁמוֹ יִשְׂרָאֵל וִישֻׁרוּן — **Because of the love with which You adored him and the joy with which You delighted in him — You named Him Yisrael and Yeshurun.** Because of your love for Yaakov, You called him Yisrael, and because of the joy that You had with him, You called him Yeshurun. The *Tanna d'Vei Eliyahu,* from which this *tefillah* is taken, customarily uses the expression מֵאַהֲבָתְךָ שֶׁאָהַבְתָּ אוֹתוֹ.

The theme there is that *HaKadosh Baruch Hu* loves those who love Him. It is not a one-sided affair. And when *HaKadosh Baruch Hu* loves someone, that person feels His love. A person once told me, "I don't feel that *HaKadosh Baruch Hu* loves me." In response, I quoted אֲנִי לְדוֹדִי וְדוֹדִי לִי, *I alone am my Beloved's and my Beloved is mine* (Shir HaShirim 6:3). *HaKadosh Baruch Hu* tells man, "I love you, if you love Me." I explained that the reason he did not feel loved by *HaKadosh Baruch Hu* was because he did not love *HaKadosh Baruch Hu*. The most marvelous emotion a person can have is feeling loved by someone. The entire *Shir HaShirim* is a *mashal* (parable) of the love between *HaKadosh Baruch Hu* and *Am Yisrael*. (See *Malbim* on *Shir HaShirim* for a detailed explanation.)

◦§ וּמִשִּׂמְחָתְךָ שֶׁשָּׂמַחְתָּ בּוֹ — *Joy* here means that in addition to the aforementioned *love,* we bring joy to *HaKadosh Baruch Hu* when we do more than is expected of us, *lifnim mishuras hadin*. When we do the will of Hashem, we are rewarded with the love of *HaKadosh Baruch Hu*. But when we do more than is expected of us, the love then becomes joy as well. This is analogous to the joy that parents have when their children bring them special gifts for special occasions. When the children are especially thoughtful, the love blossoms into joy.

קָרָאתָ אֶת שְׁמוֹ יִשְׂרָאֵל וִישֻׁרוּן — **You called him (Yaakov) two names. One is Yisrael, because of the love, and one is Yeshurun, because of the joy.** The two names Yisrael and Yeshurun are found together in *Yeshayahu* 44:2, but there they refer to the Jewish nation. As to Yaakov himself, we know that God called him Yisrael (see *Bereishis* 32:29). And the reason given there is כִּי שָׂרִיתָ עִם אֱלֹהִים וְעִם אֲנָשִׁים וַתּוּכָל, *for you have striven with the Divine and with men and have overcome,* which, paraphrased, means, "Because you overcame all obstacles, and have been successful in bringing the message of God to the world."

However, the source for God's naming Yaakov "Yeshurun" is not that clear. We find Moshe Rabbeinu calling the Jewish nation "Yeshurun": אֵין כָּאֵל יְשֻׁרוּן, *There is none like God, Yeshurun* (*Devarim* 33:26). *Sifrei* (ibid.) remarks on this: While Moshe Rabbeinu tells Yeshurun (Yisrael) there is none like God, God says to Yisrael, כָּאֵל יְשֻׁרוּן, *Yeshurun is like God,* a truly remarkable statement. Nevertheless here, Aggadically, we find God calling the Jewish nation "Yeshurun." Although this name was not given to Yaakov directly, it applies to Yaakov, the original "Yisrael," as much as it applies to his progeny.

There is a related Aggadic statement in the Gemara (*Megillah* 18a) in which Yaakov is called אֵל. On the *pasuk* וַיִּקְרָא לוֹ אֵל אֱלֹהֵי יִשְׂרָאֵל, *He called Him "God, the God of Israel"* (*Bereishis* 33:20), the Gemara remarks, "God called Yaakov, אֵל." This is indeed astounding. The following could be the explanation. The word יְשֻׁרוּן comes from ישר, meaning straight, correct, or proper. The idea is that Yisrael in its mission in the world is expected to be יָשָׁר בְּעֵינֵי ה׳, to follow the straight road and do the right and proper thing in the eyes of *HaKadosh Baruch Hu.* However, the grammatically correct term for this meaning would be יַשְׁרָן. The usage יְשֻׁרוּן is a פֻּעַל form, which conveys the thought of "having been made straight." We therefore feel that the meaning implied here is that Yaakov is the representative of *HaKadosh Baruch Hu* in this world, much as an ambassador is the representative of the *person* of his nation's leader. He is directly connected — יָשָׁר — to his president or king. Likewise, *HaKadosh Baruch Hu* says to Yaakov, "You are My 'ambassador,' you are My יְשֻׁרוּן. You are directly connected to Me. I, therefore, call you אֵל. You represent My Person in this world." If anyone wants to know what *HaKadosh Baruch Hu* wants of him, Yaakov will tell him.

אֲבָל אֲנַחְנוּ עַמְּךָ בְּנֵי בְרִיתֶךָ — **But in truth we are Your nation, Your covenanted children.** Literally, we are the "children of Your covenant," which You made with our *Avos*. In this declaration, we cite them in their roles as "representatives" of *HaKadosh Baruch Hu* in this world. They each emphasize different aspects of *Malchus Shamayim*. To Avraham this meant that *HaKadosh Baruch Hu* was Melech HaOlam, reigning over all of mankind — וְהָיָה ה׳ לְמֶלֶךְ עַל כָּל הָאָרֶץ (*Zechariah* 14:9). His concept of *HaKadosh Baruch Hu* was that of worldwide *Malchus Shamayim*. He spread the knowledge of *HaKadosh Baruch Hu* throughout the entire world.

Yitzchak recognized *HaKadosh Baruch Hu* as his own personal *melech* (king) for Whom he was prepared, at any moment, to give up his life. He concentrated on subordinating his own personal life to *Malchus Shamayim*.

Yaakov recognized *HaKadosh Baruch Hu* first as *Melech* over *Klal Yisrael* — מֶלֶךְ יִשְׂרָאֵל וְגֹאֲלוֹ (*Yeshayahu* 44:6) — and knew that this *malchus* would eventually spread throughout the entire world. יִמְלֹךְ ה' לְעוֹלָם אֱלֹהַיִךְ צִיּוֹן לְדֹר וָדֹר, *Hashem shall reign forever — your God, O Tziyon, from generation to generation* (*Tehillim* 146:10). The *Malchus Shamayim* will have its focal point in *Tziyon*, meaning the *Beis HaMikdash*, which will be the capital of the world. From there, מִצִּיּוֹן תֵּצֵא תוֹרָה (*Yeshayahu* 2:3), the whole world will be involved and accept the sovereignty of *HaKadosh Baruch Hu* as taught by the Torah. This will then remain לְדֹר וָדֹר, for every generation to come.

These three different viewpoints are all complementary. Our *Avos*, each in his own specialized approach, spread the concept of the totality of *Malchus Shamayim* throughout the world.

This explains why the mere mention of אֱלֹהֵי אַבְרָהָם אֱלֹהֵי יִצְחָק וֵאלֹהֵי יַעֲקֹב in the first *berachah* of the *Shemoneh Esrei* places that *berachah* in compliance with the requirement that: כָּל בְּרָכָה שֶׁאֵין בָּהּ מַלְכוּת אֵינָה בְּרָכָה, *Every blessing wherein Kingship is not mentioned is void* (*Berachos* 40b). One of the elements of a *berachah* is that it describes *HaKadosh Baruch Hu* as *Melech HaOlam*. However, the first *berachah* of the *Shemoneh Esrei* does not use the words *Melech HaOlam*, and yet it conveys the thought of *malchus* by utilizing the words אֱלֹהֵי אַבְרָהָם אֱלֹהֵי יִצְחָק וֵאלֹהֵי יַעֲקֹב. When we address *HaKadosh Baruch Hu* as אֱלֹהֵי אַבְרָהָם יִצְחָק וְיַעֲקֹב, we have, ipso facto, declared Him to be *Melech HaOlam* (see *Tosafos* ibid. s.v. אמר אביי).

§ לְפִיכָךְ אֲנַחְנוּ חַיָּבִים לְהוֹדוֹת לְךָ וּלְשַׁבֵּחֲךָ וּלְפָאֶרְךָ וּלְבָרֵךְ וּלְקַדֵּשׁ שֶׁבַח וְהוֹדָיָה לִשְׁמֶךָ — **Therefore**, because of this distinction, having the privilege of being the children of Avraham, Yitzchak, and Yaakov, **we are obliged to thank You, praise You, glorify You, bless, sanctify, and offer praise and thanks to Your Name.** As we previously mentioned, the seven expressions of thankfulness and praise utilized here are meant to offset the seven הֲבָלִים with which we began this *tefillah*. These expressions of thankfulness, while being generally synonymous, still convey slightly different meanings. We intend to develop the nuances of these words with the explanations of *Pesukei d'Zimrah*. It is also important to note that there is a significant difference in the sense conveyed by the words לְךָ and לִשְׁמֶךָ in this *tefillah*. We intend to deal with this shortly.

§ אַשְׁרֵינוּ — **We are fortunate.** The word אַשְׁרֵינוּ, from אֶשֶׁר, as in בְּאָשְׁרִי כִּי אִשְּׁרוּנִי בָּנוֹת, *In my good fortune! For women had deemed me fortunate*

(*Bereishis* 30:13), means how happy and fortunate we are. Rav Samson R. Hirsch explains that אָשֵׁר or אַשְׁרֵי means *to progress, to stride forward* (see R' Hirsch on *Tehillim* 1:1, 37:31 and *Bereishis* 25:3). A person is in a happy frame of mind when he is progressing toward his goals in life, and certainly upon achieving them.

◆§ **How good is our portion,** — מַה טוֹב חֶלְקֵנוּ וּמַה נָּעִים גּוֹרָלֵנוּ וּמַה יָּפָה יְרֻשָּׁתֵנוּ **how pleasant our lot, and how beautiful is our heritage.** The words חֶלְקֵנוּ, גּוֹרָלֵנוּ, יְרֻשָּׁתֵנוּ are used to characterize our unique position in the world, much as one would if he received an unearned "windfall," in one of the following three ways:

(a) Being appointed a partner in a wealthy man's business. This is חֶלְקֵנוּ. We have been selected by *HaKadosh Baruch Hu* to become His "partner" and receive the Torah — כִּי חֵלֶק ה' עַמּוֹ, *God's portion is His nation.* This "partnership" is expressed by the *Mekubalim* as קוּדְשָׁא בְּרִיךְ הוּא וְאוֹרַיְיתָא וְיִשְׂרָאֵל חַד הוּא, *HaKadosh Baruch Hu, the Torah, and Yisrael are one* (see *Zohar HaKadosh* 3:73). This is all one "company," one unit. The Torah gives us all the happiness in the world. Our lives would be totally meaningless without it. This is our portion.

(b) Winning a large lottery. גּוֹרָלֵנוּ here refers to the *mitzvos*. We find the *goral,* the drawing of lots, being used on Yom Kippur to determine which he-goat is for Hashem and which is for Azazel. However, unlike a random lot, this *goral* is actually symbolic of the conscious choice which we have to make, whether to direct our lives to Hashem or to Azazel. Do we follow the *mitzvos* or not? It is our choice. הַחַיִּים וְהַמָּוֶת נָתַתִּי לְפָנֶיךָ הַבְּרָכָה וְהַקְּלָלָה וּבָחַרְתָּ בַּחַיִּים, *I have placed life and death before you, blessing and curse, and you shall choose life* (*Devarim* 30:19). On which, *Rashi,* quoting the *Sifrei,* comments: כְּאָדָם הָאוֹמֵר לִבְנוֹ בְּחַר לְךָ חֵלֶק יָפֶה בְּנַחֲלָתִי . . . וְעַל זֶה נֶאֱמַר: ה' מְנָת חֶלְקִי וְכוֹסִי אַתָּה תּוֹמִיךְ גּוֹרָלִי, This is similar to a father who is dividing his property and directs his son to the best field, saying, "Take this one." And this is what is meant by, *God is the portion of my share and my cup, You support my lot* (*Tehillim* 16:5). מַה נָּעִים גּוֹרָלֵנוּ, then, is used here in the sense of "how pleasant and sweet is the lot which we have chosen, at Your urging." In keeping the *mitzvos,* we have chosen life.

(c) Being a beneficiary of the will of a distant relative. This is יְרֻשָּׁתֵנוּ: Our entire "Jewish heritage" of תּוֹרָה שֶׁבִּכְתָב וּבְעַל פֶּה, *the Written and Oral Torah;* מִצְוֹת דְּאוֹרַיְיתָא וּדְרַבָּנָן, *commandments of Biblical and Rabbinic origin;* נְבִיאִים, *Prophets;* כְּתוּבִים, *Writings;* מִשְׁנָה, *the Mishnah;* תַּלְמוּד, *the Talmud;* תַּקָּנוֹת חֲכָמִים, *ordinances of the Sages;* תְּפִלּוֹת, *Prayers;* דִּינִים וּמִנְהָגִים, *Laws and Customs;* פֵּירוּשֵׁי רִאשׁוֹנִים וְאַחֲרוֹנִים, *the elucidations of Rishonim and Acharonim;* פּוֹסְקִים, *decisors of halachah;* etc., has all been handed down to us as an inheritance. We acquired it without effort; it was all done for us.

And now, we come to the high point of this *tefillah,* which deals with *kiddush Hashem,* as is indicated by the ending, מְקַדֵּשׁ אֶת שִׁמְךָ בָּרַבִּים. Rav Elchanan Wasserman told me, personally, of a tradition which is connected with the famous *ger tzedek,* the Polish count, "Graf" Pototsky. At the behest of the Catholic Church, he was condemned to be burned at the stake by the Polish government for the "crime" of converting to Judaism. The Vilna Gaon had arranged to bribe the prison guards, so that he could escape. However, the *ger tzedek* refused the offer, preferring to be *mekadeish Hashem* in public. He asked the Gaon which *berachah* to make at the time of his execution, and he was told to say this *berachah,* starting with אַתָּה הוּא עַד שֶׁלֹּא נִבְרָא הָעוֹלָם and ending with מְקַדֵּשׁ אֶת שִׁמְךָ בָּרַבִּים.

A great *tzaddik,* R' Alexander Ziskind, who lived in Grodno, the author of the famous *Yesod V'Shoresh HaAvodah,* disguised himself and mingled among the crowd at the public execution, so that he could hear that *berachah* being made and answer *amen* to it. The Vilna Gaon and the ashes of the *ger tzedek* were buried next to each other, and I had the *zechus* to visit these *kevarim* in prewar Poland.

The commonly accepted text that follows is: אַשְׁרֵינוּ שֶׁאֲנַחְנוּ מַשְׁכִּימִים וּמַעֲרִיבִים עֶרֶב וָבֹקֶר וְאוֹמְרִים פַּעֲמַיִם בְּכָל יוֹם שְׁמַע יִשְׂרָאֵל ה' אֱלֹהֵינוּ ה' אֶחָד. However, the words עֶרֶב וָבֹקֶר do not seem to fit as a parenthetical phrase after מַשְׁכִּימִים וּמַעֲרִיבִים. Therefore, according to our *minhag,* we have the text:

§ — אַשְׁרֵינוּ שֶׁאֲנַחְנוּ מַשְׁכִּימִים וּמַעֲרִיבִים בְּכָל יוֹם תָּמִיד פַּעֲמַיִם בְּאַהֲבָה וְאוֹמְרִים How fortunate are we that we lovingly begin and end each and every day by twice proclaiming: שְׁמַע יִשְׂרָאֵל.

מַשְׁכִּימִים וּמַעֲרִיבִים here also has an additional, figurative meaning. The first words which a father is to teach a child, as soon as he is able to talk, are: תּוֹרָה צִוָּה לָנוּ מֹשֶׁה וּפָסוּק רִאשׁוֹן שֶׁל קְרִיאַת שְׁמַע, *Torah tzivah lanu Moshe,* and the first verse of *Krias Shema* (see *Succah* 42a). So the earliest words (מַשְׁכִּימִים) uttered by a person are *Shema Yisrael,* and as life ends (מַעֲרִיבִים), the *chevrah kaddisha* says the words of *Shema Yisrael* with the person about to die. Life begins and ends with these words. [Ed. note: Those who were present at the Rav's *petirah,* witnessed him saying *Shema Yisrael* just before his *neshamah* left him.]

Shema Yisrael here means the *mitzvah* of *Krias Shema.* It must be said early enough (מַשְׁכִּימִים) to avoid missing the time limit, and it is also the last thing we say before retiring at night (מַעֲרִיבִים). Since this *tefillah* has as its focal point the *mitzvah* of *kiddush Hashem,* the reference here is to the ensuing words: בְּכָל נַפְשְׁךָ . . . וְאָהַבְתָּ אֵת ה' אֱלֹהֶיךָ, which means that we are commanded to sacrifice our lives *al kiddush Hashem,* if necessary. כִּי עָלֶיךָ הֹרַגְנוּ כָל הַיּוֹם means literally, *We are being killed for You every day* (*Tehillim* 44:23). This is explained by the Midrash (see *Zohar HaKadosh* 1:124 in

Midrash HaNe'elam) as referring to our daily readiness to give up our lives *al kiddush Hashem.* So, here, we proclaim our good fortune and happiness at being Yisrael and Yeshurun, which leads us to such heights that we are ready at any moment, if the Torah requires it, with the words of *Shema Yisrael,* and the loud בָּרוּךְ שֵׁם כְּבוֹד מַלְכוּתוֹ לְעוֹלָם וָעֶד on our lips, to be *mekadeish Shemo b'rabbim,* to sanctify Hashem's Name in public. These are the words of *kiddush Hashem.*

Normally, this requirement for *mesiras nefesh* applies only in the cases of *avodah zarah* (idolatry), *gilui arayos* (immorality), and *shefichas damim* (bloodshed). If a person is forced, at the point of a gun, to commit any of these three *aveiros,* he is required to give up his life rather than violate them. However, during *gezeiras ha'shmad,* where the "powers to be" are coercing Jews, upon threat of death, to *publicly* violate any *din* — and, according to some opinions, even certain *minhagim* — just to prove that they do not believe in it, one is also required to give up his life *al kiddush Hashem.* (See *Sanhedrin* 74b.) This occurred during the time of Chanukah, when people were forced to publicly eat forbidden foods. The famous story of Elazar and how he was *moseir nefesh* rather than submit to these demands is told in the *piyutim* of Shabbos Chanukah. As we know, throughout our history, especially in the Middle Ages, tens of thousands of our brethren laid down their lives with the words of *Shema Yisrael* rather than violate Torah and *mitzvos.*

We find a very noteworthy pattern in our history. In the decades that followed each period where Jews were murdered *al kiddush Hashem,* there was an explosive growth of Torah and *kedushah* (holiness) in the world. This was true of the period of the *gezeiras ha'shmad* of the Greeks, which was followed by the Chashmonaim dynasty, during which time the great *nissim* (miracles) of Chanukah occurred. Then there was the martyrdom of Rabbi Akiva and the period of *Asarah Harugei Malchus,* which was followed by the *Tannaim* and the *Amoraim.* After the time of the Crusades, which we call *gezeiros Tatnu* (תתנ"ו — the year 4856 in the Jewish calendar, corresponding to the year 1096 in the general calendar), there followed a period of several hundred years during which there was an explosive growth of Torah which produced *Rashi,* the *Baalei HaTosafos,* and all the *Rishonim.* It is my opinion that the phenomenon which we find today, known as the *baal teshuvah* movement, and the great resurgence of Torah learning in the world, is the result of the *kiddush Hashem* during the Holocaust.

Kiddush Hashem means that if a person sacrifices his life, he verifies his absolute *emunah* in the existence of Hashem. This is because if he had the slightest doubt, he would have capitulated at the last moment. And if this sacrifice is made in front of ten Jews, it is called *kiddush Hashem b'rabbim.*

Therefore, we say in this *berachah* that we pride ourselves in being members of *Klal Yisrael,* through whose veins runs the blood of the thousands of our ancestors who made the "supreme sacrifice" and were killed *al kiddush Hashem*. And we affirm our *emunah* in *HaKadosh Baruch Hu* and His Torah to the extent that we, too, are ready to sacrifice our lives, if this were to become necessary according to *halachah*. Of course, the Torah demands that we do everything possible to save our lives — וְנִשְׁמַרְתֶּם מְאֹד לְנַפְשֹׁתֵיכֶם, *You shall be exceedingly careful in protecting your lives* (*Devarim* 4:15). *Mesiras nefesh* for the purpose of *kiddush Hashem* is required only under certain circumstances, as outlined above. But if and when the time comes — by this *tefillah* we affirm our readiness to do so. Once a person is ready for *kiddush Hashem,* and he affirms it twice during *Krias Shema,* then nothing else is difficult. Is it hard to get up for *shul* in the morning? Is it hard to learn Torah at night when one is tired? Is it hard to give *tzedakah* when one feels the economic "crunch"? All this pales by comparison to the readiness for the supreme sacrifice.

This *tefillah* ends with the words, בָּרוּךְ אַתָּה ה' מְקַדֵּשׁ אֶת שִׁמְךָ בָּרַבִּים, *Blessed are You, Hashem, Who sanctifies His Name among the multitudes,* meaning that we give thanks to *HaKadosh Baruch Hu* for giving us the resolve and strength to offer our lives for *kiddush Hashem,* if necessary. This readiness for *mesiras nefesh* is not only our doing. We humbly and movingly recognize that if *HaKadosh Baruch Hu* had not given us the *siyata d'Shmaya* to implant this *emunah* into our hearts, such unshakable conviction would be impossible. It is *He* Who is מְקַדֵּשׁ אֶת שִׁמְךָ בָּרַבִּים, not us. This is analogous to the *berachah* of הַמּוֹצִיא לֶחֶם מִן הָאָרֶץ, wherein we thank *HaKadosh Baruch Hu* for *bringing forth bread from the earth.* The text is based on the words: מַצְמִיחַ חָצִיר לַבְּהֵמָה וְעֵשֶׂב לַעֲבֹדַת הָאָדָם לְהוֹצִיא לֶחֶם מִן הָאָרֶץ, *He causes vegetation to sprout for the animal, and plants through man's labor, to bring forth bread from the earth* (*Tehillim* 104:14). Although the farmer plows, sows, irrigates and harvests the wheat, which is made into flour and then baked to become bread, we do not give credit to the farmer. It is אַתָּה ה' Who is מוֹצִיא לֶחֶם מִן הָאָרֶץ. It is *HaKadosh Baruch Hu* Who gives the ability and strength to the farmer and baker to finally produce the bread. So it is with this *berachah,* wherein we praise *HaKadosh Baruch Hu* for giving us the ability to be *mekadeish Shemo b'rabbim.*

The conclusion leading up to the *berachah* begins with the words:

אַתָּה הוּא עַד שֶׁלֹּא נִבְרָא הָעוֹלָם, אַתָּה הוּא מִשֶּׁנִּבְרָא הָעוֹלָם, אַתָּה הוּא בָּעוֹלָם הַזֶּה, אַתָּה הוּא לָעוֹלָם הַבָּא — You are One Who existed before the world was created, You are the same One Who has existed since Creation of the world, You are the One in this world, and You are the One Who will be there in the World to Come. The wording is לָעוֹלָם הַבָּא, not בָּעוֹלָם הַבָּא, because we look forward to the future time when we will encounter *HaKadosh Baruch Hu* in *Olam Haba.*

The most overlooked word in this sentence is הוּא. Without it, the words would read: אַתָּה עַד שֶׁלֹּא נִבְרָא הָעוֹלָם וכו׳. While this might still convey the meaning that "You are Eternal and Omnipresent," it would leave out a very profound aspect of our perception of *HaKadosh Baruch Hu*. The finite human mind is not able to perceive *HaKadosh Baruch Hu* per se. He is Infinite, בְּלִי רֵאשִׁית, בְּלִי תַכְלִית, *without beginning or end*. We can describe what our mind perceives of Him: He is the Creator, He is the First, He is Omniscient, He is Omnipresent. These words are descriptive of what we understand of Him. However, this is still not His Essence. Had *HaKadosh Baruch Hu* not revealed His existence to His creatures, we would not know it. We would know just as little as a fish swimming in a tank, who is not aware that a world exists outside. All we know of the *Ribbono Shel Olam* is what He wanted to reveal to us about His existence. His essence, though, can never be perceived. It is, therefore, not possible to praise Him. We do not know Him, so how can we praise Him? Dovid HaMelech says, לְךָ דֻמִיָּה תְהִלָּה, *Silence is Your praise* (*Tehillim* 65:2).

The word הוּא conveys the idea of "He" — what we know of Him: We know that He exists, because He revealed Himself to us. He revealed certain aspects of His existence to us. Other than that, we know nothing of Him. He is הַקָּדוֹשׁ בָּרוּךְ הוּא, meaning "He Is"; but what the essence of this "He" is, is beyond our power of conception. So when we say אַתָּה הוּא, it means, "You are the הוּא." And *HaKadosh Baruch Hu* says: אָנֹכִי ה׳ אֱלֹהֶיךָ — about Me, you know only that I am אֱלֹהֶיךָ, and what I have revealed to you about Me. Regarding the essence of My Being, the human mind can have no conception. I am בְּלִי רֵאשִׁית בְּלִי תַכְלִית. What we *can* know are His "Names," that which He wants us to know about Him.

כָּל הַתּוֹרָה כֻּלָּהּ שְׁמוֹתָיו שֶׁל הקב״ה (see *Zohar HaKadosh* 2:87, *Parashas Yisro,* and *Ramban's* Introduction to *Bereishis*). Every letter, every word in the Torah is another *Shem,* another revelation of *HaKadosh Baruch Hu*. These are the things that He wants us to know about Him. Therefore, in *birchos haTorah,* we say: וְנִהְיֶה אֲנַחְנוּ וכו׳ יוֹדְעֵי שְׁמֶךָ, *May we be knowledgeable of Your Name*. The teachings of the Torah are Your "Names." *HaKadosh Baruch Hu* has revealed to us, through Torah and *Neviim,* what His will in the world is, and we pray that we be given the proper understanding of what that will is. This is all we know of Him. This is what we mean when we say אַתָּה הוּא.

Now we can better understand the previous words: לְפִיכָךְ אֲנַחְנוּ חַיָּבִים לְהוֹדוֹת לְךָ, וּלְשַׁבֵּחֲךָ, וּלְפָאֶרְךָ. These are words of praise to *HaKadosh Baruch Hu* directed to His הוּא aspect, but we go further and add: וּלְבָרֵךְ, וּלְקַדֵּשׁ, וְלָתֵת שֶׁבַח וְהוֹדָיָה לִשְׁמֶךָ, *we give praise,* etc. *to Your Name*. The word לִשְׁמֶךָ refers to the aspects of *HaKadosh Baruch Hu* which He has revealed to us about Himself: that He is the Creator of everything, that He is the One and Only God; that He is *rishon* (first) and *acharon* (last); that He directs the affairs of the world. Here we praise the known aspects of *HaKadosh Baruch Hu*. We therefore should concentrate on the meaning of the words, בָּרוּךְ הוּא וּבָרוּךְ שְׁמוֹ, which are often just quickly mumbled while the *chazzan* makes the *berachos*. As we have now seen, these words are very specific in their meaning. Blessed be "He" and blessed be "His Name." The *chazzan* should pause for just a second after בָּרוּךְ אַתָּה ה׳ to allow the congregation to say these four words, and to be aware of their meaning.

We now understand the words: אַתָּה הוּא עַד שֶׁלֹּא נִבְרָא הָעוֹלָם, אַתָּה הוּא מִשֶּׁנִּבְרָא הָעוֹלָם, אַתָּה הוּא בָּעוֹלָם הַזֶּה, וְאַתָּה הוּא לָעוֹלָם הַבָּא. You are the same הוּא before, during and after Creation, in this world and the coming world. Nothing about "You" has changed; nor will it.

קַדֵּשׁ אֶת שִׁמְךָ עַל מַקְדִּישֵׁי שְׁמֶךָ — **Sanctify Your Name through those who [cause others to] sanctify Your Name.** It does not say עַל מְקַדְּשֵׁי שְׁמֶךָ, which would mean "Sanctify Your Name through those who make a *kiddush Hashem*." What it does say is, "Sanctify Your Name through those who *cause others* to sanctify Your Name" (מַקְדִּישֵׁי = הִפְעִיל). As we have said, *kiddush Hashem* means to verify the fact that Hashem exists. This can be done privately or publicly, and it does not necessarily have to entail giving up one's life. It can be done in the privacy of one's own room. We were all born with a *yetzer hara*, which *HaKadosh Baruch Hu* wants us to keep under control. It is nothing to be ashamed of. If a person has an urge to do an *aveirah*, and there is nothing stopping him from doing so — nobody would ever know and he would take it into his grave — and yet, he overcomes that urge, because he knows *HaKadosh Baruch Hu* does not want him to do it, and for no other reason, הֲרֵי זֶה מְקַדֵּשׁ אֶת הַשֵּׁם, *this is sanctifying the Name* (Ramban, Hil. Yesodei HaTorah Ch. 5:10). He cites the example of Yosef HaTzaddik who refused the advances of Potiphar's wife. The sin could have been done in total secrecy. She would never have told her husband, nor would anyone else have known about it; and yet, Yosef tells her: וְאֵיךְ אֶעֱשֶׂה הָרָעָה הַגְּדֹלָה הַזֹּאת וְחָטָאתִי לֵאלֹהִים, *How can I perpetrate this great evil and have sinned against God!* (Bereishis 39:9). However, if a person does commit the *aveirah*, and even if nobody ever finds out about it and he takes it into his grave, הֲרֵי זֶה מְחַלֵּל אֶת הַשֵּׁם, *this is desecrating the Name* (Rambam, ibid.). And if it is done publicly, הֲרֵי זֶה חִלֵּל אֶת הַשֵּׁם בָּרַבִּים, *this is desecrating the Name in public.*

The same applies to *kiddush Hashem*. If done privately, it verifies a person's personal *emunah* in Hashem. However, if a person *publicly* refuses to do an *aveirah*, or does a *mitzvah*, even at the risk of life and limb, and thus encourages others to verify their *emunah*, he is not only *mekadeish Hashem*, but causes others to do so as well. He is then called מַקְדִּישֵׁי שְׁמֶךָ. So we ask *HaKadosh Baruch Hu* here that the efforts of those who publicly sanctify His

Name, even at the risk of life and limb, shall be successful in encouraging others to strengthen their *emunah,* and thereby *kiddush Hashem* will spread in the world.

וְקַדֵּשׁ אֶת שִׁמְךָ בְּעוֹלָמֶךְ — **And sanctify Your Name in Your world.** Even if there are not מַקְדִּישֵׁי שְׁמֶךָ in the world, we ask that *HaKadosh Baruch Hu* Himself manifest His presence in the world through events and occurrences of נִסֶּיךָ שֶׁבְּכָל יוֹם עִמָּנוּ, *Your miracles which are with us every day,* which clearly point to Divine *hashgachah pratis,* God's intervention into the details of the events of people's lives.

וּבִישׁוּעָתְךָ תָּרוּם וְתַגְבִּיהַּ קַרְנֵנוּ — **May You uplift and hold high our horns through Your salvation.** This is a metaphoric expression conjuring up the image of a bull or buck at peace, whose horns are raised. However, when he prepares for an attack, he lowers them to forcefully strike his foe. All the power of an animal is concentrated in the horns, and the horns are therefore symbolic of power. We ask here that through *yeshuas Hashem,* our "horns be held high," symbolic of our being at peace, not only temporarily, but וְתַגְבִּיהַּ, permanently kept high, at peace, without our having to "lower our horns" to protect ourselves against danger.

בָּרוּךְ אַתָּה ה' מְקַדֵּשׁ אֶת שִׁמְךָ בָּרַבִּים — **Blessed are You, Hashem, Who sanctifies His Name among the multitudes.** This is based on the verse, וְנִקְדַּשְׁתִּי בָם לְעֵינֵי הַגּוֹיִם רַבִּים, *and I become sanctified through them in the eyes of the many nations* (Yechezkel 39:27). As time goes on, more and more people in the world will recognize the existence of *HaKadosh Baruch Hu* and do His will. However, knowledge of Hashem will still not be universally accepted. Even in the time of *Mashiach,* there will still be those who refuse to accept *Malchus Hashem.*

This is the meaning of the war of Gog and Magog. The idea, וְקַדֵּשׁ אֶת שִׁמְךָ בְּעוֹלָמֶךְ, *universal* acceptance of *HaKadosh Baruch Hu,* will take place only in God's own time. [This is what we are *mispallel* for on Rosh Hashanah and Yom Kippur, in the prayer of וְתִמְלוֹךְ אַתָּה ה' לְבַדֶּךָ עַל כָּל מַעֲשֶׂיךָ, *And may You God, alone, reign over all of Your creatures.*] But for now, only רַבִּים, increasing multitudes of people — but not all people — are *mekadeish Shemo,* sanctifying His Name.

Atah Hu Hashem Eloheinu BaShamayim U'VaAretz / אַתָּה הוּא ה' אֱלֹהֵינוּ בַּשָּׁמַיִם וּבָאָרֶץ

As we previously outlined, at this point in our *tefillos* we have passed through the Gates of Nikanor and are now standing in the Israelites' Courtyard. There we find ourselves among the *Kohanim* and *Leviim* and the *anshei maamad* (communal representatives) (see *Taanis* 26a and 27a) representing all of *Klal Yisrael,* together with other ordinary people who had the *zechus* to be present during the offering of the *korbanos.* This, then, is the fitting time in our *tefillos* for us to express our yearning for *kibbutz galuyos,* the return of our entire people to Eretz Yisrael.

This *tefillah* should actually be divided into two paragraphs, both of which deal with *kibbutz galuyos.* The first paragraph begins with אַתָּה הוּא ה' אֱלֹהֵינוּ and ends with לְכֹל מַמְלְכוֹת הָאָרֶץ. The second paragraph begins אַתָּה עָשִׂיתָ אֶת הַשָּׁמַיִם וְאֶת הָאָרֶץ and ends with בְּשׁוּבִי אֶת שְׁבוּתֵיכֶם לְעֵינֵיכֶם, אָמַר ה'.

In the first paragraph we ask God, קַבֵּץ קוֶֹיךָ, gather together those who hope to You. קוֶֹיךָ means those *tzaddikim* who "continually look to You with hope." These are the special people who place their complete hope and trust in *HaKadosh Baruch Hu,* and we pray that *HaKadosh Baruch Hu* may bring these special *tzaddikim* back to Eretz Yisrael. The origin of these words is, הֲלֹא אַתָּה הוּא ה' אֱלֹהֵינוּ וּנְקַוֶּה לָךְ, *Surely it is You, Hashem, our God, and we place our hope in You* (Yirmiyahu 14:22).

The word קוֶֹיךָ, from תִּקְוָה, has an additional meaning — rope, as in תִּקְוַת חוּט הַשָּׁנִי, *cord of scarlet thread* (Yehoshua 2:18), or נָטָה קָו, *stretches a line* (Yeshayahu 44:13). The reference here is to one who has a "tie" or direct connection to *HaKadosh Baruch Hu.* We also refer to this תִּקְוָה in the *Shemoneh Esrei,* where we say: הַטּוֹב כִּי לֹא כָלוּ רַחֲמֶיךָ וְהַמְרַחֵם כִּי לֹא תַמּוּ חֲסָדֶיךָ, מֵעוֹלָם קִוִּינוּ לָךְ. We thank *HaKadosh Baruch Hu* for all the daily *nissim* (miracles) which we experience, and ask that His goodness and mercy never come to an end, although we do not deserve this. Then we add, מֵעוֹלָם קִוִּינוּ לָךְ, *we have always placed hope in You.* We have always kept our "tie" to You, even if the outlook was totally hopeless. This is followed by עַל הַנִּסִּים, where we mention the salvation of *Klal Yisrael* on Purim and on Chanukah. Both times, the outlook for the survival of the Jewish nation was totally hopeless, but, nevertheless, we were miraculously saved.

◆§ אַתָּה הוּא ה' אֱלֹהֵינוּ בַּשָּׁמַיִם וּבָאָרֶץ וּבִשְׁמֵי הַשָּׁמַיִם הָעֶלְיוֹנִים §◆ — **It is You Who are Hashem, our God, in heaven and on earth and in the loftiest heavens.** The word שָׁמַיִם refers to the whole universe, and אָרֶץ is the one tiny planet on which *HaKadosh Baruch Hu* has willed to plant the human race, who are *baalei bechirah* (beings who are endowed with free will). This does not exist anywhere else in the whole universe. The author of this *tefillah,* who is *Tanna d'Vei Eliyahu,* mentions וּבִשְׁמֵי הַשָּׁמַיִם הָעֶלְיוֹנִים, with which he is familiar, because this is where Eliyahu HaNavi finds himself, meaning the higher world, the spiritual world, the world of the *malachim* and the *Kisei HaKavod,* the "angels," or spiritual creatures, and the "Throne" of God Himself.

◆§ אֱמֶת אַתָּה הוּא רִאשׁוֹן וְאַתָּה הוּא אַחֲרוֹן וּמִבַּלְעָדֶיךָ אֵין אֱלֹהִים §◆ — **True — You are the first and You are the last, and other than You there is no God.** It is true that before anything else existed, there was הוּא, "He," *HaKadosh Baruch Hu* existed completely unknown to anyone else but Himself.

And after everything comes to an end, there will likewise be only הוּא. But, as to the here and now, וּמִבַּלְעָדֶיךָ — besides *HaKadosh Baruch Hu,* the "הוּא" — there is no אֱלֹהִים.

These words are taken from *Yeshayahu* 44:6: כֹּה אָמַר ה' מֶלֶךְ יִשְׂרָאֵל וְגֹאֲלוֹ ה' צְבָאוֹת אֲנִי רִאשׁוֹן וַאֲנִי אַחֲרוֹן וּמִבַּלְעָדַי אֵין אֱלֹהִים, *Thus said Hashem, King of Israel and its Redeemer, Hashem, Master of Legions: I am the first and I am the last, and aside from Me there is no God.* This verse refers to the eventual redemption, and in it *HaKadosh Baruch Hu* says, "Just as I am incomprehensible, so will the redemption of *Bnei Yisrael* be incomprehensible."

Similarly, in the first *berachah* of the *Shemoneh Esrei,* we mention וְזוֹכֵר חַסְדֵי אָבוֹת, meaning that we exist only because of the oath *HaKadosh Baruch Hu* made to our Forefathers. However, וּמֵבִיא גוֹאֵל לִבְנֵי בְנֵיהֶם, when it comes to *Mashiach,* our final and complete redemption, this is beyond חַסְדֵי אָבוֹת, *the merit of the fathers.* This will happen only לְמַעַן שְׁמוֹ בְּאַהֲבָה, *for His Name's sake, with love.* We do not deserve it; even *zechus Avos* is insufficient for this. It is purely for His own Name's sake. This goes beyond any comprehension. This is purely *b'ahavah,* with love.

In this *tefillah* the *Tanna d'Vei Eliyahu* uses the word הוּא four times:

אַתָּה הוּא ה' אֱלֹהֵינוּ בַּשָּׁמַיִם וּבָאָרֶץ
אֱמֶת אַתָּה הוּא רִאשׁוֹן
וְאַתָּה הוּא אַחֲרוֹן
כִּי אַתָּה הוּא הָאֱלֹהִים לְבַדְּךָ

As we have previously discussed, the concept of הוּא, when referring to *HaKadosh Baruch Hu,* means, "He is that which He is." We only know Names of *HaKadosh Baruch Hu,* which we use to refer to Him: for instance,

י־ה־ו־ה, אֵל, בּוֹרֵא עוֹלָם, אֲדוֹן כָּל הָעוֹלָמִים, וכו׳. However, we do not know His Essence. He exists beyond the comprehensibility of any of His creations, humans or others. So when we speak of *HaKadosh Baruch Hu* in general terms, we call Him הוּא, "He," because there is no definitive name that we can give Him. He is inexplicable to the human mind. However, *HaKadosh Baruch Hu* has done us a great *chessed* in that He has revealed His presence to us. Had He not done so, we would not be aware of His existence altogether. This is actually the meaning of the words of מוֹדִים, in which we say: מוֹדִים אֲנַחְנוּ לָךְ שָׁאַתָּה הוּא ה׳ אֱלֹהֵינוּ, We thank You that You, הוּא, the Great Unknowable, have revealed Your Presence to us.

We are all familiar with the explanation in the *Pesach Haggadah* of the *pasuk*: וְעָבַרְתִּי בְאֶרֶץ מִצְרַיִם בַּלַּיְלָה הַזֶּה וְהִכֵּיתִי כָל בְּכוֹר בְּאֶרֶץ מִצְרַיִם מֵאָדָם וְעַד בְּהֵמָה וּבְכָל אֱלֹהֵי מִצְרַיִם אֶעֱשֶׂה שְׁפָטִים אֲנִי ה׳, *I shall go through the land of Egypt on this night, and I shall strike every firstborn in the land of Egypt, from man to beast; and against all the gods of Egypt I shall mete out punishments — I am Hashem* (*Shemos* 12:12).

This is explained in the *Haggadah* as:

- וְעָבַרְתִּי – אֲנִי וְלֹא מַלְאָךְ: "I shall go through" means, I and not an angel;
- וְהִכֵּיתִי – אֲנִי וְלֹא שָׂרָף: "I shall strike" means, I and not a *Seraph*;
- אֶעֱשֶׂה – אֲנִי וְלֹא הַשָּׁלִיחַ: "I shall do" means, I and not the messenger (Moshe);
- אֲנִי ה׳ – אֲנִי הוּא וְלֹא אַחֵר: "I am God" means, only I am "He," and none other.

When teaching of the personal intervention of *HaKadosh Baruch Hu* in *yetzias Mitzrayim* (the Exodus from Egypt), the *Haggadah* explains the words אֲנִי ה׳ as אֲנִי הוּא, *I am the Unknowable He*, Who is performing the miracles of *yetzias Mitzrayim*. So too, in this *tefillah* for the future *geulah*, we ask *HaKadosh Baruch Hu* as אַתָּה הוּא, You, the Incomprehensible, Who brought about the *geulah* in Egypt — from a hopeless future of slavery and eventual annihilation, as אֲנִי הוּא וְלֹא אַחֵר — may You likewise bring about our future *geulah*, which will also be miraculous. As we have previously pointed out, this is the reason why we begin the *Shemoneh Esrei* immediately after גָּאַל יִשְׂרָאֵל. We say בָּרוּךְ אַתָּה ה׳, meaning we direct our *tefillah* only to You, Who intervened personally for us at *yetzias Mitzrayim*. The same incomprehensible הוּא, Who redeemed us from Egypt, is the One to Whom we direct our *tefillos*.

If I may be very candid and frank, the situation which prevails today in Eretz Yisrael does not seem solvable. The so-called "peace talks" with the Arabs are at an impasse. The most ingenious negotiators have not been able to come up with a formula which would satisfy both sides. The future for peace looks totally hopeless. Still, קִוִּינוּ לָךְ, we hope for Your miraculous intervention.

At this point, I would like to emphasize — strange as it may sound — that we are not "hoping for *Mashiach*"; rather, *we are hoping for Hashem Yisbarach Who will send Mashiach*. As we say in the *tefillah* for *geulah*: וּמִבַּלְעָדֶיךָ אֵין לָנוּ מֶלֶךְ גּוֹאֵל וּמוֹשִׁיעַ, *we have no king, redeemer, or savior* — other than HaKadosh Baruch Hu Himself. Our unceasing hope is that *HaKadosh Baruch Hu* will send us *Mashiach,* as He has promised us. We hope that more and more people will recognize *HaKadosh Baruch Hu* in the world and, consequently, *HaKadosh Baruch Hu* will send *Mashiach.*

This is what occurred at the time of Ezra. We find Koresh, the most powerful person in the world at that time, who had conquered the unconquerable Babylonian Empire, proclaiming: כֹּה אָמַר כֹּרֶשׁ מֶלֶךְ פָּרַס כֹּל מַמְלְכוֹת הָאָרֶץ נָתַן לִי ה' אֱלֹהֵי הַשָּׁמַיִם וְהוּא פָקַד עָלַי לִבְנוֹת לוֹ בַיִת בִּירוּשָׁלַם אֲשֶׁר בִּיהוּדָה, *Thus said Koresh, king of Persia: All the kingdoms of the earth has Hashem, God of heaven, given to me and He has commanded me to build Him a Temple in Jerusalem, which is in Judah* (*Ezra* 1:2). The mighty king Koresh had heard that two hundred years earlier, there had been a *navi*, Yeshayahu, speaking in the Name of *HaKadosh Baruch Hu*, who had mentioned him and said that he, Koresh, would build the *Beis HaMikdash*: הָאֹמֵר לְכוֹרֶשׁ רֹעִי וְכָל חֶפְצִי יַשְׁלִם וְלֵאמֹר לִירוּשָׁלַם תִּבָּנֶה וְהֵיכָל תִּוָּסֵד, *Who says of Koresh, "He is My shepherd, He will fulfill all My desires," to say of Jerusalem, "It shall be built," and of the Temple, "It shall be established"* (*Yeshayahu* 44:28). He is called "My shepherd Koresh." [In Persian, the word Koresh means shepherd.] In the next chapter (45:1), we read: כֹּה אָמַר ה' לִמְשִׁיחוֹ לְכוֹרֶשׁ, *Thus said Hashem to His anointed one, to Koresh.* Here he is called "anointed one."

Koresh had heard that Hashem had spoken of him, called him His shepherd and anointed one, and foretold that he would build the *Beis HaMikdash*. So he issued an edict, in his capacity as the supreme ruler on earth, empowered by *HaKadosh Baruch Hu,* to build Him a house in Yerushalayim: מִי בָכֶם מִכָּל עַמּוֹ יְהִי אֱלֹהָיו עִמּוֹ וְיַעַל לִירוּשָׁלַם אֲשֶׁר בִּיהוּדָה וְיִבֶן אֶת בֵּית ה' אֱלֹהֵי יִשְׂרָאֵל הוּא הָאֱלֹהִים אֲשֶׁר בִּירוּשָׁלָם, *Whoever is among you of His entire people — may his God be with him — and let him go up to Jerusalem which is in Judah and build the Temple of Hashem, God of Israel — He is the God! — which is in Jerusalem* (*Ezra* 1:3).

These words, spoken by the most powerful man on earth, recognizing that ה' הוּא הָאֱלֹהִים, *Hashem, He is God,* constitute the greatest *kiddush Hashem* (sanctification of God's Name) imaginable. This, then, is what is meant by our hope for the coming of *Mashiach*. In the process of the eventual recognition of *HaKadosh Baruch Hu* in the world, there will be *Mashiach,* the ingathering of the exiles and the rebuilding of Yerushalayim. However, just how this will come about is totally unknown to us. Just as *HaKadosh Baruch*

Hu is the Great Incomprehensible, so is the future *geulah* of Israel totally unknown to us.

This first part of our *tefillah* ends with the words:

קַבֵּץ קוֹיֶךָ מֵאַרְבַּע כַּנְפוֹת הָאָרֶץ יַכִּירוּ וְיֵדְעוּ כָּל בָּאֵי עוֹלָם כִּי אַתָּה הוּא הָאֱלֹהִים לְבַדֶּךָ לְכֹל מַמְלְכוֹת הָאָרֶץ — **Gather in those who yearn for You, from the four corners of the earth. Let all who walk the earth recognize and know that You alone are the God over all the kingdoms of the earth.** With these words, we conclude the first part of this *tefillah,* in which we paraphrase the words of Koresh. In this part, first, we are *mispallel* that *HaKadosh Baruch Hu* may gather together His vanguard, that of the קוֹיֶךָ — those who have never lost their hope in His *geulah*. And this will eventually lead to a universal recognition by all the people in the world — men, women, and children — that You are the One and Only God in the world. *Kibbutz galuyos* alone is not the objective that we seek. What we ask for here is a simultaneous *kibbutz galuyos* and *gilui HaShechinah.* We ask that the recognition of Hashem become so universal that כָּל בָּאֵי עוֹלָם, all "newcomers" to the world, the newborn children, as soon as they are old enough to learn, will immediately know כִּי אַתָּה הוּא הָאֱלֹהִים לְבַדֶּךָ, *that You alone are THE God.* They will not first be taught something different, and then have to relearn the correct *emunah*. Rather, they will know of the true *emunah* as soon as they "arrive into the world." This is the end of the first paragraph of this *tefillah*.

אַתָּה עָשִׂיתָ אֶת הַשָּׁמַיִם וְאֶת הָאָרֶץ — **You have made the heavens and the earth.** We now begin the second paragraph of this *tefillah*. This part refers to the second phase of the *geulah,* which will include us, the ordinary people who are not on the level of being called קוֹיֶךָ, or who are not even worthy of the coming of *Mashiach.* It will include even those who are so far removed from Torah and *mitzvos* that they are referred to only as נִדַּחֲךָ בִּקְצֵה הַשָּׁמַיִם, *Your dispersal at the ends of heaven* (Devarim 30:4), which was interpreted by one of the chassidic greats as meaning that even if only a small spark of heavenliness remains in them, they too will be redeemed — מִשָּׁם יְקַבֶּצְךָ ה', *from there Hashem will gather you in* (ibid.).

אֶת הַיָּם וְאֶת כָּל אֲשֶׁר בָּם וּמִי בְּכָל מַעֲשֵׂה יָדֶיךָ בָּעֶלְיוֹנִים אוֹ בַתַּחְתּוֹנִים שֶׁיֹּאמַר לְךָ, מַה תַּעֲשֶׂה — **The sea and all therein; who is there among all Your creatures, in the higher world or lower world, who can say to You: "What are You doing?"** These words remind us of *krias Yam Suf* (the Splitting of the Sea), when the *sar shel yam* (the spiritual "Captain of the Sea") contended that most of *Bnei Yisrael* were not worthy of being saved, because they were no better than the pursuing Egyptians: הַלָּלוּ עוֹבְדֵי עֲבוֹדָה זָרָה וְהַלָּלוּ עוֹבְדֵי עֲבוֹדָה זָרָה, "These are idol worshipers, and those are idol worshipers" (*Zohar* Sec. II, p. 108; *Shemos Rabbah* 21:7). Similarly, now when we are *mispallel* for the general *kibbutz galuyos* of all of our nation, we invoke these words because we feel just as unworthy as our forefathers were at *yetzias Mitzrayim*. We pray that none of the עֶלְיוֹנִים or תַּחְתּוֹנִים ask: מַה תַּעֲשֶׂה — *What are You doing?* Those people are not worthy of redemption!

When we think of the Jewish population in America, approximately six million, of whom less than seven percent are Torah observant, this question is very legitimate. So we plead:

אָבִינוּ שֶׁבַּשָּׁמַיִם עֲשֵׂה עִמָּנוּ חֶסֶד — **Our Father in Heaven, do kindness with us.** We ask that our Father in Heaven have compassion on *us*, the ordinary people — even if our desire for *geulah* is not only for lofty or sublime reasons, even if we, the ordinary people, only long for *Mashiach* because we want peace and tranquility on earth. Nevertheless, we throw ourselves upon the mercy of *HaKadosh Baruch Hu* and pray for the *geulah*.

בַּעֲבוּר שִׁמְךָ הַגָּדוֹל שֶׁנִּקְרָא עָלֵינוּ — **For the sake of Your great Name that has been proclaimed upon us.** You, as אֱלֹהֵי יִשְׂרָאֵל ,ה', have promised us the *geulah* not because we deserve it, as we find in the verse, לֹא לְמַעַנְכֶם אֲנִי עֹשֶׂה בֵּית יִשְׂרָאֵל, כִּי אִם לְשֵׁם קָדְשִׁי אֲשֶׁר חִלַּלְתֶּם, *It is not for your sake that I act, O House of Israel, but for My holy Name that you have desecrated* (Yechezkel 36:22). The promised *geulah* will come to make a *kiddush Hashem* in the world.

We now end this *tefillah* by asking that *HaKadosh Baruch Hu* fulfill his promise to us:

וְקַיֵּם לָנוּ ה' אֱלֹהֵינוּ מַה שֶּׁכָּתוּב: בָּעֵת הַהִיא אָבִיא אֶתְכֶם וּבָעֵת קַבְּצִי אֶתְכֶם כִּי אֶתֵּן אֶתְכֶם לְשֵׁם וְלִתְהִלָּה בְּכֹל עַמֵּי הָאָרֶץ בְּשׁוּבִי אֶת שְׁבוּתֵיכֶם לְעֵינֵיכֶם אָמַר ה' — **Fulfill for us, Hashem, our God, what is written, "At that time I shall bring you (home), and at that time I shall gather you (in). I shall (gratuitously) make your name praiseworthy among all the nations of the earth, when I return your captives before your eyes, said Hashem"** (Tzephaniah 3:20).

This *pasuk* refers to two stages of the *geulah*, the final redemption. The first stage is described as, בָּעֵת הַהִיא אָבִיא אֶתְכֶם, *At that time I shall bring you.* This refers to the return of the vanguard of the Jewish people to Eretz Yisrael: the *tzaddikim*, the righteous people.

The second stage will be the ingathering of the entire Jewish nation to Eretz Yisrael. This second stage is what is meant by וּבָעֵת, *and at that time,* the time when קַבְּצִי אֶתְכֶם, *I will gather (the rest of) you;* לְעֵינֵיכֶם, *before your eyes,* meaning the eyes of the *tzaddikim*, who will witness the return of the rest of the Jewish nation. This accounts for the use of the word קַבְּצִי, meaning a wide ingathering, to describe the second stage of the redemption, as opposed to the use of אָבִיא, *I shall bring,* which refers only to the first, limited, stage of the *geulah*.

And at the time of the general ingathering of the Jewish nation to Eretz Yisrael, the Jewish nation will, once again, become synonymous with greatness and world leadership: כִּי אֶתֵּן אֶתְכֶם לְשֵׁם וְלִתְהִלָּה בְּכֹל עַמֵּי הָאָרֶץ, *I shall* (gratuitously) *make your name praiseworthy among all the nations of the world.*

These two phases are also referred to in the *haftarah* which we say on a *taanis tzibbur* (communal fast day): נְאֻם ה' אֱלֹהִים מְקַבֵּץ נִדְחֵי יִשְׂרָאֵל עוֹד אֲקַבֵּץ עָלָיו לְנִקְבָּצָיו, *So says Hashem, Who gathers the dispersed of Israel: I will again bring together,* to join those who are already there, *an additional group of dispersed people (Yeshayahu* 56:8). This is exactly what happened at the beginning of *Bayis Sheni* (Second Temple). First, Koresh issued a proclamation that the Jews may return to Yerushalayim and build the *Beis HaMikdash*: מִי בָכֶם מִכָּל עַמּוֹ יְהִי אֱלֹהָיו עִמּוֹ וְיַעַל לִירוּשָׁלַָם, *Who among you, from his entire nation, may his God be with him, will go to Yerushalayim (Ezra* 1:3). The first returnees consisted only of the רָאשֵׁי הָאָבוֹת (tribal leaders), the *Kohanim* and *Leviim,* and others הֵעִיר הָאֱלֹהִים אֶת רוּחוֹ, *whose spirit God had awakened* (*Ezra* 1:5). This vanguard group of *tzaddikim,* which was led by Mordechai, Nechemiah, Yehoshua *Kohen Gadol,* Zerubavel and others, totaled only about 42,000 people. It was during this period that the miracle of Purim occurred in Persia. In the meantime, the permission to rebuild the *Beis HaMikdash* had been rescinded, and was only reinstated much later by Daryavesh.

Then, much later, after the *Beis HaMikdash* had been rebuilt and dedicated, permission was granted for everyone to come back to Eretz Yisrael. This "Second Aliyah" was led by Ezra HaSofer. Although multitudes came, still, not everyone was prepared to come back. Had they all come during this second phase, this would have been the *geulah* for which we are still waiting, שֶׁיָּבוֹא בִּמְהֵרָה בְיָמֵינוּ אָמֵן.

[See *Maayan Beis HaSho'evah, Nitzavim* 30:3, for the source of this explanation of the two stages of *Kibbutz Galuyos,* the Ingathering of the Exiles.]

בִּרְכוֹת הַתּוֹרָה / Birchos HaTorah

According to our *minhag*, which follows the order of the *Tur* and *Shulchan Aruch*, we say בִּרְכוֹת הַתּוֹרָה at this point, after all the בִּרְכוֹת הַשַּׁחַר, and before the פָּרָשַׁת הַתָּמִיד. This, notwithstanding the prevailing *minhag* throughout most of the world, which is to say בִּרְכוֹת הַתּוֹרָה before the בִּרְכוֹת הַשַּׁחַר. (In fact, even the Roedelheim *Siddur* has בִּרְכוֹת הַתּוֹרָה before בִּרְכוֹת הַשַּׁחַר.)

We find this order of בִּרְכוֹת הַתּוֹרָה being said after all the בִּרְכוֹת הַשַּׁחַר in the *siddur* of R' Amram Gaon, which dates back to the period shortly after the completion of the Talmud. It is also found in this order in *Sefer HaOrah*, which is attributed to Rashi and it is also the *minhag HaGra* (see *Beur HaGra* to *Orach Chaim* 56:9). The *siddur* of the *mekubal*, R' Hertz Shaliach Tzibbur, printed about 500 years ago, which has many of the German *minhagim*, also has בִּרְכוֹת הַתּוֹרָה at this point. However, he omits יְבָרֶכְךָ and אֵלּוּ דְבָרִים and proceeds directly to the פָּרָשַׁת הַתָּמִיד. Our *minhag*, to add יְבָרֶכְךָ and אֵלּוּ דְבָרִים after the בִּרְכוֹת הַתּוֹרָה, originates from the old French *minhag*, which is found in *Tosafos* to *Berachos* 11b (end of s.v. שכבר).

Reciting בִּרְכוֹת הַתּוֹרָה, according to many opinions, is *d'Oraisa* (of Biblical origin). Therefore, since *safeik d'Oraisa l'chumrah*, a Biblical doubt is decided stringently, if one is in doubt whether he has said *birchos haTorah* or not, he must repeat at least one of them: אֲשֶׁר בָּחַר בָּנוּ, which is called מְעוּלָה שֶׁבַּבְּרָכוֹת, the highest of these *berachos* (*Berachos* 11b). However, *Rambam* in the *Sefer HaMitzvos* does not count בִּרְכוֹת הַתּוֹרָה among the *mitzvos d'Oraisa*. Rav Samson R. Hirsch in the *Chumash* gives a very ingenious explanation of this opinion of the *Rambam* (see *Devarim* 32:3).

In any event, suffice it to say that reciting בִּרְכוֹת הַתּוֹרָה is an extremely important *halachah*. *Berachos* 21a holds that the basis for it is the *pasuk*, כִּי שֵׁם ה' אֶקְרָא הָבוּ גֹדֶל לֵאלֹהֵינוּ, *When I call out the Name of Hashem, ascribe greatness to our God* (*Devarim* 32:3). Moshe Rabbeinu tells us here that when you "call the Name of Hashem," meaning when you talk about *divrei Torah*, you shall first give greatness to *HaKadosh Baruch Hu*.

According to *Nedarim* 81a, the meaning of the verse, עַל מָה אָבְדָה הָאָרֶץ . . . וַיֹּאמֶר ה' עַל עָזְבָם אֶת תּוֹרָתִי, *For what reason did the land perish . . . But Hashem has said: Because of their forsaking My Torah* (*Yirmiyahu* 9:11,12), is that the destruction of *Eretz Yisrael* and the *churban Beis HaMikdash* were the result of שֶׁאֵין מְבָרְכִין בַּתּוֹרָה תְּחִלָּה, they did not make a *berachah* first, i.e. prior to learning Torah. They considered the Torah just a science, another discipline, like any other knowledge, and therefore did not make a *berachah* before learning it. So while the Torah does certainly contain all the knowledge in the world, it is unique as תּוֹרָתִי, *My Torah*: it is *d'var Hashem*, and He has commanded us to study it. This is what we express in the בִּרְכוֹת הַתּוֹרָה.

❧ ❧ ❧

בִּרְכוֹת הַתּוֹרָה, as do all בִּרְכוֹת הַמִּצְוֹת, begin with the words:

אֲשֶׁר קִדְּשָׁנוּ בְּמִצְוֹתָיו וְצִוָּנוּ לַעֲסוֹק בְּדִבְרֵי תוֹרָה — **Who has sanctified us with His mitzvos and has commanded us to busy ourselves with the words of Torah.** Hashem has sanctified us by His *mitzvos*, and since we are thus sanctified, וְצִוָּנוּ, *He has commanded us to do* . . . whatever that particular *mitzvah* may be. We have already explained (see עַל נְטִילַת יָדָיִם) the meaning of קִדְּשָׁנוּ as *kedushas guf Yisrael*, the sanctification of the physical body of a Jew. Notwithstanding its earthly origin — and return thereto — the physical body of a Jewish person, while the *neshamah* is in it, has been sanctified. We are therefore commanded to perform *mitzvos* with the various parts of our bodies. Even after the *neshamah* leaves the physical body, the *chevrah kaddisha* (burial society) treats this physical frame, which had *kedushah*, with all the deference and dignity which a *guf Yisrael* deserves. This is why even a *Kohen Gadol* must become *tamei* for a *meis mitzvah*, to prevent the desecration of this *kedushas Yisrael*.

It is for this reason that we do not make a *berachah* on *mitzvos* which are done primarily with our mind, because אֲשֶׁר קִדְּשָׁנוּ refers to the *kedushas guf Yisrael*. An example would be קְרִיאַת שְׁמַע. We do not say . . . אֲשֶׁר קִדְּשָׁנוּ עַל מִצְוַת קְרִיאַת שְׁמַע, because the basic element of this *mitzvah* is the *kavannah*, concentration on the meaning of the words, at least on the first *pasuk*, without which one is not *yotzei*, and has not fulfilled his obligation. שְׁמַע יִשְׂרָאֵל means *hear*, i.e. put your mind to it. Obviously, if one does not understand what he is saying he has not performed this *mitzvah* at all. The same applies to *tefillah*. There is no *berachah* for the *mitzvah* of *tefillah*, because its main aspect is performed by the mind, not by the body, i.e., concentrating on the fact that we are talking to *HaKadosh Baruch Hu*. Without this, we are not *yotzei*. Similarly, the daily *mitzvah* of remembering *yetzias Mitzrayim* is primarily done by the mind, as is the *Haggadah shel Pesach*, therefore no *berachah* is made for these *mitzvos*.

However, the *mitzvah* of *limud Torah* does require *bircas hamitzvah*, because an essential part of the *mitzvah* is that we utilize our bodily power of speech, and physically speak the words of Torah — וְלִמַּדְתֶּם אֹתָם אֶת בְּנֵיכֶם לְדַבֵּר בָּם, *Teach them to your children, to discuss them* (Devarim 11:19). This requirement is manifested in the words of the *berachah* itself: בְּפִינוּ וּבְפִי עַמְּךָ בֵּית יִשְׂרָאֵל, *in our mouth and in the mouth of Your people, Israel*. While, of course, one must understand what one is learning, it is equally essential to the performance of this *mitzvah,* that one actually *speak* the words of Torah — לַעֲסוֹק בְּדִבְרֵי תוֹרָה. To busy ourselves with Torah infers talking about it. The body and mind are equal partners in this *mitzvah.* The *minhag* of the *Sefardim* is to say עַל דִּבְרֵי תוֹרָה, "about the *words* of Torah." However, as explained by the *Bach* (*Orach Chaim* 47:5), we prefer לַעֲסוֹק בְּדִבְרֵי תוֹרָה, because דִּבְרֵי תוֹרָה alone is not sufficient. The main purpose of *talmud Torah* is to learn how to fulfill the *mitzvos.* Therefore, the extended meaning of לַעֲסוֹק is to occupy our minds with Torah, expressing its learning in words, and implementing the *divrei Torah* in actual practice.

The *Taz* explains (ibid.) that the word לַעֲסוֹק refers to the great amount of effort and hard work involved in learning. Overcoming lethargy, sleepiness, limitations of one's mind, and other distractions are all necessary for *talmud Torah.* The first stage of learning Torah is לַעֲסוֹק, overcoming obstacles and difficulties which may stand in the way. It does not come easily.

The first *berachah* is לַעֲסוֹק בְּדִבְרֵי תוֹרָה. The next *berachah* is וְהַעֲרֶב נָא. There is a *machlokes* (dispute) among the *poskim* whether this is a separate *berachah* or a continuation of the first *berachah.* In this event, no *amen* would be said after לַעֲסוֹק בְּדִבְרֵי תוֹרָה. To avoid any problem, our *minhag* is that the *shaliach tzibbur* says these words in an undertone, and only raises his voice at the end of וְהַעֲרֶב נָא, which is: בָּרוּךְ אַתָּה ה' הַמְלַמֵּד תּוֹרָה לְעַמּוֹ יִשְׂרָאֵל.

We use the same procedure for the *berachah* of *tefillin* on Chol HaMoed. Following the original *minhag,* based on the Gemara, we don *tefillin* on Chol HaMoed, although most people today do not. The latter *minhag* is the opinion of the *Mechaber, Orach Chaim* 31:2, which is based on the *Zohar.* In order to avoid any arguments, the *shaliach tzibbur* says the *berachah* quietly.

וְהַעֲרֶב נָא ה' אֱלֹהֵינוּ אֶת דִּבְרֵי תוֹרָתְךָ בְּפִינוּ — **Please, Hashem, our God, sweeten the words of Your Torah in our mouth.** Once we have made an effort to apply ourselves to learning, we ask *HaKadosh Baruch Hu* to make the words of the Torah sweet to us. A very prosaic analogy would be to one who is reluctant to jump into a cold pool of water. However, once he has jumped in and "broken the ice," he enjoys the water immensely. Learning Torah is a similar experience. At first, it is very difficult to overcome the obstacles and make the necessary effort. However, as a result of the לַעֲסוֹק, the hard work which we expend, we ask *HaKadosh Baruch Hu* to make it pleasant and sweet for us. One of the benefits that a Jewish person derives from *talmud Torah* is the enjoyment of the learning, the *cheshkas haTorah.* We ask that the words of the Torah become sweet to our mouths, stressing the physical aspect of learning, that of actually saying the words of the Torah. [The author elaborates on this point in *Maayan Beis HaSho'evah, BeShalach* 16:31, with a vivid personal account of the words of the *Chofetz Chaim* concerning the sweetness of *talmud Torah.*]

וּבְפִי עַמְּךָ בֵּית יִשְׂרָאֵל — **And in the mouth of Your People, the House of Israel.** We feel responsible not only for our own learning, but for the learning of others as well. This is why we support yeshivos and Torah institutions, which is the meaning of the next phrase:

וְנִהְיֶה אֲנַחְנוּ וְצֶאֱצָאֵינוּ וְצֶאֱצָאֵי עַמְּךָ בֵּית יִשְׂרָאֵל — **May we and our offspring and the offspring of Your people, the House of Israel.** Here we express our responsibility for the Torah learning not only of ourselves and our descendants, but similarly for the entire Jewish nation and its descendants.

כֻּלָּנוּ יוֹדְעֵי שְׁמֶךָ וְלוֹמְדֵי תוֹרָתֶךָ — **All of us know Your Name and study Your Torah.** The *Tur* says that we do not say לִשְׁמָהּ, *for its own sake*, because not everyone reaches the level of תַּלְמוּד תּוֹרָה לִשְׁמָהּ. However, we hope that eventually this will follow: מִתּוֹךְ שֶׁלֹּא לִשְׁמָהּ בָּא לִשְׁמָהּ, paraphrased, this means that learning Torah, even if for ulterior motives, will lead to learning Torah for its own sake.

We have here two different requests:

יוֹדְעֵי שְׁמֶךָ — "that we will know Your Name." We ask that we become familiar with, and know, the *Torah Shebichsav*, the Written Torah. We are told by *Chazal* that כָּל הַתּוֹרָה כּוּלָהּ שְׁמוֹתָיו שֶׁל הקב״ה, The entire Torah is comprised of Names of Hashem (see *Zohar HaKadosh* 2:87, *Parashas Yisro*, and *Ramban's* Introduction to *Bereishis*). The *Chachamim* of the Kabbalah are aware of "secrets" in every letter of *Torah Shebichsav*, which have not been revealed to ordinary mortals. The *Neviim* were aware of these "secrets" and they handed them down to their *talmidim*. This is actually the meaning of the word "Kabbalah," something received *ish mipi ish* — through word of mouth, going back to the *Neviim*. So therefore, the words of *Torah Shebichsav* are called שְׁמֶךָ, because they contain hidden references to *HaKadosh Baruch Hu*.

וְלוֹמְדֵי תוֹרָתֶךָ — "and students of Your Torah." We ask that we be successful in learning and knowing *Your Torah*, referring to *Torah Shebe'al Peh*, the Oral Law.

בָּרוּךְ אַתָּה ה׳ הַמְלַמֵּד תּוֹרָה לְעַמּוֹ יִשְׂרָאֵל — **Blessed are You, Hashem, Who teaches Torah to His nation Israel.** We have already explained that the word בָּרוּךְ at the opening of all of our *berachos* is used in the sense of "increasing," meaning that we pray that more and more people will recognize *HaKadosh Baruch Hu* (in the sense of יִתְגַּדַּל וְיִתְקַדַּשׁ שְׁמֵהּ רַבָּא). Here we refer to *HaKadosh Baruch Hu* as "the One Who teaches Torah to His nation Israel." We speak of Him as a "Teacher." We find many similar references to this; some examples are: (1) In אַהֲבָה רַבָּה we say: בַּעֲבוּר אֲבוֹתֵינוּ שֶׁבָּטְחוּ בְךָ וַתְּלַמְּדֵם חֻקֵּי חַיִּים, *for the sake of our forefathers who trusted in You and whom You taught the decrees of life.* (2) בָּרוּךְ אַתָּה ה׳ לַמְּדֵנִי חֻקֶּיךָ, *Blessed are You, Hashem, teach me Your*

BIRCHOS HATORAH   77

statutes (Tehillim 119:12). According to the Gemara (Sanhedrin 99b), when a person learns Torah *l'shem Shamayim,* for the sake of Heaven, and he makes an effort to understand what he is learning, *HaKadosh Baruch Hu* helps him understand it. In the words of the Gemara, "the Torah works for him," because he worked to understand it. And when one is successful in achieving the understanding of Torah, he find sweetness and great joy in that understanding. It is this sweetness which we pray for in this *tefillah* of וְהַעֲרֶב נָא. [For a fuller treatment of this subject see *Maayan Beis HaSho'evah* p. 301b, s.v. ודרכי האדם.]

Women are also obligated to say בִּרְכוֹת הַתּוֹרָה. While *patur* (exempt) from *talmud Torah* purely for the sake of learning, women are, nevertheless, obligated to learn the *halachos* of the *mitzvos* so they can properly fulfill them. With the exception of the few time-bound *mitzvos,* women have the same obligation as men to know and keep the vast majority of the *mitzvos* of the Torah. It is therefore incumbent upon women to learn the details of these *mitzvos* in order to observe them properly. How can a woman keep Shabbos or Yom Tov properly without knowing the applicable *halachos*?

How can a woman conduct a business if she is not familiar with the *dinim* (laws) of *ribbis* (interest), *onaah* (misrepresentation or price fraud), or *gezel* (outright theft). The difference is only in the goal of the learning. For a man, in addition to the need to know the practical *halachos* in order to apply them, it is also a *mitzvah* to occupy himself with *talmud Torah* as a form of *avodas Hashem,* serving Hashem. This is so even if there is no immediate need for this knowledge in practice, either because he already knows the *dinim,* or his immediate circumstances do not require the application of what he is learning. However, for a woman, the purpose of the learning is to gain the knowledge in order to put it into practice.

The third *berachah* is:

אֲשֶׁר בָּחַר בָּנוּ מִכָּל הָעַמִּים וְנָתַן לָנוּ אֶת תּוֹרָתוֹ — **Who selected us from all the nations and gave us His Torah.** This means that *HaKadosh Baruch Hu* has selected us, *Am Yisrael,* as the beneficiary of His gift, תּוֹרָתוֹ, which He did not give to any other nation. While the nations of the world were also given laws, such as the seven Noahide *mitzvos,* and even had *derech eretz,* with its lofty concepts of *middos tovos,* which was קָדְמָה לַתּוֹרָה (preceded Torah), befitting the human being who was created *b'tzelem Elokim* (in the image of God), they were, nevertheless, not given the special gift of His Torah. With *Matan Torah* (the Giving of the Torah) at *Har Sinai,* with all its ramifications, the Jewish people received not only a "code of laws" but concurrently, *HaKadosh Baruch Hu* infused the Jewish *neshamah* with a special *kedushah* (holiness). The *Toras Hashem* was put into our system as a gift by *HaKadosh Baruch Hu* to elevate the *nishmas Yisrael* (Jewish soul).

This is what is meant when *Chazal* tell us that while a Jewish embryo is developing in the womb, a *malach* (angel) teaches it the entire Torah (*Niddah* 30b). So when the child is born, he or she, as a part of the Jewish nation, *Klal Yisrael,* already has the *kedushas nishmas Yisrael.* This, then, is what is meant by this *berachah,* and why it is called מְעוּלָה שֶׁבַּבְּרָכוֹת, *the most elevated of the* בִּרְכוֹת הַתּוֹרָה. We recognize the uniqueness of this gift, in that *HaKadosh Baruch Hu* has selected us, *Klal Yisrael,* to receive this special gift of Torah with which He has infused our *neshamah.* After *Matan Torah* we became a different nation than we were before. Our souls were infused with the holiness of Torah.

בִּרְכַּת כֹּהֲנִים / Bircas Kohanim

According to our *minhag*, the *birchos haTorah* are followed by actually "learning." This is based on the old French (*minhag haTzarfatim*), mentioned in *Tosafos* to *Berachos* 11b, which requires that immediately after *Birchos HaTorah* we "learn" selections from *Mikra*, i.e. the written part of Torah, Mishnah, and Gemara. According to *Talmidei Rabbeinu Yonah* and *Baal HaMaor* (ibid.), the three *birchos haTorah* correspond to the three parts of Torah, which are *Mikra*, Mishnah, and Gemara. For the *Mikra* portion, we recite the *Bircas Kohanim;* for the Mishnah portion, אֵלּוּ דְבָרִים שֶׁאֵין לָהֶם שִׁעוּר; and for the Gemara portion, we say the *Baraisa:* אֵלּוּ דְבָרִים שֶׁאָדָם אוֹכֵל פֵּרוֹתֵיהֶם וכו׳. [Gemara also includes *Baraisos*, discussions and opinions by various *Tannaim* pertaining to the subject matter contained in the *Mishnah*, but which were not included in the Mishnah text. This was the Gemara which the *Tannaim* learned before and after the close of the Mishnah.]

These three citations all have special references to *talmud Torah*, for which we have just made the *berachah*. We will explain their special connection to Talmud Torah as we proceed.

However, this was not the original *minhag Ashkenaz*. In the old *siddurim* of *minhag Ashkenaz*, we find בִּרְכוֹת הַתּוֹרָה followed immediately by וַיְדַבֵּר, then אֵיזֶהוּ מְקוֹמָן, and רַבִּי יִשְׁמָעֵאל אוֹמֵר. These are also renditions of *Mikra*, Mishnah, and Gemara. The reason this was changed to the three examples which we recite may be because the saying of וַיְדַבֵּר and אֵיזֶהוּ מְקוֹמָן is intended to be a substitute for *korbanos* in the absence of the *Beis HaMikdash*. Since *birchos haTorah* is often said before *alos hashachar* (daybreak), it would be too early for *korbanos*. We therefore recite three other examples of *Mikra*, Mishnah, and Gemara, with which to follow *birchos haTorah*.

In keeping with our outline of the structure of the *tefillos*, we have left the *Ezras Yisrael*, the *Israelites' Courtyard* and proceed to the *Kohanim's Courtyard*, with its three-tiered podium. This is based on the mishnah in *Middos* 82:46: רַבִּי אֱלִיעֶזֶר בֶּן יַעֲקֹב אוֹמֵר מַעֲלָה הָיְתָה בֵּין עֶזְרַת יִשְׂרָאֵל לְעֶזְרַת כֹּהֲנִים וְהַדּוּכָן נָתוּן עָלֶיהָ וּבָהּ שָׁלֹשׁ מַעֲלוֹת, *Rabbi Eliezer ben Yaakov says: The Kohanim's Courtyard was separated from the Israelites' Courtyard by an elevation, on which stood a podium with three steps.* The *Tosafos Yom Tov* explains (also see *Rashi* ibid.) that the *Bircas Kohanim* was said on these three steps. It is therefore very fitting that, at this point, we recite the three parts of the *birchos haTorah*, which are followed by recitations from *Mikra*,

Mishnah, and Gemara, beginning with the *berachah meshuleshes* of the *Bircas Kohanim*.

An additional connection between *birchos haTorah* and *Bircas Kohanim* is given by the *Avudraham*. The reason why the Sages instituted three *aliyos* for the weekday *krias haTorah*, five on Yom Tov, and seven on Shabbos, is based on the three *pesukim* of *Bircas Kohanim*: יְבָרֶכְךָ ה׳ וְיִשְׁמְרֶךָ has three words; יָאֵר ה׳ פָּנָיו אֵלֶיךָ וִיחֻנֶּךָ has five words; יִשָּׂא ה׳ פָּנָיו אֵלֶיךָ וְיָשֵׂם לְךָ שָׁלוֹם has seven words.

❦ ❦ ❦

⊷ יְבָרֶכְךָ ה׳ וְיִשְׁמְרֶךָ — **May Hashem bless you and safeguard you.** There is a deeper, inner connection between the *birchos haTorah* and the *Bircas Kohanim*. The center of *Bircas Kohanim* is a blessing for understanding the Torah as expressed by its middle *berachah*. The first *berachah* definitely refers to physical, material blessings, as explained by the Midrash (*Bamidbar Rabbah* 11:5): יְבָרֶכְךָ ה׳ בְּעוֹשֶׁר, בְּבָנִים; וְיִשְׁמְרֶךָ מִן הַלִּסְטִים — *May God bless you with riches, with children, etc., and protect you from thieves, etc.*

⊷ However, the second *berachah*, יָאֵר ה׳ פָּנָיו אֵלֶיךָ וִיחֻנֶּךָ, means: **May Hashem cause His face to shine toward you, and give you chein.** R' Samson R. Hirsch explains the meaning of וִיחֻנֶּךָ in German to mean *"geistige Begabung."* In English, this would mean a spiritual endowment or gift. Accordingly, the *berachah* is that we may be spiritually gifted by Hashem in the sense of אַתָּה חוֹנֵן לְאָדָם דַּעַת, *You bestow knowledge to man as a gift*. It is therefore not a surprise that *Midrash Rabbah* (ibid.) explains this *pasuk* as: יָאֵר ה׳ פָּנָיו אֵלֶיךָ, שֶׁיָּאִיר עֵינֶיךָ וְלִבְּךָ בַּתּוֹרָה, וְיִתֵּן לְךָ בָּנִים בְּנֵי תוֹרָה — This means that Hashem *shall enlighten your eyes and heart through your understanding of the Torah, and He shall grant you children who are bnei Torah*. The sense is the same in כִּי בְאוֹר פָּנֶיךָ נָתַתָּ לָּנוּ תּוֹרַת חַיִּים in *Shemoneh Esrei*, and וְהָאֵר עֵינֵינוּ בְּתוֹרָתֶךָ in *Ahavah Rabbah*, which are prayers for the gift of understanding the Torah.

So here, right in the middle of *Bircas Kohanim*, we have a *berachah* in which the *Kohanim* express the wish that *HaKadosh Baruch Hu* may endow upon us the gift of understanding His Torah. The Torah is the *chochmah* (wisdom) of *HaKadosh Baruch Hu*. If we study it as we would any other science, we may gain some knowledge of it. However, what we strive for is: יָאֵר ה׳ פָּנָיו אֵלֶיךָ, which means we pray that through *talmud Torah*, our mind will meet with the Mind of *HaKadosh Baruch Hu* (כִּבְיָכוֹל), and thereby become enlightened with a deep understanding of the *chochmah* of the Torah. In effect, we ask that our mind may absorb something of the *chochmah* of *HaKadosh Baruch Hu*.

Then finally, the third *berachah* is:

יִשָּׂא ה׳ פָּנָיו אֵלֶיךָ וְיָשֵׂם לְךָ שָׁלוֹם — **May Hashem turn His countenance to you and establish peace for you.** This is the inner peace of mind which comes as the result of a personal relationship with *HaKadosh Baruch Hu*. We intend to devote more time to a broader explanation of this *berachah* at the end of *Shemoneh Esrei*. This completes the *Mikra* portion of *talmud Torah*.

אֵלּוּ דְבָרִים / Eilu Devarim

We now come to the Mishnah portion. We recite the first mishnah in *Maseches Pe'ah* because of its reference to *talmud Torah*:

❦ ❦ ❦

אֵלּוּ דְבָרִים שֶׁאֵין לָהֶם שִׁעוּר — The following precepts have no limit: This means that *mi'd'Oraisa* (as a Torah obligation), these have neither a minimum nor a maximum limit.

הַפֵּאָה — The corner of a field [which must be left for the poor]. The Jewish farmer in Eretz Yisrael is required to share his field with the poor. This is based on: לֹא תְכַלֶּה פְּאַת שָׂדְךָ לִקְצֹר וכו׳ לֶעָנִי וְלַגֵּר תַּעֲזֹב אֹתָם, *You shall not complete your reaping to the corner of your field; for the poor and the proselyte shall you leave them* (*Vayikra* 19:9,10). The *halachah* requires the farmer to leave a corner, or a part of the field, for the poor, rather than give it to them. The poor man is the farmer's partner. He is taking his share. The farmer gives the poor nothing (see *Toras Kohanim* ibid., and *Pe'ah*, beginning of Ch. 4). Ownership rights of landed property in Eretz Yisrael include a share for the poor. One of these rights is *pe'ah*, which is the portion left in the field. However, the amount to be left has no minimum or maximum limit *mi'd'Oraisa*. This means that the farmer can take one stalk for himself and leave the rest of the field for the poor. Or, conversely, he can take the entire field for himself, with the exception of one stalk, which he leaves for the poor. However, to avoid abuses by the farmer, the Sages instituted a minimum *shiur* of one-sixtieth of the field to be left for the poor as *pe'ah*.

וְהַבִּכּוּרִים — The first-fruit offering. The first produce of the *shivas haminim* (seven species) in Eretz Yisrael have to be brought to the *Kohanim* in the *Beis HaMikdash*. Here too, there are no limits on the amount required to be brought up, not even *mi'd'Rabbanan*. Even the *Chachamim* never fixed a minimum amount for this. When presenting his *bikkurim* basket, no matter how simple or how elaborate, the farmer makes the following declaration upon his arrival in front of the *Mizbe'ach* (Altar): הִגַּדְתִּי הַיּוֹם לַה׳ אֱלֹהֶיךָ כִּי בָאתִי אֶל הָאָרֶץ אֲשֶׁר נִשְׁבַּע ה׳ לַאֲבֹתֵינוּ לָתֶת לָנוּ, *I declare today to Hashem, your God, that I have come to the Land that Hashem swore to our forefathers to give us* (*Devarim* 26:3). He tells the *Kohen*, "I have some good news for you: Today I arrived in Eretz Yisrael." What the farmer is telling the *Kohen* is that the real Eretz Yisrael is right here in the *Beis HaMikdash*, the place of the *Shechinah*.

My land is only the peripheral part of the country, despite the fact that I and my ancestors have lived on it for hundreds of years. Notwithstanding the fact that even if I sell it, the land will revert to me — or my heirs — at *Yovel*, I recognize that Eretz Yisrael in its purest form, at its core, is right here in the *Beis HaMikdash*.

◆§ וְהָרְאָיוֹן — **The pilgrimage,** the appearance in the *Beis HaMikdash* at the *Shalosh Regalim,* Three Festivals. We are required to present ourselves to HaKadosh Baruch Hu three times a year, *to be seen by Him.* שָׁלוֹשׁ פְּעָמִים בַּשָּׁנָה יֵרָאֶה כָל זְכוּרְךָ אֶת פְּנֵי ה' אֱלֹהֶיךָ בַּמָּקוֹם אֲשֶׁר יִבְחָר . . . וְלֹא יֵרָאֶה אֶת פְּנֵי ה' רֵיקָם, *Three times a year all your males should appear before Hashem, your God, in the place that He will choose . . . and he shall not appear before Hashem empty handed* (*Devarim* 16:16). Although the *halachah* requires that we bring along certain *korbanos*, which must have a certain minimum value (see beginning of *Maseches Chagigah*), nevertheless, our actual presence, the רְאָיוֹן, in the *Beis HaMikdash* has neither a minimum nor a maximum limit: One can fulfill this *mitzvah* by staying for just a moment, or he may spend the entire day there.

◆§ וּגְמִילוּת חֲסָדִים — **Acts of kindness.** The meaning here is not *tzedakah*, which does have limitations. For instance, one must not give away more than one-fifth of his income — הַמְבַזְבֵּז אַל יְבַזְבֵּז יוֹתֵר מֵחוֹמֶשׁ, *one must not give away more than one-fifth* (*Kesubos* 67b) because he may incur financial difficulties. Rather, the reference here is to *gemilus chassadim shebegufo*, personal favors and nonmonetary kindnesses performed by one for another, making someone else's life better, fuller, and happier than before. It can range from a simple friendly greeting, helping an infirm person to cross the street, or a telephone call inquiring of another's welfare to as much as raising an orphan child in one's home. We fulfill the *mitzvah* of *gemilus chassadim* with every little act of *chessed* we perform, and the more we do, the greater the *mitzvah*. It has no limits.

◆§ וְתַלְמוּד תּוֹרָה — **And Torah study.** If one learns even one word, explains one *dagesh* in the Torah — or lack of it — he is fulfilling this *mitzvah*. On the other hand, if one learns Torah all day long, he is cautioned against being proud of his accomplishment, because he has only done his duty. אִם לָמַדְתָּ תּוֹרָה הַרְבֵּה, אַל תַּחֲזִיק טוֹבָה לְעַצְמְךָ, כִּי לְכָךְ נוֹצַרְתָּ, *If you have studied much Torah, do not take credit for yourself, because that is what you were created to do* (*Pirkei Avos* 2:9).

As previously pointed out, this mishnah was chosen to be said after *birchos haTorah* because of its reference to the *mitzvah* of *Talmud Torah*. Interestingly, we always refer to learning as *"talmud"* Torah, "teaching" Torah, as opposed to *"limud" haTorah,* which means simply "learning"

Torah. This is so because the process of learning Torah involves a teacher and a student. The Torah is transmitted from *rebbi* to *talmid.* This starts with the father teaching his son, וְלִמַּדְתֶּם אֹתָם אֶת בְּנֵיכֶם — and then progressing through a teacher who, in turn, had been taught by his teacher. וְשִׁנַּנְתָּם לְבָנֶיךָ, אֵלוּ הַתַּלְמִידִים – *You shall teach them clearly to your children* — this refers to students (*Sifrei, Devarim* 6:7). And if one becomes able to teach others it is, likewise, a *mitzvah* for him to do so. While this is the ideal, nevertheless, in the absence of a rebbe, one must make the effort to learn Torah himself.

This completes the Mishnah portion, which is now followed by Gemara.

אֵלוּ דְבָרִים שֶׁאָדָם אוֹכֵל פֵּרוֹתֵיהֶם בָּעוֹלָם הַזֶּה

 אֵלוּ דְבָרִים שֶׁאָדָם אוֹכֵל פֵּרוֹתֵיהֶם בָּעוֹלָם הַזֶּה וְהַקֶּרֶן קַיֶּמֶת לוֹ לָעוֹלָם הַבָּא — **These are the precepts whose fruits a person enjoys in This World but whose principal remains intact for him in the World to Come.** The Gemara which we quote is actually a *baraisa*. This exact text, containing these ten "*devarim,*" is not found in our *Talmud Bavli,* although we do find similar *Baraisos.* Nevertheless, this must be an ancient text, *nusach yashan,* because it has been universally accepted in all *siddurim.*

A similar *baraisa* in the name of R' Yaakov: שְׂכַר מִצְוָה בְּהַאי עָלְמָא לֵיכָּא, *Reward for a mitzvah does not exist in this world* (*Kiddushin* 39b). A *mitzvah* is something completely spiritual. It is infinite, so to speak, and can only be rewarded spiritually, in the World to Come. Paying a physical reward for a *mitzvah* is analogous to "rewarding" someone for saving your life by giving him 50 cents. No matter what physical reward one can receive in this world, such as robust health, abundant wealth, children, fame and success, it is not adequate payment for *one mitzvah.* The reward for one *mitzvah* of *tzitzis,* for putting on *tefillin* even once, can only be given spiritually, in *Olam Haba.* However, similar to investments where one can receive dividends without touching the principal, *mitzvos,* too, pay "dividends" in this world, in addition to the קֶרֶן קַיֶּמֶת לוֹ לָעוֹלָם הַבָּא.

However, these "dividends" are similar to the principal, in that they, too, are spiritual. We have a list here of ten דְּבָרִים which yield spiritual dividends in this world, in addition to their principal, which קֶרֶן קַיֶּמֶת לוֹ לָעוֹלָם הַבָּא, *remains intact for him in the World to Come.*

 וְאֵלוּ הֵן: כִּבּוּד אָב וָאֵם — **They are: the honor due to father and mother.** This is an extremely difficult *mitzvah* to fulfill properly. It never ceases; one can never do enough. We find that Abaye, who never knew his parents — his father died before he was born, and his mother died while giving birth to him — considered himself fortunate for never having violated this very difficult *mitzvah* (*Kiddushin* 31b).

However, if a person does have the *zechus* of fulfilling this *mitzvah,* he is promised לָךְ, לְמַעַן יַאֲרִיכֻן יָמֶיךָ וּלְמַעַן יִיטַב לָךְ, *so that your days will be lengthened and so that it will be good for you* (Devarim 5:16). In accordance with the statement of R' Yaakov, שְׂכַר מִצְוָה בְּהַאי עָלְמָא לֵיכָּא, *Reward for a mitzvah does not exist in this world* (Kiddushin 39b), this promise refers to the reward in Olam Haba, and the *pasuk* is explained as: — לְמַעַן יַאֲרִיכֻן יָמֶיךָ וּלְמַעַן יִיטַב לָךְ לְעוֹלָם שֶׁכֻּלוֹ טוֹב, לְעוֹלָם שֶׁכֻּלוֹ אָרוּךְ. This means that the main reward for *kibbud av v'eim* will be realized in the world which is "everlasting and good," in *Olam Haba*, the World to Come.

However, in addition, there are also *peiros*, "fruits" or "dividends," to be realized in this world, which grow, here and now, from the principal reward which awaits one's *neshamah* in עוֹלָם שֶׁכֻּלוֹ טוֹב for the *mitzvah* of *kibbud av v'eim*. A person who merits it is rewarded spiritually even in this world, with a miniature aspect of עוֹלָם שֶׁכֻּלוֹ טוֹב, in that he gets the feeling that all is well with him; he becomes a *same'ach b'chelko*, happy with his lot; he is even *same'ach b'yissurim* — if misfortune strikes, he accepts that happily as well. A person who merits these "dividends" has the feeling that he is already in עוֹלָם שֶׁכֻּלוֹ טוֹב in this world. [See further on this point in *Maayan Beis HaSho'evah, Yisro* 2:12 (p. 202).]

וּגְמִילוּת חֲסָדִים — **Acts of kindness.** This refers to *gemilus chassadim* in all its forms; it supersedes *tzedakah*, which applies only to the needy and the poor. *Gemilus chassadim* encompasses everything which falls under the heading of וְאָהַבְתָּ לְרֵעֲךָ כָּמוֹךָ, *You shall love your fellow as yourself* (Vayikra 19:18), and involves looking out for the welfare of others, as one would for his own. If a person does this, he gets a spiritual dividend, פֵּרוֹת, in this world.

We have a *mitzvas asei* (positive commandment) to love *HaKadosh Baruch Hu*: וְאָהַבְתָּ אֵת ה' אֱלֹהֶיךָ, *You shall love Hashem, your God* (Devarim 6:5). One can reach the lofty level of *ahavas Hashem* as a reward for וְאָהַבְתָּ לְרֵעֲךָ כָּמוֹךָ. As we find, גֹּמֵל נַפְשׁוֹ אִישׁ חָסֶד, *A man of kindness brings good upon himself* (Mishlei 11:17). The man who performs acts of love and kindness to others bestows the same upon himself. *Chessed* means the love of others. If one loves the creatures of *HaKadosh Baruch Hu*, his reward is that he develops *ahavas HaKadosh Baruch Hu*. We find that David HaMelech called himself "chassid" (Tehillim 86:2). In *Berachos* 4a we learn that this is so because he made peace, and promoted love, between husbands and wives. The result was that he himself became *an oheiv HaKadosh Baruch Hu*. He became a "chassid" as a result of the *chessed* he did for others.

Similarly, we find Avraham Avinu being called אַבְרָהָם אֹהֲבִי (Yeshayahu 41:8). Avraham reached the level of being called by *HaKadosh Baruch Hu*, "One who loves Me." His many acts of *chassadim* to people — which expressed his *ahavas habriyos* — led him to *ahavas Hashem*. This thought can be inferred from a deeper understanding of the *pasuk*: וְאָהַבְתָּ לְרֵעֲךָ כָּמוֹךָ אֲנִי ה', *You shall love your fellow as yourself* — which will bring you eventually to — *I am Hashem,* love of Hashem. This is the spiritual "dividend" of *gemilus chassadim.*

וְהַשְׁכָּמַת בֵּית הַמִּדְרָשׁ שַׁחֲרִית וְעַרְבִית — **Early attendance at the house of study morning and evening.** This refers to going to the *beis hamidrash* for the purpose of *talmud Torah,* and presupposes that the person had previously been *mispallel* in a *beis haknesses.* This follows the order: הַיּוֹצֵא מִבֵּית הַכְּנֶסֶת וְנִכְנָס לְבֵית הַמִּדְרָשׁ וְעוֹסֵק בַּתּוֹרָה זוֹכֶה וּמְקַבֵּל פְּנֵי שְׁכִינָה, שֶׁנֶּאֱמַר יֵלְכוּ מֵחַיִל אֶל חָיִל יֵרָאֶה אֶל אֱלֹהִים בְּצִיּוֹן, *One who goes from the house of prayer and enters the house of study merits coming into the proximity with the face of the presence of God, as it is stated, "Go from multitude to multitude, appear before God in Zion"* (*Berachos* 64a).

Learning Torah publicly in a *beis hamidrash,* rather than doing so in private, encourages others to follow suit. This is also a form of *gemilus chassadim,* because by learning in public he encourages others to learn as well. Of course, the spiritual reward for this is that one who does this becomes a *ben Torah* himself. He lives on a much higher plane; he is a practicing Torah Jew.

וְהַכְנָסַת אוֹרְחִים — **Hospitality to guests** — inviting guests, travelers, to one's home (אוֹרְחִים comes from אוֹרַח, *road*). This is an old Jewish custom, dating back to Avraham Avinu, who exemplified it and from whom we learn: גְּדוֹלָה הַכְנָסַת אוֹרְחִין מֵהַקְבָּלַת פְּנֵי הַשְּׁכִינָה, *The reception of guests is greater than the reception of God's presence* (*Shabbos* 127a).

A person should know that each time he invites someone into his home, and he fulfills this *mitzvah,* he comes closer to *HaKadosh Baruch Hu.* He is doing the *ratzon Hashem* (will of Hashem), and thus, comes closer to Him. We find the striking statement that the guest does the host a favor by accepting his invitation: יוֹתֵר מִמַּה שֶּׁבַּעַל הַבַּיִת עוֹשֶׂה עִם הֶעָנִי, הֶעָנִי עוֹשֶׂה עִם בַּעַל הַבַּיִת, *The poor person does more for the host than the host does for the poor person* (*Midrash Rus Rabbah* 5:9). The practice of *hachnassas orchim* elevates the person to a level surpassing that of *kabbalas Pnei HaShechinah,* as shown by Avraham Avinu (see *Rashi* to *Bereishis* 18:3). This, then, is the spiritual dividend which one receives in *Olam Hazeh* for this *mitzvah.*

וּבִקּוּר חוֹלִים — **Visiting the sick.** When a person visits the sick, he not only performs an act of great kindness to the patient, but he also does something for himself. Instead of taking his own good health for granted, he becomes grateful to *HaKadosh Baruch Hu* that he is not sick. A sure cure for one who is depressed is to go to a hospital and ask the receptionist for the condition of Mr. . . ., and give his own name. When he is told that there is no one there with that name, in any of their departments, he leaves with a wonderful feeling of gratitude that he is, after all, well.

(This was told to me, in a humorous vein, by Rabbi Gross, while I was in the hospital.)

The feeling of *hakaras hatov,* of gratitude, to *HaKadosh Baruch Hu* for one's own health after visiting a sick person is a spiritual dividend in *Olam Hazeh* for doing this *mitzvah*.

וְהַכְנָסַת כַּלָּה — **Providing for a bride.** The simplest way to do this is by financially assisting a poor bride to make her wedding preparations, including the buying of clothing, furniture, and household necessities. However, it also includes anything one does to assist someone to get married. This starts with suggesting a *shidduch* (match), all the way to rejoicing at the wedding celebration. All these efforts are called *mesame'ach chassan v'kallah,* (gladdening the bride and groom), which the Gemara considers such a great *mitzvah* that the one who performs it is considered as if he had rebuilt one of the ruins of Yerushalayim (*Berachos* 6b). This is so because one of the reasons why the destruction of Yerushalayim took place was: תַּחַת אֲשֶׁר לֹא עָבַדְתָּ אֶת ה' אֱלֹהֶיךָ בְּשִׂמְחָה וּבְטוּב לֵבָב, *We did not perform our mitzvos with happiness and joy* (*Devarim* 28:47). So by being *mesame'ach chassan v'kallah,* we are performing a *mitzvah* with joy, we are doing Hashem's will with joy, and are thus rectifying one of the causes of the downfall of Yerushalayim. This is the spiritual "dividend" of this *mitzvah* in *Olam Hazeh*.

וּלְוָיַת הַמֵּת — **Escorting the dead.** This includes everything which the *chevrah kaddisha* (burial society) does, and that which is done by all those who participate in the *levayah* (funeral) and the *kevurah* (burial). The spiritual dividend in *Olam Hazeh* for this *mitzvah* can be found in the words of *Koheles*: טוֹב לָלֶכֶת אֶל בֵּית אֵבֶל מִלֶּכֶת אֶל בֵּית מִשְׁתֶּה... וְהַחַי יִתֵּן אֶל לִבּוֹ, *It is better to go to a house of mourning than to go to a house of feasting . . . and the living should take it to heart* (*Koheles* 7:2). When one goes to the house of an *aveil* (mourner), it is a sobering experience. He realizes that someday his own time of reckoning will come, and this will prompt him to do *teshuvah* (repentance).

It is striking that the order of this *baraisa* has *bikur cholim* and *levayas hameis* separated by *hachnassas kallah*. Why does *hachnassas kallah* separate the two? I heard a beautiful explanation by the Steipler Rav, who explained this as a subtle hint: If one wants a *zechus* to overcome sickness, so that it not lead to *levayas hameis,* he should do the *mitzvah* of *hachnassas kallah*. Just as the resulting new family will bring new life to the world, so may the life of the *choleh* (sick person) be restored.

וְעִיּוּן תְּפִלָּה — **Concentrating on *tefillah*.** This is the purpose of these *shiurim*: to learn the meaning of the *tefillos,* so that we can concentrate on them. The reason that this *hanhagah tovah* (good practice) is included in this list is because it includes *tefillah* for the health or welfare of others (*Rashi, Shabbos* 127b). This, then, is also an act of *gemilus chassadim,* as are the other activities on this list. The spiritual dividend in this world for being *mispallel* for others is given in *Bava Kamma* 92a: כָּל הַמְבַקֵּשׁ רַחֲמִים עַל חֲבֵירוֹ וְהוּא צָרִיךְ לְאוֹתוֹ דָּבָר הוּא נַעֲנֶה תְחִלָּה, *If someone is mispallel for the benefit of another, and he himself has that same need, HaKadosh Baruch Hu responds to his need first.* This is clearly פֵּרוֹתֵיהֶם בָּעוֹלָם הַזֶּה, the benefits one enjoys in This World.

◆§ וַהֲבָאַת שָׁלוֹם בֵּין אָדָם לַחֲבֵרוֹ — **Bringing peace between man and his fellow.** We know that the destruction of the *Beis HaMikdash* and the *galus* were due to *sinas chinam* (unfounded hatred). We know how *machlokes* (strife) can ruin lives. If a person can make peace between enemies, or between husbands and wives, it is indeed an enormous *mitzvah.* This is what Aaron HaKohen was noted for — אוֹהֵב שָׁלוֹם וְרוֹדֵף שָׁלוֹם, *loving peace and pursuing peace.* The spiritual reward in *Olam Hazeh* for being a "peacemaker" is that he himself becomes beloved by other people, and consequently receives a *kesser shem tov* (the crown of a good name), which is the highest form of adulation in this world (see *Pirkei Avos* 4:17).

◆§ וְתַלְמוּד תּוֹרָה כְּנֶגֶד כֻּלָּם — **And the study of Torah is equivalent to them all.** This means not merely *limud,* "learning," but rather *talmud,* "teaching." This is in contrast to *limud Torah,* which is mentioned earlier as הַשְׁכָּמַת בֵּית הַמִּדְרָשׁ. However, what this *baraisa* is telling us is that teaching Torah to another person is equal to all of the aforementioned acts of *chessed* together. The greatest form of *chessed* is to teach Torah to someone. This is compared to having given birth to him — כָּל הַמְלַמֵּד בֶּן חֲבֵירוֹ תּוֹרָה מַעֲלֶה עָלָיו הַכָּתוּב כְּאִילוּ יְלָדוֹ, *Whoever teaches Torah to the son of his fellow, is regarded by Scripture as if he had fathered him* (*Sanhedrin* 19b).

And if one is not able to teach Torah himself, he can fulfill this *mitzvah* by promoting, financially and otherwise, institutions which do teach Torah. Furthermore, a woman who encourages her husband to learn, or who sees to it that her children receive an education in Torah, is also practicing *talmud Torah* (see *Berachos* 17b). The spiritual dividend for this is obvious. One of the greatest forms of spiritual satisfaction is the awareness that we have imparted Torah knowledge to someone else.

We have now completed the three recitations of *Mikra,* Mishnah, and Gemara, following the *birchos haTorah,* in accordance with the aforementioned *minhag Sefardim.* The reason that we choose portions from the three divisions of the Torah is based on *Kiddushin* 30a: לְעוֹלָם יְשַׁלֵּשׁ אָדָם שְׁנוֹתָיו, שְׁלִישׁ בַּמִּקְרָא, שְׁלִישׁ בַּמִּשְׁנָה, שְׁלִישׁ בַּתַּלְמוּד, *A person should divide the years of his life into three parts, spending a third of them in the study of Mikra (Torah*

Shebichsav), a third in the study of Mishnah (Torah Shebe'al Peh), and a third in the study of Talmud. Talmud is what we know as Gemara, the explanation of the Mishnah which begins with the *Baraisos* and includes all *halachah, aggadata,* and *midrashim.*

As we pointed out, these particular selections from the three divisions of Torah were chosen because they all have some reference to *talmud Torah*, for which we have just made the *berachah*.

פָּרָשַׁת הַתָּמִיד / Parashas HaTamid

According to our outline, we are now standing in the *Ezras Kohanim*, facing the *Mizbe'ach*, where the *korbanos* are brought. It is therefore appropriate at this point in our *tefillos*, in the absence of the actual *korbanos*, to recite selections from the three divisions of Torah: *Mikra*, *Mishnah*, and *Gemara*, which refer to *korbanos*. This is an old *minhag*, albeit not mentioned in the Gemara: עַל כֵּן תִּקֵּן בְּסֵדֶר רַבִּי עַמְרָם גָּאוֹן כְּמוֹ שֶׁאָנוּ נוֹהֲגִים בְּכָל יוֹם קוֹדֶם פְּסוּקֵי דְזִמְרָה לוֹמַר מִקְרָא מִשְׁנָה וּגְמָרָא, *Rav Amram Gaon instituted, in his siddur, that we are to recite selections from Mikra, Mishnah, and Gemara before starting Pesukei d'Zimrah* (*Tosafos, Kiddushin* 30a s.v. לא). The particular selections are defined in *Tosafos* (*Avodah Zarah* 19b s.v. ישלש) as פָּרָשַׁת הַתָּמִיד for *Mikra*; פֶּרֶק אֵיזֶהוּ מְקוֹמָן, which discusses all *korbanos*, for *Mishnah*; and the *baraisa* of רַבִּי יִשְׁמָעֵאל אוֹמֵר for Gemara. This *baraisa* is actually an introduction to *Toras Kohanim*. The said *Toras Kohanim*, also known as *Sifra*, which preceded the Mishnah, is the *Torah Shebe'al Peh* on *Vayikra*, and pertains to the *halachos* of *Kohanim* and *korbanos*.

It is not our purpose here to detail the *korbanos* and their *halachos*. However, it is important to learn these *halachos* and, especially, to familiarize oneself with the meaning of the selections which we recite every morning.

A classic synopsis of the essence of the meaning of the *korbanos* and their details can be found in the "Hirsch *Siddur*" on אֵיזֶהוּ מְקוֹמָן. It is highly recommended.

※ ※ ※

וַיְדַבֵּר ה' אֶל מֹשֶׁה לֵּאמֹר. צַו אֶת בְּנֵי יִשְׂרָאֵל וְאָמַרְתָּ אֲלֵהֶם אֶת קָרְבָּנִי לַחְמִי לְאִשַּׁי רֵיחַ נִיחֹחִי תִּשְׁמְרוּ לְהַקְרִיב לִי בְּמוֹעֲדוֹ — **Hashem spoke to Moshe saying: Command the Children of Israel and tell them: My offering, My food for My fires, My satisfying aroma, you are to be scrupulous to offer Me in its appointed time.** The פָּרָשַׁת הַתָּמִיד begins with Moshe Rabbeinu being told by HaKadosh Baruch Hu to direct this commandment אֲלֵהֶם, to the entire nation of *Bnei Yisrael*, not only to the *Kohanim*. The bringing of *korbanos* is *a national responsibility*. This is the reason the *korbanos* were brought in the presence of the *anshei maamad*. These were twenty-four groups of laymen representing all parts of *Klal Ysrael*, acting as "honor guards" to stand by each one of the twenty-four *mishmaros*, or duty watches of *Kohanim*, as they went about their *avodas hakodesh*. However, the next *pasuk* says: וְאָמַרְתָּ לָהֶם זֶה הָאִשֶּׁה אֲשֶׁר תַּקְרִיבוּ לַה' וגו', *And you are to tell them, "This is the fire-offering* *that you are to bring to Hashem . . .;* this refers only to the *Kohanim,* who actually do the *avodah* and thus carry out the national obligation of bringing the *korbanos.*

The word קָרְבָּן comes from קרב, meaning *to come close.* Through the *korban,* an individual — or *Klal Yisrael* as a nation — can come as close to *HaKadosh Baruch Hu* as is humanly possible. In the absence of *korbanos,* we use *tefillah* as a substitute: וּנְשַׁלְּמָה פָרִים שְׂפָתֵינוּ, *and let our lips substitute for bulls* (Hoshea 14:3). However, it is only a substitute, and cannot bring us as close to *HaKadosh Baruch Hu* as can the *korban.*

The *korban* is called רֵיחַ נִיחֹחַ, literally, *a pleasant smell.* Rav Hirsch explains that the *korban* — representing our personality — emits its pleasant fragrance as a symbolic expression of our desire to please *HaKadosh Baruch Hu* by fulfilling His will — לְשֵׁם הֲנָחַת רוּחַ, *for the purpose of pleasing (Him)* (Zevachim 46b).

◆§ לַחְמִי לְאִשַּׁי — **My food for My fires.** We know that despite the fact that *HaKadosh Baruch Hu* is Omnipresent — מְלֹא כָל הָאָרֶץ כְּבוֹדוֹ, *the entire world is filled with His glory* (Yeshayahu 6:3) — most people do not merit to perceive His presence. However, there were a few periods in history when *HaKadosh Baruch Hu* did manifest His presence in the world. One of these times was *Matan Torah,* the giving of the Torah to Yisrael, during which, the Torah tells us: וּמַרְאֵה כְּבוֹד ה׳ כְּאֵשׁ אֹכֶלֶת בְּרֹאשׁ הָהָר, *The glory of Hashem appeared as a consuming fire on the top of the mountain* (Shemos 24:17). Rav Hirsch explains that the *fire* on the *Mizbe'ach* is symbolic of the *Shechinah,* the presence of *HaKadosh Baruch Hu* on earth, which manifested itself as fire at the time of *Matan Torah.* The *korban,* representing the desire of the individual or nation to please *HaKadosh Baruch Hu* by doing His will, *la'asos Retzono,* becomes לַחְמִי לְאִשַּׁי, "fuel" for keeping My Fire burning on earth. As long as we do the *ratzon Hashem,* the *Shechinah* remains manifest on earth.

The daily *korban tamid,* together with all the other *korbanos,* is the fuel which keeps the fire on the *Mizbe'ach* burning constantly. We are forbidden to extinguish this fire: וְהָאֵשׁ עַל הַמִּזְבֵּחַ תּוּקַד בּוֹ לֹא תִכְבֶּה, *The fire on the Altar shall be kept burning on it, it shall not be extinguished* (Vayikra 6:5). This is symbolic of the desire of the Jewish nation to remain permanently pleasing in the eyes of God, and thus to keep the "*Shechinah* fire" burning on earth.

◆§ אֶת הַכֶּבֶשׂ אֶחָד תַּעֲשֶׂה בַבֹּקֶר, וְאֵת הַכֶּבֶשׂ הַשֵּׁנִי תַּעֲשֶׂה בֵּין הָעַרְבָּיִם — **One lamb-service you are to perform in the morning and the second lamb-service you are to perform in the afternoon.** With the *korban tamid,* which is the first and last *korban* of each day, *Klal Yisrael* dedicates itself to *HaKadosh Baruch Hu* by the symbolic offering of a lamb. This represents our special relationship with *HaKadosh Baruch Hu* as our shepherd: וְאַתֵּן צֹאנִי צֹאן מַרְעִיתִי, *Now, you are My sheep, the sheep of My pasture* (*Yechezkel* 34:31). We are the flock of *HaKadosh Baruch Hu*, under his special care and guidance. This *korban* consists of a *keves* (lamb), which represents our physical existence, by means of its blood that is sprinkled on the *Mizbe'ach*, and its flesh that is consumed by the fire.

The *zerikas hadam* (blood sprinkling) of most *korbanos* consisted of the *Kohanim* taking the container of blood and dashing it, from some distance, at two diagonal corners of the *Mizbe'ach*: northeast and southwest. This is known as *shtei matnos she'hein arba,* two applications which touch all four sides of the *Mizbe'ach,* because the blood at each of the corners spreads to their respective sides. Thus the blood is applied *al hamizbe'ach saviv,* all around the *Mizbe'ach.* Rav Samson R. Hirsch explains the four sides of the *Mizbe'ach* as corresponding to the structure of the *Mishkan* and its *keilim* (vessels), as follows.

The west side faces the *Kodesh HaKadashim,* the place of the *Aron,* which held the *Torah Shebichsav,* consisting of the *shnei luchos* and the original *sefer Torah* written by Moshe Rabbeinu, as well as the *Kapores* with the *kanfei shnei Keruvim* from which *HaKadosh Baruch Hu* spoke the words of *Torah Shebe'al Peh* to Moshe Rabbeinu. So the west corresponds to the Torah.

The opposite side, the east, corresponds to the people. They enter from the east and move forward toward the Torah. The east represents *Klal Yisrael.*

The north side corresponds to the *Shulchan* in the *Heichal,* and thus represents the material element. The south side corresponds to the Menorah, and thereby represents the spiritual element.

The *korbanos* were accompanied by סוֹלֶת, שֶׁמֶן, and יַיִן. The *so'les* consisted of finely ground wheat flour, in an amount of *asiris ha'eifah,* which is sufficient for one person's daily sustenance. This amount, called *omer,* was the same volume as that of the מָן, *manna,* the miraculous heavenly food, which was allotted to each person, each day, in the desert. The *shemen,* the olive oil, representing that which is added to basic nourishment to make it palatable, is symbolic of our prosperity, which we also dedicate to *HaKadosh Baruch Hu.* And *yayin,* wine, being the symbol of joy — וְיַיִן יְשַׂמַּח לְבַב אֱנוֹשׁ, *And wine that gladdens man's heart* (*Tehillim* 104:15) — represents the joy in our lives, which we similarly dedicate to *HaKadosh Baruch Hu.*

◆§ עֹלַת תָּמִיד הָעֲשֻׂיָה בְּהַר סִינַי — **It is the continual elevation-offering that was done at Mount Sinai.** The simple meaning is that the *halachos* of the *korban tamid* were shown to Moshe Rabbeinu on *Har Sinai.* And the first time the *korban tamid* was brought was in the *Ohel Moed,* which was erected at the foot of Har Sinai.

Additionally, immediately following *Matan Torah,* we were told to symbolically reproduce *Har Sinai,* in the form of the *Mizbe'ach,* and take it with us: מִזְבַּח אֲדָמָה תַּעֲשֶׂה לִי וגו', *You shall build an earthen altar for Me* etc. (*Shemos* 20:21). The copper *Mizbe'ach HaNechoshes* was a hollow copper shell, filled with earth, on top of which was the fire. The *Mizbe'ach,* this earthen mound, is called הַרְאֵל, *the Mountain of God* (*Yechezkel* 43:15), because it is a symbolic reproduction of *Har Sinai.* This symbolic *Har Sinai* was to accompany us in the form of the *Mizbe'ach* throughout our wanderings in the *midbar* (desert), and later in Eretz Yisrael wherever there was a *Mishkan* or a *Beis HaMikdash.*

The *Mizbe'ach* was approached by way of the *kevesh,* (ramp). Although this was an integral part of the *Mizbe'ach,* it is not specifically mentioned in the Torah. It is only alluded to in the words: וְלֹא תַעֲלֶה בְמַעֲלֹת עַל מִזְבְּחִי, *You shall not use steps to ascend my Altar* (*Shemos* 20:23). Since the *kevesh* is not specifically mentioned among the *klei kodesh* (the holy furnishings and vessels of the *Mishkan*), we may assume that in the *midbar,* the actual desert floor was built up into a *kevesh* for ascending the *Mizbe'ach.* This would be a further extension of the *Har Sinai* symbolism of the *Mizbe'ach.* However, later in the *Beis HaMikdash,* a *kevesh* made of stone was used and it, too, was reminiscent of the mountain terrain of Sinai which consisted of desert rocks and sand.

In *Tehillim* we find the *pasuk:* אֲדֹנָי בָם סִינַי בַּקֹּדֶשׁ, *My Master is* (*now*) *among them, Sinai in the Sanctuary.* This means that *HaKadosh Baruch Hu* is among Israel, because Sinai is in the Sanctuary (*Tehillim* 68:18). With the symbolic representation of *Har Sinai* through the fire on the *Mizbe'ach,* the *Shechinah* is בָם, among the entire nation, wherever it may be. (See Rav Samson R. Hirsch on *Tehillim* ibid.)

The *Gemara* in *Shabbos* 116a, commenting on the verse, וַיִּסְעוּ מֵהַר ה', *They journeyed from the mountain of Hashem* (*Bamidbar* 10:33), categorizes this first leg of the journey from Sinai to Eretz Yisrael as פּוּרְעָנוּת, *a sinful occurrence,* שֶׁסָּרוּ מֵאַחֲרֵי ה', *because Bnei Yisrael turned away from Hashem.* This "turning away" is explained in *Midrash Yelamdeinu* (see *Tosafos* s.v. פורענות ibid.) as the manner in which they left Sinai: כְּתִינוֹק הַיּוֹצֵא מִבֵּית הַסֵּפֶר, *like a child leaving school.* They wanted to leave *Har Sinai* behind them. *Chazal* sensed this as a פּוּרְעָנוּת, or sinful event, because here Sinai is called *Har Hashem* instead of *Har Sinai.* We know that once the *Shechinah* departed *Har Sinai* after *Matan Torah,* the mountain itself had no further *kedushah* (*Beitzah* 5b). If, nevertheless, the Torah here still calls it הַר ה', it is a subtle indication that *Bnei Yisrael* were not yet ready to have the סִינַי בַּקֹּדֶשׁ, *Sinai in their own sanctuary,* wherever they traveled. Rather, they were more comfortable with leaving the *kedushah* on Sinai, as a "holy shrine" to which they could come back from time to time and say a *kappitel Tehillim.* They wanted it to remain as a הַר ה'.

They had failed to understand the meaning of the *Mishkan* and *ishei Hashem* (the fires of Hashem), which were to be a continuation and extension of the *eish* and the *gilui HaShechinah* which they had witnessed on *Har Sinai*. However, this sinful misunderstanding could only be felt by those who had a higher sensitivity. Their punishment, פּוּרְעָנוּת, was the sad realization that *Bnei Yisrael* had, indeed, misunderstood the purpose of the *Mishkan* and the *eish* on the *Mizbe'ach* as a continuation of the *gilui haShechinah* of *Har Sinai*.

However, the next פּוּרְעָנוּת, that of the מִתְאוֹנְנִים, *complainers* (for details of this sad episode see *Bamidbar* Ch. 11), which was a great *aveirah* with catastrophic consequences, is separated from the previous וַיִּסְעוּ מֵהַר ה׳, by brackets, נוּן הַפוּכָה (see in *Chumash*), to indicate the difference in kind between these two sinful events in the Torah. The first affected only those who were on a high spiritual level; the second, with its catastrophic consequences, was experienced by the entire nation.

Although nowadays, in the absence of *korbanos*, our *tefillos* act as a substitute for them, וּנְשַׁלְּמָה פָרִים שְׂפָתֵינוּ, *and let our lips substitute for bulls*, however, there is still a major difference between the two. The Vilna Gaon explains that while *tefillah* and *teshuvah* for an *aveirah* are accepted by HaKadosh Baruch Hu as a *kapparah* (atonement), the *aveirah* still exists. However, the *korban* completely eradicates the *aveirah,* as if it never existed. *Midrash Rabbah* (*Bamidbar* 21:21) explains the verse, צֶדֶק יָלִין בָּהּ, *righteousness lodged in her* (*Yeshayahu* 1:21), to mean that when the *korbanos* were brought in Yerushalayim, righteousness slept there, and therefore *aveiros* did not endure there. The *tamid* offering of Shacharis eradicated the *aveiros* of the previous night, and the *tamid* of *bein ha'arbayim* (twilight) eradicated those which were done during the day. This is why *tefillah* is, at most, a substitute for the *korbanos,* but it does not replace them. [For a fuller development of this subject by the author, see *Maayan Beis HaSho'evah, Bereishis* 1:4.]

◆§ וְשָׁחַט אֹתוֹ עַל יֶרֶךְ הַמִּזְבֵּחַ צָפֹנָה לִפְנֵי ה׳ וְזָרְקוּ בְּנֵי אַהֲרֹן הַכֹּהֲנִים אֶת דָּמוֹ עַל הַמִּזְבֵּחַ סָבִיב — **He is to slaughter it on the north side of the Altar before Hashem, and Aaron's sons the Kohanim are to dash its blood upon the Altar, all around.** This *pasuk*, which appears much earlier in the Torah than the פָּרָשַׁת הַתָּמִיד, is recited afterward, in accordance with the *minhag* found in *Beis Yosef, Orach Chaim, Siman* 1, originating with Rav Yaakov ben R' Yakar, who was one of the *Rebbe'im* of Rashi. By the way, I had the *zechus* of being at his *matzeivah* (memorial gravestone) in Mainz. The inscription was extremely simple, consisting only of the words: מרנא יעקב בן יקר (Rabbi Yaakov Ben Yakar), without embellishments.

The *minhag* to recite this *pasuk* was, most probably, not widespread originally. It does not appear in the *siddur* of the *mekubal* Rabbi Hertz which was printed nearly 500 years ago in Tuhingen, Germany. However, eventually, the entire *Klal Yisrael* did accept it.

The reason for reciting this *pasuk* after the פָּרָשַׁת הַתָּמִיד, as given by the *Beis Yosef*, is as follows:

טוֹב לוֹמַר עִם הַקָּרְבָּנוֹת פָּסוּק זֶה: וְשָׁחַט אֹתוֹ עַל יֶרֶךְ הַמִּזְבֵּחַ צָפֹנָה לִפְנֵי ה׳. כִּדְאַמְרִינַן בְּוַיִקְ״ר (ב:י״א-ו׳ע׳ תדב״א פ״ו): אָמַר הַקָּבָּ״ה מֵעִיד אֲנִי עָלַי שָׁמַיִם וָאָרֶץ, בֵּין גּוֹי בֵּין יִשְׂרָאֵל, בֵּין אִישׁ בֵּין אִשָּׁה, בֵּין עֶבֶד בֵּין אָמָה, בְּשָׁעָה שֶׁהֵן קוֹרִין מִקְרָא זֶה צָפֹנָה לִפְנֵי ה׳ אֲנִי זוֹכֵר עֲקֵידַת יִצְחָק בֶּן אַבְרָהָם. The *Midrash* (*Vayikra Rabbah* 2:11; see *Tanna d'Vei Eliyahu* 6) here is saying that *HaKadosh Baruch Hu* is testifying, with heaven and earth as witnesses, that when any person, be he Jew or non-Jew, man or woman, slave or maidservant, recites this *pasuk,* which contains the words צָפֹנָה לִפְנֵי ה׳, *HaKadosh Baruch Hu* will remember the *Akeidah* of Yitzchak the son of Avraham.

This startling statement needs to be explained.

There is a very important concept connected with the *Akeidah* of Yitzchak ben Avraham: that of *kabbalas yissurim* (acceptance of suffering). Through *yissurim* a person can become his own *mizbe'ach*. This concept is expressed by *Chazal* regarding a person who is suffering from *tzaraas*: כָּל מִי שֶׁיֵּשׁ בּוֹ אֶחָד מֵאַרְבָּעָה מַרְאוֹת נְגָעִים הַלָּלוּ אֵינוֹ אֶלָּא מִזְבֵּחַ כַּפָּרָה, *Anyone on whom there is one of these four appearances of tzaraas, they are nothing other than a mizbe'ach of atonement* (*Berachos* 5b). Similarly, we find in the *Shir HaYichud* for *yom rishon,* which is said by many on *Kol Nidrei* night: מִזְבֵּחַ אֶבְנֶה בְּשִׁבְרוֹן לִבִּי, *I will build a mizbe'ach with my broken heart. I myself will become a mizbe'ach.*

When one stands in the *Azarah,* heading forward from east to west, toward the *Heichal,* he is facing the place where the *Shechinah* is concentrated, the *Kodesh HaKadashim*. This is the general area which is known halachically as לִפְנֵי ה׳. However, there is another, more specific לִפְנֵי ה׳, on one's right side as he continues forward toward the *Mizbe'ach*. This is the place of the *shechitas korbanos* (slaughtering of the offerings) which is called צָפֹנָה לִפְנֵי ה׳, which, literally translated, means "north before God." The physical entity known as the human being is composed of a *guf,* the physical body, and *nefesh,* which is usually erroneously translated as soul, but is something totally different, as we shall explain. However, *nefesh,* or *ruach,* are both still physical components of the human being.

Nefesh, also known as *nefesh habeheimis,* could be translated as "psyche." This is the sum total of our emotional, nervous, and mental activities, and is something that we share with the animal. So when psychiatrists or psychologists wish to study certain human behaviors, they use guinea pigs or other animals, because these animals share behavior patterns with humans. We find the usage בְּכָל אַוַּת, אִם יֵשׁ אֶת נַפְשְׁכֶם, *If it is truly your will* (*Bereishis* 23:8); נַפְשְׁךָ תִּזְבַּח וְאָכַלְתָּ, *to your heart's desire you may slaughter and eat meat* (*Devarim* 12:15); and כִּי תְאַוֶּה נַפְשְׁךָ, *for you will have a desire* (ibid. 12:20), all having the meaning of desires, instincts, emotions, feelings, drives, and urges. All these are various levels and manifestations of *nefesh*. The *nefesh* is closely aligned with the physical apparatus, the *guf*, which *HaKadosh Baruch Hu* created with such great *chochmah*, as we previously discussed in detail at the *berachah* of *asher yatzar*.

Ruach, translated as "spirit," is the human side of the person, as in אָכֵן רוּחַ הִיא בֶאֱנוֹשׁ, *But it is a spirit in man* (*Iyov* 32:8). This can even develop to the level of *ruach hakodesh*. It is something which humans do not share with animals. It is וּמוֹתַר הָאָדָם מִן הַבְּהֵמָה, that which is above the animal. This is the source of the יֵצֶר הַטוֹב, *yetzer hatov,* and is not possessed by animals. However, the יֵצֶר הָרָע, *yetzer hara,* a part of the *nefesh,* which is implanted upon birth, includes all the normal desires and urges for gratification which *HaKadosh Baruch Hu* has placed within us for a purpose, as He has done in the animals, with great *chochmah*. However, the ability to control the *yetzer hara* is unique to the human being. Animals do not have this ability. Also, abstract thinking is not shared with the animal, and is also part of *ruach*. However, this is still not the *neshamah*.

The *neshamah* is that special entity which *HaKadosh Baruch Hu* has placed within the human being to enable him to have contact with *HaKadosh Baruch Hu*. This is what is meant by וַיִּפַּח בְּאַפָּיו נִשְׁמַת חַיִּים, *And He blew into his nostrils the soul of life* (*Bereishis* 2:7). This נְשָׁמָה שֶׁבְּמוֹחִי, *the soul that is in my brain* (from the prayer before donning *tefillin*), is the heavenly aspect of the human being, the שְׁמַיְמִית of the person. It is the ability to recognize *HaKadosh Baruch Hu,* to have *ahavas Hashem, yiras Shamayim, emunah,* and *bitachon*.

Now, using the symbolism of the structure of the *Mishkan* and its *keilim,* as previously outlined, if we picture the person himself as a *mizbe'ach*, his body is symbolized by the east which is behind him, the direction of the physical nation. The *neshamah*, the חֵלֶק אֱלוֹהַּ מִמַּעַל, or heavenly aspect, is symbolized by the opposite side, the west, the place of the *Kodesh HaKadashim*. Continuing with this symbolism, the right side, or north, is the material side, which represents the *nefesh,* and the left side represents the *ruach*.

This is what is to be understood by the words which we say in the bedtime *Krias Shema*: מִימִינִי מִיכָאֵל וּמִשְּׂמֹאלִי גַּבְרִיאֵל וּמִלְּפָנַי אוּרִיאֵל וּמֵאֲחוֹרַי רְפָאֵל וְעַל רֹאשִׁי שְׁכִינַת אֵל, *May Michael be at my right, Gavriel at my left, Uriel before me, and Rephael behind me; and above my head the Presence of God.* This means that I am making myself into a *mizbe'ach*. On my right (צָפוֹן, *north*) is Michael, of whom *Chazal* say he offers the *neshamos* of the *tzaddikim* as a *korban* to *HaKadosh Baruch Hu* (see *Chagigah* 12b and *Tosafos* to *Menachos* 110a). On my left is Gavriel, representing the ability of the *ruach* aspect to subdue the *nefesh*, to be a *gever* to overpower the physical aspect. In front of me is Uriel, literally, the "light of God," referring to my Divine aspect, the *neshamah,* the חֵלֶק אֱלוֹהַּ מִמַּעַל. Behind me is Rephael; this is my mortal and weak body, which is in constant need of *refuah.* And on my head is the *Shechinas Keil,* corresponding to the fire on the *Mizbe'ach.* This is a description of a person who becomes his own *mizbe'ach.*

A person can become his own *mizbe'ach* when he is suffering. This thought is expressed by the prayer, מִזְבֵּחַ אֶבְנֶה בְּשִׁבְרוֹן לִבִּי, *I will build an altar with my broken heart.* This may be any kind of suffering, physical pain or mental anguish. In fact, our *Chachamim* tell us that one of the ways of acquiring Torah is *kabbalas hayissurim,* acceptance of suffering (*Pirkei Avos* 6:6). No one goes through life without suffering. If, in the midst of the myriads of great benefits and miracles of our daily lives which *HaKadosh Baruch Hu* showers upon us, He decides, in His wisdom, that we must suffer — including the ultimate suffering when we leave this world — we are to accept it. And if a person does so, he becomes a *mizbe'ach kapparah,* an altar of atonement. This is what we learn from our forefather, Yitzchak ben Avraham. He epitomized this by his readiness for the *Akeidah,* the ultimate sacrifice. He accepted his suffering willingly.

In our daily *tefillah* of עֶזְרַת אֲבוֹתֵינוּ, we find the phrase: אַשְׁרֵי אִישׁ שֶׁיִּשְׁמַע לְמִצְוֹתֶיךָ וְתוֹרָתְךָ וּדְבָרְךָ יָשִׂים עַל לִבּוֹ, *Fortunate is the person who obeys your commandments and takes to his heart Your teaching and Your word.* There are two gates that lead to *HaKadosh Baruch Hu,* as it states, פִּתְחוּ לִי שַׁעֲרֵי צֶדֶק, *Open for me the gates of righteousness* (*Tehillim* 118:19). One is תּוֹרָתְךָ, through His Torah we learn how to lead our lives. This is the ideal way — מִלְּפָנַי אוּרִיאֵל. We receive our direction in life by looking straight ahead to the *Kodesh HaKadashim.* We are *mispallel* that this will be our lot in life. However, if *HaKadosh Baruch Hu* decrees that one must receive his direction in life through the other gate, דְּבָרְךָ, through *yissurim,* suffering, and he hears this message, he is also אַשְׁרֵי, fortunate. The word וּדְבָרְךָ refers to the personal messages which a person receives from *HaKadosh Baruch Hu* through the difficult *gezeiros* and suffering which he endures in his life. Fortunate is the man, אַשְׁרֵי אִישׁ, who understands the meaning of these personal messages. (See *Rambam, Shemini* 10:3, on this subject.)

If one accepts his suffering as a message from *HaKadosh Baruch Hu,* and then practices וְשָׁחַט אֹתוֹ by destroying the desire to rebel against these harsh lessons, he is, in effect, offering himself as a *korban* on his own personal *mizbe'ach.* This personal *korban* being offered at לִפְנֵי ה' could be מִזְרָחִית צְפוֹנִית, acceptance of physical suffering, symbolized by the northeast corner of the *mizbe'ach,* or צְפוֹנִית מַעֲרָבִית, acceptance of spiritual or emotional pain or anguish, symbolized by the northwest corner.

The entire *sefer* of *Iyov* describes how Iyov, the great *tzaddik hador* that he was, nevertheless, did not willingly accept his suffering. On the contrary, he rebelled against his *tzaros.* The *Midrash* says (see *Yalkut Shimoni, Iyov* 23,

508) that if Iyov had accepted his *yissurim* willingly, he would have risen to the level of *tzidkus* (righteousness) of the *Avos*, and we would have included the words *Elokei Iyov* in our *tefillah*.

וְשָׁחַט אֹתוֹ עַל יֶרֶךְ הַמִּזְבֵּחַ צָפֹנָה לִפְנֵי ה': The Torah uses the word יֶרֶךְ to mean the side of the *Mizbe'ach*. Actually, יֶרֶךְ means a thigh, a private part of the body which is hidden, *makom tzanua*. This special usage alludes to the concept that a person can become his own *mizbe'ach kapparah* through his acceptance of suffering. He privately offers his right side, his *nefesh*, characterized by the "north" side of his personal *mizbe'ach*, as a *korban* to HaKadosh Baruch Hu. This is pithily expressed as, קַבָּלָה דְּיִסּוּרֵי שְׁתִיקוּתָא וּמִבָּעֵי רַחֲמֵי, silently accepting suffering and praying (to HaKadosh Baruch Hu) for mercy (*Berachos* 62a). The *Chazon Ish* calls suffering *sheluchei d'Rachmana*, personal messengers from HaKadosh Baruch Hu to the individual.

We find a startling statement in *Bereishis Rabbah* 65:9: יִצְחָק תָּבַע יִסּוּרִין, or according to another opinion, יִצְחָק חִדֵּשׁ יִסּוּרִין (literally: Yitzchak requested — or initiated — suffering). Before Yitzchak, people died without suffering, thereby never having had the opportunity to be awakened to the need to do *teshuvah*. Yitzchak therefore asked HaKadosh Baruch Hu to send suffering to people before they die, so that they would do *teshuvah* and thereby cleanse their souls for everlasting reward in *Olam Haba*. The response given by HaKadosh Baruch Hu was: חַיֶּיךָ דָּבָר טוֹב תָּבַעְתָּ וּמִמְּךָ אֲנִי מַתְחִיל, *You have requested a good thing, and I will begin with you*. The result was: וַיְהִי כִּי זָקֵן יִצְחָק וַתִּכְהֶיןָ עֵינָיו מֵרְאֹת, *And it came to pass, when Yitzchak had become old, and his eyes dimmed from seeing* (*Bereishis* 27:1). Yitzchak became blind in his old age.

In *Eichah* (3:39) we find, מַה יִּתְאוֹנֵן אָדָם חָי, גֶּבֶר עַל חֲטָאָיו, *Why does a living person complain? Let him become a master over his sins*. Chazal explain this to mean: דַּיּוֹ שֶׁהוּא חַי, *it is sufficient that he is alive*. HaKadosh Baruch Hu is sending him a message through his suffering (see *Eichah Rabbah* ibid.).

We are all *mispallel* that we may be saved from *yissurim*, but if, *chas v'shalom*, this does befall one, the response should be שְׁתִיקוּתָא וּמִבָּעֵי רַחֲמֵי. HaKadosh Baruch Hu wants us to be quietly — privately — awakened by His messages, which are not accidents, and to be *mispallel* for deliverance from our *tzaros*. If one is sick, he asks for a *refuah* (cure); if he is poor, he asks for *parnassah* (livelihood); if he is subject to fears, he asks for *bitachon* (trust).

So, based on the foregoing, we can have some understanding of the *minhag* to say the *pasuk* of צָפֹנָה לִפְנֵי ה' after the פָּרָשַׁת הַתָּמִיד. The symbolism of *korbanos* can be extended to the creation of one's own personal *mizbe'ach*, by the acceptance of *yissurim*. What we are being told here by our Midrash is that HaKadosh Baruch Hu testifies, with heaven and earth as His witnesses, that anyone, בֵּין גּוֹי בֵּין יִשְׂרָאֵל, whether a Jew or non-Jew, who becomes a *mizbe'ach kapparah* through *kabbalas yissurim*, will thereby invoke the *zechus* of the *Akeidah* of Yitzchak ben Avraham, from whom we learn this concept.

ובְיוֹם הַשַׁבָּת שְׁנֵי כְבָשִׂים וגו׳ — On the Sabbath day, two first-year lambs etc. On Shabbos the *minhag* is to say the *pesukim* in the פָּרָשַׁת הַתָּמִיד which deal with Shabbos (see *Orach Chaim, Siman* 48). The special *korban mussaf* of Shabbos consisted of two lambs, in addition to the lambs brought in the morning and in the evening, every day, as the *korban tamid*. The two special Shabbos lambs represent the dual aspects of Shabbos: *zachor* and *shamor*. One is the basic reminder: כִּי שֵׁשֶׁת יָמִים עָשָׂה ה׳ אֶת הַשָׁמַיִם וְאֶת הָאָרֶץ וּבַיּוֹם הַשְׁבִיעִי שָׁבַת וַיִּנָּפַשׁ, *In six days did Hashem make the heaven and the earth, and on the seventh day He rested and was refreshed* (Shemos 31:17). We are to refrain from *melachah* on the seventh day of every week, to renew our *emunah* in *beriyas haOlam*, God's creation of the world. This is the mundane, or *shamor*, aspect of Shabbos. Then there is the *zachor*, or spiritual, aspect of Shabbos which is called *oneg*, as it states: וְקָרָאתָ לַשַׁבָּת עֹנֶג, *If you proclaim the Shabbos a delight* (Yeshayahu 58:13), referring to the spiritual pleasure of Shabbos, which is a foretaste of the World to Come — מֵעֵין עוֹלָם הַבָּא. (For further development of this subject, see *Maayan Beis HaSho'evah, Beshalach* 16:29.)

This "dualism" is also reflected by the *lechem mishneh*, two *challos*, *shnei neiros* (two candles), and *Kiddush* being recited twice, once at the beginning of Shabbos and once at the end, in the form of *Havdalah*, which is actually also a part of *Kiddush*.

עַל עֹלַת הַתָּמִיד וְנִסְכָּהּ — In addition to the regular elevation-offering and its wine-libation. This means that *first* the daily *korban tamid* is to be brought, followed by the *korban mussaf* of Shabbos.

The phrase עַל עֹלַת הַתָּמִיד, meaning *in addition to the daily korban*, is also used by the *korban mussaf* brought on Rosh Chodesh. However, on all other Yamim Tovim, the phrase is מִלְבַד עוֹלַת הַתָּמִיד. While these two words are somewhat synonymous, there is a difference. Shabbos and Rosh Chodesh are routine. One arrives every week, and one every month. The word עַל is appropriate when used to connote an addition to something already existing, whereas מִלְבַד, meaning *besides*, is used when referring to something relatively new and special, coming only occasionally, i.e. on Yom Tov.

[The עַל found at the end of the *korbanos* of Pesach (see *Bamidbar* 28:24) is used there because the same *korbanos* are brought for all seven days, thus making it, too, "routine."]

וּבְרָאשֵׁי חָדְשֵׁיכֶם תַּקְרִיבוּ עֹלָה לַה׳ — On the first of your months you are to bring an elevation-offering to Hashem. According to the *minhag Ashkenaz*, as codified by *Rema* in *Orach Chaim* 48:1, it is customary to say this *parashah* on Rosh Chodesh, together with the *Parashas HaTamid,* to make the day known to the *tzibbur* (congregation). However, the opinion of the author of the *Shulchan Aruch,* which is the *minhag haSefardim,* is that the *krias haTorah* on Rosh Chodesh is sufficient to publicize the day, and it is therefore not necessary to mention it in the *tefillah*.

וּשְׂעִיר עִזִּים אֶחָד לְחַטָּאת לַה׳ — **And one he-goat for a sin-offering to Hashem.** The phrase לְחַטָּאת לַה׳, *a sin-offering to Hashem,* is not found in connection with any of the other *mussafin* of Yom Tov. *Chazal* have therefore explained that the communal *korban chatas* of Rosh Chodesh comes to atone for *aveiros* which are known only to *HaKadosh Baruch Hu*: חַטָּאת לַה׳ — something which no person ever had any knowledge of, neither before nor afterwards (*Shevuos* 9a). This is identified there as טוּמְאַת מִקְדָּשׁ וְקָדָשָׁיו, the hidden and unknown defilement of the *Beis HaMikdash* or any of its *korbanos*. This can happen when a *Kohen* unknowingly comes into contact with a *kever hatehom,* a grave which is deep underground, in a place not known to contain graves. The *Kohen* becomes *tamei,* ritually unclean, because the *tumah* of the dead body, which is lying underground, radiates upwards through the earth — טוּמְאָה רְצוּצָה בּוֹקַעַת וְעוֹלָה — and contaminates the *Kohen*. He is therefore precluded from entering the *Beis HaMikdash* and is certainly unfit to bring any *korbanos* on the *Mizbe'ach*.

Over the course of thousands of years, these long-forgotten gravesites could be scattered all over the land. Consequently, it is very possible that the *Kohanim* who regularly perform the *avodah* could unknowingly be *tamei* from a *meis,* which if done בְּמֵזִיד (intentionally) would incur *kares*. So every Rosh Chodesh, the חַטָּאת לַה׳ is brought to atone for this *aveirah,* which is known only to *HaKadosh Baruch Hu.*

However, *Rashi* on *Bamidbar* 28:15 (taken from *Chullin* 60b) quotes a different explanation, of the meaning of חַטָּאת לַה׳ as follows: וּמִדְרָשׁוֹ בָּאַגָּדָה: אָמַר הַקָּבָּ"ה הָבִיאוּ כַּפָּרָה עָלַי עַל שֶׁמִּעַטְתִּי אֶת הַיָּרֵחַ. This means that *HaKadosh Baruch Hu* is asking us to bring a *korban chatas* on "His behalf" to atone for His having reduced the size of the moon. וַיַּעַשׂ אֱלֹהִים אֶת שְׁנֵי הַמְּאֹרֹת הַגְּדֹלִים אֶת הַמָּאוֹר הַגָּדֹל לְמֶמְשֶׁלֶת הַיּוֹם וְאֶת הַמָּאוֹר הַקָּטֹן לְמֶמְשֶׁלֶת הַלַּיְלָה, *And God made the two great lights, the greater light to dominate the day and the lesser light to dominate the night*. Originally, the moon is called one of the two מְאֹרֹת הַגְּדֹלִים, *great lights,* but immediately afterwards, it is called הַמָּאוֹר הַקָּטֹן, *lesser light* (*Bereishis* 1:16).

The aforementioned *aggadah* quotes a "dialogue" on this matter between *HaKadosh Baruch Hu* and the moon: אָמְרָה הַלְּבָנָה לִפְנֵי הַקָּבָּ"ה: רִבּוֹנוֹ שֶׁל עוֹלָם, אִי אֶפְשָׁר לִשְׁנֵי מְלָכִים שֶׁיִּשְׁתַּמְּשׁוּ בְּכֶתֶר אֶחָד. The moon complained that it was impossible for both the sun and the moon to perform the same function, that of providing bright light for the earth. To which, *HaKadosh Baruch Hu*

PARASHAS HATAMID ❧ 101

answered: לְכִי וּמַעֲטִי אֶת עַצְמֵךְ — *You are quite right. Go ahead and reduce your size.* It thereupon became הַמָּאוֹר הַקָּטָן. However, the moon complained that it should not have to suffer because of its "constructive criticism." So, to "console" it, *HaKadosh Baruch Hu* added the stars, וְאֵת הַכּוֹכָבִים, to accompany the light of the moon at night (see *Rashi* ibid.).

Therefore, continues the *aggadah,* every Rosh Chodesh we are asked by *HaKadosh Baruch Hu* to bring this חַטָּאת לַה׳, on His behalf, as His "atonement" for having reduced the size of the moon from being one of the הַמְּאֹרֹת הַגְּדֹלִים to becoming הַמָּאוֹר הַקָּטָן.

It is obvious that this *aggadah* is not intended as a simplistic story which children would enjoy. It is a known fact that *Chazal* often teach the most profound truths in veiled terms, which we must endeavor to understand. To do so, let us first consider how there could have been day and night, וַיְהִי עֶרֶב וַיְהִי בֹקֶר, if, originally, both the sun and moon were equally bright.

We find: וַיַּרְא אֱלֹהִים אֶת הָאוֹר כִּי טוֹב, וַיַּבְדֵּל אֱלֹהִים בֵּין הָאוֹר וּבֵין הַחֹשֶׁךְ, *God saw that the light was good, and God separated between the light and the darkness.* *Rashi* quotes the *aggadah* on this verse: רָאָהוּ שֶׁאֵינוֹ כְדַאי לְהִשְׁתַּמֵּשׁ בּוֹ רְשָׁעִים, וְהִבְדִּילוֹ לַצַּדִּיקִים לֶעָתִיד לָבֹא. This means that the original light of creation, וַיְהִי אוֹר, was not the physical light of the sun — which was not even created until the fourth day — but rather a supernatural, spiritual light, which *Chazal* call *Ohr HaShechinah.* It was this light that was taken away, because the *reshaim* (wicked people) who would inhabit the earth would not be worthy of it, and it was put aside for the *tzaddikim* to use *l'asid lavo,* in the Time to Come (*Chagigah* 12a). This is referred to in Kabbalistic terms as אוֹר הַגָּנוּז, *the light which was hidden away.*

Then, when the sun and the moon were created, the physical light of the sun illuminated the earth, just as it does today. However, the original *Ohr HaShechinah* remained, and for reasons unknown to us, the moon became its carrier. The result was that there were שְׁנֵי מְאֹרֹת הַגְּדֹלִים. One was the original *Ohr HaShechinah,* the spiritual light of creation, and the other was the physical light of the sun. Whereupon, the moon "complained" that the earth should be illuminated either by the *Ohr HaShechinah,* if it deserved it, or by the physical light of the sun. Upon which, *HaKadosh Baruch Hu* removed the spiritual light and set it aside *l'asid lavo,* for the future world, when it will be enjoyed by the *tzaddikim.* The result was that the moon, without the bright glow of the *Ohr HaShechinah,* became the מָּאוֹר הַקָּטָן, merely the physical reflector of the sun's light.

However, in the meantime, the moon's "consolation" is that the *Shechinah* is still manifested by the sky at night, when the moon is accompanied by וְאֵת הַכּוֹכָבִים, billions of stars from billions of galaxies, which bespeak the *gevuras Hashem,* the Almighty Power of the Creator. This is expressed in the verse, שְׂאוּ מָרוֹם עֵינֵיכֶם וּרְאוּ מִי בָרָא אֵלֶּה, *Raise your eyes on high and see*

Who created these (*Yeshayahu* 40:26). The moon is thereby "consoled" in that the *Shechinah* is still visible.

The monthly renewal of the moon cycle, Rosh Chodesh, is one of the *moadim* (festivals) and is reflected as such in the *korbanos*, which are the same as those of the other Yamim Tovim, except that we do not celebrate it as a Yom Tov. This celebration will come only *l'asid lavo*, with the return of the *Ohr HaShechinah*.

When we are *mekadesh levanah* (sanctify the moon), we are reminded of the absence of the *Ohr HaShechinah*, and ask *HaKadosh Baruch Hu* for its eventual restoration: וִיהִי רָצוֹן מִלְּפָנֶיךָ וגו' לְמַלֹּאת פְּגִימַת הַלְּבָנָה, וְלֹא יִהְיֶה בָּה שׁוּם מְעוּט, וִיהִי אוֹר הַלְּבָנָה כְּאוֹר הַחַמָּה, וּכְאוֹר שִׁבְעַת יְמֵי בְרֵאשִׁית כְּמוֹ שֶׁהָיְתָה קוֹדֶם מְעוּטָהּ, שֶׁנֶּאֱמַר אֶת שְׁנֵי הַמְּאֹרֹת הַגְּדֹלִים, *May it be Your will . . . to fill the flaw of the moon that there be no diminution in it. May the light of the moon be like the light of the sun and like the light of the seven days of Creation, as it was before it was diminished, as it is said: "The two great luminaries."*

Chazal tell us in various midrashim that the original *Ohr HaShechinah* was so intense that, through its light, one could see מִסּוֹף הָעוֹלָם וְעַד סוֹפוֹ, *from one end of the world to the other.* If this was the case, there was nothing hidden, and there would be no *tumas hatehom* (ritual impurity from unknown burial sites), because any such concealed *kever* would be visible. Consequently, there would be no need for a *korban chatas* for טוּמְאַת מִקְדָּשׁ וְקָדָשָׁיו, entering the *Mikdash* or eating *korbanos* while in a state of *tumah*. Therefore, every month *HaKadosh Baruch Hu* tells us: הָבִיאוּ כַּפָּרָה עָלַי, *Bring an atonement on My behalf,* because I removed the *Ohr HaShechinah,* which, in turn, was the reason for טוּמְאַת מִקְדָּשׁ וְקָדָשָׁיו, caused by *kever hatehom*.

So both reasons for the חַטָּאת לַה' are actually related. When *HaKadosh Baruch Hu* removed the *Ohr HaShechinah* from the moon, it became the מָאוֹר הַקָּטָן and, consequently, this allowed the *tumas hatehom* to remain unseen, causing טוּמְאַת מִקְדָּשׁ וְקָדָשָׁיו.

אֵיזֶהוּ מְקוֹמָן / Eizehu Mekoman

For the Mishnah portion of the three-part *talmud Torah* program, the fifth *perek* of *Zevachim* was chosen. This dates back to the *siddur* of Rav Amram Gaon, as previously mentioned. Since this is Mishnah, it must not merely be said, but it must actually be learned. In fact, the *Shelah* advises that one should say this *perek* with the *niggun* used when learning *Mishnayos*. When one is *mispallel*, even if he has only a general idea of the *tefillah*, and does not know the meaning of every word, he is at least using the words coined by *Chazal*, which are based on the words of the *Neviim*. However, merely to mouth the words of a mishnah and not understand its meaning does not constitute learning. It is not within the framework of this *shiur* to explain these *mishnayos*, but merely to make some observations. I would therefore advise everyone to learn, once and for all, the *mishnayos* of אֵיזֶהוּ מְקוֹמָן, with the *peirush* of Rav Ovadiah miBartenura, or other *mefarshim*. Then, when they are repeated each morning with knowledge of the subject matter, it will be *talmud Torah*.

The reason this *perek* was chosen is, first, because it has no *machlokes* (difference of opinion), which means it was received directly from Moshe at Sinai. Second, since at this point in our *tefillos* we are, figuratively, standing in front of the *Mizbe'ach*, it is appropriate that we recite the *halachos* which pertain to all the various *korbanos*. And third, the text of this *perek* must be very old, because we find expressions such as לִפְנִים מִן הַקְּלָעִים, which means the *Azarah*. Now, we know that once the *Beis HaMikdash* was built, there were no more קְלָעִים, curtains. These were used in the *Mishkan*, and were replaced by stone walls when Shlomo HaMelech built the *Beis HaMikdash*. So this text must have been in use since the time of the *Mishkan*.

To learn the same chapter of *Mishnayos* every day, although we may even know it by heart, constitutes *talmud Torah lishmah*, learning Torah for its own sake. Our *Chachamim* apply this idea to the *pasuk:* וְשַׁבְתֶּם וּרְאִיתֶם בֵּין צַדִּיק לְרָשָׁע, בֵּין עֹבֵד אֱלֹהִים לַאֲשֶׁר לֹא עֲבָדוֹ, *Then you will return and see the difference between the righteous and the wicked, between one who serves God and one who does not serve Him* (Malachi 3:18). This means that when *Mashiach* comes one will be able to discern between a *tzaddik* and *rasha*. In the world in which we live, we cannot make this distinction. A person may appear as a *tzaddik* and actually be a *rasha*. Also, there may be people whom we would consider *reshaim*, but who may actually be *tzaddikim* because of their hidden *mitzvos* or *ma'asim tovim* (good deeds).

The meaning of עֹבֵד אֱלֹהִים, which is seemingly a redundancy of צַדִּיק, is explained: אֵינוֹ דוֹמֶה שׁוֹנֶה פִּרְקוֹ מֵאָה פְּעָמִים לְשׁוֹנֶה פִּרְקוֹ מֵאָה פְּעָמִים וְאֶחָד, *There is no comparison between a person who reviews his learning a hundred times and one who reviews it a hundred and one times* (Chagigah 9b). The latter is called an עֹבֵד אֱלֹהִים; he serves *HaKadosh Baruch Hu* by learning. In the past, all learning was done by heart. A one hundredfold review was considered the norm for memorization. However, to review it more than that constitutes learning purely *lishmah*, learning only because *HaKadosh Baruch Hu* wants one to learn. One who practices this is called עֹבֵד אֱלֹהִים.

The repeated, daily learning of אֵיזֶהוּ מְקוֹמָן is an example of שׁוֹנֶה פִּרְקוֹ מֵאָה פְּעָמִים וְאֶחָד. Although we may know the meaning of these *mishnayos*, and have reviewed them thousands of times, nevertheless, their constant repetition is *talmud Torah lishmah,* and is therefore called *avodas Elokim,* and is a fitting part of our *tefillah,* which is *avodah shebelev*, the service of God with our heart.

❧ ❧ ❧

⊱ הָעוֹלָה קֹדֶשׁ קָדָשִׁים . . . וּטְעוּנָה הַפְשֵׁט, וְנִתּוּחַ, וְכָלִיל לָאִשִּׁים ⊰ — **The elevation-offering is among the most-holy offerings … It requires flaying and dismemberment, and it is entirely consumed by fire.** The *korban olah* requires three things: (a) הַפְשֵׁט: The animal must be skinned. (b) וְנִתּוּחַ: It must be cut into sections. (c) וְכָלִיל לָאִשִּׁים: It must be completely burned by the fire.

Since our *tefillah* is a substitute for the *olas hatamid,* its fundamental part, the *Shemoneh Esrei,* also contains these requirements:

First, similar to הַפְשֵׁט, we are mentally to practice הַפְשָׁטַת הַגַּשְׁמִיּוּת, *stripping oneself of physicality,* while saying *Shemoneh Esrei.* This means withdrawing into our own inner self. We are to disregard our outer physical frame while our inner, spiritual, true self is communicating with *HaKadosh Baruch Hu.* The transient, physical aspect of the human being as seen in a mirror is not that which is communicating with *HaKadosh Baruch Hu.* This aspect is to be removed during *tefillah.* Rather, it is our spiritual side, our *neshamah,* which is being *mispallel* (see *Shulchan Aruch, Orach Chaim* 98:1-4).

Second, just as the *olah* requires נִתּוּחַ, we too are to appear before *HaKadosh Baruch Hu* with a *lev nishbar,* a broken and humble persona. לֵב נִשְׁבָּר וְנִדְכֶּה אֱלֹהִים לֹא תִבְזֶה, *A heart broken and crushed, O God, You will despise not* (Tehillim 51:19). We are to imagine that this "little me," this little nothing that I am, with all my shortcomings, is approaching the *Ribbono Shel Olam,* the Master of the universe. What audacity, what *chutzpah*! This feeling of complete inadequacy is what is meant by *lev nishbar.* This corresponds to the נִתּוּחַ of the *olah.*

Third, the *tefillah* is to be said with *hislahavus* (fiery enthusiasm), which corresponds to כָּלִיל לָאִשִּׁים. One should feel exhilarated to be fortunate enough to be chosen by *HaKadosh Baruch Hu* as part of *Klal Yisrael*, and to say the words of his *Neviim* and *Chachamim*, together with the rest of *Klal Yisrael*.

This would explain the reason for saying ה׳ שְׂפָתַי תִּפְתָּח וּפִי יַגִּיד תְּהִלָּתֶךָ, *My Lord, open my lips, that my mouth may declare Your praise,* before beginning *Shemoneh Esrei*. At this point, we are mentally discarding our physical outer shell and standing before *HaKadosh Baruch Hu* in a state of נָתוּחַ, with our humble and broken hearts, which would make it impossible even to speak. So we ask *HaKadosh Baruch Hu* to help us express the words and thoughts of our *tefillah* with our lips and mouths.

Finally, when we are ready to begin, we throw ourselves at the mercy of *HaKadosh Baruch Hu* and say בָּרוּךְ אַתָּה ה׳ אֱלֹהֵינוּ וֵאלֹהֵי אֲבוֹתֵינוּ with fiery enthusiasm, as if we are offering ourselves on the *Mizbe'ach*, much as the *olas hatamid* is put on the *Mizbe'ach* and is כָּלִיל לָאִשִּׁים.

רַבִּי יִשְׁמָעֵאל אוֹמֵר: בִּשְׁלֹשׁ עֶשְׂרֵה מִדּוֹת הַתּוֹרָה נִדְרֶשֶׁת

For the Gemara portion of our three-part *talmud Torah* program, the *baraisa* at the beginning of *Toras Kohanim* has been selected, because it is a sort of introduction to *Torah Shebe'al Peh* and, specifically, because of its connection with the *korbanos* and the *dinim* of the *Kohanim* in the *Beis HaMikdash*.

Since this is learning and, as such, it must be understood, I can highly recommend that one use the Hirsch *Siddur*, which explains and offers examples of each of the י״ג מִדּוֹת, the thirteen methods of explaining and interpreting the Torah. This is the least one should do. However, an in-depth study can only be made by learning *Toras Kohanim* itself, with its *mefarshim*.

At the conclusion of this *baraisa,* we say:

יְהִי רָצוֹן מִלְּפָנֶיךָ ה׳ אֱלֹהֵינוּ וֵאלֹהֵי אֲבוֹתֵינוּ שֶׁיִּבָּנֶה בֵּית הַמִּקְדָּשׁ בִּמְהֵרָה בְיָמֵינוּ וְתֵן חֶלְקֵנוּ בְּתוֹרָתֶךָ, וְשָׁם נַעֲבָדְךָ בְּיִרְאָה כִּימֵי עוֹלָם וּכְשָׁנִים קַדְמוֹנִיּוֹת — **May it be Your will, Hashem, our God and the God of our forefathers, that the Holy Temple be rebuilt, speedily in our days, and grant us our share in Your Torah, and may we serve You there with reverence as in days of old and in former years.** This *tefillah* expresses the hope that we will "receive our share" of understanding of the *halachos* which are applicable in the *avodah* of the *Beis HaMikdash*. In this way, when the *Beis HaMikdash* is rebuilt — soon, in our time — they will be put into practice properly when we perform the *avodah* in the *Beis HaMikdash,* as was done in the days of yore.

עֲטִיפַת הַטַּלִית וְהַנָּחַת תְּפִלִּין /
Atifas HaTallis Vehanachas Tefillin

According to our *minhag,* which was prevalent in most of Ashkenaz, the *tallis* and *tefillin* are put on at this point, before בָּרוּךְ שֶׁאָמַר. However, in the *Tur* and *Shulchan Aruch,* the *halachos* of *tzitzis* and *tefillin* precede בִּרְכוֹת הַשַּׁחַר. It is for this reason that, in most of the Jewish world, the *tallis* and *tefillin* are put on before the beginning of the *tefillah.*

The origin of our *minhag* seems to be very simple. The prevalent custom throughout most of Ashkenaz was to begin *Shacharis* very early. Many times during the year, this was too early for putting on *tallis* and *tefillin,* which cannot be done before there is enough dawn light to "recognize a casual acquaintance at a distance of four *amos,*" about seven feet (*Orach Chaim* 30:1). By the time one reached בָּרוּךְ שֶׁאָמַר, the requisite time for *tallis* and *tefillin* had arrived.

The proof for this reason is that, on Shabbos and Yom Tov, when it is a *mitzvah* to begin the *tefillah* somewhat later (*Rema, Orach Chaim* 281), it is indeed, our *minhag* to put on the *tallis* at the beginning of *Shacharis.*

But on Rosh Hashanah and Yom Kippur, when it is a *mitzvah* to start the *tefillah* early (see *Selichos* to *Erev Rosh Hashanah* number 52: "אָעִירָה שַׁחַר וגו'", *I will awaken dawn, the dawn will not awaken me*), we wait to put on the *tallis* until just before בָּרוּךְ שֶׁאָמַר, for the same reason that we do so on weekdays.

It is important to remember that when one puts on *tallis* and *tefillin,* one should have the *kavannah* that he is fulfilling two *mitzvos asei d'Oraisa.* One is וְעָשׂוּ לָהֶם צִיצִת עַל כַּנְפֵי בִגְדֵיהֶם, *They shall make themselves tzitzis on the corners of their garments* (*Bamidbar* 15:38); the other is וּקְשַׁרְתָּם לְאוֹת עַל יָדֶךָ וְהָיוּ לְטֹטָפֹת בֵּין עֵינֶיךָ, *Bind them as a sign upon your arm and let them be ornaments between your eyes* (*Devarim* 6:8). According to some opinions, *mitzvos tzerichos kavannah,* and one would not even have fulfilled the *mitzvah* unless he has the *kavannah* to fulfill it. (See, for instance, *Beur Halachah* to *Orach Chaim* 128:1 s.v. דָּזָר.) Unfortunately, in many cases, the wearing of *tallis* and *tefillin* is done without giving any thought to the *mitzvah,* and has become מִצְוַת אֲנָשִׁים מְלֻמָּדָה, a *mitzvah* done purely by habit. Even the saying of the introductory הִנְנִי מְכֻוָּן וגו', *I have the intention* etc., which is not our *minhag,* has become a mere mouthing of words.

Rav Samson R. Hirsch explains the meaning of *tzitzis* on our clothing as an extension, or outgrowth — וְעָלָיו יָצִיץ נִזְרוֹ, *Upon him, his crown will shine* (*Tehillim* 132:18) — of the basic moral meaning of clothing to the human being. Before the *cheit* (sin) of Adam and Chavah, the Torah tells us: וַיִּהְיוּ שְׁנֵיהֶם עֲרוּמִּים הָאָדָם וְאִשְׁתּוֹ וְלֹא יִתְבּשָׁשׁוּ, *They were both naked, the man and his wife, but were not ashamed* (Bereishis 2:25). Their true selves were not identified with their bodies. Their animal bodies clothed their real being, which was their *neshamah,* their spirituality, that aspect of themselves which was superior to the animal.

However, immediately after the *cheit,* the *pasuk* says: וַיֵּדְעוּ כִּי עֵירֻמִּם הֵם וַיִּתְפְּרוּ עֲלֵה תְאֵנָה וַיַּעֲשׂוּ לָהֶם חֲגֹרֹת, *They realized that they were naked, so they sewed fig leaves for themselves* (ibid. 3:7). Once they had succumbed to their bodily desires, they became identified with their animal bodies and, consequently, felt ashamed of their nakedness. They therefore made themselves rudimentary clothing, reflecting their knowledge that they had the moral obligation to subdue their animal nature. And after their expulsion from *Gan Eden, HaKadosh Baruch Hu* clothed them with "garments of leather": וַיַּעַשׂ ה' אֱלֹהִים לְאָדָם וּלְאִשְׁתּוֹ כָּתְנוֹת עוֹר וַיַּלְבִּשֵׁם, *And Hashem God made for Adam and his wife garments of skin, and He clothed them* (ibid. 3:21). These garments were a gift of *HaKadosh Baruch Hu* to the human race.

So the idea of clothing is a reflection of the truth that יֵשׁ מוֹתַר הָאָדָם מִן הַבְּהֵמָה. Man's supremacy over animals lies in his ability to control his animal nature. While man has an animal body, with all its desires and urges, he has the unique ability to control them. He even has the ability to elevate and sanctify these urges. So the entire animal body of the human being is covered, with the exception of the head, where its spiritual faculties are concentrated, and the hands, to which *HaKadosh Baruch Hu* has given the power to control the world — וְכִבְשֻׁהָ, *and subdue it* (ibid. 1:28). This is the concept of clothing for all mankind.

However, as far as Israel is concerned, explains Rav Hirsch, man's ability to subdue his animal nature grows and flowers into an even higher moral calling, that of acceptance of the *mitzvos* of Hashem. Therefore, דַּבֵּר אֶל בְּנֵי יִשְׂרָאֵל וְאָמַרְתָּ אֲלֵהֶם וְעָשׂוּ לָהֶם צִיצִת עַל כַּנְפֵי בִגְדֵיהֶם, *Speak to the Children of Israel and say to them that they shall make themselves tzitzis on the corners of their garments* (Bamidbar 15:38). Where *derech eretz* — with which all humanity is charged — ends, עַל כַּנְפֵי בִגְדֵיהֶם, *at the corners of their garments,* there the specifically Jewish mandate begins. Torah presupposes the highest form of human decency and dignity — דֶּרֶךְ אֶרֶץ קָדְמָה לַתּוֹרָה. We, as *Bnei Yisrael,* are to make "extensions" of our clothing to symbolize our special mandate. So, when we look at our *tzitzis* we are reminded that our membership in *Klal Yisrael,* through the acceptance of the *mitzvos,* extends our humanity to a higher moral calling. The white strands represent the *mitzvos lo saaseh,* meaning being free of sin, and the blue *techeiles* represent the *mitzvos asei,* the performance of the positive commandments. Thus, וּרְאִיתֶם אֹתוֹ וּזְכַרְתֶּם אֶת כָּל מִצְוֹת ה' וַעֲשִׂיתֶם אֹתָם, *you* may see it and remember all the commandments of Hashem and perform them (Bamidbar 15:39).

While the *tzitzis* have many knots and windings, representing the restrictions placed upon us by the *mitzvos,* nevertheless, two thirds of the length of the *tzitzis* are free-flowing strands. Once our lives are controlled by the parameters of the *mitzvos* of Hashem, represented by the knots, we have much more freedom than restrictions, to enjoy that which *HaKadosh Baruch Hu* has given us in our lives. This is represented by the two-thirds length of free-flowing strings.

[Ed. note: For a fuller, more detailed exposition of the symbolism of *tzitzis,* see the full commentary of Rav Samson R. Hirsch on *Bamidbar* 15:38.)

Despite the profound importance of the *mitzvah* of *tzitzis,* women are nevertheless exempt from it, because it is a time-bound *mitzvah,* since it is applicable only during the daytime. The reason women have not voluntarily accepted this *mitzvah,* as they have many others, is because since placing *tzitzis* on a four-cornered garment is *obligatory* only for men, a garment with *tzitzis* attached becomes, in effect, "men's clothing," and as such would violate the restriction against women wearing men's clothing: לֹא יִהְיֶה כְלִי גֶבֶר עַל אִשָּׁה, *male garb shall not be on a woman* (Devarim 22:5; and see *Targum Yonasan* ibid.).

Notwithstanding this, the higher moral symbolism of Jewish clothing is very much evident in regard to Jewish women through the laws of *tzenius.* In men, the symbolism of the higher concept of clothing is evident only when they wear *tzitzis.* However, in women's clothing, it is there at all times. In addition to the simple purpose of clothing as protection against the elements, and for common decency, the appearance of the modestly dressed Jewish woman proclaims for all to see: . . . וְלֹא תָתוּרוּ אַחֲרֵי לְבַבְכֶם וְאַחֲרֵי עֵינֵיכֶם וִהְיִיתֶם קְדֹשִׁים לֵאלֹהֵיכֶם, *And you shall not explore after your heart and after your eyes . . . and be holy to your God* (Bamidbar 15:39-40). It is not only an expression of her elevated status, but it is also a message to men to be aware of their own mandate of וִהְיִיתֶם קְדֹשִׁים. Just as a Jewish male does not stress his masculinity, a Jewish woman does not flaunt her femininity. She is not merely a female; rather, she is a personality with Jewish values.

The *tallis* is put on before the *tefillin,* because the *mitzvah* of *tzitzis* is performed more frequently — we wear them on Shabbos and Yom Tov — which is not the case with *tefillin.* We thus invoke the rule: תָּדִיר וְשֶׁאֵינוֹ תָדִיר תָּדִיר קוֹדֵם, a more frequent mitzvah precedes a less frequent one. (See *Beis Yosef, Orach Chaim* 25.)

The *tefillin* are symbolic of *kedushas guf Yisrael,* the holiness of the Jewish body. This was publicly established at the time of *yetzias Mitzrayim,* and is evidenced by the *mitzvah* of *pidyon bechor,* redemption of the firstborn, which is declared in two of the four *parshiyos* of our *tefillin*:

קַדֶּשׁ לִי כָל בְּכוֹר פֶּטֶר כָּל רֶחֶם בִּבְנֵי יִשְׂרָאֵל בָּאָדָם וּבַבְּהֵמָה לִי הוּא . . . וְהָיָה לְךָ לְאוֹת עַל יָדְךָ וּלְזִכָּרוֹן בֵּין עֵינֶיךָ, *Sanctify to Me every firstborn; the first issue of every womb among the Children of Israel, of man and beast, is Mine. . . . And it shall be for you a sign on your arm and a reminder between your eyes* (Shemos 13:2,9).

. . . עַל כֵּן אֲנִי זֹבֵחַ לַה׳ כָּל פֶּטֶר רֶחֶם הַזְּכָרִים וְכָל בְּכוֹר בָּנַי אֶפְדֶּה. וְהָיָה לְאוֹת עַל יָדְכָה וּלְטוֹטָפֹת בֵּין עֵינֶיךָ כִּי בְּחֹזֶק יָד הוֹצִיאָנוּ ה׳ מִמִּצְרָיִם (ibid. 13:15-16), *Therefore I offer to Hashem all male first issue of the womb, and I shall redeem all the firstborn of my sons. And it shall be a sign upon your arm, and an ornament between your eyes, for with a strong hand Hashem removed us from Egypt* (ibid. 13:15-16).

Every Jewish firstborn male has *kedushah*, holiness, because *HaKadosh Baruch Hu* declares: לִי הוּא, *he belongs to Me*. The *kedushas bechor* is symbolic of the sanctification of all the members of the Jewish nation by *HaKadosh Baruch Hu,* which was confirmed when He declared to the world: בְּנִי בְכֹרִי יִשְׂרָאֵל, *my firstborn son, Israel* (Shemos 4:22). The *mitzvah* applies not only to the firstborn male child, but also to the firstborn animal, which reflects the sanctity of both aspects of the Jewish personality, the *guf* and the *nefesh,* which was demonstrated at the time of *yetzias Mitzrayim.*

The *tefillin,* as our אוֹת (sign) and זִכָּרוֹן (reminder) (Shemos 13:9), are reminders of *kedushas guf Yisrael.* Consequently, they must be made from the skins of animals which we are permitted to eat, and wearing them requires a *guf naki* (a clean body). This is why children are not trained in this *mitzvah* until shortly before their *bar mitzvah.*

Furthermore, the *retzuos* (straps) of the *tefillin* are tied tightly to our arm and head, as a veritable extension of our own skin. We thereby symbolically tie our body to the *ratzon Hashem* (will of Hashem).

The first two *parshiyos* of the *tefillin,* which deal with *mitzvas bechor,* correspond to the *kedushah* of the *guf* and *nefesh habeheimis* of Israel. This special *kedushas haguf* (holiness of the Jewish body) is why we have so many *mitzvos* pertaining to our bodies, e.g., *tzitzis, tefillin, matzah, korban pesach, bris milah,* etc. Therefore, even after the *neshamah* leaves the body, the *guf* must be treated as a *davar shebik'dushah,* a holy object.

The other two *parshiyos* of the *tefillin,* שְׁמַע and וְהָיָה אִם שָׁמֹעַ, which deal with *kabbalas ol malchus Shamayim* (acceptance of the Yoke of Heaven), and *sechar* (reward) and *onesh* (punishment) for the *mitzvos,* correspond to the *kedushah* of our *neshamah* and our *ruach.*

And we tie both of these aspects of personalities to the *ratzon Hashem.* With the *tefillin shel yad,* we bind our physical aspects — *guf* and *nefesh* — to the will of *HaKadosh Baruch Hu,* and with the *tefillin shel rosh,* we bind our spiritual aspects — *ruach* and *neshamah* — to the *ratzon Hashem.*

Furthermore, comparing the four-sided *batim* (housing) of the *tefillin* to the four-sided *Mizbe'ach,* we find a similar division of their symbolism. The physical aspects, the combination of *guf* and *nefesh,* which is symbolized by the northeast side of the *Mizbe'ach,* corresponds to the *tefillin shel yad;* and the combination of the spiritual aspects, that of *ruach* and *neshamah,* which is symbolized by the southwest side, corresponds to the *tefillin shel rosh.* Thus, we tie all aspects of our being, *guf, nefesh, ruach,* and *neshamah,* to HaKadosh Baruch Hu.

[Ed. note: The author details the meaning of the four aspects of the human being, as well as the symbolism of the *Mizbe'ach,* in his piece on *kabbalas yissurim,* which is found on pp. 98 (פר׳ התמיד).]

The symbolism of *kedushas haguf* for Jewish women, who are exempt from *tefillin* as a time-bound *mitzvah,* is found in the *mitzvah* of *tevilah* in the *mikveh.* With her immersion, she symbolizes *kedushas guf Yisrael* in a most profound way.

In our modern era, the idea of "feminism" has become widespread, and has even permeated some elements of our people. We hear of women who put on *tallis* and *tefillin,* and who want to have public prayer groups — even at the *Kosel.* A Jewish woman, fulfilling her role, is a true "feminist." If she wants to act as a man, she becomes a "masculinist." Actually, this is not new; *Chazal* tell us that King Shaul's daughter Michal, the wife of David HaMelech, wore *tefillin* (see *Eruvin* 96a). We find her criticizing her husband for strenuously dancing and jumping in honor of the *Aron HaKodesh* upon its being brought to Yerushalayim: מַה נִּכְבַּד הַיּוֹם מֶלֶךְ יִשְׂרָאֵל אֲשֶׁר נִגְלָה הַיּוֹם לְעֵינֵי אַמְהוֹת עֲבָדָיו כְּהִגָּלוֹת אַחַד הָרֵקִים, *How honorably you have behaved today, O Jewish king, when you debased yourself in public, in front of the servants, as an empty-headed fool would do* (Shmuel II 6:20).

Chazal tell us (ibid. *Yalkut Shimoni*) that she thought it disgraceful that while David was dancing strenuously, his royal robe had lifted, and his undergarments were visible. In her mind, she thought, "How would he like it if I behaved in this manner?" Since she had put on *tefillin,* her thought processes also worked like that of a man. She had lost her sensitivity to the difference in behaviors of men and women. She became a "masculinist."

The *pasuk* tells us: וּלְמִיכַל בַּת שָׁאוּל לֹא הָיָה לָהּ יָלֶד עַד יוֹם מוֹתָהּ, *Michal daughter of Shaul had no child until the day of her death* (ibid. 6:23). As a result of her having castigated her husband for his manner of honoring the *Aron HaKodesh,* she no longer bore children. Since she abrogated her special role as a Jewish woman, her punishment was *middah k'neged middah* in that she was no longer blessed with the ultimate fulfillment of Jewish womanhood, that of bearing children.

[Ed. note: According to the Gemara, this *pasuk* means only that from the moment she castigated her husband through the end of her life, Michal no longer bore children. However, she did have children earlier (see *Sanhedrin* 21a).]

As far as our connection to *HaKadosh Baruch Hu* through fulfilling the *mitzvos* is concerned, both men and woman are to fulfill their unique roles which have been assigned to them by *HaKadosh Baruch Hu,* in accordance with His Supreme Wisdom.

פְּסוּקֵי דְזִמְרָה / Pesukei d'Zimrah

In our outline of the order of the *tefillah*, we explained that the פְּסוּקֵי דְזִמְרָה portion of the *tefillah* corresponds to the *Ulam* in the architecture of the *Beis HaMikdash*. Interestingly, the *Ulam* did not exist in the *Mishkan*, and made its first appearance in the *Beis HaMikdash* built by Shlomo HaMelech (*Melachim I* 6:3). It also existed in the second *Beis HaMikdash,* as is described in *Middos* (3:47), and will be a part of the third *Beis HaMikdash* — may it be built speedily in our days (*Yechezkel* 40:48-49).

The *Ulam* was a very large entrance hall (אוּלָם, from אלם, meaning *powerful*), with a huge portal leading to it, and an equally huge portal at its exit leading directly into the *Heichal*. This structure separated the *Ezras Kohanim* — where the *Mizbe'ach* stood — from the *Heichal*. It was in the *Ulam* that the *Kohen* prepared himself spiritually to appear in the *Heichal*. The word *Heichal* actually means "palace" which, in the *Beis HaMikdash,* means the abode of the *Baal HaYecho'les,* the All-Powerful Ruler.

Our Sages, who organized the *tefillah,* instituted the פְּסוּקֵי דְזִמְרָה as a form of preparation for the *tefillah.* These "verses of singing" correspond to the *Ulam,* in which the *Kohen* prepared for entrance to the *Heichal,* while their introductory and concluding *berachos* of בָּרוּךְ שֶׁאָמַר and יִשְׁתַּבַּח correspond to the huge entrance and exit portals of the *Ulam.*

The *Pesukei d'Zimrah* are divided into five parts, which will be detailed later. The significance of the number five could very well be related to the fact that the *Ulam* is the next progression after the *Mizbe'ach*. The *Mizbe'ach* is represented by the number four, due to its four sides, its four corner "horns," and the fourfold application of the blood: שְׁתֵּי מַתָּנוֹת שֶׁהֵם אַרְבַּע. The *Ulam,* then, in progressive order, would be represented by the number five.

[Ed. note: Although not mentioned by Rav Schwab, it was pointed out by Rabbi D. Margareten that the number five has an additional significance in representing the *Ulam,* in that it was adorned with five מַלְתְּרָאוֹת, decoratively carved wooden cornices (*Middos* 3:7).]

Interestingly, this "numerology" progresses. The *Shulchan* and its twofold *lechem hapanim,* each of which consists of six loaves, are represented by the number *six*. This is followed by the *seven* branches of the Menorah, which is followed by the *Mizbe'ach HaZahav* and the *Paroches,* with their *eight* applications of blood, הַזָּאוֹת אַחַת וָשֶׁבַע. Then we have the *Aron HaKodesh* with its height of *nine tefachim,* and also the *nine* sounds of *tekias shofar* on Rosh Hashanah which are to be לְזִכָּרוֹן לִפְנֵי ה׳, and are representative of the *Kodesh HaKadashim* (see כְּבִפְנִים דָּמֵי [שׁוֹפָר], *Rosh Hashanah* 26a). And

PESUKEI D'ZIMRAH 113

finally, the *Kapores,* the cover of the *Aron,* which contained the *Aseres HaDibros,* was *ten tefachim* from the ground.

Jewish symbolic numerology plays a very significant role in understanding many aspects of our *mitzvos.* Rav Samson R. Hirsch explains the symbolism of many of the numbers, i.e., six, seven, eight, etc., as these numbers occur in the details of various *mitzvos.* Interestingly, *Maharal* used a very similar approach. However, it must be assumed that Rav Hirsch was not aware of it, since he does not quote *Maharal* in this regard. This is not the place for a broader study of symbolic numerology, but it is important to know of the existence of this area of *talmud Torah.*

The daily recital of *Pesukei d'Zimrah* and the *berachos* of בָּרוּךְ שֶׁאָמַר and יִשְׁתַּבַּח, as we know them, are not specifically mandated in the Mishnah or Gemara. Nevertheless, this portion of the *tefillah* must have been a very old tradition, dating back to the time of the *Amoraim* and probably even to the *Tannaim,* because it is alluded to in numerous places in the Gemara. Some references are:

אָמַר ר׳ יוֹסֵי: יְהֵא חֶלְקִי מִגּוֹמְרֵי הַלֵּל בְּכָל יוֹם, *R' Yose said: May my lot be among those who complete Hallel every day* (*Shabbos* 118b). This is explained by the Gemara there as referring to *Pesukei d'Zimrah,* which includes the last six chapters of *Tehillim.*

אָמַר ר׳ אֶלְעָזָר אָמַר רַבִּי אֲבִינָא: כָּל הָאוֹמֵר תְּהִלָּה לְדָוִד בְּכָל יוֹם שָׁלֹשׁ פְּעָמִים מוּבְטָח לוֹ שֶׁהוּא בֶּן הָעוֹלָם הַבָּא, *R' Elazar said in the name of R' Avina: Whoever says Tehillah L'David three times daily is assured that he is one of "the people of the future world"* (*Berachos* 4b). This refers to אַשְׁרֵי, which is part of the *Pesukei d'Zimrah.*

Other early references to *Pesukei d'Zimrah* are:

(1) *Pesachim* 118a refers to יִשְׁתַּבַּח as בִּרְכַּת הַשִּׁיר (according to R' Yochanan — see *Tur* 480);

(2) הַמְסַפֵּר בֵּין יִשְׁתַּבַּח לְיוֹצֵר אוֹר עֲבֵירָה הִיא בְּיָדוֹ וְחוֹזֵר עָלֶיהָ מִמַּעַרְכֵי הַמִּלְחָמָה, "One who talks between *Yishtabach* and *Yotzer Ohr,* etc." (*Talmud Yerushalmi,* cited in *Tur, Orach Chaim* 51, et al.). See also *Taz* (*Orach Chaim* 51:1) that *Pesukei d'Zimrah* was instituted by the *Anshei Knesses HaGedolah.*

There are many instances in which details of existing *halachos* are not mentioned in the Mishnah and were later expounded upon in the Gemara. These were left as *Torah Shebe'al Peh* until the time of the Gemara. Some examples are, *mezuzah, tefillin,* and *tzitzis.* Also, the specifics of the *halachos* of Chanukah are detailed in the Gemara, although they were largely omitted in the Mishnah. Similarly, the specific text of the *Pesukei d'Zimrah* and their *berachos* were omitted from the Mishnah, and even from the Gemara. Nevertheless, the text of this portion of the *tefillah* belongs to the class of very old traditions which were accepted by *Klal Yisrael,* and transmitted and perpetuated *be'al peh,* orally.

However, the general rule is that one precede *tefillah* with praises to *HaKadosh Baruch Hu:* לְעוֹלָם יְסַדֵּר אָדָם שִׁבְחוֹ שֶׁל הקב״ה וְאַחַר כָּךְ יִתְפַּלֵּל, *A person should always precede the tefillah with an ordered expression of the praises of HaKadosh Baruch Hu* (*Berachos* 32a). The *Gemara* (ibid.) finds the source for this in the *tefillah* of Moshe Rabbeinu when he beseeched *HaKadosh Baruch Hu* for permission to enter Eretz Yisrael: וָאֶתְחַנַּן אֶל ה' בָּעֵת הַהִוא לֵאמֹר. ה' אֱלֹהִים אַתָּה הַחִלּוֹתָ לְהַרְאוֹת אֶת עַבְדְּךָ אֶת גָּדְלְךָ וְאֶת יָדְךָ הַחֲזָקָה אֲשֶׁר מִי אֵל בַּשָּׁמַיִם וּבָאָרֶץ אֲשֶׁר יַעֲשֶׂה כְמַעֲשֶׂיךָ וְכִגְבוּרֹתֶךָ. אֶעְבְּרָה נָּא וְאֶרְאֶה אֶת הָאָרֶץ הַטּוֹבָה וגו׳, *I implored Hashem at that time, saying, "My Lord Hashem, You have begun to show Your servant Your greatness and Your strong hand, for what power is there in the heaven or on the earth that can perform according to Your deeds and according to Your mighty acts? Let me now cross and see the good Land . . ."* (*Devarim* 3:23-25). Thus, we see that the *tefillah* of Moshe Rabbeinu that he be allowed to enter Eretz Yisrael is preceded by words of *shevach* (praise) to *HaKadosh Baruch Hu.*

Throughout *Pesukei d'Zimrah* we find two commonly recurring words, which are seemingly synonymous: שִׁירָה, *shirah,* and זִמְרָה, *zimrah.* However, it is important to note that these words are not synonymous; rather, they are complementary of each other, as we shall explain.

The word שִׁירָה has the root שִׁיר, which really means a connection. We find this word used in the Mishnah in the sense of a leash attached to an animal: וְכָל בַּעֲלֵי הַשִּׁיר יוֹצְאִין בְּשִׁיר, *All animals which (usually) have a leash attached* etc. (*Shabbos* 51b). Utilized in the praise of *HaKadosh Baruch Hu,* the word *shirah* similarly conveys the thought of "attachment," with the meaning being that through the "song," we express our attachment to *HaKadosh Baruch Hu.*

The word זִמְרָה, on the other hand, has at its root the opposite idea — that of זָמַר, which means *cut* or *prune.*

Some examples of this are:

וְכַרְמְךָ לֹא תִזְמֹר, *Do not prune your vineyard* (*Vayikra* 25:4); קְחוּ מִזִּמְרַת הָאָרֶץ, *Take of the (cut) produce of the land* (*Bereishis* 43:11); זְמִיר עָרִיצִים, *He who cuts down the powerful ones* (*Yeshayahu* 25:5).

Rav Moshe Chaim Luzzatto, in the beginning of his *Mesillas Yesharim,* states: הָאָדָם לֹא נִבְרָא אֶלָּא לְהִתְעַנֵּג עַל ה' וְלֵיהָנוֹת מִזִּיו שְׁכִינָתוֹ שֶׁזֶּהוּ הַתַּעֲנוּג הָאֲמִיתִּי וְהָעִידּוּן הַגָּדוֹל מִכָּל הָעִידּוּנִים שֶׁיְּכוֹלִים לְהִמָּצֵא, וּמְקוֹם הָעִידּוּן הַזֶּה בֶּאֱמֶת הוּא הָעוֹלָם הַבָּא. This means that because of the *chessed* of *HaKadosh Baruch Hu,* He created man to give him an opportunity to bask in an intimate loving attachment to *HaKadosh Baruch Hu.* This highest possible state of bliss can be realized only in *Olam Haba.*

In *Shir HaShirim,* Shlomo HaMelech expresses this intimate attachment allegorically in human terms, as a blissful "love affair" between a man and a woman, reflecting the desire of *Klal Yisrael* to attach itself to *HaKadosh Baruch Hu.*

Strange as it may sound, the human being's innate desire for happiness, or even his lustful thoughts and desires for earthly pleasure, are actually only sublimations of his innate longing to become close to *HaKadosh Baruch Hu.* Now, since a person cannot reach this ultimate state of bliss in this world, he often subconsciously seeks satisfaction by pursuing forbidden and sinful activities, which are against the *ratzon* of Hashem. In order for a person to succeed and gain his ultimate reward in *Olam Haba,* he must cut out, "prune," his misdirected desires, so that he may reach life's eventual goal, that of לְהִתְעַנֵּג עַל ה׳, *to delight in Hashem.*

The meaning of *zimrah* is a happy singing to *HaKadosh Baruch Hu,* by which one can "prune" out the powers of *tumah,* those sinful subliminal substitutions, and replace them with his deep feelings of becoming close to *HaKadosh Baruch Hu.* When one does so, he can experience in this world a foretaste, מֵעֵין עוֹלָם הַבָּא, of the eventual realization of true happiness and pleasure, that of לְהִתְעַנֵּג עַל ה׳, which is the ultimate goal of creation.

The *Pesukei d'Zimrah,* then, with its combination of *shirah* and *zimrah,* becomes an appropriate preparation for the main part of the *tefillah.* We "do battle" with those powerful forces of the *yetzer hara* and "cut down" the powers of *tumah* by overwhelming them with *shirah,* expressions of our deep, innate desire to become attached to *HaKadosh Baruch Hu.*

This explains the unusual language used in the *Shulchan Aruch, Orach Chaim* 54:3, prohibiting any interruption by talking between יִשְׁתַּבַּח, which concludes the *Pesukei d'Zimrah,* and the beginning of יוֹצֵר אוֹר, which starts the *berachos* of *Krias Shema*: הַמְסַפֵּר בֵּין יִשְׁתַּבַּח לְיוֹצֵר עֲבֵירָה הִיא בְּיָדוֹ וְחוֹזֵר עָלֶיהָ מֵעוֹרְכֵי הַמִּלְחָמָה, *If one talks between* יִשְׁתַּבַּח *and* יוֹצֵר, *he has committed an aveirah for which he must return from battle.*

The term "return from battle" refers to the command of the officers to the Jewish soldiers before a battle: מִי הָאִישׁ הַיָּרֵא וְרַךְ הַלֵּבָב יֵלֵךְ וְיָשֹׁב לְבֵיתוֹ, *Whoever is afraid, and weak of heart, shall leave and return to his home (Devarim* 20:8). The Mishnah (*Sotah* 44a) explains that the soldier may be afraid that his sins will cause him to fall in battle. He is therefore disqualified from battle, because his fear may affect the courage of his fellow warriors.

So the simple meaning of this section of the *Shulchan Aruch* is that even an *aveirah* as seemingly minor as that of interrupting between *Pesukei d'Zimrah* and יוֹצֵר אוֹר is severe enough to disqualify a Jewish soldier from battle.

However, the *Chofetz Chaim* (see *Mishnah Berurah* ibid. 5) adds an allegoric interpretation of this *halachah,* in accordance with the aforesaid meaning of זמר. He says that through the *Pesukei d'Zimrah,* we are waging a battle against the powers of *tumah* which exist as a result of the influence of our *aveiros*. These forces serve as a barrier between our *tefillos* and *HaKadosh Baruch Hu*. By happily reciting these songs of praise to *HaKadosh Baruch Hu,* we cut off (זמר) these forces, thereby allowing our *tefillos* access to Him. After we have "waged this battle" we have an immediate opening to approach *HaKadosh Baruch Hu* with our *tefillah,* which begins with יוֹצֵר אוֹר. However, if we interrupt and separate these two, we are "returning from battle" without utilizing the advantage we have gained, and the powerful forces of the powers of *tumah* are again able to gain the upper hand and prevent *tefillos* from reaching *HaKadosh Baruch Hu*.

At this point in our study of *tefillah,* it is important that we explain the entire notion of praising *HaKadosh Baruch Hu*. Why is He interested in our praises or acknowledgments? Why, for example, would *HaKadosh Baruch Hu* want us to thank Him for our food, as in the *mitzvah* of וְאָכַלְתָּ וְשָׂבָעְתָּ וּבֵרַכְתָּ אֶת ה' אֱלֹהֶיךָ, *And you shall eat and you shall be satisfied and you shall bless Hashem your God* (*Devarim* 8:10), referring to *Bircas HaMazon,* the Grace After Meals.

What is the meaning of הקב"ה מתאוה לתפלתן של צדיקים, God desires the prayers of the righteous (*Chullin* 60b)? We, as human beings, due to our imperfect nature, are in need of recognition and praise. We can become deeply insulted if a favor goes unrecognized. However, *HaKadosh Baruch Hu,* in His absolute perfection, has no such need.

Some understanding of this might be gained if we look at the method which *HaKadosh Baruch Hu,* in His infinite wisdom, chose to sustain the world. We notice that there is a cycle of life in which each creature lives off another. For example, a bird eats a worm from the ground, leaving its droppings which in turn fertilize the ground, making it nourishing for other worms, which provide more food for birds. This life cycle applies to the entire physical world, which is self-sustaining.

Similarly, *HaKadosh Baruch Hu* also created the spiritual world to be self-sustaining. While He is the Source of all life, nevertheless, *HaKadosh Baruch Hu* wants the human being to initiate a relationship with him through *tefillah,* which must be preceded by *shevach v'hoda'ah,* as we have previously mentioned. Then, when *HaKadosh Baruch Hu* responds to the *tefillah,* the cycle is complete. So, for example, the purpose of וְאָכַלְתָּ וְשָׂבָעְתָּ וּבֵרַכְתָּ is that we are to thank *HaKadosh Baruch Hu* for our food, so that He, in turn, may bless us with sustenance in the future.

This is also the meaning of phrases like תְּנוּ עֹז לֵאלֹהִים, *Give strength to God* (*Tehillim* 68:35), or הָבוּ לַה' כָּבוֹד וָעֹז, *Prepare for Hashem honor and might* (ibid. 29:1), which we say in our *tefillah.* We "give strength" to *HaKadosh Baruch Hu* by expressing our desire to please him through *shirah* and *shevach,* initiating the process whereby *HaKadosh Baruch Hu* responds to us and sends *kedushah* and *yiras Shamayim* into the world. Our *tefillah* has a "cosmic influence" on all of creation.

The idea of a self-sustaining "spiritual life cycle" is inherent in the meaning of the words הוֹד וְהָדָר לְפָנָיו עֹז וְחֶדְוָה בִּמְקֹמוֹ, *Glory and majesty are before Him; might and joy are in His place* (*Divrei Hayamim I* 16:27), which we will soon find in the *Pesukei d'Zimrah*. These words are difficult to translate, especially since *lashon kodesh* does not easily lend itself to be accurately translated into English. An approximate translation of הוֹד might be *grace* or *glory*. However, these words do not accurately convey the true meaning.

The root of הוֹד is actually הֵד, which means *an echo*. We find a similar usage in, וְנָתַתָּה מֵהוֹדְךָ עָלָיו, *You shall give some of your glory to him* (*Bamidbar* 27:20). Yehoshua was to "echo," or emulate, Moshe Rabbeinu. When we say to *HaKadosh Baruch Hu*, "I love You," He answers, "I love you, too." This response is heard by our *neshamah*. The entire *Shir HaShirim* is a dialogue between *Klal Yisrael* and *HaKadosh Baruch Hu*, phrased in the language between one and his beloved. This is the meaning of אֲנִי לְדוֹדִי וְדוֹדִי לִי, *I am my Beloved's and my Beloved is mine* (*Shir HaShirim* 6:3). Furthermore, we find *tefillah* being called רִנַּת דּוֹדִים, *a joyful song of lovers* (*Kitzur Shulchan Aruch* 128:1). The expression of love between two people is the sweetest feeling in the world.

[Ed. note: This reference to *Kitzur Shulchan Aruch* was suggested by Rabbi B. Forst.]

So the meaning of הוֹד is the "echo" of *HaKadosh Baruch Hu* in response to our *tefillah*. The *tefillah* is not one sided. It starts with our praises, expressing our desire to please Him, but then *HaKadosh Baruch Hu* returns this love to us, and sends His blessings into the world. Similarly, the word הָדָר, used together with הוֹד, also has the meaning of "responding" or "returning." When we praise *HaKadosh Baruch Hu*, He returns this love to us. Therefore, עֹז וְחֶדְוָה בִּמְקֹמוֹ, *strength and joy emanate from Him*. As a result of our joyful singing to Him, *HaKadosh Baruch Hu* responds to us.

Many years ago, in Marienbad, I had the *zechus* to meet the great *tzaddik*, HaRav Hersh Henach Levine, the "Bendiner Rav," who was the brother-in-law of the Gerrer Rebbe (the *Imrei Emes*). It was related to me there that unbeknown to the Rav, while he was standing in a corner during his *tefillah*, people overheard him saying in Yiddish: *"Oy, Ribbono Shel Olam, ich hob Dich doch azoy lieb,"* meaning, "O Master of the Universe, I love You so very much." This *tzaddik* was in love with *HaKadosh Baruch Hu*! One of those present remarked that a *navi* (prophet) would have heard the response from *HaKadosh Baruch Hu*, "I love you, too."

Based on this, we can have some understanding of the Gemara in *Berachos* 6a, which says, strangely, that *HaKadosh Baruch Hu* wears *tefillin*, and that these *tefillin* contain the words: מִי כְּעַמְּךָ יִשְׂרָאֵל גּוֹי אֶחָד בָּאָרֶץ, *Who is* like Your people, one nation in the world (Divrei Hayamim I 17:21). This means that "the *tefillin* of *HaKadosh Baruch Hu,* expressing the uniqueness of *Klal Yisrael,* is His response to the declaration contained in our *tefillin* — שְׁמַע יִשְׂרָאֵל ה׳ אֱלֹהֵינוּ ה׳ אֶחָד. This, again, is the הוֹד וְהָדָר of *HaKadosh Baruch Hu.*

Similarly, we also find in the Gemara (ibid. 7a): הקב״ה מתפלל, *HaKadosh Baruch Hu prays,* and says the words, יְהִי רָצוֹן מִלְפָנַי שֶׁיִּכְבְּשׁוּ רַחֲמַי אֶת כַּעֲסִי וְיָגוֹלּוּ רַחֲמַי עַל מִדּוֹתַי, "May it be My will that My mercy may overpower My anger, and therefore My mercy will dominate My attributes." While this is obviously not to be taken simply, some understanding of it may be found in this concept of "the self-sustaining cycle of *tefillah.*" The meaning here, then, would be that *HaKadosh Baruch Hu,* anticipating our *tefillah,* expresses His own *tefillah*: He awaits our *tefillos,* by virtue of which His mercy may overcome His harsh decrees.

Although *HaKadosh Baruch Hu* does not interfere with our *bechirah* (freedom of choice), it is His desire that we approach Him with *ahavah* (love), *yirah* (awe), and *tefillah.*

This concept, that *HaKadosh Baruch Hu* is *mispallel,* is also found in, מִי יִתֵּן וְהָיָה לְבָבָם זֶה לָהֶם לְיִרְאָה אֹתִי וְלִשְׁמֹר אֶת כָּל מִצְוֹתַי כָּל הַיָּמִים, *Who can assure Me that this heart should remain theirs, to fear Me and observe all My commandments all the days* (Devarim 5:26). The idea is the same: It is His desire that through our free will, we initiate the cycle of contact with Him, serve Him, and do His will, to which He will respond.

So, if we serve *HaKadosh Baruch Hu* with joy, עִבְדוּ אֶת ה׳ בְּשִׂמְחָה, *Serve Hashem with gladness* (Tehillim 100:2) by singing His praises, He gives this joy back, and there is joy in the world. Or, for example, if we express our exalted feelings of the *kedushah* of Shabbos in our *tefillos* of Shabbos, the result is that *HaKadosh Baruch Hu* causes the holiness of Shabbos to permeate the world.

On a higher level, then, our relationship to *HaKadosh Baruch Hu* is not merely that of a *mekabal* to a *mashpia,* a recipient to a donor, similar to a baby nursing from its mother; but rather, it is that of a *mashpia* to a *mashpia,* because we ourselves become the cause of our own blessings by initiating our contact with *HaKadosh Baruch Hu.* This is a much greater form of attachment to *HaKadosh Baruch Hu* than merely being the recipient of His blessings.

This is the meaning of הַבּוֹחֵר בְּשִׁירֵי זִמְרָה, *Who chooses songs of praise.* *HaKadosh Baruch Hu* has chosen to bestow His blessings to the world by receiving man's *songs of praise.* He has chosen to relate to us as "one giver to another," This, at its core, is the underlying meaning of the *Pesukei d'Zimrah.*

[Ed. note: This concept is developed further in *Maayan Beis HaSho'evah, Eikev* 6:5, 11:14.]

The term *Pesukei d'Zimrah,* "Verses of Singing," is mentioned in *Shabbos* 118b and refers to this entire *tefillah* from בָּרוּךְ שֶׁאָמַר to יִשְׁתַּבַּח. When we recite this part of the *tefillah,* it is important that we keep in mind the words, אֵין אוֹמְרִים הַזְמִירוֹת בִּמְרוּצָה כִּי אִם בְּנַחַת, *One is not to hurriedly recite these "songs," but rather, they should be said deliberately* (Shulchan Aruch, Orach Chaim 51:8). The *Ba'er Heteiv* adds: שֶׁלֹא יְדַלֵּג שׁוּם תֵּיבָה וְלֹא יַבְלִיעֵם אֶלָּא יוֹצִיא מִפִּיו כְּאִלּוּ מוֹנֶה מָעוֹת, *None of the words should be skipped or mumbled; but each word is to be pronounced as if one were counting money.*

If there are circumstances in which it is difficult to recite the entire *Pesukei d'Zimrah* properly in this fashion, it is better to say only a small piece properly than to rush and stumble through the entire section. Thus we find: טוֹב מְעַט תַּחֲנוּנִים בְּכַוָּנָה מֵהַרְבּוֹת בְּלֹא כַּוָּנָה, *Better a few prayers with concentration than many without concentration* (Orach Chaim 1:4). This does not mean that we should skip any part of the *Pesukei d'Zimrah,* but rather, one should at least make an effort to recite one part of it with complete concentration and careful pronunciation.

Many *kehillos* have the *minhag* to say מִזְמוֹר שִׁיר חֲנֻכַּת הַבַּיִת לְדָוִד (*Tehillim* 30) before beginning the *Pesukei d'Zimrah,* immediately before בָּרוּךְ שֶׁאָמַר. However, this *minhag* is found neither in the *Shulchan Aruch* nor in the old *siddurim* to which we referred earlier, which had been printed some four hundred years ago. Apparently, this *minhag* started in Poland, and is based on the Kabbalah of the *Arizal,* which originated in Eretz Yisrael and became popular about three to four hundred years ago. We did not adopt this *minhag* because our *siddur* was completed hundreds of years before the Kabbalah became commonly known. Prior to this, the Kabbalah was known only to, and studied by, special *yechidei segulah,* individuals of great merit.

There is a uniquely "Frankfurt" *minhag* for the *chazzan* to announce, before beginning בָּרוּךְ שֶׁאָמַר: שְׁתִיקָה יָפָה בִּשְׁעַת הַתְּפִלָּה, *It is a beautiful thing to maintain silence during the tefillah.* However, this is an inaccurate portrayal of the actual *halachah.* It is not only "beautiful" to maintain silence during the *tefillah,* but rather, *it is absolutely forbidden to talk during the tefillah, from the beginning of* בָּרוּךְ שֶׁאָמַר, *until after the end of* חֲזָרַת הש"ץ. Even answering בָּרוּךְ הוּא וּבָרוּךְ שְׁמוֹ is forbidden (see *Shulchan Aruch, Orach Chaim* 51:4). However, what this announcement does mean is that we are asking our neighbors in *shul,* who may not yet have reached בָּרוּךְ שֶׁאָמַר, to please refrain from talking — and disturbing us — so that we may concentrate on our *tefillah.* This is the meaning of יָפָה. It is, indeed, "beautiful" and considerate of others to heed this request.

בָּרוּךְ שֶׁאָמַר / Baruch She'amar

In *Sefer Yuchsin* we find that upon the appointment of a new *Reish Galusa,* Exilarch, in the "Neo-Persian Empire" of Babylonia and adjacent countries, where the Jews enjoyed a certain autonomy, there would be a celebration in honor of the new leader on the Shabbos following the appointment. Part of that celebration consisted of a choir of *bachurim* who would respond to the *chazzan* as he recited the בָּרוּךְ שֶׁאָמַר.

When he said בָּרוּךְ שֶׁאָמַר וְהָיָה הָעוֹלָם, they responded: בָּרוּךְ הוּא.
When he said בָּרוּךְ עֹשֶׂה בְרֵאשִׁית, they responded: בָּרוּךְ הוּא.
When he said בָּרוּךְ אוֹמֵר וְעֹשֶׂה, they responded: בָּרוּךְ הוּא; and so on throughout the entire *tefillah* of בָּרוּךְ שֶׁאָמַר.

So it is obvious that at least as far back as this period — which was the time of the *Rabbanan Savorai* — the text of בָּרוּךְ שֶׁאָמַר as we know it was in common use.

בָּרוּךְ שֶׁאָמַר is composed of two parts. The first part consists of ten different aspects of the definition of the Ineffable Name of God, the *Shem HaMeforash*: י-ה-ו-ה. Each one of these is preceded by בָּרוּךְ.

The second part consists of the body of the *berachah* itself. Although we humans can have no understanding of the essence of *HaKadosh Baruch Hu,* the Torah has given us ten definitions of the meaning of the *Shem HaMeforash,* which are recited in the first part.

There is a *minhag* to hold the two front *tzitzis* and look at them, at least during the recitation of this part of בָּרוּךְ שֶׁאָמַר. The two *tzitzis* are composed of eight threads and five double knots each. Together, these sixteen threads and ten double knots are equal to the numerical value of י-ה-ו-ה, which is twenty-six. By looking at these *tzitzis* we are reminded to concentrate on the Name of *HaKadosh Baruch Hu.*

These ten definitions of the Ineffable Name of God follow:

❈ ❈ ❈

בָּרוּךְ שֶׁאָמַר וְהָיָה הָעוֹלָם (1) — **Blessed is He Who spoke and the world came into existence.** The first definition of the Name that we attribute to *HaKadosh Baruch Hu* is שֶׁאָמַר וְהָיָה הָעוֹלָם, *He spoke and the world came into existence.* It is this fact that is meant by the name י-ה-ו-ה, which conveys the basic concept of מְהַוֶּה כָּל הַהֲוָיוֹת, *He makes all existing things exist.* The first and foremost Name of God is that He created the world out of nothing, *yeish mei'ayin.*

The source for this definition of the Name of *HaKadosh Baruch Hu* is found in the verse, וַיְדַבֵּר אֱלֹהִים אֶל מֹשֶׁה וַיֹּאמֶר אֵלָיו אֲנִי ה', *God spoke to Moshe and said to him, "I am Hashem"* (*Shemos* 6:2), and *Mechilta* explains this as: אָמַר לוֹ הקב״ה לְמֹשֶׁה: אֲנִי הוּא שֶׁאָמַרְתִּי וְהָיָה הָעוֹלָם. Here *HaKadosh Baruch Hu* identifies Himself as *It is I, Who spoke and the world came into existence.* This is also expressed as כִּי הוּא אָמַר וַיֶּהִי הוּא צִוָּה וַיַּעֲמֹד, *For He spoke and it came to be, He commanded and it stood firm* (*Tehillim* 33:9).

This concept that *HaKadosh Baruch Hu* speaks and the world comes into being is extremely sublime. What הוּא אָמַר וַיֶּהִי really means is that it is only when He speaks that there is existence. Human speech is temporal. It exists only while it is spoken. However, with *HaKadosh Baruch Hu,* Who is beyond time, He is הָיָה, הֹוֶה, וְיִהְיֶה — there is no difference between the past, present, and future. So the אָמַר is the condition for the continuing וַיֶּהִי. All of existence is a "word of *HaKadosh Baruch Hu.*" Before He spoke, there was nothing, and if He is finished speaking there will be nothing. Since this thought is so sublime, and we cannot possibly grasp it, we follow it by simply saying, בָּרוּךְ הוּא, similar to the usage הַקָּדוֹשׁ בָּרוּךְ הוּא. We call God "the Holy One," and since this, too, is beyond our comprehension, we add a simple: בָּרוּךְ הוּא.

ও§ (2) בָּרוּךְ עֹשֶׂה בְרֵאשִׁית — Blessed is He Who constantly creates. We next define Him as *the One Who constantly creates.* עֹשֶׂה, "He makes," in the present tense, conveys the idea of an ongoing process of creation. In other words, we could say: "He keeps what exists in existence." There was not only a one-time "big bang" of Creation of יֵשׁ מֵאַיִן, but this is ongoing. It is only because He constantly keeps all of creation in existence that it continues to exist. This is expressed in our *tefillah* of יוֹצֵר אוֹר as: מְחַדֵּשׁ בְּכָל יוֹם תָּמִיד מַעֲשֵׂה בְרֵאשִׁית, *He renews daily, continuously, the work of creation.* This sense, too, is conveyed by the grammatical makeup *of the Shem HaMeforash,* י-ה-ו-ה: that of constant and continuing creation.

ও§ (3) בָּרוּךְ אוֹמֵר וְעוֹשֶׂה — Blessed is He Who makes His word into reality. We then define Him as *the One Who makes His word into reality.* I.e., he makes His word come true. וָאֵרָא אֶל אַבְרָהָם אֶל יִצְחָק וְאֶל יַעֲקֹב בְּאֵל שַׁדָּי וּשְׁמִי ה' לֹא נוֹדַעְתִּי לָהֶם. וְגַם הֲקִמֹתִי אֶת בְּרִיתִי אִתָּם לָתֵת לָהֶם אֶת אֶרֶץ כְּנָעַן ... וְגַם אֲנִי שָׁמַעְתִּי אֶת נַאֲקַת בְּנֵי יִשְׂרָאֵל ... וָאֶזְכֹּר אֶת בְּרִיתִי. לָכֵן אֱמֹר לִבְנֵי יִשְׂרָאֵל אֲנִי ה' ..., *I appeared to Avraham, to Yitzchak, and to Yaakov as El Shaddai, but with my Name* י-ה-ו-ה *I did not make Myself known to them. Moreover, I established My covenant with them to give them the land of Canaan ... Moreover, I have heard the groan of the Children of Israel ... I had remembered My covenant. Therefore, say to the Children of Israel: "I am Hashem"* (*Shemos* 6:3-6).

The *Mechilta* (ibid.) explains: אֲנִי ה': אֲנִי הוּא שֶׁאָמַרְתִּי לְיַעֲקֹב וכו', וְעַכְשָׁיו הֲרֵי

הַשְּׁבוּעָה וכו׳, וַאֲנִי מְבַקֵּשׁ לְהוֹצִיאָם, שֶׁ"אֲנִי ה׳ ", הַמְהַוֶּה וּמְאַמֵּת מַה שֶׁדִּבַּרְתִּי, וּמְקַיֵּים מַה שֶׁהִבְטַחְתִּי. This can be paraphrased as: "I am God Who promised your Forefathers that I would take their children out of slavery and bring them back to their land. That time has come now, and I will fulfill this promise. Because אֲנִי י-ה-ו-ה — My Name is: 'What I promise is what I do.' "

This is known as the מִדָּה אֲמִתִּית שֶׁלִּי, *My attribute of Truth* (see *Rashi* ibid.).

Thus, we see *HaKadosh Baruch Hu* defining His own Name as *the Keeper of Promises*. This idea is also inherent in the grammatical construction of the lettering י-ה-ו-ה, which conveys the meaning of an ongoing process, i.e. His promise will, per se, be kept. This is אוֹמֵר וְעוֹשֶׂה. Our whole hope for the eventual *geulah*, *bi'as Mashiach* and *techiyas hameisim* is based on this meaning of the *Shem HaMeforash*.

◈§ (4) בָּרוּךְ גּוֹזֵר וּמְקַיֵּם — **Blessed is He Who makes decrees and fulfills them.** "Decrees" here refers to the meting out of punishment to the *reshaim*. We find the source for this meaning in *Vayikra* 18:2. There, in the introduction to the פָּרָשַׁת הָעֲרָיוֹת, we find an ominous warning to violators: אֲנִי ה׳ אֱלֹהֵיכֶם. The *Toras Kohanim* explains: אֲנִי הוּא שֶׁפָּרַעְתִּי מִדּוֹר הַמַּבּוּל וּמֵאַנְשֵׁי סְדוֹם וּמִן הַמִּצְרִים, וְעָתִיד לִיפָּרַע מִכֶּם אִם תַּעֲשׂוּ כְּמַעֲשֵׂיהֶם, I, י-ה-ו-ה, Who punished the Mabul generation, the people of Sodom, and the Egyptians, will also punish you if you do as they did. This means that although some *reshaim* may thrive and be successful in this world, *HaKadosh Baruch Hu* says: אֲנִי ה׳: "If I decree a punishment, it will surely happen." *Chazal* have understood this concept, too, to be inherent in the *Shem HaMeforash* with the meaning: He is מְהַוֶּה גְזֵרוֹתָיו, *He brings His decrees into reality*.

The source for the usage גּוֹזֵר וּמְקַיֵּם to mean the certainty of punishment of *reshaim* is found in *Berachos* 57b. There, the Gemara suggests several *berachos* that one would make upon seeing the remnants of what was once the wicked Babylonia. This refers to the fulfillment of the prophecy of Yirmiyahu regarding the destruction of Babylonia, which starts with the ominous words, כֹּה אָמַר ה׳ הִנְנִי מֵעִיר עַל בָּבֶל, *Thus said Hashem: Behold, I am stirring up a spirit of destruction against Babylonia* (*Yirmiyahu* 51:1). The entire chapter is devoted to a prediction of the eventual utter desolation of this country, which was the site of a highly developed civilization. The last *berachah* mentioned is, בָּרוּךְ אוֹמֵר וְעוֹשֶׂה, בָּרוּךְ גּוֹזֵר וּמְקַיֵּם. During the Gulf War, when the Allied armies converged on this formerly blossoming civilization, they found mostly desert and wasteland. The *gezeirah* of Hashem was realized.

◈§ (5) בָּרוּךְ מְרַחֵם עַל הָאָרֶץ — **Blessed is He Who has mercy on the earth.**

◈§ (6) בָּרוּךְ מְרַחֵם עַל הַבְּרִיּוֹת — **Blessed is He Who has mercy on the creatures.** These two definitions belong together. כָּל מָקוֹם שֶׁנֶּאֱמַר י-ה-ו-ה זוּ

מִדַּת הָרַחֲמִים, *Whenever the four-lettered Name is used, it has the meaning of mercy, goodness, compassion* (*Sifrei, Devarim,* end of *Perek* 21). The very fact that *HaKadosh Baruch Hu,* Who is totally perfect and independent of any of His creatures, created the world and its inhabitants, is an act of *rachamim.* He, through His *middas harachamim,* wished to impart some of His goodness to others, and He therefore created recipients who can benefit from His goodness. (This philosophical concept is expounded upon by Rav Samson R. Hirsch, as well as by *Ramchal* and others.) Here *Chazal* find the meaning of *Baal HaRachamim* inherent in the four-lettered Name י-ה-ו-ה.

In this phrase we specify both the earth and its inhabitants: מְרַחֵם עַל הָאָרֶץ and מְרַחֵם עַל הַבְּרִיּוֹת. Similarly, we say, הַמֵּאִיר לָאָרֶץ וְלַדָּרִים עָלֶיהָ בְּרַחֲמִים, *He Who illuminates the earth and those who dwell upon it with compassion.* First we recognize His *rachamim* in creating the earth. The earth itself, compared to all the other heavenly bodies, is like one grain of sand out of all the sand shores on earth. For reasons of His own, *HaKadosh Baruch Hu* chose this planet, Earth, and positioned it in relation to the sun so that it would not be scorched by heat, nor frozen by the lack of it, either of which conditions would make life impossible. He then surrounded this planet with various atmospheric gases, *rekiim,* to protect it from the unhealthy effects of the sunlight, and to provide air for vegetative and organic life. So, the very fact that He created this little "grain of sand" and placed it with just the right conditions to support life is, in itself, an act of *rachamim.*

Then, we recognize His רַחֲמִים עַל הַבְּרִיּוֹת. This refers to human beings. All other life, be it animal or vegetable, is included in אָרֶץ. For reasons of His own, *HaKadosh Baruch Hu* has endowed one class of creatures, humankind, with a free will, and the ability to oppose Him.

So the אָרֶץ and the בְּרִיּוֹת were created with *rachamim,* while the rest of creation exists only by *middas hadin,* in accordance with their predetermined physical properties, with no possibility to oppose God's will.

(7) בָּרוּךְ מְשַׁלֵּם שָׂכָר טוֹב לִירֵאָיו — **Blessed is He Who gives a good reward to those who fear Him.** This refers to *Olam Haba.* The source for this definition of the four-lettered Name is found in, וַיֹּאמֶר אֵלָיו אֲנִי י-ה-ו-ה, *And He said to him, "I am Hashem"* (*Shemos* 6:2), on which *Rashi* comments: נֶאֱמָן לְשַׁלֵּם שָׂכָר טוֹב לַמִּתְהַלְּכִים לְפָנַי, *I will surely pay a good reward to those who walk before Me.* A "good reward" means an everlasting one, a continuing reward. If a person attaches his own will to that of *HaKadosh Baruch Hu,* and thereby fulfills His will, the resulting reward will last forever. This is, again, inherent in the meaning of י-ה-ו-ה: He is מְהַוֶּה אֶת הַהֲוָיוֹת. Whatever He created, including reward, He keeps in existence forever. This is what is meant by, וְחַיֵּי עוֹלָם נָטַע בְּתוֹכֵנוּ, *He implanted everlasting life among us.* This concept, eternal existence, is beyond our comprehension, but it refers to the fact that *HaKadosh Baruch Hu* gave us the opportunity to connect ourselves eternally with Him, through the fulfillment of His commandments.

∽§ (8) בָּרוּךְ חַי לָעַד וְקַיָּם לָנֶצַח — Blessed is He Who is always living, and He will exist forever. This is a verbal definition of the Eternity of *HaKadosh Baruch Hu,* as indicated in the spelling of י-ה-ו-ה. The י in the Ineffable Name indicates the future tense; the ה means the past tense; and the ו conveys the meaning of a combination of past and future, and has the sense of eternal "being." This, simply put is: הָיָה, הֹוֶה, וְיִהְיֶה, *He was, He is, and He will be.*

∽§ (9) בָּרוּךְ פּוֹדֶה וּמַצִּיל — Blessed is He Who redeems and saves. This definition of the *Shem HaMeforash* is based on the opening phrase of the *Aseres HaDibros,* Ten Commandments: אָנֹכִי ה׳ אֱלֹהֶיךָ אֲשֶׁר הוֹצֵאתִיךָ מֵאֶרֶץ מִצְרַיִם מִבֵּית עֲבָדִים, *I am Hashem, your God, Who took you out of Egypt* (*Shemos* 20:2). At the Revelation at Sinai, *HaKadosh Baruch Hu* did not reveal Himself to us by saying, "I am the Creator of heaven and earth," but rather, He relates to us in His role as Redeemer. "You know Me in this role. I am not אֱלֹהִים אֲחֵרִים אֲשֶׁר לֹא יְדַעְתָּם, *like gods of others that you did not know* (*Devarim* 13:3). You experienced My personal intervention at *yetzias Mitzrayim.* As we say in the Haggadah: אֲנִי וְלֹא מַלְאָךְ ... אֲנִי וְלֹא שָׂרָף ... אֲנִי וְלֹא הַשָּׁלִיחַ ... אֲנִי הוּא וְלֹא אַחֵר, *I and no angel ... I and no seraph ... I and no messenger ... it is I and no other.* So, it is in this directly personal way, that of Redeemer, that we relate to *HaKadosh Baruch Hu.* (See *Rambam* ibid. for further elaboration on this subject.)

We, as a nation, have experienced *HaKadosh Baruch Hu* as our פּוֹדֶה and מַצִּיל not only at *yetzias Mitzrayim,* but on many other occasions during our history as well, and we will experience Him again in this role at the *geulah sheleimah l'asid.* Without the intervention of *HaKadosh Baruch Hu,* we, as a nation, would have had no hope of survival, and we would have faced certain oblivion. These words, בָּרוּךְ פּוֹדֶה וּמַצִּיל, mean that we recognize *HaKadosh Baruch Hu* in His role as our Redeemer and, as such, He insures the continuity of our nation. He is מְהַוֶּה the *Klal Yisrael.* This is, again, a definition of י-ה-ו-ה.

∽§ (10) Then, finally, we say בָּרוּךְ שְׁמוֹ — Blessed is His Name. This is the ultimate referral to the *Shem HaMeforash.* Despite having revealed certain aspects of His Name, *HaKadosh Baruch Hu* tells us, זֶה שְׁמִי לְעֹלָם, *This is My Name forever* (*Shemos* 3:15), with the word לְעֹלָם, *forever,* written as if it could be read לְעָלַם, meaning *hidden.* Just as I am beyond your comprehension, so shall My true Name, My essence, remain unknown and hidden to the human mind. So we humbly, simply, say: בָּרוּךְ שְׁמוֹ.

[Ed. note: For a somewhat similar explanation of the definitions of the *Shem HaMeforash* in בָּרוּךְ שֶׁאָמַר, see the commentary to *Vayikra* 1:1 by Rav Dovid

Tzvi Hoffman, which is quoted by Rav Shelomoh Eliezer Danziger in *Moreshes Tzvi*, "The Living Hirschian Legacy," KAJ, 1988.]

After the recitation of these ten definitions of the Name, the main body of the *berachah* follows.

Before we begin this part, it is important to point out that the various terms utilized for the praise of *HaKadosh Baruch Hu* in this *berachah*, and in the *Pesukei d'Zimrah* in general, are not synonymous. Rather, there are fine nuances between them, with each word expressing a unique element of the praise of *HaKadosh Baruch Hu,* as we shall see.

&≈ בָּרוּךְ אַתָּה ה' אֱלֹהֵינוּ מֶלֶךְ הָעוֹלָם ≈& — **Blessed are You, Hashem, our God, King of the universe.** We have previously explained the meaning of this introduction to our *berachos*. See עַל נְטִילַת יָדָיִם.

&≈ הָאֵל הָאָב הָרַחֲמָן ≈& — **The Almighty, the merciful Father.** The word הָאֵל refers to the concept that *HaKadosh Baruch Hu* is "Almighty" in the sense that He is not governed or restricted by His *middos*. This means, in this instance, that *HaKadosh Baruch Hu* can, and does, relate to humanity with mercy even if the individuals do not deserve it. We find this expressed in the verse, וְחַנֹּתִי אֶת אֲשֶׁר אָחֹן וְרִחַמְתִּי אֶת אֲשֶׁר אֲרַחֵם, *I shall show favor when I choose to show favor, and I shall show mercy when I choose to show mercy* (*Shemos* 33:19). Although we may not understand it, *HaKadosh Baruch Hu* acts as a "Merciful Father" toward all mankind, albeit even undeservedly. Were it not for this fact, mankind would have long ago ceased to exist.

&≈ הַמְהֻלָּל בְּפִי עַמּוֹ ≈& — **Who is lauded by the mouth of His nation.** While many of the nations of the world do praise *HaKadosh Baruch Hu,* it is only עַמּוֹ, *His nation,* that praises Him as ה' אֶחָד, *the One and Only,* שֶׁאָמַר וְהָיָה הָעוֹלָם. As it states, וְאַתָּה קָדוֹשׁ יוֹשֵׁב תְּהִלּוֹת יִשְׂרָאֵל, *Yet You are the Holy One, enthroned upon the praises of Israel* (*Tehillim* 22:4). This means that the nation Israel, to whom You have revealed Your Holiness, "enthroned" You with their praises.

We find this very explicitly expressed in the *tefillah* of *Nishmas* which is said on Shabbos: וּבְמַקְהֲלוֹת רִבְבוֹת עַמְּךָ בֵּית יִשְׂרָאֵל, *In the congregations of the tens of thousands of Your nation Israel;* בְּרִנָּה יִתְפָּאַר שִׁמְךָ מַלְכֵּנוּ בְּכָל דּוֹר וָדוֹר, *With jubilation is Your Name, our King, glorified in every generation;* שֶׁכֵּן חוֹבַת כָּל הַיְצוּרִים לְפָנֶיךָ ה' אֱלֹהֵינוּ לְהוֹדוֹת לְהַלֵּל לְשַׁבֵּחַ וגו׳ . . . עַל כָּל דִּבְרֵי שִׁירוֹת וְתִשְׁבָּחוֹת דָּוִד בֶּן יִשַׁי עַבְדְּךָ מְשִׁיחֶךָ, *For it is really the duty of all Your creatures to praise You* etc., *even above and beyond all those songs and praises spoken by Your anointed servant Dovid* which we, Your people Yisrael, have adopted as our national songs of praise to *HaKadosh Baruch Hu.*

&≈ מְשֻׁבָּח וּמְפֹאָר בִּלְשׁוֹן חֲסִידָיו וַעֲבָדָיו וּבְשִׁירֵי דָוִד עַבְדֶּךָ ≈& — **He is praised and glorified in the language of both those who are dedicated to Him because of *ahavah* (חֲסִידָיו) or of *yirah* (עֲבָדָיו), and with the songs of Your servant Dovid.**

This is all one phrase, and is based on, דָּוִד הַמֶּלֶךְ כָּתַב סֵפֶר תְּהִלִּים עַל יְדֵי עֲשָׂרָה זְקֵנִים. While most of *Tehillim* was authored by Dovid HaMelech, he also included, and edited, some psalms which were composed by others. These others are the *asarah zekeinim,* who are identified by *Chazal* (ibid.) as: Adam HaRishon (psalm 139); Malchi Tzedek (psalm 110); Avraham Avinu [Aisan HaEzrachi] (psalm 89); Moshe Rabbeinu (psalms 90-100); Heiman HaEzrachi (psalm 88); Yedusun (psalm 39); Asaf (psalms 50, 73-83); Asir, Elkanah, and Aviasaf [3 sons of Korach] (psalms 42-49, 84, 85, 87).

[Ed. note: Heiman HaEzrachi, the author of psalm 88, who is referred to in *Divrei HaYamim I* 6:18 as הֵימָן הַמְשׁוֹרֵר (see Rav Samson R. Hirsch, *Tehillim* 88), was a descendant of one of the three sons of Korach. This would explain why psalm 88 begins with שִׁיר מִזְמוֹר לִבְנֵי קֹרַח.]

These ten *zekeinim,* and others, are the חֲסִידָיו וַעֲבָדָיו to whom we refer in this phrase. So this phrase ends with the clause וּבְשִׁירֵי דָוִד עַבְדֶּךָ, and not וּבְשִׁירֵי דָוִד עַבְדְּךָ נְהַלֶּלְךָ וגו'. This is so, because some parts of the *Pesukei d'Zimrah* are not שִׁירֵי דָוִד עַבְדֶּךָ, but were composed by others. The *Leviim* composed אַתָּה הוּא ה' לְבַדֶּךָ, *You alone are Hashem* (Nechemiah 9:6).

◆§ נְהַלֶּלְךָ ה' אֱלֹהֵינוּ בִּשְׁבָחוֹת — **We shall laud you, Hashem, our God, with praises.** We, too, wish to offer our praises to You, God our God, by means of the words of the aforementioned חֲסִידִים וַעֲבָדִים. The general word for praise, שֶׁבַח, appears five times in some form in this *berachah,* e.g., מְשַׁבֵּחַ, בִּשְׁבָחוֹת, וּנְשַׁבֵּחֲךָ, מְשַׁבֵּחֲךָ, בַּתִּשְׁבָּחוֹת.

◆§ וּבִזְמִרוֹת נְגַדֶּלְךָ, וּנְשַׁבֵּחֲךָ, וּנְפָאֶרְךָ, וְנַזְכִּיר שִׁמְךָ, וְנַמְלִיכְךָ מַלְכֵּנוּ אֱלֹהֵינוּ — **And with song we will declare Your greatness, praise You, glorify You, remember Your Name and declare You our King, our only God.** This section of the *berachah* contains five expressions of praise. We will show later how these five expressions correspond to the five parts of the *Pesukei d'Zimrah.* This is all in keeping with the symbolism of the *Ulam,* as we explained earlier.

First, let us explain the meaning of each word here. The wording of this *berachah* was chosen by the Sages to follow a certain order. This is in accordance with the dictum which we previously mentioned: לְעוֹלָם יְסַדֵּר אָדָם שִׁבְחוֹ שֶׁל הקב"ה וְאַחַר כָּךְ יִתְפַּלֵּל, *A person should first express the ordered praises of Hashem and then pray* (Berachos 32a). It is of the essence that the praises of HaKadosh Baruch Hu not be randomly said, but rather, they are to be ordered. The five expressions of praise in this *berachah* are different from each other, in that each one adds a thought not contained in the previous one. These praises follow a definite order.

❑ וּבִזְמִרוֹת נְגַדֶּלְךָ — *And with song we will declare Your greatness,* or, *we shall magnify You.* This term is very difficult to comprehend. How do we "magnify" HaKadosh Baruch Hu Who is infinite? The simple meaning could be

BARUCH SHE'AMAR 127

that we will stress certain aspects of *HaKadosh Baruch Hu* of which people are usually not aware. However, there is an additional meaning of the root גדל, that of "intertwined," as in גְּדִלִים תַּעֲשֶׂה לָּךְ (*Devarim* 22:12), which refers to *tzitzis*. The *tzitzis* consist of four strands each, which are pulled through a hole in the corner of the garment, and then twisted together into knots. This part of the *tzitzis,* with its knots, is called גָּדִיל. The *Gemara* says: קֶשֶׁר עֶלְיוֹן דְּאוֹרָיְיתָא (*Menachos* 39a), meaning that without the knots these strands would not be called גְּדִלִים. Also, we find the term used for the braiding of hair, as in מִרְיָם מְגַדְּלָא שֵׂיעַר (*Chagigah* 4b).

Similarly, the נְגַדֶּלְךָ technique in the *Pesukei d'Zimrah* uses combinations of various *pesukim,* and brings two or three of them together, or even only one that may just fit into the context, and makes a "bouquet" of various *shevachim.* This expresses a certain harmony of thoughts, much like a florist would make up a beautiful arrangement of flowers. In this way, we praise *HaKadosh Baruch Hu,* not by pointing out one particular relationship that we have with Him, but rather, by combining various aspects of our perception of Him.

❑ וּנְשַׁבֵּחֲךָ — *Praise You.* The word שֶׁבַח is usually translated as *praise.* However, it really means לְהַשְׁבִּיחַ, *to improve something.* If a field is underproducing, and the owner takes steps to improve it, he is said to be doing this לְהַשְׁבִּיחַ הַשָּׂדֶה. Used as praise to *HaKadosh Baruch Hu,* this expression refers to occasions and situations in life in which we cannot clearly see Him as only טוֹב וּמֵטִיב, absolutely good. There are situations when we must accept the reverse as גַּם זוֹ לְטוֹבָה [*gam zo l'tovah*], *this too is for good.* The Mishnah requires that: חַיָּיב אָדָם לְבָרֵךְ עַל הָרָעָה כְּשֵׁם שֶׁמְּבָרֵךְ עַל הַטּוֹבָה, *Man is obligated to bless (Hashem) for the bad just as he blesses (Him) for the good* (*Berachos* 54a). This acceptance, which is expressed as יְהַלְלוּ אֶת שִׁמְךָ בֶּאֱמֶת is called שֶׁבַח, *shevach.* This means that regardless of how *HaKadosh Baruch Hu* relates to us, we are מַשְׁבִּיחַ Him in the sense that we "improve" our perception of Him in all of life's occurrences, good or otherwise, as being entirely good.

❑ וּנְפָאֶרְךָ — *Glorify You.* The literal meaning of פְּאֵר is a *crown,* which is worn above the head. This word occurs in the verse, לֹא תְפָאֵר אַחֲרֶיךָ, *do not remove all the splendor behind you* (*Devarim* 24:20), prohibiting the removal of the "crown" from the top of the tree, referring to the *mitzvah* of pe'ah. Accordingly, וּנְפָאֶרְךָ is the praising of *HaKadosh Baruch Hu* concerning those aspects of Him which are higher than our minds can grasp.

❑ וְנַזְכִּיר שִׁמְךָ — *Remember Your Name.* During certain periods of our lives, it may appear as if *HaKadosh Baruch Hu* has forsaken us, so we need to remind ourselves that He never forsakes us. We reinforce our *emunah* and *bitachon* by reminding ourselves that יֵשׁ ה׳ בְּקִרְבֵּנוּ. As it states, אֵלֶּה בָרֶכֶב וְאֵלֶּה בַסּוּסִים

וַאֲנַחְנוּ בְּשֵׁם ה׳ אֱלֹהֵינוּ נַזְכִּיר, *Some with chariots, and some with horses, but as for us, we remember the Name of Hashem our God* (*Tehillim* 20:8). This thought is poignantly expressed in *Tehillim*. First Dovid HaMelech desperately calls out: אֵלִי אֵלִי לָמָה עֲזַבְתָּנִי, *My God, my God, why have You forsaken me* (*Tehillim* 22:2), but immediately upon mentioning the Name of Hashem he realizes that: וְאַתָּה קָדוֹשׁ יוֹשֵׁב תְּהִלּוֹת יִשְׂרָאֵל, *Yet You are the Holy One, enthroned upon the praises of Israel* (ibid. 22:4). "You are eternally right here"; "Whatever happens is Your doing." The same thought is expressed in, עִמּוֹ אָנֹכִי בְצָרָה, *I am with him in times of difficulty* (ibid. 91:15).

❏ וְנַמְלִיכְךָ מַלְכֵּנוּ אֱלֹהֵינוּ יָחִיד — *We declare You our King, our only God.* We subject ourselves totally and unconditionally to Your will. This is called *kabbalas ol Malchus Shamayim*. In the *Malchuyos* section of the *Rosh Hashanah Mussaf*, we use the *pasuk* of שְׁמַע יִשְׂרָאֵל ה׳ אֱלֹהֵינוּ ה׳ אֶחָד (*Devarim* 6:4) as one of the requisite ten *pesukim*, because the declaration of *Achdus Hashem* is tantamount to *malchus* (kingship).

❧ חֵי הָעוֹלָמִים — **He Who lives forever.** Or, "the source of life for all time periods," meaning that nothing would exist if *HaKadosh Baruch Hu* would not constantly give it life.

[Ed. note: See earlier on רִבּוֹן כָּל הָעוֹלָמִים for the author's broader interpretation of עוֹלָמִים.]

There are those who pronounce this חַי הָעוֹלָמִים. We do find this form in the *piyut* of הָאַדֶּרֶת וְהָאֱמוּנָה לְחַי עוֹלָמִים in the *Shacharis* of יוֹם כִּפּוּר. Also, וַאֲנִי יָדַעְתִּי גֹּאֲלִי חָי, *But I know that my Redeemer lives* (*Iyov* 19:25). However, our *minhag* prefers the form חֵי הָעוֹלָמִים.

❧ מֶלֶךְ מְשֻׁבָּח וּמְפֹאָר עֲדֵי עַד שְׁמוֹ הַגָּדוֹל — **He is the King, Whose great Name will be praised and glorified forever and ever.** This means that even if we are no longer in this world to praise *HaKadosh Baruch Hu*, His praises will continue in perpetuity. עֲדֵי עַד means literally, "until until," in the sense of forever and ever.

❧ בָּרוּךְ אַתָּה ה׳ מֶלֶךְ מְהֻלָּל בַּתִּשְׁבָּחוֹת — In conclusion, we say, **Blessed are You, Hashem, the King Who is praised by various forms of praise.** There are two similar meanings of the root הלל. One is הִלֵּל, to praise something extraordinary, as in וַיְהַלְלוּ אֹתָהּ אֶל פַּרְעֹה (*Bereishis* 12:15). The Egyptians praised Sarah as a most beautiful woman, fitting for Pharaoh. Also, תְּהִלַּת ה׳ יְדַבֶּר פִּי, *My mouth shall bespeak the praise* of the extraordinary wonders performed by *HaKadosh Baruch Hu* (*Tehillim* 145:21).

However, the other word, הֵלֶל, as explained by Rav Samson R. Hirsch, is the פָּעַל form of the word הלל, which means to shine a light on something, as in בְּהִלּוֹ נֵרוֹ עֲלֵי רֹאשִׁי, *When He shines His light on my head* (*Iyov* 29:3). However, הִלֵּל, in the פִּעֵל form, means to reflect the light away. So the פָּעַל

form is actually the reverse of the קַל form. We find this structure in דָּשֵׁן, meaning to put down ashes, while דַּשֵּׁן means to remove ashes, as in וְדִשְּׁנוּ אֶת הַמִּזְבֵּחַ, *They shall clear the ash from the Altar* (*Bamidbar* 4:13). Also, סָקַל means to throw stones, and סַקֵּל means to remove them, as in סַקְּלוּ מֵאֶבֶן, *Clear it of stones* (*Yeshayahu* 62:10).

It is in this sense that we use the words הַלֵּל or אֲהַלְלָה, and מְהַלָּל, when expressing praise to *HaKadosh Baruch Hu*. What we are saying is that we are "reflecting back to Him" all the blessings which He bestows upon us, through our expressions of praise. Our "praises" of *HaKadosh Baruch Hu*, then, are really an acknowledgment that He is the source of all our blessings.

[See Rav Samson R. Hirsch on *Tehillim* 146:1 and "Collected Writings" Vol. 8, p. 30, for further elucidation on this subject.]

הוֹדוּ / Hodu

The *Pesukei d'Zimrah* start with הוֹדוּ לַה' קִרְאוּ בִשְׁמוֹ (*Divrei HaYamim I* 16:8-36). A very similar text, with some slight variations, is found in two separate chapters of *Tehillim*: the first part is in 105:1-15, and the second part in Chapter 96.

The circumstances in which this *mizmor* was first recited are as follows. The Philistines had destroyed the *Mishkan* of Shiloh and had captured the *Aron HaKodesh*, which they kept with them for a period of seven months. During the time the *Aron* was in their possession, their population suffered horrific plagues and they consequently decided to return it.

Although the *Mishkan* had been rebuilt in Givon, Dovid HaMelech built a special tent enclosure for the *Aron* in *Ir Tziyon*, which is in Yerushalayim. To afford the *Aron* its proper dignity and protection, Dovid HaMelech designated an "honor guard" of *Leviim* for it. As part of their duties, the *Leviim* formed a "choir" to sing various *mizmorim* to HaKadosh Baruch Hu, as we find in *Divrei HaYamim* (ibid. v. 4): לְהַזְכִּיר וּלְהוֹדוֹת וּלְהַלֵּל לַה' אֱלֹהֵי יִשְׂרָאֵל, *to bring to mind, to thank, and to offer praises to Hashem, the God of Yisrael*. The head of this group of *Leviim* was Asaf, who was one of the Ten Elders who composed parts of *Tehillim*, as we mentioned earlier.

On the day that the *Aron* was brought into its special enclosure, with great festivity and honor, Dovid HaMelech composed a special *mizmor*, which Asaf and his fellow *Leviim* were to recite, as described in *Divrei HaYamim*: בַּיּוֹם הַהוּא אָז נָתַן דָּוִד בָּרֹאשׁ לְהֹדוֹת לַה' בְּיַד אָסָף וְאֶחָיו, *Then, on that day, Dovid gave Asaf and his colleagues a song of praise to Hashem to sing first* (ibid. v. 7). This *mizmor* is then cited in full, beginning with הוֹדוּ לַה' קִרְאוּ בִשְׁמוֹ, and continuing through בָּרוּךְ ה' אֱלֹהֵי יִשְׂרָאֵל מִן הָעוֹלָם וְעַד הָעֹלָם וַיֹּאמְרוּ כָל הָעָם אָמֵן וְהַלֵּל לַה'. This is exactly the text of the first part of our הוֹדוּ.

During the time that the *Aron* was in this tent, Dovid HaMelech instituted a special *korban tamid* there, which was brought twice daily, in honor of the *Aron*; this was in addition to the daily *temidim* which were brought in the *Mishkan* in Givon. This *mizmor* was then recited daily by Asaf and his fellow *Leviim* in the presence of the *Aron* (see *Divrei Hayamim I* ibid. v. 37, and *Seder Olam* Ch. 14).

This *mizmor* actually consists of two parts (see *Rashi, Divrei HaYamim I* 16:8). According to *Seder Olam* (ibid.), the first part, from הוֹדוּ לַה' through אַל תִּגְּעוּ בִמְשִׁיחָי וּבִנְבִיאַי אַל תָּרֵעוּ, was sung in the morning, in conjunction with the morning *tamid* offering; and the second part, from שִׁירוּ לַה' כָּל הָאָרֶץ through the end, וַיֹּאמְרוּ כָל הָעָם אָמֵן וְהַלֵּל לַה', was sung in the afternoon, in conjunction with the twilight *tamid*. If we analyze the *pesukim*, we see that the first part refers to the ancient past of the Jewish people, which corresponds to the *tamid* of the morning; and the second part sings of the glorious future of *Klal Yisrael,* and of the world in general, corresponding to the twilight *tamid.*

This would explain the *Sefard minhag* to say הוֹדוּ before בָּרוּךְ שֶׁאָמַר. Since the *mizmor* of הוֹדוּ was originally instituted to be sung in connection with the *korban tamid,* it should be said together with the *korbanos* portion of the *tefillah.* However, our *minhag* is based on the fact that this arrangement was only temporary. When the *Beis HaMikdash* was ultimately built, and the *Aron* was put into its designated place, then different *mizmorim* were sung together with the daily *korbanos.* (See end of *Maseches Tamid,* הַשִּׁיר שֶׁהָיוּ הַלְוִיִּם אוֹמְרִים בְּבֵית הַמִּקְדָּשׁ וְגוֹ׳.) Therefore, we recite הוֹדוּ as one of the *mizmorim* of the *Pesukei d'Zimrah,* as it was no longer associated with the *korbanos.*

[Ed. note: It was not the author's intention in these *shiurim* to translate every word of the *tefillos.* Therefore, in the *Pesukei d'Zimrah,* as well as in other parts of this work, many words are not translated, or are even omitted, because in these cases, the author only explained these words or phrases in general terms, or he expressed certain concepts regarding their broader meaning, presupposing that the students knew the simple translation of the words.]

❧ ❧ ❧

הוֹדוּ לַה׳ קִרְאוּ בִשְׁמוֹ הוֹדִיעוּ בָעַמִּים עֲלִילוֹתָיו — Give thanks to Hashem, declare His Name, make His acts known among the peoples. The first part of the *mizmor,* ending with וּבִנְבִיאַי אַל תָּרֵעוּ, reflects upon our nation's ancient history.

In saying הוֹדוּ, the composer, Dovid HaMelech, is addressing the entire Jewish nation: זֶרַע יִשְׂרָאֵל עַבְדּוֹ, as mentioned four *pesukim* later, to whom he says, *Thank Hashem, call out His Name, and make the nations know of His deeds.*

We have already explained that הוֹדוּ or מוֹדֶה comes from the word הוֹדָאָה, which means *an admission.* In thanking *HaKadosh Baruch Hu,* we "admit" that we could never possibly repay Him for all of His benevolence to us. (See earlier, on אֱלֹהַי נְשָׁמָה.)

The feeling of gratitude is not inborn in a person. For example, when we give candy to a child, his mother has to remind him to say "thank you." A human being does not have an innate sense of gratitude. From the time the child is born, he receives everything from his parents, and takes it all for granted. No child will instinctively thank its mother for its food. The sense of gratitude must be taught, and it then develops further through the maturing process.

Strikingly, the *chachamim* who instituted מוֹדִים דְּרַבָּנָן ended it with the words: עַל שֶׁאֲנַחְנוּ מוֹדִים לָךְ, which means literally, *we thank You for the fact that we thank You.* This is explained by Rashi to mean: עַל שֶׁנָּתַתָּ בְּלִבֵּנוּ לִהְיוֹת מוֹדִים לָךְ, *For putting in our hearts the sense of being grateful to You* (*Sotah* 40a). Were it not for this, we could go through life without any feeling of gratitude to *HaKadosh Baruch Hu* for giving us life and benevolence. This would be analogous to a baby which has finished nursing, and then simply turns away and disregards its mother until it feels hungry again. This is what is meant when the *navi* Yeshayahu calls the Jewish nation גְּמוּלֵי מֵחָלָב עַתִּיקֵי מִשָּׁדָיִם, *Those who are weaned of milk, and have outgrown the breasts* (*Yeshayahu* 28:9); meaning, like a thoughtless infant, you have no sense of gratitude to *HaKadosh Baruch Hu* for giving you life. The moment you are satisfied, you turn away from Him.

So the idea of הוֹדוּ לַה׳ is that we are constantly to remind ourselves not to take life, or anything that we receive, for granted. We attach ourselves to *HaKadosh Baruch Hu* by acknowledging that we are indebted to Him for our lives, and that He is the source of everything we have.

The words קִרְאוּ בִשְׁמוֹ are based on *Bereishis* (12:8) in connection with Avraham Avinu: וַיִּקְרָא בְּשֵׁם ה׳, which is usually translated, *He called out the Name of Hashem,* meaning, he proclaimed the existence of *HaKadosh Baruch Hu* to the world. However, Rav Samson R. Hirsch points out that וַיִּקְרָא בְּשֵׁם ה׳ really means, *He called everything by the Name of Hashem,* meaning that he proclaimed to the world that everything that exists was created by *HaKadosh Baruch Hu.*

And after we have absorbed the idea of הוֹדָאָה in our own minds, we are to teach it to the world. So, קִרְאוּ בִשְׁמוֹ הוֹדִיעוּ בָעַמִּים עֲלִילֹתָיו means: "Tell the world that everything that exists was created by *HaKadosh Baruch Hu,* and also make His great deeds known among the nations." This is the source of the Jewish custom to punctuate our speech with phrases like *Baruch Hashem, b'ezras Hashem,* and *im yirtzeh Hashem.*

The foremost of the עֲלִילֹתָיו, the great deeds of *HaKadosh Baruch Hu,* which we, the Jewish people, should proclaim every day, is the miracle of our existence and survival in a hostile world. This is what is meant when we say מוֹדִים דְּרַבָּנָן in עַל שֶׁהֶחֱיִיתָנוּ וְקִיַּמְתָּנוּ.

This is especially important in our Holocaust remembrances. In addition to mourning the great *churban* (destruction) of the recent past, these remembrances should focus on the miracle of our survival, rather than the negative — that of the terrible and unprecedented atrocities which were committed against us. For individuals like myself, who were in extreme mortal danger, we should never forget the *nissim* and *niflaos* connected with our escape. And for the nation as a whole, we should constantly remind ourselves and the world of the miraculous survival and revitalization of our people in the wake of the unspeakable horrors which we suffered. It is this aspect — the indestructibility of the Jewish nation — that we should publicize and keep ever fresh in the world's eyes, כִּי גָבַר עָלֵינוּ חַסְדּוֹ, and this is what is meant by הוֹדִיעוּ בָעַמִּים עֲלִילֹתָיו.

As to remembrances alone, I doubt very much if any present or future evil-minded *rasha* would be deterred from attempting to harm the Jewish nation simply because the atrocities of the Holocaust are kept ever fresh in the world's eyes.

§ שִׁירוּ לוֹ זַמְּרוּ לוֹ שִׂיחוּ בְּכָל נִפְלְאֹתָיו — **Sing to Him, make music to Him, speak of all His wondrous deeds.** Make it a topic of your conversation with the nations. We have already discussed the broader meaning of *shirah* and *zimrah* in our introduction.

§ הִתְהַלְלוּ בְּשֵׁם קָדְשׁוֹ — **Glory in His holy Name.** This is reflexive. Literally, it means *praise yourselves with His holy Name.* We pride ourselves with the knowledge that *HaKadosh Baruch Hu* is in our midst. This is similar to, אַל יִתְהַלֵּל חָכָם בְּחָכְמָתוֹ וְאַל יִתְהַלֵּל הַגִּבּוֹר בִּגְבוּרָתוֹ אַל יִתְהַלֵּל עָשִׁיר בְּעָשְׁרוֹ. כִּי אִם בְּזֹאת יִתְהַלֵּל הַמִּתְהַלֵּל הַשְׂכֵּל וְיָדֹעַ אוֹתִי וגו', *Let not a wise man praise himself for his wisdom, nor a powerful person for his power, nor a rich person for his riches. Rather, by this shall one pride himself: intelligently knowing of My existence* etc. (*Yirmiyahu* 9:22). Neither a wise man nor a powerful rich person can pride himself with his material accomplishments, for they are not of his own doing. Rather, they are gifts from *HaKadosh Baruch Hu.* However, if a person reaches the level of הַשְׂכֵּל וְיָדֹעַ אוֹתִי, when — after diligent effort — he has achieved a spiritual level of coming close to *HaKadosh Baruch Hu,* this, indeed, is something of which he can be proud.

§ יִשְׂמַח לֵב מְבַקְשֵׁי ה' — **So that the hearts of those who seek Hashem shall be gladdened.** There are many people in the world, Jews as well as non-Jews, who are utterly disgusted with the type of world they live in. They are looking for meaning in their lives. These people are seeking Hashem, some consciously, and some subconsciously. They are called מְבַקְשֵׁי ה', *those who seek God.*

I highly recommend a fascinating article detailing the metamorphosis of a Japanese man who subsequently became a *ger tzedek,* and eventually a member of the Kollel Gur Aryeh of Yeshivah Rabbi Chaim Berlin. He describes the trials and tribulations of his beginnings as an atheist, then as an agnostic, then a Christian. Turning to Judaism, he first became "Reform," then "Conservative," until he finally became a true *ben Torah.* He was a real *mevakeish Hashem,* similar to the many thousands of *baalei teshuvah* who are finding their way into our ranks.

[Ed. note: This article appeared in the January 1992 issue of the *Jewish Observer*: "Elisha Eisan, A Straight Path."]

What causes us to feel happy and proud is our relationship with *HaKadosh Baruch Hu,* and not our superiority in any other way to the rest of the world. When we are מִתְהַלֵּל בְּשֵׁם קָדְשׁוֹ, this brings us joy, and this is what attracts the *mevakshei Hashem* to us. They yearn to feel this happiness.

If this is true among non-Jews, how much more so does it apply to our own nation. Among the five or six million American Jews — most of whom are to be considered as if they were תִּינוֹקוֹת שֶׁנִּשְׁבּוּ לְבֵין הָעכּוּ״ם (captured among idolaters since infancy) — there are tens of thousands of *mevakshei Hashem*, people who are searching for Hashem. We have a responsibility to them, to present ourselves and our lifestyle in a manner which is attractive to the potential *baal teshuvah,* and thereby encourage them to fulfill their yearnings and come close to *HaKadosh Baruch Hu.*

This is what is meant by הִתְהַלְלוּ בְּשֵׁם קָדְשׁוֹ: By priding ourselves on a life that focuses on the holy Name of *HaKadosh Baruch Hu,* and by living our lives in accordance with His will, we will encourage others, especially those who are searching for Him, to come close to Him and thereby gladden their hearts — יִשְׂמַח לֵב מְבַקְשֵׁי ה׳.

§ דִּרְשׁוּ ה׳ וְעֻזּוֹ — **Seek Hashem and His strength.** According to *Ramban* (*Bereishis* 25:22), לִדְרוֹשׁ ה׳ means *tefillah*. And *Shir HaShirim Rabbah* 2:3:3 comments that עוֹז means Torah. The meaning, then, would be that if we seek Hashem, there are two ways to come close to Him, either through *tefillah* or *talmud Torah.*

§ בַּקְּשׁוּ פָנָיו תָּמִיד — **Seek His Presence always.** The term בַּקֵּשׁ פָּנִים means to look at someone's face and see what he needs. (In German, there is an expression: *"Einen ein wunsch aus den Augen ablesen,"* meaning, "To read a person's wish from his eyes.") If one is eager to please another, he can just look at his face and see what he needs. If his friend looks hungry, or tired, or sad, he will offer him some food or shelter, or perhaps cheer him up. So the meaning here is, "constantly seek ways to please *HaKadosh Baruch Hu.*"

§ זִכְרוּ נִפְלְאֹתָיו אֲשֶׁר עָשָׂה מֹפְתָיו וּמִשְׁפְּטֵי פִיהוּ — **Remember His wonders that He has done, His marvels, and the judgments of His mouth.** And all these aforesaid inspirational exhortations are directed to:

§ זֶרַע יִשְׂרָאֵל עַבְדּוֹ בְּנֵי יַעֲקֹב בְּחִירָיו. הוּא ה׳ אֱלֹהֵינוּ בְּכָל הָאָרֶץ מִשְׁפָּטָיו — **O seed of Israel, His servant, O children of Yaakov, His chosen ones. He is Hashem our God, over all the earth are His judgments.** We look at the world with the knowledge that מֶלֶךְ בְּמִשְׁפָּט יַעֲמִיד אָרֶץ, *Through justice a king establishes a land* (*Mishlei* 29:4).

§ זִכְרוּ לְעוֹלָם בְּרִיתוֹ דָּבָר צִוָּה לְאֶלֶף דּוֹר — **Remember His covenant forever, the word He commanded for a thousand generations.** The simple meaning here is that this דָּבָר, the Torah, was commanded to us for all time to come.

However, *Chazal* tell us that the Torah was originally meant to be given after one thousand generations, but *HaKadosh Baruch Hu* chose instead to give it after only twenty-six (*Chagigah* 14a).

🙠 אֲשֶׁר כָּרַת אֶת אַבְרָהָם וּשְׁבוּעָתוֹ לְיִצְחָק. וַיַּעֲמִידֶהָ לְיַעֲקֹב לְחֹק לְיִשְׂרָאֵל בְּרִית עוֹלָם 🙢 — **That he made with Avraham and His vow to Yitzchak. Then He established it for Yaakov as a statute, for Israel as an everlasting covenant.** This covenant and oath which *HaKadosh Baruch Hu* made to our forefathers was eventually realized, permanently, in their offspring Yisrael, the Jewish nation.

🙠 לֵאמֹר — **Saying.** And this promise was:

🙠 לְךָ אֶתֵּן אֶרֶץ כְּנַעַן חֶבֶל נַחֲלַתְכֶם 🙢 — **I shall give to you the land of Canaan, the territorial region of your inheritance.** Formerly, territory was measured and subdivided by means of a חֶבֶל, *string*, for accurate delineation.

In summarizing our ancient history, we first of all announce to the world that Eretz Yisrael belongs to us, through a covenant which was granted to us by *HaKadosh Baruch Hu*. This is לְיַעֲקֹב לְיִשְׂרָאֵל בְּרִית עוֹלָם. It applies regardless of who claims sovereignty to this land, be it the Romans, the Ottoman Turks, or the British; and is irrespective of whether we have a Jewish state. The fact of the matter is that this land is rightfully ours by the grant of *HaKadosh Baruch Hu*. Unfortunately, the world has not accepted this. Nevertheless, the fact is that every part of Eretz Yisrael belongs to us by right.

And this land of ours has *kedushah*: Every blade of grass, every pebble of sand in Eretz Yisrael is holy. Anything that grows in this land is subject to the *halachos* of *terumah, maaser, orlah,* and *kilayim*. If a person just walks there, he is fulfilling a *mitzvah* (*Kesubos* 111a). Since we hold this land in such high regard, as a gift from *HaKadosh Baruch Hu,* one should not complain about bad weather or other natural inconveniences there. In Eretz Yisrael, everything is good. It is אֶרֶץ חֶמְדָּה טוֹבָה וּרְחָבָה שֶׁהִנְחַלְתָּ לַאֲבוֹתֵינוּ, *the desirable, good, and broad land, which You have given as an inheritance to our Forefathers.*

We must know that there is a vast difference between a "state" and a "land." Historically, our statehood was constantly contested. Even after we had conquered Eretz Yisrael, Nevuchadnezzar and the Babylonians waged wars against us. Then the Persians, the Greeks, and the Romans followed suit. Today it is contested by the Arabs.

However, all this does not change the fact that from the time *HaKadosh Baruch Hu* gave Avraham Avinu the land, all of it belongs to us. Yerushalayim is our city, and the *makom haMikdash* (the Temple Mount) belongs to us. The world will not recognize this fact as long as there is a *galus*. When *HaKadosh Baruch Hu* sees fit to bring the final *geulah* and end the *galus,* the world will recognize our sovereignty over the land.

∽§ בִּהְיוֹתְכֶם מְתֵי מִסְפָּר — **When you were but few in number.** We find Yaakov Avinu using the expression, וַאֲנִי מְתֵי מִסְפָּר, *I am few in number* (*Bereishis* 34:30).

∽§ כִּמְעַט וְגָרִים בָּהּ — **Hardly dwelling there.** And you remained there only a short while, and even then, you were strangers in it. Although the land already belonged to us, we were still only few in number and treated as strangers in it.

∽§ וַיִּתְהַלְּכוּ מִגּוֹי אֶל גּוֹי וּמִמַּמְלָכָה אֶל עַם אַחֵר — **And,** notwithstanding their ownership of Eretz Canaan, **they wandered from nation to nation, from one kingdom to another.** Our Forefathers traveled from Aram to Mitzrayim to the land of Pelishtim, and then to the *galus Mitzrayim,* before returning to claim our land.

∽§ לֹא הִנִּיחַ לְאִישׁ לְעָשְׁקָם — **He did not permit any man to oppress them.** This refers to Lavan and Eisav, who wanted to harm Yaakov.

∽§ וַיּוֹכַח עֲלֵיהֶם מְלָכִים — **And He admonished kings concerning them.** This refers to Avimelech and Pharaoh, who wanted to harm Avraham and Yitzchak.

∽§ אַל תִּגְּעוּ בִמְשִׁיחָי וּבִנְבִיאַי אַל תָּרֵעוּ — The warning which *HaKadosh Baruch Hu* issued to the potential oppressors of our Forefathers was: **Do not touch My "anointed ones," and to My prophets do no harm.** The word מָשִׁיחַ, *anointed,* usually refers to a king or to a *Kohen Gadol,* who was anointed with oil. However, the actual meaning of the word is *distinguished.* Anointing someone with a drop of oil on the forehead was a symbolic gesture, commanded by the Torah, for the *Kohen Gadol* or the king as a sign of distinction.

We find the word מָשַׁח used in the sense of "distinction," in connection with the *matnos Kehunah,* the gifts which belong to the *Kohanim* as an honorarium: לְךָ נְתַתִּים לְמָשְׁחָה וּלְבָנֶיךָ לְחָק עוֹלָם, *I have given them to you and to your sons as a sign of distinction* (*Bamidbar* 18:8). We also find this word used in connection with the Persian king, Cyrus: כֹּה אָמַר ה׳ לִמְשִׁיחוֹ לְכוֹרֶשׁ, *Thus has God said to His anointed one, to Koresh* (*Yeshayahu* 45:1). The word is also used here in the sense of *distinguished.*

So אַל תִּגְּעוּ בִמְשִׁיחָי וּבִנְבִיאַי אַל תָּרֵעוּ means, "Don't touch or harm those whom I have distinguished." This refers to the *Avos,* who were also *Neviim,* and their children, all of whom were under the special protection of *HaKadosh Baruch Hu* in a hostile environment.

However, the Gemara says that this phrase has an additional meaning: אַל תִּגְּעוּ בִמְשִׁיחָי refers to תִּינוֹקוֹת שֶׁל בֵּית רַבָּן, *children who learn Torah* (*Shabbos* 119b). The purest *talmud Torah* that exists is that of children who have never sinned. And even if they have committed certain wrongful acts, these are not considered *aveiros,* because they are not yet held responsible for them. The Gemara (ibid.) states further, אֵין הָעוֹלָם מִתְקַיֵּם אֶלָּא בִּשְׁבִיל הֶבֶל תִּינוֹקוֹת שֶׁל בֵּית רַבָּן, *The world exists only because of the merit of the breath of children who are learning.* These little children are the מְשִׁיחָי, our *distinguished ones.*

The second part of this phrase, וּבִנְבִיאַי אַל תָּרֵעוּ, refers to *talmidei chachamim* (ibid.). This means that the Torah that they learn is the result of the *nevuah* received through Moshe Rabbeinu, which was then transmitted to the *Neviim,* and handed down further to the *talmidei chachamim,* who themselves were inspired by a prophetic spirit.

Inherent in this *pasuk* is a warning to the nations of the world: "Don't touch My *talmidei chachamim* in miniature, the little children who are learning Torah, nor My fully matured *talmidei chachamim,* who are the leaders of My people." Each of My children is a potential *Mashiach,* and each of My *talmidei chachamim* is a potential *Navi.*

As we previously explained, this *pasuk* completes the first part of הוֹדוּ. Here we give thanks to *HaKadosh Baruch Hu* for His protection, from the very beginning of our nation, in a hostile world. Despite the fact that we were only כִּמְעַט, and וַיִּתְהַלְּכוּ מִגּוֹי אֶל גּוֹי, we survived as His people — לֹא הִנִּיחַ לְאִישׁ לְעָשְׁקָם. And since this part of the *mizmor* deals with the early history of our nation, it was appropriate that it was sung by the *Leviim* at the time of the morning *tamid* offering — which corresponds to the "morning" of our existence — as is described in the aforementioned *Seder Olam.*

§ שִׁירוּ לַה' כָּל הָאָרֶץ — **Sing to Hashem, everyone on earth.** This begins the second part of this *mizmor,* which refers to the remote future of our nation and the world. We have previously pointed out that the first part of הוֹדוּ, with some slight variations, is found in *Tehillim* 105 and, similarly, much of this second part is found in *Tehillim* 96.

Here the Psalmist calls upon all the inhabitants of the world: *Sing to Hashem.*

§ בַּשְּׂרוּ מִיּוֹם אֶל יוֹם יְשׁוּעָתוֹ — **Spread the good news, from day to day, about His salvation.** Rav Samson R. Hirsch (ibid.) explains that there is a form of salvation by *HaKadosh Baruch Hu,* which occurs every day, and that is the continuation of life. Unless we "spread the news," we would tend to forget about this daily *yeshuah.*

§ סַפְּרוּ בַגּוֹיִם אֶת כְּבוֹדוֹ, בְּכָל הָעַמִּים נִפְלְאוֹתָיו — **Relate His glory among the nations, among all the peoples His wonders.** There is a difference between גּוֹיִם and עַמִּים. Rav Hirsch explains that the word גּוֹי is related to גֵּו, *gav,* and גּוּף, *guf,* and refers to a nation as a political body, while עַם comes from the word עִם, which means the society, or "togetherness" of people. One is a political term, and the other an ethnic or social term.

⋄§ כִּי גָדוֹל ה' וּמְהֻלָּל מְאֹד וְנוֹרָא הוּא עַל כָּל אֱלֹהִים §⋄ — Continue to tell the world that **Hashem is great and highly praised, and He is feared above all gods.** Eventually the time will come when all the strange religions and concepts of gods will disappear, and the nations of the world will be afraid to apply the term "god" to that which they formerly worshiped.

⋄§ כִּי כָּל אֱלֹהֵי הָעַמִּים אֱלִילִים §⋄ — **For all the gods of the peoples are nothings.** Because all the gods in which the nations believed proved to be "nonentities." The word אֱלִילִים is comprised of אַל and לֹא, literally meaning "no-no gods."

⋄§ וַה' שָׁמַיִם עָשָׂה §⋄ — **Because Hashem made heaven.** These heavens, to which they always looked as the habitat of their gods and saints, were made by *HaKadosh Baruch Hu,* the Creator and Ruler of the world.

⋄§ הוֹד וְהָדָר לְפָנָיו §⋄ — **Glory and majesty are before Him.** Do not look for dignity or beauty from any other source anymore, for these attributes are only His. Historically, people who aspired to satisfy their intellectual capacity, or their artistic ability, were drawn to various forms of religious worship. In this *mizmor*, we tell the world: All of your intellectual religious yearnings and desires can be satisfied by coming לְפָנָיו, before *HaKadosh Baruch Hu.*

⋄§ עֹז וְחֶדְוָה בִּמְקֹמוֹ. הָבוּ לַה' מִשְׁפְּחוֹת עַמִּים, הָבוּ לַה' כָּבוֹד וָעֹז §⋄ — **Might and delight are in His place. Give to Hashem, O families of the peoples, give to Hashem honor and might.** The honor and power in world affairs, which you, the combined "family of nations," the superpowers, had considered as yours, actually belong to *HaKadosh Baruch Hu.* "Give it to Hashem" means that the honor and power is not yours, but it is His.

⋄§ הָבוּ לַה' כְּבוֹד שְׁמוֹ §⋄ — **Give to Him the glory and honor.** It is rightfully His.

⋄§ שְׂאוּ מִנְחָה וּבֹאוּ לְפָנָיו, הִשְׁתַּחֲווּ לַה' בְּהַדְרַת קֹדֶשׁ §⋄ — **Carry a tribute and come before Him. Prostrate yourselves before Hashem in the beauty of the Sanctuary.** These two phrases refer to the *Beis HaMikdash* of the future. The *Neviim* speak of the time when the entire world will come streaming to the *Beis HaMikdash* to worship *HaKadosh Baruch Hu.* We find such *pesukim* as: וְהָיָה בְּאַחֲרִית הַיָּמִים נָכוֹן יִהְיֶה הַר בֵּית ה' וגו' וְנָהֲרוּ אֵלָיו כָּל הַגּוֹיִם, *It will happen in the end of days: The mountain of the Temple of Hashem will be firmly established . . . and all the nations will stream to it (Yeshayahu 2:2)*; וּבְנֵי הַנֵּכָר הַנִּלְוִים עַל ה' לְשָׁרְתוֹ וגו' וַהֲבִיאוֹתִים אֶל הַר קָדְשִׁי וגו' כִּי בֵיתִי בֵּית תְּפִלָּה יִקָּרֵא לְכָל הָעַמִּים, *And the foreigners who join themselves to Hashem to serve Him . . . and I will bring them to My holy mountain . . . for My house will be called a house of prayer for all the peoples* (ibid. 56:6-7).

Those nations that will remain and be *zocheh* to recognize *HaKadosh Baruch Hu* as the One and Only Creator — God of the universe — will come before Him in the future *Beis HaMikdash* to pay homage to Him.

Chazal tell us: אַל תִּקְרֵי "בְּהַדְרַת" אֶלָּא "בְּחֶרְדַּת" קֹדֶשׁ, *Read not (only) the "beauty" of holiness, but (also) the "trembling" of holiness* (*Berachos* 30b). This means that the *Beis HaMikdash* is not merely a place of beauty which satisfies man's aesthetic sense, but it is also the place where the highest form of fear and trembling before *HaKadosh Baruch Hu* occurs.

חִילוּ מִלְּפָנָיו כָּל הָאָרֶץ, אַף תִּכּוֹן תֵּבֵל בַּל תִּמּוֹט — **Tremble before Him all the inhabitants of the earth, so that the world of mankind shall also be firmly established and will no longer sway.** Rav Samson R. Hirsch says that the word חִיל is always used in the sense of חִיל כַּיּוֹלֵדָה, *the travail of childbirth*. It is used here to describe the "labor pangs" of the world before it gives birth to a new world order, that of ה' יִמְלֹךְ לְעוֹלָם וָעֶד, in which everyone will recognize the sovereignty of *HaKadosh Baruch Hu*. The word תֵּבֵל means the earth occupied by humanity. So the meaning here is: Once the trembling and travail of the rebirth of society is over, when all wars will cease, and crime and violence will be relegated to history, when peace is firmly established throughout the world — as is so beautifully portrayed in the verse, לֹא יָרֵעוּ וְלֹא יַשְׁחִיתוּ בְּכָל הַר קָדְשִׁי כִּי מָלְאָה הָאָרֶץ דֵּעָה אֶת ה' כַּמַּיִם לַיָּם מְכַסִּים, *They will neither injure nor destroy in all of My sacred mountain; for the earth will be as filled with knowledge of Hashem as water covering the seabed* (*Yeshayahu* 11:9) — once this "rebirth" takes place, the world of humanity, תֵּבֵל, will never again waver and revert to its previous corrupt world order — בַּל תִּמּוֹט.

יִשְׂמְחוּ הַשָּׁמַיִם וְתָגֵל הָאָרֶץ — **The heavens will be glad and the earth will rejoice.** At the time of the "new world order," there will be abundant joy, both in the spiritual world, הַשָּׁמַיִם, and the physical world, הָאָרֶץ. The first letters of these four words form the acrostic of the full שֵׁם הֲוָיָה, **the Ineffable Name.** However, until mankind reaches this point in world history, and as long as the power of Amalek is still influential in the world, the Name of *HaKadosh Baruch Hu* and His Throne will be "incomplete." נִשְׁבַּע הקב"ה שֶׁאֵין שְׁמוֹ שָׁלֵם וְאֵין כִּסְאוֹ שָׁלֵם עַד שֶׁיִּמָּחֶה שְׁמוֹ שֶׁל עֲמָלֵק כֻּלּוֹ, וּכְשֶׁיִּמָּחֶה שְׁמוֹ יִהְיֶה הַשֵּׁם שָׁלֵם, *HaKadosh Baruch Hu swore that His Name is not whole nor is His Throne whole until the name of Amalek is completely eradicated and when [Amalek's] Name is eradicated the Name will be whole* (see *Rashi, Shemos* 17:16). Then, when the power of Amalek is finally eradicated, and the world will have reached its goal of כִּי מָלְאָה הָאָרֶץ דֵּעָה אֶת ה', *the earth will be filled with knowledge of Hashem* (*Yeshayahu* 11:9), the Name of *HaKadosh Baruch Hu* will be complete, and abundant joy will fill all of creation.

וְיֹאמְרוּ בַגּוֹיִם, ה' מָלָךְ — **And it will be said among the nations: "God reigns!"** That which was predicted by the Jewish prophets, and believed by their people for so long, will then have become a reality.

And now the Psalmist waxes joyfully poetic in his description of that future time:

❧ יִרְעַם הַיָּם וּמְלֹאוֹ, יַעֲלֹז שָׂדַי וְכָל אֲשֶׁר בּוֹ ❧ — **The ocean, and all that fills it, will roar;** cultivated **fields, and everything in them, will frolic.**

❧ אָז יְרַנְּנוּ עֲצֵי הַיָּעַר ❧ — **The trees of the forest,** referring to the uncultivated part of nature on earth, **will also jubilate at that time.**

❧ מִלִּפְנֵי ה' כִּי בָא לִשְׁפּוֹט אֶת הָאָרֶץ ❧ — **Before Hashem, for He will have arrived to judge the earth.** All of creation is celebrating. Hashem has come to judge the world. The word לִשְׁפּוֹט is related to שָׁפַט, which means to put something into order. A judge puts order into the society. It is used here in the sense of restoring order to nature. At the time when the reign of *HaKadosh Baruch Hu* is recognized by all of humanity, even nature will be put back in order. All of the ecological damage done by man, by his selfish mismanagement of nature — which has polluted the air and water, destroyed so many species of animals, and damaged the ozone layer which protects us against the harmful effects of the sun — will be restored. The entire natural world will celebrate its return to its original pristine condition.

The Psalmist concludes this *mizmor* — with its beautiful picture of the restoration of the spiritual and physical world — and exclaims:

❧ הוֹדוּ לַה' כִּי טוֹב כִּי לְעוֹלָם חַסְדּוֹ ❧ — **Give thanks to Hashem for He is good, for His lovingkindness is forever.** Praise Hashem, because this total harmony of mankind and nature is due to the reign of the *Malchus Shamayim* (the Kingdom of Heaven), which will last forever.

That which the whole world has now finally seen was proclaimed by Yisrael throughout its history, although the reign of Hashem was not apparent then. יֹאמַר נָא יִשְׂרָאֵל כִּי לְעוֹלָם חַסְדּוֹ, *Say it now* (נָא means "now"), *O Israel, that His lovingkindness is forever* (*Tehillim* 118:2). *Bnei Yisrael* and the *yirei Hashem* had always held the firm conviction of כִּי לְעוֹלָם חַסְדּוֹ. The rest of the world has now finally come to experience it.

However, the Psalmist realizes that this ideal situation is not yet at hand, so in the meantime, before closing the *mizmor,* he returns to actuality, and says to Yisrael:

❧ וְאִמְרוּ הוֹשִׁיעֵנוּ אֱלֹהֵי יִשְׁעֵנוּ ❧ — **And say: Save us, O God of our salvation.** This utopian world just portrayed is far away. So for now, you, Yisrael, say to *HaKadosh Baruch Hu,* "Help us now, our God, Who has saved us in the past." You have proven Yourself to us in the past as אֱלֹהֵי יִשְׁעֵנוּ, *God of our salvation.*

❧ וְקַבְּצֵנוּ וְהַצִּילֵנוּ מִן הַגּוֹיִם לְהֹדוֹת לְשֵׁם קָדְשֶׁךָ, לְהִשְׁתַּבֵּחַ בִּתְהִלָּתֶךָ ❧ — **Gather us and rescue us from the nations, to thank Your holy Name and to glory in Your praise.** We thank *HaKadosh Baruch Hu* for the fact that we can exist among hostile nations. And we pride ourselves in that we are privileged to recognize *HaKadosh Baruch Hu* as the Source of our salvation, and therefore express His praises.

There is a very similar *pasuk* in *Tehillim* 106:47, which is incorporated in *Maariv*: הוֹשִׁיעֵנוּ ה' אֱלֹהֵינוּ וְקַבְּצֵנוּ מִן הַגּוֹיִם לְהוֹדוֹת לְשֵׁם קָדְשֶׁךָ לְהִשְׁתַּבֵּחַ בִּתְהִלָּתֶךָ, *Save us Hashem, our God, and gather us from among the peoples, to thank Your holy Name and to glory in Your praise.* There, the word וְהַצִּילֵנוּ is omitted, because that chapter of *Tehillim* describes a time when *Bnei Yisrael* has already been dispersed in the Diaspora among the nations, and are therefore asking *HaKadosh Baruch Hu* to "gather us in," and bring us back from this *galus*.

However, when Dovid HaMelech composed this *mizmor,* and asked Asaf and the other *Leviim* to sing it daily in front of the *Aron Kodesh* in conjunction with the twilight *tamid,* the Jewish nation was not in *galus*. But this *tefillah* is a plea to *HaKadosh Baruch Hu* to "bring us together" from the great hostility and discord that prevailed among the *shevatim,* as is described throughout *Shoftim* and *Melachim,* such as the great tragedies of *Pilegesh b'Givah* (see *Shoftim* Chs. 19-21) and in the secession of the ten tribes, which resulted in the two kingdoms of Yisrael and Yehudah. Likewise, during the reign of Dovid, there was the war between the tribes of Binyamin and Yehudah. Such disunity has a great weakening effect on the entire nation, and leaves us vulnerable to being attacked by our enemies. So here Dovid is asking *HaKadosh Baruch Hu* to unify the Jewish People, קַבְּצֵנוּ, to gather us together, which will strengthen us, and thereby הַצִּילֵנוּ מִן הַגּוֹיִם, save us and protect us from any evil intentions that other nations may have against us. This is certainly very relevant to our time.

The Psalmist then ends with:

בָּרוּךְ ה' אֱלֹהֵי יִשְׂרָאֵל מִן הָעוֹלָם וְעַד הָעֹלָם — **Blessed is Hashem, the God of Yisrael, from "World to World."** As we have previously explained, עוֹלָם, which is usually translated as *forever,* comes from נֶעְלָם, meaning *hidden*. The details concerning the obscure, early past of our people, and its distant future, which are the subjects of this *mizmor,* are matters to which we are not privy. So Dovid HaMelech concludes this psalm by recognizing that *HaKadosh Baruch Hu,* Who was the source of the blessings of our nation "forever," meaning at its early beginnings, will continue to be the source of our *berachah* forever — literally, "from the hidden beginnings to the hidden end."

וַיֹּאמְרוּ כָל הָעָם אָמֵן וְהַלֵּל לַה' — **And the entire assemblage said: "Amen and praise to Hashem!"** We are told in *Divrei HaYamim I* 16:36 that after this *mizmor* was completed, the entire assemblage who had heard it responded with אָמֵן וְהַלֵּל לַה׳. We find a similar *pasuk* in *Tehillim* (106:48) which, however, ends with אָמֵן הַלְלוּיָהּ.

The *Gemara* (*Pesachim* 117a) tells us that the word הַלְלוּיָהּ is the highest term for the praise of *HaKadosh Baruch Hu* found in *Tehillim*. בַּעֲשָׂרָה מַאֲמָרוֹת שֶׁל שֶׁבַח נֶאֱמַר סֵפֶר תְּהִלִּים וכו׳ גָּדוֹל מִכּוּלָן הַלְלוּיָהּ, *There are ten expressions of praise etc. in Tehillim, but* הַלְלוּיָהּ *is the greatest of them all*, שֶׁכּוֹלֵל שֵׁם וָשֶׁבַח בְּבַת אֶחָת, *because it is a combination of a Name of HaKadosh Baruch Hu* [*which is* יָהּ] *and praise, all in one word*.

This can be understood in view of our earlier explanation that the word הַלֵּל really means *to reflect light*. (See מֶלֶךְ מְהֻלָּל בַּתִּשְׁבָּחוֹת, end of *Baruch She'amar*.) By using this term to praise *HaKadosh Baruch Hu*, we express the thought that if we lead our lives in accordance with His will, as a *tzelem Elokim*, we ourselves are reflective of *HaKadosh Baruch Hu*. Our "praises" to *HaKadosh Baruch Hu* are analogous to an image in a mirror, which is a "picture" of the source of the reflection. Similarly, ideally, our lives are to be a reflection of Him. Literally, then, הַלְלוּיָהּ means *a reflection of God*. We "praise" Him by saying: "We wish to live our lives in accordance with His will." Therefore, the word הַלְלוּיָהּ itself expresses Divinity, and has *kedushah*, because it represents the idea of the reflection of *HaKadosh Baruch Hu* in our lives.

We have now concluded this opening *mizmor* which *Dovid HaMelech* instituted for daily recital by the *Leviim* in conjunction with the *korban Tamid*, while the *Aron HaKodesh* was in its special tent.

As we previously explained in בָּרוּךְ שֶׁאָמַר, the *Pesukei d'Zimrah* are divided into five sections, namely, נְגַדֶּלְךָ; נְשַׁבֵּחֲךָ; נְפָאֶרְךָ; נַזְכִּיר שִׁמְךָ; וְנַמְלִיכְךָ מַלְכֵּנוּ אֱלֹהֵינוּ יָחִיד. The following *pesukim*, beginning with רוֹמְמוּ ה׳ אֱלֹהֵינוּ, start the נְגַדֶּלְךָ section.

We previously pointed out the difficulty in translating the word נְגַדֶּלְךָ as *we wish to make You great*. We therefore took the word in its alternate sense, that of combining small units into one large mass, as in גָּדוֹל שֵׂעָר, which means the plaiting or braiding of hair, or intertwining strands into a larger unit, similar to a cord formed of several strands twisted together. (See *Devarim* 22:12, גְּדִלִים, and *Melachim I* 7:17.)

In this section of *Pesukei d'Zimrah* we shall see how various *pesukim* expressing similar ideas, but from different perspectives, are combined as גְּדִלִים [*g'dilim*], cords, in which each "cord" expresses a unique form of praise to *HaKadosh Baruch Hu*, corresponding to נְגַדֶּלְךָ in בָּרוּךְ שֶׁאָמַר.

We start with the following two *pesukim*, which are taken from *Tehillim* 99 and are combined here, although they are not contiguous in *Tehillim*:

רוֹמְמוּ ה׳ אֱלֹהֵינוּ וְהִשְׁתַּחֲווּ לַהֲדֹם רַגְלָיו, קָדוֹשׁ הוּא — **Elevate Hashem, our God, and prostrate yourselves at His footstool; He is holy!**

HODU 143

רוֹמְמוּ ה׳ אֱלֹהֵינוּ וְהִשְׁתַּחֲווּ לְהַר קָדְשׁוֹ כִּי קָדוֹשׁ ה׳ אֱלֹהֵינוּ — **Exalt Hashem, our God, and bow at His holy mountain, for holy is Hashem, our God.**

These two *pesukim* have the same beginnings and similar endings, but differ as to the object of the "bowing." The word הִשְׁתַּחֲוֶה does not mean simply to bend down before something — this would be כּוֹרֵעַ — but rather to prostrate oneself fully on the ground, with arms and legs outstretched, as a sign of one's total subservience. The Gemara (*Shevuos* 16b) calls this פִּשׁוּט יָדַיִם וְרַגְלַיִם (the spreading out of arms and legs) and, ideally, should be done on Yom Kippur in commemoration of the *avodah* of Yom Kippur in the *Beis HaMikdash*. Usually, however, in a *shul*, the constraints of space make this very difficult for the entire congregation; nevertheless the *shaliach tzibbur* certainly should do so.

By laying flat on the ground, one symbolically expresses *bitul ha'yeish*, the complete negation of his own ego. By doing so, the person is expressing the thought that: "Compared to You, HaKadosh Baruch Hu, I am nothing, I am equivalent to the ground." So, in a manner of speaking, the more one gives up of himself, vis-a-vis HaKadosh Baruch Hu, the more "elevated" He becomes. And the more the human being is conscious of his own importance, the less elevated HaKadosh Baruch Hu becomes, so to speak.

The first *pasuk*, רוֹמְמוּ ה׳ אֱלֹהֵינוּ וְהִשְׁתַּחֲווּ לַהֲדֹם רַגְלָיו, קָדוֹשׁ הוּא, is directed toward mankind in general: *Elevate Hashem, our God, in your mind, and express it by prostrating yourselves at His footstool, because He is holy.* "Holy" means He is higher than the mind can grasp. The term הֲדֹם רַגְלָיו refers to the earth, as in הַשָּׁמַיִם כִּסְאִי וְהָאָרֶץ הֲדֹם רַגְלָי, *The heaven is My throne and the earth is My footstool* (*Yeshayahu* 66:1).

However, the second *pasuk*, ending with וְהִשְׁתַּחֲווּ לְהַר קָדְשׁוֹ כִּי קָדוֹשׁ ה׳ אֱלֹהֵינוּ, is directed specifically to Yisrael: "You, Yisrael, prostrate yourselves at His holy mountain, the *Beis HaMikdash*, and thereby elevate God to an even higher level;" this is the meaning of כִּי קָדוֹשׁ ה׳ אֱלֹהֵינוּ. The הִשְׁתַּחֲוָיָה (devotional prostration) performed in the *Beis HaMikdash* is a much higher form of worship of HaKadosh Baruch Hu.

So these two *pesukim*, one directed at mankind in general, and one at Yisrael, are combined together and result in גְּדִיל, a broader strand of praise.

In the next גְּדִיל, wherein we implore HaKadosh Baruch Hu for *rachamim*, we merge the following three *pesukim*:

❏ וְהוּא **רַחוּם** יְכַפֵּר עָוֹן וְלֹא יַשְׁחִית וְהִרְבָּה לְהָשִׁיב אַפּוֹ וְלֹא יָעִיר כָּל חֲמָתוֹ ❏ — *But He, the Merciful One, is forgiving of iniquity, and does not destroy; frequently He withdraws His anger, not arousing His entire wrath* (*Tehillim* 78:38);

❏ אַתָּה ה׳ לֹא תִכְלָא **רַחֲמֶיךָ** מִמֶּנִּי חַסְדְּךָ וַאֲמִתְּךָ תָּמִיד יִצְּרוּנִי ❏ — *You, Hashem, withhold not Your mercy from me; may Your kindness and Your truth always protect me* (ibid. 40:12);

❑ זְכֹר רַחֲמֶיךָ ה׳ וַחֲסָדֶיךָ כִּי מֵעוֹלָם הֵמָּה — *Remember Your mercies, Hashem, and Your kindness, for they are from the beginning of the world* (Tehillim 25:6).

❧ וְהוּא רַחוּם יְכַפֵּר עָוֹן וְלֹא יַשְׁחִית ❧ — **But He, the Merciful One, is forgiving of iniquity, and does not destroy.**

The *pasuk* וְהוּא רַחוּם is very familiar to us, for we recite it at least four times every day: here in הוֹדוּ; in יְהִי כָבוֹד; in וּבָא לְצִיּוֹן; and in מַעֲרִיב. (On *Motza'ei Shabbos Kodesh* through Sunday, and on Mondays and Thursdays, we say it five times.) Each time it is recited, we add a thought which was not included at the earlier recital, as we shall explain.

מְרַחֵם would mean, *He is merciful.* However, וְהוּא רַחוּם, in the passive פָּעַל form, means *He responds mercifully.* If we pray for *rachamim,* he will give it to us. "He is responsive to our request for mercy." Similarly, in the *berachah* of סְלַח לָנוּ in the שְׁמוֹנֶה עֶשְׂרֵה, when we pray for forgiveness of our *aveiros,* we end with חַנּוּן הַמַּרְבֶּה לִסְלוֹחַ, He responds with graciousness to our request for forgiveness."

We know that punishment for *aveiros* is not an act of "vengeance" by *HaKadosh Baruch Hu* but is sent to purify the person. If one dares to rebel against the will of his Creator, the *middas hadin* (strict justice) would dictate that the wrongdoing be immediately and severely punished. However, וְהוּא רַחוּם, since He is responsive to our request for mercy, He will יְכַפֵּר עָוֹן, "cover over" our עָוֹן, sin, even our intentional sins; וְלֹא יַשְׁחִית, and he does not destroy the person as a result of his sins.

❧ וְהִרְבָּה לְהָשִׁיב אַפּוֹ וְלֹא יָעִיר כָּל חֲמָתוֹ ❧ — **Frequently He withdraws His anger, not arousing His entire wrath.**

Rather, His "anger," which would would result in swift, strict punishment, is often withdrawn in favor of the more lenient method of extending the punishment, in smaller doses, over a long period of time. He metes out a pain here, a sickness there, sadness, worries, disappointments, frustrations, and failures over one's lifetime, to make the punishment tolerable. All these, if given at once, would amount to a horrible punishment. But since He is רַחוּם, *merciful,* He does not awaken all of His fury at once. A person would not survive this. So we ask *HaKadosh Baruch Hu* to stretch out any punishment which we may deserve over a period of time, to make it tolerable for us. This is analogous to one who owes an overwhelming debt which he cannot possibly repay at once; but if he pays small installments, if he lives long enough it will eventually be liquidated.

This first וְהוּא רַחוּם of the day is a prayer for each individual personally, as is indicated by the second "strand" of these combined *pesukim* of *rachamim*:

❧ אַתָּה ה׳ לֹא תִכְלָא רַחֲמֶיךָ מִמֶּנִּי חַסְדְּךָ וַאֲמִתְּךָ תָּמִיד יִצְּרוּנִי ❧ — **You, Hashem, withhold not Your mercy from me; may Your kindness and Your truth always protect me.** חֶסֶד, *chessed,* and אֱמֶת, *emes,* are often mentioned together, as, e.g., חֶסֶד וֶאֱמֶת מַן יִנְצְרֻהוּ, *Appoint kindness and truth, that they may preserve him* (*Tehillim* 61:8). *Chessed,* as used here, refers to the fact that *HaKadosh Baruch Hu* overlooks one's mistakes and accepts his *teshuvah* and the person is forgiven.

However, *emes* refers to the true nature of a person's actions. While the gratification that results from an *aveirah* may taste very sweet at the time it is perpetrated, in reality, in *emes,* it is really very bitter. Conversely, a *mitzvah* can often seem bitter and fraught with difficulties. If, for example, one has to dig deep into his pockets to give *tzedakah* and thereby deprives himself of the use of the money, it can be a bitter pill to swallow. Similarly, holding oneself back from a very tempting *aveirah* can seem to be difficult and bitter. However, in truth, it is really very sweet.

So if *HaKadosh Baruch Hu* offers a person an opportunity to rehabilitate himself and, as a result, he suffers physical pain, this pain, this bitterness, is what the *aveirah* really is. The perceived sweetness has turned into the *emes* of what it really was in the first place. This contrast between perception and actuality is expressed by the verse, הוֹי הָאֹמְרִים לָרַע טוֹב וְלַטּוֹב רָע ... שָׂמִים מַר לְמָתוֹק וּמָתוֹק לְמָר, *Woe is to those who consider what is bad good, and what is good bad; . . . they make bitter that which is sweet, and sweet that which is bitter* (*Yeshayahu* 5:20).

Therefore the meaning of חַסְדְּךָ וַאֲמִתְּךָ תָּמִיד יִצְּרוּנִי is that the individual prays: "May the *chessed* of *HaKadosh Baruch Hu* protect me from punishment. However, if He finds that I am to be punished for my *aveiros,* and must consequently, experience the *emes* of my actions, may this suffering awaken my mind to repentance, and this will be my protection in the future."

And now we have the third "strand" in this *combined g'dil* of *pesukim* of *rachamim*:

זְכֹר רַחֲמֶיךָ ה' וַחֲסָדֶיךָ כִּי מֵעוֹלָם הֵמָּה — **Remember Your mercies, Hashem, and Your kindnesses, for they are from the beginning of the world.** We are not asking *HaKadosh Baruch Hu* for anything new, but rather, to remember us mercifully with His *middah* of *rachamim* with which He created the world, as is expressed in the verse, עוֹלָם חֶסֶד יִבָּנֶה, *the world was built on lovingkindness* (*Tehillim* 89:3). The entire creation of the world was an act of *chessed.* So we implore *HaKadosh Baruch Hu* to treat us mercifully, in accordance with the *chessed* and *rachamim* with which the world was created.

We now encounter a threefold combination of the use of the word עֹז, meaning strength: תְּנוּ עֹז לֵאלֹהִים עַל יִשְׂרָאֵל גַּאֲוָתוֹ וְעֻזּוֹ בַּשְּׁחָקִים. נוֹרָא אֱלֹהִים מִמִּקְדָּשֶׁיךָ אֵל יִשְׂרָאֵל הוּא נֹתֵן עֹז וְתַעֲצֻמוֹת לָעָם בָּרוּךְ אֱלֹהִים, *Ascribe power to God, Whose pride is in Yisrael and Whose might is in the high heavens. You are awesome, O God, from Your holy places, O God of Israel — It is He Who grants might and power to the people, blessed is God* (ibid. 68:35-36).

◆§ תְּנוּ עֹז לֵאלֹהִים — **Ascribe power to God.** The word עֹז has the general meaning of "strength," but there are several other words in *lashon kodesh* which also mean strength, e.g., אוֹן, חֹזֶק, עֶצֶם, כֹּחַ. However, עֹז, as explained by Rav Samson R. Hirsch (*Tehillim* 8:3), means "irresistible," or "invincible," something which cannot be overcome. This is why the Torah is called עֹז. (See *Shir HaShirim Rabbah* 2:3:3.)

The simple meaning here is: *Ascribe all the power to God.* However, there is a deeper meaning here. We have already explained the concept that *HaKadosh Baruch Hu* created the spiritual world to be self-sustaining, as is the physical world. This self-sustaining spiritual cycle is initiated by our actions. Consequently, any *mitzvah* which we do, or any *tefillah* which we express, or any Torah which we learn, results in *kedushah* and *berachah* being brought into the world. So, in a manner of speaking, we are actually enhancing the power of *HaKadosh Baruch Hu* in the world by doing His will. In this way, we are "giving power to *HaKadosh Baruch Hu*."

◆§ עַל יִשְׂרָאֵל גַּאֲוָתוֹ — **Whose pride is in Yisrael.** He is "proud" that His nation, Yisrael, is bringing His power into the world by their performance of *mitzvos* and *talmud Torah*.

◆§ וְעֻזּוֹ בַּשְּׁחָקִים — **And Whose might is in the high heavens.** *HaKadosh Baruch Hu* does not need Yisrael to bring his blessings into the world, because He is independently All-powerful. However, it is His will that His blessings of *kedushah, taharah, simchah,* and *shalom* be bestowed upon the world as a result of our Torah, *mitzvos,* and *tefillah*.

◆§ נוֹרָא אֱלֹהִים מִמִּקְדָּשֶׁיךָ — **You are awesome, O God, from Your holy places.** This refers to the *Beis HaMikdash* from whence *tefillos* go up to *shamayim*, heaven. (The plural refers to the different sections of the *Beis HaMikdash*.)

◆§ אֵל יִשְׂרָאֵל הוּא נוֹתֵן עֹז וְתַעֲצֻמוֹת לָעָם, בָּרוּךְ אֱלֹהִים — **O God of Israel — It is He Who grants might and power to the people, blessed is God.** Here we bless *HaKadosh Baruch Hu* for having given Yisrael עֹז, the power of Torah, as previously mentioned, and תַעֲצֻמוֹת, various forms of great "bone-like" strength (from the root עצם), all of which enable the Jewish people to withstand the suffering and pressures inflicted on them by the outside world.

The next *g'dil* is a threefold use of words which mean *vengeance*. The *pesukim* are taken from *Tehillim* (94:1,2):

◆§ אֵל נְקָמוֹת ה׳, אֵל נְקָמוֹת הוֹפִיעַ. הִנָּשֵׂא שֹׁפֵט הָאָרֶץ, הָשֵׁב גְּמוּל עַל גֵּאִים — **O God of vengeance, Hashem, O God of vengeance, appear! Arise, O Judge of the earth, render [a full measure of] recompense to the haughty.** The word

HODU ∽ 147

גְּמוּל, *a full measure of recompense,* also has the meaning of *revenge.* Chazal tell us, אֵל נְקָמוֹת ה׳, *God's vengeance* גְּדוֹלָה נְקָמָה שֶׁנִּתְּנָה בֵּין שְׁתֵּי אוֹתִיּוֹת, שֶׁנֶּאֱמַר אֵל נְקָמוֹת ה׳, *(punishment of the wicked) is severe, for the word "revenge" is preceded and followed by God's Names* (Berachos 33a). Here the word נְקָמוֹת appears between two Names of *HaKadosh Baruch Hu,* because revenge is restricted to His domain. לִי נָקָם וְשִׁלֵּם, *Revenge and recompense belong to Me* (Devarim 32:35), says *HaKadosh Baruch Hu.* However, in our interpersonal relationships, ordinary human vengeance is forbidden, as it states, לֹא תִקֹּם וְלֹא תִטֹּר, *You shall not take revenge and you shall not bear a grudge* (Vayikra 19:18).

The word נָקָם, which we usually translate as *revenge,* actually has the meaning of rectifying a wrong which was committed. When evil is perpetrated in the world, when millions of innocent people are tortured and killed *al kiddush Hashem* (in sanctification of the Name), as happened during the Holocaust, the natural God-ordered world goes awry. It is out of order, similar to a train which becomes "derailed" and must be put back "on track." We do not understand why it went awry, and how it could ever be "avenged." Only *HaKadosh Baruch Hu* can rectify such wrongs. The entire *tefillah* of אַב הָרַחֲמִים is a plea to *HaKadosh Baruch Hu* to "avenge" the horrible catastrophes which have befallen our people over the long *galus* years. We are convinced that *HaKadosh Baruch Hu* will not keep quiet in the face of such injustice in the world, and not a single drop of blood will go unavenged. אָשִׁיב נָקָם לְצָרָי . . . הַרְנִינוּ גוֹיִם עַמּוֹ כִּי דַם עֲבָדָיו יִקּוֹם וְנָקָם יָשִׁיב לְצָרָיו, *I shall return vengeance upon My enemies . . . O nations sing the praises of His people, for He will avenge the blood of His servants, He will bring retribution upon His foes* (Devarim 32:41,43).

Yet, in this *tefillah,* we ask *HaKadosh Baruch Hu* to show us, to let us see how such enormous wrongs will be rectified — similar to the end of *Av HaRachamim,* in which we say: יִוָּדַע בַּגּוֹיִם לְעֵינֵינוּ נִקְמַת דַּם עֲבָדֶיךָ הַשָּׁפוּךְ, *Let it be known among the nations, before our eyes, the revenge of Your servants' blood that was spilled.* A mass murderer, even if he is put to death, can only die once. Only *HaKadosh Baruch Hu* can avenge, or rectify, the many wrongs that he perpetrated. And we pray that, eventually, we will understand how such wrongs are righted. וְהָיָה מִדֵּי חֹדֶשׁ בְּחָדְשׁוֹ וּמִדֵּי שַׁבָּת בְּשַׁבַּתּוֹ וגו׳ . . . וְיָצְאוּ וְרָאוּ בְּפִגְרֵי הָאֲנָשִׁים הַפּשְׁעִים בִּי כִּי תוֹלַעְתָּם לֹא תָמוּת וְאִשָּׁם לֹא תִכְבֶּה וְהָיוּ דֵרָאוֹן לְכָל בָּשָׂר, *It shall be that every New Moon and on every Sabbath . . . And they will go out and see the corpses of the men who rebelled against Me, for their decay will not cease and their fire will not be extinguished and they will lie in disgrace before all mankind* (Yeshayahu 66:23,24).

So the meaning of אֵל נְקָמוֹת ה׳, אֵל נְקָמוֹת הוֹפִיעַ, הִנָּשֵׂא שֹׁפֵט הָאָרֶץ, is that we are asking *HaKadosh Baruch Hu* to *appear, arise,* as the *Judge of the earth* to bring order into the world, and to let us witness how He will rectify the horrific wrongs which have been perpetrated against us throughout our history. וְהָשֵׁב גְּמוּל עַל גֵּאִים, *and render recompense to the haughty*.

We follow this by adding one more "strand" to this group of *pesukim*. While the evildoers in the world are suffering under the *middas hadin*, as represented by אֵל נְקָמוֹת ה׳, we say to *HaKadosh Baruch Hu*:

☙ לַה׳ הַיְשׁוּעָה עַל עַמְּךָ בִרְכָתֶךָ סֶּלָה — **Salvation is Hashem's.** We have already suffered our full measure, and shall suffer no longer, because **upon Your people is Your blessing, Selah.**

Next we combine two *pesukim* containing the words ה׳ צְבָאוֹת:

❑ ה׳ צְבָאוֹת עִמָּנוּ מִשְׂגָּב לָנוּ אֱלֹהֵי יַעֲקֹב סֶלָה, *God of Hosts is with us, the God of Jacob is our stronghold, Selah* (*Tehillim* 46:12);

❑ ה׳ צְבָאוֹת אַשְׁרֵי אָדָם בֹּטֵחַ בָּךְ, *O God of Hosts, happy is the person who trusts in You* (ibid. 84:13).

These two *pesukim* are juxtaposed, based on לְעוֹלָם לֹא יְהֵא הַפָּסוּק הַזֶּה זָז מִפִּיךָ: ה׳ צְבָאוֹת עִמָּנוּ מִשְׂגָּב לָנוּ אֱלֹהֵי יַעֲקֹב סֶלָה, וְחַבְרַיָּיא: ה׳ צְבָאוֹת אַשְׁרֵי אָדָם בֹּטֵחַ בָּךְ, *You should always remember the pasuk of Tehillim* 46:12, *and its companion*, ibid. 84:13 (*Talmud Yerushalmi, Berachos* 5:1).

☙ ה׳ צְבָאוֹת עִמָּנוּ, מִשְׂגָּב לָנוּ אֱלֹהֵי יַעֲקֹב סֶלָה — **God of Hosts is with us, the God of Jacob is our stronghold, Selah.** The term ה׳ צְבָאוֹת, usually translated as *God of Hosts*, is one of the Names of *HaKadosh Baruch Hu* which have *kedushah* and cannot be erased. The word צְבָאוֹת actually means a large multitude of people or things, e.g., an army, as we find in connection with *Bnei Yisrael*: וַיְהִי בְּעֶצֶם הַיּוֹם הַזֶּה הוֹצִיא ה׳ אֶת בְּנֵי יִשְׂרָאֵל מֵאֶרֶץ מִצְרַיִם עַל צִבְאֹתָם, *It happened on that very day: Hashem took the Children of Israel out of the land of Egypt in their legions* (*Shemos* 12:51); מִבֶּן עֶשְׂרִים שָׁנָה וָמַעְלָה כָּל יֹצֵא צָבָא בְּיִשְׂרָאֵל תִּפְקְדוּ אֹתָם לְצִבְאֹתָם אַתָּה וְאַהֲרֹן, *From twenty years of age and up — everyone who goes out to the legion in Israel — you shall count them according to their legions, you and Aaron* (*Bamidbar* 1:3). Here the Jewish people is viewed as an "army" or a potential army.

In connection with mankind in general, הֲלֹא צָבָא לֶאֱנוֹשׁ עֲלֵי אָרֶץ, *Behold, man has an allotted time upon the earth* (*Iyov* 7:1).

The idea of ה׳ צְבָאוֹת, used as a Name of *HaKadosh Baruch Hu*, has an overwhelming connotation. It means that everything that He created has a purpose. Just as we, *Bnei Yisrael*, have a purpose in this life, so do all other people, including all the *reshaim*. Every part of the human body has a purpose. Gradually, medical science is discovering more and more about the various bodily systems, even microscopic glands, all of which are necessary for the growth, immunity protection, and healthy maintenance of the extremely complex human body. Every animal, every creature, the billions of insects and the myriads of seemingly insignificant life forms, even the smallest molecules, all were created by *HaKadosh Baruch Hu* for a purpose. We may not understand what purpose they serve but, nevertheless, they are part of the *tzavah* of *HaKadosh Baruch Hu*. This is all contrary to the theory of Evolution, which explains life as being independent of a Creator, and the result of random natural forces.

Every person, including every physically impaired person, has his purpose. The *Midrash Shocher Tov* (34) quotes Dovid HaMelech as asking *HaKadosh Baruch Hu* why He created insane people: אָמַר דָּוִד לִפְנֵי הקב"ה: כָּל מַה שֶּׁעָשִׂיתָ יָפֶה וגו' אֲבָל הַשְּׁטוּת שֶׁבָּרֵאתָ מַה הֲנָאָה יֵשׁ לְפָנֶיךָ, *Dovid said before God: Everything which You created is good . . . but what benefit is there before You for insanity, which You created*. To which *HaKadosh Baruch Hu* answers: חַיֶּיךָ שֶׁתִּצְטָרֵךְ לוֹ — *You, personally, will have a need for it*. This is followed by the narrative of how Dovid HaMelech had to disguise himself as a drooling, feeble-minded beggar to elude his enemies. After his escape, he composed psalm 34, לְדָוִד בְּשַׁנּוֹתוֹ אֶת טַעְמוֹ לִפְנֵי אֲבִימֶלֶךְ, *To David when he disguised his sanity before Avimelech* (*Tehillim* 34:1). The truth that all of creation has a purpose is expressed in the mishnah: אַל תְּהִי בָז לְכָל אָדָם וְאַל תְּהִי מַפְלִיג לְכָל דָּבָר, שֶׁאֵין לְךָ אָדָם שֶׁאֵין לוֹ שָׁעָה וְאֵין לְךָ דָּבָר שֶׁאֵין לוֹ מָקוֹם, *Do not be scornful of any person and do not be disdainful of anything, for you have no person without his hour, and you have no thing without its place* (*Pirkei Avos* 4:3).

As to the cosmos, we find in the verse: *He counts the number of the stars, assigning names to all of them* (*Tehillim* 147:4). We know that there are billions of galaxies, and each galaxy has billions of suns, and each sun has many thousands of various satellites which rotate around it. To Hashem these are all מִסְפָּר — a small number. And He has given each one of these a "name" — a purpose — for which it exists.

So the meaning of ה' צְבָאוֹת, or אֱלֹהִים צְבָאוֹת, be it *middas hadin* or *middas harachamim*, is that all of the creations of *HaKadosh Baruch Hu*, from the microscopic to the cosmic, are part of the צָבָא — the "army" — of *HaKadosh Baruch Hu*. Every component of this "army" was given its "rank," its place and purpose of existence. However, the specific purpose of each component is beyond our comprehension. This concept is indeed overwhelming.

Nevertheless, regarding each person's own view of himself, one must feel that his existence is necessary. He should know that if *HaKadosh Baruch Hu* placed him in the world, his life has a purpose; every minute of it is precious. For this reason, the *mitzvos* are called *pikudei Hashem* (assignments of Hashem), and the purpose of one's life is to fulfill these assignments.

So in the first *pasuk*, we say ה' צְבָאוֹת עִמָּנוּ . . . אֱלֹהֵי יַעֲקֹב, You, our Creator, Who has given us, as descendants of Yaakov, a special purpose in life, are with us; מִשְׂגָּב לָנוּ, You have thereby lifted us up. You are our Tower of Strength. The word מִשְׂגָּב is a combination of שַׂגִּיא, meaning *strong*, and גָּבוֹהַּ, meaning *high*.

ה' צְבָאוֹת, אַשְׁרֵי אָדָם בֹּטֵחַ בָּךְ — **God of Hosts, happy is the person who trusts in You.** In this *pasuk*, we again address *HaKadosh Baruch Hu* as ה' צְבָאוֹת; however, this time we add אַשְׁרֵי אָדָם בֹּטֵחַ בָּךְ, meaning, happy and fortunate is the person who has achieved the level of *bitachon* (trust) in which he accepts that it is ה' צְבָאוֹת, Who, in His wisdom, has created everything, notwithstanding the fact that human beings do not understand the purpose of most of creation.

Next, we have a "cord" consisting of two *pesukim* of יְשׁוּעָה, salvation:

- ה' הוֹשִׁיעָה הַמֶּלֶךְ יַעֲנֵנוּ בְיוֹם קָרְאֵנוּ — *Hashem save! The King will answer us on the day we call* (Tehillim 20:10);

- הוֹשִׁיעָה אֶת עַמֶּךָ וּבָרֵךְ אֶת נַחֲלָתֶךָ וּרְעֵם וְנַשְּׂאֵם עַד הָעוֹלָם — *Grant salvation to Your people and bless Your inheritance, tend them and elevate them forever* (Tehillim 28:9).

ה' הוֹשִׁיעָה, הַמֶּלֶךְ יַעֲנֵנוּ בְיוֹם קָרְאֵנוּ. הוֹשִׁיעָה אֶת עַמֶּךָ, וּבָרֵךְ אֶת נַחֲלָתֶךָ, וּרְעֵם וְנַשְּׂאֵם עַד הָעוֹלָם — **Hashem save! The King will answer us on the day we call. Grant salvation to Your people and bless Your inheritance, tend them and elevate them forever.**

The word יְשׁוּעָה is used for salvation from a situation that seems totally hopeless. In the first *pasuk*, we call upon *HaKadosh Baruch Hu* to answer our *tefillos* in such situations. In the second, we, as the special "heritage" of *HaKadosh Baruch Hu*, ask Him to care for us as a shepherd would, even in hopeless situations. However, we add a wish that we may be elevated to an awareness of His constant *yeshuah* and intervention in our lives.

The Torah uses the word יְשׁוּעָה to describe the salvation of *Bnei Yisrael* from the Egyptians at *krias Yam Suf* (the Splitting of the Sea): וַיּוֹשַׁע ה' בַּיּוֹם הַהוּא אֶת יִשְׂרָאֵל מִיַּד מִצְרָיִם, *On that day Hashem saved Israel from the hand of Egypt* (Shemos 14:30). The situation was seemingly hopeless. *Bnei Yisrael* were at the banks of the Red Sea, with the Egyptians in hot pursuit. They faced what would — without Divine intervention — be certain destruction.

The Torah tells us: וַיִּירְאוּ מְאֹד וַיִּצְעֲקוּ בְנֵי יִשְׂרָאֵל אֶל ה', *Bnei Yisrael were gripped with terror and they cried out to Hashem* (Shemos 14:10). On this, *Rashi* (ibid.) quotes from the *Mechilta*: תָּפְשׂוּ אוּמָּנוּת אֲבוֹתָם, *they utilized the art of their forefathers* by engaging in *tefillah*. They utilized the ancient Jewish "art form" of *tefillah* which they had inherited from their Forefathers. This "art" of *tefillah* was practiced by Avraham, who introduced the *tefillah* of Shacharis; followed by Yitzchak, who instituted the *tefillah* of Minchah; and then by Yaakov who established the *tefillah* of Maariv (see *Berachos* 26b).

But this quotation from *Mechilta* begs the question: What connection is there between the ordinary daily devotional *tefillos* of our Forefathers, and the desperate cry of the Jewish people for salvation from the seemingly hopeless situation in which they found themselves at the *Yam Suf*? My revered Rebbe, the Mirrer *Mashgiach*, Rav Yerucham Levovitz, explained this as an example of הֲרֵי זֶה בָּא לְלַמֵּד וְנִמְצָא לָמֵד, *This is an example of a source of a teaching which sheds light on another matter* (see *Pesachim* 25b). By comparing the two, the Sages have shed light on the ordinary daily *tefillos* of our *Avos*. They are describing to us how the *Avos* davened Shacharis, Minchah and Maariv. The *Avos* stood before *HaKadosh Baruch Hu* during their daily *tefillos* with the awareness that they would be totally helpless without Him. Were it not for the *chessed* of Hashem, they would not be able to think, see, hear, talk, or walk. No aspect of their physical lives would be possible. They understood that without the constant intervention of *HaKadosh Baruch Hu*, their daily existence would be totally hopeless, as hopeless as the situation in which *Bnei Yisrael* found themselves at the *Yam Suf*.

Ideally, it is with this thought that we, too, should begin our daily *tefillos*. And if a person has the *zechus* to have this *kavannah* for even a small portion of the *tefillah*, he has not only focused properly on the whole concept of *tefillah*, but it is also an elevating experience for the person himself. When he is *mispallel*, he is bringing these profound thoughts into his own mind. And this deeper awareness of the *hashgachah pratis* will result in וְנִשָּׂאֵם עַד הָעוֹלָם, the person being elevated to a higher, eternal world.

The next "intertwined cord" is a threefold combination of the concept of *bitachon*, trust. This consists of the following three *pesukim* from *Tehillim*:
נַפְשֵׁנוּ חִכְּתָה לַה' עֶזְרֵנוּ וּמָגִנֵּנוּ הוּא — *Our soul yearns for Hashem* — *He is our helper and protector* (33:20);
כִּי בוֹ יִשְׂמַח לִבֵּנוּ כִּי בְשֵׁם קָדְשׁוֹ בָטָחְנוּ — *For in Him will our hearts be glad, for in His holy Name we trusted* (33:21);
יְהִי חַסְדְּךָ ה' עָלֵינוּ כַּאֲשֶׁר יִחַלְנוּ לָךְ — *May the lovingkindness of Hashem be upon us, while we eagerly await Him* (33:22).

The word *bitachon* has become a household word, and it conveys the idea of "trust in *HaKadosh Baruch Hu*." However, it is usually misunderstood. For instance, one can be said to "have *bitachon*" and still have fears, but the true *baal bitachon* has no fear, as is found in: הִנֵּה אֵל יְשׁוּעָתִי אֶבְטַח וְלֹא אֶפְחָד, *Behold, God is my salvation, I shall trust and not fear* (*Yeshayahu* 12:2). Since most of us are afraid at times, *bitachon* seems to be just a word which we use, but very few of us succeed in actually putting it into practice.

The pamphlet *Leket Hanhagos HaChazon Ish* quotes some aphorisms of the Chazon Ish concerning the meaning of true *bitachon*. Among these is: עִנְיַן הַבִּטָּחוֹן הוּא הָאֱמוּן שֶׁאֵין מִקְרֶה בָּעוֹלָם, וְכָל הַנַּעֲשֶׂה תַּחַת הַשֶּׁמֶשׁ הַכֹּל בְּהַכְרָזָה מֵאִתּוֹ יִתְבָּרַךְ, meaning that *bitachon* is the conviction that nothing happens by accident, and everything which occurs has been previously predetermined by *HaKadosh Baruch Hu*. אֵין אָדָם נוֹקֵף אֶצְבָּעוֹ מִלְמַטָּה אֶלָּא אִם כֵּן מַכְרִיזִין עָלָיו מִלְמַעְלָה, *No one as much as cuts his finger here below, unless it has previously been "announced" above* (*Chullin* 7b). Nothing happens by accident, from the smallest to the most sublime. All occurrences are part of the plan of *HaKadosh Baruch Hu*. If one is convinced of this, he has *bitachon*.

The Chazon Ish further states: הַשְׁגָּחָתוֹ יִתְבָּרֵךְ הִיא לְפִי מִדַּת הַבִּטָּחוֹן, meaning that the *hashgachah pratis,* Divine Providence, of *HaKadosh Baruch Hu* toward a person is based on the measure of *bitachon* that person has in *HaKadosh Baruch Hu*. בָּרוּךְ הַגֶּבֶר אֲשֶׁר יִבְטַח בַּה' וְהָיָה ה' מִבְטַחוֹ, *Blessed is the man who trusts in Hashem, then Hashem becomes his trust* (*Yirmiyahu* 17:7). The moment a person has *bitachon* in the *hashgachah pratis* of *HaKadosh Baruch Hu,* then *Hashem becomes his trust.* That person's *bitachon* becomes self-rewarding. The more intense the *bitachon* the person has in *HaKadosh Baruch Hu,* the closer *HaKadosh Baruch Hu* pays attention to him. *Bitachon* is not wishful thinking, as, for instance, "things will be well with me," but it is the conviction that "if *HaKadosh Baruch Hu* wills it, things will be well with me."

Divine Providence is at the very foundation of all *tefillah*. If a person is not firmly convinced that *HaKadosh Baruch Hu* takes a personal interest in him, there would be no reason to be *mispallel*. It would be ridiculous, a meaningless gesture.

This concept of *bitachon* is expressed in our three *pesukim*:

נַפְשֵׁנוּ חִכְּתָה לַה', עֶזְרֵנוּ וּמָגִנֵּנוּ הוּא — **Our souls yearn for Hashem.** And while we have *bitachon* in Him, **He is our helper and protector.** As the result of, and at the moment of, our *bitachon* in Him, He becomes our savior and protector.

כִּי בוֹ יִשְׂמַח לִבֵּנוּ, כִּי בְשֵׁם קָדְשׁוֹ בָטָחְנוּ — **For in Him will our hearts be glad, for in His holy Name we trusted.** Using כִּי in its sense of "when" or "while," the meaning here is: "While we place our trust in His holy Name, at that time our hearts are gladdened." During the time of one's *bitachon* in *HaKadosh Baruch Hu,* he has a blissful feeling of joy: He is in God's Hands, he can relax; all fear leaves him.

יְהִי חַסְדְּךָ ה' עָלֵינוּ, כַּאֲשֶׁר יִחַלְנוּ לָךְ — **May the lovingkindness of Hashem be upon us, while** — during the time — **we eagerly await Him.** This means that at the moment we look forward to His help, and place our trust in Him, His lovingkindness is upon us.

The final "cord" in this *g'dilim* section is composed of two *pesukim* in which we ask *HaKadosh Baruch Hu* to fulfill our *bitachon*. While *bitachon* has its own rewards, and is an end in itself, we still ask *HaKadosh Baruch Hu* to show us that our *tefillos* have been answered:

◈§ הַרְאֵנוּ ה' חַסְדֶּךָ, וְיֶשְׁעֲךָ תִּתֶּן לָנוּ §◈ — **Let us see Your lovingkindness, Hashem, and give us Your salvation.** We yearn to actually experience that for which we have been praying. We then proceed, saying:

◈§ קוּמָה עֶזְרָתָה לָּנוּ, וּפְדֵנוּ לְמַעַן חַסְדֶּךָ §◈ — **Arise to our aid, and redeem us for the sake of Your lovingkindness.** We ask that *HaKadosh Baruch Hu* "arise" — as if He were, so to speak, sitting down and not paying attention — so that we may realize the fulfillment of our hopes.

The word עֶזְרָתָה is the feminine, or weaker form, of עֵזֶר, both of which mean *help*. The same usage is found in עֶזְרַת אֲבוֹתֵינוּ. While עֵזֶר or עֶזְרָה convey the idea of powerful, unassisted help, as in עֶזְרִי מֵעִם ה', *My help comes from Hashem (Tehillim* 121:2), עֶזְרָתָה has the connotation of assisting, a weaker form of help. What this *pasuk* means is that by having *bitachon,* we have done our part, and we now ask *HaKadosh Baruch Hu* to complement this, and to "do His part," that of bringing about our salvation.

In response to the aforementioned *tefillos,* we now quote the answer of *HaKadosh Baruch Hu* in the following *pasuk* which is familiar to us from the *shir* of *yom chamishi,* the psalm (*Tehillim* 81) recited every Thursday.

◈§ אָנֹכִי ה' אֱלֹהֶיךָ הַמַּעַלְךָ מֵאֶרֶץ מִצְרָיִם, הַרְחֶב פִּיךָ וַאֲמַלְאֵהוּ §◈ — **I am Hashem, your God, Who lifted you up from the land of Egypt, open wide your mouth and I will fill it.** To paraphrase this *pasuk, HaKadosh Baruch Hu* is saying: "You may rest assured that I, Hashem, your God, Who lifted you up from the land of Mitzrayim, will fulfill even the greatest requests which could possibly fill your mouth." Words similar to הַמַּעַלְךָ מֵאֶרֶץ מִצְרַיִם — meaning that *HaKadosh Baruch Hu* lifted us up above the culture of the land of Egypt — are also found in *Vayikra* (11:45). In both places they mean lifting up, or elevating, the Jewish nation from Egypt, rather than merely taking them out, as in הוֹצֵאתִיךָ מֵאֶרֶץ מִצְרַיִם (*Shemos* 20:2).

This lifting-up process, as well as this remarkable assurance that even our greatest requests of *HaKadosh Baruch Hu* will be fulfilled, can be understood by an examination of several previous *pesukim* in psalm 81: עֵדוּת בִּיהוֹסֵף שָׂמוֹ, בְּצֵאתוֹ עַל אֶרֶץ מִצְרָיִם, שְׂפַת לֹא יָדַעְתִּי אֶשְׁמָע, *As a testimony to Yehoseif He imposed it, when He went out over the land of Egypt, a language unknown to me I heard* (v. 6). Here Asaf, the composer of this *mizmor,* exclaims that at the time of *yetzias Mitzrayim,* he, as a member of *Bnei Yisrael,* heard a proclamation from *HaKadosh Baruch Hu* in a "new language," which they did not understand. This proclamation was: הֲסִירוֹתִי מִסֵּבֶל שִׁכְמוֹ, כַּפָּיו מִדּוּד תַּעֲבֹרְנָה, *Since I have removed the burden [of slavery] from his shoulder, his hands shall be removed from the cooking pot* (v. 7). These words, in the "new language" which he heard, admonished Yehoseif — meaning *Bnei Yisrael* — to forgo the "fleshpots" of Egypt upon their release from the burdens of enslavement. Now this description of "fleshpots" of the physical living conditions of *Bnei*

Yisrael in Mitzrayim hardly describes the cruel, backbreaking bondage and torture to which our forefathers were subjected in Mitzrayim. The reference to the "fleshpots" of Egypt is reminiscent of the complaints of *Bnei Yisrael* — when they reached the desert — that they missed the good food in Mitzrayim: בְּאֶרֶץ מִצְרַיִם בְּשִׁבְתֵּנוּ עַל סִיר הַבָּשָׂר בְּאָכְלֵנוּ לֶחֶם לָשֹׂבַע, *While we were in Mitzrayim, and sitting at the fleshpot and eating bread to our satisfaction* (Shemos 16:3).

Is this the same food that the *Haggadah* describes as הָא לַחְמָא עַנְיָא, the bread of slaves, because matzah bakes quickly and slaves are not allowed time to bake normal leavened bread? Later, we also find *Bnei Yisrael* yearning for the Egyptian food: זָכַרְנוּ אֶת הַדָּגָה אֲשֶׁר נֹאכַל בְּמִצְרַיִם חִנָּם, אֵת הַקִּשֻּׁאִים וְאֵת הָאֲבַטִּחִים וְאֶת הֶחָצִיר וְאֶת הַבְּצָלִים וְאֶת הַשּׁוּמִים, *We remember the fish that we ate in Egypt free of charge; and the cucumbers, melons, leeks, onions and garlic* (Bamidbar 11:5). Here they fondly remember those Egyptian delicacies, which were eaten without any restrictions — חִנָּם מִן הַמִּצְוֹת, *free of the obligation to do mitzvos.* "The fish" — they even mention their recipe for "gefilte fish." And why, throughout their wanderings in the desert, do we find *Bnei Yisrael* repeatedly expressing their desire to return to Egypt?

To explain these yearnings to return to Egypt and live the "good life" there, we must know that *Chazal* tell us (*Rosh Hashanah* 11b) that from Rosh Hashanah before the Nissan of *yetzias Mitzrayim,* the enforcement of the labor decrees and slavery against *Bnei Yisrael* were suspended due to the *makkos* (plagues). During this six-month period, our forefathers lived a relaxed and good life in Egypt. Having been spared the ravages of the ten *makkos* against the Egyptians, which our forefathers experienced as ten miracles, they enjoyed their lives of leisure there, while eating and drinking at the "fleshpots of Egypt."

This luxurious period in their experience was never forgotten and explains their yearning to return to a now "free" Egypt. All their slave masters had perished at *krias Yam Suf,* and they therefore hoped to resume living the "good life" in Egypt.

However, this was a complete misconception of the purpose of their freedom, and is what Asaf calls in his *mizmor,* שְׂפַת לֹא יָדַעְתִּי אֶשְׁמָע, a language which *Bnei Yisrael* did not understand. That "language" was a message from *HaKadosh Baruch Hu.* הֲסִירוֹתִי מִסֵּבֶל שִׁכְמוֹ — *When I removed the burden of slavery from his shoulder,* it was not for the purpose of living a carefree and luxurious life at the Egyptian fleshpots. He admonishes them: כַּפָּיו מִדּוּד תַּעֲבֹרְנָה, *his hands shall be removed from the fleshpot.*

Yetzias Mitzrayim was to be not only a physical redemption from slavery, but its goal was to spiritually elevate *Bnei Yisrael* from the depravities of Egyptian society, which was a land devoted to pleasures of the flesh. *Chazal* tell us (*Toras Kohanim, Acharei Mos, Parshasa* 8, 18:3) that Mitzrayim had sunk to the lowest levels of human debauchery and depravity.

The Psalmist, speaking in the Name of *HaKadosh Baruch Hu*, continues, אָנֹכִי ה' אֱלֹהֶיךָ הַמַּעַלְךָ מֵאֶרֶץ מִצְרָיִם: The purpose of *yetzias Mitzrayim* was to elevate *Bnei Yisrael* from the depths of Egyptian culture and society. So if your wishes are for the "meat and gefilte fish" of Mitzrayim, you have not really been elevated by the redemption, and thus, spiritually and culturally, you are still in Mitzrayim. You have misunderstood the entire "message" of *yetzias Mitzrayim.* To you these words are, indeed, a "strange language."

Therefore Asaf, continuing to speak in the Name of *HaKadosh Baruch Hu*, says further: וְלֹא שָׁמַע עַמִּי לְקוֹלִי וְיִשְׂרָאֵל לֹא אָבָה לִי, וָאֲשַׁלְּחֵהוּ בִּשְׁרִירוּת לִבָּם, יֵלְכוּ בְּמוֹעֲצוֹתֵיהֶם, *Since My people did not listen to My voice, and Yisrael did not want Me, I let them follow the dictates of their hearts, let them go in accordance with their own counsel* (Tehillim 81:12,13). The tragic result of this "misunderstood message" was: וְאַף ה' חָרָה בָעָם וַיַּךְ ה' בָּעָם מַכָּה רַבָּה מְאֹד, *the wrath of Hashem flared against the people, and Hashem struck a very mighty blow against the people* (Bamidbar 11:33). It is not known how many people died in this plague. Most probably, all of the אֲסַפְסֻף, or the *eirev rav*, were included, because we no longer find reference to them.

The place of this occurrence was then called קִבְרוֹת הַתַּאֲוָה, *the graves of lust*. This lust was not only for flesh, in terms of food, but, as *Chazal* tell us (see *Shabbos* 130a), it also refers to the lust for forbidden physical gratification, which they had learned from the Egyptians. The reason for this name is given there as: כִּי שָׁם קָבְרוּ אֶת הָעָם הַמִּתְאַוִּים, *Because it was there that they buried the people who were lustful.* It was there, in the desert "graves of lust," that the depraved Egyptian lifestyle, which *Bnei Yisrael* had brought with them, was finally buried. After this great tragedy, we no longer hear of any desire on the part of *Bnei Yisrael* to return to the destructive lifestyle of Egyptian culture. The *taavah* (desire) was buried there.

Once the Egyptian culture was left behind, the Psalmist Asaf exclaims: אָנֹכִי ה' אֱלֹהֶיךָ הַמַּעַלְךָ מֵאֶרֶץ מִצְרָיִם הַרְחֶב פִּיךָ וַאֲמַלְאֵהוּ. Now, when you accept the true purpose of *yetzias Mitzrayim* as הַמַּעַלְךָ, an elevating experience for your lofty purpose in life, then, in the furtherance of that noble cause, you are entitled to "open your mouth as wide as possible," and make the broadest possible request that will enhance and foster that high purpose.

The *Targum* (Tehillim 81:11), based on the Gemara (Berachos 50a), renders this as: אַפְתֵּי פּוּמָךְ בְּפִתְגָּמֵי אוֹרַיְיתָא וַאֲמַלֵּא יָתָהּ מִכָּל טָבְתָא, *Open your mouth with words of Torah, and I will fill it with all goodness.* So if a person who is motivated to develop his spiritual life earnestly asks *HaKadosh Baruch Hu*, פְּתַח לִבִּי בְּתוֹרָתֶךָ, *Open my heart for Your Torah*, or יַחֵד לְבָבִי לְאַהֲבָה וּלְיִרְאָה שְׁמֶךָ, *Make my heart capable of both loving and fearing Your Name,* he has the promise: וַאֲמַלְאֵהוּ, *I will fulfill* these requests.

We now prepare to conclude this part of *Pesukei d'Zimrah*, and joyfully exclaim:

אַשְׁרֵי הָעָם שֶׁכָּכָה לּוֹ, אַשְׁרֵי הָעָם שֶׁה' אֱלֹהָיו — **How happy is the people to whom such things occur, how happy is the people whose God is Hashem.** How fortunate are we, that as long as we desire to enhance our "uplifted" status by developing our Torah lives, we are encouraged to ask *HaKadosh Baruch Hu* for the greatest possible assistance in this regard, and He has promised that He will grant it to us.

וַאֲנִי בְּחַסְדְּךָ בָטַחְתִּי, יָגֵל לִבִּי בִּישׁוּעָתֶךָ, אָשִׁירָה לַה' כִּי גָמַל עָלָי — In conclusion, after having recited all of these *zemiros,* the individual proclaims: **I, who have always had trust in your lovingkindness,** ask that in the future, **my heart may jubilate because of Your salvation. I want to sing to Hashem when He brings His promises to fruition.** The word גָמַל means *ripening,* as in וַיִּגְמֹל שְׁקֵדִים, *and almonds ripened* (*Bamidbar* 17:23). When one has *bitachon,* his wishes are merely "buds," or unripened fruits. They exist, but they are incomplete. However, when *HaKadosh Baruch Hu* makes these wishes come true, גָמַל עָלָי, they become "ripened."

The words, אָשִׁירָה לַה', *I want to sing to Hashem,* are actually an introduction to מִזְמוֹר לְתוֹדָה, which follows, in that it expresses the person's deep desire to have an opportunity to give *todah,* thanks, to *HaKadosh Baruch Hu* when he is blessed with the fulfillment of his hopes and wishes. This *pasuk* is also appropriate for Shabbos and Yom Tov, although מִזְמוֹר לְתוֹדָה is omitted then, because it is an expression of the person's wish that he be granted opportunities to sing God's praises when good fortune shines on him.

מִזְמוֹר לְתוֹדָה / Mizmor L'Sodah

According to *Bava Basra* 14b, this *mizmor* (*Tehillim* 100) is one of eleven composed by Moshe Rabbeinu. In accordance with its name, it was sung by the *Leviim* as an accompaniment to a *korban todah* (*Shevuos* 15b). Since this *mizmor* is associated with a *korban*, we have a *minhag* to stand while reciting it, as one would do when actually bringing a *korban*.

A *korban todah* was brought by an individual who had been saved from one of the four perils listed in *Berachos* 54b: יוֹרְדֵי הַיָּם, *following an ocean voyage;* הוֹלְכֵי מִדְבָּרוֹת, *following journey through a desert;* חוֹלֶה וְנִתְרַפֵּא, *recovery from a serious illness;* חָבוּשׁ בְּבֵית הָאֲסוּרִים וְיָצָא, *release from imprisonment.*

The *Shulchan Aruch* (*Orach Chaim* 219:1) offers a mnemonic to remember them: וְכָל "הַחַיִּים" יוֹדוּךָ סֶלָה: חוֹלֶה, יָם, יִסּוּרִים, מִדְבָּרוֹת. These four are only examples, based on *Tehillim* 107. However, the same requirement to bring a *korban todah* — or in our time to say *bircas hagomel* — exists whenever a person is saved from any type of extreme danger.

The *korban todah* has one feature that distinguishes it from other *korbanos*. The *lachmei todah,* the breads of the accompanying *minchah* offering, consist of both *chametz* and *matzah*. The matzah symbolizes the salvation from the grave danger which the person had been facing, similar to the matzah which commemorates *yetzias Mitzrayim*. [See *Maayan Beis HaSho'evah, Bo* 12:27, for further development of this idea.]

However, the *chametz* — the everyday, usual bread — symbolizes the daily *nissim* that occur to the person, although he may not even be aware of them. This is a reminder that one should "*bensch gomeil*" עַל נִסֶּיךָ שֶׁבְּכָל יוֹם עִמָּנוּ, *for the miracles that are with us every day,* and consistently bear in mind how thankful he should be that he was not sick, or that he was not exposed to other dangers.

Since this *mizmor* is associated with the *todah,* which could not be brought on Shabbos or Yom Tov, it is omitted on these days. It is likewise not recited on *erev* Pesach, *Chol HaMoed* Pesach, and on *erev* Yom Kippur, because the *korban todah* and its accompanying bread-loaves must be eaten for "a day and a night," which would not be possible on Pesach, or on Yom Kippur.

Now, if מִזְמוֹר לְתוֹדָה has been so closely associated with the *korban todah,* one wonders why the organizers of our *tefillah* did not place it with the other *korbanos* before בָּרוּךְ שֶׁאָמַר, or with the מִזְמוֹרִים שֶׁל יוֹם, which were recited together with the daily *korbanos*.

This can be understood in light of the following Midrash: לֶעָתִיד לָבוֹא כָּל הַקָּרְבָּנוֹת בְּטֵלִין וְקָרְבַּן תּוֹדָה אֵינוֹ בָּטֵל לְעוֹלָם (see *Vayikra Rabbah,* end of 27, and *Tanchuma Emor* 14). *Chazal* tell us here that eventually, at some point during the time of *Mashiach,* when the *yetzer hara* no longer exists, there will be no further need for voluntary, private *korbanos.* Of these, only the *korban todah* will remain, along with mandated private *korbanos* such as *olos re'iyah* and *shalmei chagigah.* Shlomo HaMelech cautions against volunteering to bring *korbanos*: טוֹב אֲשֶׁר לֹא תִדֹּר מִשֶּׁתִּדּוֹר וְלֹא תְשַׁלֵּם, *Better that you do not vow at all than that you vow and not pay* (Koheles 5:4). Also, לָמָּה לִּי רֹב זִבְחֵיכֶם יֹאמַר ה', *Why do I need your numerous sacrifices? says Hashem* (Yeshayahu 1:11), meaning that in ideal times, there will be no need for private, voluntary *korbanos.*

This statement by *Chazal* is complemented by another one: כָּל הַתְּפִלּוֹת לֶעָתִיד לָבוֹא בְּטֵלוֹת וְהוֹדָיָה אֵינָהּ בְּטֵלָה, *In the future, all prayers will cease, but prayers of thanksgiving will never cease.* (See *Midrash Shocher Tov, Tehillim* and the above quoted *Vayikra Rabbah* and *Tanchuma.*)

This means that at that ideal time, in the times of *Mashiach,* when all our wishes will have come true, there will be no more reason to ask for personal or national requests. However, *tefillos* of *hoda'ah,* with which we express our thankfulness to *HaKadosh Baruch Hu,* will always exist.

In this world, in which we now live, we are acutely aware of what displeases us, e.g., pain, suffering, disappointments, etc. but we are not always aware of the good which befalls us. However, מִזְמוֹר לְתוֹדָה focuses on the Time to Come, when we will become acutely aware of all the blessings which *HaKadosh Baruch Hu* has bestowed upon us. At that time, we will sense the *lack* of pain just as clearly as we now sense pain.

The Gemara (*Taanis* 9a) quotes the verse, וַהֲרִיקֹתִי לָכֶם בְּרָכָה עַד בְּלִי דָי, *And I shall pour out upon you blessing without end* (Malachi 3:10), which is explained there to mean, עַד שֶׁיִּבְלוּ שִׂפְתוֹתֵיכֶם מִלּוֹמַר דַּי, *Until your lips are worn out from saying "dai"* (enough) — *I shall pour out upon you so much blessing that you will no longer be able to say, "Enough!"*

Now we know that saying the word *dai* even a million times will not affect the lips. It is said with the tongue. *"Vei"* or *"oy vei"* is said with the lips, but not *"dai."*

What the Sages mean here is that in this world our lips have become worn out by saying *vei* as a result of all the *tzaros* which we have suffered. But the world of *Olam Haba* will be such that instead of wearing out our lips with *vei,* we will be saying *dai."* So this is paraphrased as: "You will no longer wear out your lips from all of your *vei,* but instead, you will be saying *dai.*"

Therefore the only *tefillah* which will remain at that time will be the *tefillah* of *hoda'ah,* wherein we will continually thank *HaKadosh Baruch Hu* for all the good which He has bestowed upon us. We will say *dai,* "Enough, we are not worthy of all these blessings which You have showered upon us. We can never thank You enough."

When Moshe Rabbeinu composed the מִזְמוֹר לְתוֹדָה he intended to convey a foretaste of the future world, of that world שֶׁכֻּלוֹ טוֹב, where everything is good. He wanted the person who experiences salvation from mortal danger, and who wishes to express his thanks to *HaKadosh Baruch Hu,* either by song or *korban,* to have a feeling of what that future world will be like. He wanted such a person to experience מֵעֵין עוֹלָם הַבָּא, *a taste of the World to Come.*

It is for this reason that מִזְמוֹר לְתוֹדָה has become part of the *Pesukei d'Zimrah.* It is a glimpse into the future, when all that will remain of our personal *avodah* to *HaKadosh Baruch Hu* will be *hoda'ah.*

With this introduction we understand the meaning of the following:

❧ ❧ ❧

◈§ הָרִיעוּ לַה׳ כָּל הָאָרֶץ — **Call out to Hashem, everyone on earth.** We invite the whole world to participate in our sense of gratitude to *HaKadosh Baruch Hu.* We do not want to keep our happiness to ourselves, so we call out:

◈§ עִבְדוּ אֶת ה׳ בְּשִׂמְחָה, בֹּאוּ לְפָנָיו בִּרְנָנָה. דְּעוּ כִּי ה׳ הוּא אֱלֹהִים, הוּא עָשָׂנוּ — **Serve Hashem with joy, come before Him with jubilation. Know that Hashem, He is God, it is He Who made us.** We continue to tell the world that of all the things for which we are thankful, the greatest reason for *todah* is the fact that He, with His *middas harachamim* and *middas hadin,* has made us into His nation Yisrael.

The word עָשָׂנוּ here is used in the same sense as it is used in *Aleinu*: שֶׁלֹּא עָשָׂנוּ כְּגוֹיֵי הָאֲרָצוֹת, which, in accordance with the explanation of Rav Samson R. Hirsch, means, "He did not form us into a nation, as other nations were formed." (See *Devarim* 27:9.) All other nations developed first by holding on to a piece of land, and its system of government was based either on the consent of the governed, as in a democracy, or on the power of a king or ruler who forced his people to follow him and crown him as their leader. These became "sovereign" and independent nations.

However, the notion of "independence" for the Jewish nation is a misnomer. The opposite is true. The only nonsovereign nation is the Jewish nation. Our "nationhood" is based on the laws of *HaKadosh Baruch Hu,* and our land was granted to us by Him alone, as the ideal place to keep His laws, and on the condition that we keep His laws.

So הוּא עָשָׂנוּ means, "It was He Who made us into a nation."

◈§ וְלוֹ אֲנַחְנוּ עַמּוֹ — **And we belong to Him, His people.** A similar expression is found in, עַם זוּ יָצַרְתִּי לִי, *I have created this people for Me* (Yeshayahu 43:21), so that תְּהִלָּתִי יְסַפֵּרוּ, *they may talk of My praises.* This means that the purpose of the Jewish nation, as God's nation, is to enlighten the whole world about the existence of *HaKadosh Baruch Hu.*

Although this word is read וְלוֹ, *to Him,* in *Tehillim* (ibid.) it is written וְלֹא, meaning *and not.* However, both the *kri* and the *kesiv* have a similar meaning: either "He made us, we did not make ourselves into a people"; or, as we read it, וְלוֹ אֲנַחְנוּ, *We belong to Him, as His people.*

§ וְצֹאן מַרְעִיתוֹ — **And the sheep of His pasture.** Since we serve *HaKadosh Baruch Hu,* He takes care of our needs, as a shepherd cares for his flock.

§ בֹּאוּ שְׁעָרָיו בְּתוֹדָה, חֲצֵרֹתָיו בִּתְהִלָּה — **Enter His gates with thanksgiving, His courtyards with praise.** We invite the whole world to follow us and come through His gates with thankfulness, follow our example, and proceed into His courtyards, to express His praises. Only thanks and praises, instead of complaints, will fill His precincts.

§ הוֹדוּ לוֹ, בָּרְכוּ שְׁמוֹ. כִּי טוֹב ה׳, לְעוֹלָם חַסְדּוֹ — **Give thanks to Him, bless His Name. For Hashem is good, His kindness endures forever.** This is similar to the הוֹדוּ לַה׳ כִּי טוֹב and the response כִּי לְעוֹלָם חַסְדּוֹ, which is found in *Tehillim* 118 and 136, except that here we invite the nations of the world to join us in this הוֹדוּ, and to respond כִּי לְעוֹלָם חַסְדּוֹ.

§ וְעַד דֹּר וָדֹר אֱמוּנָתוֹ — **And from generation to generation is His faithfulness.** We tell the world that His faithfulness and lovingkindness will last from generation to generation.

An additional way of understanding this *mizmor,* with its focus on the future realization of mankind's ideal state of being — and the universal recognition of *HaKadosh Baruch Hu* — is that it alludes to the time when multitudes will be streaming to worship *HaKadosh Baruch Hu* in Yerushalayim, which will become the capital of the world, as is described in the verse, וְנָהֲרוּ עָלָיו עַמִּים. וְהָלְכוּ גוֹיִם רַבִּים וְאָמְרוּ לְכוּ וְנַעֲלֶה אֶל הַר ה׳, *And peoples will stream to it; many nations will go and say, "Come let us go up to the Mountain of Hashem"* (Michah 4:1-2). At that time, Yerushalayim will not be large enough to contain these masses of people, and it will have to be expanded. This necessity to extend the boundaries of the *Beis HaMikdash* and Yerushalayim is alluded to in, הַרְחִיבִי מְקוֹם אָהֳלֵךְ, *Expand the place of your tent* (Yeshayahu 54:2) and וְדַמֶּשֶׂק מְנֻחָתוֹ, *and Damascus will be his resting place* (Zechariah 9:1). The latter is explained in *Sifrei (Devarim* 1) to mean, שֶׁעֲתִידָה יְרוּשָׁלַיִם לִהְיוֹת מַגַּעַת עַד דַּמֶּשֶׂק, *In the future Yerushalayim will reach all the way to Damascus.*

Now, we know that the dimensions of Yerushalayim and the *Beis HaMikdash* may not be changed unless a specific procedure is followed. This is described in *Shevuos* 14a: אֵין מוֹסִיפִין עַל הָעִיר וְעַל הָעֲזָרוֹת אֶלָּא בְּמֶלֶךְ וְנָבִיא וְאוּרִים

MIZMOR LESODAH ~ 161

וְתוּמִים וְסַנְהֶדְרִין שֶׁל שִׁבְעִים וְאֶחָד וּבִשְׁתֵּי תוֹדוֹת וּבְשִׁיר וּבֵית דִּין מְהַלְּכִין וּשְׁתֵּי תוֹדוֹת אַחֲרֵיהֶן וְכָל יִשְׂרָאֵל אַחֲרֵיהֶן. This procedure involved a large procession, led by the king and a prophet, followed by the *Urim VeTumim* (the inscripted part of the breastplate of the *Kohen Gadol*), followed by the Sanhedrin with all its seventy-one members, who were followed by שְׁתֵּי תוֹדוֹת וְשִׁיר (two thanksgiving offerings) which the Gemara (ibid. 15a) explains as referring to two large *lachmei todah* (thanksgiving loaves) accompanied by music and song and all of Israel bringing up the rear. Such a procession is actually recorded in *Nechemiah* Chapter 12.

It is these *todos* and *shir* which are alluded to in our *mizmor*. We invite the nations of the world to follow us to the expanded Yerushalayim in this future great procession, and we tell them: בֹּאוּ שְׁעָרָיו בְּתוֹדָה, "Follow our *lachmei todah* into His gates; חֲצֵרוֹתָיו בִּתְהִלָּה, *into his His courtyards with praise,*" referring to the *shir*, which is the music and the singing of praises during this procession, into Yerushalayim, which will be the new capital of the world.

יְהִי כָבוֹד / Yehi Chevod

[Ed. note: As we explained in the Foreword, this series of *shiurim* was limited to the weekday *tefillah*. At this point in the *shiur*, Rav Schwab expressed the hope that if *HaKadosh Baruch Hu* gave him strength, he would like to have the opportunity to explain the *mizmorim* for Shabbos in detail, as well. Unfortunately, this was not to be. What a great loss. חֲבַל עַל דְּאָבְדִין וְלָא מִשְׁתַּכְּחִין, *Alas for those who are gone and no more to be found.*]

Before continuing, let us just briefly point out that on weekdays we recite nine *mizmorim* in the *Pesukei d'Zimrah*. These are: The first part of הוֹדוּ לַה' (*Divrei Hayamim I* 16:8-36); the second part of הוֹדוּ תְּהִלָּה לְדָוִד – אַשְׁרֵי (*Tehillim*, psalm 100); (שִׁירוּ לַה' כָּל הָאָרֶץ) מִזְמוֹר לְתוֹדָה (from *Tehillim*, psalm 144); the five psalms beginning with הַלְלוּיָהּ (*Tehillim* 146-150).

However, on Shabbos, in keeping with its "dual aspects," as we discussed earlier, at וּבְיוֹם הַשַּׁבָּת שְׁנֵי כְבָשִׂים, we double this, and add nine additional *mizmorim*. [See *Midrash Shocher Tov* on *Tehillim* 92: כָּל עִיסְקָא דְשַׁבַּתָּא כָּפוּל, *All* עוֹמֶר כָּפוּל, קָרְבָּנוֹ כָּפוּל, עוֹנְשָׁהּ כָּפוּל, שְׂכָרָהּ כָּפוּל, אַזְהָרוֹתֶיהָ כְּפוּלוֹת, מִזְמוֹרוֹ כָּפוּל, *activities of Shabbos are doubled: The Omer is double; its Korban is double; its punishment is double, its reward is double; its warnings are double and its mizmor is double.*]

These are as follows: (1) לְדָוִד בְּשַׁנּוֹתוֹ אֶת (*Tehillim* 19); (2) לַמְנַצֵּחַ מִזְמוֹר לְדָוִד (ibid. 91); (3) תְּפִלָּה לְמֹשֶׁה (ibid. 90); (4) יֹשֵׁב בְּסֵתֶר עֶלְיוֹן (ibid. 91); (5) הַלְלוּיָהּ (ibid. 34); (3) טַעֲמוּ (ibid. 136); (7) הוֹדוּ לַה' כִּי טוֹב (ibid. 136); (7) רַנְּנוּ צַדִּיקִים בַּה' (ibid. 135); (6) הַלְלוּ אֶת שֵׁם ה' (ibid. 93). This total (8) מִזְמוֹר שִׁיר לְיוֹם הַשַּׁבָּת (ibid. 92); (9) ה' מָלָךְ גֵּאוּת לָבֵשׁ (ibid. 93). This total of eighteen *mizmorim* on Shabbos serves as a substitute for the weekday *Shemoneh Esrei*. Although we omit מִזְמוֹר לְתוֹדָה on Shabbos, it is compensated for by נִשְׁמַת, so the total remains eighteen.

Also, interestingly, יְהִי כָבוֹד consists of eighteen *pesukim*, and the Name of Hashem is mentioned nineteen times, alluding to the *tefillah* of *Shemoneh Esrei*, which originally consisted of eighteen *berachos*, and later was expanded to nineteen. This is in keeping with the purpose of the *Pesukei d'Zimrah*, which is to prepare ourselves for the main *tefillah*. (Actually, the phrase ה' מֶלֶךְ ה' מָלָךְ ה' יִמְלֹךְ לְעֹלָם וָעֶד is not one *pasuk*, but rather a combination of segments of three separate *pesukim*.)

As we shall soon see, יְהִי כָבוֹד is of an especially elevated nature, and therefore one should try not to omit it, even if he must omit other *mizmorim* and only say שֶׁאָמַר, בָּרוּךְ, אַשְׁרֵי, and יִשְׁתַּבַּח in order to say *Krias Shema* on time, or to *daven Shemoneh Esrei* together with the *tzibbur*.

YEHI CHEVOD 163

We explained earlier that the *Pesukei d'Zimrah*, as a preparation for the *tefillah*, correspond to the *Ulam* of the *Beis HaMikdash*, which was the preparatory chamber before the *Heichal*. The *Ulam* had golden chains hanging from the ceiling, as is described in *Middos* (3:48): שַׁרְשָׁרוֹת שֶׁל זָהָב הָיוּ קְבוּעִין בִּתְקָרַת הָאוּלָם.

So in keeping with the נְגַדֶּלְךָ portion of the *Pesukei d'Zimrah*, the organizers of the *tefillah*, in composing יְהִי כְבוֹד, alluded to these golden chains by utilizing a paragogical style in which the various *pesukim* are linked together in chainlike fashion: Words from an earlier *pasuk* are picked up and act as links to the following *pasuk* which contains the same or a similar word. This "chain of words" is readily discernible in these *pesukim*:

May the **glory** of Hashem endure **forever**,	יְהִי כְבוֹד ה' לְעוֹלָם
Let Hashem rejoice in His works	יִשְׂמַח ה' בְּמַעֲשָׂיו
Blessed be the **Name of Hashem**,	יְהִי שֵׁם ה' מְבֹרָךְ
from this time and **forever**.	מֵעַתָּה וְעַד עוֹלָם
From the rising of the sun to its setting,	מִמִּזְרַח שֶׁמֶשׁ עַד מְבוֹאוֹ
Hashem's Name is praised.	מְהֻלָּל שֵׁם ה'
High above all nations is Hashem,	רָם עַל כָּל גּוֹיִם ה'
above **the heavens is His glory**.	עַל הַשָּׁמַיִם כְּבוֹדוֹ
Hashem is Your Name forever,	ה' שִׁמְךָ לְעוֹלָם
Hashem is Your memorial	ה' זִכְרְךָ
throughout the generations.	לְדֹר וָדֹר
Hashem has established His throne in **the heavens**,	ה' בַּשָּׁמַיִם הֵכִין כִּסְאוֹ
and His kingdom reigns over all.	וּמַלְכוּתוֹ בַּכֹּל מָשָׁלָה
The heavens will be glad	יִשְׂמְחוּ הַשָּׁמַיִם
and the earth will rejoice,	וְתָגֵל הָאָרֶץ
They will proclaim among **the nations**,	וְיֹאמְרוּ בַגּוֹיִם
"Hashem **has reigned!**"	ה' מָלָךְ
Hashem **reigns**, Hashem **has reigned**,	ה' מֶלֶךְ ה' מָלָךְ
Hashem **shall reign for all** eternity.	ה' יִמְלֹךְ לְעֹלָם וָעֶד
Hashem **reigns forever and ever**,	ה' מֶלֶךְ עוֹלָם וָעֶד
when **the nations** will have perished from His earth.	אָבְדוּ גוֹיִם מֵאַרְצוֹ
Hashem annuls **the counsel of nations**,	ה' הֵפִיר עֲצַת גּוֹיִם
He balks **the designs of** peoples.	הֵנִיא מַחְשְׁבוֹת עַמִּים
Many **designs are in** man's **heart**,	רַבּוֹת מַחֲשָׁבוֹת בְּלֶב אִישׁ
but the counsel of Hashem — only it will prevail.	וַעֲצַת ה' הִיא תָקוּם
The counsel of Hashem will endure **forever**,	עֲצַת ה' לְעוֹלָם תַּעֲמֹד
the designs of His heart	מַחְשְׁבוֹת לִבּוֹ
throughout the generations.	לְדֹר וָדֹר
For He spoke and it came to be;	כִּי הוּא אָמַר וַיֶּהִי
He commanded **and it stood firm**.	הוּא צִוָּה וַיַּעֲמֹד

For God **selected** Zion,	כִּי בָחַר ה' בְּצִיּוֹן
He desired it for His dwelling place	אִוָּהּ לְמוֹשָׁב לוֹ
For God **selected** Jacob as His own,	כִּי יַעֲקֹב בָּחַר לוֹ יָהּ
Israel as His treasure.	יִשְׂרָאֵל לִסְגֻלָּתוֹ
For Hashem will not cast off His **people**,	כִּי לֹא יִטֹּשׁ ה' עַמּוֹ
nor will He forsake His **heritage**.	וְנַחֲלָתוֹ לֹא יַעֲזֹב

[Ed. note: Rav Schwab did not translate *Yehi Chevod*. We have inserted the translation from "The Complete Artscroll Siddur" for reference purposes.]

This entire hymn, starting with יְהִי כְבוֹד ה' לְעוֹלָם, reflects the state in which the world will exist in the time of *Mashiach*, when the height of the development of mankind will have been reached, and with the entire world recognizing *HaKadosh Baruch Hu*. It continues with the three *pesukim* of the beginning of *Hallel*, in which the universal and permanent recognition of *HaKadosh Baruch Hu* is the subject. The permanence of this new world order is the theme of the following set of *pesukim*. This continues with the description of the happiness of all creatures, spiritual as well as physical — יִשְׂמְחוּ הַשָּׁמַיִם וְתָגֵל הָאָרֶץ — when *HaKadosh Baruch Hu* is finally and permanently recognized as Supreme Ruler of the Universe with the declaration, ה' מֶלֶךְ, ה' מָלָךְ, ה' יִמְלֹךְ לְעוֹלָם וָעֶד.

This is followed by ה' מֶלֶךְ עוֹלָם וָעֶד אָבְדוּ גוֹיִם מֵאַרְצוֹ, meaning, that when Hashem becomes the permanently recognized Ruler of the Universe, "nations" will disappear from His world. "Nations" are political entities which delineate themselves into self-contained, independent units. In our time, nations, or states, are the building blocks of the world. Each sovereign nation is independent of the other. However, eventually, in the time of *Mashiach*, "nations," as we know them, will disappear. Instead, the world will be united by their recognition of *HaKadosh Baruch Hu*, and their divisions will fall into "families," rather than disconnected and independent nations.

We find this definition given to Avraham Avinu by *HaKadosh Baruch Hu*: וְנִבְרְכוּ בְךָ כֹּל מִשְׁפְּחֹת הָאֲדָמָה, *All the families of the earth shall bless themselves by you* (*Bereishis* 12:3). Here Avraham is told that eventually "all the families of the world" will be blessed in his *zechus*. It is these "families," consisting of fathers and mothers, children and grandchildren, brothers and sisters, which will eventually become the building blocks of the world. It was with this structure that *HaKadosh Baruch Hu* planned His creation of the world: מַחְשְׁבוֹת לִבּוֹ לְדֹר וָדֹר, and eventually it will become realized.

However, unfortunately, in our time, not only have we seen the deterioration of the traditional family, but the opposite of "family" is becoming legitimized by "same-gender" relationships — and even marriages! The next few *pesukim* are devoted to the furtherance of the theme that all these aberrant ideas and plans will eventually be eliminated from the world.

YEHI CHEVOD ∽ 165

Then we come upon four *pesukim,* each one beginning with the word כִּי. The Gemara (*Rosh Hashanah* 3a) states that כִּי can have four different meanings, as follows:

אֲרֵי — *if;*

דִּילְמָא — *when* or *in the event of;*

אֶלָּא — *but* (used in opposition to a previous statement);

דְּהָא — *because.*

Each one of the four *pesukim* to which we refer has one of these meanings:

❏ כִּי הוּא אָמַר וַיֶּהִי הוּא צִוָּה וַיַּעֲמֹד — ***If*** He says something, it becomes reality, and if He commands, it stands up.

❏ כִּי בָחַר ה׳ בְּצִיּוֹן אִוָּהּ לְמוֹשָׁב לוֹ — (Therefore), ***When*** Hashem chose Tziyon, He wanted it to be His dwelling place.

❏ כִּי יַעֲקֹב בָּחַר לוֹ יָהּ יִשְׂרָאֵל לִסְגֻלָּתוֹ — ***Because*** HaKadosh Baruch Hu chose Yaakov, He wanted Yisrael to become His special treasure.

❏ כִּי לֹא יִטֹּשׁ ה׳ עַמּוֹ וְנַחֲלָתוֹ לֹא יַעֲזֹב — Even if we do not merit to be His treasure, nevertheless, ***But*** Hashem will not leave His people, nor will He forsake His inheritance.

❦ ❦ ❦

This is actually the conclusion of יְהִי כְבוֹד. However, we realize that due to our shortcomings, we are still very far from reaching the ideal situation portrayed in the previous *pesukim.* We therefore call upon HaKadosh Baruch Hu with the familiar words:

☙ וְהוּא רַחוּם יְכַפֵּר עָוֹן וְלֹא יַשְׁחִית, וְהִרְבָּה לְהָשִׁיב אַפּוֹ ☙ — **But He, the Merciful One, is forgiving of iniquity, and does not destroy; frequently He withdraws His anger.** The first time we quoted this *pasuk* was in הוֹדוּ, where we, as individuals, prayed, אַתָּה ה׳ לֹא תִכְלָא רַחֲמֶיךָ מִמֶּנִּי, that *You, Hashem, do not withhold Your mercy from me.*

Now, however, we approach HaKadosh Baruch Hu as the collective nation of Yaakov-Yisrael, whom He has chosen as His treasure. We ask that if we must be punished, it be in small installments,

☙ וְלֹא יָעִיר כָּל חֲמָתוֹ ☙ — **Not arousing His entire rage,** so that וְלֹא יַשְׁחִית, that despite our shortcomings, we may be preserved as His nation, to realize the purpose of our creation: to lead the world to a universal recognition of HaKadosh Baruch Hu. In *Tehillim* 20:2, we ask יַעַנְךָ ה׳ בְּיוֹם צָרָה, *May Hashem answer you on the day of distress,* and express our conviction that:

☙ ה׳ הוֹשִׁיעָה, הַמֶּלֶךְ יַעֲנֵנוּ בְיוֹם קָרְאֵנוּ ☙ — **Hashem save! The King will answer us on the day we call.** This concludes the נְגַדֶּלְךָ portion of the *Pesukei d'Zimrah,* and we now begin the נְשַׁבֵּחֲךָ portion, starting with אַשְׁרֵי.

אַשְׁרֵי / Ashrei

The Mishnah (Berachos 30b) tells us: חֲסִידִים הָרִאשׁוֹנִים הָיוּ שׁוֹהִין שָׁעָה אַחַת וּמִתְפַּלְּלִים כְּדֵי שֶׁיְּכַוְּנוּ לִבָּם לַאֲבִיהֶם שֶׁבַּשָּׁמַיִם, *The early chassidim would tarry one hour to meditate and concentrate their hearts on [HaKadosh Baruch Hu] their Father in Heaven, and then they would pray.*

The Gemara (ibid. 32b) explains that the source for this practice is the *pasuk,* אַשְׁרֵי יוֹשְׁבֵי בֵיתֶךָ עוֹד יְהַלְלוּךָ סֶּלָה, *Happy are the dwellers of Your house; they will continue to praise You, Selah* (Tehillim 84:5). As explained by *Rashi* (ibid.), these *chassidim* understood this *pasuk* to mean that before beginning the *tefillah,* יוֹשְׁבֵי בֵיתֶךָ, one is to sit and meditate in Your house; and only afterwards, עוֹד יְהַלְלוּךָ סֶּלָה, can one reach the proper state of mind for *tefillah.* This means that a prerequisite for proper *tefillah* is a period of meditation on one's relationship with *HaKadosh Baruch Hu.*

While we are not like the original *chassidim,* with the power to meditate for an hour, nevertheless, אַשְׁרֵי offers us an opportunity to concentrate, at least momentarily, about Whom, and to Whom, we are talking, before we engage in יְהַלְלוּךָ סֶּלָה, which in Tefillas *Shacharis* consists of the recitation of תְּהִלָּה לְדָוִד together with the last five chapters of *Tehillim.*

There are two ways in which a person can relate to *HaKadosh Baruch Hu.* One is through *ahavah* (love), in which a person feels very close to Him, and the other is through *yirah* (awe), in which one is awestruck by His Omnipotence and Omniscience. This may explain the ancient Jewish practice of "shokeling," swaying forward and backward during *tefillah.* The forward motion expresses one's desire to come close to *HaKadosh Baruch Hu,* but then, upon reflection, one realizes that He is the *Ribbono Shel Olam,* the Master of the universe, which causes one to reel back in awe. These thoughts are typically evoked during meditation.

These two aspects of one's relationship to *HaKadosh Baruch Hu* are reflected in the composition of the *pesukim* of תְּהִלָּה לְדָוִד. Of the twenty-one *pesukim* in this *mizmor,* eleven are בְּלָשׁוֹן נוֹכַח, in second person, where we address *HaKadosh Baruch Hu* directly, in the second person, as "You," expressing the *ahavah* relationship. In the other ten, we address Him in the third person, בְּלָשׁוֹן נִסְתָּר, as "He" or "His," expressing the *yirah* aspect of our relationship.

To introduce this *mizmor,* which we commonly call אַשְׁרֵי, but which actually begins with תְּהִלָּה לְדָוִד (from *Tehillim* 145), the organizers of our *tefillah* chose two *pesukim* beginning with the word אַשְׁרֵי as a "title" and "subtitle" to characterize the *mizmor* to follow.

The "title" is:

אַשְׁרֵי יוֹשְׁבֵי בֵיתֶךָ, עוֹד יְהַלְלוּךָ סֶּלָה — **Happy are the dwellers of Your house; they will continue to praise You, Selah.** אַשְׁרֵי, which definitely means "happiness," as in כִּי אִשְּׁרוּנִי בָּנוֹת, *I have been made happy among women* (*Bereishis* 30:13), is written in the plural, because happiness never comes in small installments. If a person is said to be "happy," he is very happy. It does not mean that he is happy and sad at the same time.

יוֹשְׁבֵי בֵיתֶךָ cannot mean "those who sit in Your house," because we know that sitting in the *Beis HaMikdash* is prohibited, with the exception of a king of the Davidic dynasty (see *Yoma* 25a). So the simple meaning would be, "those who dwell in Your house." However, Rav Samson R. Hirsch points out that יוֹשְׁבֵי בֵיתֶךָ does not mean one who merely "dwells in Your house" — even if he meditates about the *tefillah* — for this would be called יוֹשְׁבִים בְּבֵיתֶךָ, similar to הָעוֹמְדִים בְּבֵית ה׳, *Who stand in the House of Hashem* (*Tehillim* 134:1). Rather, it is a frame of mind which is descriptive of a person who lives his normal, everyday life in the House of Hashem. Wherever such a person is, or whatever he does, he has some connection with *HaKadosh Baruch Hu*. He is always in God's House, and is a veritable "citizen of that House." Because of the Torah, even the most mundane activities of life — one's livelihood, even one's body functions — have some connection with *HaKadosh Baruch Hu*. Therefore, his entire life in *Olam Hazeh* (this world) is in the *Beis Hashem*.

So the expanded meaning of this "title" is: Every type of happiness is the lot of the יוֹשְׁבֵי בֵיתֶךָ — of those who in this life, *b'Olam Hazeh*, are true "residents of Your House." And as a result of this, עוֹד יְהַלְלוּךָ סֶּלָה, they will merit to continue to praise You forever, not only in this world, but also *b'Olam Haba* (in the World to Come).

This title, then, in its full meaning, explains the declaration of the Sages: כָּל הָאוֹמֵר תְּהִלָּה לְדָוִד בְּכָל יוֹם שָׁלֹשׁ פְּעָמִים מוּבְטָח לוֹ שֶׁהוּא בֶּן הָעוֹלָם הַבָּא (*Berachos* 4b). This means that if one says this *mizmor* three times a day, not merely by "mouthing" it, but by concentrating on the meaning of the words, and living his life accordingly, he is assured of *Olam Haba*. He can then be assured עוֹד יְהַלְלוּךָ סֶּלָה, that he will always say it, meaning that he will merit to say it in the World to Come. He is מוּבְטָח לוֹ שֶׁהוּא בֶּן הָעוֹלָם הַבָּא.

The simple reference of saying this *mizmor* three times a day is to *Shacharis*, where it is said twice, and to *Minchah*, where it is recited once. However, this could also be an analogy, having the meaning of three circumstances in which a person may find himself in his life, whether this be עֶרֶב, בֹּקֶר, or צָהֳרַיִם.

❏ עֶרֶב, *evening*, would refer to a time in one's life during which he feels he is going downhill. It is "evening" for him. This could be either because of age, or lack of *mazal* in his endeavors, or difficult experiences in his life.

❑ בֹּקֶר, *morning*, is the period of his life when everything appears "sunny," and he feels he is advancing and "going uphill." He is becoming more and more successful.

❑ צָהֳרַיִם, *afternoon*, is the bright sunshine time in his life when everything he touches is successful. He has reached the height of his career. He is "on top of the world."

So a person is מוּבְטָח לוֹ שֶׁהוּא בֶּן הָעוֹלָם הַבָּא, *he is assured that he is worthy of the World to Come*, if he is properly inspired by the thoughts expressed in *Ashrei*, which we will explain as we proceed, regardless of which of life's conditions he may find himself in.

This is similar to the thanksgiving prayer expressed in *Modim*: עַל חַיֵּינוּ הַמְּסוּרִים בְּיָדֶךָ וְעַל נִשְׁמוֹתֵינוּ הַפְּקוּדוֹת לָךְ וְעַל נִסֶּיךָ שֶׁבְּכָל יוֹם עִמָּנוּ וְעַל נִפְלְאוֹתֶיךָ וְטוֹבוֹתֶיךָ שֶׁבְּכָל עֵת עֶרֶב וָבֹקֶר וְצָהֳרַיִם, *For our lives, which are committed to Your power and for our souls that are entrusted to You; for Your miracles that are with us every day; and for Your wonders and favors at all times: evening, morning, and afternoon.*

This is what Dovid HaMelech meant: עֶרֶב וָבֹקֶר וְצָהֳרַיִם אָשִׂיחָה וְאֶהֱמֶה, *Evening, morning, and noon, I speak and supplicate* (*Tehillim* 55:18). Under any of life's circumstances, be it "evening," "morning," or "noon" in my life, I will always speak and express my prayers to *HaKadosh Baruch Hu*.

We will explain how these thoughts are inspired within us by a proper recitation of אַשְׁרֵי, why this *mizmor* is in the center of the *Pesukei d'Zimrah*, and why it brings one to *Olam Haba*.

The following, second אַשְׁרֵי is the "subtitle" of תְּהִלָּה לְדָוִד. It is the last *pasuk* of *Tehillim* 144, which immediately precedes it. *Chazal* usually refer to this *mizmor* as תְּהִלָּה לְדָוִד, however we do find it called אַשְׁרֵי due to this *pasuk* which immediately precedes it (see *Berachos* 4b).

❧ אַשְׁרֵי הָעָם שֶׁכָּכָה לּוֹ, אַשְׁרֵי הָעָם שֶׁה׳ אֱלֹהָיו — **Happy is the people for whom this is so, happy is the people whose God is Hashem.** Happy is the nation to whom the aforementioned term of יוֹשְׁבֵי בֵיתֶךָ applies. Happy is the nation whose God is Hashem. Because of our practice of Torah and *mitzvos*, the Jewish nation as a whole is characterized as יוֹשְׁבֵי בֵיתֶךָ. And it is this thought which introduces the actual *mizmor* of תְּהִלָּה לְדָוִד.

In accordance with our previous division of the *Pesukei d'Zimrah* into five segments, with each one expressing praises to *HaKadosh Baruch Hu* in a different form, we now begin the נְשַׁבֵּחֲךָ portion. As we explained, *shevach* means to improve something. It also has the meaning of "improving" something in our mind, that of seeing every occurrence or situation in life as being inherently good.

ASHREI / 169

תְּהִלָּה לְדָוִד is divided into two parts. The first part, up to פּוֹתֵחַ אֶת יָדֶךָ, is a vision of the future world — עוֹלָם שֶׁכֻּלּוֹ טוֹב, *a world where everything is good.*

That world is described as: לֹא כָּעוֹלָם הַזֶּה הָעוֹלָם הַבָּא. הָעוֹלָם הַזֶּה עַל בְּשׂוֹרוֹת טוֹבוֹת אוֹמֵר בָּרוּךְ הַטּוֹב וְהַמֵּטִיב, וְעַל בְּשׂוֹרוֹת רָעוֹת אוֹמֵר בָּרוּךְ דַּיַּין הָאֱמֶת. לָעוֹלָם הַבָּא כּוּלוֹ הַטּוֹב וְהַמֵּטִיב, *The World to Come is not like this world. In this world, one blesses God for good tidings and accepts God's judgments for bad tidings; but in the World to Come, everything is seen as only good* (Pesachim 50a). At that time, even happenings which we would now consider bad or unfortunate will be clearly understood as being *kulo tov,* completely and only good. This is not yet our world, it is the world after the arrival of *Mashiach.*

The second part, beginning with פּוֹתֵחַ אֶת יָדֶךָ, reflects the realities of our world, a world where there is good and bad, happiness and suffering, laughter and tears. In this world, we also make an effort, through our *emunah* in Hashem, to consider everything we experience as being good.

We will show how these two different worlds are alluded to in the two opening *pesukim.*

◆§ תְּהִלָּה לְדָוִד — **A psalm of praise by Dovid.** Both the first and last *pasuk* of this *mizmor* open with תְּהִלָּה. As we have previously pointed out, תְּהִלָּה means to praise something extraordinary. וַיְהַלְלוּ אֹתָהּ אֶל פַּרְעֹה, *they praised her [extraordinary beauty as fitting] for Pharaoh* (Bereishis 12:15). So Dovid HaMelech is characterizing this *mizmor* as expressing something extraordinary.

◆§ אֲרוֹמִמְךָ אֱלוֹהַי הַמֶּלֶךְ — **I will exalt You, my God the King.** I wish to praise You with the highest form of praise. Here Dovid HaMelech sees *HaKadosh Baruch Hu* as the King of the world when the world has reached the state of *olam shekulo tov,* a world where everything is completely and only good, and continues:

◆§ וַאֲבָרְכָה שִׁמְךָ לְעוֹלָם וָעֶד — **And I will bless Your Name forever and ever.** This means, "I would like to continue to express my *berachah,* my wish forever, that יִתְגַּדַּל וְיִתְקַדַּשׁ שְׁמֵהּ רַבָּא, *May His great Name,* His recognition, grow exalted and sanctified forever."

In this first *pasuk,* Dovid HaMelech is visualizing the future *olam shekulo tov,* at the time of *Mashiach,* and he expresses the *tefillah* that he will continue to experience this in *Olam Haba,* the spiritual world of the *neshamah* after death, at which time, he will continue to bless *HaKadosh Baruch Hu* forever. This is the subject of the first part of the *mizmor.* However, the second *pasuk,* which follows, refers to the "here and now," and corresponds to the second part of the *mizmor:*

◆§ בְּכָל יוֹם אֲבָרְכֶךָּ — **Every day I will bless You.** But even in the present time, in the ordinary circumstances of the present world, whether they be good days or bad days, Dovid HaMelech says, "I wish to bless You every day."

◈§ וַאֲהַלְלָה שִׁמְךָ לְעוֹלָם וָעֶד §◈ — **And I will praise Your Name forever and ever.** And forever express my feelings of *Hallel*, "extraordinary goodness," to You, concerning Your blessings to us in our present day-to-day lives. [For this definition of הַלֵּל, see earlier on מֶלֶךְ מְהֻלָּל בַּתִּשְׁבָּחוֹת (in *Baruch She'amar*).]

The *mizmor* now continues with a vision of a world which is absolutely without evil:

◈§ גָּדוֹל ה' וּמְהֻלָּל מְאֹד §◈ — **Hashem is great and exceedingly praised.** The word גָּדוֹל, when used in connection with *HaKadosh Baruch Hu*, always refers to His *middah* of *chessed*. (See *Rashi* on *Devarim* 3:24; *Sifrei* ibid., *piska* 27: זֶה בִּנְיַן אָב לְכָל גָּדְלְךָ שֶׁבַּתּוֹרָה.) The manifestation of His *chessed* is such that there is no space which is devoid of Him. This is expressed as: אֵין מָקוֹם פָּנוּי מִן הַשְּׁכִינָה — *There is no space empty of God's presence* (*Shir HaShirim Rabbah* 80:3).

Therefore, in His Omnipresence, He is so close to us that when we speak to Him, we whisper. Even if we only think about Him, we can communicate with Him. This revelation of the *chessed* of *HaKadosh Baruch Hu* and His closeness applies to the whole world. And then we continue:

◈§ וְלִגְדֻלָּתוֹ אֵין חֵקֶר §◈ — **And His greatness is beyond investigation.** God's greatness is "unsearchable." The human mind cannot fathom such infinite greatness. It is beyond our capacity to comprehend His Omnipresence.

◈§ דּוֹר לְדוֹר יְשַׁבַּח מַעֲשֶׂיךָ, וּגְבוּרֹתֶיךָ יַגִּידוּ §◈ — **Each generation will praise Your deeds to the next, and of Your mighty deeds they will tell.** In this new world — *olam shekulo tov* — which will exist after the arrival of *Mashiach*, the entire world will praise the works of *HaKadosh Baruch Hu*. They will tell their children of His mighty deeds which they experienced, how all the evil powers in the world were destroyed, and how *HaKadosh Baruch Hu* established this new world order in which they now find themselves.

◈§ הֲדַר כְּבוֹד הוֹדֶךָ, וְדִבְרֵי נִפְלְאֹתֶיךָ אָשִׂיחָה §◈ — **However,** says Dovid HaMelech in the name of *Klal Yisrael, as for me,* my contribution to the מְהֻלָּל מְאֹד is that **I shall speak of the splendrous glory of Your Majesty and of Your wondrous deeds.** Rav Samson R. Hirsch (*Tehillim* ibid.) explains that while the nations of the world will tell all the details of the mighty upheavals in nature and history and the destruction of the *reshaim* — which were precursors of the coming of *Mashiach* and the establishment of *Malchus Shamayim* in the world — *Klal Yisrael* will see these events as manifestations of the beauty and the glory of God. As a result of the special insight that the Torah gives the Jewish nation, it views these world-historic events from a loftier perspective: גַּל עֵינַי וְאַבִּיטָה נִפְלָאוֹת מִתּוֹרָתֶךָ, *Unveil my eyes that I may perceive wonders from Your Torah* (*Tehillim* 119:18). For greater emphasis, this thought is repeated in the following verse:

∾ וֶעֱזוּז נוֹרְאוֹתֶיךָ יֹאמֵרוּ, וּגְדוּלָּתְךָ אֲסַפְּרֶנָּה — **And of Your awesome power they will speak, but I will tell of Your greatness.** While they, the nations of the world, will speak of the fierceness of Your awesome deeds, meaning the disasters which have befallen the *reshaim* and which prepared the way for the establishment of the kingdom of *HaKadosh Baruch Hu* in the world, Dovid HaMelech says, but *I will tell of Your greatness*. As previously mentioned, גָּדוֹל, in describing *HaKadosh Baruch Hu,* always refers to His lovingkindness, as in גָּדַל חֶסֶד. So Dovid HaMelech says here that at that momentous period in the history of the world, he will desire to stress the lovingkindness of *HaKadosh Baruch Hu,* and describe how His goodness fills the world.

∾ זֵכֶר רַב טוּבְךָ יַבִּיעוּ, וְצִדְקָתְךָ יְרַנֵּנוּ — After Dovid HaMelech has praised the גָּדַל חֶסֶד aspect of *HaKadosh Baruch Hu,* the nations of the world will also want to follow suit. Therefore, **they will express the memory of Your abundant goodness, and be jubilant about Your righteousness.**

The word יַבִּיעוּ, translated as *express,* really means to bubble over with excited talk, as in נַחַל נֹבֵעַ, *a gushing stream* (Mishlei 18:4). Similarly, we find יוֹם לְיוֹם יַבִּיעַ אֹמֶר, *Day following day brings expressions of praise* (Tehillim 19:3). So here the *pasuk* means, "The nations, too, will bubble over with excitement regarding the abundant goodness of *HaKadosh Baruch Hu.*"

The word צִדְקָתְךָ, *righteousness,* from צְדָקָה, is explained in *Zohar HaKadosh* (2:62; 3:111) as being a combination of *chessed* and *gevurah.* The nations of the world will also see the *chessed* of *HaKadosh Baruch Hu* inherent in His *gevurah.*

∾ חַנּוּן וְרַחוּם ה' — **Gracious and merciful is Hashem.** In that world of *kulo tov,* the nations will exult over the fact that Hashem is accessible to them. He is חַנּוּן, *gracious,* even to the undeserving, and He is certainly רַחוּם, *merciful,* to those who deserve His mercy and compassion.

∾ אֶרֶךְ אַפַּיִם וּגְדָל חָסֶד — The nations continue: **He is long suffering and great in [bestowing] kindness.** This means that *HaKadosh Baruch Hu* has given us the opportunity, over a long period of time, to make good the wrongs that we have committed.

∾ טוֹב ה' לַכֹּל, וְרַחֲמָיו עַל כָּל מַעֲשָׂיו — In this vision of the ideal world, *Bnei Yisrael* and the *umos ha'olam,* together, exclaim: **Hashem is good to all, and His mercy is upon all His works.** This includes not only mankind, but all animals, every butterfly, every blade of grass, and every flower. And therefore:

∾ יוֹדוּךָ ה' כָּל מַעֲשֶׂיךָ, וַחֲסִידֶיךָ יְבָרְכוּכָה — **All Your works shall thank You, Hashem, and Your devout ones,** whom You love, **will bless You.** They will express the fervent desire that the world's awareness of *HaKadosh Baruch Hu* shall continue to grow, as in יִתְגַּדַּל וְיִתְקַדַּשׁ שְׁמֵהּ רַבָּא.

ּ‌כְּבוֹד מַלְכוּתְךָ יֹאמֵרוּ, וּגְבוּרָתְךָ יְדַבֵּרוּ — **Of the glory of Your kingdom they will speak, and of Your power they will tell.** Now the nations of the world, having learned from *Bnei Yisrael,* combine both the *malchus* and the *gevurah*: They speak softly and reverently of the glory of the kingdom of *HaKadosh Baruch Hu* (*yomeiru*); and, in strong terms, (*yedabeiru*) talk of the world-shaking events which His power has brought about.

ּ‌לְהוֹדִיעַ לִבְנֵי הָאָדָם גְּבוּרֹתָיו, וּכְבוֹד הֲדַר מַלְכוּתוֹ — **To inform human beings of His mighty deeds, and the glorious splendor of His kingdom.** They will inform the people who were born after the mighty world-shaking upheavals that brought about this completely changed world, of the combination of God's greatness and the glory and beauty of His kingdom. Those decent human beings, who will deserve to be called בְּנֵי הָאָדָם, will need to know the attributes of *HaKadosh Baruch Hu,* Who brought about this ideal world in which they live.

ּ‌מַלְכוּתְךָ מַלְכוּת כָּל עֹלָמִים, וּמֶמְשַׁלְתְּךָ בְּכָל דּוֹר וָדֹר — **Your kingdom is a kingdom spanning all eternities, and Your dominion is throughout every generation.** In this vision of the future world, Dovid HaMelech sees the nations of the world, in symphony with *Bnei Yisrael,* who will conduct them, exclaiming that the kingdom of *HaKadosh Baruch Hu* will last for all time periods, extending to all future generations. The world will not revert back to the earlier period of good and evil, and ups and downs.

ּ‌סוֹמֵךְ ה' לְכָל הַנֹּפְלִים, וְזוֹקֵף לְכָל הַכְּפוּפִים — **Hashem supports all those who are about to fall and straightens those who are bowed down.** The order of the *pesukim* up to this point in the *mizmor* has followed the *aleph-beis,* beginning with אֲרוֹמִמְךָ אֱלוֹהַי הַמֶּלֶךְ, and continuing through מַלְכוּתְךָ וגו'. This *pasuk,* however, omits the נ, and begins with a ס.

The reason is given in the Gemara (*Berachos* 4b): מִפְּנֵי שֶׁיֵּשׁ בָּהּ מַפַּלְתָּן שֶׁל שׂוֹנְאֵי יִשְׂרָאֵל. The letter נ has an ominous connotation, in that it is the first letter in the *pasuk,* נָפְלָה לֹא תוֹסִיף קוּם בְּתוּלַת יִשְׂרָאֵל, *She has fallen and will no longer rise, virgin of Israel* (*Amos* 5:2), which refers to the downfall of the Jewish nation.

However, continues the Gemara, Dovid HaMelech, in his *ruach hakodesh,* envisioned an *olam shekulo tov,* in which there is no נְפִילָה, *falling,* because *HaKadosh Baruch Hu* will support all those who are weak, physically or spiritually, without exception (לְכָל הַנֹּפְלִים, לְכָל הַכְּפוּפִים). So the absence of the נ, followed by סוֹמֵךְ, alludes to a world in which there is no falling.

ּ‌עֵינֵי כֹל אֵלֶיךָ יְשַׂבֵּרוּ — **The eyes of all expectantly look forward to You.** The word יְשַׂבֵּרוּ is related to the Aramaic סָבַר, meaning *to understand,* or סָבְרִי, which is said before making *Kiddush,* and means, "Pay attention to me, I want to be *motzi* you, to include the fulfillment of your obligation with my

ASHREI ⁓ 173

berachah." The Targum of לִישׁוּעָתְךָ קִוִּיתִי ה׳ (Bereishis 49:18) is, לְפוּרְקָנָךְ סַבָּרִית ה׳, *I hopefully look forward to Your redemption.*

◆§ וְאַתָּה נוֹתֵן לָהֶם אֶת אָכְלָם בְּעִתּוֹ — **And You give them their food in its time.** There is no starvation or hunger. Whenever the need for food arises, it is there for them.

This does not reflect the realities of our world. This is the future world which all the *Neviim* have predicted. This is אֲרוֹמִמְךָ אֱלוֹהַי הַמֶּלֶךְ, our highest expectation, that of *Olam Haba,* the future, perfect world after *Mashiach* comes, which we believe with *emunah sheleimah* (complete faith), will eventually come about. And when one firmly believes that this will eventually become a reality, he has been assured by *Chazal* that indeed he will see it — מוּבְטָח לוֹ שֶׁהוּא בֶּן הָעוֹלָם הַבָּא.

However, for the time being we must deal with the realities of the "here and now," the world in which we presently live, which was referred to earlier in this *mizmor* as בְּכָל יוֹם אֲבָרְכֶךָּ, and this is the subject of the second part of אַשְׁרֵי, which follows.

◆§ פּוֹתֵחַ אֶת יָדֶךָ וּמַשְׂבִּיעַ לְכָל חַי רָצוֹן — **You open Your hand and satisfy the desire of every living thing.** "Open," by definition, indicates that sometimes the hand is closed. In our present world there are times and places where there is no food. Some people are hungry; they do not always have אָכְלָם בְּעִתּוֹ. In these cases, the hand of *HaKadosh Baruch Hu* is, so to speak, "closed." So we praise Him for opening His hand after it was closed."

This brings to mind the Gemara which says: כָּל מְזוֹנוֹתָיו שֶׁל אָדָם קְצוּבִים לוֹ מֵרֹאשׁ הַשָּׁנָה וְעַד יוֹם הַכִּפּוּרִים, *The amount of a person's livelihood for the entire year is predetermined for him during the period between Rosh Hashanah and Yom Kippur* (Beitzah 16a). However, the Gemara there lists the following exceptions: חוּץ מֵהוֹצָאַת שַׁבָּת וְיוֹם טוֹב וְהוֹצָאַת בָּנָיו לְתַלְמוּד תּוֹרָה, *except for his expenditure on Shabbos and Yom Tov and his expenditure on educating his children in Torah.* Whatever one spends for these items will be added by *HaKadosh Baruch Hu* to the "budget" — כָּל הַמּוֹסִיף מוֹסִיפִין לֵיהּ.

So, for instance, trying to save money on yeshivah tuitions will not add anything to the bottom line, because whatever expense one incurs for his children's Torah education will be reimbursed by *HaKadosh Baruch Hu.*

To understand the importance of this *pasuk,* let us again refer to the Gemara: כָּל הָאוֹמֵר תְּהִלָּה לְדָוִד בְּכָל יוֹם שָׁלֹשׁ פְּעָמִים מוּבְטָח לוֹ שֶׁהוּא בֶּן הָעוֹלָם הַבָּא, *Whoever says Tehillah L'Dovid three times every day may be assured that he is worthy of the World to Come* (Berachos 4b).

The Gemara there inquires as to what it is about אַשְׁרֵי that, if he recites it daily, assures a person of *Olam Haba.*

אִילֵימָא מִשּׁוּם דְּאָתְיָא בְּא״ב, *If its importance lies in the fact that it follows the* aleph-beis, נֵימָא אַשְׁרֵי תְּמִימֵי דָרֶךְ דְּאָתְיָא בִּתְמַנְיָא אַפִּין, then it would be better to say Tehillim 119, which contains an eightfold repetition of the aleph-beis.

The Gemara continues: אֶלָּא מִשּׁוּם דְּאִית בֵּיהּ פּוֹתֵחַ אֶת יָדֶךָ, If it is because it contains the words פּוֹתֵחַ אֶת יָדֶךָ, which praise HaKadosh Baruch Hu for giving us parnassah, then let him say הַלֵּל הַגָּדוֹל which contains similar words: נוֹתֵן לֶחֶם לְכָל בָּשָׂר כִּי לְעוֹלָם חַסְדּוֹ, He gives bread to all living creatures, for His kindness endures forever (Tehillim 136:25).

The final reason given by the Gemara is, אֶלָּא מִשּׁוּם דְּאִית בֵּיהּ תַּרְתֵּי, It has both: It follows the aleph-beis, and it contains a reference to parnassah in the pasuk, פּוֹתֵחַ אֶת יָדֶךָ.

This Gemara presents several difficulties:

First, what is the connection between the aleph-beis and one's livelihood? Second, why is this connection found only in פּוֹתֵחַ אֶת יָדֶךָ? The previous pasuk of עֵינֵי כֹל אֵלֶיךָ יְשַׂבֵּרוּ וְאַתָּה נוֹתֵן לָהֶם אֶת אָכְלָם בְּעִתּוֹ also deals with this subject, so why is it ignored?

Furthermore, the importance of פּוֹתֵחַ אֶת יָדֶיךָ is underscored by the halachah in Orach Chaim 51:7, that if one failed to have kavannah while saying פּוֹתֵחַ אֶת יָדֶךָ, he must repeat it. This means that since this mizmor follows the aleph-beis, he must repeat all the words from פּוֹתֵחַ אֶת יָדֶךָ until the end of the chapter, even if he already said it.

The role of HaKadosh Baruch Hu in a person's livelihood is described: קָשִׁין מְזוֹנוֹתָיו שֶׁל אָדָם יוֹתֵר מִן הַגְּאֻלָּה, דְּאִילּוּ בִּגְאֻלָּה כְּתִיב הַמַּלְאָךְ הַגֹּאֵל אוֹתִי מִכָּל רָע . . . וְאִילּוּ בִּמְזוֹנוֹת כְּתִיב הָאֱלֹהִים הָרוֹעֶה אוֹתִי, One's livelihood is more difficult than redemption, because Yaakov Avinu described his redemption as having been done by a malach, but as to his livelihood, he recognized that it was God Himself who provided it to him (Pesachim 118a). When Yaakov Avinu looked back on his life, he described his salvation from harm as having come through a malach, a heavenly messenger. However, as to his livelihood, he recognized that this came directly from הָאֱלֹהִים הָרוֹעֶה אוֹתִי, God Who fed and nourished me, from my beginnings until this day.

So, says the Gemara, we see that HaKadosh Baruch Hu comes into closer contact with a person in providing for his livelihood than He does in redeeming him from harm. For us, it is difficult to differentiate between being saved by a malach — who is sent by HaKadosh Baruch Hu — and being provided for directly by HaKadosh Baruch Hu. Nevertheless, there must be a difference. There must be something about providing for a person's parnassah that could not be done by a malach.

In the Bircas HaMazon, when we ask HaKadosh Baruch Hu to provide for our sustenance, we ask that it come directly from "His hand": כִּי אִם לְיָדְךָ הַמְּלֵאָה הַפְּתוּחָה הַקְּדוֹשָׁה וְהָרְחָבָה, but only of Your Hand that is full, open, holy, and generous.

Many years ago, at my own sheva berachos [Ed. note: This was early

November, 1931], I heard an explanation in the name of Rav Samson R. Hirsch that sheds a great deal of light on the matter of one's *parnassah*. One of the speakers on that occasion was Marcus Hirsch, a grandson of Rav Hirsch. He was a distant relative of my wife, the *kallah*. In expressing his good wishes to us, as *chassan* and *kallah,* he reminisced about a stroll which he had taken with his grandfather during which Rav Hirsch gave him a unique explanation of the *pasuk,* פּוֹתֵחַ אֶת יָדֶךָ וּמַשְׂבִּיעַ לְכָל חַי רָצוֹן.

In his commentary on *Tehillim,* which had already been published at that time, Rav Hirsch explained the *pasuk* to mean that *HaKadosh Baruch Hu* opens His hand and satiates the desire of all who are living. However, during that stroll, he told his young grandson that the *pasuk* also has another meaning: the word רָצוֹן means *goodwill* or *benevolence,* as in יְהִי רְצוּי אֶחָיו, *he shall be pleasing to his brothers* (*Devarim* 33:24); or יְהִי רָצוֹן מִלְפָנֶיךָ, the meaning there being that of finding favor with others or being well liked. He translated it in German as *"wohlgefallen."*

He explained that this *pasuk* means that *HaKadosh Baruch Hu* provides a person with goodwill and favorable acceptance in the eyes of others, which is the prerequisite for all *parnassah*. One's livelihood is based on whether or not he finds רָצוֹן, *favor,* in the eyes of others. This could apply to a beggar who knocks at the door, or to a professor who is applying for a position at a university. If the beggar finds favor, he will receive a donation, and if not, the owner will either close the door in his face, or if he wants to at least fulfill the *mitzvah* of *tzedakah,* he will give him only a pittance. Similarly, a professor with the highest qualifications who is not liked by the board of directors will not be given tenure by them. A salesman of goods or services who is not well liked will not get an order. There were instances of famous painters who died in poverty because nobody would buy their works; they were not well liked. Nevertheless, after their deaths, their paintings were sold for a great deal of money. The finding of favor with others, which results in one's *parnassah,* is a *neis* (miracle), which comes directly from *HaKadosh Baruch Hu*. Each time a person succeeds in selling his goods or services, or if he is well liked as a doctor, a psychiatrist, an engineer, a government worker, or even as a simple assistant in the sanitation department, he has experienced the *neis* of *parnassah,* which comes directly from *HaKadosh Baruch Hu*. If people like the way he repairs shoes, or the merchandise he sells, whether he is a small peddler or the owner of a giant department store, he has experienced the miracle of a favorable reception in the eyes of his fellow man, which comes directly from *HaKadosh Baruch Hu*. If people do not like Macy's or Wal-Mart, these stores will go out of business, and if people stop liking Coca-Cola, it too will cease to exist.

Nobody understands why and how certain people have רָצוֹן, while others do not. The secret of *parnassah* is known only to *HaKadosh Baruch Hu*.

While Divine salvation in other areas of one's life could happen by means of הַמַּלְאָךְ הַגֹּאֵל אֹתִי מִכָּל רָע, however, in the area of one's *parnassah*, it is הָאֱלֹהִים הָרוֹעֶה אוֹתִי, it is God Himself Who provides for me.

So the meaning of this *pasuk* is that *HaKadosh Baruch Hu* satiates all life with רָצוֹן, goodwill and favor in the eyes of others, which enables people to make a living.

However, whatever the explanation of רָצוֹן is, this *pasuk* begs the obvious question: What is the meaning of לְכָל חַי, *every living thing?* All life does not benefit from this miracle of finding favor and consequently having *parnassah*. A large portion of the world's population suffers from hunger and starvation. They have not been granted their *parnassah*. Indeed, the Torah itself makes reference to hunger: וַיְהִי רָעָב בָּאָרֶץ, *There was a famine in the land* (*Bereishis* 12:10, 26:1). There is even the gruesome reference to extreme hunger: וְאָכַלְתָּ פְרִי בִטְנְךָ, *You will eat the fruit of your womb* (*Devarim* 28:53-57). The same question applies to the words of *Birchas HaMazon*: כִּי הוּא אֵל זָן וּמְפַרְנֵס לַכֹּל וּמֵטִיב וּמֵכִין מָזוֹן לְכָל בְּרִיּוֹתָיו אֲשֶׁר בָּרָא, בָּרוּךְ אַתָּה ה', הַזָּן אֶת הַכֹּל, *because He is God Who nourishes and sustains and benefits all, and He prepares food for all of His creatures which He created. Blessed are You, Hashem, Who nourishes all.*

The underlying meaning of this *berachah* can be found in the text of *nusach Sefard,* which reads: כָּאָמוּר פּוֹתֵחַ אֶת יָדֶךָ וּמַשְׂבִּיעַ לְכָל חַי רָצוֹן, בָּרוּךְ אַתָּה ה', הַזָּן אֶת הַכֹּל. While this is not our *minhag,* it nevertheless reflects the underlying sense of the *berachah,* which is that the emphasis is on the word חַי. If *HaKadosh Baruch Hu* wants any creature — man or mouse — to live, He will give him the ability to do so. So this *pasuk* means, "He will satiate with His benevolence לְכָל חַי, *all those whom He wants to live."*

So, it is in the sense of מַשְׂבִּיעַ לְכָל חַי that we say *HaKadosh Baruch Hu* is: מְפַרְנֵס לַכֹּל, מֵטִיב לַכֹּל, מֵכִין מָזוֹן לְכָל בְּרִיּוֹתָיו, הַזָּן אֶת הַכֹּל. The meaning is that all those who do have sustenance and food have *HaKadosh Baruch Hu* to thank for it. If He wants a person to live, He gives him the means to survive.

As previously explained, this *pasuk* does not refer to the ideal world, which is envisioned in the first part of אַשְׁרֵי, and which will become a reality when God sees fit. It refers to the world in which we live, where we experience the hand of *HaKadosh Baruch Hu* as sometimes being "open," and at other times "closed." And when He opens His hand, it is for the purpose of מַשְׂבִּיעַ לְכָל חַי, to satiate those whom He wants to live. If a person has food, it is because *HaKadosh Baruch Hu* wants him to live. He has experienced the miracle of *parnassah*.

The aforementioned Gemara stresses the importance of אַשְׁרֵי in that it follows the alphabetical order, and includes a reference to the miracle of one's *parnassah*: פּוֹתֵחַ אֶת יָדֶךָ. However, these two dominant factors of אַשְׁרֵי are really totally different.

An alphabetical order presupposes human logic and order: א is followed by ב, and so on; the number 1 is followed by the number 2; 2 + 2 = 4, etc. This is all based on logical progression. However, the miracle of *parnassah*, as reflected by פּוֹתֵחַ אֶת יָדֶךָ, is a part of the world of *nissim*, which is outside the ordered world of logic; it is not part of the *aleph-beis* and is fully perceived only by the *neshamah*.

The same dualism also exists in the area of Torah. The Torah which we have received is a revelation from *HaKadosh Baruch Hu*. Its formulation is not based on human logic. For instance, we know that אֵין מוּקְדָם וּמְאוּחָר בַּתּוֹרָה, *there is no chronological order in the Torah;* it does not follow the *aleph-beis* but rather starts with a ב and ends with a ל. It is the *chachmah* (wisdom) of *HaKadosh Baruch Hu* and as such comes under the heading of לִתְבוּנָתוֹ אֵין מִסְפָּר, *to His mind, there are no numbers* (*Tehillim* 147:5). Numbers do not matter to *HaKadosh Baruch Hu*. The Torah teaches truths which no human mind could formulate, and includes laws which we cannot understand. In fact, our *Chachamim* tell us that Torah is the very "blueprint of the world." [See remarks on *Adon Olam*.]

However, the *learning* of Torah, the integration of its subject matter, and the understanding of its principles is, indeed, within our realm. This is הַנִּגְלֹת לָנוּ, *those things which are revealed to us;* this *does* follow a system of *aleph-beis*. We are required to use our human, logical mind to the greatest possible extent in order to understand it. It is for this reason that psalm 119, previously referred to as תְּמַנְיָא אַפֵּי (the eightfold repetition of the *aleph-beis*), which deals only with *limud haTorah*, follows the *aleph-beis*, repeating it eight times. For the same reason, *Eishes Chayil* (*Mishlei* 31), which *Chazal* tell us (see *Yalkut* ibid.) is a metaphor for the Torah, follows the order of the *aleph-beis*. The study of Torah is based on the use of the human, logical mind. Furthermore, *Chazal* tell us: לְפִיכָךְ נִקְרְאוּ רִאשׁוֹנִים סוֹפְרִים שֶׁהָיוּ סוֹפְרִים כָּל הָאוֹתִיוֹת שֶׁבַּתּוֹרָה (*Kiddushin* 30a). Our early sages counted and understood the meaning and importance of each and every letter in the Torah.

Similarly, the concept of *parnassah* also has two aspects: that of it being a *neis* from *HaKadosh Baruch Hu*, which is based strictly on *emunah*, and the human intellectual element necessary in the pursuit of one's livelihood.

Both of these aspects are referred to at the time of the Heavenly judgment: בְּשָׁעָה שֶׁמַּכְנִיסִין אָדָם לְדִין אוֹמְרִים לוֹ נָשָׂאתָ וְנָתַתָּ בֶּאֱמוּנָה, *When a person is brought to trial (after death) he is asked: Did you conduct your business affairs with faith?* (*Shabbos* 31a). This question, concerning one's business dealings with *emunah*, has two meanings.

First, it means: Did you conduct your business with the conviction that it is not your efforts that will bring about your *parnassah*? Did you firmly believe that your *parnassah* has been predetermined by *HaKadosh Baruch*

Hu for reasons, and in a manner, which we cannot understand? That when you offered your merchandise or services for sale, it was strictly up to *HaKadosh Baruch Hu* whether or not you would find favor in the eyes of your potential clients? That your *parnassah* was really a *neis* from *HaKadosh Baruch Hu*?

And it also means: Did you conduct your business honestly? Could people trust you? For this, you will have had to use your human intelligence; you will have had to learn a trade or other means of earning a livelihood.

The Torah presupposes that people must know how to calculate values. We find the phrase וְחִשַּׁב עִם קֹנֵהוּ, *He shall make a reckoning with his purchaser* (*Vayikra* 25:50), in connection with the calculation of the unearned redemption value of the purchase price of an *eved ivri*, a Jewish indentured slave. An erroneous business calculation could result in violating the prohibitions of *gezel* or *onaah*, thievery or price fraud.

When one does business, it must be *b'emunah*; other people should be able to trust him. So when *Chazal* talk of *parnassah* in terms of הַנְהֵג בָּהֶם מִנְהַג דֶּרֶךְ אֶרֶץ, *encourage them to conduct normal business affairs* (*Berachos* 35b), it means that one is to use his human intellect to conduct his business in a manner in which people can trust him. Human intellectual effort is required in completing agreements and contracts; making statements of "yes" which means "yes," or "no" which means "no"; and maintaining honesty regarding weights and measures. All of this requires the use of the *aleph-beis*.

אַשְׁרֵי was designated by our *Chachamim* as the perfect *tefillah* for one's livelihood because it contains these two aspects of *emunah* which make up the total of a person's quest for a livelihood, דְּאִית בֵּיהּ תַּרְתֵּי, *for it has both*: that of the *aleph-beis*, the orderly progression — which represents the human intellectual input into one's livelihood, his logic, his honesty, and reliability — and the aspect of pure *emunah* (faith) that Hashem will grant me goodwill in the eyes of people, expressed by the word *ratzon*, which represents the direct intervention of *HaKadosh Baruch Hu* in providing one's *parnassah*.

The *pasuk* of עֵינֵי כֹל אֵלֶיךָ יְשַׂבֵּרוּ וְאַתָּה נוֹתֵן לָהֶם אֶת אָכְלָם בְּעִתּוֹ, which is a vision of the future, ideal, world, but does not represent our present-day world, would not fully convey all the thoughts which are inherent in פּוֹתֵחַ אֶת יָדֶיךָ as we have explained them. It is therefore not mentioned in the Gemara as being the reason אַשְׁרֵי was chosen.

◆§ צַדִּיק ה' בְּכָל דְּרָכָיו וְחָסִיד בְּכָל מַעֲשָׂיו — **Righteous is Hashem in all His ways and magnanimous in all His deeds.** I heard a beautiful explanation on this from Rav Joseph Breuer. He said that this is the צִדּוּק הַדִּין (a prayer said for the acceptance of God's strict judgment) of one who is not treated by *HaKadosh Baruch Hu* the way he would wish, and he is not successful in finding רָצוֹן, *favor,* in the eyes of people, which leaves him with an inadequate livelihood.

In this case, he is מַצְדִיק עָלָיו אֶת הַדִּין. He expresses *emunah* in Hashem by saying *HaKadosh Baruch Hu* is just in all His ways. Even if he lost his job or does not succeed, it is God's will. And since He is just, there must be a reason for it.

And if, in spite of the fact that he does not deserve it, *HaKadosh Baruch Hu* hears his *tefillos* and does grant him some measure of *parnassah, lifnim mishuras hadin,* over and above what he deserves, it is only because He is חָסִיד בְּכָל מַעֲשָׂיו, He goes beyond the strict judgment and grants him חֶסֶד, *lovingkindness.*

ספ קָרוֹב ה' לְכָל קֹרְאָיו — **Hashem is close to all who call upon Him.** This represents our world, where people call out to Hashem for their sustenance. *HaKadosh Baruch Hu* is close to those who call on Him.

ספ לְכֹל אֲשֶׁר יִקְרָאֻהוּ בֶאֱמֶת — **To all who call upon Him sincerely.** However, He is close only to those who call upon Him with sincerity, as *Chazal* tell us, יָכוֹל לַכֹּל, תַּלְמוּד לוֹמַר לְכֹל אֲשֶׁר יִקְרָאֻהוּ בֶאֱמֶת, *You might think (He is close) to all, but the pasuk teaches, (He is close only) to those who call upon Him sincerely* (see *Vayikra Rabbah* 17:1). A simple routine *davening* does not help, especially not with regard to *parnassah;* it will not bring a person close to *HaKadosh Baruch Hu.*

ספ רְצוֹן יְרֵאָיו יַעֲשֶׂה וְאֶת שַׁוְעָתָם יִשְׁמַע וְיוֹשִׁיעֵם — **He will do the will of those who fear Him** — He does their will because they are *yere'im,* they are God fearing, **He will hear their cries and save them.** This reflects our world, where people need *parnassah* and call out to *HaKadosh Baruch Hu* for salvation, and they are grateful when He hears their pleas for help.

I once heard another explanation of the words רְצוֹן יְרֵאָיו יַעֲשֶׂה, as meaning, literally, *HaKadosh Baruch Hu* "creates the will" of those who fear Him. In other words, the desires of God-fearing people are there because *HaKadosh Baruch Hu* causes them to have these desires.

It took me many years to fully understand this, until I realized that this is the meaning of the saying of Rabban Gamliel the son of Rabbi Yehudah HaNasi: עֲשֵׂה רְצוֹנוֹ כִּרְצוֹנְךָ, *Do His will as if it were your will* (*Pirkei Avos* 2:4), meaning a person should perform every *mitzvah* with the same desire as if he wanted to do this for himself. And if one does this, the reward will be כְּדֵי שֶׁיַּעֲשֶׂה רְצוֹנְךָ כִּרְצוֹנוֹ, *So that HaKadosh Baruch Hu will make you want what He wants.*

This, then, is exactly the meaning of our *pasuk*: רְצוֹן יְרֵאָיו יַעֲשֶׂה, the reward of those who fear *HaKadosh Baruch Hu* will be that He will make them want what He wants. And now since these *yere'im,* God-fearing people, want only what *HaKadosh Baruch Hu* wants, וְאֶת שַׁוְעָתָם יִשְׁמַע וְיוֹשִׁיעֵם, He will hear their cries and bring them the salvation which they are seeking.

§ שׁוֹמֵר ה' אֶת כָּל אֹהֲבָיו, וְאֵת כָּל הָרְשָׁעִים יַשְׁמִיד — **Hashem protects all who love Him, but all the wicked He will destroy.** Although it is not always apparent in this world in which we live, Hashem protects all those who love Him, and will destroy the *reshaim*. This is so despite the fact that we often witness just the opposite: *tzaddikim* are destroyed and the *reshaim* are protected. However, this *pasuk* expresses our *emunah* that life in this world is limited, and all that really counts is what follows it. So the meaning here is that Hashem protects the *neshamos* of those who love Him, so that they will reap their eventual reward in *Olam Haba*. However, the *reshaim*, despite their apparent success in this world, will receive their destruction in that future world where final reward and punishment are meted out by *HaKadosh Baruch Hu*.

§ תְּהִלַּת ה' יְדַבֶּר פִּי, וִיבָרֵךְ כָּל בָּשָׂר שֵׁם קָדְשׁוֹ לְעוֹלָם וָעֶד — **May my mouth declare the praise of Hashem, and may all flesh bless His holy Name forever and ever.** Dovid HaMelech concludes this *mizmor* by referring back to the first part, which envisions the future world, *olam shekulo tov*, and says: "What I say now shall not only be a momentary expression, reflecting my mood at the present time, but these exalted feelings of praise to *HaKadosh Baruch Hu* shall remain forever, and eventually the entire world will join me in blessing His holy Name forever."

While this is actually the end of psalm 145, nevertheless the *minhag Yisrael*, dating back to the *siddur* of Rav Amram Gaon, is to follow this with the last *pasuk* of psalm 115, which is part of *Hallel*:

§ וַאֲנַחְנוּ נְבָרֵךְ יָהּ מֵעַתָּה וְעַד עוֹלָם, הַלְלוּיָהּ — **We will bless God from this time forward, Halleluyah.** This corresponds to the aforementioned saying of our *Chachamim*: כָּל הָאוֹמֵר תְּהִלָּה לְדָוִד בְּכָל יוֹם מֻבְטָח לוֹ שֶׁהוּא בֶּן הָעוֹלָם הַבָּא, *Whoever says the psalm, "A praise of Dovid," every day is assured that he is worthy of the World to Come.* We therefore express the wish through this *pasuk* that we may be *zocheh* to bless *HaKadosh Baruch Hu* not only now but forever — in the world of *Olam Haba* as well. And to this wish we add הַלְלוּיָהּ, *All of you praise God*, which means it is our wish that the whole world may chime in — together with us — and sing the praises of *HaKadosh Baruch Hu*.

However, Rav Amram Gaon gives an additional reason for adding this *pasuk*: כְּדֵי לְשַׁלְשׁוּלֵי הַלְלוּיָהּ בָּתַר הַלְלוּיָהּ, *so that this* הַלְלוּיָהּ *may be attached*, in a chainlike fashion, to the following הַלְלוּיָהּ.

The *Bach* (*Orach Chaim* 51) explains this to mean: כְּלוֹמַר שֶׁיִּהְיוּ קְשׁוּרִים כָּל הַמִּזְמוֹרִים יַחַד מִתְּחִלָּה וְעַד סוֹף כְּשַׁלְשֶׁלֶת לְהַתְחִיל בְּהַלְלוּיָהּ וּלְסַיֵּם בְּהַלְלוּיָהּ, *So that these six consecutive mizmorim will be attached from beginning to end, in a chainlike fashion, starting with* הַלְלוּיָהּ *and ending with* הַלְלוּיָהּ. Since תְּהִלָּה לְדָוִד starts, but does not end, with תְּהִלָּה (a form of הַלְלוּיָהּ), the *pasuk* of וַאֲנַחְנוּ נְבָרֵךְ יָהּ ... הַלְלוּיָהּ, was inserted as a link between תְּהִלָּה לְדָוִד and the following five *mizmorim,* which all begin and end with הַלְלוּיָהּ.

This reason is very much in accord with our explanation that the *Pesukei d'Zimrah* correspond to the *Ulam.* By linking these *mizmorim* together we are reminded of the interlocking golden chains in that preparatory chamber in which the *Kohanim* readied themselves to enter the *Heichal,* just as the *Pesukei d'Zimrah* prepare us for the actual *tefillah.*

הַלְלוּיָהּ הַלְלִי נַפְשִׁי אֶת ה' / Halleluyah Halleli Nafshi Es Hashem

With this *mizmor* we begin the five psalms, 146-150, which conclude *Sefer Tehillim*. The Gemara quotes Rabbi Yose: יְהֵא חֶלְקִי מִגּוֹמְרֵי הַלֵּל בְּכָל יוֹם, *May my portion in Olam Haba be together with those who complete Hallel every day* (Shabbos 118b). The Gemara defines the "completing of *Hallel*" in general terms to mean *Pesukei d'Zimrah,* and this is further explained by the commentators (see *Rambam, Hil. Tefillah* 7:12) as referring to the part of *Pesukei d'Zimrah* which includes the end of *Tehillim,* i.e., from תְּהִלָּה לְדָוִד through these five chapters of הַלְלוּיָהּ.

However, Rashi on the Gemara (ibid.) defines this as referring only to two of them: הַלְלוּ אֶת ה' מִן הַשָּׁמַיִם, *Praise Hashem from the heavens* (psalm 148), and הַלְלוּ אֵל בְּקָדְשׁוֹ, *Praise God in His Sanctuary* (psalm 150). Therefore, if a person did not have enough time to say all five he should at least say these two.

The aforementioned wish of Rabbi Yose that he hoped to merit the reward of those who "finish *Hallel*" every day means that he wished he could say all of these *mizmorim* every day, and not have to omit some to keep up with the *chazzan* who apparently *davened* too quickly for Rabbi Yose to have the proper *kavannah.*

We have previously explained that the *Pesukei d'Zimrah* are divided into five parts. (See notes on בָּרוּךְ שֶׁאָמַר.) Up to this point, we have shown how the first part until אַשְׁרֵי corresponds to נְגַדֶּלְךָ, and that אַשְׁרֵי (תְּהִלָּה לְדָוִד) itself corresponds to נְשַׁבֵּחֲךָ.

With these five chapters of הַלְלוּיָהּ, we have come to the third part, which corresponds to נְפָאֶרְךָ, meaning, *We will give You the crown.* The root פאר, *top,* is used here to mean a crown which is placed on top of the head. It is also found in לֹא תְפַאֵר אַחֲרֶיךָ, *Do not remove all the splendor behind you* (Devarim 24:20), where it refers to the fruits which grow on top of the tree.

The sense in which it is used here is that these five last chapters of *Tehillim* are the פְּאֵר, or the *top* — the highest — of all the תְּהִלּוֹת, שִׁירוֹת, וְתִשְׁבָּחוֹת, (various expressions of praise) which Dovid HaMelech recited. We will show how they envision the קֵץ כָּל הַיָּמִים, *End of Days,* which includes *yemos HaMashiach, techiyas hameisim,* and *olam haneshamos.* (These terms refer to the future: Epoch of *Mashiach;* Revival of the Dead; and the spiritual world of souls after death.) The sequence of these הַלְלוּיָהּ is:

❑ הַלְלוּיָהּ, הַלְלִי נַפְשִׁי אֶת ה', which corresponds to our present period, the "predawn," the time before *bi'as haMashiach.* This is the realm of *nefesh.*

❑ הַלְלוּיָהּ, כִּי טוֹב זַמְּרָה אֱלֹהֵינוּ, which is set in the period of the dawn of the epoch of *yemos haMashiach*. We will call this the period of *ruach*.

❑ הַלְלוּיָהּ, הַלְלוּ אֶת ה' מִן הַשָּׁמַיִם, which corresponds to the actual period of *yemos haMashiach*. We will show how this *mizmor* refers to the level of *ruach hakodesh*.

❑ הַלְלוּיָהּ, שִׁירוּ לַה' שִׁיר חָדָשׁ, which refers to *techiyas hameisim*, the period in which the aspect of *neshamah* becomes dominant when it is reunified with the *guf*.

❑ And then finally: הַלְלוּיָהּ, הַלְלוּ אֵל בְּקָדְשׁוֹ . . . כֹּל הַנְּשָׁמָה תְּהַלֵּל יָהּ, which refers to the *olam haneshamos*, that purely spiritual world which is the highest sublimity of our existence as creatures of *HaKadosh Baruch Hu*.

The previous *pasuk*, תְּהִלַּת ה' יְדַבֶּר פִּי וִיבָרֵךְ כָּל בָּשָׂר שֵׁם קָדְשׁוֹ וגו', describes how all of humanity expresses its gratitude, physically, for the bounty which *HaKadosh Baruch Hu* has bestowed upon the world. This is the level of *guf*. This first הַלְלוּיָהּ ascends one step higher, in that it talks of the praises offered to *HaKadosh Baruch Hu* by the *nefesh*, the spiritual aspect of the human personality.

Each of the following five *mizmorim* expresses praises to God from the standpoint of the epoch in which it is set.

❦ ❦ ❦

◆§ הַלְלוּיָהּ, הַלְלִי נַפְשִׁי אֶת ה' — **Halleluyah! Praise Hashem, O my soul.** Here the Psalmist has a dialogue with his soul. He addresses it by saying, "You, my soul, say *Hallel* to Hashem," upon which the *nefesh* answers:

◆§ אֲהַלְלָה ה' בְּחַיָּי, אֲזַמְּרָה לֵאלֹהַי בְּעוֹדִי — **Yes, I will praise Hashem during my lifetime, I will sing to my God as long as I exist.** Another explanation of this *pasuk* is based on הַשְׁאָרַת הַנֶּפֶשׁ, the principle that the soul lives on forever. As an everlasting creature, the *nefesh* answers: "I express my praises to Hashem by the fact that I am alive, and my continued endurance is an expression of song to my God."

The key to understanding the context of this psalm lies in the last sentence: יִמְלֹךְ ה' לְעוֹלָם אֱלֹהַיִךְ צִיּוֹן לְדֹר וָדֹר הַלְלוּיָהּ, *Hashem shall reign forever — your God, O Tziyon — from every generation. Halleluyah!* which is very familiar in that it is the conclusion of every *Kedushah*, be it weekday, Shabbos, or Yom Tov.

The universal reign of *Malchus Shamayim* (the sovereignty of Heaven), to which this *pasuk* refers, is the ultimate goal for which *Klal Yisrael* and all of mankind live. It is this goal that we yearn for in our *tefillah* of Rosh Hashanah: *All* וְיֹאמַר כֹּל אֲשֶׁר נְשָׁמָה בְאַפּוֹ ה' אֱלֹהֵי יִשְׂרָאֵל מֶלֶךְ וּמַלְכוּתוֹ בַּכֹּל מָשָׁלָה,

who possess a soul will say, "Hashem the God of Israel is King, and His reign encompasses everything."

What this means is that the world will not simply recognize Hashem as the King of the universe, but specifically, as אֱלֹהֵי יִשְׂרָאֵל, *the God of Israel*, Who will reign in Tziyon. This means that the *Beis HaMikdash* will have become the house of prayer for the entire world: כִּי בֵיתִי בֵּית תְּפִלָּה יִקָּרֵא לְכָל הָעַמִּים, *For My House will be called a house of prayer for all the peoples* (Yeshayahu 56:7). The rule of *HaKadosh Baruch Hu* over mankind will emanate from there as the capital of the world: כִּי מִצִּיּוֹן תֵּצֵא תוֹרָה, *For from Zion will the Torah come forth* (ibid. 2:3). (See *Avos d'Rabbi Nassan*, Chapter 35.)

At that time, the Jewish people will finally have achieved its goal, that of becoming the מַמְלֶכֶת כֹּהֲנִים וְגוֹי קָדוֹשׁ, *A kingdom of priests and a holy nation* (Shemos 19:6), the role model for the rest of the world, the light to the nations, אוֹר לַגּוֹיִם, which was its mission throughout history.

It is in this context that this הַלְלוּיָהּ was formulated by Dovid HaMelech. Since יִמְלֹךְ ה' לְעוֹלָם אֱלֹהַיִךְ צִיּוֹן וכו' is the last *pasuk*, the entire *mizmor* must be set in the period just before that takes place, and is leading up to that time.

There have been many man-made efforts to bring about *Mashiach*. This dates back to the time of the Persian king Koresh, who pronounced, in the Name of *HaKadosh Baruch Hu*, his desire to rebuild the *Beis HaMikdash*, and he encouraged anyone who wanted to help in this project to do so. (See *Ezra*, Chapter 1, for the details.) Of course, this proved to be a major disappointment. Efforts of this sort have not let up throughout history. Even the beginnings of Christianity had this as its original purpose. Mohammed had the same idea. There were well-known Jewish "false Messiahs," up to our very own time.

So the first lesson the *neshamah* expounds in this *mizmor* is:

אַל תִּבְטְחוּ בִנְדִיבִים, בְּבֶן אָדָם שֶׁאֵין לוֹ תְשׁוּעָה — **Do not rely on nobles, nor on a human being for he holds no salvation.** Do not place your trust on even the most noble-intentioned human beings, who want to bring about the dawn of a new world order. They are mere mortals, who cannot even save themselves. יְשׁוּעָה, *salvation,* is something which endures, but a human being cannot possess the ability to bring this about, because he will eventually die.

תֵּצֵא רוּחוֹ, יָשֻׁב לְאַדְמָתוֹ — **When his spirit goes out, he returns to his own earth.** This is pithily expressed: וְיָשֹׁב הֶעָפָר עַל הָאָרֶץ כְּשֶׁהָיָה, וְהָרוּחַ תָּשׁוּב אֶל הָאֱלֹהִים אֲשֶׁר נְתָנָהּ, *Thus the dust returns to the ground, as it was, and the spirit returns to God Who gave it* (Koheles 12:7).

Rav Samson R. Hirsch explains (see *Tehillim* 146:4) that the only piece of earth that one actually owns and is identified with is the four *amos* in which one is buried. This can be called אַדְמָתוֹ, *his own earth*, which is waiting for the *ben Adam* from the day he is born. Any other real estate that one owns does not truly belong to him. Ownership of property implies one's ability to alter, dispose of, or destroy it. This ability does not exist in the ownership of real estate. It was there before him, and will survive him. Therefore, the word for real estate in Hebrew is אֲחֻזָּה, for one only *holds on to it*, but does not truly "own" it.

☙ בַּיּוֹם הַהוּא אָבְדוּ עֶשְׁתֹּנֹתָיו — **On that day his big plans are lost.** These *nedivim* (noble people) may have had the grandest plans to save the world, or the Jewish nation, or to welcome the new millennium. Marxism, which was a rebellion against the *Ribbono Shel Olam*, was a plan to save the world. However, once the person dies, his plans die with him. He no longer has the power to carry them through.

The word עֶשְׁתֹּן, which is familiar from the *piyut* of Rosh Hashanah, בּוֹחֵן כָּל עֶשְׁתֹּנוֹת, comes from the root עשת, as in, אוּלַי יִתְעַשֵּׁת הָאֱלֹהִים לָנוּ, *Hopefully, God will bethink Himself, will change His plans* (Yonah 1:6). Ordinary plans would be expressed as עֶשְׁתֹּן. However, *extraordinary*, or large, plans are called עֶשְׁתֹּנוֹת. The word עשת also occurs in the Talmud, e.g., מְנוֹרָה הָיְתָה בָּאָה מִן הָעֶשֶׁת, *The Menorah was made from a solid block* (Menachos 28a), where it means strong raw material. As used here, the word עֶשְׁתֹּנוֹת means the strong and substantial plans formulated by the brain.

By the way, the word עַשְׁתֵּי עָשָׂר (the number eleven, literally: ten strengthened) is also related to the same idea. The Gemara (*Sanhedrin* 29a) says: מִנַּיִן שֶׁכָּל הַמּוֹסִיף גּוֹרֵעַ מִדִּכְתִיב (תרומה כו:ז) עַשְׁתֵּי עֶשְׂרֵה יְרִיעוֹת, An example of the dictum, "By adding something, one actually detracts," would be the words עַשְׁתֵּי עֶשְׂרֵה, which means eleven, while the shorter phrase, שְׁתֵּי עֶשְׂרֵה, means twelve. By adding the ע, you have actually taken something away. The lesson taught there is that when it comes to one's spiritual growth, one cannot take giant leaps, but rather, he should elevate himself slowly. He cannot jump from ten to twenty to thirty, etc, but must move forward slowly, step by step. After having reached his first goal, characterized as "ten," he may be tempted to take large steps, עֶשְׁתּוֹנוֹת, and jump to twenty and thirty, etc. He is therefore well advised by *Chazal* to slow down, because כָּל הַמּוֹסִיף גּוֹרֵעַ, *by adding, one detracts.* Having reached the spiritual milestone of "ten," one is advised to progress only gradually toward the next goal of "eleven"; then "twelve," and so on.

☙ אַשְׁרֵי שֶׁאֵל יַעֲקֹב בְּעֶזְרוֹ — **Happy is one whose help is Jacob's God.** Yaakov, throughout his troubles, placed his trust in his Almighty God, to help him. How happy and fortunate is the person who recognizes that his salvation is brought about by the God of Yaakov.

☙ שִׂבְרוֹ עַל ה' אֱלֹהָיו — **Whose hope is in Hashem, his God** — whose thoughts are concentrated on Hashem, His God. He knows that his salvation can come only from *HaKadosh Baruch Hu*.

In our Shabbos *Shacharis tefillah* we say, אֶפֶס בִּלְתְּךָ גּוֹאֲלֵנוּ לִימוֹת הַמָּשִׁיחַ, *Even when Mashiach comes, it will be only You Who will be our Savior.* Even Mashiach himself will be among those who are saved. We find him being called צַדִּיק וְנוֹשָׁע הוּא, *He is a righteous person who will be redeemed* (*Zechariah* 9:9). What we really mean when we say we are waiting for *Mashiach* is that we are waiting for *HaKadosh Baruch Hu* — אֶפֶס בִּלְתְּךָ גּוֹאֲלֵנוּ, *there is no redeemer but You.* In our times there is a great deal of talk about waiting for *Mashiach*, and it almost eclipses the real purpose of the *geulah*, that of the revelation of *HaKadosh Baruch Hu* in the world. *Mashiach* will be the *shaliach* (messenger) of *HaKadosh Baruch Hu* to bring this about.

Even the greatest of all of our leaders, Moshe Rabbeinu, was completely helpless when he, together with *Bnei Yisrael*, faced extreme danger at the time of *krias Yam Suf*. After the great *nissim* which saved the Jewish people, the Torah tells us, וַיַּרְא יִשְׂרָאֵל אֶת הַיָּד הַגְּדֹלָה אֲשֶׁר עָשָׂה ה' בְּמִצְרַיִם . . . וַיַּאֲמִינוּ בַּה' וּבְמֹשֶׁה עַבְדּוֹ, *Israel saw the great hand that Hashem inflicted upon Egypt . . . and they had faith in Hashem and in Moses His servant* (*Shemos* 14:31). *Bnei Yisrael* realized with total conviction that it was only *HaKadosh Baruch Hu* Who saved them, and that Moshe was merely His servant. It is for this same reason that when we recite the story of *yetzias Mitzrayim* in the *Haggadah shel Pesach*, we make no mention of Moshe Rabbeinu. It was *HaKadosh Baruch Hu* Who brought us out of Mitzrayim, and Moshe Rabbeinu was only His messenger.

And now the *mizmor* continues in the context of the anticipation of *bi'as haMashiach*, during which time a new world order will be instituted, together with the universal recognition of *HaKadosh Baruch Hu* as the King over the whole world. This has been promised to us by *HaKadosh Baruch Hu*, as is mentioned in the Torah, then repeated many times in *Neviim* and *Kesuvim*.

עֹשֶׂה שָׁמַיִם וָאָרֶץ אֶת הַיָּם וְאֶת כָּל אֲשֶׁר בָּם הַשֹּׁמֵר אֱמֶת לְעוֹלָם — **He is the Maker of heaven and earth, the sea and all that is in them, Who safeguards truth forever.** That אֱמֶת, *truth* — the promise to bring about the final redemption of Israel and to institute a new world order — was made by the Creator of heaven and earth, and it will be kept forever. This promise and its connection with the creation of the world is mentioned in the verse, לִנְטֹעַ שָׁמַיִם וְלִיסֹד אָרֶץ וְלֵאמֹר לְצִיּוֹן עַמִּי אָתָּה, *He Who plants the heavens and establishes the earth, He is the One Who says: Tziyon, you are My nation* (*Yeshayahu* 51:16).

As long as there is heaven and earth, Tziyon will be the nation of *HaKadosh Baruch Hu*.

The salvation which *HaKadosh Baruch Hu* has promised, which we call *geulah*, and which includes *bi'as haMashiach* and the building of the *Beis*

HaMikdash, which will bring about וְהָיָה ה' לְמֶלֶךְ עַל כָּל הָאָרֶץ, is just as much *emes* (truth) as the existence of the world. The world created by *HaKadosh Baruch Hu* is *emes*; there is no *sheker* (falsehood) in the entire universe with the exception of the human race, which has *bechirah chafshis* (free will).

Each month, at *kiddush levanah,* when we acknowledge God's renewal of the lunar cycle, we say: פּוֹעֵל אֱמֶת שֶׁפְּעֻלָּתוֹ אֱמֶת, וְלַלְּבָנָה אָמַר שֶׁתִּתְחַדֵּשׁ עֲטֶרֶת תִּפְאֶרֶת לַעֲמוּסֵי בָטֶן, הָעֲתִידִים לְהִתְחַדֵּשׁ כְּמוֹתָהּ. This means that *HaKadosh Baruch Hu,* the פּוֹעֵל אֱמֶת, in all His truth, will keep His promise to redeem and renew the Jewish people, just as He faithfully renews the lunar cycle each month. This promise is the *emes* that *HaKadosh Baruch Hu* will keep forever.

What follows now is the description of the new world order which *HaKadosh Baruch Hu* will institute at the time of the *geulah*. Human beings cannot possibly bring about this new world order by themselves. It will take messengers of *HaKadosh Baruch Hu,* such as Eliyahu HaNavi and *Mashiach*. And according to the *sefarim* of the *Mekubalim,* as explained by the Vilna Gaon, Moshe Rabbeinu will come back at that time.

The physical manifestations of this new world order are:

עֹשֶׂה מִשְׁפָּט לָעֲשׁוּקִים — **He does justice for the exploited.** In this new world order *HaKadosh Baruch Hu* will do justice for those who had been deprived of justice. עֹשֶׁק means to withhold something which belongs to someone else. Theretofore, the majority of the people of the world were deprived of what rightfully belonged to them.

נֹתֵן לֶחֶם לָרְעֵבִים — **He gives bread to the hungry.** He will be the One Who gives bread to the hungry. Hunger and poverty will be abolished from the world.

ה' מַתִּיר אֲסוּרִים — **Hashem releases the bound.** God will free those who are in prison. No person will be allowed to control and restrict the freedom of others.

Now there follows the spiritual side of that future world:

ה' פֹּקֵחַ עִוְרִים — **Hashem gives sight to the blind.** This does not mean only simply that He makes the blind see, but it also means He will enlighten the hitherto "blind" world to the *Malchus Hashem*. It is difficult for me to understand why every physicist or astronomer is not a *tzaddik* and a *yerei Shamayim* combined. Such people see *HaKadosh Baruch Hu* all the time in the course of their scientific work.

We are told by *Chazal* (*Midrash Tanchuma, Vezos HaBerachah* 7) that: רָשָׁע בְּחַיָּיו חָשׁוּב כְּמֵת כְּמֶת שֶׁרוֹאֶה חַמָּה זוֹרַחַת וְאֵינוֹ מְבָרֵךְ יוֹצֵר אוֹר, שׁוֹקַעַת וְאֵינוֹ מְבָרֵךְ מַעֲרִיב עֲרָבִים, *A wicked person is considered dead even while he is alive, because he sees the sun rise and does not praise God for it, and he sees the sun set and does not say the prayer of "He Who makes the evening* etc." The miraculous events of daily sunrise and sunset appear before their eyes, and they do not see *HaKadosh Baruch Hu* behind all this. They can truly be called "blind." At that time, *HaKadosh Baruch Hu* will open their eyes to His presence.

ה' זוֹקֵף כְּפוּפִים — **Hashem straightens the bent.** This refers to people who are bent down in despair, broken and depressed. These are deeply disappointed people, whose world is nothing but a vale of tears, and their lives are a completely hopeless form of existence. Only *HaKadosh Baruch Hu* can — and will — "straighten them up" and restore them to a purposeful and meaningful life, under that new world order.

ה' אֹהֵב צַדִּיקִים — **Hashem loves the righteous.** In our world, we do not always recognize that *HaKadosh Baruch Hu* loves the righteous people. The *tzaddik* feels this love, but the world does not see it. However, *l'asid lavo,* in that new world order, everyone will see clearly that *HaKadosh Baruch Hu* loves the *tzaddikim*.

ה' שֹׁמֵר אֶת גֵּרִים יָתוֹם וְאַלְמָנָה יְעוֹדֵד — **God will protect the stranger, and He will give the orphan and the widow the strength to endure.** עדד, from עוֹד, has the meaning of "again," which in our *pasuk* means endurance.

The three terms for deprived individuals — *ger, yasom,* and *almanah* (literally: the stranger, the orphan, and the widow) — which appear so often in the Torah and in the words of the *Neviim,* often serve as a *mashal,* an allegory, for three types of people:

Ger refers to the *baal teshuvah.* In connection with Yom Kippur, the Torah says, וְהָיְתָה לָכֶם לְחֻקַּת עוֹלָם בַּחֹדֶשׁ הַשְּׁבִיעִי . . . וְהַגֵּר הַגָּר בְּתוֹכְכֶם, *This shall remain for you an eternal decree: In the seventh month . . . the stranger who lives among you* (Vayikra 16:29). The Jew becomes a new person after the *teshuvah* of Yom Kippur, and he is therefore called הַגֵּר הַגָּר בְּתוֹכְכֶם, *the stranger who lives among you.* He had only been *living* among the Jewish people, but was not really Jewish. Now, after his *teshuvah,* he is a *ger;* it is as if he had converted from a different faith. So *ger* is a metaphor for a *baal teshuvah.*

Yasom refers to *tinokos shenishbu* (children who were captured among the nations), one who never had a father, or anyone else, to teach him Torah and *mitzvos.* He has been "orphaned" from Judaism. He is completely innocent.

Almanah means a generation which has been bereft of its leadership. Its leaders have died out. This is expressed in, אֵין מְנַהֵל לָהּ מִכָּל בָּנִים יָלָדָה, *Among all the children she has borne there is no one to guide her* (Yeshayahu 51:18). Our only consolation is that the Jewish people is never bereft of its God: כִּי לֹא אַלְמָן יִשְׂרָאֵל וִיהוּדָה מֵאֱלֹהָיו, *For Israel is not widowed, nor is Judea, from his*

God (*Yirmiyahu* 51:5). In our time, the number of *gedolei Yisrael* who can *pasken* a *she'elah* that is accepted by the entire Jewish world can be counted on less than the fingers of one hand, and most of those are aged.

The last generation before the coming of the *geulah* is called *almanah*. Therefore, an additional meaning of this *pasuk* is that in the generation just preceding the *geulah*, we will be a nation composed of *ger, yasom,* and *almanah,* meaning *baalei teshuvah, tinokos shenishbu,* and people without leaders. It is these people who will be among the *tzaddikim* whom *HaKadosh Baruch Hu* loves and protects, and to whom He will give the strength to endure, and to experience the new world order.

וְדֶרֶךְ רְשָׁעִים יְעַוֵּת — As a result of the love and protection which *HaKadosh Baruch Hu* affords the *tzaddikim,* **He will twist the road of the evildoers,** meaning, He will frustrate the plans of the *reshaim,* so that they will never reach their goals.

The *mizmor* up to this point is set in the "predawn" of the new world order to come at the time of the *geulah*. Now, in the following, concluding *pasuk,* Dovid HaMelech looks ahead to the dawning of this new era, in which *Mashiach* will come, the *Beis HaMikdash* will be rebuilt, and there will be *kibbutz galiyos,* the ingathering of the exiles.

יִמְלֹךְ ה' לְעוֹלָם אֱלֹהַיִךְ צִיּוֹן לְדֹר וָדֹר, הַלְלוּיָהּ — He exclaims to the world: **Hashem shall reign forever — your God, O Tziyon — for every generation. Halleluyah!** This blissful new world order will continue in perpetuity.

As we have previously explained, the *mizmor* of אַשְׁרֵי praised *HaKadosh Baruch Hu* from the physical point of view, that of the *guf*. And this first הַלְלוּיָהּ speaks in the name of the *nefesh*, in the period immediately before *bi'as haMashiach*. Now, the next two הַלְלוּיָהּ express these praises from the point of view of the *ruach*, those special spiritual qualities which will be the hallmark of the *Melech HaMashiach,* notwithstanding the fact that the name of *Mashiach* does not appear at all in these psalms. The Torah tells us: וְרוּחַ אֱלֹהִים מְרַחֶפֶת עַל פְּנֵי הַמָּיִם, *And the Divine Presence hovers upon the surface of the waters* (*Bereishis* 1:2), on which the Midrash explains: זֶהוּ רוּחוֹ שֶׁל מֶלֶךְ הַמָּשִׁיחַ, *This is a reference to the spirit of the king Mashiach* (*Bereishis Rabbah* 2:4). The *Melech HaMashiach* will have a special *ruach* endowed upon him by *HaKadosh Baruch Hu*: וְנָחָה עָלָיו רוּחַ ה' רוּחַ חָכְמָה וּבִינָה רוּחַ עֵצָה וּגְבוּרָה רוּחַ דַּעַת וְיִרְאַת ה', *The spirit of Hashem will rest upon him — a spirit of wisdom and understanding, a spirit of counsel and strength, a spirit of knowledge and fear of Hashem* (*Yeshayahu* 11:2).

הַלְלוּיָהּ כִּי טוֹב זַמְּרָה אֱלֹהֵינוּ / Halleluyah Ki Tov Zamrah Eloheinu

This psalm is set in the context of the new world order which will already have begun with *bi'as haMashiach,* the coming of *Mashiach.*

❧ ❧ ❧

❧ **הַלְלוּיָהּ, כִּי טוֹב זַמְּרָה אֱלֹהֵינוּ — Halleluyah! For it is good to sing to our God.** The form זַמְּרָה is used with poetic license. The grammatically correct form would be לְזַמֵּר.

❧ **כִּי נָעִים נָאוָה תְהִלָּה — Because it is pleasant when praise is fitting.** This means that until this era of *yemos haMashiach,* the praises of *HaKadosh Baruch Hu* were based solely on our *emunah sheleimah* (pure faith). However, now that this new idyllic world has become a reality, we see that these praises actually describe what we are experiencing in this new life.

❧ **בּוֹנֵה יְרוּשָׁלַיִם ה', נִדְחֵי יִשְׂרָאֵל יְכַנֵּס — The Builder of Yerushalyim is Hashem, the dispersed of Israel He will gather in.** We now see that Hashem, indeed, has built Yerushalayim and has gathered together the dispersed people of Israel. The *Chachamim* tell us: מָסוֹרֶת אַגָּדָה הִיא שֶׁאֵין יְרוּשָׁלַיִם נִבְנֵית עַד שֶׁיִּתְכַּנְּסוּ הַגָּלֻיּוֹת, *There is an Aggadic tradition that Yerushalayim will not be rebuilt until the exiles have entered it* (see *Midrash Tanchuma, Noach* 11).

The prerequisite for the building of Yerushalayim is the ingathering of the exiles. The meaning of our verse is that Hashem will be constantly building Yerushalayim while He is bringing back the dispersed people of Israel. Then, when the ingathering is complete, the building process of Yerushalayim will have been finished.

Now, this Yerushalayim is not the City of Jerusalem that we know today. Rather, it will be the Yerushalayim that is described in *Neviim* as being built of precious stones and gems (see *Yeshayahu* 54:11-12). These "precious stones," upon which *HaKadosh Baruch Hu* is building this future Yerushalayim, are the *tefillos* and hopes which the Jewish people has expressed throughout the millennia. The familiar *tefillos* which we have said throughout our long history — לְשָׁנָה הַבָּאָה בִּירוּשָׁלָיִם, *the coming year in Yerushalayim,* which I say every year at the *Seder* table, and which was said by my father before me, and by his father before him; יִתְגַּדַּל וְיִתְקַדַּשׁ שְׁמֵהּ רַבָּא בַּעֲגָלָא וּבִזְמַן קָרִיב..., *May His great Name grow exalted and sanctified* . . .

swiftly and soon; יְהִי רָצוֹן ... שֶׁיִּבָּנֶה בֵּית הַמִּקְדָּשׁ בִּמְהֵרָה בְיָמֵינוּ, *May it be Your will ... that the Holy Temple be rebuilt, speedily in our days* — are all everlasting. Not a single one of these *tefillos* or hopes or expressions of *emunah* in the eventual *geulah* is wasted. These *tefillos* that were so fervently expressed by the Jewish people throughout history never ceased to exist, and they are the spiritual building blocks from which the future Yerushalayim of light and fire and *gilui HaShechinah* (revelation of the Shechinah) is being built. It will be a physical city, but its foundations are spiritual.

Similarly, the Torah describes the prophetic vision beheld by Nadav and Avihu and the *Zekeinim* (Elders) before *Matan Torah* with the words: וְתַחַת רַגְלָיו כְּמַעֲשֵׂה לִבְנַת הַסַּפִּיר וּכְעֶצֶם הַשָּׁמַיִם לָטֹהַר, *And under His feet was the likeness of a brick made of sapphire, and it was as pure as heaven itself* (*Shemos* 24:10).

This vision is explained by Rav Samson R. Hirsch to mean that instead of *Bnei Yisrael* making bricks in Mitzrayim as the servants of Pharaoh, to build up and support his throne, their duty now, as the servants of Hashem, is to make "bricks" for the purpose of building up *Malchus Shamayim* on earth. The lesson being that anything physical which is done *l'Shem Shamayim* becomes just as heavenly as עֶצֶם הַשָּׁמַיִם, *Heaven itself.*

In this same way, the *tefillos* for *geulah* which *Klal Yisrael* expressed throughout the ages are the building blocks for the return of *Malchus Shamayim* to Yerushalayim. So the process with which Yerushalayim will be rebuilt consists of God's accepting the fervent prayers of the Jewish people for its reconstruction. Each one of these prayers is a building block.

The recent return of so many of our brethren from Russia and Ethiopia and many other countries, as welcome as it is, is not the subject of this *pasuk*. But rather, the *kibbutz galuyos* to which this *pasuk* refers is the eventual gathering together of all of *Klal Yisrael* into the Yerushalayim of the future, which is being built, stone by precious stone, from all the *tefillos* and hopes and *emunah* of *Klal Yisrael* throughout its long *galus*.

◆§ הָרוֹפֵא לִשְׁבוּרֵי לֵב §◆ — **He Who heals the brokenhearted.** Hashem will comfort the brokenhearted Jews who return from the *galus*. Throughout our history, we have been surrounded by oceans of hatred and anti-Semitism, sometimes benign, but mostly fatal.

◆§ וּמְחַבֵּשׁ לְעַצְּבוֹתָם §◆ — **And He dresses their wounds.** This means that *HaKadosh Baruch Hu* will remove all the traumatic effects of the *galus* from his nation.

◆§ מוֹנֶה מִסְפָּר לַכּוֹכָבִים, לְכֻלָּם שֵׁמוֹת יִקְרָא §◆ — **He Who counts the number of all the stars has also given them** [the שְׁבוּרֵי לֵב] **names.** Each one of the brokenhearted survivors of the *galus* has a purpose to fulfill; each one becomes one of the most important people in the world.

The word מִסְפָּר denotes a small number. We know that there are countless billions of galaxies in the universe; each galaxy is composed of countless billions of suns; and our earth is a satellite of one small sun in the galaxy known as the "Milky Way." To *HaKadosh Baruch Hu,* all these countless billions of heavenly bodies are merely מִסְפָּר, a small number. Notwithstanding the vastness of His creations, *HaKadosh Baruch Hu* has, nevertheless, given each one of those *galus* survivors, who were *zocheh* to experience the *yemos haMashiach,* an individual "name," or purpose to fulfill in the world.

◆§ גָּדוֹל אֲדוֹנֵינוּ וְרַב כֹּחַ — **Our Lord is great and a Master of power.** As we have previously pointed out, the word גָּדוֹל always refers to the *middah* of *chessed* of *HaKadosh Baruch Hu.*

◆§ לִתְבוּנָתוֹ אֵין מִסְפָּר — Literally, this means, **And His understanding cannot be counted.** However, Rav Samson R. Hirsch explains that since one does not "count" understanding, the sense of this *pasuk* is: Regarding the understanding of *HaKadosh Baruch Hu,* מִסְפָּר, *numbers,* are not relevant; they do not count. In the "understanding" of *HaKadosh Baruch Hu* this handful of שְׁבוּרֵי לֵב who merited to experience *yemos haMashiach* are more important than the countless numbers of heavenly bodies.

◆§ מְעוֹדֵד עֲנָוִים ה' — **Hashem encourages the humble.** These humble people who suffered during the *galus* and endured it with their *bitachon* are rewarded by *HaKadosh Baruch Hu* by "endurance," meaning eternal life.

◆§ מַשְׁפִּיל רְשָׁעִים עֲדֵי אָרֶץ — And at the same time, **He will lower the wicked to the earth.** This means that for them, the opposite is true; they will no longer live; they will merge with the earth.

◆§ עֱנוּ לַה' בְּתוֹדָה, זַמְּרוּ לֵאלֹהֵינוּ בְכִנּוֹר — When all this takes place, **respond to Hashem with thanksgiving, and play songs to our God with the harp.** These two forms for the Names of *HaKadosh Baruch Hu* represent the expressions of song to *HaKadosh Baruch Hu* for the *middah* of *rachamim* and the *middah* of *din* which the Jewish people have experienced in its history.

A further description of the events which will occur during the unfolding of the *yemos haMashiach* follows.

◆§ הַמְכַסֶּה שָׁמַיִם בְּעָבִים, הַמֵּכִין לָאָרֶץ מָטָר — **Who covers the heavens with clouds, Who prepares rain for the earth.** One of the early signs of impending disaster and the *galus* from Eretz Yisrael was that Hashem would "close" the heavens and withhold the rains: וְחָרָה אַף ה' בָּכֶם וְעָצַר אֶת הַשָּׁמַיִם וְלֹא יִהְיֶה מָטָר . . . וַאֲבַדְתֶּם מְהֵרָה מֵעַל הָאָרֶץ הַטֹּבָה וגו', *Then the wrath of Hashem will blaze against you; He will restrain the heaven so there will be no rain . . . and you will*

HALLELUYAH KI TOV ZAMRAH ELOHEINU ◆ 193

be swiftly banished from the goodly land (Devarim 11:17). However, now in the context of this *mizmor,* which is set in the beginning of the *yemos haMashiach,* this is reversed. Hashem covers the heavens with clouds in preparation for rain. The אֶרֶץ used here refers specifically to Eretz Yisrael, the land which was promised that special rain, יוֹרֶה וּמַלְקוֹשׁ, as a reward for וְהָיָה אִם שָׁמֹעַ תִּשְׁמְעוּ אֶל מִצְוֹתַי, *And it will come to pass that if you continually hearken to My commandments (Devarim* 11:13), and from which it had been withheld as a result of the *aveiros* of the Jewish people. Now that *Mashiach* has come, these rains will once again shower this land.

⧉ הַמַּצְמִיחַ הָרִים חָצִיר. נוֹתֵן לִבְהֵמָה לַחְמָהּ לִבְנֵי עֹרֵב אֲשֶׁר יִקְרָאוּ — **He makes the mountains grow grass. He gives the animal its food and to the young of the raven that for which they cry out.** Raven mother birds usually abandon their young, who must then fend for themselves at an early age. The verdant mountains, blessed by Hashem, provide the necessary food even for these raven offspring. In the world order described here there is suffering neither by man nor animal.

⧉ לֹא בִגְבוּרַת הַסּוּס יֶחְפָּץ, לֹא בְשׁוֹקֵי הָאִישׁ יִרְצֶה — **He does not take delight in the strength of the horse, nor does He want the thighs of man.** This describes the usual symbol of warfare, סוּס וְרֹכְבוֹ, which is a horseman soldier sitting with his thighs spread astride his horse. Warriors will no longer ply their trade in this world, because there will no longer be warfare.

⧉ רוֹצֶה ה' אֶת יְרֵאָיו, אֶת הַמְיַחֲלִים לְחַסְדּוֹ — **Because in this world, Hashem takes delight in those who fear Him, and those who wait for His lovingkindness.**

⧉ שַׁבְּחִי יְרוּשָׁלַיִם אֶת ה', הַלְלִי אֱלֹהַיִךְ צִיּוֹן — Now that *galus* is over and all the dispersed people of *Bnei Yisrael* have returned to Yerushalayim and have been healed of their wounds, both physical and spiritual, the Psalmist exclaims: Now, **Yerushalayim, praise Hashem, and Tziyon, praise your God.** יְרוּשָׁלַיִם — which is now comprised of the entire Eretz Yisrael — is the city surrounding צִיּוֹן, which is the *Beis HaMikdash,* the spiritual nucleus of the Jewish people, the מַמְלֶכֶת כֹּהֲנִים וְגוֹי קָדוֹשׁ, *kingdom of priests and holy nation (Shemos* 19:6).

⧉ כִּי חִזַּק בְּרִיחֵי שְׁעָרָיִךְ, בֵּרַךְ בָּנַיִךְ בְּקִרְבֵּךְ — Yerushalayim and Tziyon praise HaKadosh Baruch Hu **because He has strengthened the bars of your gates and blessed your children within your midst.** Formerly, the fortified cities were walled and the entrance portals had huge bars which reinforced them against an enemy onslaught. However, in the case of Yerushalayim of the future, this will no longer be necessary, because its security will consist of its Jewish children who will all be *talmidei chachamim,* as expressed in the verse, וְכָל בָּנַיִךְ לִמּוּדֵי ה׳, *All your children will be students of Hashem* (*Yeshayahu* 54:13). They will act as the "fortified gates."

הַשָּׂם גְּבוּלֵךְ שָׁלוֹם — **He Who makes your borders peaceful.** The boundaries of the "Greater Eretz Yisrael" which was promised to our *Avos* will be שָׁלוֹם. Peace will surround the entire country.

חֵלֶב חִטִּים יַשְׂבִּיעֵךְ — And as far as economics are concerned, there is also nothing about which to worry, for **He will satiate you with the best of wheat.** Your former concerns regarding security and economic strength will no longer exist.

And now we reach the culmination of the *yeshuah* of Hashem of the *yemos haMashiach*. Yeshayahu HaNavi (51:4) says that at the time of *Mashiach*: כִּי תוֹרָה מֵאִתִּי תֵצֵא, *Torah will come forth from Me.* This does not mean that there will be a new Torah, but rather, a new understanding of Torah will emanate from *HaKadosh Baruch Hu.* At that time we will understand Torah in a way in which we never understood it before. We will see that the entire world is nothing but ד׳ אַמּוֹת שֶׁל הֲלָכָה (literally: the four ells of *halachah,* which means the universe of Torah). We will see how the whole physical world, and its entire history, is really part of Torah.

הַשֹּׁלֵחַ אִמְרָתוֹ אָרֶץ עַד מְהֵרָה יָרוּץ דְּבָרוֹ — Because, **He sends His message down to earth; His word runs swiftly.** The word of *HaKadosh Baruch Hu* comes to mankind on earth very swiftly, despite the fact that He is *baShamayim mima'al* (in Heaven above).

Now the Psalmist offers a *mashal* (allegory) to explain how the Torah, which is the wisdom of Hashem, is transmitted by *HaKadosh Baruch Hu* to mankind.

הַנֹּתֵן שֶׁלֶג כַּצָּמֶר, כְּפוֹר כָּאֵפֶר יְפַזֵּר. מַשְׁלִיךְ קַרְחוֹ כְפִתִּים — **He places the snow as wool; He spreads the frost like ashes; He throws down His ice like little pieces.** This means that even a monumental snowfall falls in individual flakes, like so much wool. And frost comes to earth as softly as fly ash. Even a huge ice storm comes to earth in little pieces of hail.

לִפְנֵי קָרָתוֹ מִי יַעֲמֹד — This is so, **because who could withstand His cold.** This is a reference to the קֶרַח הַנּוֹרָא, the *awesome ice* of which the *Navi* speaks (see *Yechezkel* 1:22). If *HaKadosh Baruch Hu* would allow the water vapor which is frozen in the clouds to come down to earth all at once, in giant sheets of ice, all life would cease. Therefore, *HaKadosh Baruch Hu* breaks this ice into small pieces and causes it to fall on earth, either as snow, frozen rain, or hail.

יִשְׁלַח דְּבָרוֹ וְיַמְסֵם, יַשֵּׁב רוּחוֹ יִזְּלוּ מָיִם — **He sends His word and makes it melt, He makes His wind blow, and the waters flow.** Since water is a prerequisite for life on earth, *HaKadosh Baruch Hu* converts this frozen snow and ice to water. The water which we drink was originally huge sheets of ice, which were melted by the rising temperature and the winds as the result of "the word of God," which turned them into refreshing water to sustain our lives.

מַגִּיד דְּבָרָיו לְיַעֲקֹב, חֻקָּיו וּמִשְׁפָּטָיו לְיִשְׂרָאֵל — The previous *pesukim* were the *mashal* (the allegory), and now we have the *nimshal* (the analogy). Just as *HaKadosh Baruch Hu* converts the awesome sheets of ice into potable life-giving water for the earth, **He details His words to Yaakov, and His chukim and mishpatim to Israel.** The comparison means the following:

For example, in *Parashas Mishpatim* we have many and various civil laws concerning property rights and responsibilities, e.g., וְכִי יִגֹּף שׁוֹר אִישׁ אֶת שׁוֹר רֵעֵהוּ, *If one man's ox shall strike his fellow's ox* (*Shemos* 21:35); וְכִי יִפְתַּח אִישׁ בּוֹר, *If a man shall uncover a pit* (ibid. v. 33); and כִּי תֵצֵא אֵשׁ, *If a fire shall go forth* (*Shemos* 22:5); etc.; this is known as *tzedek u'mishpat*, justice between man and his fellow man. These concepts are so elementary that we teach them to our children when we introduce them to Talmud, in *Bava Kamma, Bava Metzia,* and *Bava Basra.*

However, in truth, the idea of *tzedek u'mishpat* (righteousness and justice) is a most rarefied and sublime concept, because it emanates directly from the *Kisei HaKavod,* as is expressed in, צֶדֶק וּמִשְׁפָּט מְכוֹן כִּסְאֶךָ, *Righteousness and justice are Your throne's foundation* (*Tehillim* 89:15). It is the very basis of the "Throne of *HaKadosh Baruch Hu.*" This is incomprehensible to us.

The ultimate justice and righteousness in the eyes of *HaKadosh Baruch Hu,* and how it relates to our concepts of justice, can be compared to the קֶרַח הַנּוֹרָא, that awesome mass of ice which *HaKadosh Baruch Hu* sends down to us in small bits and pieces, as snow, hail, and frost, which we can utilize. By the time these sublime concepts come to us, in broken-down form, they become so easy to understand that we can teach them even to young children.

All of the דְּבָרִים, חֻקִּים, and מִשְׁפָּטִים which *HaKadosh Baruch Hu* has taught us go back to the highest concepts upon which He has created the world. They come from Him, Who is יוֹשֵׁב עַל כִּסֵּא רָם וְנִשָּׂא (enthroned on high), and we cannot possibly have a full understanding of these concepts. All the *halachos* of the Torah which *HaKadosh Baruch Hu* has sent down to us are sublime concepts of *chochmas Elokim* (the wisdom of God) broken down for us in small bits and pieces, making it possible for us to absorb them.

[Ed. note: For a broader development of this concept by the author, see *Maayan Beis HaSho'evah, Ki Sisa* 31:18.]

So now, in the *yemos haMashiach,* we will gain a new understanding of the Torah; we will be able to "drink it like water" — אֵין מַיִם אֶלָּא תוֹרָה, *Water is a* metaphor for Torah (*Bava Kamma* 17a). We will then understand how all Torah principles go back to higher principles, and still higher principles, up to the *Kisei HaKavod*. As the *Navi* says, כִּי תוֹרָה מֵאִתִּי תֵצֵא, *Torah will come forth from Me;* at that time, *HaKadosh Baruch Hu* will reveal to us an understanding of the Torah on a level which we never understood before.

לֹא עָשָׂה כֵן לְכָל גּוֹי — **He did not do so for any other nation.** This new, higher understanding of the Torah, at the time of *yemos haMashiach*, will be revealed only to *Yisrael*, and not to any other nation. At that time our minds will be opened so that we will be able to learn Torah in its highest potential form. Even *Torah Shebe'al Peh*, which was written down as a stop-gap measure to avoid Torah being forgotten, will again be learned by heart and remembered, without having to consult the written Mishnah and Gemara.

וּמִשְׁפָּטִים בַּל יְדָעוּם, הַלְלוּיָהּ — **Such judgments — they know them not. Halleluyah!** The other nations do have civil laws — often very similar to our own. However, these are man-made and have developed over time, dating back to the Greeks, or even earlier, as Hittite or Hammurabi law.

At the time of *Mashiach*, however, only *Am Yisrael*, as the מַמְלֶכֶת כֹּהֲנִים וְגוֹי קָדוֹשׁ, will be privileged to understand the lofty underlying concepts of the *chukim* and *mishpatim*, which stem from *HaKadosh Baruch Hu* Himself.

הַלְלוּיָהּ הַלְלוּ אֶת ה' מִן הַשָּׁמַיִם / Halleluyah
Hallelu Es Hashem Min HaShamayim

This *Halleluyah* continues in the context of *yemos haMashiach*, but on an even higher level. It progresses from the level of *ruach* to *ruach hakodesh*. Here Dovid HaMelech visualizes the entire spiritual and physical universe expressing songs of praise to *HaKadosh Baruch Hu*, under the direction of the *Melech HaMashiach*, who is Dovid HaMelech reincarnated. This "reincarnation" is referred to in the הוֹשַׁעֲנוֹת where we say, הוּא דָוִד בְּעַצְמוֹ, he is Dovid himself. Also, in our *tefillos* we often refer to *Mashiach* as Dovid, e.g., עַל יְדֵי דָוִד מְשִׁיחַ צִדְקֶךָ, *through Dovid Your righteous anointed one*. (The reincarnation of Dovid as *Melech HaMashiach* is referred to in *Zohar HaKadosh*, *Lech Lecha* p. 82.)

And just as a conductor directs his baton at the various sections of his orchestra in front of him — the strings, the winds, the percussions, and other instruments — to elicit various sounds which are combined into a harmonious musical rendition, so too, does the *Melech HaMashiach* in this *mizmor* lead all of creation in a great symphony of *shevach* to *HaKadosh Baruch Hu*.

The "conductor," *Melech HaMashiach*, in his *ruach hakodesh*, now directs the entire universe in his symphony, as follows:

❧ ❧ ❧

❧ הַלְלוּיָהּ, הַלְלוּ אֶת ה' מִן הַשָּׁמַיִם, הַלְלוּהוּ בַּמְּרוֹמִים. הַלְלוּהוּ כָל מַלְאָכָיו, הַלְלוּהוּ כָל צְבָאָיו ❧ — **Halleluyah! Praise Hashem from the heavens, praise Him in the heights. Praise Him, all His angels; praise Him, all His legions.** First He directs the spiritual beings, in the highest heights of heaven, to express their praises to *HaKadosh Baruch Hu*.

❧ הַלְלוּהוּ שֶׁמֶשׁ וְיָרֵחַ, הַלְלוּהוּ כָּל כּוֹכְבֵי אוֹר — **Praise Him, sun and moon; praise Him, all stars which give light.** Then He directs his baton at the visible universe, the sun, the moon, and the stars, exhorting them to praise Him.

❧ הַלְלוּהוּ שְׁמֵי הַשָּׁמָיִם, וְהַמַּיִם אֲשֶׁר מֵעַל הַשָּׁמָיִם ❧ — **Praise Him, the heaven of the heavens and the waters that are above the heavens.** Continuing, He calls forth praise from the "heaven of the heavens," meaning the "super galaxies," which we do not see, and the primordial matter, the "plasma," from which all matter was created, which is called מַיִם אֲשֶׁר מֵעַל הַשָּׁמָיִם.

❧ יְהַלְלוּ אֶת שֵׁם ה', כִּי הוּא צִוָּה וְנִבְרָאוּ ❧ — **Let them praise the Name of Hashem, for He commanded and they were created.** He directs all these creations to join in this symphony of praise to *HaKadosh Baruch Hu* because He is the source of their existence — Hashem gave the order, and they were created.

וַיַּעֲמִידֵם לָעַד לְעוֹלָם, חָק נָתַן וְלֹא יַעֲבוֹר — **And He placed them so that they would last forever. They will not die as long as the universe exists. He declared this as law, and it cannot be changed.** The laws of nature controlling the universe are inviolable.

הַלְלוּ אֶת ה' מִן הָאָרֶץ — **Praise Hashem from the earth.** Now he points his baton at the physical earth and calls on it to join in the symphony of song to *HaKadosh Baruch Hu*.

תַּנִּינִים וְכָל תְּהֹמוֹת. אֵשׁ וּבָרָד, שֶׁלֶג וְקִיטוֹר, רוּחַ סְעָרָה עֹשָׂה דְבָרוֹ — **Sea giants and all watery depths; fire and hail, snow and smoke; stormy wind fulfilling His word.** First, he motions to the marine creatures and all the great depths of the seas; next to the fire and hail; and then to the snow and the smoke from volcanoes, and even to the storm winds. They all carry out the directives of *HaKadosh Baruch Hu* by doing what they were created to do.

הֶהָרִים וְכָל גְּבָעוֹת, עֵץ פְּרִי וְכָל אֲרָזִים — **Mountains and all hills, fruitful trees and all cedars.** Then he points his baton at the mountain ranges and great highlands of earth; and the fruit trees and the mighty cedars which have no fruit — for their participation.

הַחַיָּה וְכָל בְּהֵמָה, רֶמֶשׂ וְצִפּוֹר כָּנָף — **Beasts and all cattle, crawling things and winged fowl.** Next he points his baton at the animals, which include both the wild and the domesticated ones, as well as the creeping things and the winged birds, and asks them to join in this great symphony.

מַלְכֵי אֶרֶץ וְכָל לְאֻמִּים, שָׂרִים וְכָל שֹׁפְטֵי אָרֶץ — **Kings of the earth and all governments, princes and all judges on earth.** Now he looks in a different direction and points to the leaders of mankind, to the kings of earth and their nations, and all the noblemen and rulers of earth. He exhorts them to join with their people in praising *HaKadosh Baruch Hu* as a part of this great symphony.

בַּחוּרִים וְגַם בְּתוּלוֹת, זְקֵנִים עִם נְעָרִים — **Young men and also maidens, elders together with youths.** These great masses of people are composed of young men and also young women. (Not בַּחוּרִים "עִם" בְּתוּלוֹת, but "וְגַם"; these groups are separated.) Old and young join together in this great symphony.

יְהַלְלוּ אֶת שֵׁם ה', כִּי נִשְׂגָּב שְׁמוֹ לְבַדּוֹ — **Let them praise the Name of Hashem, for His Name alone is exalted.** All these components of the spiritual and physical universe join together to praise *HaKadosh Baruch Hu*, because now, during this period of *yemos haMashiach*, no longer does anyone recognize any other Divine force beside *HaKadosh Baruch Hu.* The word נִשְׂגָּב is a combination of שַׂגִּיא and גָּבוֹהַ, meaning *high* and *mighty.*

§ הוֹדוֹ עַל אֶרֶץ וְשָׁמָיִם. וַיָּרֶם קֶרֶן לְעַמּוֹ, תְּהִלָּה לְכָל חֲסִידָיו, לִבְנֵי יִשְׂרָאֵל עַם קְרֹבוֹ, הַלְלוּיָהּ — **His glory is above earth and heaven. And He has raised a horn for His nation; praise for all of His devout ones, for the Jewish people, His close nation. Halleluyah!** Now we arrive at the climax of the *mizmor.* At the center of this beautiful portrait of all creation in a symphonic expression of praises to *HaKadosh Baruch Hu* stands "His nation," represented by the *Melech HaMashiach,* conducting this universal "orchestra." While *HaKadosh Baruch Hu* finds His other adherents — the non-Jewish *chasidei umos ha'olam* — worthy of reward, and has even given them a share in *Olam Haba,* it is only בְּנֵי יִשְׂרָאֵל עַם קְרֹבוֹ, *the Jewish people who were consistently close to Him* throughout history, for whom He has "raised a horn," making them the spiritual leaders of the world. The Jewish nation, through its *tzaddikim* with their Torah and *mitzvos,* who have withstood all the tests to which they were subjected throughout history, has earned the title עַם קְרֹבוֹ, *His close nation,* and *HaKadosh Baruch Hu* has therefore appointed it — at this apex of world history — as the spiritual leader of the world.

הַלְלוּיָהּ שִׁירוּ לַה' שִׁיר חָדָשׁ /
Halleluyah Shiru Lashem Shir Chadash

הַלְלוּיָהּ, שִׁירוּ לַה' שִׁיר חָדָשׁ — **Halleluyah! Sing to Hashem a new song.** At this point, after having visualized the high point of the history of the development of mankind in the world, and now, nearly at the completion of the entire *Sefer Tehillim*, Dovid HaMelech calls this *mizmor* a שִׁיר חָדָשׁ, *a new song*. We are tempted to ask, "What could be new now?"

The answer, however, lies in the key words of this שִׁיר חָדָשׁ — יְרַנְּנוּ עַל מִשְׁכְּבוֹתָם, *let them sing joyously upon their beds*, which is a reference to *techiyas hameisim*, similar to the *pasuk*, הָקִיצוּ וְרַנְּנוּ שֹׁכְנֵי עָפָר, *Awaken and rejoice, you who dwell in the dust* (Yeshayahu 26:19). This, indeed, is something חָדָשׁ — even to Dovid HaMelech, and as such, this *mizmor* has gone even beyond the level of *ruach hakodesh*. It has reached the level of the realm of the *neshamah*, that of *techiyas hameisim*, meaning the reunification of the *neshamah* with the *guf*. We refer to this in our *birchos hashachar*: הַמַּחֲזִיר נְשָׁמוֹת לִפְגָרִים מֵתִים, *Who restores souls to dead bodies*.

Dovid HaMelech uses the term שִׁיר חָדָשׁ in *Tehillim* seven times, and each time there is a reason for the new *shir*. In our *mizmor*, we have the last שִׁיר חָדָשׁ in *Tehillim*, and this time, it refers to the final חָדָשׁ, that of *techiyas hameisim*.

Throughout history, our *tzaddikim* have yearned for *yemos haMashiach* — as expressed in such *tefillos* as, יִרְאוּ עֵינֵינוּ וְיִשְׂמַח לִבֵּנוּ וְתָגֵל נַפְשֵׁנוּ בִּישׁוּעָתְךָ בֶּאֱמֶת, בֶּאֱמֹר לְצִיּוֹן מָלַךְ אֱלֹהָיִךְ, *May our eyes see, our hearts rejoice and our souls jubilate, at Your real salvation, when it will be said of Tziyon "Your God reigns"* — but they have departed this world without seeing the fulfillment of these *tefillos*. These *tzaddikim* will be brought to life again at *techiyas hameisim* and will sing this שִׁיר חָדָשׁ as an expression of their *hoda'ah* to *HaKadosh Baruch Hu* for being privileged to experience this new existence of ultimate bliss.

Techiyas hameisim is referred to in *Daniel* (12:2): וְרַבִּים מִיְּשֵׁנֵי אַדְמַת עָפָר יָקִיצוּ אֵלֶּה לְחַיֵּי עוֹלָם וְאֵלֶּה לַחֲרָפוֹת לְדִרְאוֹן עוֹלָם, *Many of those who sleep in the dust of the earth will awaken, some for eternal life, and some for eternal shame and damnation.* Chazal tell us: כָּל הַנְּבִיאִים כּוּלָן לֹא נִתְנַבְּאוּ אֶלָּא לִימוֹת הַמָּשִׁיחַ, אֲבָל לָעוֹלָם הַבָּא, עַיִן לֹא רָאָתָה אֱלֹהִים זוּלָתְךָ, *While the prophets spoke of the epoch of Mashiach, none of them were privy to the "World to Come," about which it is written "No eye has seen it, except You, Elohim"* (Yeshayahu 64:3; from Berachos 34b). All the prophecies said by the *Neviim* have never gone further than that of a description of the world at the time of *yemos ha-Mashiach*. However, no one, including the *Neviim,* has even been given a description of *Olam Haba,* meaning *techiyas hameisim.* This is known only to *HaKadosh Baruch Hu.*

We do not know any details about *techiyas hameisim* other than that it will happen, and that it will not be only for Israel, but it will also include *chasidei umos ha'olam,* as we will see in the *mizmor* itself (see *Rambam, Hil. Melachim,* end of Ch. 8).

◈— תְּהִלָּתוֹ בִּקְהַל חֲסִידִים. יִשְׂמַח יִשְׂרָאֵל בְּעֹשָׂיו, בְּנֵי צִיּוֹן יָגִילוּ בְמַלְכָּם — **Let His praise be in the congregation of the devout. Let Israel exult in its Creator, let the Children of Zion rejoice in their King.** While the *chasidei umos ha'olam* will also be included in *techiyas hameisim,* and will therefore express their praise to *HaKadosh Baruch Hu* in all of their assemblies, the main focus will be on Israel: כָּל יִשְׂרָאֵל יֵשׁ לָהֶם חֵלֶק לָעוֹלָם הַבָּא, *All Israel has a share in the World to Come* (*Sanhedrin* 90a). So it will be *Klal Yisrael* who will rejoice the most at *techiyas hameisim.*

The predominance of the role of Israel in *techiyas hameisim* is based on the *pasuk,* הָקִיצוּ וְרַנְּנוּ שֹׁכְנֵי עָפָר כִּי טַל אוֹרֹת טַלֶּךָ, *Awaken and rejoice, you who dwell in the dust, a dew of light is your dew* (*Yeshayahu* 26:19). This is explained by *Chazal* as a reference to *techiyas hameisim*: זֶהוּ הַטַּל שֶׁעָתִיד הקב"ה לְהַחֲיוֹת בּוֹ מֵתִים, *This is the dew which HaKadosh Baruch Hu will utilize in the future to revive the dead* (*Yerushalmi, Berachos* 5:2). And this "dew of light" is described by *Chazal* as being the enlightenment of Torah: אוֹר תּוֹרָה מְחַיֵּיהוּ, *the light of Torah will revive him* (*Kesubos* 111b).

So, while the *chasidei umos ha'olam* will surely share in the blissful state of life of *techiyas hameisim,* they will not be privileged to share in the enhanced state of enlightenment of טַל אוֹרֹת, *a dew of light,* which can come about only through Torah, which they do not possess.

יִשְׂמַח יִשְׂרָאֵל בְּעֹשָׂיו is a difficult expression, because עֹשָׂיו is plural, and means *its creators,* whereas עוֹשֵׂהוּ would be *its Creator.* However, we do find the use of the "majestic plural" in the Names of *HaKadosh Baruch Hu* — as in אֱלֹהִים — and עֹשָׂיו could be similarly understood. (See *Rashi* to *Vayeira* 20:13, וַיְהִי כַּאֲשֶׁר הִתְעוּ אֹתִי אֱלֹהִים וגו', *And so it was when God caused me to wander.*) In fact, it was commonplace even for kings to utilize the royal "we" when referring to themselves.

However, Rav Samson R. Hirsch offers an additional explanation for the use of the plural form when referring to *HaKadosh Baruch Hu* as the Creator of the Jewish people. On the *pasuk,* כִּי בֹעֲלַיִךְ עֹשַׂיִךְ, *For your Master is your Creator* (*Yeshayahu* 54:5), where the plural form is also utilized, Rav Hirsch explains that the formation, or creation, of the Jewish people by *HaKadosh Baruch Hu* was not a one-time event; rather, it took place many times in our history. After its initial creation at *yetzias Mitzrayim*, *HaKadosh Baruch Hu* continued to expand this creation through the world-historic events that have kept the Jewish people alive as a nation ever since then. However, the culmination and final creation of the Jewish nation will be at *techiyas hameisim*, when it will have reached its highest possible state of being.

Accordingly, the sense of our word, בְּעֹשָׂיו, would be, "the One Who has — many times — created it."

יְהַלְלוּ שְׁמוֹ בְמָחוֹל, בְּתֹף וְכִנּוֹר יְזַמְּרוּ לוֹ — **They will praise His Name in a dance; they will sing to Him with drum and stringed instrument.** The drum is to maintain the beat, and the strings are for the music.

This מָחוֹל, *dance*, is described to us by *Chazal*: עָתִיד הקב"ה לַעֲשׂוֹת מָחוֹל לַצַּדִּיקִים בְּגַן עֵדֶן וְהוּא יוֹשֵׁב בֵּינֵיהֶם וְכָל אֶחָד וְאֶחָד מַרְאֶה בְאֶצְבָּעוֹ, שֶׁנֶּאֱמַר וְאָמַר בַּיּוֹם הַהוּא הִנֵּה אֱלֹהֵינוּ זֶה, *In the future, HaKadosh Baruch Hu will make a dance for the tzaddikim in Gan Eden, and He will sit in their midst, and every one of them will point his finger (at him). This is meant by the pasuk, "Behold, this is our God"* (*Yeshayahu* 25:9; from *Taanis* 31a). This means that *l'asid lavo* — in the *olam haneshamos* and afterwards at *techiyas hameisim* — there will be a perception of *HaKadosh Baruch Hu* which is not possible while we are alive.

The Chofetz Chaim explains that the idea of this מָחוֹל is that just as in a circle no part of it is closer to the center than the other, so too, *l'asid lavo*, will the *tzaddikim* realize that they are all equal in their relationship to *HaKadosh Baruch Hu*, Who is at the "center of this dancing circle."

Rav Joseph Breuer once based a very unique explanation of the reason for the *hakafos* on Simchas Torah on this *maamar Chazal*. He said we know that the *hakafos* on Succos and Hoshana Rabbah are a *zecher l'Mikdash*, in commemoration of that which was done in the *Beis HaMikdash*, to remind us of the procession around the *Mizbe'ach* with *lulavim* and *haddasim* which took place every day of Yom Tov. Our processions around the *bimah*, on which a *sefer Torah* is placed, is a commemoration of the *hakafos* around the *Mizbe'ach*. However, said Rav Breuer, on Simchas Torah the *bimah* is empty, corresponding to that fact that *HaKadosh Baruch Hu* is invisible in this world, because לֹא יִרְאַנִי הָאָדָם וָחָי, *No human can see Me and live* (*Shemos* 33:20). When we move around the *bimah* with the *sifrei Torah*, which represent the *tzaddikim* who are the personification of Torah, this is in anticipation of the time *l'asid lavo* when all the *tzaddikim* will be privileged to join in that great circle and point to *HaKadosh Baruch Hu*, Who will be "visible" at its center. Thus, we very aptly precede the *hakafos* with the aforementioned *pasuk*, וְאָמַר בַּיּוֹם הַהוּא הִנֵּה אֱלֹהֵינוּ זֶה.

כִּי רוֹצֶה ה' בְּעַמּוֹ — **For Hashem finds favor in His people.** *Techiyas hameisim* is the ultimate fulfillment of the promise made by *HaKadosh*

Baruch Hu: וִהְיִיתֶם לִי סְגֻלָּה מִכָּל הָעַמִּים, *You, [Bnei Yisrael,] will be My personal treasure — more so than all the peoples* (Shemos 19:5); and וְאַתֶּם תִּהְיוּ לִי מַמְלֶכֶת כֹּהֲנִים וְגוֹי קָדוֹשׁ, *You shall be to Me a kingdom of ministers and a holy nation* (ibid. v. 6). This is also what is meant by, וּלְתִתְּךָ עֶלְיוֹן עַל כָּל הַגּוֹיִם וגו׳ לִתְהִלָּה וּלְשֵׁם וּלְתִפְאָרֶת, *To make you supreme over all the nations that He made, for praise, for renown and for splendor* (Devarim 26:19). All the prophecies in the Torah and *Neviim* only reach their total fulfillment in the period of *techiyas hameisim*.

≈§ יְפָאֵר עֲנָוִים בִּישׁוּעָה — **He crowns the humble ones with salvation.** The more humble a person is, and the more he is aware of his shortcomings — notwithstanding all the good deeds which he has done — and is thus afraid of his ultimate judgment on the יוֹם הַדִּין הָאַחֲרוֹן, *the final day of judgment,* the more likely he is to be "crowned" with the salvation of *techiyas hameisim*.

While the word יְשׁוּעָה certainly means *salvation,* it is used here in its highest sense, that of "the ultimate salvation." It is also used in this sense in *Shemoneh Esrei* in the *berachah* of מְחַיֵּה הַמֵּתִים: מְחַיֶּה מֵתִים אַתָּה גִבּוֹר לְעוֹלָם ה׳ מְחַיֵּה מֵתִים: מֶלֶךְ מֵמִית וּמְחַיֶּה וּמַצְמִיחַ יְשׁוּעָה; and אַתָּה רַב לְהוֹשִׁיעַ.

This is so because *techiyas hameisim* will be preceded by the יוֹם ה׳ הַגָּדוֹל וְהַנּוֹרָא, *the great and awesome day of Hashem* (Malachi 3:22), as described in *Tzephaniah* (Ch. 1). This is what is known as יוֹם הַדִּין הָאַחֲרוֹן, *the final day of judgment,* of which even *tzaddikim* are afraid.

We are told (*Shmuel I* Ch. 28) of the time that Shaul HaMelech, in his desperation, asked the אֵשֶׁת בַּעֲלַת אוֹב, *a sorceress, a witch,* to conjure up Shmuel HaNavi from the dead; and when, miraculously, Shmuel did appear to Shaul, he told him, לָמָּה הִרְגַּזְתַּנִי לְהַעֲלוֹת אֹתִי, *Why did you disturb me to raise me up* (ibid. 28:15)? *Chazal* comment on this that Shmuel was disturbed because he thought, דִּילְמָא לְדִינָא מִתְבַּעֵינָא, perhaps I am being called to judgment. He feared the *yom hadin ha'acharon*.

Regarding the meaning of the *yom hadin ha'acharon*, I heard an explanation in the name of Rav Aharon Kotler. He said that when a person leaves this world and comes before the *beis din shel maalah,* the Heavenly Tribunal, he is judged only on the basis of his deeds in this world, until the day of his death. However, the effects or results of those deeds — or misdeeds — can have long-term consequences. For instance, let us say that during one's lifetime, one had a positive influence on another person, and that other person became a *tzaddik,* and his children and grandchildren also became *tzaddikim,* which may result in thousands of *tzaddikim.* At the end of time, on the *yom hadin ha'acharon,* that original influential person will receive the benefit and reward for being responsible for all those *tzaddikim* and their *ma'asim tovim* (good deeds) which resulted from his influence.

The reverse is also true. If a person makes a *chillul Hashem* in the world and others follow his example; or if someone who had the potential to become a *tzaddik,* instead became a *rasha,* because of an influential person's neglect of him, or because he observed that person in a state of disgrace and followed his example, he will have to bear the responsibility for all the *aveiros* which were perpetrated as a result of his influence — until the end of time.

So no one can know what the final result of the *yom hadin ha'acharon* will be. Therefore, if *HaKadosh Baruch Hu* saves us from the *yom hadin ha'acharon,* and we finally emerge as *bnei Olam Haba* and merit *techiyas hameisim* and to live in that world שֶׁכֻּלוֹ אָרוּךְ, which is endless, this is the ultimate *yeshuah.* This is why the expression מַצְמִיחַ יְשׁוּעָה refers to *techiyas hameisim.*

§ יַעְלְזוּ חֲסִידִים בְּכָבוֹד, יְרַנְּנוּ עַל מִשְׁכְּבוֹתָם — **Let the devout exult in glory, let them sing joyously upon their beds.** This describes the moment of the awakening of the *chassidim* who have merited *Olam Haba.* They will sing joyously on their beds. Similar words are also found in, הָקִיצוּ וְרַנְּנוּ שֹׁכְנֵי עָפָר, *Awake and shout for joy, you who rest in the dirt* (*Yeshayahu* 26:19). We have no idea how this will occur, because it was never revealed through the *Neviim,* as was previously quoted: עַיִן לֹא רָאָתָה אֱלֹהִים זוּלָתֶךָ, *No eye has ever seen it, except You, Elohim* (ibid. 64:3). All we are told here by this description is that it will be a cause for great jubilation by those who merit it — the *chassidim.*

§ רוֹמְמוֹת אֵל בִּגְרוֹנָם — **The lofty praises of God are in their throats.** And as soon as they awaken, these *chassidim* will already have the high exultation of *HaKadosh Baruch Hu* in their throats, although as yet unspoken, but they will be ready to pronounce the words of praise.

§ וְחֶרֶב פִּיפִיּוֹת בְּיָדָם — **And a double-edged sword is in their hand.** By praising *HaKadosh Baruch Hu,* the *chassidim* will hold a double-edged sword in their hands; this is all they will need to do. The punishment of the *reshaim,* which will take place at the same time, will be done by *HaKadosh Baruch Hu,* as is described in the previously quoted verse, וְרַבִּים מִיְּשֵׁנֵי אַדְמַת עָפָר יָקִיצוּ, אֵלֶּה לְחַיֵּי עוֹלָם וְאֵלֶּה לַחֲרָפוֹת לְדִרְאוֹן עוֹלָם, *Many of those who sleep in the dust of the earth will awaken, some for eternal life, and some for eternal shame and damnation* (*Daniel* 12:2). The *tzaddikim* will not be involved in meting out this punishment.

§ לַעֲשׂוֹת נְקָמָה בַּגּוֹיִם, תּוֹכֵחוֹת בַּלְאֻמִּים — **To effect revenge against certain nations, admonishments against certain states.** It will be *HaKadosh Baruch Hu* Himself Who will punish the *reshaim* who deserve חֲרָפוֹת לְדִרְאוֹן עוֹלָם, *eternal shame and damnation.* And this will be the final fulfillment of the *pesukim*: לִי נָקָם וְשִׁלֵּם, *Mine is vengeance and retribution* (*Devarim* 32:35); and אֵל נְקָמוֹת ה׳, *God of vengeance, Hashem* (*Tehillim* 94:1).

HALLELUYAH SHIRU LASHEM SHIR CHADASH ~ 205

The *chassidim* do not use their "double-edged sword"; rather, it is *HaKadosh Baruch Hu* Who will effect the final punishment on the *reshaim*. It is to this that we refer in our *tefillos*: נְקוֹם לְעֵינֵינוּ נִקְמַת דַּם עֲבָדֶיךָ הַשָּׁפוּךְ, *Avenge before our eyes the retribution for the blood of Your servants which was spilled.* Although the Jewish people has been grievously harmed by other nations throughout history, only *HaKadosh Baruch Hu* can avenge our blood; we are not capable of doing it.

ح§ לֶאְסֹר מַלְכֵיהֶם בְּזִקִּים, וְנִכְבְּדֵיהֶם בְּכַבְלֵי בַרְזֶל — **To bind their kings with chains, and their honored ones with iron ropes.** All their kings and "honored ones" who have committed these brutalities and outrages will be bound in eternal chains and iron ropes. We do not have any concept of the meaning of these Divine punishments.

ح§ לַעֲשׂוֹת בָּהֶם מִשְׁפָּט כָּתוּב — **To execute upon them written judgment,** i.e., to do justice to the *reshaim,* as is "written in the Books" of Torah and *Neviim*. We, as humans, are not capable of meting out punishment severe enough to fit the enormity of the crimes which were perpetrated against our people. When the Nazi murderer Adolph Eichmann, *yemach shemo,* was hanged, he died only once. This does not account for even one outcry of one little child who was tortured, nor for one drop of blood which was shed — and there were billions of such drops. We have no idea how this can be avenged. But we do know that it will happen, and that it will not be done by us. As this *mizmor* states, at the time of *techiyas hameisim,* while we are involved in רוֹמְמוֹת אֵל בִּגְרוֹנָם, *HaKadosh Baruch Hu* will, on our behalf, punish those responsible for all those heinous crimes throughout our history, so that it will seem as if we were actually "wielding the sword" and waging this war — וְחֶרֶב פִּיפִיּוֹת בְּיָדָם.

To explain מִשְׁפָּט כָּתוּב, I will allow myself a little "Purim Torah," since tomorrow night is Purim *Katan.*

[Ed. note: This was Purim Kattan of 1992. It was the Rav's practice to incorporate the current events of the calendar into his *shiurim*. Exactly three years later, on Purim *Katan,* would be the night of the Rav's *petirah.*]

By this, I do not mean the kind of "Purim Torah" which appears in jocular publications, or skits on Purim, but rather, I mean real Torah *min haShamayim,* which has a connection with Purim, as follows.

The *Torah Shebichsav,* or מִשְׁפָּט כָּתוּב, tells us, עַיִן תַּחַת עַיִן, *an eye for an eye* (*Shemos* 21:24), or וְקַצֹּתָה אֶת כַּפָּהּ, *you shall cut off her hand* (*Devarim* 25:12). However, the *Torah Shebe'al Peh* teaches us that the practical application of עַיִן תַּחַת עַיִן or וְקַצֹּתָה אֶת כַּפָּהּ is not the taking of the other's eye, or actually cutting off of the hand, but rather it is monetary compensation for the loss of the eye or for the public humiliation, in accordance with all the halachic principles involved in evaluating such damages. This is so even if the injury or humiliation was done purposefully — and certainly if it was done accidentally. In practical application then, the *Torah Shebichsav* can be called *middas hadin,* while the *Torah Shebe'al Peh* is *middas harachamim.* So when our *pasuk* refers to מִשְׁפָּט כָּתוּב, it means *middas hadin.*

The actual *sefer Torah* itself, the *Torah Shebichsav,* the Written Torah, is an example of *middas hadin.* The writing must be so exact that if even a small edge of the smallest letter, *yud,* קוֹצוֹ שֶׁל יוּ"ד, were to be missing, this would render the entire *sefer Torah pasul* (invalid), and it would have no greater *kedushah* than a *Chumash* possesses.

We can also find *middas hadin* in nature. For example, there are certain tiny — or even microscopic — parts of the body which are so crucial that without their proper functioning, life would be impossible.

On the other hand, the teaching of *Torah Shebe'al Peh* is done as *middas harachamim.* While the *Torah Shebichsav* must be written to exacting standards, *Torah Shebe'al Peh* can be transmitted and explained in any language; one can add a word here or subtract a word there. It was intended for a father to teach it to his son. So, in accordance with the natural instinct of a father, כְּרַחֵם אָב עַל בָּנִים, *As a father has compassion upon children* (*Tehillim* 103:13), a compassionate father teaches his child the Torah in a compassionate way, in any language, utilizing any legitimate pedagogic method — as long as the *halachah* is taught accurately in a way which will best convey the material to the child.

So when we look at the totality of Torah, we find a combination of *rachamim* and *din,* much as the world was created with a combination of *rachamim* and *din* (see *Bereishis Rabbah* 12:15, also *Rashi,* s.v. ברא אלהים).

On Purim, we read the *parashah* of Amalek, which contains the *pasuk*: כְּתֹב זֹאת זִכָּרוֹן בַּסֵּפֶר, *Write this as a remembrance in the Book* (*Shemos* 17:14). Moshe was commanded to write down the story and the *mitzvos* connected with it, בַּסֵּפֶר. Although the Torah was written by Moshe Rabbeinu after the war with *Amalek* (see disagreement in *Gittin* 60a regarding whether תוֹרָה מְגִילָה מְגִילָה נִיתְּנָה or חֲתוּמָה נִיתְּנָה), nevertheless, the *parashah* of *Amalek* was to be written immediately as a סֵפֶר, even before the entire *sefer Torah* was finished. This was so because the *mitzvah* of *mechiyas Amalek* (the blotting out of Amalek) was to be carried out by *Klal Yisrael* as the *middas hadin* of מִשְׁפָּט כָּתוּב, which does not allow for any *rachamim.*

It is for this reason that the halachah requires that *Megillas Esther* be written with שִׂרְטוּט, *line demarcations,* similar to a *sefer Torah* (see *Megillah* 16b). Since the entire *Megillah* concerns the threat of annihilation of the Jewish people ר"ל by Haman, a descendant of Amalek, by utilizing this *sefer* we are reminded of the מִשְׁפָּט כָּתוּב, the *middas hadin* which hangs over the head of the Amalek, as commanded to us in the *parashah* of Amalek, contained in the *sefer Torah.*

It is also for this reason that we are required to fulfill the *mitzvah* of זָכוֹר אֵת

אֲשֶׁר עָשָׂה לְךָ עֲמָלֵק, *Remember what Amalek did to you* (*Devarim* 25:17) by actually reading this *parashah* from a *sefer Torah* in a very careful and exacting manner. This is to underscore the מִשְׁפָּט כָּתוּב of כְּתֹב זֹאת זִכָּרוֹן בַּסֵּפֶר ... כִּי מָחֹה אֶמְחֶה אֶת זֵכֶר עֲמָלֵק, *Write this as a remembrance in the Book . . . that I shall surely erase the memory of Amalek* (*Shemos* 17:14), representing the *middas hadin* of the eventual destruction of any vestige of Amalek.

◆§ הָדָר הוּא לְכָל חֲסִידָיו, הַלְלוּיָהּ — **That will be the splendor of all His devout ones. Halleluyah!** This will be the due honor which He will bestow on all of His *chassidim* — *HaKadosh Baruch Hu* will take up their cause. Notwithstanding the grievous harm done by the *reshaim* to the *chassidim*, they will have nothing to do with the punishment of the *reshaim*, which will be meted out by *HaKadosh Baruch Hu* Himself. Just as we have no idea of the nature of the reward which is in store for the *tzaddikim* in *Olam Haba*, so do we not have any concept of the punishment of the *reshaim* at that time. We simply cannot conceptualize the עוֹמֶק הַדִּין, *the depth, or perfect application, of justice,* in the eventual punishment, and the חֲרָפוֹת לְדִרְאוֹן עוֹלָם, *eternal shame and damnation* which is in store for the *reshaim*.

הַלְלוּיָהּ הַלְלוּ אֵל בְּקָדְשׁוֹ /
Halleluyah Hallelu Eil B'Kodsho

Now, finally, with this *mizmor*, we arrive at the last chapter of *Tehillim*, which is the "crescendo" of all the praises written by Dovid HaMelech. This corresponds to the purely spiritual existence of the *olam haneshamos*, of which we do not have any understanding at all.

The Rambam (*Hil. Teshuvah* 8:2) explains that after the period of *techiyas hameisim*, there will be an existence of only *neshamos*, with no physical manifestations whatsoever. It is in that world that the *neshamos* of the *tzaddikim* will receive their ultimate reward.

This *mizmor*, too, with its constantly repeated use of the command, הַלְלוּ, *praise*, is composed as a "symphony" in which the conductor directs all the components of his orchestra to express their praise of *HaKadosh Baruch Hu*. However, in this *mizmor*, these feelings of praise are expressed from a purely spiritual point of view; it is the *neshamah* itself that pours out its devotion to *HaKadosh Baruch Hu*.

❧ ❧ ❧

הַלְלוּיָהּ הַלְלוּ אֵל בְּקָדְשׁוֹ — **Halleluyah. Praise God in His Sanctuary.** Normally, בְּקָדְשׁוֹ would refer to the *Beis HaMikdash*. In the final stages of the world's existence, the *Beis HaMikdash* and Yerushalayim will have spread throughout the entire globe. In effect, then, the entire world will have become the *mikdash* (*Yalkut Shimoni, Yeshayahu* 503). However, here "His sanctuary" refers to the souls of those human beings who have sanctified themselves during their lives by using their freedom of choice to obey God's will in this world.

הַלְלוּהוּ בִּרְקִיעַ עֻזּוֹ — **Praise Him in the firmament of His strength.** רָקִיעַ normally means the atmosphere surrounding our globe. However, here it refers to the "super world," such as is envisioned by the *Navi* Yechezkel: וּדְמוּת עַל רָאשֵׁי הַחַיָּה רָקִיעַ כְּעֵין הַקֶּרַח הַנּוֹרָא נָטוּי עַל רָאשֵׁיהֶם מִלְמָעְלָה, *There was a likeness of an expanse above the heads of the Chayah, like the color of the awesome ice, spread out over their heads from above* (*Yechezkel* 1:22). This world is even "above the heads," or comprehension level, of those spiritual beings called *Chayos* (see *Rambam, Hil. Yesodei HaTorah* 2:7).

So the conductor is calling forth the praise of Hashem first from קָדְשׁוֹ, meaning the בַּעֲלֵי בְּחִירָה, the souls of human beings who have the power of free choice, who are on a level which is even greater than *malachim,* and then from the רְקִיעַ עֻזּוֹ, from the denizens of the "super world," that spiritual world of *malachim.*

הַלְלוּהוּ בִגְבוּרֹתָיו, הַלְלוּהוּ כְּרֹב גֻּדְלוֹ — Praise Him for His mighty acts; praise Him as befits His abundant greatness. From the point of view of the *neshamah,* both the גְּבוּרָה — the *middas hadin* — and the גֻּדְלוֹ — the *middas harachamim* — are ultimately seen as one and the same. The "conductor" here wishes to evoke God's praises in the combination of *rachamim* and *din.*

[Ed. note: Undoubtedly, Rav Schwab had certain Kabbalistic concepts in mind here which he did not articulate.]

הַלְלוּהוּ בְּתֵקַע שׁוֹפָר . . . בְּנֵבֶל וְכִנּוֹר . . . בְּתֹף וּמָחוֹל . . . בְּמִנִּים וְעֻגָב . . . בְּצִלְצְלֵי שָׁמַע . . . בְּצִלְצְלֵי תְרוּעָה — Praise Him with the blast of the shofar . . . with lyre and harp . . . with drum and dance . . . with organ and flute . . . with clanging cymbals . . . with resonant trumpets. The exact identity of the various musical instruments listed here, as well as throughout *Tehillim,* whether they are wind, stringed or percussion instruments and cymbals, and their accompanying dances, is not known to us. However, we do know that each one was intended to evoke certain feelings and emotions of the *neshamah* which could best be expressed by the particular instrument called for by the composer of the *mizmor.* Just as the *guf* has various parts which serve different purposes, so does the *neshamah* have various feelings and emotions. These various musical instruments are meant to express those spiritual emotions.

Here, Dovid HaMelech is calling upon all of these instruments to accompany him in this final great crescendo of:

כֹּל הַנְּשָׁמָה תְּהַלֵּל יָהּ, הַלְלוּיָהּ — This means either, All souls shall praise Hashem, or **The totality of the** *neshamah* **shall praise Hashem.** This would include all of the various emotions and feelings of the *neshamah.*

It is with this outpouring of the emotions of his soul that Dovid HaMelech concludes the entire *Sefer Tehillim.*

Interestingly, in this symphony of praises by the *neshamah* to *HaKadosh Baruch Hu,* the directives הַלְלוּ and הַלְלוּהוּ are repeated ten times. However, in the other "symphony," that of הַלְלוּ אֶת ה' מִן הַשָּׁמַיִם (psalm 148), which we explained in the context of being conducted by *Mashiach,* there are only eight directives of הַלְלוּהוּ and הַלְלוּ.

This would correspond to, כִּנּוֹר שֶׁל מִקְדָּשׁ שֶׁל שִׁבְעַת נִימִין הָיָה, וְשֶׁל יְמוֹת מָשִׁיחַ שְׁמוֹנָה, וְשֶׁל עוֹלָם הַבָּא שֶׁל עֶשֶׂר, *The harp used in the Beis HaMikdash consisted of seven strings, and that which will be used at the time of Mashiach will have eight strings, but the one that will be used in Olam Haba will have ten* (Arachin 13b).

Accordingly, the "eight strings" are represented in the aforementioned psalm 148 by the eight commands of הַלְלוּ and הַלְלוּהוּ, given by the "conductor," *Mashiach*.

However, the present *mizmor* of הַלְלוּ אֵל בְּקָדְשׁוֹ, representing *Olam Haba*, which will be experienced exclusively by the *neshamos*, contains ten commands of הַלְלוּ and הַלְלוּהוּ, an allusion to the ten-stringed instrument of *Olam Haba*.

It is for this reason that מִזְמוֹר שִׁיר לְיוֹם הַשַּׁבָּת (psalm 92), which refers to יוֹם שֶׁכֻּלּוֹ שַׁבָּת, *a day which is totally Sabbatical*, meaning *Olam Haba*, offers praises to *HaKadosh Baruch Hu* עֲלֵי עָשׂוֹר, *on a ten-stringed instrument*.

Furthermore, we find in the *Midrash* that הַכִּנּוֹר שֶׁהָיָה דָוִד מְנַגֵּן בּוֹ הָיָה בַעֲשָׂרָה נִימִין, *The harp which David used contained ten strings* (*Pirkei d'Rabbi Eliezer* 19 and *Midrash Shocher Tov* 92). This harp could refer to psalm 150, with which *Dovid HaMelech* concludes *Sefer Tehillim*. And these ten commands of הַלְלוּ are the ten strings, representing *Olam Haba*, to which the aforementioned *Midrash* refers.

There is a universally accepted *minhag* to repeat the last sentence of this *mizmor*, כֹּל הַנְּשָׁמָה תְּהַלֵּל יָהּ הַלְלוּיָהּ. This is explained by the *Tur* (*Orach Chaim* 51), based on *Avudraham*, as an indication that this is the completion of *Sefer Tehillim*. The same applies to the *shirah* of אָז יָשִׁיר, in which we repeat the last *pasuk* of ה' יִמְלֹךְ לְעֹלָם וָעֶד. Prosaically, we could see this as being similar to a seam at the edge of a garment, which is double-stitched to strengthen it, and to prevent it from fraying at the edges. By repeating the last sentence, we make it clear that we have concluded this section, and that whatever follows does not belong to it.

Strikingly, the Name of *HaKadosh Baruch Hu* used in this last sentence is יָהּ, the same One used in the *parashah* of Amalek: כִּי יָד עַל כֵּס יָהּ, *For the hand is on the throne of God* (*Shemos* 17:16). And, as we previously mentioned, *Rashi* thereon quotes the *maamar Chazal*: נִשְׁבַּע הקב"ה שֶׁאֵין שְׁמוֹ שָׁלֵם וְאֵין כִּסְאוֹ שָׁלֵם עַד שֶׁיִּמָּחֶה שְׁמוֹ שֶׁל עֲמָלֵק כֻּלּוֹ, וּכְשֶׁיִּמָּחֶה שְׁמוֹ יִהְיֶה הַשֵּׁם שָׁלֵם, *HaKadosh Baruch Hu has sworn that His Name will not be complete and His throne will be incomplete until the name of Amalek is completely obliterated, and when Amalek's name is finally obliterated, God's Name will be complete* (from *Midrash Tanchuma*, end of *Ki Seitzei*). At this final "crescendo" of all the *mizmorim*, we would have expected to find the full שֵׁם הֲוָיָה, *Ineffable Name* of *HaKadosh Baruch Hu* used, and not the abbreviated, temporary יָהּ.

The reason can be found in an ancient *Midrash* called *Perek Shirah*, which details the expressions of songs to *HaKadosh Baruch Hu* by each creature. (It is quoted in *Yalkut Shimoni*, *Tehillim* 889.) אָמְרוּ עַל דָּוִד מֶלֶךְ יִשְׂרָאֵל בְּשָׁעָה שֶׁסִּיֵּים סֵפֶר תְּהִלִּים זָחָה דַעְתּוֹ עָלָיו, *It was said of Dovid HaMelech that when he concluded Sefer Tehillim, his mind became arrogant*. This means that after his monumental accomplishment of completing *Sefer Tehillim*, Dovid

HaMelech became aware of thoughts of his self-importance, which he normally suppressed. However, at that time these thoughts "slipped out" into his conscious mind. The word יָזַח here is used in the sense of וְלֹא יִזַּח הַחֹשֶׁן מֵעַל הָאֵפוֹד, where it has the meaning *to slip out* (*Shemos* 28:28).

The *Midrash* continues: וְאָמַר לִפְנֵי הקב״ה: יֵשׁ בְּרִיָּה שֶׁבָּרָאתָ בְּעוֹלָמְךָ שֶׁאוֹמֶרֶת שִׁירוֹת וְתִשְׁבָּחוֹת יוֹתֵר מִמֶּנִּי, *He said to HaKadosh Baruch Hu, "Is there any creature which You have created in Your world that says more songs and praises than I do?"* בְּאוֹתוֹ שָׁעָה נִזְדַּמְּנָה לוֹ צְפַרְדֵּעַ אַחַת, *At that moment, a frog appeared to him.* This probably means that this was the thought which *HaKadosh Baruch Hu* placed in his mind at that moment. וְאָמְרָה לוֹ: דָּוִד, אַל תָּזוּחַ דַּעְתְּךָ עָלֶיךָ שֶׁאֲנִי אוֹמֶרֶת שִׁירוֹת וְתִשְׁבָּחוֹת יוֹתֵר מִמְּךָ, *And it said to him: Dovid, don't be so arrogant; I, the little frog, say more praises than you and your entire Sefer Tehillim.*

The frog continues: וְלֹא עוֹד אֶלָּא שֶׁאֲנִי עוֹסֶקֶת בְּמִצְוָה גְדוֹלָה, יֵשׁ בִּשְׂפַת הַיָּם מִין אֶחָד שֶׁאֵין פַּרְנָסָתוֹ כִּי אִם בַּמַּיִם, *Not only this, but I perform a great mitzvah. There is a certain animal at the seashore which lives only from food found in the water.* וּבְשָׁעָה שֶׁהוּא רָעֵב נוֹטְלַנִי וְאוֹכְלֵנִי לְקַיֵּים מַה שֶּׁנֶּאֱמַר: אִם רָעֵב שֹׂנַאֲךָ הַאֲכִלֵהוּ לָחֶם, *And when he is hungry, he catches me and eats me, and with this I fulfill the mitzvah* (*Mishlei* 25:21), *"If your enemy is hungry, feed him."*

This *Midrash* can be explained to mean the following. The greatness and glory of a human being lies in his power of free choice, *bechirah*. Each person has a *yetzer hatov* and a *yetzer hara*. We are fascinated — if we are deserving — with the desire to come close to *HaKadosh Baruch Hu*, but we are equally fascinated in pursuing the opposite. Because even if we are successful in subduing the attraction of the *yetzer hara*, we still possess it as long as we are alive. It is for this reason that when Moshe Rabbeinu asked *HaKadosh Baruch Hu*, הַרְאֵנִי נָא אֶת כְּבֹדֶךָ, *Show me Your glory* (*Shemos* 33:18), *HaKadosh Baruch Hu* answered him, כִּי לֹא יִרְאַנִי הָאָדָם וָחָי, *for no human can see me and live* (ibid. 33:20). As long as man is alive and has a *yetzer hara*, he cannot comprehend *HaKadosh Baruch Hu*.

Therefore, if a frog were able to think and communicate as humans do, it would be able to express more songs and praises to *HaKadosh Baruch Hu* than could man, because the frog would be unencumbered by a *yetzer hara*. For man, however, despite the fact that he has the ability to overcome the attraction of the *yetzer hara*, which is his glory and his greatness, the *yetzer hara* is also his limitation. It is this limitation of the human being — even a Moshe Rabbeinu or a Dovid HaMelech — which is alluded to by the "abbreviated" form יָהּ. Regarding the perception of *HaKadosh Baruch Hu*, as long as a human being is alive, he can only reach the level of יָהּ.

Interestingly, this is borne out by the *pasuk* that the *Perek Shirah* describes as that which is expressed by the frog: צְפַרְדֵּעַ אוֹמֵר: בָּרוּךְ שֵׁם כְּבוֹד מַלְכוּתוֹ לְעוֹלָם וָעֶד, *The frog says: Blessed is the Name of His Kingdom forever.* Although we do not truly understand the meaning here, we do know that this is the *shirah* of the *malachim*, "song of the angels." (See *Tur Orach Chaim* Ch. 619.)

Here, then, in this final chapter of *Tehillim*, Dovid HaMelech, at the highest and sublimest moment of his life, yet being merely a mortal man, alludes to the human being's limited ability to express the songs and praises of *HaKadosh Baruch Hu.* For as long as one is subject to the limitations of לֹא יִרְאַנִי הָאָדָם וָחָי, he can only summarize his highest forms of the praises of *HaKadosh Baruch Hu* as כָּל הַנְּשָׁמָה תְּהַלֵּל יָהּ, which expresses the human being's inherent limitation in comprehending *HaKadosh Baruch Hu.*

בָּרוּךְ ה' לְעוֹלָם אָמֵן וְאָמֵן / Baruch Hashem L'olam Amen V'amen

Just as after הַלֵּל we have a *berachah acharonah,* a concluding blessing, so too do we conclude the saying of these *mizmorim,* which *Chazal* have called גּוֹמְרֵי הַלֵּל, *the ending of Hallel-Tehillim* (*Shabbos* 118b), with this group of *pesukim.* They contain the word בָּרוּךְ four times, and they are the same four *pesukim* that we say in *chutz la'aretz,* communities outside of Eretz Yisrael, during the weekday Maariv, before *Shemoneh Esrei.* Each one of these four *pesukim* is, in itself, a concluding verse.

❧ ❧ ❧

❧ בָּרוּךְ ה' לְעוֹלָם, אָמֵן וְאָמֵן ❧ — **Blessed is Hashem forever, Amen and Amen.** This is the last *pasuk* of *sefer shelishi,* the third book of *Tehillim,* psalm 89.

❧ בָּרוּךְ ה' מִצִּיּוֹן, שֹׁכֵן יְרוּשָׁלָיִם, הַלְלוּיָהּ ❧ — **Blessed is Hashem from Tziyon, Who dwells in Jerusalem, Halleluyah.** This is the last *pasuk* of psalm 135, which precedes הַלֵּל הַגָּדוֹל (הוֹדוּ לַה' כִּי טוֹב כִּי לְעוֹלָם חַסְדּוֹ).

❧ בָּרוּךְ ה' אֱלֹהִים אֱלֹהֵי יִשְׂרָאֵל, עֹשֵׂה נִפְלָאוֹת לְבַדּוֹ. וּבָרוּךְ שֵׁם כְּבוֹדוֹ לְעוֹלָם, וְיִמָּלֵא כְבוֹדוֹ אֶת כָּל הָאָרֶץ אָמֵן וְאָמֵן ❧ — **Blessed is Hashem, God, the God of Israel, Who alone does wonders. Blessed is His glorious Name forever, and may all the earth be filled with His glory, Amen and Amen.** These are the concluding *pesukim* of psalm 72, with which the *sefer sheini,* the second book of *Tehillim,* ends. (*Tehillim* is subdivided into five "books.")

These four *pesukim* conclude the aforementioned chapters, which encompass the various topics contained in *Tehillim*:

The topic of psalm 89, which concludes with בָּרוּךְ ה' לְעוֹלָם אָמֵן וְאָמֵן, is the depth of the *galus,* הַסְתָּרַת פָּנִים, a time during which "God's face" is hidden, and it seems as if He has relinquished control of the world. The author pleads, עַד מָה ה' תִּסָּתֵר לָנֶצַח . . . אַיֵּה חֲסָדֶיךָ הָרִאשֹׁנִים, *Until when, Hashem, will You constantly hide Yourself . . . Where are your former acts of kindness.* Yet, notwithstanding this condition of the seemingly endless *galus* in which *Klal Yisrael* finds itself, he still concludes with בָּרוּךְ ה' לְעוֹלָם אָמֵן וְאָמֵן.

The next *pasuk,* בָּרוּךְ ה' מִצִּיּוֹן, from psalm 135 — which compares the idol-worshiping world of עֲצַבֵּי הַגּוֹיִם כֶּסֶף וְזָהָב, *The idols of the nations are silver and gold,* with בֵּית יִשְׂרָאֵל בָּרְכוּ אֶת ה', *O House of Israel, bless Hashem* — expresses the satisfaction that at least in Tziyon, God reveals Himself and is recognized by *Am Yisrael*. For this, the *mizmor* concludes thankfully, בָּרוּךְ ה׳ מִצִּיּוֹן שֹׁכֵן יְרוּשָׁלָיִם הַלְלוּיָהּ.

Finally, the last two *pesukim*, בָּרוּךְ ה׳ אֱלֹהִים... וּבָרוּךְ שֵׁם כְּבוֹדוֹ לְעוֹלָם, which conclude psalm 72, and are the end of *sefer sheini*, describe the *yemos haMashiach*. The *mizmor* starts with לִשְׁלֹמֹה, *For Shlomo*, who Dovid HaMelech had hoped would be *Mashiach*. (See *Midrash Shocher Tov* 72 and *Radak* ibid.)

The entire *mizmor* talks of הֶאָרַת פָּנִים, the enlightened state of humanity in its recognition of *HaKadosh Baruch Hu*, and the blessed condition of life in the world under the leadership of the *Melech HaMashiach*. It concludes with בָּרוּךְ ה׳ אֱלֹהִים אֱלֹהֵי יִשְׂרָאֵל עֹשֵׂה נִפְלָאוֹת לְבַדּוֹ. The God of Israel, *HaKadosh Baruch Hu*, is now finally and universally recognized as the sole Source of all wonders, which will result in וְיִמָּלֵא כְבוֹדוֹ אֶת כָּל הָאָרֶץ, *the earth will be filled with His glory*.

The final words in this chapter are כָּלּוּ תְפִלּוֹת דָּוִד בֶּן יִשָׁי, *The prayers of Dovid, the son of Yishai, are ended*. Rav Samson R. Hirsch explains this by prefacing it with one word: "then." After the entire world has recognized *HaKadosh Baruch Hu*, and וְיִמָּלֵא כְבוֹדוֹ אֶת כָּל הָאָרֶץ, then, and only then, כָּלּוּ תְפִלּוֹת דָּוִד בֶּן יִשָׁי, will the prayers of Dovid the son of Yishai be concluded. Until that time, however, Dovid says he will continue to be *mispallel* for this eventual goal for humanity.

Our recitation of the conclusion of psalm 72 ends with אָמֵן וְאָמֵן. There are two meanings for the word *amen*. The first is that the respondent identifies himself with the preceding words and accepts them as truth. But it also has an additional meaning, that of a *tefillah*. For instance, when one receives a *berachah* from another, he answers *amen*, praying that the good wish be fulfilled. Also, in a מִי שֶׁבֵּרַךְ, all those who hear it respond with וְנֹאמַר אָמֵן.

Similarly, here we first say אָמֵן, meaning that we are מַאֲמִין בֶּאֱמוּנָה שְׁלֵמָה, *we believe with a perfect faith*, that eventually the whole world will recognize *HaKadosh Baruch Hu*: בָּרוּךְ ה׳ לְעוֹלָם and וְיִמָּלֵא כְבוֹדוֹ אֶת כָּל הָאָרֶץ. Then we say אָמֵן again, as a *tefillah* that this time may come soon.

With this we have concluded the וּנְפָאֶרְךָ portion of the *Pesukei d'Zimrah*, and we now begin the וַיְבָרֶךְ דָּוִיד portion with וְנַזְכִּיר שִׁמְךָ.

וַיְבָרֶךְ דָּוִיד / Vayevarech Dovid

This portion, starting with וַיְבָרֶךְ דָּוִיד, corresponds to וְנַזְכִּיר שִׁמְךָ, the fourth of the five sections of *Pesukei d'Zimrah* referred to in בָּרוּךְ שֶׁאָמַר. The simple meaning of וְנַזְכִּיר שִׁמְךָ is that should we forget the Name of *HaKadosh Baruch Hu*, we will recall it in our minds. However, at this point in our *tefillah*, it is hardly possible to have forgotten the Name of *HaKadosh Baruch Hu* when He has been the subject of the entire *Pesukei d'Zimrah* up to this point.

So it is obvious that וְנַזְכִּיר שִׁמְךָ does not mean simply, "We will remember Your Name." Rather, this is to be understood in the sense of its usage in אֵלֶּה בָרֶכֶב וְאֵלֶּה בַסּוּסִים וַאֲנַחְנוּ בְּשֵׁם ה' אֱלֹהֵינוּ נַזְכִּיר, *Some through chariots, and some through horses, but we, in the Name of Hashem, our God, call out* (*Tehillim* 20:8), which means that our happiness over our victories will focus on the fact that it was Hashem Who brought them about. While others credit the power of their armies for their victories, we will be cognizant of — and "remember" — that it is Hashem Who has brought about our success.

The next two pieces — one starting with וַיְבָרֶךְ דָּוִיד and ending with מְהַלְלִים לְשֵׁם תִּפְאַרְתֶּךָ (from *Divrei HaYamim I* Ch. 29), and the other, starting with אַתָּה הוּא ה' לְבַדֶּךָ, to וַתַּעַשׂ לְךָ שֵׁם כְּהַיּוֹם הַזֶּה (from *Nechemiah* Ch. 9) — reflect on the *yemos haMashiach*. The focus here is the fact that even when the Jewish people merit the coming of *Mashiach*, there will be the danger that this world-historic event may eclipse its ultimate purpose: that of the universal knowledge and acceptance of *HaKadosh Baruch Hu*.

Even today, when there is so much talk of *"Mashiach,"* *HaKadosh Baruch Hu* is not part of the picture. The הֲמוֹן עָם, *most people,* tend to forget that *Mashiach* is merely a tool in the hands of *HaKadosh Baruch Hu*, Who will bring about the *yeshuah*. And it is this recognition that is meant by וְנַזְכִּיר שִׁמְךָ.

Historically, this *tefillah* was said by Dovid HaMelech at the public coronation of his son Shlomo (see *Divrei HaYamim I* Ch. 29). It was the hope of Dovid HaMelech that Shlomo would become the *Mashiach*. This is alluded to by the words, וַיֵּשֶׁב שְׁלֹמֹה עַל כִּסֵּא ה', *Shlomo sat upon the throne of Hashem* (ibid. 29:23), an expression that we find only with respect to Shlomo. If Shlomo HaMelech had not committed certain acts, which for him were considered *aveiros*, this hope would have indeed been realized. Instead, three thousand years after this coronation, we are still waiting for *Mashiach*.

Dovid HaMelech was concerned that upon his son's elevation to the כִּסֵּא ה', which would begin the *yemos haMashiach*, the epoch of *Mashiach*, with all its glory, the people would lose sight of the purpose of it all: that of the הִתְגַּלּוּת אֱלֹהִים, *the revelation of the existence of God*, in the world. So Dovid had to remind them that it was שֵׁם תִּפְאַרְתֶּךָ, *Your glorious Name*, which would be behind all of the splendor of the reign of Shlomo Ha-Melech.

The same applies to Moshe Rabbeinu at *krias Yam Suf*, the splitting of the *Yam Suf*, which is described by Nechemiah in the next piece, starting with אַתָּה הוּא ה' לְבַדֶּךָ. In this speech, Nechemiah declares publicly to the assembled people, lest they forget, that: וַתַּעַשׂ לְךָ שֵׁם כְּהַיּוֹם הַזֶּה, *You brought Yourself renown as clear as this very day* (Nechemiah 9:10). It was not because Moshe Rabbeinu raised his rod that the *Yam Suf* had split, but rather, it was *HaKadosh Baruch Hu* Who performed that historic miracle. And He also reminded them that, וְהַיָּם בָּקַעְתָּ לִפְנֵיהֶם וַיַּעַבְרוּ בְתוֹךְ הַיָּם בַּיַּבָּשָׁה, *It was You Who split the sea before them and they crossed in the midst of the sea on dry land.* Moshe was merely Your servant. This is expressed in the words of the Torah: וַיַּאֲמִינוּ בַּה' וּבְמֹשֶׁה עַבְדּוֹ, *And they had faith in Hashem and in Moshe His servant* (Shemos 14:31).

When we read the account of the death of Dovid HaMelech (*Melachim I*, Ch. 2), we find only a brief portion of his final words. Furthermore, a significant segment of Dovid's speech is devoted to his seemingly cruel last wish, in which he commands his son and successor, Shlomo, that Yoav ben Tzeruyah and Shimi ben Geira not be allowed to die natural deaths. Rather, Shlomo was to see to it that they would die violent deaths. The reason for this is unknown to me.

However, in *Divrei HaYamim I* (Chap. 28) we find a much more detailed account of the last words of Dovid HaMelech, and of his many speeches to Shlomo HaMelech and to *Klal Yisrael* before he closed his eyes forever. *Divrei HaYamim*, which was written by Ezra (*Bava Basra* 14b), is a *peirush* (commentary) on the *Sifrei HaNeviim*, and includes many details which were left out of the *Sifrei HaNeviim*. I really do not know why these facts, and many details of other events, were not included in the *Sifrei HaNeviim*, but there must be a reason.

In one of these final speeches, recorded in *Divrei HaYamim I*, Chs. 28-29, Dovid HaMelech, shortly before his death, assembled the leaders of the nation and told them of his preparations to build the *Beis HaMikdash*. He informed them that all of the vast treasures which he had won as a result of his victorious battles against his many enemies had been set aside for the purpose of building the *Beis HaMikdash*. Dovid had taken none of the wealth for himself.

At this time, Dovid HaMelech reaffirmed to the nation that his young son, Shlomo was the rightful heir to the throne, despite the fact that he was only 12 years of age at the time. He told the assemblage that it was the will of *HaKadosh Baruch Hu* that young Shlomo would bring about the recognition of *Malchus Shamayim* in the entire world, and that it would be Shlomo who would direct the building of the *Beis HaMikdash,* utilizing the vast fortune which Dovid HaMelech had accumulated. This was especially important in view of the failed attempt by another of his sons, Adoniyahu ben Chagis, to assume his father's throne.

Dovid HaMelech goes on to describe to the assembled people what the huge fortune that he had accumulated consisted of, but he made it very clear to them that this great glittering hoard of gold and silver and other precious materials was not the result of his great prowess in battle, but rather, of *HaKadosh Baruch Hu* delivering it all into his hands. Furthermore, in addition to this fortune which he dedicated for the building of the *Beis HaMikdash,* he also invited every Israelite to contribute to it as well, just as was done at the time of the building of the *Mishkan* in the desert. Then he was *mispallel* to *HaKadosh Baruch Hu* that He accept these donations as a great and everlasting *zechus* for the Jewish people: ה׳ אֱלֹהֵי אַבְרָהָם יִצְחָק וְיִשְׂרָאֵל אֲבוֹתֵינוּ שָׁמְרָה זֹאת לְעוֹלָם לְיֵצֶר מַחְשְׁבוֹת לְבַב עַמֶּךָ וְהָכֵן לְבָבָם אֵלֶיךָ, *Hashem, God of our Forefathers Avraham, Yitzchak, and Yisrael, preserve this forever to be the product of the thoughts of the hearts of Your people, and set their hearts towards You* (*Divrei HaYamim I* 29:18).

It was in the context of contemplating this huge store of amassed wealth, and its source, that Dovid HaMelech spoke these words:

※ ※ ※

וַיְבָרֶךְ דָּוִיד אֶת ה׳ לְעֵינֵי כָּל הַקָּהָל — **And Dovid blessed Hashem in the presence of the entire congregation.** With these words, Dovid HaMelech begins his touching and extensive *tefillah* on this occasion. We recite only a small segment of it and, unfortunately, even these few verses are said so routinely that we may overlook some of their fine points.

The usage of the word לְעֵינֵי כָּל הַקָּהָל instead of לִפְנֵי כָּל הַקָּהָל strikes us immediately as being quite unusual. One could say that the simple reason for this is that only those of this vast audience who were in close proximity were able to hear Dovid HaMelech — there were no amplifiers at that time. The others could only see him, but could not hear him, thus the use of לְעֵינֵי.

However, on a deeper level, the reason it was important to mention the word לְעֵינֵי was to convey the idea that this *tefillah* contained matters of such great significance that even if the people in that audience did not grasp their full meaning immediately, they nevertheless understood that there was a message here which, to be properly understood, required that they be מְעַיֵּין, *look into,* each word at a later time.

It is important that we attempt to uncover the profound significance of these words which the organizers of the *tefillah* at the time of the *Geonim* singled out to be recited as a part of our daily *Pesukei d'Zimrah*. We also need to understand the reason for the *minhag Yisrael* that one is to recite this *tefillah* while standing. We will suggest our explanations as we proceed.

וַיֹּאמֶר דָּוִיד: בָּרוּךְ אַתָּה ה' אֱלֹהֵי יִשְׂרָאֵל אָבִינוּ — **Dovid said: Blessed are You, Hashem, the God of our father Yisrael.** In this *tefillah*, Dovid HaMelech invokes the memory of Yaakov Avinu because he had hoped that with the beginning of the reign of Shlomo HaMelech, and the imminent building of the *Beis HaMikdash*, the nation named after "our father Yisrael" would finally have accomplished its task: that of promulgating *Malchus Shamayim* in the world. The Jewish nation would finally be worthy of the name Yisrael, which *HaKadosh Baruch Hu* gave our Forefather Yaakov Avinu: כִּי שָׂרִיתָ עִם אֱלֹהִים וְעִם אֲנָשִׁים וַתּוּכָל, *For you have striven with the Divine and with man and have overcome* (*Bereishis* 32:29). This corresponds to the words of *Chazal* that the image "Yisrael" is etched into the *Kisei HaKavod* (*Bereishis Rabbah* 78:3).

[Ed. note: The Rav did not elaborate on this saying of *Chazal* and its connection here. He said he intended to do so at the next *shiur*. Unfortunately, he did not. We can only speculate on what he meant. Rabbi D. Margareten, in the Hebrew version of this *sefer*, offers an explanation. Please refer to it.]

מֵעוֹלָם וְעַד עוֹלָם — **Literally, "from World to World."** The meaning here is: from the unknown beginnings of time until the unknown future.

[Ed. note: For a broader treatment of the concept of עוֹלָם, see above on עַל נְטִילַת יָדַיִם in the *berachah* of מֶלֶךְ הָעוֹלָם.]

לְךָ ה' הַגְּדֻלָּה וְהַגְּבוּרָה וְהַתִּפְאֶרֶת וְהַנֵּצַח וְהַהוֹד כִּי כֹל בַּשָּׁמַיִם וּבָאָרֶץ — **Yours, Hashem, is the greatness, the strength, the glory, the victory, and the majesty, even everything in heaven and earth.** In accordance with the dictum of the *Rambam* (*Hil. Yesodei HaTorah*, Ch. 1) that one cannot possibly describe the attributes of *HaKadosh Baruch Hu* since they are beyond the perception of the human mind, most of the commentators of the *Tanach* have given a simple *p'shat* to these words. They explain them as referring to the acknowledgment by Dovid HaMelech that all the many blessings which he and his nation received were bestowed upon them by *HaKadosh Baruch Hu*.

Accordingly, Dovid HaMelech is referring here to his having finally been recognized as the undisputed leader of the entire Jewish nation, and having been victorious over all his enemies, which left him in possession of enormous wealth. He is especially grateful that his son Shlomo, despite all of the obstacles to his succession, has now finally been recognized as his successor. He attributes all of these successes to "You Hashem," Who brought this all about. He lists these blessings as:

הַגְּדֻלָּה — *the greatness,* meaning his vast wealth;

וְהַגְּבוּרָה — *the strength* to subdue his enemies;

וְהַתִּפְאֶרֶת — *the glory,* meaning his undisputed sovereignty;

וְהַנֵּצַח — *the victory,* as in נִצָּחוֹן, referring to his having been victorious over all of his enemies, within and without;

וְהַהוֹד — *and the majesty* which he now enjoys in all his surroundings.

כִּי כֹל בַּשָּׁמַיִם וּבָאָרֶץ — This, too, refers back to the subject לְךָ ה׳, meaning "because everything in heaven and earth comes from You."

However, in delving deeper into the meaning of these words, as was seemingly intended by Dovid HaMelech through his use of the phrase לְעֵינֵי כָּל הַקָּהָל, we can gain a little understanding of their meaning, in accordance with the teaching found in the *Zohar* and other *sefarim* of Kabbalah.

In Kabbalistic terms, the words גְּדֻלָּה, גְּבוּרָה, תִּפְאֶרֶת, נֵצַח and הוֹד are components of the שֶׁבַע סְפִירוֹת, *seven counts,* a concept regarding the seven ways in which *HaKadosh Baruch Hu* has revealed Himself to His creations. And while we are not even at the "entrance door" of understanding the meaning of these *sefiros,* we know some of the "headlines" of their definitions.

גְּדֻלָּה is a reference to the infinite *chessed* of *HaKadosh Baruch Hu,* as in וְגָדָל חָסֶד, *And great in kindness* (*Tehillim* 145:8). So, the meaning of לְךָ ה׳ הַגְּדֻלָּה, in this term of reference, would be: *Yours is the absolute, infinite chessed.*

In contrast, גְּבוּרָה refers to the "strength" of pure justice, *din,* which knows no *chessed* whatsoever. This is the revelation of absolute, infinite *din.*

The harmony between these two extremes is תִּפְאֶרֶת, *tiferes,* the beautiful synthesis of *chessed* and *din.*

Parenthetically, these three *sefiros* are symbolically represented by our *Avos* (Patriarchs).

Avraham is associated with *chessed* = גְּדֻלָּה, because he is the greatest *baal chessed* known to us, as is described in the Torah: תִּתֵּן אֱמֶת לְיַעֲקֹב חֶסֶד לְאַבְרָהָם, *Grant truth to Yaakov, kindness to Avraham* (*Michah* 7:20).

Yitzchak is associated with *middas hadin* = גְּבוּרָה; he was prepared to offer his life at the *Akeidah.*

Yaakov is the combination of the two. He combines the attributes of his father and his grandfather. This beautiful synthesis is called *tiferes,* which is also known as *middas ha'emes,* and is expressed as, תִּתֵּן אֱמֶת לְיַעֲקֹב, *Grant truth to Yaakov* (ibid.). The *emes,* or reality, of the existence of the world is a result of the combination of *rachamim* and *din,* which is expressed by *Chazal* as שִׁתֵּף הקב״ה מִדַּת הָרַחֲמִים לְמִדַּת הַדִּין, *HaKadosh Baruch Hu mitigated the attribute of strict justice by adding to it the attribute of mercy* (*Bereishis Rabbah* 12:15 and *Rashi,* beginning of *Parashas Bereishis*).

In fact, the word אֱמֶת itself is an illustration of the harmonious combination of *rachamim* and *din*. The first two letters, אמ, means "mother," the epitome of *rachamim*, which is derived from רֶחֶם, *womb*. The second and third letters together form מת, *death*, which is the ultimate form of *din*. The synthesis of these two opposites combine to form the word אֱמֶת.

This *tiferes* is actually *what* Moshe Rabbeinu wanted to see when he asked HaKadosh Baruch Hu, הַרְאֵנִי נָא אֶת כְּבֹדֶךָ, *Show me now Your glory* (*Shemos* 33:18). But the answer came back, לֹא יִרְאַנִי הָאָדָם וָחָי, *No human can see Me and live* (ibid. v. 20). The physical conceptualization of the *tiferes* of HaKadosh Baruch Hu is impossible for a living human being: וּפָנַי לֹא יֵרָאוּ, *But My face may not be seen* (ibid. v. 23). However, he was told, וְרָאִיתָ אֶת אֲחֹרָי, *And you will see My back* (ibid. v. 23). The Gemara (*Berachos* 7a) comments: שֶׁהֶרְאָה הקב״ה לְמֹשֶׁה קֶשֶׁר שֶׁל תְּפִילִין, *HaKadosh Baruch Hu showed Moshe the knot of His tefillin,* which is at the "back of His head."

The knot of the *tefillin shel rosh* which is placed at the back of the head is formed by two *retzuos*. In accordance with our Kabbalistic reference, one of these represents נֵצַח, *eternity*, which comes from the higher world to the lower, הַשְׁפָעָה מִלְמַעְלָה לְמַטָּה. This is symbolized by Moshe Rabbeinu, because he brought the Torah from its highest abode down to earth for all future generations. The other *retzuah* represents הוֹד, *the reflected glory*, meaning the reflection back to HaKadosh Baruch Hu of our *avodah* in this world. This is the הַשְׁפָעָה מִלְמַטָּה לְמַעְלָה, through the *avodah* of the *korbanos* of which Aharon HaKohen, as the representative of *Klal Yisrael,* is symbolic.

[Ed. note: These definitions of *netzach* and *hod* are Kabbalistic, and are to be understood as complementary to the *p'shat,* or simple meaning, of the words which are used in our translation. See, also, the Rav's detailed explanation of הוֹד as a reflection back to HaKadosh Baruch Hu in his introduction to *Pesukei d'Zimrah.*]

כִּי כֹל בַּשָּׁמַיִם וּבָאָרֶץ — This refers to the "totality" of the universe: the supremacy of the spiritual world over what had been the as yet uncreated physical world. This is called יְסוֹד, *yesod*.

[Ed. note: This esoteric concept is discussed earlier in the Rav's piece on אֲדוֹן עוֹלָם.]

This connection between כֹל and יְסוֹד is mentioned by *Ramban* (*Bereishis* 24:1) on the words, וַה׳ בֵּרַךְ אֶת אַבְרָהָם בַּכֹּל. He explains this *pasuk* to mean that HaKadosh Baruch Hu blessed Avraham Avinu by revealing to Him His attribute of כֹל, which, he says, is one of the secrets of the Torah: כִּי בַּכֹּל תִּרְמוֹז עַל עִנְיָן גָּדוֹל וְהוּא שֶׁיֵּשׁ בהקב״ה מִדָּה תִּקָּרֵא ״כֹּל״ מִפְּנֵי שֶׁהִיא יְסוֹד הַכֹּל, *The word "bakol" alludes to an esoteric matter, which is that HaKadosh Baruch Hu has an attribute which is called "Kol" — ALL — because it is the basis of everything.* The result of this *berachah* was that Avraham Avinu lived a completely spiritual life even in this world. My Rebbe, HaRav Yerucham Levovitz, the

Mirrer *Mashgiach,* once remarked that when he thought of *Olam Haba* for his *neshamah,* his wish was that he would have in *Olam Haba* that which Avraham Avinu had in *Olam Hazeh.*

The *middas hayesod* is also known in Kabbalistic terms as צַדִּיק, *tzaddik,* because this is the name given to a person whose spiritual aspect dominates his physical side. He is a completely spiritual person. The symbol of such a person is Yosef.

And, finally, there is the attribute of מַלְכוּת, *malchus,* which is indicated by לְךָ ה' הַמַּמְלָכָה, *Yours, Hashem, is the sovereignty.* This refers to the physical universe, which is so vast that it appears to us as being almost infinite. But it is nonetheless finite. It was all created by the Infinite Creator. The person who symbolizes the physical *malchus* in this world is Dovid.

Furthermore, these seven *sefiros,* which are personified by the seven personalities — Avraham, Yitzchak, Yaakov, Moshe, Aharon, Yosef, and Dovid — are referred to as *ushpizin* of Succos. On each one of the seven days of Succos, we "invite" one of the special "guests" to our *succah.* By doing so, each day we are symbolically emphasizing one of the seven *sefiros* — although we do not separate the others from it — through the personality that most closely represents that particular attribute.

This is also the symbolism of the seven *hakafos* of Hoshana Rabbah. There are many *siddurim* which have, in small print, a *pasuk* referring to one of these *sefiros* after each *hakafah.* In Frankfurt, however, these *pesukim* were not said.

This same symbolism is represented by the seven-stringed musical instrument that was used in the *Beis HaMikdash* (*Arachin* 13b).

The reunion between the physical and spiritual worlds takes place when we are *mekabel Shabbos* or accept upon ourselves the sanctity of Shabbos. The famous Kabbalist, R' Shlomo Alkabetz, who composed לְכָה דוֹדִי, used "code words" to allude to this, e.g., the word כַּלָה is an abbreviation for כִּי לַהּ; דוֹדִי refers to *HaKadosh Baruch Hu* in the spiritual world (see *Yeshayahu* 5:1). With *kabbalas Shabbos,* the spiritual world, so to speak, "invades" the physical world, thus: לְכָה דוֹדִי לִקְרַאת כַּלָה, *Come my Beloved to greet the bride.* This is why Shabbos is called מֵעֵין עוֹלָם הַבָּא, *a foretaste of the World to Come.* It also accounts for the prohibition of *melachos* on Shabbos which precludes us from making any changes to the physical-material world during this day of domination by the spiritual world.

Of course, our understanding of the aforementioned Kabbalistic concepts is very limited. Rav Samson R. Hirsch, in his commentary on *Tehillim,* calls our knowledge of the attributes of *HaKadosh Baruch Hu* as only "their very beginnings."

He explains the *pasuk* (ibid. 139:17), וְלִי מַה יָּקְרוּ רֵעֶיךָ אֵל, as: *How precious are to me my thoughts of You, God.* The word רֵעֶיךָ, from רַעְיוֹן, means *thoughts*. Dovid HaMelech is saying here that just to think about *HaKadosh Baruch Hu* is so very dear to him. The *pasuk* continues, מֶה עָצְמוּ רָאשֵׁיהֶם, which Rav Hirsch explains as, *how overwhelming are their very beginnings.* This means that all the thoughts which *HaKadosh Baruch Hu* allows us to understand about Him, which He has revealed about Himself, are only the very beginnings, "the headlines," the entrance door, to understanding His essence. Yet, even these very "beginnings" of such knowledge are overwhelming.

It is therefore understandable that the organizers of our *tefillah* singled out the *pesukim* from וַיְבָרֶךְ דָּוִיד through לְשֵׁם תִּפְאַרְתֶּךָ וּמְהַלְלִים and why the *minhag* is to stand while they are recited.

These *pesukim* begin the וַיְנַזְכִּיר שִׁמְךָ portion of *Pesukei d'Zimrah* because they contain some of the most sublime thoughts regarding the attributes of *HaKadosh Baruch Hu*. Still, these are only שֵׁם תִּפְאַרְתֶּךָ, only the "Name" of Your glory, only that little which was revealed to us about *HaKadosh Baruch Hu*. However, we still have no perception of the Essence of *HaKadosh Baruch Hu*, nor of His attributes. These are merely "Names" which we apply to the glory of *HaKadosh Baruch Hu*.

It is in this sense that Dovid HaMelech pronounced these words לְעֵינֵי כָּל הַקָּהָל. While this *berachah* could be understood simply, it also has an additional, deeper meaning, as we outlined, which requires a great deal of "insight" to comprehend.

§ לְךָ ה' הַמַּמְלָכָה וְהַמִּתְנַשֵּׂא לְכֹל לְרֹאשׁ § — **Yours, Hashem, is the sovereignty and the rulership of every leader.** In addition to the Kabbalistic way of understanding these words, as we have previously outlined, this too has a simple explanation similar to that which we applied to the earlier words in this sentence.

There are two kinds of governments. One is מַמְלָכָה, a legitimate authority which governs by the consent of the governed. The other is מִתְנַשֵּׂא, a dictatorship, in which one person "raises himself up" and imposes his power on others. In this *tefillah*, Dovid HaMelech is saying that any kind of leadership or government which exists — לְכֹל לְרֹאשׁ, any appointed head or authority figure — is attributable to "You, Hashem."

In *Berachos* 58a we learn that even רֵישׁ גַּרְגִּיתָא, the head of a local water distribution authority, a minor civil servant, מִן שְׁמַיָּא מַנּוּ לֵיהּ, is appointed by Heaven. Any kind of leadership, large or small — whether one becomes a *gabbai* of a *shul,* or the head of the union, or the president of a country — is all determined by *HaKadosh Baruch Hu*.

An additional, and more insightful, meaning of the לְכֹל לְרֹאשׁ is given by *Rashi* on *Divrei HaYamim I* 29:11. (However, most probably this was not written by *Rashi*, but rather by his *talmidim,* because the writer attributes his explanation, which follows, to R' Elazar bar R' Meir bar Yitzchak from Orleans. We know that this person lived during the time of the *Baalei Tosafos,* so obviously, the writer could not be *Rashi.*)

He explains the words לְכֹל לְרֹאשׁ to mean that even if one offers so many praises to *HaKadosh Baruch Hu* that he feels he has exhausted all possible expressions of praise, and has no more words to add without repeating himself, he is, nevertheless, only at the רֹאשׁ, the very beginning, of such praises; he has not even started: עֲדַיִין אֵינוּ כְלוּם שֶׁהַמְשַׁבֵּחַ עוֹמֵד לְרֹאשׁ הַשְּׁבָחוֹת, *This is still not anything for if someone praises (God) he can only begin such praises (for he has no real conception of God).* In other words, all of these expressions of praise — גְּדֻלָּה, גְּבוּרָה, תִּפְאֶרֶת etc., hardly even begin to describe the greatness of *HaKadosh Baruch Hu.*

וְהָעשֶׁר וְהַכָּבוֹד מִלְּפָנֶיךָ — Wealth and honor come from You. The thought in this *pasuk* is actually completed three *pesukim* later in this chapter, although we do not quote it in this *tefillah*: כִּי מִמְּךָ הַכֹּל וּמִיָּדְךָ נָתַנּוּ לָךְ, *For everything is from You, and from Your hand have we given to You (Divrei HaYamim I 29:14).* The meaning is that whatever we give to *HaKadosh Baruch Hu* is actually His. If we give money to *tzedakah,* or spend it in the performance of a *mitzvah,* we are giving His money. This holds true not only for money, but also when we give of ourselves, our energy and time, for *mitzvos* and *chessed.* These, too, have been given to us by *HaKadosh Baruch Hu.* And certainly when we utilize our thought processes — thinking about *HaKadosh Baruch Hu* or learning His Torah — we are utilizing the mind which He gifted to us.

וְאַתָּה מוֹשֵׁל בַּכֹּל — And You rule everything. By presenting his son Shlomo as his successor, Dovid HaMelech hoped that after Shlomo HaMelech had built the *Beis HaMikdash,* he would be designated the *Mashiach,* and Yerushalayim would become the capital of the whole world, with the *Beis HaMikdash* as its epicenter. In fact, we see that Shlomo himself, in his *tefillah* at the dedication of the newly constructed *Beis HaMikdash,* intended it to be the focal point of *tefillah* for the entire world: וְגַם אֶל הַנָּכְרִי אֲשֶׁר לֹא מֵעַמְּךָ יִשְׂרָאֵל הוּא וּבָא מֵאֶרֶץ רְחוֹקָה לְמַעַן שְׁמֶךָ. כִּי יִשְׁמְעוּן אֶת שִׁמְךָ הַגָּדוֹל וְאֶת יָדְךָ הַחֲזָקָה וּזְרֹעֲךָ הַנְּטוּיָה וּבָא וְהִתְפַּלֵּל אֶל הַבַּיִת הַזֶּה, *Also a gentile who is not of Your people Israel, but will come from a distant land, for Your Name's sake — for they will hear of Your great Name and Your strong hand and Your outstretched arm — and will come and pray toward this House (Melachim I 8:41-42).*

Dovid HaMelech here is saying to Hashem that this sovereignty, which he was now turning over to his son, belongs in reality "to You." His *tefillah* was that the greatness of Shlomo HaMelech in the eyes of the world shall not — so to speak — eclipse that of *HaKadosh Baruch Hu.* For even as *Mashiach,* Shlomo HaMelech would be only an *eved Hashem,* servant of Hashem, for You are the real Ruler — וְאַתָּה מוֹשֵׁל בַּכֹּל.

◆§ וּבְיָדְךָ כֹּחַ וּגְבוּרָה §◆ — **In Your hand is power and strength.** When Dovid HaMelech looked at his young 12-year-old son, and the immense power — spiritual, physical, economic, and political — that he would wield as king, he attributed it all to *HaKadosh Baruch Hu*. He saw it all as בְּיָדְךָ; it was all due to the power of *HaKadosh Baruch Hu*.

◆§ וּבְיָדְךָ לְגַדֵּל וּלְחַזֵּק לַכֹּל §◆ — **And it is in Your hand to make anyone great or strong.** With this Dovid HaMelech summarizes his *tefillah* by saying that the future of the *Beis HaMikdash* as the symbol of both *Malchus Yisrael* and *Malchus Shamayim* on earth is in Your hands to sustain.

◆§ וְעַתָּה אֱלֹהֵינוּ מוֹדִים אֲנַחְנוּ לָךְ §◆ — **So now, our God, we thank You.** This means that now, after we have realized all this, we "thank You." מוֹדִים, from הוֹדָאָה, admission, means we admit that we will never be able to repay our debt to You. (See earlier comments on this concept in הוֹדוּ לַה' קִרְאוּ בִשְׁמוֹ.)

◆§ וּמְהַלְלִים לְשֵׁם תִּפְאַרְתֶּךָ §◆ — **And glorify Your beautiful Name.** Dovid Ha-Melech is saying that the descriptions which we have just sketched in a few words are the "Name," our perception, of the glory of *HaKadosh Baruch Hu*. All of these aforementioned attributes of *HaKadosh Baruch Hu* constitute וְנַזְכִּיר שְׁמֶךָ.

We now continue with the second part of the וְנַזְכִּיר שְׁמֶךָ portion of the *Pesukei d'Zimrah*, with the selection from a *tefillah* found in *Nechemiah* Chapter 9, starting with אַתָּה הוּא ה' לְבַדֶּךָ.

In *Nechemiah* we find most of the names of the *Anshei Knesses HaGedolah*, and eight of them were the *Leviim* who composed this *tefillah*.

This *tefillah* was said on a *taanis*, fast day, that was observed on the twenty-fourth day of Tishrei. It was a day of *teshuvah* to atone for the sins that *Bnei Yisrael* had committed during the early period of the Second *Beis HaMikdash*. For these, they suffered greatly at the hands of their enemies, who had broken down and burned the walls and entrance gates of Yerushalayim.

The situation was grave, and the leadership of the Jews in Eretz Yisrael asked Nechemiah to come from Persia to give them encouragement and to oversee the rebuilding of the walls of Yerushalayim. As a part of their *teshuvah* process, the leadership of the Jews in Eretz Yisrael drafted a כְּתַב אֲמָנָה, a written oath and declaration of their renewed acceptance of תּוֹרַת אֱלֹהִים. (See *Nechemiah* Ch. 10.) This document was signed by all the members of the *Anshei Knesses HaGedolah* and placed in the *Beis HaMikdash* for safekeeping. *Chazal* tell us (see *Rus Rabbah* 4:5) that the next day, they found an additional signature next to the others with the word אֱמֶת. This is in accordance with the Gemara (*Sanhedrin* 64a) which remarks, חוֹתָמוֹ שֶׁל הקב"ה אֱמֶת, *The seal of HaKadosh Baruch Hu is emes, truth.*

VAYEVARECH DOVID ⌒ 225

It was in the context of this *taanis* and "declaration of faith" that this *tefillah* was said.

For the purposes of inclusion in our *Pesukei d'Zimrah,* the organizers of the *tefillah* selected the part of this *tefillah* that begins with אַתָּה הוּא ה׳ לְבַדֶּךָ, as a continuation of the thought with which we ended the previous part: וּמְהַלְלִים לְשֵׁם תִּפְאַרְתֶּךָ, which reflected on the attributes of *HaKadosh Baruch Hu* regarding His creation, in general.

However, in this part, we focus on the relationship of *HaKadosh Baruch Hu* to Yisrael, as His עַם הַנִּבְחָר, *chosen people.* Eventually, as a result of the influence of Yisrael, the entire world will recognize the veracity of the existence of *HaKadosh Baruch Hu.*

§ אַתָּה הוּא ה׳ לְבַדֶּךָ — **It is You alone, Hashem.** We have previously discussed the meaning of הוּא with regard to *HaKadosh Baruch Hu.* This has the sense of "He, the Great Unknowable." The meaning here is: "You, the Great Unknowable 'He,' were alone." Before there was any creation whatsoever, לְבַדֶּךָ, You alone existed.

§ אַתָּה עָשִׂיתָ אֶת הַשָּׁמַיִם, שְׁמֵי הַשָּׁמַיִם וְכָל צְבָאָם — **You have created the heavens, the heaven of heavens and all their hosts.** The *heaven of heavens and all their hosts* refers to the rest of the universe, which is invisible to us, with its billions of galaxies inhabited by billions of stars.

§ הָאָרֶץ וְכָל אֲשֶׁר עָלֶיהָ, הַיַּמִּים וְכָל אֲשֶׁר בָּהֶם — **The earth and everything upon it, the seas and everything in them.** Out of this immensity of Your creation, You chose this little speck, "Earth," and made all which is on it (עָלֶיהָ), which is visible to us; You also made the oceans and everything which is in them (בָּהֶם). Much of this marine life is invisible to us.

§ וְאַתָּה מְחַיֶּה אֶת כֻּלָּם — **And You give them all life.** Not only did You create them, but You are their constant source of life. They exist only because You sustain them.

§ וּצְבָא הַשָּׁמַיִם לְךָ מִשְׁתַּחֲוִים — **And the hosts of heaven bow down to You.** These hosts of heaven are the *malachim.* They recognize that *HaKadosh Baruch Hu* is their Creator, and they bow to Him in homage. Hopefully, we will expand on this topic in the *berachah* of יוֹצֵר אוֹר.

§ אַתָּה הוּא ה׳ הָאֱלֹהִים אֲשֶׁר בָּחַרְתָּ בְּאַבְרָם — **It is You, Hashem, the God, Who selected Avram.** Up to this point, the *tefillah* reflected on the Creator of the awe-inspiring universe, with its billions of galaxies and "supergalaxies," and their billions of suns. The sun of our solar system is only a medium-sized star on the rim of one of these galaxies called the "Milky Way." And our little "Earth," with its several billion human inhabitants, is one of the planets which revolve around our sun.

All of the aforesaid leads up to a dramatic change in focus. The *tefillah* now focuses on a 3-year-old child, named Avram, whom *HaKadosh Baruch Hu* selected from the myriads of inhabitants of the earth, out of the vastness of all of His creation, to teach humanity about the existence of *HaKadosh Baruch Hu*. This little boy, following his father's example, at first worshiped the sun and the moon, as did most of the people in the world in his time. Eventually, through his astronomical observations, when he reasoned that these heavenly bodies were not deities but rather, must have been created by a Creator, he fell to his knees and exclaimed, "There is a *Ribbono Shel Olam.*" He thus rediscovered *HaKadosh Baruch Hu*, Whose existence had been all but forgotten as a result of the erroneous worship of stars and *mazalos* (constellations), by most of the inhabitants of the earth. These people worshiped the creations rather than the Creator (see *Rambam, Hil. Avodah Zarah* Ch. 1). To be sure, there were still people alive who knew the truth, such as Avram's ancient ancestors Shem and Ever, but they were many hundreds of years old, relics of the past, and had no influence in the "modern world" in which Avram lived.

So here is *HaKadosh Baruch Hu,* the Creator of this vast universe, Who is worshiped and adored by myriads of צְבָא הַשָׁמַיִם, His spiritual creatures: *Malachim, Serafim, Ofanim, Chayos HaKodesh;* and He, so to speak, puts all of this aside and focuses His attention on this little child named Avram, whom He has chosen to re-educate the world. The meaning here is that it was worth the entire creation to produce one little Avram.

וְהוֹצֵאתוֹ מֵאוּר כַּשְׂדִּים — **You took him out of the city of Kasdim.** The word אוּר means "city," similar to עִיר, although it is spelled with an *aleph*. Kasdim are the people who descended from a man called Kessed. Indeed, we do find an individual with this name who was a relative of Avram (*Bereishis* 22:22).

Chazal tell us that this refers to the great *neis* (miracle) that happened to Avram. Although it is not mentioned in the Torah, we know from *Torah Shebe'al Peh* that he was thrown into a burning lime kiln, אוּר, as a punishment for having destroyed his father's idols, but *HaKadosh Baruch Hu* miraculously saved Avram from the fire (*Rashi, Bereishis* 11:28).

וְשַׂמְתָּ שְּׁמוֹ אַבְרָהָם — **And You made his name Avraham.** This young man, Avram, was no longer only an individual, the jewel chosen by *HaKadosh Baruch Hu* from the billions of creatures which He created, but "Avraham," who would eventually become אַב הֲמוֹן גּוֹיִם, *the father of a multitude of nations* (*Bereishis* 17:5). The recognition of *HaKadosh Baruch Hu*, for which this young child almost paid with his life, will eventually become the common heritage of all mankind. This is inherent in the *pasuk*,

וְנִבְרְכוּ בְךָ כֹּל מִשְׁפְּחֹת הָאֲדָמָה, *And all the families of the earth shall bless themselves by you* (*Bereishis* 12:3).

Chazal comment on the *pasuk*, אֵלֶּה תוֹלְדוֹת הַשָּׁמַיִם וְהָאָרֶץ בְּהִבָּרְאָם, *These are the products of the heaven and the earth when they were created* (*Bereishis* 2:4), that the letters of the word בְּהִבָּרְאָם are the same as בְּאַבְרָהָם, which alludes to the fact that the world was created in the merit of Avraham (see *Bereishis Rabbah* 12:9). Rav Samson R. Hirsch, referring to this *Midrash*, explains that the role of Avraham was to teach the world that the universe did not always exist, but rather, בְּהִבָּרְאָם, heaven and earth were created out of nothing by a Creator.

‎6‏ וּמָצָאתָ אֶת לְבָבוֹ נֶאֱמָן לְפָנֶיךָ 6‏ — **You found his heart faithful before You.** This is based on the *pasuk*, וְהֶאֱמִן בַּה' וַיַּחְשְׁבֶהָ לּוֹ צְדָקָה, *And he trusted in Hashem, and He reckoned it to him as righteousness* (*Bereishis* 15:6). He kept his heart faithful to *HaKadosh Baruch Hu*. For some ninety years this *emunah* was tested ten times, and Avraham had not yet seen the fulfillment of the promises that *HaKadosh Baruch Hu* had made to him. He was promised Eretz Yisrael, from which he had to flee due to famine; he had to wage war to drive out conquerors of this land. He was promised children whom he had not yet fathered. He was taken advantage of in this land — even when buying a grave for his wife. But during all this time his heart remained faithful to *HaKadosh Baruch Hu*.

We are told by *Chazal* (*Bereishis Rabbah* 29:3), שָׁלֹשׁ מְצִיאוּת מָצָא הקב״ה אַבְרָהָם דָּוִד וְיִשְׂרָאֵל, *HaKadosh Baruch Hu found three* מְצִיאוּת (valuable finds): One was *Avraham*, based on our present *pasuk*, וּמָצָאתָ אֶת לְבָבוֹ נֶאֱמָן לְפָנֶיךָ; the second was *Dovid*, based on the *pasuk*, מָצָאתִי דָּוִד עַבְדִּי, *I have found Dovid, My servant* (*Tehillim* 89:21); and the third was *Israel*, which is based on the *pasuk*, כַּעֲנָבִים בַּמִּדְבָּר מָצָאתִי יִשְׂרָאֵל, *I found Israel like grapes in the desert* (*Hoshea* 9:10).

The word מְצִיאָה, *metziah*, means a valuable object which has been discovered. The sense of our *pasuk* is that Avraham Avinu is compared to a jewel lost in the sand, for which the owner sifts through the sands until he finds it: וּמָצָאתָ אֶת לְבָבוֹ נֶאֱמָן, *You found him!* The purpose of the entire creation was to produce one Avraham Avinu. *HaKadosh Baruch Hu*, so to speak, sifted through "all the sands of creation" until he found one Avraham Avinu. The same applies to Yisrael, that was the "jewel sifted out of the sands of the nations" for the purpose of receiving the Torah in the desert. Then, finally, comes Dovid, who had an extremely difficult life before he emerged in his pristine beauty as the undisputed *Melech Yisrael*, the father of *Mashiach*. Finally, *HaKadosh Baruch Hu* could say: מָצָאתִי דָּוִד עַבְדִּי.

‎6‏ וְכָרוֹת עִמּוֹ הַבְּרִית 6‏ — **And You established the covenant with him.** Then, finally, after all of his trials and tribulations, *HaKadosh Baruch Hu* made a covenant with Avraham. This refers to the *bris milah*. The *Midrash* (*Bereishis Rabbah* 49:2) tells of a dialogue in which Avraham asks *HaKadosh Baruch Hu*, "Who will perform the *milah* on me?" *HaKadosh Baruch Hu* answered him, "You do it on yourself." Since Avraham was an old man, *HaKadosh Baruch Hu* helped him to do the *milah*. Hence, literally, וְכָרוֹת עִמּוֹ הַבְּרִית, he established the covenant "with" him, meaning that *HaKadosh Baruch Hu* helped him to perform the *bris milah*.

According to our *minhag*, during *tefillas Shacharis* before a *bris*, the *mohel* says the *pasuk* וְכָרוֹת עִמּוֹ הַבְּרִית loudly, to invoke the memory of Avraham Avinu, as a prayer that in the merit of Avraham Avinu he may have *siyata d'Shmaya* (God's help), when performing the *bris*.

הַבְּרִית, *the covenant,* unquestionably refers to the *bris milah*. However, the first result of it was *HaKadosh Baruch Hu's* giving of *Eretz Yisrael* to Avraham and his descendants:

◈ **To — לָתֵת אֶת אֶרֶץ הַכְּנַעֲנִי הַחִתִּי הָאֱמֹרִי וְהַפְּרִזִּי וְהַיְבוּסִי וְהַגִּרְגָּשִׁי לָתֵת לְזַרְעוֹ give the land of the Canaanites, Hittites, Emorites, Perizzites, Jebusites, and Girgashites, to give it to his offspring.** The בְּרִית is first described as the promise by *HaKadosh Baruch Hu* to grant the entire land of Canaan to Avraham and his descendants: בַּיּוֹם הַהוּא כָּרַת ה' אֶת אַבְרָם בְּרִית לֵאמֹר לְזַרְעֲךָ נָתַתִּי אֶת הָאָרֶץ הַזֹּאת מִנְּהַר מִצְרַיִם עַד הַנָּהָר הַגָּדֹל נְהַר פְּרָת. אֶת הַקֵּינִי וְאֶת הַקְּנִזִּי וְאֶת הַקַּדְמֹנִי. וְאֶת הַחִתִּי וְאֶת הַפְּרִזִּי וְאֶת הָרְפָאִים. וְאֶת הָאֱמֹרִי וְאֶת הַכְּנַעֲנִי וְאֶת הַגִּרְגָּשִׁי וְאֶת הַיְבוּסִי, *On that day Hashem made a covenant with Avram, saying, "To your descendants have I given this land, from the river of Mitzrayim to the great river, the Euphrates River: the Kennite, the Kenizzite, and the Kadmonite, the Hittite, the Perizzite and the Rephaim; the Emorite, the Canaanite, the Girgashite and the Jebusite"* (*Bereishis* 15:18-21).

This grant of land is further reinforced: וְנָתַתִּי לְךָ וּלְזַרְעֲךָ אַחֲרֶיךָ אֵת אֶרֶץ מְגֻרֶיךָ אֵת כָּל אֶרֶץ כְּנַעַן לַאֲחֻזַּת עוֹלָם וְהָיִיתִי לָהֶם לֵאלֹהִים, *And I will give to you and to your offspring after you the land of your sojourns — the whole of the land of Canaan — as an everlasting possession; and I shall be a God to them* (ibid. 17:8).

However, the next two *pesukim* describe the *bris* as the requirement to circumcise all males: וַיֹּאמֶר אֱלֹהִים אֶל אַבְרָהָם וְאַתָּה אֶת בְּרִיתִי תִשְׁמֹר אַתָּה וְזַרְעֲךָ אַחֲרֶיךָ לְדֹרֹתָם. זֹאת בְּרִיתִי אֲשֶׁר תִּשְׁמְרוּ בֵּינִי וּבֵינֵיכֶם וּבֵין זַרְעֲךָ אַחֲרֶיךָ הִמּוֹל לָכֶם כָּל זָכָר, *God said to Avraham, "And as for you, you shall keep My covenant — you and your offspring after you throughout their generations. This is My covenant which you shall keep between Me and you and your descendants after you: Every male among you shall be circumcised"* (ibid. 17:9,10).

We must understand the relationship between the granting of the land and the requirement to perform the *bris milah*.

In the previously quoted *pesukim* as well as in our *pasuk* of וּמָצָאתָ אֶת לְבָבוֹ נֶאֱמָן לְפָנֶיךָ, the words וְנָתַתִּי and לָתֵת are mentioned twice. This is to

VAYEVARECH DOVID ⸺ 229

underscore that the earlier grant to the previous inhabitants, קֵינִי קְנִזִּי קַדְמֹנִי, etc., was only temporary. It was to be held by them for the purpose of לָתֵת לְזַרְעוֹ, to eventually give it to the descendants of Avraham.

These earlier inhabitants of Eretz Canaan had perfected and practiced the most deviate and perverse sexual aberrations imaginable. They were masters at the dehumanization of the *tzelem Elokim*. Indeed, the *parashas arayos*, the section of the Torah which deals with forbidden sexual relations, makes reference to this: כְּמַעֲשֵׂה אֶרֶץ מִצְרַיִם וגו׳ . . . וּכְמַעֲשֵׂה אֶרֶץ כְּנַעַן אֲשֶׁר אֲנִי מֵבִיא אֶתְכֶם שָׁמָּה לֹא תַעֲשׂוּ וּבְחֻקֹּתֵיהֶם לֹא תֵלֵכוּ, *Do not perform the practice of the land of Egypt etc., and do not perform the practice of the land of Canaan to which I bring you and do not follow their traditions* (Vayikra 18:3); וַתִּטְמָא הָאָרֶץ וָאֶפְקֹד עֲוֹנָהּ עָלֶיהָ וַתָּקִא הָאָרֶץ אֶת יֹשְׁבֶיהָ. וּשְׁמַרְתֶּם אַתֶּם אֶת חֻקֹּתַי וְאֶת מִשְׁפָּטַי וְלֹא תַעֲשׂוּ מִכֹּל הַתּוֹעֵבֹת הָאֵלֶּה. . ., *The land became contaminated and I recalled its iniquity upon it; and the land disgorged its inhabitants. But you shall safeguard My decrees and My judgments, and not commit any of these abominations* (ibid. 25-26).

This very land, which was occupied by these most depraved people — and which eventually "vomited them out" — was promised by God to the descendants of Avraham. And under his descendants this very land would be sanctified with עֶשֶׂר קְדוּשׁוֹת, *the ten levels of sanctity* which are operative in Eretz Yisrael (Keilim 1:6), and would be the place of the dwelling of the *Shechinah* on earth.

Similarly, the *bris milah* is performed on the member of the body with which man expresses his most animalistic desires. It is just this spot on which *HaKadosh Baruch Hu* has placed his covenant and called it *bris kodesh*. He has taken the most physical part of the human body and sanctified it.

Now, the connection between the *bris milah* and the granting of the land to *Bnei Yisrael* is clear. The sanctification of the land of Canaan after its occupancy by *Bnei Yisrael* is similar to the sanctification of the people of Yisrael by the *bris milah*. Just as *HaKadosh Baruch Hu* has taken that part of the human body with which man expresses his most animalistic desires and stamped it with his *bris kodesh* and thereby sanctified it, so does the nation of Yisrael, under the laws of God, sanctify the land of Canaan, which had been so totally defiled by the depravity of its previous inhabitants, and gives it its ten "levels of sanctity."

ַ וַתָּקֶם אֶת דְּבָרֶיךָ כִּי צַדִּיק אָתָּה — **You have kept Your word because You are just.** We have previously mentioned that the term צַדִּיק refers to the spiritual control over the physical. (See on כִּי כֹל בַּשָּׁמַיִם וּבָאָרֶץ and the Kabbalistic explanation there.)

ַ וַתֵּרֶא אֶת עֳנִי אֲבוֹתֵינוּ בְּמִצְרָיִם — **You saw the poverty of our forefathers in Mitzrayim.** It does not say עִנּוּי or עוֹנִי, which would mean *torture* or *pain*, but rather, עֳנִי, which means *poverty*. While *HaKadosh Baruch Hu* certainly saw the physical torture and pain of our forefathers in Mitzrayim, this *pasuk* focuses on the spiritual poverty of our forefathers while they languished in Mitzrayim. *HaKadosh Baruch Hu* saw that they were losing their *kedushas avos*. They had already descended through forty-nine of the fifty "gates of *tumah*," and had almost sunk to the lowest level of the abominations of Mitzrayim. (See *Mechilta d'Pischa* 5 and other *Midrashim*.)

Were it not for their "sudden" redemption from Mitzrayim, בְּחִפָּזוֹן, *in haste,* our forefathers might have continued in their downward spiral and passed through the fiftieth — and ultimate — gate of defilement, from which there would have been no return.

וְאֶת זַעֲקָתָם שָׁמַעְתָּ עַל יַם סוּף — **You heard their outcry at the** *Yam Suf*. After their sudden release from Mitzrayim, they again faced mortal danger at the banks of the *Yam Suf*. It was there that you heard their outcry.

וַתִּתֵּן אֹתֹת וּמֹפְתִים בְּפַרְעֹה וּבְכָל עֲבָדָיו וּבְכָל עַם אַרְצוֹ, כִּי יָדַעְתָּ כִּי הֵזִידוּ עֲלֵיהֶם — **You imposed signs and wonders upon Pharaoh and upon all his servants, and upon all the people of his land. For You knew that they sinned flagrantly against them.** Despite the fact that *HaKadosh Baruch Hu* had long ago told Avraham Avinu that his descendants would be enslaved and made to suffer in Mitzrayim — וַעֲבָדוּם וְעִנּוּ אֹתָם, *and they will serve them, and they will oppress them* (*Bereishis* 15:13) — nevertheless, in carrying out their evil plans, Pharaoh and his countrymen inflicted much greater suffering on the Jewish people than *HaKadosh Baruch Hu* had decreed. And for this they were severely punished by these miraculous punishments.

וַתַּעַשׂ לְךָ שֵׁם כְּהַיּוֹם הַזֶּה — **And You brought Yourself renown as it is to this very day.** Through this miraculous redemption You made for Yourself the Name of גֹּאֵל יִשְׂרָאֵל, *redeemer of Israel,* to this very day.

The greatest of all the signs and wonders is that You, *HaKadosh Baruch Hu,* allow us to continue to exist today — as You did in the Middle Ages and in ancient times — despite the ocean of hatred which surrounds us. Your Name, גֹּאֵל יִשְׂרָאֵל, continues throughout our history.

With these words of וַתַּעַשׂ לְךָ שֵׁם, we conclude the וְנַזְכִּיר שִׁמְךָ portion. The following *pasuk* introduces the fifth — and final — portion of *Pesukei d'Zimrah* called וְנַמְלִיכְךָ.

וְהַיָּם בָּקַעְתָּ לִפְנֵיהֶם, וַיַּעַבְרוּ בְתוֹךְ הַיָּם בַּיַּבָּשָׁה — **You split the sea before them,** in plain view of them, **and they crossed in the midst of the sea on dry land.** First they went into the sea, and then it split and became dry land.

וְאֶת רֹדְפֵיהֶם הִשְׁלַכְתָּ בִמְצוֹלֹת, כְּמוֹ אֶבֶן בְּמַיִם עַזִּים — **And their pursuers You threw, as stones, into the shadowy depths of powerful waters.** This *tefillah* of Nechemiah goes on to describe the miraculous events of the survival of the Jewish people through their wanderings in the desert and the conquest of Eretz Yisrael. It describes the history of the *melachim* and the *Neviim*, including the shortcomings of *Bnei Yisrael* leading to the *churban* (destruction) of the *Beis HaMikdash,* and it praises *HaKadosh Baruch Hu* for the continuing survival of our people.

However, for the purposes of *Pesukei d'Zimrah* we end our quote from *Nechemiah* here, because this leads into the next — and final — portion of the *Pesukei d'Zimrah* which is referred to in בָּרוּךְ שֶׁאָמַר, that of וְנַמְלִיכְךָ מַלְכֵּנוּ אֱלֹהֵינוּ. In this portion, which follows, we proclaim the *Malchus Hashem.* It focuses entirely on *krias Yam Suf* and the consequent *Shiras HaYam,* which culminates with ה' יִמְלֹךְ לְעֹלָם וָעֶד. In our Maariv *tefillah* we make reference to this as well: מַלְכוּתְךָ רָאוּ בָנֶיךָ.

At the time of the miracle of *krias Yam Suf,* the *Malchus Shamayim* became clearly evident in the physical universe. With the ocean in front of them, and the Egyptians pursuing them, *Bnei Yisrael* suddenly became aware of the *Malchus Shamayim* which had intervened on their behalf to effect their salvation.

אָז יָשִׁיר / Az Yashir

וַיּוֹשַׁע ה' בַּיּוֹם הַהוּא אֶת יִשְׂרָאֵל מִיַּד מִצְרָיִם — Hashem saved — on that day — Israel from the hand of Mitzrayim. With this introduction to the *shirah* (from *Shemos* 14:30), we stand up. We stand for וַיְבָרֶךְ דָּוִיד through לְשֵׁם תִּפְאַרְתֶּךָ, to underscore the significance and Kabbalistic concepts of the various attributes of *HaKadosh Baruch Hu*, as we explained there. And here, too, we stand up in recognition of the central point of this *shirah*, that of *kabbalas Malchus Shamayim* (the acceptance of God's sovereignty).

Although most people remain standing for אַתָּה הוּא through בְּמַיִם עַזִּים, there is really no reason to do so, other than to avoid the inconvenience of sitting down for this short piece and then standing up again for וַיּוֹשַׁע ה'.

וַיַּרְא יִשְׂרָאֵל אֶת מִצְרַיִם מֵת עַל שְׂפַת הַיָּם וַיַּרְא יִשְׂרָאֵל אֶת הַיָּד הַגְּדֹלָה אֲשֶׁר עָשָׂה ה' בְּמִצְרַיִם וַיִּירְאוּ הָעָם אֶת ה' — Israel saw, at the seashore, that Mitzrayim had perished. Israel saw the great hand that Hashem inflicted upon Mitzrayim and the people feared Hashem. The outcome of witnessing this miraculous event was *yiras Hashem*.

וַיַּאֲמִינוּ בַּה' וּבְמֹשֶׁה עַבְדּוֹ — And they had faith in Hashem and in Moshe His servant. Moshe was not perceived by them as some sort of "miracle worker," but rather as the *eved Hashem*.

We must understand that אֱמוּנָה (faith) is something different than יְדִיעָה (knowledge). One can speak of his *emunah* that *HaKadosh Baruch Hu* created the world, that there was *yetzias Mitzrayim*, and that the Torah was given from *Shamayim*, although he was not there. However, one does not say that he has *emunah* that right now, in this *shul*, he is participating in a *shiur*. He does not have to "believe" it; he *knows* it. It is reality.

When Israel saw that the sea split open and the waters became solidified as a wall on their right and left sides, and they walked through it on dry land, they did not require *emunah* to believe this. It was reality; it was happening in front of them. They could point and say: זֶה אֵלִי, *This is my God*.

Therefore, the *emunah* mentioned here refers not to the actual experience of *krias Yam Suf* — they knew that — but rather, to the *result* of this world-shaking event, which would have a continuing effect on them.

So the meaning of this *pasuk* is: וַיִּירְאוּ הָעָם אֶת ה', *the people feared Hashem*. When they became aware of the fact that *HaKadosh Baruch Hu* conducts the affairs of the world and can change nature at His will, they were overcome with the fear that at any moment He could end all of existence. And after they had experienced the *neis*, the miracle of the parting of the sea and the subsequent destruction of their enemies, during which they clearly saw the hand of *HaKadosh Baruch Hu,* and could point and say זֶה אֵלִי וְאַנְוֵהוּ, the result of it was, וַיַּאֲמִינוּ בַּה׳, they *remained faithful* to that level of *yediah,* the *knowledge* of the reality of *HaKadosh Baruch Hu* in the conduct of world events.

Similarly, we find in connection with *Matan Torah:* וְגַם בְּךָ יַאֲמִינוּ לְעוֹלָם, *Their faith in you shall remain forever* (*Shemos* 19:9). Long after the miracles seen by *Bnei Yisrael* at *Matan Torah,* they will continue to have the *emunah,* the conviction, that Moshe is the *Navi Hashem.*

Also, we find in connection with Avraham Avinu: וְהֶאֱמִן בַּה׳, *And he had faith in Hashem* (*Bereishis* 15:6). He had personally experienced the existence and intervention of *HaKadosh Baruch Hu* when he was miraculously saved from the fiery furnace, and he *remained faithful* to that same level of *yediah* that he experienced, even after all of his trials and tribulations.

◆§ אָז יָשִׁיר מֹשֶׁה ◆§ — **Then Moshe sang.** It is important to know that the word שִׁיר, *shir,* does not mean a melody or tune, which is expressed by voice or a musical instrument. This would be called זִמְרָה, *zimrah. Shirah,* or *shir,* means the text of a poem, as in, וַיְדַבֵּר דָּוִד לַה׳ אֶת דִּבְרֵי הַשִּׁירָה הַזֹּאת, *Dovid spoke to Hashem the words of this song* (*Shmuel II* 22:1). To accompany a poem with music is called *mizmor shir.*

This is the first *shirah* that we find in the Torah and, as such, it is certainly appropriate that we include it in the שִׁירוֹת וְתִשְׁבָּחוֹת, *songs and praises,* of the *Pesukei d'Zimrah.* However, we must understand why the organizers of the *tefillah* placed this *shirah,* from the Torah, *after* all the other songs and praises that were composed hundreds of years after the Torah was written.

The reason the organizers of the *tefillah* placed אָז יָשִׁיר after the other songs and praises is because the *very recitation* by the *Bnei Yisrael* of this *shirah* in response to Moshe Rabbeinu — who led them in it — was a *neis* (miracle). It was part of the miracle of *krias Yam Suf.* This recitation of the *shirah* here elevates the level of *Pesukei d'Zimrah.*

Short of a *neis,* how would it have been possible, before the advent of loudspeakers, for the voice of Moshe Rabbeinu — who even had difficulty speaking (*Shemos* 4:10) — to be amplified so loudly? Six hundred thousand men and their wives and children could hear him well enough to affirmatively respond by *at least* repeating the first words of each sentence (see *Sotah* 30b).

This miracle is even greater according to the opinion of R' Eliezer the son of R' Yose HaGlili (ibid.), who says that they repeated every word of the *shirah* after Moshe. And it was clearly a *neis* according to the opinion of R' Nechemiah, as explained by *Rashi* (ibid.), that, שָׁרְתָה רוּחַ הַקֹּדֶשׁ עַל כֻּלָּם וְכִוְּנוּ יַחַד אֶת הַשִּׁירָה כִּכְתָבָהּ, *The Holy Spirit came over all of them, and they* were all inspired to express the words of the *shirah* at the same time exactly as it is written.

It is therefore obvious that the communal recitation of this *shirah* by *Bnei Yisrael* was a miraculous event in itself. And by repeating it in our *Pesukei d'Zimrah* after the other songs and praises, we raise our level of praise to *HaKadosh Baruch Hu* by remembering the miraculous way in which He assisted our forefathers in expressing their feelings of joy and thankfulness to Him through this *shirah,* at the time of their miraculous *geulah* from Mitzrayim.

It is not the purpose of this *shiur* of *iyun Tefillah* to give a word-by-word translation of the *shirah*. This should be done in conjunction with the weekly learning of *parashas hashavua*, or on *Shevii Shel Pesach,* when it is read during the *krias HaTorah*. However, I would just like to point out some of the highlights of the *shirah.*

Before we continue, it is interesting to know that in the entire *shirah*, which consists of some twenty verses, the miraculous event of the parting of the sea, *krias Yam Suf,* is referred to only once: וּבְרוּחַ אַפֶּיךָ נֶעֶרְמוּ מַיִם נִצְּבוּ כְמוֹ נֵד נוֹזְלִים קָפְאוּ תְהֹמֹת בְּלֶב יָם, *At a blast from Your nostrils the waters were heaped up; straight as a wall stood the running water, the deep waters congealed in the heart of the sea.* And even there, no mention is made of the actual miracle of the Splitting of the Sea. The focus of the *shirah* is on the returning of the sea to its natural state, thereby destroying the Egyptians. In Miriam's version of the *shirah* for the women, *only* this aspect is mentioned: וַתַּעַן לָהֶם מִרְיָם שִׁירוּ לַה' כִּי גָאֹה גָּאָה סוּס וְרֹכְבוֹ רָמָה בַיָּם, *And Miriam led them: Sing to Hashem for He is infinitely exalted. Horse and rider did He throw into the sea* (Shemos 15:21).

Chazal tell us, קָשִׁין מְזוֹנוֹתָיו שֶׁל אָדָם כִּקְרִיעַת יַם סוּף, *One's sustenance is as difficult as the parting of the sea* (Pesachim 118a). Obviously, this cannot mean that *krias Yam Suf* was "difficult" for *HaKadosh Baruch Hu*. What it means is that it is difficult for us to comprehend. The human mind cannot grasp the miraculous. Our minds can comprehend natural events; but a supernatural event, such as *krias Yam Suf,* although witnessed by millions of people, defies human understanding.

The *neis* of *krias Yam Sur* consisted of two parts. The first was the supernatural phenomenon of the parting of the water, with the seabed underneath becoming dry land on which *Bnei Yisrael* passed. This miraculous event was beyond the comprehension of *Bnei Yisrael*. It cannot be described in human terms in a *shirah*.

However, the second part of this event was readily comprehensible. This is when Moshe Rabbeinu lifted his arm toward the sea, and the waters miraculously returned to their original state, drowning the pursuing Egyptian army. It is this part — in which *HaKadosh Baruch Hu* returned the laws of nature to their normal functions for the benefit of *Bnei Yisrael* — that is the main theme of the *shirah*.

∾§ עָזִּי וְזִמְרָת יָהּ — **God is my strength and my song.** The Name יָהּ usually describes the perception of *HaKadosh Baruch Hu* during a period of incomplete recognition of *Malchus Shamayim*, as in כִּי יָד עַל כֵּס יָהּ, *For the hand is on the throne of God* (see *Shemos* 17:16 and *Rashi* there). The sense here is: While I was enslaved in Egypt, and the Name of *HaKadosh Baruch Hu* was not recognized in the world — which resulted in our enslavement — nevertheless, He was my strength and my song.

∾§ וַיְהִי לִי לִישׁוּעָה — **And He was a salvation for me.** Meaning, my faith in *HaKadosh Baruch Hu* developed into my salvation, which our nation has now experienced at the shores of the *Yam Suf*.

We must know that the life of our forefathers in Egypt was not one of only tears and pain. Nor was the life of our forefathers in the ghettos of prewar Europe one of only suffering. There were many among our brethren, both in Egypt and throughout our *galus*, whose *bitachon* (faith) in Hashem elevated their lives above the suffering and degradation of the slavery in Egypt and in their ghetto restrictions.

It was this tenacious adherence to their *bitachon* in *HaKadosh Baruch Hu*, even while they were building Pisom and Raameses (see *Shemos* 1:11) — during which He showed Himself to them only as יָהּ — which eventually led to their *yeshuah*.

This combination of suffering and the joy-bringing *bitachon* in *HaKadosh Baruch Hu* is beautifully symbolized at our *Seder* tables when we dip the *marror* into the *charoses*. Surprisingly, the *charoses,* which symbolizes the mortar which our forefathers had to make for their bricks — with its cinnamon strips symbolizing the straw — is to be composed of sweet ingredients instead of bitter ones. But it is just the sweetness of this dip which reminds us that the bitterness of the slavery of our forefathers, the וַיְמָרְרוּ אֶת חַיֵּיהֶם, *and they embittered their lives* (*Shemos* 1:14), was mitigated and sweetened by their *bitachon* that *HaKadosh Baruch Hu* would eventually redeem them.

In his *peirush* on the *Shir HaMaalos* that we sing before *Bircas HaMazon* (*Tehillim* 126), Rav Samson R. Hirsch offers a beautiful explanation on the *pesukim,* אָז יֹאמְרוּ בַגּוֹיִם הִגְדִּיל ה׳ לַעֲשׂוֹת עִם אֵלֶּה, *Then they will declare among the nations, "Hashem has done greatly with these"* (ibid. v. 2). This means that at the time of the coming of *Mashiach,* it will be said among the nations that Hashem has done a great deed for the Jewish people, in that He has redeemed them from their suffering. However, to this, the Jewish people respond, הִגְדִּיל ה׳ לַעֲשׂוֹת עִמָּנוּ, *Hashem has done greatly with us* (ibid. v. 3). What you nations do not know nor understand is that God has done an even greater thing for us, and that is: הָיִינוּ שְׂמֵחִים, which he translates as, "*Wir sind heiter geblieben,*" meaning that through God's gift of *bitachon, we remained happy,* even during the darkest time of our *galus* experience.

This inner happiness of the Jewish people is reflected in the beautiful *niggunim* for Shabbos and *Shalosh Regalim*, most of which originate from the *Maharil*, who composed them while he lived in the ghetto! (*Maharil*, R' Yaakov Moelin, Germany, 1365-1427).

זֶה אֵלִי — This is my God. He is אֵל — His power is limitless, as we saw through this miracle.

וְאַנְוֵהוּ — The simple meaning, the *p'shat*, here is, **And I wish to serve Him in a beautiful way.** Our *Chazal* find in these words the source for *hiddur mitzvah*, the concept of performing the *mitzvos* in a beautiful way (see *Nazir* 2b). When one does something in a beautiful way, it is an indication that he enjoys doing it. On the topic of מִצְוֹת לַאו לֵהָנוֹת נִתְּנוּ, *Mitzvos were not given for physical benefit* (*Rosh Hashanah* 28a), *Rashi* explains the reason: לֹא לֵהָנוֹת נִתְּנוּ לְיִשְׂרָאֵל לִהְיוֹת קִיּוּמָם לָהֶם הֲנָאָה אֶלָא לְעוֹל עַל צַוָּארֵיהֶם נִתְּנוּ, *The mitzvos were not given to Israel for enjoyment, so that their observance could be considered as pleasure, but rather, they were given as a mandatory yoke on their necks.*

Based on this, we are led to the conclusion that when we observe *hiddur mitzvah*, and perform the *mitzvos* beautifully, it shows that we willingly accept having this "yoke" of *mitzvos* placed on our necks.

On the level of *derush* (the secondary, yet complementary meaning), however, וְאַנְוֵהוּ is explained by *Targum Onkelos* as having the meaning of a dwelling, as in נָוֶה. He therefore renders this as, וְאֶבְנֵי לֵהּ מַקְדְּשָׁא, *And I will build for Him a Beis HaMikdash.* Rav Samson R. Hirsch expands on this idea and translates it to mean, "I wish to *become* a dwelling for Him," meaning, I wish to live my life so that it becomes an abode for His *Shechinah* in this world.

אֱלֹהֵי אָבִי, וַאֲרֹמְמֶנְהוּ — The God of my father, and I will exalt Him. The generation of those who went out of Mitzrayim is saying that while our fathers had *bitachon* that HaKadosh Baruch Hu would eventually redeem them, we, who actually experienced the redemption, will extol Him on an even higher level.

ה' אִישׁ מִלְחָמָה, ה' שְׁמוֹ — Hashem is Master of war; His Name is Hashem. The four-letter Name י-ה-ו-ה of *HaKadosh Baruch Hu* is used here twice to convey the thought that despite the fact that He *appears* here as a man of war, Who has suddenly become a ravaging destroyer, nevertheless, His Name still remains י-ה-ו-ה. He is waging this war with His *middas harachamim*.

[Ed. note: See further on this subject, on יְמִינְךָ ה' נֶאְדָּרִי בַּכֹּחַ וגו'.]
This is borne out by the Gemara: אָמַר ר' יוֹחָנָן מַאי דִכְתִיב וְלֹא קָרַב זֶה אֶל זֶה כָּל הַלַּיְלָה בִּקְשׁוּ מַלְאֲכֵי הַשָּׁרֵת לוֹמַר שִׁירָה. אָמַר הקב"ה מַעֲשֵׂה יָדַי טוֹבְעִין בַּיָּם וְאַתֶּם אוֹמְרִים שִׁירָה, R' *Yochanan commented on the pasuk, "and one did not come near to the other all night" (Shemos 14:20): The angels wanted to say praises (upon the miracle of the Yam Suf), however, God said to them, "My creations are*

AZ YASHIR 237

drowning and you wish to say praises?" (*Megillah* 10b). This is a manifestation of *middas harachamim*. This concept that *HaKadosh Baruch Hu* destroys the *reshaim* as a result of His *middas harachamim* is very difficult for us to comprehend.

The question arises, if the *malachim* were precluded from saying *shirah* over the destruction of the Egyptians, how could Moshe Rabbeinu and the entire *Bnei Yisrael* do so? I heard an answer while I was in the yeshivah, but I do not recall if it was said in the name of a *gadol,* nor who told it to me. However, the explanation is perfectly understandable. The Midrash tells us, אֵין מַלְאָךְ אֶחָד עוֹשֶׂה שְׁתֵּי שְׁלִיחוּיוֹת, *One malach cannot perform two tasks* (see *Bereishis Rabbah* 50:2). A *malach* can do only one thing at a time; he cannot experience two things together. This is based on, וְרַגְלֵיהֶם רֶגֶל יְשָׁרָה, *their feet are one* (*Yechezkel* 1:7). (Emulating this, we put our feet together during *Shemoneh Esrei,* as if they were one.) A human being has the ability to do two contrasting things at the same time. He can feel sorry for the drowning Egyptians, while he rejoices over his own redemption. However, a *malach* has no such capability. He has a "one-track mind"; his singular purpose is the completion of the mission for which he was sent by *HaKadosh Baruch Hu.* He therefore cannot say *shirah* for the redemption of the *Bnei Yisrael* while his mission is the destruction of the Egyptians.

[Ed. note: This explanation presumes that the מַלְאֲכֵי הַשָּׁרֵת referred to above (*Megillah* 10a) were the ones who were sent to destroy the Egyptians.]

◆§ יְמִינְךָ ה' נֶאְדָּרִי בַּכֹּחַ, יְמִינְךָ ה' תִּרְעַץ אוֹיֵב — **Your right hand, Hashem, is adorned with strength; Your right hand, Hashem, smashes the enemy.** This thought of *middas harachamim* is expanded upon here by the use of the Name י-ה-ו-ה, coupled with the expression יְמִין ה', *the right hand of Hashem.* The right hand of Hashem is a metaphor for His *rachamim,* and the left hand metaphorically represents *middas hadin.* By twice using the Name י-ה-ו-ה together with the right hand in this phrase, the *shirah* extols the fact that in His destruction of the Egyptians, *HaKadosh Baruch Hu,* so to speak, had two right hands. Not only is the כֹּחַ, or *strength,* which He displayed in the salvation of Israel a manifestation of His *rachamim,* but even תִּרְעַץ אוֹיֵב, the smashing of the enemy, was the result of יְמִינְךָ ה', meaning the *middas harachamim.*

Chazal tell us: עֲשָׂרָה נִסִּים נַעֲשׂוּ לַאֲבוֹתֵינוּ בְּמִצְרַיִם וַעֲשָׂרָה עַל הַיָּם. עֶשֶׂר מַכּוֹת הֵבִיא הקב"ה עַל הַמִּצְרִים בְּמִצְרַיִם וְעֶשֶׂר עַל הַיָּם, *Ten miracles were performed for our ancestors in Mitzrayim and ten at the sea. Ten plagues did the Holy One, Blessed is He, bring upon the Egyptians in Mitzrayim and ten at the sea* (*Pirkei Avos* 5:5). What this means is that *the very same events* that *Bnei Yisrael* experienced as *nissim* in Mitzrayim and at the sea were *makkos* to the Egyptians. There were ten *nissim* and ten *makkos. Bnei Yisrael* experienced them as their salvation, while at the same time, the Egyptians felt them as pain and suffering. The very same *middas harachamim* that is manifested to the *tzaddik* as a *neis* is to the *rasha* a *makkah*.

It is noteworthy that the four-letter Name of *HaKadosh Baruch Hu*, יְ־הֹ־וָ־ה, which always denotes *middas harachamim*, is mentioned ten times in the *shirah*. This could very well be a reference to these ten *makkos* and ten *nissim*. Notwithstanding the fact that the main result of *krias Yam Suf* was the destruction of the myriads of Egyptian soldiers by drowning in the sea, it is still viewed as an act of *rachamim*. This concept is very difficult to understand.

§ נָשַׁפְתָּ בְרוּחֲךָ כִּסָּמוֹ יָם, צָלְלוּ כַּעוֹפֶרֶת בְּמַיִם אַדִּירִים — **You blew with Your wind — the sea enshrouded them; the mighty ones sank like lead in the waters.** The simple translation of the second phrase would be, "they sank like lead in the mighty waters." This would be similar to, מִקֹּלוֹת מַיִם רַבִּים אַדִּירִים, *More than the roars of mighty waters* (*Tehillim* 93:4), and this is the way it is taken by *Targum Onkelos* on the *shirah*.

However, the Gemara (*Menachos* 53a), based on the *Mechilta* on this *pasuk,* explains the meaning to be, "They, the strong ones (the Egyptians), sank like lead in the water." This is borne out by the cantillation of a טִפְחָא, *tippcha,* under the word בְּמַיִם, indicating a separation between it and אַדִּירִים. However, this in itself is not definitive, because we also find the *tippcha* under לֹא before תִגְנֹב in the *taam ha'elyon* (the special accentuation of the notes for the public Torah Reading of the *Aseres HaDibros,* the Ten Commandments) where it does not indicate a separation. However, since the Gemara and *Mechilta* say that the Egyptians are called אַדִּירִים, it should be read with a pause after בְּמַיִם to indicate this meaning.

The historical fact arising out of the enslavement in Mitzrayim, as well as all the great persecutions that *Bnei Yisrael* suffered, is that *HaKadosh Baruch Hu* permits *reshaim* to become אַדִּירִים, powerful people, who can inflict great suffering on them. This is dealt with in the following *pasuk*.

§ מִי כָמֹכָה בָּאֵלִם ה', מִי כָּמֹכָה נֶאְדָּר בַּקֹּדֶשׁ — **Who is like You among the heavenly powers, Hashem! Who is like You, mighty in holiness.** This is one of the two *pesukim* that the organizers of the *tefillah* have quoted in the *berachah* of גָּאַל יִשְׂרָאֵל in the *tefillos* of Shacharis and Maariv, apparently as a summary of the entire *shirah*. The other is ה' יִמְלֹךְ לְעֹלָם וָעֶד.

The Gemara states: "דְּבֵי ר' יִשְׁמָעֵאל תָּנָא: מִי כָמֹכָה בָּאֵלִם ה': מִי כָמֹכָה בָּאִלְּמִים ה'", which is further explained in the *Mechilta,* מִי כָמֹכָה בָּאִלְּמִים, שׁוֹמֵעַ עֶלְבּוֹן בָּנֶיךָ וְשׁוֹתֵק (*Gittin* 56b). The *Chazal* see in the word אֵלִם, which is spelled without a *yud* in this *pasuk,* an allusion to the meaning, אִלֵּם, mute, and explain it to mean: *Who is like You among the mutes; You hear the suffering of Your children, but You remain silent* as if You were mute.

What *Chazal* are conveying with this *derush* is the following: The word אֵלִם

AZ YASHIR ⤳ 239

means the powerful forces of nature. (See Rav Samson R. Hirsch on the *shirah* for this meaning of אֵלִם.) The forces of nature are completely silent to the outcries of tortured human beings. On the days when tens of thousands of our brethren were screaming in terror and pain while being brutally and sadistically murdered in Auschwitz, the birds continued their chirping, the flowers still blossomed, and the sun still shone. Nature did not take notice of all the indescribable torture and the screams of innocent people. The natural forces of the world remain mute and do not cry out when such outrages are committed.

While *Bnei Yisrael* were suffering under the yoke of their enslavement and torture in Mitzrayim, they could not understand how *HaKadosh Baruch Hu* could remain silent in the face of all of their suffering. They understood that the forces of nature, the אֵלִם, are really אִלֵּם, deaf and mute to all of the world's suffering. But how could *HaKadosh Baruch Hu*, Who created them, also be אִלֵּם, deaf and mute, to the cries of the Jewish mothers and fathers while their children were being thrown into the Nile River? Is He, too, silent as are the forces of nature? This is impossible to understand.

However, at the time of *krias Yam Suf*, when their redemption from Egypt was finalized, *Bnei Yisrael* had reached a level in their *emunah* in which they accepted the *tzaar* of the *galus*, together with the *geulah*. *Chazal* see in the peculiar spelling of מִי כָמֹכָה בָּאֵלִם ה׳ a reference to the acceptance by *Bnei Yisrael* of the fact that *HaKadosh Baruch Hu* remained אִלֵּם, silent, in the face of their long suffering. In the *shirah*, then, *Bnei Yisrael* did not only exult over their *geulah*, but they also praised *HaKadosh Baruch Hu* Whose will had caused their suffering in the *galus*. They understood that the Egyptians had become אַדִּירִים over them because it was the will of *HaKadosh Baruch Hu*. This thought continues: מִי כָמֹכָה נֶאְדָּר בַּקֹּדֶשׁ — *Who is as mighty in holiness as You*. *Kedushah* is something which is separated (see *Rashi, Kedoshim* 19:2). There is nothing as powerful and far removed from our understanding as You are. While we praise You and accept our suffering, we simply cannot have any answers to the questions of מִי כָמֹכָה בָּאֵלִם ה׳.

נוֹרָא תְהִלֹּת עֹשֵׂה פֶלֶא — **Awesome to praise when He performs wondrous deeds.** It is awesome to praise *HaKadosh Baruch Hu* when He performs wondrous deeds. We tend to offer praises only for the good things, but actually we are required to do so for both the good and the bad, as the Mishnah says: חַיָּב אָדָם לְבָרֵךְ עַל הָרָעָה כְּשֵׁם שֶׁמְּבָרֵךְ עַל הַטּוֹבָה, שֶׁנֶּאֱמַר וְאָהַבְתָּ אֵת ה׳ אֱלֹהֶיךָ בְּכָל לְבָבְךָ וּבְכָל נַפְשְׁךָ וּבְכָל מְאֹדֶךָ – בְּכָל מִדָּה וּמִדָּה שֶׁהוּא מוֹדֵד לְךָ הֱוֵי מוֹדֶה לוֹ, *A person is obligated to bless (Hashem) for the bad just as he does for the good. As the pasuk says, "You shall love Hashem with all of your heart, with all your soul (life), with all of your might," and for every measure (good or bad) which He metes out to you, be thankful to Him* (Berachos 54a). While we can appreciate and offer praise to *HaKadosh Baruch Hu* for the *nissim* that result in our redemption, we tend not to understand the lack of those *nissim* when we cry out for help and are apparently not answered, which is also פֶּלֶא. The words נוֹרָא תְהִלֹּת mean, therefore, that it is with trepidation that we offer praises to *HaKadosh Baruch Hu* for the good things that happen to us, because in doing so we may lose sight of our obligation to praise *HaKadosh Baruch Hu* even for that which we cannot understand. However, with מִי כָמֹכָה, *Bnei Yisrael* did finally express their full acceptance of the *galus*.

With this explanation, we can well understand why the organizers of the *tefillah* selected this *pasuk* in the *berachah* of *geulah* of the *tefillos* of Shacharis and Maariv as a "summary" of the *shirah*. It was through the *shiras hayam* that *Bnei Yisrael* finally — and with great joy — expressed their acceptance of the suffering which they and their forefathers endured during the *galus*, together with the joyous celebration of their *geulah*.

This was the שִׁירָה חֲדָשָׁה, *the new song,* which became clear to *Bnei Yisrael* at the time of *krias Yam Suf,* and which they expressed in the *shirah*. Not only did they discover through *ruach hakodesh* that the punishment of the *reshaim* comes from *middas harachamim* — which defies our limited comprehension — but also, they had finally reached the level in their *emunah* in which they could happily accept the fact that the Egyptians had become the אַדִּירִים, under whom they suffered, because it was the will of מִי כָמֹכָה בָּאֵלִם (בָּאִלְמִים) ה׳. They came to understand that they were required to thank *HaKadosh Baruch Hu* even for the *galus*.

This acceptance of both the enslavement and the redemption is symbolized by the matzah on the *Seder* night when we say, מַצָּה זוּ שֶׁאָנוּ אוֹכְלִים עַל שׁוּם מָה, עַל שׁוּם שֶׁלֹּא הִסְפִּיק בְּצֵקָם שֶׁל אֲבוֹתֵינוּ לְהַחֲמִיץ עַד שֶׁנִּגְלָה עֲלֵיהֶם מֶלֶךְ מַלְכֵי הַמְּלָכִים הקב״ה וּגְאָלָם, *Why do we eat this matzah? It is because there was not enough time for the dough of our forefathers to become leavened before Hashem revealed His presence to them and redeemed them.* The matzah here is a reminder of the *geulah*. However, before we begin the *Seder,* we refer to the matzah as a symbol of our slavery, when we say, הָא לַחְמָא עַנְיָא דִי אֲכָלוּ אַבְהָתָנָא בְּאַרְעָא דְמִצְרָיִם, *This is the bread of suffering which our forefathers ate in the land of Egypt.* In the middle of their work, there was no time to make actual bread. All they had time to do was to slap together a little flour and water and throw it into the hot oven to be baked and quickly eaten so they could go back to work.

The matzah eaten during our *Seder,* then, celebrates both our enslavement and our redemption, and with it we express our thanks to *HaKadosh Baruch Hu* for the *geulah,* as well as for the enslavement, although the latter may be difficult to understand.

In fact, the Torah itself asks us to remember both the *geulah* from Mitzrayim and the enslavement, as we find: . . . שִׁבְעַת יָמִים תֹּאכַל עָלָיו מַצּוֹת

לְמַעַן תִּזְכֹּר אֶת יוֹם צֵאתְךָ מֵאֶרֶץ מִצְרַיִם, *For seven days you shall eat matzos because of it . . . so that you will remember the day of your departure from the land of Mitzrayim* (Devarim 16:3). Here the *mitzvah* is to remember the *geulah*. Then, at the end of the next chapter, the Torah tells us that we are to remember our enslavement in Egypt: וְזָכַרְתָּ כִּי עֶבֶד הָיִיתָ בְּמִצְרָיִם, *You shall remember that you were a slave in Egypt* (ibid. v.12). This means that we are to accept the enslavement in Egypt in the same manner as we rejoice over our redemption from it.

This concept of acceptance of suffering *b'simchah*, with joy, refers to *Klal Yisrael* in general, and to every individual in particular who suffers pain or other *tzaar* that he does not understand.

The *Mechaber*, the author of the *Shulchan Aruch*, goes into uncharacteristic length in explaining this halachah: חַיָּב אָדָם לְבָרֵךְ עַל הָרָעָה בְּדַעַת שְׁלֵמָה וּבְנֶפֶשׁ חֲפֵצָה, כְּדֶרֶךְ שֶׁמְּבָרֵךְ בְּשִׂמְחָה עַל הַטּוֹבָה, כִּי הָרָעָה לְעוֹבְדֵי הַשֵּׁם הִיא שִׂמְחָתָם וְטוֹבָתָם, כֵּיוָן שֶׁמְּקַבֵּל מֵאַהֲבָה מַה שֶּׁגָּזַר עָלָיו הַשֵּׁם, נִמְצָא שֶׁבְּקַבָּלַת רָעָה זוֹ הוּא עוֹבֵד אֶת הַשֵּׁם שֶׁהִיא שִׂמְחָה לוֹ, *A person is obligated to bless for the bad with complete knowledge and willing spirit just as he blesses with joy for the good, because the bad for those who serve God is their joy and goodness, because he accepts with love whatever was decreed for him by God. It emerges that with the acceptance of this bad he serves God, which is a joy for him* (Shulchan Aruch, Orach Chaim 222:3).

What the *Mechaber* means here is that the acceptance of suffering becomes a form of *avodas Hashem* and, as with all *avodas Hashem*, it must be done *b'simchah* in accordance with the dictum: עִבְדוּ אֶת ה' בְּשִׂמְחָה, *Serve Hashem with gladness* (Tehillim 100:2).

The last part of the *shirah*, which follows, beginning with נָחִיתָ בְחַסְדְּךָ עַם זוּ גָּאָלְתָּ, can best be understood in the light of the *pasuk*, אַחַד עָשָׂר יוֹם מֵחֹרֵב דֶּרֶךְ הַר שֵׂעִיר עַד קָדֵשׁ בַּרְנֵעַ, *Eleven days from Chorev by way of Mount Seir to Kadesh-barnea* (Devarim 1:2). There Moshe Rabbeinu is telling *Bnei Yisrael* that their entire stay in the *midbar*, after *Matan Torah*, should have lasted a mere eleven days, which would have been the normal traveling time to reach the boundary of Eretz Yisrael. The following anticipates their imminent entrance into *Eretz Yisrael*:

נָחִיתָ בְחַסְדְּךָ עַם זוּ גָּאָלְתָּ, נֵהַלְתָּ בְעָזְּךָ אֶל נְוֵה קָדְשֶׁךָ. שָׁמְעוּ עַמִּים יִרְגָּזוּן, חִיל אָחַז יֹשְׁבֵי פְּלָשֶׁת — **You guide, in Your lovingkindness, this nation which You have redeemed. You lead it with Your power to Your holy dwelling. The nations heard and they became agitated; trembling possessed the inhabitants of Pileshes.** The awesome *nissim* in connection with *yetzias Mitzrayim*, culminating with *krias Yam Suf*, had plunged the nations of the entire region into fear for their lives. The Philistines were the people who lived in the territory directly between Egypt and Eretz Yisrael, and thus, in their minds, they feared being the first nation to be overrun by *Bnei Yisrael*.

However, the route of *Bnei Yisrael* was not known to the nations of the region, so that Edom (הַר שֵׂעִיר) and Moav also feared the possibility that *Bnei Yisrael* might pass through their territory and conquer it on the way to their land. Thus, the following *pasuk*:

אָז נִבְהֲלוּ אַלּוּפֵי אֱדוֹם, אֵילֵי מוֹאָב יֹאחֲזֵמוֹ רָעַד, נָמֹגוּ כֹּל יֹשְׁבֵי כְנָעַן — **Then the princes of Edom became disturbed; the powerful people of Moav were possessed with trembling. All the inhabitants of Canaan melted (from fear).** Of course, these people had the most to fear, because they knew that they were about to lose their land, which had been promised by *HaKadosh Baruch Hu* to *Bnei Yisrael*.

תִּפֹּל עֲלֵיהֶם אֵימָתָה וָפַחַד בִּגְדֹל זְרוֹעֲךָ יִדְּמוּ כָּאָבֶן עַד יַעֲבֹר עַמְּךָ ה' עַד יַעֲבֹר עַם זוּ קָנִיתָ. תְּבִאֵמוֹ וְתִטָּעֵמוֹ בְּהַר נַחֲלָתְךָ, מָכוֹן לְשִׁבְתְּךָ פָּעַלְתָּ ה'. מִקְּדָשׁ ה' כּוֹנְנוּ יָדֶיךָ — **Fear and terror befall them. They fall silent as a stone when You show the power of Your arm. Until Your people cross, Hashem, until this nation which You have acquired shall cross. You will bring them home, and You will plant them on the mountain of Your inheritance. The place of Your dwelling which You have created, Hashem. The holy place, Hashem, which Your hands have prepared.** This part of the *shirah* reflects the original plan in which everything was prepared so that after *yetzias Mitzrayim*, *Bnei Yisrael* would proceed immediately to Eretz Yisrael after *shivah asar b'Tammuz* (17th day of Tammuz), when Moshe Rabbeinu would return from his forty days spent on *Har Sinai* for *kabbalas haTorah*. And upon their arrival in the land, Moshe Rabbeinu would build the *Beis HaMikdash*. This was to have been the final *geulah* — for which we are still waiting.

However, at this point, something happened that changed the course of history. This occurred when *Bnei Yisrael* exclaimed:

ה' יִמְלֹךְ לְעֹלָם וָעֶד — **Hashem shall reign for all eternity.** We find the following statement in the *Mechilta* (Shemos 15:18): ר' יוֹסֵי הַגְּלִילִי אוֹמֵר: אִלּוּ אָמְרוּ יִשְׂרָאֵל עַל הַיָּם "ה' מֶלֶךְ לְעֹלָם וָעֶד" לֹא הָיָה אוּמָה וְלָשׁוֹן שׁוֹלֶטֶת בָּהֶם לְעוֹלָם, אֶלָּא אָמְרוּ ה' יִמְלֹךְ לְעֹלָם וָעֶד – לֶעָתִיד לָבֹא, *Said R' Yose HaGlili: If Israel would have said at the sea, "Hashem is King forever," no nation would ever have been powerful enough to dominate them. But (since) they said only, "Hashem will be King," this referred to the future to come.* At that moment of their lofty conceptualization of *HaKadosh Baruch Hu*, *Bnei Yisrael* should have declared, ה' מֶלֶךְ לְעֹלָם וָעֶד, *Hashem is the King forever*. Instead, strangely, they only expressed the wish that ה' יִמְלֹךְ לְעֹלָם וָעֶד, meaning that at some time in the future, Hashem *will reign* forever.

The *Mechilta* (ibid.) tells us that at the moment of *krias Yam Suf*, *Bnei Yisrael* had reached a degree of closeness to *HaKadosh Baruch Hu* that even exceeded that of the *Navi* Yechezkel: רָאֲתָה שִׁפְחָה עַל הַיָּם מַה שֶּׁלֹּא רָאָה יְחֶזְקֵאל

וְכָל שְׁאָר הַנְּבִיאִים, *A mere handmaiden saw more (of the presence of God) than did Yechezkel and all the other Neviim.* They had reached such a lofty level of *ruach hakodesh* that even the lowliest handmaiden saw more of the revelation of *HaKadosh Baruch Hu* than did the greatest of our *Neviim*. The reference here is to the vivid description by the *Navi* Yechezkel of the *Kisei HaKavod*, Throne of Glory, and the *malachim* (angels) known as *maaseh merkavah* (*Yechezkel,* Ch. 1). It is read in the *haftarah* of Shavuos, and it defies our understanding. (The honor of reading this *haftarah* is usually given to the Rav, because, at least, *he knows* that he does not understand one word of it!) Why, then, did *Bnei Yisrael* not declare right there and then, ה׳ מֶלֶךְ לְעֹלָם וָעֶד!

To understand the reason for this, let us look back for a moment at Adam HaRishon in *Gan Eden*. Although he had the opportunity to eat from the *eitz hachaim,* Tree of Life (מִכֹּל עֵץ הַגָּן אָכֹל תֹּאכֵל, *Of every tree of the garden you may freely eat; Bereishis* 2:16), and this would have assured him everlasting life, he did not do so. The reason was because he knew that by doing so he would lose his *bechirah,* his freedom of choice.

[Ed. note: Unfortunately, the Rav did not explain the reason for this. One can only presume he meant that an *assurance* of everlasting life would presuppose that he — and the rest of mankind — would not have the ability to sin. And this would mean that man would not possess a moral freedom of choice, with which he would have the ability to freely choose to avoid evil and practice goodness without any compulsion. However, this unavoidably presupposes that he could also not sin. And the avoidance of sin by his own free will is man's greatest superiority over all other of *HaKadosh Baruch Hu's* creatures. Adam HaRishon did not want to lose this by partaking of the *eitz hachaim*. See Rav Samson R. Hirsch to *Bamidbar* 28:15.]

Similarly, after *Matan Torah,* we find *HaKadosh Baruch Hu* saying to Moshe Rabbeinu, מִי יִתֵּן וְהָיָה לְבָבָם זֶה לָהֶם לְיִרְאָה אֹתִי וְלִשְׁמֹר אֶת כָּל מִצְוֹתַי כָּל הַיָּמִים, *If only their hearts would remain as they are presently: (resolved) to fear Me and to keep all of My commandments all of the days (Devarim* 5:26). Paraphrasing, Hashem said: If only ("it is to be wished that") this level of *yiras Shamayim* would remain with *Bnei Yisrael* forever! This means that *HaKadosh Baruch Hu,* although He has the ability to control everything, has restricted Himself in the area of *bechirah,* and does not interfere with the human being's freedom of choice. He can "only wish" that *Bnei Yisrael* will maintain their present level of *yiras Shamayim.* The Gemara (*Avodah Zarah* 5a) comments on this that *Bnei Yisrael* should have responded to *HaKadosh Baruch Hu*: תֵּן אַתָּה, "We agree; please fulfill this wish!" The reason they did not do so was because they did not want to have their *yiras Shamayim* preordained by *HaKadosh Baruch Hu*. Rather, they wanted to rise to this level on their own, through their *bechirah*.

It is for this same reason, then, that *Bnei Yisrael* at *krias Yam Suf* did not say ה' מֶלֶךְ לְעוֹלָם וָעֶד, but rather, ה' יִמְלֹךְ לְעוֹלָם וָעֶד. By saying ה' מֶלֶךְ לְעוֹלָם וָעֶד, they would have forfeited their *bechirah*. *HaKadosh Baruch Hu* would have been recognized as King of the universe, and this would have resulted in their immediate and unopposed settlement of *Eretz Yisrael* and the building of the *Beis HaMikdash* as the capital of the *Malchus Shamayim* on earth. This would have brought about the euphoric period of *yemos haMashiach*, which is the ultimate goal of mankind in the world.

However, *Bnei Yisrael*, fearing the loss of their *bechirah*, preferred to say only ה' יִמְלֹךְ לְעֹלָם וָעֶד, that the universal recognition of *Malchus Shamayim* will occur at some time in the future. But for now, they wished to continue to use their *bechirah* in their *avodas Hashem*.

In accordance with our *minhag*, we do not say the *pasuk*, כִּי בָא סוּס פַּרְעֹה וגו', which follows the opinion of the *Ramban*, who says that it is not a part of the *shirah* (see *Ramban, Shemos* 15:19). However, those who do say it follow other opinions that include the reciting of this *pasuk* since they hold it is a part of the *shirah*.

[Ed. note: For further comments by the Rav on the *shirah*, please refer to *Maayan Beis HaSho'evah, Beshalach.*]

What follows now are several *pesukim* of *malchus*, which we say as a substitute for ה' מֶלֶךְ לְעֹלָם וָעֶד, something which our forefathers at the *Yam Suf* failed to do. And with these *pesukim* we close the וְנַמְלִיכְךָ, and final, portion of *Pesukei d'Zimrah*.

❧ כִּי לַה' הַמְּלוּכָה, וּמוֹשֵׁל בַּגּוֹיִם ❧ — **For the sovereignty is Hashem's, and He rules over nations** (*Tehillim* 22:29). There is a difference between *melech* and *mosheil*. A *melech* is a king who is accepted by the consensus of the governed. One can speak with him; he is capable of being influenced by reasonable discussions. (In Aramaic, we find the related word אִימְלִיךְ, *I will discuss it,* i.e., get an agreement, etc.) However, *mosheil* means a ruler, a dictator. It is in this sense that the brothers of Yosef said to him, הֲמָלֹךְ תִּמְלֹךְ עָלֵינוּ אִם מָשׁוֹל תִּמְשֹׁל בָּנוּ, *Do you think we will accept you as our king; and if not, do you wish to force yourself upon us a ruler?* (*Bereishis* 37:8).

So what we say in this *pasuk* is, כִּי לַה' הַמְּלוּכָה, we accept Hashem as our King (מֶלֶךְ). But, as to those nations that do not accept Him, וּמוֹשֵׁל בַּגּוֹיִם, for them He will be a ruler (מוֹשֵׁל).

However, eventually, this will change, and at that time:

❧ וְעָלוּ מוֹשִׁעִים בְּהַר צִיּוֹן לִשְׁפֹּט אֶת הַר עֵשָׂו, וְהָיְתָה לַה' הַמְּלוּכָה ❧ — **And saviors will ascend *Har Tziyon* to judge the mountain of *Eisav*, and the kingdom will be Hashem's** (*Ovadiah* 1:21). According to *Radak* and the other *mefarshim*, the meaning of מוֹשִׁיעִים, *saviors,* is הַמֶּלֶךְ מָשִׁיחַ וַחֲבֵרָיו. This refers to שִׁבְעָה רֹעִים וּשְׁמֹנָה נְסִיכֵי אָדָם, *Seven shepherds and eight officers* (*Michah* 5:4).

After *techiyas hameisim,* these *tzaddikim,* who will be the helpers of *Mashiach,* will ascend *Har Tziyon* to sit in judgment of *Har Eisav.* Then, after the elimination of the evil in the world, represented by Eisav, Hashem will reign supreme. As long as Eisav has any power in the world, the throne of *HaKadosh Baruch Hu* will be incomplete.

Next, we quote:

וְהָיָה ה' לְמֶלֶךְ עַל כָּל הָאָרֶץ, בַּיוֹם הַהוּא יִהְיֶה ה' אֶחָד וּשְׁמוֹ אֶחָד — **Then Hashem will be King over all the world, on that day Hashem will be One and His Name will be One** (*Zechariah* 14:9). There are different ways in which people perceive *HaKadosh Baruch Hu.* His "Name" is different to different people. There are people and nations who believe in "One God," but have a different way of understanding this. However, this *pasuk* refers to the time when the whole world will understand *HaKadosh Baruch Hu* the way we do: שְׁמוֹ אֶחָד, *His Name will be One.* This means that the whole world will share our understanding of the One and Only Universal God, as taught to us by the Torah.

In most *kehillos* the following *pasuk* is not said. However, in our *kehillah,* following *minhag* Frankfurt, we conclude with this fourth *pasuk*:

וּבְתוֹרָתְךָ כָּתוּב לֵאמֹר שְׁמַע יִשְׂרָאֵל ה' אֱלֹהֵינוּ ה' אֶחָד — **And in Your Torah it is written: Hear O Israel: Hashem is our God, Hashem, the One and Only** (*Devarim* 6:4).

This is explained by *Rashi* (ibid.): ה' שֶׁהוּא אֱלֹהֵינוּ עַתָּה וְלֹא אֱלֹהֵי הָאֻמּוֹת הוּא עָתִיד לִהְיוֹת ה' אֶחָד. This means although now *Hakadosh Baruch Hu* is only אֱלֹהֵינוּ, *our God,* eventually He will be recognized by the entire world as the One God.

The *Maharam Schick* in his responsa (*Orach Chaim* 43) in the name of his rebbe, the *Chasam Sofer* — who was originally from Frankfurt — concurs with this *minhag* to quote this fourth *pasuk* of *malchus* at this point, and gives the reason.

[Ed. note: Although the Rav did not quote the reason, see *Maharam Schick* (ibid.) for the explanation. Also see *Beis Yosef* (*Orach Chaim,* end of *Siman* 51) for an additional reason to say this *pasuk.*]

And now, in concluding *Pesukei d'Zimrah,* which we close with the *berachah* of יִשְׁתַּבַּח, we express the thought that while we end our rendition of the songs and praises at this point, so that we may continue with our *tefillah,* this does not mean that this concludes the praises of *HaKadosh Baruch Hu.* On the contrary, we immediately say יִשְׁתַּבַּח שִׁמְךָ לָעַד מַלְכֵּנוּ, *May Your Name be praised forever.*

יִשְׁתַּבַּח / Yishtabach

As we have explained in our outline, בָּרוּךְ שֶׁאָמַר -- which begins the *Pesukei d'Zimrah* — corresponds to the entrance door of the preparatory *Ulam*, and the *Pesukei d'Zimrah* themselves correspond to the *Ulam*. Now, as we conclude *Pesukei d'Zimrah* with יִשְׁתַּבַּח, we will have figuratively passed through the exit door of the *Ulam*, and will find ourselves facing the entrance to the *Heichal*.

The *Heichal* is the repository of the three main *keilim* (vessels) of the *Beis HaMikdash*. As we enter, we find the *Shulchan* (Table) on the right (northern) side; the *Menorah* on the left (southern) side; and the *Mizbe'ach HaKetores* (Incense, or Golden Altar) is in the middle. The organizers of the *tefillah* instituted that the *berachos* of יוֹצֵר אוֹר and אַהֲבָה רַבָּה, which follow in the next part of the *tefillah*, be recited there to correspond to the *Shulchan* and the *Menorah* respectively, and these *berachos* are followed by *Kerias Shema* which corresponds to the *Mizbe'ach HaKetores*. [For a more detailed explanation of the symbolism here, see Author's Introduction pps: xxxii-xxxiii]

In יִשְׁתַּבַּח, as we figuratively take leave of the *Ulam* and prepare to enter the *Heichal* of the King, with its three major *keilim*. We find an allusion to this in the thrice-combined words אֵל and מֶלֶךְ, as follows:

- יִשְׁתַּבַּח שִׁמְךָ לָעַד מַלְכֵּנוּ **הָאֵל הַמֶּלֶךְ**
- בָּרוּךְ אַתָּה ה' **אֵל מֶלֶךְ** גָּדוֹל בַּתִּשְׁבָּחוֹת
- אֵל הַהוֹדָאוֹת
- **מֶלֶךְ אֵל** חֵי הָעוֹלָמִים

The reason יִשְׁתַּבַּח does not start with בָּרוּךְ אַתָּה ה' is because it is the counterpart of בָּרוּךְ שֶׁאָמַר and, as such, is a בְּרָכָה הַסְּמוּכָה לַחֲבֶרְתָּהּ, a blessing which follows another blessing, which does not open with בָּרוּךְ אַתָּה ה'. The *tefillah* of יִשְׁתַּבַּח is the closing *berachah* of *Pesukei d'Zimrah*, similar to יְהַלְלוּךְ, the closing *berachah* of *Hallel*, which also does not begin with בָּרוּךְ for the same reason.

Interestingly, in the case of the reading of the *Megillah*, the *berachah* of הָרָב אֶת רִיבֵנוּ, which is said afterwards, *does* begin with בָּרוּךְ. This is so because it is not a closing *berachah*, but rather, it was instituted separately, to be said *b'tzibbur*, as a public thanksgiving pronouncement to *HaKadosh Baruch Hu* for saving the Jewish people from their enemies.

Therefore, if one were to read the *Megillah* privately, he would not say the *berachah* of הָרָב אֶת רִיבֵנוּ afterwards (see *Rema*, *Orach Chaim* 692:1).

יִשְׁתַּבַּח and the *berachah acharonah* of *Hallel*, however, are said privately as well as publicly. Since they are grouped with their respective opening *berachos*, they are considered סְמוּכָה לַחֲבֶרְתָּהּ and do not start with בָּרוּךְ.

≈ ≈ ≈

◆§ We — יִשְׁתַּבַּח שִׁמְךָ לָעַד מַלְכֵּנוּ – הָאֵל הַמֶּלֶךְ הַגָּדוֹל וְהַקָּדוֹשׁ – בַּשָּׁמַיִם וּבָאָרֶץ §◆ have indicated the proper syntax of these words with hyphens; and the meaning is as follows: **May Your Name, our King, be praised forever — the All-Powerful Great and Holy King — in heaven and earth.**

◆§ בִּי לְךָ נָאֶה ה׳ אֱלֹהֵינוּ וֵאלֹהֵי אֲבוֹתֵינוּ §◆ — **Because for You is fitting — O Hashem, our God, and the God of our forefathers.** The word נָאֶה is usually translated *beautiful*. However, the real meaning is *fitting* or *appropriate*, similar to its usage in the phrase כַּלָּה נָאָה וַחֲסוּדָה. In the opinion of *Beis Hillel,* this means a *fitting kallah for this chassan* (see *Kesubos* 17a). Similarly, in this phrase we will list fifteen expressions of praise of *HaKadosh Baruch Hu,* all of which we say are "befitting of You."

◆§ שִׁיר וּשְׁבָחָה, הַלֵּל וְזִמְרָה, עֹז וּמֶמְשָׁלָה §◆ — **Song and praise, lauding and hymns, power and dominion,** There are fifteen expressions of praise in this sentence, and they should be said without interruption (see *Magen Avraham,* beginning of *Siman* 53). This does not mean they must be said in one breath as is required when reading the listing of the ten sons of Haman in the *Megillas Esther,* but, rather, that these fifteen words are to be said as one unit, corresponding to the numerical value of the Name יָהּ.

These fifteen terms of praise, while closely resembling synonyms, actually have individual meanings of their own. However, the exact definition of each one of these words as it applies to the praises of *HaKadosh Baruch Hu* eludes us. Even the various *mefarshim* differ as to the specific meaning of each of these — and of other expressions of praise.

Interestingly, we have שֶׁבַח, which is masculine, and שְׁבָחָה, which is feminine. According to the Vilna Gaon, when reciting the קְדֻשָּׁה, one should say וּשְׁבָחֲךָ, which is a derivative of שְׁבָחָה, rather than וְשִׁבְחֲךָ, which is derived from שֶׁבַח. Similarly, we have here הַלֵּל, which is masculine, and זִמְרָה, which is feminine; עֹז is masculine, and מֶמְשָׁלָה is feminine. Obviously, there are different nuances regarding these expressions, and the exact meaning of each one regarding its application as praise to *HaKadosh Baruch Hu* is unclear. We continue the fifteen terms:

◆§ נֶצַח גְּדֻלָּה וּגְבוּרָה תְּהִלָּה וְתִפְאֶרֶת קְדֻשָּׁה וּמַלְכוּת בְּרָכוֹת וְהוֹדָאוֹת מֵעַתָּה וְעַד עוֹלָם §◆ — **Triumph, greatness and strength, praise and splendor, holiness and sovereignty, blessings and thanksgivings from this time and forever.** This grouping of the fifteen forms of praise belongs together, with the meaning, "An immortal perpetuation of שִׁיר וּשְׁבָחָה הַלֵּל וְזִמְרָה עֹז וּמֶמְשָׁלָה נֶצַח (לְךָ נָאֶה) befits You גְּדֻלָּה וּגְבוּרָה תְּהִלָּה וְתִפְאֶרֶת קְדֻשָּׁה וּמַלְכוּת בְּרָכוֹת וְהוֹדָאוֹת from now to eternity." Sometimes when we praise something over and over again, we eventually become tired of it. For instance, if one stands in front of a beautiful view, whether this be a man-made picture or a structure, or even a natural sight or wonder, and he praises it over and over again, eventually, it will lose its appeal. Not so in the case of *HaKadosh Baruch Hu,* Whose praises go on in perpetuity.

It is a commonly accepted practice that the *chazzan* starts from בְּרָכוֹת וְהוֹדָאוֹת מֵעַתָּה וְעַד עוֹלָם. This is not technically correct because, as we previously stated, these fifteen forms of praise are to be said as one unit. This would account for the *minhag* Frankfurt that on Rosh Hashanah and Yom Kippur the *chazzan* starts with בָּרוּךְ אַתָּה ה'. Nevertheless, the practice for the *chazzan* to begin with בְּרָכוֹת וְהוֹדָאוֹת prevails despite the fact that all fifteen expressions should be said together.

בָּרוּךְ אַתָּה ה', אֵל מֶלֶךְ גָּדוֹל בַּתִּשְׁבָּחוֹת, אֵל הַהוֹדָאוֹת, אֲדוֹן הַנִּפְלָאוֹת — **Blessed are You, Hashem, God, King great in praises, God of thanksgivings, Master of wonders.** This closing *berachah* of *Pesukei d'Zimrah* contains three statements.

The first is that *HaKadosh Baruch Hu* is גָּדוֹל בַּתִּשְׁבָּחוֹת, *great in praises.* In human terms, when one is highly praised and is extolled as the "best," the "smartest," or the "most wonderful," etc. the subject of such acclamation becomes lost under these praises; in the end the person's praises have been exhausted. Not so with *HaKadosh Baruch Hu,* for the more we praise Him, the more we realize that we have really not said anything. He becomes גָּדוֹל בַּתִּשְׁבָּחוֹת. He is greater than any possible praises could describe.

This is illustrated when Moshe Rabbeinu, the greatest of our *Neviim,* exclaimed at the end of his life, at the age of 120 years, that he had *only begun* to see God's greatness: אֲדֹנָי ה' (אֱלֹהִים) אַתָּה הַחִלּוֹתָ לְהַרְאוֹת אֶת עַבְדְּךָ אֶת גָּדְלְךָ וְאֶת יָדְךָ הַחֲזָקָה וגו', *My Lord, Hashem/Elohim, You have begun to show Your servant Your greatness and Your strong hand* etc. (*Devarim* 3:24). "After all this time, You have just *started* to show me Your greatness."

The second statement of this *berachah* is that He is אֵל הַהוֹדָאוֹת, *God of thanksgivings.* This means that not only do we offer thanksgiving to *Ha-Kadosh Baruch Hu,* we *thank Him for giving us the idea of thanksgiving.*

We have previously pointed out, in our comments on הוֹדוּ לַה' כִּי טוֹב, that in מוֹדִים דְּרַבָּנָן, we say, עַל שֶׁאֲנַחְנוּ מוֹדִים לָךְ, which is explained by *Rashi* to mean, עַל שֶׁנָּתַתָּ בְּלִבֵּנוּ לִהְיוֹת דְּבוּקִים בָּךְ וּמוֹדִים לָךְ, *We thank you for putting the concept of being grateful to You in our hearts* (*Sotah* 40a). And there, as here, we bless *HaKadosh Baruch Hu* by saying, בָּרוּךְ אֵל הַהוֹדָאוֹת. No one is born with a natural impulse of gratitude for being alive. The natural feeling is to take life for granted, because for as long as one can remember he has always been alive. The feeling of gratitude comes gradually with maturity and is, in itself, a gift from *HaKadosh Baruch Hu.*

If one's life became endangered, and he survives, then he feels grateful; then he exclaims, "*Baruch Hashem,* I am alive." Here we thank Hashem for giving us the gift of feeling gratitude to Him for life and its blessings, without having to be reminded by the threat of losing them.

The third statement is that *HaKadosh Baruch Hu* is אֲדוֹן הַנִּפְלָאוֹת, *the Master of wonders*. Throughout history, He has shown the world myriads of wonders and miracles. This could continue at any moment. He is an inexhaustible source of wonders and miracles.

⋅≤ הַבּוֹחֵר בְּשִׁירֵי זִמְרָה — **Who chooses songs of praise.** *HaKadosh Baruch Hu* has chosen *Bnei Yisrael* to deliver His praises. This is based on, וְאַתָּה קָדוֹשׁ יוֹשֵׁב תְּהִלּוֹת יִשְׂרָאֵל, *You, Holy One, are enthroned by the praises of Israel* (*Tehillim* 22:4). [See translation of Rav Samson R. Hirsch, ibid.]

After completing *Pesukei d'Zimrah*, which express the praises of *HaKadosh Baruch Hu* in the name of all of creation, from its highest forms to its lowest forms, עֶלְיוֹנִים וְתַחְתּוֹנִים, we thank *HaKadosh Baruch Hu* in this *berachah* for having chosen us, *Bnei Yisrael,* to deliver His praises.

⋅≤ מֶלֶךְ אֵל חֵי הָעוֹלָמִים — **King, God, Life-source of all periods of existence.** *HaKadosh Baruch Hu* is the life-source of all time periods of existence. עוֹלָמוֹת would mean *worlds,* but עוֹלָמִים expresses the idea of for all times — forever.

As a child in Frankfurt, I can still remember that on the *yahrzeit* of the *Chazzan* Frieslander, when his son would serve as the *shaliach tzibbur* in the "*Klauss,*" he would say "חַי" הָעוֹלָמִים, because this was his father's *minhag*.

However, the generally accepted *minhag* is to say חֵי הָעוֹלָמִים (see *Tosefos Yom Tov* end of *Tamid* in the name of *Rambam, Hil. Yesodei HaTorah* 2:10 and commentaries to *Shulchan Aruch, Orach Chaim* 207).

[Ed. note: See similar comments by the Rav on חֵי הָעוֹלָמִים at the end of בָּרוּךְ שֶׁאָמַר.]

קַדִּיש וּבָרְכוּ / Kaddish U'Barchu

Our *Chachamim* have instituted the saying of *Kaddish* at least seven times daily, and any additional *Kedeishim* are voluntary. Some authorities have found a *remez* (allusion) for this in the words of *Tehillim* (119:164): שֶׁבַע בַּיּוֹם הִלַּלְתִּיךָ, *I praise you seven times daily* (*Roke'ach* 322 and *Levush HaTecheiles* 57). These seven mandated *Kedeishim* are: three times during *Shacharis*, and twice each during *Minchah* and *Maariv*.

The *mesadrei hatefillah*, organizers of the *tefillah*, instituted that *Kaddish* be said before and after each *Shemoneh Esrei*, which is the main *tefillah b'tzibbur* (communal prayer), because the purpose of *Kaddish* is the sanctification of Hashem's Name by the entire *tzibbur*, by saying, יִתְגַּדַּל וְיִתְקַדַּשׁ שְׁמֵהּ רַבָּא. During *Shacharis*, since *Kaddish* cannot be said before *Shemoneh Esrei* — because of the requirement that *tefillah* is to follow *geulah* without any interruption — it is said afterwards instead.

[Ed. note: See *Mishnah Berurah* 236:5 for the reason *Kaddish* is said at *Maariv* between *geulah* and *tefillah*. Also, see ibid. 55:5, in which these seven *Kedeishim* are apportioned somewhat differently. However, the Rav's apportionment of only three *Kedeishim* at *Shacharis* is based on *Magen Avraham* to 25:13 on *Rema* ibid.; see *Mishnah Berurah* 56 ibid.]

The *Kaddish* with which we are dealing now is the one following יִשְׁתַּבַּח, as a conclusion to the *Pesukei d'Zimrah*.

What is commonly known as חֲצִי קַדִּישׁ was originally the entire *Kaddish*. The *tefillos* of תִּתְקַבֵּל and עַל יִשְׂרָאֵל וְעַל רַבָּנָן and עַל שְׁלָמָא רַבָּא and יְהֵא were later additions, instituted during the time of the *Geonim*. This is similar to the addition of the הָרַחֲמָן group to the *Bircas HaMazon* which actually concludes with אַל יְחַסְּרֵנוּ.

Kaddish is one of the *tefillos* called *davar shebik'dushah*, which are required to be said with a *minyan*. The others are קְרִיאַת הַתּוֹרָה, קְדֻשָּׁה, בָּרְכוּ, and הַפְטָרָה. The Gemara (*Megillah* 23b) bases this halachah on the *pasuk*, וְנִקְדַּשְׁתִּי בְּתוֹךְ בְּנֵי יִשְׂרָאֵל, *I will be sanctified among Bnei Yisrael* (*Vayikra* 22:32), on which *Chazal* comment: כָּל דָּבָר שֶׁבִּקְדוּשָּׁה לֹא יְהֵא פָּחוֹת מֵעֲשָׂרָה, *All words of kedushah — special holiness — can be said only if there are no less than ten (males) present.* The Gemara explains there why בְּתוֹךְ בְּנֵי יִשְׂרָאֵל means at least ten people.

Originally, *Kaddish* was said in *lashon hakodesh*, as we see from the language of the Gemara (*Berachos* 3a), which cites the original words used as יְהֵא שְׁמֵיהּ הַגָּדוֹל מְבוֹרָךְ. During some later period, when the Jewish vernacular was no longer pure *lashon hakodesh*, but rather, a colloquial mixture of *lashon hakodesh* and Aramaic — which no Aramean would have

KADDISH U'BARCHU 251

understood — it was changed to the form that we have today. It is this form of "Aramaic" that is used in most of the Gemara, and even in some parts of the Mishnah.

This usage is similar to Yiddish, or, in our time, when Torah is learned in English (sometimes called "Yinglish") the language used is actually a mixture of Hebrew and English, most of which would not be understood by a non-Jew.

Some of the words of *Kaddish* are pure *lashon hakodesh,* such as: יִתְבָּרַךְ, וְיִשְׁתַּבַּח, יִתְגַּדַּל, וְיִתְפָּאַר, etc., while others are Aramaic, such as בְּעָלְמָא דִּי בְרָא כִרְעוּתֵהּ, שְׁמֵהּ רַבָּא, etc. This mixture of language characterized the vernacular, which the common people understood best.

Some authorities attribute an esoteric reason to the changing of the language of *Kaddish* by the *Chachamim* from pure *lashon kodesh* to the vernacular Aramaic (see *Tosafos, Berachos* 3a, s.v. ועונין). However, the simple reason given by *Tosafos* (ibid.) is based on the great importance of the public participation in *Kaddish,* as expressed by the Gemara: וְאֶלָּא עָלְמָא אַמַּאי קָא מְקַיַּים אַקְּדוּשָׁה דְסִידְרָא וְאִיְהֵא שְׁמֵיהּ רַבָּא דְּאַגַּדְתָּא, *The world exists only in the merit of the saying of the "Order of Kedushah"* (referring to the *Kedushah* in the prayer *Uvah L'Tziyon*), *and of the public pronouncement: "May His Great Name, etc", from Kaddish, following the study of Aggadah* (*Sotah* 49a). Since the *tzibbur* is composed of all elements of Jewish society, some learned and others not, the *Kaddish* had to be said in the vernacular, so that even the common folk could understand it and join in the response of יְהֵא שְׁמֵהּ רַבָּא מְבָרַךְ וגו'.

By the way, the word צִבֻּר, *tzibbur,* can be seen as an acronym which reflects its components: צַדִּיקִים, בֵּינוֹנִים, רְשָׁעִים (*reshaim* probably means *baalei teshuvah* who were once *reshaim*).

This same concept of communal *tefillah* applies also to בָּרְכוּ. We say בָּרְכוּ in the morning and evening at the beginning of the *berachos* of *Krias Shema,* and also when one is called up to the Torah. The *shaliach tzibbur* — or the *oleh laTorah* — is saying to the *tzibbur*: בָּרְכוּ אֶת ה' הַמְבֹרָךְ, "This is not only my private affair; I invite the entire *tzibbur* to join me in making a communal sanctification of Hashem's Name." While the *berachos* of *Krias Shema* can also be said without a *minyan,* the invitation of בָּרְכוּ אֶת ה' הַמְבֹרָךְ is said only with a minyan indicating that the blessing of Hashem by each individual (הַמְבֹרָךְ) will be elevated to a much higher level when the entire *tzibbur* combines their individual *berachos*. And the *tzibbur* combines their *berachos* by responding: בָּרוּךְ ה' הַמְבֹרָךְ לְעוֹלָם וָעֶד.

As previously explained, the invitation by the *chazzan* of בָּרְכוּ אֶת ה' הַמְבֹרָךְ and its communal response בָּרוּךְ ה' הַמְבֹרָךְ לְעוֹלָם וָעֶד are considered *davar shebik'dushah,* and thus must be said in the presence of ten adult males, representing the entire *Bnei Yisrael.*

Therefore, the *chazzan* should join the *tzibbur* in the response of בָּרוּךְ ה׳ הַמְבֹרָךְ לְעוֹלָם וָעֶד and not say it separately after the *tzibbur,* because as a *davar shebik'dushah,* it must be said together with the *tzibbur.* In many congregations the *chazzan* says בָּרוּךְ ה׳ הַמְבֹרָךְ לְעוֹלָם וָעֶד *after* the *tzibbur* has finished saying it. This is not correct. I am very pleased that the *minhag* in our *kehillah* is for the *chazzan* to say it together with the *tzibbur,* as is proper.

The same applies also to one who is called up to the Torah. By saying בָּרְכוּ אֶת ה׳ הַמְבֹרָךְ, he tells the *tzibbur* that this *parashah* to which he is called up is being read not only for him, but rather it is being read for the entire *tzibbur* as well, and he invites them to join him in honoring the Torah. Therefore, the *oleh laTorah* should also join the *tzibbur* in saying בָּרוּךְ ה׳ הַמְבֹרָךְ לְעוֹלָם וָעֶד, to include himself with them. Whenever I am called up to the Torah, I make sure to say בָּרוּךְ ה׳ הַמְבֹרָךְ לְעוֹלָם וָעֶד together with the *tzibbur.*

Therefore, I would like to point out that the practice of teaching *bar mitzvah* boys to repeat בָּרוּךְ ה׳ הַמְבֹרָךְ לְעוֹלָם וָעֶד after the *tzibbur* has said it — while sounding very nice — is, nevertheless, not proper. Rather, they should be taught that since this is a *davar shebik'dushah,* it should be said together with the *tzibbur.*

קַדִּישׁ יָתוֹם

[Ed. note: The following explanation of *Kaddish* was not part of the *Iyun Tefillah* series of lectures, but was given by the Rav during his speech at the annual *seudah* of the *Chevrah Kaddisha* of K'hal Adath Jeshurun in 1992. We have included it here but have omitted those parts which were covered in the previous section.]

We have three similar words which convey the general concept of "holiness":

❑ קִדּוּשׁ, *kiddush,* means *sanctification,* pertaining to Shabbos and Yom Tov;
❑ קְדֻשָּׁה, *kedushah,* means *sanctify,* pertaining to the *shirah* that the *malachim* sing to *HaKadosh Baruch Hu;*
❑ קַדִּישׁ, *kaddish,* is the Aramaic translation of the word קָדוֹשׁ, *kadosh,* which refers to *HaKadosh Baruch Hu* Himself, and it is this meaning that is employed when we say the word *kaddish.*

Based on an age-old *takanah* (institution), the so-called *Kaddish Yasom* is the *Kaddish* said by an "orphan," in honor of his father or mother who have departed this world. This is a form of *kibbud av v'eim,* a *mitzvah* which does not cease when father and mother are no longer with us in the flesh, as *Chazal* teach, מְכַבְּדוֹ בְּחַיָּיו וּמְכַבְּדוֹ בְּמוֹתוֹ, *One is to honor his father or mother during their lifetimes, and after their deaths* (*Kiddushin* 31b).

There are various Midrashim which tell of the important significance of a son saying *Kaddish* in honor of his father or mother after they have passed away, while their *neshamos* are purified in *Gehinnom,* or are subjected to some other form of Heavenly punishment for any wrongdoing and *aveiros* during their lifetime. These *neshamos* are greatly benefited by the son saying *Kaddish* and causing ten Jews to say יְהֵא שְׁמֵהּ רַבָּא וגו'.

The *Zohar Chadash* (*Acharei Mos,* p. 49) relates the story of one of the *Chazal* who communicated with a *neshamah* that was undergoing purification in the other world. That *neshamah* told him: בְּשַׁעְתָּא דְּאָמַר בְּנִי קַדִּישׁ קוֹרְעִין לִי גְזַר דִּין מִכֹּל וָכֹל, *Whenever my son says Kaddish for me they tear up the evil decree completely.*

The reason for this is because the son, or any child, is an "extension" of his father or mother, בְּרָא כַּרְעֵיהּ דַּאֲבוּהּ. The child represents what is left of the father or mother in this world, after they have died. By virtue of the existence of his children, a part of the parent's body still exists. Therefore, at the moment when the *aveil* (mourner) says *Kaddish* in honor of his father or mother, he may not realize it, but he is really speaking in the name of his father or mother. It is his father or mother who is imploring the assembled congregation יִתְגַּדַּל וְיִתְקַדַּשׁ שְׁמֵהּ רַבָּא. And when the congregation responds, יְהֵא שְׁמֵהּ רַבָּא מְבָרַךְ לְעָלַם וּלְעָלְמֵי עָלְמַיָּא, this is a great *zechus* for the *neshamah* of his parents, and the highest form of *kibbud av v'eim.*

Originally, there were seven mandated *Kadeishim,* and three more were added by the generally accepted *minhag,* making a minimum of ten *Kadeishim* recited in our three daily *tefillos.* Any additional *Kadeishim* are only voluntary, subject to local *minhagim.* These additional *Kedeishim* are usually reserved for the orphan, which includes an *aveil* or one observing *yahrzeit* for his parents.

The essence of *Kaddish* is, undoubtedly, the congregation's response: יְהֵא שְׁמֵהּ רַבָּא מְבָרַךְ וגו', and the meaning of it is as follows:

❧ ❧ ❧

יְהֵא שְׁמֵהּ רַבָּא מְבָרַךְ לְעָלַם וּלְעָלְמֵי עָלְמַיָּא — May His great Name be blessed throughout all of the four worlds of existence. The words לְעָלַם וּלְעָלְמֵי עָלְמַיָּא could not mean "eternity of eternities of eternity." It would not make sense. Therefore, עָלַם, in this phrase, must be used with its other meaning, which is "world." Accordingly, *Nefesh HaChaim* (1:20) translates this to mean "in the world, and in the worlds of the world." This is a reference to the four "worlds" of existence (world = 1; worlds = 2; world = 1). These are as follows:

First, there is the physical universe, called *Olam Ha'asiyah.* This is the world in which we live. Then, there is a higher, spiritual universe called *Olam Hayetzirah.* Then, still higher, is the third world, called *Olam Haberiyah,* which is the world of the *malachim.* Finally, the highest of these worlds is called *Olam Ha'atzilus,* which means a world which is *eitzel* (near)

HaKadosh Baruch Hu. It is the "heaven" above the *malachim.* This is something beyond human comprehension.

[Ed. note: For the meaning of *berachah,* or blessing of *HaKadosh Baruch Hu,* and its connection to *Kaddish,* please refer to the Rav's explanation in the *berachah* of עַל נְטִילַת יָדַיִם.]

We also refer to these "four worlds" in אֱלֹהַי נְשָׁמָה, which we say each morning: אֱלֹהַי נְשָׁמָה שֶׁנָּתַתָּ בִּי טְהוֹרָה הִיא, *My God, the soul You placed within me is pure.* This refers to the *neshamah* before it was created — in the *Olam Ha'atzilus,* right next to *HaKadosh Baruch Hu;* אַתָּה בְרָאתָהּ — It was then brought to the *Olam Haberiyah for creation;* אַתָּה יְצַרְתָּהּ — It was then formed by *HaKadosh Baruch Hu,* with its individual characteristics, for placement within the *guf.* This is a reference to the *Olam Hayetzirah;* אַתָּה נְפַחְתָּהּ בִּי וְאַתָּה מְשַׁמְּרָהּ בְּקִרְבִּי — Then finally, *HaKadosh Baruch Hu* placed it into my body. This refers to our physical world, the *Olam Ha'asiyah.*

[Ed. note: The Rav made previous reference to this esoteric concept in his explanations of אֱלֹהַי נְשָׁמָה and אֲדוֹן עוֹלָם.]

The Gemara (*Shabbos* 119b) places extremely great importance on the saying of הָעוֹנֶה יְהֵא שְׁמֵיהּ רַבָּא with one's fullest concentration: כָּל הָעוֹנֶה יְהֵא שְׁמֵיהּ רַבָּא מְבָרַךְ בְּכָל כֹּחוֹ קוֹרְעִין לוֹ גְּזַר דִּינוֹ — The responding of יְהֵא שְׁמֵהּ רַבָּא with all one's strength is so powerful that it can cause the *beis din shel maalah* (the Heavenly Court) to "tear up" a decree of punishment for one's *aveiros,* and give him another chance to make good for them.

Rashi (ibid.) explains בְּכָל כֹּחוֹ to mean בְּכָל כַּוָּנָתוֹ, *with his complete concentration of mind.* There are others (see *Tosafos* ibid.) who explain it to mean simply בְּקוֹל רָם, *with a loud voice.* It is certainly true that when one says something loudly, it increases his concentration on the meaning of what he is saying. According to this opinion, יְהֵא שְׁמֵהּ רַבָּא would be an exception to the rule that the response to a *berachah* may not be louder than the *berachah* itself: הָעוֹנֶה אָמֵן לֹא יַגְבִּיהַּ קוֹלוֹ יוֹתֵר מִן הַמְבָרֵךְ (cf. *Berachos* 45a). However, even according to this opinion, one must be careful not to shout it so loudly as to make himself look ridiculous (see *Mishnah Berurah* 56:5).

The previously mentioned statement (*Shabbos* 119b) concerning having the greatest possible concentration while saying יְהֵא שְׁמֵהּ רַבָּא is supported there by a *pasuk* from *Shiras Devorah* which, on the surface, has nothing to do with *Kaddish.* It is essential to the meaning of *Kaddish* that we understand this connection.

The *pasuk* is as follows: בִּפְרֹעַ פְּרָעוֹת בְּיִשְׂרָאֵל בְּהִתְנַדֵּב עָם בָּרְכוּ ה׳, *When things get out of control in Israel, and then the people voluntarily dedicate themselves, then you bless Hashem* (*Shoftim* 5:2).

However, *Rashi* (on the Gemara ibid.) explains this *pasuk* as if the phrases were reversed: כְּשֶׁמִּתְנַדְּבִין יִשְׂרָאֵל לְבָרֵךְ אֶת בּוֹרְאָן means, בְּהִתְנַדֵּב עָם בָּרְכוּ ה׳,

KADDISH U'BARCHU 255

When the people of the nation (Israel) voluntarily dedicate themselves with all their strength to bless their Maker; בִּפְרֹעַ פְּרָעוֹת בְּיִשְׂרָאֵל, then, בְּטוּל פּוּרְעָנִיּוֹת, the punishments against Israel become annulled.

This *pasuk* was said by Devorah HaNeviah in her *shirah* following the Jewish victory over Yavin the king of Canaan, and refers to בְּהִתְנַדֵּב עָם, the voluntary dedication of the people, in that battle. Yavin, with his powerful army equipped with nine hundred iron chariots — equivalent to tanks today — had already made inroads into the northern part of Eretz Yisrael and was threatening the rest of the country. To counter this threat, Barak, heeding the command of Devorah which came to her in the Name of Hashem, went to war against Yavin. The entire army that he recruited for this battle consisted of only ten thousand volunteers from the tribes of Naftali and Zevulun. These were joined by other volunteers, who were mainly *talmidei chachamim* from Yissachar and Ephraim. Some who refused to join in this effort were criticized by Devorah.

In this *shirah,* Devorah praises these volunteers, who risked their lives in this cause: זְבֻלוּן עַם חֵרֵף נַפְשׁוֹ לָמוּת וְנַפְתָּלִי עַל מְרוֹמֵי שָׂדֶה, *Zevulun is a people that risked its life to the death, and so did Naftali, on the heights of the battlefield* (Shoftim 5:18). The soldiers from Zevulun and Naftali had brought themselves into the utmost danger, and were ready to die in this battle, which had been mandated by *HaKadosh Baruch Hu* against His enemies.

According to this, בְּהִתְנַדֵּב עָם means to dedicate oneself fully, with every ounce of one's strength, to *HaKadosh Baruch Hu,* even if it becomes necessary to give one's life for this purpose.

Similarly, our *Chazal* view the saying of יְהֵא שְׁמֵהּ רַבָּא with total concentration and dedication, בְּכָל כֹּחוֹ, as a verbal form of *mesiras nefesh,* which has the same power to annul potential danger to the Jewish people as did the life-risking dedication of the Jewish soldiers at the time of Devorah HaNeviah. This resulted in בִּפְרֹעַ פְּרָעוֹת, the annulment of the evil decree of the imminent mortal threat posed by the Canaanite king. Similarly, when one says יְהֵא שְׁמֵהּ רַבָּא מְבָרַךְ לְעָלַם וּלְעָלְמֵי עָלְמַיָּא with total concentration, it means he is ready to give his soul back through all the four worlds, to *HaKadosh Baruch Hu,* from whence it came, for the purpose of יִתְגַּדַּל וְיִתְקַדַּשׁ שְׁמֵהּ רַבָּא, making a *Kiddush Hashem* in the world. Such a person is truly worthy of קוֹרְעִין לוֹ גְּזַר דִּינוֹ, having his evil decree torn apart.

The last word of this phrase, יִתְבָּרַךְ, is a reference to בָּרְכוּ ה', the last words of the aforementioned *pasuk,* בָּרְכוּ ה' ... בִּפְרֹעַ פְּרָעוֹת בְּיִשְׂרָאֵל, with which this entire part of *Kaddish* is so closely connected.

If the central theme of *Kaddish* is the saying of יְהֵא שְׁמֵהּ רַבָּא with total concentration, בְּכָל כֹּחוֹ, it is no mere coincidence that the structure of the words and sentences of *Kaddish* correspond to the number 28, the numerical value of כ״ח: There are 28 words from יִתְגַּדַּל through וּלְעָלְמֵי עָלְמַיָּא; 28 words from יְהֵא שְׁמֵהּ רַבָּא through דַּאֲמִירָן בְּעָלְמָא; and 28 letters in יְהֵא שְׁמֵהּ רַבָּא מְבָרַךְ לְעָלַם וּלְעָלְמֵי עָלְמַיָּא.

Then in addition to *Yisbarach* which is the central theme, we add seven more elevated stages: וְיִשְׁתַּבַּח, וְיִתְפָּאַר, וְיִתְרוֹמַם, וְיִתְנַשֵּׂא, וְיִתְהַדָּר, וְיִתְעַלֶּה, וְיִתְהַלָּל, and each one of these is further enhanced by four forms of praise, which correspond to the "four worlds": לְעֵלָּא מִן כָּל בִּרְכָתָא וְשִׁירָתָא תֻּשְׁבְּחָתָא וְנֶחֱמָתָא. This combination also totals 28.

[Ed. note: For an explanation of these four forms of praise, see *Maayan Beis HaSho'evah* on *Yisro* 20:12.]

It is abundantly clear from all of this that the organizers of the *tefillah* structured the entire *Kaddish* around the central theme of כ״ח, to convey the importance of saying it with total concentration and dedication.

When the *shaliach tzibbur*, or the *aveil*, or the one who has *yahrzeit* who becomes the *shaliach tzibbur*, says יִתְגַּדַּל וְיִתְקַדַּשׁ שְׁמֵהּ רַבָּא בְּעָלְמָא דִּי בְרָא כִרְעוּתֵהּ, he is expressing the wish and prayer that the great Name of *HaKadosh Baruch Hu* shall become even greater and more holy "in the world which He has created according to His will." This "world which He has created according to His will" is detailed in the *Kaddish* which is said after a *kevurah* (burial), as follows:

❑ בְּעָלְמָא דִּי הוּא עָתִיד לְאִתְחַדָּתָא — In the world which He will renew, in the future. Not this world of ours, with all its negative aspects.

❑ וּלְאַחֲיָאָה מֵתַיָּא וּלְאַסָּקָא יָתְהוֹן לְחַיֵּי עָלְמָא — And when He will make the dead come alive and bring them up to eternal life.

❑ וּלְמִבְנֵא קַרְתָּא דִּי יְרוּשְׁלֵם — And He will build the city of Yerushalayim.

❑ וּלְשַׁכְלָלָא הֵיכְלֵהּ בְּגַוַּהּ — And He will establish His palace in it (meaning the Beis HaMikdash).

❑ וּלְמֶעְקַר פָּלְחָנָא נֻכְרָאָה מִן אַרְעָא — And all forms of idol worship will be eliminated from the world.

❑ וְלַאֲתָבָא פָּלְחָנָא דִּי שְׁמַיָּא לְאַתְרֵהּ — And the worship of *HaKadosh Baruch Hu* will be reestablished in its own place.

❑ וְיַמְלִיךְ קֻדְשָׁא בְּרִיךְ הוּא בְּמַלְכוּתֵהּ וִיקָרֵהּ — And *HaKadosh Baruch Hu* will rule in His kingdom and His glory.

Then the *shaliach tzibbur* expresses the wish that all this shall not take place solely at some distant and future time, but rather, he tells the congregation that all this shall take place:

❑ בְּחַיֵּיכוֹן וּבְיוֹמֵיכוֹן וּבְחַיֵּי דְכָל בֵּית יִשְׂרָאֵל — In your lifetime and in the lifetime of all of the house of Israel.

❑ בַּעֲגָלָא וּבִזְמַן קָרִיב — And this shall come about quickly and in the near future.

י§ וְאִמְרוּ אָמֵן — **Now respond, Amen.** The *shaliach tzibbur* now exhorts the congregation to say *Amen,* as an expression of agreement with all of the aforesaid. To which they respond, אָמֵן, "Yes, we agree," and therefore, we say: יְהֵא שְׁמֵהּ רַבָּא מְבָרַךְ לְעָלַם וּלְעָלְמֵי עָלְמַיָּא.

Now, after all this, when we think about the exalted nature of *Kaddish,* and how we are to respond to it, we are reminded of how *Chazal* (*Berachos* 6b) interpret the *pasuk,* כְּרֻם זֻלּוּת לִבְנֵי אָדָם, *When the basest of men are elevated* (*Tehillim* 12:9): There are certain things which are עוֹמְדִים בְּרוּמוֹ שֶׁל עוֹלָם, of primary importance in the world, but unfortunately, people still belittle them, מְזַלְזְלִים בָּהֶם. If one would understand the true meaning of *Kaddish,* he would certainly treat it as one of those things which are of supreme importance, as we have now seen.

When an entire congregation listens to the *shaliach tzibbur* who may be representing the *neshamah* of his deceased parent beseeching them to give their lives, if necessary, for the purpose of יִתְגַּדַּל וְיִתְקַדַּשׁ שְׁמֵהּ רַבָּא, and they respond affirmatively with יְהֵא שְׁמֵהּ רַבָּא מְבָרַךְ לְעָלַם וּלְעָלְמֵי עָלְמַיָּא, this is the highest form of a verbal *kiddush Hashem* in this world.

בִּרְכוֹת קְרִיאַת שְׁמַע / Birchos Krias Shema

בִּרְכַּת יוֹצֵר אוֹר

The *Chachamim* instituted the recital of three *berachos* each morning in conjunction with *Krias Shema*: יוֹצֵר אוֹר and אַהֲבָה רַבָּה before *Krias Shema*, and אֱמֶת וְיַצִּיב, or גְּאוּלָה, afterwards (see Mishnah, *Berachos* 11a).

The text of these *berachos* is so familiar that we tend to forget to focus on their meaning. According to our outline of the *tefillah*, we are now — figuratively speaking — standing inside the *Heichal*. The *Shulchan*, representing the material side of *Klal Yisrael*, is on the right; the *Menorah*, representing its spiritual side, is to the left; and the *Mizbach HaKetores*, also known as the *Mizbach HaZahav*, representing *kabbalas ol Malchus Shamayim*, is in the middle.

Accordingly, as we begin the *berachos* of *Krias Shema*, the first *berachah* focuses our attention on the revelation of *HaKadosh Baruch Hu* in the material universe, as symbolized by the *Shulchan*. This *berachah* begins with בָּרוּךְ אַתָּה ה' אֱלֹהֵינוּ מֶלֶךְ הָעוֹלָם, as do all of our *berachos*, except those that are *semuchah lachavertah*, which follow another full *berachah*.

❧ ❧ ❧

יוֹצֵר אוֹר וּבוֹרֵא חֹשֶׁךְ — He forms light and creates darkness. Since this *berachah* is said in the morning, we mention the light before the darkness, although, at their creation, the opposite was true. First there was וְחֹשֶׁךְ עַל פְּנֵי תְהוֹם, *darkness upon the surface of the deep* (*Bereishis* 1:2), and only later was light created: וַיֹּאמֶר אֱלֹהִים יְהִי אוֹר, *God said, "Let there be light"* (ibid. v.3). Similarly, in Maariv, we first thank *HaKadosh Baruch Hu* for the darkness: גּוֹלֵל אוֹר מִפְּנֵי חֹשֶׁךְ, *He rolls away the light in the face of the oncoming darkness,* and then we add, וְחֹשֶׁךְ מִפְּנֵי אוֹר, *and [He rolls away] the darkness in the face of the oncoming light.*

The reason we mention both light and darkness in the morning as well as the evening is: לְהַזְכִּיר מִדַּת יוֹם בַּלַּיְלָה וּמִדַּת לַיְלָה בַּיּוֹם, *One is to make reference to the daytime at night, and to the nighttime by day* (*Berachos* 11b). We are to mention the creation of light during the *tefillah* of Maariv, while we praise *HaKadosh Baruch Hu* for the creation of darkness. And, during the *tefillah* of Shacharis, we do the opposite. We mention the creation of darkness, while we thank *HaKadosh Baruch Hu* for creating the light.

עֹשֶׂה שָׁלוֹם וּבוֹרֵא אֶת הַכֹּל — **Makes peace and creates everthing.** He makes the two harmonize, and He creates the totality of the universe.

Chazal tell us: רְשָׁעִים בְּחַיֵּיהֶם חֲשׁוּבִים כְּמֵתִים מִפְּנֵי שֶׁרוֹאִים חַמָּה זוֹרַחַת וְאֵינָם מְבָרְכִים יוֹצֵר אוֹר וְחַמָּה שׁוֹקַעַת וְאֵינָם מְבָרְכִים מַעֲרִיב עֲרָבִים, Paraphrased, this means: The wicked are considered dead even in their lifetimes, because they see the continuous cycle of sunrise and sunset, light and darkness, and yet, they do not bless God for creating this cycle (*Midrash Tanchuma, Berachah* 7). The marvel of our solar system, with its sunrises and sunsets, is such that if one does not see the work of the Creator behind it, he is considered a *rasha*. Such people consider this cycle as merely a predictable statistic that can be found in the daily newspapers. They give no thought to the יוֹצֵר of this אוֹר, Who established this cycle of light and darkness. It has nothing to do with them personally. These *reshaim* are considered dead, because they fail to see *HaKadosh Baruch Hu*, the living God, at work when they go to bed while it is dark, and awaken to find that the light of the sun has, once again, illuminated the earth.

This is in stark contrast to *Bnei Yisrael* who *are alive,* and recognize that *HaKadosh Baruch Hu* is the cause of the daily cycles of light and darkness: וְאַתֶּם הַדְּבֵקִים בַּה' אֱלֹהֵיכֶם חַיִּים כֻּלְּכֶם הַיּוֹם, *But you who cling to Hashem, your God, you are all alive today* (*Devarim* 4:4). Despite the fact that we know exactly when to expect sunrise and sunset, this miraculous cycle affects each one of us personally to the extent that we enthusiastically thank *HaKadosh Baruch Hu* for it daily with the *berachah* of יוֹצֵר אוֹר וּבוֹרֵא חֹשֶׁךְ, as if this were the first time we had witnessed this marvel.

It is noteworthy that the previous statement by *Chazal* that מַזְכִּירִין מִדַּת יוֹם בַּלַּיְלָה וּמִדַּת לַיְלָה בַּיּוֹם refers not only to the physical aspect of sunset and sunrise as it affects the whole world; rather, מִדַּת יוֹם literally means "the measure of light," which symbolizes the *middas harachamim* of *HaKadosh Baruch Hu* Who makes the sun shine and awakens the world. Similarly, darkness, מִדַּת לַיְלָה, means "the measure of darkness," which represents the *middas hadin* of *HaKadosh Baruch Hu*. We will find references to this as we continue with the *berachos*.

Now let us examine the *berachah* itself. The words are taken from *Yeshayahu* (45:7): יוֹצֵר אוֹר וּבוֹרֵא חֹשֶׁךְ עֹשֶׂה שָׁלוֹם וּבוֹרֵא רָע אֲנִי ה' עֹשֶׂה כָל אֵלֶּה, *The One Who forms light and creates darkness; Who makes peace and creates evil; I am Hashem, Maker of all these.* The chapter in which this *pasuk* is found has given many headaches to those cynics who do not believe in the veracity of the *Neviim*. It opens with the words כֹּה אָמַר ה' לִמְשִׁיחוֹ לְכוֹרֶשׁ, *Thus said Hashem to His anointed one, to Koresh* (ibid. v.1). Hashem is sending a message to His "anointed one," Koresh (Cyrus), who lived about two hundred years after these words were spoken by Yeshayahu HaNavi. Therefore, these people conveniently invented a "Deutero-Isaiah," a second

Isaiah (Yeshayahu), who was to have lived during the time of Koresh, at the beginning of *Bayis Sheni* (the Second Temple), which was some two hundred years after the "first Isaiah," and this chapter was supposedly written at that time. They scoffed at the old Jews who were so naive that they actually believed that Yeshayahu was a real *navi,* with real prophetic powers; that he was not a faker like the other prophets, that he actually was told by *HaKadosh Baruch Hu* that there would be a king Koresh who would live two hundred years later; and that he would have a major influence on the world, especially on Jewish life. Or else, they explain away the prophecy by saying, "Koresh," which means "shepherd" in Persian, could refer to another king as, in fact, there were many kings who were called Koresh.

However, in truth, this *pasuk* is the *nevuah* (prophecy) of the one and only Yeshayahu HaNavi, who had a prophetic vision about the famous Persian king, Koresh, who would live about two hundred years later, at the time of the beginning of *Bayis Sheni.* And it was this Koresh who issued a proclamation encouraging the Jews to begin rebuilding the *Beis HaMikdash*: כֹּה אָמַר כֹּרֶשׁ מֶלֶךְ פָּרַס כֹּל מַמְלְכוֹת הָאָרֶץ נָתַן לִי ה' אֱלֹהֵי הַשָּׁמַיִם וְהוּא פָקַד עָלַי לִבְנוֹת לוֹ בַיִת בִּירוּשָׁלַיִם אֲשֶׁר בִּיהוּדָה, *Thus said Koresh the king of Persia: Hashem the God of heaven has given unto me all the governments of the world, and He issued a command directing me to build for Him a House in Yerushalayim which is in Yehudah* (Ezra 1:2).

Koresh had been told by the Jews of his time that there had been a Jewish prophet, named Yeshayahu, who lived about two hundred years before him, and that he had foretold, in the Name of Hashem, that Koresh would be chosen as God's instrument to rebuild Yerushalayim and the *Beis HaMikdash,* and to bring the Jewish people back from *Galus Bavel* (*Yeshayahu* 45:4-8).

Continuing his prophetic message to Koresh, Yeshayahu says, All of your power and success and dominion over the world is לְמַעַן עַבְדִּי יַעֲקֹב וְיִשְׂרָאֵל בְּחִירִי, *for the sake of my servant Yaakov and Israel My chosen one.* He is told here that the reason *HaKadosh Baruch Hu* gave him so much power in the world was for the purpose of rebuilding the *Beis HaMikdash* and bringing the Jews back from *Bavel* to Eretz Yisrael.

The *nevuah* continues (ibid. v.4): אֶקְרָא לְךָ בִּשְׁמֶךָ אֲכַנְּךָ וְלֹא יְדַעְתָּנִי, *I call you by your name, but you don't know Me.* (Part of this *pasuk* has been paraphrased in אֲדַמְּךָ אֲכַנְּךָ וְלֹא יְדַעְתִּיךָ: אֲנָעִים זְמִירוֹת.) This is followed by v.5, אֲנִי ה' וְאֵין עוֹד זוּלָתִי אֵין אֱלֹהִים אֲאַזֶּרְךָ וְלֹא יְדַעְתָּנִי, *I am Hashem, and there is no other; besides Me there is no god; I strengthen you, but you do not know Me* [because you were not even born when these words were said]. This is followed by v.6, לְמַעַן יֵדְעוּ מִמִּזְרַח שֶׁמֶשׁ וּמִמַּעֲרָבָה כִּי אֶפֶס בִּלְעָדָי אֲנִי ה' וְאֵין עוֹד, *That they [the nations of the world] may know, from east and from west there is none other besides me; I am God, and there is no other.* And now we come

BIRCHOS KRIAS SHEMA 261

to the *pasuk* on which our *berachah* is based: יוֹצֵר אוֹר וּבוֹרֵא חֹשֶׁךְ עֹשֶׂה שָׁלוֹם וּבוֹרֵא רָע אֲנִי ה' עֹשֶׂה כָל אֵלֶּה, *The One Who forms light and creates darkness; Who makes* [them co-exist in harmonious] *peace, and creates evil; I am Hashem, Maker of all these.*

To put this prophetic message in its proper context, and to understand the words וּבוֹרֵא רָע, *Who creates evil,* we must know that this was spoken against a background of "multideism," when the whole world believed in a multitude of gods — thousands of them. There were "demigods," "male-gods," and "female gods." In fact, all of nature had been deified. Then, prior to the time of Yeshayahu, a Far Eastern philosopher by the name of Zarathustra, or Zoroaster, as the Greeks called him, postulated a dualistic religious system in which he reduced all these gods to only two: a god of light and a god of darkness. The god of light was the one who gives light, health, happiness, success, and victory, while the god of darkness was responsible for all evil: sickness, death, and all other negative events in the world. This was already considered religious progress, and was later adopted by Koresh and the Persian Empire.

This would explain an event which occurred during the transition of power from the Babylonians to the Persians (*Daniel* 6:8-9). There we learn of an edict that was enacted whereby there was to be a thirty-day moratorium on prayer to any god or person. This was done to allow the temples to be converted from the old Babylonian-style worship of nature and multitudinous gods, to the new and "progressive" dualistic form of religious worship, "Zoroasterism," which Koresh had proclaimed as the new Persian religion.

Given this "dualistic" religious belief that prevailed at the time of Koresh, we now understand the meaning of the language of our *pasuk*. Yeshayahu sends his prophetic message to Koresh in the Name of the One and Only God, *HaKadosh Baruch Hu*, Who is the source of everything in the world. Light and darkness, good and evil, all emanate from Him; אֲנִי ה' וְאֵין עוֹד זוּלָתִי אֵין אֱלֹהִים, *I am Hashem and there is no other; other than Me there is no God* (*Yeshayahu* 45:5). And it is this One God Who is commanding him to build the *Beis HaMikdash* and bring the Jews back from Bavel to their land.

This concept that *HaKadosh Baruch Hu* "creates evil" is not easy to understand. Unfortunately, we in this century have experienced more evil than many past centuries combined. It is very hard even for one who believes *be'emunah sheleimah* to imagine that it is *HaKadosh Baruch Hu*, as בּוֹרֵא רָע, Who empowered a Dr. Mengele to inflict severe torture and pain on women and children as he conducted his evil experiments on them. Since there is no other power but *HaKadosh Baruch Hu,* then it was He Who made Mengele's mind and heart — and those of the Nazis — continue to function while they tortured and murdered our people in the ghettos and concentration camps. Who made Hitler's ימ"ש brain work? Who made the lungs of

Haman breathe air? Isn't it the same *HaKadosh Baruch Hu* Who gives us life and makes the sun shine Who is also the בּוֹרֵא רָע? How is this possible?

The answer to this age-old question, as paraphrased in *Tehillim* (92:8), בִּפְרֹחַ רְשָׁעִים כְּמוֹ עֵשֶׂב וַיָּצִיצוּ כָּל פֹּעֲלֵי אָוֶן, *When the wicked bloom like grass and all the iniquitous blossom,* has not been revealed to us. This secret remains with *HaKadosh Baruch Hu* only — at least in this world, in which He has revealed to us only segments of His creation, but not the totality of it. The answer to this question is not part of His revelation to the human world.

The *Anshei Knesses HaGedolah,* who composed the *berachah* of יוֹצֵר אוֹר, did not want to use the words וּבוֹרֵא רָע, so they substituted וּבוֹרֵא אֶת הַכֹּל, meaning, "He created the totality of the universe, including evil." While we do not understand this, at least not in this world, we believe *be'emunah sheleimah* that it is the same ה' אֶחָד, *One God,* Who created everything, be it good or bad. Eventually, *l'asid lavo,* we will lead the world in understanding this heretofore unknown explanation. That future time is described: לֹא כָּעוֹלָם הַזֶּה הָעוֹלָם הַבָּא הָעוֹלָם הַזֶּה עַל בְּשׂוֹרוֹת טוֹבוֹת אוֹמֵר בָּרוּךְ הַטּוֹב וְהַמֵּטִיב וְעַל בְּשׂוֹרוֹת רָעוֹת אוֹמֵר בָּרוּךְ דַּיָּין הָאֱמֶת לָעוֹלָם הַבָּא כּוּלוֹ הַטּוֹב וְהַמֵּטִיב, *The World to Come is unlike this world. In this world, upon [hearing] good tidings one says, Blessed [are You, Hashem, Our God, King of the universe,] Who is good and does good; and upon [hearing] bad tidings one says: Blessed [are You etc.] the true Judge. But, in the World to Come, everything will be understood as being only good* (*Pesachim* 50a). At that time, even happenings that we consider as bad or unfortunate in this world will be clearly understood as being *kulo tov.* This is not yet our world; it is the world that will exist after the coming of *Mashiach.*

To the unschooled mind, the words וּבוֹרֵא חֹשֶׁךְ, *He creates darkness,* seem strange. One thinks that darkness is merely the absence of light, and thus, it would not be called a "creation." However, the language of this *berachah* reflects the teaching of the *Chachamim* that darkness is not merely the absence of light, but rather, it is matter in itself (see *Oros HaGra* 149). It is very interesting that modern astrophysicists have almost reached this point in their research.

Before the Creation there was absolutely nothing, *yeish mei'ayin,* and if so, there was no darkness, either. The Torah tells us that at the beginning of the Creation, the earth was in a condition of chaos — תֹּהוּ וָבֹהוּ — and was covered with darkness, וְחֹשֶׁךְ עַל פְּנֵי תְהוֹם. This means that darkness was also included in the creation by *HaKadosh Baruch Hu.* Furthermore, if darkness did not "exist," we would not know that light exists. The only way we can perceive the light is because there is darkness.

The fact that the universe is dark — despite the billions and billions of galaxies from which so much light emanates — is proof that the darkness is so overwhelming that even these billions of enormously powerful light sources — many of which are millions of times more luminous than our own sun — cannot light up the universe.

In summary, the meaning of the *berachah* is: יוֹצֵר אוֹר , He "forms" light, meaning He creates various forms of light; וּבוֹרֵא חֹשֶׁךְ, after He had created darkness, as the background for the light to be perceived; עֹשֶׂה שָׁלוֹם וּבוֹרֵא אֶת הַכֹּל, He makes harmony between the two. Both light and darkness exist, but *HaKadosh Baruch Hu* separated their functions: וַיַּבְדֵּל אֱלֹהִים בֵּין הָאוֹר וּבֵין הַחֹשֶׁךְ.

And now we continue this *berachah* by thanking *HaKadosh Baruch Hu* for illuminating the earth, without which life, as we know it, would be impossible.

ও§ הַמֵּאִיר לָאָרֶץ וְלַדָּרִים עָלֶיהָ בְּרַחֲמִים — **He makes light shine upon the earth, and to those who live upon it with mercy.** The illumination of the earth — for itself, and for the benefit of all human, animal, and vegetable life which inhabit it — is described here as coming from the *middas harachamim* of *HaKadosh Baruch Hu*. This is so because the exact position of the sun vis-a-vis the earth is critical to the life on it, and is therefore a manifestation of the *middas harachamim* of *HaKadosh Baruch Hu*. Were the sun closer to earth, its heat would scorch everything, and if it were farther away from earth, everything on the planet would freeze; life would not be possible either way. Life on earth is therefore dependent on *middas harachamim*.

ও§ וּבְטוּבוֹ מְחַדֵּשׁ בְּכָל יוֹם תָּמִיד מַעֲשֵׂה בְרֵאשִׁית — **And in His goodness He constantly renews, every day, the act of Creation.** The thought of *middas harachamim* is continued here with וּבְטוּבוֹ. This is a reference not only to וַיַּרְא אֱלֹהִים אֶת הָאוֹר כִּי טוֹב, but also to the recurrence of the word and concept of טוֹב in connection with each day of the שֵׁשֶׁת יְמֵי הַמַּעֲשֶׂה, *six days of Creation* (with the exception of the second day). The entire creation is an act of טוֹב by *HaKadosh Baruch Hu*. One tends to take the daily, recurring cycle of sunrise and sunset for granted. However, upon reflection, we must know that the fact that *HaKadosh Baruch Hu* made the earth rotate on its axis today does not mean that it will, necessarily, do so tomorrow. *HaKadosh Baruch Hu* is not compelled by what He created. So we say to *HaKadosh Baruch Hu* here that when we see the sun rise again, we recognize that this is not an automatic natural phenomenon, but וּבְטוּבוֹ, *in His goodness*, He renews His Creation daily. And since the time of sunrise varies as the earth rotates, this daily reenactment of מַעֲשֵׂה בְרֵאשִׁית is תָּמִיד, a constant and continuing process of Creation.

ও§ מָה רַבּוּ מַעֲשֶׂיךָ ה', כֻּלָּם בְּחָכְמָה עָשִׂיתָ — **How manifold are Your works, Hashem, You have made them all with wisdom.** The word עָשִׂיתָ means the way You have finished it; the way in which Your creations present themselves to us. The more we study nature, the more we discover the enormous intelligence behind it. We see that nature is not chaotic, but that each and every aspect of it follows its own set of rules and laws by which it exists.

מָלְאָה הָאָרֶץ קִנְיָנֶךָ — This is normally translated as: **The earth is filled with Your possessions.** However, the word קִנְיָן, *kinyan*, in the language of the *Chachamim* is an act one does to acquire something. For example, if one finds an object which is *hefker* (ownerless), or he purchases something, he actually acquires it only when he makes a *kinyan* on it. This could be done by picking it up (*hagbaah*); by pulling it towards him (*meshichah*); by paying for it (*kesef*); or by other acts of acquisition. All these acts are proofs of possession. Similarly, we say in this *tefillah*, "the world is filled with proofs of Your possession."

If an *apikorus,* nonbeliever, studies nature, he explains the origin of the universe as having come from a spontaneous "Big Bang" which occurred at a given moment, some 20 billion years ago. And as a result of many accidents, coincidences, and random developments, the world as we know it came into existence.

However, the believer looks at the world and says, "The entire world is filled with proofs of Your ownership." When one studies any aspect of nature — whether astronomy, anatomy of the human or animal body, botany, biology, chemistry, physics, or zoology, etc. — he sees that מָלְאָה הָאָרֶץ קִנְיָנֶךָ, the proofs of God's ownership are clearly evident throughout the universe. These fly in the face of any theories of the random development of life.

In this connection, I would like to relate a personal experience. I had traveled overseas many times on slow, conventional, propeller-driven airplanes, which flew at relatively low altitudes. One could clearly see the ocean below, and I would make the requisite *berachah* of עֹשֶׂה מַעֲשֵׂה בְרֵאשִׁית upon seeing it. However, the first time I traveled in a jet aircraft, I was greatly impressed by the fact that the plane flew above the clouds. "Imagine, I am above the clouds!" I thought. When it came time for Shacharis, I asked for, and was given, a small cubicle in which I could put on my *tallis* and *tefillin* and *daven* in privacy. During my *tefillah,* as I gazed down at the clouds, and out at the vastness of the clear, sun-drenched sky, I was greatly moved as I said, יוֹצֵר אוֹר וּבוֹרֵא חֹשֶׁךְ . . . הַמֵּאִיר לָאָרֶץ וְלַדָּרִים עָלֶיהָ בְּרַחֲמִים . . . מָה רַבּוּ מַעֲשֶׂיךָ ה׳, כֻּלָּם בְּחָכְמָה עָשִׂיתָ.

When I returned, I told Rav Breuer that never had I had such *kavannah* and *hisorerus* (awareness) while saying מָה רַבּוּ מַעֲשֶׂיךָ ה׳ as I did on that flight. He listened quietly to my enthusiastic report, and responded with a smile, "I have the same feeling when I look at a simple daisy." (He used the German word "*gensenblumchen.*") Viewing the growth and structure of a simple flower that emanated from a tiny seed tells us just as clearly, מָה רַבּוּ מַעֲשֶׂיךָ ה׳.

My Rebbe, Reb Yerucham Levovitz, the Mirrer *Mashgiach,* would say that just as one is impressed by a very loud, crashing, clap of thunder, and consequently trembles while saying the *berachah* of שֶׁכֹּחוֹ וּגְבוּרָתוֹ מָלֵא עוֹלָם, so should one also tremble and be awe inspired when making the *berachah* שֶׁהַכֹּל נִהְיֶה בִּדְבָרוֹ before drinking a glass of water. The creation of water is just as much a result of the strength and power of *HaKadosh Baruch Hu* as is thunder or lightening.

We need not wait for something extraordinary to happen to us to be inspired by the great intelligence behind the creation, but rather, we should see מָה רַבּוּ מַעֲשֶׂיךָ ה׳ in even the smallest particle of nature.

◆§ הַמֶּלֶךְ הַמְרוֹמָם לְבַדּוֹ מֵאָז, הַמְשֻׁבָּח וְהַמְפֹאָר וְהַמִּתְנַשֵּׂא מִימוֹת עוֹלָם — **The King Who was exalted in solitude before Creation, Who is praised, glorified, and elevated since days of old.** With this introductory sentence, we return to the beginnings of Creation and again refer to the Kabbalistic concept of the "four worlds of Creation." We elaborated upon this in our explanation of אֲדוֹן עוֹלָם, and briefly mentioned it again in our comments on *Kaddish*. These "worlds" are alluded to in the following phrases:

❏ לְבַדּוֹ מֵאָז: The King Who was highly praised then, when He was all alone, before the origin of Creation — this refers to the *Olam Ha'atzilus*;

❏ הַמְשֻׁבָּח: Who was praised in the *Olam Haberiyah*, as *HaKadosh Baruch Hu* developed the Creation *yeish mei'ayin*;

❏ וְהַמְפֹאָר: Who was glorified in the *Olam Hayetzirah*;

❏ וְהַמִּתְנַשֵּׂא מִימוֹת עוֹלָם — Who is elevated in the world as we see it, since the time of the hidden beginning of the *Olam Ha'asiyah*.

◆§ אֱלֹהֵי עוֹלָם, בְּרַחֲמֶיךָ הָרַבִּים רַחֵם עָלֵינוּ — **Eternal God, with Your abundant compassion be compassionate to us.** Now we focus on the world in which we find ourselves, *Olam Hazeh*, for whatever time period *HaKadosh Baruch Hu* has allotted to us. Appropriately, during the morning, the time of sunrise, which is a manifestation of the *middas harachamim*, we appeal to *HaKadosh Baruch Hu,* the God of the world in which we live, to have mercy upon us. בְּרַחֲמֶיךָ הָרַבִּים, with the great compassion you have shown by allowing us to awaken and live another day, רַחֵם עָלֵינוּ, have mercy on us during our entire lifetimes. Then, we proceed to give four "titles" to *HaKadosh Baruch Hu*:

◆§ אֲדוֹן עֻזֵּנוּ, צוּר מִשְׂגַּבֵּנוּ — **Lord Who strengthens us. Rock of our stronghold.** The word מִשְׂגָּב, which really means "a tower of strength," is a combination of שַׂגִּיא, strong, and גָּבוֹהַּ, high.

◆§ מָגֵן יִשְׁעֵנוּ, מִשְׂגָּב בַּעֲדֵנוּ — **Shield of our Salvation, our Tower of Strength.** In the *Siddur HaGra* there is a commentary called *Avnei Eliyahu,* consisting of *peirushim* in the name of the Vilna Gaon and his son R' Avraham. In this commentary, the above four phrases are explained as referring to the four stages of a person's life, during which one is in need of the mercy of *HaKadosh Baruch Hu*.

❏ אֲדוֹן עֻזֵּנוּ refers to infancy. A human being, unlike an animal, is born totally helpless. If its mother, or another nurturer, would not pay attention to it, it could not survive. A young child lacks immunities to illnesses and thus is very vulnerable to disease. If one survives infancy despite all these weaknesses, it is because *HaKadosh Baruch Hu* has been "the Lord of our strength," the One Who has given us our עוֹז, the resistance against the overwhelming forces which could destroy a helpless human life in infancy.

❏ צוּר מִשְׂגַּבֵּנוּ — Then we progress to childhood and adolescence, the time when one "grows up." Having developed from a tiny infant to a grown person, we laud *HaKadosh Baruch Hu* as the Rock upon which our "tower of strength," our physical bodies, have developed, until we become fully mature people.

❏ מָגֵן יִשְׁעֵנוּ — This refers to mature manhood, or womanhood. During this time, *HaKadosh Baruch Hu* serves as the Shield which saves us. We may not even be aware of the dangers from which He has shielded us during this period of our lives. It is a time when we are raising our families in a world filled with manifold dangers, which could shorten our lives and interfere with our health and livelihood and that of our families. If, despite these dangers, we survive through this period into old age, it is only because *HaKadosh Baruch Hu* is our מָגֵן יִשְׁעֵנוּ.

❏ מִשְׂגָּב בַּעֲדֵנוּ — If *HaKadosh Baruch Hu* allows us to reach old age, He is our "stronghold," which provides the strength to continue to live on despite the frailties and weaknesses of advanced age.

When I saw this explanation, it immediately occurred to me that this corresponds exactly to the four periods of the *mitzvah* of *arachin* (valuation; *Vayikra* 27). There the Torah details the amount one would be required to give to the *Beis HaMikdash* if he made a *neder* (oath) to donate to it an amount based on the "value" of a human being. The Torah prescribes a "value" for each of four categories that are based on the age and gender of the person who is the object of the *neder*. The monetary value of each group symbolically evaluates the relationship that *HaKadosh Baruch Hu* has with a person during each of the four periods of his life.

The first group starts at 30 days — when the newborn reaches the age of viability — and goes until 5 years of age. אֲדוֹן עֻזֵּנוּ refers to this period.

The second group is from 5 to 20 years of age. It is to this period that צוּר מִשְׂגַּבֵּנוּ refers.

The third group is from 20 to 60 years of age. This is referred to when we say מָגֵן יִשְׁעֵנוּ.

BIRCHOS KRIAS SHEMA 267

And, finally, the fourth age group is from 60 and over. When we say that *HaKadosh Baruch Hu* is מִשְׂגָּב בַּעֲדֵנוּ, we are referring to this period.

The connection of these four phrases to the four periods of our lives, as reflected in the *mitzvah* of *arachin*, is alluded to in the continuation of this *tefillah*, which is said on Shabbos: אֵין כְּעֶרְכְּךָ וְאֵין זוּלָתֶךָ . . . אֵין כָּמוֹךָ ה׳ אֱלֹהֵינוּ . . ., *There is no comparison to You, there is nothing except for You . . . There is no comparison to You, Hashem, our God . . .* This means that the aforementioned allusion to the concept of *arachin* refers only to human beings, but as to You, *HaKadosh Baruch Hu*, there is no valuation possible.

The following sentence, which begins with אֵל בָּרוּךְ גְּדוֹל דֵּעָה, follows the order of the entire *aleph-beis*. The first word is אֵל, and every word thereafter begins with the succeeding letter, until תָּמִיד, which completes the entire alphabet in its proper sequence. This *tefillah* is structured as a ladder that rises from the physical world and leads directly upwards to the spiritual world. It is noteworthy that this entire *tefillah*, with the *Kedushah d'yeshivah* as its focal point, emphasizes the בָּרוּךְ aspect of *HaKadosh Baruch Hu*. We will develop this thought further as we progress.

[Ed. note: Regarding the meaning of *Kedushah d'yeshivah* see further on בָּרוּךְ כְּבוֹד ה׳ מִמְּקוֹמוֹ.]

◆§ אֵל בָּרוּךְ גְּדוֹל דֵּעָה — **The Almighty, Blessed, the One of Great Knowledge.** The first "step" on this "ladder" describes *HaKadosh Baruch Hu* as the One Who created human beings on earth and has given them דֵּעָה, *intelligence,* as we say in *Shemoneh Esrei*: אַתָּה חוֹנֵן לְאָדָם דַּעַת, *You mercifully bestow knowledge to man.* Here, we address *HaKadosh Baruch Hu* as the One from Whom all intelligence originates; He is the גְּדוֹל דֵּעָה, the One with the Supreme Knowledge.

◆§ הֵכִין וּפָעַל זָהֳרֵי חַמָּה — **He has prepared, and made work, the rays of the sun.** The rungs of this ladder now rise from Earth to our solar system, in which *HaKadosh Baruch Hu* has planted our sun to shine on all its planets.

◆§ טוֹב יָצַר כָּבוֹד לִשְׁמוֹ — **He formed all this goodness as glory for His Name.** We now climb yet higher on this ladder, and gain an overview of the entire physical universe, with all its heavenly bodies. According to Rav Samson R. Hirsch the word טוֹב here is a metaphor for all of creation: וַיַּרְא אֱלֹהִים אֶת כָּל אֲשֶׁר עָשָׂה וְהִנֵּה טוֹב מְאֹד, *And God saw all that He had made, and behold it was very good* (*Bereishis* 1:31). The phrase then means, *He formed all this goodness as glory for His Name.* This corresponds to the saying of *Chazal*: כָּל מַה שֶּׁבָּרָא הקב״ה בְּעוֹלָמוֹ לֹא בְרָאוֹ אֶלָּא לִכְבוֹדוֹ, *All that the Holy One, Blessed is He, created in His world, He created solely for His glory* (*Pirkei Avos* 6:11). The word כָּבוֹד, as used here, does not have the usual meaning, "honor," of which *HaKadosh Baruch Hu*, in his perfection, has no need; rather, it means "glory," with the meaning, "an affirmation that He exists." He makes His presence known by virtue of His creations. This is similar to וְאִכָּבְדָה בְּפַרְעֹה, *I wish to make Pharaoh know that I exist* (Shemos 14:4).

מְאוֹרוֹת נָתַן סְבִיבוֹת עֻזּוֹ — He has, therefore, placed luminaries surrounding His power. The concept of a hidden Creator is so elusive that the only way one can recognize that *HaKadosh Baruch Hu* exists is through His creations. When we look at the multitude of billions of luminaries in the universe, we recognize that a most powerful Creator brought all this into existence. It is this conclusion that is the "glory" that *HaKadosh Baruch Hu* seeks.

Continuing up the ladder, having passed through our solar system and the entire starry physical universe, we now reach the metaphysical, spiritual world of the *malachim,* which is reflected in the following:

פִּנּוֹת צְבָאָיו קְדוֹשִׁים רוֹמְמֵי שַׁדַּי — The masters (officers) of His spiritual hosts, those Holy beings, are the ones who praise Hakadosh Baruch Hu as שַׁדַּי. Only *malachim* can truly comprehend the meaning of שַׁדַּי as the Name of *HaKadosh Baruch Hu* in which He reveals Himself as having completed His Creation of the universe: שֶׁאָמַר לְעוֹלָמוֹ דַּי, *He announced to His world: Enough!* The Gemara (*Chagigah* 12a) talks of the universe expanding until *HaKadosh Baruch Hu* declared it complete and stopped its further development. בְּשָׁעָה שֶׁבָּרָא הקב״ה אֶת הָעוֹלָם הָיָה מַרְחִיב וְהוֹלֵךְ ... עַד שֶׁגָּעַר בּוֹ הקב״ה וְהֶעֱמִידוֹ, *During the Creation of the universe it was constantly expanding, until God demanded that it stop.*

However, we human beings have only a limited view of the Creation. When we view the universe through mighty telescopes, we see what appears to be a still-expanding universe, with galaxies moving away from each other. This is so because what we observe today is how the universe looked during the six days of Creation, which, to the scientists, appears as if it occurred many millions of light years ago. However, we cannot observe what is happening now, we cannot see the universe in its completed state of דַּי. Only the *malachim* can have this overview.

[Ed. note: The Rav wrote a detailed essay called "How Old is the Universe?" in which he deals with the apparent contradiction between scientific theory regarding the age of the universe and the Torah. This can be found in *Selected Writings,* p. 251, published by C.I.S. — 1988.]

תָּמִיד מְסַפְּרִים כְּבוֹד אֵל וּקְדֻשָּׁתוֹ — Constantly relate the honor of God and His sanctity. We have now reached the ת of the *aleph-beis,* representing the pinnacle of our ascent on this "ladder," which spans the distance between the human-material world and the spiritual world. The previously referred to *malachim* who exist in this spiritual world live forever, and thus are able to "constantly tell of the glory of the Almighty and His Holiness."

However, these spiritual creatures have no free will, and they are compelled by the nature of their being to function in the way they were created. These *malachim* were created to express כְּבוֹד אֵל וּקְדֻשָּׁתוֹ, and they can do no less.

Now, the following sentence shifts our focus back to human beings, who, unlike the *malachim,* are endowed by *HaKadosh Baruch Hu* with free will. We can study nature through a microscope or a telescope, and can recognize Him as the Creator of all this, or ח"ו deny that He exists (see *Rambam, Hil. Teshuvah* Ch. 5). And when, nevertheless, we do recognize *HaKadosh Baruch Hu* as the Creator of the world, and are *mekabel ol Malchus Shamayim* with our free will, this brings us to a higher level than that of the previously referred-to *malachim*. Therefore, from the human point of view, we say:

תִּתְבָּרַךְ ה' אֱלֹהֵינוּ עַל שֶׁבַח מַעֲשֵׂה יָדֶיךָ, וְעַל מְאוֹרֵי אוֹר שֶׁעָשִׂיתָ, יְפָאֲרוּךָ, סֶּלָה — **You, our God, shall be blessed higher than the praise of the work of Your hands, and higher than the luminaries that You have made, which constantly glorify You, Selah.** We, with our *bechirah chafshis,* have freely chosen You as אֱלֹהֵינוּ, and therefore, our praise of You is on a higher level than that of the spiritual beings and physical heavenly bodies which You have created, who are compelled by their very nature to praise Your glory.

The aforementioned sentence — and its meaning — refers to all human beings, but the following refers to *Bnei Yisrael,* from the point of view of their special relationship with *HaKadosh Baruch Hu.*

תִּתְבָּרַךְ צוּרֵנוּ מַלְכֵּנוּ וְגֹאֲלֵנוּ, בּוֹרֵא קְדוֹשִׁים — **May our Rock, our King, and our Redeemer be blessed. He is the One Who created the holy beings,** the *malachim.*

יִשְׁתַּבַּח שִׁמְךָ לָעַד מַלְכֵּנוּ — **May Your Name be praised forever, our King.** We have accepted *HaKadosh Baruch Hu* as our King; we have made the free-willed choice to accept His *ol Malchus Shamayim.* This is the essence of קְרִיאַת שְׁמַע, toward which this *berachah* is leading.

יוֹצֵר מְשָׁרְתִים — **Who forms servants.** These servants include various types of *malachim,* some of which are known to us as *Ofanim, Chayos, Serafim, Keruvim.* However, the commentators have explained that the מְשָׁרְתִים in this *tefillah* are those special *malachim* (*Chagigah* 14a) that are created daily for the purpose of expressing *shirah* to *HaKadosh Baruch Hu.* And when they have fulfilled their purpose, they cease to exist. The Gemara there bases this on the words, חֲדָשִׁים לַבְּקָרִים, *They are new every morning* (*Eichah* 3:23). These spiritual beings are not the same as certain other *malachim* who have existed since Creation, and who live forever.

We know the names of several of these, such as Michael and Gavriel.

However, in my opinion, these מְשָׁרְתִים also include those *tzaddikim* who lived in this world with the hope that after their *neshamos* were transferred by *HaKadosh Baruch Hu* from their physical environment in this world to *Olam Haba,* their *neshamos* would merit to be placed near the *Kisei HaKavod,* next to the *malachim.* This would be the fulfillment of the words of *Kedushah,* in which we express our desire to emulate the *malachim* and come close to *HaKadosh Baruch Hu:* נְקַדֵּשׁ אֶת שִׁמְךָ בָּעוֹלָם כְּשֵׁם שֶׁמַּקְדִּישִׁים אוֹתוֹ בִּשְׁמֵי מָרוֹם, *We shall sanctify Your Name in this world, just as they sanctify It in heaven above.* This means that we have the desire to sanctify *HaKadosh Baruch Hu* in the same way as the *malachim* do in heaven. Whereupon, we quote, קָדוֹשׁ קָדוֹשׁ קָדוֹשׁ ה' צְבָאוֹת מְלֹא כָל הָאָרֶץ כְּבוֹדוֹ, *Holy, holy, holy is Hashem, Master of Legions, the whole world is filled with His glory* (*Yeshayahu* 6:3). During *Kedushah* in *Shemoneh Esrei,* we symbolize our desire to emulate the *malachim* by raising ourselves up from the ground while saying these words, similar to the flying motion of the *malachim,* described there by Yeshayahu (see *Rema, Orach Chaim* 125).

This explanation of the expanded meaning of מְשָׁרְתִים to include the *neshamos* of the *tzaddikim* is supported by the text of this *tefillah,* תִּתְבָּרֵךְ צוּרֵנוּ. The word כֻּלָּם is repeated eight times, underscored by יַחַד and כֻּלָּם כְּאֶחָד, making a total of ten references to this broad and disparate group of מְשָׁרְתִים.

◆§ וַאֲשֶׁר מְשָׁרְתָיו כֻּלָּם עוֹמְדִים בְּרוּם עוֹלָם §◆ — **And that all of His servants stand at the heights of the world.** This includes the *malachim* and the *neshamos* of *tzaddikim.*

◆§ וּמַשְׁמִיעִים בְּיִרְאָה יַחַד בְּקוֹל דִּבְרֵי אֱלֹהִים חַיִּים וּמֶלֶךְ עוֹלָם §◆ — **And, in fear, they loudly proclaim together** — both the *malachim* and the *neshamos* of *tzaddikim* — **the words of the living God and King of the world.**

◆§ כֻּלָּם אֲהוּבִים §◆ — **They are all beloved.** They all love each other. Notwithstanding the difference between these two groups, there is mutual love between them. Both the *malachim* who never knew sin, and the *neshamos* of the *tzaddikim* who had encountered sin and overcame it — or who were *baalei teshuvah* — through their own *bechirah,* have united for one purpose.

◆§ כֻּלָּם בְּרוּרִים, כֻּלָּם גִּבּוֹרִים §◆ — **They are all pure; they are all mighty.** They are all pure, and are given the same powers by *HaKadosh Baruch Hu.*

◆§ וְכֻלָּם עוֹשִׂים בְּאֵימָה וּבְיִרְאָה רְצוֹן קוֹנָם §◆ — **And all of them** — the *malachim* and the *neshamos* of *tzaddikim* — **carry out the will of their Creator in awe and fear.**

וְכֻלָּם פּוֹתְחִים אֶת פִּיהֶם בִּקְדֻשָּׁה וּבְטָהֳרָה, בְּשִׁירָה וּבְזִמְרָה, וּמְבָרְכִים וּמְשַׁבְּחִים וּמְפָאֲרִים וּמַעֲרִיצִים וּמַקְדִּישִׁים וּמַמְלִיכִים — **And they all open their mouth in holiness and purity, in song and hymn — and bless, praise, glorify, acknowledge His strength, sanctify and declare the kingship of —** This combined group of exalted spiritual beings joins together, and they all open their mouths in holiness and purity with these ten expressions of praise to *HaKadosh Baruch Hu*. The word וּמַעֲרִיצִים, from עָרִיץ, *powerful,* means they praise *HaKadosh Baruch Hu* as the "All-Powerful."

[Ed. note: The Rav twice pointed out that the number ten was reflected in the words of this *tefillah*. However, unfortunately, he did not explain its significance here.]

אֶת שֵׁם הָאֵל הַמֶּלֶךְ הַגָּדוֹל הַגִּבּוֹר וְהַנּוֹרָא קָדוֹשׁ הוּא — **The Name of God, the great, mighty, and awesome King; holy is He.** This phrase is a continuation of the previous וּמַמְלִיכִים.

וְכֻלָּם מְקַבְּלִים עֲלֵיהֶם עֹל מַלְכוּת שָׁמַיִם זֶה מִזֶּה וְנוֹתְנִים רְשׁוּת זֶה לָזֶה — **Then they all accept upon themselves the yoke of Heavenly sovereignty from one another, and grant permission to one another.** And these two groups of spiritual beings, the *malachim* and the *neshamos* of the *tzaddikim,* accept upon themselves the rule of Heaven, and harmoniously accept each other's invitation to sanctify their Maker. Each of these two groups has an advantage in its level of *kedushah* that the other does not have. Nevertheless, they harmoniously grant their counterparts permission:

לְהַקְדִּישׁ לְיוֹצְרָם בְּנַחַת רוּחַ — **To sanctify their Creator with calmness of the mind.** This is the world where everything is calm. This is what is called קוֹרַת רוּחַ בָּעוֹלָם הַבָּא, *spiritual bliss in the World to Come. Chazal* tell us, יָפָה שָׁעָה אַחַת שֶׁל קוֹרַת רוּחַ בָּעוֹלָם הַבָּא מִכֹּל חַיֵּי הָעוֹלָם הַזֶּה, *Even one moment of spiritual bliss in the World to Come is greater than all of the pleasures of this world* (Pirkei Avos 4:22).

בְּשָׂפָה בְרוּרָה וּבִנְעִימָה. קְדֻשָּׁה כֻּלָּם כְּאֶחָד עוֹנִים וְאוֹמְרִים בְּיִרְאָה — **With a purified language, in a sweet melody. Together, in awe, they all proclaim the words of holiness** (קָדוֹשׁ קָדוֹשׁ קָדוֹשׁ) that follow.

קְדֻשָׁה דִישִׁיבָה / Kedushah D'Yeshivah

קָדוֹשׁ קָדוֹשׁ קָדוֹשׁ ה' צְבָאוֹת מְלֹא כָל הָאָרֶץ כְּבוֹדוֹ. וְהָאוֹפַנִּים וְחַיּוֹת הַקֹּדֶשׁ בְּרַעַשׁ גָּדוֹל מִתְנַשְּׂאִים לְעֻמַּת שְׂרָפִים. לְעֻמָּתָם מְשַׁבְּחִים וְאוֹמְרִים: בָּרוּךְ כְּבוֹד ה' מִמְּקוֹמוֹ — Holy, holy, holy is Hashem, Master of Legions, the whole world is filled with His glory. Then the *Ofanim* and the holy *Chayos* with great noise raise themselves toward the *Serafim*. Facing them they give praise, saying: Blessed is the glory of Hashem from His place.

There are three times in the *tefillah* when we incorporate these *pesukim* of *Kedushah*, which are taken from the *Neviim*. The first *pasuk*, קָדוֹשׁ קָדוֹשׁ קָדוֹשׁ ה' צְבָאוֹת מְלֹא כָל הָאָרֶץ כְּבוֹדוֹ, is from *Yeshayahu* 6:3, and the second *pasuk*, בָּרוּךְ כְּבוֹד ה' מִמְּקוֹמוֹ, from *Yechezkel* 3:12.

The reciting of these two *pesukim* is of such great importance that one may even interrupt *Krias Shema* to join the *tzibbur* in saying them.

The *Kedushah* in the *berachah* of יוֹצֵר אוֹר is called קְדֻשָׁה דִישִׁיבָה, *Kedushah d'yeshivah*, because it is said while sitting. In fact, one *should* sit while saying all of the *berachos* of *Krias Shema*, so that one may purposefully stand up for the *Shemoneh Esrei* to show that it is the high point of the entire *tefillah*. This is often characterized by the words *omdim b'tefillah* (one stands up for the *tefillah*). As we proceed to explain the *Kedushah*, we will offer an additional reason for sitting while reciting it here. (See *Ba'er Heitev*, to *Orach Chaim* 59:3, specifically with regard to sitting while saying this *Kedushah*.)

The second time, the *Kedushah* is recited in conjunction with the *shaliach tzibbur* during the repetition of the *Shemoneh Esrei*. There it is called קְדֻשָּׁה דַעֲמִידָה, *Kedushah da'amidah*, because it is said while standing, as a part of the *Amidah*, or *Shemoneh Esrei*.

The third time it is said after the *Shemoneh Esrei* in וּבָא לְצִיּוֹן גּוֹאֵל, and there it is called קְדֻשָּׁה דְסִדְרָא, *Kedushah d'sidra*.

These quotations from the *Neviim* describe what is happening in *Olam Haba*, in the *shmei marom* (the spiritual "heaven above"): the world where the *neshamos* of Avraham, Yitzchak, Yaakov and all the other *tzaddikim* and *chassidim* exist. These *neshamos*, together with the *malachim*, express these exalted words of praise concerning *HaKadosh Baruch Hu*. We have no understanding of that world other than that it exists.

I have explained many times that when we discuss subjects such as these details of the *malachim* and *Maaseh Merkavah*, which were revealed to the *Neviim*, we can have no real conception of the true meaning of the subject matter. Such a discussion is analogous to people who were born sightless discussing traffic lights. They may say that red means "stop" and green means "go," but since such people have never seen light or colors, they can have no real conception of what these words mean. Similarly, we can have no conception of the various spiritual creatures known as *Ofanim, Chayos, Serafim, Keruvim, Eilim* or *Shinanim,* nor of their functions and activities which are described in the prophecies of Yeshayahu and Yechezkel.

Notwithstanding this, we can have some limited understanding of what these *pesukim* mean.

The threefold repetition, קָדוֹשׁ קָדוֹשׁ קָדוֹשׁ ה׳ צְבָאוֹת, can be interpreted in two ways. One is that *HaKadosh Baruch Hu* is extolled here by the *malachim* and the *neshamos* of the *tzaddikim* in terms of *ascending* levels of sanctity. In accordance with this interpretation of קָדוֹשׁ, the idea here is that the higher any creature — spiritual or physical — elevates itself toward *HaKadosh Baruch Hu,* the higher the conception it has of *HaKadosh Baruch Hu.* This is so because *HaKadosh Baruch Hu* Himself is totally removed from any of His creatures; He is the ultimate קָדוֹשׁ. This way of understanding it is in accordance with: אָדָם מְקַדֵּשׁ עַצְמוֹ מְעַט מְקַדְּשִׁין אוֹתוֹ הַרְבֵּה; מִלְּמַטָּה מְקַדְּשִׁין אוֹתוֹ מִלְמַעְלָה, *If a person sanctifies himself in a small measure, he will be sanctified in a large measure; if one sanctifies himself here on earth, he will become sanctified in the world above* (Yoma 39a).

מְלֹא כָל הָאָרֶץ כְּבוֹדוֹ does not refer to our earth, but rather, it is to be understood as that place where this pronouncement is made. This would be in the same sense as, וָאֵרֶא הַחַיּוֹת וְהִנֵּה אוֹפַן אֶחָד בָּאָרֶץ, *I saw the Chayos — and behold! one Ofan was on the surface* (Yechezkel 1:15); and וּבְהִנָּשֵׂא הַחַיּוֹת מֵעַל הָאָרֶץ יִנָּשְׂאוּ הָאוֹפַנִּים, *and when the Chayos were lifted from upon the surface, the Ofanim were lifted* (ibid. v.19). There it means that as they praise *HaKadosh Baruch Hu,* the *malachim* elevate themselves higher than their previous level of *kedushah.* Similarly, מְלֹא כָל הָאָרֶץ כְּבוֹדוֹ here refers to the place where these *malachim* and *neshamos* of *tzaddikim* are when they make this pronouncement of קָדוֹשׁ קָדוֹשׁ קָדוֹשׁ ה׳ צְבָאוֹת, which includes the entirety of creation, from the spiritual world down to our physical world.

The other way of understanding it is in a *descending* order of holiness. Rav Samson R. Hirsch, in accordance with the *Targum Yonasan ben Uziel,* which is quoted in וּבָא לְצִיּוֹן גּוֹאֵל, explains that the *Navi* is visualizing the *kedushah* descending from the highest level to a lower level. It is thus קְדֻשָּׁה דְסִדְרָא, *Kedushah d'sidra,* because it descends in the ordinary world order of things:

First, there is the highest level: קַדִּישׁ בִּשְׁמֵי מְרוֹמָא עִלָּאָה בֵּית שְׁכִינְתֵּהּ, *He is holy in the highest world of heaven, the place of His Presence.* Then, descending to our world: קַדִּישׁ עַל אַרְעָא עוֹבַד גְּבוּרְתֵּהּ, *He is holy on earth which was created by His power.* Finally, referring to the future: קַדִּישׁ לְעָלַם וּלְעָלְמֵי עָלְמַיָּא, ה׳ צְבָאוֹת, מַלְיָא כָל אַרְעָא זִיו יְקָרֵהּ, *He is holy for all future times, the God of Hosts; the entire world* (our world) *is filled with the splendor of His* glory. This *splendor of His glory* is what moves people, sometimes to tears or to singing, when they see the beauty of nature, or are fascinated when they see the sun setting into the ocean, or rising at the top of a mountain. We cannot see the *Shechinah*, but we can see and appreciate the זִיו יְקָרֵהּ, *splendor of His glory* — which is the reflection of His *Shechinah* — in the beauty of nature that He has created.

These *pesukim* of *Kedushah* are taken from the *Maaseh Merkavah*, prophetic revelations regarding the *Kisei HaKavod*, which were stated in two different forms by the *Neviim*.

The first one, קָדוֹשׁ קָדוֹשׁ קָדוֹשׁ, which was said by Yeshayahu, is read as the *haftarah* of *Parashas Yisro*: בִּשְׁנַת מוֹת הַמֶּלֶךְ עֻזִּיָּהוּ וָאֶרְאֶה אֶת אֲדֹנָי יֹשֵׁב עַל כִּסֵּא רָם וְנִשָּׂא וְשׁוּלָיו מְלֵאִים אֶת הַהֵיכָל. שְׂרָפִים עֹמְדִים מִמַּעַל לוֹ, שֵׁשׁ כְּנָפַיִם שֵׁשׁ כְּנָפַיִם לְאֶחָד, בִּשְׁתַּיִם יְכַסֶּה פָנָיו וּבִשְׁתַּיִם יְכַסֶּה רַגְלָיו וּבִשְׁתַּיִם יְעוֹפֵף. וְקָרָא זֶה אֶל זֶה וְאָמַר קָדוֹשׁ קָדוֹשׁ קָדוֹשׁ ה' צְבָאוֹת, מְלֹא כָל הָאָרֶץ כְּבוֹדוֹ, *In the year of King Uzziahu's death, I saw the Lord sitting upon a high and lofty throne, and its legs filled the Temple. Serafim were standing above, at His service. Each one had six wings; with two it would cover its face, with two it would cover its legs, and with two if would fly. And one would call to another and say, "Holy, holy, holy, is Hashem, Master of Legions, the whole world is filled with His glory"* (*Yeshayahu* 6:1-3).

The second revelation, בָּרוּךְ כְּבוֹד ה' מִמְּקוֹמוֹ, is read as the *haftarah* of the first day of Shavuos: וַיְהִי בִּשְׁלֹשִׁים שָׁנָה בָּרְבִיעִי בַּחֲמִשָּׁה לַחֹדֶשׁ וַאֲנִי בְתוֹךְ הַגּוֹלָה עַל נְהַר כְּבָר נִפְתְּחוּ הַשָּׁמַיִם וָאֶרְאֶה מַרְאוֹת אֱלֹהִים, *It happened in the thirtieth year, in the fourth month, on the fifth of the month, as I was among the exile by the River Chebar; the heavens opened and I saw visions of God* (*Yechezkel* 1:1).

In the third chapter, Yechezkel tells how he was directed by *HaKadosh Baruch Hu* to bring his message of *teshuvah* to the people who were in exile in Babylonia, whether they wanted to listen or not: וַיֹּאמֶר אֵלַי בֶּן אָדָם אֶת כָּל דְּבָרַי אֲשֶׁר אֲדַבֵּר אֵלֶיךָ קַח בִּלְבָבְךָ וּבְאָזְנֶיךָ שְׁמָע. וְלֵךְ בֹּא אֶל הַגּוֹלָה אֶל בְּנֵי עַמְּךָ וְדִבַּרְתָּ אֲלֵיהֶם וְאָמַרְתָּ אֲלֵיהֶם כֹּה אָמַר אֲדֹנָי אֱלֹהִים אִם יִשְׁמְעוּ וְאִם יֶחְדָּלוּ, *Then He said to me, "Son of man, all my words that I will speak to you, take into your heart and hearken with your ears; and go come to the exile, to the children of your people, and speak to them. Say to them, "Thus says the Lord, whether they will heed or whether they will refrain"* (ibid. 3:10-11).

As Yechezkel HaNavi was preparing to deliver his message, he suddenly became aware of another *nevuah*, which he describes as follows: וַתִּשָּׂאֵנִי רוּחַ וָאֶשְׁמַע אַחֲרַי קוֹל רַעַשׁ גָּדוֹל בָּרוּךְ כְּבוֹד ה' מִמְּקוֹמוֹ, *A spirit lifted me up, and I heard a great noise behind me, saying, "Blessed be the glory of Hashem from His place"* (ibid. v. 12).

He continues in the next sentence, where he describes the source of this "noise" as the wings of certain *malachim*, called *Chayos* and *Ofanim*, knocking against each other, creating "opposing noises": וְקוֹל כַּנְפֵי הַחַיּוֹת מַשִּׁיקוֹת אִשָּׁה אֶל אֲחוֹתָהּ, וְקוֹל הָאוֹפַנִּים לְעֻמָּתָם, וְקוֹל רַעַשׁ גָּדוֹל, *And the sound of wings*

KEDUSHAH D'YESHIVAH ~ 275

of the Chayos knocking against one another, and the sound of the Ofanim opposite them, and the sound of a great noise (ibid. v. 13).

Unquestionably, this קוֹל רַעַשׁ גָּדוֹל, which literally means an earthquake or major upheaval of some sort, must have great significance in this *nevuah*. The organizers of the *tefillah* considered it powerful enough to incorporate it in the *Kedushah d'yeshivah* of יוֹצֵר אוֹר (וְהָאוֹפַנִּים וְחַיּוֹת הַקֹּדֶשׁ בְּרַעַשׁ גָּדוֹל וגו'), and also in the *Kedushah da'amidah* of Shabbos Shacharis (אָז בְּקוֹל רַעַשׁ גָּדוֹל אַדִּיר וְחָזָק מַשְׁמִיעִים קוֹל וגו').

The *nevuah* describes this קוֹל רַעַשׁ גָּדוֹל that the *Ofanim* and *Chayos HaKodesh* create as being לְעֻמָּתָם, *in opposition to them*. This seems to indicate that the new pronouncement of בָּרוּךְ כְּבוֹד ה' מִמְּקוֹמוֹ is the opposite message — a total reversal of the earlier one of קָדוֹשׁ קָדוֹשׁ — found in Yeshayahu. This would account for the great noise, or upheaval, which this new message embodies. We must now attempt to understand the meaning of these two opposite messages.

The first message of קָדוֹשׁ קָדוֹשׁ קָדוֹשׁ expresses the idea of the total separation of *HaKadosh Baruch Hu* from any of His creations. The underlying meaning of קָדֵשׁ is "separation." For instance, קְדֹשִׁים תִּהְיוּ, normally translated as *You shall be holy* (*Vayikra* 19:2), is explained by Rashi to mean, הֱווּ פְרוּשִׁים מִן הָעֲרָיוֹת וּמִן הָעֲבֵירָה, *Keep yourselves far away from immorality and from sin,* which, in any case, conveys the thought: "Remove yourselves away from prohibited unions." When we refer to *HaKadosh Baruch Hu* as קָדוֹשׁ, we mean that He is elevated above, and removed from, our power of perception. This concept of God's total separation from his creations is applicable not only to human beings but also to the spiritual beings, the *malachim*.

This is the meaning of אַתָּה קָדוֹשׁ, or קָדוֹשׁ אַתָּה. It conveys the thought that *HaKadosh Baruch Hu* is removed from, and higher than, the perception of any creature, be it a human being or a *malach*. This total separation remains intact no matter how high any physical or spiritual creature raises itself. The higher the creatures elevate themselves, the more they perceive that *HaKadosh Baruch Hu* is ever higher. Even if the *malachim* "flap their wings," which represents their raising themselves מִן הָאָרֶץ, from their present levels, they find that *HaKadosh Baruch Hu* is still higher and higher; He is קָדוֹשׁ קָדוֹשׁ קָדוֹשׁ, far removed and higher than is comprehensible to any creature. This is expressed in the *Kedushah* of Mussaf on Shabbos, where we say מְשָׁרְתָיו שׁוֹאֲלִים זֶה לָזֶה, *His servants ask each other,* אַיֵּה מְקוֹם כְּבוֹדוֹ, *Where is the place of His glory?* In their attempt to come closer to *HaKadosh Baruch Hu,* they have come to the conclusion that no matter how high they go, *HaKadosh Baruch Hu* is still higher than they are.

We understand very little of the meaning of "wings of the *Chayos,*" and the differences between the "six-winged" creatures mentioned in Yeshayahu, and those with "four wings," described by Yechezkel. Nevertheless, it seems clear that the thought conveyed by the "wings" is related to the idea of an elevation from a lower position to a higher one. The Gemara states that the *malachim* of Yeshayahu had six wings because the *Beis HaMikdash* still existed at that time, while those of Yechezkel had only four wings, because his *nevuah* was said shortly before the *churban Beis HaMikdash,* in Babylonia, where a substantial portion of the Jewish people had already been exiled (*Chagigah* 13b).

The commentaries which we can understand (others are Kabbalistic in nature and are extremely difficult to understand) give us some idea of the symbolism of those "wings." They say that the "six wings" of these creatures correspond to the six words of בָּרוּךְ שֵׁם כְּבוֹד מַלְכוּתוֹ לְעוֹלָם וָעֶד. And after the destruction of the *Beis HaMikdash,* the two "middle wings" — corresponding to כְּבוֹד מַלְכוּתוֹ — were removed, leaving them with only four wings, as depicted in Yechezkel. This is why in the Mussaf of the *Shalosh Regalim,* when we are *mispallel* for the restoration of the *Beis HaMikdash,* we say גַּלֵּה כְּבוֹד מַלְכוּתְךָ עָלֵינוּ מְהֵרָה,,, *Reveal to us the glory of Your Kingship soon.*

The unique *minhag* Frankfurt in the *piyut* of Rosh Hashanah and Yom Kippur, which introduces the *Kedushah,* is to leave out the words עַל יַד נְבִיאֶךָ, and say only the six words כַּכָּתוּב וְקָרָא זֶה אֶל זֶה וְאָמַר, because this alludes to the six wings of the *malachim* that exist during the time when the *Beis HaMikdash* is in existence.

After the conclusion of the *Kedushah* in *Shemoneh Esrei,* we say, לְדוֹר וָדוֹר נַגִּיד גָּדְלֶךָ וּלְנֵצַח נְצָחִים קְדֻשָּׁתְךָ נַקְדִּישׁ, *From generation to generation we shall relate Your greatness and for eternity of eternities we shall proclaim Your holiness.* The meaning of נֵצַח נְצָחִים here is a reference to the *malachim* and the *neshamos* of the *tzaddikim* who are already in a life of נֵצַח, eternity. These spiritual beings express their desire to proclaim Your *kedushah* from one state of נֵצַח to a yet higher level, נֵצַח נְצָחִים, *eternity of eternities.*

But upon doing so, they become increasingly aware that *HaKadosh Baruch Hu* is still higher and higher, and that He will always remain הָאֵל הַקָּדוֹשׁ, incomprehensible and far removed from any of His creatures. Therefore, the meaning of קָדוֹשׁ קָדוֹשׁ קָדוֹשׁ is that *HaKadosh Baruch Hu* is still higher, higher, and ever higher than we can possibly comprehend.

However, the other message of בָּרוּךְ כְּבוֹד ה' מִמְּקוֹמוֹ teaches the *very opposite* — לְעֻמָּתָם — that *HaKadosh Baruch Hu* is as *close* as possible to His creatures. The message of בָּרוּךְ teaches that notwithstanding the fact that *HaKadosh Baruch Hu* is far removed from our comprehension, the *malachim* sense that, nevertheless, He is coming closer, closer, and closer to them. And they excitedly announce His presence by saying בָּרוּךְ כְּבוֹד ה' מִמְּקוֹמוֹ. Paraphrased, this means the *malachim* say that "*HaKadosh Baruch Hu* has come from the incomprehensible and unfathomable to a place so close to us that we sense His presence, and therefore we loudly proclaim בָּרוּךְ."

KEDUSHAH D'YESHIVAH ⁓ 277

This, then, is the meaning of the רַעַשׁ גָּדוֹל, this "loud noise," which is made as the *Ofanim* and the *Chayos HaKodesh* express the בָּרוּךְ attribute — which is the very opposite of what the *Serafim* had said, לְעֻמָּתָם שְׂרָפִים, לְעֻמָּתָם. The *Ofanim* and the *Chayos HaKodesh* excitedly declare that, notwithstanding the fact that *HaKadosh Baruch Hu* is קָדוֹשׁ, incomprehensible and unreachable, as the *Serafim* had stressed, the opposite is also true. He is also בָּרוּךְ — very, very close to His creatures.

This explanation, in addition to the earlier one, affords us a better understanding of the reason for the *minhag* to sit down while saying the *Kedushah d'yeshivah*, as we shall explain.

Midrash Rabbah (*Bereishis* 48:6) states the following with regard to the verse: וַיֵּרָא אֵלָיו ה' בְּאֵלֹנֵי מַמְרֵא וְהוּא יֹשֵׁב פֶּתַח הָאֹהֶל כְּחֹם הַיּוֹם, *Hashem appeared to him in the Plains of Mamre while he was sitting at the entrance of the tent in the heat of the day* (*Bereishis* 18:1). The *Midrash* comments: בִּקֵּשׁ לַעֲמוֹד, אָמַר לוֹ הקב"ה שֵׁב וְאַתָּה סִימָן לְבָנֶיךָ, מָה אַתָּה יוֹשֵׁב וּשְׁכִינָה עוֹמֶדֶת, כָּךְ בָּנֶיךָ יוֹשְׁבִים וּשְׁכִינָה עוֹמֶדֶת עַל גַּבָּן, כְּשֶׁיִּשְׂרָאֵל נִכְנָסִים לְבָתֵּי כְּנֵסִיּוֹת וּלְבָתֵּי מִדְרָשׁוֹת וְקוֹרִין קְרִיאַת שְׁמַע וְהֵן יוֹשְׁבִים וַאֲנִי בִּכְבוֹדִי עוֹמֵד עַל גַּבָּן, שֶׁנֶּאֱמַר אֱלֹהִים נִצָּב בַּעֲדַת אֵל, *He wanted to rise, but Hashem said to him: Sit, and you will be an example to your descendants. Just as you sit and the Holy Presence stands, so are your children to sit when they are in their houses of prayer or study and they read the Shema while I in My honor stand before them. This is based on the pasuk: God stands in the Divine Tribunal* (*Tehillim* 82:1).

Rashi (ibid.) quotes a slightly different version of this *Midrash*: וְהוּא יֹשֵׁב יָשַׁב כְּתִיב, בִּקֵּשׁ לַעֲמוֹד אָמַר לוֹ הקב"ה שֵׁב וַאֲנִי אֶעֱמוֹד וְאַתָּה סִימָן לְבָנֶיךָ שֶׁעָתִיד אֲנִי לְהִתְיַצֵּב בַּעֲדַת הַדַּיָּנִין וְהֵן יוֹשְׁבִין, שֶׁנֶּאֱמַר אֱלֹהִים נִצָּב בַּעֲדַת אֵל, יָשֵׁב *is spelled without a* ו, *as if it read* יָשַׁב, "*sat.*" *This teaches us that Avraham wanted to stand out of respect for the Divine Presence. The Holy One said to him: Sit, and I will stand; you are a foretoken for your children, for I am destined to stand in the assembly of the judges, while they are sitting, as it says: God stands in the Divine Tribunal.*

An understanding of the meaning of our sitting at the *Kedushah d'yeshivah* is closely related to the reason judges sit while hearing a case of Torah law. And both, in turn, are related to an understanding of the meaning of the two main *pesukim* of the *Kedushah*: קָדוֹשׁ קָדוֹשׁ קָדוֹשׁ ה' צְבָאוֹת מְלֹא כָל הָאָרֶץ כְּבוֹדוֹ, and בָּרוּךְ כְּבוֹד ה' מִמְּקוֹמוֹ.

Nobody can imagine how close *HaKadosh Baruch Hu* came to Avraham Avinu, who, at the age of 90, had performed the *bris milah* on himself; and who, on the third day after the *milah*, aching with pain, sitting in front of his tent in the unbearable heat — instead of staying inside in the shade — was looking for exhausted, hungry, and thirsty wayfarers, whom he could invite for a refreshing drink and a meal in the shade of his trees. When *HaKadosh Baruch Hu* appeared to him at that exalted moment, Avraham wanted to stand up, but *HaKadosh Baruch Hu* told him, "No, don't stand up, I have come so close to you that I am right here with you; remain seated as you are."

Similarly, when the *dayanim* (judges), as representatives of *Klal Yisrael,* sit down to judge a case involving Torah law — even one as mundane as Reuven not having paid his rent to Shimon — *HaKadosh Baruch Hu* comes so extremely and overpoweringly close to them *that they cannot even stand up!* When the *adas keil* (a tribunal hearing a case involving Torah law) is engaged in trying to determine what *HaKadosh Baruch Hu* says in a particular matter, *HaKadosh Baruch Hu* comes close and closer, until He is standing right there. At that moment, *HaKadosh Baruch Hu* is נִצָּב בַּעֲדַת אֵל.

This is the thought expressed by בָּרוּךְ כְּבוֹד ה' מִמְּקוֹמוֹ. Notwithstanding the קָדוֹשׁ aspect of *HaKadosh Baruch Hu* — that He is totally removed from our comprehension — He is, nevertheless, closer to us than anything else. One may think that one is close to oneself; however, *HaKadosh Baruch Hu* is even closer. This is the meaning of the בָּרוּךְ aspect of *HaKadosh Baruch Hu,* and is the reason one says בָּרוּךְ שֵׁם כְּבוֹד מַלְכוּתוֹ לְעוֹלָם וָעֶד quietly. Since these words express a similar idea to that of בָּרוּךְ כְּבוֹד ה' מִמְּקוֹמוֹ, there is no need to say them out loud. In saying . . . בָּרוּךְ שֵׁם כְּבוֹד, we express the idea that *HaKadosh Baruch Hu* is so close to us that we can fairly whisper these words to Him.

These two contrasting *nevuos* of Yeshayahu and Yechezkel belong together. Yeshayahu's prophecy stresses the קָדוֹשׁ attribute of *HaKadosh Baruch Hu*: He is unreachable and incomprehensible. Yechezkel sees the opposite. *HaKadosh Baruch Hu* is בָּרוּךְ: He is as close as possible to His creatures. Despite the apparent contradiction, both attributes coexist; and they should be expressed together. Notwithstanding the fact that *HaKadosh Baruch Hu* is so far away from us that He is unreachable, He is nevertheless breathtakingly close to us.

In our *tefillah* of *Kedushah d'yeshivah,* as a part of the *berachos* of *Krias Shema,* we recite both *nevuos,* and remain seated while doing so. This emphasizes the בָּרוּךְ aspect, which expresses the thought that when saying these words with the proper *kavannah* we become aware that *HaKadosh Baruch Hu* comes closer, closer, and closer to us — so close that we can hardly breathe! We are overwhelmed with the extreme proximity of *HaKadosh Baruch Hu* and cannot stand up. This corresponds with the silent whispering of בָּרוּךְ שֵׁם כְּבוֹד מַלְכוּתוֹ in *Krias Shema,* which also invokes the same idea.

However, in *Kedushah da'amidah* during the *chazzan's* repetition of the *Shemoneh Esrei,* we emphasize the other aspect of the *nevuos,* that of קָדוֹשׁ, by standing up while reciting these *pesukim*. Incomprehensible as it may be, these two opposite *nevuos* teach us that both aspects, קָדוֹשׁ and בָּרוּךְ, are true, and both equally coexist.

[Ed. note: Regarding the *Kedushah d'sidra,* which is said in וּבָא לְצִיּוֹן, the Rav expressed the hope that if *HaKadosh Baruch Hu* would give him life and health, he would explain its particular significance in וּבָא לְצִיּוֹן when the *shiur* reached that point. Unfortunately, this was not to be. However, some reference is made to it in the *Shemoneh Esrei,* at *Kedushah da'amidah.* Please refer to it.]

◆§ לְאֵל בָּרוּךְ נְעִימוֹת יִתֵּנוּ §◆
L'Eil Baruch Ne'imos Yiteinu

As previously explained, the *Ofanim* and *Chayos HaKodesh* have proclaimed, בָּרוּךְ כְּבוֹד ה', meaning that they envision *HaKadosh Baruch Hu* as extending His Divinity further and further, מִמְּקוֹמוֹ, from wherever He is, to come closer and closer to His creatures — both the spiritual and physical ones. The *berachah* of יוֹצֵר אוֹר now continues to describe the special perception that these aforementioned spiritual beings have of *HaKadosh Baruch Hu* as בָּרוּךְ, meaning His extreme proximity to His creatures — and how this relates to our physical world.

❦ ❦ ❦

◆§ לְאֵל בָּרוּךְ נְעִימוֹת יִתֵּנוּ. לְמֶלֶךְ אֵל חַי וְקַיָּם, זְמִרוֹת יֹאמֵרוּ וְתִשְׁבָּחוֹת יַשְׁמִיעוּ, כִּי הוּא לְבַדּוֹ פּוֹעֵל גְּבוּרוֹת — **They give forth sweet melodies in praise of Him Whom they have defined as** בָּרוּךְ. **To the Almighty King, Who lives eternally, they speak songs and proclaim praises, for it is He alone Who performs mighty deeds.**

The *malachim*, who have visualized *HaKadosh Baruch Hu* as so exceedingly close to His creatures, now sing a chorus of praise to Him as אֵל בָּרוּךְ, in which they express recognition of the fact that *HaKadosh Baruch Hu* is the sole source of all the great achievements in the world.

This refers, among other things, to the mighty deeds, inventions, and accomplishments which the human race has succeeded in doing throughout its history. The *malachim* see the role of mankind in these great accomplishments merely as instruments of *HaKadosh Baruch Hu*. In reality, it is *HaKadosh Baruch Hu*, in His extreme closeness to our world, Who has done all this, because He has given man the intelligence, energy, drive, and ingenuity to conquer the physical world.

◆§ עֹשֶׂה חֲדָשׁוֹת — The *malachim* continue: **He alone is the Maker of new inventions.** Since the beginning of the world, man has continually developed his life with new inventions. Beginning with the very primitive Stone Age, graduating to the Bronze Age, and later to the Dark and Middle Ages, mankind has made constant innovations, which rendered the previous ones obsolete. Even the work of the great inventors of the recent past has been made obsolete in our modern computerized age. Who gave all these people the ideas and intelligence to make all these innovations? It is הוּא לְבַדּוֹ, only *HaKadosh Baruch Hu*.

◆§ בַּעַל מִלְחָמוֹת — **He is the Master of wars.** When people wage war, evil as it may be, nevertheless, it is *HaKadosh Baruch Hu* Who gives them the power to do so. Thus, if wicked people exercise their God-given *bechirah*, freedom of choice, and wage an evil war, it is only *HaKadosh Baruch Hu* Who gives them the ability to destroy and to conquer. This is expressed by our *Chachamim* as בָּא לִיטַמֵּא פּוֹתְחִין לוֹ, *If one wants to become defiled, Hashem will give him the opportunity to do so* (*Shabbos* 104a). This is a difficult concept for us to comprehend.

◆§ זוֹרֵעַ צְדָקוֹת — **He sows righteousness.** On the other hand, *HaKadosh Baruch Hu* is seen here as the *Baal HaRachamim*. The *mitzvos* and *maasim tovim* of the *tzaddikim* are "sown" by *HaKadosh Baruch Hu* for their future growth.

◆§ מַצְמִיחַ יְשׁוּעוֹת — **He makes salvation grow.** One's acts of *chessed* become "seeds" that are nurtured by *HaKadosh Baruch Hu* to become a source of salvation in the future. For example, if a great *tzaddik* writes a *sefer* on *lashon hara* (evil speech), and one hundred years later thousands of people are still influenced by it and refrain from talking *lashon hara*, this seed of *chessed* was nurtured by *HaKadosh Baruch Hu* until it "sprouted forth" its goal, that of the salvation of potential sinners.

◆§ בּוֹרֵא רְפוּאוֹת — **He creates cures.** Man's ingenuity in the field of medicine is such that almost every day we hear of new medicines and cures that are being developed by medical science, many of which render the previously accepted practices obsolete. So much so, that if a surgeon of yesteryear — even one so highly regarded as having had a university named after him — would perform an operation in a modern operating room, using his outdated knowledge and techniques, he might very well be charged with malpractice. On a personal note, when I was 26 years old and living in Germany, I contracted scarlet fever after having visited someone who had the disease. The doctor told me that he had a new *"wunder"* medicine (I think it was penicillin) that would quickly cure me. It was given to me in powdered form mixed with a solution which smelled and tasted awful. However, as he had predicted, I was cured in three days. This "wonder drug" is one of hundreds of antibiotics that are now almost indispensable and taken for granted in the field of medicine.

The aforementioned *malachim* look at all of the countless "wonders" and advances of medical knowledge, which have extended and improved the lives of millions of people on earth, and burst forth in songs of praise to *HaKadosh Baruch Hu,* because He is the ultimate Creator of all these innovations. It is הוּא לְבַדּוֹ, only He, Who is the בּוֹרֵא רְפוּאוֹת. He has given the scientists the gift of intelligence and insight with which to find new cures for illnesses and ways to prevent them.

◆§ נוֹרָא תְהִלּוֹת — **Awesome of praise.** One praises *HaKadosh Baruch Hu* in trepidation and fear. It is quite easy to praise Him for the good that happens to people. However, by doing so, and neglecting to praise Him even when His will necessitates suffering and evil in the world, one could indicate that he is thankful only for the good that occurs. This would be the opposite of praising *HaKadosh Baruch Hu*. We must be very careful when praising Him to be cognizant of the fact that when there is suffering in the world, this too is His doing. When God's will is done, whether we see it as good or bad, we are to praise Him for it. As *Chazal* tell us: חַיָּיב אָדָם לְבָרֵךְ עַל הָרָעָה כְּשֵׁם שֶׁמְּבָרֵךְ עַל הַטּוֹבָה, *A person is obligated to bless God for the bad just as he does for the good* (*Berachos* 54a). Although we may not understand the reasons for the evil and suffering in the world, nevertheless, since we recognize that it is הוּא לְבַדּוֹ, it is only He Who has brought this about for reasons of His own, we must therefore praise Him for it.

◆§ אֲדוֹן הַנִּפְלָאוֹת — **Master of wonders.** On the other hand, if we do see wonders in the world, we must know that He alone is the master of these wonders. We recently witnessed the miraculous events in Eretz Yisrael when numerous "Scud" missiles were fired at our land. The results could have been catastrophic, but, *baruch Hashem*, they were either intercepted by "Patriot" antimissile missiles, or fell to the ground with minimal injuries and damage. *This was not mere happenstance.* These were נִפְלָאוֹת, and it was only הוּא לְבַדּוֹ Who was the Master of these miracles.

[Ed. note: This is a reference to the Gulf War in Jan.-Feb. 1991.]

◆§ הַמְחַדֵּשׁ בְּטוּבוֹ בְּכָל יוֹם תָּמִיד מַעֲשֵׂה בְרֵאשִׁית — **In His goodness He renews daily, perpetually, the work of Creation.** From their vantage point, the *malachim* see that *HaKadosh Baruch Hu,* in His goodness, on a continuing daily basis, renews the Creation. The Torah tells us, וַיַּרְא אֱלֹהִים אֶת כָּל אֲשֶׁר עָשָׂה וְהִנֵּה טוֹב מְאֹד, *And God saw all that He had made and behold it was very good* (*Bereishis* 1:31). Rav Samson R. Hirsch explains that טוֹב, as used here, means that *HaKadosh Baruch Hu* keeps His creation in a constant state of existence only because He finds it "good" that it should continue to exist. And it only exists so long as He continues to find it "good" that it should exist. (See commentary of Rav Hirsch, *Bereishis* 1:4).

◆§ כָּאָמוּר, לְעֹשֵׂה אוֹרִים גְּדֹלִים, כִּי לְעוֹלָם חַסְדּוֹ — **As it is written, "[Give praise] to Him Who makes great luminaries, for His lovingkindness lasts forever"** (*Tehillim* 136:7). The *tefillah* quotes this *pasuk* to prove the aforementioned statement of הַמְחַדֵּשׁ בְּטוּבוֹ בְּכָל יוֹם תָּמִיד מַעֲשֵׂה בְרֵאשִׁית, that *HaKadosh Baruch Hu* constantly re-creates the world. This proof seems to be derived from the fact that this sentence is constructed in the present tense, with the meaning that *HaKadosh Baruch Hu* "constantly makes" great luminaries. However, a review of this psalm, which is also known as הַלֵּל הַגָּדוֹל, shows that other *pesukim* in it are also written in the present tense, using poetic license, although the past tense is clearly intended. For example: לְגֹזֵר יַם סוּף לִגְזָרִים; לְמַכֵּה מִצְרַיִם בִּבְכוֹרֵיהֶם.

To understand how the organizers of the *tefillah* read into this psalm that it is extolling *HaKadosh Baruch Hu* for His constant re-creation of the world, let us look at the statements of *Chazal* in explaining the *pesukim* in the Torah regarding the original creation of the heavenly bodies of light.

At the very beginning of Creation, the Torah tells us: וַיֹּאמֶר אֱלֹהִים יְהִי אוֹר. וַיְהִי אוֹר. וַיַּרְא אֱלֹהִים אֶת הָאוֹר כִּי טוֹב וַיַּבְדֵּל אֱלֹהִים בֵּין הָאוֹר וּבֵין הַחֹשֶׁךְ, *God said, "Let there be light," and there was light. God saw that the light was good, and God separated between the light and the darkness* (Bereishis 1:3-4). Rashi (ibid.), quoting *Chazal*, explains the meaning of the second *pasuk*: רָאָהוּ שֶׁאֵינוּ כְדַאי לְהִשְׁתַּמֵּשׁ בּוֹ רְשָׁעִים וְהִבְדִּילוֹ לַצַּדִּיקִים לֶעָתִיד לָבֹא, *He saw that it was too precious to be used by evil people, so He put it aside for the use of the tzaddikim in the World to Come.* This means that when *HaKadosh Baruch Hu* saw that Adam HaRishon would commit the sin of the *eitz hadaas* (Tree of Knowledge), and that there would be many generations of evildoers in the world such as those of the period of the Flood, etc., who would not be worthy of benefiting from this light, He therefore put it aside, וַיַּבְדֵּל, *separated it,* to be used by the *tzaddikim,* who would be worthy of benefiting from it in the World to Come.

We learn here that the original light which *HaKadosh Baruch Hu* called into being by the pronouncement יְהִי אוֹר, on the first day of Creation, was not the light of our sun, but rather, it was the "light of Creation." It was this light that *HaKadosh Baruch Hu* put aside to be enjoyed by the *tzaddikim* in the future.

On the fourth day of Creation, the Torah states: וַיַּעַשׂ אֱלֹהִים אֶת שְׁנֵי הַמְּאֹרֹת הַגְּדֹלִים אֶת הַמָּאוֹר הַגָּדֹל לְמֶמְשֶׁלֶת הַיּוֹם וְאֶת הַמָּאוֹר הַקָּטֹן לְמֶמְשֶׁלֶת הַלַּיְלָה, *And God made the two great luminaries, the greater luminary to dominate the day and the lesser luminary to dominate the night* (Bereishis 1:16). And Rashi, quoting from the words of *Chazal,* remarks: שָׁוִים נִבְרְאוּ; וְנִתְמַעֲטָה הַלְּבָנָה עַל שֶׁקִּטְרְגָה וְאָמְרָה אִי אֶפְשָׁר לִשְׁנֵי מְלָכִים שֶׁיִּשְׁתַּמְּשׁוּ בְּכֶתֶר אֶחָד (Chullin 60a). Paraphrased, this means that originally, the sun and moon were created equal. However, when the moon complained that it was not possible "for two kings to use the same crown" — for both to illuminate the earth — it was told by *HaKadosh Baruch Hu,* "You are absolutely correct, and therefore you are to reduce your size and become הַמָּאוֹר הַקָּטֹן, *the lesser luminary.*"

The *pasuk* continues, וְאֵת הַכּוֹכָבִים, *and* [God also created] *the stars.* On this, Rashi, again quoting *Chazal,* explains: עַל יְדֵי שֶׁמִּיעֵט אֶת הַלְּבָנָה הִרְבָּה צְבָאֶיהָ לְהָפִיס דַּעְתָּהּ, *Since He reduced the size of the moon, He increased the number of its accompanying hosts, in order to console it.* Literally, this means that *HaKadosh Baruch Hu* gave the stars to the moon as auxiliary luminaries, to assist it in illuminating the earth at night.

In attempting to understand these statements by *Chazal,* we must keep in mind that this explanation is not some sort of legend that is told to children, but rather, it is part and parcel of *talmud Torah,* and as such, requires *birchos haTorah* before learning it, as is the case with any other aspect of Torah learning. It therefore behooves us to attempt to understand these profound thoughts.

Based on even an elementary knowledge of astronomy, we know that this characterization by *Chazal* of the billions of enormous stars as merely "accompanying hosts," or auxiliaries, to the moon, and the complaint by the moon to *HaKadosh Baruch Hu* about its competing role with the sun, must be understood in the Aggadic sense, whereby *Chazal* intended to convey profound thoughts in simplistic terms.

We suggest that the meaning of these statements by *Chazal* is based on an explanation of the שְׁנֵי הַמְּאֹרֹת הַגְּדֹלִים, *two great luminaries.* Originally, these two heavenly bodies, the sun and the moon, radiated two forms of light. The sun radiated its physical light, and the moon became the carrier of the original "light of creation." The moon was the same size and shape as it is today. However, instead of merely reflecting the sun's light, as it does today, the moon radiated the *Ohr HaShechinah,* the light emanating from the presence of *HaKadosh Baruch Hu,* which illuminated the world. We had small glimpses of this light from time to time in our history: the עַמּוּד אֵשׁ, *pillar of fire,* which lighted the night for *Bnei Yisrael* at the time of *yetzias Mitzrayim* (*Shemos* 13:21); the fire which burned on *Har Sinai* at the time of *Matan Torah* (*Shemos* 24:19); and the fire over the *Mishkan* during the travels of *Bnei Yisrael* in the *midbar* (desert) (*Shemos* 40:38).

This "dual illumination" of the earth prompted the moon to "complain" that the single function of illuminating the earth — the כֶּתֶר אֶחָד — cannot be performed by two "kings." Either *HaKadosh Baruch Hu* should reveal Himself by means of the spiritual light of the *Ohr HaShechinah* that emanated from the moon, or *HaKadosh Baruch Hu* should reveal His existence by means of the physical light of the sun.

Thereupon, *HaKadosh Baruch Hu* said to the moon, "You are quite right, the present arrangement is impossible. Therefore, 'Reduce your size.' Let the physical light of the sun rule during the day — shining directly on the earth — and at night, you will reflect the sun's light to the earth."

The condition of the moon as merely a reflector of the sun's light — without the *Ohr HaShechinah* emanating from it — is called פְּגִימַת הַלְּבָנָה, *the imperfection of the moon.* Since the moon was relegated to a purely physical reflector of light, instead of it being the carrier of the *Ohr HaShechinah,* it

L'EIL BARUCH NE'IMOS YITEINU 285

was "comforted" by *HaKadosh Baruch Hu* by the accompaniment of the stars that serve with it.

True, the moon had become relegated to a purely physical reflector of light, but when one gazes at the heavens and sees it "accompanied by its hosts" of the billions of stars, he immediately becomes aware of the *Shechinah,* the Great and Powerful Creator of the cosmos. This is expressed in, כִּי אֶרְאֶה שָׁמֶיךָ מַעֲשֵׂי אֶצְבְּעֹתֶיךָ, *When I behold Your heavens, the work of Your fingers* (*Tehillim* 8:4); and in, שְׂאוּ מָרוֹם עֵינֵיכֶם וּרְאוּ מִי בָרָא אֵלֶּה, *Raise your eyes on high and see Who created these things* (*Yeshayahu* 40:26). (The letters of מִי and אֵלֶּה form the word א־ל־ה־יִם.)

So while the *Ohr HaShechinah* has been hidden away for the *tzaddikim* in the World to Come, nevertheless, we can still see a manifestation of the *Shechinah* in the starry skies. During the period when the moon carried the "light of Creation" it was so bright that it eclipsed the view of the stars. However, when the light of Creation was removed from the moon, its physical light was not bright enough to illuminate the darkness. Therefore, in the absence of the *Ohr HaShechinah* from the moon, we become aware of the billions of stars in the cosmos, which is evidence of the presence of *HaKadosh Baruch Hu* in the universe.

Chazal say, עַל יְדֵי שֶׁמִּיעֵט אֶת הַלְּבָנָה הִרְבָּה צְבָאֶיהָ לְהָפִיס דַּעְתָּהּ, *Paraphrased, this means: By reducing the light of the moon, Hashem effectively made its myriads of hosts visible, and thus "consoled" it.* The meaning is: When the moon appears, we also become aware of the billions of stars in the sky, whose immensity in size and numbers testify to the existence of their Creator. This is so aptly expressed: הַשָּׁמַיִם מְסַפְּרִים כְּבוֹד אֵל וּמַעֲשֵׂה יָדָיו מַגִּיד הָרָקִיעַ, *The heavens declare the glory of God, and the expanse of the sky tells of His handiwork* (*Tehillim* 19:2). This manifestation of the *Shechinah,* then, is a "consolation" to the moon for its "reduction in stature," its having lost its own *Ohr HaShechinah.*

With this introduction, we can now better understand the meaning of the words of our *tefillah*: הַמְחַדֵּשׁ בְּטוּבוֹ בְּכָל יוֹם תָּמִיד מַעֲשֵׂה בְרֵאשִׁית, כָּאָמוּר, לְעֹשֵׂה אוֹרִים גְּדֹלִים וגו׳. When we look at *Tehillim* Ch. 136, where this *pasuk* is found, we see that the *pasuk* we quote in the *tefillah* is only the first of three that belong together: (1) לְעֹשֵׂה אוֹרִים גְּדֹלִים כִּי לְעוֹלָם חַסְדּוֹ; (2) אֶת הַשֶּׁמֶשׁ לְמֶמְשֶׁלֶת בַּיּוֹם כִּי לְעוֹלָם חַסְדּוֹ; (3) אֶת הַיָּרֵחַ וְכוֹכָבִים לְמֶמְשְׁלוֹת בַּלַּיְלָה כִּי לְעוֹלָם חַסְדּוֹ.

The *malachim* are aware that *HaKadosh Baruch Hu* daily re-enacts *maasei Bereishis.* They see how He re-creates, daily, the original sequence of events, which started with the creation of the אוֹרִים גְּדֹלִים, and was followed with the sun being utilized only for daytime illumination, and the moon and stars for illumination at night.

And it is this thought that is expressed by these three *pesukim.* The first *pasuk* extols *HaKadosh Baruch Hu* for לְעֹשֵׂה, for the daily re-creation of the "great lights." First, *HaKadosh Baruch Hu* creates the two large luminaries: the sun, with its physical light, and the moon, which carries the spiritual light. Then, after removing the spiritual light from the moon and replacing it with the physical reflection of the sun, He divides the functions of the physical light so that the sun rules during the day, and the moon and stars rule at night.

The proof that הַמְחַדֵּשׁ בְּטוּבוֹ בְּכָל יוֹם תָּמִיד מַעֲשֵׂה בְרֵאשִׁית lies in the first of these three *pesukim*: כָּאָמוּר לְעֹשֵׂה אוֹרִים גְּדֹלִים כִּי לְעוֹלָם חַסְדּוֹ, which is written in the present tense, notwithstanding the fact that these "great luminaries" were subsequently changed to הַמָּאוֹר הַקָּטֹן and הַמָּאוֹר הַגָּדוֹל, and we see only the practical result: the sun illuminating the day, and the moon and stars shining at night. The psalm, however, thanks *HaKadosh Baruch Hu* for the *daily re-creation of the entire process*: first, that of שְׁנֵי הַמְּאוֹרֹת הַגְּדֹלִים, and then for אֶת הַיָּרֵחַ וְכוֹכָבִים לְמֶמְשְׁלוֹת בַּלָּיְלָה and אֶת הַשֶּׁמֶשׁ לְמֶמְשֶׁלֶת בַּיּוֹם.

It is this daily process seen by the *malachim* that is the subject of their "sweet song," נְעִימוֹת, to *HaKadosh Baruch Hu,* extolling Him for the daily reenactment of *maaseh Bereishis.*

✦ אוֹר חָדָשׁ עַל צִיּוֹן תָּאִיר — **May You shine a new light on Zion.** We ask *HaKadosh Baruch Hu* here to bring the *geulah*, which was described as "light": וְהָיָה לְעֵת עֶרֶב יִהְיֶה אוֹר, *but it will happen towards evening time that there will be light* (Zechariah 14:7). This wish, very appropriately, follows immediately after the mention of *maaseh Bereishis,* because the אוֹר חָדָשׁ to which we refer here is our *tefillah* for the return of the *Ohr HaShechinah*, which was removed by *HaKadosh Baruch Hu* during *maaseh Bereishis* for the benefit of the future world.

Each month, during the *berachah* of *Kiddush Levanah*, when we witness the new moon-cycle, we see it as a constant reminder that just as the moon-cycle is renewed, so will *HaKadosh Baruch Hu* renew our relationship with Him, and return the *Ohr HaShechinah* to the world. וְלַלְּבָנָה אָמַר שֶׁתִּתְחַדֵּשׁ עֲטֶרֶת תִּפְאֶרֶת לַעֲמוּסֵי בָטֶן שֶׁהֵם עֲתִידִים לְהִתְחַדֵּשׁ כְּמוֹתָהּ, *To the moon He said that it should renew itself as a crown of splendor for those borne [by Him] from the womb, those who are destined to renew themselves like it.*

This is followed by an additional *tefillah* that makes a direct reference to the return of the *Ohr HaShechinah* to the world: וִיהִי רָצוֹן מִלְּפָנֶיךָ ה' אֱלֹהַי וֵאלֹהֵי אֲבוֹתַי, לְמַלֹּאת פְּגִימַת הַלְּבָנָה וְלֹא יִהְיֶה בָּהּ שׁוּם מִעוּט. וִיהִי אוֹר הַלְּבָנָה כְּאוֹר הַחַמָּה וּכְאוֹר שִׁבְעַת יְמֵי בְרֵאשִׁית, כְּמוֹ שֶׁהָיְתָה קֹדֶם מִעוּטָהּ, שֶׁנֶּאֱמַר: אֶת שְׁנֵי הַמְּאֹרֹת הַגְּדֹלִים, *May it be Your will, Hashem, my God, and the God of my forefathers, to fill the flaw of the moon that there be no diminution in it. May the light of the moon be like the light of the sun and like the light of the seven days of creation, as it was before it was diminished, as it is said: "the two great luminaries."*

The moon has been a symbol of our hope for the renewal of our relationship with *HaKadosh Baruch Hu,* through the *geulah,* ever since He gave us the first *mitzvah* in the Torah at the time of *geulas Mitzrayim,* that of קִדּוּשׁ הַחֹדֶשׁ עַל פִּי הָרְאִיָּה, as the verse says: הַחֹדֶשׁ הַזֶּה לָכֶם רֹאשׁ חֳדָשִׁים, *This month shall be for you the beginning of the months* (Shemos 12:2).

וְנִזְכֶּה כֻלָּנוּ מְהֵרָה לְאוֹרוֹ — **May we all merit seeing His light.** We ask *HaKadosh Baruch Hu* to allow us all to see the previously mentioned אוֹר חָדָשׁ, which will be "His light," meaning the *Ohr HaShechinah.*

בָּרוּךְ אַתָּה ה׳ יוֹצֵר הַמְּאוֹרוֹת — **Blessed are You, Hashem, Who fashions the luminaries.** In concluding this *berachah,* we thank *HaKadosh Baruch Hu* not only for the יוֹצֵר אוֹר, with which we began — referring to the physical light of the sun, which for us is the source of life and health — but also for the spiritual light, the *Ohr HaShechinah.* We therefore conclude by saying יוֹצֵר הַמְּאוֹרוֹת, He creates both forms of light, the physical and the spiritual.

אַהֲבָה רַבָּה / Ahavah Rabbah

In accordance with our outline of the "architecture" of the *tefillah,* the *berachah* of אַהֲבָה רַבָּה corresponds to the *Menorah* in the *Heichal.* The spiritual life of *Klal Yisrael* is represented by the *Menorah,* which symbolizes *limud haTorah* and *havanas haTorah,* and *ruach daas* and *yiras Shamayim* (learning Torah and understanding its letter and spirit, which lead to the fear of Heaven). [Ed. note: See Rav Samson R. Hirsch, *Shemos* 25:31, for a very lengthy and detailed treatise on the spiritual symbolism of the *Menorah.*]

Accordingly, אַהֲבָה רַבָּה — corresponding to the *Menorah* — properly belongs before קְרִיאַת שְׁמַע, in which we accept upon ourselves *ol Malchus Shamayim,* the obligation to accept the yoke of heaven upon ourselves, which corresponds to the *Mizbach HaZahav,* the Golden Altar in the center of the *Heichal.*

The *Mizbach HaNechoshes* (Copper Altar) outside the *Heichal* in the *Azarah* was the place where the *korbanos,* which represent our physical lives, were offered to *HaKadosh Baruch Hu.* The blood and flesh of the animals, the wine, the oil, and the flour, all are symbolic of various aspects of our physical lives. However, the *Mizbach HaZahav,* inside the *Heichal,* was the place where the *ketores hasamim* (incense spices) was offered, the ingredients of which produce a רֵיחַ נִיחוֹחַ לַה׳, *a pleasant scent for Hashem,* indicating the nation's desire to be pleasing to *Hakadosh Baruch Hu.* Through this means, we symbolically offer our inner, spiritual lives to *HaKadosh Baruch Hu,* including our feelings, sentiments, and thoughts.

It is noteworthy that the *Menorah* and the *ketores* always function together. The Torah tells us that each morning while the *Menorah* is prepared for its lighting the following evening, the *ketores* is to be brought on the *Mizbach HaZahav:* וְהִקְטִיר עָלָיו אַהֲרֹן קְטֹרֶת סַמִּים בַּבֹּקֶר בַּבֹּקֶר בְּהֵיטִיבוֹ אֶת הַנֵּרֹת יַקְטִירֶנָּה, *Aaron shall burn upon it the incense-spices every morning; when he cleans the lamps he is to burn it* (Shemos 30:7). And again, in the evening, at the time of the actual lighting of the *Menorah,* the *ketores* is offered on the *Mizbach Ha-Zahav:* וּבְהַעֲלֹת אַהֲרֹן אֶת הַנֵּרֹת בֵּין הָעַרְבַּיִם יַקְטִירֶנָּה קְטֹרֶת תָּמִיד לִפְנֵי ה׳ לְדֹרֹתֵיכֶם, *And when Aaron ignites the lamps in the afternoon, he is to burn it, as continual incense before Hashem, throughout your generations* (ibid. v. 8).

Although the *Menorah* and the *ketores* function only during the time when the *Beis HaMikdash* exists, the word לְדֹרֹתֵיכֶם is a subtle *remez* (allusion) for all generations to come that a connection shall remain between the *hatavos haneiros* and *ketores hasamim* (the institution of the *Menorah* and that of the *Mizbe'ach* of *ketores*). The organizers of the *tefillah* have expressed this connection by placing אַהֲבָה רַבָּה, which corresponds to the *Menorah,* just before the *kabbalas ol Malchus Shamayim* of *Krias Shema,* which corresponds to the *Mizbach HaZahav.*

❧ ❧ ❧

☙ אַהֲבָה רַבָּה אֲהַבְתָּנוּ ה' אֱלֹהֵינוּ ❧ — **You have loved us with ever-increasing love, Hashem, our God.** Actually, the phrase אַהֲבָה רַבָּה does not appear in *Tanach.* The closest we have is אַהֲבַת עוֹלָם אֲהַבְתִּיךְ, *I have loved you with an eternal love* (*Yirmiyahu* 31:2). We use this expression in the *tefillah* of Maariv in the corresponding *berachah* before *Krias Shema*: אַהֲבַת עוֹלָם בֵּית יִשְׂרָאֵל עַמְּךָ אָהָבְתָּ. However, the *Sefardim* (but not all of *nusach Sefard*) do have the text אַהֲבַת עוֹלָם in Shacharis, instead of אַהֲבָה רַבָּה.

Our text, אַהֲבָה רַבָּה, was instituted during the time of the *Geonim.* The term רַבָּה is used in the sense of "constantly increasing," similar to רַבָּה וְהוֹלֶכֶת. The meaning is that *HaKadosh Baruch Hu,* in His ever-increasing love of *Am Yisrael,* constantly expanded the chain of Torah knowledge throughout all of our generations. Each generation expounded further on the Torah knowledge handed to them from their predecessors: from the *Tannaim* to the *Amoraim* to the *Geonim* to the *Rishonim* and to the *Acharonim,* up to our own lifetimes. This, notwithstanding the fact that our generations have constantly become diminished in terms of their Torah knowledge. This historical fact is commonly known as *yeridas hadoros* (literally: the decline of the generations). And this, together with the absence of the Sanhedrin, has resulted in many *halachos* being forgotten, and has left many halachic issues unresolved.

☙ חֶמְלָה גְדוֹלָה וִיתֵרָה חָמַלְתָּ עָלֵינוּ ❧ — **You have shown us great and overwhelming compassion.** The word חֶמְלָה, meaning compassion, appears in the Torah twice. The first is when the daughter of Pharaoh saw the little baby Moshe in the basket, and her emotional state is described as וַתַּחְמֹל עָלָיו, *and she pitied him* (*Shemos* 2:6). The second time it is found in connection with the *halachah* of מֵסִית לַעֲבוֹדָה זָרָה, referring to one who attempts to convince others to worship idols. If he is convicted of this crime and is consequently sentenced to death, the Torah forbids the judges to look for mitigating circumstances which might make it possible for him to evade the death penalty. The Torah expresses this law as וְלֹא תַחְמֹל וְלֹא תְכַסֶּה עָלָיו, *you shall not be compassionate nor conceal him* (*Devarim* 13:9). In both of these examples חמל is used to express compassion, in which the *rachamim* replaces the *din.* When the daughter of Pharaoh saved Moshe, she acted contrary to the prevailing Egyptian law, which required that כָּל הַבֵּן הַיִּלּוֹד הַיְאֹרָה תַּשְׁלִיכֻהוּ, *Every son that will be born — into the river shall you throw him* (*Shemos* 1:22). Therefore, her act of saving him is described as

וַתַּחְמֹל עָלָיו: She changed the *din* to *rachamim*. Similarly, when a judge attempts to allow leniency regarding the death sentence of a *meisis* (one who induces others to idol worship), contrary to the *din Torah* which does not allow for *rachamim* for a *meisis* — as would be the case in other instances of the death penalty — the Torah warns the judge: לֹא תַחְמֹל ... עָלָיו.

Similarly, the meaning of חֶמְלָה גְדוֹלָה is as follows: Notwithstanding the fact that we may not have deserved Hashem's compassion, because there were periods in Jewish history when large segments of our nation neglected the learning of Torah, and much of it was forgotten by large sectors of the Jewish people, nevertheless, instead of treating us with *din* for the neglect of Torah learning, *HaKadosh Baruch Hu*, in His abundant compassion, changed the *middas hadin* to the *middas harachamim*. He did this by providing our people with great Torah scholars, *talmidei chachamim*, and *poskim* in every generation, who kept the Torah alive throughout our history.

◆§ אָבִינוּ מַלְכֵּנוּ, בַּעֲבוּר אֲבוֹתֵינוּ שֶׁבָּטְחוּ בְךָ, וַתְּלַמְּדֵם חֻקֵּי חַיִּים, כֵּן תְּחָנֵּנוּ וּתְלַמְּדֵנוּ §◆ — The opening words of this phrase, אָבִינוּ מַלְכֵּנוּ, indicate that this must be a very important *tefillah*: **Our Father, our King, for the sake of our forefathers who had faith in You, and You taught them the laws of life, so may You also endow us spiritually and teach us.** The word תְּחָנֵּנוּ comes from חן, which always means a spiritual endowment, as in אַתָּה חוֹנֵן לְאָדָם דַּעַת, *You endow man with knowledge* (from the *Amidah* prayer). [Ed. note: See earlier on *Bircas Kohanim* at *birchos hashachar*.]

The entire Torah here is called חֻקֵּי חַיִּים, or "the ground rules of life." חֻקִּים in the Torah usually refers to those laws whose reason we do not understand, but we accept them as the will of *HaKadosh Baruch Hu*. However, חֻקֵּי חַיִּים here is to be understood in the sense, הַטְרִיפֵנִי לֶחֶם חֻקִּי, *allow me my daily ration of food* [without which I could not live] (*Mishlei* 30:8). In this *tefillah* we ask *HaKadosh Baruch Hu* to teach us His Torah, containing His will, which is the basis on which our lives depend.

It is important that we understand the connection between *bitachon* in *HaKadosh Baruch Hu* and *limud haTorah*. We know that Torah learning requires יְגִיעָה, *effort*, but true success in learning and understanding the Torah is based on *bitachon*, trust that *HaKadosh Baruch Hu* will crown one's efforts in *limud haTorah* with success.

Torah learning really means the comprehension of the *chochmah* of *HaKadosh Baruch Hu* by our physical minds. How can we humans, with our limited understanding, dare to attempt to comprehend the intelligence of *HaKadosh Baruch Hu* as revealed to us in the Torah? Nevertheless, the very existence of the *mitzvah* of *talmud Torah* means that it is possible, and it assures us that in the *zechus* of our effort to learn the Torah, *HaKadosh Baruch Hu* will crown our effort with success. At first, all Torah learning is similar to חֻקִּים, for one does not really comprehend a thing. But if one makes a sincere effort to learn and understand *Toras Hashem,* and has *bitachon* that *HaKadosh Baruch Hu* will give him the proper understanding, He will do so.

For this reason, *Chazal* tell us: אִם יֹאמַר לְךָ אָדָם: יָגַעְתִּי וְלֹא מָצָאתִי, אַל תַּאֲמִין. לֹא יָגַעְתִּי וּמָצָאתִי, אַל תַּאֲמִין, *If one tells you, "I made an effort to learn but was unsuccessful," [or,] "I was successful without effort," do not believe either statement.* However, if he tells you, יָגַעְתִּי וּמָצָאתִי, תַּאֲמִין, *"I made an effort and was successful in finding understanding of Torah,"* believe him. The use of the word מָצָאתִי is very significant in that it connotes a מְצִיאָה, the finding of a lost article. The מְצִיאָה in this case is the gift of understanding the Torah that *HaKadosh Baruch Hu* has given him as a result of his efforts in learning it.

The effortless, "instant coffee" type of Torah study is not called *talmud Torah,* and the knowledge thus gained will not remain with the person. It is similar to the reading of a newspaper article, which is forgotten almost as soon as it is read. However, true Torah learning is not easy. It requires יְגִיעָה, a great deal of effort. And when one makes this effort with the expectation that *HaKadosh Baruch Hu* will grant him success in his learning, he is utilizing *bitachon* in this *talmud Torah*. We therefore ask *HaKadosh Baruch Hu* in this *tefillah* to grant us success in our *limud haTorah,* in the merit of the total trust that our forefathers had that *HaKadosh Baruch Hu* would grant them the proper understanding of His Torah: בַּעֲבוּר אֲבוֹתֵינוּ שֶׁבָּטְחוּ בְךָ וַתְּלַמְּדֵם חֻקֵּי חַיִּים כֵּן תְּחָנֵּנוּ וּתְלַמְּדֵנוּ.

"Our forefathers" referred to here by the organizers of our *tefillah* here are the *Tannaim* and *Amoraim,* whose intense efforts at *talmud Torah* and their *bitachon* that *HaKadosh Baruch Hu* would crown these efforts with success, resulted in their being able to plumb the depths of the Torah and to find sources for the *Torah Shebe'al Peh* in every letter and word of the *Torah Shebichsav.*

The connection between the effort invested in Torah learning and *bitachon* in *HaKadosh Baruch Hu* that He will grant us the proper understanding of it is found in the following mishnah: כֹּל שֶׁחָכְמָתוֹ מְרֻבָּה מִמַּעֲשָׂיו לְמָה הוּא דוֹמֶה, לְאִילָן שֶׁעֲנָפָיו מְרֻבִּין וְשָׁרָשָׁיו מוּעָטִין, *One whose knowledge exceeds his deeds is compared to a tree whose branches outnumber is roots* (Pirkei Avos 3:22). This describes a person whose learning ("branches") consists of offering beautiful ideas, *peirushim* and *chiddushim* (explanations and novellae), on various parts of Torah, but his actual Torah learning is very meager. This person's מַעֲשָׂיו, *deeds,* do not refer to his general *maasim tovim,* but rather, specifically, to his "deeds of learning." The time spent in effort-filled learning, the מַעֲשִׂים, are characterized as the "roots" of any *talmid chacham.*

Torah learning that is not properly "rooted" in time and effort will eventually disappear. This is expressed by the mishnah: וְהָרוּחַ בָּאָה וְעוֹקַרְתּוֹ וְהוֹפַכְתּוֹ עַל פָּנָיו, *a wind will uproot it and turn it upside down* (ibid.). This is because this "tree," this gifted person who can — with very little effort — produce beautiful explanations and novel ideas, but has not worked very hard at actual *limud haTorah,* can easily be "blown over" when he is faced with a רוּחַ, a "storm," of heretical thoughts, *apikorsus,* or peer pressure of anti-Torah sentiments. Having made very little effort in his learning, such a person will not be able to withstand these "hurricane winds," and will easily be uprooted by them.

And the source that the aforementioned mishnah uses to support this saying is taken from a *pasuk* that does not even refer to *talmud Torah*: שֶׁנֶּאֱמַר, וְהָיָה כְעַרְעָר בָּעֲרָבָה וְלֹא יִרְאֶה כִּי יָבוֹא טוֹב, וְשָׁכַן חֲרֵרִים בַּמִּדְבָּר, אֶרֶץ מְלֵחָה וְלֹא תֵשֵׁב, *As it is said: And he shall be like an isolated tree in an arid land and shall not see when good comes; he shall dwell on parched soil in the wilderness, on a salted land, uninhabited (Yirmiyahu 17:6).*

In quoting this *pasuk,* the mishnah compares the person who has very few effort-filled deeds of Torah learning ("roots") to a lonely, dried-up bush in the desert which has no hope that anything good will ever come of it. However, in its context in *Yirmiyahu,* this lonely bush is used to exemplify one who lacks *bitachon* in *HaKadosh Baruch Hu.* Such a person שָׂם בָּשָׂר זְרֹעוֹ, relies on the strength of his brain, which is really only "flesh," and sees no need to have trust in *HaKadosh Baruch Hu.* כֹּה אָמַר ה' אָרוּר הַגֶּבֶר אֲשֶׁר יִבְטַח בָּאָדָם וְשָׂם בָּשָׂר זְרֹעוֹ וּמִן ה' יָסוּר לִבּוֹ, *Thus said Hashem: Accursed is the man who trusts in people and makes flesh and blood his strength and turns his heart away from Hashem (Yirmiyahu 17:5).* It is obvious, therefore, that by making this comparison, the *Chachamim* of the Mishnah viewed *limud haTorah* as being based on *bitachon.*

We therefore ask *HaKadosh Baruch Hu* to teach us Torah just as He did to our forefathers, because we could never be successful in learning *Toras Hashem* unless he teaches it to us: . . . כֵּן תְּחָנֵּנוּ וּתְלַמְּדֵנוּ. אָבִינוּ מַלְכֵּנוּ *Endow us —* אַתָּה חוֹנֵן לְאָדָם דַּעַת *— and teach us Your Torah.*

⊱ אָבִינוּ, הָאָב הָרַחֲמָן הַמְרַחֵם, רַחֵם עָלֵינוּ — **Our Father, the merciful Father, Who acts mercifully, have mercy upon us.** Remarkably, we have four expressions through which we plead with *HaKadosh Baruch Hu* to mercifully give us the ability to understand His Torah. In these four pleas, we ask *HaKadosh Baruch Hu* to allow us to understand the totality of His Torah, which consists of four parts:

The first level of understanding Torah is *p'shat*: This refers to the basic meaning of the subject matter under study.

The second level is *derash,* which is the exegetical method of studying the words and letters of the text, through which the *Chachamim* have arrived at its meaning. Indeed, many *halachos* and *aggados* were derived solely from this method of learning.

The third, *remez,* is a higher form of learning, in which various *halachos* and concepts are only alluded to in certain words and sentences. An example would be *gematrios,* which are based on the numerical values of letters and words.

And the fourth, and highest, form of learning is called *sod.* This encompasses the secrets and mysteries hidden in the Torah, which are known as *sisrei haTorah* (secrets of the Torah). Very few people are privileged to reach this level of learning.

One could compare these four levels of Torah learning to the body. The *p'shat* is analogous to the skin, which is only the outward appearance and covers that which lies beneath it. It is only "skin deep." The *derash* is comparable to the muscle tissue that lies underneath the skin. The *remez* can be compared to the bone structure, the skeleton, which is underneath the muscle tissue. And, finally, the *sod* — the covered and hidden secrets of the Torah — is analogous to the organs enclosed by the skeleton: the heart, lung, kidneys, intestines, stomach, etc.

• וְתֵן בְּלִבֵּנוּ לְהָבִין — **Instill in our hearts a depth of perception.** לְהָבִין, from בִּינָה, is the highest form of understanding. This level was achieved by the *Neviim* and the *anshei ruach hakodesh* who understood the *sisrei Torah.* It is the understanding by the *neshamah* of the depths of Torah.

• וּלְהַשְׂכִּיל — **And to understand.** And if we cannot rise to the level of לְהָבִין, we are *mispallel* that *HaKadosh Baruch Hu* may allow us to have, at least, a full understanding of Torah, utilizing our full physical, intellectual powers, that of our brain. This corresponds to the next highest level of Torah learning, that of *remez.*

Normally, in our requests and *tefillos* to *HaKadosh Baruch Hu,* we do not ask Him for an abundance of anything. However, with regard to the understanding of Torah, in this *tefillah* we plead with *HaKadosh Baruch Hu* to grant us the greatest possible understanding, לְהָבִין וּלְהַשְׂכִּיל, of all aspects of His Torah. The Gemara (*Berachos* 50a) tells us that one may, indeed, ask for an abundance of Torah knowledge.

This is based on the words, הַרְחֶב פִּיךָ וַאֲמַלְאֵהוּ, *Open your mouth (with the widest possible request) and I shall fulfill it* (*Tehillim* 81:11). And the Gemara comments thereon: הַהוּא בְּדִבְרֵי תוֹרָה כְּתִיב, *This is a request for the fullest possible understanding of Torah.*

• לִשְׁמוֹעַ — **To hear.** If we do not merit the achievement of the two highest forms of understanding the Torah, then we pray to *HaKadosh Baruch Hu* that He may allow us לִשְׁמוֹעַ, to "hear" the Torah. The word לִשְׁמוֹעַ, *to hear,* encompasses two meanings.

The first is to hear something and commit it to memory with such intensity that one will never forget it. An example of this definition is: וַיֵּלֶךְ רְאוּבֵן וַיִּשְׁכַּב אֶת בִּלְהָה פִּילֶגֶשׁ אָבִיו, *Reuven went and lay with Bilhah, his father's concubine* (*Bereishis* 35:22). Reuven committed a subtle misdeed with regard to Bilhah to protest against the way his father had treated his mother Leah following Rochel's death. It is not entirely clear what the indiscretion actually was — it is described as בִּלְבֵּל יְצוּעֵי אָבִיו — he re-arranged the bed of his father, and *Chazal* tell us that this was not really a sin: כָּל הָאוֹמֵר רְאוּבֵן חָטָא אֵינוֹ אֶלָּא טוֹעֶה, *Whoever says Reuven committed a sin is making an error* (*Shabbos* 55b).

But whatever this misdeed was, the Torah records Yaakov's reaction as, וַיִּשְׁמַע יִשְׂרָאֵל, *Yisrael heard,* but no mention is made there that he did anything about it. However, on his deathbed, Yaakov tells his son Reuven, רְאוּבֵן בְּכֹרִי אַתָּה . . . פַּחַז כַּמַּיִם אַל תּוֹתַר כִּי עָלִיתָ מִשְׁכְּבֵי אָבִיךְ אָז חִלַּלְתָּ יְצוּעִי עָלָה, *Reuven, you are my firstborn . . . Waterlike impetuosity — you cannot be foremost, because you mounted your father's bed; then you desecrated Him Who ascended my couch* (*Bereishis* 49:3-4). "Your hasty and ill-advised action, when you violated the sanctity of my bed, shows that you are not fit for higher leadership. I cannot give you this *berachah*." With these words, at the end of Yaakov's life, he showed what was meant when the Torah describes his reaction as וַיִּשְׁמַע יִשְׂרָאֵל. It meant: "Yisrael heard it and never forgot it." And at the end of his life, Yaakov showed that, indeed, he had never forgotten it.

The second meaning of לִשְׁמוֹעַ is for each individual to hear the words of Torah as being directed toward him — personally. For instance, when the Torah says וְאָהַבְתָּ אֵת ה׳ אֱלֹהֶיךָ, *You shall love Hashem, your God* (*Devarim* 6:5), each person is to "hear" it and understand that this is a direct command to *him.* He is to think, "This means me!"

As an illustration, the first time I used the streetcar on Broadway in New York City, after my arrival from Germany, I assumed that, as in Europe, it was customary first to sit down and then to pay the conductor as he came through the car to collect the fare. After taking my seat, a loud voice called out, "Hey you, you forgot to drop your nickel into the box." Being blissfully unaware of the local custom, I did not "hear," and understand, that the conductor was calling to me, until my fellow passengers made me aware of it.

So, in this *tefillah,* we ask HaKadosh Baruch Hu that when we learn His Torah, we be given the ability לִשְׁמוֹעַ, to "hear," the subject matter, both in the sense of learning it and never forgetting it, and also, that we be given the awareness that the words of Torah are directed towards us. For instance, when one learns the mishnah which asks מֵאֵימָתַי קוֹרִין אֶת שְׁמַע בָּעֲרָבִין, *When does the time for reading of the Shema begin in the evening* (*Berachos* 1:1), or בַּמֶּה מַדְלִיקִין וּבַמָּה אֵין מַדְלִיקִין, *Which [fuels] are, and are not, suitable for kindling of the Sabbath lights* (*Shabbos* 2:1), he should be aware of the fact that these teachings are directed toward him personally. The Torah talks to each individual when he learns it. If one has this awareness while learning, he can possibly achieve the level of *derash*.

ללמוד — To learn. But, if we are not privileged to achieve the previously mentioned three deeper levels of learning, we ask *HaKadosh Baruch Hu* to grant us, at least, the opportunity to learn the simple *p'shat* of Torah. We ask for the privilege of being allowed just to learn Torah, even if it is on a very basic level.

וּלְלַמֵּד — And to teach. In the learning of Torah, the object is not only to know it and understand it personally, but to teach it: first to one's children, and then to others.

לִשְׁמֹר — To safeguard. This does not mean "keeping the Torah" in the colloquial sense. That would be called לַעֲשׂוֹת, which is the next word. Rather, it is to be understood in the sense of וּלְמַדְתֶּם אֹתָם וּשְׁמַרְתֶּם לַעֲשֹׂתָם, *learn them, and be careful to perform them* (*Devarim* 5:1), which is explained by *Rashi* in the name of *Chazal*: הֱווּ עֲמֵלִים בַּתּוֹרָה עַל מְנָת לִשְׁמוֹר וּלְקַיֵּים, *Be laboring in the Torah in order to safeguard and to fulfill that which you learn* (see *Rashi* on *Vayikra* 26:3). One keeps and preserves the Torah by learning it over and over again, so that he will be able to apply his learning immediately when the occasion arises. This is expressed by *Chazal* as וּשְׁמַרְתֶּם זוֹ מִשְׁנָה, *You shall safeguard; this is study* (see *Rashi*, *Devarim* 4:6).

וְלַעֲשׂוֹת — To observe. The object of Torah learning is its practical application, as *Chazal* teach, תַּלְמוּד גָּדוֹל שֶׁהַתַּלְמוּד מֵבִיא לִידֵי מַעֲשֶׂה, *Learning is greater, because it causes one to act* (observe *mitzvos*) (*Kiddushin* 40b); and לֹא הַמִּדְרָשׁ הוּא הָעִקָּר אֶלָּא הַמַּעֲשֶׂה, *Study is not the main thing, but rather it is the practice* (the performance of *mitzvos*) (*Pirkei Avos* 1:17). By "keeping" and storing the Torah in one's mind, he will have immediate access to the *halachos* when the occasion to apply them arises.

וּלְקַיֵּם — To uphold the *mitzvos*. This is not the same as לַעֲשׂוֹת, which means to observe the *mitzvos*. לְקַיֵּם means to strengthen and uphold the observance of *mitzvos* even if this involves hardships that may cause one to neglect them for various reasons. Some *mitzvos* may even interfere with one's livelihood or other important aspects of one's life. We ask *HaKadosh Baruch Hu* to give us the strength, in the face of all odds, to uphold those *mitzvos* that are about to fall and be trampled upon.

אֶת כָּל דִּבְרֵי תַלְמוּד תּוֹרָתֶךָ — All the words of Your Torah's teaching. We ask here that we may be privileged to keep the *mitzvos* as a result of learning about them in the Torah. We do not wish to keep the Torah and *mitzvos* merely as a "tradition." This relegates such observance to some kind of routine folk culture or superstition. We wish to keep the *mitzvos because we have learned about them in the Torah. Chazal* tell us: לֹא עַם הָאָרֶץ חָסִיד, *An unlearned person cannot be scrupulously pious* (*Pirkei Avos* 2:6). If one is ignorant of Torah learning, the *mitzvos* that he keeps as a "tradition" can never be performed properly.

בְּאַהֲבָה — **With love.** We ask *HaKadosh Baruch Hu* to grant us the frame of mind to practice the *mitzvos* not out of compulsion, or with a feeling of restriction, but out of love for Him and His Torah.

וְהָאֵר עֵינֵינוּ בְּתוֹרָתֶךָ — **Enlighten our eyes through Your Torah.** We ask *HaKadosh Baruch Hu* to give us the ability to find the hidden treasures in His Torah. It is not necessary to be a genius or a *gaon* to find something new in the Torah. Every Jewish *neshamah* has a share in the Torah. As David HaMelech said, גַּל עֵינַי וְאַבִּיטָה נִפְלָאוֹת מִתּוֹרָתֶךָ, *Open my eyes, so that I may see wonders in Your Torah* (*Tehillim* 119:18). There is no end to new knowledge that can be found in the Torah. For example, notwithstanding the fact that the popular *Chumash Mikraos Gedolos* contains dozens of *mefarshim* of *Rishonim* and *Acharonim*, Rav Samson R. Hirsch still found new insights to the Torah that had not been explained before. This holds true for other commentators, such as *Malbim* and *Ha'amek Davar*, who were also privileged by *HaKadosh Baruch Hu* to be enlightened with *chiddushei Torah* that had never been known before. And it applies equally to the commentators on the Mishnah and Gemara, and *Shulchan Aruch*.

The Torah describes Moshe Rabbeinu, in the following *pesukim*, as the greatest human being who ever lived. עַבְדִּי מֹשֶׁה בְּכָל בֵּיתִי נֶאֱמָן הוּא. פֶּה אֶל פֶּה אֲדַבֶּר בּוֹ וּמַרְאֶה וְלֹא בְחִידֹת וּתְמֻנַת ה' יַבִּיט, *My servant Moshe; in My entire house he is the trusted one. Mouth to mouth do I speak to him; in a clear vision and not in riddles, at the image of Hashem does he gaze* (*Bamidbar* 12:7-8); וְלֹא קָם נָבִיא עוֹד בְּיִשְׂרָאֵל כְּמֹשֶׁה אֲשֶׁר יְדָעוֹ ה' פָּנִים אֶל פָּנִים, *Never again has there arisen in Israel a prophet like Moshe, whom Hashem had known face to face* (*Devarim* 34:10).

Moshe Rabbeinu had the greatest insight into *HaKadosh Baruch Hu* that is humanly possible; three times he had spent forty days on *Har Sinai* in the closest proximity to *HaKadosh Baruch Hu* that is humanly possible; and yet, after having seen and experienced all this, at the age of 120 years, he expresses a *tefillah* to *HaKadosh Baruch Hu* in which he says: אַתָּה הַחִלּוֹתָ לְהַרְאוֹת אֶת עַבְדְּךָ אֶת גָּדְלְךָ וְאֶת יָדְךָ הַחֲזָקָה אֲשֶׁר מִי אֵל בַּשָּׁמַיִם וּבָאָרֶץ אֲשֶׁר יַעֲשֶׂה כְמַעֲשֶׂיךָ וְכִגְבוּרֹתֶךָ, *You have just begun to show Your servant Your greatness,* etc. (*Devarim* 3:24).

Moshe Rabbeinu recognized that all of the exalted experiences of his entire life were but the *beginning* of his insight into the way in which *HaKadosh Baruch Hu* reveals Himself. He realized that there is so much more to see.

A person may have been learning Torah for forty years, and may have reviewed the same Gemara many times, and yet all of a sudden he gains a new insight that he had never understood before. He has then received הֶאָרַת עֵינַיִם, *enlightenment,* from *HaKadosh Baruch Hu* on that particular part of the Torah.

A similar thought is expressed in the *haftarah* we read yesterday. [Ed. note: The reference is to the *haftarah* of *Bereishis,* October 24, 1992.] הַחֵרְשִׁים שְׁמָעוּ וְהַעִוְרִים הַבִּיטוּ לִרְאוֹת. מִי עִוֵּר כִּי אִם עַבְדִּי וְחֵרֵשׁ כְּמַלְאָכִי אֶשְׁלָח, מִי עִוֵּר כִּמְשֻׁלָּם וְעִוֵּר כְּעֶבֶד ה׳, *Listen, you deaf ones; take a good look, you blind ones. Who is as blind as my servant, or as deaf as the messenger whom I am sending? Who is as blind as the perfect person, as blind as the servant of God?* (*Yeshayahu* 42:18-19). And the *pasuk* continues, רָאוֹת רַבּוֹת וְלֹא תִשְׁמֹר פָּקוֹחַ אָזְנַיִם וְלֹא יִשְׁמָע, *There is so much to see, but you did not observe; your ears are wide open, but you did not hear.*

The meaning of these *pesukim* is that even the *Neviim,* who had heard and seen revelations that *HaKadosh Baruch Hu* revealed to them, can always find new and deeper meanings of these revelations, so much so, that once they discover their deeper meaning, they realize that they had previously been deaf and blind to the message that *HaKadosh Baruch Hu* wanted to give them. And the greater the *navi,* the more he can discover in the messages of Hashem: מִי עִוֵּר כִּמְשֻׁלָּם וְעִוֵּר כְּעֶבֶד ה׳, *Who is as blind as the perfected ones, or the servant of Hashem?* Even with his greater insight, the *eved Hashem* realizes that, nevertheless, there is yet so much more to see. He is still blind to all that can be known from a message of *HaKadosh Baruch Hu.* The *pasuk* (ibid. v. 21) concludes with, ה׳ חָפֵץ לְמַעַן צִדְקוֹ יַגְדִּיל תּוֹרָה וְיַאְדִּיר, *It is the will of Hashem for [Israel's] righteousness that the Torah become greater and stronger.* He wants every generation to gain new insights into His Torah through diligent study of it, which former generations did not see. This is expressed in the Gemara as: מָקוֹם הִנִּיחוּ לִי אֲבוֹתַי לְהִתְגַּדֵּר בּוֹ, *My forefathers have left room for me to become great in* (Torah novellae) (*Chullin* 7a). An ordinary person who begins to learn, and does so in earnest, may be able to find something new in the Torah that will astound even a seasoned *talmid chacham.* I have experienced many instances where simple people began to learn and have asked very astute questions, or have offered novel answers to difficult questions. Their eyes were enlightened by *HaKadosh Baruch Hu;* they found their share in the Torah. This is the meaning of וְהָאֵר עֵינֵינוּ בְּתוֹרָתֶךָ.

◆§ וְדַבֵּק לִבֵּנוּ בְּמִצְוֹתֶיךָ — **Attach our hearts to Your commandments.** Once our eyes have been enlightened through Torah learning, our hearts become attached to its *mitzvos.* This attachment is known as *dikduk b'mitzvos.* The more one learns, the more he is able to fulfill the *mitzvos* properly. And even on a simple level, one may think that he is doing the *mitzvos* properly, but without learning he cannot possibly do so, especially with regard to the *mitzvos* of Shabbos and Yom Tov, the *halachos* of *tzitzis* and *tefillin*, *berachos* — even *Kiddush* and *Bircas HaMazon*.

The result of diligent Torah learning is not only that we become more desirous of doing the *mitzvas asei* as, for instance, Shabbos and Yamim Tovim, but we become equally desirous of avoiding even the slightest *aveirah*. Our hearts become attached to every aspect of Torah and *mitzvos*.

וְיַחֵד לְבָבֵנוּ לְאַהֲבָה וּלְיִרְאָה אֶת שְׁמֶךָ — **Unite our hearts to love and fear Your Name.**

When we speak of the "Name" of *HaKadosh Baruch Hu* we mean *HaKadosh Baruch Hu* Himself. We can only understand "His Name," that which He reveals to us, but we cannot, as human beings, comprehend His essence, which is בְּלִי רֵאשִׁית וּבְלִי תַכְלִית, *without beginning and without end*. In fact *Chazal* tell us, כָּל הַתּוֹרָה כֻּלָּהּ שְׁמוֹתָיו שֶׁל הקב״ה, *the entire Torah consists of the Names of HaKadosh Baruch Hu,* meaning the revelation to us of His will. (See *Zohar HaKadosh, Yisro* 87 and Intro. to *Ramban Al HaTorah.*) Also, in the Torah (*Devarim* 28:58) we find the *pasuk:* לְיִרְאָה אֶת הַשֵּׁם הַנִּכְבָּד וְהַנּוֹרָא הַזֶּה, אֶת ה׳ אֱלֹהֶיךָ, *to fear this honored and awesome Name, Hashem your God.* Here the Torah identifies for us the "Name" of Hashem, as meaning Hashem Himself.

לְבָבֵנוּ is a plural-like form, and alludes to the "double heart." The heart can have two relationships with *HaKadosh Baruch Hu*. Some people can love *HaKadosh Baruch Hu,* however, they lack *yiras Shamayim*. For instance, one could love to learn Torah — even as God's Torah — but may not be fearful of doing things which could possibly constitute an *aveirah*. These are separate parts of the heart's relationship with *HaKadosh Baruch Hu*. Love of *HaKadosh Baruch Hu* and *yiras Shamayim* do not necessarily go together. And that is why we ask in this *tefillah* that *HaKadosh Baruch Hu* may unite our hearts to both love and fear Him.

This idea is beautifully illustrated by the Torah at *Akeidas Yitzchak*. First, Avraham Avinu is told by *HaKadosh Baruch Hu*: קַח נָא אֶת בִּנְךָ אֶת יְחִידְךָ אֲשֶׁר אָהַבְתָּ אֶת יִצְחָק... וְהַעֲלֵהוּ שָׁם לְעֹלָה, *Take your only and beloved son Yitzchak . . . and bring him as an offering [to me]* (*Bereishis* 22:2). I once heard from a great *talmid chacham* in Baltimore, Rabbi Michael HaKohen Forshlager, a *talmid* of the *Avnei Nezer,* that if *HaKadosh Baruch Hu* calls him "beloved" and "one and only," this *d'var Hashem* created a bond of love between father and son the likes of which did not exist previously. *At that moment, no father loved his son, or felt that he was unique, more than Avraham loved and felt the uniqueness of Yitzchak!* And yet, by performing the will of *HaKadosh Baruch Hu,* he was to demonstrate that his love of *HaKadosh Baruch Hu* was even greater than his love for Yitzchak. Then, after Avraham Avinu withstood the test, instead of simply being relieved that his beloved son's life was spared, he was afraid that the *d'var Hashem* would remain unfulfilled. He therefore wanted to fulfill the *d'var Hashem* in some symbolic manner, and offered a ram on the *mizbe'ach* in place of Yitzchak. This was a demonstration of *yiras Shamayim*. And when the *malach* called to him afterwards, he said, עַתָּה יָדַעְתִּי כִּי יְרֵא אֱלֹהִים אַתָּה וְלֹא חָשַׂכְתָּ אֶת בִּנְךָ אֶת יְחִידְךָ מִמֶּנִּי (ibid. v.12), *Now I know that you are a true* יְרֵא אֱלֹהִים: You have demonstrated not only your abundant love of *HaKadosh Baruch Hu*, but also your fear of violating His command.

The combination of *ahavas Hashem* and *yiras Hashem* can be achieved only through learning Torah. Without *limud haTorah*, any feelings of longing that a person may have for the Jewish way of life as practiced in the old *kehillos* of the towns and villages of Europe do not represent the love or fear of *HaKadosh Baruch Hu*. Rather, they are mostly nostalgic sentiments, somewhat like that which is expressed by the song "*Mein Shtetele Belz.*" They have no real connection with *HaKadosh Baruch Hu*. Such a connection can be achieved only through *limud haTorah*. One cannot fear or love something that is only an idea. By learning Torah, we recognize the reality of *HaKadosh Baruch Hu* and, consequently, can achieve both *ahavas Hashem* and *yiras Hashem*.

Love and fear are really contradicting relationships. One either fears another, or loves him. Love draws one to something, and fear repels one from it. We therefore ask *HaKadosh Baruch Hu* in this *tefillah* that in our relationship to Him, He allow us to have both sentiments, that of our love for Him, together with our fear of violating His will. This is the meaning of וְיַחֵד לְבָבֵנוּ.

To "fear" *HaKadosh Baruch Hu* does not mean that one must constantly tremble before Him. Rather, it means that one is to be afraid to violate His will. This is similar to the fear a driver has of going through a red light, which does not mean that he sits in his car and trembles. On the contrary, he can be very relaxed, while at the same time being acutely aware of the danger to his life should he go through that red light. This "fear" actually makes driving very safe. Similarly, we ask *HaKadosh Baruch Hu* to unify our hearts, לְיַחֵד, to love Him, while at the same time, to make us afraid of transgressing His will.

This *tefillah* for *ahavah* and *yirah* is a very appropriate introduction to our daily *Krias Shema*, which consists of both these aspects of *avodas Hashem*. The *halachah* requires that, on the one hand, it be said, בְּאֵימָה וּבְיִרְאָה בְּרֶתֶת וּבְזִיעַ, *with fear, trepidation, trembling, and shuddering,* similar to the moment of *Matan Torah*, where the Torah tells us that וַיֶּחֱרַד כָּל הָעָם אֲשֶׁר בַּמַּחֲנֶה, *And the entire people that was in the camp trembled* (Shemos 19:16; see Berachos 22a). At the same time, *Krias Shema* teaches us to love *HaKadosh*

וְאָהַבְתָּ אֵת ה' אֱלֹהֶיךָ בְּכָל לְבָבְךָ וּבְכָל נַפְשְׁךָ וּבְכָל מְאֹדֶךָ, **And You shall love Hashem, your God, with all your heart, with all your soul, and with all your resources.** This is also similar to *Matan Torah*, where the people had to be warned to restrain their desire to come too close to the *Shechinah* as a result of their *ahavas Hashem*. They were at once fascinated by their desire to come close to *HaKadosh Baruch Hu*, as an expression of their *ahavah*, while at the same time they trembled in awe and fear of Him. These two emotions are not contradictory. We need them both in the service of *HaKadosh Baruch Hu*.

§ וְלֹא נֵבוֹשׁ לְעוֹלָם וָעֶד — **So that we will not be put to shame for all eternity.** This refers to the World to Come, where everybody, sooner or later — we all hope and pray that it will be later — will have to come to *HaKadosh Baruch Hu* and give an account of his life. A *sefer Torah* is opened and the person is asked, "What did you keep, and what didn't you keep?" Therefore, we express the *tefillah* here that at that moment of truth, we will not be put to shame about how we lived our lives here on earth, because we are trying our very best to "love and fear Your Name." Hopefully, we will be able to say at that hidden, but certain, time, לְעוֹלָם וָעֶד: "We loved and feared *HaKadosh Baruch Hu* to the best of our ability." And then we will have no reason to be ashamed of the way we lived our lives here on earth. [Ed. note: For an explanation of this interpretation of עוֹלָם וָעֶד — with עוֹלָם meaning "hidden," and וָעֶד meaning "certain" — see Rav Samson R. Hirsch to *Shemos* 15:18.]

§ כִּי בְשֵׁם קָדְשְׁךָ הַגָּדוֹל וְהַנּוֹרָא בָּטָחְנוּ § — **Because we have trusted in Your great and awesome holy Name.** As we have explained, the "Name" of *HaKadosh Baruch Hu* is what we know about Him, because we cannot know His essence. Here we refer to His revelation to us that He is גָּדוֹל, in the sense of גְּדָל חֶסֶד — His greatness lies in the fact that He is full of mercy, kindness. At the same time, He is נוֹרָא, meaning the One Who inspires awe and fear in His creatures. This again emphasizes *ahavah* and *yirah*.

We have *bitachon*, full trust, that if we try our very best to love and fear *HaKadosh Baruch Hu*, we will succeed in this endeavor, and will have nothing to be ashamed of when we are faced with our moment of truth. This is again preparatory to *Krias Shema*, wherein we accept the command: וְאָהַבְתָּ אֵת ה' אֱלֹהֶיךָ בְּכָל לְבָבְךָ וּבְכָל נַפְשְׁךָ וּבְכָל מְאֹדֶךָ, which tells us that our love of *HaKadosh Baruch Hu* is to be so great that we are to be prepared even to sacrifice everything we have, including our lives if necessary, to follow His commands.

§ נָגִילָה וְנִשְׂמְחָה בִּישׁוּעָתֶךָ § — **May we exult and rejoice in Your salvation.** We have full *bitachon* that if we do what is right in this world, we can then look forward to rejoice in Your salvation. Salvation here refers to the *ultimate salvation of man*: to be saved from all the pitfalls of *Olam Hazeh* and earn an everlasting life of heavenly bliss in *Olam Haba*. We pray to *HaKadosh Baruch*

Hu here that we shall not be excluded from the blissful reward which awaits the *tzaddikim* in that future world, because life in this world is only a preparation for eternal life in *Olam Haba*. This is expressed in *Mesillas Yesharim* (Ch. 1): הָאָדָם לֹא נִבְרָא אֶלָּא לְהִתְעַנֵּג עַל ה׳, Man was created only to have the opportunity to enjoy a blissful eternal life in the proximity of *HaKadosh Baruch Hu* in *Olam Haba*.

וַהֲבִיאֵנוּ לְשָׁלוֹם מֵאַרְבַּע כַּנְפוֹת הָאָרֶץ — **Bring us home to peace from the four corners of the earth.** Earlier, we expressed our desire to come to *Olam Haba* without having to feel ashamed of ourselves at our moment of truth. However, in this phrase, we ask *HaKadosh Baruch Hu* to allow us, already in this world, to realize the blessings promised by the Torah, and that is to experience the *yemos haMashiach*.

וְתוֹלִיכֵנוּ קוֹמְמִיּוּת לְאַרְצֵנוּ — **And lead us upright to our land.** According to the custom of the *Arizal,* which was adopted all over *Ashkenaz,* at this point we gather our four *tzitzis,* to symbolize our desire to see and experience the *kibbutz galuyos* at the time of *Mashiach.* Although one is prohibited from engaging in any other activity during *tefillah,* to avoid a disruption of *kavannah,* nevertheless, since this act is symbolic of the words of this particular *tefillah,* it does not interfere with one's concentration on it.

The word קוֹמְמִיּוּת occurs only once in all of *Tanach,* and besides its use here in this *tefillah,* we also use it in the series of הָרַחֲמָן, which we say after *Bircas HaMazon*: הָרַחֲמָן הוּא יִשְׁבּוֹר עֻלֵּנוּ מֵעַל צַוָּארֵנוּ וְהוּא יוֹלִיכֵנוּ קוֹמְמִיּוּת לְאַרְצֵנוּ. The singular occurrence of קוֹמְמִיּוּת in *Tanach* is: וָאֶשְׁבֹּר מֹטֹת עֻלְּכֶם וָאוֹלֵךְ אֶתְכֶם קוֹמְמִיּוּת, and I broke the poles of your yoke, and I led you upright (*Vayikra* 26:13). *Rashi* (ibid.) explains קוֹמְמִיּוּת as בְּקוֹמָה זְקוּפָה, *an upright and erect posture.* The simple meaning of this *pasuk* is that *HaKadosh Baruch Hu* is telling *Bnei Yisrael* that He took them out of Mitzrayim and broke the yoke of Egyptian slavery for the purpose of their receiving the Torah on *Har Sinai,* toward which He led them in an "upright posture."

The translation, "I led you in an upright posture," provided by *Rashi,* presents a difficulty in light of the statement that one should not walk even four *amos* with a קוֹמָה זְקוּפָה, an overly erect posture, because it is a sign of arrogance (*Kiddushin* 31a). I remember, when I was in the Mirrer Yeshivah, my revered Rebbe, the *Mashgiach,* HaRav Yerucham Levovitz, was troubled by this, and offered a prize of 10 *zlotys* to any *bachur* who could explain this *Rashi* to his satisfaction. I would have loved to earn the 10 *zlotys* at that time, but it took me many years to understand the true meaning of קוֹמְמִיּוּת. I finally came to the realization that *Rashi's* explanation of קוֹמְמִיּוּת as בְּקוֹמָה זְקוּפָה means he understood it as having the meaning of *stretching oneself up to one's full height.* This would be similar to what one would do while his height is being measured at the doctor's office.

Based on this, the meaning of the *pasuk* is as follows. *HaKadosh Baruch Hu* is telling *Bnei Yisrael* that in addition to the actual redemption from Egypt, *I broke the poles of your yoke,* meaning, "Not only did I redeem you from slavery in Egypt, but I completely severed any vestiges of your connection to the swamp of Egyptian culture, which had dragged you down through the מ״ט שַׁעֲרֵי טוּמְאָה, *the forty-nine gates of tumah.* During the long years of enslavement, our forefathers languished in the swamp of Egyptian culture, and were deprived of any spiritual growth. However, when the redemption came, *HaKadosh Baruch Hu* whisked this former horde of slaves away from Egypt as "quickly as the eagle flies," וָאֶשָּׂא אֶתְכֶם עַל כַּנְפֵי נְשָׁרִים, and within forty-nine days they found themselves standing at the foot of *Har Sinai* on a spiritual level elevated enough to receive the Torah. During this brief time period, *HaKadosh Baruch Hu* had brought *Klal Yisrael* up from the depths of depravity, and raised them to the highest possible level that they could ever reach.

Accordingly, וָאוֹלֵךְ אֶתְכֶם קוֹמְמִיּוּת means that at the time of *Matan Torah*, *HaKadosh Baruch Hu* had raised the Jewish nation up to their fullest potential. They had experienced all the *nissim* and *niflaos* that were associated with *yetzias Mitzrayim* and *krias Yam Suf* and the *manna*. And when, after all these great revelations of *HaKadosh Baruch Hu*, the Jewish people finally stood at the foot of *Har Sinai* and uttered the words, כֹּל אֲשֶׁר דִּבֶּר ה׳ נַעֲשֶׂה וְנִשְׁמָע, *Whatever Hashem has said we will do and we will listen* (*Shemos* 24:7), they had been raised to the highest level of spiritual development they could ever possibly reach. At that moment, they had achieved the spiritual level of Adam before the sin, and were at their highest level of spiritual development. This is the בְּקוֹמָה זְקוּפָה that *Rashi* understood to be the meaning of קוֹמְמִיּוּת.

I believe this explanation would have satisfied my Rebbe, and he would have awarded me the 10 *zlotys*.

Therefore, it is in this sense that we say in our *tefillah* here, וַהֲבִיאֵנוּ לְשָׁלוֹם מֵאַרְבַּע כַּנְפוֹת הָאָרֶץ וְתוֹלִיכֵנוּ קוֹמְמִיּוּת לְאַרְצֵנוּ. We ask *HaKadosh Baruch Hu* that we shall not have to wait until we come to *Olam Haba* to receive our full reward and not be put to shame; rather, we ask that we achieve our highest spiritual potential here and now, with the ingathering of our people to Eretz Yisrael and the coming of *Mashiach*.

This *tefillah* of our redemption and return to Eretz Yisrael in peace follows the previous *tefillah* for success in the learning of Torah and fulfilling its *mitzvos*. In the words וַהֲבִיאֵנוּ לְשָׁלוֹם, we express the *tefillah* for the actual *kibbutz galuyos,* which will bring all of our people home together in peaceful coexistence, based on Torah, through *Mashiach*. This will be the time when תַּלְמִידֵי חֲכָמִים מַרְבִּים שָׁלוֹם בָּעוֹלָם, *Torah scholars increase peace in the world* (Conclusion, *Berachos* 64a), because we will all learn the same Torah, and that will bring us together. שֶׁנֶּאֱמַר וְכָל בָּנַיִךְ לִמּוּדֵי ה׳, וְרַב שְׁלוֹם בָּנָיִךְ, *As the pasuk* says: *And all of your children will be students of Hashem, and great will be the peace of your children* (*Yeshayahu* 54:13). And *Chazal* tell us, אַל תִּקְרֵי בָּנַיִךְ, אֶלָּא בּוֹנַיִךְ, *Do not read "your children," but rather, read "your knowledgeable ones,"* meaning, we will bring our diversified strengths together, and build one big political structure with its foundation firmly resting on the Torah. We refer to this in the *Shemoneh Esrei*: תְּקַע בְּשׁוֹפָר גָּדוֹל לְחֵרוּתֵנוּ . . . וְקַבְּצֵנוּ יַחַד מֵאַרְבַּע כַּנְפוֹת הָאָרֶץ, *Sound the great shofar for our freedom . . . and gather us together from the four corners of the earth.* The word יַחַד, *together,* connotes the nation coming together in peaceful harmony, which will be brought about through *limud haTorah*. At that time we will again have reached our highest potential greatness, and will once again stand proudly upright, קוֹמְמִיּוּת, in our land.

Although in our time *Eretz Yisrael* has become a haven of refuge for millions of our brethren from all over the world, this is in no way the fulfillment of the *kibbutz galuyos,* under *Mashiach,* for which we have been praying for thousands of years. That coming together, under *Mashiach,* will be לְשָׁלוֹם, "toward peace", the peace which results from adherence to Torah, without the bitter polarization and factional infighting that exists in *Eretz Yisrael* today.

By asking *HaKadosh Baruch Hu* to reunify His nation in *Eretz Yisrael*, we introduce the central theme of *Krias Shema*, that of the absolute "Oneness" of *HaKadosh Baruch Hu*. The words ה׳ אֶחָד mean that, in reality, nothing else exists besides Hashem, אֵין עוֹד מִלְבַדּוֹ. All other existence is but a manifestation of His will. To properly express this profound and overwhelming thought, it is necessary for all of *Klal Yisrael* to be together in *Eretz Yisrael*. The Torah — and its core truth, that ה׳ אֶחָד — was given to the entire *Klal Yisrael* and not to individuals. When the Jewish nation prepared to receive the Torah, we are told that the people were unified as one: וַיִּחַן שָׁם יִשְׂרָאֵל נֶגֶד הָהָר, *And Israel encamped there opposite the mountain* (*Shemos* 19:2). *Rashi* (ibid.), quoting *Chazal*, remarks, כְּאִישׁ אֶחָד בְּלֵב אֶחָד, *As if they were one person with one mindset.*

כִּי אֵל פּוֹעֵל יְשׁוּעוֹת אָתָּה — Because You are the Almighty Who does works of salvation. In the previous *berachah* of יוֹצֵר אוֹר we had the phrase כִּי הוּא לְבַדּוֹ פּוֹעֵל גְּבוּרוֹת, and there it referred to material strength. However, in the present *berachah*, we are referring to the spiritual "work" of *HaKadosh Baruch Hu* in bringing us salvation. As we already explained, this consists of *yemos haMashiach* in this world, and *chayei haolam haba,* in the future World to Come.

וּבָנוּ בָחַרְתָּ מִכָּל עַם וְלָשׁוֹן — And You have chosen us from all nations and tongues. This refers to *Matan Torah*. The Jewish nation was chosen by *HaKadosh Baruch Hu* from all the world's nations to receive His Torah. We also find the expression, "אֲשֶׁר בָּחַר בָּנוּ מִכָּל הָעַמִּים", which means that *HaKadosh Baruch Hu* has chosen us out of all the nations of the world, from the most primitive to the most highly developed, good and bad, great and small. However, "אֲשֶׁר בָּחַר בָּנוּ מִכָּל עָם", and "וְלָשׁוֹן מִכָּל עָם וּבָנוּ בָחַרְתָּ" means, "He has chosen us from even the most highly developed nations and sophisticated cultures." The word לָשׁוֹן, *tongue,* in this sentence conveys the idea of "culture."

וְקֵרַבְתָּנוּ לְשִׁמְךָ הַגָּדוֹל סֶלָה בֶּאֱמֶת — **You have brought us close to Your Great Name in truth.** Many philosophers and theologians have ideas and conceptions of God, but these are not בֶּאֱמֶת; they are ideas developed by man. However, through the Torah, *HaKadosh Baruch Hu* has revealed to us the truth of His existence and the attributes of His Being.

לְהוֹדוֹת לְךָ — **To thank You.** The first result of our having received the Torah is to thank You. Not even for one day are we to forget that *HaKadosh Baruch Hu* selected us from all the nations of the world and gave us His Torah. The בִּרְכַּת הַתּוֹרָה of אֲשֶׁר בָּחַר בָּנוּ מִכָּל הָעַמִּים וְנָתַן לָנוּ אֶת תּוֹרָתוֹ is a *berachah* of thanksgiving, *bircas hoda'ah,* thanking *HaKadosh Baruch Hu* for giving us the Torah, which we are to say every day of our lives.

These last few phrases actually contain the elements of *birchos haTorah.* Therefore, if one forgot to say *birchos haTorah* at the beginning of his *tefillah,* by saying אַהֲבָה רַבָּה he has in effect said the *berachah* over the Torah. But since *birchos haTorah* require that one learns some Torah afterwards, he should learn something after *Shemoneh Esrei,* and he will thus have satisfied his obligation of saying *birchos haTorah* (see *Shulchan Aruch, Orach Chaim* 47:7).

וּלְיַחֶדְךָ בְּאַהֲבָה — **And to declare Your Unity, Your Oneness, with love.** The love we are referring to here is our love of *HaKadosh Baruch Hu,* and His reciprocal love.

Interestingly, the numerical value of אַהֲבָה is 13, which is the same as אֶחָד. And the combination of the two is 26, which is the numerical value of the Name י־ה־ו־ה.

בָּרוּךְ אַתָּה ה׳ הַבּוֹחֵר בְּעַמּוֹ יִשְׂרָאֵל בְּאַהֲבָה — **Blessed are You, Hashem, Who chooses His people Israel with love.** The greatest act of love that *HaKadosh Baruch Hu* has shown us is the giving to us of His Torah. And we are obligated to respond by loving Him, which obligation is contained in the first part of *Krias Shema*: וְאָהַבְתָּ אֵת ה׳ אֱלֹהֶיךָ בְּכָל לְבָבְךָ וּבְכָל נַפְשְׁךָ וּבְכָל מְאֹדֶךָ.

The *Midrash Rabbah* (*Va'eschanan* 2:31) explains the connection between *Krias Shema* and *Matan Torah* as follows:

How did *Bnei Yisrael* merit the *mitzvah* of reading the *Shema*? Rabbi Pinchas ben Chama said that the first words which Hashem spoke on Sinai were when He told them: "Hear, Yisrael, I am Hashem, your God." Upon which they all responded, "Hashem is our God; Hashem is One." And Moshe said, "Blessed be the Name of the glory of His Kingdom forever."

During *Matan Torah,* every Jewish soul — even the yet unborn — was present when 600,000 men, their wives and children — a total of several million people — heard the voice of *HaKadosh Baruch Hu* articulating His words in the sound of a powerful *shofar* blast, speaking directly to them: פָּנִים בְּפָנִים דִּבֶּר ה' עִמָּכֶם בָּהָר מִתּוֹךְ הָאֵשׁ, *Face-to-face did Hashem speak with you on the mountain, from amid the fire* (*Devarim* 5:4). They heard clearly the words of the first two of the *Aseres HaDibros,* face-to-face, directly from *HaKadosh Baruch Hu.*

This Midrash is telling us here that the twice-daily repetition of *Krias Shema* reminds us of *Matan Torah,* when the entire Jewish nation declared, ה' אֱלֹהֵינוּ, *Hashem is our God,* in response to the voice of *HaKadosh Baruch Hu* saying, in the first statement: אָנֹכִי ה' אֱלֹהֶיךָ אֲשֶׁר הוֹצֵאתִיךָ מֵאֶרֶץ מִצְרַיִם וגו', *I am Hashem, your God, Who has taken you out of the land of Egypt* (ibid. v. 6); and ה' אֶחָד, *Hashem, the One and Only,* in response to the second statement, לֹא יִהְיֶה לְךָ אֱלֹהִים אֲחֵרִים עַל פָּנָי, *You shall not recognize the gods of others in My Presence* (ibid. v. 7).

Therefore, by saying *Krias Shema,* we are fulfilling the *mitzvah* of never forgetting that moment when we stood at Sinai and accepted the Torah: פֶּן תִּשְׁכַּח אֶת הַדְּבָרִים אֲשֶׁר רָאוּ עֵינֶיךָ . . . יוֹם אֲשֶׁר עָמַדְתָּ לִפְנֵי ה' אֱלֹהֶיךָ בְּחֹרֵב, *lest you forget the things that Your eyes have beheld . . . the day that you stood before Hashem, your God, at Chorev* (ibid. 4:9-10).

This is why, as we have mentioned previously, it is necessary to say *Krias Shema* with the utmost seriousness, בְּאֵימָה וּבְיִרְאָה בְּרֶתֶת וּבְזִיעַ, *with fear, trepidation, trembling, and shuddering.*

Whenever we learn Torah we must remember that we are not merely listening to an interesting *shiur* or covering an interesting topic, but rather, we must keep in mind that *we are learning God's Torah!* Even the *takanos Chachamim* (Rabbinic enactments) or their various *gezeiros* (decrees) are all based upon the *Torah Shebe'al Peh* or the *Torah Shebichsav.*

We learn (*Pirkei Avos* 3:10): רַבִּי דּוֹסְתָּאִי בַּר יַנַּאי מִשּׁוּם רַבִּי מֵאִיר אוֹמֵר: כָּל הַשּׁוֹכֵחַ דָּבָר אֶחָד מִמִּשְׁנָתוֹ מַעֲלֶה עָלָיו הַכָּתוּב כְּאִלּוּ מִתְחַיֵּב בְּנַפְשׁוֹ, שֶׁנֶּאֱמַר (דברים ד:ט-י) "רַק הִשָּׁמֶר לְךָ וּשְׁמֹר נַפְשְׁךָ מְאֹד פֶּן תִּשְׁכַּח אֶת הַדְּבָרִים אֲשֶׁר רָאוּ עֵינֶיךָ (. . . יוֹם אֲשֶׁר עָמַדְתָּ לִפְנֵי ה' אֱלֹהֶיךָ בְּחֹרֵב. . . "). יָכוֹל אֲפִילוּ תָּקְפָה עָלָיו מִשְׁנָתוֹ, תַּלְמוּד לוֹמַר "וּפֶן יָסוּרוּ מִלְּבָבְךָ כֹּל יְמֵי חַיֶּיךָ," הָא אֵינוֹ מִתְחַיֵּב בְּנַפְשׁוֹ עַד שֶׁיֵּשֵׁב וִיסִירֵם מִלִּבּוֹ. Paraphrasing, this means that if one forgets *one thing* of his learning, it is considered as if he had forfeited his life. This is based on the *pesukim* (*Devarim* 4:9-10), *Watch yourself and guard your life carefully, lest you lose it, by forgetting the things that your eyes have seen: the day on which you stood before HaKadosh Baruch Hu at Chorev and He taught you the Torah.* This means the paramount and overriding דָּבָר אֶחָד, the "one thing" which one must never forget is *the fact that the Torah we are learning is God's Torah.* To forget this is playing with one's life!

Besides underlining the importance of always remembering this cardinal foundation of all Torah learning, this mishnah also stresses the importance of retaining Torah knowledge in one's heart, and the danger of "sitting down and purposefully removing it." A sure way of such purposeful removal of Torah knowledge from one's mind would be by sitting down in front of a television set. Viewing most of the material there is a sure-fire method of overriding and erasing the *divrei Torah* from one's mind.

קְרִיאַת שְׁמַע / Krias Shema

The twice-daily recitation of *Krias Shema* is a fulfillment of a *mitzvah* of the Torah. One is required to say *Krias Shema* at night and to repeat it in the morning during the first three hours of the day, the time when most people arise. The commandment, וְדִבַּרְתָּ בָּם . . . בְּשָׁכְבְּךָ וּבְקוּמֶךָ, *And speak of them . . . when you retire and when you arise* (*Devarim* 6:7 and 11:19), which is the basis for this *mitzvah*, is contained in the first two *parshiyos* of *Krias Shema*. However, there is a difference of opinion as to what parts of the Torah are to be recited to fulfill this *mitzvah d'Oraisa* (see *Mishnah Berurah* 67:2).

According to most opinions, only the first *pasuk*, שְׁמַע יִשְׂרָאֵל ה׳ אֱלֹהֵינוּ ה׳ אֶחָד, is *d'Oraisa*, and all the rest of *Krias Shema* is *d'Rabbanan* (see *Sefer HaChinuch* 420; *Ba'er Heitev* 67:1; *Magen Avraham* ibid., among others).

A second opinion is that the saying of the entire first *parashah* is from the Torah (see *Talmidei Rabbeinu Yonah* to *Berachos* 16a [folio 9a of *Rif*, s.v. למימרא]; *Mishnah Berurah* 64:15).

A third opinion is that both the *parshiyos* of שְׁמַע and וְהָיָה אִם שָׁמֹעַ are Torah obligations (see *Pri Chadash, Orach Chaim* beginning of 67).

And according to a fourth opinion, there is no specific *parashah* which has been stipulated from the Torah for the fulfillment of the *mitzvah* of וְדִבַּרְתָּ בָּם . . . בְּשָׁכְבְּךָ וּבְקוּמֶךָ. The Torah left it up to the *Chachamim* to decide which parts of the Torah should be recited at night and in the morning in fulfillment of this *mitzvah*. The *Chachamim* selected the three *parshiyos* that we call *Krias Shema* with which to fulfill this *mitzvah* (see *Talmidei Rabbeinu Yonah* to *Berachos* 21a [folio 12b of *Rif*, s.v. גמ׳ אמר רב יהודה]).

Be that as it may, since the *mitzvah* of *Krias Shema* can be performed only at specific times in the morning, and again only at night, it falls under the category of *mitzvas asei shehazeman gerama*, a time-bound positive commandment from which women are exempt. However, the underlying meaning of *Krias Shema*, that of *kabbalas ol Malchus Shamayim*, applies to men and women equally, and this can be fulfilled at any time, by women as well as by men.

Therefore, if a person misses the specific times for reading the *Shema*, while he has forfeited the *mitzvas asei* of *Krias Shema*, he still should read the *parshiyos*, because by doing so he has at least fulfilled a *mitzvah* of reading the Torah, and can, at the same time, also fulfill the *mitzvah* of *kabbalas ol Malchus Shamayim*.

Our *Chachamim* have ordained that *Krias Shema* be accompanied by the recitation of *birchos Krias Shema*. These consist of two *berachos* before the *Shema*, both in the morning and in the evening; two *berachos* afterwards in the evening; and one *berachah* afterwards in the morning. (The *berachah* of בָּרוּךְ ה' לְעוֹלָם אָמֵן וְאָמֵן in the Maariv prayer was instituted at a later period, is not said on Shabbos or Yom Tov, and is said only in *chutz la'aretz* (outside Eretz Yisrael).

The question arises: Since *Krias Shema* is a *mitzvah*, why do we not recite a *berachah*, לִקְרוֹא אֶת שְׁמַע, before we say it, as we do before reciting *Hallel*, לִקְרוֹא אֶת הַהַלֵּל; or עַל מִקְרָא מְגִילָה before reading the *Megillah*? This question is valid even according to those opinions that consider the saying of the specific three *parshiyos* a *mitzvah d'Rabbanan*, because *Hallel* and the reading of the *Megillah* are also *mi'd'Rabbanan*, and yet, we make the aforementioned *berachos*.

The answer is this: The essence of the *mitzvah* of *Krias Shema* is *kabbalas ol Malchus Shamayim*, which is the intent of the first *pasuk*, שְׁמַע יִשְׂרָאֵל ה' אֱלֹהֵינוּ ה' אֶחָד. If one were simply to read these words without the *kavannah* of the acceptance of God's existence and Oneness, and His sovereignty over the world, he would not have performed the *mitzvah* at all. This is because the meaning of שְׁמַע is "hear," "listen," "intellectualize." The mere קְרִיאָה, physical reading, of the *pasuk* does not fulfill this *mitzvah*. It requires concomitant thought. As to the rest of *Krias Shema*, if one were to merely read it, without concentrating on its meaning — which is certainly not ideal — he would still be fulfilling the *mitzvah* of קְרִיאָה, reading. This would be similar to reading the *Megillas Esther* or *Hallel* without *kavannah*, in which case he would still be *yotzei* (have fulfilled) these *mitzvos* (*Megillah* 18a).

Therefore, it is the *kavannah* that makes *Krias Shema* into a *mitzvah* and there is no *berachah* for *kavannah*. The *berachos* were instituted only for *maaseh hamitzvah* (the physical act of performing a *mitzvah*), and not for *kavannah* alone. It is for this reason that we do not make a *berachah* over the *mitzvah* of *tefillah*, אֲשֶׁר קִדְּשָׁנוּ בְּמִצְוֹתָיו וְצִוָּנוּ לְהִתְפַּלֵּל, even according to the Rambam, who considers *tefillah* a *mitzvas asei d'Oraisa*. Thus, if one were to say *Shemoneh Esrei* without, at least, concentrating on the first *berachah*, he would not be *yotzei* the *mitzvah*. (See *Shulchan Aruch, Orach Chaim* 101:1).

The Midrash says: אָמַר רַבִּי לֵוִי: צָרִיךְ אָדָם לִהְיוֹת זָהִיר בִּקְרִיאַת שְׁמַע, שֶׁהִיא שְׁקוּלָה כְּנֶגֶד כָּל הַקָּרְבָּנוֹת, *Rabbi Levi said: One should be very careful with the reading of Shema for it is the equivalent of all the Korbanos* (see *Devarim Rabbah* [*Yerushalayim*] p. 63). The idea of a *korban* is that a person offers his life to *HaKadosh Baruch Hu*. Symbolically, the animal represents the person, and it is offered instead of him. Similarly, the meaning of *Krias Shema* is that by accepting the "yoke of heaven" upon himself (*kabbalas ol Malchus Shamayim* — which is the essence of *Krias Shema*), one expresses the thought that, if necessary, he is ready to offer his life to *HaKadosh Baruch Hu*. Incidentally, the word ש־מ־ע, in reverse order, is the abbreviation of עוֹל מַלְכוּת שָׁמַיִם.

In the *Zohar Chadash* (Rus, p. 77), we find the statement: אָמַר רַבִּי נְחֶמְיָה אָמַר רַבִּי נְהוֹרַאי: אַסְוָותָא לְבַר נָשׁ בְּהַאי עָלְמָא, בְּכָל יוֹמָא, מַאן דְּקָרָא קְרִיאַת שְׁמַע עַל תִּקּוּנֵיהּ, A sure, daily, remedy for a person in this world is the regular and timely reading of the *Shema*. This means that the proper saying of *Krias Shema* is a remedy for any doubts that a person may have concerning the veracity of the existence of *HaKadosh Baruch Hu* or *Torah min haShamayim*. The proper saying of *Krias Shema* is a *refuas hanefesh,* a cure for the spirit, and serves to recharge the battery and strengthen the *emunah* of a person.

Furthermore: אָמַר רַבִּי מָנִי: לֹא תְהֵא קְרִיאַת שְׁמַע קַלָּה בְּעֵינֶיךָ, *Rabbi Mani said: Do not treat Krias Shema lightly* (*Midrash Tanchuma, Kedoshim* 6). This means that despite the fact that קְרִיאַת שְׁמַע is a very easy *mitzvah* to fulfill — it takes only a brief amount of time and does not cost money — do not take it lightly; מִפְּנֵי שֶׁיֵּשׁ בָּהּ מָאתַיִם וְאַרְבָּעִים וּשְׁמוֹנָה תֵּיבוֹת, כְּמִנְיַן אֵבָרִים שֶׁבָּאָדָם, *because it has 248 words* (including בָּרוּךְ שֵׁם כְּבוֹד מַלְכוּתוֹ לְעוֹלָם וָעֶד), *corresponding to the 248 parts of the human body*. The Midrash continues: אָמַר הקב״ה: אִם שָׁמַרְתָּ אֶת שֶׁלִּי לִקְרוֹת קְרִיאַת שְׁמַע כְּתִיקְנָהּ, אֲנִי אֶשְׁמוֹר אֶת שֶׁלָּךְ, It is as if *HaKadosh Baruch Hu* is saying, "If you watch over all of the 248 words of My *mitzvah* of *Krias Shema*, I will watch over all the 248 members of your body."

However, as a matter of fact, there are only 245 words in *Krias Shema*, even if we include בָּרוּךְ שֵׁם כְּבוֹד מַלְכוּתוֹ לְעוֹלָם וָעֶד. The three missing words are compensated for, either by the generally accepted *minhag* of the saying אֵל מֶלֶךְ נֶאֱמָן by an individual who is not *davening* with the *tzibbur* (these words begin with the letters א־מ־ן) or by hearing the *chazzan* concluding with ה׳ אֱלֹהֵיכֶם אֱמֶת. However, according to *minhag* Frankfurt and some other *kehillos Ashkenaz* — in which the *chazzan* does not repeat אֲנִי ה׳ אֱלֹהֵיכֶם, but rather announces the end of *Krias Shema* only by saying אֱמֶת — the two other missing words are compensated for by the saying of *Amen* after הַבּוֹחֵר בְּעַמּוֹ יִשְׂרָאֵל בְּאַהֲבָה, and the addition of the word אֱמֶת by each individual at the end of *Krias Shema*.

The *mitzvah* of *Krias Shema* has an interesting correlation to the *mitzvah* to establish עָרֵי מִקְלָט [*arei miklat*] (cities of refuge) in *Eretz Yisrael*. The Torah mandates that if a person kills another person accidentally, under certain circumstances he is to flee to one of these cities to escape the wrath of the גּוֹאֵל הַדָּם, a relative who would seek to avenge the inadvertent death of his family member. However, once the murderer reaches and remains in one of these cities, the relative is prohibited from killing him.

The *ir miklat* is קוֹלֶטֶת: It protects the accidental killer from being killed by a bereaved relative. This *mitzvah* is repeated several times in the Torah. After listing the three cities which Moshe selected as *arei miklat* in *eiver layardein* (the Jewish territory given to the Tribes of Reuven, Gad, and half of Menashe) [in all there were six *arei miklat*], the Torah immediately adds the words וְזֹאת הַתּוֹרָה אֲשֶׁר שָׂם מֹשֶׁה לִפְנֵי בְּנֵי יִשְׂרָאֵל, *This is the teaching that Moshe placed before the Bnei Yisrael* (*Devarim* 4:41-44). And the Gemara points out: אָמַר רַבִּי יוֹחָנָן: מִנַּיִן לְדִבְרֵי תוֹרָה שֶׁהֵן קוֹלְטִין, שֶׁנֶּאֱמַר: אֶת בֶּצֶר בַּמִּדְבָּר וגו' ... וְזֹאת הַתּוֹרָה וגו', *Said Rabbi Yochanan: The source for the fact that words of Torah are protective is that immediately following the names of the three cities of refuge we find the verse: "This is the Torah, which Moshe placed before the Jewish people"* (*Makkos* 10a). Rav Yochanan views the juxtaposition of the *pasuk* of וְזֹאת הַתּוֹרָה וגו' to the *parashah* of *arei miklat* expressing the idea that just as the *arei miklat* serve to protect and save the accidental killer from death, so do the words of Torah save a person from death.

The cities of refuge serve to save someone who accidentally killed another person from being killed. Similarly, if a person accidentally condemns himself to death by doing *aveiros* which carry the penalty of *misah b'yedei Shamayim* or *kares* (these are forms of capital punishment which are meted out by Heaven, and not by human courts), although this was not his intention when he did these *aveiros,* similar to one who killed another accidentally, a return to and acceptance of *divrei Torah* can serve to save him from the fatal consequences of his own actions, just as surely as an *ir miklat* saves an accidental murderer from being killed.

The *divrei Torah* expressed in *Krias Shema* have a special relationship with *arei miklat*. Both שְׁמַע יִשְׂרָאֵל ה' אֱלֹהֵינוּ ה' אֶחָד, from *Torah Shebichsav,* and its counterpart, בָּרוּךְ שֵׁם כְּבוֹד מַלְכוּתוֹ לְעוֹלָם וָעֶד, from *Torah Shebe'al Peh,* contain six words. This corresponds to the six *arei miklat*. And the first *parashah,* beginning with וְאָהַבְתָּ, contains exactly 42 words, corresponding to the 42 cities of the *Leviim,* which also served as *arei miklat* (see *Bamidbar* Ch. 35).

Therefore, וְזֹאת הַתּוֹרָה אֲשֶׁר שָׂם מֹשֶׁה לִפְנֵי בְּנֵי יִשְׂרָאֵל, mentioned immediately after the *mitzvah* of *arei miklat,* expresses the thought that Torah itself plays the same role as *arei miklat,* and one can save himself from his own inadvertent "suicide" by "fleeing" back to, and accepting upon himself, *divrei Torah* which will protect him. This is especially true regarding those basic tenets of Torah that are expressed in *Krias Shema.*

The ideal way to say the *pasuk* שְׁמַע יִשְׂרָאֵל is to do so together with the other *mispallelim,* in a loud voice, as a national declaration of our faith (see *Shulchan Aruch, Orach Chaim* 61:4). I remember that this was the way it was said by the *kehillos* in Ashkenaz. I also remember, laudatorily, that in Shearith Israel Congregation of Baltimore, the entire congregation would sing שְׁמַע יִשְׂרָאֵל together, in a loud voice. However, for some unknown reason, here, even in our *kehillah,* it is said quietly and without enthusiasm. I do not know who started this practice, but it would be well to have it corrected.

However, בָּרוּךְ שֵׁם כְּבוֹד מַלְכוּתוֹ לְעוֹלָם וָעֶד is to be said quietly. This is based on, כְּבֹד אֱלֹהִים הַסְתֵּר דָּבָר, *It is the honor of God to conceal a matter* (*Mishlei* 25:2). When one speaks of God, hide things. This means that discussions about *HaKadosh Baruch Hu* are not to be preached in the marketplace. These are esoteric topics, which can be discussed only among people with elevated minds who are striving for a more spiritual life. However, וּכְבֹד מְלָכִים חֲקֹר דָּבָר, *but it is the honor of kings to search out a matter,* meaning when it comes to discussions about kings, you are to explore things publicly in all details and talk openly of the splendor and accomplishments of the king (see *Peirush HaGra, Mishlei* 25:2).

Therefore, שְׁמַע יִשְׂרָאֵל, with its *kabbalas ol Malchus Shamayim*, is to be said publicly and out loud, as a declaration of the general concept of the acceptance of the rule of *HaKadosh Baruch Hu* over ourselves. This is כְּבֹד מְלָכִים, *honor of kings,* and it is to be rightfully publicized.

However, בָּרוּךְ שֵׁם כְּבוֹד מַלְכוּתוֹ לְעוֹלָם וָעֶד, which Moshe Rabbeinu heard from the *malachim* while he was near the *Kisei HaKavod* during the thrice-repeated forty days on *Har Sinai*, is כְּבֹד אֱלֹהִים, *honor of God,* which is to be said quietly in deference to its very esoteric nature. In fact, the Midrash compares the reciting of these words to a piece of jewelry which was "stolen from the King's palace": לְמָה הַדָּבָר דּוֹמֶה, לְאֶחָד שֶׁגָּנַב קוּזְמִין מִתּוֹךְ פַּלְטִין שֶׁל מֶלֶךְ, נְתָנָהּ לָהּ לְאִשְׁתּוֹ וְאָמַר לָהּ: אַל תִּתְקַשְּׁטִי בָּהּ בְּפַרְהֶסְיָא אֶלָּא בְּתוֹךְ בֵּיתֵךְ, *This can be compared to one who stole a piece of jewelry from the king's palace and gave it to his wife with instructions to wear it only in her house, but not publicly* (see *Devarim Rabbah* 2:36 and *Midrash Tanchuma, Kedoshim* 6).

The meaning is that the *malachim* did not know that Moshe Rabbeinu had heard them say these exalted words, and that he would later transmit them to *Bnei Yisrael* through *Torah Shebe'al Peh*. We therefore say בָּרוּךְ שֵׁם כְּבוֹד מַלְכוּתוֹ לְעוֹלָם וָעֶד quietly to ourselves, to stress the very exalted nature of the meaning of these words.

Another reason for the saying of בָּרוּךְ שֵׁם כְּבוֹד מַלְכוּתוֹ לְעוֹלָם וָעֶד is: When Yaakov Avinu was on his deathbed, he called his children together for the purpose of telling them what the future would hold in store for them at *acharis hayamim,* the End of Days: הֵאָסְפוּ וְאַגִּידָה לָכֶם אֵת אֲשֶׁר יִקְרָא אֶתְכֶם בְּאַחֲרִית הַיָּמִים, *Assemble yourselves and I will tell you what will befall you in the End of Days* (*Pesachim* 56a, based on *Bereishis* 49:1-2).

However, in the next sentence, instead of talking about the *acharis hayamim,* he begins with the *berachos.* And the Gemara explains: בִּיקֵּשׁ יַעֲקֹב לְגַלּוֹת לְבָנָיו קֵץ הַיָּמִין וְנִסְתַּלְּקָה מִמֶּנּוּ שְׁכִינָה, *Yaakov had intended to reveal what would happen at the end of Jewish History,* when Mashiach would come, *but the Heavenly Presence left him.* He wanted to reveal to them when the End of Days would occur (meaning *Mashiach, geulah,* and *techiyas hameisim*), but the *Shechinah,* the presence of *HaKadosh Baruch Hu,* left him and he was therefore unable to reveal the *acharis hayamim.*

Troubled by this, Yaakov Avinu asked his children: שֶׁמָּא חַס וְשָׁלוֹם יֵשׁ בְּמִטָּתִי פְּסוּל, כְּאַבְרָהָם שֶׁיָּצָא מִמֶּנּוּ יִשְׁמָעֵאל, וְאָבִי יִצְחָק שֶׁיָּצָא מִמֶּנּוּ עֵשָׂו, *Is it possible that there is a fault in my bed [one of my children is a sinner], similar to Avraham who fathered Yishmael, or my father Yitzchak who fathered Eisav?* Yaakov Avinu was afraid that the reason the *Shechinah* had left him was because perhaps one or more of his children were not following in his footsteps, as had occurred to his father and grandfather before him. Upon which, his children, calling him by his God-given name, Yisrael, answered: שְׁמַע יִשְׂרָאֵל ה' אֱלֹהֵינוּ ה' אֶחָד, כְּשֵׁם שֶׁאֵין בְּלִבְּךָ אֶלָּא אֶחָד, כָּךְ אֵין בְּלִבֵּנוּ אֶלָּא אֶחָד, which means: *Just as there is only One God in your heart, so is there only One God in our hearts* (Gemara, ibid.).

When Yaakov Avinu heard this and looked around and saw his twelve sons — all of whom were *tzaddikim* who had long ago forgiven each other for any wrongs that they had committed — and saw that here, in Egypt, he was surrounded by their families, who were all *tzaddikim* and *tzidkaniyos* and were now united in brotherly love around his deathbed, he felt as if he was having a preview of the *acharis hayamim*. To Yaakov Avinu, this was the *kibbutz galuyos* in miniature. And the Gemara (ibid.) tells us that at that moment Yaakov Avinu said the words בָּרוּךְ שֵׁם כְּבוֹד מַלְכוּתוֹ לְעוֹלָם וָעֶד.

However, these exalted words were not heard by the children of Yaakov Avinu, and it was not until Moshe Rabbeinu heard them from the *malachim* that we became aware of them. It is a prayer of the *neshamah* and reflects the world of the *malachim*, from which the *neshamah* emanates.

The meaning of these words is very difficult to comprehend, but we will make an attempt at understanding them as we proceed.

The Gemara (ibid.) continues, and asks, הֵיכִי נַעֲבִיד, *What shall we do?* Shall we say בָּרוּךְ שֵׁם כְּבוֹד מַלְכוּתוֹ לְעוֹלָם וָעֶד, or not? On the one hand, since Moshe Rabbeinu did not write it in the Torah, how can we say it? However, on the other hand, Yaakov Avinu did say it. Therefore, the Gemara concludes, הִתְקִינוּ שֶׁיְּהוּ אוֹמְרִים אוֹתוֹ בַּחֲשַׁאי, *they* [the Chachamim] *instituted that it be said, but only quietly.*

Regarding the *pasuk* of שְׁמַע יִשְׂרָאֵל, it is written in the *sefer Torah* with a large ע at the end of the first word, and a large ד at the end of the last word:

שְׁמַע יִשְׂרָאֵל ה' אֱלֹהֵינוּ ה' אֶחָד

The large ד in אֶחָד is to insure that it not be misread as ר (forming the word אַחֵר). And the word אַחֵר in the *pasuk* לֹא תִשְׁתַּחֲוֶה לְאֵל אַחֵר, *For you shall not prostrate yourselves to an alien god* (Shemos 34:14), is written with a large ר at the end, to avoid the mistake of misreading it as a ד (which would form the word אֶחָד).

Rav Samson R. Hirsch (on *Devarim* 6:4) remarks: The ר of the polytheistic thought is accommodatingly rounded, while the ד of the Jewish truth is sharply angular. With the loss of a little sharpness, the אֶחָד becomes אַחֵר. The meaning is quite clear: ה' אֶחָד is a sharply defined concept, *it is this way, and there are no other possibilities.*

Rav Hirsch continues, and explains that the reason for the large ע in שְׁמַע is to emphasize that the word be read correctly as שְׁמַע, *hear,* and that the ע not be mistaken for an א, which would result in the word שֶׁמָּא, *perhaps.* Also, the combination of these two large letters forms the word עֵד, *witness.* In his words: "The contents of שְׁמַע יִשְׂרָאֵל are a testimony by Israel to Israel, and everybody who utters it stands forth thereby as a witness of God to himself and to the world."

He also suggests that perhaps the emphasis on the letter עַיִן, *eye,* is to underscore that the nation was an eyewitness to *Matan Torah,* as is expressed by אַתָּה הָרְאֵתָ לָדַעַת כִּי ה' הוּא הָאֱלֹהִים . . . מִן הַשָּׁמַיִם הִשְׁמִיעֲךָ אֶת קֹלוֹ לְיַסְּרֶךָּ, *Your were shown in order to know that Hashem is The God . . . He allowed you to hear His voice from heaven to teach you* (Devarim 4:35-36).

I would like to add that this is supported by the *pasuk,* וְכָל הָעָם רֹאִים אֶת הַקּוֹלֹת, *the entire people saw the thunder* (Shemos 20:15), on which Rashi (ibid.) comments: רוֹאִין אֶת הַנִּשְׁמָע שֶׁאִי אֶפְשָׁר לִרְאוֹת בְּמָקוֹם אַחֵר, *They "saw sounds,"* an impossibility in any other situation. This means that at *Matan Torah* the Jewish nation *saw what they heard,* a phenomenon that does not occur elsewhere. Therefore, the Jewish nation does not have to "believe" that *Matan Torah* occurred, for it is an eyewitness to it. This is emphasized by the large עַיִן.

When one says שְׁמַע יִשְׂרָאֵל, he is saying to himself that he, as a member of the nation of Israel, who witnessed *Matan Torah,* accepts ה' אֱלֹהֵינוּ as ה' אֶחָד, as did our nation from its inception through this very moment.

When we say ה' אֱלֹהֵינוּ, we pronounce the Name of *HaKadosh Baruch Hu* as אֲדֹנָי, *my Lord,* which expresses each individual's acceptance of *HaKadosh Baruch Hu* as his own personal Lord. (We commented on this subject in our remarks on אֲדוֹן עוֹלָם.)

This is what is meant by *kabbalas ol Malchus Shamayim,* and it includes being ready to sacrifice one's life for *HaKadosh Baruch Hu,* if necessary. At that moment, a person should think that one day his life will end anyway; and just as he has lived with ה' אֱלֹהֵינוּ, he will die with ה' אֱלֹהֵינוּ. This is the essence of one's whole existence.

Notwithstanding the pronunciation אֲדֹנָי, one should also think of the meaning of the written form, י-ה-ו-ה, which is הָיָה, הֹוֶה, וְיִהְיֶה, *He was, He is, and He will be;* he constantly calls everything into existence. The true meaning of the Ineffable Name י-ה-ו-ה is מְהַוֶּה כָּל הַהֲוָיוֹת, that He makes all existence exist. Without Him nothing would exist. This is why this Name is called שֵׁם הַוָיָה, *Existence.* And it was this Name which *Bnei Yisrael* heard on *Har Sinai*, in the words of אָנֹכִי יְ־הֹ־וָ־ה אֱלֹהֶיךָ, *I am Hashem, your God* (*Shemos* 20:2).

So when one says שְׁמַע יִשְׂרָאֵל he should imagine himself, as a member of *Klal Yisrael*, standing at *Har Sinai* and hearing *HaKadosh Baruch Hu* saying אָנֹכִי יְ־הֹ־וָ־ה אֱלֹהֶיךָ, *I am Hashem, your God*, and לֹא יִהְיֶה לְךָ אֱלֹהִים אֲחֵרִים, *You shall not recognize the gods of others* (ibid. 20:3). This does not mean simply, "I am Hashem your God," but rather, "Accept Me as your God." And the *mitzvah* is to do so without any questions or reservations. By saying ה׳ אֱלֹהֵינוּ, he has accepted the first commandment, אָנֹכִי יְ־הֹ־וָ־ה אֱלֹהֶיךָ, and by saying ה׳ אֶחָד, he has accepted the second commandment, that of לֹא יִהְיֶה לְךָ אֱלֹהִים אֲחֵרִים.

Despite the fact that every human being has a free choice, *bechirah*, to accept or deny *HaKadosh Baruch Hu* as His God, the saying of שְׁמַע יִשְׂרָאֵל is a declaration that he has given away this freedom, and has accepted *ol Malchus Shamayim*. This does not mean simply the acceptance of the fact of *Malchus Shamayim*, that there is a Heavenly King, similar to the way one accepts the election of a new president of the United States, whether one likes it or not. Rather, "the acceptance of the *yoke* of Heaven" means that he has given away his *bechirah* and accepts *HaKadosh Baruch Hu* unconditionally, similar to locking himself up and throwing away the key. This conviction is to be so strong that nothing in the world can ever take it away from him.

The covering of one's eyes during the recitation of שְׁמַע יִשְׂרָאֵל is to indicate our exclusion of every possible argument for not accepting *HaKadosh Baruch Hu* — and there are thousands of them — and to concentrate one's thoughts on this truth: ה׳ אֱלֹהֵינוּ ה׳ אֶחָד.

The *Talmud Yerushalmi* (*Berachos*, beginning of Ch. 2) states: צָרִיךְ לְהַאֲרִיךְ בְּאֶחָד, *one is required to draw out the word* אֶחָד. This is qualified by Rav Nachman bar Yaakov: וּבִלְבַד בְּדָלֶת, *this [requirement applies] only to the* ד. One is to linger only on the sound of the ד.

However, Rav Ashi cautions: וּבִלְבַד שֶׁלֹּא יַחֲטוֹף בְּחֵי״ת, *that when attempting to stress the* ד *sound, one should [be careful] not to slur the* ח (*Berachos* 13b). (This would result in the word אֲחַד, *echd*, which is meaningless.)

This requirement to extend the saying of אֶחָד is considered so important that the Gemara (ibid.) states: כָּל הַמַּאֲרִיךְ בְּאֶחָד מַאֲרִיכִין לוֹ יָמָיו וּשְׁנוֹתָיו, *One who properly draws out the word Echad will have his days and years lengthened.*

But Rav Nachman bar Yaakov in the *Talmud Yerushalmi* declares: וְלֵית אַתְּ צָרִיךְ [לְהַאֲרִיךְ] כָּל הָכֵין אֶלָּא כְּדֵי שֶׁתַּמְלִיכֵיהּ בַּשָּׁמַיִם וּבָאָרֶץ וּבְאַרְבַּע רוּחוֹת הָעוֹלָם, *You do not have to draw it out longer than it takes to conceptualize HaKadosh Baruch Hu as the King of heaven and earth, and in all four directions.* This does not have to take too long. One should just think that he is surrounded by

HaKadosh Baruch Hu, that nothing else but the will of HaKadosh Baruch Hu surrounds him.

The three letters of אֶחָד are to be pronounced as follows:

א is said quickly, because this refers to the *absolute unity* of *HaKadosh Baruch Hu,* a concept on which we cannot dwell, because it is incomprehensible to the human mind. To us, the number "1" in the mathematical sense is also divisible. However, as regards *HaKadosh Baruch Hu,* His "Oneness" is absolute and indivisible; it is *achdus peshutah.* We therefore do not dwell on the א, since we cannot comprehend this concept. However, it should not be said so quickly as to miss the sound altogether, and produce a word which would sound like חָד.

ח is said with a slight lingering sound to emphasize the sound ח, and to avoid it sounding like ה (see *Rashi* to *Berachos* 13b). The letter ח corresponds to the number eight, referring to the relationship of *HaKadosh Baruch Hu* with our world, which comes down to us through the שִׁבְעָה רְקִיעִים, *seven heavens.* The *seven heavens* is a symbolic expression for the seven attributes of *HaKadosh Baruch Hu.* (See our comments on וַיְבָרֶךְ דָּוִיד, and specifically, לְךָ ה' הַגְּדֻלָּה, וְהַגְּבוּרָה, וְהַתִּפְאֶרֶת, וְהַנֵּצַח, וְהַהוֹד, כִּי כֹל בַּשָּׁמַיִם וּבָאָרֶץ, לְךָ ה' הַמַּמְלָכָה.)

By pronouncing the ח clearly, and lingering on it slightly, we express the thought that this ineffable, inexplicable, inconceivable concept of the Absolute Oneness of *HaKadosh Baruch Hu* has come all the way down to us through the שִׁבְעָה רְקִיעִים, *seven layers* of the revelation of *HaKadosh Baruch Hu* to us, and is accepted by us here in this world.

ד is said with a lingering emphasis (by holding one's tongue against his upper teeth), although not to the extent that it would sound like ך. It is here that each person should have the thought that this Absolute Oneness of *HaKadosh Baruch Hu* relates to him personally. מַאֲרִיךְ בְּדָלֶת means that each person is to clarify in his own mind that *HaKadosh Baruch Hu* is absolutely and uniquely One throughout all of existence. Be this right, left, up or down, *HaKadosh Baruch Hu* is the only true existence, and anything else which exists does so only because He wants it to exist. Even the evil in the world exists only because He wants it to exist. One is to concentrate on the thought that he is surrounded on all sides by revelations of *HaKadosh Baruch Hu.*

This truth is expressed in the Torah: וְיָדַעְתָּ הַיּוֹם וַהֲשֵׁבֹתָ אֶל לְבָבֶךָ, *You shall know today, and you shall continually bring this thought back to your heart;* כִּי י־ה־ו־ה הוּא הָאֱלֹהִים בַּשָּׁמַיִם מִמַּעַל וְעַל הָאָרֶץ מִתָּחַת, *that* י־ה־ו־ה *is the God in the heavens above and on the earth below* (*Devarim* 4:39). One needs to be reminded of this constantly, because it is a very elusive thought. When one looks at nature and sees the magnificence of the heavens, the moon, the starry sky, the oceans, and the mountains, it is comparatively easy to recognize the existence of *HaKadosh Baruch Hu.* However, when one sees slum buildings inhabited by drug dealers and other criminals, it is quite difficult to recognize that this, too, exists only by the will of *HaKadosh Baruch Hu*. It is only *HaKadosh Baruch Hu* Who makes the drug dealer's heart beat and his mind work. For reasons which we do not understand, *HaKadosh Baruch Hu* has allowed evil people to exist in the world, whether they be Nazis or any other criminals or evildoers. The *Navi* exclaims this in the Name of *HaKadosh Baruch Hu*: אָנֹכִי בָּרָאתִי מַשְׁחִית לְחַבֵּל, *I created the destroyer to destroy* (*Yeshayahu* 54:16). However, the evil in the world will eventually disappear, as expressed in the verse, יִתְפָּרְדוּ כָּל פֹּעֲלֵי אָוֶן, *all doers of iniquity shall be dispersed* (*Tehillim* 92:10).

The aforementioned *pasuk* (*Devarim* 4:39) ends with אֵין עוֹד, *There is nothing else*. One may think: "Well, I am here, with my *yetzer hara*, with all my doubts, with all my resentments." But since one is required to negate his own existence by being ready to give up all of his desires and instincts, even his life, if this is required according to *halachah*, for *HaKadosh Baruch Hu*, then he is really not "there"; there is no עוֹד. This is the meaning of אֵין עוֹד, and it is this concept which is called *kabbalas ol Malchus Shamayim*.

Rav Moshe Chaim Luzzatto explains that while we cannot understand — and should not even attempt to understand — the *middos* of *HaKadosh Baruch Hu*, the Torah does require that we think about His unique Oneness, אֵין עוֹד מִלְבַדּוֹ, and אַחְדוּתוֹ יִתְבָּרַךְ.

Rashi on the *pasuk* שְׁמַע יִשְׂרָאֵל gives a very prosaic explanation of its meaning, as follows: ה' שֶׁהוּא אֱלֹהֵינוּ עַתָּה וְלֹא אֱלֹהֵי הָאֻמּוֹת הוּא עָתִיד לִהְיוֹת ה' אֶחָד, *Hashem Who is now only our God, and not the God of the rest of the world, will eventually become recognized as the One and Only God*. For now, only שְׁמַע יִשְׂרָאֵל, only Israel knows that Hashem is God. However, eventually, He will be accepted by the whole world. Even gentiles who believe in God combine the Deity with some other entity or entities. This is called *shituf*. So שְׁמַע יִשְׂרָאֵל means that what we believe today with *emunah sheleimah* that אֵין עוֹד מִלְבַדּוֹ, will one day become universal: בַּיּוֹם הַהוּא יִהְיֶה ה' אֶחָד וּשְׁמוֹ אֶחָד, *On that day Hashem will be One and His Name will be One* (*Zechariah* 14:9).

One day, when there is no more evil, no more *yetzer hara*, no more sin, everybody will clearly see that ה' אֶחָד. However, in the meantime, we, as Israel, through our power of *emunah*, can see this even today.

בָּרוּךְ שֵׁם כְּבוֹד מַלְכוּתוֹ לְעוֹלָם וָעֶד /
Baruch Shem Kevod Malchuso LeOlam Va'ed

As we explained earlier, these words are composed of language which the *malachim* use. They express thoughts which defy simple explanations, and are therefore to be said quietly, in the spirit of כְּבוֹד ה' הַסְתֵּר דָּבָר. And by using these words, we join the *malachim* in their praise of *HaKadosh Baruch Hu*.

❧ ❧ ❧

The approximate meaning is:

בָּרוּךְ שֵׁם כְּבוֹד מַלְכוּתוֹ — **May the Name of the glory of His Kingdom be increasingly expanded,** until, eventually, all human beings will recognize the existence of *HaKadosh Baruch Hu*.

לְעוֹלָם וָעֶד — **At a hidden, but certain, time in the future.** I was once asked what thought a person should have while saying בָּרוּךְ שֵׁם כְּבוֹד מַלְכוּתוֹ. I answered that while doing so, he should imagine himself in the *Beis HaMikdash*, prostrated before *HaKadosh Baruch Hu*, with arms and legs outstretched, in total submission to the will of *HaKadosh Baruch Hu*, just as we do on Yom Kippur during the *avodah* in the *tefillah* of Mussaf.

The idea of prostrating oneself, with arms and legs outstretched in the *Beis HaMikdash,* is that the person doing so becomes part of the *Beis HaMikdash,* which is dedicated completely to the service of *HaKadosh Baruch Hu*. As such, the person expresses the thought that he is prepared to give up his ego, his self, completely to *HaKadosh Baruch Hu*, and is even ready to sacrifice his life, if necessary, for *HaKadosh Baruch Hu*.

[Ed. note: The Rav left a handwritten page of notes, with the heading כְּבוֹד ה' הַסְתֵּר דָּבָר, regarding the meaning of the words בָּרוּךְ שֵׁם כְּבוֹד מַלְכוּתוֹ לְעוֹלָם וָעֶד. There he explains the words שֵׁם, כְּבוֹד, and מַלְכוּתוֹ in highly Kabbalistic and esoteric language. It is difficult to decipher, and we have therefore not included it in this work.]

While all of these concepts connected with *Krias Shema* are very profound, the actual recitation of *Krias Shema* need not take inordinately long. Once a person becomes accustomed to the twice-daily repetition of the text, with the proper concentration on its basic elements, it can be said rather quickly.

The *mitzvah* of *Krias Shema* requires that one pronounce each and every word clearly in accordance with the rules of *dikduk:* for instance, to clearly differentiate between a *sheva na* and a *sheva nach*. Some examples of this are: וְאָהַבְתָּ is to be pronounced "*ve'ahavta,*" because the *sheva* under the ב is *nach;* וּקְשַׁרְתָּם should be pronounced "*ukeshartam,*" because the *sheva* under the ר is a *sheva nach* (and not "*ukesharetom,*" as it would be if it were a *sheva na*); לְבָבְךָ should be pronounced "*levavecha,*" because in this case the *sheva* is *na*.

Furthermore, one must separate words which, if said quickly, could sound as if they are combined into one word, resulting in a different meaning. An example would be the words וְחָרָה אַף, which, if said quickly, would sound like וְחָרֵף (this actually means blasphemy). Or, in the case of words that follow each other when the letter ending the first word also begins the next word, e.g. וַאֲבַדְתֶּם מְהֵרָה, care must be taken not to drop the second מ and make a combined sound of וַאֲבַדְתְּמְהֵרָה. Similarly, the words וְשַׂמְתֶּם אֶת must be clearly separated to avoid producing a sound like וְשַׂמְתֶּם מֵת. For a fuller list of many possible reading errors, see *Orach Chaim* 61:22. Fortunately, according to the *halachah* cited there, if one is unfamiliar with the rules of *dikduk,* or mispronounces these or similar words, he is still *yotzei* the *mitzvah* of reciting *Krias Shema*. However, it is proper that one familiarize himself with the proper reading of the *Shema* in order to be *yotzei* the *mitzvah* in its best possible way.

There is a very beautiful explanation for the *mitzvah* of *Krias Shema* in *Sefer HaChinuch* (420), which we quote as follows: כִּי בִּהְיוֹת הָאָדָם בַּעַל חוֹמֶר, נִפְתֶּה אַחַר הַבְלֵי הָעוֹלָם וְנִמְשָׁךְ לְתַאֲוֹתָיו, צָרִיךְ עַל כָּל פָּנִים זִכָּרוֹן תְּמִידִי בְּמַלְכוּת שָׁמַיִם. וְנִצְטַוֵּינוּ לְזָכְרוֹ בִּשְׁנֵי הָעִתִּים שֶׁל יוֹם וָלַיְלָה, מֵחֲמַת שֶׁבְּדֶרֶךְ כְּלָל כָּל מַה שֶׁרוֹאֶה הָאָדָם בְּמֶשֶׁךְ הַיּוֹם וְהַלַּיְלָה נִרְאָה כְּהֵיפֶךְ הָאֱמוּנָה בַּה׳ חַס וְשָׁלוֹם, לָכֵן עָלָיו לְהִתְחַזֵּק עֶרֶב וָבֹקֶר בְּהַזְכָּרַת שְׁמַע יִשְׂרָאֵל, שֶׁיִהְיוּ עֵינָיו פְּקוּחוֹת לְפַלֵּס אוֹרְחוֹתָיו וּלְכַוֵּן צְעָדָיו עַל פִּי רְצוֹנוֹ יִתְבָּרַךְ. In summary, this means that since, generally, the impressions which a person receives from the world in which he lives seem to convey the opposite of the basic truths of our faith, it is therefore necessary to "recharge the batteries" regularly to reinforce one's *emunah*. One's "storage battery" of *emunah* is usually at full capacity for only half a day before it needs "recharging." The twice-daily recitation of *Krias Shema* serves as a reinforcement of the basic truths of our faith.

As we previously explained, one is to recite *Krias Shema* while in a frame of mind of the utmost seriousness, and in awe of *HaKadosh Baruch Hu,* similar to that which our forefathers experienced at the time of *Matan Torah* (see *Berachos* 22a). מַה לְּהַלָּן בְּאֵימָה וּבְיִרְאָה וּבְרֶתֶת וּבְזִיעַ. אַף כָּאן בְּאֵימָה וגו׳, *Just as at Matan Torah, there was fear, trepidation, trembling, and shuddering, here, too (while saying the Shema), one should be in a similar frame of mind.* The awesome events described in the Torah during *Matan Torah* inspired awe and fear in the hearts of *Bnei Yisrael* to the extent that they feared for their lives. They thought that the whole world was coming to an end. And amidst all of this fear, they suddenly heard the sound of *HaKadosh Baruch Hu* saying, אָנֹכִי ה' אֱלֹהֶיךָ ... לֹא יִהְיֶה לְךָ אֱלֹהִים אֲחֵרִים, *I am Hashem, your God ... You shall not recognize the gods of others in My Presence* (Devarim 5:6-7). Notwithstanding this frame of mind while saying *Krias Shema*, one is to temper this feeling of *yiras Hashem* with *ahavas Hashem*, which is the subject of the next sentence: וְאָהַבְתָּ אֵת ה' אֱלֹהֶיךָ. The saying of *Krias Shema* is to evoke a combination of *ahavas Hashem* and *yiras Hashem*. This combination is referred to in אַהֲבָה רַבָּה with the words וְיַחֵד לְבָבֵנוּ לְאַהֲבָה וּלְיִרְאָה אֶת שְׁמֶךָ, *Enable our hearts to both love and fear Your Name.*

וְאָהַבְתָּ אֵת ה' אֱלֹהֶיךָ

As we previously mentioned, there is a difference of opinion among our *Chachamim* as to whether the reciting of this entire parsha of *Krias Shema* is a *mitzvas asei d'Oraisa* or *mi'd'Rabbanan*. However, be that as it may, the *mitzvah* to love *HaKadosh Baruch Hu* is certainly *mi'd'Oraisa*, as is clearly evidenced by our *pasuk*, וְאָהַבְתָּ אֵת ה' אֱלֹהֶיךָ, **You shall love Hashem, Your God.** And this *mitzvah* is repeated several times in the Torah.

The Gemara tells us: כָּל הַקּוֹרֵא קְרִיאַת שְׁמַע בְּלֹא תְּפִלִּין כְּאִילּוּ מֵעִיד עֵדוּת שֶׁקֶר בְּעַצְמוֹ, *If someone reads the Shema without wearing tefillin, [which is mandated in it,] it is akin to giving false testimony to HaKadosh Baruch Hu* (Berachos 14b). If one merely exercises "lip service" of the *mitzvos*, and does not perform them, he is lying to *HaKadosh Baruch Hu*. It is said in the name of the Chafetz Chaim that similarly, if one merely mouths the words וְאָהַבְתָּ אֵת ה' אֱלֹהֶיךָ, but he does not feel any love towards *HaKadosh Baruch Hu* at that moment, he, too, is lying.

We are commanded to love *HaKadosh Baruch Hu*: בְּכָל לְבָבְךָ וּבְכָל נַפְשְׁךָ וּבְכָל מְאֹדֶךָ, *with all your heart, with all your soul, and with all your resources.* We will attempt to explain the meaning of these three relationships.

◆§ בְּכָל לְבָבְךָ — **With all your heart.** The love of *HaKadosh Baruch Hu* is based first and foremost on the knowledge that *HaKadosh Baruch Hu* exists. One cannot love an idea or a philosophical concept. One can love only something that actually exists. And not only does *HaKadosh Baruch Hu* exist, but He relates to each individual personally, because He created each individual. This personal relationship is described in the Torah (Devarim 5:4) in connection with the revelation at Sinai: פָּנִים בְּפָנִים דִּבֶּר ה' עִמָּכֶם, *Face-to-face did Hashem speak to You.* *HaKadosh Baruch Hu* spoke to us as if He were a person!

The *Chovos HaLevavos* explains that the basic reason for *ahavas Hashem* is out of gratitude for the fact that He created us. Each person is to think, *HaKadosh Baruch Hu* created me — although He did not need me. The world existed previously without me, and will continue to exist after me. When I came to live in Washington Heights some thirty-three years ago, many of the people who are here now did not even exist yet. There was the same street, the same *shul* building. And there were older people at that time, who were born before I existed. So we love *HaKadosh Baruch Hu,* firstly, because He created us gratuitously.

Furthermore, we love *HaKadosh Baruch Hu* not only in gratitude for creating us as human beings who can eat, sleep, earn a living, procreate, and generally enjoy life, but especially, because He created us as members of *Bnei Yisrael.*

And even more, we love *HaKadosh Baruch Hu* not only for creating us as human beings who are members of Israel to live in this world — which is of a limited duration — but also because He created each and every one of us with the potential of earning eternal life, לְהִתְעַנֵּג עַל ה׳, *to enjoy the pleasure of closeness to Hashem* (from *Mesillas Yesharim* Ch. 1) in *Olam Haba,* where one can enjoy the highest possible form of bliss and happiness, and total peace and serenity.

We love *HaKadosh Baruch Hu* because He created us for all this, and for no other reason than to bestow some of His ultimate goodness to another entity. We love *HaKadosh Baruch Hu* because He gave us a purpose in life. And if we look carefully, we can see His *hashgachah pratis,* how He constantly watches over us.

The Torah tells us, וְאָהַבְתָּ אֵת ה׳ אֱלֹהֶיךָ בְּכָל לְבָבְךָ. The word for heart is written in a plural-like form: a "double heart." And *Chazal* tell us that this refers to the *yetzer hatov* and the *yetzer hara* (see *Berachos* 54a).

The love for *HaKadosh Baruch Hu* with one's *yetzer hatov* is that which is described by the *Rambam* (*Hil. Teshuvah* 10:3) as a love that is even greater than the love that a man has for a woman. If a man is in love with a woman, he cannot think of anything else; no matter what he does, she is always on his mind. This is so, because he knows that she is personally interested in him as an individual.

The comparison is quite obvious. If I know that *HaKadosh Baruch Hu* is interested in me personally — otherwise I wouldn't wake up in the morning — and that He is forgiving of me, despite the fact that I have done so many things that were wrong, I become overwhelmed with love for Him because of His goodness toward me.

While most people do not have the *zechus* to reach this level of *ahavas Hashem,* nevertheless, by saying the *pasuk* וְאָהַבְתָּ אֵת ה׳ אֱלֹהֶיךָ, we express the wish that our love of *HaKadosh Baruch Hu* may eventually reach this level. This is the desire of our *yetzer hatov.* However, the *yetzer hara* has another agenda, namely, to urge us to do the opposite of what *HaKadosh Baruch Hu* wants us to do. And it is not simply an urge, it is a fascination, a strong desire, to oppose the will of *HaKadosh Baruch Hu.* And through the *yetzer hara,* one can even derive a sense of momentary pleasure for opposing the will of *HaKadosh Baruch Hu.*

How can one love *HaKadosh Baruch Hu* with His *yetzer hara*? To understand this, I wish to refer to the explanation of Rav Samson R. Hirsch on the words which *HaKadosh Baruch Hu* directed to Cain (*Kayin*), when he became angry and jealous after *HaKadosh Baruch Hu* had rejected his *korban,* and accepted that of his brother Hevel: וַיֹּאמֶר ה' אֶל קָיִן . . . הֲלוֹא אִם תֵּיטִיב שְׂאֵת, *And Hashem said to Cain . . . Surely, if you improve yourself, you will be forgiven* (*Bereishis* 4:6,7). Paraphrasing the translation of Rav Hirsch, this means, "If you will do good, and control your urge to harm your brother, you will rise to a high level, you will become a great person." The desire to do something bad is nothing to be ashamed of. If one has the urge — and the opportunity — to steal, or to cheat, or to commit an immoral act with impunity, and he overcomes his desire and does not do so, he becomes a greater person for it. Each time he overcomes these desires, he rises to a higher level; he becomes "שְׂאֵת."

However, וְאִם לֹא תֵיטִיב לַפֶּתַח חַטָּאת רֹבֵץ, *but if you do not improve yourself, sin rests at the door* (ibid.). Continuing to paraphrase Rav Hirsch: "If you do not do good, then, as soon as you open the door, the sin will be quietly lying there." He explains that the word רֹבֵץ does not mean lying in ambush, ready to spring forth and attack. Rather, it means "lying down peacefully, quietly," e.g., בִּנְאוֹת דֶּשֶׁא יַרְבִּיצֵנִי, *In lush meadows He lays me down* (*Tehillim* 23:2); רֹבֵץ תַּחַת מַשָּׂאוֹ, *crouching under its burden* (*Shemos* 23:5).

And Rav Hirsch continues to explain the *pasuk,* וְאֵלֶיךָ תְּשׁוּקָתוֹ וְאַתָּה תִּמְשָׁל בּוֹ, *its desire is toward you, and you shall rule over it* (*Bereishis* 4:7). The *yetzer hara* is not our deadly enemy, per se, but rather, *HaKadosh Baruch Hu* created this force for the purpose of being subjugated by man. By nature, it is רֹבֵץ, it wants to lie peacefully, under the control of man. Rav Hirsch calls our attention to the fact that the same applies to the relationship of a man and a woman. There, too, we find the words: וְאֶל אִישֵׁךְ תְּשׁוּקָתֵךְ וְהוּא יִמְשָׁל בָּךְ, *yet your craving shall be for your husband, and he shall rule over you* (*Bereishis* 3:16). The normal relationship between husband and wife should be such that the wife wants the husband to be someone for her to look up to. She wants him to guide her.

The same relationship that applies to husband and wife also exists between the *yetzer hatov* and the *yetzer hara*: The *yetzer hara,* by its normal nature, has the desire to be controlled by the *yetzer hatov.* The *yetzer hara,* with all its fascination with evil, wants by its created nature to be controlled by man's ability to overcome it with his *yetzer hatov.*

And if man does not rule over the *yetzer hara,* it becomes his deadly enemy. If man relinquishes his rule over it, it is waiting "outside the door" for an opportunity to attack him.

This, then, is the meaning of וְאָהַבְתָּ אֵת ה' אֱלֹהֶיךָ בְּכָל לְבָבְךָ, which *Chazal* explain as meaning בִּשְׁנֵי יְצָרֶיךָ, with both your good and evil inclinations. Even the *yetzer hara*, which is part of man's personality, is to become a part of our love for *HaKadosh Baruch Hu*. By subjugating one's evil inclinations, one has fulfilled the natural desire of the *yetzer hara* — that of being subjugated by man's *yetzer hatov*. Thus, one can express his gratitude and love for *HaKadosh Baruch Hu* even with his *yetzer hara,* when its innate desire to be subjugated by man's *yetzer hatov* is fulfilled.

Our *Chachamim* expand the meaning of וְאָהַבְתָּ אֵת ה' אֱלֹהֶיךָ to include causing others to love *HaKadosh Baruch Hu*: שֶׁיְּהֵא שֵׁם שָׁמַיִם מִתְאַהֵב עַל יָדְךָ, *That that Name of Heaven shall become beloved by others through you* (*Yoma* 86a). If a person truly loves *HaKadosh Baruch Hu,* he wants everyone to love *HaKadosh Baruch Hu.* This is similar to the words: עַל כֵּן עֲלָמוֹת אֲהֵבוּךָ, *therefore maidens love you* (*Shir HaShirim* 1:3). Just as a woman is proud if other people love and admire her husband, just so are we very proud and happy if other people also love *HaKadosh Baruch Hu*. And this dictum of שֶׁיְּהֵא שֵׁם שָׁמַיִם מִתְאַהֵב עַל יָדְךָ, to spread the love of *HaKadosh Baruch Hu*, even includes having our *yetzer hara* love *HaKadosh Baruch Hu* by subjugating it to His will.

Another explanation for the meaning of the double form for heart, בְּכָל לְבָבְךָ, is given by Rashi: שֶׁלֹּא יִהְיֶה לִבְּךָ חָלוּק עַל הַמָּקוֹם, אֶלָּא שֶׁתִּהְיֶה הָאַהֲבָה אֵלָיו יִתְבָּרַךְ בְּכָל לְבָבְךָ. This means, *Your heart shall not be divided toward HaKadosh Baruch Hu, but rather, the love for HaKadosh Baruch Hu shall be with the "wholeness" of your heart* (*Sifrei, Va'eschanan Piska* 32). The meaning of the "heart being divided toward *HaKadosh Baruch Hu*" is a function of one's free will.

HaKadosh Baruch Hu has implanted within us a freedom of choice. On one hand, we can be very intrigued and fascinated with the desire to come close to *HaKadosh Baruch Hu*, and to live a life that is worthy of His presence, for which we will be rewarded with eternal life in *Olam Haba*.

On the other hand, our hearts are חָלוּק עַל הַמָּקוֹם, *divided toward HaKadosh Baruch Hu*. For some very strange reasons that we do not understand, every one of us is a question mark. Why is it that we are also intrigued and fascinated with doing the very opposite of coming close to *HaKadosh Baruch Hu*? Why do we desire to do those things that *HaKadosh Baruch Hu* has forbidden and are abominable in His eyes?

The fact that we do have a *yetzer hara* should not frighten us; on the contrary, this is our distinction. The ability to control the *yetzer hara* is the crown which *HaKadosh Baruch Hu* has placed on our heads. The only creature that *HaKadosh Baruch Hu* created with שְׁנֵי יְצָרִים, *two yetzarim,* is the human being. This is why the word וַיִּיצֶר, referring to the creation of man, is spelled with two *yuds* (*Bereishis* 2:7). One *yud* refers to the *yetzer hatov*, and the other to the *yetzer hara*. And if, in spite of the pull of our *yetzer hara* which is innate within us — the *yetzer hatov* develops in man later — and causes us to be חָלוּק עַל הַמָּקוֹם, we overcome it by allowing our *cheilek hatov* (our good aspect) to control our *cheilek hara* (our evil inclination), we have realized the crowning distinction of the human being over any other creation of *HaKadosh Baruch Hu*. No animal has been given the power to control its basic instincts, and if we do so, we are worthy of the *neshamah* which *HaKadosh Baruch Hu* has placed within us.

However, when it comes to וְאָהַבְתָּ אֵת ה׳ אֱלֹהֶיךָ, we are obligated to do this בְּכָל לְבָבְךָ, which *Chazal* say means שֶׁלֹּא יְהֵא לִבְּךָ חָלוּק עַל הַמָּקוֹם. The greatest form of *ahavas Hashem,* love of Hashem, and the supreme act of freedom of will is the giving up of one's *bechirah* to *HaKadosh Baruch Hu*. In doing so, we take the crown of the human species, our *bechirah,* off our heads and place it in front of *HaKadosh Baruch Hu* and say, "We renounce our *bechirah!*" This voluntary relinquishing of our *bechirah* to *HaKadosh Baruch Hu* is called *kabbalas ol Malchus Shamayim*.

[Ed. note: This extremely profound thought is also explained by the Rav in *Maayan Beis HaSho'evah, Devarim* 11:13-14. It requires much insight to be truly understood.]

Therefore, in אַהֲבָה רַבָּה we say וְדַבֵּק לִבֵּנוּ בְּמִצְוֹתֶיךָ, not לְבָבֵנוּ, because that is a *tefillah* for the fulfillment of our desire to ovecome any and all objections by our *yetzer hara,* so that our hearts become "one" regarding the love of *Hakadosh Baruch Hu*. The word for heart is therefore expressed in the singular referring to our undivided and totally committed heart. Similarly, we find the expression in the Gemara regarding the meaning of the *lulav*: מַה תָּמָר זֶה אֵין לוֹ אֶלָּא לֵב אֶחָד אַף יִשְׂרָאֵל אֵין לָהֶם אֶלָּא לֵב אֶחָד לַאֲבִיהֶם שֶׁבַּשָּׁמַיִם, *Just as a palm branch has but one "heart," so does Yisrael have but one heart toward its Father in Heaven* (Succah 45b). The *lulav,* with its one "heart" (stem) from which all the branches emerge, symbolizes the ideal of the Jewish people, that of having only "one heart" in their total commitment to the will of *HaKadosh Baruch Hu*. The *netilas lulav* symbolizes our giving our "one heart" to *HaKadosh Baruch Hu*.

All of these explanations of *ahavas Hashem* are based on our gratitude to Him for our being the recipients of the bounty of His goodness. We are thankful to Him for our existence, from our conception, our gestation in our mother's womb, our birth, our parents' nurturing, our childhood and development, and for saving us from all the various dangers which surround a person constantly. Then *HaKadosh Baruch Hu* gives each person his own history of *chassadim* (acts of great kindness) that he has received, continues to receive, and expects to receive in the future, as we say in *Bircas HaMazon*: הוּא גְמָלָנוּ, הוּא גוֹמְלֵנוּ, הוּא יִגְמְלֵנוּ, *He has favored us, He presently favors us, and He will favor us . . .*

In all of this gratitude, for which we love *HaKadosh Baruch Hu,* we look at

Him as the *Mashpia,* the Giver, and ourselves as the *mekablim,* the *recipients* of His beneficence. And this love is to be בְּכָל לְבָבְךָ, meaning בִּשְׁנֵי יְצָרֶיךָ, with both our good and evil inclinations. This love is to be so intense as to include the voluntary giving up of our *bechirah* for it, as explained.

We may think there is no higher form of love of *HaKadosh Baruch Hu* than this. However, there is another, higher, level of love for *HaKadosh Baruch Hu,* and that is the love of one *mashpia* to another *mashpia.* This is what the Torah calls בְּכָל נַפְשְׁךָ, and its explanation follows.

וּבְכָל נַפְשְׁךָ — With all your soul. *Chazal* tell us that . . . וְאָהַבְתָּ אֵת ה' אֱלֹהֶיךָ בְּכָל נַפְשְׁךָ means אֲפִילוּ הוּא נוֹטֵל אֶת נַפְשְׁךָ, *even if He takes your soul* (*Berachos* 54a). This refers to the moment of death, when *HaKadosh Baruch Hu* takes one's soul away from his body. According to the *halachah,* there are certain *mitzvos* that are inviolable, even at the pain of death. These cardinal *aveiros* are: *gilui arayos, shefichas damim, avodah zarah* (having forbidden relations, murder, and idolatry). If a person is confronted with the choice of violating these three *mitzvos* or be killed, he must be prepared to die rather than violate them.

We find: כִּי עָלֶיךָ הֹרַגְנוּ כָל הַיּוֹם, *We are killed for Your sake every day* (*Tehillim* 44:23). *Chazal* say that this refers to the daily *Krias Shema,* in which we resolve to allow ourselves to be killed, if necessary, in fulfillment of וְאָהַבְתָּ אֵת ה' אֱלֹהֶיךָ . . . בְּכָל נַפְשְׁךָ. At the moment when a person resolves to allow himself to be killed for *kiddush Hashem* — and hundreds of thousands of Jews have done it — the *resolution* itself is considered as if the person had already offered his life for *HaKadosh Baruch Hu* (see *Gittin* 57a; also *Midrash Hane'elam, Zohar* 1:124). When a person offers himself for *kiddush Hashem,* he is no longer a *mekabel,* but rather, he rises to the level of a *mashpia.* He has become a "giver," rather than a "taker," because he has brought *kedushah* into the world.

The definition of אַהֲבָה is found in the Torah's description of the depth of Yaakov's love for his son Binyamin (וְאָבִיו אֲהֵבוֹ, *and his father loved him; Bereishis* 44:20), which Yehudah describes as וְנַפְשׁוֹ קְשׁוּרָה בְנַפְשׁוֹ, *His soul is tied to his soul* (ibid. v. 30). Yaakov and Binyamin, as human beings and father and son, are equals in their relationship to each other. However, *HaKadosh Baruch Hu,* in His perfection, has no needs; He does not need our love. He is purely a Giver, not a receiver. Although we use the words וְקַבֵּל בְּרַחֲמִים וּבְרָצוֹן אֶת תְּפִלָּתֵנוּ, . . . *and receive our prayers with mercy and good will* (from *Shema Koleinu* in *Shemoneh Esrei*), this is only a metaphor for "acceptance." *HaKadosh Baruch Hu* has no *need* for our *tefillah;* He is not a *mekabel* (a receiver of anything). Human beings by nature are needy and cannot exist without receiving. We are *mekablim,* but *HaKadosh Baruch Hu* is a *Mashpia.*

Usually, the relationship between man and *HaKadosh Baruch Hu* is that of two *unlike* entities: one is a *mashpia* and the other, a *mekabel*. But when a person gives his life for *HaKadosh Baruch Hu*, and he is *mekadeish Hashem*, he is no longer a *mekabel*. He, too, becomes a *mashpia*, because he has brought *kedushah* into the world and, in this respect, he is similar to *HaKadosh Baruch Hu*. And the similar characteristics of a *mashpia* and another *mashpia* create a much closer relationship between them than that of two entities with the opposite characteristics, of a *mashpia* and a *mekabel*. This relationship is akin to the נַפְשׁוֹ קְשׁוּרָה בְנַפְשׁוֹ of Yaakov and Binyamin, who were equals because they were humans, who were father and son, and were as close as possible to each other.

Therefore, the bond that one forms with *HaKadosh Baruch Hu*, by loving Him בְּכָל נַפְשְׁךָ, is much closer than that which he has with Him by loving Him בְּכָל לְבָבְךָ.

As previously stated, one is required to give his life for *HaKadosh Baruch Hu* rather than violate the three cardinal sins of *gilui arayos, shefichas damim*, and *avodah zarah*. However, it is not commonly known that there is a fourth circumstance in which one is also required to forfeit his life *al kiddush Hashem*. That occurs if one is forced, *bish'as hashemad* (during times of forced conversions), to publicly admit and show that he has abandoned his faith. This is known as לְהַעֲבִיר עַל הַדָּת (to transgress the Jewish faith).

If one is forced by a non-Jew to eat *tereifah* at the pain of death, he is not required to lose his life, and he should eat the *tereifah*. However, if the non-Jew is making a public demonstration out of forcing the Jew to eat the *tereifah*, as a sign that he has abandoned his faith — with at least ten people of Israel knowing about it — the Jew is required to give his life *al kiddush Hashem*, rather than eat the *tereifah*.

And this attempt to force a Jew to publicly display his abandonment of Judaism does not have to apply only to a *mitzvah* — it can apply equally to any commonly known Jewish custom. The Gemara gives an example: לְשַׁנּוּיֵי עַרְקְתָא דִמְסָאנָא, *even only to change the way one ties his shoes* (Sanhedrin 74b). If one is publicly forced, as an act of *shemad*, just to change the way he would normally tie his shoes, to conform to the non-Jewish style, and thereby to demonstrate that he has abandoned his faith, he is required to give up his life rather than to accede to this demand.

I remember that in the Frankfurt Yeshivah there was a *baal teshuvah* by the name of Meyer, הי״ד, who eventually died *al kiddush Hashem*. He was once approached by a Nazi who demanded that he pronounce the Name of *HaKadosh Baruch Hu* together with an obscene word. To enforce his demand, the Nazi bully pulled out his revolver and held it to Meyer's heart and said, "Will you do it, yes or no?" The young Meyer shouted with all his strength, "No!" Upon which the Nazi returned his revolver to its holster and said, "I just wanted to find out if you were a Jewish coward." Those barbaric and satanic Nazis, who were the lowest scum of the earth, were used by *HaKadosh Baruch Hu* as His agents to give us the opportunity to fulfill נוֹטֵל אֶת נַפְשְׁךָ, *even if one has to offer his life,* and consequently, myriads of our brethren became מַקְדִּישֵׁי שְׁמֶךָ, showing publicly that they loved *HaKadosh Baruch Hu* more than their lives.

Therefore, during the twice-daily recitation of *Krias Shema*, while saying the words וְאָהַבְתָּ אֵת ה׳ אֱלֹהֶיךָ . . . וּבְכָל נַפְשְׁךָ, a person is required to resolve that if he is confronted with a situation in which he must give up his life to show the world that he really does believe in *HaKadosh Baruch Hu*, and that the Jewish nation has really accepted His Torah, he is ready to do so. And the making of a firm resolution to make a public *kiddush Hashem*, if the need arises, is in itself considered as if one had actually offered his life for *kiddush Hashem*, because מַחֲשָׁבָה טוֹבָה הקב״ה מְצָרְפָהּ לְמַעֲשֶׂה, *God considers one's good resolution as if he had actually done the good deed* (Kiddushin 40a). This, therefore, is the meaning of כִּי עָלֶיךָ הֹרַגְנוּ כָל הַיּוֹם, *We are killed for Your sake every day.*

[For sources on the *mitzvah* of *mesiras nefesh al kiddush Hashem*, see *Rambam, Hilchos Yesodei HaTorah* Ch. 5; *Chidushei HaRan, Sanhedrin* end of Ch. 6; also see *Bach, Taz,* and *Shach* to *Yoreh Deah* 157.]

Notwithstanding everything we have said about the extremely high level of *ahavas Hashem,* first בְּכָל לְבָבְךָ and then the higher level of וּבְכָל נַפְשְׁךָ, there is a form of *ahavas Hashem* which is even higher, and that is וּבְכָל מְאֹדֶךָ. The explanation follows.

וּבְכָל מְאֹדֶךָ — With all your possessions. The word מְאֹד means *very much,* and the literal meaning of וְאָהַבְתָּ אֵת ה׳ אֱלֹהֶיךָ is that we are commanded to love *HaKadosh Baruch Hu* with all the means at our disposal, including everything that we love very much. It is therefore usually translated as *with all your possessions.* This means that one is to love *HaKadosh Baruch Hu* so much that if circumstances arise under which one must lose all his possessions in order to abide by His will, he must do so.

The Gemara explains that this *pasuk* refers to a person who loves his money even more than his life: יֵשׁ לְךָ אָדָם שֶׁמָּמוֹנוֹ חָבִיב עָלָיו מִגּוּפוֹ לְכָךְ נֶאֱמַר: בְּכָל מְאֹדֶךָ, *There are people who love their money more than their lives, therefore it states: with all your possessions* (Berachos 61b).

The simple understanding of this Gemara is that this *pasuk* is addressing those individuals who would rather risk their lives than give up their possessions. And if one of these people is confronted with a similar situation to וּבְכָל נַפְשְׁךָ, in which he is publicly forced to commit any of the three cardinal sins — *gilui arayos, shefichas damim, avodah zarah,* or *leha'avir al hadas,* as described earlier — at the risk of losing all of his possessions,

KRIAS SHEMA 327

including his money, his house, his clothing, and his livelihood, and he is facing a lifetime ahead of abject poverty — which to him is a fate worse than death — he is required, under the *mitzvah* of וּבְכָל מְאֹדֶךָ, to lose everything that he has rather than violate these cardinal commandments.

This applies even if the mindset of this person is based on the fact that all of his possessions were acquired as the result of hard and honest work which was based on *shemiras Shabbos;* not a penny was obtained through devious means; he never violated the laws of *ribbis* (interest) or *ona'ah* (price misrepresentation), and he always gave *maaser* (tithes) and *tzedakah*. This person is so closely identified with his "kosher" possessions that he would rather die than lose them. It is to him that the Torah says, וְאָהַבְתָּ אֵת ה' אֱלֹהֶיךָ וּבְכָל מְאֹדֶךָ .... You are required to love Hashem so much that you must relinquish all of your possessions — which to you is a greater sacrifice than death — rather than violate the cardinal commandments of the Torah. However, most of the *Rishonim* are of the opinion that the requirement to relinquish all of one's possessions, rather than transgress a law, applies not only to the cardinal sins, but also to any of the *mitzvos lo saaseh* (negative commandments) (*Ran, Succah* Ch. 3; *Shulchan Aruch, Yoreh Deah* 157:1).

An example of this would be if a person is forced into eating one *kezayis* of *tereifah* (an olive-size quantity of forbidden food), or losing all of his possessions. In such a case, he would be required to lose everything, short of his life, rather than violate the law of *tereifah*. (It is possible that this could apply even to less than a *kezayis,* under the rule of חֲצִי שִׁעוּר אָסוּר מִן הַתּוֹרָה, *even a part of the minimum quantity is forbidden*.) The *mitzvah* of וְאָהַבְתָּ אֵת ה' אֱלֹהֶיךָ ... וּבְכָל מְאֹדֶךָ would apply equally to the wearing of a garment with *shaatnez* (a forbidden mixture of wool and linen), or even to the telling of a lie, or to the taking of another's property illegally.

This is expressed in the verse, טוֹב לִי תוֹרַת פִּיךָ מֵאַלְפֵי זָהָב וָכָסֶף, *The Torah of Your mouth is better for me than thousands in gold and silver* (*Tehillim* 119:72). When *HaKadosh Baruch Hu* says, "I do not want you to eat *neveilah* or *tereifah,*" and someone comes to force a Jew to violate this command, his answer is to be, "My money means nothing compared to violating a direct command of *HaKadosh Baruch Hu.*"

However, with regard to *mitzvos asei* (positive commandments), one is not required to relinquish all of his possessions to enable him to perform them (see *Shulchan Aruch, Yoreh Deah* 157; *Orach Chaim* 656 in *Rema*). In fact, *Chazal* tell us: הַמְבַזְבֵּז אַל יְבַזְבֵּז יוֹתֵר מֵחוֹמֶשׁ, which means that one should not spend more than a fifth of his money for a *mitzvas asei*. This is why most people do not perform the *mitzvah* of writing a *sefer Torah*. (The minimum price for such an undertaking today is about $25,000, which would require that one have at least $125,000 in his possession in order to fulfill this *mitzvah*.)

[Ed. note: This difference between a *mitzvas asei* and *lo saaseh* is discussed at length by the *Rishonim* and *Acharonim,* with the main distinction being that the violation of a *mitzvas asei* is done בְּשֵׁב וְאַל תַּעֲשֶׂה, by passively doing nothing, while that of a *mitzvas lo saaseh* represents a positive act of violation, בְּקוּם וַעֲשֵׂה.]

I would like to suggest an additional meaning of וּבְכָל מְאֹדֶךָ. I would translate the phrase as, "You shall love Hashem your God with all of your "very-muchness." This would refer to the extra talents or abilities which *HaKadosh Baruch Hu* has given a person, מְאֹד, more than that which he has given to other people. Examples would be utilizing one's great intelligence, or musical or artistic ability, or building skills, to demonstrate his love for *HaKadosh Baruch Hu*.

An additional meaning of וּבְכָל מְאֹדֶךָ is found in the mishnah: בְּכָל מִדָּה וּמִדָּה שֶׁהוּא מוֹדֵד לְךָ הֱוֵי מוֹדֶה לוֹ, *For every measure which He metes out to you, be thankful to Him* (*Berachos* 54a). Rashi on *Devarim* 6:5 renders this dictum: בְּכָל מִדָּה וּמִדָּה שֶׁמּוֹדֵד לְךָ, בֵּין בְּמִדָּה טוֹבָה בֵּין בְּמִדַּת פּוּרְעָנוּת, meaning *we are to love HaKadosh Baruch Hu, regardless of which measure He assigns to us; be that a good measure, or one which involves punishment.*

We have previously explained that *ahavas Hashem* on the level of בְּכָל לְבָבְךָ — which is the love of a *mekabel* for its *mashpia* — is exceeded by the level of love of וּבְכָל נַפְשְׁךָ, which is the love of one *mashpia* for another *mashpia*. Although this is the level of *ahavas Hashem* on which one is ready to give his life for *HaKadosh Baruch Hu,* there is still a higher level: that of וּבְכָל מְאֹדֶךָ, when one loves *HaKadosh Baruch Hu* equally in every circumstance in which he may find himself, בְּכָל מִדָּה וּמִדָּה שֶׁהוּא מוֹדֵד לְךָ, as we shall explain.

Every human being is totally unique; he is different from any other person that was ever created, and no one will ever be exactly like him. For example, if one has a feeling of happiness, it is so intimately personal that nobody in the world — even his best friend — can possibly have an understanding of it. True, his friend may be happy for him in his moment of happiness. Nevertheless, one's feeling of happiness is so completely unique that no one can know exactly what he is feeling. Or, if one is in pain, no one, even one's best friend who may shed tears when he sees his friend in agony, can fully feel that pain. It is totally personal. This is expressed in the *pasuk,* לֵב יוֹדֵעַ מָרַת נַפְשׁוֹ וּבְשִׂמְחָתוֹ לֹא יִתְעָרַב זָר, *The heart knows the bitterness of itself, and no stranger will be mixed into its happiness* (*Mishlei* 14:10). This uniqueness of each human being has been implanted into each person by *HaKadosh Baruch Hu,* the Absolutely Unique יָחִיד וּמְיוּחָד. He has invested some of His Uniqueness into each human being that He created. And this is what is meant by, וַיִּבְרָא אֱלֹהִים אֶת הָאָדָם בְּצַלְמוֹ בְּצֶלֶם אֱלֹהִים בָּרָא אֹתוֹ, *God created Man in His image, in the image of God He created* him (*Bereishis* 1:27). The human being, as a unique creature, is a reflection of *HaKadosh Baruch Hu*.

Therefore, if one loves *HaKadosh Baruch Hu* regardless of which of life's circumstances he may find himself in, בְּכָל מִדָּה וּמִדָּה — whether this is in his most personal moments of happiness, or during his private excruciating pain — and he recognizes that these unique emotions or sensations come directly from the אֶחָד יָחִיד וּמְיוּחָד, *the Absolutely Unique One,* Who through His *hashgachah pratis* wants him to experience this happiness or this pain — which no other person can feel — he has experienced some of the Uniqueness of *HaKadosh Baruch Hu*. And it is this which is meant by וְאָהַבְתָּ אֵת ה' אֱלֹהֶיךָ .. וּבְכָל מְאֹדֶךָ, the loving of *HaKadosh Baruch Hu* with one's unique nature, בְּכָל מִדָּה וּמִדָּה, which is the highest level of *ahavas Hashem* of which a human being is capable.

Sometimes, *HaKadosh Baruch Hu* inflicts pain upon a person to cleanse him from his sins, similar to *hechsher keilim*, the purification of vessels to rid them of the *tamei* material absorbed in them. Sometimes pain and suffering are inflicted upon a person to test his *emunah*. Whatever the reason, during a person's suffering, he has a direct connection with *HaKadosh Baruch Hu*.

Rashi (ibid.), based on the Gemara (*Berachos* 54a), after quoting the aforesaid וְכֵן דָּוִד הָיָה אוֹמֵר כּוֹס יְשׁוּעוֹת אֶשָּׂא בְּכָל מִדָּה וּמִדָּה שֶׁמּוֹדֵד לְךָ, ends with וּבְשֵׁם ה' אֶקְרָא; צָרָה וְיָגוֹן אֶמְצָא וּבְשֵׁם ה' אֶקְרָא, *And thus did Dovid say: "When I lift up my cup of salvation, I call on the Name of Hashem"* (*Tehillim* 116:13); *"and when I faced trouble and sorrow, I called on the Name of Hashem"* (ibid. vs. 3-4). He points out that Dovid HaMelech uses the same expression, וּבְשֵׁם ה' אֶקְרָא, in reacting to his sublimest moments of happiness, as he does in his times of suffering and anguish. This is a perfect example of בְּכָל מִדָּה וּמִדָּה שֶׁהוּא מוֹדֵד לְךָ הֱוֵי מוֹדֶה לוֹ.

Each individual was created by *HaKadosh Baruch Hu* as a unique entity, and no one else ever was, or ever will be, exactly the same. *Chazal* tell us: כָּל מַה שֶּׁבָּרָא הקב"ה בְּעוֹלָמוֹ לֹא בְרָאוֹ אֶלָּא לִכְבוֹדוֹ, *All that the Holy One, Blessed is He, created in His world, He created solely for His glory* (*Pirkei Avos* 6:11), and somewhere in the master plan of the Creation, each person has a specific purpose, as the mishnah states: לְפִיכָךְ נִבְרָא הָאָדָם יְחִידִי . . . כָּל אֶחָד וְאֶחָד חַיָּיב לוֹמַר בִּשְׁבִילִי נִבְרָא הָעוֹלָם, *Man (Adam HaRishon) was created as a single person (no other humans existed yet) . . . and therefore each person is to imagine that the world was created only for him* (*Sanhedrin* 37a). And if *HaKadosh Baruch Hu* decrees that one should suffer, and he accepts his suffering as the will of *HaKadosh Baruch Hu*, and he loves *HaKadosh Baruch Hu* for it — because at the moment of his pain, *HaKadosh Baruch Hu* Who is the אֶחָד יָחִיד וּמְיוּחָד connects Himself to the unique human being, the יְחִידִי — it is an even higher form of *ahavas Hashem* than וּבְכָל נַפְשְׁךָ.

It is therefore understandable that in the second *parashah* of *Krias Shema*, which addresses the nation as a whole, rather than each individual and unique creation of *HaKadosh Baruch Hu*, no mention is made of וּבְכָל מְאֹדְכֶם.

◆§ וְהָיוּ הַדְּבָרִים הָאֵלֶּה אֲשֶׁר אָנֹכִי מְצַוְּךָ הַיּוֹם — **Let these words that I am commanding you today.** The phrase, *these words*, refers to the immediately preceding *pesukim* of שְׁמַע and וְאָהַבְתָּ. Rashi (ibid.) explains that הַדְּבָרִים הָאֵלֶּה refers specifically to the *mitzvah* of וְאָהַבְתָּ אֵת ה' אֱלֹהֶיךָ, and he states as follows: וּמַהוּ הָאַהֲבָה, *And what is the love?* How does one achieve this *mitzvah* to love *HaKadosh Baruch Hu*? Rashi continues: וְהָיוּ הַדְּבָרִים הָאֵלֶּה ... שֶׁמִּתּוֹךְ כָּךְ אַתָּה מַכִּיר בהקב״ה וּמִדַּבֵּק בִּדְרָכָיו. There is only one way for a person to recognize and to love God, and that is for one to be aware of the fact that "these words" — שְׁמַע and וְאָהַבְתָּ — are directed at him *personally*: אֲשֶׁר אָנֹכִי מְצַוְּךָ, *that I am commanding you.* A person may think that he is the אָנֹכִי, the "I," but in reality, it is *HaKadosh Baruch Hu* Who is the only true "I." And once a person recognizes that *HaKadosh Baruch Hu* is addressing him personally, he becomes attached to Him. This is what is meant by "loving *HaKadosh Baruch Hu*."

Although a person may think that he does not deserve to be addressed personally by *HaKadosh Baruch Hu* because of his shortcomings and mistakes, nevertheless, אֲשֶׁר אָנֹכִי מְצַוְּךָ הַיּוֹם teaches us that if a person makes up his mind that starting today, הַיּוֹם, he wishes to accept the commandments of *HaKadosh Baruch Hu*, then he has established a personal relationship with *HaKadosh Baruch Hu* in which he personally receives those commandments — מְצַוְּךָ — directly from *HaKadosh Baruch Hu*.

Rashi, quoting from *Sifrei* (ibid.), states that הַיּוֹם tells us that with each new day a person can make a new beginning and reaccept the *mitzvos* upon himself as if they were brand new. לֹא יִהְיוּ בְעֵינֶיךָ כְּדִיּוֹטַגְמָא יְשָׁנָה ... אֶלָּא כַּחֲדָשָׁה שֶׁהַכֹּל רָצִים לִקְרָאתָהּ, *He should not consider the mitzvos of HaKadosh Baruch Hu as some ancient proclamations, but rather, one is encouraged to embrace them as if they were newly ordained laws which people are eager to accept.*

◆§ עַל לְבָבֶךָ — **Upon your heart.** These laws are to be accepted upon the heart of each person as binding on himself to the extent that as a result of God's laws, he gives up his freedom of choice concerning them. His commitment is to be so strong that he voluntarily gives up his *bechirah* and consequently, as a part of God's world, he voluntarily agrees to become forced to abide by the personal mandate of *HaKadosh Baruch Hu* to abide by His commandments.

The following story will illustrate the meaning of אֲשֶׁר אָנֹכִי מְצַוְּךָ הַיּוֹם. Many years ago, in Baltimore, the president of the Conservative synagogue, Chizuk Emunah, and his wife came to see me about a certain matter. (This congregation was originally founded about 150 years ago as an Orthodox demonstration against the Reform movement in Baltimore, but it was later changed to Conservative.) This meeting occurred at the time of the coronation of Queen Elizabeth of England, and all the news reports were filled with descriptions of the pageantry and pomp of the ancient traditions, and the use of the historic artifacts stored in museums, all of which were associated with royal coronations in England. My visitor was very impressed with all of this, and drew a parallel with the interest of the Conservative movement in maintaining the ancient Jewish traditions. He therefore asked me why I was opposed to Conservatism. "After all," he said, "we keep traditional Judaism. And," he added, "I even put on my *tefillin*, every day." When I told him I was interested only mildly in "traditional Judaism," and that I could even do without it altogether, he moved to the edge of his chair in astonishment. "Tradition leaves me cold," I continued. "Just because my father did something, doesn't mean I have to do the same thing. If my father wore long wool stockings, does that mean I cannot wear cotton socks?" By this time, he was totally exasperated. "If you are not interested in upholding Jewish tradition, why then would you put on *tefillin* every day?" he asked. "I'll tell you why I wear *tefillin*," I answered. "Because God wants me, personally, at that moment, to put on *tefillin*. The mere tradition of wearing *tefillin* means nothing to me. While I am very proud and happy that my ancestors for countless generations before me kept the same Torah laws as I do, however, this is not the reason I keep them."

The declaration of שְׁמַע יִשְׂרָאֵל and the corresponding *mitzvah* of וְהָיוּ הַדְּבָרִים הָאֵלֶּה אֲשֶׁר אָנֹכִי מְצַוְּךָ הַיּוֹם עַל לְבָבֶךָ, which contains the first and second persons, "you" and "I," are representative of a personal relationship between man and *HaKadosh Baruch Hu*. Each person is to feel that *HaKadosh Baruch Hu* is addressing him personally, with a fresh and new message, every day of our lives, הַיּוֹם. We do not keep the *mitzvos* as "tradition," but rather, we carry on a new personal relationship with *HaKadosh Baruch Hu* whenever we learn His Torah and keep His *mitzvos*.

Our *Chachamim* tell us that with the completion of this sentence, we have fulfilled our obligation of concentrating on the meaning and the message of the words of *Krias Shema*: עַל לְבָבֶךָ – עַד כָּאן כַּוָּנַת הַלֵּב, *Concentration of the heart is required up to this point* (*Berachos* 13b). To be sure, the rest of *Krias Shema* must also be read carefully, but deep concentration is not required, because the rest is really a commentary on the basic tenets that are contained in the first three *pesukim*.

⇨ וְשִׁנַּנְתָּם לְבָנֶיךָ — **Teach** [literally: **sharpen**] **them** [these words] **thoroughly to your children.** This is explained by *Chazal* to mean, שֶׁיְּהוּ דִבְרֵי תוֹרָה מְחוּדָּדִים בְּפִיךָ, *The words of Torah are to be sharply expressed by your mouth* (*Kiddushin* 30a). The idea is that the teaching of Torah is to be done in a "sharp" and precise manner, to produce a clear understanding by the student of the subject matter under study. The goal of such learning and teaching should be to enable one to respond clearly to questions of *halachah*: אִם יִשְׁאַל לְךָ אָדָם דָּבָר, אַל תְּגַמְגֵּם וְתֹאמַר לוֹ אֶלָּא אֱמוֹר לוֹ מִיָּד, *If a person asks you something don't stammer, but rather, give him an immediate and clear answer* (ibid.).

The Gemara (ibid.) offers an additional interpretation of וְשִׁנַּנְתָּם, which is אַל תִּקְרֵי וְשִׁנַּנְתָּם אֶלָּא וְשִׁלַּשְׁתָּם, meaning that it is necessary to learn the subject matter at least three times. For a teacher to teach a subject, he must himself have learned it at least twice to absorb the knowledge. (The word שִׁנּוּן, *to study,* comes from שְׁנַיִם, meaning *two,* or *to repeat.*) The Gemara compares the learning of something only once to a hunter who has captured a bird and, although does not render it unfit to fly, expects it to stay with him. Repeating a subject matter captures it in one's mind for a long period of time (see *Eruvin* 54b). Therefore, when one is teaching a subject, it will be the third time the teacher has studied it.

Although the word לְבָנֶיךָ means *to your children, Chazal* tell us that in the context of learning Torah, the meaning of לְבָנֶיךָ is extended to include one's students — אֵלּוּ תַּלְמִידֶיךָ (*Sifrei,* ibid.). In other words, the *mitzvah* here is for one to teach Torah to his children and to his students. Usually, though, one's first *talmidim* are his own children.

וְדִבַּרְתָּ בָּם — And speak of them. Rashi (ibid.), quoting from the *Sifrei,* gives the meaning here as: שֶׁלֹּא יְהֵא עִיקַּר דִּבּוּרְךָ אֶלָּא בָּם, עֲשֵׂם עִקָּר וְאַל תַּעֲשֵׂם טָפֵל, *Your main conversation shall be about them* [the Torah and *mitzvos*]. *Make them primary; do not make them secondary.* Rav Samson R. Hirsch finds in this *Sifrei* a source for the teaching of secular subjects, so long as the Torah remains primary, and the secular subjects remain secondary to it. If secular subjects were totally excluded from study, *Chazal* would have said something to the effect that: וְדִבַּרְתָּ בָּם: שֶׁלֹּא יְדַבֵּר אֶלָּא בָּם.

בְּשִׁבְתְּךָ בְּבֵיתֶךָ וּבְלֶכְתְּךָ בַדֶּרֶךְ — While you sit in your home, and while you are traveling on the road. The Gemara (*Berachos* 16a) derives from here that the obligation to read the *Shema* in one's home, or while traveling, refers only to those times when he is engaged in his own personal pursuits (בְּשִׁבְתְּךָ, וּבְלֶכְתְּךָ). However, if one is occupied with a *d'var mitzvah,* whether at home or while traveling, he is *patur* (exempt) from the *mitzvah* of *Krias Shema.* This is the source of the general rule: הָעוֹסֵק בְּמִצְוָה פָּטוּר מִן הַמִּצְוָה, *While one is occupied with doing a mitzvah, he is exempt from other mitzvos* (*Succah* 25a).

This obligation of Torah study applies not only to the teaching of Torah to others, but also to one's own learning of Torah. One is to engage in Torah learning wherever he finds himself, whether this be at home or on the road. Regarding וּבְלֶכְתְּךָ בַדֶּרֶךְ, let me refer to the mishnah: רַבִּי יַעֲקֹב אוֹמֵר: הַמְהַלֵּךְ בַּדֶּרֶךְ וְשׁוֹנֶה, וּמַפְסִיק מִמִּשְׁנָתוֹ וְאוֹמֵר מַה נָּאֶה אִילָן זֶה וּמַה נָּאֶה נִיר זֶה מַעֲלֶה עָלָיו הַכָּתוּב כְּאִלּוּ מִתְחַיֵּב בְּנַפְשׁוֹ, *Rabbi Yaakov said: One who walks on the road while* reviewing [a Torah lesson], but interrupts his review and exclaims, "How beautiful is this tree! How beautiful is this plowed field!" — Scripture considers it as if he bears guilt for his soul (Pirkei Avos 3:9). This means that if one is learning while traveling and he interrupts by remarking on the beautiful nature surrounding him, he is worthy of "having forfeited his life." Let us attempt to understand what great harm there could be in this. On the contrary, our Chachamim have even instituted a special berachah, שֶׁכָּכָה לוֹ בְּעוֹלָמוֹ, when one sees beautiful creations of HaKadosh Baruch Hu (Berachos 58b).

This mishnah alludes to a very interesting phenomenon, as follows. If one is engaged in the learning of Torah while traveling through an area of natural beauty, he may suddenly become aware of the glory of HaKadosh Baruch Hu in the natural scene. While he is learning, he has a different view of nature, because its beauty has become greatly enhanced as a result of the Torah which he is learning. If naturalists or botanists study natural science, they may be able to see the chochmah of HaKadosh Baruch Hu in nature. But if one views nature while studying Torah, he becomes aware of a special kind of beauty spreading over the world. So the mishnah tells us: "Don't interrupt your learning now. What you are seeing is the kavod Hashem in the world, which is directly attributable to the Torah that you are now learning." And if one stops learning just to gaze at the beautiful scenery, he has totally missed the point. He is replacing an enhanced appreciation of natural beauty, triggered by Torah learning, with the ordinary human sense of esthetics. In doing so, he has missed a golden opportunity to see the kavod of HaKadosh Baruch Hu in nature.

[Ed. note: The Rav records a personal experience of this kind in his diary of June 1969, while on vacation in Locarno, Italy. He writes that on Shabbos of Parashas Behaalosecha, while he was discussing some Torah topic with his brother, Rav Moshe, on the balcony of the hotel, he gazed out over the lake and surrounding mountains and suddenly became aware of beauty, brightness, and glory on top of the mountains, the likes of which he had never seen in his life. He writes that he did not tell this to his brother, with whom he was conversing at the time, nor did he reveal it to anyone else.]

§ וּבְשָׁכְבְּךָ וּבְקוּמֶךָ — **When you lie down and when you arise.** Although it is not implicit in the text, the Torah Shebe'al Peh teaches us that this refers to the mitzvah of Krias Shema of Shacharis and Arvis, which is to be performed at the time when people usually go to sleep, and when they normally arise. The time for the latter has been defined by the Chachamim as the first three hours of the day (Berachos 10b). Even if one's own personal habits and schedules differ from the norm, he is still obligated to recite the Krias Shema at the same time the general public does.

As we mentioned earlier, the words וְהָיוּ הַדְּבָרִים הָאֵלֶּה refer to the pesukim of שְׁמַע and וְאָהַבְתָּ. These include the obligation to give away one's freedom of choice, his life, and all of his possessions in the pursuit of *ahavas Hashem,* to promote *kiddush Hashem* in the world. It is this obligation which we are to teach our children and students; we are obligated to talk about this with them, and teach them that this is our main task in life. And furthermore, these truths are to be written and attached to the doorposts of our houses and placed in our *tefillin.*

Regarding the *mitzvah* of giving one's life for *HaKadosh Baruch Hu,* I heard a beautiful explanation from my Rebbe, HaRav Shlomo Breuer, in Frankfurt. When Yaakov Avinu finally met his beloved son Yosef in Egypt after twenty-two years, during which period he thought that Yosef had died, the Torah, in describing their first meeting, tells us: וַיִּפֹּל עַל צַוָּארָיו, וַיֵּבְךְּ עַל צַוָּארָיו עוֹד, *He fell on his neck, and he continued to cry on his neck* (*Bereishis* 46:29). Rashi (ibid.), quoting *Chazal,* explains that it was only Yosef who hugged and kissed his father, but Yaakov, at that exalted moment — instead of embracing his beloved son — was saying *Shema*: אֲבָל יַעֲקֹב לֹא נָפַל עַל צַוְּארֵי יוֹסֵף וְלֹא נְשָׁקוֹ, וְאָמְרוּ רַבּוֹתֵינוּ שֶׁהָיָה קוֹרֵא אֶת שְׁמַע, *Our Rabbis have taught: But Yaakov did not fall upon Yosef's neck, nor did he kiss him — He was reciting the Shema.* And then Yaakov speaks: אָמוּתָה הַפַּעַם אַחֲרֵי רְאוֹתִי אֶת פָּנֶיךָ, *Now that I have seen your face I can die* (ibid. v. 30).

[Ed. note: The source of this *Rashi* is obscure. *Zecher L'Avraham* on *Rashi* attributes this to R' Yehuda'i Gaon and this is mentioned in *Teshuvos HaGeonim,* Ch. 45 of *Likkutim.*]

To explain this remarkable saying of *Chazal,* Rav Breuer said as follows: During the twenty-two years when Yaakov Avinu, dressed in sackcloth, mourned and cried over what he thought was the loss of his beloved son Yosef, his life was not worth much to him. Like the other *Avos,* Yaakov kept all the *mitzvos* before they were given, including the daily saying of *Krias Shema,* and when he said the words וְאָהַבְתָּ אֵת ה' אֱלֹהֶיךָ בְּכָל... נַפְשְׁךָ, it was not very difficult for him to offer his life for *HaKadosh Baruch Hu.* In his state, he would not be giving up very much. Life was almost worthless to him. However, after seeing that Yosef was not only alive, but wearing the Egyptian crown on his head, surrounded by the trappings of royalty, Yaakov's life took on new meaning. Now that he was reunited with his beloved son, his life had become precious again. And it was precisely at that exalted moment, when his life had taken on such great value, that he offered to give it to *HaKadosh Baruch Hu* if the need arose. Now he was really offering his most precious possession: his life in its most exalted state! It was therefore necessary for him to recite *Krias Shema* at that moment, and say אָמוּתָה הַפַּעַם, I am prepared to offer everything — including my very precious life — for *HaKadosh Baruch Hu* if the need arises.

From these words of my late Rebbe, I was inspired to say the following. On

Yamim Tovim, when we read of the *moadim* (festivals) from the *parashah* [*Emor*], we begin the *krias haTorah* with the small *parashah* of שׁוֹר אוֹ כֶשֶׂב אוֹ עֵז, which precedes the *parashas hamoadim* and is, apparently, unrelated to the subject of the *moadim*. The reason for this, however, is not to allow enough *pesukim* for the five or seven *aliyos* on Yom Tov and Shabbos, because there are more than enough *pesukim* to allow for all the *aliyos* in the *parashas hamoadim* itself.

In order to understand the connection between the two *parshiyos*, let us examine the highlights of the *parashah* of . . . שׁוֹר אוֹ כֶשֶׂב אוֹ עֵז:

שׁוֹר אוֹ כֶשֶׂב אוֹ עֵז כִּי יִוָּלֵד וְהָיָה שִׁבְעַת יָמִים תַּחַת אִמּוֹ — *When an ox or a sheep or a goat is born, it shall remain under its mother for seven days* (*Vayikra* 22:27). When an animal is born, it must remain with its mother for seven days before it can be offered as a *korban*.

וְשׁוֹר אוֹ שֶׂה אֹתוֹ וְאֶת בְּנוֹ לֹא תִשְׁחֲטוּ בְּיוֹם אֶחָד — *A mother and its offspring may not be slaughtered on the same day* (ibid. v.28). Both of these laws teach us that the Torah values the maternal instincts of even an animal towards its offspring, and that even animal life is very highly regarded by the Torah.

וְכִי תִזְבְּחוּ זֶבַח תּוֹדָה לַה' וגו' — *When you slaughter a feast thanksgiving-offering to Hashem* (ibid. v.29). This is the law the Torah prescribes regarding a *korban todah*, a thanksgiving offering, which is brought in gratitude to Ha-Kadosh Baruch Hu when a person's own physical life had been in mortal danger and was saved.

וְלֹא תְחַלְּלוּ אֶת שֵׁם קָדְשִׁי וְנִקְדַּשְׁתִּי בְּתוֹךְ בְּנֵי יִשְׂרָאֵל — *You shall not desecrate My holy Name, rather I should be sanctified among Bnei Yisrael* (ibid. v.32). Rashi explains מְסוֹר עַצְמְךָ וְקַדֵּשׁ שְׁמִי, which is a reference to the *mitzvah* of *kiddush Hashem* in cases of *avodah zarah*, *gilui arayos*, and *shefichas damim*. If there are ten Jews present, there is the even greater *mitzvah* of וְנִקְדַּשְׁתִּי בְּתוֹךְ בְּנֵי יִשְׂרָאֵל, which is a *kiddush Hashem b'rabbim*, a public *kiddush Hashem*. And if one does not offer his life rather than violate these laws, he transgresses the *mitzvah* of וְלֹא תְחַלְּלוּ אֶת שֵׁם קָדְשִׁי.

This *pasuk* ends with אֲנִי ה' מְקַדִּשְׁכֶם, *I am Hashem Who gives you holiness*. This supersedes all, despite the previously demonstrated fact that physical life is of such great importance — an animal's birth and life is one of the wonders of *HaKadosh Baruch Hu,* and human life is a thousand times more so. If one's physical life was in danger and it was spared, he is to celebrate that with a *korban todah* to HaKadosh Baruch Hu. Nevertheless, HaKadosh Baruch Hu tells us in this *parashah*, וְנִקְדַּשְׁתִּי בְּתוֹךְ בְּנֵי יִשְׂרָאֵל אֲנִי ה' מְקַדִּשְׁכֶם, that if need be, your physical life, which is one of the wonders of My creation and is so dear and cherished by Me, must be given up to sanctify My Name.

הַמּוֹצִיא אֶתְכֶם מֵאֶרֶץ מִצְרַיִם לִהְיוֹת לָכֶם לֵאלֹהִים אֲנִי ה' — *Who took you out of the land of Egypt to be a God unto you; I am Hashem* (ibid. v.33). The connection between *yetzias Mitzrayim* and the aforesaid laws is explained by Rashi as עַל

מְנַת כֵּן. This means that *HaKadosh Baruch Hu* is saying, "I took you out of Mitzrayim on the condition that you would sanctify My Name. If you have to, give Me your physical life."

All of the aforementioned is of the essence in introducing the *parashas hamoadim*. Throughout the *parashah* of *moadim*, we have the expression מִקְרָאֵי קֹדֶשׁ, *a call for holiness*. This means that all of our Shabbasos and Yamim Tovim are "calls to us for *kiddush Hashem*." Despite the fact that it is a *mitzvah* to physically enjoy Shabbos and Yom Tov, we are told by the Torah, "Be cognizant of the fact that notwithstanding the value of human life, if the time comes, on a moment's notice, that you must give up the pleasures of this physical life *al kiddush Hashem*, you must be ready to do so." This is the condition on which we were redeemed from Egypt.

This explains the reason we always include the words מִקְרָא קֹדֶשׁ זֵכֶר לִיצִיאַת מִצְרָיִם, *a holy convocation, a memorial of the Exodus from Egypt*, in our *tefillah* and *Kiddush* on Yamim Tovim, as well as on Shabbos. The connection between Shabbos and *yetzias Mitzrayim* is clear — it is referred to in the *Aseres HaDibros* in *Parashas Va'eschanan*: וְזָכַרְתָּ כִּי עֶבֶד הָיִיתָ בְּאֶרֶץ מִצְרַיִם וַיֹּצִאֲךָ ה' אֱלֹהֶיךָ מִשָּׁם, וגו', *And you shall remember that you were a slave in the land of Egypt, and Hashem, your God, has taken you out from there* etc. (*Devarim* 5:15). But what possible connection does Rosh Hashanah or Shemini Atzeres have with *yetzias Mitzrayim*? The answer lies in the proper reading of this phrase. Our Yamim Tovim are called מִקְרָא קֹדֶשׁ, *a call for holiness*, which itself is a זֵכֶר לִיצִיאַת מִצְרַיִם, a reminder of the condition whereby we were taken out of Mitzrayim. We were taken out of Mitzrayim for the purpose of making a *kiddush Hashem* in the world. All of our Shabbasos and Yamim Tovim serve as regular reminders of the condition under which we were redeemed from Mitzrayim, that of וְנִקְדַּשְׁתִּי בְּתוֹךְ בְּנֵי יִשְׂרָאֵל אֲנִי ה' מְקַדִּשְׁכֶם.

וּקְשַׁרְתָּם לְאוֹת עַל יָדֶךָ — Bind them as a sign upon your hand.

We have already made some observations on the *mitzvah* of *tefillin*. (See at הַנָחַת טַלִּית וּתְפִלִּין, before בָּרוּךְ שֶׁאָמַר.) However, at this time, I would just like to add one point. We know that the *tefillah shel yad* is to be tied on the muscle of the upper arm, and yet, the words of the Torah commanding us to perform this *mitzvah* are וּקְשַׁרְתָּם לְאוֹת עַל יָדֶךָ. The word יָדֶךָ means *hand*, not *arm*. However, the *Torah Shebe'al Peh* teaches us that it is not to be placed on the hand, but rather, on the biceps which control the function of the hand.

Also, in the יְהִי רָצוֹן which is said according to some *minhagim* before putting on the *tefillin*, there is the phrase וְצִוָּנוּ לְהָנִיחַ עַל הַיָּד לְזִכְרוֹן זְרוֹעַ הַנְּטוּיָה, meaning that the *tefillah shel yad*, which is placed on the upper part of the arm, called זְרוֹעַ (the lower part is called קָנֶה), is to remind us of the "outstretched arm" of *HaKadosh Baruch Hu* which manifested itself during *yetzias Mitzrayim*. Furthermore, וְשֶׁהִיא נֶגֶד הַלֵּב, it is near the heart, לְשַׁעְבֵּד בָּזֶה,

KRIAS SHEMA 337

תַּאֲוַת וּמַחְשְׁבוֹת לִבֵּנוּ לַעֲבוֹדָתוֹ, יִתְבָּרַךְ שְׁמוֹ, to help us control the urges and instincts of our heart for the purpose of serving *HaKadosh Baruch Hu*.

The connection between the human biceps and the זְרוֹעַ נְטוּיָה of *HaKadosh Baruch Hu,* which is a metaphor for His Almightiness and His power over the forces of nature, is that *HaKadosh Baruch Hu* has *given us* a זְרוֹעַ נְטוּיָה as well. Just as *HaKadosh Baruch Hu* controls nature, so has He given us the power to control our own nature. This is the meaning of נֶגֶד הַלֵּב. The power of the human being to control his animal urges and instincts is symbolically expressed by our placing our *tefillin* on the muscle which controls the movement of our hand. It is expressed in the Torah as עַל יָדֶךָ, *over your hand,* because the primary lesson of the *tefillah shel yad* is for us to utilize the power that we have to control our activities, our "hands."

ונּ⌘ **וְהָיוּ לְטֹטָפֹת בֵּין עֵינֶיךָ — And let them be *tefillin* between your eyes.** The word טֹטָפֹת is explained by *Tosafos* (*Menachos* 34b, s.v. לטוטפת) as having the meaning of a headgear, or crown, which identifies it as something worn on the head. However, it is to be worn בֵּין עֵינֶיךָ, which is the front part of the head directly above the space between the eyes. This area of the head is called the "fontanelle," the membrane over the hollow between the bones of the skull in an infant, which eventually fuses together in the months after birth. In a young baby, the pulse is palpable at this soft spot on the head. The symbolism here, again, is that our "crown" is our *bechirah,* our ability to make free moral choices, utilizing our mind.

The unusual word טֹטָפֹת, as explained by the Gemara (ibid.), is a compound word consisting of two words from two different languages, both of which mean "two": טט in the Caspian language means *two,* and פת in one of the African languages likewise means *two.* This is a reference to the double set of two *parshiyos* in the *tefillin.* The two different languages correspond to the two different messages of the *tefillin.*

We have previously remarked [see on עֲטִיפַת הַטַּלִּית וַהֲנָחַת תְּפִילִּין] that the two *parshiyos* in the *tefillin,* קַדֶּשׁ לִי כָל בְּכוֹר and וְהָיָה כִּי יְבִיאֲךָ, correspond to the *kedushah* of the *guf,* the holiness of the body of a member of the Jewish nation. This is why we have so many *mitzvos* pertaining to our bodies, e.g., *tzitzis, tefillin, matzah, korban pesach, milah, shaatnez,* laws regulating the shaving of our hair, etc. Therefore, even after the *neshamah* leaves the body, the *guf* must be treated as a *davar shebik'dushah,* a holy object.

The other two *parshiyos* of the *tefillin,* שְׁמַע and וְהָיָה אִם שָׁמֹעַ, which deal with *kabbalas ol Malchus Shamayim* and reward and punishment for the *mitzvos,* correspond to the *kedushah* of our *neshamah* and our *ruach.*

And we tie them both to the *ratzon Hashem.* With the תְּפִלָּה שֶׁל יָד, we bind our physical aspects — *guf* and *nefesh* — to the will of *HaKadosh Baruch Hu,* and with the תְּפִלָּה שֶׁל רֹאשׁ, we bind our spiritual aspects — *ruach* and *neshamah* — to the *ratzon Hashem*. The combined meaning is that we bind our entire existence, physical and spiritual, to the will of *HaKadosh Baruch Hu*.

As far as women are concerned, in the absence of the *mitzvah* of *tefillin*, these ideas are expressed by the woman's use of the *mikveh*. Upon immersing herself in the *mikveh*, she is surrounded by the *mitzvah*, and thereby expresses the dedication of her physical and spiritual aspects to the *ratzon Hashem*.

וּכְתַבְתָּם עַל מְזֻזוֹת בֵּיתֶךָ — **And write them on the doorposts of your house.** The *Torah Shebe'al Peh* teaches us that the two *parshiyos* of the *mezuzah* are to be written on a piece of parchment and placed on the doorpost. The *halachah* further stipulates that only one of the doorposts within each doorway requires a *mezuzah*. This is alluded to by the fact that the word מְזֻזוֹת is written with only one ו (and not with two, as in מְזוּזוֹת).

The *mitzvah* of *mezuzah* applies only to a house where one lives or works. Therefore, a *beis haknesses*, which is used only for *tefillah* or Torah, does not fall under the category of בֵּיתֶךָ, and therefore would not require a *mezuzah*. However, a *beis hamidrash*, where people also eat and drink, would require a *mezuzah*.

The parchment on which the *mezuzah* is written requires *sirtut* which means the scrolling of straight horizontal lines into the material with a knife prior to the writing, as an outline, to ensure that each line of writing will be straight. This *halachah* of *sirtut* applies also to *Megillas Esther*. The Gemara (*Megillah* 16b) says that this is alluded to in the *Megillah* by the words דִּבְרֵי שָׁלוֹם וֶאֱמֶת, *Words of peace and truth* (ibid.), which means that the *Chachamim* instituted that it be written with *sirtut*, similar in form to a *sefer Torah*, כַּאֲמִיתָהּ שֶׁל תּוֹרָה, *as the truth of the Torah*, which in most opinions requires *sirtut*.

However, in the opinion of Rabbeinu Tam (*Tosafos Gittin* 6b; *Sotah* 17b; *Menachos* 32b), a *sefer Torah* does not require *sirtut*. Only *mezuzah* and *Megillas Esther* require it. According to this opinion, the אֲמִתָּהּ שֶׁל תּוֹרָה referred to in *Megillah* 16b means *mezuzah*, because in its two *parshiyos* it contains the basic truths of the Torah. The commonality of *mezuzah* and *Megillas Esther* is based on הִנֵּה לֹא יָנוּם וְלֹא יִישָׁן שׁוֹמֵר יִשְׂרָאֵל, *Behold the Guardian of Israel neither slumbers nor sleeps* (*Tehillim* 121:4). The *mezuzah* represents our individual protection by *HaKadosh Baruch Hu* (see further in the narrative regarding *Onkelos*), and the chain of events detailed in *Megillas Esther* is an example of our national protection by *HaKadosh Baruch Hu*.

At the end of *Rambam, Hil. Mezuzah*, there is a remarkable statement: כָּל זְמַן שֶׁיִּכָּנֵס וְיֵצֵא יִפְגַּע בְּיִחוּד ה', שְׁמוֹ שֶׁל הקב"ה, וְיִזְכֹּר אַהֲבָתוֹ וְיֵעוֹר מִשְּׁנָתוֹ וּשְׁגִיּוֹתָיו

KRIAS SHEMA ⚬ 339

בְּהַבְלֵי הַזְּמָן, When he comes and goes, he should become aware of the existence of the One God, and remember his Love for God, and this will awaken him from his "sleep" and his erroneous way in his fleeting life. This means that most people are usually not "fully awake," and do not think of the important things in the world. But when one passes a *mezuzah*, it should remind him of *HaKadosh Baruch Hu*, which will "wake him up" so that he can correct the errors of his ways in a temporal and fleeting world. The only other place where the Rambam uses the expression וְיֵעוֹר מִשְּׁנָתוֹ is in connection with the message of *tekias shofar* (see *Hil. Teshuvah* Ch. 3, halachah 4).

The Rambam continues in *Hilchos Mezuzah*: וְיֵדַע שֶׁאֵין דָּבָר הָעוֹמֵד לְעוֹלָם וּלְעוֹלְמֵי עוֹלָמִים אֶלָּא יְדִיעַת צוּר הָעוֹלָם וּמִיָּד הוּא חוֹזֵר לְדַעְתּוֹ וְהוֹלֵךְ בְּדַרְכֵי מֵישָׁרִים. When he passes the *mezuzah*, he should remind himself that nothing is permanent except the knowledge of *HaKadosh Baruch Hu*, meaning His knowledge of us and our knowledge of Him, if we make a connection with Him.

The *mezuzah* is the doorpost which witnesses the comings and goings of a person. Since everything in life is constantly changing, there will come a time when neither the person nor the house will be there any longer. The only thing that does not change is ה' אֱלֹהֵינוּ ה' אֶחָד. When one leaves his house, and thinks of the permanence of *HaKadosh Baruch Hu*, he "wakes up" and becomes aware of his own mortality, and that maybe this will be the last time he will walk out of his house. Maybe he will not come home; and even if he does, maybe he will be carried out at the next time! This will certainly "wake him up" and make him think of what *HaKadosh Baruch Hu* wants of him in the world. The message of the *mezuzah* is that one's house and possessions are fleeting, and the only real permanence is יְדִיעַת צוּר הָעוֹלָמִים, the awareness of the Rock of all Times, meaning the "rocklike" permanence of *HaKadosh Baruch Hu*.

∽§ וּבִשְׁעָרֶיךָ — **And upon your gates.** These are the public gates of the streets or the cities of *Eretz Yisrael*. We will fulfill this *mitzvah* when *Eretz Yisrael* is under the control of *Malchus Hashem*.

The first *parashah* of *Krias Shema* contains three *mitzvos* in addition to שְׁמַע and וְאָהַבְתָּ, and these are: וְשִׁנַּנְתָּם לְבָנֶיךָ: the *mitzvah* to learn and teach the Torah; וּקְשַׁרְתָּם לְאוֹת עַל יָדֶךָ וְהָיוּ לְטֹטָפֹת בֵּין עֵינֶיךָ: the *mitzvah* of *tefillin*; וּכְתַבְתָּם עַל מְזֻזוֹת בֵּיתֶךָ וּבִשְׁעָרֶיךָ: the *mitzvah* of *mezuzah*.

The Gemara, in three narratives to which we shall refer, illustrates for us that our *Chachamim* considered these three *mitzvos* to be absolutely vital to the very existence of our individual and national life.

Regarding the *mitzvah* of teaching Torah, the Gemara tells us that Rabbi Akiva publicly defied a governmental edict prohibiting the teaching of

Torah, for which he was subsequently imprisoned and brutally martyred. We are told there that Papus ben Yehudah, a *tzaddik* and *talmid chacham,* asked Rabbi Akiva why he would endanger his life to teach Torah, and he answered with the famous "fox and fish" parable. The fox advised the fish to avoid the fishermen's nets by coming out of the water onto the dry land. The fish answered, "If you are so smart, you should know that if we cannot be sure of our lives in our own element, we certainly cannot be protected when we are out of it." Said Rabbi Akiva, "The same applies to the Jewish nation; we simply cannot exist without Torah" (*Berachos* 61b).

כִּי הֵם חַיֵּינוּ וְאֹרֶךְ יָמֵינוּ is not simply a nice phrase; it is literally true. The Jewish nation cannot exist without Torah. Despite the fact that his life was in danger, Rabbi Akiva placed the survival of the Jewish people, whose lives would be absolutely worthless without Torah, over his own life, and he taught Torah publicly to insure their survival. For this, he paid the ultimate price.

Regarding the *mitzvah* of *tefillin,* the Gemara tells of Elisha, who was called בַּעַל כְּנָפַיִם (the winged one), because of the following occurrence.

When the government prohibited the Jews to wear *tefillin,* he continued to wear his *tefillin* in direct violation of that governmental order. When he noticed that a local law enforcement official had seen him, he fled, and while he was running he removed the *tefillin* from his head and held it in his hand. (The *tefillin* on the arm are easily concealed by a garment.) When the policeman caught him, he asked, "What is that in your hand?" "These are the wings of a dove," he answered. "Let me see," said the officer, and the Gemara states that Elisha opened his hand and, miraculously — *al pi neis* — there actually were dove wings in his hand. Although Elisha had no idea that a *neis* would occur to save him, he considered the *mitzvah* of *tefillin,* which contains the basic tenets of our *emunah,* of such vital importance, that to be without them — and their constant reminders — is analogous to a dove which cannot survive without wings. The Jewish nation, without the basic tenets of its faith, cannot survive (*Shabbos* 49a).

Regarding the *mitzvah* of *mezuzah,* the Gemara tells of a *ger tzedek* (a proselyte) by the name of Onkelos bar Klonymous who was related to the Roman emperor. (It is questionable whether this man was the one who composed *Targum Onkelos.*) When the emperor heard that he had converted to Judaism, he sent several detachments of Roman soldiers to attempt to force him to reconvert to his former religion. The first few times he convinced the soldiers themselves to convert. However, subsequently this proved impossible, and his continued refusal to reconvert placed him in mortal danger. For Onkelos, that was a true *she'as hashemad,* and he was prepared to give up his life, if necessary, rather than give up his *geirus.* As the soldiers were taking him out of his house, for what he thought would be his torture and execution, he placed his hand on the *mezuzah*. Puzzled by this strange act, they asked him, "What is the idea of that?" And he answered them, "Normally, a king's bodyguard keeps watch over him on the outside, while he is safely inside the palace. However, with the Jews, our King keeps watch over us on the outside, while we are inside." Hearing this, the soldiers became so enthralled by this idea that they wanted to hear more about the Jewish religion. Eventually, they, too, converted to Judaism, and the life of Onkelos was saved because of the *mitzvah* of *mezuzah* (*Avodah Zarah* 11a). (By the way, the Gemara does not talk of "kissing the *mezuzah,*" but rather, one is encouraged to simply place his hand on it to associate himself with the meaning of its contents.)

This story, too, teaches us about our survival. We live in a hostile world, and we cannot survive without the protection of *HaKadosh Baruch Hu*. *Mezuzah* reminds us of the fact that הִנֵּה לֹא יָנוּם וְלֹא יִישָׁן שׁוֹמֵר יִשְׂרָאֵל, *Behold, the Guardian of Israel neither slumbers nor sleeps,* and our survival is based on our *kabbalas ol Malchus Shamayim* and our acceptance of *mitzvos,* which are the contents of the *mezuzah*.

וְהָיָה אִם שָׁמֹעַ

The Gemara states: אָמַר רַבִּי יְהוֹשֻׁעַ בֶּן קָרְחָה: לָמָּה קָדְמָה פָּרָשַׁת ״שְׁמַע״ לְ״וְהָיָה אִם שָׁמֹעַ״, כְּדֵי שֶׁיְּקַבֵּל עָלָיו עוֹל מַלְכוּת שָׁמַיִם תְּחִלָּה וְאַחַר כָּךְ מְקַבֵּל עָלָיו עוֹל מִצְוֹת, *Said Rabbi Yehoshua ben Korchah: The reason the chapter of Shema precedes that of Vehaya Im Shamoa is to encourage one to accept upon himself the yoke of God's reign before accepting the yoke of the mitzvos* (*Berachos* 13a). In *parashas Shema* we accept the "yoke" of the rule of heaven over ourselves, which is a prerequisite to the *parashah* of וְהָיָה אִם שָׁמֹעַ, in which we take upon ourselves the "yoke" of the obligation to perform the *mitzvos*. This obligation can be very difficult, and the *chachamim* have therefore characterized it as a "yoke."

It is proper to pause somewhat between the end of *parashas Shema* and the beginning of וְהָיָה אִם שָׁמֹעַ, to indicate a change of subject.

As we explained, *parashas Shema,* with its *kabbalas ol Malchus Shamayim,* mandates us to be ready to offer our very lives for *HaKadosh Baruch Hu* if it is required, as in cases of *gilui arayos, avodah zarah,* and *shefichas damim,* or during periods of *shemad*. However, with regard to the *parashah* of וְהָיָה אִם שָׁמֹעַ, whose subject is *kabbalas ol mitzvos,* the opposite is true. We are told, וָחַי בָּהֶם, *and live through them* (*Vayikra* 18:5), וְלֹא שֶׁיָּמוּת בָּהֶם. This means one is to live by the mitzvos and not to die because of them (*Yoma* 85b), meaning that in cases of life or death — except in the specific cases previously detailed — we are permitted, nay, obligated, to violate the *mitzvos* rather then give our lives to uphold them, יַעֲבוֹר וְאַל יֵהָרֵג. It is for this reason that one may eat on Yom Kippur or have *chametz* on Pesach, or be *mechallel Shabbos,* and certainly do any other *aveirah,* if his life is at stake.

וְהָיָה אִם שָׁמֹעַ תִּשְׁמְעוּ אֶל מִצְוֹתַי אֲשֶׁר אָנֹכִי מְצַוֶּה אֶתְכֶם הַיּוֹם — **And it will come to pass that if you continually hearken to My commandments that I command you today.** *Listening to the mitzvos* means that the *mitzvos* have a message. And that message is that *HaKadosh Baruch Hu* is telling us, "These are מִצְוֹתַי, *My mitzvos.*" One eats kosher, or puts on *tefillin,* not because "Jews eat kosher" or "Jews put on *tefillin,*" but rather, because *HaKadosh Baruch Hu* has commanded that we eat kosher and put on *tefillin.* One can give the most beautiful explanation for the *mitzvah* of *tefillin,* but this is not the reason one puts on *tefillin.* The reason one does a *mitzvah* is simply because *HaKadosh Baruch Hu* has commanded us to do so: אֲשֶׁר קִדְּשָׁנוּ בְּמִצְוֹתָיו וְצִוָּנוּ. We have previously pointed out that this is similar to the "laws of nature." Scientists, for instance, have long tried to explain gravity, and every so often another explanation is offered. But whatever the reason may be, gravity exists because it is a law of nature, and not because of any explanation which scientists may give for it. Similarly, while we attempt to discover the underlying meaning of the *mitzvos,* they exist not because of their meaning, but because God has ordained that they exist.

שָׁמֹעַ תִּשְׁמְעוּ — **Continually hearken.** Our *Chachamim* (*Succah* 46b) have explained that this double expression tells us, אִם שָׁמוֹעַ בַּיָּשָׁן, תִּשְׁמַע בֶּחָדָשׁ, *If you hear the old (subject matter), you will merit hearing the new.* This refers to reviewing one's learning, because when one reviews his Torah learning, he gains a new insight into it. And the more one learns about a *mitzvah,* the better he can observe it. Learning without observing the *mitzvah* is only half of the job.

Learning about the *mitzvos* consists of two parts: First, learning that a particular act or behavior — or prohibition — is a *mitzvah;* second, learning the details of the *mitzvah,* which includes an attempt to understand its meaning.

To be sure, there are *mitzvos* which, by their nature, cannot be observed by every person; for instance, the *mitzvos* pertaining to a *melech* or a *Kohen* or the *avodah* in the *Beis HaMikdash,* etc. In those cases the learning itself is the fulfillment of the *mitzvah.* However, if one can fulfill a *mitzvah,* his learning is incomplete unless he has actually performed the *mitzvah.* As *Chazal* tell us: תַּלְמוּד מֵבִיא לִידֵי מַעֲשֶׂה, *Learning brings one to act,* to carry out that which he had learned (*Kiddushin* 40b), and this is incorporated in the *berachah* of אַהֲבָה רַבָּה, as it states, לִלְמוֹד וּלְלַמֵּד לִשְׁמֹר וְלַעֲשׂוֹת וּלְקַיֵּם.

לְאַהֲבָה אֶת ה' אֱלֹהֵיכֶם — **To love Hashem, your God.** The *kabbalas ol mitzvos* has as its ultimate purpose the development of the love of *HaKadosh Baruch Hu.* If a person keeps the *mitzvos* properly, he will eventually develop *ahavas Hashem*. But, the prerequisite for keeping the *mitzvos* is learning how to fulfill them properly. Therefore, this sentence describes the chain of events once one has accepted upon himself the *ol mitzvos*. First, אִם שָׁמֹעַ תִּשְׁמְעוּ, one must learn Torah, which will lead him to the proper fulfillment of the *mitzvos,* אֶל מִצְוֹתַי, which, in turn, will lead him to the ultimate goal of לְאַהֲבָה אֶת ה', the development of a love relationship with *HaKadosh Baruch Hu.*

◆§ וּלְעָבְדוֹ בְּכָל לְבַבְכֶם וּבְכָל נַפְשְׁכֶם — **And to serve Him with all your heart and with all your soul.** What does this add? Does the fulfillment of the *mitzvos* not constitute *avodas Hashem*? And is this not already included in וְאָהַבְתָּ אֵת ה' אֱלֹהֶיךָ בְּכָל לְבָבְךָ וּבְכָל נַפְשְׁךָ וּבְכָל מְאֹדֶךָ, contained in the first *parashah*?

The simple answer is that this sentence, in the plural, addresses the Jewish people, and commands us, as a matter of "national policy," to serve *HaKadosh Baruch Hu* with our whole hearts and lives. The sentence in the first *parashah,* וְאָהַבְתָּ וגו', is addressed to each individual.

However, there is more to this. Our *Chazal* see in the words וּלְעָבְדוֹ בְּכָל לְבַבְכֶם the basis for the *mitzvah* of *tefillah* : אֵיזוֹ הִיא עֲבוֹדָה שֶׁהִיא בְּלֵב, הֱוֵי אוֹמֵר זוֹ תְּפִלָּה, *What constitutes "service of the heart"? — The answer is, prayer* (Taanis 2a). Usually, the word עֲבוֹדָה in the Torah, in the sense of the service of *HaKadosh Baruch Hu,* is used in connection with *korbanos*. However, here the *avodah* is described as something which is done only with the heart, בְּכָל לְבַבְכֶם, which is *tefillah.*

However, merely thinking the *tefillah* is insufficient, הִרְהוּר לָאו כְּדִבּוּר דָּמֵי, *Mere thinking of the words does not satisfy the requirement that one is to actually speak them* (*Berachos* 20b; codified for *tefillah* in *Orach Chaim* 101:2); and the *halachah* requires that one must actually verbalize his *tefillah,* unless this is impossible due to sickness or the impurity of the place in which one may find himself (see *Beur Halachah* 62:4). Nevertheless, the verbalization of the *tefillah* is only the way the *mitzvah* is done, but it does not constitute the *mitzvah* itself. The *mitzvah* of *tefillah* itself is בְּלֵב [*b'leiv*], *with the heart*. It is to be רַחֲמִים וְתַחֲנוּנִים לִפְנֵי הַמָּקוֹם, placing ourselves at the mercy of God.

Furthermore, *tefillah* — although it is essentially *avodah sheb'lev,* service of the heart — is greatly enhanced when it is said together with others as part of *tefillah b'tzibbur*. The Torah emphasizes this by the use of the plural form וּלְעָבְדוֹ בְּכָל לְבַבְכֶם וּבְכָל נַפְשְׁכֶם. When one thinks about it, it is really quite presumptuous for an individual person, with all of his shortcomings and faults, to address the *Ribbono Shel Olam*! Even *Avraham Avinu,* in his *tefillah,* said וְאָנֹכִי עָפָר וָאֵפֶר, *I am dust and ashes* (*Bereishis* 18:27). It is for this reason that when we address *HaKadosh Baruch Hu* at the beginning of the *Shemoneh Esrei,* we do so by saying אֱלֹהֵינוּ וֵאלֹהֵי אֲבוֹתֵינוּ, meaning, "We come to you, not as individuals, but rather, as children of our parents, and we are all bound together as descendants of the Forefathers of our nation."

There is a big difference if one addresses *HaKadosh Baruch Hu* as an individual or as part of a *tzibbur*. Every *beis haknesses*, or even every small *minyan*, represents a segment of *Klal Yisrael*. And, with the *tzibbur*, each individual approaches *HaKadosh Baruch Hu* as a segment of His nation, which has been assured of His closeness: כִּי מִי גוֹי גָּדוֹל אֲשֶׁר לוֹ אֱלֹהִים קְרֹבִים אֵלָיו כַּה' אֱלֹהֵינוּ בְּכָל קָרְאֵנוּ אֵלָיו, *For which nation is so great that it has a God Who is close to it, as is Hashem, our God, whenever we call to Him?* (*Devarim* 4:7).

Rambam, at the beginning of *Hilchos Tefillah*, states clearly that *tefillah* is a *mitzvas asei d'Oraisa*: מִצְוַת עֲשֵׂה לְהִתְפַּלֵּל בְּכָל יוֹם, שֶׁנֶּאֱמַר: וַעֲבַדְתֶּם אֶת ה' אֱלֹהֵיכֶם, מִפִּי הַשְּׁמוּעָה לָמְדוּ שֶׁעֲבוֹדָה זוֹ הִיא תְפִלָּה, שֶׁנֶּאֱמַר וּלְעָבְדוֹ בְּכָל לְבַבְכֶם, אָמְרוּ חֲכָמִים: אֵיזוֹ הִיא עֲבוֹדָה שֶׁבַּלֵּב, זוֹ תְּפִלָּה, *It is a Torah obligation to pray every day. For it says: "You shall serve Hashem, your God"* (*Shemos* 23:25). *Our Sages have received an oral tradition that "service" means prayer, for it says: "And to serve Him with all your heart"* (*Devarim* 11:13). *Which service is done with the heart? This is prayer* (from Rambam, *Hilchos Tefillah* 1:1).

However, according to most of the *poskim*, *tefillah* is *d'Rabbanan*, and the reference to the *pasuk* of וּלְעָבְדוֹ בְּכָל לְבַבְכֶם is אַסְמַכְתָּא בְּעָלְמָא, *homiletically supported by the text*, although not exegetic. And, according to the Rambam, who holds that *tefillah* is *d'Oraisa*, the details of the *mitzvah* of *tefillin* are *d'Rabbanan*: how, what, when, and where one is to be *mispallel* are all *d'Rabbanan*.

Regarding the obligation of women to fulfill the *mitzvah* of *tefillah*, the basic *mitzvah* to be *mispallel* to *HaKadosh Baruch Hu* is not time-bound, and therefore women are obligated, just as men are, to fulfill this *mitzvah*. This is clearly set forth in the Mishnah (*Berachos* 20b); and the Gemara (ibid.) explains that since the essence of *tefillah* consists of רַחֲמִים, *prayers for mercy*, and women are just as dependent on the mercy of *HaKadosh Baruch Hu* as are men, they are equally obligated to be *mispallel*. Furthermore, *tefillah*, as *avodah*, consists of the realization that one is totally dependent on *HaKadosh Baruch Hu* every moment of one's life, and women are as obligated as men to serve *HaKadosh Baruch Hu* in this manner. However, women are exempt from being *mispallel* at specific times, such as Shacharis, Minchah, and Maariv, because this falls under the category of *mitzvas asei shehazeman gerama*, from which women are exempt.

❏ וּלְעָבְדוֹ . . . בְּכָל נַפְשְׁכֶם — *And to serve Him . . . with all your soul.* This phrase tells us that in addition to *tefillah b'leiv*, service of the heart, there is another form of *tefillah*, which is called *tefillah b'nefesh*. Ordinary *tefillah* is characterized by the word מִתְפַּלֵּל, a reflexive verb indicating that the purpose of the *tefillah* is to benefit the one who is praying. However, in *tefillah b'nefesh* we do not focus on our own personal needs, physical or even spiritual, but rather, the object of that *tefillah* is to increase *kiddush Hashem* in the world. An example of this form of *tefillah* is found in the *Shemoneh Esrei*. After having asked *HaKadosh Baruch Hu* for all of our needs, personal and national, including *daas, teshuvah, selichah, geulah, refuah, parnassah,* etc. we end this portion of the *tefillah* with בָּרוּךְ אַתָּה ה׳ שׁוֹמֵעַ תְּפִלָּה. Then, immediately afterwards, we seem to start all over again by saying רְצֵה ה׳ אֱלֹהֵינוּ בְּעַמְּךָ יִשְׂרָאֵל וּבִתְפִלָּתָם וגו׳. However, this is not so. The previous part of the *tefillah*, ending with שׁוֹמֵעַ תְּפִלָּה, consists of *tefillah b'leiv*, in which we ask *HaKadosh Baruch Hu* for our own needs. However, the *tefillah* of רְצֵה, in which we ask *HaKadosh Baruch Hu* for the return of the *avodah* in the *Beis HaMikdash,* is purely *l'shem Shamayim*. There we express the thought that regardless of whether *HaKadosh Baruch Hu* accepts our *tefillos* for our physical or spiritual needs, we nevertheless ask Him, for His sake, that He increase the amount of *kiddush Hashem* in the world through the return of the *avodah* in the *Beis HaMikdash*. This form of *tefillah* is called *tefillah b'nefesh,* because we are, so to speak, giving away our own *nefesh* — placing our own personal needs in the background — and focusing only on our desire to see the level of *kiddush Hashem* increase in the world through the means of the *avodah* in the *Beis HaMikdash,* which has as its primary purpose the creation of a רֵיחַ נִיחוֹחַ לַה׳, to express our desire to be pleasing in the eyes of *HaKadosh Baruch Hu.*

Even a *korban chatas,* which is brought as part of the *kapparah* (atonement) process for committing a sin, together with *teshuvah,* has as its primary purpose the eradication of the *tumah* and the evil in the world engendered by the *aveirah* which was committed, and its replacement with *taharah* and goodness. Instead of the *chillul Hashem* which was caused by the sin, the *korban chatas* will bring *kiddush Hashem* into the world.

This thought is incorporated in the text of רְצֵה in the words: וּתְפִלָּתָם בְּאַהֲבָה תְקַבֵּל בְּרָצוֹן, *And their tefillah out of love, may You willingly accept.* (The words וּתְפִלָּתָם בְּאַהֲבָה תְקַבֵּל בְּרָצוֹן belong together. It does not say וּתְפִלָּתָם תְקַבֵּל בְּאַהֲבָה וּבְרָצוֹן.) The meaning is that this *tefillah* is based purely on our love for *HaKadosh Baruch Hu,* and we are *mispallel* that His Name shall be honored and sanctified and not be desecrated in the world, that the entire world may recognize Him. This is similar to the thought which is expressed by: יְהִי שֵׁם ה׳ מְבֹרָךְ מֵעַתָּה וְעַד עוֹלָם, *Blessed be the Name of Hashem from this time forth and forever* (*Tehillim* 113:2).

◈ וְנָתַתִּי מְטַר אַרְצְכֶם בְּעִתּוֹ יוֹרֶה וּמַלְקוֹשׁ — **Then I will provide rain for your land in its proper time, the early and late rains.** The reward for the fulfillment of the previously stated וְהָיָה אִם שָׁמֹעַ תִּשְׁמְעוּ וגו׳ will be the timely rainfalls in *Eretz Yisrael*, which will result in plentiful produce. יוֹרֶה is the early rain in the fall; מַלְקוֹשׁ, is the late rain in the spring.

A representative of a Conservative synagogue once remarked to me, "We have eliminated the second part of the *Shema*, because it focuses on the needs of the Jewish people when they were mainly an agricultural society, in which the reward for the observance of the commandments is said to be adequate rainfall which will produce plentiful food for man and animal. This is a primitive notion, which was applicable to a largely agricultural society, but it is no longer applicable in our modern age."

Whereupon, I answered him, "If this is your understanding of this chapter, you have never really read it properly. Look at the words: וְהָיָה אִם שָׁמֹעַ תִּשְׁמְעוּ אֶל מִצְוֹתַי . . . לְאַהֲבָה אֶת ה' אֱלֹהֵיכֶם וּלְעָבְדוֹ וגו'. The text clearly states that the purpose of keeping the commandments is to demonstrate our love of *HaKadosh Baruch Hu* and thereby to serve Him."

When one performs the *mitzvos*, he should forget about himself and his needs, and concentrate on complying with God's commandments, as a form of service to Him. Notwithstanding this, however, *HaKadosh Baruch Hu* promises us in this second *parashah* of *Krias Shema* that if we do perform the *mitzvos* properly, we will be blessed with rain and produce of the land. However, this is not the purpose of observing the *mitzvos*.

This concept is underscored by Rashi (ibid.), quoting the *Sifrei*, which paraphrases the Heavenly response to our observance of the *mitzvos*: עֲשִׂיתֶם מַה שֶׁעֲלֵיכֶם, אַף אֲנִי אֶעֱשֶׂה מַה שֶׁעָלַי, *If you fulfill your obligation, I will fulfill my obligation.*

Unquestionably, the importance of timely rainfall to our existence cannot be underestimated. The welfare of nations depend on it; the lack of rainfall and its consequences can topple kings. מֶלֶךְ לְשָׂדֶה נֶעֱבָד, *A king is a servant of the field* (*Koheles* 5:8). Even a king's power is dependent on the produce of the fields. If nothing grows in the fields, the king might as well abdicate his throne, because his population will either rise up against him or flee the country.

Even the *tefillos* of מוֹרִיד הַגֶּשֶׁם וּמוֹרִיד הָרוּחַ מַשִּׁיב and לִבְרָכָה וּמָטָר טַל וְתֵן are so much of the essence that if one forgets to say them one must repeat the entire *Shemoneh Esrei*. This would not be necessary if one were to leave out any of the other words or phrases within each *berachah* of the *Shemoneh Esrei*.

However, we must understand the significance of the fact that adequate rainfall is given here as the main reward for our performance of *mitzvos* and *tefillah*.

The first reference to *tefillah* in the Torah is found in connection with rain. In *Bereishis* 2:5 we find the statement: וְכָל שִׂיחַ הַשָּׂדֶה טֶרֶם יִהְיֶה בָאָרֶץ וְכָל עֵשֶׂב הַשָּׂדֶה טֶרֶם יִצְמָח כִּי לֹא הִמְטִיר ה' אֱלֹהִים עַל הָאָרֶץ וְאָדָם אַיִן לַעֲבֹד אֶת הָאֲדָמָה, *Now all the trees of the field were not yet on the earth and all the herb of the field had not yet sprouted, for Hashem God has not sent rain upon the earth and there was no man to work the soil.*

מְלַמֵּד שֶׁיָּצְאוּ דְשָׁאִים וְעָמְדוּ עַל פֶּתַח קַרְקַע עַד שֶׁבָּא Rashi explains this as follows: אָדָם הָרִאשׁוֹן וּבִקֵּשׁ עֲלֵיהֶם רַחֲמִים וְיָרְדוּ גְשָׁמִים וְצָמְחוּ. לְלַמֶּדְךָ שֶׁהקב"ה מִתְאַוֶּה לִתְפִלָּתָן שֶׁל צַדִּיקִים (Chullin 60b). Paraphrased, this means that no vegetation grew from the earth until Adam HaRishon prayed for it, because "HaKadosh Baruch Hu desires the prayers of the *tzaddikim*." And in answer to these prayers, HaKadosh Baruch Hu showered the earth with rain, which produced the vegetation on the earth.

We have already discussed in our "Introduction to *Pesukei d'Zimrah*" the concept of שֶׁל צַדִּיקִים לִתְפִלָּתָן מִתְאַוֶּה הקב"ה. [Please refer to it.] We pointed out there that the "need" that HaKadosh Baruch Hu has for *tefillah* is based on the fact that in His infinite wisdom, He created the world to be self-sustaining, not only physically but spiritually as well. It is the will of HaKadosh Baruch Hu that we initiate our relationship with Him through *tefillah*, and His response completes this self-sustaining cycle. This is the purpose of our שִׁירוֹת, תְּפִלּוֹת, זְמִירוֹת, וְתִשְׁבָּחוֹת, בְּרָכוֹת, וְהוֹדָאוֹת.

The blessing of rainfall in וְהָיָה אִם שָׁמֹעַ as a reward for our keeping of the *mitzvos* and our *tefillah*, besides its literal meaning, is symbolic of the entire system of the *hashpa'ah*, the means through which HaKadosh Baruch Hu grants His blessing to us in this self-sustaining world.

Rain develops when the moisture of the oceans and from other parts of the earth evaporates and rises up and collects in clouds. Eventually, the stored-up moisture in the clouds returns to earth in the form of rain. The moisture in the clouds is referred to as "storehouses," as in נֹתֵן בָּאוֹצָרוֹת תְּהוֹמוֹת, *He places deep waters in storehouses* (*Tehillim* 33:7); or יִפְתַּח ה' לְךָ אֶת אוֹצָרוֹ הַטּוֹב אֶת הַשָּׁמַיִם לָתֵת מְטַר אַרְצְךָ בְּעִתּוֹ, *He* [HaKadosh Baruch Hu] *will open His good storage chamber,* etc. (*Devarim* 28:12).

Just as the cycle of rain begins with the evaporation of water from the earth, so do all of our blessings from HaKadosh Baruch Hu, physical as well as spiritual, begin with our initiatives in the form of the observance of the *mitzvos* and *tefillah*. The response of HaKadosh Baruch Hu is the continuation of this self-sustaining cycle, just as rain results from the evaporation of water from the earth, which will then again evaporate and develop into more rain. This symbolism is expressed by Yechezkel HaNavi as וְזָרַקְתִּי עֲלֵיכֶם מַיִם טְהוֹרִים, *Then I will sprinkle pure water upon you* (*Yechezkel* 36:25). All of the *kedushah* and *taharah* which HaKadosh Baruch Hu will bestow upon *Bnei Yisrael* is expressed as מַיִם טְהוֹרִים, symbolizing the self-sustaining cycle, which will continue if it is sustained by our "gifts" of *mitzvos* and *tefillah*.

While on the subject of rainfall, as a side comment, I wish to point out that the *minhag Ashkenaz*, as practiced in our *kehillah*, is that the fasts of שֵׁנִי חֲמִישִׁי וְשֵׁנִי, Monday, Thursday, and Monday (see explanation below), after Succos, begin in the second half of Marcheshvan, instead of during the first, as is practiced in most *kehillos*. The reason for this could simply be based on the fact that the days are shorter in the latter half of the month, which makes it easier for those who wish to complete a full day's fast.

[Ed. note: This is a reference to the customary, voluntary fasts, after Pesach and Succos, on the first Monday, Thursday, and the following Monday, which are practiced in most *kehillos* after Rosh Chodesh of Iyar and of Marcheshvan.]

However, a more significant reason is based on the Mishnah, which tells us that in Eretz Yisrael one begins to pray for rain, שׁוֹאֲלִין אֶת הַגְּשָׁמִים, on the seventh of Marcheshvan. And if there is no rain by the seventeenth of Marcheshvan, the *talmidei chachamim*, יְחִידִים (individuals), begin to fast. If the drought lingers on, a general fast is declared (*Taanis* 10a). Therefore, our observance of תַּעֲנִית שֵׁנִי חֲמִישִׁי וְשֵׁנִי begins on the Monday either on, or after, the seventeenth of Marcheshvan, corresponding to the beginning of the period of *taaniyos* prescribed by the Mishnah.

◆§ וְאָסַפְתָּ דְגָנֶךָ וְתִירשְׁךָ וְיִצְהָרֶךָ — **That you may gather in your grain, your wine, and your oil.** The change from the plural to the singular reflects the fact that not everyone is a farmer. This phrase is directed to those individuals who grow crops. תִּירוֹשׁ, the liquid of the grape, refers to wine. יִצְהָר, from צהר, meaning *light,* refers to olives, which were grown chiefly to produce oil for lighting purposes.

There is a difference of opinion in the Gemara (*Berachos* 35b) regarding this *pasuk* of וְאָסַפְתָּ דְגָנֶךָ, which apparently presupposes that one pursue a worldly occupation. This is apparently in opposition to the *mitzvah* of *talmud Torah,* which obligates a person to constantly study Torah: לֹא יָמוּשׁ סֵפֶר הַתּוֹרָה הַזֶּה מִפִּיךָ וְהָגִיתָ בּוֹ יוֹמָם וָלַיְלָה, *This Book of the Torah shall not depart from your mouth; rather you should contemplate it day and night* (*Yehoshua* 1:8). According to the opinion of R' Yishmael, the *pasuk* of וְאָסַפְתָּ דְגָנֶךָ teaches us that הַנְהֵג בָּהֶן מִנְהַג דֶּרֶךְ אֶרֶץ, one is to include a normal livelihood within the framework of *talmud Torah,* as it is needed.

However, R' Shimon bar Yochai is of the opinion that it is impossible to combine an agricultural livelihood with Torah learning: אֶפְשָׁר אָדָם חוֹרֵשׁ בִּשְׁעַת חֲרִישָׁה וְזוֹרֵעַ בִּשְׁעַת זְרִיעָה וְקוֹצֵר בִּשְׁעַת קְצִירָה וְדָשׁ בִּשְׁעַת דִּישָׁה וְזוֹרֶה בִּשְׁעַת הָרוּחַ, תּוֹרָה מַה תְּהֵא עָלֶיהָ, *If one plows during plowing time, sows during planting time, harvests during harvest time, threshes during threshing time, and winnows during winnowing time, what will become of Torah learning (when will he have the time to learn)?* If one is involved with the agricultural cycle, it will leave him very little time for learning Torah. Therefore, R' Shimon bar Yochai remarks: בִּזְמַן שֶׁיִּשְׂרָאֵל עוֹשִׂין רְצוֹנוֹ שֶׁל מָקוֹם מְלַאכְתָּן נַעֲשֵׂית עַל יְדֵי אֲחֵרִים, שֶׁנֶּאֱמַר וְעָמְדוּ זָרִים וְרָעוּ צֹאנְכֶם וגו' (*Yeshayahu* 61:5). The prophet Yeshayahu prophesies that if the Jewish people live in accordance with the will of *HaKadosh Baruch Hu,* circumstances will be such that they will be free to pursue their Torah studies, because others will come and do the work of their fields.

As to the practical application of this dispute, the Gemara (ibid.) quotes Abaye who observed that: הַרְבֵּה עָשׂוּ כְּרַבִּי יִשְׁמָעֵאל וְעָלְתָה בְיָדָן, כְּרַבִּי שִׁמְעוֹן בֶּן יוֹחַי וְלֹא עָלְתָה בְיָדָן, *Many people followed the opinion of R' Yishmael and were successful, and many followed that of R' Shimon bar Yochai and were not successful.* What this means is that the lofty goal of studying Torah exclusively is a path for the selected few outstanding individuals only, where others will do their work for them, but it is not for the הַרְבֵּה, the general population. On the other hand, the program suggested by R' Yishmael, הַנְהֵג בָּהֶן מִנְהַג דֶּרֶךְ אֶרֶץ, of combining Torah learning with the pursuit of a livelihood, has proven successful for הַרְבֵּה, the masses.

The mention here of דְּגָנֶךָ וְתִירֹשְׁךָ וְיִצְהָרֶךָ, the three types of produce of Eretz Yisrael is not without significance.

דָּגָן, meaning grain, refers only to the five kinds of grain from which there is a Torah obligation to take *terumah* and *maasros*: חִטָּה, שְׂעוֹרָה, כּוּסְמִין, שִׁבּוֹלֶת שׁוּעָל, וְשִׁיפּוֹן, *wheat, barley, rye, "spelt" (the exact species is unclear), and oats.*

The Gemara says that a child begins to develop its דַּעַת, its mental capacity, only after it begins to eat grain: אֵין הַתִּינוֹק יוֹדֵעַ לִקְרוֹת אַבָּא וְאִמָּא עַד שֶׁיִּטְעוֹם טַעַם דָּגָן (*Berachos* 40a). The eating of grain has the effect of stimulating mental growth. Furthermore, the Gemara tells us that the excrement of a child who has not yet eaten cereals is not considered "filth" in the halachic sense, and its presence would not prohibit one from saying words of Torah, *berachos,* and *tefillah* (see *Yerushalmi, Berachos* 3:5).

The grain grown in Eretz Yisrael has a special quality. When one eats this grain — which was grown in an atmosphere of *kedushah* and *taharah,* and from which the requisite *terumah, maasros,* and *challah* are taken — it promotes a higher level of intelligence than ordinary grain would, that of *daas Elokim.*

Similarly, תִּירוֹשׁ, *wine,* from the grapes of Eretz Yisrael, from which *nesachim* in the *avodas hakorbanos* can be brought, has a special quality — it creates happiness: וְיַיִן יְשַׂמַּח לְבַב אֱנוֹשׁ, *and wine that gladdens man's heart* (*Tehillim* 104:15). One can become intoxicated from any alcohol, but the wine of Eretz Yisrael has the special quality of inducing a feeling of spiritual happiness, which is not related to simple frivolity.

יִצְהָר, *olive oil,* similarly grown in Eretz Yisrael, which is used in the sacrificial service together with flour for *menachos,* and is the fuel for the light of the *Menorah* in the *Beis HaMikdash,* has the special quality of enlightening one's mind to a higher level of understanding of the Torah. It promotes the *ohr haTorah* in the human personality, of which the highest form is *ruach hakodesh*.

These three forms of vegetation, and their spiritual effect on the human personality in Eretz Yisrael, are alluded to in the words, תַּדְשֵׁא הָאָרֶץ דֶּשֶׁא, *Let the earth sprout vegetation* (*Bereishis* 1:11): the letters of דֶּשֶׁא stand for דַּעַת [*daas*], *knowledge;* שִׂמְחָה [*simchah*], *joy;* אוֹר [*ohr*], *light*.

Furthermore, this explains the statement in *Bircas Me'ein Shalosh* (*al hamichyah*): וְעַל אֶרֶץ חֶמְדָּה טוֹבָה וּרְחָבָה שֶׁרָצִיתָ וְהִנְחַלְתָּ לַאֲבוֹתֵינוּ לֶאֱכוֹל מִפִּרְיָהּ וְלִשְׂבּוֹעַ מִטּוּבָהּ, which means that the purpose for which *HaKadosh Baruch Hu* gave us the land was to eat from its produce! This is a truly remarkable statement. In other words, it is a *mitzvah* for us to eat the fruit of the land, and to satiate ourselves from its goodness! In view of our explanation, this is very understandable, because the Torah wants us to absorb the produce of Eretz Yisrael, and thereby to enhance our *daas, simchah,* and *ohr,* as a result of the special qualities of its produce (see *Bach, Orach Chaim* 208).

This also explains the comment on the repeated pleas of Moshe Rabbeinu to enter Eretz Yisrael: מִפְּנֵי מָה נִתְאַוָּה מֹשֶׁה רַבֵּנוּ לִיכָּנֵס לְאֶרֶץ יִשְׂרָאֵל, וְכִי לֶאֱכוֹל מִפִּרְיָהּ הוּא צָרִיךְ וגו', *Why was Moshe Rabbeinu so desirous of entering Eretz Yisrael? Did he need to eat of its fruits?* (*Sotah* 14a). This is truly astounding. Is eating the produce of Eretz Yisrael the main reason for entering the land? But, following our explanation, what our *Chachamim* mean here is that Moshe Rabbeinu indeed *did not* need to eat the fruits of Eretz Yisrael to gain a heightened sense of *daas Elokim, simchah, ohr,* and *ruach hakodesh*.

It is very possible that the effect which the produce of Eretz Yisrael has on the human personality may exist even in today's Eretz Yisrael. This would be borne out by the ending עַל הָאָרֶץ וְעַל פְּרִי גַפְנָהּ and עַל הָאָרֶץ וְעַל פֵּרוֹתֶיהָ, of the בִּרְכַּת מֵעֵין שָׁלֹשׁ which is said in Eretz Yisrael, because this expresses thanks to *HaKadosh Baruch Hu* for having given one the *zechus* to eat the specially endowed produce of Eretz Yisrael.

וְנָתַתִּי עֵשֶׂב בְּשָׂדְךָ לִבְהֶמְתֶּךָ וְאָכַלְתָּ וְשָׂבָעְתָּ — **I will provide grass in your field for your cattle and you will eat and be satisfied.** Again, this is written in the singular, because not everyone owns animals. We learn from this sentence structure that one must feed his animals before he himself eats. Therefore, while one may not interrupt between a *berachah* and the beginning of the eating — and if he does so, he must make the *berachah* again — an interruption for the purpose of ordering that his animal be fed is not considered an interruption, because it is a *tzorech berachah,* a prerequisite for his own meal (see *Berachos* 40a).

Many years ago, I was invited to have breakfast with Rav Breuer, and I remember that he placed some bird food into a birdcage before he sat down for breakfast.

❑ וְאָכַלְתָּ וְשָׂבָעְתָּ — *You will eat and be satisfied.* We all have animal desires, and the most powerful is the desire to satiate one's hunger. However, Rashi, quoting from *Chazal* (*Toras Kohanim,* cited in *Rashi, Vayikra* 26:5), tells us that שֶׁתְּהֵא בְרָכָה מְצוּיָה בַּפַּת בְּתוֹךְ הַמֵּעַיִם, *This is an additional gift,* זוֹ בְּרָכָה אַחֶרֶת, *that a blessing will exist in the bread within the intestines;* אוֹכֵל קִמְעָה וְהוּא מִתְבָּרֵךְ בְּמֵעָיו, the food will be so richly endowed with the blessings of HaKadosh Baruch Hu that one will eat only a little, and yet be satisfied.

The Rambam (*Hil. Dei'os* 4:2) warns one to use moderation in eating and not to eat to full satiation. He advises that one should leave about one quarter of his intestinal capacity unfilled. Today, many people are health conscious, and they follow similar guidelines. Once one has fulfilled his nutritional needs, the remaining "hunger" is only the animal desire to eat, which should be controlled. The special *berachah* in Eretz Yisrael will be that as soon as one has eaten enough to meet his nutritional needs, he will feel completely satiated.

This explains: יְראוּ אֶת ה' קְדשָׁיו כִּי אֵין מַחְסוֹר לִירֵאָיו, which literally means, *Fear God, you, His holy ones, because those who fear Him lack nothing* (*Tehillim* 34:10). Since one cannot become קְדוֹשָׁיו without fearing God, why would one who is already *kadosh* have to be told to fear Him? The answer lies in the proper interpretation of this *pasuk.* קְדשָׁיו here refers to those who sanctify themselves by abstaining and limiting even their permissible activities, in the sense of קַדֵּשׁ עַצְמְךָ בַּמּוּתָּר לָךְ (*Yevamos* 20a; *Ramban Vayikra* 19:2).

Applied to eating, this means that when one has an appetite to continue to eat or drink after fulfilling his nutritional needs, and he curbs his appetite as an exercise in controlling his purely animal instinct, he is called a *kadosh.* In this sense, the paraphrased sense of this *pasuk* is: "You, holy ones of God, fill the void left by your suppressed appetite for worldly pleasures with *yiras Shamayim,* because those who fear Him do not feel anything lacking."

In fact, *ahavas Hashem* and *yiras Shamayim* are possible only if one does not fully satiate his desire for food and other earthly pleasures. [For an explanation on this subject, see *Maayan Beis HaSho'evah, Va'eschanan* 6:5, p. 395 s.v. וּמֵעוֹלָם תמהתי.]

◈§ הִשָּׁמְרוּ לָכֶם, פֶּן יִפְתֶּה לְבַבְכֶם — **Beware, lest your heart be seduced.** This *pasuk* warns us that once we have achieved satiation of our earthly needs, וְאָכַלְתָּ וְשָׂבָעְתָּ, as a result of living in Eretz Yisrael amid God's abundant blessings, danger lurks not far behind. So long as a person controls his earthly desires and does not fully satiate them, there is still room within him for *yiras Shamayim.* However, we are told here, "Watch yourselves, your heart may be tempted, etc." Unless one curbs his animal desires, and does not fully satiate them, there is the real danger that he will be subverted by illicit temptation. A person who is fully satiated with earthy pleasures has no room for *yiras Shamayim*.

◈§ וְסַרְתֶּם וַעֲבַדְתֶּם אֱלֹהִים אֲחֵרִים וְהִשְׁתַּחֲוִיתֶם לָהֶם — **And you turn astray and serve gods of others and bow to them.** And as soon as one is fully satiated with earthly pleasure, the first result is that he will be influenced to worship "other gods." This raises some difficulty.

Rashi (ibid.), quoting the *Sifrei*, explains this as follows: וְסַרְתֶּם, לִפְרוֹשׁ מִן הַתּוֹרָה, וּמִתּוֹךְ כָּךְ וַעֲבַדְתֶּם אֱלֹהִים אֲחֵרִים, שֶׁכֵּיוָן שֶׁאָדָם פּוֹרֵשׁ מִן הַתּוֹרָה הוֹלֵךְ וּמִדַּבֵּק בַּעֲבוֹדָה זָרָה. Rashi is conveying the thought that אֱלֹהִים אֲחֵרִים does not mean only "other gods," but it also means "another God," meaning *HaKadosh Baruch Hu*. Even if one "believes in God" and keeps all the *mitzvos*, but he is פּוֹרֵשׁ מִן הַתּוֹרָה, meaning, he removes *limud haTorah* from his life, he is, in effect, practicing another religion; he is worshiping "another God."

In attempting to worship God without *limud haTorah,* he is no longer worshiping the *Ribbono Shel Olam*. Judaism without Torah is "another religion," similar to all others, which have prayers, rituals, observances and prohibitions, and, in former times, animal sacrifices. The attempt to worship God without *limud haTorah* is called אֱלֹהִים אֲחֵרִים. If a non-Jew wishes to embrace Judaism, and is willing to accept everything except learning Torah, he may just as well stay with his own religion, because a "Torahless" form of Judaism is not Judaism at all.

Rashi (ibid.) further explains the meaning of אֱלֹהִים אֲחֵרִים as follows: שֶׁהֵם אֲחֵרִים לְעוֹבְדֵיהֶם. They are called other gods, because *they are strangers to those who worship them;* צוֹעֵק אֵלָיו וְאֵינוֹ עוֹנֵהוּ, *one pleads with it but it does not answer;* נִמְצָא עָשׂוּי לוֹ כְּנָכְרִי, *consequently, this "other god" is a "stranger" to the person who prays to it."*

What Rashi means here is that the first step toward actual *avodah zarah* is when a person is פּוֹרֵשׁ מִן הַתּוֹרָה, he abandons Torah learning, but yet, attempts to maintain a relationship with *HaKadosh Baruch Hu*. This relationship will be as cool as if it were with a stranger. Without Torah leaning, *HaKadosh Baruch Hu* is אֱלֹהִים אֲחֵרִים.

This person may believe in ה' אֶחָד, and he is certainly not an idol worshiper, but, as the result of his separation from Torah, he feels no contact with *HaKadosh Baruch Hu,* he does not have the feeling that someone is listening to his *tefillos*. And, as in the time of the *Tanach,* when there was a fascination with *avodah zarah*, this relationship with *HaKadosh Baruch Hu* as a "stranger," without *limud haTorah,* will dissipate altogether and deteriorate into actual *avodah zarah,* in which people have a mystical experience and imagine that someone really is listening to them. Even today, there still exist many forms of actual *avodah zarah.*

It is also true — and very frightening — that although a person may *daven* and *shokel,* and say all the words, bow where necessary, and sing all the beautiful *niggunim,* if he does not have the proper *kavannah* and awareness that he is standing before the *Ribbono Shel Olam,* he is actually praying to אֱלֹהִים אֲחֵרִים, "a stranger," *who does not hear his tefillos.* When praying without *kavannah,* one is really not talking to anybody. It is similar to praying to actual אֱלֹהִים אֲחֵרִים of whom it is said: עֲצַבֵּיהֶם כֶּסֶף וְזָהָב מַעֲשֵׂה יְדֵי אָדָם. פֶּה לָהֶם וְלֹא יְדַבֵּרוּ עֵינַיִם לָהֶם וְלֹא יִרְאוּ. אָזְנַיִם לָהֶם וְלֹא יִשְׁמָעוּ וגו', *Their idols are silver and gold, the handiwork of man. They have a mouth but cannot speak; they have eyes but cannot see; they have ears, but cannot hear (Tehillim* 115:4-6).

❧ וְחָרָה אַף ה' בָּכֶם, וְעָצַר אֶת הַשָּׁמַיִם וגו' — **Then the anger of Hashem will burn against you. He will restrain the heavens, etc.** The result of וְסַרְתֶּם וַעֲבַדְתֶּם אֱלֹהִים אֲחֵרִים, in all its broad ramifications, will be that the anger of God will burn against you. *HaKadosh Baruch Hu* is not subject to good or bad "moods," and frustration resulting in outbursts of anger, as human beings are. The expression of "burning anger" here, as well as elsewhere in the Torah, is used only as a manner of speech to relate to us humans, דִּבְּרָה תוֹרָה כִּלְשׁוֹן בְּנֵי אָדָם.

The Rambam in *Moreh Nevuchim* 1:36 writes that we never find the expression חֲרוֹן אַף attributed to *HaKadosh Baruch Hu* except in connection with *avodah zarah.* [Ed. note: See *Maayan Beis HaSho'evah, Shemos* 4:14 for an explanation of the few exceptions to this.] The meaning of burning anger, when attributed to *HaKadosh Baruch Hu,* is the application of the *middas hadin* without the mitigation of *middas harachamim.*

❧ וְעָצַר אֶת הַשָּׁמַיִם, וְלֹא יִהְיֶה מָטָר — **And He will restrain the heavens and there will be no rain.** These are two phrases. First, there will be a closing of the heavens in the meteorological sense of an absence of rain, producing a drought; and furthermore, when you pray for rain, the "heavens will be closed," your *tefillos* will remain unanswered, and there will still be no rain.

In *Maseches Taanis* there are detailed *halachos* about how and when to pray and fast for rain in the event of drought. This *pasuk* is telling us that, as the result of *avodah zarah,* these *tefillos* will find a "closed heaven," and they will be refused.

❧ וְהָאֲדָמָה לֹא תִתֵּן אֶת יְבוּלָהּ — **And the soil will not give its produce.** Rashi, quoting *Sifrei (Eikev* 43), says: אַף מַה שֶּׁאַתָּה מוֹבִיל לָהּ, *it will not even produce as much as the seed which you put into it.*

❧ וַאֲבַדְתֶּם מְהֵרָה מֵעַל הָאָרֶץ הַטֹּבָה — Literally: **You will be completely lost, very soon, from being on the good land.** The word הַטֹּבָה is written deficient, without a ו. This is a reference to the fact that when the Jewish nation was driven out of Eretz Yisrael by the Babylonians, the land lost some of its "goodness" in that the land become devoid of its *kedushah,* just as it had been before the Jews took possession of it. Consequently, the laws of *terumos u'maasros* and other *mitzvos* that are linked to the land were suspended. During the seventy years of *galus Bavel*, Eretz Yisrael lost its *kedushah*, thus diminishing the "goodness of the land," as is indicated by the missing ו in the word הַטֹּבָה. The initial *kedushas Eretz Yisrael* was lost for those seventy years. קָדְשָׁה רִאשׁוֹנָה קִדְּשָׁה לְשַׁעְתָּהּ וְלֹא קִדְּשָׁה לֶעָתִיד לָבֹא, *The original sanctification of the land was temporary, and it was not sanctified for all time to come* (while the Jewish people were in exile) (see *Rambam, Hil. Terumos* 1:5).

The phrase וַאֲבַדְתֶּם מְהֵרָה means, "You will completely and permanently lose the land very quickly." This refers to the historic fact that the Jewish nation lost the land, which was to be theirs forever, in a relatively short period of time: after only 850 years. Regarding וַאֲבַדְתֶּם, meaning "to lose permanently," the Gemara (*Gittin* 88a) tells us that the Jewish nation was, in fact, in danger of losing the land permanently, as a result of their *avodah zarah* and other *aveiros*. Quoting the *pesukim* וְנוֹשַׁנְתֶּם בָּאָרֶץ וְהִשְׁחַתֶּם. . .וַעֲשִׂיתֶם הָרַע וגו׳ כִּי אָבֹד תֹּאבֵדוּן מַהֵר מֵעַל הָאָרֶץ, *When you will have been long in the land, you will grow corrupt. . . and you will do evil . . . You will surely perish quickly from the land* (*Devarim* 4:25-26), the Gemara there says that the word וְנוֹשַׁנְתֶּם, which has a numerical value of 852, alludes to the fact that if the Jewish nation had remained in Eretz Yisrael for two more years — and continued to do these *aveiros* — they would have reached the full limit of וְנוֹשַׁנְתֶּם, or 852 years, and there would have been no way to avoid the full fury of אָבֹד תֹּאבֵדוּן, the permanent loss of the land. However, since the Jewish nation was driven out of Eretz Yisrael after only 850 years, the full force of וַאֲבַדְתֶּם was mitigated, and the loss of the land was not permanent: צְדָקָה עָשָׂה הקב״ה עִם יִשְׂרָאֵל. . .שֶׁהִקְדִּים שְׁתֵּי שָׁנִים לְ״וְנוֹשַׁנְתֶּם״.

The Gemara there remarks that from here we see that מְהֵרָה, *quickly*, in the eyes of *HaKadosh Baruch Hu*, to Whom time means nothing, is 852 years: שְׁמַע מִינָהּ ״מְהֵרָה״ דְּמָרֵי עָלְמָא תַּמְנֵי מְאָה וְחַמְשִׁין וְתַרְתֵּי הוּא.

As an aside, when we express the wish that *Mashiach* may come soon, we always express it as בִּמְהֵרָה בְיָמֵינוּ, meaning, not quickly in the eyes of *HaKadosh Baruch Hu* — which could take a long time — but "quickly" in our way of reckoning, which means, literally, "soon."

When the Jews returned to Eretz Yisrael from *Galus Bavel*, under the leadership of Zerubavel and Ezra, the land became resanctified, and this *kedushah sheniyah* remains forever: קָדְשָׁה שְׁנִיָּה קִדְּשָׁה לְשַׁעְתָּהּ וְלֶעָתִיד לָבֹא. (See *Rambam* ibid.)

Eretz Yisrael belongs to the Jewish nation, despite the many rulers who have governed it for the past 2,000 years. Nevertheless, every blade of grass, every stone, has *kedushah,* and whatever grows there is subject to the laws of *terumah* for the *Kohanim,* and *maasros* (tithes), for the *Leviim* and the poor.

The reason for the difference between the first *kedushah,* which was temporary, and the second, which was permanent — *kedushah l'asid lavo* — is as follows. When the Jews entered the land the first time, under Yehoshua, they conquered it by force of arms *al pi Hashem* — otherwise they could not have done it. Now, when the opposite happened, and they lost the land to the Babylonians as the result of armed conflict, the Jewish conquest was nullified. Since the *kedushah* was acquired when the Jewish nation conquered the land, it was also lost when the Babylonians conquered it and drove the Jews out of the land.

However, when the Jews returned to Eretz Yisrael after *Galus Bavel,* they took possession of the land peacefully. The king of Persia, who ruled Eretz Yisrael at that time, gave the Jewish people permission to reoccupy their land, and the land then became theirs permanently through their legal occupancy, *chazakah.* In keeping with the rule of קַרְקַע אֵינָהּ נִגְזֶלֶת, *Legally owned land can never be stolen,* the land remains in possession of the Jewish nation forever. Therefore, the *kedushah sheniyah* remains forever, regardless of who rules over Eretz Yisrael (see *Rambam, Hil. Beis HaBechirah* 6:16).

אֲשֶׁר ה׳ נֹתֵן לָכֶם — **That which Hashem is giving to you.** The use of the present tense here is very comforting. It does not say נָתַן, in the past tense, but rather, נֹתֵן, *He is giving it to us.* This alludes to the fact that the loss of the land will not be permanent, and *HaKadosh Baruch Hu* will eventually give it back to us.

וְשַׂמְתֶּם אֶת דְּבָרַי אֵלֶּה עַל לְבַבְכֶם וְעַל נַפְשְׁכֶם — **Place these words of Mine upon your heart and upon your soul.** The Torah here tells us that although we would lose our land and be driven into *galus,* and the majority of our people would be living in *Bavel,* with some in Mitzrayim and other lands, we nevertheless are to place דְּבָרַי אֵלֶּה, *these words of Mine* — meaning the aforementioned conditions for keeping Eretz Yisrael — עַל לְבַבְכֶם וְעַל נַפְשְׁכֶם, *on your hearts and souls.*

We are told here that while we are in *galus* we are to desire, with all our heart and soul, the reinstatement of the conditions described here, in which the Jewish nation lives on its land under the rule of *HaKadosh Baruch Hu.* וְעַל נַפְשְׁכֶם is to be understood here as "a deep longing of the heart," as in לְשִׁמְךָ וּלְזִכְרְךָ תַּאֲוַת נָפֶשׁ, *Your Name and Your mention, the yearning of our soul* (*Yeshayahu* 26:8). The longing for *HaKadosh Baruch Hu* is the desire of the soul.

We are to constantly look forward to and long for the fulfillment of the immediately preceding words of אֲשֶׁר ה׳ נֹתֵן לָכֶם, in which *HaKadosh Baruch Hu* tells us that He will eventually give Eretz Yisrael back to us. Our *Chazal* call this never-ending hope for the reunion of *HaKadosh Baruch Hu* with the Jewish people in Eretz Yisrael under the rule of Torah — צִפִּיָּה לִישׁוּעָה, *longing for salvation.*

Therefore, in this longing for the certainty of its fulfillment, we study the laws of those *mitzvos* which are linked to the land, the *Beis HaMikdash* and *korbanos,* and of ritual purity, as if the *Beis HaMikdash* were already rebuilt, and we were performing the sacrificial service and fulfilling all of the practical applications of the laws that depend on our living in Eretz Yisrael.

On this *pasuk* Rashi, quoting *Sifrei,* says as follows: אַף לְאַחַר שֶׁתִּגְלוּ הֱיוּ מְצֻיָּנִים בַּמִּצְוֹת, *Even after you are exiled, continue to distinguish yourselves by the mitzvos.* When the Jewish people are in exile, living in a non-Jewish environment, speaking the language of the host country, and participating in the social life of that country, there is the real danger of assimilation. In fact, when the first group of Jews was exiled to *Bavel* during the time of King Yechoniah, Yirmiyahu HaNavi sent them a letter advising them to be good citizens to their host country: כֹּה אָמַר ה' צְבָאוֹת אֱלֹהֵי יִשְׂרָאֵל לְכָל הַגּוֹלָה אֲשֶׁר הִגְלֵיתִי. . .וְדִרְשׁוּ אֶת שְׁלוֹם הָעִיר אֲשֶׁר הִגְלֵיתִי אֶתְכֶם שָׁמָּה וְהִתְפַּלְּלוּ בַעֲדָהּ אֶל ה' כִּי בִשְׁלוֹמָהּ יִהְיֶה לָכֶם שָׁלוֹם, *Thus said Hashem, Master of Legions, God of Israel, to all of the exile whom I have exiled. . .Seek the peace of the city to which I have exiled you and pray for it to Hashem, for through its peace will you have peace* (Yirmiyahu 29:4-7).

It is for this reason that we are told here to "distinguish ourselves" as a separate nation by performing the *mitzvos* during our stay in *galus.*

And the *Sifrei* continues: הַנִּיחוּ תְּפִלִּין עֲשׂוּ מְזוּזוֹת כְּדֵי שֶׁלֹּא יְהוּ לָכֶם חֲדָשִׁים כְּשֶׁתַּחְזְרוּ, *put on tefillin and mezuzos so that when you return from exile, these will not seem like new mitzvos to you.* And thus does the *pasuk* say: הַצִּיבִי לָךְ צִיֻּנִים, *Set up signposts for yourself* (Yirmiyahu 31:20). Astonishingly, the reason given here for continuing to keep the *mitzvos* of *tefillin* and *mezuzos* in exile is to prevent them from being forgotten. In our travels through the *galus,* these *mitzvos* are to act as "road markers" to insure that we will find our way back to Eretz Yisrael. [See Rashi to *Devarim* 11:18.]

Ramban (ibid.) raises the obvious question: This *Sifrei* seems to indicate that *tefillin* and *mezuzah* are really only operative in Eretz Yisrael, and they are only practiced in *galus* to insure that they not be forgotten. What connection is there between these *mitzvos* and Eretz Yisrael? These are not operative only in Eretz Yisrael. Ramban does not answer this question, and he ends the matter by saying: יֵשׁ בַּמִּדְרָשׁ הַזֶּה סוֹד עָמוֹק, *This Midrash contains a deep secret.*

However, even simple people like us, who are not privy to this "secret," must try to understand this *Sifrei.* I would like to suggest the following explanation.

The three *mitzvos* referred to here — *talmud Torah, tefillin,* and *mezuzah* — although not land based, are not practiced in their ideal way while we are in *galus.* We practice them meanwhile, but in an imperfect way, as צִיֻּנִים, *signposts, or road markers,* to help us stay the course, until they can be practiced

KRIAS SHEMA 357

again with every detail being fulfilled at the time of the coming of *Mashiach*. The explanation follows.

❑ תַּלְמוּד תּוֹרָה: The way we learn *Torah Shebe'al Peh* today is not the optimal way of doing so. Nowadays even the most outstanding *gaon* who learns Torah uses *sefarim*. He has access to printed *Shas Bavli* and *Yerushalmi,* and *Beis Yosef, Tur, Rambam,* and thousands of other *sefarim*. However, ideally, *Torah Shebe'al Peh* is intended to be transmitted orally, from teacher to student, and then studied orally by the students: דְּבָרִים שֶׁבְּעַל פֶּה אִי אַתָּה רַשַּׁאי לְאוֹמְרָן בִּכְתָב (*Gittin* 60b). The use of *sefarim* as a means of learning Torah was instituted as an emergency measure by *Rabbeinu HaKadosh* when he compiled the Mishnah, so that the Torah would not be forgotten. He based his ruling on the *pasuk*: עֵת לַעֲשׂוֹת לַה' הֵפֵרוּ תּוֹרָתֶךָ, *When it was time to act in Hashem's Name, they voided Your Torah* (*Tehillim* 119:126). Following the lead of *Rabbeinu HaKadosh*, eventually all of *Torah Shebe'al Peh* was reduced to writing.

However, when *Mashiach* comes, the *Shas* and other printed *sefarim* will be relegated to the museums, and the original — and ideal — system of learning *Torah Shebe'al Peh* orally will be reinstituted. For now, Torah learning from written *sefarim* is only a temporary measure, a "marker," to stay the course, and keep us familiar with the Torah, until *bi'as HaMashiach,* when the ideal way of learning *be'al peh,* orally, will be reinstituted.

Interestingly, the printing press, on which the propagation of Torah among the Jewish people has depended so heavily for the past 500 years, was invented by a non-Jew named Gutenberg, from the City of Mainz in Germany. This invention was really a very simple idea, and was in no way comparable to the great inventions and discoveries of history as, for instance, the harnessing of electric power. In fact, the Chinese had already invented printing 1,000 years earlier, but it never reached Europe. Nevertheless, this simple invention impacted on Jewish life so greatly that without it Judaism would have come to a standstill. The availability of printing was immediately seized upon by our people, and some of the earliest printed books were *Chumash* with Rashi and *Talmud Bavli.* Imagine not having printed Gemaras, and having to refer to a few handwritten copies, with Rashi in a separate "*Kuntreis,*" or notebook. If a person had ten children, he would have to write ten copies of the *Shas* by hand to enable his children to learn.

Why did *HaKadosh Baruch Hu* not give the *zechus* of inventing this means of propagating the Torah among our people to a Jew, rather than to Gutenberg? The reason is because learning *Torah Sheb'al Peh* from a written book is not the ideal way of doing so. It is only an emergency measure, which was necessitated in *galus,* to insure that Torah would not be forgotten. For now, our method of learning *mitoch hak'sav* is only a "road marker" until

Mashiach comes, when the ideal method of learning *Torah Sheb'al Peh* orally will be reinstituted.

❏ תְּפִלִּין: This *mitzvah,* too, is not practiced fully while we are in *galus.* Originally, *tefillin* were not meant to be worn for a half hour or so doing *davening,* but rather, they were to be worn all day long, at home as well as in our place of business. Today, due to our *galus* environment, it is not possible to practice this *mitzvah* optimally. The *Sifrei* therefore tells us to do the best we can for the time being, so that, when *Mashiach* comes, and the *mitzvah* of *tefillin* is reinstituted in its optimal form, it will not be something strange to us. This will be so, because all through the *galus* years we will have kept it — albeit minimally — as a "signpost," and we will therefore feel perfectly familiar with it when it is practiced again in its full optimal form.

❏ מְזוּזָה: Here again, in *galus,* we do not practice this *mitzvah* in its fullest form. The *mitzvah* requires that we not only place *mezuzos* on our homes and businesses, but also וּבִשְׁעָרֶיךָ, *on your city gates.* In a Jewish city, every city gate or every street or neighborhood which had an entranceway leading to it (subject to the halachic definitions of שַׁעַר) is required to have a *mezuzah* placed in a niche inside the gateway, בִּשְׁעָרֶיךָ. For instance, the Jaffa Gate in Yerushalayim will need a *mezuzah.* Here in America, one does not see city or street gates very often. However, I remember seeing some of the old cities in Europe which did have such gates. The Brandenburg Gate in Berlin comes to mind. I specifically remember seeing the *mezuzos,* still intact, in the gate of the old city of Rottenburg, in Germany, where the *Maharam MiRottenburg* — the Rebbe of the *Rosh* — lived. The *mitzvah* of *mezuzah* was optimally to be a public affair, not relegated merely to one's private quarters. Compared to this, the way we practice it today is only a partial fulfillment of the *mitzvah* — a "signpost" — a reminder of the optimal form of the *mitzvah.* When *Mashiach* comes and it is reinstituted in its full form, with *mezuzos* proudly displayed in public, it will appear to us as a natural progression of the *mitzvah* from the minimal form which is practiced today, to its fulfillment in its optimal form.

§ וּקְשַׁרְתֶּם אֹתָם לְאוֹת עַל יֶדְכֶם וְהָיוּ לְטוֹטָפֹת בֵּין עֵינֵיכֶם — **Bind them for a sign upon your arm and let them be *tefillin* between your eyes.** Here the *mitzvah* of *tefillin* is written in the plural — as opposed to the earlier וּקְשַׁרְתָּם לְאוֹת עַל יָדֶךָ — to teach us that not only is each individual obligated to put on *tefillin,* but he is also obligated to see to it that others do so as well: כָּל יִשְׂרָאֵל עֲרֵבִים זֶה בָּזֶה (*Shevuos* 39a).

§ וְלִמַּדְתֶּם אֹתָם אֶת בְּנֵיכֶם — **Teach them to your children.** לִמּוּד, as opposed to שִׁנּוּן, means to become accustomed to something. The *mitzvah* here is to not only learn with one's sons, but also to educate them to become accustomed to learning Torah. The *mitzvah* referred to here is that of intensive learning. This entails not only knowing the *halachah* — that would be called שנון — but also learning Torah solely for the sake of learning, *Torah lishmah.* And this *mitzvah* applies only to men and not to women. For instance, if a woman were to know and never forget all the practical *halachos* of Shabbos, it would not be a *mitzvah* for her to learn them over again. However, men are obligated to learn for the sake of learning, as a form of worship of *HaKadosh Baruch Hu.* Even if one has a fabulous memory and never forgets a single *halachah,* he still has a *mitzvah* to continue to learn and delve into all the details of the Torah.

The weekly repetition of the chapter of *Mishnayos* of בַּמֶּה מַדְלִיקִין on Friday nights is a case in point. Even if a man would know it all by heart, it is still a *mitzvah* for him to repeat it.

It is this form of *talmud Torah* — learning purely for the sake of learning — to which our *Chachamim* refer when they say: וְלֹא – וְלִמַּדְתֶּם אֹתָם אֶת בְּנֵיכֶם בְּנוּתֵיכֶם.

However, women are obligated to learn the laws of the *mitzvos* of the Torah — most of which apply to women as well as men — for the purpose of fulfilling them properly. It is for this reason that women say the *birchos haTorah,* just as men do. Furthermore, women are also obligated to learn about the basics of our faith, *yiras Shamayim* and *hashkafos,* no less than are men.

[Ed. Note: For more details on this subject, see the Rav's explanation of the *berachah* of שֶׁעָשַׂנִי כִּרְצוֹנוֹ in the בְּרְכוֹת הַשַּׁחַר.]

∽ לְדַבֵּר בָּם, בְּשִׁבְתְּךָ בְּבֵיתֶךָ, וּבְלֶכְתְּךָ בַדֶּרֶךְ, וּבְשָׁכְבְּךָ, וּבְקוּמֶךָ ⸺ **To discuss them, while you sit in your home, while you travel, when you retire, and when you arise.** Ramban (ibid.) explains that in this second *parashah* of *Shema* the *mitzvah* of teaching Torah adds the element of לְדַבֵּר בָּם. This means that one is to teach Torah to his children to the extent that they will be capable of conversing and discussing matters of Torah among themselves: שֶׁבָּא לְהוֹסִיף כָּאן "לְדַבֵּר בָּם", כִּי שָׁם [בְּפָרָשַׁת וְאָהַבְתָּ] צִוָּה "וְדִבַּרְתָּ" – אַתָּה – בָּם בְּשִׁבְתְּךָ בְּבֵיתֶךָ", וְכָאן אָמַר שֶׁנְּלַמֵּד אוֹתָם אֶת בָּנֵינוּ עַד שֶׁיְדַבְּרוּ בָם הַבָּנִים בְּכָל שָׁעָה. . . לְדַבֵּר עִמְּךָ בָּם בְּכָל הָעִתִּים.

An additional comment on לְדַבֵּר בָּם is given by Rashi, quoting the *Sifrei:* מִשָּׁעָה שֶׁהַבֵּן יוֹדֵעַ לְדַבֵּר לַמְּדֵהוּ "תּוֹרָה צִוָּה לָנוּ מֹשֶׁה" שֶׁיְהֵא זֶה לִמּוּד דִּבּוּרוֹ. Paraphrased, this means that the child should learn to talk by saying words of Torah, and its first words should be תּוֹרָה צִוָּה לָנוּ מֹשֶׁה. Moshe Rabbeinu, shortly before his death, tells the Jewish people יִשָּׂא מִדַּבְּרֹתֶיךָ, *It becomes uplifted by Your words* (*Devarim* 33:3-4). The Jewish people are lifted up on a high pedestal by the fact that the first words which parents teach their children is תּוֹרָה צִוָּה לָנוּ מֹשֶׁה מוֹרָשָׁה קְהִלַּת יַעֲקֹב. This sentence contains the basic credo of Judaism which parents hand down to their children: *The Torah which Moshe Rabbeinu commanded to us is the heritage of the community of Yaakov.*

Continuing to quote the *Sifrei*, Rashi says: מִכָּאן אָמְרוּ כְּשֶׁהַתִּינוֹק מַתְחִיל לְדַבֵּר אָבִיו מֵשִׂיחַ עִמּוֹ בִּלְשׁוֹן הַקֹּדֶשׁ וּמְלַמְּדוֹ תּוֹרָה, וְאִם לֹא עָשָׂה כֵן הֲרֵי הוּא כְּאִילּוּ קוֹבְרוֹ, שֶׁנֶּאֱמַר וְלִמַּדְתֶּם אוֹתָם אֶת בְּנֵיכֶם לְדַבֵּר בָּם. . . לְמַעַן יִרְבּוּ יְמֵיכֶם וגו׳. When a father neglects to teach his child that Torah is the priority of his life, this neglect could result in losing the child physically — or spiritually, when the child matures into a life without Torah as his guiding force.

◆§ וּכְתַבְתָּם עַל מְזוּזוֹת בֵּיתֶךָ וּבִשְׁעָרֶיךָ — **And write them on the doorpost of your house and upon your gates.** The first person singular form is used here in contrast to the previously used plural: וְשִׂמַּחְתֶּם אֶת דְּבָרַי אֵלֶּה, וּקְשַׁרְתֶּם אֹתָם. This is not insignificant. Whenever there is a *mitzvah* of writing a *sefer Torah*, *tefillin*, *mezuzah*, or *megillah*, there is the halachic requirement that the writing be done בִּכְתִיבָה תַּמָּה, with *perfectly formed letters*. This rule is alluded to in the word וּכְתַבְתָּם, which contains the abbreviation of כְּתִיבָה תַּמָּה. Compliance with this requirement of writing and spacing the letters and words properly in accordance with the *halachah* can easily be determined by looking at the writing. However, there is the additional requirement that these *parashos* must be written לִשְׁמָהּ, which cannot be detected by looking at the writing. While writing these *kisvei kodesh*, the *sofer* must concentrate on the fact that this work is being done for the purpose of the *mitzvah* of *sefer Torah*, *tefillin*, *mezuzah*, or *Megillah*. Furthermore, when he writes the שֵׁם, the Holy Name, he must do so לְשֵׁם קְדֻשַּׁת הַשֵּׁם. This *kavannah* exists only within the mind of the individual *sofer*.

Therefore, the Torah addresses each *sofer* personally, וּכְתַבְתָּם: Whenever you write *kisvei kodesh* for use in performing a *mitzvah* — whether this be for a *sefer Torah*, *tefillin*, or a *mezuzah* — you, the *sofer*, must write these *parashos* in accordance with all the halachic requirements, including those which are up to your own personal integrity and *yiras Shamayim*. Nobody but the *sofer* can know for sure if a given work has been done in accordance with this requirement.

The *mitzvah* of *mezuzah* applies equally to women as well as to men. The Gemara refutes the argument that women should be exempt from *mezuzah* as they are from the *mitzvah* of וְלִמַּדְתֶּם אֹתָם אֶת בְּנֵיכֶם, intensive Torah study, which precedes it, because *mezuzah* is followed by לְמַעַן יִרְבּוּ יְמֵיכֶם, which blesses one with long life as a result of performing the *mitzvah* of *mezuzah*: גַּבְרֵי בָּעֵי חַיֵּי, נָשֵׁי לֹא בָּעֵי חַיֵּי?, *Don't women need life as much as men do?*

This is alluded to in *Megillas Rus*. When Naomi attempted to dissuade Ruth from joining her and accepting Judaism, she provided examples of

Jewish laws. The Midrash (*Rus Rabbah* 2:22) quotes Naomi as telling her that among these laws is: בִּתִּי, אֵין דַּרְכָּן שֶׁל בְּנוֹת יִשְׂרָאֵל לָדוּר בְּבַיִת שֶׁאֵין שָׁם מְזוּזָה, *Jewish women do not live in houses in which there is no mezuzah.* Upon which, Ruth answers her, וּבַאֲשֶׁר תָּלִינִי אָלִין, *Where you live, I will live* (Ruth 1:16).

&ז לְמַעַן יִרְבּוּ יְמֵיכֶם וִימֵי בְנֵיכֶם עַל הָאֲדָמָה אֲשֶׁר נִשְׁבַּע ה' לַאֲבֹתֵיכֶם לָתֵת לָהֶם &ז — **In order to prolong your days and the days of your children upon the land that Hashem has sworn to your ancestors to give them.** This refers back to the beginning of this *parashah*: וְהָיָה אִם שָׁמֹעַ תִּשְׁמְעוּ אֶל מִצְוֹתַי, and everything contained in it. And the meaning is that all the aforesaid commandments are given to you to insure that your days, and the days of your children, will be increased *on the land* which Hashem has sworn by an oath to give to your Forefathers. It does not say בָּאֲדָמָה, "in" the land, but rather עַל הָאֲדָמָה. We have been promised longevity *"on" the land* — while we are in control of the land — and not merely *in the land,* while it is contested by others. There will be no שִׁעְבּוּד מַלְכִיּוֹת (non-Jewish political control) in any form over Eretz Yisrael.

This assurance of longevity in the land, based on the condition of וְהָיָה אִם שָׁמֹעַ תִּשְׁמְעוּ אֶל מִצְוֹתַי, refers both to the time before the *galus,* and also during the *galus* when וְשַׂמְתֶּם אֶת דְּבָרַי אֵלֶּה וגו', keeping of the *mitzvos,* will eventually result in our return to the land and our longevity there.

&ז כִּימֵי הַשָּׁמַיִם עַל הָאָרֶץ &ז — **Like the days of the heaven on the earth,** meaning, as long as the world exists.

The Gemara (*Sanhedrin* 90b) points out that this *pasuk* does not say לָתֵת לָכֶם, *to give to you,* but rather, it says לָתֵת לָהֶם, *to give to them.* Eretz Yisrael was promised not only to the children of our Forefathers, but it was also promised to our *Forefathers themselves!* Based on this, the Gemara says: מִכָּאן לִתְחִיַּת הַמֵּתִים מִן הַתּוֹרָה, *This is the source for techiyas hameisim in the Torah.* This means that Avraham, Yitzchak, and Yaakov will live again, and they will be present in the land.

This statement refers to the mishnah in *Sanhedrin* 90a: כָּל יִשְׂרָאֵל יֵשׁ לָהֶם חֵלֶק לָעוֹלָם הַבָּא וְאֵלּוּ שֶׁאֵין לָהֶם חֵלֶק לָעוֹלָם הַבָּא הָאוֹמֵר אֵין תְּחִיַּת הַמֵּתִים מִן הַתּוֹרָה, *All of Israel has a share in the World to Come. But these have no share: One who says there is no tenet of techiyas hameisim in the Torah.* This means that if one denies that *techiyas hameisim* is foretold by the Torah, he will not have a share in the World to Come. This is explained by Rashi as follows: שֶׁכּוֹפֵר בַּמִּדְרָשִׁים דְּדָרְשִׁינָן בַּגְּמָרָא לְקַמָּן מִנַּיִן לִתְחִיַּת הַמֵּתִים מִן הַתּוֹרָה. וַאֲפִילוּ יְהֵא מוֹדֶה וּמַאֲמִין שֶׁיִּהְיוּ הַמֵּתִים אֶלָּא דְּלֹא רְמִיזָא בְּאוֹרַיְיתָא כּוֹפֵר הוּא. Even if a person believes — as do many religions — that there will be some form of resurrection of the dead, but he does not believe that a source for this belief is found in the Torah, he is still considered a כּוֹפֵר, a nonbeliever, and will therefore not have any share in *techiyas hameisim.*

The concept of Resurrection of the Dead is a universal belief based on man's desire to live on forever, and is comforting for those who have lost loved ones, because they can look forward to being reunited with them again. However, the Jewish concept of *techiyas hameisim* is not based on some human wishful thinking, but rather, it is from the Torah; the Torah tells us that it will happen.

Rashi (ibid.) put it this way: הוֹאִיל וְעוֹקֵר שֶׁיֵּשׁ תְּחִיַּת הַמֵּתִים מִן הַתּוֹרָה מַה לָּנוּ וְלֶאֱמוּנָתוֹ, וְכִי מֵהֵיכָן הוּא יוֹדֵעַ שֶׁכֵּן הוּא, הִלְכָּךְ כּוֹפֵר גָּמוּר הוּא, *Since he denies that the source for techiyas hameisim is found in the Torah, of what value is his belief (that it will happen)? How does he know that it is true? Therefore, such a person is a complete heretic.* If his belief is not *min haTorah*, it is worthless.

Thus, the mishnah is telling us that even if a person firmly believes, as we do, that the dead will rise again — not only spiritually, but also physically, in the sense that the body will be re-created and come out of the ground and live again — but he denies that there are sources for *techiyas hameisim* in the Torah, he is a *kofer*, a heretic, who will have no share in that future life.

פָּרָשַׁת צִיצִית

According to some opinions, the inclusion of this *parashah* in קְרִיאַת שְׁמַע is *d'Oraisa*. However, according to most *poskim*, it is only *mi'd'Rabbanan*, except for the reference to *yetzias Mitzrayim*, which is a fulfillment of the *mitzvas asei d'Oraisa* requiring one to remember this event once each day and night (*Pri Megadim* intro. to *Hil. Krias Shema*; *Aruch HaShulchan Orach Chaim* 58:16; *Sefer HaChinuch* 420; *Ba'er Heitev* 67:1; *Magen Avraham* ibid.; *Tosafos Berachos* 20b s.v. בעל קרי, et al.).

The Gemara (*Berachos* 12b) states as follows:

פָּרָשַׁת צִיצִית מִפְּנֵי מָה קְבָעוּהָ אָמַר רַבִּי יְהוּדָה בַּר חֲבִיבָא: מִפְּנֵי שֶׁיֵּשׁ בָּהּ חֲמִשָּׁה דְּבָרִים: מִצְוַת צִיצִית, יְצִיאַת מִצְרַיִם, עוֹל מִצְוֹת, וְדַעַת מִינִים, הִרְהוּר עֲבֵירָה, וְהִרְהוּר עֲבוֹדָה זָרָה.
The reason the *parashah* of *tzitzis* was incorporated into *Krias Shema* is because it contains five other *mitzvos* in addition to the *mitzvah* of *tzitzis*:

(1) אֲנִי ה' אֱלֹהֵיכֶם אֲשֶׁר הוֹצֵאתִי אֶתְכֶם מֵאֶרֶץ מִצְרַיִם: יְצִיאַת מִצְרַיִם. The remembrance of *yetzias Mitzrayim* every day and every night;

(2) וּזְכַרְתֶּם אֶת כָּל מִצְוֹת ה': עוֹל מִצְוֹת. When one looks at the *tzitzis*, he is to remember that he is obligated to fulfill all of God's commandments;

(3) לֹא תָתוּרוּ אַחֲרֵי לְבַבְכֶם: דַּעַת מִינִים. To avoid the influence of nonbelievers and atheists;

(4) וְאַחֲרֵי עֵינֵיכֶם: הִרְהוּר עֲבֵירָה. To avoid immoral thoughts which are triggered by what the eyes see;

(5) אַתֶּם זֹנִים: הִרְהוּר עֲבוֹדָה זָרָה. To avoid thoughts of worshiping false gods.

The word *tzitzis* is usually translated as *fringes,* similar to *curls,* as in וַיִּקָּחֵנִי בְּצִיצִת רֹאשִׁי, *and took me by a lock of my head* (*Yechezkel* 8:3). Or, based on the *mitzvah* of וּרְאִיתֶם אֹתוֹ, it could be related to the word מֵצִיץ, *to look,* as in מֵצִיץ מִן הַחֲרַכִּים, *peering through the lattices* (*Shir HaShirim* 2:9). (See *Rashi, Bamidbar* 15:38.) This is why the ornament worn on the forehead of the *Kohen Gadol* is called צִיץ, *tzitz,* meaning "something to look at."

Rav Samson R. Hirsch explains that *tzitzis* is related to the word for flower, צִיץ, as in צִיץ הַשָּׂדֶה, *a flower which sprouts from the ground* (*Tehillim* 103:15). He therefore explains that *tzitzis* sprouting from our clothing is an extension of the higher moral significance of clothing to the human being. This is based on the first reference to clothing in the Torah, with regard to Adam and Chavah.

The Torah tells us that before their sin, Adam and Chavah did not wear clothing, nevertheless, they had no sense of being ashamed of their nakedness: וַיִּהְיוּ שְׁנֵיהֶם עֲרוּמִּים הָאָדָם וְאִשְׁתּוֹ וְלֹא יִתְבֹּשָׁשׁוּ, *They were both naked, the man and his wife, and they were not ashamed* (*Bereishis* 2:25). They felt no sense of shame because their true selves were not identified with their bodies. Their animal bodies clothed their real being, which was their *neshamah,* their spirituality — that aspect of themselves which was superior to the animal.

However, immediately after their sin, the Torah tells us: וַיֵּדְעוּ כִּי עֵירֻמִּם הֵם, וַיִּתְפְּרוּ עֲלֵה תְאֵנָה וַיַּעֲשׂוּ לָהֶם חֲגֹרֹת, *They realized that they were naked, so they sewed together a fig leaf and made themselves aprons* (ibid. 3:7). Once they had succumbed to their bodily desires, they became identified with their animal bodies and, consequently, felt ashamed of their nakedness. Therefore, they made rudimentary clothing for themselves, which reflected their sense that they had the moral obligation to subdue their animal nature. And after their expulsion from *Gan Eden,* וַיַּעַשׂ ה' אֱלֹהִים לְאָדָם וּלְאִשְׁתּוֹ כָּתְנוֹת עוֹר וַיַּלְבִּשֵׁם, *And Hashem God made for Adam and his wife garments of skin, and he clothed them* (ibid. 3:21). These garments were a gift of *HaKadosh Baruch Hu* to the human race.

So the idea of clothing for all human beings is a reflection of the truth that יֵשׁ מוֹתַר הָאָדָם מִן הַבְּהֵמָה. Man's supremacy over animals lies in his ability to control his animal nature. While man has an animal body, with all its desires and urges, he has the unique ability to control them. He even has the ability to elevate and sanctify these urges. By covering our bodies, we emphasize that our body is not the essence of our being. What makes the human being "human" is the *neshamah.* So we cover the animal side of our personality, with the exception of the head, where our spiritual faculties are concentrated, and the hands, to which *HaKadosh Baruch Hu* has given the power to control the world: וְכִבְשֻׁהָ, *and subdue it* (ibid. 1:28). This is the concept of clothing for all human beings.

However, as far as Israel is concerned, explains Rav Hirsch, man's ability to subdue his animal nature is extended; it becomes צִיצִית: it grows and flowers into an even higher moral calling, that of the acceptance of God's *mitzvos*.

Therefore, the Torah (*Bamidbar* 15:37) tells us as follows:

※ ※ ※

וַיֹּאמֶר ה' אֶל מֹשֶׁה לֵּאמֹר: דַּבֵּר אֶל בְּנֵי יִשְׂרָאֵל וְאָמַרְתָּ אֲלֵהֶם וְעָשׂוּ לָהֶם צִיצִת עַל כַּנְפֵי בִגְדֵיהֶם — **Hashem said to Moshe, saying: Speak to the Children of Israel and say to them that they shall make for themselves *tzitzis* on the corners of their garments.**

The Jewish people are to make *tzitzis* at the corners — ends — of their garments. This reflects the idea that where *derech eretz* — with which all humanity is charged — ends, עַל כַּנְפֵי בִגְדֵיהֶם, there the specifically Jewish mandate begins. Torah presupposes the highest form of human decency and dignity, דֶּרֶךְ אֶרֶץ קָדְמָה לַתּוֹרָה. But we, as *Bnei Yisrael,* are to make "extensions" of our clothing to symbolize our higher calling of וִהְיִיתֶם קְדֹשִׁים לֵאלֹהֵיכֶם, *and be holy to your God.* We are told here לֹא תָתוּרוּ אַחֲרֵי לְבַבְכֶם וְאַחֲרֵי עֵינֵיכֶם, not only are we not to act like an animal, but we are also not to *think* like an animal.

So, when we look at our *tzitzis* we are reminded that our membership in *Klal Yisrael,* through the acceptance of the *mitzvos,* extends our humanity to a higher moral calling. The white strands represent the *mitzvos lo saaseh,* signifying freedom from sin, and the blue *techeiles* strands represent the *mitzvos asei,* the performance of the positive commandments. Thus: וּרְאִיתֶם אֹתוֹ וּזְכַרְתֶּם אֶת כָּל מִצְוֹת ה' וַעֲשִׂיתֶם אֹתָם, *You may see it and remember all the commandments of Hashem and perform them* (*Bamidbar* 15:39).

While the *tzitzis* have many knots and windings, representing the restrictions placed upon us by the *mitzvos,* nevertheless, two thirds of the length of the *tzitzis* are free-flowing strands. Once our lives are controlled by the parameters of the *mitzvos* of Hashem represented by the *kesharim,* we have much more freedom than restrictions, enabling us to enjoy that which *HaKadosh Baruch Hu* has given us in our lives. This is represented by the two-thirds length of free-flowing strands.

[Ed. Note: The Rav previously expressed these thoughts in the section on *atifas tallis.*]

Despite the profound importance of the *mitzvah* of *tzitzis,* women are nevertheless exempt from it, because it is a *mitzvas asei shehazeman gerama,* a time-bound *mitzvah,* since it is applicable only during the daytime. The reason women have not voluntarily accepted this *mitzvah* as they have many others is because since placing *tzitzis* on a four-cornered garment is *obligatory* only for men, a garment with *tzitzis* attached becomes, in effect, "men's clothing" and, as such, would violate the restriction against wearing men's clothing: לֹא יִהְיֶה כְלִי גֶבֶר עַל אִשָּׁה, *Male garb shall not be on a woman* (*Devarim* 22:5 and see *Targum Yonasan* ibid.).

Notwithstanding this, the higher moral symbolism of Jewish clothing is very much evident in regard to Jewish women through the laws of *tzenius*. In men, the symbolism of the higher concept of clothing is evident only when they wear *tzitzis*. However, in women's clothing, it is there all the time. In addition to the simple purpose of clothing, as protection against the elements, and for common decency, the appearance of the modestly dressed Jewish woman proclaims for all to see: וְלֹא תָתוּרוּ אַחֲרֵי לְבַבְכֶם וְאַחֲרֵי עֵינֵיכֶם . . . וִהְיִיתֶם קְדֹשִׁים לֵאלֹהֵיכֶם. The wearing of modest clothing by women is the equivalent of a man wearing a *tallis* with *tzitzis*.

Based on the profound ideas expressed by the *mitzvah* of *tzitzis*, Rav Hirsch explains דַּבֵּר אֶל בְּנֵי יִשְׂרָאֵל וְאָמַרְתָּ אֲלֵהֶם וְעָשׂוּ לָהֶם צִיצִת. He points out that it does not say דַּבֵּר אֶל בְּנֵי יִשְׂרָאֵל וְיַעֲשׂוּ לָהֶם צִיצִת, *make tzitzis for yourselves*, which would be the normal command for a *mitzvah*. But rather, it says, *Speak to the Jewish people and say to them and they will make tzitzis for themselves*. The meaning is, "Once you have explained to the Jewish people the great distinction and *kedushah* of wearing *tzitzis*, they will eagerly make *tzitzis* for themselves." Despite the fact that the obligation of *tzitzis* applies only to a four-cornered garment, and one could thus easily avoid the obligation altogether by not wearing this type of garment, nevertheless, the Jewish people will look for opportunities to fulfill this *mitzvah*, which expresses its higher calling.

Three meanings of the word *tzitzis* are utilized in this *parashah*:

❑ וְעָשׂוּ לָהֶם צִיצִת עַל כַּנְפֵי בִגְדֵיהֶם: This has the meaning of something sprouting out of the corners of the garments, corresponding to the Jewish extension of the general concept of "clothing";

❑ וְנָתְנוּ עַל צִיצִת הַכָּנָף פְּתִיל תְּכֵלֶת: Here it has the meaning of fringes or curls; defining the meaning of *tzizis* as fringes;

❑ וְהָיָה לָכֶם לְצִיצִת וּרְאִיתֶם אֹתוֹ: And you shall see it — in the singular — referring to the כָּנָף with its attachments, as something for you to look at; and you shall, indeed, look at it and thereby: וּזְכַרְתֶּם אֶת כָּל מִצְוֹת ה׳.

☙ **וְעָשׂוּ לָהֶם צִיצִת עַל כַּנְפֵי בִגְדֵיהֶם לְדֹרֹתָם וְנָתְנוּ עַל צִיצִת הַכָּנָף פְּתִיל תְּכֵלֶת** ❧ — **They are to make for themselves *tzitzis* on the corners of their garments, throughout their generations. And they are to place upon the *tzitzis* of each corner a thread of *techeiles*.**

The *tzitzis* are composed of four doubled strands which are to be placed on each of the four corners of the garment. Two of these strands are to be white, or *lavan*, and two are to be blue, or *techeiles*. And, as is the case in our time — and has been for many hundreds of years — if the dye necessary for making the *techeiles* color is unavailable, the *mitzvah* of *tzitzis* can be fulfilled by placing four *lavan* strands on the corners of the garment without any *techeiles*: הַתְּכֵלֶת אֵינָהּ מְעַכֶּבֶת אֶת הַלָּבָן (*Menachos* 38a).

The dye for making the *techeiles* was derived from the blood of a fishlike creature called *chilazon,* which appears only once in seventy years (*Menachos* 44a; *Rambam, Hil. Tzitzis* 2:2).

Many people have attempted to find this creature to produce the dye from its blood. Among them was the famous Radziner Rebbe, who did produce what he said was *techeiles,* and he and his followers placed the blue strands made from this dye in their *tzitzis.*

It is noteworthy that the word לְדֹרֹתָם appears after וְעָשׂוּ לָהֶם צִיצִת עַל כַּנְפֵי בִגְדֵיהֶם, because the *lavan* strands are always available and therefore the *mitzvah* is operative throughout all of our generations. However, since the *techeiles* is dependent on a specific dye which is not always available, the Torah does not use the word לְדֹרֹתָם in connection with the *mitzvah* of *techeiles.*

The Gemara tells us: הַתְּכֵלֶת דּוֹמָה לַיָּם וְיָם דּוֹמֶה לָרָקִיעַ וְרָקִיעַ דּוֹמֶה לְכִסֵּא הַכָּבוֹד, *The sky-blue color which this dye produces is similar to the color of the sea, which reflects the color of the sky, which is similar to the "Throne of Glory"* (*Sotah* 17a). (A beautiful version of this sky-blue area is readily visible along the northern coast of Eretz Yisrael, near Natanya or Haifa.) Although we have no conception of the meaning of *Kisei HaKavod,* and certainly not of its "color," we can understand why the sky is blue.

We pointed out in our comments on יוֹצֵר אוֹר וּבוֹרֵא חֹשֶׁךְ that the vast majority of the space of the universe is dark, and that the billions of light sources and reflectors in it are only small points of light, which, however, do not illuminate the darkness of space. Our sun illuminates the darkness of space surrounding the earth, *and the mixture of the darkness of the universe with the light of the sun produces the sky-blue color.* As we have also pointed out there, darkness is representative of the *middas hadin,* and the light of the sun represents *middas harachamim.*

When we speak of the *Kisei HaKavod,* we mean the supervision of the world by *HaKadosh Baruch Hu,* whereby He combines His *middas hadin* with His *middas harachamim.* And what better symbolism can we have for this than sky-blue *techeiles,* the color which is representative of the combination of darkness (= *din*) and light (= *rachamim*).

The white strands of the *tzitzis* represent the ideal person, free of sin, as a result of his following the dictum: וְלֹא תָתוּרוּ אַחֲרֵי לְבַבְכֶם וְאַחֲרֵי עֵינֵיכֶם. [The symbolism is based on בְּכָל עֵת יִהְיוּ בְגָדֶיךָ לְבָנִים, *Let your garments always be white* (*Koheles* 9:8).] The freedom from sin is the negative aspect of *tzitzis.* And the *mitzvah* of *techeiles* is the symbolic expression of the positive aspect of *tzitzis,* that of וִהְיִיתֶם קְדֹשִׁים לֵאלֹהֵיכֶם . When one looks at the *techeiles* of the *tzitzis,* he should be reminded of the *Kisei HaKavod,* with its combination of *din* and *rachamim,* before which he will eventually have to offer an account of his life, לִפְנֵי מֶלֶךְ מַלְכֵי הַמְּלָכִים הקב״ה, *in front of the King of kings, HaKadosh Baruch Hu.*

The color *techeiles* was also used in the *Mishkan* and the *bigdei Kehunah,* to express the same idea as the *tzitzis:* וִהְיִיתֶם קְדֹשִׁים לֵאלֹהֵיכֶם.

The *mitzvah* of *tzitzis,* with its blue and white colors, is the origin of the use of blue and white as a Jewish nationalistic symbol. However, the people who adopted these colors for this purpose were not aware of their symbolism, that of וִהְיִיתֶם קְדֹשִׁים לֵאלֹהֵיכֶם, nor of אֲנִי ה׳ אֱלֹהֵיכֶם, but ideally, these colors really do have a place in the context of *a truly Jewish* national emblem.

⋅≈ וְהָיָה לָכֶם לְצִיצִת — Paraphrased, this means **These are to be your *tzitzis*;** wear them all the time; they are to be yours to be seen and held as your protection and "lifeline" against impure thoughts and impulses which may arise during the day. It is for this purpose that we wear our *tallis katan.*

The word לָכֶם means that the *mitzvah* of *tzitzis* carries its special message "for you" only if you wear the requisite four-cornered garment and place the *tzitzis* on its corners. However, the same garment even with *tzitzis* attached carries no significance while lying in a drawer. It carries its symbolism only when it is an adornment of the actual clothing worn, and the *tzitzis* become an extension of the higher concept of the clothing of the human being.

⋅≈ וּרְאִיתֶם אֹתוֹ וּזְכַרְתֶּם אֶת כָּל מִצְוֹת ה׳ — **That you may see it and remember all the commandments of Hashem.** The symbolism of the *tzitzis* which reminds us of all of Hashem's *mitzvos* lies in the way we knot the strands. The four doubled strands on each corner are each configured into five double knots separated by various level of tight windings, called גְּדִיל; the rest of the length of the strands remain loose and unknotted. The loose portion is called עָנָף. Actually, only the first double knot is required by Torah law; the others were added by the *Chachamim.* (See קֶשֶׁר עֶלְיוֹן דְּאוֹרַיְיתָא, *Menachos* 39a.) The windings and knots portion of the *tzitzis* are to take up only one third of their total length, and the remaining two thirds are left to hang down freely.

It is the configuration of the *tzitzis* which reminds us of כָּל מִצְוֹת ה׳. The knots and windings of the *tzitzis* represent the restrictions and obligations placed upon us by the Torah. The Gemara tells us, תַּנְיָא אִידָךְ וּרְאִיתֶם אֹתוֹ וּזְכַרְתֶּם אֶת כָּל מִצְוֹת ה׳ שְׁקוּלָה מִצְוָה זוֹ כְּנֶגֶד כָּל הַמִּצְוֹת כּוּלָן, the *mitzvah* of *tzitzis* is equal to all the other *mitzvos* of the Torah combined (*Menachos* 43b). The meaning is that the *mitzvah* of *tzitzis* — with its knots and windings — carries the message that our lives are guided and delineated by the *mitzvos Hashem.*

Nevertheless, the remaining two thirds of the length of the *tzitzis* — the free-flowing strands — represent the freedom which we may enjoy once our lives are controlled by the *mitzvos Hashem*. After a person has accepted the restrictions and obligations placed upon him by the Torah, he is free to live his life in accordance with his own individual inclinations: to marry and earn his livelihood in accordance with his own individual abilities and tastes. Some people become leaders, others become followers; some are public-spirited, others prefer a private life; some strive to ennoble their character traits, others are content to remain the way they are. People are free to live and enjoy the blessings which *HaKadosh Baruch Hu* has bestowed upon them in their lives in the way which they deem appropriate to their own individual tastes. The blessings of *HaKadosh Baruch Hu* which we are free to enjoy are far greater than the restrictions and obligations which the Torah places upon us.

❏ וּרְאִיתֶם אֹתוֹ — *That you may see it.* This could also mean, literally, that one is to look at the *tzitzis* before making the *berachah* to see if they are still intact. The woolen strands could easily have become snagged and torn off during their last use, which would render them unfit to use. It is therefore prudent to check them before each new use, to avoid reciting a *berachah* in vain (see *Orach Chaim* 8:9).

❦ וַעֲשִׂיתֶם אֹתָם — **And perform them.** Remembering the *mitzvos* is insufficient if it does not lead to their actual fulfillment.

Our *pasuk* is divided into two parts.

First, וּרְאִיתֶם אֹתוֹ וּזְכַרְתֶּם אֶת כָּל מִצְוֹת ה', when we look at the *tzitzis,* we are to *remember all of the mitzvos of Hashem.* This means that we are obligated to learn and remember the entire Torah, even those parts which we, as individuals, could never fulfill. Indeed, formerly all Torah learning was done through וּזְכַרְתֶּם, by remembering the material, which was transmitted from *rebbi* to *talmid.* Torah was not learned from a written text. In fact, it was prohibited to learn *Torah Shebe'al Peh* from a written text, *mitoch hakesav.* (See earlier וְשַׂמְתֶּם אֶת דְּבָרַי אֵלֶּה in וְהָיָה אִם שָׁמֹעַ.)

We are told here that by looking at the *tzitzis* we will be aided in our efforts to remember all of the *mitzvos,* וּרְאִיתֶם אֹתוֹ וּזְכַרְתֶּם אֶת כָּל מִצְוֹת ה'. It is very possible that as long as we do not have the *techeiles* as part of our *tzitzis,* we will not get the full benefit of remembering the Torah which we have learned by looking at the *tzitzis.*

However, the second part of the *pasuk,* וַעֲשִׂיתֶם אֹתָם, tells us *You shall perform them.* This means that, as a practical matter, we are obligated to perform only those *mitzvos* which apply to us as individuals. No one can possibly perform all of the *mitzvos* of the Torah. For example, certain *mitzvos* apply only to *Kohanim;* certain ones are only for the *melech;* others are only for *shoftim.* There are many more examples of *mitzvos* which can be done only under certain circumstances, and by certain individuals, and no one individual can perform all of them.

In the introduction to the *Chovos HaLevavos,* the author divides the *mitzvos* of the Torah into the categories of מִצְוֹת הָאֵבָרִים — commandments which we perform with our physical faculties — and מִצְוֹת הַלְּבָבוֹת — commandments which are performed with our hearts and minds.

The aforementioned difference between learning the entire Torah and the practical application of the *mitzvos* to individuals and circumstances applies only to the מִצְוֹת הָאֵבָרִים, those *mitzvos* which we perform with our bodies. However, with regard to the מִצְוֹת הַלְּבָבוֹת, the *mitzvos* which are incumbent on our minds and thinking process, these are universally applicable to all individuals under all circumstances.

The difference is recognizable in the subtlety of the construction of the following *pasuk*: לֹא תָתוּרוּ אַחֲרֵי לְבַבְכֶם וְאַחֲרֵי עֵינֵיכֶם. Here we are warned against following the temptations and dictates of our hearts and eyes. This refers to thoughts of apostasy, *avodah zarah,* and *arayos.* However, the ending is לְמַעַן תִּזְכְּרוּ וַעֲשִׂיתֶם אֶת **כָּל מִצְוֹתָי** וִהְיִיתֶם קְדֹשִׁים לֵאלֹהֵיכֶם, *You shall remember and perform* **all of My mitzvos,** *and be holy to your God.* When it comes to *mitzvos* of the heart, controlling our thoughts and character, and elevating ourselves to the level of וִהְיִיתֶם קְדֹשִׁים לֵאלֹהֵיכֶם, there are no exceptions, and no circumstances in which these *mitzvos* do not apply. For this category of *mitzvos*, we are obligated not only to remember them but also *to do all of them.*

§ וְלֹא תָתוּרוּ אַחֲרֵי לְבַבְכֶם וְאַחֲרֵי עֵינֵיכֶם — **And not explore after your heart and after your eyes.** Rashi explains that the word תָתוּרוּ is to be understood in the sense of וַיָּשֻׁבוּ מִתּוּר הָאָרֶץ, *they returned from spying out the land* (*Bamidbar* 13:25), which conveys the thought of "to spy out," or to investigate something. Just as we, in our natural curiosity, investigate the world to find out about nature, history, or our social environment, to determine what we are and what surrounds us, so did the *meraglim* — whom we would call today "intelligence agents" — attempt to investigate Eretz Yisrael.

Rashi (ibid. 15:39) continues: הַלֵּב וְהָעֵינַיִם הֵם מְרַגְּלִים לַגּוּף מְסַרְסְרִים לוֹ אֶת הָעֲבֵרוֹת, *The heart and the eyes are the investigators for the body, and they solicit the sins for it.* In other words, they look around and they receive a wrong impression of the world, similar to the *meraglim,* who came to Eretz Yisrael and misinterpreted what they saw. Regarding their visit to Chevron, they did not report that they saw the place where Avraham Avinu performed the *bris milah* at the age of 99; nor did they report that they saw the *aishel* that Avraham Avinu planted in Be'er Sheva; nor did they report that they saw the *Har HaMoriyah* on which Yitzchak Avinu offered his life to *HaKadosh Baruch Hu.* However, what they did report was that in Chevron they found an extremely well-fortified, ancient city populated by a race of giants. And wherever they traveled in the land they saw only the external features, which caused them to give a totally inaccurate picture of the land.

Similarly, our eyes and heart are our *meraglim*. They receive an external impression of what they see, which causes them to solicit within us certain desires which we may not even have without their assistance. This is analogous to a catalogue from a mail-order house which offers us many things that we never knew we needed. A case in point would be a computer for our kitchen, or an electric peeler! Were it not for these solicitations, it would never occur to us that we should have any of these items. This is what Rashi meant in his conclusion: הָעַיִן רוֹאָה הַלֵּב חוֹמֵד וְהַגּוּף עוֹשֶׂה אֶת הָעֲבֵרָה, *The eye sees it, and the heart desires it, and the body does the aveirah.*

The Torah tell us here that in the course of our investigation of the world around us, we are neither to follow אַחֲרֵי עֵינֵיכֶם, our physical desires, nor אַחֲרֵי לְבַבְכֶם, the superficial impressions which these investigations have had upon us. The world is not what it appears to be. For instance, the world appears to be hundreds of billions of years old (this number changes every few years), because this is the way *HaKadosh Baruch Hu* created the world to appear. However, in reality it is not so. Similarly, life *appears* to scientists to have evolved from a single-celled amoeba, which eventually developed into monkeys and apes, which eventually evolved into human beings.

Our *Chachamim* tell us לְבַבְכֶם refers to *meenus,* apostasy or heresy, which means the rejection of *HaKadosh Baruch Hu* or the Torah (*Berachos* 12b). However, this raises a difficulty because the word לְבַבְכֶם is actually a metaphor which means "your desires," but heresy or apostasy is something which is associated with one's mind, and not one's "heart." When one comes to the conclusion, after his philosophical investigations, that he does not accept the concept of a Creator, this is the "mind" at work, not the "heart."

HaRav Elchonon Wasserman (see *Kovetz Maamarim — Maamar al Ha-Emunah*) offers the following explanation for this. No rational person would doubt the existence of the Creator, *Yisbarach Shemo,* if we were not born with the desire for instant gratification of our urges — a desire we share with the animals. Even the proponents of the "Big Bang" theory of the origin of the world must admit that the energy and matter which exploded must have come from somewhere. Or, they must admit that the DNA programming found in living organisms, which dictates how that particular form of life will develop, had to derive from somewhere. Who created the energy which caused the explosion? Who created the program for the DNA? All rational signs point to a Creator. But the apostate, or the *apikores,* who tries to explain everything away, is not following the intellectual or philosophical impulses. Rather, he is employing these faculties to rationalize his desire to gratify his physical urges. If there is no absolute right or wrong, no purpose in life, לֵית דִּין וְלֵית דַּיָּן, no accounting of one's action to a Creator, why should he not fully gratify all of his desires as he sees fit? It is for this reason that our *Chachamim* see the word לְבַבְכֶם, *your desires,* as the root which promoted the *meenus* and apostasy.

Our *Chachamim* tell us further that אַחֲרֵי עֵינֵיכֶם זֶה הִרְהוּר עֲבֵירָה (ibid.). The Torah is telling us here that when we look at a fellow human being, what we should see is the fact that here stands another human personality with a *tzelem Elokim,* and a *neshamah,* and not allow our eyes to focus on the aspect of that person which appeals to our animal desires. When one goes to a zoo and sees an elephant, he is not conscious of whether this is a male or female, because it makes no difference to him. Similarly, the appeal of one human being to another should not be based on one's sensual aspects. Whether one is looking at a male or a female human being should be irrelevant.

§ אֲשֶׁר אַתֶּם זֹנִים אַחֲרֵיהֶם — **After which you stray.** Paraphrased, this means that if you follow the external impressions of your heart and eyes, you will eventually become זֹנִים, unfaithful to *HaKadosh Baruch Hu.* Moreover, this *pasuk* teaches us that, unlike other *aveiros,* where the thought of possibly perpetrating a wrongful act is not punishable because the thought in itself is not an *aveirah* (see *Kiddushin* 40a), thoughts of *zenus* and *meenus* in and of themselves are *aveiros.* A violation of וְלֹא תָתוּרוּ אַחֲרֵי לְבַבְכֶם וְאַחֲרֵי עֵינֵיכֶם is ipso facto an *aveirah.* As soon as one allows himself thoughts of apostasy or forbidden sexual relations, he immediately joins the זֹנִים, those who are unfaithful to *HaKadosh Baruch Hu.*

§ לְמַעַן תִּזְכְּרוּ וַעֲשִׂיתֶם אֶת כָּל מִצְוֹתָי — **So that you may remember and perform all My commandments.**

So, in summary, this sentence, וְלֹא תָתוּרוּ אַחֲרֵי לְבַבְכֶם וְאַחֲרֵי עֵינֵיכֶם אֲשֶׁר אַתֶּם זֹנִים אַחֲרֵיהֶם, warns us not to follow the external impressions which we receive when we are investigating our surroundings here on earth, whether this be in the area of *meenus* or *zenus.*

And this commandment, which is a *Chovos HaLevavos,* applies to all of us, men and women, at all times, and under all circumstances, as is indicated by לְמַעַן תִּזְכְּרוּ וַעֲשִׂיתֶם אֶת כָּל מִצְוֹתָי.

§ וִהְיִיתֶם קְדֹשִׁים לֵאלֹהֵיכֶם — **And be holy to your God.** The Torah here tells us that it is incumbent upon a person to continually elevate himself. After a person is born, his body and mind grow and develop until the maximum possible maturation. One's body usually stops growing at 18 or 20 years of age, and his intellectual capacity probably continues to develop for a few more years, but then all growth stops. However, as far as one's moral and ethical development is concerned, this is a lifelong process. Under the mandate of וִהְיִיתֶם קְדֹשִׁים לֵאלֹהֵיכֶם, as long as *HaKadosh Baruch Hu* gives one life, he is required to keep on elevating himself and come closer and closer to *HaKadosh Baruch Hu*. The word קְדֹשִׁים means "separated." We are to separate ourselves from what we were before and continually elevate ourselves to become more and more devoted to *HaKadosh Baruch Hu*.

The ladder which Yaakov Avinu saw in his dream actually represents the human personality. It starts off as סֻלָּם מֻצָּב אַרְצָה, *a ladder was set earthward* (*Bereishis* 18:12) and, throughout the person's life, he is to climb upwards, step by step, towards its zenith, וְרֹאשׁוֹ מַגִּיעַ הַשָּׁמָיְמָה, *and its top reached heavenward* (ibid.). Of course, no one can actually reach *HaKadosh Baruch Hu*, but one is required to strive upwards toward that goal.

אֲנִי ה' אֱלֹהֵיכֶם אֲשֶׁר הוֹצֵאתִי אֶתְכֶם מֵאֶרֶץ מִצְרַיִם לִהְיוֹת לָכֶם לֵאלֹהִים — **I am Hashem, your God, Who has taken you out of the land of Egypt to be a God to you.** By reciting this sentence, we fulfill the *mitzvah* of remembering our exodus from Egypt every day and every night of our lives: לְמַעַן תִּזְכֹּר אֶת יוֹם צֵאתְךָ מֵאֶרֶץ מִצְרַיִם כֹּל יְמֵי חַיֶּיךָ, *so that you will remember the day of your departure from the land of Egypt all the days of your life* (*Devarim* 16:3). In fact, this entire *parashah* is called *yetzias Mitzrayim* in the Gemara: מַזְכִּירִין יְצִיאַת מִצְרַיִם בַּלֵּילוֹת וְגוּ' (*Berachos* 12b).

The use of the four-lettered name יְ-ה-וָ-ה is always a reference to the *middas harachamim*. And Rashi (ibid.) quoting the *Sifrei*, says that אֲנִי ה' here means נֶאֱמָן לְשַׁלֵּם שָׂכָר which, paraphrased, means "You can rely on Me to reward you for every good thought that you have, for every evil thought that you suppress, for every *mitzvah* that you do, for every kind deed that you perform, and for every unkind deed or word that you refrain from doing." On the other hand, as Rashi continues, אֱלֹהֵיכֶם is a reference to *middas hadin*: נֶאֱמָן לְהִפָּרַע, *You can also be assured that I will punish you for your misdeeds*.

❏ אֲשֶׁר הוֹצֵאתִי אֶתְכֶם מֵאֶרֶץ מִצְרָיִם — *Who has removed you from the land of Egypt*. Here again, following Rashi, this means, עַל מְנָת כֵּן פָּדִיתִי אֶתְכֶם שֶׁתְּקַבְּלוּ עֲלֵיכֶם גְּזֵרוֹתַי, *I redeemed you from the land of Egypt on the condition that you accept My decrees upon yourselves*. In the narrative of *yetzias Mitzrayim* in the Torah, we do not find any mention of a "conditional redemption." What we do find is the fact that our forefathers were persecuted and enslaved in Egypt under severe oppression, and were about to be completely obliterated by the Egyptians, until *HaKadosh Baruch Hu* in His mercy intervened and redeemed us.

Every *Seder* night we repeat עֲבָדִים הָיִינוּ לְפַרְעֹה בְּמִצְרָיִם . . . וַיּוֹצִיאֵנוּ ה' וְגוּ'. We were enslaved to Pharaoh in Egypt under his total control, and we had absolutely no voice or rights to determine our own lives. And when we were redeemed by *HaKadosh Baruch Hu*, He told us, "What you were to Pharaoh you are now to Me. You are now under My total control." This is what is meant by: כִּי לִי בְנֵי יִשְׂרָאֵל עֲבָדִים, עֲבָדַי הֵם אֲשֶׁר הוֹצֵאתִי אוֹתָם מֵאֶרֶץ מִצְרָיִם, *For the Children of Israel are servants to Me, they are My servants, Whom I have taken out of the land of Egypt* (Vayikra 25:55). Freedom for the Jew means to be aware that he is under total control of *HaKadosh Baruch Hu*. This includes life, death, health, happiness, prosperity, failures, and successes. And this awareness itself has made us free.

At the Pesach *Seder* we point to the matzah and say הָא לַחְמָא עַנְיָא דִי אֲכָלוּ אַבְהָתָנָא בְּאַרְעָא דְמִצְרָיִם, *This is the slave-bread which our forefathers ate in Mitzrayim*. Our enslaved forefathers had no time to bake regular loaves of bread — they were not given a "lunch hour" — but rather, when it came time to eat, they just slapped together some flour and water, threw it on hot oven bricks where it baked for a few minutes, quickly removed it and ate it, and immediately returned to work. This was the לֶחֶם עוֹנִי, *the bread of misery*, upon which our forefathers subsisted during their slavery.

And as they left Egypt, extremely wealthy with Egyptian gold and silver, but without time to properly prepare provisions for their journey, our forefathers hurriedly took along dough with which to bake bread. The journey out of Egypt into the wilderness probably took several hours, during which time they expected their dough to rise, but when they opened their cloth bags containing the dough they found that, miraculously, it had not risen. And now, as free people, they baked these unleavened pieces of dough into the same kind of bread that they had eaten in Egypt while they were being kicked by their overseers and "Gestapo" slavemasters in Egypt.

The eating of this "slave-bread" *immediately after their redemption from Egypt* brought to our forefathers' attention the idea that now, and forever afterward, they had become transformed into servants of God instead of servants of Pharaoh. And it is this total domination of *HaKadosh Baruch Hu* over us that we Jews call freedom. Our destiny is totally in the hands of *HaKadosh Baruch Hu,* and no human being has any power to change this. And it is this that is meant by the aforementioned "condition of our redemption," עַל מְנָת כֵּן פָּדִיתִי אֶתְכֶם שֶׁתְּקַבְּלוּ עֲלֵיכֶם גְּזֵירוֹתַי. Our redemption from Egypt was actually a transformation of our total domination by Pharaoh to that of *HaKadosh Baruch Hu*.

[Ed note: See *Maayan Beis HaSho'evah, Bo* 12:39 for a broader commentary on וַיֹּאפוּ אֶת הַבָּצֵק אֲשֶׁר הוֹצִיאוּ מִמִּצְרַיִם עֻגֹת מַצּוֹת כִּי לֹא חָמֵץ.]

§ אֲנִי ה' אֱלֹהֵיכֶם — **I am Hashem, your God.** The repetition of this phrase at the end of this sentence is of the essence here. There are two ways in which *HaKadosh Baruch Hu* relates to us. One is that of *gilui Shechinah*. The word *Shechinah* comes from שכן, which means *close* or *neighbor*. There were times in world history — which will recur in the future — in which *HaKadosh Baruch Hu* showed His presence in the world through miraculous events:

nissim (miracles), *niflaos* (wonders) and *nevuah* (prophecy). The most outstanding example of this was the period of *yetzias Mitrayim,* during which the presence of *HaKadosh Baruch Hu* was clearly evident. This was the period of the greatest *gilui Shechinah* that ever existed, starting from the ten plagues, followed by *krias Yam Suf,* which was then followed by the highest level of *gilui Shechinah* in world history, that of *Matan Torah,* during which *HaKadosh Baruch Hu* communicated directly with the Jewish nation: פָּנִים בְּפָנִים דִּבֶּר ה' עִמָּכֶם בָּהָר מִתּוֹךְ הָאֵשׁ, *Face-to-face did Hashem speak with you on the mountain from amid the fire* (*Devarim* 5:4).

It is this series of events to which the first part of our *pasuk* refers: אֲנִי ה' אֱלֹהֵיכֶם אֲשֶׁר הוֹצֵאתִי אֶתְכֶם מֵאֶרֶץ מִצְרַיִם לִהְיוֹת לָכֶם לֵאלֹהִים, *I am Hashem, your God, Who took you out of Egypt for the purpose of becoming your God.* This purpose was fulfilled at *Matan Torah,* as is evidenced by the first words of the *Aseres HaDibros*: אָנֹכִי ה' אֱלֹהֶיךָ אֲשֶׁר הוֹצֵאתִיךָ מֵאֶרֶץ מִצְרַיִם, *I am Hashem, your God, Who has taken you out of the land of Egypt* (*Shemos* 20:2). And this *galui Shechinah* toward the Jewish people, albeit on a somewhat reduced level, continued during their stay in the *midbar* as was evidenced by the many *nissim* which occurred during this period.

However, for most of world history, the relationship of *HaKadosh Baruch Hu* with the world has been that of עוֹלָם כְּמִנְהָגוֹ נוֹהֵג, *the world follows its natural order.* And the world in which we find ourselves today seems to follow its normal and natural order, during which the presence of *HaKadosh Baruch Hu* is veiled or hidden. This veiled relationship of *HaKadosh Baruch Hu* to the world is expressed as יֹשֵׁב בְּסֵתֶר עֶלְיוֹן בְּצֵל שַׁדַּי יִתְלוֹנָן, *He, the Most High, dwells in secret; in the shadow, does Shaddai dwell* (*Tehillim* 91:1). Paraphrased, this means: "The One on High dwells hidden in the shade." To be sure, the *Shechinah* is very close to us, especially during the learning of Torah or during *tefillah,* and certainly in a house which is dedicated solely for these purposes, but we are not aware of it, because *HaKadosh Baruch Hu* is יֹשֵׁב בְּסֵתֶר.

It is this latter relationship which is referred to by the repetition of אֲנִי ה' אֱלֹהֵיכֶם. *HaKadosh Baruch Hu* is thereby telling the Jewish people that the *gilui Shechinah* which they experienced at *yetzias Mitzrayim* and *Matan Torah* will not last forever. They are to know that when they come to Eretz Yisrael, they should expect to live a normal life of עוֹלָם כְּמִנְהָגוֹ נוֹהֵג, during which time the *Shechinah* will be hidden. Therefore, *HaKadosh Baruch Hu* ends this *parashah* by saying אֲנִי ה' אֱלֹהֵיכֶם: "Although you may not be aware of My presence in your future daily lives, nevertheless, I am the same God Who related to you through the world-shaking *nissim* and *niflaos* of *yetzias Mitzrayim* and *Matan Torah.* I shall continue to be ה' אֱלֹהֵיכֶם, under all circumstances of My management of the world."

This thought is also expressed in the *pasuk*: אֲנִי אֲנִי דִּבַּרְתִּי אַף קְרָאתִיו, *I, only*

KRIAS SHEMA ∽ 375

I, have spoken and even summoned him (*Yeshayahu* 48:15). As evidenced by the accents on these two words, the meaning is "I, the same 'I,' call to you." I, Whom you recognized through the *nissim* and *niflaos* of *yetzias Mitzrayim* and *Matan Torah*, call out to you: אֲנִי ה׳ אֱלֹהֵיכֶם; "every time you perform a *mitzvah*, you are to hear My call: I am your God."

Rav Samson R. Hirsch offers a deeply introspective explanation of a seemingly difficult use of the phrase אֲנִי ה׳ אֱלֹהֵיכֶם during one of the final speeches of Moshe Rabbeinu. The Torah records the following speech to the assembled *Bnei Yisrael* as they prepare for their entry into Eretz Yisrael. There Moshe Rabbeinu reminds the Jewish people of the great *nissim* that they experienced during *yetzias Mitzrayim* and their forty-year sojourn in the desert: אַתֶּם רְאִיתֶם אֵת כָּל אֲשֶׁר עָשָׂה ה׳ לְעֵינֵיכֶם בְּאֶרֶץ מִצְרַיִם וגו׳ הַמַּסּוֹת הַגְּדֹלֹת אֲשֶׁר רָאוּ עֵינֶיךָ . . . וָאוֹלֵךְ אֶתְכֶם אַרְבָּעִים שָׁנָה בַּמִּדְבָּר וגו׳, *You have seen everything that Hashem did before your eyes in the land of Egypt; the great trials that your eyes beheld . . . I led you for forty years in the Wilderness etc.* (*Devarim* 29:1-5). And Moshe Rabbeinu ends with לְמַעַן תֵּדְעוּ כִּי אֲנִי ה׳ אֱלֹהֵיכֶם, *So that you would know that I am Hashem, your God,* instead of the expected ending לְמַעַן תֵּדְעוּ כִּי ה׳ אֱלֹהֵיכֶם so that you would know that Hashem is your God. Moshe Rabbeinu continues with his own words: וַתָּבֹאוּ אֶל הַמָּקוֹם הַזֶּה, *Then you arrived at this place* (ibid. v.6), indicating that the words אֲנִי ה׳ אֱלֹהֵיכֶם are also his words.

To my knowledge, this highly unusual usage is not commented upon by any of the *mefarshim*, except for Rav Hirsch. His explanation is pithily contained in the English translation of Rav Hirsch on *Chumash* which contains two Hebrew words: "So that you should know that אֲנִי ה׳ is your God." He explains that Moshe Rabbeinu is here utilizing אֲנִי ה׳ as the expanded Name of *HaKadosh Baruch Hu*.

The Name אֲנִי ה׳ conveys the idea that *HaKadosh Baruch Hu* is not some concept, idea or philosophy, but rather He is אֲנִי־יְ־הֹ־וָ־ה; an "Entity," the One and only One Who can truly say, אֲנִי אֲנִי הוּא, *I alone Am "I"* (*Devarim* 32:39). I alone Am the One Personality Whose absolutely free will controls every present and future moment of all existence in heaven and on earth. Rav Hirsch explains that the purpose of all the miraculous events which *Bnei Yisrael* experienced, starting from *yetzias Mitzrayim* right through the end of the forty years in the desert, was to impress upon them this idea of אֲנִי ה׳.

Therefore, while *Bnei Yisrael* were experiencing the miraculous events of *yetzias Mitzrayim* and *Har Sinai*, and during the forty years of God's personal intervention in their lives in the desert, the "Personality" of *HaKadosh Baruch Hu* as אֲנִי ה׳ became quite clear to them. But with their anticipated transition to a "normal" life in Eretz Yisrael — in which נוֹהֵג כְּמִנְהָגוֹ עוֹלָם, where they would wake up in the morning and go about the ordinary routine of one's daily life (i.e., earning a livelihood) — the presence of *HaKadosh Baruch Hu* would not be so obvious. Therefore, the "second" אֲנִי ה׳ at the end of *parashas tzitzis* teaches *Bnei Yisrael* to remember that אֲנִי ה׳ אֱלֹהֵיכֶם: "I am just as present now in your 'normal' and routine lives in Eretz Yisrael — although I choose now to veil My presence — as I was during the miraculous experiences of *yetzias Mitzrayim* and the forty years in the *midbar.*"

The last words of *Krias Shema*, אֲנִי ה׳ אֱלֹהֵיכֶם, are a reaffirmation of its very beginning: שְׁמַע יִשְׂרָאֵל ה׳ אֱלֹהֵינוּ ה׳ אֶחָד. This usage of חֲתִימָה מֵעֵין הַפְּתִיחָה is similar to the composition of *berachos.*

אֲנִי ה׳ אֱלֹהֵיכֶם is immediately followed by the word אֱמֶת, which is actually the beginning of the next paragraph, אֱמֶת וְיַצִּיב וְנָכוֹן וגו׳. This is based on halachah: אָמַר רַבִּי אַבָּהוּ אָמַר רַבִּי יוֹחָנָן: הֲלָכָה כְּרַבִּי יְהוּדָה דְּאָמַר בֵּין אֱלֹהֵיכֶם לֶאֱמֶת וְיַצִּיב לֹא יַפְסִיק (*Berachos* 14a), meaning that one should not interrupt, or even pause, between the words ה׳ אֱלֹהֵיכֶם and אֱמֶת. This includes even the saying of *amen* (see *Orach Chaim* 6:5). The reason given by the Gemara (ibid.) for the attachment of ה׳ אֱלֹהֵיכֶם to אֱמֶת is that it corresponds, with וַה׳ אֱלֹהִים אֱמֶת (*Yirmiyahu* 10:10).

The following paragraph, beginning with אֱמֶת וְיַצִּיב וְנָכוֹן and having as its object הַדָּבָר הַזֶּה, *this matter,* is an affirmation by us of the aforementioned basic truth that אֲנִי ה׳ אֱלֹהֵיכֶם is absolutely and inviolably אֱמֶת.

אֱמֶת וְיַצִּיב / Emes V'Yatziv

The Gemara (*Berachos* 21a) states that reciting the *tefillah* beginning with אֱמֶת וְיַצִּיב is a fulfillment of the *mitzvas asei d'Oraisa* of *zechiras yetzias Mitzrayim,* the commandment to verbally remember the Exodus from Egypt every day, in that it contains the sentence מִמִּצְרַיִם גְּאַלְתָּנוּ וגו׳. Although *yetzias Mitzrayim* was just referred to in the previous *parashah* of *tzitzis,* nevertheless the *Chachamim* composed this *tefillah* as a further remembrance of, and to express our gratitude to *HaKadosh Baruch Hu* for, *yetzias Mitzrayim.*

The Torah does not specify how we are to remember *yetzias Mitzrayim,* but the *Chachamim* have told us that we are to fulfill this *mitzvah* by the saying of *parashas tzitzis* and אֱמֶת וְיַצִּיב. This is similar to the *mitzvah* of זָכוֹר אֶת יוֹם הַשַּׁבָּת לְקַדְּשׁוֹ, *Remember the Shabbos to sanctify it* (*Shemos* 20:8), for which the Torah does not specify a particular way of fulfilling it. However, the *Chachamim* have told us that we are to fulfill the *mitzvah* of sanctifying Shabbos by "making *Kiddush,*" זוֹכְרֵהוּ עַל הַיַּיִן (*Pesachim* 106a).

In our outline of the "architecture" of the *tefillah,* we explained that *Krias Shema* corresponds to the *Mizbach HaZahav* (Golden Altar), the inner *mizbe'ach,* on which the *ketores* — symbolizing our feelings, emotions, and all of our intellectual faculties — was offered. The *Mizbach HaNechoshes* (Copper Altar), the outer *mizbe'ach,* is where we symbolically dedicate the physical part of our existence to *HaKadosh Baruch Hu.*

Following our outline, this *tefillah* of אֱמֶת וְיַצִּיב corresponds to the *Paroches* which separates the *Kodesh* from the *Kodesh HaKadashim.* Similarly, אֱמֶת וְיַצִּיב is the dividing line between the preparatory part of the *tefillah* and the main *tefillah* itself — the *Shemoneh Esrei.* And just as in the second *Beis HaMikdash* the *Paroches* consisted of two parts (*Yoma* 51b), this *tefillah* also consists of two parts. The first part, beginning with אֱמֶת וְיַצִּיב and ending with אֵין אֱלֹהִים זוּלָתֶךָ, affirms all of the truths which we have expressed in the *parshiyos* of קְרִיאַת שְׁמַע. And the second part, beginning with עֶזְרַת אֲבוֹתֵינוּ, focuses on the *geulah* of *yetzias Mitzrayim.*

The symbolism of the *Paroches* is alluded to in this *tefillah* by the fact that the word אֱמֶת appears six times. This corresponds to the *halachah* that every strand of each of the four types of material used in the *Paroches* had to be composed of six twisted strings of its type. Furthermore, all four types of these sixfold strands had to be combined to form each completed thread (see *Yoma* 71b). And corresponding to the twenty-four strings in each completed thread which went into the weaving of the *Paroches,* the *mesadrei hatefillah* composed twenty-four sentences from אֱמֶת וְיַצִּיב through גָּאַל יִשְׂרָאֵל. Upon counting them, you may not arrive at this total because the printers have placed the periods ending each sentence in the wrong places. A careful study of the words and phrases, however, will show that there are definitely twenty-four sentences in this *tefillah*.

Just as אֲנִי ה' אֱלֹהֵיכֶם is to be followed immediately by אֱמֶת without interruption, the *halachah* requires that this *berachah* of *geulah* also be followed immediately — and without any interruption — by the *Shemoneh Esrei*. This is called *semichus geulah l'tefillah* (*Berachos* 9b; *Shulchan Aruch, Orach Chaim* 111). In preparation for the *Shemoneh Esrei* we focus our minds on the miraculous events of *geulas Mitzrayim* which were clearly a manifestation of the personal involvement of *HaKadosh Baruch Hu* Himself in our redemption: אֲנִי וְלֹא מַלְאָךְ, אֲנִי וְלֹא שָׂרָף, אֲנִי וְלֹא הַשָּׁלִיחַ, אֲנִי הוּא וְלֹא אַחֵר. It is in this frame of mind that we begin our *tefillah* with our thoughts directed toward *HaKadosh Baruch Hu* Himself, and not to any form of intermediary. This is the meaning of the statement in the Gemara, הַמִּתְפַּלֵּל צָרִיךְ שֶׁיִּרְאֶה כְּאִלּוּ שְׁכִינָה כְּנֶגְדּוֹ (*Sanhedrin* 22a). One who prays is to imagine that he is standing in the *Kodesh HaKadashim* and addressing *HaKadosh Baruch Hu* Himself.

[Ed. note: See the Introduction to *Shemoneh Esrei* for a broader explanation of *semichus geulah l'tefillah*.]

The words אֱמֶת וְיַצִּיב וְנָכוֹן וגו' express essentially the same thought sixteen times. They all convey the idea of an affirmation of the previously mentioned truth, הַדָּבָר הַזֶּה, that אֲנִי ה' אֱלֹהֵיכֶם, which is the subject of all of these affirmations. We are affirming that this truth of אֲנִי ה' אֱלֹהֵיכֶם applies at all times, whether the presence of the *Shechinah* is openly apparent as in *yetzias Mitzrayim,* or in circumstances of עוֹלָם כְּמִנְהָגוֹ נוֹהֵג, where the *Shechinah* is hidden.

The 16 words of this affirmation actually consist of 8 pairs of expressions: אֱמֶת וְיַצִּיב; וְנָכוֹן וְקַיָּם; וְיָשָׁר וְנֶאֱמָן; וְאָהוּב וְחָבִיב; וְנֶחְמָד וְנָעִים; וְנוֹרָא וְאַדִּיר; וּמְתֻקָּן וּמְקֻבָּל; וְטוֹב וְיָפֶה. This was composed in this style to correspond to the eight double strands of the *tzitzis,* each of which is made up of at least two smaller strands (see *Eruvin* 96b; *Orach Chaim* 11:2 with *Taz*). Each pair of words contains affirmations of the truth of אֲנִי ה' אֱלֹהֵיכֶם, which are reflective of both the world of *gilui Shechinah* and that of *hester panim,* the times when God's Presence is hidden, as follows:

❊ ❊ ❊

⊱ אֱמֶת וְיַצִּיב — **True and certain.** The word וְיַצִּיב is the Aramaic translation of אֱמֶת. This conveys the idea that we affirm the truth of אֲנִי ה' אֱלֹהֵיכֶם, both in an environment of *gilui Shechinah,* or אֱמֶת, and during the periods of *hester panim,* which is conveyed by the Aramaic translation, וְיַצִּיב.

📓 **וְנָכוֹן וְקַיָּם — It is established and enduring.** Similarly, וְנָכוֹן, meaning it is clear and apparent, refers to times of *gilui Shechinah*, but וְקַיָּם meaning enduring, or long lasting, refers to times of *hester panim*. What was נָכוֹן to us when we had *gilui Shechinah* is קַיָּם, and endures even now when we live in a world of *hester panim*.

📓 **וְיָשָׁר וְנֶאֱמָן — Fair and faithful.** The same applies to יָשָׁר וְנֶאֱמָן. During times of *gilui Shechinah* we see the יָשָׁר, or the "straightness," of *HaKadosh Baruch Hu*, which is not apparent during times of *hester panim*, when we sometimes wonder why *HaKadosh Baruch Hu* punishes *tzadikkim* and why innocent people suffer. So we affirm here that that which is יָשָׁר, or apparent and clear, during times of *gilui Shechinah*, is נֶאֱמָן, faithfully accepted by us during times of *hester panim*.

📓 **וְאָהוּב וְחָבִיב — Beloved and cherished** conveys the same idea. The *ahavas Hashem* which one experiences during times of *gilui Shechinah* is overwhelming and indescribable. This is why at the time of *Matan Torah*, despite the awe-inspiring thunder, lightning, fire, smoke, and loud shofar blasts (see *Shemos* 19:16-19), the people had an overwhelming desire to come closer to the place where *HaKadosh Baruch Hu* was manifesting His presence, disregarding the danger to their lives which this would have entailed.

This was evident when Moshe Rabbeinu was told by *HaKadosh Baruch Hu* to repeatedly warn the people to stay away from the mountain, lest they die: וְהִגְבַּלְתָּ אֶת הָעָם סָבִיב לֵאמֹר הִשָּׁמְרוּ לָכֶם עֲלוֹת בָּהָר וּנְגֹעַ בְּקָצֵהוּ, כָּל הַנֹּגֵעַ בָּהָר מוֹת יוּמָת, *You shall set boundaries for the people roundabout, saying, "Beware of ascending the mountain or touching its edge; whoever touches the mountain shall surely die!"* and רֵד הָעֵד בָּעָם פֶּן יֶהֶרְסוּ אֶל ה' לִרְאוֹת וְנָפַל מִמֶּנּוּ רָב, *Descend, warn the people, lest they break through to Hashem to see, and a multitude of them will fall* (ibid. vs. 12 and 21). This overwhelming *ahavas Hashem* is expressed as: יִשָּׁקֵנִי מִנְּשִׁיקוֹת פִּיהוּ, *Communicate Your innermost wisdom to me again in loving closeness* (*Shir HaShirim* 1:2), which describes the yearning of Jewish people to experience again that great love which *HaKadosh Baruch Hu* showed us at the time of *Matan Torah*, when פָּנִים בְּפָנִים דִּבֶּר ה' עִמָּכֶם, *Face-to-face did Hashem speak with you* (*Devarim* 5:4). See *Targum Shir HaShirim* there: וְהוּא מִתְמַלֵּל עִמָּן אַפִּין בְּאַפִּין כִּגְבַר דְּנָשֵׁק לְחַבְרֵיהּ וגו'.

The *pasuk* שְׁמַע יִשְׂרָאֵל ה' אֱלֹהֵינוּ ה' אֶחָד, which reminds us of *Matan Torah* (see above), is always introduced by words of *ahavah* (הַבּוֹחֵר בְּעַמּוֹ יִשְׂרָאֵל and אוֹהֵב עַמּוֹ יִשְׂרָאֵל בְּאַהֲבָה), because of the great love which existed between *HaKadosh Baruch Hu* and *Am Yisrael* at the time of the *gilui Shechinah* connected with *Matan Torah*.

However, in times of *hester panim*, this great love is only חָבִיב, a still cherished memory which we hope will be repeated.

‎וְנֶחְמָד וְנָעִים‎ — **Delightful and pleasant** repeats the same concept. In times of *gilui Shechinah*, we have the feeling of great desire, ‎חֶמְדָּה‎, to be close to *HaKadosh Baruch Hu*, but in times of *hester panim* this desire exists only on the level of being ‎נָעִים‎, sweet or pleasant.

‎וְנוֹרָא וְאַדִּיר‎ — **Awesome and powerful.** In times of *gilui Shechinah*, such as *Matan Torah*, the awareness of *HaKadosh Baruch Hu* among us instills in us ‎נוֹרָא‎, feelings of awe and trepidation: ‎וַיֶּחֱרַד כָּל הָעָם אֲשֶׁר בַּמַּחֲנֶה‎, *the entire people that was in the camp shuddered* (*Shemos* 19:16). However, for us, in the world of *hester panim*, this awareness can be described only as ‎אַדִּיר‎, powerful.

‎וּמְתֻקָּן וּמְקֻבָּל‎ — **Correct and accepted.** In times of *gilui Shechinah*, the truths of the Torah are clearly evident from the text itself. During such times, one can clearly see how every *halachah* is indicated in the words and letters of the Torah. During times of Divine enlightenment, it becomes evident how each *mitzvah* and *halachah* is ‎מְתֻקָּן‎, *well established* and documented within the text of the Torah. One could clearly see the details of the *Torah Shebe'al Peh* alluded to in the wording and lettering of the *Torah Shebichsav*.

However, in our times of *hester panim,* when we cannot see the *halachos* in the wording of the Torah, it is only ‎מְקֻבָּל‎: we accept that which our *Chachamim* — who were closer to the source than we are — understood from the text of the Torah to be its true meaning. Although we are not privileged to see and understand the nuances which Rabbi Akiva found in each ‎קוֹצוֹ שֶׁל יוּ"ד‎, even the tiny extension of a *yud*, from which he derived innumerable *halachos* (see *Menachos* 29b), we nevertheless accept the authenticity of these *derashos*. That which was ‎מְתֻקָּן‎ and clear to Rabbi Akiva is ‎מְקֻבָּל‎ to us. The Torah was transmitted to us from Moshe Rabbeinu, who received it from Sinai, down through the *Neviim*, the *Rishonim*, and the *Acharonim*, until our time, and we have accepted it as the absolutely authentic Torah.

‎וְטוֹב וְיָפֶה‎ — **Good and beautiful.** The fact that everything that *HaKadosh Baruch Hu* does is absolutely good, ‎טוֹב‎, is clearly discernible at times of *gilui Shechinah*. However, for us, in our times of *hester panim*, it is ‎יָפֶה‎, beautiful, when we come to the recognition, through a great deal of *emunah*, that everything that *HaKadosh Baruch Hu* does is absolutely good.

‎הַדָּבָר הַזֶּה עָלֵינוּ לְעוֹלָם וָעֶד‎ — **Is this affirmation to us forever and ever.** This "thing," the fact that ‎אֲנִי ה' אֱלֹהֵיכֶם‎, is accepted by us forever and ever, regardless of whether there is a *gilui Shechinah* or *hester panim*.

‎אֱמֶת אֱלֹהֵי עוֹלָם מַלְכֵּנוּ‎ — **It is true that the God of the Universe is our King.** Our King, *HaKadosh Baruch Hu*, is not only our God, but He is the God of the entire universe, physical and spiritual. In *Krias Shema*, we, the Jewish nation, by accepting His rule upon ourselves, *ol Malchus Shamayim,* confirm that He is our King.

ঌ§ צוּר יַעֲקֹב מָגֵן יִשְׁעֵנוּ — **The Rock of Jacob is the Shield of our salvation.** We, the children of Yaakov who relied on *HaKadosh Baruch Hu* to protect him from danger, הַמַּלְאָךְ הַגֹּאֵל אֹתִי מִכָּל רָע, *the angel who redeems me from all evil* (Bereishis 48:16), also see *HaKadosh Baruch Hu* as the Shield of our salvation. When *HaKadosh Baruch Hu* protects us, he does so as צוּר יַעֲקֹב.

ঌ§ לְדֹר וָדֹר הוּא קַיָּם — **From generation to generation He endures.** This is so, because *HaKadosh Baruch Hu* endures for all generations.

ঌ§ וּשְׁמוֹ קַיָּם — **And His Name endures.** We cannot understand *HaKadosh Baruch Hu;* we can only know His "Name," meaning the fact of His existence, and those attributes which He chose to reveal to us in His Torah.

ঌ§ וְכִסְאוֹ נָכוֹן — **And His throne** in heaven **is well established,** with the attendance of the myriads of spiritual creatures, such as *Ofanim* and *Chayos HaKodesh,* etc., and this endures forever and ever.

ঌ§ וּמַלְכוּתוֹ וֶאֱמוּנָתוֹ לָעַד קַיָּמֶת — **And His sovereignty and His reliability** — in our world — **endures forever.**

ঌ§ וּדְבָרָיו חָיִים — **And His words,** contained in the Torah, **live.** In our times we do not have the benefit of the open and clear manifestations of the Presence of *HaKadosh Baruch Hu* among us through *nissim geluyim.* Although our daily lives are filled with God's "hidden miracles," נִסֶּיךָ שֶׁבְּכָל יוֹם עִמָּנוּ, we nevertheless tend to explain these away as natural occurrences or coincidences. However, what we do have — and always will have — is the Torah, "the word of *HaKadosh Baruch Hu,*" אֵין לָנוּ שִׁיּוּר רַק הַתּוֹרָה הַזֹּאת (*Selichos* to *erev Rosh Hashanah* [42], *Zechor Bris Avraham*), and this will endure forever.

Every letter and every word, ever *din* and every *halachah* of the Torah is alive. Its words are חָיִים, they pulse with life. In simple terms, the words of Torah are analogous to a live electric wire which may appear quite dead until one comes into contact with it, then he immediately senses the enormous energy surging within it. And, like a live wire, if one attempts to touch the Torah, to tamper with it, he does so at the risk of his eternal life.

ঌ§ וְקַיָּמִים — **The words of Torah endure.** We have the same Torah today which Moshe Rabbeinu presented to the Jewish people. וְזֹאת הַתּוֹרָה אֲשֶׁר שָׂם מֹשֶׁה לִפְנֵי בְּנֵי יִשְׂרָאֵל, *This is the Torah that Moshe placed before the Children of Israel* (Devarim 4:44).

ঌ§ נֶאֱמָנִים — **They are believed.** We have *emunah,* absolute trust, that these are the authentic words of the Torah as we received them.

וְנֶחֱמָדִים לָעַד וּלְעוֹלְמֵי עוֹלָמִים. עַל אֲבוֹתֵינוּ וְעָלֵינוּ, עַל בָּנֵינוּ וְעַל דּוֹרוֹתֵינוּ — **They are cherished by us for all times to come. For our forefathers and for us, for our children and for our generations.** This same accepted and treasured Torah which was binding on our forefathers is binding on us, and will also bind our children and our children's children.

וְעַל כָּל דּוֹרוֹת יִשְׂרָאֵל, עֲבָדֶיךָ — **And for all the generations of Yisrael, Your servants.** It will bind all future generations of the Jewish people so long as they wish to remain עֲבָדֶיךָ, *Your servants.* Unfortunately, there are millions of Jews who do not wish to be עֲבָדֶיךָ, and for them all this means nothing.

עַל הָרִאשׁוֹנִים וְעַל הָאַחֲרוֹנִים, דָּבָר טוֹב וְקַיָּם לְעוֹלָם וָעֶד — **Upon the earlier and upon later generations, this affirmation is good and enduring forever.** The Torah of *HaKadosh Baruch Hu* was cherished as "the good word" by the earlier generations, and will continue to endure as such, for all later generations, forever.

אֱמֶת וֶאֱמוּנָה, חֹק וְלֹא יַעֲבֹר — **True and faithful, it is an unbreachable decree.** The Jewish people have accepted the Torah which they saw clearly as אֱמֶת, absolute truth, during the "daylight" of its history, the times of *gilui Shechinah*. They then continued to uphold it as absolute truth, through their unshakable *emunah,* even during the "night" of Jewish history, when the presence of the *Shechinah* was veiled.

During the period of *hester panim* in which we live, our *emunah* that the Torah is true is based on our acceptance of the *emes* which our forefathers experienced during the time of *gilui Shechinah,* and for us, it is accepted as *emunah,* for we have absolute faith that the Torah is חֹק וְלֹא יַעֲבֹר, "The Law," and it will never disappear. Though some of the *mitzvos* of the Torah may sound old-fashioned, outdated, or impossible to understand, yet we accept them *b'emunah sheleimah* to be absolutely true and valid, whether we understand them or not. This is what is meant by *kabbalas ol Malchus Shamayim,* which is the central message of *Krias Shema*.

אֱמֶת שָׁאַתָּה הוּא ה' אֱלֹהֵינוּ וֵאלֹהֵי אֲבוֹתֵינוּ — **It is true that You are Hashem, our God and the God of our forefathers.** The repetition of *emes* here follows the previously mentioned אֱמֶת וֶאֱמוּנָה חֹק וְלֹא יַעֲבֹר, to express the thought that just as we accept the Torah as the same unchanged law which our forefathers accepted, so too is our concept of אַתָּה הוּא ה' אֱלֹהֵינוּ unchanged from that of our forefathers. We have no new perceptions of *HaKadosh Baruch Hu.*

מַלְכֵּנוּ מֶלֶךְ אֲבוֹתֵינוּ, גֹּאֲלֵנוּ גֹּאֵל אֲבוֹתֵינוּ — **Our King and the King of our forefathers, our Redeemer, the Redeemer of our forefathers.** We reiterate here our total *emunah* that *HaKadosh Baruch Hu,* Whom we accept as our King and Redeemer, is the same as He Who redeemed our forefathers and Who was King at the time of *yetzias Mitzrayim.*

EMES V'YATZIV

אֶ **יוֹצְרֵנוּ, צוּר יְשׁוּעָתֵנוּ — He is our Creator, the Rock of our salvation.** This is a very clear statement that Judaism excludes any idea of a new concept of *Mashiach,* or a *savior* to bring about a בְּרִית חֲדָשָׁה, a *New Testament,* as in the Christian religion, on whom to rely in times of need or danger. Rather, it is *HaKadosh Baruch Hu* Himself, our Creator, on Whom we rely for our salvation.

אֶ **פּוֹדֵנוּ וּמַצִּילֵנוּ מֵעוֹלָם שְׁמֶךָ, אֵין אֱלֹהִים זוּלָתֶךָ — He, our Redeemer and Saviour, has been known to us by this Name forever. There is no God besides You.** With this phrase, which contains an affirmation of the basic elements of our *emunah,* we conclude the first part of אֱמֶת וְיַצִּיב. Inasmuch as this *tefillah* contains the basic elements of our *emunah,* it would behoove us to recite it with deliberation and concentration, and not simply to skim over the words.

The Chafetz Chaim suggests a beautiful parable which has a definite application in connection with this *tefillah.* A person was once stranded on an island far from civilization. He noticed that the ground of this forlorn island was covered with thousands of precious stones. The aborigines who lived there had no idea of their value and considered them simply worthless pebbles. When he was finally about to be rescued and returned to civilization, he scooped up a handful of these precious stones and put them in his pocket. When he arrived back home, he took one of these little "pebbles" out of his pocket, and sold it for a great deal of money, which made him a wealthy man for life.

The point of the parable is that we live in a world which is filled with unused and unrecognized opportunities for a person to earn everlasting life in *Olam Haba.* This *tefillah* is an example. If one says these exalted words with the proper *kavannah,* it can bring him to *Olam Haba.* And when he is asked, after he leaves this world, what he had to show for his life on Earth, he can point to this *tefillah* and say, "I said these words and believed them with my whole heart." This person will surely not be put to shame, וְלֹא נֵבוֹשׁ, when he comes to עוֹלָם וָעֶד.

I read once, though I cannot recall exactly where, that when the Nazis were taking a group of Jews to be murdered, one of the *gedolim* among them told them to say this *tefillah* as their last words before being shot to death, as an expression of their total affirmation and acceptance of their *emunah* in *HaKadosh Baruch Hu* and His Torah.

עֶזְרַת אֲבוֹתֵינוּ / Ezras Avoseinu

As we have previously explained, the two words אֱמֶת וְיַצִּיב correspond to the *Paroches* which leads into the *Kodesh HaKadashim*. In the second *Beis HaMikdash*, there were two *Perachos* (see *Yoma* 51b), and correspondingly, this *tefillah* consists of two parts: The first starts with אֱמֶת וְיַצִּיב and ends with אֵין אֱלֹהִים זוּלָתֶךָ; and the second part begins with עֶזְרַת אֲבוֹתֵינוּ and ends with the *berachah* of גָּאַל יִשְׂרָאֵל.

The first part of this *tefillah* consists of our affirmation of the truths contained in *Krias Shema*. This second part, from עֶזְרַת אֲבוֹתֵינוּ until *Shemoneh Esrei*, is called *geulah*, because its contents focus on *yetzias Mitzrayim* (the redemption from Egypt), and it ends with גָּאַל יִשְׂרָאֵל. This is in compliance with the *halachah* of *semichus geulah l'tefillah*, which requires us to express our recognition and gratitude to *HaKadosh Baruch Hu* for our redemption from Egypt immediately before beginning the main part of the *tefillah*.

❧ ❧ ❧

עֶזְרַת אֲבוֹתֵינוּ אַתָּה הוּא מֵעוֹלָם — You are the same One Who has been the help of our Forefathers since times immemorial. (מֵעוֹלָם, from נֶעְלָם, has the meaning of "from the hidden past.") "Our Forefathers" refers to Avraham, Yitzchak, and Yaakov, as *Chazal* tell us, אֵין קוֹרִין אָבוֹת אֶלָּא לִשְׁלֹשָׁה, The honorific, *Avos*, or Forefathers, is applied only to these three: Avraham, Yitzchak, and Yaakov (*Berachos* 16b). And these Forefathers lived in times which no one can remember (*mei'olam*), and we know of them only because their history is recorded in the Torah.

The word עֶזְרַת, from עֶזְרָה, similar to קוּמָה עֶזְרָתָה לָּנוּ, *Arise, help us* (*Tehillim* 44:27), is the weaker, feminine form of עֵזֶר, which is the stronger, masculine, form of the word meaning "help," as in עֶזְרֵנוּ וּמָגִנֵּנוּ הוּא, *Our help and our shield is He* (ibid. 33:20).

The weaker form עֶזְרַת, which is used here, very subtly expresses the thought that our *Avos*, by their own *zechuyos*, *emunah*, and *bitachon*, did their own part to help bring about their salvation. Consequently, *HaKadosh Baruch Hu* had only to be their עֶזְרַת, and not their עֵזֶר, because they, too, participated in their own salvation by their *ma'asim tovim*. Thus, the weaker form עֶזְרַת is employed here.

Interestingly, a wife is called עֵזֶר כְּנֶגְדּוֹ, utilizing the masculine, stronger, form of the word, despite her femininity. This is so because that which a wife does, the husband cannot do. For instance, she bears the children and nurses them, and in this respect she is a full-fledged עֵזֶר, because the husband relies on her completely to perform her own part in complementing the marriage;

Just as You protected and saved our Forefathers,

מָגֵן וּמוֹשִׁיעַ לִבְנֵיהֶם אַחֲרֵיהֶם בְּכָל דּוֹר וָדוֹר — **You also shield and save their children after them in every generation.** *HaKadosh Baruch Hu* acts as a מָגֵן, a Shield, to protect us from mishaps; and if, because of our *aveiros*, adverse things do happen in our lives, *HaKadosh Baruch Hu* is also our מוֹשִׁיעַ, to Whom we can look for salvation from our *tzaros*.

לִבְנֵיהֶם אַחֲרֵיהֶם — *Their children after them* means those who adopt their lifestyle of keeping Torah and *mitzvos*. The word אַחֲרֵיהֶם is used here in the same sense as in: וַהֲקִמֹתִי אֶת בְּרִיתִי בֵּינִי וּבֵינֶךָ וּבֵין זַרְעֲךָ אַחֲרֶיךָ לְדֹרֹתָם לִבְרִית עוֹלָם, לִהְיוֹת לְךָ לֵאלֹהִים וּלְזַרְעֲךָ אַחֲרֶיךָ, *I will rectify My covenant between Me and you and between your offspring after you, throughout their generations as an everlasting covenant, to be a God to you and to your offspring after you* (*Bereishis* 17:7); and וְהָיְתָה לּוֹ וּלְזַרְעוֹ אַחֲרָיו בְּרִית כְּהֻנַּת עוֹלָם, *And it shall be for him and his offspring after him a Covenant of eternal priesthood* (*Bamidbar* 25:13).

The Gemara (*Yevamos* 42a, 100b) understands the words זַרְעֲךָ אַחֲרֶיךָ used here as generally describing children who follow in the footsteps of their parents. The covenant that *HaKadosh Baruch Hu* made with Avraham Avinu included Avraham and those of his offspring who follow in his footsteps.

בְּרוּם עוֹלָם מוֹשָׁבֶךָ, וּמִשְׁפָּטֶיךָ וְצִדְקָתְךָ עַד אַפְסֵי אָרֶץ — **Although Your dwelling place is in the hidden spheres above the universe, nevertheless, Your strict judgment and Your mitigated judgment reach the very ends of the world,** until such time as the world ceases to exist.

The word אַפְסֵי, from אֶפֶס, *nothing,* expresses the meaning, "ending, becoming nothing."

There are two kinds of judgments. One is מִשְׁפָּטֶיךָ, from שָׁפַט, which means *order,* and it refers to the harsh judgments of those people who deserve to be treated with strict justice. The other is צִדְקָתְךָ, from צְדָקָה, which means *charity,* and it refers to the mild or mitigated judgments which are charitable to those who have earned a milder form of punishment, *lifnim mi'shuras hadin*. In the upcoming *Shemoneh Esrei*, we refer to *HaKadosh Baruch Hu* as the King Who metes out both forms of justice, מֶלֶךְ אוֹהֵב צְדָקָה וּמִשְׁפָּט.

אַפְסֵי אָרֶץ, *the ends of the earth,* includes two opposite groups of people who, while they live on this earth, really exist on its outer fringes. These are the *tzaddikim* who live above the world. Although they inhabit the earth, they do not live a worldly existence because they have elevated themselves above the mundane. On the other hand, there are *reshaim* who do not deserve to dwell on earth, for they have lowered themselves below the minimum standard of human decency.

So while *HaKadosh Baruch Hu* is high and mighty, and inconceivable and inexplicable, nevertheless His *tzedakah* and *mishpat* reach everyone on earth, with reward and punishment — from one extreme to the other — and will continue to do so as long as the world exists.

אַשְׁרֵי אִישׁ שֶׁיִּשְׁמַע לְמִצְוֹתֶיךָ — **Happy is the man who will listen to Your mitzvos.** The term used is not שֶׁשׁוֹמֵעַ, "who listens," but rather, שֶׁיִּשְׁמַע, *who will listen,* one who has decided to abide by the *mitzvos*. This refers to the *baal teshuvah* who has made up his mind that he will listen to the *mitzvos* of *HaKadosh Baruch Hu* in the future. This alludes to the *pasuk,* אַשְׁרֵי אִישׁ יָרֵא אֶת ה׳, *Happy is the man who fears Hashem* (*Tehillim* 112:1), on which our *Chachamim* remark: אָמַר רַבִּי עַמְרָם אָמַר רַב, אַשְׁרֵי מִי שֶׁעוֹשֶׂה תְשׁוּבָה כְּשֶׁהוּא אִישׁ, *Rabbi Amram said in the name of Rav: Happy is the person who does teshuvah while he is still a "man,"* in his full virility and strength (*Avodah Zarah* 19a). This, of course, applies to a woman as well. Many people do *teshuvah* as a last resort, when they are old and feeble and have no strength left to do anything wrong — so they decide that they might as well do things right. But how fortunate and happy is the person who recognizes his mistakes while he is still young and strong enough to do *aveiros,* and yet he struggles with his temptations and overcomes them.

To be sure, *HaKadosh Baruch Hu* waits for a person's *teshuvah* until his last breath, as we say in *U'Nesaneh Tokef*: וְעַד יוֹם מוֹתוֹ תְּחַכֶּה לוֹ, אִם יָשׁוּב מִיַּד תְּקַבְּלוֹ. Nevertheless, the *teshuvah* of a person in his full vigor is on a much higher level.

וְתוֹרָתְךָ וּדְבָרְךָ יָשִׂים עַל לִבּוֹ — **And he will take to heart Your Torah and Your Word.** Even those people who do not deserve to be on earth, who exist at its "outer fringes," אַפְסֵי אָרֶץ — the *reshaim* — can do *teshuvah* and turn their lives around when they accept God's Torah and His word. Indeed, they are called אַשְׁרֵי, fortunate and happy.

The word וּדְבָרְךָ, *and Your word,* needs to be explained. What is the *word* of *HaKadosh Baruch Hu,* other than the Torah, which a person is to take to heart? Does *HaKadosh Baruch Hu* speak to people, other than possibly to a *navi*?

To understand this, I wish to refer to an explanation given by the *Ramban* in *Parashas Shemini.* After the two sons of Aharon, the *tzaddikim* Nadav and Avihu, died on the day of the dedication of the *Ohel Moed,* the Tabernacle of Assembly, Moshe Rabbeinu addressed him in the Name of *HaKadosh Baruch Hu* as follows: הוּא אֲשֶׁר דִּבֶּר ה׳ לֵאמֹר בִּקְרֹבַי אֶקָּדֵשׁ וגו׳, *This is what God said to say: I will become holy through My close ones* (*Vayikra* 10:3).

Inasmuch as we do not know of any such statement by God in the Torah, Rashi explains in the name of the Gemara (*Zevachim* 115b) that this refers to the statement by Hashem: וְנִקְדַּשׁ בִּכְבֹדִי, *And it* [the *Ohel Moed*] *will become holy with My honor* (*Shemos* 29:43). Rashi continues: אַל תִּקְרֵי בִּכְבֹדִי אֶלָּא בִּמְכֻבָּדַי, *Do not read this, "with My honor" but rather "with those whom I honor."* According to this, this *pasuk* means that the *Ohel Moed* would be sanctified by those whom *HaKadosh Baruch Hu* honors, meaning Nadav and Avihu. And this is "the word of God," which is meant by הוּא אֲשֶׁר דִּבֶּר ה' לֵאמֹר בִּקְרֹבַי אֶקָּדֵשׁ וגו'.

However, the Ramban (ibid.) explains that הוּא אֲשֶׁר דִּבֶּר ה' does not refer, literally, to a specific "word" of Hashem. Rather, it means the "decrees" of Hashem: כִּי דְבַר ה' גְּזֵירוֹתָיו וּמַחְשַׁבְתּוֹ וְעִנְיַן דְּרָכָיו. If a person experiences a difficult occurrence in his life, a גְּזֵירָה מִן הַשָּׁמַיִם, this decree is a "word of Hashem"; Hashem is speaking to him, and it means something. He has to become a different person afterwards. Here Moshe is telling Aharon that the enormous tragedy that befell him was a message to him from *HaKadosh Baruch Hu,* and that this message should especially be heeded by him because of בִּקְרֹבַי אֶקָּדֵשׁ, his closeness to *HaKadosh Baruch Hu.*

Any person who goes through tragedies and difficult periods in his life — and, unfortunately, most of us have — is experiencing a private conversation with *HaKadosh Baruch Hu*: a wake-up call from *HaKadosh Baruch Hu* to him to examine his life.

This, then, is the meaning of our *tefillah*: Happy and fortunate is the person who takes to heart not only God's Torah, but also His "word," the message, which *HaKadosh Baruch Hu* sends him, and he not only hears it, but he improves his life accordingly.

And now, a statement of another truth, אֱמֶת, is introduced.

אֱמֶת אַתָּה הוּא אָדוֹן לְעַמֶּךָ וּמֶלֶךְ גִּבּוֹר לָרִיב רִיבָם — True — You are the Master for Your people and a mighty King to take up their grievance. In peacetime and under normal circumstances, *HaKadosh Baruch Hu* is the "Master" of His people. As such, He provides for and offers them His special care, *hashgachah,* although He may not make His Presence in our affairs known, and we may not even be aware of His protection. Nevertheless, He is always there, He never sleeps: הִנֵּה לֹא יָנוּם וְלֹא יִישָׁן שׁוֹמֵר יִשְׂרָאֵל, *Behold, the Guardian of Israel neither slumbers nor sleep* (*Tehillim* 121:4).

However, under abnormal circumstances, when there were wars and disputes, *HaKadosh Baruch Hu* acted, and will act again, as our "powerful King" Who wages our wars. Then His Presence becomes known, as, for example, at the time of Chanukah.

[Ed. note: This particular *shiur* was given on the Sunday before Chanukah, 1993.]

The "statement of truth" is an introduction to the focus of this *tefillah*, that of the remembrance of *yetzias Mitzrayim*, in fulfillment of the *mitzvas asei d'Oraisa* of לְמַעַן תִּזְכֹּר אֶת יוֹם צֵאתְךָ מֵאֶרֶץ מִצְרַיִם כֹּל יְמֵי חַיֶּיךָ, *So that you will remember the day of your exodus from Mitzrayim all the days of your life* (*Devarim* 16:3). As we have explained previously, our *Chachamim* have directed us to fulfill this *mitzvah* by saying פָּרָשַׁת צִיצִית and אֱמֶת וְיַצִּיב.

◆§ אֱמֶת אַתָּה הוּא רִאשׁוֹן וְאַתָּה הוּא אַחֲרוֹן §◆ — **True — You are the First and You are the Last.** This second "statement of truth" is a declaration that *HaKadosh Baruch Hu* is the One Who has waged our battles (referring back to לָרִיב רִיבָם), from the very first one at *yetzias Mitzrayim* until the *geulah acharonah* at the time of *bi'as HaMashiach*.

◆§ וּמִבַּלְעָדֶיךָ אֵין לָנוּ מֶלֶךְ גּוֹאֵל וּמוֹשִׁיעַ §◆ — **And other than You we have no king, redeemer, or savior.** And in between, meaning during all of Jewish history, all the other redemptions were and are also only entirely the result of the personal intervention of *HaKadosh Baruch Hu* on our behalf. Although throughout the long periods of *hester panim* in Jewish history it may have seemed as if *HaKadosh Baruch Hu* was only indirectly involved in our delivery from evil forces, however, in reality, מִבַּלְעָדֶיךָ אֵין לָנוּ מֶלֶךְ גּוֹאֵל וּמוֹשִׁיעַ, it was also only *HaKadosh Baruch Hu* Himself Who fought our wars and saved us from destruction, and no one else.

The word גּוֹאֵל means a complete redemption, while מוֹשִׁיעַ is only a partial salvation, the relief of the immediate problem at hand, but not a complete resolution of the overriding problem. An example of this is Purim, on which we do not say *Hallel*, because it was not a *geulah*. Despite the fact that the immediate danger had been averted, the Jewish nation still remained subjects of the Persian Empire, אֲכַתִּי עַבְדֵי אֲחַשְׁוֵרוֹשׁ אֲנָן (*Megillah* 14a). It was therefore only a *yeshuah*, a partial salvation.

However, the *neis* Chanukah was a *geulah*, in which the Jewish people were redeemed and freed from the rule of any outside government. Rambam (*Hil. Chanukah* Ch. 3) states that after the *neis* Chanukah, the Jewish kingdom was reestablished, and it lasted for over two hundred years. By the way, this does not mean that Rambam is very happy with all that transpired during those two hundred years. After the first generation of the Chashmonaim, their kingdom deteriorated and was eventually destroyed. This later period also gave rise to the movement of the *Tzedukim*. (See *Bava Basra* 3b; *Ramban, Bereishis* 49:10, regarding the reason the Chashmonaim were punished with the loss of their dynasty.)

Notwithstanding this, the *neis* Chanukah, with its *geulah*, had created an opportunity for two hundred years for the Jewish people to reestablish themselves as the nation that would deserve the *geulah sheleimah* at the end. Unfortunately, this opportunity was missed.

All of this is an introduction to the next piece: the commemoration of *yetzias Mitzrayim*.

ממצרים גאלתנו ה׳ אלהינו — You, Hashem, our God, have redeemed us from Egypt. This statement is in accordance with the requirement that each person is to imagine that *he personally experienced yetzias Mitzrayim*: חַיָּב אָדָם לִרְאוֹת אֶת עַצְמוֹ כְּאִילוּ הוּא יָצָא מִמִּצְרַיִם (*Pesachim* 116b).

[Ed. Note: It is noteworthy that the Rav understands this requirement as being applicable every day — and not only on *Seder* night, as is usually assumed.]

ומבית עבדים פדיתנו — And from the house of slavery You liberated us. This is an additional statement. The *Mechilta* tells us that the borders of Egypt were so tightly guarded that, prior to the exodus of the Jewish people from Egypt, no slave had ever escaped from there (see *Rashi* in *Shemos* 18:9). It is for this reason that the land of *Mitzrayim* was called בֵּית עֲבָדִים.

The word פדיתנו describes an additional aspect of *yetzias Mitzrayim*. פִּדְיוֹן always means *an exchange,* as, for instance, פִּדְיוֹן שְׁבוּיִים [*pidyon shevuyim*], redemption of captives. When one ransoms a captive, the money is an exchange for his freedom. *Pidyon haben* and *pidyon maaser* are exchanges of one thing for another. Similarly, when *HaKadosh Baruch Hu* redeemed us from Mitzrayim, He exchanged us, His *bechor,* for the *bechorei Mitzrayim*:

כל בכוריהם הרגת, ובכורך גאלת — All their firstborn You slew, but Your firstborn You redeemed. On his first mission to Pharaoh, *HaKadosh Baruch Hu* told Moshe to declare that the Jewish people were the *bechor* of *HaKadosh Baruch Hu*: כֹּה אָמַר ה׳ בְּנִי בְכֹרִי יִשְׂרָאֵל. And this declaration continued: וָאֹמַר אֵלֶיךָ שַׁלַּח אֶת בְּנִי וְיַעַבְדֵנִי וַתְּמָאֵן לְשַׁלְּחוֹ הִנֵּה אָנֹכִי הֹרֵג אֶת בִּנְךָ בְּכֹרֶךָ, *So I say to you, Release My son so that he may serve Me and if you refuse to release My firstborn, I shall kill your firstborn* (*Shemos* 4:22-23).

In Egypt, all firstborn sons were sanctified to be ministrants to the various gods that the Egyptians worshiped. At *makkas bechoros, HaKadosh Baruch Hu* "exchanged" these firstborn Egyptians for His own nation of "firstborn," *Am Yisrael,* whose mission in life would be to promulgate the worship of The One and Only God. The *mitzvah* of קַדֶּשׁ לִי כָל בְּכוֹר פֶּטֶר כָּל רֶחֶם בִּבְנֵי יִשְׂרָאֵל בָּאָדָם וּבַבְּהֵמָה לִי הוּא, *Sanctify to Me every firstborn, the first issue of every womb among the Children of Israel of man and beast, is Mine* (*Shemos* 13:2), in which the firstborn Jewish son and firstborn male animal have special requirements, is a symbolic expression of the status of the entire nation, that of בְּנִי בְכֹרִי יִשְׂרָאֵל, *My firstborn son, Yisrael.*

Rav Samson R. Hirsch explains that the role of a firstborn son is that of a leader: He is to set the example for the other children to follow. Similarly, the Jewish nation is called בְּנִי בְכֹרִי יִשְׂרָאֵל because they were the first people to recognize the existence of *HaKadosh Baruch Hu*. Eventually, *b'acharis hayamim*, all of humanity will follow their lead and recognize and worship The One and Only God, *HaKadosh Baruch Hu*. The eventual recognition and acceptance of *HaKadosh Baruch Hu* by the nations of the world is mentioned in the *pasuk* וְנִלְווּ גוֹיִם רַבִּים אֶל ה' בַּיּוֹם הַהוּא וְהָיוּ לִי לְעָם, *Many nations will join themselves to Hashem on that day, and they will become a people unto Me* (Zechariah 2:15). This is also the focus of the *tefillah* of עַל כֵּן נְקַוֶּה לְךָ ה' אֱלֹהֵינוּ וְגוֹ' in which we pray: יַכִּירוּ וְיֵדְעוּ כָּל יוֹשְׁבֵי תֵבֵל וְגוֹ'.

[Ed. note: See *Maayan Beis HaSho'evah, Bo* 12:12, for an in-depth explanation of the meaning of *bechorah* in general, and the special significance of *makkas bechoros*.]

⋦ וְיַם סוּף בָּקַעְתָּ — **And You split the *Yam Suf*.** Without *krias Yam Suf*, the full effect of *yetzias Mitzrayim* on *Bnei Yisrael* would have been canceled. The purpose of *krias Yam Suf* was to dispel the notion that the Egyptian people were being helpful in the release of *Bnei Yisrael* from their country. After all, did they not show themselves as being courteous and helpful to the Jewish people at the last moments of their stay in their country? Did they not give *Bnei Yisrael* presents of gold and silver and other valuables? Had they not held the Jewish leader, Moshe, in the highest esteem: גַּם הָאִישׁ מֹשֶׁה גָּדוֹל מְאֹד בְּאֶרֶץ מִצְרַיִם בְּעֵינֵי עַבְדֵי פַרְעֹה וּבְעֵינֵי הָעָם, *Moreover, the man Moshe was very great in the land of Egypt, in the eyes of the servants of Pharaoh and in the eyes of the people* (Shemos 11:3). And Pharaoh even sent along an escort to make sure *Bnei Yisrael* would be going in the right direction. (See *Mechilta* and *Midrash Tanchuma*, beginning of *Parashas Beshalach*.)

It was therefore necessary to cancel this misconception by having the Egyptians show themselves for what they really were: the deadly enemies of *Bnei Yisrael*, who were now pursuing them with the intention of completely annihilating them. And this final confrontation resulted in the total destruction of the pursuing Egyptian forces through the miracle of *krias Yam Suf*.

And this, the last of the miraculous events surrounding *yetzias Mitzrayim*, impressed upon the Jewish mind, once and for all, that *yetzias Mitzrayim* had been accomplished against the will of the Egyptians, by the personal intervention of *HaKadosh Baruch Hu*.

⋦ וְזֵדִים טִבַּעְתָּ, וִידִידִים הֶעֱבַרְתָּ — **You drowned the wicked ones, and You led Your beloved ones across.** Actually, the order should have been the opposite: First *Your beloved ones* were brought across and then, *You drowned the wicked ones*. Besides, the drowning of the enemies is repeated in the next phrase: וַיְכַסּוּ מַיִם צָרֵיהֶם.

This phrase, however, describes a separate *neis* within the *neis* of *krias Yam Suf*. When the pursuing Egyptians saw that the sea had split, and a completely dry path had opened before *Bnei Yisrael*, the Egyptians followed them into this dry path, into the middle of the sea. Even if the Egyptians rationalized this phenomenon away as a combination of high winds and low tide, were they not afraid that the wind and tide could shift at any moment, and the sea would swallow them up?

However, *Chazal* tell us that at this stage the Egyptian officers were no longer in control of the army, because their horses pulled their chariots forward against their drivers' will into the dry land within the parted sea, and the rest of the army obediently followed (see *Mechilta Beshalach* 15:1).

This miraculous event is incorporated into the *piyutim* of *Shevii shel Pesach* (אוֹמֶץ גְּבוּרוֹתֶיךָ), and is also meant by: לְסֻסָתִי בְּרִכְבֵי פַרְעֹה דִּמִּיתִיךְ רַעְיָתִי (*Shir HaShirim* 1:9). (See *Shir HaShirim Rabbah* 1:9:4.) Here *HaKadosh Baruch Hu* is saying, "*I have compared you, My friend, [Israel] to My horse leading the chariots of Pharaoh. Just as those horses followed My command, and pulled Pharaoh and his army into the sea, so do I follow your requests, My friend, Israel, when you pray to Me.*" This is expressed in the *pasuk*: רְצוֹן יְרֵאָיו יַעֲשֶׂה וְאֶת שַׁוְעָתָם יִשְׁמַע וְיוֹשִׁיעֵם, *He does the will of those who revere Him and He hears their cry and saves them* (*Tehillim* 145:19); and by our *Chachamim*: צַדִּיק גּוֹזֵר וְהַקָּבָּ"ה מְקַיֵּם, *the tzaddik decrees it, and HaKadosh Baruch Hu fulfills it* (see *Moed Katan* 16b).

And at the same time that *Bnei Yisrael* were walking through the *Yam Suf* on dry land, their oppressors behind them were already being covered by the returning waters of the sea. While the Egyptians were drowning on one side of the *Yam Suf*, *Bnei Yisrael* were still walking on dry land on the other side.

Therefore, the sense of וְיַם סוּף בָּקַעְתָּ וְזֵדִים טִבַּעְתָּ וִידִידִים הֶעֱבַרְתָּ is *After You split the Yam Suf, You drowned the wicked ones, who were miraculously being pulled forward by their horses, while You led Your beloved ones through.*

The reason *Bnei Yisrael* were called יְדִידִים, *beloved,* is because they had full *bitachon* in *HaKadosh Baruch Hu* and followed His directive, which was given through Moshe Rabbeinu: דַּבֵּר אֶל בְּנֵי יִשְׂרָאֵל וְיִסָּעוּ, *Speak to Bnei Yisrael and let them journey forth* (*Shemos* 14:15), and proceeded directly into the sea. First Nachshon ben Aminadav showed the way, and he was followed by the tribe of Binyamin, who, in turn, were followed by all the rest of *Bnei Yisrael*. Only after they had demonstrated their complete *bitachon,* and were already in the water, did the great miracle occur, and the *Yam Suf* split.

§ וַיְכַסּוּ מַיִם צָרֵיהֶם אֶחָד מֵהֶם לֹא נוֹתָר — **And the water covered their foes — not one of them was left.** This phrase is a quotation from *Tehillim* 106:11. However, there is a statement in *Yalkut Shimoni* (*Beshalach*, Ch. 14, 239) that Pharaoh survived *krias Yam Suf;* he was not pulled forward by his horses. This was in accordance with the previous pronouncement of Moshe Rabbeinu, in the Name of *HaKadosh Baruch Hu,* that he, Pharaoh, would be spared so that he would publicize the great *nissim* connected with *yetzias*

וְאוּלָם בַּעֲבוּר זֹאת הֶעֱמַדְתִּיךָ בַּעֲבוּר הַרְאֹתְךָ אֶת כֹּחִי וּלְמַעַן סַפֵּר שְׁמִי בְּכָל־ *Mitzrayim*: הָאָרֶץ, *However, for this have I let you endure, in order to show you My strength and so that My Name may be declared throughout the world* (Shemos 9:16).

Therefore, in accordance with this Midrash, the meaning of this *pasuk* is: *The waters covered their pursuing enemies; not one of them survived.* Since Pharaoh, at the last moment, was protected by *HaKadosh Baruch Hu* — although he did not deserve it, for the aforementioned reason — he was therefore not among the pursuing enemies. He was not one of *them,* of which none survived.

“עַל זֹאת שִׁבְּחוּ אֲהוּבִים וְרוֹמְמוּ אֵל” — **By reason of this occurrence, the beloved ones praised You and they exalted You as the Almighty.** This mention of *exalting* or *praising HaKadosh Baruch Hu* is a reference to the *Shiras HaYam* in which *Bnei Yisrael* said אֱלֹהֵי אָבִי וַאֲרֹמְמֶנְהוּ, *He is the God of my forefathers, and I shall raise Him up even higher.* In the *Shirah,* they reached a higher level of praising *HaKadosh Baruch Hu* than they had ever reached before.

“וְנָתְנוּ יְדִידִים זְמִרוֹת שִׁירוֹת וְתִשְׁבָּחוֹת, בְּרָכוֹת וְהוֹדָאוֹת, לְמֶלֶךְ אֵל חַי וְקַיָּם” — **The dear ones offered hymns, songs, praises, blessings, and thanksgiving to the King, the living and enduring God.** Therefore, following the example of the אֲהוּבִים, who praised *HaKadosh Baruch Hu* with the *Shiras HaYam,* "the dear ones," meaning our *Chachamim,* have instituted songs, poetry and praises, blessings, and expressions of gratitude to the King, the Living God.

In the famous *siddur* of R' Pinchus ben R' Yehudah MiPalatchik, which has the approval of the Vilna Gaon, there is the explanation that this sentence, with its various expressions of praises to *HaKadosh Baruch Hu,* is a summary of the entire *tefillah*:

❏ זְמִירוֹת is an obvious reference to *Pesukei d'Zimrah;*

❏ שִׁירוֹת refers to אָז יָשִׁיר;

❏ וְתִשְׁבָּחוֹת refers to יִשְׁתַּבַּח;

❏ בְּרָכוֹת refers to *bircas yotzer;*

❏ וְהוֹדָאוֹת refers to אַהֲבָה רַבָּה, in which we recognize the abundant love that *HaKadosh Baruch Hu* has shown, and continues to show, toward us, and we praise Him for it (the concluding phrase of אַהֲבָה רַבָּה contains the words לְהוֹדוֹת לְךָ);

❏ לְמֶלֶךְ אֵל חַי וְקַיָּם refers to *Krias Shema* with its *kabbalas ol Malchus Shamayim,* and to *Shemoneh Esrei* with its חַי (18) *berachos.*

The entire *tefillah* of עֶזְרַת אֲבוֹתֵינוּ, up to this point, has been an introduction to the *Bircas HaGeulah,* which now begins with the following ten attributes of *HaKadosh Baruch Hu* which *Bnei Yisrael* recognized at *krias Yam Suf.* These correspond to the ten *nissim* that were done for our forefathers by *HaKadosh Baruch Hu* in connection with *krias Yam Suf* (*Pirkei Avos* 5:5).

‎עש רָם — **High,** so high that none of His creatures, even the *malachim,* can comprehend Him;

‎עש וְנִשָּׂא — **Exalted,** meaning "carried" by the *malachim* who are the *merkavah* of the *Shechinah,* the "Chariots" of God's Presence (a highly esoteric concept);

‎עש גָּדוֹל — **Great,** which is always a reference to His *middas harachamim,* His lovingkindness, as in גְּדָל חָסֶד;

‎עש וְנוֹרָא — **Awesome,** referring to *middas hadin;*

‎עש מַשְׁפִּיל גֵּאִים — **He lowers the arrogant,** a reference to the *middas hadin* which HaKadosh Baruch Hu applied to the Egyptians;

‎עש וּמַגְבִּיהַּ שְׁפָלִים — **He raises the lowly,** a reference to the *middas harachamim* which He showed *Bnei Yisrael.*

‎עש מוֹצִיא אֲסִירִים, וּפוֹדֶה עֲנָוִים, וְעוֹזֵר דַּלִּים — **He takes out those who are imprisoned; and He redeems the humiliated ones; and He helps the helpless.**

Here the word עוֹזֵר (the masculine form) is used, as opposed to עֶזְרַת (see above), because דַּל always means one who has no means to help himself, and therefore a full ("masculine") measure of help is required to save him. This refers to all people, but as to *Bnei Yisrael*:

‎עש וְעוֹנֶה לְעַמּוֹ בְּעֵת שַׁוְעָם אֵלָיו — **He answers His people when they call Him for help.** The word שַׁוְעָם, from which we get the word יְשׁוּעָה, is used in the sense of "calling for help."

There is a statement in the *Zohar HaKadosh* (*Bamidbar, Balak:* 195) that when a person prepares himself for *Shemoneh Esrei,* he should imagine himself as poor and helpless. In this connection I would like to repeat the following thought which I heard from my revered Rebbe, Harav Yerucham Levovitz, the Mirrer *Mashgiach.*

The Torah tells us that just prior to *Kriyas Yam Suf:* וַיִּירְאוּ מְאֹד וַיִּצְעֲקוּ בְנֵי יִשְׂרָאֵל אֶל ה', *Bnei Yisrael* were gripped with terror and they cried out to Hashem (*Shemos* 14:10). Rashi (ibid.), quoting from the *Mechilta,* comments on this: תָּפְשׂוּ אוּמָּנוּת אֲבוֹתָם, by engaging in *tefillah,* "they emulated the art of their forefathers." They utilized the ancient Jewish "art form" of *tefillah* which they had inherited from their Forefathers. This "art" of *tefillah* was practiced by Avraham, who instituted *tefillas* Shacharis, followed by Yitzchak who instituted *tefillas* Minchah, and then by Yaakov who established *tefillas* Maariv.

But this quotation from *Mechilta* begs the question: What connection is there between the ordinary daily devotional *tefillos* of our Forefathers, and the desperate cry of the Jewish people for salvation from the seemingly hopeless situation in which they found themselves at the *Yam Suf*?

My Rebbe explained this as an example of הֲרֵי זֶה בָּא לְלַמֵּד וְנִמְצָא לָמֵד. By comparing the two, the *Chachamim* have shed light on the ordinary daily *tefillos* of our *Avos*. They are describing to us how the *Avos* davened Shacharis, Minchah, and Maariv. The *Avos* stood before *HaKadosh Baruch Hu* during their daily *tefillos* with the awareness that they were totally helpless without Him. Were it not for *chasdei Hashem,* they would not be able to think, see, hear, talk, walk, or even live for another second. No aspect of their lives would be possible. They understood that without the will of *HaKadosh Baruch Hu* and without His *chassadim,* one's daily existence would be as hopeless as the situation in which *Bnei Yisrael* found themselves at the *Yam Suf*.

In times of their greatest despair, *Bnei Yisrael* emulated that which their Forefathers, Avraham, Yitzchak, and Yaakov, did in their ordinary daily *tefillos,* and which they wanted their offspring to follow.

Therefore, as we prepare ourselves for *Shemoneh Esrei,* we stand before *HaKadosh Baruch Hu* and concentrate on our total dependence on Him for our very existence. We realize that without this we are as helpless שְׁפָלִים, as our forefathers were when they were confronted by the Egyptian גֵּאִים, who still considered *Bnei Yisrael* as their slaves, אֲסִירִים; during which confrontation we were עֲנִיִּים and דַּלִּים, helpless and powerless to defend ourselves. It is in this frame of mind that we, too, approach *HaKadosh Baruch Hu* and ask Him to answer our *tefillos* just as He answered our forefathers: וְעוֹנֶה לְעַמּוֹ בְּעֵת שַׁוְּעָם אֵלָיו.

תְּהִלּוֹת לְאֵל עֶלְיוֹן בָּרוּךְ הוּא וּמְבֹרָךְ — Praises to the Supreme God, the blessed One Who is blessed. This phrase introduces a new thought into the *tefillah,* and the *minhag* is to rise at this point, in preparation for *Shemoneh Esrei,* because in this phrase lies the highest part of the *tehillos* which *Bnei Yisrael* expressed in the *shirah*. We now describe *HaKadosh Baruch Hu* as אֵל עֶלְיוֹן, meaning, He is so high as to be incomprehensible to us. *HaKadosh Baruch Hu* does things which we simply do not — and cannot — understand. We do not understand why *HaKadosh Baruch Hu* permitted so many Jewish children to be thrown into the *Yam Suf;* why He allowed the Egyptians to enslave and brutalize entire generations of our forefathers, who lived and died in conditions which the Torah describes as וַיַּעֲבִדוּ מִצְרַיִם אֶת בְּנֵי יִשְׂרָאֵל בְּפָרֶךְ. וַיְמָרְרוּ אֶת חַיֵּיהֶם וגו׳, *Egypt enslaved the Children of Israel with crushing harshness. They embittered their lives* . . . (*Shemos* 1:13-14); and certainly not why He allowed six million Jews to die in the Holocaust.

Nevertheless, what *Bnei Yisrael* meant by this in the *Shirah* is that we praise *HaKadosh Baruch Hu,* Who is אֵל עֶלְיוֹן, "above our understanding," even for the things which we do not understand; we accept these as absolutely right and only good. This will be explained further when we discuss מִי כָמֹכָה בָּאֵלִם ה׳.

The proper phrasing here is תְּהִלּוֹת לְאֵל עֶלְיוֹן בָּרוּךְ הוּא, *Praises to God Who*

EZRAS AVOSEINU 395

is high beyond our comprehension, the blessed One (already having been blessed), וּמְבֹרָךְ, And He will continue to be blessed by us.

[Ed. note: The Rav discusses בָּרוּךְ וּמְבֹרָךְ in his comments on Kaddish and Barchu. The basic concept of "blessing" HaKadosh Baruch Hu, and of berachos in general, are dealt with in the section on בִּרְכַּת עַל נְטִילַת יָדַיִם. Please refer to these sections.]

מֹשֶׁה וּבְנֵי יִשְׂרָאֵל לְךָ עָנוּ שִׁירָה — **Moshe and the Children of Israel exclaimed a song to You.** We have previously explained that the communal saying of the *Shirah* by *Bnei Yisrael* together with Moshe was a miraculous event in itself. Short of a *neis,* how would it have been possible, before the advent of loudspeakers, for the voice of Moshe Rabbeinu — who was a *kevad peh* — to be amplified so loudly that six hundred thousand people and their children could hear him well enough to affirmatively respond by, at least (see *Sotah* 30b), repeating the first words of each sentence?

This miracle is even greater according to the opinion of Rabbi Eliezer the son of Rabbi Yosi HaGelili (ibid.), who says that *Bnei Yisrael* repeated every word of the *Shirah* after Moshe.

And it was clearly a *neis* according to the opinion of Rabbi Nechemiah, as explained by Rashi (ibid.), that: שָׁרְתָה רוּחַ הַקֹּדֶשׁ עַל כֻּלָּם וְכִוְּנוּ יַחַד אֶת הַשִּׁירָה כִּכְתָבָהּ; Moshe and the Jewish people were the beneficiaries of *ruach hakodesh* which enabled them, although unrehearsed, to say the same words of the *Shiras HaYam* together.

The *Alshich HaKadosh (Beshalach* 15:1) sees a reference to this miracle in the words of the Torah: וַיַּאֲמִינוּ בַּה׳ וּבְמֹשֶׁה עַבְדּוֹ, *And they had faith in Hashem and in Moshe, His servant (Shemos* 14:31), which is followed immediately by אָז יָשִׁיר מֹשֶׁה וּבְנֵי יִשְׂרָאֵל, *Then Moshe and the Children of Israel chose to sing this song (Shemos* 15:1). He explains this to mean that as a result of the *emunah* of *Bnei Yisrael,* they were blessed with *ruach hakodesh* which enabled them to simultaneously say the words of the *Shirah* together with Moshe Rabbeinu.

בְּשִׂמְחָה רַבָּה, וְאָמְרוּ כֻלָּם — **With great joy, and they all said.** Moshe and *Bnei Yisrael,* all of them together, with great joy said the following *pasuk,* which was previously referred to as תְּהִלּוֹת לְאֵל עֶלְיוֹן:

מִי כָמֹכָה בָּאֵלִם ה׳ — **Who is like You among the heavenly powers, Hashem!** This is one of the two *pesukim* of the *Shirah* which the *mesadrei hatefillah* have quoted in בִּרְכַּת גָּאַל יִשְׂרָאֵל in *tefillas* Shacharis and Maariv, apparently as a summary of the entire *Shirah.* The other one is ה׳ יִמְלֹךְ לְעֹלָם וָעֶד.

This *pasuk,* מִי כָמֹכָה וגו׳, was singled out because it incorporates the concept of giving praise to *HaKadosh Baruch Hu* for the *galus* as well as the *geulah.* We refer back to our comments on אָז יָשִׁיר, where we quoted the

(*Gittin* 56b). דְּבֵי ר' יִשְׁמָעֵאל תָּנָא: מִי כָמֹכָה בָּאֵלִם ה': מִי כָמֹכָה בָּאִלְּמִים. This Gemara: is further explained in the *Mechilta:* מִי כָמֹכָה בָּאִלְּמִים, שׁוֹמֵעַ עֶלְבּוֹן בָּנָיו וְשׁוֹתֵק.

The *Chazal* see in the word אֵלִם, which is spelled without a י in this *pasuk,* an allusion to the meaning אִלֵּם, *mute,* and explain it to mean: "Who is like You among the mutes; You hear the suffering of Your children, but You remain silent as if You were mute."

What *Chazal* are conveying with this *derush* is the following: The word אֵלִם means the powerful forces of nature. (See Rav Samson R. Hirsch on the *Shirah* for this meaning of אֵלִים.) The forces of nature are completely silent to the outcries of tortured human beings. A writer once wrote that on the days when tens of thousands of our brethren were screaming in terror and pain while being brutally and sadistically murdered in Auschwitz, the birds continued their chirping, the flowers still blossomed, and the sun still shone. Nature took no notice of all the indescribable torture and screaming of innocent people. The natural forces of the world remain mute and do not cry out when such outrages are committed.

While *Bnei Yisrael* were suffering under the yoke of their enslavement and torture in Mitzrayim, they could not understand how *HaKadosh Baruch Hu* could remain silent in the face of all of their suffering. They understood that the forces of nature, the אֵלִם, are really אִלֵּם, deaf and mute to all of the world's suffering. But how could *HaKadosh Baruch Hu,* Who heard the cries of the Jewish mothers and fathers while their children were being thrown into the Nile River, also be אִלֵּם, deaf to their pleas, and not respond? This was impossible for them to understand.

However, our *Chazal* see in the unusual spelling of מִי כָמֹכָה בָּאֵלִם ה' a reference to the fact that at the time of *krias Yam Suf,* when their redemption from Egypt was complete, *Bnei Yisrael* had finally reached a level in their *emunah* in which they praised *HaKadosh Baruch Hu* even for the *tzaar* of the *galus,* while they gave thanks to Him for their *geulah. Bnei Yisrael* accepted the silence of *HaKadosh Baruch Hu* in the face of their suffering as a manifestation of His will — and praised Him for it — as surely as they thanked and praised Him for their redemption.

◆§ מִי כָמֹכָה נֶאְדָּר בַּקֹּדֶשׁ §◆ — **Who is as powerful in holiness as You.** *Kedushah* is something which is separated (see *Rashi, Vayikra* 19:2). "There is nothing as powerful and far removed from our understanding as You are." We simply cannot have any answers to the questions of מִי כָמֹכָה "בָּאֵלִם" ה'. Nevertheless, through this *Shirah,* the Jewish people expressed not only their joy at their redemption, בְּשִׂמְחָה רַבָּה, but they also accepted *b'simchah* the judgment of *HaKadosh Baruch Hu* for their suffering. This thought continues:

◆§ נוֹרָא תְהִלֹּת עֹשֵׂה פֶלֶא §◆ — **It is awesome to praise *HaKadosh Baruch Hu* when He performs wondrous deeds.** We tend to offer praises only for the good things, but actually we are required to do so for both the good and the bad: חַיָּב אָדָם לְבָרֵךְ עַל הָרָעָה כְּשֵׁם שֶׁמְּבָרֵךְ עַל הַטּוֹבָה, שֶׁנֶּאֱמַר וְאָהַבְתָּ אֵת ה' אֱלֹהֶיךָ בְּכָל לְבָבְךָ וּבְכָל נַפְשְׁךָ וּבְכָל מְאֹדֶךָ – בְּכָל מִדָּה וּמִדָּה שֶׁהוּא מוֹדֵד לְךָ הֱוֵי מוֹדֶה לוֹ (Berachos 54a). While we can appreciate and offer praise to *HaKadosh Baruch Hu* for the *nissim* which result in our redemption, we tend not to understand the lack of those *nissim* when we cry out for help, and are apparently not answered, which is also פֶּלֶא, *wondrous*. נוֹרָא תְהִלֹּת means, therefore, that it is with trepidation that we offer praises to *HaKadosh Baruch Hu* for the good things that happen to us, because while doing so we may lose sight of our obligation to praise *HaKadosh Baruch Hu* even for that which we cannot understand. However, with מִי כָמֹכָה, *Bnei Yisrael* finally expressed their full and joyful acceptance of the *galus,* and praised *HaKadosh Baruch Hu* for it, while at the same time they celebrated their *geulah:* בְּשִׂמְחָה רַבָּה וְאָמְרוּ כֻלָּם מִי כָמֹכָה בָּאֵלִם ה' וגו'.

שִׁירָה חֲדָשָׁה שִׁבְּחוּ גְאוּלִים לְשִׁמְךָ עַל שְׂפַת הַיָּם — **With a new song, the redeemed ones praised Your Name at the seashore.** This "new song," that of praising Hashem for the bad as well as the good, resulted from their heightened awareness of the sovereignty of God's rule of the world. After *Bnei Yisrael* crossed the sea, having been miraculously redeemed, and were standing safely at its outer banks, they achieved a heightened awareness of the concept of *Malchus Shamayim,* and therefore ended their song of praise by declaring the Name of *HaKadosh Baruch Hu* as their *Melech.*

יַחַד כֻּלָּם הוֹדוּ וְהִמְלִיכוּ וְאָמְרוּ: ה' יִמְלֹךְ לְעֹלָם וָעֶד — **All of them in unison gave thanks, acknowledged [Your] sovereignty and said: "Hashem will reign for all eternity."** At that moment, Moshe and *Bnei Yisrael,* all together, acknowledged that *HaKadosh Baruch Hu* is their *Melech* by saying, "God will reign forever." We have already quoted the explanation of Rav Samson R. Hirsch that עֹלָם means "the hidden future," and וָעֶד, "the certain future." ה' יִמְלֹךְ לְעֹלָם וָעֶד, therefore, means that nobody knows how or when, but it is certain that eventually the sovereignty of *HaKadosh Baruch Hu* will be recognized by the entire world.

This sublime moment is described in Maariv with these words: מַלְכוּתְךָ רָאוּ בָנֶיךָ בּוֹקֵעַ יָם לִפְנֵי מֹשֶׁה זֶה אֵלִי עָנוּ וְאָמְרוּ: ה' יִמְלֹךְ לְעֹלָם וָעֶד, *When Your children saw Your sovereignty as You split the sea in front of Moshe, they exclaimed, "This is my God," He will rule forever.* At that miraculous moment they could "point" to *HaKadosh Baruch Hu,* as clearly as *Neviim* (see *Mechilta Shemos* 15:18), and say, *This is my God.* At that moment, they saw clearly that it was *HaKadosh Baruch Hu,* as their All-Powerful Ruler, *Melech,* Who caused the sea to part in front of them; the waters on each side of them to form walls of ice; and the sea to close in and envelop their mortal enemies and pursuers behind them, while they were passing safely through the opening in front of them on dry land.

The culmination of the *Shirah* is ה' יִמְלֹךְ לְעֹלָם וָעֶד, on which the *Mechilta*

ר' יוֹסִי הַגְּלִילִי אוֹמֵר: אֵלּוּ אָמְרוּ יִשְׂרָאֵל עַל הַיָּם ה' מֶלֶךְ לְעוֹלָם וָעֶד לֹא (.ibid) comments: הָיָה אוּמָה וְלָשׁוֹן שׁוֹלֶטֶת בָּהֶם לְעוֹלָם, אֶלָּא אָמְרוּ ה' יִמְלֹךְ לְעוֹלָם וָעֶד — לֶעָתִיד לָבֹא. Had Bnei Yisrael said ה' מֶלֶךְ לְעוֹלָם וָעֶד, Hashem is the King forever, this moment would have been the beginning of yemos haMashiach. [Please refer to the Rav's comments on the words in the Shirah.]

Since the two pesukim, מִי כָמֹכָה וגו' and ה' יִמְלֹךְ לְעוֹלָם וָעֶד, are the high points of the Shirah, the minhag is for the entire kahal to say them together, as our forefathers did, יַחַד כֻּלָּם הוֹדוּ וְהִמְלִיכוּ וְאָמְרוּ.

◆ צוּר יִשְׂרָאֵל, קוּמָה בְּעֶזְרַת יִשְׂרָאֵל — **Rock of Israel, arise to the salvation of Israel.** This final portion of this tefillah is a plea to HaKadosh Baruch Hu that He may repeat for us that which He did for our forefathers at the time of yetzias Mitzrayim, namely, to bring about our geulah.

In asking HaKadosh Baruch Hu to bring about our geulah, we address Him as צוּר יִשְׂרָאֵל, which is based on ה' צוּרִי וְגֹאֲלִי, Hashem, my Rock and my Redeemer (Tehillim 19:15).

❏ קוּמָה בְּעֶזְרַת יִשְׂרָאֵל — *Arise in the salvation of Israel.* The word עֶזְרַת, as we have already explained, connotes salvation in which the subject participates in the salvation. The Jewish people participate in their geulah by their steadfast bitachon that HaKadosh Baruch Hu will bring it about soon. We have nothing else to offer HaKadosh Baruch Hu but our bitachon, and this entitles us to be mispallel for the geulah. The Jewish people throughout the millennia have maintained their unshakable bitachon in HaKadosh Baruch Hu in the face of all their trials and suffering in the galus, and have never given up hope that HaKadosh Baruch Hu will bring the geulah soon through bi'as Mashiach.

◆ וּפְדֵה כִנְאֻמֶךָ יְהוּדָה וְיִשְׂרָאֵל — **Redeem Yehudah and Yisrael in accordance with Your spoken word.** The phrase נְאֻם ה' is used frequently in the addresses of HaKadosh Baruch Hu to the Neviim. פְּדֵה, meaning redemption, is used here again in the sense of an exchange: the destruction of the reshaim in order to save the tzaddikim. The name Yehudah probably refers to the special tzaddikim, and Yisrael to the ordinary אַחֵינוּ כָּל בֵּית יִשְׂרָאֵל.

◆ גֹּאֲלֵנוּ ה' צְבָאוֹת שְׁמוֹ, קְדוֹשׁ יִשְׂרָאֵל — **Our Redeemer, Whose Name is God of Hosts, Who is the Holy One of Israel** (Yeshayahu 47:4). This quotation has been added and accepted almost universally, even in Germany, as a part of this tefillah. However, according to minhag Frankfurt, the original tefillah is retained and this pasuk is omitted. This omission is supported by the Rokeach and Maharitz Gei'us.

The Rokeach explains that צוּר יִשְׂרָאֵל contains the name Yisrael four times to correspond to the four expressions of geulah (Shemos 6:6-7). The addition of this pasuk, which also contains the name Yisrael, would have added a fifth, and thus interfered with this symbolism. Furthermore, says the Rokeach, without this *pasuk,* this *tefillah* contains fourteen words and sixty letters, which corresponds to the שִׁשִּׁים רִבּוֹא, *six hundred thousand,* who were redeemed on the fourteenth of Nissan.

However, in all other *kehillos* this *pasuk* is said, based on the *kabbalah* of the *Arizal.* In the *geulah* of Maariv we also quote a *pasuk*: כִּי פָדָה ה' אֶת יַעֲקֹב וּגְאָלוֹ מִיַּד חָזָק מִמֶּנּוּ, *For Hashem will have redeemed Yaakov and delivered him from a hand mightier than he* (*Yirmiyahu* 31:10), which has been accepted by everyone.

§ בָּרוּךְ אַתָּה ה', גָּאַל יִשְׂרָאֵל — **Blessed are You Hashem, Who has redeemed Israel.** With this *berachah* we conclude the *geulah.* גָּאַל in the past tense refers to the Jewish national experience of *geulas Mitzrayim.* We exist as a nation only because of the seminal event of *yetzias Mitzrayim.* Without it, we would have been completely assimilated into the Egyptian nation and we would have eventually disappeared together with it from the world scene. However, the *berachah* רְאֵה בְעָנְיֵנוּ, in *Shemoneh Esrei,* which ends with גּוֹאֵל יִשְׂרָאֵל, is a prayer for present and future redemptions from our *tzaros* (see *Pesachim* 117b, also *Rashi* to *Megillah* 17b, s.v. אתחלתא דגאולה).

The *halachah* of *semichus geulah l'tefillah* requires that we now, immediately, without any interruption, begin *Shemoneh Esrei* (see *Berachos* 9b and *Shulchan Aruch Orach Chaim* 111). This even precludes the saying of *amen* between גָּאַל יִשְׂרָאֵל and the beginning of *Shemoneh Esrei.* It is therefore advisable to finish the *berachah* together with the *chazzan,* who says it audibly, but with a lowered voice, as a signal for those who are with him not to answer *amen,* but yet loud enough for the benefit of those who have not yet reached this point in their *tefillah,* who should answer *amen.*

The *halachah* of *semichus geulah l'tefillah* is based on the ending and beginning of two consecutive chapters of *Tehillim,* both having the introduction לַמְנַצֵּחַ מִזְמוֹר לְדָוִד. Psalm 19 ends with ה' צוּרִי וְגֹאֲלִי, *Hashem, my Rock and my Redeemer,* which is followed by יַעַנְךָ ה' בְּיוֹם צָרָה, *May Hashem answer you on the days of distress,* the beginning of Chapter 20. To put oneself into the proper frame of mind before asking *HaKadosh Baruch Hu* to answer his *tefillos,* one must recognize and repeat the truth that it is only *HaKadosh Baruch Hu* — Who has answered our *tefillos* and redeemed us from Mitzrayim — Who has the power to answer our present and future *tefillos.* (See *Yerushalmi Berachos* 1:1-6; and *Rashi, Berachos* 4b s.v. זה הסומך.)

The characterization of *tefillah* as יַעַנְךָ ה' בְּיוֹם צָרָה is especially understandable in view of our earlier explanation that one should consider himself completely helpless, בְּצָרָה, while he is being *mispallel.* Based on this, according to some opinions (see *Rema* או״ח ס' קי״א), on Shabbos and Yom Tov there is no requirement for *semichus geulah l'tefillah,* for it would be inappropriate to call these days יוֹם צָרָה.

הַקְדָּמָה לשמונה עשרה / Hakdamah L'Shemoneh Esrei

סְמִיכוּת גְּאֻלָּה לִתְפִלָּה

We have already called attention to the fact that our *Chachamim* have placed great importance on סְמִיכוּת גְּאֻלָּה לִתְפִלָּה [*semichus geulah l'tefillah*], meaning that the *berachah* of גָּאַל יִשְׂרָאֵל should be immediately followed, without any interruption, by the *Shemoneh Esrei* (see *Talmud Yerushalmi, Berachos* 81:1-6 and *Rashi, Berachos* 4b s.v. זה הסומך).

The Gemara (*Berachos* 4b) states: אֵיזֶהוּ בֶּן הָעוֹלָם הַבָּא? זֶה הַסּוֹמֵךְ גְּאֻלָּה לִתְפִלָּה. I once explained that the meaning of one who is described as a בֶּן הָעוֹלָם הַבָּא [*ben Olam Haba*] is that in addition to the reward for his *mitzvos* in *Olam Haba*, he is a *ben Olam Haba* even in this world, meaning that he receives a taste of his future reward, מֵעֵין עוֹלָם הַבָּא, *mei'ein Olam Haba*, already in this world. This includes one who is *someich geulah l'tefillah*.

The Gemara (ibid. 9b) recounts an occurrence in the life of Rav Beruna, who is described there as אָדָם גָּדוֹל הוּא וְשָׂמֵחַ בְּמִצְוֹת, *a great person because he was happy when he did mitzvos*. The Gemara continues: זִימְנָא חֲדָא סָמַךְ גְּאֻלָּה לִתְפִלָּה וְלֹא פָּסִיק חוּכָא מִפּוּמֵיהּ כּוּלֵיהּ יוֹמָא. *Once, he was someich geulah l'tefillah* and this made him so happy *that the smile did not disappear from his mouth all day*. This is an indication that the *mitzvah* of *semichus geulah l'tefillah* is not easily accomplished, and it is not the mere lip service of beginning *Shemoneh Esrei* immediately after גָּאַל יִשְׂרָאֵל. Rather, it must involve concentrating on the deeper meaning of attaching *geulah* and *tefillah*. And this happened to the great *tzaddik*, Rav Beruna, only once.

Furthermore, we find a statement in the *Talmud Yerushalmi* which also points to the high level of achievement of *semichus geulah l'tefillah*. The Gemara there tell us: אָמַר רַבִּי יוֹסֵי בַּר בּוּן: כָּל שֶׁהוּא תּוֹכֵף גְּאֻלָּה לִתְפִלָּה אֵין הַשָּׂטָן מְקַטְרֵג בְּאוֹתוֹ הַיּוֹם, *Rabbi Yose bar Boon says: If one immediately follows the geulah with tefillah, the Satan will not accuse him all that day* (*Berachos* 1:1). Here, again, we see that the actual accomplishment of *semichus geulah l'tefillah* is no simple task, and it is the exception rather than the norm.

The *Talmud Yerushalmi* there adds: כָּל מִי שֶׁאֵינוֹ תּוֹכֵף גְּאֻלָּה לִתְפִלָּה לְמָה הוּא דּוֹמֶה? לְאוֹהֲבוֹ שֶׁל מֶלֶךְ שֶׁבָּא וְהִרְתִּיק עַל פִּתְחוֹ שֶׁל מֶלֶךְ, יָצָא לֵידַע מַה הוּא מְבַקֵּשׁ וּמְצָאוֹ שֶׁהִפְלִיג, עוֹד הוּא הִפְלִיג, *One who does not immediately follow geulah with tefillah can be compared to a friend of the king who knocks on the king's door,* but by the time the king comes to find out what he wants, he sees that he has already left, so the king also leaves him.

The idea is that once one has made an approach to *HaKadosh Baruch Hu* through *geulah,* and he does not use this opportunity to come closer to Him by immediately following it with *tefillah,* he is, in effect, moving away from *HaKadosh Baruch Hu,* with the result that *HaKadosh Baruch Hu* moves away from him.

To understand the deeper meaning of *semichus geulah l'tefillah,* let us first examine the meaning of the word *geulah,* which is used in the *bircas geulah* in reference to both the *geulah* from Mitzrayim and the future *geulah* through the arrival of *Mashiach,* for which we are *mispallel.*

In the Torah, the word גאל is used to describe a close relative who shows his concern for his relative. For example: וּבָא גֹאֲלוֹ הַקָּרֹב אֵלָיו, *His redeemer who is closest to him shall come (Vayikra 25:25);* אֶחָד מֵאֶחָיו יִגְאָלֶנּוּ, אוֹ דֹדוֹ אוֹ בֶן דֹּדוֹ וגו׳, *One of his brothers shall redeem him; or his uncle or his cousin* (ibid. vs. 48-49); וְאִם אֵין לָאִישׁ גֹּאֵל, *If the man has no redeemer (Bamidbar 5:8).*

Similarly, וְגָאַלְתִּי אֶתְכֶם, *I shall redeem you,* used at *yetzias Mitzrayim,* means that *HaKadosh Baruch Hu* told *Bnei Yisrael* that He has a close personal relationship with us and He will thus act as our "close relative" and redeem us. Through the miraculous events of *yetzias Mitzrayim, HaKadosh Baruch Hu* came as close to us as He will ever come. This close, personal relationship is expressed by the *Baal Haggadah* (the composer/compiler of the *Haggadah*) as: אֲנִי וְלֹא מַלְאָךְ אֲנִי וְלֹא שָׂרָף אֲנִי וְלֹא הַשָּׁלִיחַ אֲנִי הוּא וְלֹא אַחֵר. Paraphrased, this means, "I personally effected your redemption. It occurred not through a *malach* or a *saraf,* but rather through Me personally, and not through the messenger. It was I Who brought this about, and none other."

At the revelation at *Har Sinai, HaKadosh Baruch Hu* "introduces Himself" as: אָנֹכִי ה׳ אֱלֹהֶיךָ אֲשֶׁר הוֹצֵאתִיךָ מֵאֶרֶץ מִצְרַיִם. He does not say אָנֹכִי ה׳ אֱלֹהֶיךָ הַבּוֹרֵא שָׁמַיִם וָאָרֶץ, because that event was far removed from us; we were not there, and it is hard for us to even imagine the concept of creation *yeish mei'ayin* (*ex nihilo*). However, through *geulas Mitzrayim* we had the opportunity to experience the closest possible proximity of *HaKadosh Baruch Hu* to man. *From the viewpoint of HaKadosh Baruch Hu, His closest relationship to Israel is through geulah.*

Correspondingly, from the viewpoint of Israel, the highest form of *avodas Hashem,* that which brings us into the closest possible proximity of *HaKadosh Baruch Hu,* is the *korban.* The word *korban* comes from קרב, meaning to come close. Through the *korban,* an individual — or *Klal Yisrael* as a nation — can come as close to *HaKadosh Baruch Hu* as is humanly possible (see *Ramban, Vayikra* 1:9; also *Maayan Beis HaSho'evah, Bereishis* 1:4).

The highest form of *tefillah,* the essence of which is *Shemoneh Esrei,* is when one offers himself as a *korban* to *HaKadosh Baruch Hu.* The source for this is in the *Midrash Tanchuma (Korach* 12) on the verse: כָּל תִּשָּׂא עָוֹן וְקַח טוֹב, *May You forgive all iniquity and accept good (Hoshea* 14:3). אָמְרוּ יִשְׂרָאֵל: רִבּוֹנוֹ שֶׁל עוֹלָם בִּזְמַן שֶׁבֵּית הַמִּקְדָּשׁ קַיָּים הָיִינוּ מַקְרִיבִין קָרְבָּן וּמִתְכַּפֵּר וְעַכְשָׁיו אֵין בְּיָדֵינוּ אֶלָּא תְּפִלָּה, *Yisrael said: Ribbono Shel Olam, when the Beis HaMikdash existed, we would bring a korban and be forgiven, but now we have only tefillah.* This means that in the absence of *korbanos, tefillah* itself is the *korban.* If, in his *tefillah,* one has the *zechus* to be on the *madreigah* (level) of *kavannah* that when saying בָּרוּךְ אַתָּה ה' אֱלֹהֵינוּ וֵאלֹהֵי אֲבוֹתֵינוּ, he means, "I am offering to You, *HaKadosh Baruch Hu,* my body and soul — I am Your *korban,*" he has then come as close as humanly possible to *HaKadosh Baruch Hu.*

As we have explained in our outline of the "architecture" of the *tefillah,* the *Shemoneh Esrei* corresponds to the *Kodesh HaKadashim.* This is because through *tefillah* — of which *Shemoneh Esrei* is the essence — we bring our *neshamah* from the mundane world symbolically into the *Kodesh HaKadashim,* just as the *Kohen Gadol* on Yom Kippur brought the blood of the *se'ir* (goat) from the *Azarah* through the *Ulam* into the *Heichal,* and then into the *Kodesh HaKadashim.* Correspondingly, before beginning the *Shemoneh Esrei,* we take three steps forward symbolizing that we are leaving the mundane world and entering the world of the *Kodesh HaKadashim* with our *dam* (blood) and our *nefesh* (soul). In this frame of mind, as we begin the *Shemoneh Esrei* with בָּרוּךְ אַתָּה ה', we give ourselves completely up to *HaKadosh Baruch Hu* as a *korban.* And just as a *korban* is bound, we too place our feet together and fold our hands (see *Shulchan Aruch, Orach Chaim* 95), as if to say to *HaKadosh Baruch Hu,* "I am completely tied up, I can't move anymore, I offer myself completely to You as a *korban.*"

And it is this that our *Chachamim* mean when they say that the *malach* Michael offers the *neshamos* of the *tzaddikim* as a *korban* to *HaKadosh Baruch Hu* (see *Chagigah* 12b with *Hagahos HaBach; Ein Yaakov* ibid.; *Tosafos Menachos* 110a, s.v. ומיכאל).

The meaning, then, of *semichus geulah l'tefillah* is the connection between the closest possible relationship of *HaKadosh Baruch Hu* to us — through *geulah* — with our closest possible relationship to Him — through *tefillah* — in which we offer ourselves as a *korban* to *HaKadosh Baruch Hu.*

There is a remarkable statement in the Gemara (*Berachos* 10b) regarding the great *tzaddik* Chizkiyahu HaMelech, the champion of *talmud Torah,* of whom *Chazal* tell us that he impaled a sword into the *beis hamidrash* as a symbol that those who do not learn Torah deserve to be run through with a sword. He was so successful in promulgating *talmud Torah* that, during his reign, a test was conducted throughout Eretz Yisrael which proved that every man, woman and child was thoroughly familiar with the laws of *tumah* and *taharah* (see *Sanhedrin* 94b). This was the man to whom the *Chazal* applied the *pasuk*: וְחֻבַּל עֹל מִפְּנֵי שָׁמֶן, *The yoke was broken because of the oil* (*Yeshayahu* 10:27), meaning the yoke of Sancheriv was broken because of the oil that was burned to illuminate the *battei midrashos*. This was the great *tzaddik* whom *HaKadosh Baruch Hu* even wanted to make the *Melech HaMashiach*, had his generation merited it (see *Sanhedrin* 94a).

And yet we find this great *tzaddik*, who was still a young man, deathly ill, being visited by Yeshayahu HaNavi who tells him, in the Name of *HaKadosh Baruch Hu*, that he should make his last will known to his family, because he was about to die (*Yeshayahu* 38:1). And *Chazal* tell us (ibid.) that the reason he was being punished with death was that he had never married. He opted not to marry because he saw in *ruach hakodesh* that he would have a son, Menasheh, who would be a *rasha* of such magnitude that the *Beis HaMikdash* would eventually be destroyed because of his actions. But Yeshayahu HaNavi rebuked him: בַּהֲדֵי כַּבְשֵׁי דְּרַחֲמָנָא לָמָּה לָךְ, *The secrets of HaKadosh Baruch Hu are not your concern*. Despite your visions of the future, you were obligated to marry and leave the future up to *HaKadosh Baruch Hu*. And since you did not do so, you have forfeited your life: כִּי מֵת אַתָּה וְלֹא תִחְיֶה.

But Chizkiyahu HaMelech refused to accept the death sentence he received from Yeshayahu HaNavi as irrevocable. He turned to the wall and was *mispallel* to *HaKadosh Baruch Hu*: וַיֹּאמֶר אָנָּה ה' זְכָר נָא אֵת אֲשֶׁר הִתְהַלַּכְתִּי לְפָנֶיךָ בֶּאֱמֶת וּבְלֵב שָׁלֵם וְהַטּוֹב בְּעֵינֶיךָ עָשִׂיתִי וַיֵּבְךְּ חִזְקִיָּהוּ בְּכִי גָדוֹל, *He said, "Please, Hashem, remember now that I have always walked before You faithfully and wholeheartedly and I have done what is good in Your eyes." And Chizkiyahu wept an intense weeping* (*Yeshayahu* 38:3).

This tearful *tefillah* was accepted by *HaKadosh Baruch Hu*, and He granted Chizkiyahu HaMelech an additional fifteen years of life (see *Yeshayahu* ibid.). Remarkably, the Gemara (ibid.) tells us that of all the great *mitzvos* done by Chizkiyahu HaMelech, the mitigating factor and overriding *zechus* on which he based his plea — וְהַטּוֹב בְּעֵינֶיךָ עָשִׂיתִי — was that he was *someich geulah l'tefillah*. This *maamar Chazal* begs clarification.

I saw an explanation that הַטּוֹב בְּעֵינֶיךָ עָשִׂיתִי is a reference to לֹא טוֹב הֱיוֹת הָאָדָם לְבַדּוֹ, *It is not good that man be alone* (*Bereishis* 2:18), for which reason *HaKadosh Baruch Hu* created Chavah and the institution of marriage. In attempting to mitigate his not being married, Chizkiyahu HaMelech declared in his *tefillah* that while he did not fulfill the טוֹב of marriage, nevertheless, he fulfilled another form of טוֹב בְּעֵינֶיךָ, through the attachment of *geulah* to *tefillah*. However, my source for this did not explain why the טוֹב of *semichus geulah l'tefillah* is of such great importance that it served in place of the לֹא טוֹב of not being married.

Based on our explanation that through *semichus geulah l'tefillah* we respond to the closeness of *HaKadosh Baruch Hu* to us — as expressed by *geulah* — by offering ourselves as a *korban* to Him, one can understand the rationale of Chizkiyahu HaMelech in which he substituted *semichus geulah l'tefillah* for marrying and having children.

By seizing the moment of the *Birchas HaGeulah*, which he followed by offering himself as a *korban* to *HaKadosh Baruch Hu* through his *tefillah*, Chizkiyahu emulated Yitzchak Avinu at the time of the *Akeidah* — he too, was not yet married, and *HaKadosh Baruch Hu* requested that he become a *korban*. Therefore, Chizkiyahu HaMelech said in his *tefillah*, הַטּוֹב בְּעֵינֶיךָ עָשִׂיתִי, I have fulfilled that which is even greater than marrying and having children: I offered myself as a *korban* to *HaKadosh Baruch Hu* by means of סְמִיכוּת גְאוּלָה לִתְפִלָּה, seizing the moment of remembering God's closeness to us by redeeming us from Mitzrayim, with my readiness to come as close as is humanly possible to *HaKadosh Baruch Hu* by being prepared to offer my life to *HaKadosh Baruch Hu* if that occasion should arise.

Obviously, based on our explanation, the ideal form of *semichus geulah l'tefillah* is very difficult for the average person to achieve. That is why Rav Beruna showed his inner happiness all day when he was successful in doing it properly once, which he had never done before. Nevertheless, it is incumbent upon every individual to make an effort to work toward the goal of achieving the closest possible proximity to *HaKadosh Baruch Hu* by connecting the concepts of *geulah* and *tefillah*, as we have explained.

≈{ The Origin of Shemoneh Esrei }≈

שִׁמְעוֹן הַפָּקוּלִי הִסְדִּיר שְׁמוֹנֶה עֶשְׂרֵה בְּרָכוֹת לִפְנֵי רַבָּן גַּמְלִיאֵל עַל הַסֵּדֶר בְּיַבְנֶה, The *Tanna Shimon HaPakuli* recited the order of the "Eighteen Berachos" before *Rabban Gamliel in Yavneh* (Megillah 17b). This occurred either immediately prior to *Churban Bayis Sheni*, or, most likely, directly afterwards.

The Gemara there continues: מֵאָה וְעֶשְׂרִים זְקֵנִים וּבָהֶם כַּמָּה נְבִיאִים תִּקְנוּ שְׁמוֹנֶה עֶשְׂרֵה בְּרָכוֹת עַל הַסֵּדֶר, *One hundred twenty zekeinim, among whom were a number of Neviim, composed the eighteen berachos and placed them in their order.* This group of one hundred twenty Elders comprised the *Anshei Knesses HaGedolah*, who lived at the beginning of the Second Temple, approximately four hundred twenty years before Rabban Gamliel in Yavneh. The only *Neviim* among the *Anshei Knesses HaGedolah* who are known to us are: Chaggai, Zechariah, and Malachi; according to some opinions Ezra was also a *navi*. However, the version of this Gemara in the Yerushalmi is וּמֵהֶם שְׁמוֹנִים וְכַמָּה נְבִיאִים *among them were some eighty Neviim* (*Yerushalmi, Berachos* 2:34). This means that the vast majority of the *Anshei Knesses HaGedolah*, who composed and arranged the *Shemoneh Esrei*, were *Neviim*.

The obvious question asked by the Gemara there is: If the *Shemoneh Esrei* had already been composed and set in order four hundred years earlier by the *Anshei Knesses HaGedolah,* including many *Neviim* — and presumably was in regular use by the people three times a day — why was it necessary for Shimon HaPakuli to recite the *berachos* in their proper order before Rabban Gamliel to obtain his approval and the acceptance of the *Sanhedrin* in Yavneh?

The answer given by the Gemara (ibid. 18a) is: שְׁכָחוּם וְחָזַר וְסִדְּרוּם. While the eighteen *berachos* had been in use since the *Anshei Knesses HaGedolah* composed them, their exact text and proper order had been largely forgotten over the course of time, until Shimon HaPakuli recited them again in their original form and proper order. This text and order was accepted by Rabban Gamliel and the Sanhedrin in Yavneh, and is essentially the *Shemoneh Esrei* that we know today.

The only way we can explain why the general population forgot the proper order of the *Shemoneh Esrei* is that originally the *tefillos* were said by heart, because the *berachos* and *tefillos* were considered a part of *Torah Shebe'al Peh,* and thus were prohibited from being committed to writing. The generally accepted institution of the written *siddur* had to await a much later period: after *Rabbeinu HaKadosh* (R' Yehudah HaNasi) instituted the writing of *Torah Shebe'al Peh,* some 170 years after the *Churban Beis HaMikdash.* There were, however, individuals who did transcribe the *tefillos* — probably out of ignorance of the *halachah* — but these were the exceptions rather than the rule.

The fact that the *tefillos* were considered *Torah Shebe'al Peh,* and thus were prohibited from being written down, is borne out by the Gemara (*Shabbos* 115b). In discussing the *halachos* concerning which *kisvei hakodesh* may be saved from a burning building on Shabbos (under certain circumstances), the Gemara there quotes the following *Baraisa*: תָּנוּ רַבָּנָן: הַבְּרָכוֹת וְהַקְּמֵיעִין, אַף עַל פִּי שֶׁיֵּשׁ בָּהֶן אוֹתִיּוֹת שֶׁל שֵׁם וּמֵעִנְיָנוֹת הַרְבֵּה שֶׁבַּתּוֹרָה, אֵין מַצִּילִין אוֹתָן מִפְּנֵי הַדְּלֵיקָה אֶלָּא נִשְׂרָפִים בִּמְקוֹמָן [הֵן וְאַזְכָּרוֹתֵיהֶן]. מִכַּאן אָמְרוּ: כּוֹתְבֵי בְרָכוֹת כְּשׂוֹרְפֵי תוֹרָה. Paraphrased, this means that if a *siddur* containing *berachos* and *tefillos* is endangered by fire on Shabbos — even if it contains *pesukim* and *Shemos* — one may not violate any of the prohibitions of Shabbos, even those that are only *mi'd'Rabbanan,* in order to save it. And, continues the Gemara, this is the source for the saying כּוֹתְבֵי בְרָכוֹת כְּשׂוֹרְפֵי תוֹרָה, *Those who write down berachos are comparable to those who burn a Torah.* By writing down the *berachos* and *tefillos,* they create the possibility that the *Shemos HaKedoshim* contained in them may not be fully protected from fire (if it occurs on Shabbos) and would thus be burned. The writer is therefore considered responsible for the burning of the *Shemos* and *pesukim* contained in the *siddur.*

Before the written *Torah Shebe'al Peh* — which included the *berachos* and *tefillos* — we must assume that people had fabulous memories with which they could retain all of the Mishnah, Gemara, etc., and the text and order of the *berachos* and *tefillos*. The reason the *chazaras hashatz* was instituted was to help those who were אֵינוֹ בָּקִי, whose memories were not so excellent, and they did not know the *berachos* of the *Shemoneh Esrei* by heart (see *Rosh Hashanah* 34b).

It is understandable that in the course of some four hundred years — with faltering memories, and different recollections — divergent texts and *nuschaos* of the *Shemoneh Esrei berachos* developed. It was not until Rabban Gamliel and the Sanhedrin in Yavneh accepted and verified that the text and order recited by Shimon HaPakuli was in fact the authentic original and proper text and order of the *Shemoneh Esrei berachos,* as composed by the *Anshei Knesses HaGedolah,* that the *Shemoneh Esrei* as we know it today was established once and for all.

To be sure, in the course of the approximately two thousand years since Rabban Gamliel and his Sanhedrin reestablished the authentic original text of the *Shemoneh Esrei,* some variations did develop — for instance, *minhag Sefard* and *minhag Ashkenaz* — but these variations are relatively minor. However, the order of the berachos remains unchanged since Shimon HaPakuli.

The root from which the *Shemoneh Esrei* grows is the first *berachah,* and this goes back to Moshe Rabbeinu.

The Midrash (*Shocher Tov, Tehillim* 19) states: מֹשֶׁה תִּקֵּן סֵדֶר תְּפִלָּה, *Moshe established the order of tefillah.* The Midrash bases this on *Devarim* 10:17, where Moshe Rabbeinu addresses *HaKadosh Baruch Hu* as הָאֵל הַגָּדֹל הַגִּבּוֹר וְהַנּוֹרָא, *the great, mighty, and awesome God.* The *Chachamim* call these words מַטְבֵּעַ שֶׁל תְּפִלָּה, *the coin of tefillah* (*Yerushalmi Berachos* 7:3 and *Megillah* end of Ch. 3). Just as a coin contains only a few words — the country, its ruler, and a few other selected words — so do these few words which were used by Moshe Rabbeinu act as the basic foundation of the text of the *tefillah.*

Moshe Rabbeinu addressed *HaKadosh Baruch Hu* with these words because they are based on certain miraculous events which he experienced in his lifetime:

❏ הַגָּדוֹל: עָשָׂה גְּדֹלוֹת בְּמִצְרַיִם, *Who has done great things in Egypt* (*Tehillim* 106:21). The word גָּדוֹל means *middas hachessed,* as in גְּדָל־חָסֶד (ibid. 145:8). The greatest form of *chessed* which *HaKadosh Baruch Hu* showed us was at *yetzias Mitzrayim.*

❏ הַגִּבּוֹר: שֶׁעָשָׂה גְּבוּרוֹת עַל הַיָּם, *Who performed mighty deeds at the sea* (see *Tehillim* 106:8-9). גִּבּוֹר refers to *middas hadin.* The greatest form of *din* which *HaKadosh Baruch Hu* showed us was the final punishment of the *Mitzriyim* at *krias Yam Suf.*

❏ **וְהַנּוֹרָא**: נוֹרָא אֱלֹהִים מִמִּקְדָּשֶׁיךָ, *You are awesome, O God, from Your sanctuaries* (*Tehillim* 68:36). This refers to the awe-inspiring event at the completion of the *Mishkan,* when fire came down from heaven.

[Ed. note: See the *siddur Shaar HaRachamim* by the *Maggid* Pinchas of Polotzk, which is the source for the explanations of הַגָּדֹל הַגִּבּוֹר וְהַנּוֹרָא.]

But the Midrash adds that after the *Churban Beis HaMikdash* some of these three words were omitted from the *tefillah*:

We find הָאֵל הַגָּדוֹל הַגִּבּוֹר, *the great and mighty God* (*Yirmiyahu* 32:18), with the word נוֹרָא omitted; and we find *Daniel* saying הָאֵל הַגָּדוֹל וְהַנּוֹרָא, *The Great and Awesome One* (*Daniel* 9:4), and גִּבּוֹר is omitted.

The *Chachamim* point out (see *Yoma* 69b) that these words were left out because the people could not perceive *HaKadosh Baruch Hu* as נוֹרָא, *awesome,* nor as גִּבּוֹר, *mighty,* when the *Beis HaMikdash* lay in ruins and the Jewish people were suffering. How could they say *HaKadosh Baruch Hu* was נוֹרָא when his enemies were not afraid to vandalize, besmirch, and defile His holy abode? אַיֵּה נוֹרְאוֹתָיו, *Where is His awesomeness?* Could they address *HaKadosh Baruch Hu* as גִּבּוֹר when He allows His people to suffer and be taken away into captivity, and He does not defend them? אַיֵּה גְּבוּרוֹתָיו, *Where is His power?*

But, continues the Midrash: וְכֵיוָן שֶׁעָמְדוּ אַנְשֵׁי כְּנֶסֶת הַגְּדוֹלָה הֶחֱזִירוּ אֶת הַגְּדוּלָּה לְיוֹשְׁנָהּ, *When the Anshei Knesses HaGedolah arose they restored the greatness to its old glory.*

It was not until the beginning of the Second *Beis HaMikdash* that the "Great Assembly," *Anshei Knesses HaGedolah* — consisting of one hundred and twenty *zekeinim,* among whom were many *Neviim* — reinstituted the use of the full phrase הָאֵל הַגָּדֹל הַגִּבּוֹר וְהַנּוֹרָא in the *tefillah,* and thus restored the crown of *HaKadosh Baruch Hu* to its former glory. In fact, it was because of this that they were called אַנְשֵׁי כְּנֶסֶת הַגְּדוֹלָה (Midrash ibid.).

Indeed, we do find the use of all three words by Nechemiah who was one of the members of the *Anshei Knesses HaGedolah*: וְעַתָּה אֱלֹהֵינוּ הָאֵל הַגָּדוֹל הַגִּבּוֹר וְהַנּוֹרָא, *And now, our God — the great, powerful and awesome God* (*Nechemiah* 9:32).

The Gemara (*Yoma* 69b) tells us that the reason the *Anshei Knesses HaGedolah* restored the words גִּבּוֹר and נוֹרָא, with which Moshe Rabbeinu addressed *HaKadosh Baruch Hu,* was because they understood גִּבּוֹר to mean that the real strength of *HaKadosh Baruch Hu* is shown not when He destroys His enemies, but when He withholds His retribution and remains silent in the face of the enormous suffering and pain endured by his people, זוֹ הִיא גְּבוּרַת גְּבוּרָתוֹ שֶׁכּוֹבֵשׁ אֶת יִצְרוֹ שֶׁנּוֹתֵן אֶרֶךְ אַפַּיִם לָרְשָׁעִים; and נוֹרָא, what really inspires "fear" of *HaKadosh Baruch Hu* is that His nation, *Bnei Yisrael,* despite their being in a miserable state of helplessness, have survived in the face of all the powerful nations who have attempted to destroy them, וְאִלּוּ הֵן נוֹרְאוֹתָיו

שֶׁאִלְמָלֵא מוֹרָאוֹ שֶׁל הקב"ה הֵיאַךְ אֻמָּה אַחַת יְכוֹלָה לְהִתְקַיֵּים בֵּין הָאֻמּוֹת. If it were not for fear in the hearts of our enemies, how would it be possible for "one sheep to survive among seventy wolves"? (see *Tosafos Yeshanim* ibid. from *Midrash Tanchuma*).

Therefore, in spite of the fact that during times of *galus*, persecution, suffering, and holocausts, we see neither the גְּבוּרָה nor the נוֹרָאוֹת of *HaKadosh Baruch Hu*, the *Anshei Knesses HaGedolah*, nevertheless, reinstituted the words used by Moshe Rabbeinu in the Torah, הָאֵל הַגָּדוֹל הַגִּבּוֹר וְהַנּוֹרָא, in addressing *HaKadosh Baruch Hu* in our *tefillah*.

These first words of the first *berachah* of the *Shemoneh Esrei* are the basic מַטְבֵּעַ שֶׁל תְּפִלָּה, the foundation upon which the *Anshei Knesses HaGedolah* structured all of the eighteen *berachos*.

◆{ The Symbolism of "Eighteen" in Tefillah }◆

It behooves us to understand why the *Anshei Knesses HaGedolah* composed eighteen *berachos* to comprise the *tefillah*, and what significance the number eighteen has in our *tefillah*. Quite a few reasons have been cited by our *Chachamim*:

❏ (*Berachos* 28b): ... רַב יוֹסֵף אָמַר: כְּנֶגֶד שְׁמוֹנֶה עֶשְׂרֵה אַזְכָּרוֹת שֶׁבִּקְרִיאַת שְׁמַע Corresponding to the eighteen times the Name of *HaKadosh Baruch Hu* appear in *Krias Shema*.

❏ (*Talmud* רַבִּי חֲנִינָא בְּשֵׁם רַבִּי פִּנְחָס: כְּנֶגֶד שְׁמוֹנֶה עֶשְׂרֵה פְּעָמִים שֶׁאָבוֹת כְּתוּבוֹת בַּתּוֹרָה *Yerushalmi, Berachos* 4:3): ... Corresponding to the eighteen times the names Avraham, Yitzchak, and Yaakov appear as a unit in the Torah.

❏ רַבִּי שְׁמוּאֵל בַּר נַחְמָנִי בְּשֵׁם רַבִּי יוֹחָנָן: כְּנֶגֶד שְׁמוֹנֶה עֶשְׂרֵה צִוּוּיִין שֶׁכָּתוּב בְּפָרָשַׁת מִשְׁכָּן שֵׁנִי (ibid.): ... Corresponding to the eighteen times the phrase כַּאֲשֶׁר צִוָּה ה' אֶת מֹשֶׁה, *As Hashem had commanded Moshe* (*Shemos* 40:27), appears at the end of *Parashas Pekudei*. In the description of how Moshe Rabbeinu erected the *Mishkan*, the phrase כַּאֲשֶׁר צִוָּה ה' אֶת מֹשֶׁה appears after each action that he took in its construction.

❏ רַבִּי שִׁמְעוֹן אוֹמֵר: כְּנֶגֶד שְׁמוֹנָה עָשָׂר מִזְמוֹרִים שֶׁמֵּרֹאשׁ סֵפֶר תְּהִלִּים עַד יַעַנְךָ ה' בְּיוֹם צָרָה (*Midrash Tanchuma, Vayeira* 1): ... Corresponding to the eighteen chapters of *Tehillim*, from its beginning until the *mizmor* which begins with יַעַנְךָ ה' בְּיוֹם צָרָה, which is a reference to *tefillah*, as we have explained earlier. Actually this *mizmor* is known to us as Psalm 20; the Gemara, however, says that the *mizmorim* אַשְׁרֵי הָאִישׁ and לָמָּה רָגְשׁוּ גוֹיִם (Chapters 1 and 2) are to be counted as one *mizmor*. When the *Chachamim* subsequently added the *Bircas HaMinim* to make a total of nineteen *berachos*, they correspondingly separated the first chapter of *Tehillim* into two to equal nineteen until יַעַנְךָ ה'

בְּיוֹם צָרָה. Perhaps, one could say that eventually, when the *reshaim* disappear from the world, and the *Bircas HaMinim* becomes unnecessary, the first two chapters will again be combined to keep the total at eighteen.

אָמַר רַב הִלֵּל בְּרֵיהּ דְּרַב שְׁמוּאֵל בַּר נַחְמָנִי: כְּנֶגֶד שְׁמוֹנָה עֶשְׂרֵה אַזְכָּרוֹת שֶׁאָמַר דָּוִד בְּ"הָבוּ לַה' בְּנֵי אֵלִים" (*Berachos* 29b): . . . *Corresponding to the eighteen times David mentioned the Name of God in the mizmor, "Prepare for Hashem, you sons of the powerful"* (*Tehillim* 29:1).

This מִזְמוֹר לְדָוִד, which is said Friday nights at *Kabbalas Shabbos* and also on Shabbos when the *sefer Torah* is brought back to the *Aron Kodesh* following *krias haTorah,* contains the Name of *HaKadosh Baruch Hu* eighteen times. And the reason why many *kehillos* have the *minhag* to stand while saying this *mizmor* is because its eighteen אַזְכָּרוֹת, mentions of God's Name, take the place of the eighteen *berachos* in the weekday *Shemoneh Esrei.*

Interestingly, Rav Saadia Gaon in his *siddur* says that he counted eighteen times in which the Torah mentions that somebody said a *tefillah* to *HaKadosh Baruch Hu.* He also mentions the fact that the Torah designated eighteen days in the year as Yamim Tovim: seven days of Pesach; one day of Shavuos; one day of Rosh Hashanah; one day of Yom Kippur; and eight days of Succos and Shemini Atzeres.

All of these sources are instances in which there is a factor of eighteen. However, this still begs the question: *What is the significance of the number eighteen?*

The significance of the number eighteen in *tefillah* is given by *Midrash Tanchuma, Vayeira* 1, as follows: כְּנֶגֶד שְׁמוֹנָה עֶשְׂרֵה חוּלְיוֹת שֶׁבַּשִּׁדְרָה, *to correspond to the eighteen joints in the spine.* שֶׁבְּשָׁעָה שֶׁאָדָם מִתְפַּלֵּל וְכוֹרֵעַ צָרִיךְ שֶׁיִּכְרַע עַד שֶׁיִּתְפַּקְּקוּ כָּל חֻלְיוֹת שֶׁבַּשִּׁדְרָה, שֶׁנֶּאֱמַר: כָּל עַצְמוֹתַי תֹּאמַרְנָה ה' מִי כָמוֹךָ, *During tefillah, when a person bends his knees, he must bow down to a point at which all of the joints of his spine are opened, as it says, "All my limbs will say: Hashem, Who is like You"* (*Tehillim* 35:10). When one says בָּרוּךְ he is to bend his knees; at אַתָּה he is to bend his back until all the eighteen joints are involved. In this way, all of one's bones, כָּל עַצְמוֹתַי, are involved in the *tefillah.*

Based on this, all of the aforementioned instances where the number eighteen is cited as the source for the *hakdamah l'shemoneh esrei berachos* are based on the fact that the number eighteen represents the physical framework of the human being, and thus the number eighteen is the ideal symbolism to express the essence of *tefillah,* namely:

We are offering, as we have explained, the entirety of our body — and our soul — as a *korban* to *HaKadosh Baruch Hu* through *tefillah.* This is the meaning of כָּל עַצְמוֹתַי תֹּאמַרְנָה ה' מִי כָמוֹךָ, and that is why we begin the

Shemoneh Esrei by bowing down and involving our entire body in the tefillah.

The following two halachos embody the thoughts we have expressed, and will help put one into the proper frame of mind as he begins the Shemoneh Esrei.

(1) The Chachamim tell us: הַמִּתְפַּלֵּל צָרִיךְ שֶׁיְּכַוֵּין אֶת רַגְלָיו שֶׁנֶּאֱמַר: וְרַגְלֵיהֶם רֶגֶל יְשָׁרָה (Berachos 10b). When one is mispallel, he is to keep his feet together similar to the malachim, who have only רֶגֶל יְשָׁרָה, one "straight foot," as it says, their feet were one straight foot (Yechezkel 1:7). Rav Samson R. Hirsch explains that malachim, unlike human beings, do not have freedom of choice; they have only "one foot." They must do only that for which they were created by HaKadosh Baruch Hu. Human beings, on the other hand, have total freedom of choice to go to the "right" or to the "left." (See Rambam, Hil. Teshuvah, beginning of Ch. 5; also, our comments on בְּכָל פָּרָשַׁת וְאָהַבְתָּ in לְבָבֶךָ.)

Similarly, in accordance with our explanation, when one stands before HaKadosh Baruch Hu in tefillah and places his feet together as one, emulating the malachim, he is expressing the thought that he is relinquishing his free will and thus offering himself as a korban to HaKadosh Baruch Hu. In so doing, he has performed the greatest act of free choice of which a human being is capable: that of voluntarily relinquishing that choice to HaKadosh Baruch Hu.

(2) As we begin the Shemoneh Esrei with בָּרוּךְ אַתָּה ה׳, we bend our knees, followed by our whole body, as if we were falling down before HaKadosh Baruch Hu, expressing the thought that without Him, we would not have the ability to exist. But before we say אֲדֹנָי, we arise from our bow and stand before Him erectly, and then say אֲדֹנָי, expressing the thought that ה׳ זוֹקֵף כְּפוּפִים, it is He Who keeps us up and prevents us from falling. (See Orach Chaim 113:7.)

Notwithstanding the fact that we relinquish our free will to HaKadosh Baruch Hu and are offering ourselves as a korban to Him, HaKadosh Baruch Hu does not want us to leave this world. On the contrary, HaKadosh Baruch Hu wants us to be alive in this world; He wants us to live our lives here in accordance with His will. This thought is expressed in Maariv: הַשָּׂם נַפְשֵׁנוּ בַּחַיִּים וְלֹא נָתַן לַמּוֹט רַגְלֵנוּ, He keeps us alive and does not allow our feet to slip. By living our lives here in this world in accordance with His will, and by dedicating our lives to Him and longing for Him, our lives have, in effect, become a living korban to HaKadosh Baruch Hu. It is with these thoughts that we begin the Shemoneh Esrei.

תְּפִלַּת הָעֲמִידָה – שְׁמוֹנֶה עֶשְׂרֵה / Tefillas HaAmidah — Shemoneh Esrei

ה' שְׂפָתַי תִּפְתָּח וּפִי יַגִּיד תְּהִלָּתֶךָ

Before beginning the *Shemoneh Esrei,* we quote this *pasuk* from *Tehillim* 51:17. The Gemara (*Berachos* 4b) tells us that saying this *pasuk* is not considered an interruption between *geulah* and *tefillah* because the *Chachamim* instituted it to become a part of the *tefillah* itself, כִּתְפִלָּה אֲרִיכְתָּא.

The concept of beginning the *Shemoneh Esrei* by asking *HaKadosh Baruch Hu* to "open our lips" so that our mouths can speak His praises, can be better understood in the light of our explanation that through *tefillah,* we are offering ourselves as a *korban* to *HaKadosh Baruch Hu.* And, as such, just as the *korban olah* involves the three steps of הֶפְשֵׁט, וְנִתּוּחַ, וְכָלִיל לָאִשִּׁים (see Mishnah, *Perek* איזהו מקומן), so does *tefillah*:

❏ הֶפְשֵׁט — The animal must be skinned.

❏ וְנִתּוּחַ — It must be cut into sections.

❏ וְכָלִיל לָאִשִּׁים — It is then completely burned on the *Mizbe'ach.*

First, similar to הֶפְשֵׁט, we are mentally to practice הַפְשָׁטַת הַגַּשְׁמִיּוּת while saying the *Shemoneh Esrei* (see *Shulchan Aruch, Orach Chaim* 98:1-4). This means that we are to withdraw from our external physical existence into our own inner self. We are to disregard our outer, physical frame, while our inner, spiritual, true self is communicating with *HaKadosh Baruch Hu.* The transient, physical aspect of the human being that can be seen in a mirror is not the real person, but merely a capsule of one's "real self." Our outward appearance is similar to the hands of a clock, which is only its external feature. However, these hands are controlled by a very complicated system of wheels and movements which are hidden. The external manifestations of the human being are to be removed during *tefillah.* And it is our spiritual essence, our *neshamah,* our true "self," which is communicating with *HaKadosh Baruch Hu* during *tefillah.* This being the case, we ask *HaKadosh Baruch Hu*: ה' שְׂפָתַי תִּפְתָּח, *Open my lips,* because we have symbolically withdrawn from our physical frame and are communicating with Him through our *neshamah.*

Second, as is pointed out by the *Shulchan Aruch* (ibid.), one should concentrate on humbling thoughts as he stands before the *Ribbono Shel Olam* in *tefillah.* This is similar to the נִתּוּחַ of the *korban olah,* as we appear before *HaKadosh Baruch Hu* with a *lev nishbar,* a broken and humble persona, as is expressed in the *pasuk*: לֵב נִשְׁבָּר וְנִדְכֶּה אֱלֹהִים לֹא תִבְזֶה, *A heart broken and humbled, O God, You will not despise* (*Tehillim* 51:19). We are to imagine that "little me," this little nothing that I am, with all my shortcomings, is approaching the *Ribbono Shel Olam,* the Master of the universe. What audacity! What chutzpah! This feeling of complete inadequacy is what is meant by *lev nishbar.* This second condition corresponds to וּפִי יַגִּיד תְּהִלָּתֶךָ, meaning, "May my mouth, unworthy as it is, nevertheless be permitted to speak Your praises."

And third, the *tefillah* is to be said with *hislahavus,* fiery enthusiasm, which corresponds to כָּלִיל לָאִשִּׁים (see *Shulchan Aruch* ibid., 4: הַתְּפִלָּה הוּא בִּמְקוֹם הַקָּרְבָּן וגו׳). One should feel exhilarated to be fortunate enough to be chosen by *HaKadosh Baruch Hu* as part of *Klal Yisrael,* and to say the words of His *Neviim* and *Chachamim,* together with the rest of *Klal Yisrael.* And in this frame of mind, we bow and start: בָּרוּךְ אַתָּה ה׳ וגו׳.

In light of this explanation, it is clear why ה׳ שְׂפָתַי תִּפְתָּח is part and parcel of the *tefillah,* תְּפִלָּה אֲרִיכְתָּא, and is therefore not an interruption between *geulah* and *tefillah.*

אָבוֹת

‖ — בָּרוּךְ אַתָּה ה׳ אֱלֹהֵינוּ וֵאלֹהֵי אֲבוֹתֵינוּ, אֱלֹהֵי אַבְרָהָם, אֱלֹהֵי יִצְחָק, וֵאלֹהֵי יַעֲקֹב
Blessed are You, Hashem, our God and the God of our Forefathers, God of Avraham, God of Yitzchak, and God of Yaakov.

The *Chachamim* tell us (*Mechilta, Bo* 13:3) that the language of this first *berachah* of the *Shemoneh Esrei* has its origin in the Torah itself:
מִנַּיִן שֶׁאוֹמְרִים בָּרוּךְ אַתָּה ה׳ אֱלֹהֵינוּ וֵאלֹהֵי אֲבוֹתֵינוּ אֱלֹהֵי אַבְרָהָם אֱלֹהֵי יִצְחָק וֵאלֹהֵי יַעֲקֹב, שֶׁנֶּאֱמַר: וַיֹּאמֶר עוֹד אֱלֹהִים אֶל מֹשֶׁה כֹּה תֹאמַר אֶל בְּנֵי יִשְׂרָאֵל ה׳ אֱלֹהֵי אֲבֹתֵיכֶם אֱלֹהֵי אַבְרָהָם אֱלֹהֵי יִצְחָק וֵאלֹהֵי יַעֲקֹב שְׁלָחַנִי אֲלֵיכֶם, זֶה שְׁמִי לְעוֹלָם וְזֶה זִכְרִי לְדֹר דֹּר.
Here *HaKadosh Baruch Hu* (*Shemos* 3:15) is telling Moshe that when *Bnei Yisrael* wish to address Him, they should do so with the expression of ה׳ אֱלֹהֵי אֲבֹתֵיכֶם אֱלֹהֵי אַבְרָהָם אֱלֹהֵי יִצְחָק וֵאלֹהֵי יַעֲקֹב. This is also the way *HaKadosh Baruch Hu* "introduced" Himself to Moshe: וַיֹּאמֶר אָנֹכִי אֱלֹהֵי אָבִיךָ אֱלֹהֵי אַבְרָהָם אֱלֹהֵי יִצְחָק וֵאלֹהֵי יַעֲקֹב (ibid. v. 6).

Rashi, quoting *Bereishis Rabbah,* explains that when we invoke the merit of our Forefathers in our *tefillah,* the merit of our original Forefather, Avraham, has special significance. This comment is made on the following *pasuk*. וְאֶעֶשְׂךָ לְגוֹי גָּדוֹל וַאֲבָרֶכְךָ וַאֲגַדְּלָה שְׁמֶךָ וֶהְיֵה בְּרָכָה, *And I will form you into a great nation, and I will bless you, and I will make your name greater and greater; and you will become a (source of) blessing* (*Bereishis* 12:2). Rashi, citing *Bereishis Rabbah,* comments on this: וְאֶעֶשְׂךָ לְגוֹי גָּדוֹל זֶה שֶׁאוֹמְרִים אֱלֹהֵי אַבְרָהָם; וַאֲבָרֶכְךָ זֶה שֶׁאוֹמְרִים אֱלֹהֵי יִצְחָק; וַאֲגַדְּלָה שְׁמֶךָ זֶה שֶׁאוֹמְרִים אֱלֹהֵי יַעֲקֹב. This means that in our *Shemoneh Esrei* the phrase, *I will form you into a great nation,* is the basis for saying, *the God of Avraham; and I will bless you* is the basis for saying *the God of Yitzchak; and I will make your name greater and greater* is the basis for saying *the God of Yaakov.*

Rashi continues to quote: יָכוֹל יִהְיוּ חוֹתְמִין בְּכוּלָן ת"ל וֶהְיֵה בְּרָכָה, בְּךָ חוֹתְמִין וְלֹא בָהֶם. One might think that the *berachah* of *Avos* should conclude with all three *Avos* to correspond with its beginning. It is for this reason that the *pasuk* ends with וֶהְיֵה בְּרָכָה, *and you (Avraham) will become a (source of) blessing,* to teach us: בְּךָ חוֹתְמִין וְלֹא בָהֶם, the *berachah* is to conclude only with Avraham's name.

The connection between the *berachos* given here to Avraham and the language of the first *berachah* of the *Shemoneh Esrei* is difficult to understand.

Earlier we mentioned that the words מֶלֶךְ הָעוֹלָם are missing from this *berachah,* which, apparently, places it in noncompliance with the generally accepted rule of *berachos* that כָּל בְּרָכָה שֶׁאֵין בָּהּ מַלְכוּת אֵינָהּ בְּרָכָה, *Every blessing wherein God's Kingship is not mentioned is not a proper berachah* (see *Berachos* 40b).

However, notwithstanding the missing מֶלֶךְ הָעוֹלָם, *Bircas Avos* is nevertheless in full compliance with the requirement of mentioning *Malchus Hashem.* This is so because by addressing *HaKadosh Baruch Hu* as אֱלֹהֵי אַבְרָהָם יִצְחָק וְיַעֲקֹב, we thereby declare that He is the *Melech HaOlam,* the King of the universe (see *Tosafos* ibid. s.v. אמר אביי). This can be understood as follows.

Our *Avos* — Avraham, Yitzchak, and Yaakov — recognized *HaKadosh Baruch Hu* as *Melech HaOlam.* However, there are three aspects of *Malchus Shamayim,* and each one of the *Avos* emphasized one of them in their lives:

Avraham spread the knowledge of *HaKadosh Baruch Hu* in the world. In his own lifetime, he convinced thousands of people to become believers in *HaKadosh Baruch Hu.* And eventually, in *yemos HaMashiach,* when נְדִיבֵי עַמִּים נֶאֱסָפוּ (*Tehillim* 47:10), the noblemen of the nations gather and recognize that *HaKadosh Baruch Hu* is the *Melech HaOlam,* this universal recognition of *HaKadosh Baruch Hu* will be based on the historic influence of עַם אֱלֹהֵי אַבְרָהָם, *the nation of the God of Avraham* (ibid.). When the time comes that וְהָיָה ה' לְמֶלֶךְ עַל כָּל הָאָרֶץ, *Hashem will be the King over all the land* (*Zechariah* 14:9), and the whole world finally recognizes the *Malchus Shamayim,* it will be because Avraham Avinu, the אַב הֲמוֹן גּוֹיִם, *the father of a multitude of nations* (*Bereishis* 17:5), spread the knowledge of *HaKadosh Baruch Hu* throughout the world. This is what is meant by אֱלֹהֵי אַבְרָהָם.

Yitzchak emphasized the recognition of *HaKadosh Baruch Hu* as his own personal *Melech.* Yitzchak demonstrated through the *Akeidah* that not only is *HaKadosh Baruch Hu* the מֶלֶךְ עַל כָּל הָאָרֶץ, as his father Avraham had taught, but He is especially his own *Melech* for Whom he was prepared, at any moment, to give up his life. This is what is meant when *Chazal* tell us:

אָמְרוּ לְפָנַי ... מַלְכֻיּוֹת כְּדֵי שֶׁתַּמְלִיכוּנִי עֲלֵיכֶם, *Say the words of kingship before Me to express the fact that you have accepted me as your king* (*Rosh Hashanah* 16a). The *Rema*, quoting *Rambam* in *Moreh Nevuchim*, emphasizes that one should be aware that every moment of his life he is constantly being watched by הַמֶּלֶךְ הַגָּדוֹל, *the great King, HaKadosh Baruch Hu* (see *Rema, Shulchan Aruch, Orach Chaim* 1). This special awareness that Yitzchak had is what is meant by, וַאֲבָרְכֶךָ זֶהוּ שֶׁאוֹמְרִים אֱלֹהֵי יִצְחָק.

Yaakov embodied וַאֲגַדְּלָה שְׁמֶךָ, *I will make your Name grow [gradually] greater and greater* (*Bereishis* 12:2). The teaching of *Malchus Shamayim* that Avraham brought to the world spread gradually to the rest of the world. The contribution of Yaakov in furthering this ideal was to emphasize first the full and unequivocal acceptance of *Malchus Shamayim* among his own people, *Klal Yisrael*. *HaKadosh Baruch Hu* had first to become מֶלֶךְ יִשְׂרָאֵל וְגֹאֲלוֹ, *The King of Yisrael and its Redeemer* (*Yeshayahu* 44:6), and then the concept of *Malchus Shamayim* would eventually be recognized throughout the entire world: יִמְלֹךְ ה' לְעוֹלָם אֱלֹהַיִךְ צִיּוֹן לְדֹר וָדֹר, *Hashem shall reign forever — your God, O Tziyon, from generation to generation* (*Tehillim* 146:10).

These three different viewpoints are all complementary. Our *Avos*, each in his own specialized approach, spread the concept of the totality of *Malchus Shamayim* throughout the world.

In summary, therefore, the *Bircas Avos* is very much in compliance with the rule requiring *Malchus* in our *berachos*, because it contains:

אֱלֹהֵי אַבְרָהָם, meaning מֶלֶךְ עַל הָעוֹלָם, *King of the universe;*

אֱלֹהֵי יִצְחָק, meaning מֶלֶךְ עַל הַיָּחִיד, *King of each individual;*

אֱלֹהֵי יַעֲקֹב, meaning מֶלֶךְ עַל כְּלַל יִשְׂרָאֵל, *King of the Jewish people.*

The *berachah* continues:

ఆ§ הָאֵל — **The Almighty.** *HaKadosh Baruch Hu* is not bound by His *middos*, therefore His power transcends even His own attributes. He can pardon the worst *reshaim*, and *chas v'shalom* punish the greatest *tzaddikim* for the slightest infraction. The name אֵל, although connoting "power," nevertheless expresses *middas harachamim* (see Rashi on *Shemos* 34:6; also חֶסֶד אֵל כָּל הַיּוֹם, *The kindness of God is all day long* [*Tehillim* 52:3]), because the greatest sign of power by which *HaKadosh Baruch Hu* has revealed Himself is the fact that He created the world. *HaKadosh Baruch Hu*, Who is Perfection per se, has no need to create the world. However, as the *Baal HaRachamim*, the ultimate merciful One, His purpose was to create objects, "vessels," which would be the recipients of His goodness. (See Rabbi Moshe Chaim Luzzatto, in the beginning of his *Mesillas Yesharim*.)

ఆ§ הַגָּדוֹל — **Great** here refers to His unbounded kindness (as in גְּדָל חֶסֶד), which is symbolized by Avraham. We serve *HaKadosh Baruch Hu* in love, as did אַבְרָהָם אֹהֲבִי, *Avraham who loved Me* (*Yeshayahu* 41:8).

◈§ הַגִּבּוֹר — **Powerful.** We serve *HaKadosh Baruch Hu* in fear of His power, as did Yitzchak — פַּחַד יִצְחָק (*Bereishis* 31:42).

◈§ וְהַנּוֹרָא — **Awesome.** This is a combination of גָּדוֹל and גִּבּוֹר. Emulating Yaakov, who said מַה נּוֹרָא הַמָּקוֹם הַזֶּה, *How awesome is this place* (*Bereishis* 28:17), we serve *HaKadosh Baruch Hu* with a combination of love and fear.

◈§ אֵל עֶלְיוֹן — **The Almighty, Who is above our understanding.** None of His creations can conceive of Him. While we can have some understanding of the underlying concepts of גָּדוֹל, גִּבּוֹר, וְנוֹרָא, and can say that *HaKadosh Baruch Hu* is קוֹנֵה שָׁמַיִם וָאָרֶץ, *Master of heaven and earth* (*Bereishis* 14:19,22), the human mind cannot possibly comprehend the essence of *HaKadosh Baruch Hu,* or His conduct of world affairs. For instance, it is beyond our comprehension that the wicked can prosper and grow, בִּפְרֹחַ רְשָׁעִים כְּמוֹ עֵשֶׂב וַיָּצִיצוּ כָּל פֹּעֲלֵי אָוֶן, *When the wicked bloom like grass and all the iniquitous blossom* (*Tehillim* 92:8), while *tzaddikim* suffer; or that perfectly innocent children are born with deformities or are afflicted with suffering and diseases. The Holocaust which claimed six million Jews, in addition to the suffering that our people has had to endure for thousands of years, is beyond our ability to explain. All attempts to explain it will be futile. The אֵל עֶלְיוֹן has not revealed this to us.

◈§ גּוֹמֵל חֲסָדִים טוֹבִים — **Who bestows beneficial kindnesses.** However, this same אֵל עֶלְיוֹן, Whose seemingly harsh judgment is beyond our comprehension, is also the source of constant benefaction to His creations: He constantly grants "good kindness." חֲסָדִים alone benefit only the recipients, but חֲסָדִים טוֹבִים describes the kindness with which the recipients can benefit others. All of us who were able to escape from Europe or who survived the Holocaust are alive only because *HaKadosh Baruch Hu* is גּוֹמֵל חֲסָדִים טוֹבִים.

◈§ וְקוֹנֵה הַכֹּל — **He is the owner of everything.** Every day of our lives we are the beneficiaries of the multitudinous benefits and kindnesses bestowed upon us by *HaKadosh Baruch Hu,* which sustain us. Every second of our lives is filled with these favors; from the moment we awaken in the morning we are the beneficiaries of the gifts of *HaKadosh Baruch Hu*: we can see; we can hear; we can move; we can walk; we can think; our bodily functions work; we can go about our business, etc. We do not have the means to adequately express our gratitude to *HaKadosh Baruch Hu* for even one of these favors, as is so beautifully expressed in *Nishmas*: אִלּוּ פִינוּ מָלֵא שִׁירָה כַּיָּם . . . אֵין אֲנַחְנוּ מַסְפִּיקִים לְהוֹדוֹת לְךָ ה' אֱלֹהֵינוּ . . . עַל אַחַת מֵאֶלֶף אֶלֶף אַלְפֵי אֲלָפִים וְרִבֵּי רְבָבוֹת פְּעָמִים הַטּוֹבוֹת שֶׁעָשִׂיתָ עִם אֲבוֹתֵינוּ וְעִמָּנוּ, *Were our mouth as full as song as the sea . . . we still could not thank You sufficiently, Hashem our God . . . for even one of the thousand thousand, thousands of thousands and myriad myriads of favors that You performed for our ancestors and for us.*

The words וְקוֹנֵה הַכֹּל express the same idea. Since we are at a loss to adequately express our gratitude to *HaKadosh Baruch Hu,* we declare, וְקוֹנֵה הַכֹּל, meaning, "We have nothing to offer You, for You own everything; we are therefore Your servants."

There is an interesting illustration of this in *Parashas Vayigash* (*Bereishis* 47:13-23) in the narrative of how Yosef managed the distribution of the stored grain and food in Egypt during the famine. The Torah tells us there that in the first year of the famine alone, the Egyptians and Canaanites used all of their money and traded all of their livestock to buy enough grain and food to sustain themselves. And in the second year, with no wherewithal to buy food, the populace approached Yosef and offered to exchange themselves, together with their land, in servitude to Pharaoh for food. This offer was accepted by Yosef on behalf of Pharaoh. The result was that, in exchange for feeding the Egyptian population, Pharaoh acquired all of their money, livestock, land, and even their bodies as indentured slaves, in exchange for their sustenance.

The reason the Torah relates this piece of Egyptian history — which, on the surface, has no connection with the development of the Jewish people in Egypt — is to illustrate for us how we are to approach the concept of gratitude to *HaKadosh Baruch Hu* when we are utterly devoid of the means to do so. Just as the Egyptians of old declared, וְנִהְיֶה . . . עֲבָדִים לְפַרְעֹה, *and we will become slaves to Pharaoh* (*Bereishis* 47:19), when they lacked any other means of repayment for their sustenance, we too say to *HaKadosh Baruch Hu,* we offer ourselves as Your servants: וְקוֹנֵה הַכֹּל, "You own everything — even ourselves."

◆§ וְזוֹכֵר חַסְדֵי אָבוֹת §◆ — **He remembers the merits of the *Avos.*** *Chessed,* here, is used in the sense of *zechus avos,* the reward that our Forefathers earned. It is this reward that *HaKadosh Baruch Hu* "remembers" when He blesses us as their beneficiaries.

◆§ וּמֵבִיא גוֹאֵל לִבְנֵי בְנֵיהֶם §◆ — **He brings the redeemer** [*Mashiach*] **to their children's children.** This means us. This is expressed in the present tense, because the *geulah* does not happen all at once, but rather, it is an ongoing process which culminates with *bi'as HaMashiach.*

◆§ לְמַעַן שְׁמוֹ בְּאַהֲבָה §◆ — **For His own sake, out of love.** One of the Names of *HaKadosh Baruch Hu* is גוֹאֵל יִשְׂרָאֵל, *Redeemer of Israel,* because He promised us that He would eventually redeem us. This redemption will come even if we don't deserve it, purely out of the love of *HaKadosh Baruch Hu* for *Bnei Yisrael.* The Gemara states (*Shabbos* 55a) that *zechus avos* has limits — תָּמָה זְכוּת אָבוֹת, when the benefits to us of the *ma'asim tovim* of our forefathers have been exhausted. Nevertheless, *HaKadosh Baruch Hu* will bring the *geulah* for

His own sake, purely out of love for *Bnei Yisrael*. [Ed. note: See *Tosafos* ibid. s.v. ושמואל אמר, explaining that while *zechus avos* has been exhausted, *bris avos* continues forever. This is expressed as לְמַעַן שְׁמוֹ בְּאַהֲבָה.]

During the *Aseres Yemei Teshuvah*, at this point, we add: זָכְרֵנוּ לְחַיִּים מֶלֶךְ חָפֵץ בַּחַיִּים וְכָתְבֵנוּ בְּסֵפֶר הַחַיִּים לְמַעַנְךָ אֱלֹהִים חַיִּים. This means, we ask *HaKadosh Baruch Hu* to let us live to actually witness the occurrence of וּמֵבִיא גּוֹאֵל לִבְנֵי בְנֵיהֶם.

≈§ מֶלֶךְ עוֹזֵר וּמוֹשִׁיעַ וּמָגֵן — **O King, Helper, Savior, and Shield.** Meanwhile, before the actual coming of *Mashiach*, in the absence of *zechus avos*, we recognize that it is only due to the love of *HaKadosh Baruch Hu* Who, as our King, helps, saves, and protects us.

Here we have the first use of מֶלֶךְ in the *Shemoneh Esrei*. We recognize *HaKadosh Baruch Hu* first as מֶלֶךְ, the King, Who is our Redeemer. We then describe Him as עוֹזֵר, Who "helps" us. This means that when we make an effort to make ourselves worthy of the *geulah*, He helps us in this effort. However, there are times when we, as a nation, make no — or very little — effort to make ourselves worthy of being redeemed. It is for those times that we refer to *HaKadosh Baruch Hu* as מוֹשִׁיעַ, *Savior*. He saves us even when we are helpless and have made no effort toward deserving our *geulah*.

And מָגֵן means that *HaKadosh Baruch Hu* protects us during the *galus* from the evil which our enemies plan for our destruction. Sometimes *HaKadosh Baruch Hu* protects us in very strange ways. Anti-Semitism is an example of this. Had there been no anti-Semitism in Russia, not a single Russian Jew would have remained Jewish. It was only because of the blatant anti-Semitism that existed in Russia that the Russian Jews were reminded that they were, in fact, Jews.

However, the concept of *HaKadosh Baruch Hu* as our מָגֵן extends much further. During the end of the *galus,* at the time before the coming of *Mashiach* — the so-called עִקְבְתָא דִמְשִׁיחָא, *the footsteps of Mashiach* — our *Chachamim* tell us that conditions will exist that will make this the darkest epoch of the *galus*. The *galus* will never have been as dark as during the time immediately before the break of the dawn of *Mashiach* (see Sotah 49b). Interestingly, the word שַׁחַר, *morning,* has the same letters as שָׁחֹר, *black,* because it is just before the break of dawn that the night is at its blackest.

Some of our *Chachamim* dreaded this period to the extent that they expressed the wish, יֵיתֵי וְלֹא אַחֲמִינֵיהּ, *It is my hope that he* [Mashiach] *will come, but I do not want to see him* (Sanhedrin 98b). They did not want to witness the *chillul Hashem* and the spread of *kefirah* (apostasy) throughout the world which our *Chachamim* have predicted will exist during the time just before the coming of *Mashiach* (see *Sotah* ibid.).

We live in a world in which there is the threat not only of our physical annihilation — in Eretz Yisrael and throughout the world — but also of our spiritual destruction. The description that our *Chachamim* have given for the time immediately before the coming of *Mashiach,* in which the world would be filled with the darkness of immorality and apostasy, seems to apply to our times. The disbelief that there is *HaKadosh Baruch Hu* in the world started a few hundred years ago, and has developed now to the extent that a large segment of the world's population — from the highest echelons of government to the lowest level of human society — lacks moral values. These people believe in nothing: לֵית דִּין וְלֵית דַּיָּן, *There is no moral law and there is no Supreme Judge.* For the Jewish nation to have survived in such a world is due only to the example shown us by Avraham Avinu, who, as "אַבְרָהָם "הָעִבְרִי, taught us that even if the whole world is against us on one side, we can successfully remain firm in our convictions on the other side.

After Avraham Avinu had returned victorious from the battle with the four kings and restored the king of Sodom to his rule, *HaKadosh Baruch Hu* told him: אַל תִּירָא אַבְרָם אָנֹכִי מָגֵן לָךְ, *Fear not, Avram, I am a shield for you* (*Bereishis* 15:1). Despite the fact that you have come into contact with the most depraved of societies, that of Sodom, you have nothing to fear; I will protect you from the influence of the Sodomite way of life, for "I am your shield."

Similarly, when *HaKadosh Baruch Hu* brings about our final redemption, מֵבִיא גוֹאֵל לִבְנֵי בְנֵיהֶם, it will be possible only because *HaKadosh Baruch Hu* protected us physically as well as spiritually throughout the long *galus* night, in which immorality is rampant, and a culture has developed where even "sodomism" has been legalized.

It is in this world of immorality where we need the help of *HaKadosh Baruch Hu* as our עוֹזֵר וּמוֹשִׁיעַ וּמָגֵן.

And all of this goes back to Avraham Avinu. Our *Chachamim* tell us that Avraham Avinu recognized the existence of *HaKadosh Baruch Hu* at the age of 3 (see *Nedarim* 32a). Yet, there is a midrash that states that he recognized *HaKadosh Baruch Hu* when he was 40 years of age, at the time of the building of the Tower of Bavel (see *Bereishis Rabbah* 64:4; *Kesef Mishneh, Hil. Avodah Zarah* 1:3).

These two statements, however, are not contradictory. While it is true that Avraham Avinu first recognized the existence of *HaKadosh Baruch Hu* at the age of 3, it was not until he was 40 — and witnessed how Nimrod built the mighty tower of Bavel as an act of defiance against the rule of *HaKadosh Baruch Hu* in the world — that he had to take a stand and separate himself from his King and the rest of the world.

This Jewish determination of separating oneself from the evils of the world, no matter how popular they may be, is expressed in *Hallel*: אֲנִי אָמַרְתִּי בְחָפְזִי כָּל הָאָדָם כֹּזֵב, *I said in my hurrying* [through the *galus*], *"All of mankind* is lying" (*Tehillim* 116:11). Israel proudly says, "I stood steadfast against all of mankind who tried to influence me with their beliefs and immorality." As He did for *Avraham Avinu* of old, we are confident that *HaKadosh Baruch Hu* will protect us, too, from falling prey to the prevailing immorality and apostasy of the times.

This, then, is the meaning of the statement of our *Chachamim*: וֶהְיֵה בְּרָכָה, *and you shall be a blessing* (*Bereishis* 12:2): בְּךָ חוֹתְמִין וְאֵין חוֹתְמִין בְּכוּלָן (*Pesachim* 117b). When we thank *HaKadosh Baruch Hu* for being our protector against the evil influences of the world, it is because we have taken our example from *Avraham Avinu*. And *HaKadosh Baruch Hu*, Who protected him from being influenced by the prevailing idolatry in the world, protects us as well in our efforts to maintain our *emunah*. We therefore finish the *berachah* with:

⊷ בָּרוּךְ אַתָּה ה' מָגֵן אַבְרָהָם — **Blessed are You, Hashem, Shield of Avraham.** Our *Chachamim* have instituted that we are to bow down at the beginning and end of the *berachah* of *Avos* (see *Berachos* 34a; *Shulchan Aruch, Orach Chaim* 113). The fact that we are to bow at the beginning and again at the end of this *berachah* indicates that each of these acts of bowing must express a slightly different meaning than the other.

Most probably, the bowing at the beginning of the *berachah* expresses the thought that we accept *HaKadosh Baruch Hu* as אֱלֹהֵינוּ וֵאלֹהֵי אֲבוֹתֵינוּ. We accept Him as our God because our Forefathers recognized *HaKadosh Baruch Hu* and accepted Him as their God, and this recognition and belief in Him was handed down to us by our parents, who received it from their parents, all the way back to the original *Avos*. To us, *HaKadosh Baruch Hu* is the same אֱלֹהֵינוּ He was to our Forefathers, וֵאלֹהֵי אֲבוֹתֵינוּ.

However, the bowing at the end of the *berachah* expresses the thought that there are some people who do not have an unbroken chain of a relationship with *HaKadosh Baruch Hu* through their ancestors. When they say אֱלֹהֵינוּ וֵאלֹהֵי אֲבוֹתֵינוּ they do not mean their immediate ancestors, because they have had to work out their own relationship with the *Ribbono Shel Olam* just as *Avraham Avinu* had to discover *HaKadosh Baruch Hu* by himself. Once *Avraham Avinu* recognized the existence of *HaKadosh Baruch Hu*, he had the courage and the wisdom and the *emunah* to firmly resist the negative influences of his parents and grandparents — and of the entire world at that time — who attempted to shake him from his conviction that there was One *Ribbono Shel Olam*, the Creator, Whom mankind must serve. Our *Chachamim* tell us that he was called אַבְרָם הָעִבְרִי (*Bereishis* 14:13), because כָּל הָעוֹלָם כֻּלּוֹ מֵעֵבֶר אֶחָד וְהוּא מֵעֵבֶר אַחֵר (*Bereishis Rabbah* 42:8) — there was no one else in the whole world who was on his side regarding the recognition of the *Ribbono Shel Olam*.

In our times, the Jews of Russia and the myriads of *baalei teshuvah* who are returning to the faith of our people in great numbers are examples of those who cannot say that *HaKadosh Baruch Hu* is the "God of their forefathers." Therefore, when we bow down at the end of the *berachah* while saying בָּרוּךְ אַתָּה ה' מָגֵן אַבְרָהָם, we thank *HaKadosh Baruch Hu* especially for protecting and strengthening those of our people who, like Avraham, have had to discover *HaKadosh Baruch Hu* themselves without the benefit of an attachment to the tradition of their immediate forebears.

In truth, this concept really applies to everyone, even those with a heritage of אֱלֹהֵי אֲבוֹתֵינוּ. We say in the *Haggadah*: מִתְּחִלָּה עוֹבְדֵי ע״ז הָיוּ אֲבוֹתֵינוּ, וְעַכְשָׁיו קֵרְבָנוּ הַמָּקוֹם לַעֲבוֹדָתוֹ, *Originally, our forefathers were idol worshipers, and now HaKadosh Baruch Hu has brought us close to His service*. It does not say וְאָז, *and then,* He brought us close; but rather, עַכְשָׁיו, *now,* as members of the Jewish nation, *HaKadosh Baruch Hu* has brought us, each individual, close to His service. This means that, notwithstanding the fact that a person may have the example of pious parents and grandparents, and may have been given an excellent Jewish education in Torah and *mitzvos,* he still lives in a world filled with seduction and attractions which oppose everything that he has inherited and has been taught. Unfortunately, there are many examples of those who have come from the finest Jewish homes but have, nevertheless, deviated from Judaism and gone far astray.

We are surrounded by a culture that has rejected, in large part, the sacred Jewish concept of עַיִן רוֹאָה וְאוֹזֶן שׁוֹמַעַת, *an eye is watching, and an ear is listening,* which teaches that a human being is held accountable for his actions. Public schools are even prohibited from teaching the existence of God. Therefore, in the world in which we live, each individual has his own *nisyonos* (challenges) that he must overcome in working out his own relationship with *HaKadosh Baruch Hu*.

Therefore, especially in our times, we should have the *kavannah,* when bowing to *HaKadosh Baruch Hu* at מָגֵן אַבְרָהָם, that in addition to אֱלֹהֵינוּ וֵאלֹהֵי אֲבוֹתֵינוּ, we thank Him for protecting us, as He did Avraham Avinu, against the onslaught and pressure of the powerful influences of the world filled with *kefirah* surrounding us, which could have a devastating effect on our *emunah* and *bitachon* in *HaKadosh Baruch Hu*. Similarly, on *Seder* night, in every generation, each individual expresses thanks to *HaKadosh Baruch Hu* that He has assisted him in his own efforts to come close to Him: וְעַכְשָׁיו קֵרְבָנוּ הַמָּקוֹם לַעֲבוֹדָתוֹ, *And now, constantly, HaKadosh Baruch Hu has brought us close to His service.*

The three *berachos* at the beginning of the *Shemoneh Esrei,* מָגֵן אַבְרָהָם, מְחַיֵּה הַמֵּתִים, הָאֵל הַקָּדוֹשׁ, are all considered one unit. Therefore, if one makes a substantial mistake in their wording — for instance, if he omits מַשִּׁיב הָרוּחַ וּמוֹרִיד הַגֶּשֶׁם — he is required to start again from the beginning of the first berachah (see *Orach Chaim* 114:4). Similarly, in *Aseres Yemei Teshuvah*, if one says הָאֵל הַקָּדוֹשׁ instead of הַמֶּלֶךְ הַקָּדוֹשׁ, he is required to start again from the beginning of the first *berachah*. This is in contrast to the omission of טַל וּמָטָר, where one has to begin again only from בָּרֵךְ עָלֵינוּ (see ibid. 117:5 for specifics on this).

The interconnection of the first three *berachos* is alluded to in the wording of the beginning of the first *berachah*: הָאֵל הַגָּדוֹל הַגִּבּוֹר וְהַנּוֹרָא. As we explained earlier, הַגָּדוֹל, corresponding to Avraham, refers to מָגֵן אַבְרָהָם; הַגִּבּוֹר, corresponding to Yitzchak, refers to אַתָּה גִבּוֹר; and הַנּוֹרָא, corresponding to Yaakov, refers to הָאֵל הַקָּדוֹשׁ [as is found in, נוֹרָא אֱלֹהִים מִמִּקְדָּשֶׁיךָ, *You are awesome, O God, from Your sanctuaries* (*Tehillim* 68:36)].

גְּבוּרוֹת

This second *berachah* of *Shemoneh Esrei* is called variously תְּחִיַּת הַמֵּתִים (*Berachos* 33a), because it ends with בָּרוּךְ אַתָּה ה' מְחַיֵּה הַמֵּתִים, or גְּבוּרוֹת (*Megillah* 17b), because it starts with אַתָּה גִבּוֹר. As we proceed, we will explain how both of these names actually express the same idea.

◆ אַתָּה גִבּוֹר לְעוֹלָם אֲדֹנָי — **You are eternally all-powerful, my Master.** The opening of this *berachah*, following immediately after מָגֵן אַבְרָהָם, utilizes the name אֲדֹנָי, which was first used to address *HaKadosh Baruch Hu* by Avraham Avinu (see *Berachos* 7b). In our study of *Adon Olam*, we explained the difference between מֶלֶךְ and אָדוֹן. We pointed out there that while a מֶלֶךְ, a king or ruler, has a general relationship with his subjects, because he has an entire nation to govern and knows very few of his people personally, an אָדוֹן, a master, has a personal relationship with his servants, and knows each one. So in our *berachos*, we start with בָּרוּךְ אַתָּה אֲדֹנָי, through which each person expresses the thought that *HaKadosh Baruch Hu* is "my personal Master" — He knows me, and I have a personal relationship with Him.

So while the earlier great *tzaddikim* — for instance, Adam, Mesushelach, Noach, and Shem — recognized *HaKadosh Baruch Hu* as the Universal Ruler, מֶלֶךְ הָעוֹלָם, it was Avraham Avinu who first taught that while *HaKadosh Baruch Hu* is the מֶלֶךְ הָעוֹלָם, nevertheless, He is also our *Adon* and, as such, He is aware of each individual, akin to the relationship of a master to His servant. Therefore each individual has a personal relationship with *HaKadosh Baruch Hu*.

The name אֲדֹנָי, meaning "My Master," describes the *middas hadin* of *HaKadosh Baruch Hu* (it contains the letters ד-נ); and י-ה-ו-ה, which we pronounce the same way, expresses His *middas harachamim* as the One Who is מְהַוֶּה כָּל הַהֲוָיוֹת, for He calls everything into existence. As we explained earlier, the only reason *HaKadosh Baruch Hu* created the world was to imbue His creatures with His goodness. Everything that was created was brought into existence as a vessel to receive the bounty of the מְהַוֶּה, *the One Who brings everything into existence.*

This combination of the written Name, which expresses the *middas harachamim* of *HaKadosh Baruch Hu,* and the pronounced Name, which expresses His *middas hadin,* reflects the idea that while we are a product of the *rachamim* of *HaKadosh Baruch Hu* — He created us and keeps us alive out of *rachamim* — we nevertheless call Him, "My Master," the One to Whom we are strictly accountable for our actions, because we accept upon ourselves the strict standard of conduct that "My Master" has laid down for us here in this world.

Our *Chachamim* tell us: יֵשׁ דִּין לְמַטָּה אֵין דִּין לְמַעְלָה (see *Devarim Rabbah* 5:4). This means that if we apply the *din* to ourselves here in this world, there will be no need for *HaKadosh Baruch Hu* to apply the *middas hadin* to us in *Olam Haba,* leaving only *rachamim* to be applied to us. While it is true that we have been placed here through the *middas harachamim* of *HaKadosh Baruch Hu,* nevertheless, the benefit of that *rachamim* can only be received by us if we do the will of *HaKadosh Baruch Hu* while we are alive.

The meaning of אַתָּה גִּבּוֹר לְעוֹלָם אֲדֹנָי is *You are eternally all-powerful, my Master.* גִּבּוֹר conveys the idea of being more powerful than something else — overpowering. As applied to *HaKadosh Baruch Hu,* it means "the absolutely superior strength." This absolute strength manifests itself through the fact that *HaKadosh Baruch Hu* calls all life into existence and, by the same token, can — and will eventually — also overpower and negate all of existence. This basic truth is at the root of the declaration by Yeshayahu HaNavi: כֹּה אָמַר ה' מֶלֶךְ יִשְׂרָאֵל וְגֹאֲלוֹ ה' צְבָאוֹת אֲנִי רִאשׁוֹן וַאֲנִי אַחֲרוֹן וּמִבַּלְעָדַי אֵין אֱלֹהִים, *Thus said Hashem, King of Israel and its Redeemer, Hashem, Master of Legions: I am the first and I am the last, and aside from Me there is no God* (Yeshayahu 44:6). It has also been incorporated into the *piyutim* (*Shir HaYichud,* Thursday): כֻּלָּם יִבְלוּ אַף יַחֲלוֹפוּ, הֵם יֹאבֵדוּ וְאַף יָסוּפוּ; וְאַתָּה תַעֲמוֹד וּתְבַלֶּה כֻּלָּם, כִּי חַי וְקַיָּם אַתָּה לְעוֹלָם, *They will all wither and pass on, they will be lost and cease to exist, but You will remain and outlive them all, because You live and exist forever.*

The power that *HaKadosh Baruch Hu* created to extinguish life is called the מַלְאַךְ הַמָּוֶת [*malach hamaves*], and the phrase אַתָּה גִּבּוֹר **לְעוֹלָם** אֲדֹנָי means that even this power of destruction that *HaKadosh Baruch Hu* created will eventually be overpowered by Him and be negated: בִּלַּע הַמָּוֶת לָנֶצַח, *He will eliminate death forever* (Yeshayahu 25:8). The *malach hamaves,* too, is only a creation of *HaKadosh Baruch Hu,* and is subject to the negation of its existence. This idea is likewise expressed in the *Haggadah* in *Chad Gadya*: וְאָתָא הקב"ה וְשָׁחַט לְמַלְאַךְ הַמָּוֶת, *and then HaKadosh Baruch Hu will come and slaughter the angel of death.*

This thought leads directly to the next phrase:

מְחַיֶּה מֵתִים אַתָּה — The Resurrector of the dead are You. The *gevurah* of *HaKadosh Baruch Hu* in negating the *malach hamaves* is in preparation for the creation of a new, higher form of life, that of *techiyas hameisim*. Thus, אַתָּה גִּבּוֹר לְעוֹלָם means, Your *gevurah* does not stop at extinguishing the existence of the *malach hamaves*, but rather, it lasts forever as manifested by *techiyas hameisim*.

Therefore, in this *tefillah*, each person expresses the thought: "You are eternally all-powerful, my Master." This means, I am here to serve You, and I know that at some point my life here on earth will end; but Your eternal power is such that eventually You will even negate the power You created that ended my life, and then I will live again by Your power of *techiyas hameisim*. Based on this, it is understandable that the names of this *berachah*, תְּחִיַּת הַמֵּתִים and גְּבוּרוֹת, actually convey the same idea.

רַב לְהוֹשִׁיעַ — The Master of salvation. *Techiyas hameisim* is the ultimate *yeshuah*, and it is described repeatedly as such in our *tefillos*: at the end of this *berachah*, וְאֵין דּוֹמֶה לְּךָ מוֹשִׁיעֵנוּ, and in הַכֹּל יוֹדוּךָ on Shabbos, מַצְמִיחַ יְשׁוּעָה לִתְחִיַּת הַמֵּתִים. Rav Samson R. Hirsch explains that the root of יְשׁוּעָה is יֵשׁ, which means "something" or "existence." It conveys the idea of something substantive, whereas, תְּשׁוּעָה means simply "victory." Therefore, *techiyas hameisim* is called יְשׁוּעָה in that *HaKadosh Baruch Hu* grants everlasting existence to those who have merited it, based on their *emunah* and conviction during their lifetime that יֵשׁ תְּחִיַּת הַמֵּתִים מִן הַתּוֹרָה, the tenet of the revival of the dead is promised to us in the Torah. (See *Rashi, Sanhedrin* 90a, s.v. האומר אין תחיית המתים מן התורה.)

Techiyas hameisim is described: וְרַבִּים מִיְּשֵׁנֵי אַדְמַת עָפָר יָקִיצוּ אֵלֶּה לְחַיֵּי עוֹלָם וְאֵלֶּה לַחֲרָפוֹת לְדִרְאוֹן עוֹלָם, *Many of those who sleep in the dust of the earth will awaken, some for eternal life, and some for eternal shame and damnation* (*Daniel* 12:2). This awesome event is called יוֹם הַדִּין הָאַחֲרוֹן or יוֹם הַדִּין הַגָּדוֹל וְהַנּוֹרָא, the most awesome day that ever existed (cf. *Malachi* 3:23), as described in *Tzephaniah* Ch. 1.

I heard an explanation in the name of Rav Aharon Kotler regarding the *yom hadin ha'acharon*, or "Final Day of Judgment," the judgment that each person must face in addition to the *din* following one's death. He explained that when one leaves this world and comes before the Heavenly Court, he is judged only on the basis of his deeds in *Olam Hazeh*, up to the day of his death. However, the effects or results of those deeds — or misdeeds — can have long-term consequences. For instance, let us say that during one's lifetime, one had a positive influence on another person who had doubts in his *emunah*. By inviting him and befriending him, he was successful in imparting his own strong *emunah* to the other person, who eventually became a *tzaddik* and whose children and grandchildren also became *tzaddikim*. Over the years, and over many generations, this could have resulted in thousands of *tzaddikim*. After hundreds of years, one friendly word could have resulted in an enormous amount of *kedushah* being brought into the world.

At the end of time, on the *yom hadin ha'acharon,* that original influential person will receive the benefit and reward for having been responsible for all those *tzaddikim* and their *maasim tovim* and the additional *kedushah* in the world, all of which is traceable to his beneficial influence.

And the reverse is also true. If a person causes a *chillul Hashem* in this world and others follow his example, or someone who might have become a *tzaddik* becomes an *apikores* because of an influential person's neglect of him, or because he observed an influential person in a state of disgrace and followed his example, these influential people will be held accountable. These people will have to bear the responsibility for the *aveiros* that were perpetrated as a result of their wrong example — or by their neglect — which could affect not only an individual but also his children and grandchildren who follow in his footsteps, and whose *aveiros* can be traced back to the omission or commission of that one influential person. It is for this reason that even *tzaddikim* fear the eventual *yom hadin ha'acharon*. Similarly, one friendly inquiry by Yosef of his coprisoners in jail — מַדּוּעַ פְּנֵיכֶם רָעִים הַיּוֹם, *Why do you appear downcast today?* — set into motion a chain of events which eventually led to *yetzias Mitzrayim* and *Matan Torah*. Without the simple friendly question of "Why are you looking so sad this morning? You don't look so good to me," the entire history of the world may well have been different.

Therefore, if *HaKadosh Baruch Hu* allows us to finally emerge successfully from the *yom hadin ha'acharon,* and we are raised from the dead and are judged as being worthy of אֵלֶּה לְחַיֵּי עוֹלָם (*Daniel* 12:2), it will be an everlasting life. This will, indeed, be יֵשׁ — the יְשׁוּעָה — because if we exist then, we will exist forever.

This is meant by the words מֶלֶךְ מֵמִית וּמְחַיֶּה וּמַצְמִיחַ יְשׁוּעָה — when *HaKadosh Baruch Hu* makes us live again, it will be the ultimate *yeshuah*.

מַשִּׁיב הָרוּחַ וּמוֹרִיד הַגֶּשֶׁם — **Who makes the wind blow and makes the rain descend.** This is said during the winter months only, and if one mistakenly says מוֹרִיד הַגֶּשֶׁם in the summer, or he forgets to say it in the winter, he is required to repeat the *Shemoneh Esrei*. (See *Shulchan Aruch, Orach Chaim* 114:4-5 for specifics of this *halachah*.)

We must understand why this phrase is suitable only for the winter. After all, מוֹרִיד הַגֶּשֶׁם means "He makes the rain fall." Life would be impossible without rain. What harm can there be in recognizing all year round that *HaKadosh Baruch Hu* creates rain?

Actually, though, rain represents both *din* and *rachamim*. If it rains in Eretz Yisrael during the summer months, it is very harmful to agriculture. At that time, rain does not represent *rachamim,* but rather *din*. A hurricane that brings a huge amount of rain can be catastrophic. The deluge of the *Mabul* was an example of rain that represented *middas hadin*. But in the winter months, rain in Eretz Yisrael represents *middas harachamim,* with its life-giving waters for drinking and growing food.

Therefore, the untimely mentioning of מוֹרִיד הַגֶּשֶׁם would represent *middas hadin,* and would be a distortion of the context of this *berachah* which expresses the *middas harachamim* of *HaKadosh Baruch Hu,* with *techiyas hameisim* — the ultimate in *middas harachamim* — as its central thought.

The reason the *mesadrei hatefillah* inserted מַשִּׁיב הָרוּחַ in the *berachah* of *techiyas hameisim* is given in the Gemara: אָמַר מַזְכִּירִין גְּבוּרוֹת גְּשָׁמִים מַאי טַעְמָא? רַב יוֹסֵף: מִתּוֹךְ שֶׁשְּׁקוּלָה כִּתְחִיַּית הַמֵּתִים, לְפִיכָךְ קְבָעוּהָ בִּתְחִיַּית הַמֵּתִים (*Berachos* 33a). Paraphrased, this means, Rav Yosef said that the reason we mention the "Strength of Rainfall" in the *berachah* of *techiyas hameisim* is because rainfall is equivalent to the revival of the dead. The basic similarity between the effect of rainfall and *techiyas hameisim* is quite obvious. When a seed is placed into the ground, it first disintegrates. When it becomes saturated with rain, it slowly begins to develop and sprout its growth out of the earth. A large apple tree, capable of producing thousands of apples, can develop from the decaying seed of a rotten apple. Similarly, when the human body is placed into the ground, it first disintegrates, but at *techiyas hameisim* it will come to life again: וּמַצְמִיחַ יְשׁוּעָה, He causes the "ultimate salvation," *techiyas hameisim,* to sprout forth from the ground.

However, on an esoteric level, our *Chachamim* have called the life-giving force with which *HaKadosh Baruch Hu* will revive those who are worthy of *chayei olam,* everlasting life, allegorically as טַל וְגֶשֶׁם שֶׁל תְּחִיָּה, which is based on the verse, גֶּשֶׁם נְדָבוֹת תָּנִיף אֱלֹהִים, *A generous rain did You lavish, O God* (*Tehillim* 68:10). (See *Yalkut Shimoni, Tehillim* 68, Para. 795; also see *Shabbos* 88b.) Reference is made to this concept repeatedly in the *piyutim* of תְּפִלַּת טַל and תְּפִלַּת גֶּשֶׁם.

It is for these reasons that the *mesadrei hatefillah* have incorporated מַשִּׁיב הָרוּחַ וּמוֹרִיד הַגֶּשֶׁם in the *tefillah* of תְּחִיַּת הַמֵּתִים.

מְכַלְכֵּל חַיִּים בְּחֶסֶד, מְחַיֵּה מֵתִים בְּרַחֲמִים רַבִּים — He provides life to the living with kindness, He resurrects the dead out of abundant mercy. Our *Chachamim* tell us: כָּל הַנְּבִיאִים כּוּלָן לֹא נִתְנַבְּאוּ אֶלָּא לִימוֹת הַמָּשִׁיחַ, אֲבָל לָעוֹלָם הַבָּא, "עַיִן לֹא רָאָתָה אֱלֹהִים זוּלָתְךָ" (*Berachos* 34b). All the prophecies of the *Neviim* have never gone farther than that of a description of the world at the time of *yemos haMashiach*. However, no one, including the *Neviim,* has ever been given a description of *Olam Haba,* meaning *techiyas hameisim*. This is known only to *HaKadosh Baruch Hu*. This statement is based on the *pasuk*, עַיִן לֹא רָאָתָה אֱלֹהִים זוּלָתְךָ, *No eye had ever seen it — except for You, O God.* (*Yeshayahu* 64:3).

While we can have no conception of the world of *techiyas hameisim*, our world is filled with "*techiyas hameisim*-like" events, which have certain similarities to that future world. The *mesadrei hatefillah* have included מְכַלְכֵּל חַיִּים בְּחֶסֶד in the *berachah* of מְחַיֵּה הַמֵּתִים to illustrate some of the "*techiyas hameisim*-like" events which we experience here in this world, and the *tefillah* will cite some examples.

However, first we must understand the nuances of the phrase itself. מְכַלְכֵּל חַיִּים בְּחֶסֶד means that He provides life to the living with חֶסֶד, *kindness;* but, מְחַיֵּה מֵתִים בְּרַחֲמִים רַבִּים, what He does for the dead is done בְּרַחֲמִים רַבִּים, *with abundant mercy.*

The word מְכַלְכֵּל expresses the idea of a limitation. While *HaKadosh Baruch Hu* sustains life with *chessed,* He does so with limits. מְכַלְכֵּל is related to כָּלָא, restrain, or כּוּל, contain, both having the meaning of limitation, which is also the root of כַּלְכָּלָה, *basket* — a limited amount.

An example of this usage would be כַּלְכָּלַת שַׁבָּת, *a basket [of fruit] for Shabbos* (*Eduyos* 4:4), meaning limited for a specific purpose; or וַיְכַלְכֵּל יוֹסֵף אֶת אָבִיו וְאֶת אֶחָיו וְאֵת כָּל בֵּית אָבִיו לֶחֶם לְפִי הַטָּף, *Yosef sustained his father and his brothers and all of his father's household with food according to the children* (*Bereishis* 47:12). While Joseph provided his family with the necessary means for their livelihood, this is described as וַיְכַלְכֵּל, meaning he rationed their provisions, based on the number of people and their ages — children tend to waste more food than adults — to avoid the appearance of their living a luxurious life while the rest of the country was starving. [Also see הִנֵּה הַשָּׁמַיִם וּשְׁמֵי הַשָּׁמַיִם לֹא יְכַלְכְּלוּךָ, *Behold, the heavens and the highest heavens cannot contain You* (*Melachim I* 8:27).]

The meaning of מְכַלְכֵּל חַיִּים בְּחֶסֶד, therefore, can be paraphrased as: "He mercifully provides food and provisions sufficient for the sustenance of life."

While *HaKadosh Baruch Hu* sustains life בְּחֶסֶד — and all of life is filled with His *chassadim* — this kindness is, nevertheless, limited. To be sure, it is by the *chessed* of *HaKadosh Baruch Hu* that we are able to get up in the morning, and think, and see, and hear, and earn a livelihood, but not every person has been given these abilities. And even among those who have, there are differences among them, with some being more blessed than others. However, מְחַיֵּה מֵתִים is done בְּרַחֲמִים רַבִּים, meaning רַחֲמִים פְּשׁוּטִים, with absolute, unlimited, and boundless lovingkindness.

So the sense of this phrase is: That which *HaKadosh Baruch Hu* does for life in this world in a limited and measured form, He does at *techiyas hameisim* in an unlimited way, בְּרַחֲמִים רַבִּים.

What follows now are examples of the *chassadim* of *HaKadosh Baruch Hu* that transcend the ordinary day-to-day merciful sustenance of life by *HaKadosh Baruch Hu,* and are "*techiyas hameisim*-like" events that can be experienced in this world.

פּוֹמֵךְ נוֹפְלִים — **He supports the falling.** There are people who experience a constant series of "falling down" in their lives. They have one failure or disappointment after another. They see the bottom falling out from under them. And then, suddenly, *HaKadosh Baruch Hu* lifts them up, and they experience a turnaround in their lives. This is an example of a "*techiyas hameisim*-like" event. However, these events are still only examples of מְכַלְכֵּל חַיִּים בְּחֶסֶד, measured and limited acts of kindness, but not בְּרַחֲמִים רַבִּים, because such cases are rare and, even if one experiences such a turnaround, he could lose his livelihood again.

וְרוֹפֵא חוֹלִים — **He heals the sick.** Consider the case of someone who falls seriously ill, with the doctors abandoning all hope for his recovery, and he, himself, believing he will never get well. But then, he experiences a sudden, inexplicable recovery, and lives for many years. This is an example of an event of *techiyas hameisim* in this world, as a result of the *chessed* of *HaKadosh Baruch Hu.* Yet, such cases cannot be described as occurring בְּרַחֲמִים רַבִּים, because first, such recoveries are not universal, and furthermore, one could become sick again. In addition, every person will eventually reach the point when he will not recover and will experience death.

וּמַתִּיר אֲסוּרִים — **He releases the confined.** If one is in prison — or in a concentration camp — without hope of release and he suddenly receives a pardon, or the American army captures the concentration camp and frees all the prisoners, he has experienced a *techiyas hameisim*-like event. However, while this event is an example of the *chessed* of *HaKadosh Baruch Hu,* there is no guarantee that this person will not once again lose his freedom.

We have already pointed out in the *berachah* of הַמַּחֲזִיר נְשָׁמוֹת לִפְגָרִים מֵתִים that in our daily cycle of sleeping and awakening we experience something of the miracle of *techiyas hameisim.* While we are asleep, our consciousness leaves us and, upon our awakening, it returns. In fact, *Chazal* call sleep "one sixtieth of death" (see *Berachos* 57b). If sleep is one sixtieth of death, then awakening is one sixtieth of *techiyas hameisim.* The very fact that we awaken in the morning is an act of *techiyas hameisim.* Therefore, if one forgot to say the *berachah* of הַמַּחֲזִיר נְשָׁמוֹת לִפְגָרִים מֵתִים, and has already completed the *Shemoneh Esrei,* he need not say it later, because he has affirmed his *emunah* by saying בָּרוּךְ אַתָּה ה' מְחַיֵּה הַמֵּתִים (see *Mishnah Berurah* 6:12).

These are examples of מְכַלְכֵּל חַיִּים בְּחֶסֶד, in which *HaKadosh Baruch Hu* metes out His acts of kindness in this world which, while they are not limitless, are nevertheless *mei'ein Olam Haba.*

§❧ וּמְקַיֵּם אֱמוּנָתוֹ לִישֵׁנֵי עָפָר — **And He maintains His faith to those asleep in the dust.** This means that at the actual event of *techiyas hameisim*, *HaKadosh Baruch Hu* will fulfill His faithfulness to those "who sleep in the dust," בְּרַחֲמִים רַבִּים, with boundless and endless mercy, unlike the מְכַלְכֵּל חַיִּים in this world, which is limited and measured. Those who merit *chayei Olam Haba* after *techiyas hameisim* will live on forever, as a result of the רַחֲמִים רַבִּים of *HaKadosh Baruch Hu*. He will maintain His faithfulness to them, וּמְקַיֵּם אֱמוּנָתוֹ, forever.

Interestingly, it does not say here לִישֵׁנֵי בֶעָפָר, those who sleep *in* the dust, but rather לִישֵׁנֵי עָפָר, literally: those who sleep the dust. This is a reference to the *pasuk*, כִּי עָפָר אַתָּה וְאֶל עָפָר תָּשׁוּב, *For you are dust, and to dust shall you return* (*Bereishis* 3:19). It means that those who have died have, themselves, become nothing but dust, and yet *HaKadosh Baruch Hu* will make them live again forever at *techiyas hameisim*.

§❧ מִי כָמוֹךָ בַּעַל גְּבוּרוֹת — **Who is like You, Master of strengths.** "Strengths," in the plural here, refers to both aspects of the *gevurah* of *HaKadosh Baruch Hu*: the strength of destroying life, and of destroying the destroyer of life, וְשָׁחַט לְמַלְאַךְ הַמָּוֶת, which will result in *techiyas hameisim*. (See above on גְּבוּרוֹת.)

§❧ וּמִי דוֹמֶה לָךְ — **Who can be compared to You.** We have no frame of reference for *HaKadosh Baruch Hu*. He is incomprehensible.

§❧ מֶלֶךְ מֵמִית וּמְחַיֶּה — **The same King Who puts to death also brings to life.** This is based on אֲנִי אָמִית וַאֲחַיֶּה, *I put to death and I bring life* (*Devarim* 32:39). The Gemara (*Pesachim* 68a) offers this *pasuk* as one of the sources of *techiyas hameisim*.

The act of taking away life is itself the beginning of *techiyas hameisim*, as it is stated: הַיִּלּוֹדִים לָמוּת וְהַמֵּתִים לִחְיוֹת, *The newborn will die; the dead will live again* (*Pirkei Avos* 4:29). From the moment a person is created, his heart begins to beat, and it beats throughout his life, but, like a clock, eventually the beating will stop, and his life will end. A very prosaic example can be found in our modern-day telephones. A phone is programmed to emit loud tones to attract attention if it is left off the hook. However, after a certain period of time, the tones are programmed to stop and the line will be disconnected. Similarly, we must know that life is programmed — for eventual death.

And the same thing applies to death: וְהַמֵּתִים לִחְיוֹת, death is also programmed — for eventual life. The process of dying, בַּר מִנָּן (may it be far removed from us), is a preparation for the eventual life of *techiyas hameisim*.

§❧ וּמַצְמִיחַ יְשׁוּעָה — **He makes salvation sprout.** צֶמַח means a slow process of growth. When the *neshamah* and the *guf* are separated at the time of death, both go through a purification process. The *neshamah* is purified in the higher world, and the *guf* is purified by its disintegration in the *kever*. By turning into עָפָר, dust of the earth, it is cleansed of all its sins and *tumah*. Then, at *techiyas hameisim,* the two purified entities are reunited. Therefore, מַצְמִיחַ יְשׁוּעָה means that at the time of a person's death, HaKadosh Baruch Hu begins a slow purification process of both *guf* and *neshamah,* and this process will eventually grow into the "ultimate *yeshuah,*" when the purified *guf* and *neshamah* are reunited at *techiyas hameisim.*

וְנֶאֱמָן אַתָּה לְהַחֲיוֹת מֵתִים — **And You are faithful to resurrect the dead.** We have full *emunah* that this is going to take place.

We have already made reference to the explanation given by Rashi to the Mishnah: כָּל יִשְׂרָאֵל יֵשׁ לָהֶם חֵלֶק לָעוֹלָם הַבָּא . . . וְאֵלוּ שֶׁאֵין לָהֶם חֵלֶק לָעוֹלָם הַבָּא הָאוֹמֵר אֵין תְּחִיַּת הַמֵּתִים מִן הַתּוֹרָה. (*Sanhedrin* 90a.) If one denies that there are sources for *techiyas hameisim* in the Torah, he will, indeed, not have a share in that world of *techiyas hameisim.*

This is explained by Rashi as follows: שֶׁכּוֹפֵר בַּמִּדְרָשִׁים דְּדַרְשִׁינָן בַּגְּמָרָא לְקַמָּן מִנַּיִן לִתְחִיַּת הַמֵּתִים מִן הַתּוֹרָה. וַאֲפִילוּ יְהֵא מוֹדֶה וּמַאֲמִין שֶׁיִּהְיוּ הַמֵּתִים אֶלָּא דְּלֹא רְמִיזָא בְּאוֹרַיְיתָא, כּוֹפֵר הוּא. This means that even if a person believes — as do many religions — that there will be some form of resurrection of the dead, but he does not believe that there are sources for this in the Torah, he is still considered a *kofer,* a nonbeliever, and will therefore not have any share in *techiyas hameisim.*

The concept of resurrection of the dead is a universal belief based on man's desire to live on forever, and is comforting for those who have lost loved ones, because they can look forward to being reunited with them again. However, the Jewish concept of *techiyas hameisim* is not based on some human wishful thinking, but rather, it is *min haTorah*; the Torah tells us that it will happen.

And Rashi (ibid.) continues to explain this statement: הוֹאִיל וְעִיקָּר שֶׁיֵּשׁ תְּחִיַּת הַמֵּתִים מִן הַתּוֹרָה, מַה לָּנוּ וְלֶאֱמוּנָתוֹ, וְכִי מֵהֵיכָן הוּא יוֹדֵעַ שֶׁכֵּן הוּא, הִלְכָּךְ כּוֹפֵר גָּמוּר הוּא, *Since he denies that the source for techiyas hameisim is found in the Torah, of what value is his belief? How does he know that it is true? Therefore, such a person is a complete heretic.*

Thus, the Mishnah is telling us that even if a person firmly believes, as we do, that the dead will rise again — not only spiritually, but also physically, in the sense that the body will be re-created and emerge from the earth and live again — but he denies that there are sources for *techiyas hameisim* in the Torah, he is a *kofer,* a heretic, who will have no share in that future life. *If his belief is not rooted in the Torah, it is worthless.*

בָּרוּךְ אַתָּה ה' מְחַיֵּה הַמֵּתִים — **Blessed are You, Hashem, Who resurrects the dead.** Our belief in *techiyas hameisim* is so strong that we make this *berachah* — in the present tense — as if we had witnessed it ourselves.

There is a *halachah* that if one sees his friend, whom he has not seen in a year, he says בָּרוּךְ אַתָּה ה' מְחַיֵּה הַמֵּתִים (*Orach Chaim* 225:1). The reason is because when this happens, one can get some idea of *techiyas hameisim*.

During the *Aseres Yemei Teshuvah*, at this point, we add: מִי כָמוֹךָ אַב הָרַחֲמִים זוֹכֵר יְצוּרָיו לְחַיִּים בְּרַחֲמִים, meaning that we are asking *HaKadosh Baruch Hu* in his mercy to allow us to experience *techiyas hameisim* and live again.

קְדֻשַּׁת הַשֵּׁם

❧ אַתָּה קָדוֹשׁ וְשִׁמְךָ קָדוֹשׁ וּקְדוֹשִׁים בְּכָל יוֹם יְהַלְלוּךָ סֶּלָה — *You are Kadosh; and Your Name is Kadosh; and holy beings praise You every day forever.* The word קָדוֹשׁ has at its core the meaning of "separation." קְדֹשִׁים תִּהְיוּ, *You shall be holy* (*Vayikra* 19:2), is explained by *Chazal* to mean הֱווּ פְּרוּשִׁים מִן הָעֲרָיוֹת וּמִן הָעֲבֵירָה. Thus, when we speak of an אִישׁ קָדוֹשׁ, we mean a person who has separated and raised himself above most other people.

We also find this root used in the opposite sense: הַקְּדֵשָׁה, *the harlot* (*Bereishis* 38:21). The sense there is of one who is separated and designated for a lewd purpose.

Also, there are numerous examples of various border cities that were called קָדֵשׁ, with the meaning "boundary," because they separated one country from another: קָדֵשׁ עִיר קָצֶה גְבוּלֶךָ (*Bamidbar* 20:16); קָדֵשׁ בַּרְנֵעַ (ibid. 32:8), the southern boundary from which the *meraglim* (spies) were sent; קֶדֶשׁ נַפְתָּלִי (*Shoftim* 4:6), the northern border of Eretz Yisrael. And there are many more such examples.

As it relates to *HaKadosh Baruch Hu*, the concept קָדוֹשׁ conveys the thought of His being far removed from our sphere of understanding. Our phrase contains קָדוֹשׁ three times, and this is based on the pronouncement of the *malachim* in the *nevuah* of Yeshayahu: קָדוֹשׁ קָדוֹשׁ קָדוֹשׁ ה' צְבָאוֹת (*Yeshayahu* 6:3).

❏ וּקְדוֹשִׁים בְּכָל יוֹם יְהַלְלוּךָ סֶּלָה — *And holy beings praise You every day forever.* This latter phrase refers to the *malachim* who are called *kedoshim*, as in בּוֹרֵא קְדוֹשִׁים in בִּרְכַּת יוֹצֵר. These beings are not *kedoshim* by their own doing — as we are obliged to become by the mandate קְדֹשִׁים תִּהְיוּ; rather, they were created as *kedoshim*.

The *malachim*, in their pronouncement קָדוֹשׁ קָדוֹשׁ קָדוֹשׁ, convey both the concept of God's incomprehensibility, and also that He has revealed certain aspects of His Being to His creatures. This is alluded to by the *taamim*, which accent and enhance the meaning of the words, as we shall explain.

❏ אַתָּה קָדוֹשׁ, *You are holy,* corresponds to the first קָדוֹשׁ, which is accented by a דַּרְגָּא, *darga,* the rising tone, expressing the total incomprehensibility of

SHEMONEH ESREI ✦ 431

any conception of *HaKadosh Baruch Hu* in our minds; He is completely separated and removed from our understanding.

We discussed this earlier in explaining the word אַתָּה הוּא, which conveys the idea that to us, *HaKadosh Baruch Hu* can only be thought of in terms of "He," meaning what we know of "Him," but we are incapable of knowing His essence. We know only that He exists, and that He is the בּוֹרֵא כָּל הַמַּעֲשִׂים, *Creator of everything which exists;* that He is יָחִיד, *absolutely One;* that He is רִאשׁוֹן and that He is אַחֲרוֹן, *that He is the first and the last of existence;* that He is מַשְׁגִּיחַ עַל הָעוֹלָם, *that He supervises the entire world.* He revealed these aspects of His existence to us. Other than that, we know nothing of Him. He is הַקָּדוֹשׁ בָּרוּךְ הוּא, *the holy One, Blessed is He;* but what the essence of this "He" is, is beyond our power of conception. The human mind cannot comprehend something that has no beginning and no end. He is simply — קָדוֹשׁ.

❑ וְשִׁמְךָ קָדוֹשׁ, *Your Name is holy.* This corresponds to the second קָדוֹשׁ which is accented by a תְּבִיר, *tevir,* a falling sound, indicating that *HaKadosh Baruch Hu* has revealed to us certain aspects of His Being: His Names. This means that while we have no conception of Him, nevertheless, *HaKadosh Baruch Hu* has revealed to us His "Names," His attributes, that aspect of His Being that He wishes us to know. Rav Samson R. Hirsch explains that the word שֵׁם, *name,* is related to שָׁם, meaning *there.* In the realm of the mind, by naming and defining something, one puts it in its "proper place."

When *HaKadosh Baruch Hu* said אָנֹכִי ה' אֱלֹהֶיךָ, He meant: Regarding Me, you know only that I am אֱלֹהֶיךָ, and what I have revealed to you about Me. Regarding the essence of My Being, the human mind can have no conception, I am בְּלִי רֵאשִׁית וּבְלִי תַכְלִית, *without a beginning and without an end.* However, what you can know about Me are My "Names," that which I revealed to you through the Torah. This is what is meant by כָּל הַתּוֹרָה כֻּלָּהּ שְׁמוֹתָיו שֶׁל הקב״ה (see *Zohar HaKadosh* 3:13b and *Ramban, Introduction to Bereishis*). Every letter, every word in the Torah is another *Shem,* another revelation of *HaKadosh Baruch Hu.*

These are the things that He wants us to know about Him. Therefore, in *birchos haTorah,* we say: וְנִהְיֶה אֲנַחְנוּ וכו' יוֹדְעֵי שְׁמֶךָ, *May we be knowledgeable of Your Name.* The teachings of the Torah are Your "Names." *HaKadosh Baruch Hu* has revealed to us, through the Torah and *Neviim,* what His will in the world is, and we pray that we be given the proper understanding of what that will is. (See below on נְקַדֵּשׁ אֶת שִׁמְךָ בָּעוֹלָם.)

❑ וּקְדוֹשִׁים בְּכָל יוֹם יְהַלְלוּךָ סֶּלָה, *and holy beings praise You every day forever.* This corresponds to the third קָדוֹשׁ, of צְבָאוֹת, קָדוֹשׁ ה' צְבָאוֹת, *the God of the heavenly hosts,* and refers to the holy beings, the *malachim,* the *Serafim,* the *Ofanim,* the *Chayos HaKodesh,* and the other *mesharsim,* spiritual ministrant beings, to whom "the Names of *HaKadosh Baruch Hu*" — meaning Torah — was revealed first. These spiritual beings have a somewhat higher comprehension of *HaKadosh Baruch Hu* than we do, but, they, too, recognize that His essence is far above them. [Ed. note: The Rav here touched on the Kabbalistic concept of חָכְמָה בִּינָה וָדַעַת, referring to the existence of the Torah before the world was created, and which was known only to the *malachim* who surrounded the Throne of Glory. He did not elaborate on it.]

The Torah tells us, קְדֹשִׁים תִּהְיוּ, *You shall be holy* (*Vayikra* 19:2), which is explained by *Chazal* to mean הֱווּ פְּרוּשִׁים מִן הָעֲרָיוֹת וּמִן הָעֲבֵירָה (see *Rashi* ibid.), which in this case conveys the thought: *You shall remove yourselves far away from prohibited unions.* The reason given by the Torah is כִּי קָדוֹשׁ אֲנִי ה׳ אֱלֹהֵיכֶם, *Because I Hashem, your God, am holy* (ibid.). The difficulty here is obvious. It is analogous to a demand by a king that "You shall be a king because I am a king"; or by a philosopher that, "You shall be a philosopher because I am one." How can *HaKadosh Baruch Hu* ask us to be holy because He is holy? We are human beings; *HaKadosh Baruch Hu* created us with a *yetzer hara* and placed us in a material world with all its attractions and enticements.

But *HaKadosh Baruch Hu* is telling us here קְדֹשִׁים תִּהְיוּ, which means, פְּרוּשִׁים תִּהְיוּ, separate yourselves from your animal urges, כִּי קָדוֹשׁ אֲנִי ה׳ אֱלֹהֵיכֶם, because I have placed within you a spark of my own *kedushah*, the *tzelem Elokim*, which is the ability of the human being to overpower and separate himself from his *yetzer hara*. Just as *HaKadosh Baruch Hu* is קָדוֹשׁ above and not bound by His nature, He has imbued the human being with a similar power of *kedushah*, that of being able to transcend his own urges and inclinations, and separate himself from them.

And we thank *HaKadosh Baruch Hu* for giving us this ability of transcending our animal urges, and thereby assuming an aspect of *kedushah*, by saying, **בָּרוּךְ אַתָּה ה׳ הָאֵל הַקָּדוֹשׁ — Blessed are You, Hashem, the holy God.** As we explained earlier, the name אֵל, *Almighty*, denotes the *middas harachamim* of *HaKadosh Baruch Hu*. The greatest *rachamim* that *HaKadosh Baruch Hu* has shown us is that He gave us the ability to become *kedoshim*. And this is true even if someone has already succumbed to his desires and tasted the *aveiros*, and has developed a desire to do more *aveiros*; he still has within him the capacity for *kedushah* that *HaKadosh Baruch Hu* granted to him, to overcome his nature, and to become a person whom the Torah can call *kadosh*.

During the *Aseres Yemei Teshuvah*, we substitute הַמֶּלֶךְ הַקָּדוֹשׁ for הָאֵל הַקָּדוֹשׁ, because during this period, the time of *din*, we apply much stricter standards to ourselves and do not rely only on the וְחַנֹּתִי אֶת אֲשֶׁר אָחֹן וְרִחַמְתִּי אֶת אֲשֶׁר אֲרַחֵם, *And I will gratuitously grant mercy and have compassion to those whom I wish to favor* (*Shemos* 33:19), denoted by the name אֵל, which could sometimes result in a person being favored even if he does not deserve it. However, during the *Aseres Yemei Teshuvah,* if one does not do *teshuvah* and relies only on the *middas harachamim,* he will not pass the test of the *yemei hadin.* Therefore, during this time, we do not stress the הָאֵל aspect of *HaKadosh Baruch Hu,* but rather, we are encouraged to look fearfully at *HaKadosh Baruch Hu* as הַמֶּלֶךְ, the King, Who decides our fate based on our actions — and not on mercy alone.

קְדֻשָּׁה דַעֲמִידָה

We will now discuss the *Kedushah* said by the *shaliach tzibbur* during the repetition of the *Shemoneh Esrei.* The pronouncement of קְדֻשַּׁת הַשֵּׁם in public — that is, among ten adult Jewish males — is a fulfillment of the *mitzvah* of וְנִקְדַּשְׁתִּי בְּתוֹךְ בְּנֵי יִשְׂרָאֵל, *I should be sanctified among Bnei Yisrael* (*Vayikra* 22:32; see *Berachos* 21b). The saying of the public *Kedushah* is of such great importance that one is required to interrupt even *Krias Shema* and its blessings in order to join the *tzibbur* in the public pronouncement of the words of the *malachim* as reported by the *Neviim.*

The saying of the words of *Kedushah,* specifically, קָדוֹשׁ קָדוֹשׁ קָדוֹשׁ ה' צְבָאוֹת מְלֹא כָל הָאָרֶץ כְּבוֹדוֹ, and בָּרוּךְ כְּבוֹד ה' מִמְּקוֹמוֹ (from *Yeshayahu* 6:3 and *Yechezkel* 3:12), is an expression of our yearning to eventually merit *Olam Haba,* where we will join the *malachim* as one of the *mesharsim* who express these words of *kedushah* to *HaKadosh Baruch Hu.* [Ed. Note: This is a reference to the Rav's earlier explanation at *Bircas Yotzer* of the meaning of these מְשָׁרְתִים and קְדוֹשִׁים, and the repeated use of כֻּלָּם in that *tefillah*. A review of that section would be very useful in understanding this thought.] The *minhag* to lift oneself up on one's toes during the *Kedushah* when quoting the words קָדוֹשׁ קָדוֹשׁ קָדוֹשׁ and בָּרוּךְ כְּבוֹד ה' מִמְּקוֹמוֹ (and according to some opinions, יִמְלֹךְ ה' לְעוֹלָם) is symbolic of the flying motions of the *malachim* described there by the *Neviim,* and expresses our desire to emulate those *malachim* here, in this world, and — eventually, in *Olam Haba* — to be among the *malachim* who express these lofty concepts of the *kedushah* of *HaKadosh Baruch Hu* (see *Rema, Orach Chaim* 125).

◆§ נְקַדֵּשׁ אֶת שִׁמְךָ בָּעוֹלָם §◆ — **We wish to declare the Holiness of Your Name in this world.** We cannot actually "declare the Holiness" of *HaKadosh Baruch Hu* Himself; the most we can do is to "declare the Holiness" of His Name, that which He has revealed about Himself to us through the Torah. Actually, we know that כָּל הַתּוֹרָה כֻּלָּהּ שְׁמוֹתָיו שֶׁל הקב״ה, everything in the Torah — especially all the *mitzvos* — is a description of what *HaKadosh Baruch Hu* wants of us and our purpose in life. As far as we are concerned, this is all that we know of Him. To us, His Torah is His Name. When we express the *kedushah* of *HaKadosh Baruch Hu,* we can do so concerning what we know about Him — His "Name."

ۘ *כְּשֵׁם שֶׁמַּקְדִּישִׁים אוֹתוֹ בִּשְׁמֵי מָרוֹם* — **In the same way as they sanctify Him in the heavens on high.** We have already suggested in our explanations of *Bircas Yotzer* that the meaning of מְשָׁרְתִים of *HaKadosh Baruch Hu*, and the often-repeated כֻּלָּם in that *berachah*, is a reference not only to the *malachim*, but also to the *tzaddikim* who lived in this world, with the hope that after their *neshamos* would be transferred by *HaKadosh Baruch Hu* from their physical environment in this world to *Olam Haba*, these *neshamos* would have the *zechiyah* to be placed near the *Kisei HaKavod*, to join the *malachim*. It is this thought that is meant by: נְקַדֵּשׁ אֶת שִׁמְךָ בָּעוֹלָם כְּשֵׁם שֶׁמַּקְדִּישִׁים אוֹתוֹ בִּשְׁמֵי מָרוֹם. We express the desire to sanctify *HaKadosh Baruch Hu* already in this world, in the same way as the *malachim* do in heaven, and eventually to be *zocheh* to join them near the *Kisei HaKavod*. Thereupon, we quote קָדוֹשׁ קָדוֹשׁ ה׳ (*Yeshayahu* 6:3) and בָּרוּךְ כְּבוֹד ה׳ מִמְּקוֹמוֹ (*Yechezkel* 3:12), which are the words of *Kedushah* that these *Neviim* reported that they heard in the spiritual world.

ۘ *כַּכָּתוּב עַל יַד נְבִיאֶךָ, וְקָרָא זֶה אֶל זֶה וְאָמַר: קָדוֹשׁ קָדוֹשׁ קָדוֹשׁ ה׳ צְבָאוֹת, מְלֹא כָל הָאָרֶץ כְּבוֹדוֹ. לְעֻמָּתָם בָּרוּךְ יֹאמֵרוּ. בָּרוּךְ כְּבוֹד ה׳ מִמְּקוֹמוֹ* — **As it is written by Your prophet, "And an (angel) will call another and say: 'Holy, Holy, Holy is Hashem, Masters of Legions, the whole world is filled with His glory.'" Those facing them say, "Blessed": "Blessed is the glory of Hashem from His place."**

[Ed. note: At this point, the Rav reiterated his deeply insightful explanation of the meaning of בָּרוּךְ כְּבוֹד ה׳ מִמְּקוֹמוֹ and קָדוֹשׁ קָדוֹשׁ ה׳ וגו׳ which he detailed in *Bircas Yotzer* at *Kedushah d'yeshivah*. Please refer to it there, especially with regard to the Rav's unique interpretation of the significance of the *minhag* to sit during *Kedushah d'yeshivah* and to stand during *Kedushah da'amidah*. Also please refer to the Rav's remarks on בָּרוּךְ שֵׁם כְּבוֹד מַלְכוּתוֹ לְעוֹלָם וָעֶד in *Bircas Yotzer*.]

ۘ *וּבְדִבְרֵי קָדְשְׁךָ כָּתוּב לֵאמֹר: יִמְלֹךְ ה׳ לְעוֹלָם, אֱלֹהַיִךְ צִיּוֹן לְדֹר וָדֹר הַלְלוּיָהּ* — **And in Your holy writings the following is written: "Hashem shall reign forever — your God, O Tziyon — from generation to generation, Halleluyah!"** This *pasuk* (*Tehillim* 146:10) is a part of the *Kedushah* but is not as important as the previous two *pesukim*, בָּרוּךְ כְּבוֹד וגו׳ and קָדוֹשׁ וגו׳, and therefore does not warrant the interruption of *Krias Shema* and its blessings in order to say it together with the *tzibbur* (see *Mishnah Berurah* 66:17).

We should know that the *pesukim* that we quote in the *Kedushah* correspond to the words שֵׁם כְּבוֹד מַלְכוּתוֹ לְעוֹלָם וָעֶד from בָּרוּךְ שֵׁם כְּבוֹד מַלְכוּתוֹ, which Moshe Rabbeinu heard the *malachim* saying in praise of *HaKadosh Baruch Hu* (see *Devarim Rabbah* 2:36; *Midrash Tanchuma*, *Kedoshim* 6).

The correlation is as follows:

קָדוֹשׁ קָדוֹשׁ קָדוֹשׁ ה׳ צְבָאוֹת מְלֹא כָל הָאָרֶץ כְּבוֹדוֹ — in which we mention the exalted Name of *HaKadosh Baruch Hu* — corresponds to בָּרוּךְ כְּבוֹד ה׳; מִמְּקוֹמוֹ corresponds to כְּבוֹד; and the *pesukim* of *malchus*, which are either ה׳ יִמְלֹךְ לְעֹלָם וָעֶד or יִמְלֹךְ ה׳ לְעוֹלָם אֱלֹהַיִךְ צִיּוֹן, correspond to מַלְכוּתוֹ.

It is important that we understand why the *mesadrei hatefillah* chose the *pasuk*, יִמְלֹךְ ה׳ לְעוֹלָם אֱלֹהַיִךְ צִיּוֹן לְדֹר וָדֹר הַלְלוּיָהּ, which is from *Tehillim*, rather than a similar *pasuk* from the Torah, ה׳ יִמְלֹךְ לְעֹלָם וָעֶד, *Hashem shall reign for all eternity* (Shemos 15:18). And, indeed, at the *Kedushah d'sidra* in וּבָא לְצִיּוֹן, the *pasuk* ה׳ יִמְלֹךְ לְעֹלָם וָעֶד is used to end that *Kedushah*. *Avudraham* says that the reason יִמְלֹךְ ה׳ לְעוֹלָם אֱלֹהַיִךְ צִיּוֹן was chosen is because *Tziyon* is mentioned there in connection with *Malchus Hashem*, which is not the case in the Torah *pasuk*, ה׳ יִמְלֹךְ לְעֹלָם וָעֶד.

This begs the question: What is the significance of *Tziyon* and its meaning in connection with *Malchus Hashem*? And if it is so significant, why is this *pasuk* not used in the *Kedushah d'sidra*?

The answer to this lies in the fact that the broader meaning of צִיּוֹן, which is usually taken to refer to the *Beis HaMikdash* (as in צִיּוֹן מִשְׁכַּן כְּבֹדֶךָ), includes *Bnei Yisrael*. We find the following statement in the *Pesikta DeRav Kahana* [Rav Kahana wrote a series of essays in his *Pesikta* on the *haftaros*. This one is on the *haftarah* of *Parashas Shoftim* which begins אָנֹכִי אָנֹכִי: (*Yeshayahu* 51:12-52:12)]: חָזַרְנוּ עַל כָּל הַמִּקְרָא וְלֹא מָצִינוּ מָקוֹם שֶׁנִּקְרְאוּ יִשְׂרָאֵל צִיּוֹן, *We perused the entire Tanach and did not find that Israel is called Tziyon*; וְהֵיכָן מָצִינוּ? כָּאן, *but where did we find it? Here* לִנְטֹעַ שָׁמַיִם וְלִיסֹד אָרֶץ וְלֵאמֹר לְצִיּוֹן עַמִּי אָתָּה, *He Who plants the heavens and establishes the earth is the One Who says, "Tziyon, You are My nation"* (Yeshayahu 51:16). Thus, the Jewish nation, which considers *Tziyon* — the *Beis HaMikdash* — as its capital, is itself designated by the name *Tziyon*.

Therefore, while the subjects of the first two *pesukim* of the *Kedushah* are the praises that the *malachim*, as seen by the *Neviim*, express to *HaKadosh Baruch Hu*, the *pasuk* יִמְלֹךְ ה׳ לְעוֹלָם אֱלֹהַיִךְ צִיּוֹן is an expression of the yearning of the Jewish people for the time, *b'yemos HaMashiach*, when the entire world will recognize *HaKadosh Baruch Hu* as אֱלֹהַיִךְ צִיּוֹן: the recognition and acceptance of *Malchus Hashem* as taught by the Torah, which was given to the Jewish nation by *HaKadosh Baruch Hu*. This is the meaning of אֱלֹהַיִךְ צִיּוֹן.

This yearning for the eventual universal recognition of *HaKadosh Baruch Hu* as אֱלֹהַיִךְ צִיּוֹן is constantly expressed in our *tefillos* of the *Yamim Noraim*: וְתִמְלוֹךְ אַתָּה; and וְיֹאמַר כָּל אֲשֶׁר נְשָׁמָה בְאַפּוֹ ה׳ אֱלֹהֵי יִשְׂרָאֵל מֶלֶךְ וּמַלְכוּתוֹ בַּכֹּל מָשָׁלָה ה׳. לְבַדְּךָ עַל כָּל מַעֲשֶׂיךָ בְּהַר צִיּוֹן מִשְׁכַּן כְּבוֹדֶךָ וּבִירוּשָׁלַיִם עִיר קָדְשֶׁךָ. In these *tefillos*, we yearn for the time when the whole world will recognize *HaKadosh Baruch Hu* as אֱלֹהַיִךְ צִיּוֹן — *because it was the Jewish nation* — *Tziyon* — *which taught the world about the existence of HaKadosh Baruch Hu and of His relationship with His creatures*. *Yerushalayim* will be the capital of the united world, and the *Beis HaMikdash* will become the בֵּית תְּפִלָּה . . . לְכָל הָעַמִּים, *A house of prayer . . . of all the nations* (*Yeshayahu* 56:7).

Even today, a non-Jew who accepts the *sheva mitzvos bnei Noach* (the seven Noahide laws) is considered to be among the *chassidei umos ha'olam*, and can look forward to *Olam Haba*. However this is only so if such a person practices the *sheva mitzvos bnei Noach* because they are ordained by God, as revealed to the Jewish people by Moshe Rabbeinu, through the Torah, and not merely because this individual lives a "decent" life and does not violate any of the *sheva mitzvos*. This is clearly set forth by the Rambam: כָּל הַמְקַבֵּל שֶׁבַע מִצְוֹת וְנִזְהָר לַעֲשׂוֹתָן הֲרֵי זֶה מֵחֲסִידֵי אֻמּוֹת הָעוֹלָם וְיֵשׁ לוֹ חֵלֶק לָעוֹלָם הַבָּא, וְהוּא, שֶׁיְּקַבֵּל אוֹתָן וְיַעֲשֶׂה מִפְּנֵי שֶׁצִּוָּה בָּהֶן הקב"ה בַּתּוֹרָה וְהוֹדִיעָנוּ עַל יְדֵי מֹשֶׁה רַבֵּנוּ שֶׁבְּנֵי נֹחַ מִקֹּדֶם נִצְטַוּוּ בָּהֶן. **אֲבָל אִם עֲשָׂאָן מִפְּנֵי הֶכְרֵעַ הַדַּעַת אֵין זֶה גֵּר תּוֹשָׁב וְאֵינוֹ מֵחֲסִידֵי אֻמּוֹת הָעוֹלָם וְלֹא מֵחַכְמֵיהֶם** (*Hil. Melachim* 8:11).

The universal concept of *Malchus HaKadosh Baruch Hu* that will exist at the time of the arrival of *Mashiach* will be that which has been taught by the Torah, and not that which will be arrived at by human reasoning. It will be the acceptance of the rule of *HaKadosh Baruch Hu* as אֱלֹהַיִךְ צִיּוֹן, the God of the Jewish nation.

It is for this reason that the *mesadrei hatefillah* chose the *pasuk*, יִמְלֹךְ ה' לְעוֹלָם אֱלֹהַיִךְ צִיּוֹן לְדֹר וָדֹר הַלְלוּיָהּ. This *pasuk*, although from *Tehillim*, and not from the Torah, expresses the hopes and yearning of the Jewish people for the *universal acceptance of HaKadosh Baruch Hu based on the teachings of the Torah that was revealed to the Jewish people, who are called Tziyon.*

However, in *Kedushah d'sidra*, the *mesadrei hatefillah* chose the *pasuk*, ה' יִמְלֹךְ לְעֹלָם וָעֶד, from the Torah. This is because the concept of *Tziyon* is already mentioned at the beginning, וּבָא לְצִיּוֹן גּוֹאֵל, and is referred to again in the *Targum* of בָּרוּךְ כְּבוֹד ה' מִמְּקוֹמוֹ, where מִמְּקוֹמוֹ is rendered as מֵאֲתַר בֵּית שְׁכִינְתֵּהּ, *the place of His Presence*, referring to the *Beis HaMikdash*, the capital of the Jewish nation: *Tziyon*.

We conclude the *Kedushah* in the *chazaras hashatz* by picking up the words לְדֹר וָדֹר הַלְלוּיָהּ from the last *pasuk*, and continue:

לְדוֹר וָדוֹר נַגִּיד גָּדְלֶךָ ❖— **We will tell of Your greatness from one generation to the next.** This is said in the context of the previous *pasuk*, יִמְלֹךְ ה' לְעוֹלָם אֱלֹהַיִךְ צִיּוֹן לְדֹר וָדֹר הַלְלוּיָהּ, which refers to the world of *yemos HaMashiach*, which will last for generations, with one generation teaching the next, in detail, about *gadlus Hashem*.

[Ed. note: The Rav's reference to *yemos HaMashiach* in connection with this *pasuk* is based on his earlier explanation in *Pesukei d'Zimrah* on the *mizmor*, הַלְלוּיָהּ הַלְלִי נַפְשִׁי אֶת ה'. He explains there that Psalm 146, of which this is the last *pasuk,* is set in the period just before *bi'as Mashiach,* and that this final *pasuk* coincides with the moment of *bi'as Mashiach.*]

וּלְנֵצַח נְצָחִים קְדֻשָּׁתְךָ נַקְדִּישׁ — We will declare Your sanctity for "eternity of eternities." "Eternity," by definition, cannot be extended to an even longer period. However, this phrase is referring to an even higher world than that of *yemos HaMashiach,* and that is the world of the *neshamos,* or *Olam Haba.* The *neshamah* itself has *nitzchiyus,* permanence, but if it is elevated to a higher level, then the *netzach* that it had on a lower level is elevated to a higher level. When a person has *yahrtzeit,* the *neshamah* goes through another *din,* and the *neshamah* reaches a higher level; it has an *aliyah* in the *Olam Haneshamos.* Therefore, the *netzach* becomes *netzachim,* as it is regularly elevated to a higher and higher level. And since *HaKadosh Baruch Hu* is unreachable, this elevation continues forever. This phrase, then, expresses the wish to sanctify *HaKadosh Baruch Hu* in the *Olam Haneshamos* together with the *malachim* on an ever-increasing level.

וְשִׁבְחֲךָ אֱלֹהֵינוּ מִפִּינוּ לֹא יָמוּשׁ לְעוֹלָם וָעֶד — Your praise shall not move from our mouths forever. However, in the meantime, while we are still here on this earth, and not yet in the *Olam Haneshamos* and *Mashiach* has not yet come, we promise that: *Your praise shall not move from our mouths forever.* Notwithstanding the fact that the prayer — for the future — has not yet been realized, we will continue to offer the "praise" to *HaKadosh Baruch Hu,* which is:

כִּי אֵל מֶלֶךְ גָּדוֹל וְקָדוֹשׁ אָתָּה — For You, O God, are a great and holy King. אֵל is always a reference to absolute *rachamim,* and מֶלֶךְ means *middas hadin.* The world was created by *HaKadosh Baruch Hu* with a synthesis of *din* and *rachamim,* as reflected in the combination of אֵל מֶלֶךְ.

The praise begins with the concept that *HaKadosh Baruch Hu* is אֵל מֶלֶךְ, and continues with the concept, גָּדוֹל, meaning that He is unlimited. There is no space that is empty of His Being, לֵית אֲתַר פָּנוּי מִנֵּיהּ (see *Shir HaShirim Rabbah* 3:8:2; *Bamidbar Rabbah* 12:4).

The concept of גָּדוֹל in connection with *HaKadosh Baruch Hu* means that He is so close to us that there is nothing closer, and this is inherent in the meaning of the *pasuk,* כִּי קָרוֹב אֵלֶיךָ הַדָּבָר מְאֹד בְּפִיךָ וּבִלְבָבְךָ לַעֲשׂתוֹ, *Rather, the matter is very near to you — in your mouth and your heart — to perform it* (*Devarim* 30:14). Whenever one pronounces the Name of *HaKadosh Baruch Hu* in a *berachah;* or says a word of Torah — which is *HaKadosh Baruch Hu* addressing man; or a word of *tefillah* — which is man addressing *HaKadosh Baruch Hu;* or if one even thinks about *HaKadosh Baruch Hu,* he has experienced the closest possible connection with Him. While גָּדוֹל expresses the proximity of *HaKadosh Baruch Hu,* קָדוֹשׁ expresses the opposite: *HaKadosh*

Baruch Hu is unreachable. The more we think about Him, the more elusive He becomes. Based on this, this praise says that we recognize that Ha-Kadosh Baruch Hu is both גָּדוֹל, extremely close to us, and, at the same time, He is קָדוֹשׁ. We express the promise here that we will continue to praise HaKadosh Baruch Hu as both גָּדוֹל and קָדוֹשׁ forever.

בָּרוּךְ אַתָּה ה' הָאֵל הַקָּדוֹשׁ — **Blessed are You, Hashem, the holy God.** This means that *HaKadosh Baruch Hu* in His "Almightiness" (הָאֵל, meaning *middas harachamim*) has given us the *mitzvah* of תִּהְיוּ קְדֹשִׁים, *You shall be holy* (*Vayikra* 19:2), as an act of *rachamim,* even if people do not deserve it. *HaKadosh Baruch Hu* has given us this *mitzvah* כִּי קָדוֹשׁ אֲנִי ה' אֱלֹהֵיכֶם, *For holy am I, Hashem, your God* (ibid.). *HaKadosh Baruch Hu* tells us here that the reason we are commanded to "be holy" is because "I am holy." This *berachah* goes to the source of our *kedushah*: the fact that He is הָאֵל הַקָּדוֹשׁ.

The connection between the *kedushah* of *HaKadosh Baruch Hu* and that of *Bnei Yisrael* is the subject of the following Midrash (*Vayikra Rabbah* 24:9): אָמַר רַבִּי שִׁמְעוֹן בֶּן לָקִישׁ: שְׁתֵּי פַרְשִׁיּוֹת הִכְתִּיב לָנוּ מֹשֶׁה בַּתּוֹרָה וְאָנוּ לְמֵדִין אוֹתָן מִפָּרָשַׁת פַּרְעֹה הָרָשָׁע, *Rabbi Shimon ben Lakish said: Moshe Rabbeinu wrote two parshiyos for us in the Torah, the explanations of which are derived from that which was said by the wicked Pharaoh.* The first *parashah* is וְהָיִיתָ רַק לְמַעְלָה, *You will be only highly exalted* (*Devarim* 28:13). Asks the Midrash, יָכוֹל כָּמוֹנִי, *Does this mean, as High as I am?*, and the answer comes: תַּלְמוּד לוֹמַר רַק לְשׁוֹן מִעוּט, גְּדֻלָּתִי לְמַעְלָה מִגְּדֻלַּתְכֶם, [*No*], *it is for this reason that the Torah uses the exclusionary word,* רַק, *to indicate that "My greatness is above your greatness."*

The Midrash continues: וְאָנוּ לְמֵדִין אוֹתָהּ מִפַּרְעֹה הָרָשָׁע שֶׁנֶּאֱמַר "אַתָּה תִּהְיֶה עַל בֵּיתִי", יָכוֹל כָּמוֹנִי תַּלְמוּד לוֹמַר, "רַק הַכִּסֵּא אֶגְדַּל מִמֶּךָּ", גְּדֻלָּתִי לְמַעְלָה מִגְּדֻלָּתְךָ, *We learn this from the wicked Pharaoh who declared that Yosef "will rule over my house."* He installed Yosef as the ruler of Egypt. Asks the Midrash, *"Does this mean that you will be equal to me?"* and the answer comes, *"[No], by my throne I will be greater than you"* (*Bereishis* 41:40). *My greatness is above yours.*

The Midrash then continues to our *parashah*. וְהָדֵין: קְדֹשִׁים תִּהְיוּ יָכוֹל כָּמוֹנִי, *The other one is* קְדֹשִׁים תִּהְיוּ, תַּלְמוּד לוֹמַר "כִּי קָדוֹשׁ אָנִי", קְדֻשָּׁתִי לְמַעְלָה מִקְּדֻשַּׁתְכֶם, *You shall be holy. Does this mean as holy as I am? (No), because the pasuk adds* כִּי קָדוֹשׁ אֲנִי, *I am holy; My holiness is above your holiness.*

The Midrash continues, עוֹד אָנוּ לְמֵדִים מִפַּרְעֹה הָרָשָׁע, *This, too, is learned from the parashah of Pharaoh:* וַיֹּאמֶר פַּרְעֹה אֶל יוֹסֵף "אֲנִי פַרְעֹה" יָכוֹל כָּמוֹנִי תַּלְמוּד לוֹמַר אֲנִי פַרְעֹה גְּדֻלָּתִי לְמַעְלָה מִגְּדֻלָּתְךָ. *Paraphrased, this means, "I am Pharaoh; my greatness is above yours"* (ibid. 41:44).

The difficulties with the comparisons between *HaKadosh Baruch Hu* and *Bnei Yisrael*, and the consequent questions and answers, as well as the proofs from Pharaoh, are obvious.

However, this Midrash, and the connection between the *kedushah* of *Bnei*

Yisrael and *HaKadosh Baruch Hu*, can be understood as follows. As long as Egypt was ruled by an assortment of "witch doctors" and *chartumim*, Pharaoh was the king of a very primitive country. However, with the advent of Yosef — the נָבוֹן וְחָכָם, *discerning and wise* (*Bereishis* 41:39), the man whom Pharaoh proudly declared to be אִישׁ אֲשֶׁר רוּחַ אֱלֹהִים בּוֹ, *a man who has the spirit of God within him* (ibid. v.38), — as the ruler of Egypt, Pharaoh's kingdom had suddenly taken on a new and much higher dimension. He was now the king of a nation that was ruled by the great Yosef.

Similarly, this is what the *Midrash* says we learn from Pharaoh: The holier we become, the greater our conception of *HaKadosh Baruch Hu* becomes. The question, יָכוֹל כָּמוֹנִי, conveys the idea that "the more you strive to elevate yourselves in My direction, the higher your conception of Me will become. By elevating yourselves, you are elevating Me." The more *kadosh* we become, the greater our conception of the *Kedushah* of *HaKadosh Baruch Hu*.

This is the meaning of הָאֵל הַקָּדוֹשׁ.

The first three *berachos* and the last three *berachos* of the *Shemoneh Esrei* are said every day at Shacharis, Minchah and Maariv, whether these be ordinary weekdays or Shabbos and Yamim Tovim. However, now we begin the actual body of the *Shemoneh Esrei*, which is replaced by other *berachos* on Shabbos and Yom Tov. Originally, the body, or intermediate, part of the *Shemoneh Esrei* consisted of twelve *berachos*. Later, a thirteenth was added, as we shall explain at the *berachah* of *V'Lamalshinim*. The subject of the first six is our life now, before the *geulah*, and the latter six refer to the *geulah*. The added *berachah*, *V'Lamalshinim*, was placed with this latter group, as we shall explain. We will now begin the first *berachah*.

בִּינָה

אַתָּה חוֹנֵן לְאָדָם דַּעַת — **You bestow knowledge to man, as a gift.** Before any requests, we thank *HaKadosh Baruch Hu* for giving us our mind — the ability to think. Anyone who has seen a person who has lost his mind realizes that of all the gifts that *HaKadosh Baruch Hu* has given to the human being, the ability to think is the greatest.

The word חוֹנֵן comes from חֵן, which Rav Samson R. Hirsch translates in German to mean "*geistige begabung.*" In English, this would mean "spiritual endowment," or gift. The word חֵן is related to חִנָּם, as in מַתְּנַת חִנָּם, an *undeserved gift*. *HaKadosh Baruch Hu* gives knowledge to man even if he does not deserve it. A human being — as wicked as he may be — is, nevertheless, given *daas* by *HaKadosh Baruch Hu*.

The basic meaning of the word דַּעַת is the ability to think. However, in the Torah, it can also refer to the intimate connection or relationship between a man and a woman, as in וְהָאָדָם יָדַע אֶת חַוָּה אִשְׁתּוֹ (*Bereishis* 4:1). So the extended meaning of דַעַת is "connection." This is based on the fact that "knowing," or thinking about something, means that there is a connection between one's mind and the object of the knowledge. דַעַת, the ability to think, is a combination of *chochmah* and *binah.* For one to think of something, he must first learn that it exists, which is *chochmah,* and then he draws a conclusion from this knowledge, which is *binah.* This gift of *daas,* or the ability to think, is given only to humans. Although animals may have some form of intelligence, this is limited only to intelligence that is necessary for their survival. But abstract thinking that has no connection with any physical object — that two and two equals four, the abstract "idea" of four, not four apples — was given only to human beings.

וּמְלַמֵּד לֶאֱנוֹשׁ בִּינָה — **And teach insight to a frail mortal.** אֱנוֹשׁ, from אָנַשׁ, meaning *sickness,* is the name of the grandson of Adam HaRishon, whose generation had sunk down to a much lower level than that of his forebears. (See *Rambam, Hilchos Avodah Zarah* 1:1. Also see commentary of Rav Samson R. Hirsch on *Bereishis* 4:26.)

The previous phrase referred to man as אָדָם, which is a term of honor. However, here we add that even if man does not deserve the honorable name, אָדָם, he still is given the gift of understanding.

This gift is the source for what is called "the development of civilization." Since man was created, *HaKadosh Baruch Hu* has taught each generation something that the previous generation did not know. בִּינָה means מֵבִין דָּבָר מִתּוֹךְ דָּבָר, *understanding something from something else.* Throughout the ages, each generation has inherited the knowledge of the previous one and added to it. In our times this process has proceeded very rapidly. Today, one can see in his own lifetime the rapid and momentous strides that human intelligence has made in physics, technology, computer science, astronomy, space travel, etc. One hundred years ago people simply were not aware of certain forces in nature that have been discovered and utilized by our generation. And one hundred years from now the knowledge that we possess will be considered primitive. This is an ongoing process, because *HaKadosh Baruch Hu* has given man the ability to rise to higher and higher levels of knowledge and understanding.

This, however, has nothing to do with man's moral development. One can be on the lowest possible level of human depravity and still be endowed by *HaKadosh Baruch Hu* with enormous knowledge. Human beings have been endowed by God with *binah,* regardless of their moral worth.

The aforementioned refers to human beings in general, but now we, the Jewish people, say to *HaKadosh Baruch Hu*:

חָנֵּנוּ מֵאִתְּךָ דֵּעָה בִּינָה וְהַשְׂכֵּל — **Grant us from You *dei'ah, binah,* and *haskeil*.** We ask *HaKadosh Baruch Hu* here to favor us with the understanding of

His Torah. Grant *us,* from *You,* דֵּעָה בִּינָה וְהַשְׂכֵּל. Human intelligence alone is not sufficient for an in-depth understanding of Torah. It requires a special endowment from *HaKadosh Baruch Hu.* According to *minhag* Frankfurt, the order of the text here is בִּינָה דֵּעָה וְהַשְׂכֵּל, which is in conformity with the very old *siddur* of the kabbalist Rav Hertz *Shaliach Tzibbur* printed in the year ש״כ (1560).

The meaning of these words is as follows:

❏ דֵּעָה means דַּעַת הַשֵּׁם, the knowledge about *HaKadosh Baruch Hu* that comes down to us through the Torah, as in כִּי מָלְאָה הָאָרֶץ דֵּעָה אֶת ה׳, *For the earth will be filled with knowledge of Hashem (Yeshayahu* 11:9).

❏ בִּינָה means מֵבִין דָּבָר מִתּוֹךְ דָּבָר, in this case, the understanding of Torah that results from דַּעַת הַשֵּׁם.

In *Tanach,* there are many examples in which בִּינָה comes before דֵּעָה, as well as דֵּעָה before בִּינָה, and, basically, the order really makes no difference. Either it means that through the בִּינָה of Torah one recognizes *HaKadosh Baruch Hu,* which is called דֵּעָה; or, the reverse is also true: As a result of the recognition of *HaKadosh Baruch Hu,* דֵּעָה, one proceeds to learn His Torah, which is called בִּינָה.

❏ הַשְׂכֵּל means practical, applied wisdom. If one has wisdom in theory only but does not apply it to his practical life, behavior, and character, this wisdom is not called הַשְׂכֵּל. If one knows all the *halachos* of a particular subject, but does not apply them in practice, he would not be possessed of הַשְׂכֵּל. We find לְמַעַן תַּשְׂכִּיל, *so that you will be successful (Yehoshua* 1:7), which means, in accordance with the context there, that by the practical application of the *mitzvos HaTorah,* you will be successful in your endeavors. To be sure, לְמַעַן תַּשְׂכִּיל, from שֵׂכֶל, also refers simply to the use of one's intellect. When one is referred to as an *ish maskil,* it describes a person who is intelligent and also successful.

There is a very telling use of the word מַשְׂכִּיל in the *pasuk,* אֱלֹהִים מִשָּׁמַיִם הִשְׁקִיף עַל בְּנֵי אָדָם לִרְאוֹת הֲיֵשׁ מַשְׂכִּיל דֹּרֵשׁ אֶת אֱלֹהִים. כֻּלּוֹ סָג יַחְדָּו נֶאֱלָחוּ אֵין עֹשֵׂה טוֹב אֵין גַּם אֶחָד *(Tehillim* 53:3-4). Paraphrased, this means that *HaKadosh Baruch Hu* looks down, probingly, from heaven at the human race to see if there is anyone who is a *doreish es Elokim,* one who seeks Hashem, who is also a *maskil,* but He finds only that all of humanity has turned sour and become rotten.

What this means is that *HaKadosh Baruch Hu* is seeking within mankind the combination of מַשְׂכִּיל דֹּרֵשׁ אֶת אֱלֹהִים, people to whom the search for God means the intelligent and practical application of the will of *HaKadosh Baruch Hu* to any situation that may arise in their lives. There may be people who are *doreish es Elokim* in that they *daven* fervently, learn Torah in depth, and may even be the source of *chidushei Torah;* and yet, they could still lack the element of *maskil.* If such people are confronted with some test to do something inconsistent with their דָּרֵשׁ אֶת אֱלֹהִים, they may very well fail, because the element of *maskil* was not combined with their דָּרֵשׁ אֶת אֱלֹהִים. All of their learning will not help them; it will all blow away in the wind, because they are not *maskil*: they did not have, as the primary goal of their *doreish es Elokim*, the practical application of that which *HaKadosh Baruch Hu* wants of them.

Therefore, in this *tefillah* we ask *HaKadosh Baruch Hu* to grant us not only דֵּעָה and בִּינָה, but also הַשֵּׂכֶל, the intelligence to successfully apply these levels of wisdom to our daily lives.

On *motza'ei Shabbos* and *Yom Tov* we are more specific and say אַתָּה חוֹנַנְתָּנוּ לְמַדַּע תּוֹרָתֶךָ וַתְּלַמְּדֵנוּ לַעֲשׂוֹת (בָּהֶם) חֻקֵּי רְצוֹנֶךָ, *You have granted us the ability to understand Your Torah, and You have taught us to fulfill the commandments of Your will*. While mankind in general has been given the ability to understand the creations of *HaKadosh Baruch Hu*, the Jewish nation has been granted the Torah, which contains knowledge of the Creator and what He wants of us. Rav Samson R. Hirsch justifies the use of the word בָּהֶם in the phrase וַתְּלַמְּדֵנוּ לַעֲשׂוֹת בָּהֶם חֻקֵּי רְצוֹנֶךָ, because, he explains, בָּהֶם refers to the previously mentioned דַּעַת and בִּינָה. The phrase would then mean, "*You have taught us to use these talents,* דַּעַת *and* בִּינָה, *in the fulfillment of Your commandments.*"

Every generation is faced with new halachic problems and *she'eilos* that did not exist in previous generations. When we are faced with the *she'eilah* of whether one may wear a hearing aid on Shabbos, we must access all the *halachos* of Shabbos that were given thousands of years ago on *Har Sinai*, and apply our God-given talents of דַּעַת and בִּינָה to understand how these *halachos* apply in a given case.

Despite the fact that in the development of civilization each generation rises to a higher level of scientific knowledge than the previous one, the opposite is true with regard to Torah knowledge. This is known as יְרִידַת הַדּוֹרוֹת, *decline of the generations*. The greatest people of our generation would have been considered small two hundred years ago.

A *posek hador* of today may not have merited to be the *shammas* of the Vilna Gaon. And the Vilna Gaon said of himself that even if he would become ten times as great as he was, he would not reach קַרְסוּלֵי הָרַמְבַּ"ן, "the ankles of the Ramban." And the Ramban himself would not reach anywhere near the level of the greatness of the *Geonim*, and the *Geonim* to the *Savoraim*, and the *Savoraim* to even the last of the *Amoraim*, Mar bar Rav Ashi. And the *Amoraim* themselves would not reach the level of the *Tannaim*, and the *Tannaim* to the *Sofrim*, and the *Sofrim* to the *Neviim Acharonim*, and the *Neviim Acharonim* to the *Rishonim*. And Yehoshua, who was the first of the *Neviim Rishonim*, was only like the moon in comparison to the sun of Moshe Rabbeinu.

The continuing upward development of human scientific knowledge — as opposed to the gradual decline in understanding the Torah — is at the heart of the statement of our *Chachamim* (*Eichah Rabbah* 2:17): אִם יֹאמַר לְךָ אָדָם יֵשׁ חָכְמָה בַּגוֹיִם תַּאֲמִין, *If a person says there is knowledge among the nations, believe it.* The Midrash derives this from the *pasuk*: וְהַאֲבַדְתִּי חֲכָמִים מֵאֱדוֹם וּתְבוּנָה מֵהַר עֵשָׂו, *I will eradicate wise men from Edom and understanding from the Mountain of Esau* (*Ovadiah* 1:8). The *Chachamim* continue: יֵשׁ תּוֹרָה בַּגוֹיִם אַל תַּאֲמִין, *[However, if one says] there is Torah knowledge among the nations, do not believe it.* And this is derived from the *pasuk*: מַלְכָּהּ וְשָׂרֶיהָ בַגּוֹיִם אֵין תּוֹרָה, *Her king and her officers are among the nations, there is no Torah* (*Eichah* 2:9).

The use of the word תַּאֲמִין in this Midrash requires an explanation. חָכְמָה בַּגוֹיִם is general knowledge, and is not something that has to be "believed," because it says so in the *pasuk*.

However, what is derived from this *pasuk* is as follows. *HaKadosh Baruch Hu* has endowed man with great intelligence. He has the capacity to have the highest and loftiest philosophical thoughts possible, and the most subtle concepts of physics. The fact that the *pasuk* attributes the term *chachamim* to the non-Jewish world, which possesses this great intelligence, indicates that man's innate capacity for great intellectual achievements will eventually bring him to the conclusion that there is a Creator, a *borei olam*. Otherwise, human intelligence would not be called חָכְמָה.

This we firmly believe, תַּאֲמִין, because it is derived from this *pasuk*. The scientific theory that the universe began to develop spontaneously some 15 billion years ago as a result of a colossal explosion of some primordial mass — known as the "Big Bang" theory — is simply preposterous. *This is not chochmah, but rather, it is shtus.*

This *pasuk* teaches us that eventually, by the sheer process of אַתָּה חוֹנֵן לְאָדָם דַּעַת וּמְלַמֵּד לֶאֱנוֹשׁ בִּינָה, the scientists and the philosophers of the world will reach the conclusion that there is a Creator. Otherwise, all human knowledge would not be dignified with the term חָכְמָה.

Torah, on the other hand, is the opposite. It comes down to us from the Ultimate Source, *Mipi HaGevurah. HaKadosh Baruch Hu* revealed His will through the Torah, which was given to Moshe Rabbeinu with the commandment וְשִׁנַּנְתָּם לְבָנֶיךָ, that we are to teach it to our children and others, and they to others, from there on down through the ages. Naturally, the further the Torah is removed from its source, the lower the level of its understanding. This is true even of the *aleph-beis* that is taught to the little child, which was originally taught to Moshe Rabbeinu by *HaKadosh Baruch Hu*.

But, states the Midrash, יֵשׁ תּוֹרָה בַּגוֹיִם אַל תַּאֲמִין, the understanding of Torah is not based on innate human reasoning, חָכְמָה. Rather, it is achieved by receiving the knowledge from its source, that of *Matan Torah* by *HaKadosh Baruch Hu* on *Har Sinai*.

The level of this knowledge naturally deteriorates with the passing of time. Yisro is an example of a non-Jew who arrived at the truth of the existence of *HaKadosh Baruch Hu* by the process of חָכְמָה. After having practiced every form of *avodah zarah* in the world, and studying all the other religions, he finally debunked them with the realization that they were all nonsense. By his process of intellectual elimination of all *avodah zarah,* he was left only with the concept of ה׳ אֶחָד, Hashem is the One and Only.

He had arrived at the recognition of *HaKadosh Baruch Hu* through the intellectual process of חָכְמָה (see *Rashi, Shemos* 18:11).

However, when Yisro experienced *Matan Torah* together with the Jewish people, having heard אָנֹכִי ה׳ אֱלֹהֶיךָ directly from *HaKadosh Baruch Hu,* he came to the realization that, unlike חָכְמָה, the understanding of Torah cannot be arrived at simply by reason and intellectual cognition, תּוֹרָה בַגּוֹיִם אַל תַּאֲמִין. He recognized that the level of understanding the Torah is dependent on how close one is to its source, and not simply on natural human reasoning. The understanding of Torah as received by Moshe Rabbeinu on *Har Sinai* began at its highest possible level, and the depth of its understanding diminishes gradually as it is distanced from its source.

בָּרוּךְ אַתָּה ה׳ חוֹנֵן הַדָּעַת — **Blessed are You, Hashem, the One Who endows wisdom.** We summarize this *tefillah* by thanking *HaKadosh Baruch Hu* for granting דַּעַת, *intelligence,* to human beings. All of human intelligence was granted by *HaKadosh Baruch Hu* for the ultimate purpose of finally reaching the conclusion that *HaKadosh Baruch Hu* exists. However, as far as we, the Jewish people are concerned, with these same words we thank *HaKadosh Baruch Hu* for granting us, through the Torah, the knowledge of what *HaKadosh Baruch Hu* wants of us. The Torah was not revealed to us for the purpose of teaching us what occurs in *Shamayim* or *Shmei Shamayim,* for these are הַנִּסְתָּרֹת לַה׳ אֱלֹהֵינוּ, *that which is hidden belongs to Hashem, our God* (*Devarim* 29:28). The purpose of all of Torah is to teach us what to do in this world: וְהַנִּגְלֹת לָנוּ וּלְבָנֵינוּ עַד עוֹלָם לַעֲשׂוֹת אֶת כָּל דִּבְרֵי הַתּוֹרָה הַזֹּאת, *But that which has been revealed belongs to us and to our children for the purpose of complying with all the words of this Torah* (ibid.), and for this we thank *HaKadosh Baruch Hu* in this *berachah.*

תְּשׁוּבָה

The *tefillah* for a proper understanding of Torah is followed by this *tefillah* in which we seek the help of *HaKadosh Baruch Hu* in achieving *teshuvah* based on an understanding of the true meaning of our practice of Torah and *mitzvos.*

The more בִּינָה דֵעָה וְהַשְׂכֵּל we have, the greater the realization that there is usually a very glaring deficiency in our Torah learning and *avodas Hashem*. Are we really aware that it is God's Torah that we are learning; that this is *HaKadosh Baruch Hu* talking to us; that we are observing the *mitzvos* because *HaKadosh Baruch Hu* wants us to do so?

This common deficiency exists regardless of whether we learn Torah superficially, or even if we engage in yeshivahlike, in-depth, learning. Whatever our motive for learning Torah — that we are intellectually curious, or so that we will not be considered *amei ha'aretz* (ignoramuses) by our peers, or because Torah learning is one aspect of being *frum* — it is still *shelo lishmah* unless we do so with the awareness that it is God's Torah that we are now learning, and it His will that we study His Torah. This acute awareness is very rare in the average person.

In fact, the Gemara tells us that the the destruction of Eretz Yisrael and *churban Beis HaMikdash* was the result of שֶׁלֹּא בֵּרְכוּ בַּתּוֹרָה תְּחִלָּה, *They did not make a berachah before learning Torah* (cf. *Nedarim* 81a). This is explained, שֶׁלֹּא הָיְתָה הַתּוֹרָה חֲשׁוּבָה בְּעֵינֵיהֶם כָּל כָּךְ שֶׁיְּהֵא רָאוּי לְבָרֵךְ עָלֶיהָ שֶׁלֹּא הָיוּ עוֹסְקִים בָּהּ לִשְׁמָהּ וּמִתּוֹךְ כָּךְ הָיוּ מְזַלְזְלִין בְּבִרְכָתָהּ (*Ran* ibid.). The Torah was considered just another science, another discipline, like any other knowledge, and therefore a *berachah* was not deemed necessary before learning it. While the Torah does certainly contain all the knowledge in the world, it is *unique* as תּוֹרָתִי; it is the *devar Hashem,* and it is to be learned because *HaKadosh Baruch Hu* commanded us to study it.

The Gemara there bases this on the following *pesukim*: מִי הָאִישׁ הֶחָכָם וְיָבֵן אֶת זֹאת וַאֲשֶׁר דִּבֶּר פִּי ה' אֵלָיו וְיַגִּדָהּ עַל מָה אָבְדָה הָאָרֶץ נִצְּתָה כַמִּדְבָּר מִבְּלִי עֹבֵר. וַיֹּאמֶר ה', עַל עָזְבָם אֶת תּוֹרָתִי אֲשֶׁר נָתַתִּי לִפְנֵיהֶם וְלֹא שָׁמְעוּ בְקוֹלִי וְלֹא הָלְכוּ בָהּ, *Who is the wise man who will understand this? Who is he to whom the mouth of Hashem speaks, that he may explain this? For what reason was the land devastated and become parched like the desert, without a passerby? Hashem has said: Because they have forsaken My Torah that I put before them; moreover, they did not heed My voice nor follow it* (Yirmiyahu 9:11-12).

The Gemara continues: דָּבָר זֶה נִשְׁאַל לַחֲכָמִים וְלַנְּבִיאִים וְלֹא פֵּרְשׁוּהוּ, *This question was asked of the wise men and the prophets, and none could explain it.* There was so much Torah learning in Eretz Yisrael at that time, no one understood why this did not protect the Jewish people from the destruction. עַד שֶׁפֵּרְשׁוּ הקב"ה בְּעַצְמוֹ, דִּכְתִיב: "וַיֹּאמֶר ה' עַל עָזְבָם אֶת תּוֹרָתִי וְגו' ", Nobody could explain this, until *HaKadosh Baruch Hu,* Himself, gave the reason for the destruction of the land: *"Because they have forsaken My Torah."* True, Torah was learned, but it was not learned as *"My Torah."* During the period before the *churban,* there was a great deal of Torah learning in Eretz Yisrael. However, the students of the Torah engaged in its study without the awareness that they were learning it because it is God's Torah, the *devar Hashem,* and that it is His will that we study His Torah. They considered it a science, another discipline, like any other knowledge, and, therefore, they did not consider it necessary to make a *berachah* over it. And this, *Chazal* tell us, was the cause of the destruction of the land.

הֲשִׁיבֵנוּ אָבִינוּ לְתוֹרָתֶךָ — **Bring us back, our Father, to Your Torah.** Paraphrased, this means: Return us to the awareness that it is Your Torah that we are learning. The lack of awareness of the true meaning of learning Torah and observing *mitzvos* is so common that the *Chachamim* instituted this *berachah* as a *tefillah* to ask *HaKadosh Baruch Hu* to help us stay focused on the true meaning of our *talmud Torah* and *avodas Hashem*.

וְקָרְבֵנוּ מַלְכֵּנוּ לַעֲבוֹדָתֶךָ — **And bring us close, our King, to Your service** similarly means: Help us to become aware that *we are serving You in our avodah*. This refers both to *tefillah* and the observance of *mitzvos*. While we are *mispallel,* we are not usually aware that we are talking directly to *Hashem Yisbarach*. So here we ask *HaKadosh Baruch Hu* for help in elevating our *tefillah* to the level of עֲבוֹדָתֶךָ, *Your service,* in which we are clearly aware that we are communicating directly with *HaKadosh Baruch Hu.* The same thing applies to *kiyum hamitzvos,* which are often performed perfunctorily without the awareness that by these acts we are fulfilling the will of *HaKadosh Baruch Hu* and thereby serving Him, our King. We therefore ask *HaKadosh Baruch Hu* for His help in elevating our *avodah* to the level where it becomes עֲבוֹדָתֶךָ.

May I suggest the following parable for this. There was a son who embezzled a huge amount of money from his father and then disappeared. After many years of not communicating with his father — during which time the son had lost all of this ill-gotten money — he tearfully telephoned his father begging for forgiveness and for permission to return home. The father, having compassion for his long-lost son, readily welcomed him back. However, said the son, "Unfortunately, I am penniless, Dad, so could you please send me a ticket to come home?"

Similarly, we too are asking *HaKadosh Baruch Hu* for help in coming "back home" to Him. We want to make our Torah and *tefillah* meaningful and come close to *HaKadosh Baruch Hu,* but we need help from Him to bring us back. We cannot do it on our own.

The *Chovos HaLevavos* (*Shaar Avodas HaElokim*), in explaining one's obligation to serve *HaKadosh Baruch Hu* from the point of view of gratitude, contrasts the blessings that *HaKadosh Baruch Hu* bestows upon man, which are given without any ulterior motive, with the kindness which even a good and compassionate person would bestow on another.

For instance, if one sees a person who is suffering from hunger and shivering in the cold, begging for food and warm clothing, which Jew would not help him alleviate his suffering? And when this this poor unfortunate soul offers his thanks to his benefactor, he receives great satisfaction from having done a "good deed"; he has satisfied his conscience by having helped someone in dire need and, had he refused, he would have a very guilty conscience. However, says the *Chovos HaLevavos,* the הַטָבָה (beneficence) of *HaKadosh Baruch Hu* is done for absolutely no other reason than that *HaKadosh Baruch Hu* is *tov u'meitiv* (Goodness, per se).

Ideally, in our own lives, in order to elevate a "good deed" to its highest level, that of *Avodas Hashem,* the benefactor should perform such acts of charity not merely out of the goodness of his heart, or to satisfy his conscience, but because these acts of *gemilus chassadim* are the fulfillment of the will of *HaKadosh Baruch Hu* in the *mitzvah* of וְאָהַבְתָּ לְרֵעֲךָ כָּמוֹךָ אֲנִי ה׳ (*Vayikra* 19:18). Paraphrased, this means: Love that which pertains to your fellow as if it were your own; and do so for the reason that I, Hashem, have willed that you do so.

וְהַחֲזִירֵנוּ בִּתְשׁוּבָה שְׁלֵמָה לְפָנֶיךָ — **Bring us back with a perfect *teshuvah* before You.** The *teshuvah* process must be initiated by ourselves. We must "pull ourselves up by our own bootstraps." If a person has done something wrong, he has the ability to make good for it, but he must begin the process of *teshuvah.* This is the meaning of כֹּה אָמַר ה׳ צְבָאוֹת שׁוּבוּ אֵלַי... וְאָשׁוּב אֲלֵיכֶם (*Zechariah* 1:3). Paraphrased, this means: *HaKadosh Baruch Hu* declares: "You do yours, and I will do Mine." If we begin the *teshuvah* process, *HaKadosh Baruch Hu* will respond and help us in our efforts to atone for our misdeeds.

However, there is a higher level of *teshuvah,* and that is called *teshuvah sheleimah,* "perfect *teshuvah,"* which is to return to *HaKadosh Baruch Hu* for no other reason than because it is a *mitzvah* to do *teshuvah:* וְשַׁבְתָּ עַד ה׳ אֱלֹהֶיךָ, *And you will return to Hashem, your God* (*Devarim* 30:2), We ask *HaKadosh Baruch Hu* here to help us achieve this *teshuvah sheleimah.*

A person may do *teshuvah* because he is aware of the horrible punishments for *aveiros;* because he may lose his *Olam Haba;* and because he may both suffer greatly while he is alive in this world and also at the moment of his death — and afterwards in *Gehinnom* — as a result of those *aveiros.* To be sure, *teshuvah* for these reasons is acceptable, but it does not rise to the level of *teshuvah sheleimah,* perfect *teshuvah, which is done for the sole reason that it is the will of HaKadosh Baruch Hu that a sinner do teshuvah!* This is the highest level of *teshuvah* that one can attain, and it is this that we ask *HaKadosh Baruch Hu* in this *tefillah* to help us achieve. (See *Sforno, Devarim* 30:2: וְשַׁבְתָּ עַד ה׳ אֱלֹהֶיךָ תִּהְיֶה תְשׁוּבָתְךָ כְּדֵי לַעֲשׂוֹת רְצוֹן קוֹנְךָ בִּלְבַד, וְזוֹ הִיא הַתְּשׁוּבָה שֶׁאָמְרוּ ז״ל [יוֹמָא פֶּרֶק יוֹם הַכִּפּוּרִים] שֶׁמַּגַּעַת עַד כִּסֵא הַכָּבוֹד.)

The *mitzvah* of *teshuvah* can be done at any time in one's life, even on one's deathbed. However, our *Chachamim* tell us: אָמַר רַבִּי עַמְרָם אָמַר רַב, אַשְׁרֵי מִי שֶׁעוֹשֶׂה תְּשׁוּבָה כְּשֶׁהוּא אִישׁ, *Said Rav Amram in the name of Rav: Happy is the person who does teshuvah while he is still a "man"* (*Avodah Zarah* 19a), in his full virility and strength. Many people do *teshuvah,* as a last resort, when they are old and feeble and have no strength left to do anything wrong — so they decide that they might as well do things right. But how fortunate and happy is the person who recognizes his mistakes while he is still young and still strong enough to do *aveiros,* and yet he struggles with his temptations and overcomes them.

While *teshuvah* helps atone for *aveiros* at any time, even on one's deathbed, it reaches its highest level only if one does *teshuvah* while he is in his full vigor and strength, fully capable of doing *aveiros*. If one overcomes his desires to do *aveiros* at that time, because he has made a commitment to do *teshuvah,* this, naturally, is a much higher form of *teshuvah* than the deep regret of an old sick man on his deathbed. Nevertheless, the *teshuvah* of a dying person is effective and, in fact, such a person is also called a *baal teshuvah* (see *Rambam, Hil. Teshuvah* 2:1).

In our *tefillah* of *Ne'ilah* at the waning moments of Yom Kippur, we say: אַתָּה נוֹתֵן יָד לַפּוֹשְׁעִים וִימִינְךָ פְּשׁוּטָה לְקַבֵּל שָׁבִים, *You offer a hand to sinners; Your right arm is outstretched to receive those who return*. I heard a beautiful *mashal* from Rav Carlebach, comparing the last moments of Yom Kippur to a train that has already slowly started leaving the station, and some late-coming passengers are running alongside to jump aboard. The conductor standing on the stairs of the moving train stretches out his arm to help them jump aboard. Similarly, even when Yom Kippur is almost over — or even if one's life is coming to an end — the opportunity for *teshuvah* still exists. *HaKadosh Baruch Hu* offers an outstretched arm to receive even late-coming *baalei teshuvah*.

≈§ בָּרוּךְ אַתָּה ה׳, הָרוֹצֶה בִּתְשׁוּבָה — **Blessed are You, Hashem, Who desires repentance.** *HaKadosh Baruch Hu* wants repentance; He eagerly waits for people to return to Him until the last moment of their lives — עַד יוֹם מוֹתוֹ תְּחַכֶּה לוֹ; and once they return to Him, they are immediately accepted: וְאִם יָשׁוּב מִיַּד תְּקַבְּלוֹ. [Ed. note: Both quotes above are from וּנְתַנֶּה תֹּקֶף.] No matter how much of a *rasha* one has been, no matter how much he has sinned, *HaKadosh Baruch Hu* still eagerly awaits his *teshuvah*.

And even if one's sins have been so egregious that *teshuvah* alone will not atone for them, *HaKadosh Baruch Hu* still wants him to do *teshuvah*: to stop committing *aveiros,* to feel deep contrition for them, and to ask *HaKadosh Baruch Hu* for forgiveness. *Teshuvah* in this case is done strictly for the purpose of doing the will of *HaKadosh Baruch Hu*: וְשַׁבְתָּ עַד ה׳ אֱלֹהֶיךָ, which applies even to a *rasha*.

סְלִיחָה

The next step in the *teshuvah* process, after the cessation of the *aveiros* and the firm commitment never to repeat them, is *vidui* confession. The act of *vidui* itself is a *mitzvas asei*, as we find in *Rambam* (*Hil. Teshuvah* 1:1): כְּשֶׁיַּעֲשֶׂה תְּשׁוּבָה וְיָשׁוּב מֵחֶטְאוֹ חַיָּב לְהִתְוַדּוֹת לִפְנֵי הָאֵל בָּרוּךְ הוּא, שֶׁנֶּאֱמַר "אִישׁ אוֹ אִשָּׁה כִּי יַעֲשׂוּ מִכָּל חַטֹּאת הָאָדָם . . . וְהִתְוַדּוּ אֶת חַטָּאתָם אֲשֶׁר עָשׂוּ" זֶה וִדּוּי דְּבָרִים, וִדּוּי זֶה מִצְוַת עֲשֵׂה, When a person does *teshuvah*, and he ceases doing his sin, he is required to make a confession before God, Blessed is He, as the Torah says, "A man or woman who has committed any sin, which human beings do, they shall confess their sins which they have committed." This is what is called a verbal confession. This confession is a positive Torah commandment.

Vidui means to admit to wrongdoing. In common usage, when someone is said to be *modeh*, it means that after having been accused of some impropriety, and denying it, he finally admits that he, in fact, did do that of which he was accused. Therefore, the sense of the opening phrase of this *berachah* is:

◆§ סְלַח לָנוּ אָבִינוּ כִּי חָטָאנוּ — **Forgive us our Father; we certainly did sin.** סְלַח — related to צָלַח, which means to jump over something and proceed further — is used here in connection with חֵטְא, which means an inadvertent sin, שׁוֹגֵג: a sin that one does without realizing that it is wrong, or without realizing that it is so bad as to constitute an *aveirah*. Here, we ask *HaKadosh Baruch Hu*, as our Father, to סְלַח, "overlook," our *chataim* that we did inadvertently, much as a father overlooks the misdeeds of his children who were not aware that they were doing anything wrong.

◆§ מְחַל לָנוּ מַלְכֵּנוּ כִּי פָשָׁעְנוּ — **Forgive us, our King, for we have committed acts of rebellion.** Here we address *HaKadosh Baruch Hu* as our King, because, in this phrase, we ask *HaKadosh Baruch Hu* for forgiveness for acts of פֶּשַׁע, rebellious acts, which we knew were wrong, but which we did anyway. From the point of view of *din*, justice, we know that the *aveiros* that we did require strict punishment, but nevertheless, we approach *HaKadosh Baruch Hu* as our "King," and beg Him for a "royal pardon."

◆§ כִּי מוֹחֵל וְסוֹלֵחַ אָתָּה — **For You pardon and forgive.** מוֹחֵל refers to the *aveiros* that were done with full knowledge, as a פּוֹשֵׁעַ, and סוֹלֵחַ to those that were done *b'shogeig*, inadvertently. When a person does *teshuvah*, *HaKadosh Baruch Hu* forgives him in stages. The Gemara states: אָמַר רֵישׁ לָקִישׁ גְּדוֹלָה תְּשׁוּבָה שֶׁזְּדוֹנוֹת נַעֲשׂוֹת לוֹ כִּשְׁגָגוֹת. The power of *teshuvah* is such that first, one's *aveiros* that were done purposely, *b'meizid*, are mitigated and reduced to the level of inadvertent acts, *shogeig* (*Yoma* 86b). But, continues the Gemara, as he continues to elevate his *teshuvah* to the level of *teshuvah* *mei'ahavah,* and he does *teshuvah* also for the *aveiros* that were done *b'shogeig,* his sins that were done *b'meizid* are treated by *HaKadosh Baruch Hu* as if they were actually meritorious acts, וְדוֹנוֹת נַעֲשׂוֹת לוֹ כְּזָכִיּוֹת. If a person has tasted the sweetness of the *aveirah,* and now he realizes how bitter it actually was, the *aveirah* itself is considered by *HaKadosh Baruch Hu* as a meritorious act.

The Torah tells us repeatedly that Yisro was *Kohen Midyan,* a "Midyanite priest." What great *yichus* is this for the father-in-law of Moshe? But the idea is that the Torah is pointing out that since this former leader of an idol-worshiping religion — whom *Chazal* portray as one who had experimented with every form of idolatry in the world (see *Rashi, Shemos* 18:11) — did *teshuvah* at its highest level, and even became a member of the Jewish nation, his very idolatry became a *zechus* for him!

Based on this, כִּי מוֹחֵל וְסוֹלֵחַ אָתָּה conveys the meaning of "You are a forgiver of very serious sins (מוֹחֵל), which, through *teshuvah,* become mitigated to the level of inadvertent sins (סוֹלֵחַ), which You will then overlook and forgive."

בָּרוּךְ אַתָּה ה', חַנּוּן הַמַּרְבֶּה לִסְלוֹחַ — **Blessed are You, Hashem, the gracious One Who pardons abundantly.** חַנּוּן, as opposed to חוֹנֵן, is the *pu'al* form, and means, "You graciously grant the requests that are made of You." If we pray for forgiveness, *HaKadosh Baruch Hu* "allows Himself to be entreated," and even adds to the forgiveness, He is הַמַּרְבֶּה לִסְלוֹחַ: He increases His forgiveness to the point that He considers the *aveiros* that were done *b'shogeig* to have been *zechuyos.*

[Ed. note: See *Maayan Beis HaSho'evah, Acharei,* 16:30 for a broader development of this subject.]

גְּאוּלָה

After we have asked *HaKadosh Baruch Hu* for forgiveness, we can approach Him and ask that He see our suffering and alleviate it. Sometimes, we ourselves are not even aware that we are living in perilous circumstances. Human nature is such that when one is in a very serious and dangerous situation, he may tend to minimize or overlook it. I remember the Germany of the early 30's, when Hitler ימ״ש first came to power. There never was a person as evil as he was. If we were to take all the *reshaim* in history and bundle them together on one side of a scale, and put Hitler on the other side, he would outweigh them all combined. While a small number of Jews left Germany immediately, most people thought that Hitler's government, with its virulent anti-Semitic policies, was an aberration that would soon "blow over," and normal democratic conditions would quickly return to Germany. This general attitude existed in Germany, and certainly in "faraway" Eastern

Europe. I saw a description by a *bachur* in the Mirrer Yeshivah of his life during the years 1936-1938, in which he says that he felt quite safe in Poland, although he knew that he could not travel to Germany because of the political situation there. How blind these people were to the extremely menacing situation in which they lived.

When I came to America [in December 1936], this country was known as the *"Goldene Medinah."* However, today, we realize that it is not "golden" at all, but rather, it is based on "paper money." As free as we seem to be here, nevertheless, we should know that here too, in America, we are living in *galus*. There is hate all around us. This was a big surprise about fifteen years ago, but now we realize that even here in America we are not secure. We came here because we were disliked in Europe, and if we were suddenly forced to leave America, where would we find security? In Eretz Yisrael? There we are faced with the so-called "Palestinians," a relatively new entity, who don't like us there either, and who want the land for themselves. Who says we will be secure there? Where shall we go? To the moon? There is no place on earth where Jews are *"erwunsched"* (welcome), where the general population desires and would welcome an influx of Jews. Therefore, as long as we are in *galus,* we ask *HaKadosh Baruch Hu* to protect us from the danger that lurks all around us, although such danger may be quite unbeknown to us.

רְאֵה בְעָנְיֵנוּ, וְרִיבָה רִיבֵנוּ — **See our affliction, fight our battle.** Paraphrased, this means: See our misery; we are weak, we have no real power to guarantee our survival, so therefore we ask that You, *HaKadosh Baruch Hu,* fight our battle for survival.

This underlying meaning — that danger is lurking all around us — is expressed clearly on a *taanis tzibbur,* in the special *tefillah* that the *shaliach tzibbur* inserts into this *berachah:* עֲנֵנוּ ה׳ עֲנֵנוּ בְּיוֹם צוֹם תַּעֲנִיתֵנוּ כִּי בְצָרָה גְדוֹלָה אֲנָחְנוּ, *Answer us, O God, answer us, on this day of our fast on which we afflict ourselves, as we are in great distress.* This *tefillah,* which was composed well before the Middle Ages, and possibly dates all the way back to the *Anshei Knesses HaGedolah,* when our people still lived in Eretz Yisrael, refers to the great dangers that exist all around us. And just as it was true when this *tefillah* was composed, so has it been true throughout the millennia since then, up to this very day.

This special *tefillah* continues: אַל תֵּפֶן אֶל רִשְׁעֵנוּ וְאַל תַּסְתֵּר פָּנֶיךָ מִמֶּנּוּ וְאַל תִּתְעַלַּם מִתְּחִנָּתֵנוּ, *Do not turn toward the evil which we have done, and do not hide Your face from us and avoid our pleas,* whereby we blame only ourselves for all of our *tzaros.* People may give many reasons for the Jew-hatred and suffering of our people throughout the ages; these could be political, economic, or ethnic in nature. However, the crux of the matter is, there is only one reason:

מִפְּנֵי חֲטָאֵינוּ גָּלִינוּ מֵאַרְצֵנוּ, *We were driven from our land because of our sins.* This was predicted long ago in the Torah: אִם לֹא תִשְׁמֹר לַעֲשׂוֹת אֶת כָּל דִּבְרֵי הַתּוֹרָה הַזֹּאת . . . וּבַגּוֹיִם הָהֵם לֹא תַרְגִּיעַ וגו׳, *If you will not be careful to perform all the words of this Torah . . . And among those nations you will not be tranquil* etc. (*Devarim* 28:58,65). We will find no rest among the nations as long as we continue to violate God's commandments in the Torah.

Therefore, we feel that we do not have any right to ask *HaKadosh Baruch Hu* to protect us from the dangers that lurk all around us unless we have done *teshuvah* first. Thus, סְלַח לָנוּ is followed by רְאֵה בְעָנְיֵנוּ.

◆§ וּגְאָלֵנוּ מְהֵרָה לְמַעַן שְׁמֶךָ — **And redeem us speedily for Your Name's sake.** This does not refer to the eventual *geulah sheleimah* at the time of *yemos HaMashiach*. Rather, this is a *tefillah* for protection against the daily assaults, fears, apprehensions, and persecutions that our people face, whether in Eretz Yisrael or anywhere else in the world.

The *geulah* to which we refer here is the *aschalta d'geulah*, the beginning of the *geulah*, which started as soon as the *galus* began. The Gemara tell us: וּמָה רָאוּ לוֹמַר גְּאוּלָה בַּשְּׁבִיעִית, אָמַר רָבָא: מִתּוֹךְ שֶׁעֲתִידִין לִיגָּאֵל בַּשְּׁבִיעִית. The reason *geulah* is said as the seventh *berachah* of the *Shemoneh Esrei* is because the future redemption will take place in the *Sheviis* year (*Megillah* 17b). But the Gemara immediately says that this contradicts an accepted tradition that the *geulah* will take place on *motza'ei Sheviis,* the year after *Sheviis,* but that during *Sheviis* itself there will be *milchamos,* wars. And the answer is given there: מִלְחָמָה נַמִי אַתְחַלְתָּא דִגְאוּלָה הִיא, the wars during *Sheviis* — while still part of the *galus* — are nevertheless considered as the beginning of the *geulah.*

Similarly, what we refer to here in our *berachah* as *geulah* is the constant protection of *HaKadosh Baruch Hu* against our enemies while we are in *galus* — the *geulah* within the *galus* — which the Gemara calls *aschalta d'geulah* (see *Rashi, Megillah* 17b s.v. אתחלתא דגאולה).

◆§ כִּי גּוֹאֵל חָזָק אָתָּה — **For You are a powerful Redeemer.** Paraphrased, this means: Because Your Name is the "Strong Redeemer." During our entire *galus*, *HaKadosh Baruch Hu* has shown us, again and again, how He is the גּוֹאֵל יִשְׂרָאֵל, the constant redeemer of Israel.

◆§ בָּרוּךְ אַתָּה ה׳, גּוֹאֵל יִשְׂרָאֵל — **Blessed are You, Hashem, Constant Redeemer of Israel.** The words גּוֹאֵל יִשְׂרָאֵל, *Constant Redeemer of Israel,* refer to the continuing redeeming action of *HaKadosh Baruch Hu* while we are in *galus.* While we are in *galus,* hated and despised by the world, we look to *HaKadosh Baruch Hu,* our גּוֹאֵל, for protection against our enemies. This is not the same as גָּאַל יִשְׂרָאֵל, *He Who has redeemed Israel,* said before the *Shemoneh Esrei,* which refers to *geulah* from *Mitzrayim* .

When I first came to America — having just left the virulent Nazi

Jew-hatred in Germany — I inquired of someone who had already been here for some forty years about the anti-Semitism in America. He responded, "Nobody likes us, but some don't hate us."

This was borne out a few years later during World War II, when the highest military authorities in Washington were asked to bomb the railroad tracks leading to Auschwitz and other concentration camps, where thousands upon thousands of our brethren were brought, daily, to be murdered in the most brutal way. A few bombs would have been enough to interdict those railroad tracks and save countless numbers of Jews. However, these pleas fell upon deaf ears, because nobody liked us enough to save thousands of Jewish lives.

Our situation in *galus* is a tenuous one — despite the fact that we may feel quite secure — replete with potential dangers that are not always known to us. This is analogous to one who feels quite healthy, except for some minor discomforts. However, when his doctor examines him, he discovers that he is indeed seriously ill.

Throughout our *galus,* we have existed by *nissim.* In spite of the animosity all around us, our nation continues to exist as one sheep among seventy wolves. So we end this *berachah* with, בָּרוּךְ אַתָּה ה' גּוֹאֵל יִשְׂרָאֵל, thanking *HaKadosh Baruch Hu* for His continuing *geulah* throughout our *galus,* for the many hundreds of thousands of instances where individuals — and whole communities — were saved.

This thought also lies behind the words of *Modim* in which we thank *HaKadosh Baruch Hu* for נִסֶּיךָ שֶׁבְּכָל יוֹם עִמָּנוּ, *Your miracles that are with us every day.* And, indeed, the Jewish nation says שֶׁהֶחֱיָנוּ every day for the fact that we are still existing: עַל שֶׁהֶחֱיִיתָנוּ וְקִיַּמְתָּנוּ, which is added in *Modim D'Rabbanan.*

Up to this point, we have learned the first four of the middle *berachos* of *Shemoneh Esrei*: the requests for *daas, teshuvah, selichah,* and the *geulah* within the *galus* — the *aschalta d'geulah.* There are two more *berachos* remaining in this middle section that deal with our present time — one is the *berachah* for *refuah* and the other is the *berachah* for *parnassah* — before we come to the second part of the בִּרְכוֹת הָאֶמְצָעִיּוֹת (*middle berachos*) which deals with the *geulah asidah,* the future, final, redemption of the Jewish nation.

רְפוּאָה

§ רְפָאֵנוּ ה' וְנֵרָפֵא, הוֹשִׁיעֵנוּ וְנִוָּשֵׁעָה — **Heal us, Hashem, so we may be healed; help us so that we may be saved.** These words are a paraphrase of: רְפָאֵנִי ה' וְאֵרָפֵא הוֹשִׁיעֵנִי וְאִוָּשֵׁעָה כִּי תְהִלָּתִי אָתָּה, *I will be healed only if You, Hashem, heal me; I will be helped only if You save me, and therefore I will praise only You* (*Yirmiyahu* 17:14). Put into our terms, Yirmiyahu is saying, "If I am healed, I will not praise the doctor, nor the medicine, but only You, because it is You Who saved me."

When we look at this *pasuk* (which is part of the *haftarah* of *Parashas Bechukosai*) in its proper context, we immediately recognize that רְפָאֵנִי ה׳ וְאֵרָפֵא is not a *tefillah* for the cure of physical ailments, but rather, it is a *tefillah* for the cure of moral or spiritual ailments. Earlier (ibid. v. 9), Yirmiyahu declares in the Name of *HaKadosh Baruch Hu*: עָקֹב הַלֵּב מִכֹּל וְאָנֻשׁ הוּא מִי יֵדָעֶנּוּ, *The heart is crooked — more than any other organ, and it is very sick; who would know it!* If taken literally, this would mean that a person may think he is in perfect health, but in reality he has a very sick heart. The heart is a very shrewd organ — more so than any other organ. It can deceive one into thinking that he is perfectly healthy.

However, as evidenced by the next *pasuk*, this declaration is not referring to the physical condition of the heart. Rather, it refers to the spiritual-moral deterioration of people's "hearts," meaning their minds, feelings and emotions. One's own mind and character can be very deceiving, so that others — and even oneself — can be easily fooled into thinking there is nothing wrong with him: מִי יֵדָעֶנּוּ, *Who would know it?*

The *Navi* continues: אֲנִי ה׳ חֹקֵר לֵב בֹּחֵן כְּלָיוֹת, *Only I, God — Who searches the heart, and examines the kidneys — know the truth;* וְלָתֵת לְאִישׁ כִּדְרָכָיו כִּפְרִי מַעֲלָלָיו, *and I will mete out the punishment fitting each person's misdeeds.*

Here Yirmiyahu HaNavi is chastising people who have a "sick heart" in a moral sense, possessing very detrimental character traits, *middos ra'os*, which causes them to pursue a morally corrupt way of life. A person such as this may not only offend and cause harm to others, but he may actually fool himself into thinking that he is "lily white" and upright — a *"bekovediger"* businessman — and he has a very clear conscience. In reality, though, he may be a scoundrel.

To illustrate this, the *Navi* offers a parable. קוֹרֵא דָגַר וְלֹא יָלָד, *The cuckoo hatches eggs that it has not laid.* Eventually, the chicks will sense that this bird that is hovering over them is not their mother and they will flee from it. He then compares this to people who accumulate wealth, but not in accordance with the law, עֹשֶׂה עֹשֶׁר וְלֹא בְמִשְׁפָּט. The word מִשְׁפָּט here could refer either to the laws of the Torah, or to the law of the land, the *dina d'malchusa*, which they violate. They have made themselves rich (עֹשֶׂה עֹשֶׁר) dishonestly and unjustly. But, like the cuckoo who cannot hold on to chicks that are not hers, these people, too, will eventually lose their wealth in the midst of their lives: בַּחֲצִי יָמָיו יַעַזְבֶנּוּ, and וּבְאַחֲרִיתוֹ יִהְיֶה נָבָל, *and at the end of his life he will be a morally dead person.*

While the example given by the *Navi* of a morally "sick heart" is of a person who is dishonest in business, this "heart disease" could also refer to other *middos ra'os* that one may possess and still fool himself into thinking that he has an excellent character. For example, he may be an egotist, but he thinks, I give *tzedakah*, so how can I be an egotist? Only

אֲנִי ה׳ חֹקֵר לֵב בֹּחֵן כְּלָיוֹת, Hashem knows the inner workings of one's heart.

All of this leads up to the *tefillah* of Yirmiyahu HaNavi: רְפָאֵנִי ה׳ וְאֵרָפֵא הוֹשִׁיעֵנִי וְאִוָּשֵׁעָה כִּי תְהִלָּתִי אָתָּה. Paraphrased, this means: Since the heart is so deceptive, עָקֹב הַלֵּב מִכֹּל, everyone is suspect, and I, myself, may be suffering from this same "heart disease," and my character may have deteriorated unbeknown to me. Only You, *HaKadosh Baruch Hu,* know the truth, and therefore, "Cure me, Hashem, and I will be cured." The cure for spiritual "diseases" is called *refuas hanefesh.* The thrust of the entire *sefer Chovos HaLevavos* is to make a person aware of such "spiritual diseases," and to seek their cures. A person may think of himself as basically a good person, and it could very well be true, but he may overlook the fact that he has certain spiritual "illnesses." This is similar to an ostensibly healthy person who visits a cardiologist and is told that he has heart disease, yet he had never been aware of it.

Therefore, in our *tefillah* of רְפָאֵנוּ ה׳ וְנֵרָפֵא, which is based on Yirmiyahu's *tefillah* for a spiritual *refuah,* we pray for exactly the same thing. We, too, are asking *HaKadosh Baruch Hu* for a *refuas hanefesh.* The purpose of all physical illness is to make a person aware that his *nefesh,* his spiritual existence, is sick. The reason why we ask in our רְפוּאַת הַנֶּפֶשׁ וּרְפוּאַת הַגּוּף for a מִי שֶׁבֵּרַךְ לְחוֹלֶה is because the purpose of the physical sickness is to make a person do *teshuvah* to cleanse his *nefesh* of its spiritual sickness. Therefore, we pray that through the *refuas hanefesh,* the *choleh* may also be granted a *refuas haguf.*

And just as Yirmiyahu did, we add: הוֹשִׁיעֵנוּ וְנִוָּשֵׁעָה, *help us and we will be helped.* This refers to spiritual diseases of which we *are* aware: emotional disturbances, such as fears, apprehensions, frustration, and bitterness. These illnesses are the result of one's lack of *bitachon* in *HaKadosh Baruch Hu.* If a person does not have *emunah* in *hashgachas pratis* — that *HaKadosh Baruch Hu* knows him personally and watches over him — he can be beset with all of these fears and worries. The cure for this disease is *emunah* and *bitachon.* It is for this that we seek the help of *HaKadosh Baruch Hu* in this *tefillah* of הוֹשִׁיעֵנוּ וְנִוָּשֵׁעָה.

If someone has true *bitachon,* he will lose all his fears and apprehensions. When one realizes that whatever happens to him is not an accident, but rather, the will of *HaKadosh Baruch Hu,* he will no longer have fears, worries, and apprehensions. If he is convinced that *HaKadosh Baruch Hu* has a purpose for any difficulty that he may face, he will be totally accepting of it, as part of the educational process that he is being put through. כִּי אֶת אֲשֶׁר יֶאֱהַב ה׳ יוֹכִיחַ, *If HaKadosh Baruch Hu loves a person, He will chastise him* [so that he will improve himself] (Mishlei 3:12). If the chastisement consists of an emotional "sickness of the *nefesh,*" its purpose is to make one improve his *emunah* and *bitachon.*

Dovid HaMelech says: אֲנִי אָמַרְתִּי ה׳ חָנֵּנִי רְפָאָה נַפְשִׁי כִּי חָטָאתִי לָךְ, *As for me* [when I was sick] I said, "O Hashem, show me favor! Heal my soul because I have sinned to You" (Tehillim 41:5). He recognizes that his sins were the cause of the sickness of his soul. He therefore asks *HaKadosh Baruch Hu* to forgive him and thus remove the sickness of his soul.

The *Navi* declares in the Name of Hashem, פָּחֲדוּ בְצִיּוֹן חַטָּאִים, *Tremble in fear, you sinners* (Yeshayahu 33:14). This is referring to the impending assault by Sancheriv which evoked great fear among *Bnei Yisrael*. The *Navi* tells Yisrael that only the sinners will tremble, but those who have *bitachon* in *HaKadosh Baruch Hu* will not fear.

Reinforcing one's *emunah* and *bitachon* requires a great deal of help from *HaKadosh Baruch Hu,* and for this we are *mispallel*: רְפָאֵנוּ ה׳ וְנֵרָפֵא הוֹשִׁיעֵנוּ וְנִוָּשֵׁעָה. Just as Yirmiyahu HaNavi was *mispallel* for his own *refuas hanefesh* for known and unknown spiritual ailments, so do we, as *Klal Yisrael,* ask *HaKadosh Baruch Hu* to cure us of them.

◆§ כִּי תְהִלָּתֵנוּ אָתָּה — **Because our whole praise will be You.** If we are cured, we will not give ourselves credit for "pulling ourselves up by our own bootstraps." It will be strictly because of Your help. If we are healed, it will not be because of our own actions, or because of the doctor, the operation, or the medicine, but only because *HaKadosh Baruch Hu* saved us.

The Gemara tells us: דְּתָנֵי דְּבֵי רַבִּי יִשְׁמָעֵאל "וְרַפֹּא יְרַפֵּא" מִכָּאן שֶׁנִּתְּנָה רְשׁוּת לָרוֹפֵא לְרַפְּאוֹת (Berachos 60a). While *HaKadosh Baruch Hu* expects a physician to apply his knowledge of medicine to heal and cure — and the physician thereby performs the great *mitzvos* of *hatzalas nefashos,* וְאָהַבְתָּ לְרֵעֲךָ כָּמוֹךָ, *of caring for others as he would for himself,* and *gemilas chessed* — nevertheless, the doctor should know that he is merely a *shaliach* (messenger) of *HaKadosh Baruch Hu,* Who gives him the intelligence and skill to effect the cure. Both doctor and patient must know that כִּי תְהִלָּתֵנוּ אָתָּה, praise for the cure is due only to *HaKadosh Baruch Hu* Himself.

Dovid HaMelech asks *HaKadosh Baruch Hu*: חֶסֶד וֶאֱמֶת מַן יִנְצְרֻהוּ, *Appoint mercy and truth to be my guardian* (Tehillim 61:8). This means that while *HaKadosh Baruch Hu* is a *gomeil chessed,* some *chessed* comes in a form in which we feel its sweetness — be it in our family life, our financial dealings, or other successes that we experience in life, such as *osher* (wealth), *kavod* (honor), *banim* (children), etc. However, there is another form of God's mercy to His creatures, which is called *emes,* truth, where we do not feel the *chessed* — in fact, it is sometimes bitter. This *chessed,* in the form of pain, is utilized by *HaKadosh Baruch Hu* to save the person from a much harsher punishment following his death.

The *Navi* exclaims: הוֹי הָאֹמְרִים לָרַע טוֹב וְלַטּוֹב רָע, שָׂמִים חֹשֶׁךְ לְאוֹר וְאוֹר לְחֹשֶׁךְ שָׂמִים מַר לְמָתוֹק וּמָתוֹק לְמָר, *Woe to those who say evil is good and good is evil; who make darkness into light and light into darkness; they make bitter into sweet and sweet into bitter* (*Yeshayahu* 5:20). When a person has a desire to do something that is against the Torah, and he carries it out, the gratification to his senses that he achieves is "sweet." This is a natural phenomenon, and it is expressed as מַיִם גְּנוּבִים יִמְתָּקוּ, *stolen waters are sweet* (*Mishlei* 9:17). Normally, water is tasteless, but if one steals it, it becomes forbidden, and this makes it taste "sweet." But this sweetness is an illusion; it is actually bitter, because one has violated the *ratzon Hashem* to obtain it.

But when a person becomes sick and suffers pain, what is happening is that he is getting his *aveiros* back in their true, bitter form. He is experiencing the reality of the מַר, which he previously sensed — illusively — as מָתוֹק. He is experiencing the אֱמֶת rather than its sweetness, which was a lie. If he recognizes this and does *teshuvah*, his suffering will take away the *aveirah* in this world, and there will be no need for punishment in *Olam Haba*.

Now we pray for the cure of our physical ailments.

וְהַעֲלֵה רְפוּאָה שְׁלֵמָה לְכָל מַכּוֹתֵינוּ — **Effect a complete cure for all of our illnesses;** this includes our physical ailments. The first part of this *tefillah* referred to *refuas hanefesh* in which we asked Hashem to cure our spiritual ills, and this part refers to *refuas haguf*, in which we ask Hashem to cure our physical ailments.

The Gemara tells us: אָמַר רַב חִיָּיא בַּר אַשִׁי אָמַר רַב: אַף עַל פִּי שֶׁאָמְרוּ שׁוֹאֵל אָדָם צְרָכָיו בְּשׁוֹמֵעַ תְּפִלָּה, אִם יֵשׁ לוֹ חוֹלֶה בְּתוֹךְ בֵּיתוֹ אוֹמֵר בְּבִרְכַּת חוֹלִים, וְאִם צָרִיךְ לְפַרְנָסָה אוֹמֵר בְּבִרְכַּת הַשָּׁנִים (*Avodah Zarah* 8a). If someone has a specific request for *refuah* or *parnassah,* for himself or someone else in his household, he should include a brief *tefillah* for this in the appropriate *berachah*, and in many *siddurim* a text is offered for these *tefillos*.

When asking for *refuah* or *parnassah* for an individual, or a group of individuals, it is proper to add the words, בְּתוֹךְ שְׁאָר חוֹלֵי (נִצְרָכֵי) יִשְׂרָאֵל. And when one is asking for a *refuah* for himself or another person, he should always add, רְפוּאַת הַנֶּפֶשׁ וּרְפוּאַת הַגּוּף, because, as we have explained, the purpose of all physical sickness is to make a person aware that his *nefesh,* his spiritual existence, is sick. We therefore pray that with the *refuas hanefesh,* the *choleh* may be granted a *refuas haguf*.

In our *kehillah* we have a *minhag* that when there is a *choleh* in our midst the *shaliach tzibbur* raises his voice during the saying of רְפָאֵנוּ as a signal for the congregation to say a brief *tefillah* for the *choleh*.

If one does not know how to express these additional *tefillos* properly in Hebrew, he should wait until the end of *Shemoneh Esrei* and add these *tefillos* in אֱלֹהַי נְצוֹר, just before . . . יִהְיוּ לְרָצוֹן אִמְרֵי פִי וגו׳, in his or her own words and language.

The Gemara tells us: הַנִּכְנָס לְבַקֵּר אֶת הַחוֹלֶה לֹא יֵשֵׁב לֹא עַל גַּבֵּי מִטָּה וְלֹא עַל גַּבֵּי כִּסֵּא אֶלָּא מִתְעַטֵּף וְיוֹשֵׁב לְפָנָיו מִפְּנֵי שֶׁשְּׁכִינָה לְמַעְלָה מְרַאֲשׁוֹתָיו שֶׁל חוֹלֶה שֶׁנֶּאֱמַר ה׳

יִסְעָדֶנּוּ עַל עֶרֶשׂ דְּוָי (Shabbos 12b). *One who enters to visit a sick person should not sit on a bed or a chair, but rather wrap himself and sit before him, for the Divine Presence is above the sick person's head, as it says: God will fortify him on the bed of misery* (Tehillim 41:4).

Chazal here are referring to a *choleh* who is a *yerei Shamayim* and is doing *teshuvah* for his *aveiros* — which he recognizes as having been the cause of his illness. In the company of such a *choleh* the visitor should be aware of the fact that the *Shechinah* is above the head of the sick person, and the visitor should therefore comport himself accordingly.

We find the following: פְּנֵי ה' בְּעֹשֵׂי רָע לְהַכְרִית מֵאֶרֶץ זִכְרָם, *The face of Hashem is turned against those who do evil* (עֹשֵׂי רָע means to purposely do wrong), *in order to cut off* (exterminate) *their memory from the earth* (Tehillim 34:17). However, this is followed by: צָעֲקוּ וַה' שָׁמֵעַ וּמִכָּל צָרוֹתָם הִצִּילָם, *But, if they* [these *reshaim*] *cry out, Hashem will listen, and He will save them from all of their suffering*. And the reason follows in the next *pasuk*: קָרוֹב ה' לְנִשְׁבְּרֵי לֵב וְאֶת דַּכְּאֵי רוּחַ יוֹשִׁיעַ, *Hashem is close to those who are brokenhearted, and He will save those who are crushed in spirit*.

These *pesukim* can best be understood in the context of a person who becomes sick. Hashem afflicts a person with sickness as a punishment for his *aveiros*, to save him from a much worse fate: that of a heavenly punishment. The pain that this sick person experiences can be compared to the method of purification used for eating utensils that have been rendered unfit for use, commonly known as *kashering*. Pain sent by *HaKadosh Baruch Hu* as a punishment for *aveiros* serves to purify the person much as scalding water expunges the absorbed material in a metal vessel.

There is an even stronger form of pain, in which one is beset with emotional and psychological turmoil, fears, and anxieties, which in many ways is even worse than physical pain. [See עַרְבּוּבִיתָא דְּמָאנֵי מַתְיָא לִידֵי שַׁעֲמוּמִיתָא (Nedarim 81a; see *Rashi* and *Ran* ibid.).] These afflictions can be compared to a stronger form of *kashering* called לִבּוּן, the burning out of the prohibited absorbed material by fire, as for example with a blowtorch.

If a person has to undergo either of these forms of suffering *chas v'shalom*, he should consider them as a means of expunging the impression that the *aveiros* had on him.

There is a highly significant passage in נִשְׁמַת, which has great relevance in connection with the *tefillah* for *refuah*. כָּל עַצְמוֹתַי תֹּאמַרְנָה ה' מִי כָמוֹךָ מַצִּיל עָנִי מֵחָזָק מִמֶּנּוּ וְעָנִי וְאֶבְיוֹן מִגֹּזְלוֹ, *All of my bones shall say, "Hashem, who is like You, Who saves the poor from one who is stronger, and the poor and destitute from one who wants to steal from him"* (Tehillim 35:10). On the surface, there seems to be no connection between the first part of this *pasuk*, which thanks *HaKadosh Baruch Hu* for good health, and the second part which thanks Him for protection from muggers and robbers.

However, upon reflection, we realize that the two segments of this *pasuk* are very much connected, and the second part also refers to the body. The *pasuk* begins by praising *HaKadosh Baruch Hu* for a healthy body, with all its marvelous and wondrous complexity, fairly shouting out to its Creator: מִי ה׳ כָמוֹךְ. This awesome creation, the body, has a marvelous digestive system, which distributes the nutrients via the bloodstream to its various parts. For instance, amazingly, the body "knows" that the bones need calcium, so it sends the calcium derived from the food to the bones. It "knows" that the nervous system needs phosphorous so it extracts that from the food and delivers it to the nervous system. Furthermore, the body has inherent internal controls that protect the smaller organs from being overwhelmed by the demands of the larger ones. Therefore, the greater demand for calcium by the bones does not "rob" the smaller organs — for example, the teeth — of their necessary share of the calcium.

Through the amazing mechanisms of the body, *HaKadosh Baruch Hu* protects the needs of even the "poorest" and smallest of the organs from being overwhelmed by the demands of the larger organs, so that they, too, can receive their necessary nourishment. This is what is meant by מַצִּיל עָנִי מֵחָזָק מִמֶּנּוּ וְעָנִי וְאֶבְיוֹן מִגֹּזְלוֹ which, as explained, is one of the most miraculous functions of the body, which calls out to its Creator: כָּל עַצְמוֹתַי תֹּאמַרְנָה ה׳ מִי כָמוֹךְ.

All of this is true of the healthy body, but what of the sick body with an illness where the systems have broken down and one organ grows so large that it overwhelms the ability of the other organs to function? This body is bereft of its power, and the person possessing it is truly an עָנִי וְאֶבְיוֹן.

In this case there is another meaning to this *pasuk,* which we could paraphrase as follows: All of my bones declare: Hashem, who is like You. In the healthy body, You protect even the smallest and poorest organs from being "robbed" of their needs, מַצִּיל עָנִי מֵחָזָק מִמֶּנּוּ. And in the sick body, You save this poor, defenseless person, the עָנִי וְאֶבְיוֹן, by means of his suffering, from the other alternative, *Gehinnom* — which is characterized as מִגֹּזְלוֹ, his kidnaper — which would rob him of his *Olam Haba*. In this sense, the *pasuk* incorporates the meaning that by punishing a person in *Olam Hazeh*, *HaKadosh Baruch Hu* saves him from a much harsher fate after his death:

[Ed. note: This esoteric concept — that *Gehinnom* desires to "rob" one of his reward in *Olam Habah* — is based on *Avodah Zarah* 17a in its Aggadic interpretation of *Mishlei* 3:15: לַעֲלוּקָה שְׁתֵּי בָנוֹת הַב הַב, *Alukah* (*Gehinnom*) has two daughters (denizons) [who issue the call in this world] "give, give". See also *Zohar* 303.]

These are the thoughts that a sick person lying in bed should have. And if he does focus his mind on these thoughts, this will help him have a רְפוּאָה שְׁלֵמָה לְכָל מַכּוֹתֵינוּ, either in this world or in *Olam Haba*.

‎כִּי אֵל מֶלֶךְ רוֹפֵא נֶאֱמָן וְרַחֲמָן אָתָּה — **For You are God, King, the faithful and compassionate Healer.** We have already mentioned that אֵל always refers to *HaKadosh Baruch Hu* in the sense of absolute *rachamim,* while מֶלֶךְ expresses the concept of absolute *din.* Only *HaKadosh Baruch Hu* can be called רוֹפֵא נֶאֱמָן וְרַחֲמָן, *The Healer Who is both* נֶאֱמָן, practicing *din,* and רַחֲמָן, Who, at the same time is practicing *rachamim,* mercy. He is a combination of *din* and *rachamim.* A doctor who is "merciful" may opt not to operate on the patient because he does not want him to suffer the pain connected with the surgery. However, this doctor would not be called נֶאֱמָן, a reliable doctor. On the other hand, a doctor who is "reliable," and who practices medicine and surgery without regard to the pain and suffering of the patient, would not be called רַחֲמָן.

From the Jewish viewpoint, the Torah teaches us to relate to sickness as a message from *HaKadosh Baruch Hu* to do *teshuvah.* And if we do so, we can look to *HaKadosh Baruch Hu* — our "Reliable Healer," the Ultimate רַחֲמָן — for our cure. *HaKadosh Baruch Hu* has sent us the sickness — out of *rachamim* — for the purpose of curing our *nefesh,* and in the merit of taking this to heart, and doing *teshuvah,* we look to *HaKadosh Baruch Hu* for our *refuas haguf.*

‎בָּרוּךְ אַתָּה ה׳, רוֹפֵא חוֹלֵי עַמּוֹ יִשְׂרָאֵל — **Blessed are You, Hashem, Who heals the sick of His people, Yisrael.** Although *HaKadosh Baruch Hu* is רוֹפֵא כָּל בָּשָׂר, not only חוֹלֵי יִשְׂרָאֵל — as we say in אֲשֶׁר יָצַר — nevertheless, the concept that *refuas hanefesh* comes before *refuas haguf* is a purely Jewish one, based on the teachings of the Torah. Accordingly, sickness should be viewed as a message from *HaKadosh Baruch Hu* to the patient to do *teshuvah.*

By the way, the proper inflection of the wording of this *berachah* is: בָּרוּךְ **רוֹפֵא חוֹלֵי עַמּוֹ יִשְׂרָאֵל** אַתָּה ה׳ and not רוֹפֵא חוֹלֵי, עַמּוֹ יִשְׂרָאֵל as many people erroneously say.

בִּרְכַּת הַשָּׁנִים

‎בָּרֵךְ עָלֵינוּ ה׳ אֱלֹהֵינוּ אֶת הַשָּׁנָה הַזֹּאת — **Bless on our behalf — O Hashem, our God — this year.** After *refuah* comes the *tefillah* for *parnassah.* The Gemara tells us that the extent of one's livelihood is decided upon by *HaKadosh Baruch Hu* between Rosh Hashanah and Yom Kippur: כָּל מְזוֹנוֹתָיו שֶׁל אָדָם קְצוּבִים לוֹ מֵרֹאשׁ הַשָּׁנָה וְעַד יוֹם הַכִּפּוּרִים (*Beitzah* 16a). The term מְזוֹנוֹתָיו refers not only to one's food, but to his entire livelihood. If a person is a *beinoni,* average, neither *tzaddik* nor *rasha,* he is given an opportunity to tip the scales in his favor until Yom Kippur (*Rosh Hashanah* 16b). In the *tefillah* of וּנְתַנֶּה תֹּקֶף, we refer to the fact that our *parnassah* hangs in the balance during this period: מִי יֵעָנִי וּמִי יֵעָשֵׁר

whose livelihood will decline and whose will increase. We must therefore understand the meaning of this *berachah*. If all of one's livelihood is already decided by *HaKadosh Baruch Hu* between Rosh Hashanah and Yom Kippur, what is the purpose of the thrice-daily *tefillah* for *parnassah*, בָּרֵךְ עָלֵינוּ אֶת הַשָּׁנָה הַזֹּאת? No matter how much effort one exerts, he will not make one penny more than *HaKadosh Baruch Hu* has decided. And, conversely, if *HaKadosh Baruch Hu* has decreed that a person will become wealthy, this will happen even if the individual does nothing to bring this about. Shlomo HaMelech tells us: לֹא לַחֲכָמִים לֶחֶם, *one's livelihood is not based on his intelligence* (*Koheles* 9:11). There are many very smart people who do not earn a livelihood, no matter how hard they try, and there are many people with limited intelligence who become wealthy. This is so because all *parnassah* is preordained by *HaKadosh Baruch Hu,* and is not the result of one's abilities or efforts.

This question is highlighted all the more by the fact that even on *erev* Rosh Hashanah afternoon, in our *tefillah* of Minchah, we also say בָּרֵךְ עָלֵינוּ אֶת הַשָּׁנָה הַזֹּאת. What can the words *this year* mean? There are only a few minutes left in *"this year"*! What can we earn during this time?

It is apparent by the fact that our *Chachamim* instituted a *tefillah* for *parnassah* to be recited daily, that they understood that the predetermination of the extent of one's livelihood — which occurs between Rosh Hashanah and Yom Kippur — has an inherent potential for enhancement.

The potential for the enhancement of one's *parnassah* is referred to in the other half of the previously quoted *maamar Chazal:* חוּץ מֵהוֹצָאַת שַׁבָּתוֹת וְהוֹצָאַת יָמִים טוֹבִים וְהוֹצָאַת בָּנָיו לְתַלְמוּד תּוֹרָה שֶׁאִם פָּחַת פּוֹחֲתִין לוֹ וְאִם הוֹסִיף מוֹסִיפִין לוֹ. This means that the predetermination of one's *parnassah* can be changed by the amount one spends for Shabbos and Yom Tov, or the amount he spends for the Torah education of his children.

Taken in its broadest sense, this means that in order to make a beautiful Shabbos or Yom Tov, one has to make a decent living, and he has to do so without violating any of the Torah's laws of commerce, such as *gezel* (theft), *ona'ah* (unethical business conduct), *ribbis* (prohibited interest), or withholding the pay of employees, etc. Then, one can sit at his Shabbos or Yom Tov table and say, "This was all honestly earned with kosher money." In order to do this, one requires a *berachah* in his *parnassah*.

The *Navi* tells us: שֹׁמֵר שַׁבָּת מֵחַלְּלוֹ וְשֹׁמֵר יָדוֹ מֵעֲשׂוֹת כָּל רָע, *He keeps the Shabbos, avoiding its violation, and he keeps his hands (away) from doing all evil* (*Yeshayahu* 56:2). Keeping one's hands from *doing all evil* refers not only to the laws of *muktzeh* — which our *Chachamim* instituted to prevent one from moving forbidden objects with his hands on Shabbos — but also to keeping our hands away from all evil and forbidden activities during the entire week, so that we can provide for the keeping of Shabbos in an honest and dignified way. It is not enough simply to make a "beautiful Shabbos;" rather, it has to be made with money that was earned by hands that are clean of *any* violation, מֵעֲשׂוֹת כָּל רָע.

The same is true regarding הוֹצָאַת בָּנָיו לְתַלְמוּד תּוֹרָה, expenditures for teaching one's children Torah. This does not mean only that one pays tuition and supports the yeshivos where his own children learn, but it means also that he supports the yeshivos and *mosdos haTorah* where other children learn. Because if one's children grow up in a vacuum of Torah learning, where there is no educational system for other boys and girls, or men and women, they will have no one to whom to relate, and with whom to study and share their Torah values. הוֹצָאַת בָּנָיו לְתַלְמוּד תּוֹרָה means, therefore, the support of *all talmud Torah*, all institutions where Torah is studied.

Based on this, the statement that כָּל מְזוֹנוֹתָיו שֶׁל אָדָם קְצוּבִים לוֹ מֵרֹאשׁ הַשָּׁנָה וְעַד יוֹם הַכִּפּוּרִים, with the exception of הוֹצָאַת שַׁבָּתוֹת וְהוֹצָאַת יָמִים טוֹבִים וְהוֹצָאַת בָּנָיו לְתַלְמוּד תּוֹרָה, taken in its broadest sense, means that the more one extends his activities in the areas of *shemiras Shabbos* and in supporting Torah learning, the more money he will earn. This does not mean merely that one will make up his additional expenditures, but rather, אִם הוֹסִיף מוֹסִיפִין לוֹ, which means, "If a person increases *his* expenditures in these areas, *HaKadosh Baruch Hu* will increase *His* benefits to this individual, and he will receive much more in return."

Therefore, the meaning of בָּרֵךְ עָלֵינוּ ה׳ אֱלֹהֵינוּ אֶת הַשָּׁנָה הַזֹּאת — which is said until the last minute of the year — is that we ask *HaKadosh Baruch Hu* to bless the efforts that we have made in earning our livelihood, the benefits of which we used for expanded expenditures for Shabbos and Yom Tov, and for the support of Torah.

[Ed. note: See *Tosafos* to *Rosh Hashanah* 16a s.v. כמאן מצלינן, which also deals with the question of how *tefillah* can change the predetermination of one's livelihood.]

◆§ וְאֶת כָּל מִינֵי תְבוּאָתָהּ לְטוֹבָה — **And all of its various crops, for our benefit.** The word תְּבוּאָה here does not refer only to "grain" or "produce" — that is the focus of the next phrase — but rather, it means all forms of "production," which means all business, manufactured goods, and services to others that we produce.

◆§ וְתֵן טַל וּמָטָר לִבְרָכָה / וְתֵן בְּרָכָה עַל פְּנֵי הָאֲדָמָה — **And give dew and rain for a blessing / and give blessing on the face of the earth.** Now we ask for a *berachah* for the agricultural produce of the land. פְּנֵי הָאֲדָמָה, *the face of the earth,* means the soil where growth takes place. Our *tefillah* here is that there will be enough food to feed all the hungry people in the world.

Sufficient agricultural production is an absolute necessity for the economy of any land. *Koheles* 5:8 says: מֶלֶךְ לְשָׂדֶה נֶעֱבָד, *even a king is a*

SHEMONEH ESREI ◆ 463

servant to his field, meaning that if nothing grows in the fields, all political leadership is in jeopardy. The people will either rise up against their government or flee the country.

וְשַׂבְּעֵנוּ מִטּוּבֶךָ — **Satiate us with** *Your* **Goodness.** There are others who have the text as וְשַׂבְּעֵנוּ מִטּוּבָהּ (see *Mishnah Berurah* 117:1), which means *satiate us with its goodness,* referring either to *adamah* or to *berachah.*

However, in the *tefillos* of Shabbos and Yom Tov, everyone agrees that the proper wording is שַׂבְּעֵנוּ מִטּוּבֶךָ, because there it refers to spiritual satisfaction.

שַׂבְּעֵנוּ מִטּוּבֶךָ here is meant in the same sense as וַאֲכַלְתֶּם לַחְמְכֶם לָשֹׂבַע (*Vayikra* 26:5), which Rashi there explains as meaning, אוֹכֵל קִמְעָא וְהוּא מִתְבָּרֵךְ בְּמֵעָיו, *One eats only a little, but that satiates him.* The *berachah* there is that even a little bit of food will be enough to satisfy us. This is similar to what Yaakov Avinu meant when he told his brother, וְכִי יֶשׁ לִי כֹל, *[I don't need much;] I have everything* (*Bereishis* 33:11).

Our *Chachamim* tell us (see *Sanhedrin* 97a and *Sotah* 49b) דּוֹר שֶׁבֶּן דָּוִד בָּא הַגֶּפֶן תִּתֵּן פִּרְיָהּ וְהַיַּיִן בְּיוֹקֶר .... Before the coming of *Mashiach,* there will be such greed that despite the fact that the grape crop will be abundant, the wine producers will demand high prices for it; they would rather waste it than sell it cheaply. People will have huge appetites for riches which can never be satiated.

[Ed. note: The Rav, in his *Sefer Beis HaSho'evah* (Shulsinger, 1941) — not to be confused with *Maayan Beis HaSho'evah,* Mesorah Publications, 1994 — makes reference to this *maamar Chazal* on p. 129, and offers a broader interpretation of it.]

Despite the fact that the world overproduces food, millions of people are still starving. If it would not be for greed, all the food in the world would be properly distributed among the population, and everybody would have enough to eat. However, since the טוב ה' is missing, people are never satisfied; they can never get enough. And therefore we ask Hashem שַׂבְּעֵנוּ מִטּוּבֶךָ, *Satiate us with Your goodness.* Give us enough food and money and possessions for our needs, and give us that feeling of being satisfied, which will obviate our greed and lust for more and more — a desire that can never be satisfied.

The source for our text of, וְשַׂבְּעֵנוּ מִטּוּבֶךָ, *Satiate us with Your goodness,* is: וּבָאוּ וְרִנְּנוּ בִמְרוֹם צִיּוֹן וְנָהֲרוּ אֶל טוּב ה' עַל דָּגָן וְעַל תִּירֹשׁ וְעַל יִצְהָר וְעַל בְּנֵי צֹאן וּבָקָר וגו' (*Yirmiyahu* 31:11). Our late Rav, Rav Joseph Breuer, explained this *pasuk* — which refers to the Jewish homecoming at the time of the *geulah* — as follows: *And they will come and sing joyously on the height of Tziyon; they will stream* אֶל, *to, the goodness that comes from Hashem, which is* עַל, *above, that of grain, wine, oil, and young sheep and cattle.* And then, וְהָיְתָה נַפְשָׁם כְּגַן רָוֶה, *their souls will be [satiated] as a saturated garden.* At the time of the *geulah* our people will become *spiritually satisfied*. The *Navi* continues — and this is the wording on which our text is based — וְעַמִּי אֶת טוּבִי יִשְׂבָּעוּ, *My nation will be satiated with My goodness* (ibid. v. 13). So in saying שַׂבְּעֵנוּ מִטּוּבֶךְ, we ask Hashem to satiate us not only with His physical blessings, which are necessary for our sustenance, but also with His spiritual goodness.

Similarly, in *Bircas HaMazon* we say: . . ., וְכָל **טוּב**, וּמִכָּל **טוּב** לְעוֹלָם אַל יְחַסְּרֵנוּ, which is a reference to the future time when the Jewish people will be spiritually satiated with the טוּב הַשֵּׁם. We ask Hashem in *Bircas HaMazon* to bless us with רַחֲמִים וְחַיִּים וְשָׁלוֹם וְכָל טוֹב, which are all physical blessings; but in closing we say וּמִכָּל טוּב לְעוֹלָם אַל יְחַסְּרֵנוּ, by which we pray that we may also have a part in that future blissful existence of וְעַמִּי אֶת טוּבִי יִשְׂבָּעוּ, that spiritual satiation which is more than food and drink, עַל דָּגָן וְעַל תִּירוֹשׁ וְעַל יִצְהָר.

⊷ וּבָרֵךְ שְׁנָתֵנוּ כַּשָּׁנִים הַטּוֹבוֹת — **Bless our Year** — we are referring only to the present year, because next year will have another determination — **as the good years.** The reference to *the good years* is not to those which have already passed, but rather, to the *future years*. A description of those future *good years* can be found in *Yoel* 2:18-25: וַיְקַנֵּא ה׳ לְאַרְצוֹ וַיַּחְמֹל עַל עַמּוֹ. וַיַּעַן ה׳ וַיֹּאמֶר לְעַמּוֹ הִנְנִי שֹׁלֵחַ לָכֶם אֶת הַדָּגָן וְהַתִּירוֹשׁ וְהַיִּצְהָר וּשְׂבַעְתֶּם אֹתוֹ וְלֹא אֶתֵּן אֶתְכֶם עוֹד חֶרְפָּה בַּגּוֹיִם . . . וּמָלְאוּ הַגֳּרָנוֹת בָּר . . . וְשִׁלַּמְתִּי לָכֶם אֶת הַשָּׁנִים אֲשֶׁר אָכַל הָאַרְבֶּה הַיֶּלֶק וְהֶחָסִיל וְהַגָּזָם . . ., *Then Hashem will take up the cause of His land and take pity on His people. Hashem will reply and say to His people: Behold, I am sending you the grain, and the wine and the oil, and you will be sated from it, and I will no longer make you a disgrace among the nations . . . The granaries will be filled with grain . . . I will repay you for the years that the abundant locust, the chewing locust, the demolishing locust, and the cutting locust consumed.*

In these *pesukim* we have a description of the future שָׁנִים הַטּוֹבוֹת, which will be a repayment to us for all the bad years during which we suffered throughout our history. Imagine how many bad years we have had!

This description of these blissful *good years* continues: וַאֲכַלְתֶּם אָכוֹל וְשָׂבוֹעַ, *You will eat and be satiated* (ibid. v. 26), which describes the feeling of satisfaction while eating even a little bit, אוֹכֵל קִמְעָא וְהוּא מִתְבָּרֵךְ בְּמֵעָיו.

The *Navi* continues:
וְהִלַּלְתֶּם אֶת שֵׁם ה׳ אֱלֹהֵיכֶם אֲשֶׁר עָשָׂה עִמָּכֶם לְהַפְלִיא וְלֹא יֵבֹשׁוּ עַמִּי לְעוֹלָם. וִידַעְתֶּם כִּי בְּקֶרֶב יִשְׂרָאֵל אָנִי, וַאֲנִי ה׳ אֱלֹהֵיכֶם וְאֵין עוֹד וְלֹא יֵבֹשׁוּ עַמִּי לְעוֹלָם, *You will praise the Name of Hashem Who has done marvels with you . . . and you will know that I am in the midst of Israel . . . and My nation will never again have to be put to shame* (ibid. vs. 26-27).

These *pesukim* describe those future שָׁנִים הַטּוֹבוֹת for which we pray in this *tefillah*.

In *Bircas HaMazon*, we say וְנָא אַל תַּצְרִיכֵנוּ ה׳ אֱלֹהֵינוּ, לֹא לִידֵי מַתְּנַת בָּשָׂר וָדָם, וְלֹא לִידֵי הַלְוָאָתָם, כִּי אִם לְיָדְךָ הַמְּלֵאָה הַפְּתוּחָה הַקְּדוֹשָׁה וְהָרְחָבָה, **שֶׁלֹּא נֵבוֹשׁ וְלֹא נִכָּלֵם**

לְעוֹלָם וָעֶד. And this is followed by וּבְנֵה יְרוּשָׁלַיִם עִיר הַקֹּדֶשׁ בִּמְהֵרָה בְיָמֵינוּ. When we ask *HaKadosh Baruch Hu* to provide us, individually, with a dignified livelihood, in which we will not have any need for gifts or loans, we immediately add a similar *tefillah* for our entire nation, that the time may soon come when we, as a nation, will no longer have the shame of need and dependency on other nations — a reference to the aforementioned promise, וְלֹא יֵבֹשׁוּ עַמִּי לְעוֹלָם, which will be realized at the time of the *geulah*.

Just as we ask that our individual livelihoods be given to us not by other people, but by *HaKadosh Baruch Hu* Himself, so do we ask that וּבְנֵה יְרוּשָׁלַיִם עִיר הַקֹּדֶשׁ בִּמְהֵרָה בְיָמֵינוּ not be a gift that is granted to us by the grace of the "superpowers" of the world, but rather, by *HaKadosh Baruch Hu* Himself, so that שֶׁלֹּא נֵבוֹשׁ וְלֹא נִכָּלֵם לְעוֹלָם וָעֶד, *we not feel inner shame nor be humiliated forever and ever.*

In summary, then, our *tefillah* of וּבָרֵךְ שְׁנָתֵנוּ כַּשָּׁנִים הַטּוֹבוֹת is a request to *HaKadosh Baruch Hu* to bless *our year* — this year — with the blessings of those future "good years" that He promised us through His *Navi*.

❧ בָּרוּךְ אַתָּה ה׳, מְבָרֵךְ הַשָּׁנִים — **Blessed are You, Hashem, Who blesses the years.** This is said in the present tense, in expression of our *emunah sheleimah* that *HaKadosh Baruch Hu* will fulfill His promise to bless the future years. We ask in this *tefillah* that He will also bless הַשָּׁנָה הַזֹּאת, *the present year*, with those blessings.

Although our livelihood for the present year has already been decided on Rosh Hashanah, as we have mentioned, nevertheless, we ask *HaKadosh Baruch Hu* here to increase the predetermined amount, in the merit of our extensive expenditures in the areas of Shabbos and Yom Tov, and for the support and promotion of Torah learning. The more we expand our efforts for these objectives, and practice them on a large scale, the more we can expect the blessings of *HaKadosh Baruch Hu* in return: אִם הוֹסִיף מוֹסִיפִין לוֹ.

If a person has difficulties with his *parnassah*, he should add his own personal *tefillah* here just before בָּרוּךְ אַתָּה ה׳ מְבָרֵךְ הַשָּׁנִים.

With this *berachah*, we complete the first part of the middle *berachos* of the *Shemoneh Esrei*. Now we begin the second part: the seven *berachos* that focus on the future redemption, *geulah ha'asidah*. According to the order of these *berachos*, *Mashiach* will come at the end of this period, and therefore וְלִירוּשָׁלַיִם עִירְךָ was placed after אֶת צֶמַח דָּוִד.

Rav Samson R. Hirsch, in his *Siddur*, explains the correlation between the *berachos* for the individual in the *Shemoneh Esrei* and those for the nation as a whole. Please refer to it.

[Ed. note: The Rav explains these correlations slightly differently than Rav Hirsch, which will become apparent as we proceed. Also see *Avudraham, Seder Shacharis Shel Chol U'feirusheha* p. 107.]

קִבּוּץ גָּלֻיּוֹת

תְּקַע בְּשׁוֹפָר גָּדוֹל לְחֵרוּתֵנוּ — Sound the big *shofar* for our freedom. This is based on the *pasuk*, וְהָיָה בַּיּוֹם הַהוּא יִתָּקַע בְּשׁוֹפָר גָּדוֹל וגו', *It shall be on that day that a great shofar will be blown* (Yeshayahu 27:13). This *berachah* refers to the onset of the *geulah,* which will begin with *HaKadosh Baruch Hu* making us free from dependency on any other nation.

As we have said, the latter seven *berachos* which refer to the final *geulah sheleimah* correspond to the first six. Based on this, the *berachah* of תְּקַע בְּשׁוֹפָר גָּדוֹל corresponds to אַתָּה חוֹנֵן לְאָדָם דַּעַת. Just as we have asked *HaKadosh Baruch Hu* to grant us דֵּעָה individually, we ask Him in this *tefillah* to begin the *geulah,* at which time מָלְאָה הָאָרֶץ דֵּעָה אֶת ה', *the world will be filled with the knowledge of Hashem* (Yeshayahu 11:9).

The words שׁוֹפָר גָּדוֹל, "the large, or very loud, *shofar,*" could be meant literally — we will not fully understand the language of this *nevuah* until it is actually realized. שׁוֹפָר גָּדוֹל could be a metaphor for the time in world history when, as if by a loud proclamation, there will be a worldwide universal recognition of *HaKadosh Baruch Hu.* At the time of *kibbutz galuyos,* the ingathering of the Jewish people and their return to Eretz Yisrael, there will be a worldwide recognition of *HaKadosh Baruch Hu.* And this will be a signal for our freedom, לְחֵרוּתֵינוּ, freedom from future dependency on any nation of the world.

We make reference to that time in our pre-Shacharis *tefillah* of יַכִּירוּ וְיֵדְעוּ כָּל בָּאֵי עוֹלָם כִּי אַתָּה הוּא הָאֱלֹהִים לְבַדְּךָ לְכֹל מַמְלְכוֹת הָאָרֶץ. [Ed. Note: From the *tefillah* beginning with אַתָּה הוּא ה'... קַבֵּץ קוֶיךָ. See the Rav's explanation there.]

An example of that שׁוֹפָר גָּדוֹל, which did occur once before in world history, is alluded to in the aforementioned *tefillah* of אַתָּה הוּא ה'...קַבֵּץ קוֶיךָ. In this *tefillah* we ask: יַכִּירוּ וְיֵדְעוּ כָּל בָּאֵי עוֹלָם כִּי אַתָּה הוּא הָאֱלֹהִים לְבַדְּךָ לְכֹל מַמְלְכוֹת הָאָרֶץ, which is a paraphrase of a proclamation made by the Persian king Koresh, who was the most powerful person in the world in his time. He had conquered the theretofore unconquerable Babylonian Empire, and ruled the entire then-known world. After establishing his world rule, he issued the following proclamation ordering the rebuilding of the *Beis HaMikdash,* which effectively ended *galus Bavel*: כֹּה אָמַר כֹּרֶשׁ מֶלֶךְ פָּרַס כֹּל מַמְלְכוֹת הָאָרֶץ נָתַן לִי ה' אֱלֹהֵי הַשָּׁמַיִם וְהוּא פָקַד עָלַי לִבְנוֹת לוֹ בַיִת בִּירוּשָׁלַם אֲשֶׁר בִּיהוּדָה, *Thus said Koresh king of Persia: All the kingdoms of the earth has Hashem, God of heaven, given to me and He has commanded me to build Him a Temple in Yerushalayim which is in Judah* (Ezra 1:2).

The mighty king Koresh had heard that two hundred years earlier the prophet Yeshayahu, speaking in the Name of *HaKadosh Baruch Hu,* had mentioned him and had said that he, Koresh, would eventually rebuild the *Beis HaMikdash*. The *Navi* had declared: הָאֹמֵר לְכוֹרֶשׁ רֹעִי וְכָל חֶפְצִי יַשְׁלִם וְלֵאמֹר לִירוּשָׁלַםִ תִּבָּנֶה וְהֵיכָל תִּוָּסֵד, *Who says of Koresh, "He is My shepherd, He will fulfill all My desires," to say of Yerushalayim, "It shall be built," and of the Temple, "It shall be established"* (Yeshayahu 44:28).

And, indeed, in the next chapter we find: כֹּה אָמַר ה׳ לִמְשִׁיחוֹ לְכוֹרֶשׁ, *Thus said Hashem to His anointed one, to Koresh* (45:1). Here *HaKadosh Baruch Hu* calls Koresh, מְשִׁיחִי, *My anointed one*. He was anointed by *HaKadosh Baruch Hu* to carry out His will to initiate the rebuilding of the Second *Beis HaMikdash*.

Since Koresh had heard that that ה׳ אֱלֹהֵי הַשָּׁמַיִם spoke of him two hundred years earlier — referring to him as His anointed one — and foretold that he would one day build the *Beis HaMikdash* in Yerushalayim, Koresh issued an edict, in his capacity as the supreme ruler on earth, to build the "House of God" in Yerushalayim: מִי בָכֶם מִכָּל עַמּוֹ יְהִי אֱלֹהָיו עִמּוֹ וְיַעַל לִירוּשָׁלַםִ אֲשֶׁר בִּיהוּדָה וְיִבֶן אֶת בֵּית ה׳ אֱלֹהֵי יִשְׂרָאֵל הוּא הָאֱלֹהִים אֲשֶׁר בִּירוּשָׁלָםִ, *Whoever is among you of His entire people — May his God be with him — let him go up to Yerushalayim which is in Judah and build the Temple of Hashem, God of Israel — He is the God — which is in Jerusalem* (Ezra 1:3).

These words, spoken by the most powerful man on earth, based on the recognition that ה׳ הוּא הָאֱלֹהִים, and the acceptance of the *nevuah* of Yeshayahu, constituted the greatest worldwide *kiddush Hashem* imaginable. This was an example of שׁוֹפָר גָּדוֹל. Unfortunately, we did not merit for that event to have developed into the *yemos HaMashiach*.

The era of תֵּקַע בְּשׁוֹפָר גָּדוֹל will begin when the world's rulers, presidents, prime ministers, kings and potentates finally recognize that ה׳ הוּא הָאֱלֹהִים, *Hashem, He is the God*: יַכִּירוּ וְיֵדְעוּ כָּל בָּאֵי עוֹלָם כִּי אַתָּה הוּא הָאֱלֹהִים לְבַדְּךָ לְכֹל מַמְלְכוֹת הָאָרֶץ.

&ᴥ **וְשָׂא נֵס לְקַבֵּץ גָּלֻיּוֹתֵינוּ** ᴥ& — **Raise a banner to gather our exiles.** We ask here that the nations of the world shall see — as if by a signal — that it is *HaKadosh Baruch Hu* Who is gathering our exiles together from all parts of the world.

&ᴥ **וְקַבְּצֵנוּ יַחַד** ᴥ& — **Gather us together.** During the *galus*, the Jewish people is split, not only physically-geographically, but also ideologically. One group does not see eye to eye with the other. This disparity exists not only in that the non-religious segment of our nation does not understand those who are religious, but even the people who do keep Torah and *mitzvos* are divided, and subdivided many times among themselves.

The Torah tells us that when Yaakov Avinu called his children together to tell them his final words, he said: הֵאָסְפוּ וְאַגִּידָה לָכֶם אֵת אֲשֶׁר יִקְרָא אֶתְכֶם בְּאַחֲרִית הַיָּמִים, *Assemble yourselves and I will tell you what will call you in the End of Days* (Bereishis 49:1). The word יִקְרָא is spelled with an א, meaning, something will *call* you at the end of time (and not יִקְרָה, which would mean "that which will *happen* to you"). The "call" to which Yaakov Avinu was referring is contained in the next *pasuk*: הִקָּבְצוּ וְשִׁמְעוּ בְּנֵי יַעֲקֹב, *Gather together and listen, children of Yaakov*. At the *acharis hayamim,* this "call" will consist of the recognition of *Bnei Yaakov* that a new time has come — the whole world has recognized *HaKadosh Baruch Hu* — so now we too must gather together, הִקָּבְצוּ וְשִׁמְעוּ.

⁂ מֵאַרְבַּע כַּנְפוֹת הָאָרֶץ — **From the four corners of the earth.** The use of the word כַּנְפוֹת, *wings,* to connote all parts of the world is noteworthy, and it is based on: מִכְּנַף הָאָרֶץ זְמִרֹת שָׁמַעְנוּ צְבִי לַצַּדִּיק, *From the "wing" of the earth, we have heard songs: "Beauty belongs to the tzaddik"* (*Yeshayahu* 24:16). This means that when that time comes, not only the Jewish people, but the whole world, will recognize *HaKadosh Baruch Hu,* and וּמָלְאָה הָאָרֶץ דֵּעָה אֶת ה', it will have lifted itself up to a higher level. The earth will have "sprouted wings." The earth, in every direction, will experience an uplifting of the spirit. People will understand that they have to change their lives; there will be a moral uplifting in the world.

So we ask *HaKadosh Baruch Hu* to gather us together, and unite us, from all parts of this newly uplifted world.

⁂ בָּרוּךְ אַתָּה ה', מְקַבֵּץ נִדְחֵי עַמּוֹ יִשְׂרָאֵל — **Blessed are You, Hashem, Who gathers together the dispersed of Israel.** These words are based on: נְאֻם אֲדֹנָי אֱלֹהִים מְקַבֵּץ נִדְחֵי יִשְׂרָאֵל עוֹד אֲקַבֵּץ עָלָיו לְנִקְבָּצָיו, *The word of Hashem/ Elokim, Who gathers in the dispersed of Israel: I shall gather to it even more than those who are already gathered to it* (*Yeshayahu* 56:8).

However, upon reflection, the word נִדְחֵי, from נדח, really means *pushed out*. One who is outside of a particular group or circle is called נִדָּח. And this meaning is very closely connected with the beginning of the *berachah*, תְּקַע בְּשׁוֹפָר גָּדוֹל, which is taken from: וְהָיָה בַּיּוֹם הַהוּא יִתָּקַע בְּשׁוֹפָר גָּדוֹל וּבָאוּ הָאֹבְדִים בְּאֶרֶץ אַשּׁוּר וְהַנִּדָּחִים בְּאֶרֶץ מִצְרַיִם וגו', *On that day, a great shofar will be blown and the lost ones in the land of Ashur, and those who were pushed away in the land of Mitzrayim, will return* (*Yeshayahu* 27:13). This *pasuk* refers to the ingathering of all of *Bnei Yisrael* from the four corners of the earth, and the names *Ashur* and *Mitzrayim* are used here in a figurative sense, describing the two factors that were the causes of the great losses that the Jewish people suffered during the *galus* history.

אַשּׁוּר means happiness; and in fact, the Jews who were exiled into Assyria by Sancheriv were not enslaved or persecuted. On the contrary, they were promised, and did enjoy, a very good life.

But מִצְרַיִם, from the root צר, means a land of צָרוֹת, where the Jews did suffer in their exile.

אַשּׁוּר represents those lands in the *galus* where the Jewish people had a happy and prosperous life. However, it was this prosperity that caused them to assimilate and become lost. As far as the Jewish nation is concerned, they became אֹבְדִים בְּאֶרֶץ אַשּׁוּר, *lost because of the good life in a happy country.*

מִצְרַיִם represents those lands in the *galus* where the Jewish people suffered greatly. And because of their suffering, many of them were "turned off" and, in desperation, gave up their religion. This was done either for philosophical reasons — because they could not understand why *HaKadosh Baruch Hu* would not help them, as we have witnessed from some Holocaust victims — or simply to survive physically or economically. The people in this group became נִדָּחִים בְּאֶרֶץ מִצְרָיִם, they were "pushed away because of their suffering," and remained outside of the fold of the Jewish nation.

It is these two groups to which the *Navi* refers when he envisions the day of the final *geulah*, when all segments of the Jewish people will return, regardless of whether they are אֹבְדִים בְּאֶרֶץ אַשּׁוּר or נִדָּחִים בְּאֶרֶץ מִצְרָיִם.

Therefore, while we end this *berachah* with בָּרוּךְ אַתָּה ה' מְקַבֵּץ נִדְחֵי עַמּוֹ יִשְׂרָאֵל — which refers to the *pasuk* נְאֻם ה' אֱלֹהִים מְקַבֵּץ נִדְחֵי יִשְׂרָאֵל וגו' — it is to be taken in its broader sense, which includes the אֹבְדִים, together with the נִדָּחִים, as alluded to at the beginning of the *berachah*, תְּקַע בְּשׁוֹפָר גָּדוֹל. And this is based on the *nevuah* of Yeshayahu: וְהָיָה בַּיּוֹם הַהוּא יִתָּקַע בְּשׁוֹפָר גָּדוֹל וּבָאוּ הָאֹבְדִים בְּאֶרֶץ אַשּׁוּר וְהַנִּדָּחִים בְּאֶרֶץ מִצְרָיִם. On that great day, *HaKadosh Baruch Hu* will bring back all of our people who are "outside the fold," regardless of whether they are אֹבְדִים or נִדָּחִים.

And we have such *emunah* that this will take place, that we end this *tefillah* with the *berachah* in the present tense, as if we have already experienced the ingathering of the exiles.

The concept of נִדָּחִים and אֹבְדִים, describing those of our people who — for whatever reason — have left the fold, also goes back to a very significant chapter in *Yechezkel* (34). This is a lengthy chapter, and its complete explanation is not within the scope of this *shiur*. However, one would be well advised to study it carefully on his own. In this chapter, the *Navi* addresses the shepherds, the leaders of Israel, who are remiss in their leadership duties. He tells them: הוֹי רֹעֵי יִשְׂרָאֵל, *Woe to the shepherds of Israel!* Instead of leading their people, הֲלוֹא הַצֹּאן יִרְעוּ הָרֹעִים, they allow *the sheep to lead the shepherds* (*Yechezkel* 34:2).

The *Navi* lists the following derelictions of their pastoral duties: אֶת הַנַּחְלוֹת לֹא חִזַּקְתֶּם וְאֶת הַחוֹלָה לֹא רִפֵּאתֶם וְלַנִּשְׁבֶּרֶת לֹא חֲבַשְׁתֶּם וְאֶת הַנִּדַּחַת לֹא הֲשֵׁבֹתֶם וְאֶת הָאֹבֶדֶת לֹא בִקַּשְׁתֶּם, *The weak ones you did not strengthen, the sick you did not heal, the broken ones you did not bind up, those which were outside the flock you did not return, and those which were lost you did not seek* (*Yechezkel* 34:4).

I once heard an explanation of the differences of these five categories of misdeeds from Rav Elchonon Wasserman, הי"ד — whom I had the great zechus to have as a guest in my house for one Shabbos in Baltimore [ca. 1939]. If memory serves me correctly, he said the following:

❏ נַחֲלוֹת, the *weak ones,* are Jews who keep the *mitzvos,* but do not learn Torah. Consequently, they go through the motions of keeping the *mitzvos* by rote, but without any enthusiasm. They are not too punctilious about *davening* with a *minyan,* nor are they too careful about the level of their *kashrus.* A conscientious רֹעֵה יִשְׂרָאֵל would have the duty of teaching them Torah and thus strengthening their religious observance. But they neglected this duty.

❏ חוֹלָה are the *sick* Jews, who, while they purportedly keep Torah and *mitzvos,* are very lax in the areas of *gezel* and *arayos.* There are many "*frum*" Jews who fall prey to the *yetzer hara* of greed, thievery, and unsavory business practices. Similarly, many fall prey to immorality in their sexual practices. This is a sick form of *Yiddishkeit.* A conscientious רֹעֵה יִשְׂרָאֵל would have the duty of healing these sick Jews. But they just did not care.

❏ נִשְׁבֶּרֶת, *broken,* means one of their limbs has been broken, and the fracture is in need of being reset. This refers to a Jew who keeps *mitzvos* selectively, and he simply *breaks off* the others. He may give a great deal of *tzedakah,* and send his children to yeshivos, but he does not keep Shabbos or the laws of family purity. Some may have only "one broken bone" — he keeps everything except one *mitzvah,* מוּמָר לְדָבָר אֶחָד — and some may have many "fractures" in their practice of Judaism. Nevertheless, these are people in need of a conscientious רֹעֵה יִשְׂרָאֵל who would attempt to "reset these fractures," and make the structure of their Judaism whole. But the leaders failed in this regard.

❏ נִדַּחַת refers to those Jews who are "*outside the fold,*" in the sense that they do not believe in every one of the thirteen basic principles of Judaism, י"ג עִקָּרִים. An example would be a person who may keep all the *mitzvos,* but he does not believe that the Torah was given to Moshe Rabbeinu in the form we have it today. Or, he may not believe in *bi'as Mashiach* or *techiyas hameisim.* It is the duty of a conscientious רֹעֵה יִשְׂרָאֵל to attempt to convince these Jews, who are נִדְחֵי יִשְׂרָאֵל, the outsiders, to come back into the fold (הֲשֵׁבֹתֶם) by accepting all the basic principles of Judaism. But, they did not do so.

And finally, there are the אֹבֶדֶת, those who are *lost.* These people could be *tinokos shenishbu,* who do not even know that there is a "flock" to which they belong. They have become assimilated into the secular life of the country in which they live, as a result of living in the atmosphere of an אֶרֶץ אַשּׁוּר. America is an example of this. And these אֹבֶדֶת could also include those who are lost to Judaism as a result of a life of suffering, characterized as אֶרֶץ מִצְרַיִם. These are the "lost sheep" about which the *Navi* chastises the Jewish "shepherds": לֹא בִקַּשְׁתֶּם, *You haven't even looked for them!* Regardless of the

SHEMONEH ESREI ෴ 471

cause of their being lost, it is the duty of the Jewish leaders to make every effort to seek them out (בְּקַשְׁתֶּם) and return them to the fold. This is the basis of the *kiruv rechokim* movement. However, the "Jewish shepherds" to whom the *Navi* refers have failed to bring these lost souls back.

All of this ties in very well with the next *berachah*. If the leaders do not perform their duties as they are required to do, and the Jewish people remain נִדָּחִים and אוֹבְדִים, we ask *HaKadosh Baruch Hu* to bring back to us the leaders who did lead the Jewish people on the right path: הָשִׁיבָה שׁוֹפְטֵינוּ וְאָשִׁיבָה שֹׁפְטַיִךְ כְּבָרִאשׁנָה וְיֹעֲצַיִךְ כְּבַתְּחִלָּה, as He promised us through His *Navi*: בְּבָרִאשׁוֹנָה, *I will restore your judges as we had formerly and your advisers as in the beginning* (Yeshayahu 1:26).

דִין

This is the *tefillah* for communal *teshuvah*, and it corresponds to הֲשִׁיבֵנוּ אָבִינוּ לְתוֹרָתֶךָ, which is a *tefillah* for each individual's *teshuvah*. The first thing that will occur after the "signal" is given for our return to Eretz Yisrael is that there will be a mass *teshuvah* movement. Following the previous *berachah*, in which we asked *HaKadosh Baruch Hu* to gather the Jewish people together — including all the lost souls who were outside the fold — we now ask *HaKadosh Baruch Hu* to provide us with the proper leadership of שׁוֹפְטִים and יוֹעֲצִים, who can lead the Jewish people in this general *teshuvah* movement. This movement would include every Jew, from all the different strata of the people, regardless of whether they are נַחֲלוֹת, חוֹלָה, נִשְׁבֶּרֶת, נִדַּחַת or even אֹבֶדֶת.

§ הָשִׁיבָה שׁוֹפְטֵינוּ כְּבָרִאשׁוֹנָה וְיוֹעֲצֵינוּ כְּבַתְּחִלָּה — **Restore our judges as we had formerly and our advisers as in the beginning.** This is based on: וְאָשִׁיבָה שֹׁפְטַיִךְ כְּבָרִאשֹׁנָה וְיֹעֲצַיִךְ כְּבַתְּחִלָּה, *I will return your judges, as we had formerly, and your advisers as in the beginning* (Yeshayahu 1:26). The simple explanation here is that for matters of civil law — *choshen mishpat* — which involve *bein adam l'chaveiro*, we will need proper שׁוֹפְטִים. And for matters involving *bein adam laMakom*, which involve questions of *Chovos HaLevavos*, the duties of our hearts, and how we are to serve *HaKadosh Baruch Hu*, we will need יוֹעֲצִים, advisers. We ask *HaKadosh Baruch Hu* here to once again let us have judges and advisers of the caliber which our people once possessed.

Furthermore, this also has the following meaning. יוֹעֲצַיִךְ, *your advisers*, refers to the return of our *Neviim*, such as Eliyahu HaNavi, or Elisha, etc., whose role it will be to advise and counsel the people to do *teshuvah*, so they can avoid wrongdoing and the necessity of facing the *shoftim*.

כְּבַתְּחִלָּה, *as in the beginning* — as opposed to כְּבָרִאשׁוֹנָה, *as we had formerly* — refers to the priority of the *teshuvah* process which requires that we first have יוֹעֲצִים, *advisers* — such as Eliyahu HaNavi and Elisha — who will advise and counsel us in our quest to do *teshuvah*. And if we do not heed the advice of our advisers, it will then be the role of the *shoftim* to apply justice as needed, כְּבָרִאשׁוֹנָה, *as we had formerly,* meaning that these be of the quality of those who judged us in former times. The word *shoftim* comes from שָׁפַט, which means to create order. A judge is one who creates order by righting the wrongs that were done.

The Midrash states that the meaning of וְאָשִׁיבָה שֹׁפְטַיִךְ כְּבָרִאשֹׁנָה וְיֹעֲצַיִךְ כְּבַתְּחִלָּה is that Moshe and Aharon, Dovid and Shlomo will come back to us (see *Yalkut Shimoni* to *Yeshayahu,* Ch. 1, 391).

The *Navi* tells us: בְּשׁוּבְבִי אוֹתָם מִן הָעַמִּים וְקִבַּצְתִּי אֹתָם מֵאַרְצוֹת אֹיְבֵיהֶם וְנִקְדַּשְׁתִּי בָם לְעֵינֵי הַגּוֹיִם רַבִּים . . . אֲשֶׁר שָׁפַכְתִּי אֶת רוּחִי עַל בֵּית יִשְׂרָאֵל נְאֻם אֲדֹנָי אֱלֹהִים, *When I return them from the peoples and gather them in from the land of their enemies and I become sanctified through them in the eyes of the many nations . . . I will pour out My spirit upon the House of Israel — so says Hashem* (*Yechezkel* 39:27-29).

With these words, *HaKadosh Baruch Hu* has promised us that He will again "pour His spirit" upon the Jewish people, meaning He will again endow us with *Neviim,* people who are imbued with the spirit of *HaKadosh Baruch Hu.* Whether these *nevuos* refer to the *geulah* or to *techiyas hameisim,* we do not know. This was not revealed to us.

וְהָסֵר מִמֶּנּוּ יָגוֹן וַאֲנָחָה — **Remove from us grief and sighing.** This is based on the *pasuk,* וּפְדוּיֵי ה׳ יְשֻׁבוּן וּבָאוּ צִיּוֹן בְּרִנָּה וְשִׂמְחַת עוֹלָם עַל רֹאשָׁם שָׂשׂוֹן וְשִׂמְחָה יַשִּׂיגוּ וְנָסוּ יָגוֹן וַאֲנָחָה, *Then the redeemed of Hashem will return and come to Tziyon with rejoicing, and with eternal gladness on their heads. They will attain joy and gladness; and grief and sighing will flee* (*Yeshayahu* 35:10). At the time of the *geulah,* grief and sighing will flee before the joy of the redemption. The term יָגוֹן means the grief that one carries inside of him, and אֲנָחָה is the loud sighing (like *"oy"*), or moaning, when the grief cannot be contained any longer.

הָשִׁיבָה שׁוֹפְטֵנוּ is followed immediately by וְהָסֵר מִמֶּנּוּ יָגוֹן וַאֲנָחָה, because the reason we have יָגוֹן וַאֲנָחָה is that we do not have leadership. If we look at our own generation compared to one hundred years ago, we are almost bereft of leaders.

There is almost no one who can issue a decree, a *p'sak din,* which would be universally accepted. During our lifetime, there were still a few left, but these are gradually disappearing. Our generation could be described in the words of the *Navi*: אֵין מְנַהֵל לָהּ מִכָּל בָּנִים יָלָדָה, *She has no leader — of all the children to whom she has given birth* (*Yeshayahu* 51:18).

Therefore, the meaning of this *tefillah* is that we ask *HaKadosh Baruch Hu* to return our leaders to us — our judges and advisers — and these authentic voices will bring an end to our grief, so much of which was caused by a lack of leadership of the Jewish nation.

Unfortunately, our generation has become such an "orphaned generation" that in our times we can no longer recite the *berachah,* שֶׁחָלַק מֵחָכְמָתוֹ לִירֵאָיו, which is required when seeing one of the *chachmei Yisrael* (*Orach Chaim* 224:6). As great as our present-day leaders are, no one would say that *berachah* when seeing them. When I had the *zechus* to meet the Chafetz Chaim, I did make that *berachah.* [Ed. note: This took place on the weekend of *Shabbos* פרשת החדש תר"צ — ca. 3/30/30.]

The Ponevizher Rav, in his *hesped* of the Chazon Ish, said, "We have lost the person of whom we were afraid." This means that during the lifetime of the Chazon Ish, we were always careful not to do anything for which he might censure us. But now that he has left us, our wrongdoings could often go uncorrected. In the meantime, before the return of the *shoftim* and *yo'atzim,* we ask *HaKadosh Baruch Hu,*

ּוּמְלוֹךְ עָלֵינוּ אַתָּה לְבַדְּךָ בְּחֶסֶד וּבְרַחֲמִים — **Rule over us — You, Hashem, alone — with kindness and mercy.**

We have already explained in מְכַלְכֵּל חַיִּים that חֶסֶד refers to the kindness of *HaKadosh Baruch Hu* in this world, and בְּרַחֲמִים רַבִּים, *His abundant mercy,* refers to the world of *techiyas hameisim.* Similarly, in this *berachah,* too, which refers to the world of the *geulah* — on which we began to focus in תְּקַע בְּשׁוֹפָר גָּדוֹל — we ask *HaKadosh Baruch Hu* to rule over us *b'chessed* in this world, and also later *b'rachamim* in the world of *techiyas hameisim.*

וְצַדְּקֵנוּ בַּמִּשְׁפָּט — **And treat us charitably in judgment.** צֶדֶק means a mitigated form of justice (as in צְדָקָה, *charity*), and מִשְׁפָּט means strict justice. We ask *HaKadosh Baruch Hu* here to judge us with charity.

By the way, the word צְדָקָה, when used to mean charity, also conveys the meaning of justice, because *HaKadosh Baruch Hu* has created a world in which He has given some people much more than they can ever need or use, and others much less than they need. However, *HaKadosh Baruch Hu* has given the overendowed the mandate of *tzedakah,* whereby they are commanded to "do justice" and "right this wrong," by giving some of their excess means to those who are underendowed. (See Rav Samson R. Hirsch to *Devarim* 15:8 where he expresses a similar thought.)

בָּרוּךְ אַתָּה ה', מֶלֶךְ אוֹהֵב צְדָקָה וּמִשְׁפָּט — **Blessed are You, Hashem, the King Who loves both forms of justice.** The Torah tells us in connection with Avraham Avinu: לְמַעַן אֲשֶׁר יְצַוֶּה אֶת בָּנָיו וְאֶת בֵּיתוֹ אַחֲרָיו וְשָׁמְרוּ דֶּרֶךְ ה' לַעֲשׂוֹת צְדָקָה וּמִשְׁפָּט, *Because he commands his children and his household after him that they keep the way of Hashem, doing charity and justice* (*Bereishis* 18:19). The *derech Hashem* is to mete out justice as charitably as possible.

Sometimes it is necessary to employ *mishpat,* strict justice, as when a *beis din* must sentence a person to death. But, as we know, this did not happen very often, because *beis din,* following the *derech Hashem,* attempts to mitigate its justice by treating the accused charitably, לַעֲשׂוֹת צְדָקָה וּמִשְׁפָּט, and finding means to avoid the application of strict justice.

Similarly, we find that Dovid HaMelech is described as a king who עֹשֶׂה מִשְׁפָּט וּצְדָקָה לְכָל עַמּוֹ, *administered justice and kindness to his entire people* (*Shmuel II* 8:15). His main occupation as a king was to judge disputes among his people. The Gemara tells us that after finding one party liable (*mishpat*), he would pay the judgment out of his own pocket (*tzedakah*) if the litigant was unable to do so (*Sanhedrin* 6b).

As an example, if a poor tenant cannot pay his wealthy landlord his monthly rent, strict justice, *mishpat*, would nevertheless dictate that the tenant must leave his apartment. This is in accordance with וְדָל לֹא תֶהְדַּר בְּרִיבוֹ, *You shall not give preference to a poor person in his argument* (*Shemos* 23:3). However, in the interest of *tzedakah*, after deciding the case in accordance with *mishpat*, Dovid HaMelech would provide the poor man with enough money to settle the judgment of the court.

Similarly, *HaKadosh Baruch Hu,* as מֶלֶךְ אוֹהֵב צְדָקָה וּמִשְׁפָּט, loves both forms of justice, but He prefers to apply *tzedakah,* whenever it is possible, over *mishpat* alone.

If this is our conception of Heavenly judgment, we may become complacent in our efforts to do *teshuvah* — always relying on the *tzedakah* of *HaKadosh Baruch Hu.* It is for this reason that during *Aseres Yemei Teshuvah* we end this *berachah* with הַמֶּלֶךְ הַמִּשְׁפָּט, instead of מֶלֶךְ אוֹהֵב צְדָקָה וּמִשְׁפָּט, because during this period, we apply a much stricter standard of *mishpat* to ourselves if we are to expect *rachamim* from *HaKadosh Baruch Hu.*

Furthermore, the Torah tells us בְּצֶדֶק תִּשְׁפֹּט עֲמִיתֶךָ, *Judge your fellowman with righteousness* (*Vayikra* 19:15). Our *Chachamim* learn from here הֱוֵי דָן אֶת חֲבֵירְךָ לְכַף זְכוּת (*Shavuos* 30a). If a person sees another doing something which, on the surface, appears wrong, he should not assume the worst, but rather, he should "judge" him favorably in his own mind. Although the average person is not a judge, nevertheless, we all form our own opinions, "judgments," of our fellow man.

It is in this sense that we say to *HaKadosh Baruch Hu* in this *berachah*, וְצַדְּקֵנוּ בַּמִּשְׁפָּט. Since now — before the *geulah* — we do not have the high caliber of judges and advisors to lead and advise us how to avoid our pitfalls, because we are an orphaned and leaderless people, we ask *HaKadosh Baruch Hu* to judge us favorably, to judge us *lechaf zechus* and thereby to apply *tzedakah* to our *mishpat*.

בִּרְכַּת הַמִּינִים

The *berachah* וְלַמַּלְשִׁינִים, known as בִּרְכַּת הַצְּדוֹקִים or בִּרְכַּת הַמִּינִים, *the berachah regarding heretics,* begins with a "ו," because its meaning is closely

SHEMONEH ESREI ❧ 475

associated with the sense of the previous *berachah,* הָשִׁיבָה שׁוֹפְטֵינוּ, the *tefillah* for communal *teshuvah.* Therefore, וְלַמַּלְשִׁינִים also corresponds to הֲשִׁיבֵנוּ אָבִינוּ לְתוֹרָתֶךָ, the individual's *tefillah* for *teshuvah.* After asking *HaKadosh Baruch Hu* to be lenient in His judgment, מֶלֶךְ אוֹהֵב צְדָקָה וּמִשְׁפָּט, we follow this immediately with: וְלַמַּלְשִׁינִים אַל תְּהִי תִקְוָה ... כְּרֶגַע יֹאבֵדוּ, which can be paraphrased as: But as to these evildoers, may they be dealt with harshly.

The *Bircas HaMinim* is not one of the original *Shemoneh Esrei berachos* that were instituted by the *Anshei Knesses HaGedolah* at the time of the beginning of the Second *Beis HaMikdash;* it was added much later. The Gemara tells us: בִּרְכַּת הַצְּדוּקִים בְּיַבְנֶה תִּקְנוּהָ, the *berachah regarding the heretics was instituted in Yavneh* (Berachos 28b). This could have occurred either at the time of the end of the Second *Beis HaMikdash,* or after its destruction, depending on which *Rabban Gamliel* is referred to in the statement there: שִׁמְעוֹן הַפָּקוּלִי הִסְדִּיר שְׁמוֹנֶה עֶשְׂרֵה בְּרָכוֹת לִפְנֵי רַבָּן גַּמְלִיאֵל עַל הַסֵּדֶר בְּיַבְנֶה. אָמַר לָהֶם רַבָּן גַּמְלִיאֵל לַחֲכָמִים: כְּלוּם יֵשׁ אָדָם שֶׁיּוֹדֵעַ לְתַקֵּן בִּרְכַּת הַצְּדוּקִים? עָמַד שְׁמוּאֵל הַקָּטָן וְתִקְּנָהּ.

This could be Rabban Gamliel HaZakein, who lived before the *churban,* or a later Rabban Gamliel, who lived after the *churban.*

The word מִין is used by the *Chachamim* as a general term to describe individuals or members of the various sects and offshoots of Judaism who did not accept the basic tenet of *Torah min HaShamayim,* which includes *Torah Shebichsav* and *Torah Shebe'al Peh.* Some say that מִין is an acronym for מַאֲמִינֵי יֵשׁוּ נוֹצְרִי.

The *minim* (see *Yerushalmi,* ibid.) — or *tzedukim,* as the text has it in the Babylonian Talmud, Tractate *Berachos* [probably to satisfy censorship] — who are the subject of this *berachah,* were a group of people, a sect, known as "Judeo-Christians," who believed in אוֹתוֹ הָאִישׁ, "that man." They considered this person to be *mashiach* and, eventually, part of the deity, ח"ו. This group did not have a "New Testament," but rather, they used the *Tanach,* which they misinterpreted to further their beliefs, because they did not accept the *Torah Shebe'al Peh.* Their religion was a kind of a "Reform Judaism," whose main tenets consisted of love, kindness, and forgiveness. To them, the *mitzvos* — especially those that were *mi'd'Rabbanan* — were unimportant so long as a person lived a life filled with kindness, love, and forgiveness.

Eventually, this sect became quite influential among Jews and represented a great danger to the core belief of the Jewish people (see *Rambam, Hil. Tefillah* 2:1). As a result of this, Rabban Gamliel and his court instituted a special *berachah* in the *Shemoneh Esrei* for the destruction of this pervasive influence on the Jewish people.

Despite the fact that this additional *berachah* is about two thousand years old, and constitutes a nineteenth *berachah,* we still call our *tefillah Shemoneh*

Esrei, because it is our hope that eventually, when the threat of *apikorsus* disappears, we will eliminate this additional *berachah.*

Interestingly, in Eretz Yisrael there was a *minhag* to combine אֶת צֶמַח דָּוִד with וְלִירוּשָׁלַיִם עִירְךָ because of the similarity of content, to maintain the number of *berachos* at eighteen. This is evidenced by the *Krovetz* on Purim, written by the famous *paytan,* R' Elazar HaKalir, in which there is no stanza for the *berachah* of אֶת צֶמַח דָּוִד. In accordance with this *minhag,* there were always eighteen *berachos,* including the בִּרְכַּת הַמִּינִים. [See *Yerushalmi Berachos* 4:3: אִם יֹאמַר לְךָ אָדָם תֵּשַׁע עֶשְׂרֵה אֵינָן וכו'; also see *Tosefta Berachos* 3:5, וְכוֹלֵל ... שֶׁל דָּוִד בְּבוֹנֵה יְרוּשָׁלַיִם.]

Returning to the origin of the *Bircas HaMinim,* the previously cited Gemara (*Berachos* 28b) states that Shmuel HaKatan was the one who composed it. The Gemara tells us that this same Shmuel HaKatan was a *tzaddik* who merited a *bas kol* that announced that he was worthy of the Divine presence: (See יֵשׁ כָּאן אֶחָד שֶׁרָאוּי שֶׁתִּשְׁרֶה עָלָיו שְׁכִינָה ... נָתְנוּ חֲכָמִים אֶת עֵינֵיהֶם בִּשְׁמוּאֵל הַקָּטָן *Sanhedrin* 11a). Apparently, this *tefillah,* which was composed by this great *tzaddik,* did have the desired effect, because the sect of "Judeo-Christians" existed only for a short duration in Jewish history, after which it disappeared completely. Thereafter, Christianity became a non-Jewish religion.

The result was that the remaining individuals who wanted to continue this new religion had to go to Paul, who was one of the *meshumadim,* to promote their newly created religion among the gentiles, who eagerly accepted it. During this time the intelligentia in Rome discarded the paganism of the Roman gods, and were seeking some other religious philosophy and practice. This newly formed religion, which they believed to be Judaism, was therefore eagerly adopted by those under Roman influence. The leaders of this new religion based their beliefs on their misinterpretation of *Tanach.* They discarded the *mitzvos* as old-fashioned and nonbinding on them, and substituted concepts of humanism instead. They replaced their former *avodah zarah* for a new form of *avodah zarah* which they called "the trinity."

This disappearance of the Judeo-Christians as a result of this *tefillah* explains the following anomaly in *Pirkei Avos.* There, the *Tannaim* usually offered sayings that were not *pesukim* from *Tanach,* but rather, words of wisdom that they had learned from the teachings of the Torah. However, Shmuel HaKatan, the composer of *Bircas HaMinim,* quotes an actual *pasuk* from *Mishlei* 24:17: בִּנְפֹל אוֹיִבְךָ אַל תִּשְׂמָח וּבִכָּשְׁלוֹ אַל יָגֵל לִבֶּךָ, *When your foe falls, be not glad, and when he stumbles, let your heart not be joyous* (*Pirkei Avos* 4:24). This can be very well understood in light of his having witnessed the success of his *tefillah.* In the aftermath of the downfall of the *minim,* the Judeo-Christians, this *tzaddik* cautioned the people against gloating. He quoted this *pasuk* to convey the message that the downfall of the Judeo-Christians was not the doing of the Jewish people, but rather, that *HaKadosh*

Baruch Hu, in His mercy, had heard their *tefillos* and eliminated this evil influence from their midst. This is an example of the efficacy of *tefillah* if it is offered with all of one's heart.

It is important that we know that the text of this *berachah* is completely different from the original. The text of this *berachah,* as we have it today, was born out of fear, because the Christians accused the Jews of cursing their religion every day in their synagogues. The result was that a watered-down, innocuous, and harmless version of the original *berachah* was formulated.

וְלַמַּלְשִׁינִים אַל תְּהִי תִקְוָה — **And for slanderers let there be no hope.** There have been many variations of the wording of this *tefillah* over the years, and it is very difficult to reconstruct the original text. However, from old sources, it seems that the original text began approximately as follows: וְלַמְשֻׁמָּדִים עַל תְּהִי תִקְוָה (*Rambam, Venice Print, Seder HaTefillos*) The reference is to those Jews who converted to that new belief, Judeo-Christianity, or later, to those who converted to Christianity itself.

As a result of pressure by the Church, וְלַמְשֻׁמָּדִים, *heretics,* or *converts,* became וְלַמַּלְשִׁינִים, *slanderers,* who everybody could agree were deplorable and deserved condemnation. This substitution — while satisfying the critics — was really not that far from the original, וְלַמְשֻׁמָּדִים, because these people were actually the מַלְשִׁינִים! These converts, who could read the language of the Talmud, misconstrued it as being anti-Christian, and slandered the Jews by reporting this false information to the local Church authorities. Often, the result would be a mass confiscation and burning of all copies of Gemaras that the Church authorities found. Rav Meir of Rottenberg (*Maharam MeRothenberg*) [1215—1293] composed a special *kinah* for *Tishah B'Av,* שַׁאֲלִי שְׂרוּפָה בָאֵשׁ, to bemoan the public burning of twenty-four wagonloads of handwritten Gemaras and commentaries in Paris in the year 1242. Obviously, the writing of a Gemara by hand — and certainly an entire *Shas* — is a very time-consuming and tedious process, and it was almost miraculous for anyone to have an entire *Shas*. But thousands of these volumes went up in flames at that time.

וְכָל הַמִּינִים כְּרֶגַע יֹאבֵדוּ — **And may all the heretics perish in an instant.** According to our *minhag* Frankfurt, this version is retained. (It is also used today in *nusach Sefard.*) However, the more commonly used phrase in *nusach Ashkenaz* (see Roedelheim *Siddur*) is: וְכָל עוֹשֵׂי רִשְׁעָה כְּרֶגַע יֹאבֵדוּ, which was instituted as a seemingly harmless and innocuous replacement for מִינִים, which offended the Church. In reality, עוֹשֵׂי רִשְׁעָה *is* a veiled reference to מִינִים. However, *minhag* Frankfurt viewed it differently: The phrase וְכָל עוֹשֵׂי רִשְׁעָה seemed too harsh. It asked that anyone who ever did anything wrong כְּרֶגַע יֹאבֵדוּ, should perish instantly! Obviously, this could not be the intention. Therefore, *minhag* Frankfurt retained the original wording of וְכָל הַמִּינִים.

◆§ וְכֻלָּם מְהֵרָה יִכָּרֵתוּ — **And may they all be cut down soon.** This is our text, which was changed from the older text of וְכָל אֹיְבֶיךָ מְהֵרָה יִכָּרֵתוּ or וְכָל אוֹיְבֵי עַמְּךָ, which is really the same (see *Rashi, Bamidbar* 31:3). The nations among whom we lived — especially in the Middle Ages, and to some extent even now — openly considered themselves our enemies, and an effort was made to avoid angering them by praying for their destruction. Therefore the veiled phrase, וְכֻלָּם מְהֵרָה יִכָּרֵתוּ, was formulated, which could be explained to them as referring back to the innocuous וְכָל עוֹשֵׂי רִשְׁעָה, or to וְלַמַּלְשִׁינִים.

We ask here that *Your enemies* (or *our enemies*) *shall be cut down soon.* The degree of hatred for us by our enemies varies. There are those who consider us as sheep ready for slaughter: נֶחְשַׁבְנוּ כַּצֹּאן לַטֶּבַח יוּבָל, לַהֲרֹג; others are not quite as violent, and to them we are a people who would best be lost, לְאַבֵּד; others only want to severely hurt us, לְמַכָּה; and some want only to humiliate us, לְחֶרְפָּה. Unfortunately, the אוֹיְבֵי יִשְׂרָאֵל, of whatever ilk, will not go away כְּרֶגַע, in an instant, but we ask that they may be removed quickly, meaning in the near future.

◆§ וְהַזֵּדִים מְהֵרָה תְעַקֵּר וּתְשַׁבֵּר וּתְמַגֵּר וְתַכְנִיעַ בִּמְהֵרָה בְיָמֵינוּ — **May you uproot, break, cut up, and humble the evildoers quickly, in our time.** Before explaining the meaning of these various words — which all have the general meaning of "elimination" — it is important that we know that וְהַזֵּדִים, meaning criminals, or *purposeful evildoers,* as used here, refers to another kind of enemy. It relates to those who attempt to influence Jews away from our *emunah,* and convert these Jews to their religion.

One of the tenets of Fundamentalist Christianity is that as long as there are "nonbelievers" who have not converted to their religion, the "second coming" of their "messiah" will not take place. Consequently, proselytizing was widely practiced in the Middle Ages by the Church, often by means of forced conversions. Sometimes, Jews were forced to sit in their *shuls* and listen to hours of preaching about the Christian religion. Many of the preachers who delivered these "sermons" were *meshumadim* themselves. And even today, there are missionaries of various types, especially the group called "Jews for J-s," who, unfortunately, are very successful at their evil craft.

Another form of זֵדִים is Communism. Under its rule, Jews were not permitted to study Torah or practice their religion. People who were caught teaching students under the age of 18 were either sentenced to death or to exile in Siberia, which was sometimes even worse.

And concerning these aforementioned זֵדִים, we ask *HaKadosh Baruch Hu* to eliminate them בִּמְהֵרָה בְיָמֵינוּ, *quickly, in our time,* so that we shall not have to suffer further losses to them.

The terms תְּעַקֵּר, וּתְשַׁבֵּר, וּתְמַגֵּר, וְתַכְנִיעַ, were chosen very carefully:

❑ תְּעַקֵּר means *to uproot,* to prevent any future growth. It is our *tefillah* that

SHEMONEH ESREI ⟡ 479

any movement that attempts, בְּזָדוֹן, (with evil intent, thus "zeidim"), to take Jews away from Judaism — either by force or by persuasion — shall be uprooted, and grow no further;

❑ וּתְשַׁבֵּר means here *that they may break into various factions,* each with differing approaches to converting Jews, thus rendering them ineffective in their evil objective;

❑ וּתְמַגֵּר, *and cut them up into small pieces.* We ask that these factions be divided into individuals who, while not as effective as a group, are nevertheless still dangerous on their own;

❑ וְתַכְנִיעַ, *and humble them.* We ask that these remaining individual זֵדִים be humbled and rendered harmless.

◆§ בָּרוּךְ אַתָּה ה', שׁוֹבֵר אוֹיְבִים וּמַכְנִיעַ זֵדִים — **Blessed are You, Hashem Who breaks enemies, and humbles evildoers.** אוֹיְבִים means enemies who wish to destroy us physically. מַכְנִיעַ זֵדִים refers to the humbling of those evildoers who wish to destroy us spiritually. If they are humbled, they will not have the audacity to attempt to proselytize us. What we are asking for here is that eventually all the movements that are bent on destroying the Jewish people, physically or spiritually, shall be eliminated. This *berachah,* too, is said in the present tense — as if it is happening now — because we have absolute faith that this eventually will be realized.

With this *berachah,* we end our *tefillos* concerning *teshuvah.* When the Jewish nation does *teshuvah,* encouraged and guided by the return of the *shoftim* and *yo'atzim,* HaKadosh Baruch Hu will judge us favorably, וְצַדְּקֵנוּ בַּמִּשְׁפָּט, and eliminate the *reshaim,* who have caused so much grief to the Jewish people.

צַדִּיקִים

◆§ עַל הַצַּדִּיקִים וְעַל הַחֲסִידִים — **On the righteous, on the devout.** This *berachah* for *tzaddikim* and *chassidim* corresponds to the *berachah* of סְלַח לָנוּ אָבִינוּ כִּי חָטָאנוּ in that it refers to people who have already done *teshuvah* and have been forgiven. The word צַדִּיק describes the highest level of human perfection. This is borne out by the words of Yeshayahu HaNavi in describing the Jewish people at the time of the final redemption, when their sins will have been forgiven by HaKadosh Baruch Hu: וְעַמֵּךְ כֻּלָּם צַדִּיקִים לְעוֹלָם יִירְשׁוּ אָרֶץ נֵצֶר מַטָּעַי מַעֲשֵׂה יָדַי לְהִתְפָּאֵר, *Your nation will all be tzaddikim, they will inherit the land forever; a shoot of My planting, My handiwork, of whom I shall be proud* (*Yeshayahu* 60:21). It is apparent from here that the highest level one can achieve is that of *tzaddik.* We also find: וְצַדִּיק יְסוֹד עוֹלָם, *And the tzaddik is the foundation of the world* (*Mishlei* 10:25).

Tzaddikim means people who live exactly the way HaKadosh Baruch Hu wants them to live. It is used when *HaKadosh Baruch Hu* tells Noach: כִּי אֹתְךָ רָאִיתִי צַדִּיק לְפָנַי בַּדּוֹר הַזֶּה, *For it is you that I have seen to be a tzaddik (righteous) before Me in this generation* (*Bereishis* 7:1). Further, the Torah also describes exactness of measure in terms of *tzedek:* מֹאזְנֵי צֶדֶק, אַבְנֵי צֶדֶק, אֵיפַת צֶדֶק, וְהִין צֶדֶק (*Vayikra* 19:36). In our language we would say, "A pound is to be exactly a pound and an inch is to be exactly an inch."

The *tzaddikim* are those outstanding individuals who, nevertheless, may make a mistake once in a while: כִּי אָדָם אֵין צַדִּיק בָּאָרֶץ אֲשֶׁר יַעֲשֶׂה טוֹב וְלֹא יֶחֱטָא, *Because there is no righteous person on earth who does only good, and never errs* (*Koheles* 7:20). However he is, nonetheless, still called a *tzaddik*.

Chassidim refers to the next highest level of righteousness. While not rising to the level of *tzaddikim*, this group consists of those outstanding individuals who love *HaKadosh Baruch Hu* to such an extent that they act *lifnim mishuras hadin;* they do more in the area of *mitzvos* and *maasim tovim* than people are required to do. This explains the usage of the phrase חֲסִידֵי אֻמּוֹת הָעוֹלָם used by our *Chachamim* to describe non-Jews who keep the Noahide laws the way the Torah prescribes them. They are called *chassidim* because they do more than most other non-Jews in this regard.

וְעַל זִקְנֵי עַמְּךָ בֵּית יִשְׂרָאֵל — **On the elders of Your people, the family of Israel.** This is the next category for whom we are *mispallel*.

These "elders" are not necessarily more advanced in years, but are the *talmidei chachamim* and *gedolei haTorah* of our people: אֵין זָקֵן אֶלָּא שֶׁקָּנָה חָכְמָה (*Kiddushin* 32b). These are the people to whom we can turn to answer our questions, and who instruct us as to the letter and spirit of the Torah.

וְעַל פְּלֵיטַת סוֹפְרֵיהֶם — **And on the remaining teachers [of Torah].** The word סוֹפְרֵיהֶם refers to people who teach children the *sefer*, meaning the *Torah Shebichsav:* סוֹפְרִים וּמַשְׁנִים שֶׁמְּלַמְּדִים תִּינוֹקוֹת לַאֲמִתָּן (*Vayikra Rabbah* 30:2). However, in its extended form, it includes all teachers of Torah.

Those select individuals who choose to teach Torah are called פְּלֵיטִים, *the few remaining ones,* because most people do not become Torah teachers, since their task is usually not appreciated and it does not pay well. Nevertheless, the *sofrim,* the Torah teachers of the Jewish nation, are of such importance that without them we would cease to exist as *Am Yisrael*.

Before we begin reading from the *sefer Torah* on weekdays, we say a special *tefillah* for the "remaining ones" of the Jewish people: וְיָחֹן פְּלֵיטָתֵנוּ וּפְלֵיטַת עַמּוֹ בֵּית יִשְׂרָאֵל. These "remaining ones" are our Torah teachers. It is fitting and proper that before we read the Torah in public, we pay homage to, and pray for, our Torah teachers who propagate the words of the Torah. In former times, before the advent of printing, teachers actually taught children directly from a *sefer Torah* or from a *Chumash,* which was one of the five individual scrolls of a *sefer Torah*.

After we are *mispallel* for the זִקְנֵי בֵּית יִשְׂרָאֵל, who are indispensable to us in our efforts to lead our lives in accordance with the letter and spirit of the Torah, in deed and thought, we are *mispallel* for the select few remaining Torah teachers of our children, the פְּלֵיטַת סוֹפְרֵיהֶם, the *rebbeim* who practice their holy craft with *mesiras nefesh*, out of love of teaching Torah.

We would summarize these two categories as *gedolei Torah* and *marbitzei Torah*.

ا۔ **וְעַל גֵּרֵי הַצֶּדֶק — And on the righteous converts.** The next category of people for whom we are *mispallel* is *geirim*. The *Navi* tells us that when *Mashiach* comes, the nations of the world will flock to *Am Yisrael* to join them: וּבָאוּ עַמִּים רַבִּים וְגוֹיִם עֲצוּמִים לְבַקֵּשׁ אֶת ה׳ צְבָאוֹת בִּירוּשָׁלַיִם וּלְחַלּוֹת אֶת פְּנֵי ה׳. כֹּה אָמַר ה׳ צְבָאוֹת בַּיָּמִים הָהֵמָּה אֲשֶׁר יַחֲזִיקוּ עֲשָׂרָה אֲנָשִׁים מִכֹּל לְשֹׁנוֹת הַגּוֹיִם וְהֶחֱזִיקוּ בִּכְנַף אִישׁ יְהוּדִי לֵאמֹר נֵלְכָה עִמָּכֶם כִּי שָׁמַעְנוּ אֱלֹהִים עִמָּכֶם, *Many people and mighty nations will come to seek out Hashem, Master of Legions, in Yerushalayim, and to supplicate before Hashem. Thus said Hashem, Master of Legions: In those days it will happen that ten men, of all the different languages of the nations, will take hold, they will take hold of the corner of the garment of a Jewish man, saying, "Let us go with you, for we have heard that God is with you"* (Zechariah 8:22-23). There will be so many who want to join us that we will have to determine who wants to join us because of the honor that we will have attained in the world at that time, and who wants to join us for purely spiritual reasons. But even before that time, in every generation, there are always individual *gerei hatzedek* who join our people only out of a desire to become part of the *Am Hashem*, and it is these for whom we are *mispallel* in this *tefillah*.

Importantly, this *tefillah* does not refer only to the external *geirim*, but it also includes our "internal *geirim*" — the *baalei teshuvah*. In connection with Yom Kippur, the Torah says: וְהָיְתָה לָכֶם לְחֻקַּת עוֹלָם בַּחֹדֶשׁ הַשְּׁבִיעִי . . . וְהַגֵּר הַגָּר בְּתוֹכְכֶם, *This shall remain for you an eternal decree: In the seventh month . . . the proselyte who dwells among you* (Vayikra 16:29).

The Jew becomes a new person after the *teshuvah* of Yom Kippur, and he is therefore called הַגֵּר הַגָּר בְּתוֹכְכֶם. Formerly, he had only been *living* among the Jewish people, but was not truly a Jew. Now, after his *teshuvah*, he is a *ger*; it is as if he had converted from a different faith. Similarly, in this *tefillah*, we are referring to those people who were Jews by birth only, who had lived a completely non-Jewish life in thought and in action; they have now "joined" the Jewish people as active members. These *baalei teshuvah* are the *gerei hatzedek* who are included in this *tefillah*.

ا۔ **וְעָלֵינוּ — And on ourselves.** Finally, we come to the last level of the aforementioned list: "ourselves," the simple, ordinary, everyday Jew.

◆§ יֶהֱמוּ רַחֲמֶיךָ ה׳, אֱלֹהֵינוּ — **May Your mercy be activated, Hashem, our God.** We ask that *HaKadosh Baruch Hu* "activate" His mercy. We know that *HaKadosh Baruch Hu* is *malei rachamim*, mercy per se, but we do not always feel His mercy. The *rachamim* of *HaKadosh Baruch Hu,* like the air that we breathe, is always there — we could not live without it. However, we feel the air only when the wind blows. We ask here that *HaKadosh Baruch Hu* make His mercy evident to all of the aforementioned.

◆§ וְתֵן שָׂכָר טוֹב לְכָל הַבּוֹטְחִים בְּשִׁמְךָ בֶּאֱמֶת §◆ — **And give a good reward to those who truly trust in Your Name.** Here we add an additional category: that of "those who truly trust in Your Name." The "Name" of *HaKadosh Baruch Hu* always means that which He reveals to us about Himself. The human mind cannot conceive of the essence of *HaKadosh Baruch Hu.* The meaning of *bitachon be'emes* is that the person "truly" places his trust in *HaKadosh Baruch Hu* in good times as well as bad. But if one experiences fear when facing a dangerous situation, his *bitachon* cannot be called *be'emes,* because he has not *truly* placed his trust in *HaKadosh Baruch Hu.* Rather, that would be called *bitachon b'sheker.* If a person can truthfully say הִנֵּה אֵל יְשׁוּעָתִי אֶבְטַח וְלֹא אֶפְחָד, *Behold, God is my salvation, I shall trust and not fear* (*Yeshayahu* 12:2), and ה׳ לִי וְלֹא אִירָא (*Adon Olam;* see *Tehillim* 118:6), and he has no fear under any circumstances, because he has trust in *HaKadosh Baruch Hu,* he can be called one who has "*bitachon be'emes.*"

Who are those people who have developed their trust in *HaKadosh Baruch Hu* to such a high level, that they know no fear — no matter what happens in their lives? I believe that these are the ל״ו צַדִּיקִים, *the thirty-six tzaddikim,* of whom the *Chachamim* tell us: לֹא פָּחוּת עָלְמָא מִתְּלָתִין וְשִׁיתָּא צַדִּיקֵי דִּמְקַבְּלֵי אַפֵּי שְׁכִינָה בְּכָל יוֹם, *There are no less than thirty-six tzaddikim who receive the awareness of the Heavenly Presence each day* (*Succah* 45b).

We ask here that *HaKadosh Baruch Hu* give these people who are בּוֹטְחִים בְּשִׁמְךָ בֶּאֱמֶת "a good reward," meaning a reward that can be shared with others. This is similar to our explanation of גּוֹמֵל חֲסָדִים טוֹבִים, which describes the kindness that *HaKadosh Baruch Hu* bestows upon a person with which the recipient can also benefit others. In the case of *bitachon,* the "good reward" is that one is so filled with *bitachon* in *HaKadosh Baruch Hu* that he can inspire others to have true *bitachon.*

◆§ וְשִׂים חֶלְקֵנוּ עִמָּהֶם §◆ — **May our lot be with them.** Unquestionably, every believing Jew has some measure of *bitachon;* our whole way of life is an education in *bitachon;* we start and end our day with ה׳ לִי וְלֹא אִירָא. However, most people have not yet developed *bitachon* to the level where it can be called *bitachon be'emes.* So we ask *HaKadosh Baruch Hu* here to help us attach ourselves to those who have *bitachon be'emes,* so that they may inspire us to likewise elevate our own level of *bitachon.*

◈§ וּלְעוֹלָם לֹא נֵבוֹשׁ כִּי בְךָ בָּטָחְנוּ — **May we never be put to shame by the level of our *bitachon* in You.** Our *minhag* is to include לְעוֹלָם in this phrase (see *Avudraham*). Others have the text וְשִׂים חֶלְקֵנוּ עִמָּהֶם לְעוֹלָם. This means that we are asking *HaKadosh Baruch Hu* here to help us achieve a level of *bitachon* that will allow us to face the Heavenly Tribunal in *Olam Haba* without shame when we are asked, "Did you truly have *bitachon* in *HaKadosh Baruch Hu*?" We pray here that our answer can be in the affirmative.

◈§ בָּרוּךְ אַתָּה ה', מִשְׁעָן וּמִבְטָח לַצַּדִּיקִים — **Blessed are You, Hashem, Support and Source of trust for the righteous.** We conclude this *berachah* by making reference to the *tzaddikim*, about whom the *berachah* began. *You are the support and the source of trust for the righteous.*

As little as we may think of ourselves, and as much as we are aware of our shortcomings, we should nevertheless aspire to become *tzaddikim*. Being a *tzaddik* is not something that we should think we have achieved, but rather, something for which we are to strive.

Prior to saying *Pirkei Avos*, in which we quote the great sayings of our *Chachamim* which incorporate rules for the proper conduct of one's life *al pi haTorah*, we preface it by quoting the *pasuk*: כָּל יִשְׂרָאֵל יֵשׁ לָהֶם חֵלֶק לָעוֹלָם הַבָּא, שֶׁנֶּאֱמַר וְעַמֵּךְ כֻּלָּם צַדִּיקִים לְעוֹלָם יִירְשׁוּ אָרֶץ נֵצֶר מַטָּעַי מַעֲשֵׂה יָדַי לְהִתְפָּאֵר, *Every member of Israel has a share in the World to Come, as it is said: "Your nation will all be tzaddikim; they will inherit the land forever; a shoot of My planting, My handiwork, of whom I shall be proud"* (*Yeshayahu* 60:21).

The quoting of this *pasuk* was instituted to drive home the point that, while we are not Hillel or Shammai, nor anywhere near the level of those who are quoted in *Pirkei Avos*, nevertheless this shall not deter us from having the desire to become *tzaddikim*. When one comes before the *beis din shel maalah*, the Heavenly Court, he will not be asked, "Why did you not become a Hillel or a Shammai?" Rather, he will be asked, "Why did you not become what *you* could have become?"

In modern-day language, we could say that כָּל יִשְׂרָאֵל יֵשׁ לָהֶם חֵלֶק לָעוֹלָם הַבָּא is the station-identification announcement of the Torah: This is station *Olam Haba* talking.

It is the goal of the Torah that all of Israel shall become *tzaddikim*, in whom *HaKadosh Baruch Hu* will take pride, מַעֲשֵׂה יָדַי לְהִתְפָּאֵר, and thus, they will inherit their well-earned share in *Olam Haba*.

When one says *Shema Yisrael*, or starts the *Shemoneh Esrei* with בָּרוּךְ אַתָּה ה', he should mentally ask *HaKadosh Baruch Hu* to help him become a *tzaddik*. The best wish one can give parents upon the birth of a child is, "I hope your child will become a *tzaddik*." However, we cannot accomplish this ourselves. To become a *tzaddik* requires a "crutch," that of the support of *HaKadosh Baruch Hu*.

The same applies to *bitachon*. The achievement of true *bitachon*, in which one has absolutely no fear of anything, is an accomplishment that cannot be done alone; it requires the help of *HaKadosh Baruch Hu*. Normal human beings are beset with anxieties and fears of the dangers that surround them. We are not "supermen" who can simply wish away our fears. But if a person makes a sincere effort to have true *bitachon*, *HaKadosh Baruch Hu* will help him achieve his goal. It is this which is meant by the *Navi*, בָּרוּךְ הַגֶּבֶר אֲשֶׁר יִבְטַח בַּה׳ וְהָיָה ה׳ מִבְטַחוֹ (*Yirmiyahu* 17:7). Loosely translated, this means, if the person places his trust in *HaKadosh Baruch Hu*, he will be blessed with a sense of total confidence and trust in *HaKadosh Baruch Hu* which will remove all of his fears and anxieties. But, to achieve this measure of *bitachon* in *HaKadosh Baruch Hu* requires His help, for we cannot do it alone.

And it is for this help that we are *mispallel* in this *berachah*, as we acknowledge that *HaKadosh Baruch Hu* is a מִשְׁעָן and מִבְטָח. For one who makes an effort to become a *tzaddik*, *HaKadosh Baruch Hu* is his מִשְׁעָן, and for one who makes an effort to become a *baal bitachon*, *HaKadosh Baruch Hu* will be his מִבְטָח, the One Who provides him with a sense of security when he places his full trust in *HaKadosh Baruch Hu*.

בִּנְיַן יְרוּשָׁלַיִם

The *Shemoneh Esrei* has only two *berachos* that begin with a "ו". We have already explained that the "ו" at וְלַמַּלְשִׁינִים expresses the fact that that *berachah* was added to the *Shemoneh Esrei*, to follow immediately after הָשִׁיבָה שׁוֹפְטֵינוּ, because the two are connected. Please refer to it there. Now we must understand the significance of the "ו" at the beginning of וְלִירוּשָׁלַיִם עִירְךָ, meaning "*And* to Your city Yerushalayim etc."

The simple reason for the "ו" is based on *Midrash Shocher Tov* to *Tehillim* 122:6, which tells us that מִשְׁעָן וּמִבְטָח לַצַּדִּיקִים follows וְלִירוּשָׁלַיִם עִירְךָ because the two are connected. The Midrash there says: מָה רָאוּ לוֹמַר וְלִירוּשָׁלַיִם אַחַר בִּרְכַּת הַצַּדִּיקִים? דִּכְתִיב "שַׁאֲלוּ שְׁלוֹם יְרוּשָׁלָיִם". וְהֵיכָן מִתְרוֹמְמוֹת קַרְנֵי הַצַּדִּיקִים? בִּירוּשָׁלָיִם. Paraphrased, this means that the reason the *Chachamim* placed וְלִירוּשָׁלַיִם עִירְךָ after עַל הַצַּדִּיקִים is because the *tzaddikim* achieve their full greatness only in Yerushalayim. This is based there on the *pasuk*, שַׁאֲלוּ שְׁלוֹם יְרוּשָׁלָיִם יִשְׁלָיוּ אֹהֲבָיִךְ, *Pray for the peace of Yerushalayim, those who love you will be serene* (*Tehillim* 122:6). According to this Midrash, therefore, the connection between the two *berachos*, מִשְׁעָן וּמִבְטָח לַצַּדִּיקִים and וְלִירוּשָׁלַיִם עִירְךָ בְּרַחֲמִים תָּשׁוּב is: "Hashem is the One on Whom the *tzaddikim* rely in their conviction that He, in His mercy, will return to Yerushalayim."

However, there is also a deeper meaning, based on a very "mysterious" Gemara: אָמַר הקב״ה לֹא אָבוֹא בִּירוּשָׁלַיִם שֶׁל מַעְלָה עַד שֶׁאָבוֹא לִירוּשָׁלַיִם שֶׁל מַטָּה, *HaKadosh Baruch Hu says: I will not come into "Yerushalayim on High" until I* have come to Yerushalayim below (Taanis 5a). And this is based there on: בְּקִרְבְּךָ קָדוֹשׁ וְלֹא אָבוֹא בְּעִיר, the Holy One is in your midst, and I will not enter another city (Hoshea 11:9).

Apparently, there are two Yerushalayims. There is the physical city of Yerushalayim, Yerushalahim shel mattah, for the rebuilding of which we beseech HaKadosh Baruch Hu here in this tefillah. However, there is also a Yerushalayim shel maalah. This is the place of the existence of the neshamos of the hundreds of thousands — perhaps millions — of tzaddikim who, during the past two thousand years, hoped and prayed for the rebuilding of Yerushalayim here on earth. And when the time comes that Yerushalayim here on earth is rebuilt, together with binyan Beis HaMikdash, those neshamos will experience it bashamayim together with the people who are physically experiencing the rebuilding here on earth. Those neshamos will have "preferred seats" to witness and experience this event.

In the Shiras HaYam, we find the phrase מָכוֹן לְשִׁבְתְּךָ פָּעַלְתָּ ה' מִקְּדָשׁ אֲדֹנָי כּוֹנְנוּ יָדֶיךָ, the foundation of Your dwelling-place that You, Hashem, have made — the Sanctuary, my Lord, that Your hands have established (Shemos 15:17). Paraphrased, this means, "Your hands have created the Beis HaMikdash, a place for Your dwelling." And our Chachamim comment on the words מָכוֹן לְשִׁבְתְּךָ, as follows: מִכָּאן דְּבֵית קָדְשֵׁי קָדָשִׁים שֶׁלְּמַטָּה מְכֻוָּן כְּנֶגֶד בֵּית קָדְשֵׁי קָדָשִׁים שֶׁל מַעְלָה, Paraphrased, this means: This pasuk indicates that the Beis HaMikdash on earth corresponds to the Beis HaMikdash in Heaven (Yerushalmi Berachos 4:5; Tanchuma Pekudei 1-2). Also, Rashi on Shemos 15:17 says: מִקְדָּשׁ שֶׁל מַטָּה מְכֻוָּן כְּנֶגֶד כִּסֵּא שֶׁל מַעְלָה.

This concept that there is a Yerushalayim shel maalah, which encompasses a Beis HaMikdash shel maalah, is mentioned many times in the Midrashim. In fact, in Midrash Rabbah (Shemos 35:6) we find that Moshe Rabbeinu was commanded to make the Mishkan as a replica of the Mikdash shel maalah: כָּךְ אָמַר הקב"ה לְמֹשֶׁה "וּרְאֵה וַעֲשֵׂה" ... כְּשֵׁם שֶׁאַתָּה רוֹאֶה לְמַעְלָה כָּךְ עֲשֵׂה לְמַטָּה, שֶׁנֶּאֱמַר: "עֲצֵי שִׁטִּים עוֹמְדִים" ... וְאִם תַּעֲשֶׂה כְּאוֹתָהּ שֶׁל מַעְלָה לְמַטָּה, אֲנִי ... מַשְׁרֶה שְׁכִינָתִי בֵּינֵיכֶם לְמַטָּה. מַה לְמַעְלָן "שְׂרָפִים עוֹמְדִים" אַף לְמַטָּן "עֲצֵי שִׁטִּים עוֹמְדִים". In building the Mishkan Moshe was to symbolize that which he had seen On High. Just as On High there are "Serafim standing," so will the Mishkan have "standing shittim wood." Moshe was told by HaKadosh Baruch Hu: "If you build your Mishkan corresponding to the one On High, I will cause My Presence to be among you."

And Chazal tell us that there are even korbanos brought on the Mizbe'ach shel maalah, as the malach Michael offers the neshamos of the tzaddikim as a korban to HaKadosh Baruch Hu (see Chagigah 12b; Tosafos, Menachos 110a).

The Beis HaMikdash shel maalah is surrounded by malachim and neshamos of tzaddikim. These environs are called Yerushalayim shel maalah.

As I have stated on many occasions, we can have no real concept of esoteric matters such as *Beis HaMikdash shel maalah* and *Yerushalayim shel maalah*. To explain these to those uninitiated, as we are, is analogous to describing the various colors of traffic lights and their functions to one who is blind from birth. These people can have no conception of lights, nor the meaning of red, amber, or green. However, when they hear sighted people describing this, they can repeat the words, although they really do not perceive their meaning. It is in this way that we talk of, or learn about, the concepts of *Beis HaMikdash shel maalah* and *Yerushalayim shel maalah*.

The extra "ו" at the beginning of וְלִירוּשָׁלַיִם עִירְךָ alludes to the concept that *HaKadosh Baruch Hu* will come to the *Yerushalayim shel maalah,* from which He has been "absent," only after He has been at the *Yerushalayim shel mattah*. And we are *mispallel* here that *HaKadosh Baruch Hu* may return to Yerushalayim, meaning *Yerushalayim shel mattah,* and consequently, this return will result in His return also to *Yerushalayim shel maalah.*

While we do not now understand the meaning of the statement that *HaKadosh Baruch Hu* will return to the *Yerushalayim shel maalah* only after He has returned to the *Yerushalayim shel mattah,* we hope that one day *HaKadosh Baruch Hu* may give us the *zechus* to do so, and if not in this world, then in the World to Come. After all, this statement is not hidden in the *Zohar* or other Kabbalistic sources; it is stated openly in the Gemara (*Taanis* 5a). It is for this reason that we learn it.

This applies as well to the many *Aggados* throughout the Talmud which, on the surface, seem incomprehensible. The Gemara tells us: אָמַר רָבָא לְעוֹלָם לִיגְרוֹס אִינִישׁ וְאַף עַל גַּב דְּלֹא יָדַע מַאי קָאָמַר, *Rava said: A person should learn* [literally: *say the words*] *even if he does not understand what he is saying* (*Avodah Zarah* 19a). This is because hopefully one day he will have the *zechiyah* to understand what is meant.

וְלִירוּשָׁלַיִם עִירְךָ בְּרַחֲמִים תָּשׁוּב ≥ — **May You return to Your city Yerushalayim with mercy.** This means that we ask *HaKadosh Baruch Hu* to do so even if we do not deserve it, because of His mercy. In asking *HaKadosh Baruch Hu* here to "return to *Your city Yerushalayim,"* we mean the city of Yerushalayim which can truly be called *"Your City."*

Not only can the present, mostly secular, Yerushalayim not be described as *"Your City,"* but even its holy yeshivos, and great *tzaddikim* — who arise at midnight to say *Tikkun Chatzos,* learn Torah until dawn, and then go to the *mikveh* before proceeding to the *Kosel HaMaaravi* to *daven* Shacharis *k'vasikin,* at the instant of sunrise — are only a relatively small segment of the population, and thus do not give the city the characteristic of עִירְךָ, *"Your City."* This will become a reality only when the vast majority of Yerushalayim is populated by men, women, and children who serve *HaKadosh Baruch Hu.*

We therefore ask *HaKadosh Baruch Hu* here: וְלִירוּשָׁלַיִם עִירְךָ בְּרַחֲמִים תָּשׁוּב, that we may have the *zechus* to witness Your return to a Yerushalayim that will have been transformed into "Your city."

And this idea lies at the core of our *tefillah* in Maariv: יִרְאוּ עֵינֵינוּ וְיִשְׂמַח לִבֵּנוּ וְתָגֵל נַפְשֵׁנוּ בִּישׁוּעָתְךָ בֶּאֱמֶת. This sentence, which refers to Yerushalayim, has the paraphrased meaning of, ". . .we will rejoice in your 'truthful salvation.' " Is there a salvation that is not *be'emes*, not a "real salvation"? The answer is yes, as is evidenced by today's Yerushalayim. To be sure, our whole existence there — or anywhere in Eretz Yisrael — is based on יְשׁוּעָתְךָ — we could not live there without it. Nevertheless, יְשׁוּעָתְךָ בֶּאֱמֶת is realized only בֶּאֱמֹר לְצִיּוֹן מָלַךְ אֱלֹהָיִךְ, *when it is said of Tziyon: Your God reigns* (Yeshayahu 52:7), when the rule of *HaKadosh Baruch Hu* will be clearly evident in *Tziyon*.

As long as *HaKadosh Baruch Hu* does not rule in *Tziyon* — even if the Jewish people are in a safe situation, politically, or otherwise — we have not experienced יְשׁוּעָתְךָ בֶּאֱמֶת, God's "True" Salvation.

וְתִשְׁכּוֹן בְּתוֹכָהּ כַּאֲשֶׁר דִּבַּרְתָּ — **And may You dwell in it as You have spoken.** This is based on the promise spoken in the Name of *HaKadosh Baruch Hu* by the *Navi*: שַׁבְתִּי אֶל צִיּוֹן וְשָׁכַנְתִּי בְּתוֹךְ יְרוּשָׁלָָם, *I will return to Tziyon, and I will dwell in Yerushalayim* (Zechariah 8:3). The return of *HaKadosh Baruch Hu* to Yerushalayim will be realized when it again becomes עִירְךָ. Then there is the next step, that of וְתִשְׁכּוֹן בְּתוֹכָהּ, when *HaKadosh Baruch Hu* will again "dwell" in Yerushalayim. And this is still before the following step, that of וּבְנֵה אוֹתָהּ, the permanent rebuilding of Yerushalayim which will follow.

This step of וְתִשְׁכּוֹן בְּתוֹכָהּ, the return of the *Shechinah* within Yerushalayim, will be initiated when the sacrificial service is resumed, *and this can be done even before the Beis HaMikdash is rebuilt*. The Gemara tells us: מַקְרִיבִין אַף עַל פִּי שֶׁאֵין בַּיִת. This means that *korbanos* can be brought even without the existence of the *Beis HaMikdash* (Zevachim 62a). However, in order to do so, the precise location of the Altar on the Temple Mount must be identified, and this can be done only by a prophet (see Gemara, ibid.). The exact site of the Altar is so important because this is the place from which *HaKadosh Baruch Hu* took part of the soil and created Adam, the first man. And our *Chachamim* say, אָדָם מִמְּקוֹם כַּפָּרָתוֹ נִבְרָא, *The human being was created from the place of his atonement* (Bereishis Rabbah 14:9).

This exact spot is alluded to many times in the Torah. A few examples are: כִּי אִם אֶל הַמָּקוֹם אֲשֶׁר יִבְחַר ה׳ אֱלֹהֵיכֶם. . ., *Rather, only at the place that Hashem, your God, will choose* (Devarim 12:5); . . .וְהָיָה הַמָּקוֹם אֲשֶׁר יִבְחַר ה׳ אֱלֹהֵיכֶם בּוֹ, *It shall be that the place where Hashem, your God, will choose* (ibid. v. 11); כִּי אִם בַּמָּקוֹם אֲשֶׁר יִבְחַר ה׳ בְּאַחַד שְׁבָטֶיךָ. . ., *Rather, only in the place that Hashem will choose* (ibid. v. 14).

According to our tradition, this is also the exact place where Noach built his *mizbe'ach* when he emerged from the ark, and where the *Akeidah* of Yitzchak took place (see *Rambam, Hil. Beis HaBechirah* 2:2).

The identification of this exact place for the purpose of building a *mizbe'ach* is described in *Divrei HaYamim I* 21:18-26. There we learn that a *malach* instructed the prophet Gad to tell Dovid HaMelech to build a *mizbe'ach* on the particular place that was being used at that time as a threshing floor by Aravnah HaYevusi. Consequently, Dovid HaMelech purchased this place from Aravnah and he built a *mizbe'ach* on it. Eventually, Shlomo HaMelech built the permanent *mizbe'ach* on this precise location, as part of the *Beis HaMikdash*.

So in saying וְתִשְׁכּוֹן בְּתוֹכָהּ כַּאֲשֶׁר דִּבַּרְתָּ, we pray that *HaKadosh Baruch Hu* may again "dwell" in Yerushalayim, through the reestablishment of the sacrificial service, which is the first step toward the "permanent Presence" of *HaKadosh Baruch Hu* in His city.

And following this, comes the rebuilding of Yerushalayim:

וּבְנֵה אוֹתָהּ בְּקָרוֹב בְּיָמֵינוּ — **And build it soon, in our time.** We ask that this may take place "soon," in our reckoning of soon, which is during our lifetime.

בִּנְיַן עוֹלָם — **As an eternal structure.** The prophet Yeshayahu states in the Name of *HaKadosh Baruch Hu* that the Yerushalayim of the future will be completely rebuilt using, sapphires, rubies, and other precious stones: הִנֵּה אָנֹכִי מַרְבִּיץ בַּפּוּךְ אֲבָנַיִךְ וִיסַדְתִּיךְ בַּסַּפִּירִים. וְשַׂמְתִּי כַּדְכֹד שִׁמְשֹׁתַיִךְ וּשְׁעָרַיִךְ לְאַבְנֵי אֶקְדָּח. וְכָל גְּבוּלֵךְ לְאַבְנֵי חֵפֶץ, *Behold, I will set down gems as your flooring stones and lay your foundation with sapphires. I will set your window frames with ruby and make your gates of carbuncle stones, and your entire boundary of precious stones* (*Yeshayahu* 54:11-12).

A further description of the future Yerushalayim: וַאֲנִי אֶהְיֶה לָּהּ נְאֻם ה׳ חוֹמַת אֵשׁ סָבִיב, וּלְכָבוֹד אֶהְיֶה בְתוֹכָהּ, *And I will be for it — the word of Hashem — a wall of fire all around and for glory will I be in its midst* (*Zechariah* 2:9). The *Navi* is telling us here that at the time of the *geulah*, the presence of the *Shechinah* in Yerushalayim will be visible as a fiery wall. Since it was *HaKadosh Baruch Hu* Who set the fire that destroyed Yerushalayim, it will be He Who will rebuild it through fire. The Gemara (*Bava Kamma* 60b) homiletically bases this on the *pasuk*: שַׁלֵּם יְשַׁלֵּם הַמַּבְעִר אֶת הַבְּעֵרָה, *The one who kindled the fire shall make restitution* (*Shemos* 22:5), and expresses it as follows: אָמַר הקב״ה: עָלַי לְשַׁלֵּם אֶת הַבְּעֵרָה שֶׁהִבְעַרְתִּי. אֲנִי הִצַּתִּי אֵשׁ בְּצִיּוֹן, שֶׁנֶּאֱמַר: ״וַיַּצֶּת אֵשׁ בְּצִיּוֹן וַתֹּאכַל יְסֹדֹתֶיהָ״ וַאֲנִי עָתִיד לִבְנוֹתוֹ בָּאֵשׁ, שֶׁנֶּאֱמַר: ״וַאֲנִי אֶהְיֶה לָּהּ נְאֻם ה׳ חוֹמַת אֵשׁ סָבִיב וּלְכָבוֹד אֶהְיֶה בְתוֹכָהּ״, *HaKadosh Baruch Hu said: I must make good for the fire which I set. I set the fire in Tziyon, as it says, "He kindled a fire in Tziyon which consumed its foundations"* (*Eichah* 4:11), *and I will in the future rebuild it through* fire, as it says, "And I will be for it — the word of Hashem — a wall of fire all around and for glory will I be in its midst" (Zechariah 2:9).

The Gemara tells us that the precious stones from which Yerushalayim will be rebuilt will be of enormous size: דְּיָתִיב רַבִּי יוֹחָנָן וְקָא דָּרִישׁ: עָתִיד הקב"ה לְהָבִיא אֲבָנִים טוֹבוֹת וּמַרְגָּלִיּוֹת שֶׁהֵם שְׁלֹשִׁים עַל שְׁלֹשִׁים וְחוֹקֵק בָּהֶן עֶשֶׂר עַל עֶשְׂרִים וּמַעֲמִידָן בְּשַׁעֲרֵי יְרוּשָׁלַיִם, Rabbi Yochanan expounded: At the time of the rebuilding of Yerushalayim, HaKadosh Baruch Hu will bring precious stones and pearls the size of thirty by thirty (amos), and He will engrave them in an area of ten wide and twenty high, and He will place them at the gates of Yerushalayim (Bava Basra 75a).

Upon hearing this description of the size of these stones by R' Yochanan, one of his *talmidim* ridiculed it: לִגְלֵג עָלָיו אוֹתוֹ תַלְמִיד, הַשְׁתָּא כְּבֵיעֲתָא דְצִיצְלָא לֹא מַשְׁכְּחִינָן, כּוּלֵי הַאי מַשְׁכְּחִינָן? *Nowadays, we cannot even find precious stones that are the size of a small bird's egg, so can there exist stones of the size which you described?* (In our time, the most famous of the largest known diamonds is the "Kohinoor" stone, which, when mined, weighed approximately 190 carats.)

The Gemara continues: Subsequently, this particular *talmid* embarked on an ocean voyage. During the trip, he had a dream about the *malachim* who serve Hashem. They were cutting huge precious stones of the size described by R' Yochanan. (As a *talmid* of R' Yochanan, it is no wonder that he could have such dreams.) And when, in his *ruach hakodesh* dream, he asked these *malachim* whom these stones were for, they told him that these were the stones that *HaKadosh Baruch Hu* would, in the future, erect at the gates of Yerushalayim. When he returned, he told his Rebbe, R' Yochanan, that he had, indeed, seen those stones that he had described, and the *talmid* complimented him, לְךָ נָאֶה לִדְרוֹשׁ, *You are fit to lecture;* you did not exaggerate in describing the size of those stones.

Upon hearing this, R' Yochanan responded: רֵיקָא, אִלְמָלֵא (לֹא) רָאִיתָ לֹא הֶאֱמַנְתָּ, מְלַגְלֵג עַל דִּבְרֵי חֲכָמִים אַתָּה, *You empty-headed one, had you not seen it, you would not have believed it; you scoff at the words of the Chachamim!* Whereupon, the Gemara continues: נָתַן עֵינָיו בּוֹ וְנַעֲשָׂה גַּל שֶׁל עֲצָמוֹת, *R' Yochanan gazed at him, and he became a heap of bones.* In other words, here we have a person who was elevated enough to be a *talmid* of R' Yochanan and who was great enough to have a vision in which he conversed with *malachim*, yet all of this did not help him. He perished because he lacked *emunas chachamim*.

While we can have no real conception of the actual meaning of these sayings of *Chazal*, nor of the aforementioned prophecies — these are all analogous to the "traffic lights" to which we referred earlier — it is nevertheless evident from all of this that the Yerushalayim of the future will be rebuilt *al pi neis* by the hand of *HaKadosh Baruch Hu*, as the *Navi* says: עוֹד אֶבְנֵךְ וְנִבְנֵית, *I will build it, and it will be built* (Yirmiyahu 31:3).

Rashi (*Succah* 41a, s.v. אי נמי), understands this miraculous rebuilding of Yerushalayim to include also the future *Beis HaMikdash:* אֲבָל מִקְדָּשׁ הֶעָתִיד שֶׁאָנוּ מְצַפִּים, בָּנוּי וּמְשׁוּכְלָל הוּא יִגָּלֶה וְיָבֹא מִשָּׁמַיִם שֶׁנֶּאֱמַר: "מִקְּדָשׁ אֲדֹנָי כּוֹנְנוּ יָדֶיךָ", *The future Beis HaMikdash for which we are hoping will appear fully built and finished from heaven, as it says, "The Sanctuary, my Lord, that Your hands established"* (Shemos 15:17).

Each year as we sit down at the *Seder* table, we begin by saying, הָשַׁתָּא הָכָא, לְשָׁנָה הַבָּאָה בְּאַרְעָא דְיִשְׂרָאֵל, *This year we are here, next year in the land of Israel,* and we end the *Seder* with לְשָׁנָה הַבָּאָה בִּירוּשָׁלַיִם, *next year in Yerushalayim.* I can remember my father saying it; my grandfather and great-grandfather said it, and so on back through the generations for thousands of years. In every *Bircas HaMazon* we say: וּבְנֵה יְרוּשָׁלַיִם עִיר הַקֹּדֶשׁ; and in our *Shemoneh Esrei,* three times a day, we ask וְלִירוּשָׁלַיִם עִירְךָ בְּרַחֲמִים תָּשׁוּב.

Is it possible that all of these hopes and *tefillos* are just words? Can these fervent prayers said for thousands of years simply be lost?

They are by no means lost. All of the *tefillos,* hopes and yearnings, the tears that were shed on *Tishah B'Av* throughout the ages, and the unshakable *emunah* of Israel that Yerushalayim would one day be rebuilt, have not been in vain. These spiritual "diamonds and precious stones" are all kept and treasured by *HaKadosh Baruch Hu,* and these spiritual entities will be the building blocks from which *HaKadosh Baruch Hu* will build the future Yerushalayim.

וְכִסֵּא דָוִד מְהֵרָה לְתוֹכָהּ תָּכִין — **And may You establish the throne of David and quickly bring it into it (Yerushalayim).** This does not say, may You establish the throne of David בְּתוֹכָהּ, *in it* (Yerushalayim), but rather לְתוֹכָהּ, which means, for the purpose of bringing it into Yerushalayim.

The word תָּכִין is usually taken to mean *establish.* However, it also has the meaning *prepare.* According to this meaning, the sense of this phrase would be: "May You prepare the throne of David for it." This means that we are asking *HaKadosh Baruch Hu* here to prepare the throne of Dovid for its placement in Yerushalayim.

כִּסֵּא דָוִד here refers to *Mashiach ben Dovid,* who will be a direct descendant of Dovid HaMelech.

The usage of the name Dovid for his descendants is based on *Tanach,* which uses the name Dovid in referring to the future king at the time of the *geulah:* וְעַבְדִּי דָוִד מֶלֶךְ עֲלֵיהֶם, *My servant Dovid rules over them* (Yechezkel 37:24). In our *tefillos* we often refer to *Mashiach* as Dovid, e.g., עַל יְדֵי דָוִד מְשִׁיחַ צִדְקֶךָ. On *Hoshana Rabbah* in the *piyut* of קוֹל מְבַשֵּׂר, we say הוּא דָוִד בְּעַצְמוֹ, the future *Melech HaMashiach* will be *Dovid himself!* This means that the *neshamah* of Dovid HaMelech will be incarnated into the body of one of his descendants, who will be the *Melech HaMashiach.* This is what is meant by

וְיָצָא חֹטֶר מִגֵּזַע יִשַׁי, *A staff will emerge from the stump of Yishai* (*Yeshayahu* 11:1). [The reincarnation of Dovid as *Mashiach* is also referred to in *Zohar HaKadosh, Lech Lecha* p. 82b.]

The Rambam in his י"ג עִיקָרִים, thirteen principles of our faith (*Peirush HaMishnayos, Sanhedrin, Perek Cheilek*), states that the criteria for *Mashiach* must include his being not only a descendant of Dovid, but he must also be a descendant of Shlomo. This is so because Dovid HaMelech designated his son, Shlomo, as his successor (see *I Malachim* 1:35).

We do not know whether the *Chachamim* who composed this *berachah* meant to list the future events connected with the rebuilding of Yerushalayim, as we have explained them, in the actual chronological order in which they will occur; most probably they did. However, this is irrelevant because, as we have previously pointed out, one should not dwell on the details of the time or the order of the future *geulah*. We are simply not privy to these details. We know only that there will be a *geulah*, but the details of how and when were not revealed to us.

The *Chachamim* say: אִם יֹאמַר לְךָ אָדָם מָתַי יָבוֹא קֵץ הַגְאֻלָּה, אַל תַּאֲמִין, שֶׁנֶּאֱמַר "כִּי יוֹם נָקָם בְּלִבִּי" לְפוּמָא לֹא גַּלֵּי, פּוּמָא לְמַאן גַּלֵּי?, *If a person tells you when the final redemption will occur, don't believe him, because the Torah says, "The day of revenge is in My heart." If the heart does not tell the mouth, to whom can the mouth reveal it?* (*Midrash Shocher Tov, Tehillim* 9). The Vilna Gaon explains that the "mouth" here refers to the *Neviim*, and it means that HaKadosh Baruch Hu did not reveal the details of the final *geulah* even to the *Neviim*. We then close this *berachah* with:

בָּרוּךְ אַתָּה ה', בּוֹנֵה יְרוּשָׁלַיִם — **Blessed are You, Hashem, Who is the builder of Yerushalayim.** It does not say, יִבְנֶה יְרוּשָׁלַיִם, *He will build Yerushalayim*, but rather, בּוֹנֵה יְרוּשָׁלַיִם, *He is the builder of Yerushalayim*. The building of Yerushalayim is a process that is ongoing throughout the *galus*. And just as a deep foundation must be placed in the ground before a very large structure can rise, so too have the historical events of the *galus* been preparatory for, and the "foundation" of, the rebuilding of the future Yerushalayim. Our entire *galus* experience — and it is longer than we had thought and hoped it would be — is the deep, dark underground pit into which the foundation of the future city of Yerushalayim is being placed.

This can be compared to a construction site of a large building, which is enclosed by a wall. If one manages to peek behind that wall, all he will see is a huge hole in the ground for the foundation. The higher the planned structure, the deeper the foundation must be. However, eventually, the structure will begin rising above the wall until it reaches its completion. Similarly, *HaKadosh Baruch Hu,* the בּוֹנֶה יְרוּשָׁלַיִם, has been digging the foundations of the future Yerushalayim ever since the *churban Beis HaMikdash,* and the rebuilding process has never ceased throughout the *galus.* At the time of *bi'as Mashiach,* the structure will be completed.

מַלְכוּת בֵּית דָּוִד

אֶת צֶמַח דָּוִד עַבְדְּךָ מְהֵרָה תַצְמִיחַ — **May You speedily cause the outgrowth of Dovid Your servant to sprout forth.** This is the *tefillah* for *Mashiach.* There are many places in *Tanach* where the *Melech HaMashiach,* a descendant of Dovid HaMelech, is referred to as his *tzemach,* or "sprout."

Some examples are: כִּי הִנְנִי מֵבִיא אֶת עַבְדִּי צֶמַח, *Behold, I am bringing My servant, Tzemach, the flourishing one* (Zechariah 3:8); וַהֲקִמֹתִי לְדָוִד צֶמַח צַדִּיק, *when I will establish a righteous sprout for Dovid* (Yirmiyahu 23:5); שָׁם אַצְמִיחַ קֶרֶן לְדָוִד, *There I shall cause pride to sprout for Dovid* (Tehillim 132:17).

Mashiach is called the "sprout," or outgrowth, of Dovid, because, like a seed germinating in the ground, the process of *bi'as Mashiach* is a slow but steady one. Just as a tiny seed gradually grows, bit by bit, until it breaks through the ground and then develops into a fully grown tree, so is the coming of *Mashiach* an ongoing and slowly developing process, which will not stop until the actual *bi'as Mashiach* becomes a reality.

And just as one would water a plant to make it grow, so does the *tzemach Dovid* develop and grow as the result of the tears of those who mourn over Tziyon and Yerushalayim, who are continually being *mispallel* for *binyan Yerushalayim* and *bi'as Mashiach.*

We explained earlier how the last seven *berachos* of the middle part of the *Shemoneh Esrei* correspond to the first six, and we reiterate:

אַתָּה חוֹנֵן corresponds to תְּקַע בְּשׁוֹפָר;
הֲשִׁיבָה שׁוֹפְטֵינוּ correspond to הֲשִׁיבֵנוּ אָבִינוּ - וְלַמַּלְשִׁינִים;
סְלַח לָנוּ corresponds to עַל הַצַּדִּיקִים.

Similarly, the *berachah* of בּוֹנֵה יְרוּשָׁלַיִם, which refers to the *sof hageulah,* the final and complete *geulah,* corresponds to the *berachah* of גּוֹאֵל יִשְׂרָאֵל, which refers to the *aschalta d'geulah* — the constant, ongoing *geulah* during the *galus,* which has protected the Jewish nation from extinction for the last 2,000 years. And just as in the first part of the *Shemoneh Esrei,* רְפוּאָה comes after גְּאוּלָה, in the second part, בּוֹנֵה יְרוּשָׁלַיִם is followed by אֶת צֶמַח דָּוִד, the *tefillah* for *bi'as Mashiach,* which is the ultimate *refuah* for what ails the Jewish people. The sickness that has beset the Jewish nation for the past 2,000 years is the *galus,* and its only real cure is *Mashiach.*

In *galus* the Jewish people has become very sick. As a result of our dispersion among the nations and of our mingling with them, we have learned non-Jewish values and mores from them. וַיִּתְעָרְבוּ בַגּוֹיִם וַיִּלְמְדוּ מַעֲשֵׂיהֶם, *But they mingled with the nations and learned their deeds* (Tehillim 106:35).

Unfortunately, we did not similarly absorb some of the good *middos* that are found among the *goyim*.

First, we have learned to hate each other. In the world at large, there is a great deal of ethnic hate and racial hate, and we have likewise absorbed this. For example, Jews born in one country often look down upon those from another country.

Second, we have lost two of the three distinguishing characteristics by which a Jew was always recognizable: בַּיְשָׁנִים, רַחֲמָנִים, וְגוֹמְלֵי חֲסָדִים.

בַּיְשָׁנִים: As long as a sense of *tzenius* existed in the world at large, we excelled in this trait. But, when the sense of personal modesty and decency was lost among the *goyim*, we too lost our *bushah*. When I was a child in pre-World War I Germany, no decent *goy* would swim in a mixed swimming pool. Men and women had separate swimming facilities. After World War I, this sense of personal decency was slowly lost among the *goyim* and unfortunately this trend found its way into Jewish life as well. We lost the *bushah*, not only in our mode of dressing, but also in our behavior and in the relationship between men and women.

רַחֲמָנִים: We have observed how cruel the *goyim* are to each other — not to speak of their cruelty to us — and, consequently, we too developed cruelty. I do not wish to go into details about this. Jews did not kill; Jews did not use violence; our *Neviim* and leaders did not advocate violent demonstrations. But, unfortunately, in the *galus*, we have learned these things from the *goyim*.

But, *Baruch Hashem*, one characteristic, that of *gemilus chassadim*, remains intact among the Jewish nation even during the *galus*.

Generally, though, we have contracted the "sickness of the *galus*" during our long exile. First there was the desire to associate with the "upper class" of non-Jewish society, the poets, the artists, the writers, the philosophers, the intelligentsia of the world. The desire to assimilate with the non-Jewish world then deteriorated into a desire to associate with and copy the lifestyle of the lower element of world society. Unfortunately, we now even have a "Jewish underworld."

This is a sickness, and it is getting, ח״ו, worse and worse. And, *most unfortunately*, there are even some of our people who are otherwise *shomrei Torah u'mitzvos* (observant Jews), who were historically "immune" to the diseases of the *galus*, but who now have also been "infected" by these *galus* diseases.

Therefore the "sick body" of the Jewish nation needs a *refuah sheleimah* and that cure will be realized with אֶת צֶמַח דָּוִד עַבְדְּךָ מְהֵרָה תַצְמִיחַ.

§ וְקַרְנוֹ תָּרוּם בִּישׁוּעָתֶךָ — **And his horn (power) shall be raised through Your salvation.** It does not say וְקַרְנוֹ תָּרִים, *You shall raise his horn*, but rather, תָּרוּם, *it shall be raised*. The sense of this phrase is, "The horn of *Mashiach ben Dovid* will rise only through Your *yeshuah*." The word *horn* is a metaphor for power, because an animal expresses its power by goring its perceived enemies with its horns.

In addition to the meaning *horn*, the word *keren* also has the meaning of *ray*, as in קָרַן עוֹר פְּנֵי מֹשֶׁה, *The skin of the face of Moshe radiated light* (Shemos 34:35). The people could perceive the spiritual rays of light that emanated from the face of Moshe.

The future *Mashiach* — as did Moshe Rabbeinu — will have a dual rule. First, he will bring order into the world: וְהִכָּה אֶרֶץ בְּשֵׁבֶט פִּיו וּבְרוּחַ שְׂפָתָיו יָמִית רָשָׁע, *He will strike the world with the rod of his mouth and with the breath of his lips he will slay the wicked* (Yeshayahu 11:4). This means that *Mashiach* will not be some sort of a "superman" who will simply overpower the *reshaim*, but rather, he will use *tefillah* as his staff, and will ask *HaKadosh Baruch Hu* that the *reshaim* may cease to exist, and they will cease to exist. *HaKadosh Baruch Hu* will cause the horn of the *Melech HaMashiach* to rise by empowering him to rid the world of *reshaim*

The other function of the future *Melech HaMashiach* will be his spiritual influence on the Jewish people. He will purify us, and like Moshe Rabbeinu, he will radiate spiritual light to his people. He will bring us back to Eretz Yisrael and cause a mass movement of *teshuvah* in our nation to elevate *Bnei Yisrael* to the level of וְעַמֵּךְ כֻּלָּם צַדִּיקִים, *Your people will all be righteous* (Yeshayahu 60:21).

"His horn," therefore, refers to *Mashiach* in his dual role: that of the destroyer of the *reshaim*, and of the mentor of the Jewish people by enlightening them with the spiritual rays of the Torah and bringing them back to the *Ribbono Shel Olam*.

Our *Chachamim* tell us that one of the questions that a person will be asked when he comes to *Olam Haba* is צִפִּיתָ לִישׁוּעָה, *Did you look forward to, and eagerly await, the yeshuah?* (Shabbos 31a). When one comes to *Olam Haba*, he will not be asked, "Did you wait for *Mashiach*?" or, "Did you belong to the Organization to bring *Mashiach*?"

[However, he will probably be asked, "Did you ever swindle the government on your tax return?" And he will be asked, "Were you honest in your business practices?" "Did you talk *lashon hara*?" "Did you control your *yetzer hara*?"]

But the question צִפִּיתָ לִישׁוּעָה means, "Did you eagerly await *yeshuas Hashem*?" It will not be the *Melech HaMashiach* who will bring the *yeshuah*. He will not be the savior; without the *yeshuas Hashem*, he will be completely helpless. Rather, it will be *HaKadosh Baruch Hu* Who will be the Savior, and the *Melech HaMashiach* himself will be among those who are saved. We find *Mashiach* being called צַדִּיק וְנוֹשָׁע הוּא (Zechariah 9:9). The *Melech Mashiach* will be the *tzaddik* "per se" who leads the Jewish people, and he, himself, will be one of those who are redeemed.

SHEMONEH ESREI ∽ 495

The line of the descent of *Mashiach* is highly noteworthy. He will be a descendant of Peretz, the product of the union of Yehudah and Tamar. Yehudah cohabited with Tamar, thinking she was a harlot. Further down the line, *Mashiach* will be a descendant of Dovid HaMelech, whose ancestor was Rus HaMoaviah (see end of *Megillas Ruth*); the Moavites are the product of the outrage that Lot committed with his daughters (see *Bereishis* 19:37). Then, *Mashiach* will have to have descended through the line of Shlomo HaMelech whose mother was Batsheva, with whom Dovid had a relationship, and subsequently married (*II Shmuel* Ch. 11). The *aveirah* that Dovid did at that time is not entirely clear — in fact, our *Chachamim* say that technically it was not an *aveirah* (see *Shabbos* 56a) — but, nevertheless, he was deeply remorseful for what he had done, and he did *teshuvah* for it (see ibid. Ch. 12). Our daily *tefillah* of *Tachanun* (from Psalm 6) reflects this remorse. Indeed, half of *sefer Tehillim* contains expressions of the *teshuvah* of Dovid HaMelech.

As if to underscore the ancestry of Dovid HaMelech, the Gemara (*Yevamos* 77b) juxtaposes the two *pesukim*, מָצָאתִי דָּוִד עַבְדִּי, *I have found Dovid, My servant* (*Tehillim* 89:21), and שְׁתֵּי בְנֹתֶיךָ הַנִּמְצָאֹת, *Your two daughters who are present* (*Bereishis* 19:15). The first *pasuk* refers to the exalted level of greatness of Dovid HaMelech, and the latter to the fact that his ancestry was the product of the *aveirah* that Lot committed with his daughters.

The reason for this, and consequently, for the origins of *Mashiach,* is that every one of these ancestors of Dovid HaMelech — and Dovid HaMelech himself — who was involved in these questionable acts did *teshuvah* for them. The road to *Mashiach* is paved with *teshuvah.* We can assume that Lot did *teshuvah*, for after all, he was a nephew of Avraham Avinu; Yehudah make a public confession, shaming himself: צָדְקָה מִמֶּנִּי, *She is more righteous than I* (*Bereishis* 38:26), and he did *teshuvah* for the rest of his life; and Dovid HaMelech certainly did *teshuvah* for the rest of his life, as is borne out throughout the *sefer Tehillim.*

HaKadosh Baruch Hu chose as the future *Melech HaMashiach* a person whose ancestry is replete with famous *baalei teshuvah*. The function of *Mashiach* is to make the whole world into *baalei teshuvah* : first the Jewish people, and then all the decent people among the gentiles. This is expressed in the *tefillah* of *Aleinu:* וְכָל בְּנֵי בָשָׂר יִקְרְאוּ בִשְׁמֶךָ, לְהַפְנוֹת אֵלֶיךָ כָּל רִשְׁעֵי אָרֶץ, *Then all humanity will call upon Your Name, to turn all the earth's wicked toward You.*

While the Melech HaMashich himself — similar to Dovid HaMelech before his debacle — will be (צַדִּיק וְנוֹשָׁע הוּא) בְּלִי חֵטְא, a righteous person, who will be saved, he must have a connection with, or understanding of, the special needs of *baalei teshuvah* in order for him to successfully institute a worldwide *teshuvah* movement.

‎כִּי לִישׁוּעָתְךָ קִוִּינוּ — **Because, it is for Your salvation that we hope.** What we really mean when we say we are waiting for *Mashiach* is that *we are waiting for HaKadosh Baruch Hu*; as we have previously expressed, ‎אֶפֶס בִּלְתְּךָ גּוֹאֲלֵנוּ, *There is no redeemer but You.*

Whenever we repeat this *tefillah*, ‎אֶת צֶמַח דָּוִד, in which we ask *HaKadosh Baruch Hu* to bring *Mashiach*, we should have the thought that we are eagerly awaiting the *yeshuah* of *HaKadosh Baruch Hu* in which He will bring *Mashiach*. This hope and anticipation is called ‎מְצַפִּים לִישׁוּעָה. These words were probably written as a marginal note in some old *siddurim* — as a reminder that this is the thought that one should have while saying this *tefillah*, and it later found its way into the actual text according to *nusach Sefard*.

‎כָּל הַיּוֹם — **The whole day.** This does not mean "every day," but rather, *the whole day*. This means that our whole being is permeated with the hope for *yeshuas Hashem*. The *yeshuah* that *HaKadosh Baruch Hu* has promised will come through *bi'as Mashiach*.

‎בָּרוּךְ אַתָּה ה׳, מַצְמִיחַ קֶרֶן יְשׁוּעָה — **Blessed are You, Hashem, Who makes the horn (power) of salvation sprout forth.** We end this *berachah* with an expression of our *emunah* that *HaKadosh Baruch Hu* will bring the *geulah*. We have previously compared the process of *bi'as Mashiach* to a structure being built behind an enclosure. At first, nothing is visible except the wall of the enclosure. However, suddenly, as it were, the structure begins to appear above the enclosure.

Similarly, the *Navi* describes the coming of *Mashiach* as a sudden event, ‎בְּהֶיסֵּח הַדַּעַת, which will occur at a moment when no one expects it: ‎הִנְנִי שֹׁלֵחַ מַלְאָכִי וּפִנָּה דֶרֶךְ לְפָנָי, וּפִתְאֹם יָבוֹא אֶל הֵיכָלוֹ, הָאָדוֹן אֲשֶׁר אַתֶּם מְבַקְשִׁים, *I will send My messenger and he will clear the way before Me, and the Master Whom you are seeking will suddenly come into His Palace* (Malachi 3:1). The Gemara (*Sanhedrin* 97a) includes the coming of *Mashiach* among the things that come unexpectedly: ‎שְׁלֹשָׁה בָּאִין בְּהֶיסֵּח הַדַּעַת, אֵלּוּ הֵן מָשִׁיחַ, מְצִיאָה, וְעַקְרָב, *Three things come when they are not expected. They are: Mashiach, finding a lost object, and the bite of a scorpion.*

‎קַבָּלַת תְּפִלָּה

This is the last of the twelve intermediate *berachos* of the *Shemoneh Esrei*. We have explained how these twelve *berachos* correspond to each other. And just as ‎אֶת צֶמַח דָּוִד corresponds to ‎רְפָאֵנוּ, the *berachah* of ‎שְׁמַע קוֹלֵנוּ corresponds to ‎בָּרֵךְ עָלֵינוּ, which is the *tefillah* for sustenance of the body. Correspondingly, the *berachah* of ‎שְׁמַע קוֹלֵנוּ addresses the needs of the *neshamah*. Since the *neshamah* comes from *HaKadosh Baruch Hu*, it naturally wants to be connected to Him. This connection is effected through *tefillah*, which establishes a close relationship with *HaKadosh Baruch Hu*. This is what the *neshamah* craves.

The *Chasam Sofer* says that *tefillah* is related to *nevuah* (*Teshuvos Chasam Sofer* vol. 1 *Orach Chaim* 16) [source provided by Rabbi Binyomin Forst]. Through the experience of *nevuah*, *HaKadosh Baruch Hu* communicates with the human being, either directly or by means of *malachim*. However, while the *navi* can have a dialogue with *HaKadosh Baruch Hu*, we ordinary human beings can have only a monologue with Him. This communication with *HaKadosh Baruch Hu* is accomplished through *tefillah*.

The Ramban in several places says that the Torah is replete with examples of *nissim*, miraculous events, albeit hidden miracles. The entire history of the *Avos* consists of a chain of hidden miracles, without which we could not have emerged as a nation.

Furthermore, the fact that the Torah promises physical rewards or punishments for keeping or violating the *mitzvos* — a sign of God's direct management of human events — is in itself nothing short of miraculous (see *Ramban, Bereishis* 17:1; 46:7; *Shemos* 6:3-4; *Vayikra* 27:9-11; also see *Maayan Beis HaSho'evah, Bechukosai* 26:42).

Similarly, the fact that *HaKadosh Baruch Hu* hears our *tefillos* and responds to them is among those hidden miracles with which our natural world is filled. Unless it is a miracle, the concept of *tefillah* for God's help is completely senseless. Let us say someone is very sick, and is in need of an operation in a hospital. The doctors who will perform the surgery are not observant Jews; some are simply not religious, and some may be atheists. While they are performing the operation, a close relative or friend opens a *sefer Tehillim*, mentions the sick person's name, and is *mispallel* for him, in the hope that this is going to help the doctors perform the operation successfully and save the patient's life. If the efficacy of *tefillah* were not a *neis*, it would be totally senseless to say *Tehillim* and expect this to help the patient. What possible influence could one's *tefillah* have on the doctors' performance during this surgery? But through the *neis* of *tefillah*, a person could be sitting in his private room — far removed from the operating room where the surgeons are working — pleading with *HaKadosh Baruch Hu* to save the patient's life, and if his *tefillah* is accepted, and the patient's life is saved, this result is nothing short of a *neis*. The total concept of *tefillah* is within the realm of *nissim*; otherwise, it would be totally meaningless to engage in it.

We should know that there is a difference between *tefillah* and *techinah*. The former comes from the mind, and the latter from the heart. We mention both in this *berachah*: כִּי אֵל שׁוֹמֵעַ תְּפִלּוֹת וְתַחֲנוּנִים אָתָּה. The *Shemoneh Esrei* is *tefillos*, and *tachanunim* refers to the *tachanun* that follows it. The difference between the two is as follows.

Tefillah, from פלל, has the connotation of "thinking," as in רְאֹה פָנֶיךָ לֹא פִלָּלְתִּי, I never thought I would see your face (Bereishis 48:11); or וְנָתַן בִּפְלִלִים, He shall pay by order of the judges (Shemos 21:22). The root פלל, in describing judges, conveys the idea that they "think" about the case and then render their decision. Tefillah by definition means the use of our process of thinking. Therefore, just "saying tefillos" without kavannah, without thinking about them, means absolutely nothing. Without thought and concentration, the essence of tefillah is missing. One's general kavannah, and mindset, during tefillah should be that he is aware that every minute of his life, and all of his sustenance, is totally dependent on HaKadosh Baruch Hu. One does not know what the next moment may bring, either for himself, or for the world at large. One is completely dependent on the help of HaKadosh Baruch Hu for his survival and sustenance. When one stands before HaKadosh Baruch Hu in tefillah, he should be aware that he is but one heartbeat away from oblivion! It is only HaKadosh Baruch Hu Who makes his heart beat, and Who makes him see, hear, talk, think, walk, feel, and act, and Who provides him with his daily sustenance. The process of thinking is at the root of the meaning of tefillah.

Then there is a form of prayer called tachanunim, supplications, which come from the heart, from one's feelings and emotions. This was used by Chanah — in addition to her tefillah — when she poured out her soul to HaKadosh Baruch Hu: וְחַנָּה הִיא מְדַבֶּרֶת עַל לִבָּהּ ... וָאֶשְׁפֹּךְ אֶת נַפְשִׁי לִפְנֵי ה', Chanah was speaking to her heart ... I have poured out my soul before Hashem (I Shmuel 1:13-15); also by Dovid HaMelech when he said, אֶשְׁפֹּךְ לְפָנָיו שִׂיחִי צָרָתִי לְפָנָיו אַגִּיד, I pour out my plaint before Him, I declare my suffering before Him (Tehillim 142:3). In this form of prayer, one pours out his heart, his bitterness, his frustrations, his disappointments, and his hopes and yearnings, to HaKadosh Baruch Hu.

Our Chachamim tell us, אַל תַּעַשׂ תְּפִלָּתְךָ קֶבַע, Do not make your tefillah as something which is a set routine (Pirkei Avos 2:18). This is done, for example, when one has a daily shiur from 9 to 10 a.m., and he keeps this regularly, no matter what the circumstances. The emphasis is on its regularity, as in קָבַעְתָּ עִתִּים לַתּוֹרָה, Did you have definite set times for learning Torah? However, with tefillah, the emphasis is not merely its daily routine, whereby one repeats the same words, over and over again, at the same time. Rather, one should emphasize the aspect of רַחֲמִים וְתַחֲנוּנִים לִפְנֵי הַמָּקוֹם, pleas and supplications for mercy before God.

A human being is to stand before God with the realization that he is dependent on the mercy of HaKadosh Baruch Hu every minute of his life. He may appear successful, rich and powerful, but in his heart of hearts he knows that he is as dependent on the rachamim of HaKadosh Baruch Hu as is the helpless unborn child on the nourishment provided by the רֶחֶם, womb, of its mother. (Hence, the derivation רַחֲמִים, from רֶחֶם.)

If one merely repeats the same *Shemoneh Esrei* every day, and has the same thoughts — or lack of them — he has not fulfilled the ideal form of *tefillah*. Unfortunately, most people — including myself — fall into the category of making their *tefillah* a קֶבַע, a set routine. Actually, and ideally, every *Shemoneh Esrei* should be a unique experience. One *Shemoneh Esrei* should not be the same as the other. Just as, for instance, Rosh Hashanah and Yom Kippur are not considered, by most thinking Jews, as "routine" — one thinks and worries about the year that lies ahead — so should our daily *tefillah* be a special experience each time, rather than merely a repetitious exercise in the mouthing of words.

שְׁמַע קוֹלֵנוּ ה׳ אֱלֹהֵינוּ — **Hear our voice, Hashem, our God.** We do not say, "Hear our *tefillah*." Rather, we ask *HaKadosh Baruch Hu* to hear our voice. And "voice" could not mean the *sound* of our *tefillah,* because the *Shemoneh Esrei* is said quietly. Rather, the voice of our *tefillah* refers to the *kavannah* and thought that we put into our *tefillah.* We ask *HaKadosh Baruch Hu* to listen not merely to the words we say, but to our *kavannah,* our intent, while we say them. It is the "voice," the thought and emphasis, which one puts into the words of *tefillah* that give them their true meaning.

An analogy for this would be a son who sends a terse telegram to his father: "Father, send me money." Upon receipt of this seemingly audacious note, the father becomes very upset and goes to his Rav to complain about his inconsiderate and brash son, and asks him for guidance in dealing with him. Whereupon the Rav asks to see the telegram. Upon reading it, he tells the father, "You did not read this properly. Here is what it says." And in a trembling and pleading voice, the Rav imitates the tone of the words of the young son to his father: "*Father . . . send me money!*" Upon hearing the Rav's rendition of his son's tearful and pleading request for money, the father says, "I cannot refuse such a heartrending appeal from my son to help him with some money." Similarly, we ask *HaKadosh Baruch Hu* to hear the tone and meaning that we have placed into the words of our *tefillah.* The words שְׁמַע קוֹלֵנוּ ה׳ אֱלֹהֵינוּ חוּס וְרַחֵם עָלֵינוּ take on a completely different meaning if they are said pleadingly and with supplication rather than if they are merely "rattled off" as if one were reading a newspaper.

חוּס וְרַחֵם עָלֵינוּ — **Spare us and have mercy on us.** The word חוּס is different than רַחֵם, which means *have mercy.* The Vilna Gaon explains that חוּס is used to express the feeling one would have to save or spare something that he himself made with great care and forethought. If one is an artist or a gardener and created something of beauty, he has a special interest in conserving his handiwork. We find examples of this usage in many places, for instance:

חוּסָה עַל עֲמָלָךְ, *Have pity on Your handiwork* (*Selichos*); עַל בָּנִים לֹא תָחוּס עֵינָם,

Their eyes will not have pity on children (Yeshayahu 13:18); וְעֵינְכֶם אַל תָּחֹס עַל כְּלֵיכֶם, *And let your eyes not take pity on your belongings* (Bereishis 45:20).

We ask *HaKadosh Baruch Hu,* the "Master Craftsman" Who created us, to hear our pleas and spare us, חוּס, because we are His own handiwork.

And from our standpoint, we ask *HaKadosh Baruch Hu* to have mercy on us, רַחֵם עָלֵינוּ, because we cannot exist without His *rachamim.* (See *Avnei Eliyahu,* from *Siddur Ishei Yisrael,* on *Shema Koleinu.*)

וְקַבֵּל בְּרַחֲמִים וּבְרָצוֹן אֶת תְּפִלָּתֵנוּ — **And accept with mercy and favor — our prayer.** Some *tefillos* are accepted by *HaKadosh Baruch Hu* only because of His *rachamim,* in spite of the fact that the person does not deserve it, and would otherwise be helpless.

However, there are people, *tzaddikim,* whose *tefillah deserves* to be answered, and *HaKadosh Baruch Hu* "wants" to accept these בְּרָצוֹן, with His Will, and not merely out of *rachamim.* רָצוֹן conveys the idea of liking something or, in German *"wohlgefallen,"* which means having *satisfaction and pleasure* with something. This is what is meant by our *Chachamim* when they say: הקב״ה מִתְאַוֶּה לִתְפִלָּתָן שֶׁל צַדִּיקִים, *God desires and looks forward to the prayers of the righteous* (Yevamos 64a).

Interestingly, in this phrase, it does not say תְּפִלּוֹתֵנוּ, in the plural, but rather, תְּפִלָּתֵנוּ, because while we all say the same text of the *tefillah* which our *Chachamim* instituted, each person places a different emphasis on these same words.

But, then, we continue:

כִּי אֵל שׁוֹמֵעַ תְּפִלּוֹת וְתַחֲנוּנִים אָתָּה — **For God Who always listens to prayers and pleadings are You.** Here we use the plural form, *tefillos,* because it refers to the prayers of all mankind, not just the *tefillah* of Israel. We find, שֹׁמֵעַ תְּפִלָּה, עָדֶיךָ כָּל בָּשָׂר יָבֹאוּ, *You hear prayer; to You come all people* (Tehillim 65:3). (In *nusach Sefard,* the text clearly indicates this: כִּי אַתָּה שׁוֹמֵעַ תְּפִלַּת כָּל פֶּה.) Focusing once again on Israel, we say,

וּמִלְּפָנֶיךָ מַלְכֵּנוּ רֵיקָם אַל תְּשִׁיבֵנוּ — **And do not turn us away empty-handed from before You, our King.** We hope that *HaKadosh Baruch Hu* answers our *tefillah* in the affirmative, and He gives us health, sustenance, and whatever else we ask Him for. However, sometimes, for reasons of His own, *HaKadosh Baruch Hu* says "no" to our *tefillah.* We therefore ask *HaKadosh Baruch Hu* here that if the answer to our *tefillah* is "no," then, at least "do not send us away empty-handed," with a feeling of total rejection. At least let our hearts be filled with *emunah* and *bitachon,* that we have had the *zechus* to talk to *HaKadosh Baruch Hu,* and that He has heard our *tefillah,* whether or not He answers us in the affirmative.

An illustration of this is found in the description of Chanah after she had cried her heart out to *HaKadosh Baruch Hu*, begging Him for a son. When she finished, her demeanor is described as, וּפָנֶיהָ לֹא הָיוּ לָהּ עוֹד, *Her face was no longer sad* (*Shmuel I* 1:18). Although she was not sure that her *tefillah* would be answered, she nevertheless left with a feeling that *HaKadosh Baruch Hu* had heard her *tefillah*, and she relied on His judgment.

כִּי אַתָּה שׁוֹמֵעַ תְּפִלַּת עַמְּךָ יִשְׂרָאֵל בְּרַחֲמִים — **Because You hear the communal prayers of Your nation Israel with mercy.** The ending of this *berachah* is similar to its beginning, following the rule of חֲתִימָה מֵעֵין הַפְּתִיחָה.

Here, again, we use תְּפִלַּת, in the singular, as it refers to the standardized language of the *tefillah* which was instituted by our *Chachamim* for use by עַמְּךָ יִשְׂרָאֵל.

This phrase is based upon the importance of *tefillah b'tzibbur*. Even if one considers himself unworthy of having the *Ribbon Kol HaOlamim* hear his own *tefillah*, nevertheless, by including himself in *Klal Yisrael*, who all use the same *tefillah* wherever they may be throughout the globe (with very slight textural variations), he can expect to be heard by *HaKadosh Baruch Hu*.

So we ask *HaKadosh Baruch Hu* in this *berachah* to hear our *tefillah* as part of the Jewish nation: כִּי אַתָּה שׁוֹמֵעַ תְּפִלַּת עַמְּךָ יִשְׂרָאֵל, *Because You hear the communal prayer of Your nation Israel*.

בְּרַחֲמִים, even if individuals are unworthy, but, because of His mercy, *HaKadosh Baruch Hu* "listens" to the *tefillah* of the nation as a whole.

The special relationship that the Jewish nation has with *HaKadosh Baruch Hu* when it is united in *tefillah* is pointed out for us in the Torah: כִּי מִי גוֹי גָּדוֹל אֲשֶׁר לוֹ אֱלֹהִים קְרֹבִים אֵלָיו כַּה' אֱלֹהֵינוּ בְּכָל קָרְאֵנוּ אֵלָיו, *For which is a great nation that has a God Who is close to it, as is Hashem, our God, whenever we call to Him* (*Devarim* 4:7).

If someone does not have the *zechus* to attend *tefillas tzibbur*, he should try to be *mispallel* at the same time as the *tzibbur* or, at least, he should think of himself as part of *Klal Yisrael* — and not merely as an individual — while he is being *mispallel*, and in these ways his *tefillah* becomes a part of the communal *tefillah* of *Am Yisrael*, which, God, in His mercy, hears.

בָּרוּךְ אַתָּה ה', שׁוֹמֵעַ תְּפִלָּה — **Blessed are You, Hashem, Who hears prayer.** We close by expressing our *emunah* that *HaKadosh Baruch Hu* hears our *tefillah* and, as we have said, this is nothing short of a *neis nistar* (hidden miracle).

עֲבוֹדָה

With this *berachah* we begin the last part of the *Shemoneh Esrei*, which consists of three *berachos*:

The first is רְצֵה, which our *Chachamim* call *Avodah* (see *Megillah* 18a etc.).

In fact, the word עֲבוֹדָה is mentioned twice in this *berachah*. In the course of our explanation, it will become clear why this *berachah* is more characteristic of עֲבוֹדָה than the rest of the *tefillah*, which is is also called (שֶׁבַּלֵּב) עֲבוֹדָה (see *Taanis* 2a).

The second is מוֹדִים, which our *Chachamim* call *Hoda'ah*.

And the third and final *berachah* of the *Shemoneh Esrei* is שִׂים שָׁלוֹם, which our *Chachamim* call בִּרְכַּת כֹּהֲנִים — although the *Kohen's* blessing is said only in the *Chazaras HaShatz* — for the reason that we will explain.

Rav Samson R. Hirsch, in his commentary on the *siddur*, explains how the order of the *berachos* of the *Shemoneh Esrei* corresponds to the various *avodos* that are part of the *korbanos*, because תְּפִלּוֹת כְּנֶגֶד תְּמִידִין תִּקְנוּם, *The prayers were instituted to correspond to the daily sacrificial offerings* (*Berachos* 26b). He explains, accordingly, that the *berachah* of רְצֵה which we have before us now corresponds to the *menachos* that are a part of the sacrificial service. The *menachos*, which consisted of flour and oil, were brought after most of the *korbanos*, as an adjunct thereto.

The *tefillah* of רְצֵה, corresponding to the *menachos*, expresses a thought that has not yet been expressed at all in the *Shemoneh Esrei*, just as the *menachos* express a new thought that was not yet expressed by the *korban* proper.

By the way, the meaning of *tefillas* Minchah is not related to the *menachos* of the *korbanos*, because the *menachos* were offered in conjunction with the morning *tamid* as well as the evening *tamid*. Rather, it is derived from the word נָחֹה, *resting*, and it describes the *tefillah* that is said in the afternoon at the time when the sun is setting, or "resting," מְנוּחַת הַשֶּׁמֶשׁ (see *Ramban* to *Shemos* 12:6 on בֵּין הָעַרְבָּיִם).

The word *minchah*, as used in connection with *korbanos*, is used to convey the idea of a *token* gift. However, an actual gift — given to someone who needs it, or will make good use of it — is called *matanah*. The best example of this would be *matanos l'evyonim*, gifts to the poor. But מִנְחָה means a token, or introductory, gift, which forms a bond between two individuals or ingratiates one person to another. If someone is invited as a guest, and he brings flowers or a bottle of wine — regardless of whether the host needs it — he is said to have given his host a *minchah*, as an expression of his friendship. It is this idea, the expression of our love to *HaKadosh Baruch Hu*, which lies at the root of the meaning of the *berachah* of רְצֵה.

✥ רְצֵה ה׳ אֱלֹהֵינוּ בְּעַמְּךָ יִשְׂרָאֵל וּבִתְפִלָּתָם — **Be favorable, Hashem, our God, toward Your people Israel and their prayer.** On the surface, these opening words seem to be a redundancy of the words of the previous *berachah*: כִּי אַתָּה שׁוֹמֵעַ תְּפִלַּת עַמְּךָ יִשְׂרָאֵל בְּרַחֲמִים; we seem now to be starting all over again. Furthermore, in the previous *berachah* we said תְּפִלַּת עַמְּךָ יִשְׂרָאֵל, but here we have the wording בְּעַמְּךָ יִשְׂרָאֵל וּבִתְפִלָּתָם, in which the emphasis is on עַמְּךָ יִשְׂרָאֵל.

However, the *tefillah* of רְצֵה was formulated to express a new idea, not previously included in the *Shemoneh Esrei*. Here we request that *HaKadosh Baruch Hu* willingly accept "Your nation Israel and its prayers." It is our *tefillah* here that *HaKadosh Baruch Hu* accept the Jewish nation in its mission of instilling a *kiddush Hashem* in the world.

We have previously made reference to the Gemara (*Taanis* 2a) that tells us that the source of the *mitzvah* of *tefillah* is וּלְעָבְדוֹ בְּכָל לְבַבְכֶם, *and to serve Him with all your heart and with all your soul* (*Devarim* 11:13). Whether this is a Biblically ordained *mitzvah* or an *asmachta* (a Scriptural allusion to a Rabbinic law) is the subject of a dispute among the *Rishonim* (early Sages). According to the Rambam it is a *mitzvas asei d'Oraisa* (see beginning of *Hil. Tefillah*). The *tefillah* up to this point has been one of בְּכָל לְבַבְכֶם, in which we have asked *HaKadosh Baruch Hu*, with all our heart, that we be the recipients of a whole list of blessings from Him for our spiritual and physical well-being, both on the individual and communal levels.

However, the subject of the *tefillah* of רְצֵה is based on the words that follow the aforementioned phrase of וּלְעָבְדוֹ בְּכָל לְבַבְכֶם, that of וּבְכָל נַפְשְׁכֶם, to serve *HaKadosh Baruch Hu* by means of our *nefesh*. This refers to a new area of *tefillah*, in which we do not ask *HaKadosh Baruch Hu* to give us anything. Rather, *we are mispallel to HaKadosh Baruch Hu for HaKadosh Baruch Hu*. This is expressed in the *pasuk*, לֹא לָנוּ ה' לֹא לָנוּ כִּי לְשִׁמְךָ תֵּן כָּבוֹד, *Not for our sake, Hashem, not for our sake, but for Your Name give glory* (*Tehillim* 115:1).

And it is also the meaning of the saying of our *Chachamim*: הֱווּ כַעֲבָדִים הַמְשַׁמְּשִׁין אֶת הָרַב שֶׁלֹּא עַל מְנָת לְקַבֵּל פְּרָס, *Be like servants who serve their master not for the sake of receiving a reward* (*Pirkei Avos* 1:3).

A servant who serves his master not for the purpose of receiving payment does so only because he wants to be close to his master; he wants to please his master, and his master's satisfaction is his greatest reward. His master will surely pay him, but that is not the reason the servant serves him. The reason he serves him is because the servant wishes to establish a close and personal relationship and friendship with his master.

In the *tefillah* of רְצֵה we do not ask to receive anything, but rather, we are attempting to "give" something to *HaKadosh Baruch Hu*. Instead of being a *mekabel* (recipient), we wish to become a *mashpia* (giver, the source of a gift). We want to make a *kiddush Hashem* in the world. This is the *tefillah* of בְּכָל נַפְשְׁכֶם.

[Ed. note: For a broader explanation of the concepts of *mekabel* and *mashpia*, see the Rav's remarks on the first *parashah* of *Krias Shema*.]

With this explanation, we can understand that רְצֵה ה׳ אֱלֹהֵינוּ בְּעַמְּךָ יִשְׂרָאֵל וּבִתְפִלָּתָם is by no means a redundancy of כִּי אַתָּה שׁוֹמֵעַ תְּפִלַּת עַמְּךָ יִשְׂרָאֵל בְּרַחֲמִים, because the latter is a summary of our earlier *tefillos* in which we requested something from *HaKadosh Baruch Hu*. However, in רְצֵה, we do not ask to receive anything from *HaKadosh Baruch Hu*. Rather, it is an expression of our desire that we, as עַמְּךָ בְּנֵי יִשְׂרָאֵל, shall merit to bring *kiddush Hashem* into the world.

וְהָשֵׁב אֶת הָעֲבוֹדָה לִדְבִיר בֵּיתֶךָ — **And restore the service to the Holy of Holies of Your Temple.** The means by which the Jewish nation expresses its closest connection with *HaKadosh Baruch Hu* is the *avodas hakorbanos*, and its reinstitution in the *Beis HaMikdash* will bring about the greatest *kiddush Hashem* in the world.

The term *avodah* means serving *HaKadosh Baruch Hu* without expecting any payment in return, שֶׁלֹּא עַל מְנָת לְקַבֵּל פְּרָס, and this characterizes the *korbanos* in general. But here we ask not only for the return of the *avodah*, but rather, הָעֲבוֹדָה, *the Avodah,* which refers to the *Avodah* of Yom Kippur, which is the highest level of the sacrificial service. This phrase definitely refers to the *avodas Yom HaKippurim* because we ask that the service be returned to דְּבִיר בֵּיתֶךָ, which means the *Kodesh HaKadashim* (see *Melachim I* 8:6; *Divrei HaYamim II* 5:7).

Rav Samson R. Hirsch renders דְּבִיר בֵּיתֶךָ in German as *"wortstatte,"* or "residence of His word." The "word" of *HaKadosh Baruch Hu* is represented by the *Aron HaKodesh* which "resides" in the *Kodesh HaKadashim*. The *Aron HaKodesh* contains the *Shnei Luchos HaEidus* (Two Tablets of the Testimony) — the testimony that *HaKadosh Baruch Hu* spoke to the Jewish nation — and the *sefer Torah* that was written by Moshe Rabbeinu, both of which represent *Torah Shebichsav*. And the *Torah Shebe'al Peh*, containing the entire Torah, which was spoken to Moshe Rabbeinu by *HaKadosh Baruch Hu,* is represented by the *Kapores* (Cover) and the *Keruvim* (Cherubs) that cover the *Aron*: וְדִבַּרְתִּי אִתְּךָ מֵעַל הַכַּפֹּרֶת מִבֵּין שְׁנֵי הַכְּרֻבִים אֲשֶׁר עַל אֲרוֹן הָעֵדֻת אֵת כָּל אֲשֶׁר אֲצַוֶּה אוֹתְךָ אֶל בְּנֵי יִשְׂרָאֵל, *I shall speak with you from atop the Cover, from between the Cherubim that are on the Ark of the Testimonial Tablets, everything that I shall command you to the Children of Israel* (*Shemos* 25:22).

The entirety of Torah is the דְּבָר שֶׁל הקב״ה, and the place that is built especially to house its representation is called דְּבִיר בֵּיתֶךָ [*D'vir Beisecha*].

However, during the Second *Beis HaMikdash*, the *Aron HaKodesh* was not in the *Kodesh HaKadashim* (see *Yoma* 53b), and therefore, in its absence, the *Kodesh HaKadashim* would not be called *D'vir Beisecha*. We are *mispallel* here that *HaKadosh Baruch Hu* may reinstate not only the *avodah,* but, especially, הָעֲבוֹדָה, the *Avodah* of Yom Kippur, which is the one unique

SHEMONEH ESREI 505

Avodah which is done אַחַת בַּשָּׁנָה, *once yearly,* in the *D'vir Beisecha* with the return of the *Aron HaKodesh* to its midst. During this special event, the blood of the *korban* and the *ketores* (incense-spices) are brought into the *Kodesh HaKadashim*, an act that represents both the *guf* and the *neshamah*, the material and spiritual aspects of Israel. These are brought into the inner sanctum לִפְנַי וְלִפְנִים (literally: inside of the inside), to express the idea that both the physical and spiritual life of the Jewish nation comes from the Torah and serves the Torah.

We are therefore *mispallel* here for the return of the greatest *kiddush Hashem* in the world: the performance of the *Avodah* of Yom Kippur in the *D'vir Beiseicha*. The *Kodesh HaKadashim* is the place of the reflection of the *Kisei HaKavod* in this world (*Shemos Rabbah* 35:6), and from the *Kodesh HaKadashim* the *Shechinah* radiates to the whole world.

Therefore, the meaning of רְצֵה is completely different than that of the *berachos* we offered up to this point in the *Shemoneh Esrei*. In רְצֵה, we ask nothing for ourselves. Rather, we ask that through the return of the *avodah* — especially the *Avodah* of Yom Kippur — the purpose of Creation shall be realized when the *Shechinah* will permeate the world, and *Malchus Shamayim* shall be recognized by all of mankind.

◈ וְאִשֵּׁי יִשְׂרָאֵל וּתְפִלָּתָם בְּאַהֲבָה תְקַבֵּל בְּרָצוֹן — **May You accept with goodwill, the fire offerings of Yisrael and their prayers offered out of love.** This refers to the ordinary daily *korbanos*, which were accompanied by *tefillos*. The once-a-year event of the *Avodah* of Yom Kippur is the wellspring from which all the *avodah* of the *korbanos* throughout the year draw their spirit and meaning.

The language of this phrase, וּתְפִלָּתָם בְּאַהֲבָה תְקַבֵּל בְּרָצוֹן, is noteworthy. We would have expected it to read, וּתְפִלָּתָם תְקַבֵּל בְּאַהֲבָה וּבְרָצוֹן, similar to בְּאַהֲבָה וּבְרָצוֹן הִנְחַלְתָּנוּ. It therefore seems, at least to me — and I say it this way in my *tefillah* — that this phrase should be read: וְאִשֵּׁי יִשְׂרָאֵל, וּתְפִלָּתָם בְּאַהֲבָה, תְקַבֵּל בְּרָצוֹן. In this way the meaning is: *May you accept with goodwill, the fire offerings of Israel and their prayers offered out of love.* Prayers offered out of love are those in which we ask nothing for ourselves — in which we are not *mekablim* — but rather, through which we want to be *mashpi'im*. Out of our love of *HaKadosh Baruch Hu*, we ask only that His *Shechinah* may permeate the world, as was His intention originally. This idea is expressed in *Bereishis Rabbah* 19:13 as: עִיקַּר שְׁכִינָה בַּתַּחְתּוֹנִים הָיְתָה.

And it is noteworthy that we do not say תְקַבֵּל בְּרַחֲמִים, but rather תְקַבֵּל בְּרָצוֹן here, because we are not asking anything for ourselves — for which the term "mercy" would be appropriate. Rather, all we ask here is that we may be pleasing in the eyes of *HaKadosh Baruch Hu*, and that He grant our wish that His *Shechinah* shall return to this world.

וּתְהִי לְרָצוֹן תָּמִיד עֲבוֹדַת יִשְׂרָאֵל עַמֶּךָ — **May the service of Your people Israel always be favorable to You.** However, as long as there is no *Beis HaMikdash*, no *D'vir*, and no *korbanos*, we substitute our *tefillos* for them: וּנְשַׁלְּמָה פָרִים שְׂפָתֵינוּ, *Let our lips substitute for bulls* (*Hoshea* 14:3). And we are therefore *mispallel* that our *avodah*, our *tefillah*, even without the benefit of the *korbanos*, always, *tamid*, be willingly accepted by *HaKadosh Baruch Hu*. In this context, עֲבוֹדַת יִשְׂרָאֵל refers specifically to our *tefillah* for the return of *kiddush Hashem* to the world, which will remove the vast *chillul Hashem* which is currently so prevalent. This means we are asking *HaKadosh Baruch Hu* to allow His Name to be recognized, first by all of עַמֶּךָ יִשְׂרָאֵל and consequently, following our example, by the whole world. It is for this reason that the *berachah* of רְצֵה is referred to by our *Chachamim* as *avodah*. It is a *tefillah* that has as its main purpose the enhancement of *kiddush Hashem* in the world.

יַעֲלֶה וְיָבֹא

[Ed. note: The Rav made note of the fact that this *shiur* was being delivered on Rosh Chodesh, making it all the more appropriate to offer some comments on יַעֲלֶה וְיָבֹא. The date was א׳ ר״ח אדר תשנ״ג — February 21, 1993.]

Our *Chachamim* instituted the inclusion of יַעֲלֶה וְיָבֹא in רְצֵה, during weekdays on which a *korban mussaf* is brought in the *Beis HaMikdash*, because יַעֲלֶה וְיָבֹא is an extension of the *avodah* characteristic of רְצֵה, in which we are *mispallel* בְּאַהֲבָה, not for ourselves, but rather, for a worldwide *kiddush Hashem*, which will come about as a result of the return of the *avodah* to the *Beis HaMikdash*.

The central theme of יַעֲלֶה וְיָבֹא seems to be the idea of *zachor*, in which we ask *HaKadosh Baruch Hu* to "remember" us: וְיִפָּקֵד וְיִזָּכֵר זִכְרוֹנֵנוּ וּפִקְדוֹנֵנוּ וְזִכְרוֹן אֲבוֹתֵינוּ, וְזִכְרוֹן מָשִׁיחַ בֶּן דָּוִד עַבְדֶּךָ וְזִכְרוֹן יְרוּשָׁלַיִם עִיר קָדְשֶׁךָ וְזִכְרוֹן כָּל עַמְּךָ בֵּית יִשְׂרָאֵל לְפָנֶיךָ . . . זָכְרֵנוּ ה׳ אֱלֹהֵינוּ בּוֹ לְטוֹבָה וּפָקְדֵנוּ בוֹ לִבְרָכָה. What is meant when we ask *HaKadosh Baruch Hu* to "remember" us? Human beings can forget and need to be reminded, but how does this apply to *HaKadosh Baruch Hu*?

Perhaps we can understand it in the following way. The word זֵכֶר is related to זָכָר, *a male*. In procreation, the function of the male is very fleeting, only a few seconds, but has a lasting effect. Similarly, זֵכֶר is the permanent impression on the brain of something that took but seconds to occur.

It is one of the basic tenets of our *emunah* that our every action, word, or even thought is permanently recorded and is subject to either reward or punishment: וְכָל מַעֲשֶׂיךָ בְּסֵפֶר נִכְתָּבִים, *And all your deeds are recorded in a Book* (*Pirkei Avos* 2:1), which is based on the *pasuk*, אָז נִדְבְּרוּ יִרְאֵי ה׳ אִישׁ אֶת

SHEMONEH ESREI 507

רֵעֵהוּ וַיַּקְשֵׁב ה' וַיִּשְׁמָע וַיִּכָּתֵב סֵפֶר זִכָּרוֹן לְפָנָיו וגו', *Then those who fear Hashem spoke to one another and Hashem listened and heard and a book of remembrance was written before Him* etc. *(Malachi 3:16). Midrash Tanchuma* tells us that כָּל דִּבּוּר וְדִבּוּר שֶׁיָּצָא מִפִּיךָ בַּסֵּפֶר נִכְתָּבִים, *Every spoken word that leaves your mouth is recorded (Metzora* 1). Even seemingly trivial acts are permanently recorded: putting a few pennies in a *pushke,* or a few friendly words spoken to someone to cheer him up. And certainly occupying one's mind with thoughts of holiness; or a *hirhur* of *yiras Shamayim,* a fleeting thought of the fear of Heaven; the suppression of anger or of the desire to say some words of *lashon hara;* the performance of *mitzvos* and the learning of Torah are activities that are permanently recorded by *HaKadosh Baruch Hu.* So the idea of זֵכֶר is the permanent recording of events. Even seemingly unimportant and fleeting events or episodes have permanence.

However, the permanent recording of *mitzvos* has limitations. *Chazal* tell us: עֲבֵירָה מְכַבָּה מִצְוָה, the "fire" of a mitzvah can be extinguished by an aveirah (Sotah 21a). A *mitzvah* can be lost as the result of an *aveirah,* and it will not יַעֲלֶה, *rise up,* to *HaKadosh Baruch Hu* to be recorded and rewarded. This is what is meant by the concept that *HaKadosh Baruch Hu* "forgets." If a person has created a cesspool of *tumah* and *rishus,* uncleanliness and evildoing, his *mitzvos* "go down the drain," instead of rising up to *HaKadosh Baruch Hu* to be rewarded.

We therefore ask *HaKadosh Baruch Hu* in this *tefillah* of יַעֲלֶה וְיָבֹא that, through *teshuvah,* those *mitzvos* that were lost as the result of our *aveiros* may rise up again to Him to be rewarded. So, first we ask *HaKadosh Baruch Hu* that our *mitzvos* may rise up to Him, יַעֲלֶה.

What follows יַעֲלֶה are seven expressions, which are not redundant — each one has its own unique meaning — in which we ask *HaKadosh Baruch Hu* to favorably "remember" us. The Vilna Gaon explains (*Siddur Ishei Yisrael,* following *Gra's* teachings) that the seven words: וְיָבֹא, וְיַגִּיעַ, וְיֵרָאֶה, וְיֵרָצֶה, וְיִשָּׁמַע, וְיִפָּקֵד, וְיִזָּכֵר, correspond to the Kabbalistic concept of the seven Heavens, which are: וִילוֹן, רָקִיעַ, שְׁחָקִים, זְבוּל, מָעוֹן, מָכוֹן, עֲרָבוֹת (*Chagigah* 12b). The only one of these that we can understand is וִילוֹן, *curtain,* which refers to the physical universe, the sky, and this separates us from the spiritual *rekiim.* Similarly, the word *Shamayim* has a physical connotation, that of sky, but it also refers to the spiritual heaven, of which we have no understanding.

❧ אֱלֹהֵינוּ וֵאלֹהֵי אֲבוֹתֵינוּ, יַעֲלֶה, וְיָבֹא, וְיַגִּיעַ, וְיֵרָאֶה, וְיֵרָצֶה, וְיִשָּׁמַע, וְיִפָּקֵד, וְיִזָּכֵר — Our God and the God of our forefathers, may there rise, come, reach, be seen, be willingly received, be heard, receive special attention, and be remembered. Based on the aforementioned, the *tefillah* of יַעֲלֶה וְיָבֹא is a plea to *HaKadosh Baruch Hu* that our *mitzvos,* that may have been drowned and sullied by our *aveiros,* may first rise out of the swamp of our *aveiros.* And then we pray that the acceptance of our *mitzvos* will rise steadily upwards through the various levels of heavenly spheres to be remembered by *HaKadosh Baruch Hu*. These levels of acceptance are expressed as: וְיָבֹא, *and come*; וְיַגִּיעַ, *and reach*; וְיֵרָאֶה, *and be seen*; וְיֵרָצֶה, *and be willingly received*; וְיִשָּׁמַע, *and be heard*; וְיִפָּקֵד, *and shall receive special attention*. And finally, we come to the seventh level which is expressed as וְיִזָּכֵר, corresponding to the *Kisei HaKavod* where, hopefully, our *mitzvos* will be recorded and rewarded by *HaKadosh Baruch Hu*.

§ זִכְרוֹנֵנוּ וּפִקְדוֹנֵנוּ — **The remembrance and consideration of us.** And because of our *teshuvah* may those *mitzvos* that were once destroyed by our *aveiros*, and have now been "reconstructed," receive special attention by *HaKadosh Baruch Hu*. One could also say that זִכְרוֹנֵנוּ refers to *tzaddikim* who have sinned and forfeited *mitzvos*, and וּפִקְדוֹנֵנוּ, "to pay special attention," refers to *baalei teshuvah*.

§ וְזִכְרוֹן אֲבוֹתֵינוּ — **The remembrance of our Forefathers.** This is a reference to the *Avos HaKedoshim* and their *zechuyos*, merits.

§ וְזִכְרוֹן מָשִׁיחַ בֶּן דָּוִד עַבְדֶּךָ — **The remembrance of Mashiach, son of Dovid, Your servant.** We ask *HaKadosh Baruch Hu* to remember *Mashiach*. This is a reference to the words of our *Chachamim*, which are shrouded in mystery, that *Mashiach* was born on the day the *Beis HaMikdash* was destroyed, בַּיּוֹם שֶׁחָרַב בֵּית הַמִּקְדָּשׁ נוֹלַד הַגּוֹאֵל (*Talmud Yerushalmi, Berachos* 2:4, p. 17a). In this sense, *Mashiach* exists now (which would make him several thousand years old!), and we ask that he be revealed to us.

§ וְזִכְרוֹן יְרוּשָׁלַיִם עִיר קָדְשֶׁךָ — **The remembrance of Jerusalem, the city of Your Holiness.** And we ask *HaKadosh Baruch Hu* to remember the holy Yerushalayim of old, filled with *mitzvos*, a place where one could learn *yiras Shamayim* as was its purpose: לְמַעַן תִּלְמַד לְיִרְאָה אֶת ה׳ אֱלֹהֶיךָ, *So that you will learn to fear Hashem, your God* (*Devarim* 14:23). We ask for the reestablishment of Yerushalayim *ir hakodesh*.

§ וְזִכְרוֹן כָּל עַמְּךָ בֵּית יִשְׂרָאֵל לְפָנֶיךָ — **The remembrance of Your entire people, the Family of Israel before You.** This refers to all the *mitzvos* and *maasim tovim* of the entire Jewish nation throughout history. We ask that none of these good deeds be lost to the Jewish nation.

§ לִפְלֵיטָה וּלְטוֹבָה וּלְחֵן וּלְחֶסֶד וּלְרַחֲמִים וּלְחַיִּים וּלְשָׁלוֹם — **For deliverance, for goodness, for grace, for kindness, and for compassion, for life and for peace.** We ask that all of these "memories," the high levels of achievement of the Jewish nation, will not be diminished by our *aveiros*, and that they be לִפְלֵיטָה וגו׳, saved from oblivion and rewarded in these seven ways. Here, again, we have seven expressions that correspond to the seven *rekiim*.

And then we make mention of whichever special day it is, מֵעֵין הַמְּאוֹרָע (the *halachic* requirement to always make note, in the *tefillah,* of a special day of the Jewish calendar on the day it occurs) (*Shabbos* 24a).

We call Rosh Hashanah *Yom HaZikaron,* because on the *Yom HaDin* not only do our *mitzvos* and *maasim tovim* and *zechuyos* go up for review by *HaKadosh Baruch Hu,* but our evil deeds and *aveiros* also come before the *Kisei HaKavod* for judgment on that day. This is the seriousness of the *Yom HaDin.*

This is emphasized in the *Zichronos* of Mussaf of Rosh Hashanah, in which we mention the fact that on the *Yom HaDin,* all of our actions — everything we ever did, good or bad — are brought before *HaKadosh Baruch Hu* for His judgment. Even our thoughts are subject to scrutiny on that day: כִּי זֵכֶר כָּל הַיְצוּר לְפָנֶיךָ בָּא מַעֲשֵׂה אִישׁ וּפְקֻדָּתוֹ וַעֲלִילוֹת מִצְעֲדֵי גָבֶר מַחְשְׁבוֹת אָדָם וְתַחְבּוּלוֹתָיו וְיִצְרֵי מַעַלְלֵי אִישׁ.

Continuing with יַעֲלֶה וְיָבֹא, not only on Rosh Hashanah where it has a special meaning, but at every one of the occasions on which we say it, we ask *HaKadosh Baruch Hu* to remember us, as *He has said He would:*

זָכְרֵנוּ ה' אֱלֹהֵינוּ בּוֹ לְטוֹבָה, וּפָקְדֵנוּ בוֹ לִבְרָכָה, וְהוֹשִׁיעֵנוּ בוֹ לְחַיִּים. וּבִדְבַר יְשׁוּעָה וְרַחֲמִים חוּס וְחָנֵּנוּ וְרַחֵם עָלֵינוּ וְהוֹשִׁיעֵנוּ — **Remember us on it, Hashem, our God, for goodness, consider us on it for blessing, and save us on it for life. And (based on Your) words of salvation and compassion, have mercy and be gracious to us, and have compassion on us and, thus, effect our salvation.** "Words" of salvation and compassion is a reference to the promises that *HaKadosh Baruch Hu* made to us that He will "remember" us and have mercy on us. Some examples are: וְזָכַרְתִּי לָהֶם בְּרִית רִאשֹׁנִים אֲשֶׁר הוֹצֵאתִי אֹתָם מֵאֶרֶץ מִצְרַיִם לְעֵינֵי הַגּוֹיִם, *I will remember for them the covenant of the ancients, those whom I have taken out of the land of Egypt before the eyes of the nations* (Vayikra 26:45); זָכֹר אֶזְכְּרֶנּוּ עוֹד . . . רַחֵם אֲרַחֲמֶנּוּ נְאֻם ה', *I remember him more and more . . . . I will surely take pity on him — the word of Hashem* (Yirmiyahu 31:19); וְזָכַרְתִּי אֲנִי אֶת בְּרִיתִי אוֹתָךְ בִּימֵי נְעוּרָיִךְ וַהֲקִמוֹתִי לָךְ בְּרִית עוֹלָם, *But, I will remember My covenant with you in the days of your youth, and I will establish for you an everlasting covenant* (Yechezkel 16:60).

And here again, in יַעֲלֶה וְיָבֹא, in keeping with the underlying meaning of רְצֵה, we are *mispallel* for a *kiddush Hashem* in the world. At the time of the fulfillment of the promises of דְּבַר יְשׁוּעָה וְרַחֲמִים, when *HaKadosh Baruch Hu* remembers us and brings about the *geulah,* it will cause a worldwide *kiddush Hashem* similar to that which occurred at *yetzias Mitzrayim:* כִּימֵי צֵאתְךָ מֵאֶרֶץ מִצְרַיִם אַרְאֶנּוּ נִפְלָאוֹת, *As in the days when you left the land of Egypt I will show it wonders* (Michah 7:15); The world will once again recognize כִּי אֲנִי ה' אֱלֹהֵיכֶם, *for I am Hashem their God* (Shemos 6:7; also Vayikra 26:44), as it did at the time of *yetzias mitzrayim.* This will be the time when all of mankind will recognize and serve *HaKadosh Baruch Hu*, as we express in our *tefillah* of *Aleinu*: לְתַקֵּן עוֹלָם בְּמַלְכוּת שַׁדַּי וְכָל בְּנֵי בָשָׂר יִקְרְאוּ בִשְׁמֶךָ לְהַפְנוֹת אֵלֶיךָ כָּל רִשְׁעֵי אָרֶץ, *To perfect the universe through the Almighty's sovereignty. Then all humanity will call upon Your Name to turn all the earth's wicked toward You.*

❧ כִּי אֵלֶיךָ עֵינֵינוּ כִּי אֵל מֶלֶךְ חַנּוּן וְרַחוּם אָתָּה ❧ — **For our eyes are turned to You, because You are God, the gracious and compassionate King.**

Let us now return to רְצֵה, and complete the *berachah*.

❧ וְתֶחֱזֶינָה עֵינֵינוּ בְּשׁוּבְךָ לְצִיּוֹן בְּרַחֲמִים ❧ — **May our eyes see Your merciful return to Tziyon.** Rav Breuer once told me that the use of the word חִזָּיוֹן always means to "see with prophetic eyes." This is unlike the usage of יִרְאוּ עֵינֵינוּ וְיִשְׂמַח לִבֵּנוּ וְתָגֵל נַפְשֵׁנוּ בִּישׁוּעָתְךָ בֶּאֱמֶת in *Maariv*, which refers to the physical, visual experience of seeing the rebuilding of *Yerushalayim* and the *Beis HaMikdash*. But to actually conceptualize the return of the *Shechinah* to *Tziyon*, one needs the vision of a *Navi*.

Our *Chachamim* tell us, עֲשָׂרָה נִסִּים נַעֲשׂוּ לַאֲבוֹתֵינוּ בְּבֵית הַמִּקְדָּשׁ, *Ten miracles were performed for our ancestors in the Holy Temple* (*Pirkei Avos* 5:7). In addition to those that are listed, it is obvious upon reflection that much of the *avodah* in the *Beis HaMikdash* could only be possible as *nissim*. For instance, the *mitzvah* of *korban pesach* requires everyone to eat at least a *kezayis,* including children who have reached the age of *chinuch*. Imagine, there would be millions of Jews who would have to have their *korban pesach* brought to the *Mizbe'ach,* and all the necessary *avodos* performed for each lamb, all in the span of several hours in the afternoon of the 14th of Nissan. To accomplish this, even if fifty people were to participate in bringing one lamb, it would be nothing short of a *neis*.

[Ed. note: See *Pesachim* 64b where King Agrippas ordered the counting of the *pesachim*. The total found at that time was כִּפְלַיִם כְּיוֹצְאֵי מִצְרָיִם (1,200,000). Assuming at least ten people per lamb, as the Gemara there says, this would represent a Jewish population of at least 12,000,000, חוּץ מִטָּמֵא וְשֶׁהָיָה בְדֶרֶךְ רְחוֹקָה, besides those who were not able to participate. Imagine the processing of 1,200,000 lambs in a matter of a few hours on the afternoon of 14 Nissan!]

The *mitzvah* of *aliyah l'regel* three times a year likewise presumes a *neis*. This *mitzvah* requires every Jewish male to appear in the *Beis HaMikdash* bearing *korbanos* such as *olos re'iyah, shalmei chagigah, shalmei simchah,* etc., to comply with the *mitzvah* of וְלֹא יֵרָאוּ פָנַי רֵיקָם, *Do not appear before Me empty-handed* (*Shemos* 23:15). Even if everyone's *korbanos* were brought over a period of seven days, the practical application of this *mitzvah* is hardly imaginable, unless this, too, is a *neis*.

Another example of a *neis* that occurred in the *Beis HaMikdash* is the *mitzvah* of *Hakheil*. Once in seven years every Jewish man, woman, and child, including infants who have to be carried, are obligated to be present while the *melech* reads selections from *Sefer Devarim* in the courtyard (*Ezras Nashim*) of the *Beis HaMikdash*. How is it possible for many millions of Jews to fit into this relatively small area? Such a mass of people would hardly fit into the entire city of Yerushalayim! This, too, is nothing short of a *neis*.

To see these occurrences for what they are — open *nissim* which are a manifestation of the Presence of the *Shechinah* in Yerushalayim — requires visionary eyes similar to that of a *navi*. And it is this insight that we ask for when we say וְתֶחֱזֶינָה עֵינֵינוּ בְּשׁוּבְךָ לְצִיּוֹן. However, we add the word בְּרַחֲמִים because without *rachamim* we would be unworthy of being blessed with the ability to see all of these activities surrounding the *avodah* in the *Beis HaMikdash* for what they really are, obvious open miracles.

ס**ּ בָּרוּךְ אַתָּה ה', הַמַּחֲזִיר שְׁכִינָתוֹ לְצִיּוֹן — Blessed are You, Hashem, Who restores His Presence to Tziyon.** This *berachah* is said in the present tense, although it has not happened yet, because we have such *emunah* that *HaKadosh Baruch Hu* will return His presence to Tziyon that we can visualize it before our eyes, as if it has already taken place.

Usually, the word Tziyon refers to the *Beis HaMikdash*, as in מִשְׁכַּן צִיּוֹן כְּבוֹדֶךָ, and Yerushalayim means the city, וְלִירוּשָׁלַיִם עִירְךָ. [*Tanach* is replete with examples of this.]

Tziyon conveys the idea of the "outstanding" aspect of the Jewish nation. It describes the *Beis HaMikdash*, with its focal point being the *Kodesh HaKadashim*, which contains evidence of the *Torah Shebichsav* and *Torah Shebe'al Peh*. It radiates the truth of Torah to the world through the Sanhedrin that sits within its portals, כִּי מִצִּיּוֹן תֵּצֵא תוֹרָה (*Yeshayahu* 2:3). Therefore we could say that Tziyon, the *Beis HaMikdash*, represents the *neshamah* of the Jewish nation.

And Yerushalayim, the city, could be said to represent the *guf* of the Jewish nation. It is the embodiment of the *Torah miTziyon* in the physical life of *Am Yisrael*. Accordingly, Yerushalayim, as the incorporation of the *Torah miTziyon* — with all the mundane activities of the physical life of the Jewish nation — has *kedushah*. The *Navi* describes it as: וְהָיָה כָּל סִיר בִּירוּשָׁלַיִם וּבִיהוּדָה קֹדֶשׁ לַה׳ צְבָאוֹת, *And it will happen that every pot in Yerushalayim and in Yehudah will be holy unto Hashem, Master of Legions* (*Zechariah* 14:21). Even the cooking pots will be קֹדֶשׁ לַה׳. The entire walled city of Yerushalayim is the place where *kadashim kalim* are to be eaten, including the *korban pesach;* and *maaser sheni* is likewise to be eaten there.

However, in the Mussaf of Yamim Tovim, we find the usage: וַהֲבִיאֵנוּ לְצִיּוֹן עִירְךָ בְּרִנָּה וְלִירוּשָׁלַיִם בֵּית מִקְדָּשְׁךָ בְּשִׂמְחַת עוֹלָם. This says that Tziyon is the city, and the *Beis HaMikdash* is called Yerushalayim. This is so because when we are first brought back to Yerushalayim after the *galus*, וַהֲבִיאֵנוּ, we will want to begin bringing the *korbanos* immediately, even before the *Beis HaMikdash* is built, in keeping with the dictum: מַקְרִיבִין אַף עַל פִּי שֶׁאֵין בַּיִת, *Korbanos can be brought even in the absence of the Beis HaMikdash* (*Zevachim* 62a). Therefore, upon our return, the place in Yerushalayim on the desolate *Har HaBayis* where the *Korbanos* will first be brought will be called צִיּוֹן עִירְךָ, and בֵּית מִקְדָּשְׁךָ יְרוּשָׁלַיִם, *Yerushalayim Your Beis HaMikdash,* because the *Korbanos* will be brought only within the "walls of Yerushalayim", and not yet within the enclosure of the *Beis HaMikdash*. However, this will only be temporary, at the moment of וַהֲבִיאֵנוּ. However, afterwards, when the *Beis HaMikdash* is built, Tziyon will be the *Beis HaMikdash,* and the rest of the city will be called יְרוּשָׁלַיִם עִירְךָ.

[Ed. note: For a broader explanation of the concept of צִיּוֹן, see the Rav's comments on *Kedushah* — יִמְלֹךְ ה׳ לְעוֹלָם אֱלֹהַיִךְ צִיּוֹן. And see also the Rav's comments on הוֹדָאָה — וְתִשְׁכּוֹן בְּתוֹכָהּ in the *berachah* of וְלִירוּשָׁלַיִם עִירְךָ, for a broader explanation of מַקְרִיבִין אַף עַל פִּי שֶׁאֵין בַּיִת.]

הוֹדָאָה

֎ מוֹדִים אֲנַחְנוּ לָךְ — **We gratefully thank You.** This second *berachah* of the last part of *Shemoneh Esrei* is called הוֹדָאָה (see *Megillah* 18a etc.). Following our earlier explanation that רְצֵה corresponds to the *menachos,* מוֹדִים corresponds to the *nesachim,* the wine libations that accompany the *menachos.* The wine expresses the idea that we attribute all of the joy in our lives to the special blessings that *HaKadosh Baruch Hu* has bestowed upon us, and we thereby give thanks to Him for it. This is inherent in the idea of עִבְדוּ אֶת ה׳ בְּשִׂמְחָה, *Serve Hashem with gladness* (*Tehillim* 100:2).

Our *Chachamim* tell us that while the *nesachim* were being offered on the *Mizbe'ach,* the *Leviim* accompanied the service with their songs of praise to *HaKadosh Baruch Hu:* הַשִּׁיר שֶׁהָיוּ הַלְוִיִּם אוֹמְרִים בְּבֵית הַמִּקְדָּשׁ, *The daily song that the Leviim would recite in the Temple* (*Tamid* 7:4). Similarly, in reciting the *berachah* of מוֹדִים אֲנַחְנוּ לָךְ, we too "sing songs of praise" to express our gratitude to *HaKadosh Baruch Hu* for bestowing His blessings upon us. We now list these blessings:

֎ שָׁאַתָּה הוּא ה׳ אֱלֹהֵינוּ — **For it is You Who are Hashem, our God.** First and foremost, we thank *HaKadosh Baruch Hu* for revealing to us that He exists. Had *HaKadosh Baruch Hu* not done so, we would never have known. We would know just as little about His existence as a fish swimming in a tank knows about the world outside his tank. To the fish, the tank is the whole world. He does not know that there are people outside the tank looking in. We would be in the same predicament were it not for the fact that *HaKadosh Baruch Hu* revealed His existence to us. So the first blessing for which we thank *HaKadosh Baruch Hu* is that He has bestowed upon us the knowledge that there is a *Borei Olam*, a Creator.

The *sefer Torah* starts with בְּרֵאשִׁית בָּרָא אֱלֹהִים אֵת הַשָּׁמַיִם וְאֵת הָאָרֶץ. The *taamei hamikrah*, the cantillation mark at the word *Elohim* is an *asnachta*, whose function is similar to a comma ending a phrase. One wonders why this simple sentence consists of two phrases. However, this separation conveys the fact that the first and foremost truth in the Torah is בְּרֵאשִׁית בָּרָא אֱלֹהִים, which means that there is a Creator, *Elohim*, Who created everything out of nothing. Nothing existed before He created it. If one does not accept and believe this first phrase, he might as well close the *sefer Torah* and not continue any further.

◆§ וֵאלֹהֵי אֲבוֹתֵינוּ לְעוֹלָם וָעֶד — **And the God of our Forefathers for all eternity.** Second, we thank *HaKadosh Baruch Hu* for giving our Forefathers, Avraham, Yitzchak, and Yaakov, the ability and wisdom to hand down to us the details of the knowledge of *HaKadosh Baruch Hu* which they had received when He revealed Himself to them. And this knowledge remains with us forever.

◆§ צוּר חַיֵּינוּ — **Rock of our lives.** In thanking Him we call Him the *Rock of our lives*, because He is the basis of all existence. We would not exist if there were no *Ribbono Shel Olam*.

◆§ מָגֵן יִשְׁעֵנוּ — **Shield of our salvation.** We express the idea here that not only is *HaKadosh Baruch Hu* the basis of our existence, but also if it would not be for His constant protection at every stage of our lives, we could not survive in this world. Human life, starting from its very conception until the last moment of our physical existence, is fraught with danger. We live in an environment that is also inhabited by billions of bacteria and microscopic organisms, many of which are extremely dangerous. In our daily interaction with other people, we are exposed to all sorts of dangerous diseases and contaminants. Our *Chachamim* tell us that the world is filled with *mazikim*, destructive forces, which, if we could see them, would frighten us to death, אִלְמָלֵי נִתְּנָה רְשׁוּת לָעַיִן לִרְאוֹת וגו' (*Berachos* 6a). Therefore, were it not for *HaKadosh Baruch Hu*, Who constantly shields us from all of these dangers, we could not survive.

◆§ אַתָּה הוּא לְדוֹר וָדוֹר נוֹדֶה לְּךָ וּנְסַפֵּר תְּהִלָּתֶךָ — **Are You — from generation to generation. We thank You and tell of Your praise.** This is one of those phrases in the *tefillah* that could be read in two ways, אֵין לוֹ הֶכְרֵעַ.

It could be read: אַתָּה הוּא לְדוֹר וָדוֹר, referring back to צוּר חַיֵּינוּ and מָגֵן יִשְׁעֵנוּ. Or it could be read as אַתָּה הוּא לְדוֹר וָדוֹר נוֹדֶה לְּךָ וּנְסַפֵּר תְּהִלָּתֶךָ. Each of these readings is correct.

The meaning of נוֹדֶה לְךָ means more than "we thank You." It conveys the thought: "We confess our thanks to You." This meaning is similar to מוֹדֶה בִּשְׁטָר שֶׁכָּתְבוֹ, *he admits that he wrote the document* (see *Kesubos* 19a), where it has the meaning of admission, or acknowledgment of a fact. The idea expressed is that we "confess" that we owe immense gratitude to *HaKadosh Baruch Hu,* but we have no way of repaying Him. While we cannot pay our debt to *HaKadosh Baruch Hu,* what we can do is נְסַפֵּר תְּהִלָּתֶךָ, "tell of Your praises." We praise *HaKadosh Baruch Hu* whenever the situation warrants it. This is the reason for the Jewish *minhag* to respond to inquiries about one's well being with, "*Baruch Hashem,*" "Thank God I'm fine."

Continuing here, we "confess" our indebtedness to *HaKadosh Baruch Hu* especially for the following:

≈§ עַל חַיֵּינוּ הַמְּסוּרִים בְּיָדֶךָ §≈ — **For our lives which are entrusted into Your hand.** First, we thank *HaKadosh Baruch Hu* that we are alive. He holds our entire life in His hand, from birth until our last breath. We live and die by His will.

≈§ וְעַל נִשְׁמוֹתֵינוּ הַפְּקוּדוֹת לָךְ §≈ — **For our souls which are in Your care.** Before we were born our *neshamah* was a *pikadon,* "on deposit," with *HaKadosh Baruch Hu;* while we are alive *HaKadosh Baruch Hu* keeps our *neshamah* within our body, אַתָּה מְשַׁמְּרָהּ בְּקִרְבִּי (see above on אֱלֹהַי נְשָׁמָה); and after our *neshamah* leaves our body at death, it is still entrusted in the hands of *HaKadosh Baruch Hu.*

≈§ וְעַל נִסֶּיךָ שֶׁבְּכָל יוֹם עִמָּנוּ §≈ — **For Your miracles which are with us every day.** This refers to the *nissim nistarim* (hidden miracles) with which our lives are filled, although we may not even be aware of them, אֵין בַּעַל הַנֵּס מַכִּיר בְּנִסּוֹ (see *Niddah* 31a). In our daily lives, we are the constant recipients of these "hidden miracles." A person could contract a major illness which, were it seen by a doctor, would be diagnosed as such, but then it miraculously passes and he is never aware of it, and is none the worse for it. Who knows how many dangerous situations a person goes through in his daily life without even being aware of it. He may ride the subway and be confronted by a dangerous criminal who had evil intentions for him, which were averted; or he may be in an airplane that had a bomb planted in it which did not detonate. Our lives are filled with such examples.

We refer here only to *nissim nistarim.* However, regarding the *nissim geluyim,* open and obvious miracles, that we have experienced, these are the subjects of *tefillos* at other occasions. But on Purim and Chanukah, by adding עַל הַנִּסִּים, we do include our thanks for the miraculous events that occurred on those occasions, because these, too, consisted of *nissim nistarim.* Interestingly, on Chanukah we do not mention the *neis* of the *pach hashemen* (flask of oil), because that was a *neis nigleh,* and would not fit into the general tone of *Modim.*

וְעַל נִפְלְאוֹתֶיךָ וְטוֹבוֹתֶיךָ שֶׁבְּכָל עֵת, עֶרֶב וָבֹקֶר וְצָהֳרָיִם **— And for Your wondrous deeds and bestowal of goodness, which occurs at all times — evening, morning, and afternoon.** This has a double meaning. The first is its simple, literal, meaning of thanking *HaKadosh Baruch Hu* for all the hidden miraculous events, which constantly occur all the time, for which we express our thanks *evening, morning, and afternoon,* referring to the *tefillos* of Maariv, Shacharis, and Minchah. In this sense it would be similar to that which was said by Dovid HaMelech: עֶרֶב וָבֹקֶר וְצָהֳרַיִם אָשִׂיחָה וגו׳, *I pray to You evening, morning, and afternoon (Tehillim 55:18).*

However, עֶרֶב וָבֹקֶר וְצָהֳרָיִם also has a secondary meaning, that of the moods or circumstances in which one may find himself.

❏ עֶרֶב: One may find himself in an "emotional state of *erev.*" He feels that his life is declining, either because of age or lack of *mazal;* everything is getting darker and darker, he feels more and more hopeless, until eventually it will all come to an end.

❏ בֹּקֶר: Or a person may be in a *boker* state of life, in which he sees some light coming into his life, and little by little things begin to turn around for him.

❏ צָהֳרָיִם: Or one may be experiencing the *tzaharayim* of his life; there is bright sunshine all around him; he is successful in whatever he does; he has the feeling that he is "on top of the world."

In this sense, we give thanks to *HaKadosh Baruch Hu* for עַל חַיֵּינוּ הַמְּסוּרִים בְּיָדֶךָ, for our lives which You hold in Your hand, and נִפְלְאוֹתֶיךָ וְטוֹבוֹתֶיךָ שֶׁבְּכָל עֵת, whether we are experiencing, or have experienced, a life of *erev,* or *boker,* or *tzaharayim.*

Another, deeper explanation is that עֶרֶב וָבֹקֶר וְצָהֳרָיִם is a characterization of the three forms of our existence.

This world, *Olam Hazeh,* is characterized as *erev,* evening, because it eventually ends up with לַיְלָה, nighttime, at the time of death. No matter how happy a person is in life, eventually he faces his inevitable demise when his *neshamah* leaves his *guf.*

After the *neshamah* is separated from the *guf,* there follows an existence of *boker,* in which the *neshamah* — as well as the *guf* — must go through a purification process, the *neshamah* in *Gan Eden,* and the *guf* in the earth. This is the "break of dawn" for the ultimate form of everlasting life, that of *techiyas hameisim,* the *tzaharayim,* the "bright noontime" of existence.

In this sense, we give thanks to *HaKadosh Baruch Hu* for the three forms of our existence, עֶרֶב וָבֹקֶר וְצָהֳרָיִם, which He holds in His hand.

[Ed. note: See *Maayan Beis HaSho'evah, Bereishis* 4:16 for the source of this way of explaining עֶרֶב וָבֹקֶר וְצָהֳרָיִם, and a further explanation of it.]

The underlying idea of all these interpretations is that regardless of which station of life, physical or spiritual, we may find ourselves in, we express our

עַל חַיֵּינוּ הַמְּסוּרִים בְּיָדֶךָ וְעַל existence, our for *HaKadosh Baruch Hu* to מוֹדִים
נִפְלְאוֹתֶיךָ וְטוֹבוֹתֶיךָ שֶׁבְּכָל עֵת and נִסֶּיךָ שֶׁבְּכָל יוֹם עִמָּנוּ and, נִשְׁמוֹתֵינוּ הַפְּקוּדוֹת לָךְ.

§ הַטּוֹב — Here we call *HaKadosh Baruch Hu*, **The Good One,** per se, and the reason follows.

§ כִּי לֹא כָלוּ רַחֲמֶיךָ — **Because Your mercies never come to an end.** The best example of this is that if one does not use his freedom of choice for the purpose for which it was created, and he does an *aveirah,* by right his life should be forfeited. However, he continues to live. And the reason his life does not end is because the mercy of *HaKadosh Baruch Hu* is boundless, and He will continue to grant this person life. If someone steals, who gives him the ability to steal? Who makes this person's heart beat and empowers his brain to function so that he can carry out his crime? The *rachamim* of *HaKadosh Baruch Hu* is absolute; it is not limited by our violating His will. It is for this reason that we call Him הַטּוֹב.

§ וְהַמְרַחֵם — Further, we call *HaKadosh Baruch Hu,* **The Merciful One,** per se. And the reason follows.

§ כִּי לֹא תַמּוּ חֲסָדֶיךָ — **Because Your kindness is never exhausted.** No matter how many times we ask *HaKadosh Baruch Hu* for mercy, we can count on Him to respond, whether we deserve it or not, because His goodness and mercy never come to an end. In human experience, how many times can one ask another to lend him some money? After a few times the response will be, "I have already given you money so many times; that is enough!" However, with *HaKadosh Baruch Hu* we ask for His mercy — and can look forward to its fulfillment — time and time again, every day as long as we live. He is therefore called *The Merciful One.*

§ מֵעוֹלָם קִוִּינוּ לָךְ — (Since we can remember) **we have always hoped for You.** One of the greatest *chassadim* that *HaKadosh Baruch Hu* has shown us is that He has given us the ability to sustain hope and never to give up, even in the face of the greatest adversity. Historically, the Jewish nation has found strength in putting its hope in *HaKadosh Baruch Hu.* The words קִוִּינוּ and תִּקְוָה stem from the word קַו, meaning a piece of string or rope that attaches two objects. We find this use in תִּקְוַת חוּט הַשָּׁנִי, *cord of scarlet thread* (*Yehoshua* 2:18); and נָטָה קָו, *stretches a "line"* (*Yeshayahu* 44:13).

Therefore, the underlying meaning of מֵעוֹלָם קִוִּינוּ לָךְ is that throughout our history we have maintained an unbroken attachment to *HaKadosh Baruch Hu* through our unshakable hope that He would answer our *tefillos,* even if the outlook was totally hopeless. This is followed by *al hanissim* on Purim and Chanukah, when we mention the salvation of *Klal Yisrael.* At each of these times, the outlook for the survival of the Jewish nation was extremely bleak; nevertheless, we were miraculously saved.

וְעַל כֻּלָּם יִתְבָּרַךְ וְיִתְרוֹמַם שִׁמְךָ מַלְכֵּנוּ תָּמִיד לְעוֹלָם וָעֶד — **For all of the aforementioned** (meaning the *tovos* and *chassadim* and *nissim*) **is Your Name, our King, blessed and held in the highest esteem, constantly, forever and ever.** With this, we end the first part of מוֹדִים, in which we express our thanks to *HaKadosh Baruch Hu* for the goodness and blessings that we have received from Him. We now come to the second part of מוֹדִים. Although it is much shorter than the first part, it is no less important.

וְכֹל הַחַיִּים יוֹדוּךָ סֶּלָה — **The totality of life shall praise You, Selah.** Thanking *HaKadosh Baruch Hu* is only possible while one is alive: בִּשְׁאוֹל מִי יוֹדֶה לָּךְ, *In the grave who will praise You* (*Tehillim* 6:6)? Nobody thanks *HaKadosh Baruch Hu* after death, although life does not cease at that time; only the external, physical, aspect of life ceases. However, the act of *hoda'ah* is a function only of physical life.

It does not say וְכָל הַחַיִּים, *all life,* but rather, וְכֹל הַחַיִּים, which means *the totality of life shall praise You.* סֶלָה means absolutely and unendingly. The "totality of life" includes every living person, even the blind, the sick, the lame, the deaf, and the unhappy, as well as those who are wracked by pain or fears and other psychological or emotional disorders.

When people who are suffering praise *HaKadosh Baruch Hu,* they fulfill the dictum of our *Chachamim,* חַיָּב אָדָם לְבָרֵךְ עַל הָרָעָה כְּשֵׁם שֶׁמְּבָרֵךְ עַל הַטּוֹבָה, *A person is obligated to bless Hashem for the bad just as he does for the good* (*Berachos* 54a). This is based there on וְאָהַבְתָּ אֵת ה' אֱלֹהֶיךָ בְּכָל ... מְאֹדֶךָ, which the Mishnah there explains to mean, בְּכָל מִדָּה וּמִדָּה שֶׁהוּא מוֹדֵד לְךָ הֱוֵי מוֹדֶה לוֹ. We are to love and praise *HaKadosh Baruch Hu* under all circumstances, good or bad, which He metes out to us in life.

The *Mechaber, Shulchan Aruch Orach Chaim* 222:3, goes into uncharacteristic length in explaining this *halachah*: חַיָּב אָדָם לְבָרֵךְ עַל הָרָעָה בְּדַעַת שְׁלֵמָה וּבְנֶפֶשׁ חֲפֵצָה, כְּדֶרֶךְ שֶׁמְּבָרֵךְ בְּשִׂמְחָה עַל הַטּוֹבָה, כִּי הָרָעָה לְעוֹבְדֵי הַשֵּׁם הִיא שִׂמְחָתָם וְטוֹבָתָם כֵּיוָן שֶׁמְּקַבֵּל מֵאַהֲבָה מַה שֶּׁגָּזַר עָלָיו הַשֵּׁם, נִמְצָא שֶׁבְּקַבָּלַת רָעָה זוֹ הוּא עוֹבֵד אֶת הַשֵּׁם שֶׁהִיא שִׂמְחָה לוֹ.

What the *Mechaber* intends here is that the acceptance of suffering becomes a form of *avodas Hashem* and, as with all *avodas Hashem,* must be done *b'simchah,* in accordance with the dictum: עִבְדוּ אֶת ה' בְּשִׂמְחָה, *Serve Hashem with gladness* (*Tehillim* 100:2).

We find the statement, נַעַר הָיִיתִי גַּם זָקַנְתִּי וְלֹא רָאִיתִי צַדִּיק נֶעֱזָב וְזַרְעוֹ מְבַקֶּשׁ לָחֶם, *I have been a youth and also aged; but I have not seen a righteous man forsaken, whose children were begging for bread* (*Tehillim* 37:25). This is understood by some of our *Chachamim* to mean, "I have never seen a *tzaddik* forsaken — even if he sees that his children are looking for bread."

[Ed. note: See *Maharash Di Ozidah,* quoted in "*Beis HaKnesses,*" in the *sefer Mikdash Me'at* on *Tehillim* for this way of explaining it.]

Whatever the circumstances, a *tzaddik* never feels that he is נֶעֱזָב, *forsaken by HaKadosh Baruch Hu*. In accepting the will of *HaKadosh Baruch Hu* in all conditions of his life, he feels as close to *HaKadosh Baruch Hu* in times of deprivation as he does in the good times of his life. This is what is meant by וְכֹל הַחַיִּים יוֹדוּךָ סֶּלָה. All of life, good — or seemingly bad — shall praise You.

In quoting this, I am reminded of a very personal incident that occurred when I was 5 or 6 years old. In Germany, during the First World War, there were severe food shortages, and rationing was instituted by the government. Each family was allotted only one *"kommissbrot"* — a large loaf of black bread, which was a mixture of flour, potato peels, and other ingredients — per week, for each person in the household. In our family, the name of each child was written on his own loaf so that each family member had his full ration. My mother, ע״ה, cut a slice of my black bread — which tasted awful; nobody would eat it today — and gave it to me. After hungrily swallowing it, I asked: "Please give me another slice of bread, I'm hungry." Whereupon she reprimanded me, in seeming anger, "You don't need it; you've eaten enough!" However, unbeknown to my dear, sensitive, mother, I noticed that she turned around and shed a tear, and that tear dropped onto the bread and made a slight indentation in it, as occurs when liquid falls on a soft surface. I have never forgotten the impression of that tear on my loaf of bread, when my mother could not satisfy her hungry child, וְזַרְעוֹ מְבַקֶּשׁ לָחֶם. However, being the *tzaddekes* that she was, I am sure she did not feel נֶעֱזָב, forsaken by *HaKadosh Baruch Hu*, at that moment. She saw this deprivation as the will of *HaKadosh Baruch Hu*, and lovingly accepted it as such.

וִיהַלְלוּ אֶת שִׁמְךָ בֶּאֱמֶת — **And praise Your Name sincerely.** The Name of *HaKadosh Baruch Hu* referred to here is י-ה-ו-ה, which means He is the prime מְהַוֶּה; He causes everything to exist, good and seemingly not good. Although *HaKadosh Baruch Hu* created the world in order to bestow goodness to His creatures — He is the ultimate *tov* and *meracheim* — nevertheless, for reasons of His own, He created people who suffer from birth, and there are others who suffer in their old age. Others live a life of poverty and deprivation. For most people, life is composed of a combination of happiness and pain. There are very few who do not suffer at all during their lives. Nevertheless, we accept His judgment and praise Him בֶּאֱמֶת, under all circumstances of life.

הָאֵל יְשׁוּעָתֵנוּ וְעֶזְרָתֵנוּ סֶלָה — **O God our Savior and Helper forever.** Often, people who suffer see יְשׁוּעָה in their lives. The sick person starts to feel better; the poor person suddenly finds an unexpected source of sustenance; the desperate person sees "light at the end of the tunnel." Therefore, in the first part of this phrase, we address *HaKadosh Baruch Hu* as our "Savior."

However, there are also people for whom there is no alleviation of their suffering. And, recognizing this, we add וְעֶזְרָתֵנוּ סֶלָה, *You are our Helper*

What this means is that if *HaKadosh Baruch Hu* decides that a person's suffering should not be alleviated, and he suffers in this world, it should be viewed as עֶזְרָתֵנוּ, as being instrumental in helping him achieve the blissful everlasting existence of the World to Come, סֶלָה. Our *Chachamim* say, יִסּוּרִים מְמָרְקִין כָּל עֲוֹנוֹתָיו שֶׁל אָדָם, *Suffering cleanses all of a person's sins* (*Berachos* 5a), and יִסּוּרִין מְבִיאִין אֶת הָאָדָם לְחַיֵּי הָעוֹלָם הַבָּא, *Suffering (helps) to bring a person to the World to Come* (*Pesikta Zutrasi,* beginning of *Eikev*). Suffering in this world is a means of cleansing and purifying a person of his sins, in preparation for his reward in *Olam Haba.* This is what is meant by עֶזְרָתֵנוּ סֶלָה.

In keeping with our explanation that the *berachah* of מוֹדִים corresponds to the *shirah* that accompanied the *nesachim,* this second part of מוֹדִים constitutes an even higher form of *shirah* — in which we praise God for the seemingly bad as well as the good. This is similar to that which was sung by the psalmist Assaf: הַרְנִינוּ לֵאלֹהִים עוּזֵּנוּ הָרִיעוּ לֵאלֹהֵי יַעֲקֹב, *Jubilate to God Who is our strength; blow a teruah to the God of Yaakov* (*Tehillim* 81:2). *Teruah* is a sound of anguish and pain (see גְּנוּחֵי גָנַח, יַלּוּלֵי יַלִּיל, *Rosh Hashanah* 33b). The Psalmist exclaims here that even when the Jewish nation, as "Yaakov," cries out in pain, it still jubilates before God, and happily accepts His will. "Yaakov" is the name of our nation while it is in a condition of suffering, reminiscent of the life of suffering of Yaakov Avinu. The joyful acceptance of the will of *HaKadosh Baruch Hu* is the source of our strength.

Based on this, we now conclude the *berachah*:

₪ בָּרוּךְ אַתָּה ה׳, הַטּוֹב שִׁמְךָ וּלְךָ נָאֶה לְהוֹדוֹת ₪ — **Blessed are You, Hashem, The Good One is Your Name, and it is (therefore) fitting to thank You.** Even if we suffer, *chas v'shalom, it is fitting to thank You.* This means that even if we are afflicted with suffering and pain, we accept it as a *tovah* — although we may not understand it — because *HaKadosh Baruch Hu* is pure *tov.* By accepting suffering as such, we become very close to *HaKadosh Baruch Hu.*

While ending this *berachah,* we bow down as an expression of our thankfulness to *HaKadosh Baruch Hu.* Our *Chachamim* have instituted that we bow down twice at מוֹדִים, once here at the end, and once at the beginning (see *Berachos* 34a and *Shulchan Aruch, Orach Chaim* 121:1).

In bowing at the beginning, we express our thanks to *HaKadosh Baruch Hu* for all the good that we have received from Him. And in bowing here, at the second part of מוֹדִים, in which we included וְכֹל הַחַיִּים יוֹדוּךָ סֶּלָה, the totality of life, even the seemingly bad in the world, we fulfill the requirement of thanking *HaKadosh Baruch Hu* for the bad with the same love and enthusiasm as we thank Him for the good: חַיָּב אָדָם לְבָרֵךְ עַל הָרָעָה בְּדַעַת שְׁלֵמָה וּבְנֶפֶשׁ חֲפֵצָה, כְּדֶרֶךְ שֶׁמְּבָרֵךְ בְּשִׂמְחָה עַל הַטּוֹבָה (cf. *Berachos* 54a; *Shulchan Aruch, Orach Chaim* 222:3).

Interestingly, the Gemara states: שִׁדְּרוֹ שֶׁל אָדָם לְאַחַר שֶׁבַע שָׁנִים נַעֲשֶׂה נָחָשׁ וַהֲנֵי

מִילֵּי דְּלֹא כָּרַע בְּמוֹדִים, If one does not bow at *Modim,* his spine will turn into a snake after seven years (*Bava Kamma* 16a). It is common knowledge that every piece of *Aggadata* has a profound meaning, but it is not always simple to decipher its true explanation. In this case, it is possible that our *Chachamim* intended to convey the idea that if one does not show his gratitude to *HaKadosh Baruch Hu* and bow at מוֹדִים, he is acting in a way similar to the *nachash hakadmoni,* the serpent in Gan Eden, whose ingratitude caused it to be downgraded from a highly intelligent animal to a lowly snake which, like other animals, does not have the capacity to show its gratitude to the Source of its existence.

The *nachash hakadmoni* referred to in the Torah, in connection with the *cheit* (sin) of Adam and Chavah, was by no means identical with the snakes with which we are familiar. This was the one creature that was given the highest intelligence of all the animals, including the power of speech. וְהַנָּחָשׁ הָיָה עָרוּם מִכֹּל חַיַּת הַשָּׂדֶה, *Now the serpent was cunning beyond any beast of the field* (*Bereishis* 3:1). However, this creature, in an act of profound ingratitude, utilized its great intelligence against its Creator, *HaKadosh Baruch Hu.*

In meting out its punishment, *HaKadosh Baruch Hu* decreed, among other things, עָפָר תֹּאכַל כָּל יְמֵי חַיֶּיךָ, *You shall eat dust as long as you live* (ibid. 3:14). And our *Chachamim* tell us (*Yoma* 75a) that because of this, whatever the snake eats — even the greatest delicacy — tastes like dust, as it says, וְנָחָשׁ עָפָר לַחְמוֹ, *A snake's food will be dust* (*Yeshayahu* 65:25). But, the *Chachamim* add, this curse of the *nachash* also makes it possible for it to find food wherever it may be, because dust is available everywhere, עוֹלֶה לַגַּג מְזוֹנוֹתָיו עִמּוֹ, יוֹרֵד לְמַטָּה מְזוֹנוֹתָיו עִמּוֹ. We may therefore conclude that this constant availability of its food is a part of the curse and downgrading of the *nachash hakadmoni.* It was reduced from a highly intelligent animal — which recognized *HaKadosh Baruch Hu,* and could appreciate that He provides it with its food — עֵינֵי כֹל אֵלֶיךָ יְשַׂבֵּרוּ וְאַתָּה נוֹתֵן לָהֶם אֶת אָכְלָם בְּעִתּוֹ — to that of a common snake, which does not possess this ability. Because of its ingratitude, it was condemned forever to a life of unawareness and ingratitude similar to other animals. It lost the ability to recognize *HaKadosh Baruch Hu* as the Source of its sustenance, and therefore to have the opportunity to be grateful to Him for it.

One of man's greatest blessings is that he is able to recognize the *hashgachah pratis* of *HaKadosh Baruch Hu* in his daily existence and express his gratitude to Him for it.

מוֹדִים דְּרַבָּנָן

Our *Chachamim* tell us that during *chazaras hashatz,* while the *chazzan* is saying מוֹדִים, the people are expected to express their own words of thanksgiving. בִּזְמַן שֶׁהַשָּׁלִיחַ צִבּוּר אוֹמֵר מוֹדִים הָעָם מַה הֵם אוֹמְרִים, *While the Chazan is* saying Modim, what do the people say? (Sotah 40a). This is a strange question. During the recitation of all the other *berachos* during *chazaras hashatz*, the people are expected merely to listen and say *amen*. The reason that the people are expected to add their own words of thanksgiving while the *chazzan* is saying מוֹדִים is given by *Avudraham* (*Seder Shacharis shel Chol* 115): שֶׁאֵין דֶּרֶךְ הָעֶבֶד לְהוֹדוֹת לְרַבּוֹ וְלוֹמַר לוֹ אֲדוֹנִי אַתָּה עַל יְדֵי שָׁלִיחַ. If one wishes to properly express his thanks and show servitude to his master, he must do so personally; it is inappropriate to express one's gratitude to his master through a third party.

The מוֹדִים that the *chazzan* says is a part of *chazaras hashatz* which was instituted by our *Chachamim* to represent those people who, for various reasons, could not say their own *Shemoneh Esrei*. However, this does not absolve each individual who is able to do so from saying his own *tefillah* (see *Rosh Hashanah* 34b-35a). It is of utmost importance that the entire מוֹדִים — as is the case with the rest of the *Shemoneh Esrei* — be said aloud by the *chazzan*. It is absolutely improper for the *chazzan* to begin מוֹדִים quietly, only to be heard once again somewhere in the middle thereof, for example, at הַטּוֹב כִּי לֹא כָלוּ רַחֲמֶיךָ.

While the מוֹדִים which is part of the regular *Shemoneh Esrei* represents the collective expression of the gratitude of *Klal Yisrael* for all the blessings listed in it, it also includes the personal thanks of each individual for all those blessings as they affect him. מוֹדִים דְּרַבָּנָן, however, is the communal מוֹדִים of *Klal Yisrael* as a nation, and therefore it is said only in a *tzibbur,* and not when one *davens* alone.

There are five different opinions listed in the previously quoted Gemara (*Sotah* 40a) as to exactly what the *tzibbur* should say as its *hoda'ah* while the *chazzan* is saying מוֹדִים. However, all five agree that the common refrain in each of these *hoda'os* should be מוֹדִים אֲנַחְנוּ לָךְ עַל שֶׁאָנוּ מוֹדִים לָךְ. In *Yerushalmi, Berachos* 1:1, we find a slightly different version: עַל שֶׁאָנוּ חַיָּבִים לְהוֹדוֹת לָךְ, *We thank You for the fact that we are thankful to You* (or *we are obligated to be thankful to You*). This is explained by Rashi there: עַל שֶׁנָּתַתָּ בְּלִבֵּנוּ לִהְיוֹת דְּבוּקִים בָּךְ וּמוֹדִים לָךְ, *[We are thankful to You] because You have placed in our minds the idea that we should be attached to You — and be thankful to You.* Remarkably, here we are thanking *HaKadosh Baruch Hu* for instilling the concept of gratitude into our minds! And it is for this reason that we end the entire מוֹדִים דְּרַבָּנָן with בָּרוּךְ אֵל הַהוֹדָאוֹת, *Blessed is the God of thanksgiving.*

We are born as ingrates; the trait of gratitude is not instinctive. Natural life is taken for granted, because one has been alive for as long he can remember. No one is born with a natural impulse of gratitude for being alive. The form of "gratitude" evidenced by animals to their master — or even in small children toward their parents — is only a reciprocal arrangement, because the beneficiary knows that by showing gratitude it will continue to receive its benefits. This is a sort of "business arrangement," similar to saying "thank you" to a customer in the hope of receiving more of his patronage in the future.

The concept of gratitude for its own sake is a gift from *HaKadosh Baruch Hu,* and it comes gradually with maturity. It would never occur to a child — who had never been told to do so — to say "thank you" to his mother or father for what they do for him. Gratitude must be learned. Unfortunately, in many cases, the child has not learned gratitude because it never hears the father say "thank you" to the mother when she brings the food to the table; the mother is treated as a mere waitress. Of course, a *ben Torah,* knowing the importance of *hakaras hatov,* does say thank you even to a waitress — and certainly expresses his gratitude to his wife.

The aforementioned explanation of Rashi, עַל שֶׁנָּתַתָּ בְּלִבֵּנוּ לִהְיוֹת דְּבוּקִים בָּךְ וּמוֹדִים לָךְ, contains the idea that the sense of gratitude to *HaKadosh Baruch Hu* is a form of attachment to Him. The *Chovos HaLevavos* (*Shaar Ahavas Hashem,* Ch. 2) explains that one of the bases of the *mitzvah* of *ahavas Hashem* is gratitude. In other words, love is a form of gratitude. One loves another out of gratitude for the kindness and concern shown by the other person toward him. The result is that the mere presence of the object of one's love makes him happy. This feeling is true as well in one's relationship with *HaKadosh Baruch Hu.* Therefore, when one feels gratitude to *HaKadosh Baruch Hu,* he has, in effect, fulfilled the mitzvah of וְאָהַבְתָּ אֵת ה' אֱלֹהֶיךָ.

This broader definition of *ahavah,* that of attachment, is found in Yehudah's description of the depth of Yaakov's love for his son Binyamin. Yehudah tells Yosef, וְאָבִיו אֲהֵבוֹ, *His father loves him,* which he later defines as וְנַפְשׁוֹ קְשׁוּרָה בְנַפְשׁוֹ, *His soul is attached to his soul* (*Bereishis* 44:20,30).

The aforementioned five opinions in the Gemara (*Sotah* 40a) regarding the *hoda'ah* of the *tzibbur,* in addition to עַל שֶׁאָנוּ מוֹדִים לָךְ ... מוֹדִים אֲנַחְנוּ לָךְ, on which they all agree, are as follows:

(1) In the opinion of Rav, the *tzibbur* should say: מוֹדִים אֲנַחְנוּ לָךְ ה' אֱלֹהֵינוּ. (In our version of this מוֹדִים, it has been extended to read מוֹדִים אֲנַחְנוּ לָךְ שָׁאַתָּה הוּא ה' אֱלֹהֵינוּ וֵאלֹהֵי אֲבוֹתֵינוּ.) As we have already explained in the first מוֹדִים, the first and foremost reason that we thank *HaKadosh Baruch Hu* is because He revealed His existence to us, His nation. Without this revelation, we would never know that He, in fact, exists.

Without the firm knowledge that there is a *Borei Olam,* a Creator of the world to Whom we are answerable, life would not make sense at all. Without a Creator, there is no basis for absolute values or morality. One would commit every crime imaginable — so long as he is not caught — with impunity and without remorse. In revealing to us that He exists,

HaKadosh Baruch Hu has given us the basis of all morality in life. And the knowledge of the existence of HaKadosh Baruch Hu is the basis of our endeavors to study and understand as much as is humanly possible about Him.

(2) This is followed by the opinion of Shmuel who says the *hoda'ah* should include אֱלֹהֵי כָּל בָּשָׂר. This means that our gratitude should not be confined merely to the fact that HaKadosh Baruch Hu is ה' אֱלֹהֵינוּ, *our God,* the God of the Jewish people. Rather, it should also include the fact the He is the *God of all flesh,* because, eventually, all of humanity will also realize the truth of the existence of HaKadosh Baruch Hu.

(3) And this, in turn, is followed by the opinion of Rabi Simai, who says that we should add יוֹצְרֵנוּ יוֹצֵר בְּרֵאשִׁית. While it is true that HaKadosh Baruch Hu is אֱלֹהֵי כָּל בָּשָׂר, nevertheless, we should not lose sight of the fact that He *formed us,* the Jewish nation, at the moment of creation. This means, as our Chachamim tell us, that all of creation was brought about בִּשְׁבִיל יִשְׂרָאֵל, *for the sake of Yisrael.* The ideal for which the world was created was to produce human beings who would be called "Yisrael" (see *Rashi, Bereishis* 1:1, based on קֹדֶשׁ יִשְׂרָאֵל לַה' רֵאשִׁית תְּבוּאָתֹה, *Yirmiyahu* 2:3). And here in this phrase of מוֹדִים, we thank HaKadosh Baruch Hu for giving us the privilege of being members of that nation which, of all the nations of the world, has brought the knowledge of the existence of HaKadosh Baruch Hu into the world.

(4) Then come the Nehardeans, who state in the name of Rabi Simai that we should say: בְּרָכוֹת וְהוֹדָאוֹת לְשִׁמְךָ הַגָּדוֹל עַל שֶׁהֶחֱיִיתָנוּ וְקִיַּמְתָּנוּ. They point out that since the previous *hoda'ah* makes special mention of the Jewish people, we should take this opportunity to "make *Shehecheyanu*" for the fact that we continue to exist as a nation. As individuals, we say *Shehecheyanu* on special occasions, such as *Shalosh Regalim,* etc. when we have survived to see, yet again, another one of the great occasions of the year. This is true also when one eats of the new fruit of the year, or acquires a very valuable possession, each of which is sufficient cause for gratitude and rejoicing. By this *hoda'ah* we, as a nation, offer our collective *Shehecheyanu* for our survival despite thousands of years of persecution, שֶׁבְּכָל דּוֹר וָדוֹר עוֹמְדִים עָלֵינוּ לְכַלּוֹתֵינוּ.

This is especially true in our time. There has never been a century so filled with murderous monsters who were — and are — bent on destroying the Jewish nation. Imagine, in our time alone, there arose murderers the likes of Hitler, Mussolini, Stalin, Idi Amin, Khomeini, Khaddafi, Saddam Hussein, etc. יִמַּח שְׁמָם וְזִכְרָם. And yet, despite all of these, we have survived as a nation. So when we look back on our history, we come to the realization that we have to "make a *Shehecheyanu*" every day for our survival.

(5) And finally, Rav Acha bar Yaakov says that we should add to this *Shehecheyanu* the following: כֵּן תְּחַיֵּינוּ וּתְחָנֵּנוּ וְתִקַבְּצֵנוּ וְתֶאֱסוֹף גָּלֻיּוֹתֵינוּ לְחַצְרוֹת

קָדְשֶׁךָ לִשְׁמוֹר חֻקֶּיךָ וְלַעֲשׂוֹת רְצוֹנְךָ בְּלֵבָב שָׁלֵם, so will You continue to keep us alive and be gracious to us, bring us together and gather in our exiles to Your holy Courtyards for the purpose of keeping Your laws and to abide by Your will with a full heart. Just as we thank HaKadosh Baruch Hu for having seen to the survival of our nation in the face of all the hateful murderers throughout history, we also thank Him — in advance — for our continued survival until the end of the galus. כֵּן תְּחַיֵּינוּ וּתְחָנֵּנוּ is not a prayer for our continued survival, but rather, is based on our absolute certainty of the geulah, and is the expression of our gratitude for it.

We look forward to returning to חַצְרוֹת קָדְשֶׁךָ, which means not only the holy Courtyards of the Beis HaMikdash, but is also a beautiful description of all of Eretz Yisrael in its pristine and ideal state after the geulah. The kedushah of the Courtyards of the Beis HaMikdash, which will be the capital of Eretz Yisrael, will be mirrored in the countless courtyards of the entire nation living in kedushah and taharah all across the land. Every private house will have the distinction of being called חַצְרוֹת קָדְשֶׁךָ.

And the reason we look forward to returning to Eretz Yisrael and binyan Beis HaMikdash, the building of the Beis HaMikdash, is first, לִשְׁמוֹר חֻקֶּיךָ, to be able again to keep all of the mitzvos, as opposed to the time of galus when we can keep only some of them. And to this we add לַעֲשׂוֹת רְצוֹנְךָ, we wish to do Your will, even that which is not mandatory, but לִפְנִים מִשּׁוּרַת הַדִּין, voluntary acts of mitzvos and maasim tovim which please HaKadosh Baruch Hu. And finally, we look forward to the performance of all the mitzvos, including those that are lifnim mishuras hadin, with a full and complete heart, without doubts or reservations.

Regretfully, we must admit that while we are in galus, many of us do not perform Torah and mitzvos with a complete heart. We live in a world replete with kefirah (apostasy), and while we have chosen the path of emunah over that of kefirah with which to live our lives, we cannot help but be influenced somewhat by the prevailing heretical thought, or agnosticism. Consequently, our emunah is incomplete. Therefore, we look forward to the time when we will be privileged to serve HaKadosh Baruch Hu with a complete heart, בְּלֵבָב שָׁלֵם, when there will be no questions nor a single moment of doubt in our emunah.

In וּבָא לְצִיּוֹן we say: וְיָשֵׂם בְּלִבֵּנוּ אַהֲבָתוֹ וְיִרְאָתוֹ וְלַעֲשׂוֹת רְצוֹנוֹ וּלְעָבְדוֹ בְּלֵבָב שָׁלֵם לְמַעַן לֹא נִיגַע לָרִיק וְלֹא נֵלֵד לַבֶּהָלָה. We are asking HaKadosh Baruch Hu there to help us serve Him with a complete heart, because, otherwise all our efforts would be for naught. One could scrupulously keep all the mitzvos and regularly say שְׁמַע יִשְׂרָאֵל ה' אֱלֹהֵינוּ ה' אֶחָד, and yet, because he harbors lingering doubts in his heart about the veracity of Judaism, he would give it up under duress. History has shown that there were many Jews — the Spanish Inquisition is a prime example — who chose baptism rather than

SHEMONEH ESREI 525

living a life of exile and hardship. Thousands of our brethren forfeited their Judaism this way. Unfortunately, those Jews lived "for naught." However, the myriads of *acheinu Bnei Yisrael* who gave up their lives *al kiddush Hashem* proved thereby that their *emunah* was indeed בְּלֵבָב שָׁלֵם.

עַל שֶׁאֲנַחְנוּ מוֹדִים לָךְ is, as we said, the refrain that is common to all of the above expressions of *hoda'ah,* and was originally added to each one of them.

After quoting the aforementioned five expressions of *hoda'ah,* the Gemara concludes by saying, אָמַר רַב פָּפָּא: הִילְכָּךְ נֵימְרִינְהוּ לְכוּלְהוּ, *Rav Pappa said: We say them all* (Sotah 40a). Therefore, our present-day version of this communal מוֹדִים includes, with slight textual variations, all five of these expressions of *hoda'ah.* And since this מוֹדִים consists of various expressions of *hoda'ah* which were composed by different *rabbanan,* as set forth in the Gemara, it is commonly known as מוֹדִים דְּרַבָּנָן, *Modim d'Rabbanan.*

We conclude מוֹדִים דְּרַבָּנָן with בָּרוּךְ אֵל הַהוֹדָאוֹת. We call *HaKadosh Baruch Hu* the God of Thanksgiving, because, as we explained earlier, He instilled in us the entire concept of thanksgiving, עַל שֶׁנָּתַתָּ בְּלִבֵּנוּ לִהְיוֹת דְּבוּקִים בְּךָ וּמוֹדִים לָךְ.

In the opinion of the Vilna Gaon, this מוֹדִים should conclude with the full *berachah,* בָּרוּךְ אַתָּה ה' אֵל הַהוֹדָאוֹת. However, we follow the opinion of *Shulchan Aruch* (*Orach Chaim* 127) that it should end with only בָּרוּךְ אֵל הַהוֹדָאוֹת. The difference of these two opinions is based on a dispute among the *Rishonim,* and therefore, in practice, as it is a *safek berachah,* we conclude with only בָּרוּךְ אֵל הַהוֹדָאוֹת.

עַל הַנִּסִּים / Al HaNissim

A D'var Torah on Purim

[Ed. note: This *shiur* was given just before Purim, so the Rav included the following remarks regarding Purim, following his custom of talking about current Yamim Tovim in his lectures and speeches.]

On Purim, in עַל הַנִּסִּים, we add the piece בִּימֵי מָרְדְּכַי וְאֶסְתֵּר as our *hoda'ah* for the *nissim* that occurred at that time. A brief synopsis of the historical events surrounding Purim is included there, and it ends with the death of Haman: וְתָלוּ אוֹתוֹ וְאֶת בָּנָיו עַל הָעֵץ, *They hanged him and his sons on a tree.* This "tree" gives us no rest; it is mentioned in the *Megillah* several times. Let us try to find its underlying significance in the story of Purim.

The tree on which Haman was hanged was actually a gallows, and it is described in the *Megillah* as being fifty *amos* high (*Esther* 7:9), which was the Persian custom for executions of important people.

According to the *Megillah,* only Haman died by hanging, and his execution took place approximately on the sixteenth of Nissan. His sons, however, were killed by the sword in the capital city of Shushan one year later on the thirteenth of Adar, when the Jews rose up and killed their enemies. And on the next day, the fourteenth of Adar, in accordance with the request of Esther, the bodies of the ten sons of Haman were hanged from the tree (see *Esther* 9:6-14). Our *Chachamim* make a point of telling us that their dead bodies were hanged on the same tree, one underneath the other, together with the body of Haman (see *Targum, Megillas Esther* 9:14; *Megillah* 16b). This, despite the fact that Haman had died nearly one year earlier! We even mention this tree on Chanukah in *Maoz Tzur*: רֹב בָּנָיו וְקִנְיָנָיו עַל הָעֵץ תָּלִיתָ. It remains for us to understand why our *Chachamim* placed such importance on this tree.

I would like to suggest that it has its origin in the statement: הָמָן מִן הַתּוֹרָה מִנַּיִן, *Where does Haman appear in the Torah* (*Chullin* 139b). And the answer given there is that *HaKadosh Baruch Hu* asked Adam HaRishon after he had eaten of the *eitz hadaas,* when he realized that he was naked, הֲמִן הָעֵץ אֲשֶׁר צִוִּיתִיךָ לְבִלְתִּי אֲכָל מִמֶּנּוּ אָכָלְתָּ, *Did you eat of the tree which I commanded you not to eat?* (*Bereishis* 3:11). Taken simply, this means that in this narrative, the letters of הָמָן are identical with הֲמִן, and this is the source of הָמָן מִן הַתּוֹרָה. It is obvious, however, that this statement of our *Chachamim* has a much deeper meaning.

The most heinous crime imaginable is genocide, the murder of an entire class or race of people — men, women, and children. And the most egregious form of genocide is when it is practiced against *Klal Yisrael,* as was attempted by Haman. This is the most profound *aveirah* that anyone could ever contemplate, as was done by Hitler, ימ"ש, in his "Final Solution of the Jewish Problem."

And conversely, the smallest, slightest *aveirah* — which is almost no *aveirah* — is that which was done when Adam and Chavah ate of the *eitz hadaas.* In enticing them to eat of the forbidden tree, the serpent told them that if they would eat it, they would "become like God": וִהְיִיתֶם כֵּאלֹהִים יֹדְעֵי טוֹב וָרָע, *And you will be like God, knowing good and bad* (ibid. v. 5). The desire of Adam and Chavah to eat the fruit of this tree was not one of simple animal lust — as sensual *aveiros* usually are — but rather, it was a desire to raise themselves up toward the level of *HaKadosh Baruch Hu.* Nevertheless, it was an *aveirah* because *HaKadosh Baruch Hu* forbade them to eat the fruit of this tree, and they did not use their moral freedom of choice to decide to abide by the will of God. Rather, they succumbed to the appeal which the fruit had to their senses — albeit a lofty appeal. We may therefore conclude that this was the most exalted form of an *aveirah* ever committed.

The *yetzer hara*, in the form of the *nachash*, wanted to entice Adam and Chavah to "become like God." And when they succumbed to this desire, they committed the first *aveirah*. All other *aveiros* of the human race are the result of this *aveirah*, because once one violates the will of God and experiences the "sweet taste" of sin, he has the desire to continue to do so. Consequently, Adam and Chavah, after their *cheit*, had the continuing desire for *aveiros*, and this was inherited by the human race.

The desire for the most idealistic *aveirah* — to become like *HaKadosh Baruch Hu* — which was committed by Adam and Chavah, escalated in their offspring, step by step, until it eventually reached the worst of all sins, that which was contemplated by Haman: וגו' היהודים כָּל אֶת וּלְאַבֵּד לַהֲרֹג לְהַשְׁמִיד, *To destroy, to slay, and to exterminate all the Jews* (Esther 3:13). The worst *aveirah* has its origin in the slightest *aveirah*. And this is what our *Chazal* meant when they said, הָעֵץ הָמָן – מִנַּיִן הַתּוֹרָה מִן הָמָן.

Therefore, one could say that הָעֵץ עַל בָּנָיו וְאֶת אוֹתוֹ וְתָלוּ, *And they hanged him and his sons on the gallows* (Esther 9:25), symbolically conveys the idea that the wickedness of Haman and his sons is attributable to the "tree." With this thought, we can readily understand the importance of this עֵץ which is so prominent in the story of Purim.

בִּרְכַּת כֹּהֲנִים – שָׁלוֹם

The third and final *berachah* of the last part of *Shemoneh Esrei* is שִׂים שָׁלוֹם. It is called בִּרְכַּת כֹּהֲנִים by our *Chachamim* — although the Priestly Blessing is recited in the *Shemoneh Esrei* only in the *chazzan's* repetition — for the reason that we will explain.

The *mitzvas asei* of *Bircas Kohanim* is: וַיְדַבֵּר ה' אֶל מֹשֶׁה לֵּאמֹר: דַּבֵּר אֶל אַהֲרֹן וְאֶל בָּנָיו לֵאמֹר כֹּה תְבָרְכוּ אֶת בְּנֵי יִשְׂרָאֵל אָמוֹר לָהֶם, *Hashem spoke to Moshe, saying, Speak to Aharon and his sons, saying: So shall you bless the Children of Israel, say to them* (Bamidbar 6:22-23). This *mitzvah* requires the *Kohanim* to bless the Jewish people with the following three *pesukim*: יְבָרֶכְךָ ה' וְיִשְׁמְרֶךָ, *May Hashem bless you and safeguard you* (ibid. v. 24); יָאֵר ה' פָּנָיו אֵלֶיךָ וִיחֻנֶּךָּ, *May Hashem cause His face to shine toward you, and give you grace* (v. 25); יִשָּׂא ה' פָּנָיו אֵלֶיךָ וְיָשֵׂם לְךָ שָׁלוֹם, *May Hashem lift up His face toward you and grant you peace* (v. 26). And the Torah continues: וְשָׂמוּ אֶת שְׁמִי עַל בְּנֵי יִשְׂרָאֵל וַאֲנִי אֲבָרְכֵם, *Let them place My Name upon the Children of Israel and I shall bless them* (ibid. v. 27). This means that the *Kohanim* do not "bless" the people; rather, they are commanded to express their wish that *HaKadosh Baruch Hu* may bestow His blessings of יְבָרֶכְךָ; יָאֵר; יִשָּׂא וגו' on His people. And when they do so, *HaKadosh Baruch Hu* promises that *He* will bless the

Jewish people, וַאֲנִי אֲבָרְכֵם. The Gemara describes this as: כֹּהֲנִים מְבָרְכִים לְיִשְׂרָאֵל והקב״ה מַסְכִּים עַל יָדָם (*Chullin* 49a).

אֱלֹהֵינוּ וֵאלֹהֵי אֲבוֹתֵינוּ בָּרְכֵנוּ בַבְּרָכָה הַמְשֻׁלֶּשֶׁת בַּתּוֹרָה וגו׳ — **Our God and the God of our Forefathers, bless us with the threefold blessing in the Torah.** The *Bircas Kohanim* is called *berachah hameshulleshes baTorah*, the threefold blessing in the Torah, because it consists of three *pesukim* in the Torah: יְבָרֶכְךָ וגו׳, which consists of three words; יָאֵר וגו׳, which consists of five words; and יִשָּׂא וגו׳, which consists of seven words. As a part of his repetition of the *Shemoneh Esrei*, the *chazzan* merely quotes these *pesukim* as a *tefillah*, when no actual *Bircas Kohanim* takes place. It is for this reason that the congregation responds to each *pasuk* with כֵּן יְהִי רָצוֹן, *So may it be,* rather than *Amen,* because it is merely a prayerful reference to the *Bircas Kohanim,* and not a *berachah* in itself.

הָאֲמוּרָה מִפִּי אַהֲרֹן וּבָנָיו, כֹּהֲנִים — **Which was said by Aharon and his sons, the Kohanim.** Originally *Bircas Kohanim* was said only by Aharon and his sons, and ultimately their descendants, the *Kohanim,* inherited this *mitzvah*. These *berachos* are called *meshulleshes* for an additional reason: When they were said in the *Beis HaMikdash* by Aharon and his descendants, there was a threefold response by the people. Each one of these three *berachos* contains the Ineffable Name י-ה-ו-ה, which we normally pronounce אֲדֹנָי. However, in the *Beis HaMikdash,* the *Kohanim* would pronounce this Name of *HaKadosh Baruch Hu* as it is written, and at each mention of the *Shem HaMeforash,* those people who heard it would prostrate themselves and say בָּרוּךְ שֵׁם כְּבוֹד מַלְכוּתוֹ לְעוֹלָם וָעֶד. The simple response, *Amen,* was not used in the *Beis Ha-Mikdash* (see *Sotah* 37b-38a; *Taanis* 16b; *Berachos* 63a).

In practice, in the *Beis HaMikdash,* the *Bircas Kohanim* evoked a threefold response by the people, once for each time they heard the pronouncement of the *Shem HaMeforash* as a part of the *Bircas Kohanim.* However, outside of the *Beis HaMikdash,* as during our *duchenen,* the congregation merely answers *Amen* after the *Kohanim* say each one of these *pesukim*.

עַם קְדוֹשֶׁךָ — **Your holy nation.** The *Kohanim* are called עַם קְדוֹשֶׁךָ, *Your nation of holy people* (see *Ba'er Heitev, Orach Chaim* 127:2 [4]). We also find the *Kohanim* being called עַם קְדוֹשֶׁךָ in the *vidui* of Yom Kippur (*Yoma* 41b, see mishnah there).

An additional reason why the *Bircas Kohanim* is called *berachah hameshulleshes* is because each one of the three *berachos* refers to another aspect of our lives, as we will show by quotations from various *Midrashim* (*Yalkut, Midrash Rabbah, Midrash Tanchuma, Sifrei*).

כָּאָמוּר: יְבָרֶכְךָ ה׳ וְיִשְׁמְרֶךָ — **As it is said: May Hashem bless you and safeguard you.** This first *berachah*, with its three words, refers to physical, material blessings. And וְיִשְׁמְרֶךָ is a *berachah* that *HaKadosh Baruch Hu* should protect us from losing these material blessings once we have acquired them. Here are several quotations from the *Midrashim* containing examples of these material blessings, and their retention (וְיִשְׁמְרֶךָ).

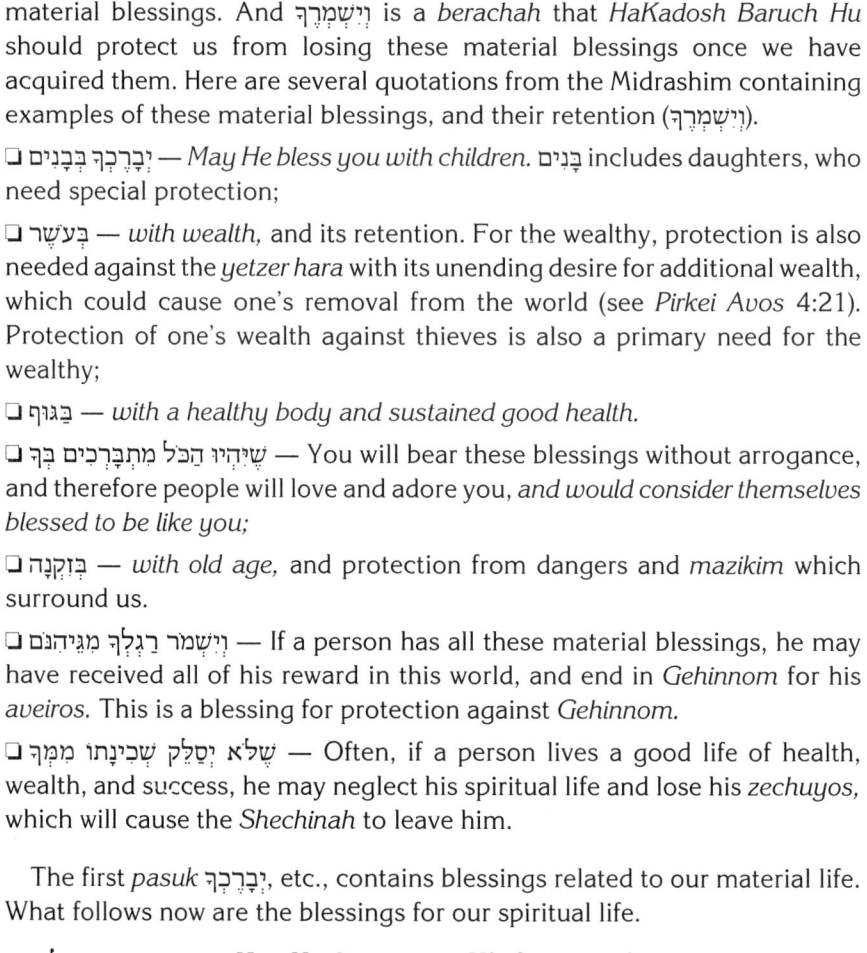

❏ יְבָרֶכְךָ בְּבָנִים — *May He bless you with children.* בָּנִים includes daughters, who need special protection;

❏ בְּעֹשֶׁר — *with wealth,* and its retention. For the wealthy, protection is also needed against the *yetzer hara* with its unending desire for additional wealth, which could cause one's removal from the world (see *Pirkei Avos* 4:21). Protection of one's wealth against thieves is also a primary need for the wealthy;

❏ בַּגּוּף — *with a healthy body and sustained good health.*

❏ שֶׁיִּהְיוּ הַכֹּל מִתְבָּרְכִים בְּךָ — *You will bear these blessings without arrogance, and therefore people will love and adore you, and would consider themselves blessed to be like you;*

❏ בְּזִקְנָה — *with old age,* and protection from dangers and *mazikim* which surround us.

❏ וְיִשְׁמוֹר רַגְלְךָ מִגֵּיהִנֹּם — If a person has all these material blessings, he may have received all of his reward in this world, and end in *Gehinnom* for his *aveiros.* This is a blessing for protection against *Gehinnom.*

❏ שֶׁלֹּא יְסַלֵּק שְׁכִינָתוֹ מִמְּךָ — Often, if a person lives a good life of health, wealth, and success, he may neglect his spiritual life and lose his *zechuyos,* which will cause the *Shechinah* to leave him.

The first *pasuk* יְבָרֶכְךָ, etc., contains blessings related to our material life. What follows now are the blessings for our spiritual life.

❏ יָאֵר ה׳ פָּנָיו אֵלֶיךָ — **May Hashem cause His face to shine toward you.** This second *berachah,* with its five words, is for spiritual gifts. We continue to quote from the various *Midrashim* for examples of the meaning of this *berachah* for spiritual blessings.

❏ יַעֲמִיד מִמְּךָ בָּנִים בְּנֵי תּוֹרָה — *May HaKadosh Baruch Hu give you children who are talmidei chachamim.*

❏ וְיָאֵר עֵינֶיךָ וְלִבְּךָ בַּתּוֹרָה — *May He illuminate your eyes and heart by giving you insights into Torah.*

❏ שֶׁיַּבִּיט בְּךָ בְּפָנִים מְאִירוֹת וְלֹא בְּפָנִים זְעוּמוֹת — *May He look at you with a "friendly face" and not with an "angry face."*

❏ וִיחֻנֶּךָּ — **And give you *chein*.** This word is difficult to translate. However, it conveys the thought of the gift (*matnas chinam*) of being well liked by God and man. We have quoted earlier the explanation of *chein* by Rav Samson R.

Hirsch as having the meaning of spiritual endowment. In German, he called it *"geistige begabung."* A prime example of this use would be אַתָּה חוֹנֵן לְאָדָם דַּעַת, *You endow man with knowledge*, as a gift.

Again, some examples of these spiritual gifts from the Midrashim are:

❏ יַחֲנֶה ה' אֶצְלְךָ — *May Hashem dwell with you;*

❏ יָחְנְךָ בְּמִשְׁאֲלוֹתֶיךָ — *may He grace you in granting your wishes;*

❏ שֶׁיִּשְׁמַע תְּפִלָּתְךָ — *may He hear your prayers;*

❏ יִתֵּן חִנְּךָ בְּעֵינֵי הַבְּרִיּוֹת — *may He cause you to find favor and be well liked by people.*

❏ בְּדַעַת וּבְחָכְמָה וּבְהַשְׂכֵּל וּמוּסָר וּבִינָה — With *daas, chochmah*, etc. — these are all gifts of different levels of knowledge.

❏ דַּעַת בְּתַלְמוּד תּוֹרָה — *May He give you the proper understanding when you learn Torah;*

❏ יִתֵּן בָּכֶם דַּעַת שֶׁתְּהוּ מְחוֹנְנִים זֶה אֶת זֶה, וּמְרַחֲמִים זֶה אֶת זֶה — *may He give you understanding and compassion for each other.* This is a blessing for the Jewish people to find mutual *chein* in each other's eyes.

The third *berachah* — with its seven words — which follows, concerns our personal relationship with *HaKadosh Baruch Hu*.

§ וִישָּׂא ה' פָּנָיו אֵלֶיךָ — **May Hashem lift up His face towards you.** This *berachah* refers to personal matters between man and *HaKadosh Baruch Hu*. The following examples from the Midrashim bear this out:

❏ יִתֵּן לְךָ נְשִׂיאוּת פָּנִים — *May He give you individual attention.*

❏ יַעֲבִיר כַּעֲסוֹ מִמְּךָ וְיַהֲפוֹךְ פָּנָיו אֶצְלְךָ — *May Hashem remove His anger from you and turn His face back to you*, meaning He will "change His attitude" toward you. This would refer to one who has done an *aveirah* and wishes to come back to *HaKadosh Baruch Hu*.

❏ בְּשָׁעָה שֶׁאַתָּה עוֹמֵד וּמִתְפַּלֵּל — This is the most personal of relationships between the human being and *HaKadosh Baruch Hu*. This is a *berachah* that *HaKadosh Baruch Hu* will turn His face toward you and listen to your *tefillah*.

❏ יַכְרִיעַ לְךָ לְכַף זְכוּת — Every person has *mitzvos* and *aveiros*, and this *berachah* asks *HaKadosh Baruch Hu* to look at us favorably and judge us so that our *mitzvos* outweigh our *aveiros*.

§ וְיָשֵׂם לְךָ שָׁלוֹם — **And grant you peace.** The word *shalom*, meaning *peace*, has three connotations.

The simple, and literal, meaning of *shalom* is *peace*, in the sense of the absence of war, as in וְנָתַתִּי שָׁלוֹם בָּאָרֶץ . . . וְחֶרֶב לֹא תַעֲבֹר בְּאַרְצְכֶם, *I will provide peace in the land . . . and a sword will not cross your land* (Vayikra 26:6). According to this meaning, *HaKadosh Baruch Hu* is blessing the Jewish

SHEMONEH ESREI ❧ 531

people with the absence of enemies who will attack them or endanger them. This also includes the absence of other forms of external disturbances of the peace, such as שָׁלוֹם מִן הַחַיּוֹת וּמִן הַמַּזִּיקִים, *peace from wild animals and from harmful natural forces* (see *Midrash Lekach Tov*).

But *shalom* also includes a second form of peace, that of peaceful relations between man and man, the absence of *machlokes* within the nation. This form of peace is expressed in the Midrash: בִּכְנִיסָתְךָ שָׁלוֹם, בִּיצִיאָתְךָ שָׁלוֹם עִם כָּל אָדָם (*Yalkut Shimoni, Naso* 711). This form of peace also includes *shalom bayis*, peace between husband and wife and between parents and children, as is expressed in the same Midrash: וְיָשֵׂם לְךָ שָׁלוֹם בְּבֵיתֶךָ.

And then, there is the finest and highest form of *shalom*, that of inner peace, one's own personal peace of mind. This is the peace of the *neshamah*.

The *Bircas Kohanim* is followed by שִׂים שָׁלוֹם.

שָׁלוֹם

The Gemara (see *Megillah* 18a) tells us: מָה רָאוּ לוֹמַר שִׂים שָׁלוֹם אַחַר בִּרְכַּת כֹּהֲנִים דִּכְתִיב "וְשָׂמוּ אֶת שְׁמִי עַל בְּנֵי יִשְׂרָאֵל וַאֲנִי אֲבָרֲכֵם״ בְּרָכָה דְּהקב״ה שָׁלוֹם, שֶׁנֶּאֱמַר: "ה׳ יְבָרֵךְ אֶת עַמּוֹ בַשָּׁלוֹם", *The Chachamim were prompted to institute the saying of Sim Shalom after Bircas Kohanim because the Torah says: "Let them place My Name upon the Children of Israel, and I shall bless them"* (Bamidbar 6:27). And the blessing of HaKadosh Baruch Hu is peace, as it says, "Hashem will bless His nation with peace" (Tehillim 29:11).

The *mesadrei hatefillah* instituted that שִׂים שָׁלוֹם be said after *Bircas Kohanim*, because the purpose of *Bircas Kohanim* is the placement of the Name of *HaKadosh Baruch Hu* on *Bnei Yisrael*, which will cause Him to bless us with His ultimate blessing, that of *shalom*. This is explained: אֵין לְךָ כְּלִי שֶׁמַּחֲזִיק בְּרָכָה יוֹתֵר מִן הַשָּׁלוֹם (*Talmud Yerushalmi, Berachos* Ch. 2:4), the "vessel" into which all the *Bircas Kohanim* are "poured," and which holds them intact, is *shalom*. We will now show how the various forms of *shalom* which we have explained are woven into the fabric of שִׂים שָׁלוֹם.

⊱§ שִׂים שָׁלוֹם, טוֹבָה, וּבְרָכָה, חֵן, וָחֶסֶד, וְרַחֲמִים — **Establish peace, goodness, blessing, graciousness, kindness, and mercy.** Since *Bircas Kohanim* ends with וְיָשֵׂם לְךָ שָׁלוֹם, the composers of this *tefillah* have picked up these words with which to begin this final *berachah* of the *Shemoneh Esrei*. The same is true of the composition of שִׂים שָׁלוֹם רָב עַל יִשְׂרָאֵל עַמְּךָ תָּשִׂים, which is said at *Minchah* and *Maariv*.

The opening phrase, beginning with שִׂים שָׁלוֹם, is a prayer for inner peace, or peace of mind, in which one is at peace with himself. This is, as we have said, the highest form of peace. We ask here for טוֹבָה וּבְרָכָה חֵן וָחֶסֶד וְרַחֲמִים,

532 ⦃ RAV SCHWAB ON PRAYER

which are all blessings through which a person can recognize that *HaKadosh Baruch Hu* loves him. By receiving these blessings, he has the wonderful feeling that his soul is at peace with *HaKadosh Baruch Hu*.

עָלֵינוּ וְעַל כָּל יִשְׂרָאֵל עַמֶּךָ — **Upon us and upon all of Your people, Yisrael.** But we are not satisfied to merely obtain this form of peace for ourselves. Rather, we pray that *HaKadosh Baruch Hu* may extend this serenity and peace עָלֵינוּ, to all our loved ones, and then to all of יִשְׂרָאֵל.

The foregoing is the first form of peace. This is now followed by a prayer for peace between one person and another.

בָּרְכֵנוּ, אָבִינוּ, כֻּלָּנוּ כְּאֶחָד בְּאוֹר פָּנֶיךָ — **Bless us, our Father, all together, with the light of Your face** or, with Your friendly face. We find: הָאֵר פָּנֶיךָ וְנִוָּשֵׁעָה, *Shine Your face (upon us), and we will be saved* (*Tehillim* 80:4,20), on which our *Chachamim* remark, אֵין לָנוּ אֶלָּא הֶאָרַת פָּנִים, *All we need [for our salvation is for HaKadosh Baruch Hu to offer us] the "light of His face"* (*Midrash Shocher Tov* 80). *HaKadosh Baruch Hu* shows us a "friendly face" when we have *shalom* among ourselves. But, as long as there is discord among us, *HaKadosh Baruch Hu* shows us an angry face.

Our *Chachamim* tell us that when *Bnei Yisrael* assembled at *Har Sinai* to receive the Torah, וַיִּחַן שָׁם יִשְׂרָאֵל נֶגֶד הָהָר, *And the Bnei Yisrael encamped there, opposite the mountain*, they did so in complete unity of purpose, כְּאִישׁ אֶחָד בְּלֵב אֶחָד, *as one man with one heart* (see *Rashi, Shemos* 19:2). This was in contrast to all of the other encampments of the *Bnei Yisrael* in the wilderness, which are described in the plural, וַיַּחֲנוּ, which subtly hints at their disunity and discord. However, at *Matan Torah*, the Jewish nation encamped as "one person." They were completely at peace with each other.

Shalom was the the precondition for the giving of the Torah to Israel. This idea lies behind the words: ה' עֹז לְעַמּוֹ יִתֵּן ה' יְבָרֵךְ אֶת עַמּוֹ בַשָּׁלוֹם, *Hashem will give strength to His nation, Hashem will bless His nation with peace* (*Tehillim* 29:11), which conveys the thought that *HaKadosh Baruch Hu* gives His עֹז, *strength*, meaning His Torah, to His nation only if He has blessed them with *shalom* (see *Tehillim* 78:61; 132:8).

At the moment of *Matan Torah*, everyone who heard the Heavenly Voice became a *talmid* of *HaKadosh Baruch Hu*: פָּנִים בְּפָנִים דִּבֶּר ה' עִמָּכֶם בָּהָר מִתּוֹךְ הָאֵשׁ, *Face-to-face did Hashem speak with you on the mountain from amid the fire* (*Devarim* 5:4). Since they heard words of Torah directly from *HaKadosh Baruch Hu*, they were verily *talmidei chachamim*. And, as *talmidei chachamim* who were at peace with each other at the moment of *Matan Torah*, our forefathers were living examples of that which our *Chachamim* tell us: תַּלְמִידֵי חֲכָמִים מַרְבִּים שָׁלוֹם בָּעוֹלָם, *Torah scholars increase peace in the world* (end of *Mesechta Berachos* and elsewhere). To be a true *talmid chacham*, one must be at peace with his fellowman.

עס **כִּי בְאוֹר פָּנֶיךָ נָתַתָּ לָּנוּ, ה' אֱלֹהֵינוּ, תּוֹרַת חַיִּים** — **Because by the light of Your face have You given us, our God, a living Torah.** This description of the Torah as something alive conveys the idea that it was not meant to be accepted only by individuals. Rather, the Torah was given to be taught by fathers and mothers to their children; by *rabbeim* to *talmidim;* and to be learned by *chaverim* with each other. It is not stagnant; it lives; it is to pulsate with life. It requires people to engage in it together, and thereby to enhance each other's understanding of it. And by doing so it also enhances peace between man and man.

עס **וְאַהֲבַת חֶסֶד** — **The love of doing kindness.** The desire to do kindness to others is a special blessing of *HaKadosh Baruch Hu,* and it is a part of the *berachah* of *shalom* among people.

עס **וּצְדָקָה, וּבְרָכָה, וְרַחֲמִים, וְחַיִּים** — **Righteousness, blessing, mercy and life.** Continuing to detail the blessings of *shalom* among people, we list here: *tzedakah,* charitable deeds to each other; *berachah,* each one's presence is a blessing to the other; *rachamim* and *chaim,* when one is in need, the other offers him his merciful assistance, thus enabling the one in need to continue living his life normally.

עס **וְשָׁלוֹם** — **And peace.** The word *shalom* is mentioned here a second time to add circumstances where people were angry with one another — for good cause, or not — and there was a *"berogez,"* a severance of relationship; nevertheless, the blessing of *shalom* makes it possible for people to forgive each other — וְשָׁלוֹם, *and* to reestablish the *shalom.*

What follows now is a reference to the third kind of *shalom*: that of the absence of war, of not being attacked or endangered.

עס **וְטוֹב בְּעֵינֶיךָ לְבָרֵךְ אֶת עַמְּךָ יִשְׂרָאֵל, בְּכָל עֵת וּבְכָל שָׁעָה בִּשְׁלוֹמֶךָ** — **And may it be good in Your eyes to bless Your people Yisrael, in every season and in every hour, with your peace.** At all times, at every hour, there is warfare and bloodshed going on somewhere in the world. If one could observe the entire globe from space at one time, he would not find one moment when the earth is free of strife, when there is no incidence of bloodshed or when no one is endangering someone else's life.

Therefore, at every moment of our lives, בְּכָל עֵת וּבְכָל שָׁעָה, we are dependent on שְׁלוֹמֶךָ, *Your peace,* meaning the protection from wars, dangers, pogroms, and Holocausts.

And then, we close שִׂים שָׁלוֹם — and the entire *Shemoneh Esrei* — with:

עס **בָּרוּךְ אַתָּה ה', הַמְבָרֵךְ אֶת עַמּוֹ יִשְׂרָאֵל בַּשָּׁלוֹם** — **Blessed are You, Hashem, Who blesses His people Yisrael with peace.** In accordance with our explanation of the composition of שִׂים שָׁלוֹם, that of the three forms of peace, this final *berachah* of שִׂים שָׁלוֹם means, "He Who blesses His nation Israel בַּשָּׁלוֹם, with *the Peace*," meaning, this threefold peace.

It is now quite clear why the *berachah* of שִׂים שָׁלוֹם is called *Bircas Kohanim* by our *Chachamim* (see *Megillah* 18a), although the actual *Bircas Kohanim* is said only by the *chazzan* during his repetition. The reason is because the threefold meaning of *shalom,* with which the *Bircas Kohanim* ends, is woven into the fabric of the composition of the entire *berachah* of שִׂים שָׁלוֹם. Therefore, שִׂים שָׁלוֹם is actually an extension of *Bircas Kohanim.*

When שִׂים שָׁלוֹם is not said, at such times when *Bircas Kohanim* is not recited, for instance, at Minchah or Maariv, a shortened version, שָׁלוֹם רָב, is said instead, and this also makes reference to the three kinds of peace:

❧ שָׁלוֹם רָב עַל יִשְׂרָאֵל עַמְּךָ תָּשִׂים לְעוֹלָם — **Establish abundant peace upon Your people Yisrael forever.** This is a reference to the שְׁלָמָא רַבָּא, *the great peace,* meaning peace of mind and soul.

❧ כִּי אַתָּה הוּא מֶלֶךְ אָדוֹן לְכָל הַשָּׁלוֹם — **For You are King, Master of all peace.** The phrase *all peace* refer to the *shalom* between man and man.

And שָׁלוֹם רָב concludes with the same wording as שִׂים שָׁלוֹם:

❧ וְטוֹב בְּעֵינֶיךָ לְבָרֵךְ אֶת עַמְּךָ יִשְׂרָאֵל, בְּכָל עֵת וּבְכָל שָׁעָה בִּשְׁלוֹמֶךָ. בָּרוּךְ אַתָּה ה', הַמְבָרֵךְ אֶת עַמּוֹ יִשְׂרָאֵל בַּשָּׁלוֹם.
Your peace, as explained before, refers to the absence of war and danger.

Although we have concluded *Shemoneh Esrei,* the Gemara (*Berachos* 9b) tells us that before we actually conclude, we should add the *pasuk,* יִהְיוּ לְרָצוֹן אִמְרֵי פִי וְהֶגְיוֹן לִבִּי לְפָנֶיךָ, ה' צוּרִי וְגֹאֲלִי, *May the expressions of my mouth and the thoughts of my heart find favor before You, Hashem, my Rock and my Redeemer* (*Tehillim* 19:15). According to our *minhag,* however, the saying of this *pasuk* is deferred until the end of אֱלֹהַי נְצוֹר.

אֱלֹהַי נְצוֹר

The Gemara (*Berachos* 17a) lists several *tefillos* that different *Amoraim* would say after they had finished their own *Shemoneh Esrei.* The one that has been incorporated into our *siddur* for daily use is that of Mar the son of Ravina, who was one of the last of the Amoraim, and it begins:

❧ אֱלֹהַי, נְצוֹר לְשׁוֹנִי מֵרָע, וגו' — **My God, guard my tongue from evil, etc.** This is in contrast to אֱלֹהַי נְשָׁמָה וגו', which we say during *Birchos HaShachar.* The word אֱלֹהַי, *My God,* begins a personal *tefillah,* after one has completed the *Shemoneh Esrei,* which was said on behalf of all of *Klal Yisrael.*

This personal *tefillah,* נְצוֹר לְשׁוֹנִי מֵרָע וּשְׂפָתַי מִדַּבֵּר מִרְמָה, which is based on: נְצֹר לְשׁוֹנְךָ מֵרָע וּשְׂפָתֶיךָ מִדַּבֵּר מִרְמָה, *Guard your tongue from evil, and your lips from speaking deceit (Tehillim 34:14),* is not a prayer to merit the performance of a voluntary "good deed." Rather, it reflects the actual Biblical prohibition against *lashon hara.*

The reason a special *tefillah* for the avoidance of *lashon hara* is added is because the temptation to violate it is very strong. In fact, our *Chachamim* tell us that this *aveirah* is so pervasive, that הַכֹּל בַּאֲבַק לְשׁוֹן הָרַע, *Everybody violates the "dust" of lashon hara* (Bava Basra 165a). This means that even if one is careful not to talk actual *lashon hara,* nevertheless, he cannot avoid its "dust," which is *lashon hara* in its most subtle form. Each person, therefore, asks *HaKadosh Baruch Hu,* in a most personal way, אֱלֹהַי נְצוֹר לְשׁוֹנִי מֵרָע, *My God, please help me avoid lashon hara.*

I can only relate to you that I received the shock of my life when I learned *Rambam, Hil. Teshuvah,* and found that *baalei lashon hara,* people who constantly talk *lashon hara,* are listed among the groups of people whose *aveiros* are so severe as to cause them to lose their *Olam Haba.*

Here is the language of the Rambam:

וְאֵלּוּ הֵן שֶׁאֵין לָהֶן חֵלֶק לָעוֹלָם הַבָּא אֶלָּא נִכְרָתִין וְאוֹבְדִין: וְנִדּוֹנִין עַל גּוֹדֶל רִשְׁעָם וְחַטָּאתָם לְעוֹלָם וּלְעוֹלְמֵי עוֹלָמִים. הַמִּינִים וְהָאֶפִּיקוֹרְסִין וְהַכּוֹפְרִים בַּתּוֹרָה וְהַכּוֹפְרִים בִּתְחִיַּית הַמֵּתִים וּבְבִיאַת הַגּוֹאֵל הַמּוּמָּרִים וּמַחְטִיאֵי הָרַבִּים וְהַפּוֹרְשִׁים מִדַּרְכֵי צִבּוּר וְהָעוֹשֶׂה עֲבֵירוֹת בְּיָד רָמָה בְּפַרְהֶסְיָא כִּיהוֹיָקִים וְהַמּוֹסְרִים וּמְטִילֵי אֵימָה עַל הַצִּבּוּר שֶׁלֹּא לְשֵׁם שָׁמַיִם וְשׁוֹפְכֵי דָּמִים וּבַעֲלֵי לָשׁוֹן הָרַע וְהַמּוֹשֵׁךְ עָרְלָתוֹ." (פ"ג מהל' תשובה הל' ו.), *The following have no share in the World to Come, but rather they are cut off and destroyed and are punished because of their great evil and sins for all eternity: minim and apostates; those who deny the veracity of the Torah, the revival of the dead, or the arrival of the redeemer; rebels; and those who cause the public to sin; and those who separate themselves from the public; those who do sin publicly and brazenly as did Yehoyakim; those who inform on others; those who instill fear unnecessarily in the public not for the sake of Heaven; murderers; those who make a practice of engaging in lashon hara; and he who attempts to undo his circumcision by stretching his foreskin* (Rambam, Hil. Teshuvah 3:6).

The *aveirah* of *lashon hara* is classified among the worst offenses that a Jew can do; it is in the same category as *minim, apikorsim,* and *kofrim.* It is therefore very understandable that we include this special plea, אֱלֹהַי נְצוֹר לְשׁוֹנִי מֵרָע, in which we ask *HaKadosh Baruch Hu* to help us avoid this terrible *aveirah* which can have such devastating consequences.

§ וּשְׂפָתַי מִדַּבֵּר מִרְמָה — **And my lips from speaking deceitfully.** The avoidance of *lashon hara* can lead to מִרְמָה, when, in an effort to conceal the details of something derogatory that was said about another, a person would invent something, and tell him an untruth. This would be a מִרְמָה, *deceit.* And therefore, we include a prayer for this as well, וּשְׂפָתַי מִדַּבֵּר מִרְמָה, in which we ask *HaKadosh Baruch Hu* to help us avoid circumstances where we might be tempted to be deceitful and tell an untruth, no matter how noble the purpose.

The *tefillah* continues:

וְלִמְקַלְלַי נַפְשִׁי תִדּוֹם — **And to those who curse me, may my soul be silent.** This means, may I remain calm and silent as the dust of the earth in the face of my tormentors. I pray that I shall not react if I am cursed or tormented.

However, we also pray for the other side of the coin:

וְנַפְשִׁי כֶּעָפָר לַכֹּל תִּהְיֶה — **And may my soul be as dust toward everything.** This means, let me not become haughty if I am praised. Although everyone likes to be praised, nevertheless, we ask here that such praises should not cause us to feel proud and arrogant, but rather, we pray that they may make as little an impression on us as the curses which we ignore.

[Ed. note: At a large gathering where the Rav was being honored, he was heard quietly whispering, וְנַפְשִׁי כֶּעָפָר לַכֹּל תִּהְיֶה, as he entered the hall.] This phrase also means: May I serve everyone, לַכֹּל, even if this means that I may be stepped upon as dust of the earth; may I not be affected even if some abuse me or exploit me, and consider me as if I were dust of the earth.

However, *Tosafos* (ibid.) explains that נַפְשִׁי כֶּעָפָר תִּהְיֶה is a prayer for the uninterrupted continuity of one's progeny, based on the *pasuk*, וְשַׂמְתִּי אֶת זַרְעֲךָ כַּעֲפַר הָאָרֶץ, *I will make your offspring as the dust of the earth* (*Bereishis* 13:16). And the meaning would be, just as dust is never eradicated, so may my offspring never come to an end — יְהִי רָצוֹן שֶׁזַּרְעִי לֹא יְכַלֶּה לְעוֹלָם. However, the difficulty with this way of explaining it is the word לַכֹּל, which apparently was not included in the text that *Tosafos* had.

Rav Samson R. Hirsch explains that extreme humility and disinterest in our own importance, for which we pray here — considering ourselves as "dust of the earth" — applies only to one's personal life and relationship with others. However, when it comes to Torah, we ask that we may have the ability to be keenly interested and aware of all its details — as follows:

פְּתַח לִבִּי בְּתוֹרָתֶךָ — **May my heart be wide open to** every nuance, every detail of **Your Torah.**

וּבְמִצְוֹתֶיךָ תִּרְדּוֹף נַפְשִׁי — **May my soul pursue Your commandments.** May I become energetic in the pursuit of Your *mitzvos*.

וְכָל הַחוֹשְׁבִים עָלַי רָעָה, מְהֵרָה הָפֵר עֲצָתָם וְקַלְקֵל מַחֲשַׁבְתָּם — **And quickly upset and destroy the bad plans which others have about me.** If, because of one's extreme humility, he is unsuspecting and not curious to find out what other people think of him, good or bad, he could at times be unaware and fall into a trap. He therefore asks *HaKadosh Baruch Hu* to protect him from the evil designs of others.

This is followed in our *siddurim* with the added *tefillah* for oneself and for the Jewish nation:

עֲשֵׂה לְמַעַן שְׁמֶךָ, עֲשֵׂה לְמַעַן יְמִינֶךָ, עֲשֵׂה לְמַעַן קְדֻשָּׁתֶךָ, עֲשֵׂה לְמַעַן תּוֹרָתֶךָ — Act for Your Name's sake, act for Your right hand's sake, act for Your sanctity's sake, act for Your Torah's sake. The *Tur* (122) quotes this *tefillah* and attributes it to an Aggadic saying: אָמַר שְׁמוּאֵל, כָּל הַזָּרִיז לוֹמַר אַרְבָּעָה דְבָרִים הַלָּלוּ זוֹכֶה וּמְקַבֵּל פְּנֵי שְׁכִינָה, *Said Shmuel: If one says these four things carefully and with concentration, he will merit to receive the Presence of Hashem.*

What this means is that if one feels that he is really unworthy of having his own *tefillos* heard by *HaKadosh Baruch Hu,* and he says, "I am nothing, but nevertheless, please respond to my *tefillos* for Your sake, for the honor of the Torah," and thereby wishes to make a *kiddush Hashem* in the world, he is worthy of having his *tefillos* heard. Because if one is a *yerei Shamayim* and an adherent of the Torah, and people see that his *tefillos* are answered, this will create a *kiddush Hashem* in the world.

After this, we quote:

לְמַעַן יֵחָלְצוּן יְדִידֶיךָ, הוֹשִׁיעָה יְמִינְךָ — For the sake of freeing Your beloved ones, may Your right hand act as their salvation (*Tehillim* 60:7). The right hand of *HaKadosh Baruch Hu* is always a reference to *nissim,* and this applies to יְדִידֶיךָ, *the beloved ones* of *HaKadosh Baruch Hu,* who deserve these *nissim* if they are necessary for their salvation. And the *pasuk* ends with the plea:

וַעֲנֵנִי — And answer me too. As for me, an ordinary person, answer me, too, in the process of answering others.

Since the previous *tefillos* were offered for the propagation of *kiddush Hashem* in the world, and for the benefit of יְדִידֶיךָ, those special *tzaddikim* who are called God's beloved ones, we add the final plea, וַעֲנֵנִי, for ourselves, in accordance with the statement of our *Chachamim*: כָּל הַמְבַקֵּשׁ רַחֲמִים עַל חֲבֵירוֹ וְהוּא צָרִיךְ לְאוֹתוֹ דָבָר הוּא נַעֲנֶה תְּחִלָּה, *Whoever pleads for God's mercy on behalf of another, while he, himself, is in need of the same thing, is answered first* (*Bava Kamma* 92a).

At this point, according to the generally accepted *minhag,* we add, יִהְיוּ לְרָצוֹן אִמְרֵי פִי וְהֶגְיוֹן לִבִּי לְפָנֶיךָ ה׳ צוּרִי וְגֹאֲלִי (*Tehillim* 19:15), which concludes the *tefillah.*

Following our outline of the "architecture" of the *tefillah,* we explained that the *Shemoneh Esrei* corresponds to the *Kodesh HaKadashim.* Now, after the completion of the *Shemoneh Esrei,* we take our leave from the *Kodesh HaKadashim* by taking three steps backwards, which symbolically brings us back, first into the *Heichal,* then to the *Ulam,* and then to the *Azarah,* from where we came.

These three steps backwards are to be taken while bowing, as one would reverentially do when taking leave of his master (see *Yoma* 53b). After the third step, while still bowing, one says the following *tefillah*, consisting of three phases, each one said while facing in different directions:

First, we direct our bowed body to the left and say:

עֹשֶׂה שָׁלוֹם בִּמְרוֹמָיו — **He Who makes peace in His heights.** There is only peace in the spiritual world of the *malachim* — and also in nature.

Then, bowing to the right we say:

הוּא יַעֲשֶׂה שָׁלוֹם עָלֵינוּ — **May He make peace "on" us.** Interestingly, it does not say בֵּינֵינוּ, *among us,* which would be similar to בִּמְרוֹמָיו, but rather, we ask *HaKadosh Baruch Hu* to impose His peace "on us," because we cannot do it ourselves.

And then, finally extending this to all of the Jewish people, we bow to the front and say:

וְעַל כָּל יִשְׂרָאֵל וְאִמְרוּ אָמֵן — **And upon all Yisrael. Now respond: Amen.** This is somewhat problematic. If וְאִמְרוּ אָמֵן is said by a *shaliach tzibbur,* it is an exhortation to the congregation to join and express its agreement with whatever *tefillah* is said. However, as an ending to the individual's silent *tefillah,* it must express another thought. May I suggest that וְאִמְרוּ אָמֵן, as used here, is a statement made to the *malachim* whom *HaKadosh Baruch Hu* has appointed to protect the Jewish people: כִּי מַלְאָכָיו יְצַוֶּה לָּךְ לִשְׁמָרְךָ בְּכָל דְּרָכֶיךָ, *He will charge His angels for you, to protect you in all your ways* (*Tehillim* 91:11). Accordingly, the meaning of this last phrase would be as follows: "I ask that you, the *malachim* — whom *HaKadosh Baruch Hu* has appointed to protect us — say Amen to my *tefillah* that *HaKadosh Baruch Hu* impose peace on us and all of Israel."

And since *tefillah* is meant to take the place of the *korbanos,* it is very appropriate that we add the epilogue:

יְהִי רָצוֹן מִלְּפָנֶיךָ ה' אֱלֹהֵינוּ וֵאלֹהֵי אֲבוֹתֵינוּ, שֶׁיִּבָּנֶה בֵּית הַמִּקְדָּשׁ בִּמְהֵרָה בְיָמֵינוּ, וְתֵן חֶלְקֵנוּ בְּתוֹרָתֶךָ. וְשָׁם נַעֲבָדְךָ בְּיִרְאָה, כִּימֵי עוֹלָם וּכְשָׁנִים קַדְמוֹנִיּוֹת. וְעָרְבָה לַה' מִנְחַת יְהוּדָה וִירוּשָׁלָיִם, כִּימֵי עוֹלָם וּכְשָׁנִים קַדְמוֹנִיּוֹת — *May it be Your will, Hashem, our God and the God of our Forefathers, that the Holy Temple be rebuilt, speedily in our days. Grant us our share in Your Torah, and may we serve You there with reverence, as in days of old and in former years. Then the offering of Judah and Jerusalem will be pleasing to Hashem, as in days of old and in former years.*

בריך רחמנא דסייען

הַגָּדָה שֶׁל פֶּסַח / Haggadah Shel Pesach

[Editor's note: During the two years that the Rav zt"l gave his lectures on *tefillah*, he devoted three *shiurim* in the weeks before Pesach to explanations on the *Haggadah*. This section is an adaptation of those *shiurim*.]

From my earliest youth, I remember that the children would ask each other on the first morning of Pesach, "How long did your *Seder* last?" This was true in my youth, and it is still the case today.

If the children were to ask me this now, I would answer them, "I made sure to eat the *afikoman* before *chatzos* (midnight)." According to some *poskim*, even the recitation of *Hallel* should be completed before *chatzos*. I must point out that the present-day practice in which all the children read from their prepared sheets which they received in school is not exactly in accordance with the mitzvah of וְהִגַּדְתָּ לְבִנְךָ, *and you shall tell to your children,* etc. (*Shemos* 13:8) The children have started a new *mitzvah* of וְהִגַּדְתָּ לְאָבִיךָ וּלְאִמֶּךָ, *you shall teach your father and mother,* which makes it extremely difficult to reach the *mitzvah* of *achilas matzah* — and certainly the *afikoman* — before *chatzos*.

Rather than discourage the children from actively participating, they should keep their remarks brief, so the father, or other leader of the *Seder,* can read the text of the *Haggadah* and explain the *nissim* of *yetzias Mitzrayim*. However, the children should be encouraged to say their *divrei Torah* during the meal if there is time or, otherwise, during the daytime meals of Yom Tov.

The *Haggadah shel leil Pesach* is probably the most popular *sefer,* after the *siddur,* in the Jewish home. There are at least a thousand commentaries on the *Haggadah,* each with different explanations and interpretations. It is not the purpose of this *shiur* to add another one, but rather to share a few thoughts on various parts of the *Haggadah.*

On *Seder* night, it is a *mitzvas asei d'Oraisa* to retell to one's children the events surrounding *yetzias Mitzrayim*. If one has the *zechus* to have children or grandchildren, it is a *mitzvah* for the father or grandfather to hand down to them the details of *yetzias Mitzrayim*. The saying of so-called *"gute vertlach," good, short pieces of Torah,* is very nice, but if these are not details of the narrative of *yetzias Mitzrayim* — or its meaning and message — they are not a part of this *mitzvah*. On *Seder* night, the children are encouraged to ask any question relevant to *yetzias Mitzrayim,* and the father has a special *mitzvah d'Oraisa* to respond to these questions, and tell his children about the miracles *HaKadosh Baruch Hu* did for us. This is based on the *pasuk*: וְהִגַּדְתָּ לְבִנְךָ בַּיּוֹם הַהוּא לֵאמֹר בַּעֲבוּר זֶה עָשָׂה ה' לִי בְּצֵאתִי מִמִּצְרָיִם, *And you shall tell your son on that day, saying, "It is because of this that Hashem acted on my behalf when I left Egypt"* (Shemos 13:8).

The Gemara says: תַּנְיָא רַבִּי אֱלִיעֶזֶר אוֹמֵר: חוֹטְפִין מַצּוֹת בְּלֵילֵי פְסָחִים בִּשְׁבִיל תִּינוֹקוֹת שֶׁלֹּא יִשְׁנוּ, *It is stated in a Baraisa that Rabbi Eliezer said: One is "choteif" the matzah on Pesach nights for the benefit of the small children, lest they fall asleep* (Pesachim 109a). The phrase חוֹטְפִין מַצּוֹת, which has the literal meaning of "snatching" the matzos, is explained by *Rashi* and *Rashbam* (ibid.) as having either of the following meanings:

It could mean מַגְבִּיהִין אֶת הַקְּעָרָה בִּשְׁבִיל תִּינוֹקוֹת שֶׁיִּשְׁאֲלוּ, the *ke'arah* (*Seder* plate containing the matzah) is raised (snatched away) to arouse the children's interest in the matzah and the other objects on the *Seder* plate.

The other explanation, which *Rashi* calls עִיקָר, the main explanation, is that אוֹכְלִים מַהֵר, the matzah is eaten early in the evening (literally: one grabs the matzos) so that the children, with their short attention span, will be awake when the matzah and *maror* are eaten. They will not be too tired when they see the father holding the matzah and hear him explain: "This is the kind of bread that our forefathers ate while they were slaves in Mitzrayim and also soon after they were redeemed." They will also hear the father explain that the *maror* reminds us of the bitterness of the lives of our forefathers while they were enslaved in Egypt.

In practice, we follow both explanations: We raise the *ke'arah* while saying הָא לַחְמָא עַנְיָא to pique the children's curiosity, and we also endeavor to eat the meal early enough so that the children can participate in performing — and understanding — all the *mitzvos* and *minhagim* of the evening. [See *Orach Chaim* 472:1 with *Mishnah Berurah* 3 and particularly *Shaar HaTziyun* 2.]

There is another explanation for חוֹטְפִין מַצּוֹת, which takes it to mean, literally: the matzos are snatched from one another (see *Rambam, Hil. Chametz U'Matzah* 7:3). While this is not our *minhag,* the reason for it is the same: to arouse the children's curiosity.

A related, and quite universal, form of חוֹטְפִין מַצּוֹת is the *minhag* that the children take the matzah that will be used for the *afikoman* while the father is distracted — and are offered a reward for its return. This little game keeps the children awake and interested until the reward is offered at the end of the meal.

I, personally, do not care for the term "stealing the matzah." *It is un-Jewish to steal* — even the *afikoman*! לֹא תִּגְנֹבוּ, the prohibition against theft, includes לֹא תִגְנֹב עַל מְנָת לְמֵיקַט, even if it is done as a prank (see *Bava*

Metzia 61b). Notwithstanding the fact that the children taking the *afikoman* is not stealing, because it is not removed from the premises, it would still be the wrong *chinuch* to call it "stealing." Rather, I would call it "hiding" the matzah, to be used later as the *afikoman,* which is called צָפוּן, hidden.

There is an oft-quoted saying, although not found in any original halachic source, מִנְהָג יִשְׂרָאֵל תּוֹרָה הִיא, that all Jewish *minhagim* have a deep meaning. For instance, the wearing of masks on Purim is an allusion to the words of *Chazal*: "רֶמֶז לְאֶסְתֵּר מִן הַתּוֹרָה מִנַּיִן . . . "וְאָנֹכִי הַסְתֵּר אַסְתִּיר פָּנַי", *Where do we find an allusion to Esther in the Torah? . . . But I will surely have concealed My face* (*Devarim* 31:18; *Chullin* 139b). The wearing of masks on Purim alludes to the fact that Hashem's "face was hidden" during the miracle of Purim. It was a *neis nistar: . . . But I will surely have concealed My face* (*Devarim* 31:18).

Thoughtful Jewish parents of old, in playing with their children, always incorporated a Torah lesson into their children's games. The story is told that the Chazon Ish, while walking with his young nephews through the streets of Bnei Brak (he never had children of his own), told the boys that he would like to play a game where he would close his eyes, pretending to be blind, and they would have to lead him. The purported object of this little game would be to see how many times he could guess which street they were on. When these boys matured, they realized that the real object of this "game" was that the Chazon Ish avoid seeing immodestly dressed women.

Similarly, the *minhag* of יַחַץ, whereby we break the matzah into a larger and smaller piece, with each being used for its special purpose, is also deeply symbolic. The smaller piece, the לַחְמָא עַנְיָא, the poor man's bread, is left in the *Seder* plate along with the *maror* and the *charoses*. However, the larger piece is hidden away for the *afikoman* by the children, who will ask for a reward for its return, and it is then eaten at the end of the meal, עַל הַשּׂוֹבַע.

I heard a beautiful explanation for the symbolism of this *minhag* from my father ז״ל. He explained that the smaller piece of matzah, the לַחְמָא עַנְיָא, represents *Olam Hazeh,* with all its trials and tribulations. This piece is left in the *Seder* plate along with the *maror* and *charoses,* reflecting life in this world, with all its sweet and bitter experiences. However, the larger, main piece, which is hidden away during the *Seder,* to be eaten after the meal as the *afikoman,* represents *Olam Haba,* which is hidden from us during our lives in this world. The eating of this piece עַל הַשּׂוֹבַע, after the meal, when one is satiated, is symbolic of our reward in *Olam Haba,* which can be obtained only if we have first satiated ourselves in this world with a life of Torah and *mitzvos.* The children's request for a reward before giving up the *afikoman* is symbolic of our reward in *Olam Haba,* which is granted to us by *HaKadosh Baruch Hu* if we have earned it.

The Haggadah was put into its present, universally accepted form by the *baal Haggadah* — his name is not known — who lived at the time of the

Geonim. The Rambam follows this order, with some slight variations. My father זצ"ל suggested that the *baal Haggadah*, in formulating the order of the *Haggadah*, followed the *pasuk*, וְהִגַּדְתָּ לְבִנְךָ בַּיּוֹם הַהוּא לֵאמֹר בַּעֲבוּר זֶה עָשָׂה ה' לִי בְּצֵאתִי מִמִּצְרָיִם, *And you shall tell your son on that day, saying, "It is because of this that Hashem acted on my behalf when I left Egypt"* (Shemos 13:8). The sections therefore follow this order:

- וְהִגַּדְתָּ לְבִנְךָ corresponds to אַרְבָּעָה בָנִים;
- בַּיּוֹם הַהוּא corresponds to יָכוֹל מֵרֹאשׁ חֹדֶשׁ ת"ל בַּיּוֹם הַהוּא;
- לֵאמֹר corresponds to מִתְחִלָּה עוֹבְדֵי עֲבוֹדָה זָרָה and all historical details;
- בַּעֲבוּר זֶה corresponds to רַבָּן גַּמְלִיאֵל הָיָה אוֹמֵר . . . פֶּסַח מַצָּה וּמָרוֹר;
- עָשָׂה ה' לִי וגו' corresponds to בְּכָל דּוֹר וָדוֹר . . . לִרְאוֹת אֶת עַצְמוֹ כְּאִלּוּ הוּא יָצָא מִמִּצְרָיִם;
- בְּצֵאתִי מִמִּצְרָיִם corresponds to הַלֵּל – בְּצֵאת יִשְׂרָאֵל מִמִּצְרָיִם.

The first part of the *Haggadah* begins with the child asking, מַה נִּשְׁתַּנָּה הַלַּיְלָה הַזֶּה מִכָּל הַלֵּילוֹת. The unusual order of things at the *Seder* is designed to pique the curiosity of the child. He has observed the father making *Kiddush* as he does every Yom Tov. But then, instead of making *hamotzi* and beginning the meal, he washes his hands — without a *berachah* — and eats the *karpas* vegetable, which he has dipped in saltwater. Then, finally, the father reaches for the matzah and, instead of making *hamotzi* and eating it, he breaks it in half and does not eat it. Then, lo and behold, the second cup is poured! By this time, the child is totally confused. And, as *Chazal* tell us, כָּאן הַבֵּן שׁוֹאֵל. The child, rightfully, says, "This is going too far. You call this סֵדֶר, order? This is the complete opposite of any order!" He then proceeds to detail his questions: מַה נִּשְׁתַּנָּה הַלַּיְלָה הַזֶּה מִכָּל הַלֵּילוֹת.

This series of questions, the מַה נִּשְׁתַּנָּה, is a quotation from the Mishnah (Pesachim 116a), and is usually the first *mishnayos be'al peh* that the child learns. If there is no child present, a grownup asks the questions. Even *talmidei chachamim* are required to ask each other these questions in the absence of children. And even if one finds himself all alone, it is a *mitzvah* to ask himself these questions (see *Baraisa* ibid.).

The number "four" plays a very prominent role in this *Seder* night. We have the four cups of wine, the four questions of the מַה נִּשְׁתַּנָּה, and the four sons. And we also have four regulations regarding the *achilas korban Pesach*: הַפֶּסַח אֵינוֹ נֶאֱכָל אֶלָּא בַּלַּיְלָה, וְאֵינוֹ נֶאֱכָל אֶלָּא עַד חֲצוֹת, וְאֵינוֹ נֶאֱכָל אֶלָּא לִמְנוּיָיו, וְאֵינוֹ נֶאֱכָל אֶלָּא צָלִי, *The korban Pesach is not eaten except at night and it is eaten only till chatzos, and it is eaten only by those who registered for it and it is eaten only roasted* (Zevachim 56b).

The significance of the number four at the *Seder* — besides being a reference to the four expression of redemption: וְהוֹצֵאתִי . . . וְהִצַּלְתִּי . . . וְגָאַלְתִּי . . . וְלָקַחְתִּי, *I shall take you out . . . I shall rescue you . . . I shall* redeem you . . . I shall take you . . . (Shemos 6:6) — is especially important in our commemoration of *yetzias Mitzrayim,* in that it corresponds to the four letters of the Ineffable Name: י־ה־ו־ה, which is contained in the *pasuk:* וְעָבַרְתִּי בְאֶרֶץ מִצְרַיִם בַּלַּיְלָה הַזֶּה, וְהִכֵּיתִי כָל בְּכוֹר בְּאֶרֶץ מִצְרַיִם מֵאָדָם וְעַד בְּהֵמָה, וּבְכָל אֱלֹהֵי מִצְרַיִם אֶעֱשֶׂה שְׁפָטִים, אֲנִי י־ה־ו־ה, *I shall go through the land of Egypt on this night, and I shall strike every firstborn in the land of Egypt, from man to beast, and against all the gods of Egypt I shall mete out punishment — I am Hashem* (Shemos 12:12).

The *baal Haggadah* divides this *pasuk* into four declarations of God's personal intervention at *yetzias Mitzrayim* :

❑ "אֲנִי וְלֹא מַלְאָךְ": וְעָבַרְתִּי בְאֶרֶץ מִצְרַיִם בַּלַּיְלָה הַזֶּה
❑ "אֲנִי וְלֹא שָׂרָף": וְהִכֵּיתִי כָל בְּכוֹר בְּאֶרֶץ מִצְרַיִם
❑ "אֲנִי וְלֹא הַשָּׁלִיחַ": וּבְכָל אֱלֹהֵי מִצְרַיִם אֶעֱשֶׂה שְׁפָטִים
❑ "אֲנִי הוּא וְלֹא אַחֵר": אֲנִי י־ה־ו־ה

The questions of the מַה נִּשְׁתַּנָּה are asked by the child who is a *chacham.* This is evidenced by the answer עֲבָדִים הָיִינוּ וגו', which the *baal Haggadah* gives as the general response to the מַה נִּשְׁתַּנָּה. This is the answer found in the Torah to the question of the *chacham:* כִּי יִשְׁאָלְךָ בִנְךָ מָחָר לֵאמֹר מָה הָעֵדֹת וְהַחֻקִּים וְהַמִּשְׁפָּטִים אֲשֶׁר צִוָּה ה' אֱלֹהֵינוּ אֶתְכֶם (*Devarim* 6:20). [Also, see חָכָם בְּנוֹ שׁוֹאֲלוֹ (*Pesachim* 116a).]

If this is so, we must understand the wisdom that lies behind the question מַה נִּשְׁתַּנָּה הַלַּיְלָה הַזֶּה?. On the surface, it does not take profound wisdom to ask, on *Seder* night, "Why is this night different from all other nights?" One could ask the same question on Succos — or any other event in the Jewish calendar. Furthermore, the child does not ask, "Why do we eat matzah, or *maror?*" etc. Rather, he is stressing that there is something different about this night.

It is therefore clear that מַה נִּשְׁתַּנָּה הַלַּיְלָה הַזֶּה is not simply the question, "Why is this night different?" This would be expressed as לָמָה or עַל מַה. Rather, מַה נִּשְׁתַּנָּה is to be understood as a rhetorical question which makes the statement: *"How different is this night from all other nights!"* The word מַה here is similar to מָה רַבּוּ מַעֲשֶׂיךָ ה', *How great are Your deeds, Hashem!*

The wisdom of the *chacham* is evidenced by the fact that he recognizes that, on this night, the most trivial things assume enormous importance. After all, on any other night, one does not care if he eats bread or matzah, sweet vegetables or bitter ones, whether one dips or not, or whether one leans or sits straight. It is totally irrelevant.

However, on *Seder* night he recognizes that these normally insignificant objects — and actions — take on a special meaning. Tonight's observance is totally unlike other *mitzvos* such as *succah, esrog, lulav,* and *shofar* which require specific objects for their fulfillment. And it is about this which the *chacham* remarks: מַה נִּשְׁתַּנָּה הַלַּיְלָה הַזֶּה, "How different is this night, when usually trivial matters take on such major significance."

And the father responds to his son's very intelligent observation: "You know why all these normally trivial matters are so important tonight? It is because tonight, we have a special guest at our table: *The guest is the Ribbono Shel Olam Himself!* Tonight is the night of Hashem; tonight Hashem pays special attention to us." לֵיל שִׁמֻּרִים הוּא לַה' לְהוֹצִיאָם מֵאֶרֶץ מִצְרָיִם הוּא הַלַּיְלָה הַזֶּה לַה' שִׁמֻּרִים לְכָל בְּנֵי יִשְׂרָאֵל לְדֹרֹתָם, *It is a night of anticipation for Hashem to take them out of the land of Egypt, this was the night for Hashem, a protection for all the Children of Israel for their generations* (Shemos 12:42).

The father explains, "From the beginning of our creation as a nation, *HaKadosh Baruch Hu* paid special attention to us on this night. He appeared to our forefathers on this night when He redeemed them from Egypt. And every year, on this night, He comes to you, the ensuing generations. It is only on one night a year (or two in *chutz la'aretz*) that we have this experience, and that is why it is so special."

This way of explaining it is borne out by the wording of the paragraph עֲבָדִים הָיִינוּ לְפַרְעֹה בְּמִצְרַיִם וַיּוֹצִיאֵנוּ ה' מִמִּצְרַיִם, which is a paraphrase: עֲבָדִים הָיִינוּ בְּיָד חֲזָקָה, *We were slaves to Pharaoh in Egypt, and Hashem took us out of Egypt with a strong hand* (Devarim 6:21), with which the *baal Haggadah* begins the father's response. However, upon reaching the words וַיּוֹצִיאֵנוּ ה', he adds his own words: אֱלֹהֵינוּ מִשָּׁם בְּיָד חֲזָקָה וּבִזְרוֹעַ נְטוּיָה וגו', to complete the narrative.

This is so, because having reached the word י-ה-ו-ה, the *baal Haggadah* interrupts and expresses the thought: "Before we go any further, let us know that at the core of our *emunah* lies the fact that our redemption was effected by *HaKadosh Baruch Hu* Himself, as אֱלֹהֵינוּ; He personally redeemed us — *bichvodo u'v'atzmo* — *He, Himself, Personally,* from Egypt. Tonight we are to remember that it is לֵיל שִׁמֻּרִים הוּא לַה'. *Tonight is God's night.*

So the father tells his son, "You rightfully pointed out that tonight everything is different. *And how is it different!* Tonight is dedicated to אֲנִי וְלֹא מַלְאָךְ, אֲנִי וְלֹא שָׂרָף, אֲנִי וְלֹא הַשָּׁלִיחַ, אֲנִי הוּא וְלֹא אַחֵר to י-ה-ו-ה. Tonight is לֵיל שִׁמֻּרִים הוּא לַה' ... לְדֹרֹתָם; it is the night when we transmit the basic elements of our *emunah* to you, the next generation."

We then continue, אִלּוּ לֹא הוֹצִיא הַקָּדוֹשׁ בָּרוּךְ הוּא אֶת אֲבוֹתֵינוּ מִמִּצְרַיִם הֲרֵי אָנוּ וּבָנֵינוּ וּבְנֵי בָנֵינוּ מְשֻׁעְבָּדִים הָיִינוּ לְפַרְעֹה בְּמִצְרָיִם. This means that if *yetzias Mitzrayim* had not been done by *HaKadosh Baruch Hu bichvodo u'v'atzmo,* through the personal involvement of *HaKadosh Baruch Hu,* the entire concept of human freedom would never have been implanted in the mind of mankind, and *Bnei Yisrael* would have been permanently enslaved to the Egyptian Pharaohs, or to any subsequent governing power. The accepted norm would have been for the Jews to be slaves.

This is a remarkable statement. It means that without *yetzias Mitzrayim al yedei HaKadosh Baruch Hu*, the event of the Exodus from Egypt as an act of God's personal intervention, there would never have been a notion of human rights, whereby the Egyptians and other civilized peoples would eventually have freed their slaves. The now commonly accepted principle that all human beings have an inherent right to freedom had its birth at *yetzias Mitzrayim al yedei HaKadosh Baruch Hu*. Without the personal intervention of *HaKadosh Baruch Hu* in *yetzias Mitzrayim*, it never would have occurred to anyone that there is any evil in one group of people subjugating or exploiting another. Therefore *yetzias Mitzrayim* was a world-historic event, not only for *Bnei Yisrael*, but also for all of mankind.

The acceptance of this basic human right of freedom from bondage, which modern civilized society now takes for granted, has taken thousands of years to be accepted in the world. Indeed, the entire Greek culture was based on slavery. The middle class relied on slaves to do all of their work, which allowed the Greek masters to pursue intellectual and physical pleasures. There was a similar situation in the Middle Ages in Europe. And without *yetzias Mitzrayim al yedei HaKadosh Baruch Hu*, there never would have been an abolitionist movement here in America, which resulted in President Abraham Lincoln freeing the slaves only some 125 years ago. In fact, even in our time, slavery has not been totally abolished; it still exists in certain parts of the world.

Therefore, the *baal Haggadah* continues, since we are talking about the miraculous personal involvement of *HaKadosh Baruch Hu* in *yetzias Mitzrayim*, it makes no difference if we already know the entire story, and we are כֻּלָּנוּ חֲכָמִים כֻּלָּנוּ נְבוֹנִים כֻּלָּנוּ זְקֵנִים כֻּלָּנוּ יוֹדְעִים אֶת הַתּוֹרָה, *even if we are all highly intelligent, all elders who are thoroughly familiar with the Torah*, . . . it is still a *mitzvah*, לְסַפֵּר בִּיצִיאַת מִצְרַיִם, *to tell* all the details *of yetzias Mitzrayim*, and, therefore, וְכָל הַמַּרְבֶּה . . . הֲרֵי זֶה מְשֻׁבָּח, *The more one tells . . . the more he is praiseworthy*. Just as *HaKadosh Baruch Hu* is Infinite, so is there never an end to talking about the *nissim v'niflaos* that He brought about in connection with *yetzias Mitzrayim*.

This is further illustrated by the next paragraph:
מַעֲשֶׂה בְּרַבִּי אֱלִיעֶזֶר וְגוֹ׳ . . . שֶׁהָיוּ . . . מְסַפְּרִים בִּיצִיאַת מִצְרַיִם. The *baal Haggadah* uses the term בִּיצִיאַת מִצְרַיִם, rather than עַל יְצִיאַת מִצְרַיִם, to emphasize that these great *Chachamim* — among the greatest of our sages after the *churban* — who were gathered in Bnei Brak instead of Yerushalayim, in the absence of the *korban Pesach*, *delved into each and every detail* of the events surrounding *yetzias Mitzrayim* during that entire night. I am sure they had eaten the matzah and said *Hallel* before *chatzos*, and later, these all-night discussions centered around the details of *yetzias Mitzrayim*, and the many *hilchos Pesach*. All the discussions of *yetzias Mitzrayim* — and even *hilchos*

Pesach — have one goal: to see ever more clearly that *yetzias Mitzrayim* occurred through the personal involvement of *HaKadosh Baruch Hu*, and not through any intermediaries, be they *malach, saraf*, or *hashaliach*, "the messenger" (Moshe Rabbeinu). Consequently, these discussions on this לֵיל שִׁמֻּרִים לַה׳ can be limitless, in accordance with the wisdom of the participants.

Then, at the end of the night, as these great Torah sages had reached the pinnacle of their perception of *HaKadosh Baruch Hu's* personal intervention in the events of *yetzias Mitzrayim,* their *talmidim* arrived and announced: "Now is the time for *Krias Shema shel Shacharis.*" What could be a more natural culmination of these lofty discussions than for them to reaffirm, in their heightened state of awareness: שְׁמַע יִשְׂרָאֵל ה׳ אֱלֹהֵינוּ ה׳ אֶחָד.

Our entire *emunah* is based on אָנֹכִי ה׳ אֱלֹהֶיךָ אֲשֶׁר הוֹצֵאתִיךָ מֵאֶרֶץ מִצְרָיִם, *I am Hashem, your God, Who has taken you out of the land of Egypt* (Devarim 5:6), and not on בְּרֵאשִׁית בָּרָא אֱלֹהִים אֵת הַשָּׁמַיִם וְאֵת הָאָרֶץ, *In the beginning of God's creating the heavens and the earth* (Bereishis 1:1). Although the creation of the world by *HaKadosh Baruch Hu,* ex nihilo, is one of the basic elements of our *emunah,* however, we cannot relate to it because we were not there when it occurred. But *yetzias Mitzrayim* is something to which we can relate, because we, as a nation, actually experienced how *HaKadosh Baruch Hu* personally redeemed us from Mitzrayim. *This is the focal point of the entire Seder night.*

It is these thoughts that the father conveys to his son — if he is a *chacham* — in response to his keen observation that tonight is מַה נִּשְׁתַּנָּה, how very different, from any other night!

וְהִגַּדְתָּ לְבִנְךָ בַּיּוֹם הַהוּא /
Vehigadeta Levincha Bayom Hahu

We now proceed to the וְהִגַּדְתָּ לְבִנְךָ section of the *Haggadah*. This details the methods that a father is to use in dealing with the אַרְבָּעָה בָנִים, the four different kinds of children envisioned by the Torah.

However, before beginning this section, the *baal Haggadah* introduces it with: בָּרוּךְ הַמָּקוֹם בָּרוּךְ הוּא בָּרוּךְ שֶׁנָּתַן תּוֹרָה לְעַמּוֹ יִשְׂרָאֵל בָּרוּךְ הוּא, *Blessed is HaMakom (Hashem), blessed is He; blessed is the One Who gave the Torah to His nation Yisrael, blessed is He.* It is important for us to understand the significance of this introduction.

The Name used here for *HaKadosh Baruch Hu* is מָקוֹם, which really means *place.* This Name is usually reserved for sad occasions, as in הַמָּקוֹם יְנַחֵם אֶתְכֶם, *May HaMakom comfort you,* or הַמָּקוֹם יְרַחֵם עֲלֵיהֶם, *may HaMakom have mercy on them,* where it is meant to convey the thought that in times of trouble and difficulties it may appear to those affected by such difficulties that *HaKadosh Baruch Hu* is absent. So we give them encouragement and hope by reaffirming our faith in the Omnipresence of *HaKadosh Baruch Hu,* and telling them that there is no empty place: *HaKadosh Baruch Hu* is the מְקוֹמוֹ שֶׁל עוֹלָם, *the "Place" of the world.* He is הַמָּקוֹם, *the "Place."* He is with us here, בְּכָל מָקוֹם, even in times of difficulty and sadness, just as surely as "place" is here with us.

Before beginning the section dealing with the *arbaah banim,* the *baal Haggadah,* too, envisions people who may be sitting at their *Seder* tables in circumstances that are less than happy. This may be because *HaKadosh Baruch Hu* has not blessed them with children, and they are there without a child to ask מַה נִּשְׁתַּנָּה, and no one with whom to be *mekayeim* the *mitzvah* of וְהִגַּדְתָּ לְבִנְךָ. In such circumstances, one is to be מַצְדִּיק עָלָיו אֶת הַדִּין, *accepting of God's judgment,* when he says the words בָּרוּךְ הַמָּקוֹם בָּרוּךְ הוּא, with which he accepts the will of *HaKadosh Baruch Hu* in not granting him children.

Or, one may have children, but either one or more have not followed in the parents' way, and ridicule their parents as "old fashioned" or superstitious in their "rigid" observance of *Torah u'mitzvos.* For this case, the *baal Haggadah* prescribes the words: בָּרוּךְ שֶׁנָּתַן תּוֹרָה לְעַמּוֹ יִשְׂרָאֵל בָּרוּךְ הוּא, God gave the Torah for *all of Yisrael;* it has an answer even for the *rasha,* and a method that may bring him back on the proper path.

The Torah has answers for any person, regardless of whether he is a *chacham, rasha, tam,* or *she'eino yodei'a lishol.* Rav Samson R. Hirsch translates: תּוֹרַת ה' תְּמִימָה מְשִׁיבַת נָפֶשׁ, *The Torah of Hashem is all-encompassing; it answers the questions asked by the soul* (Tehillim 19:8). מְשִׁיבַת נָפֶשׁ here is used in the sense of *she'eilah u'teshuvah,* answers to questions. If questions of religion torment one's soul, it will be satisfied and refreshed by the answers found in a proper understanding of the Torah, which directs man in every aspect of his existence.

⊰• — חָכָם מָה הוּא אוֹמֵר? מָה הָעֵדֹת וְהַחֻקִּים וְהַמִּשְׁפָּטִים אֲשֶׁר צִוָּה ה' אֱלֹהֵינוּ אֶתְכֶם. **What does the wise child say? (He says:) What are the testimonial laws, and the statutes, and the civil laws which Hashem has commanded you?** This question, utilizing the words of *Devarim* 6:20, is attributed to the *chacham,* not only because he categorizes the *mitzvos* of Pesach into groups — *eidos, chukim,* and *mishpatim* — but also because he wonders why the *halachos* connected with *korban Pesach* and *issur chametz* are so stringent that one violates them at the peril of the worst of all punishments, *kares*: כִּי כָּל אֹכֵל מַחְמֶצֶת וְנִכְרְתָה הַנֶּפֶשׁ הַהִוא מֵעֲדַת יִשְׂרָאֵל, *Anyone who eats leavening — that soul shall be cut off from the assembly of Israel* (Shemos 12:19); . . . וְחָדַל לַעֲשׂוֹת הַפֶּסַח וְנִכְרְתָה הַנֶּפֶשׁ הַהִוא מֵעַמֶּיהָ . . . , . . . *And he refrained from making the pesach-offering, that soul shall be cut off from its people* (Bamidbar 9:13).

The *chacham* is the first to understand the necessity for *hakaras hatov* and of remembering the great kindness that *HaKadosh Baruch Hu* showed to His people by redeeming them from slavery with great miracles. He knows that it is very fitting and proper for the people to thank *HaKadosh Baruch Hu* on this day and remember it by eating matzah and *maror,* and the *korban pesach.* However, he is puzzled by the צִוּוּי, demand, by *HaKadosh Baruch Hu* that *yetzias Mitzrayim* be remembered, and that it be remembered precisely the way it is detailed in the Torah, and why the failure to adhere to these exacting demands would result in the severest of all punishments, *kares.* His question, therefore, is מָה הָעֵדֹת וְהַחֻקִּים וְהַמִּשְׁפָּטִים אֲשֶׁר צִוָּה ה' וגו'. What is the underlying reason for the *exacting demands* by *HaKadosh Baruch Hu* in connection with Pesach? This same question could likewise be asked concerning other *mitzvos* of the Torah, as well.

It is to this insightful question that the father is to give the answer found in the Torah: וְאָמַרְתָּ לְבִנְךָ עֲבָדִים הָיִינוּ לְפַרְעֹה בְּמִצְרָיִם וגו', *You shall say to your child, "We were slaves to Pharaoh in Egypt . . ."* (Devarim 6:21). The father tells his son that our origin as *avadim* to Pharaoh served as the training for our national destiny. When *HaKadosh Baruch Hu* redeemed us from Egyptian slavery by force, וַיּוֹצִיאֵנוּ ה' מִמִּצְרַיִם בְּיָד חֲזָקָה, *Hashem took us out of Egypt with a strong hand*, it was with the intention that we become His *avadim.*

This basic truth lies at the heart of the answer (ibid. 6:22-24), which continues: וַיִּתֵּן ה' אוֹתֹת וּמֹפְתִים גְּדֹלִים וְרָעִים בְּמִצְרַיִם בְּפַרְעֹה וּבְכָל בֵּיתוֹ לְעֵינֵינוּ. וְאוֹתָנוּ הוֹצִיא מִשָּׁם לְמַעַן הָבִיא אֹתָנוּ לָתֶת לָנוּ אֶת הָאָרֶץ אֲשֶׁר נִשְׁבַּע לַאֲבֹתֵינוּ. **וַיְצַוֵּנוּ ה' לַעֲשׂוֹת אֶת כָּל הַחֻקִּים הָאֵלֶּה** וגו', *Hashem placed signs and wonders, great and harmful, against Egypt, against Pharaoh and against his entire household, before our eyes. And He took us out of there in order to bring us, to give us the land that He swore to our Forefathers.* **And Hashem commanded us to comply with all of these laws** *etc.* The Torah here is telling us that while we may have some understanding of the reasons for some of the *mitzvos*, nevertheless, a father is to tell his son that, in the final analysis, all of God's commandments are *chukim* (laws and statutes), which we are to accept solely because וַיְצַוֵּנוּ ה' . . . לְיִרְאָה אֶת ה' אֱלֹהֵינוּ, *Hashem commanded us . . . to fear Hashem, our God.* This is not an explanation of the *mitzvos*, but rather, it is the reason for the commandment to perform them. We became free of the domination of Pharaoh to become *avadim* to *HaKadosh Baruch Hu*, and He has commanded us to fulfill His will. And if we fulfill His will solely לְיִרְאָה אֶת ה' אֱלֹהֵינוּ, then we are promised לְטוֹב לָנוּ כָּל הַיָּמִים, that we will obtain the ultimate and everlasting goodness in *Olam Haba.* This will be in addition to לְחַיֹּתֵנוּ כְּהַיּוֹם הַזֶּה, keeping us alive, with a satisfying life, in this world.

The concluding sentence of the answer (ibid. 6:25) summarizes its essence: וּצְדָקָה תִּהְיֶה לָנוּ כִּי נִשְׁמֹר לַעֲשׂוֹת אֶת כָּל הַמִּצְוָה הַזֹּאת לִפְנֵי ה' אֱלֹהֵינוּ **כַּאֲשֶׁר צִוָּנוּ**, *And it will be a merit for us if we are careful to perform this entire commandment before Hashem, our God,* **as He commanded us.** This means that it will be considered *especially righteous* on our part if we keep the *mitzvos* only because *HaKadosh Baruch Hu* commanded us to do so. *This is the ultimate reason for all mitzvos.* We may understand a most beautiful explanation for the *mitzvah* of *tefillin* that satisfies our intellectual curiosity, but at the moment we put them on, we are told here to do so לִפְנֵי ה' אֱלֹהֵינוּ כַּאֲשֶׁר צִוָּנוּ, solely for the purpose of fulfilling the commandment of Hashem. This thought is expressed in all of our *birchos hamitzvos*, when we say: אֲשֶׁר קִדְּשָׁנוּ בְּמִצְוֹתָיו וְצִוָּנוּ וגו'.

This is analogous to the laws of nature. Gravity, for instance, is the force that draws matter to the earth. While there have been many attempts by physicists to explain the reason for this phenomenon, in the final analysis, the reason for it is because it is a law of nature. It exists because the One Who created the world wants this law to exist. Very tellingly, we refer to the laws of nature as חֻקּוֹת שָׁמַיִם וָאָרֶץ (*Yirmiyahu* 33:25). The words וַיְצַוֵּנוּ ה' לַעֲשׂוֹת אֶת כָּל הַחֻקִּים הָאֵלֶּה are to be taken in the same sense. The laws of Torah exist — just as the laws of nature do — because that is what *HaKadosh Baruch Hu* wants.

To be sure, the understanding of the meaning of the *mitzvos* is an important aspect of *talmud Torah* — as is evident in many parts of the Mishnah and Gemara, and Rambam and *Chinuch*, as well as many other *Rishonim* and *Acharonim*, especially Rav Samson R. Hirsch. Very tellingly, however, the literal meaning of *taamei hamitzvos* is "the taste of the *mitzvos*," but it is not its essence. One could make an analogy with the taste of food. *HaKadosh Baruch Hu* made the taste of food appealing and pleasurable to our taste buds, so that we would eat it and by eating it, our bodies would benefit from the nutrients therein, and that is its ultimate purpose. The body gains these nutrients even if the food is eaten because it tastes good and one enjoys it, and not because it keeps him alive. And if one were to eat without tasting the food, the body would still derive the same benefits from it. Similarly, the *taamei hamitzvos* are the "tastes" of the *mitzvos*, which appeal to our intellectual and emotional "taste buds" — which *HaKadosh Baruch Hu* gave us, so that we will derive pleasure from the understanding and performance of the *mitzvos*. However, the real essence of the *mitzvah* is, literally, what the word means, the fulfillment of God's commandment: וַיְצַוֵּנוּ ה' לַעֲשׂוֹת אֶת כָּל הַחֻקִּים הָאֵלֶּה לְיִרְאָה אֶת ה' אֱלֹהֵינוּ. Philosophically, it is important to understand that a human being and his will are totally separate. If a person has no will, he still exists. However, with regard to *HaKadosh Baruch Hu*, He and His will are one and the same. His will is a revelation of Himself. Therefore, if a person — with his free will — subjects his will to that of *HaKadosh Baruch Hu*, he has made direct contact with *HaKadosh Baruch Hu*. One cannot come closer to *HaKadosh Baruch Hu* than this.

The day before *Matan Torah* on *Har Sinai*, the Jewish people voluntarily accepted the Torah when they said נַעֲשֶׂה וְנִשְׁמָע. However, on the very next day, the Torah describes (*Shemos* 19:16) the awesome scene at the actual lawgiving, of thunder and lightning, fire and smoke, accompanied by loud *shofar* sounds. The Torah tells us there that Moshe Rabbeinu brought the nation, trembling with fear, to the foot of the mountain: וַיִּתְיַצְּבוּ בְּתַחְתִּית הָהָר (ibid. v.17). And *Chazal* see in these words an indication that the Jewish nation was forced to accept the Torah, שֶׁכָּפָה הקב"ה עֲלֵיהֶם אֶת הָהָר כְּגִיגִית, *HaKadosh Baruch Hu* held the mountain over them as if it were a huge vat (*Shabbos* 88a).

Nevertheless, these two forms of *kabbalas HaTorah* are not contradictory. The frightful events accompanying the actual *Matan Torah* were intended to instill a sense of *yirah*, fear of the supremacy of God's commandments, into the hearts of our people. The previous declaration of *"na'aseh venishma,"* when the Jewish people voluntarily agreed to fulfill the *mitzvos* of the Torah, was done out of their love for *HaKadosh Baruch Hu*, but this was only the first step of *kabbalas haTorah*. However, the highest form of fulfilling the *mitzvos* of the Torah is to do so out of *yirah*, simply because God commanded us to do so. This was impressed upon the minds of the awe-struck people at the time of the actual lawgiving. It was with fear and trepidation that the Torah was presented by *HaKadosh Baruch Hu* to the Jewish people at *Har Sinai*. Their descendants were to be — forever after — in fear of violating it. The purpose of the lawgiving was for the Jewish people to fear *HaKadosh Baruch Hu*.

The Gemara comments on the *pasuk*, מָה ה׳ אֱלֹהֶיךָ שֹׁאֵל מֵעִמָּךְ כִּי אִם לְיִרְאָה אֶת ה׳ אֱלֹהֶיךָ, *What does Hashem, your God, ask of you? Only to fear Hashem, your God* (*Devarim* 10:12): הַכֹּל בִּידֵי שָׁמַיִם חוּץ מִיִּרְאַת שָׁמַיִם, *Everything is in the hands of Heaven except for the fear of Heaven* (*Berachos* 33b). Since human beings have free will, their fear of heaven is not in God's hands. The frightful events accompanying *Matan Torah* were intended to impress upon our hearts a sense of *yirah*, fear of God, to teach us that the ultimate purpose of Torah is *yiras Shamayim*.

It is this that the father tells his wise son: After everything has been said, the ultimate answer to the question of מָה הָעֵדֹת וְהַחֻקִּים וְהַמִּשְׁפָּטִים אֲשֶׁר צִוָּה ה׳ אֱלֹהֵינוּ אֶתְכֶם is simply: וַיְצַוֵּנוּ ה׳ לַעֲשׂוֹת אֶת כָּל הַחֻקִּים הָאֵלֶּה **לְיִרְאָה** אֶת ה׳ אֱלֹהֵינוּ לְטוֹב לָנוּ כָּל הַיָּמִים לְחַיֹּתֵנוּ כְּהַיּוֹם הַזֶּה. וּצְדָקָה תִּהְיֶה לָּנוּ כִּי נִשְׁמֹר לַעֲשׂוֹת אֶת כָּל הַמִּצְוָה הַזֹּאת לִפְנֵי ה׳ אֱלֹהֵינוּ **כַּאֲשֶׁר צִוָּנוּ**.

[Ed. note: The thought developed by the Rav in this section — that the ultimate and ideal form of performing the *mitzvos* of the Torah is on the level of *yirah* — is not in conflict with *Yoma* 86b, where the statement is made that *teshuvah mei'ahavah* is on a higher level than *teshuvah mi'yirah*. The reference in the Gemara there is to *yiras ha'onesh*, the pragmatic fear of punishment for the *aveirah*. This is quite different than *yiras haRomemus*, which is meant by וַיְצַוֵּנוּ ה׳ לַעֲשׂוֹת אֶת כָּל הַחֻקִּים הָאֵלֶּה לְיִרְאָה אֶת ה׳ אֱלֹהֵינוּ: the awe-inspiring awareness that we, as *Bnei Yisrael*, have been chosen by *HaKadosh Baruch Hu*, the All-Powerful Creator, to fulfill His commandments, and we do so because He has commanded us to do so (see *Maayan Beis HaSho'evah, Acharei* 16:30, *Sforno, Devarim* 30:1-2: תִּהְיֶה תְּשׁוּבָתְךָ כְּדֵי לַעֲשׂוֹת רְצוֹן קוֹנְךָ בִּלְבָד).]

This answer to the *chacham* is summarized in the *Haggadah* as:

§ וְאַף אַתָּה אֱמָר לוֹ כְּהִלְכוֹת הַפֶּסַח, אֵין מַפְטִירִין אַחַר הַפֶּסַח אֲפִיקוֹמָן — **You shall also tell him that, in accordance with the laws of Pesach, one is not permitted to eat anything after partaking of the *korban pesach*.** The *Maharal* explains that this is an abbreviated version of the answer. The father must first give him the full answer as detailed in the Torah, beginning with עֲבָדִים הָיִינוּ (from *Devarim* 6:21); and then וְאַף אַתָּה אֱמָר לוֹ וגו׳, the father should illustrate the true meaning of this answer through one of the *hilchos hapesach*, which is אֵין מַפְטִירִין אַחַר הַפֶּסַח אֲפִיקוֹמָן. The *korban pesach*, or in our days, the matzah, must be eaten at the end of the meal. No sweet or dessert may be eaten afterward, so that the taste of the matzah may linger on in our mouths throughout the night. The lesson that the father gives his son here is that the dessert of a *mitzvah* is the *mitzvah* itself. There is nothing sweeter than the *mitzvah* itself. The true answer to the question מָה הָעֵדֹת וגו׳ is that the keeping of Torah and *mitzvos* is the will of *HaKadosh Baruch Hu*, and its ultimate meaning is to do so only because He commanded us to fulfill His will, כַּאֲשֶׁר צִוָּנוּ.

The next son is the *rasha*:

רָשָׁע מָה הוּא אוֹמֵר? מָה הָעֲבֹדָה הַזֹּאת לָכֶם — **What does the *rasha* say? What does this service mean to you?** This is derived from: וְהָיָה כִּי תָבֹאוּ אֶל הָאָרֶץ אֲשֶׁר יִתֵּן ה׳ לָכֶם כַּאֲשֶׁר דִּבֵּר וּשְׁמַרְתֶּם אֶת הָעֲבֹדָה הַזֹּאת. וְהָיָה כִּי יֹאמְרוּ אֲלֵיכֶם בְּנֵיכֶם מָה הָעֲבֹדָה הַזֹּאת לָכֶם. וַאֲמַרְתֶּם זֶבַח פֶּסַח הוּא לַה׳... וַיִּקֹּד הָעָם וַיִּשְׁתַּחֲווּ, *It shall be that when you come to the land that Hashem will give you, as He has spoken, you shall observe this service. And it shall be that when your children say to you, "What is this service to you?" You shall say, "It is a pesach feast-offering to Hashem"... and the people bowed* (*their heads*) *and prostrated themselves* (*Shemos* 12:25-28).

On the face of it, this son seems to be asking a nonhostile and legitimate question. He is asking his father: "What is the meaning of this service which you are performing?" *Avodah,* meaning "service to *HaKadosh Baruch Hu,*" is the word generally used in connection with *korbanos,* and specifically for the *korban pesach,* as in וְעָבַדְתָּ אֶת הָעֲבֹדָה הַזֹּאת בַּחֹדֶשׁ הַזֶּה (*Shemos* 13:5). Furthermore, the Torah prescribes a proper answer to this normal question by this inquisitive child: וַאֲמַרְתֶּם זֶבַח פֶּסַח הוּא לַה׳ אֲשֶׁר פָּסַח הוּא עַל בָּתֵּי בְנֵי יִשְׂרָאֵל בְּמִצְרַיִם בְּנָגְפּוֹ אֶת מִצְרַיִם וְאֶת בָּתֵּינוּ הִצִּיל, *You shall say, "It is a pesach feast-offering to Hashem, Who passed over the houses of the Children of Israel in Egypt when He smote the Egyptians, but He saved our households"* (ibid. 12:27).

In fact, this message itself was received by *Bnei Yisrael* as very good tidings, *besorah tovah,* which is evident from the end of it: וַיִּקֹּד הָעָם וַיִּשְׁתַּחֲווּ, they bowed down in gratitude to *HaKadosh Baruch Hu.* And Rashi comments, in the name of the *Mechilta,* that they were grateful to *HaKadosh Baruch Hu* because inherent in this message were His promises to redeem them, to bring them to their land, and to give them offspring: עַל בְּשׂוֹרַת הַגְּאֻלָּה וּבִיאַת הָאָרֶץ וּבְשׂוֹרַת הַבָּנִים שֶׁיִּהְיוּ לָהֶם.

However, notwithstanding its basic and simple meaning, our *Chachamim* find in the words מָה הָעֲבֹדָה הַזֹּאת לָכֶם additional circumstances whereby this question could be asked sarcastically by a hostile and rebellious child who does not accept the validity of the historic reason given by the Torah for this *avodah.* He sees it merely as an old-fashioned, superstitious ritual which is nothing but a burden. To him it is just "work."

The basis for this way of understanding the question is found in its introduction: וְהָיָה כִּי תָבֹאוּ אֶל הָאָרֶץ... כַּאֲשֶׁר דִּבֵּר וּשְׁמַרְתֶּם אֶת הָעֲבֹדָה הַזֹּאת. This envisions *Bnei Yisrael* as having long been settled in the land, and the *korban*

Pesach as having been brought annually for many generations. כַּאֲשֶׁר דִּבֶּר is a reference to the earlier promise וְהֵבֵאתִי אֶתְכֶם אֶל הָאָרֶץ . . . וְנָתַתִּי אֹתָהּ לָכֶם מוֹרָשָׁה אֲנִי ה׳, *I shall bring you to the land . . . and I shall give it to you as a heritage — I am Hashem* (*Shemos* 6:8). This son has witnessed his father and his grandfather offering the *korban pesach* year in and year out, and he has heard the explanation many times. However, now, for reasons of his own, he has decided that he does not wish to take part in this "ritual" any longer. He has rejected his heritage, הוֹצִיא אֶת עַצְמוֹ מִן הַכְּלָל, and he mocks his father and his family with the words: מָה הָעֲבֹדָה הַזֹּאת לָכֶם. "To me this old-fashioned ritual means nothing; why do you persist in keeping it!" Under these circumstances, this question — or rather, statement — takes on a completely different meaning, that of רָשָׁע מָה הוּא אוֹמֵר.

The answer to the *rasha* prescribed in the *Haggadah* is: וְאַף אַתָּה הַקְהֵה אֶת שִׁנָּיו. וֶאֱמָר לוֹ בַּעֲבוּר זֶה עָשָׂה ה׳ לִי בְּצֵאתִי מִמִּצְרָיִם. לִי וְלֹא לוֹ. אִלּוּ הָיָה שָׁם לֹא הָיָה נִגְאָל, *And you shall also blunt his teeth by quoting the pasuk, "Because of this did Hashem act on my behalf when I left Egypt"* (*Shemos* 13:8). *This means "for me (on my behalf) — but not for him." Had he been there, he would, indeed, not have been redeemed.* Simply, this could mean that since the *rasha* has asked a sarcastic question, in which he has excluded himself from *Klal Yisrael,* and does not really seek an explanation, he deserves this sarcastic response.

However, the meaning of this question goes much farther. It could be asked also by a person who does not really want to cut himself off from his people, one who still wants to be "Jewish," albeit not a religious Jew; even one who associates himself with Jewish charitable causes, and sincerely feels the pain of Jews who are oppressed in the world, but just refuses to accept the *mitzvos* as binding on him. Nevertheless, this person is still referred to as a *rasha.* By his refusal to accept the mandatory nature of the entire Torah and its *mitzvos,* he has, in effect, excluded himself from the essence (*ikkar*) of Judaism. לְפִי שֶׁהוֹצִיא אֶת עַצְמוֹ מִן הַכְּלָל כָּפַר בְּעִקָּר. The father tells him that there can be no "Judaism" or "Jewishness" without the acceptance of the *Torah u'mitzvos* as binding. If he is to be considered part of the body of the Jewish nation, he must accept the Torah and all of its *mitzvos.*

Rambam, in his *peirush* on the Mishnah (*Sanhedrin, Perek Chelek*), in detailing the thirteen essential principles of Judaism, the י״ג עִיקָרִים, states the following:

וְכַאֲשֶׁר יַאֲמִין הָאָדָם אֵלֶּה הַיְסוֹדוֹת כֻּלָּם וְנִתְבָּרְרָה בָּם אֱמוּנָתוֹ בָּהֶם, הוּא נִכְנָס בִּכְלַל יִשְׂרָאֵל וּמִצְוָה לְאָהֲבוֹ וּלְרַחֵם עָלָיו . . . וַאֲפִילוּ עָשָׂה מַה שֶּׁיָּכוֹל מִן הָעֲבֵירוֹת מֵחֲמַת הַתַּאֲוָה וְהִתְגַּבְּרוּת הַטֶּבַע הַגָּרוּעַ הוּא נֶעֱנָשׁ כְּפִי חֲטָאָיו אֲבָל יֵשׁ לוֹ חֵלֶק לָעוֹלָם הַבָּא וְהוּא מִפּוֹשְׁעֵי יִשְׂרָאֵל. וּכְשֶׁנִּתְקַלְקֵל לָאָדָם יְסוֹד מֵאֵלֶּה הַיְסוֹדוֹת הֲרֵי יָצָא מִן הַכְּלָל וְכָפַר בְּעִיקָּר. וְנִקְרָא מִין וְאֶפִּיקוֹרוֹס וְקוֹצֵץ בִּנְטִיעוֹת וּמִצְוָה לִשְׂנֹאוֹ וּלְאַבְּדוֹ וְגוֹ׳

Paraphrased, this means if one accepts the thirteen essential tenets of our faith, even if he does *aveiros* — he may even be a *mechallel Shabbos* — while he is called a *poshei'a Yisrael,* and will be punished for his *aveiros,* he, nevertheless, is still considered a part of the Jewish people in every respect, and is entitled to be rewarded for his *mitzvos* and *maasim tovim* in *Olam Haba.* However, if he does not accept all of the י״ג עִיקָרִים he is considered יָצָא מִן הַכְּלָל וְכָפַר בְּעִיקָּר. By refusing to accept all of the thirteen essential elements of Judaism, he has effectively removed himself from the body of the Jewish people.

To illustrate this concept, I would like to relate a brief personal story. When I was a child, approximately 5 years of age, I contracted whooping cough, which made my breathing very difficult. The doctor, not having the benefit of today's antibiotics, prescribed hot steam vapor to help me breathe easier. Unfortunately, the boiling hot kettle on the stove which provided the steam inadvertently tipped over and scalded my left arm, causing me to scream in pain. The scar remained visible for almost one year, at first red, then brownish, until it finally disappeared. This was due to the fact that the cells of the living body constantly renew themselves; the old ones die and are replaced by new ones. Despite the fact that the scar has completely healed, and my arm has, in the meantime, grown to about three times the size it was at the time of the burn, and consists of completely new tissue, I can still point to a spot on my left arm, and say, in all honesty, "Here is where I was severely burned as a child."

The analogy is clear. The body of the Jewish people, *Klal Yisrael,* personally experienced *yetzias Mitzrayim.* And, for all future generations, when a descendant of the Jewish people relates the story of the miraculous events connected with it, he is doing so as a part of the "body" of the Jewish people. Although he was not personally there, and neither was his father or grandfather, nevertheless, he, as a part of the body of the Jewish people, was there. This is conveyed by the statement later in the *Haggadah:* בְּכָל דּוֹר וָדוֹר חַיָּב אָדָם לִרְאוֹת אֶת עַצְמוֹ כְּאִלּוּ הוּא יָצָא מִמִּצְרַיִם, *In every generation a person is obligated to consider himself as having experienced the Exodus from Egypt.*

Therefore, the father tells his son, "If you don't accept the *korban pesach,* or the other *mitzvos* connected with our commemoration of *yetzias Mitzrayim,* or, for that matter, any other *mitzvah* mandated by the Torah, as binding on you, you are not Jewish. You are not a part of the Jewish people." There is no "ethnic Judaism." This son is therefore told: "There were people like you in Mitzrayim, and, indeed, they were not redeemed."

The father tells his son that which the son does not want to hear: "My dear son, I want you to be Jewish, but I also want you to know that you cannot be a Jew without a firm commitment to uphold all of the *mitzvos* of the Torah. And if you do not accept this basic tenet of Judaism, then I must tell you לִי וְלֹא לוֹ, you are not a part of our nation and its history. Make up your mind:

either you are Jewish in the full sense of the word, or you are not at all Jewish."

The advice given by the Torah to a father who wants to see his son become a *baal teshuvah* is not to countenance in him some watered-down, "ethnic" form of Judaism without the acceptance of the *mitzvos,* but rather, he must make it absolutely clear to him that there can be no *"klal"* of *Yisrael* without a full and unconditional commitment to Torah and *mitzvos.*

However, once one admits that there is a Judaism without a full commitment to Torah, he has effectively closed the door to potential *baalei teshuvah.* Why should such a person want to accept the full weight of Torah and *mitzvos* if he can be a Jew without it? Furthermore, a form of Judaism that is not fully committed to Torah and *mitzvos* could lead to one marrying a non-Jew, and having children who consequently are not Jewish, but still be buried with a *tallis* on *Har HaZeisim,* with a "rabbi" offering a *hesped,* because "after all, he was a good Jew."

This method of unequivocally and clearly defining the nature of the Jewish people was practiced by Yehoshua before his death, in his fiery speech (*Yehoshua* 24:2,15), part of which is quoted later in the *Haggadah*: וַיֹּאמֶר יְהוֹשֻׁעַ אֶל כָּל הָעָם כֹּה אָמַר ה׳ אֱלֹהֵי יִשְׂרָאֵל בְּעֵבֶר הַנָּהָר יָשְׁבוּ אֲבוֹתֵיכֶם מֵעוֹלָם . . . וְאִם רַע בְּעֵינֵיכֶם לַעֲבֹד אֶת ה׳ בַּחֲרוּ לָכֶם הַיּוֹם אֶת מִי תַעֲבֹדוּן אִם אֶת אֱלֹהִים אֲשֶׁר עָבְדוּ אֲבוֹתֵיכֶם אֲשֶׁר מֵעֵבֶר הַנָּהָר . . . וְאָנֹכִי וּבֵיתִי נַעֲבֹד אֶת ה׳, Yehoshua *said to the entire nation, "Thus said Hashem, the God of Israel: 'Your forefathers historically dwelt beyond the river' . . . If it is evil in your eyes to serve Hashem, choose today whom you will serve: the gods your forefathers served across the river . . . But as for me and my house, we will serve Hashem."*

It was also practiced by Eliyahu HaNavi when he said: עַד מָתַי אַתֶּם פֹּסְחִים עַל שְׁתֵּי הַסְּעִפִּים אִם ה׳ הָאֱלֹהִים לְכוּ אַחֲרָיו וְאִם הַבַּעַל לְכוּ אַחֲרָיו, *"How long will you dance between two opinions? If Hashem is the God, go after Him! And if the Baal, go after it"* (*Melachim I* 18:21).

The Torah does not want any child to be lost from the fold of our people, as is evident by the words of our *Chachamim,* כְּנֶגֶד אַרְבָּעָה בָנִים דִּבְּרָה תוֹרָה, *The Torah speaks to all four categories of children.* But the previously described method of bringing a child back to Torah-true Judaism is tried and proven, and will give a child who is now a *rasha* — or has the potential to become one — pause for thought, so that hope can exist that one day he will return to his people.

Following the *rasha,* we would have expected the next son to be the opposite: the *tzaddik.* However, he does not appear at all, and the next son listed is the *tam.* The word *"tam"* is used in the Gemara to denote a tame ox, *tam* (the word "tame" means the same as *tam*), as opposed to a wild ox, *muad.* The Torah tells us וְיַעֲקֹב אִישׁ תָּם יֹשֵׁב אֹהָלִים, *Yaakov was a wholesome man, abiding in tents* (*Bereishis* 25:27), on which Rashi says that תָּם

describes a person who is honest, and it is not within his nature to outsmart people.

The absence of the *tzaddik* from the listing of the children is a very significant lesson in the education of our children: *One cannot be a tzaddik unless he is a chacham.* One who attempts to be a *tzaddik* without Torah knowledge can be — at most — a *tam,* "a simple Jew." We would call such a person *"frum"* (in German, *"fromm"*). He tries his best to do the right thing, and he does not purposely do anything wrong, but since he does not learn Torah, his activities are not guided by Torah knowledge.

Accordingly, the question of the *tam* is a simple one, as opposed to the *chacham* who has already, in his mind, subdivided the Torah into *eidos, chukim,* and *mishpatim.* He asks a very unsophisticated question: מַה זֹאת "What is this?" or "What are we commemorating by this *Seder?"* And the answer the father gives him is also a very general statement: בְּחֹזֶק יָד הוֹצִיאָנוּ ה' מִמִּצְרַיִם מִבֵּית עֲבָדִים, *With a strong hand Hashem took us out of Egypt from the house of bondage* (Shemos 13:14).

Upon reflection, though, we must understand why our *Chachamim* have attributed this question, מַה זֹאת, to a תָם, a "simple-minded" person. On the surface, it seems to be a very legitimate question in the context in which it is framed in the Torah, which is the *mitzvah* of *bechor.* The Torah states: וְהָיָה כִּי יְבִאֲךָ ה' אֶל אֶרֶץ הַכְּנַעֲנִי . . . וְהַעֲבַרְתָּ כָל פֶּטֶר רֶחֶם לַה' . . . וְכָל פֶּטֶר חֲמֹר תִּפְדֶּה, *And it shall come to pass, when Hashem will bring you to the land of the Canaanites . . . then you shall set apart every first issue of the womb to Hashem . . . every first-issue donkey you shall redeem* (ibid. vs. 11-14).

This paragraph continues: וְהָיָה כִּי יִשְׁאָלְךָ בִנְךָ מָחָר לֵאמֹר מַה זֹאת, *When, tomorrow, your child will ask you, "What is the meaning of this?",* וְאָמַרְתָּ אֵלָיו, *say to him,* בְּחֹזֶק יָד הוֹצִיאָנוּ ה' מִמִּצְרַיִם מִבֵּית עֲבָדִים, *With a strong hand Hashem removed us from Egypt from the house of bondage.* This is the *pasuk* that is quoted in the *Haggadah.*

However, the quotation in the *Haggadah* is missing the notation וגו' after it, because this sentence is only the beginning of the answer. The answer continues, and explains the reason why the חֹזֶק יָד was necessary: וַיְהִי כִּי הִקְשָׁה פַרְעֹה לְשַׁלְּחֵנוּ וַיַּהֲרֹג ה' כָּל בְּכוֹר בְּאֶרֶץ מִצְרַיִם מִבְּכֹר אָדָם וְעַד בְּכוֹר בְּהֵמָה, עַל כֵּן אֲנִי זֹבֵחַ לַה' כָּל פֶּטֶר רֶחֶם הַזְּכָרִים וְכָל בְּכוֹר בָּנַי אֶפְדֶּה.

With this, the father tells his son that in commemoration of this miraculous event — in which Pharaoh was forced, by the sudden death of all male firstborn offspring of men and animals, to let us leave Mitzrayim — we were given the *mitzvah* of *bechor.*

Therefore, in its proper context, the question מַה זֹאת quoted in the *Haggadah* is only peripherally related to *yetzias Mitzrayim.* The same question could actually be asked of any *mitzvah.* But since the answer is connected with *yetzias Mitzrayim* it is included in the *Haggadah.*

It remains for us to understand what is so simple minded about the question, מַה זֹּאת, that it prompted our *Chachamim* to characterize the son who asks it as a *tam*. Furthermore, in the *Talmud Yerushalmi* (*Pesachim* 10:4), this son is actually called a *tipeish,* a fool! In its proper context, it is a perfectly intelligent question.

To explain this, I would like to offer an insight which I heard from my saintly Rebbe, Rav Yosef Leib Bloch, the Telzer Rav and *Rosh Yeshivah.* He illustrated the meaning of the *pesukim,* מַה גָּדְלוּ מַעֲשֶׂיךָ ה' מְאֹד עָמְקוּ מַחְשְׁבֹתֶיךָ. אִישׁ בַּעַר לֹא יֵדָע וּכְסִיל לֹא יָבִין אֶת זֹאת. בִּפְרֹחַ רְשָׁעִים כְּמוֹ עֵשֶׂב וַיָּצִיצוּ כָּל פֹּעֲלֵי אָוֶן וגו', *How great are Your deeds, Hashem, exceedingly profound are Your thoughts. A boor cannot know, nor can a fool understand this: When the wicked bloom like grass and all the doers of iniquity blossom,* etc. (*Tehillim* 92:6-8). My Rebbe depicted a setting which I will update to reflect our modern-day world. Imagine an uneducated person standing before the control panel of a spacecraft, with its many rows of lights, dials, switches, clocks, and counter clocks, of many sizes and shapes, illuminated by different colored lights. Noticing that one of the lights is flickering, the person asks the chief engineer, "Why is the light in the fourth row, seventh from the left, flickering?" Knowing that his visitor is totally unschooled in engineering, electronics, flight or space science, the engineer would tell him, "You are asking me about that one particular light while not being schooled in even the basic sciences needed to understand this. Without your knowledge of these sciences, I cannot begin to explain any of this to you."

My Rebbe explained this *pasuk* in a similar way. An intelligent person who looks at nature and the vast cosmos, with all of its wonders, can only marvel and exclaim: מַה גָּדְלוּ מַעֲשֶׂיךָ ה'. And when he looks at the events of world history, and the development of human civilization, his mind cries out מְאֹד עָמְקוּ מַחְשְׁבֹתֶיךָ.

And אִישׁ בַּעַר לֹא יֵדָע, *the unlearned person, does not know.* An unthinking person is not even aware of his marvelous surroundings.

But the fool, וּכְסִיל, does not understand one thing, לֹא יָבִין אֶת זֹאת: This unlearned person, who is devoid of knowledge, has only one question — only one thing, זֹאת, bothers him: בִּפְרֹחַ רְשָׁעִים כְּמוֹ עֵשֶׂב וַיָּצִיצוּ כָּל פֹּעֲלֵי אָוֶן, Why does *HaKadosh Baruch Hu* permit the *reshaim* to attain such success and to flourish? My Rebbe explained that he is called "a fool" because he picks out and expects to understand this one particular aspect of the overall plan of *HaKadosh Baruch Hu* in the management of the affairs of the world, when he has absolutely no concept at all of that master plan.

I would like to apply this same idea to the question מַה זֹּאת of the *tam.* He looks at the Torah with its hundreds of *mitzvos* — sixty-two of which apply to *korban pesach* alone — and thousands of *halachos,* but he does not say, "I would like to start learning Torah and broaden my knowledge of it; there are

HAGGADAH SHEL PESACH   559

so many things I don't understand." Instead, he picks out one *mitzvah,* and asks, מַה זֹאת?, "What is this particular law for?" And when he receives an answer for his very narrow inquiry, he is satisfied. That, indeed, is the sign of a *tam,* a simpleton, or as the *Yerushalmi* calls him, a *tipeish,* fool.

Nevertheless, if a father happens to have such a son, he is obligated to teach him on his level, one *mitzvah* at a time, and then, hopefully, he will ask another question, מַה זֹאת, and another, until slowly but surely his interest in the broader spectrum of Torah will be awakened.

Our *Chachamim* tell us, לְפִי דַעְתּוֹ שֶׁל בֶּן אָבִיו מְלַמְּדוֹ, *a father must teach his son in accordance with his abilities and mindset* (*Pesachim* 116a, in the Mishnah). Therefore, if a child is not too bright, the father, or teacher, must concentrate on teaching the subject matter to him in a form that is suitable to that particular child.

The next son is the שֶׁאֵינוֹ יוֹדֵעַ לִשְׁאוֹל, the one *who does not know enough to ask.*

On the surface of it, the father is faced here with a child who is not even interested enough to ask any questions. And to deal with this child, the *Chachamim* tell the father, אַתְּ פְּתַח לוֹ, *You must begin the conversation,* in fulfillment of the *pasuk:* וְהִגַּדְתָּ לְבִנְךָ בַּיּוֹם הַהוּא לֵאמֹר בַּעֲבוּר זֶה עָשָׂה ה' לִי בְּצֵאתִי מִמִּצְרָיִם, *And you shall tell your son on that day, saying "It is because of this that Hashem acted on my behalf when I left Egypt"* (*Shemos* 13:8).

(By the way, the word אַתְּ, in the language of the *Mechilta,* from which it comes, is the same as אַתָּה, in standard *lashon hakodesh,* and, therefore, does not suggest that this child is best dealt with gently by the mother and not the father — as has erroneously been taught.)

An attempt should be made to prompt this child to ask questions by drawing his attention to the especially beautiful and unusual table setting. For instance: "Look at the table and how it is set. Don't you see anything different here tonight?" And if, after piquing his interest by gifts of candy and nuts, he still does not ask anything, then simply begin by telling him, as the Torah prescribes: וְהִגַּדְתָּ לְבִנְךָ בַּיּוֹם הַהוּא לֵאמֹר בַּעֲבוּר זֶה עָשָׂה ה' לִי בְּצֵאתִי מִמִּצְרָיִם. The father is to tell his child that this night is dedicated to remembering and talking about *yetzias Mitzrayim* and the great *nissim* that *HaKadosh Baruch Hu* did for our forefathers to free them from Egyptian bondage.

And, as the *Haggadah* subsequently details, בַּיּוֹם הַהוּא teaches us that it must be told on the fifteenth of Nissan; בַּעֲבוּר זֶה teaches us that it be told in the presence of matzah and *maror;* and when *korbanos* are brought, the narrative is told in the presence of the *korban pesach.* Pointing to these objects, the father is to tell his son, *"Because of this,* did Hashem act for me when I left Egypt." And further on in the *Haggadah,* Rabban Gamliel explains the specific meaning of each of these objects, based on our experiences before and during *yetzias Mitzrayim.*

However, in addition to its simple meaning, שֶׁאֵינוֹ יוֹדֵעַ לִשְׁאוֹל has a secondary and deeper meaning, which is borne out by the answer given: בַּעֲבוּר זֶה עָשָׂה ה' לִי בְּצֵאתִי מִמִּצְרָיִם, as we shall explain. And this secondary meaning applies not only to a child, but also to most of us. שֶׁאֵינוֹ יוֹדֵעַ לִשְׁאוֹל does not mean only *He who does not know enough to ask,* but it also means, *He who does not know enough to ask the right question.* And the unasked question to which we are referring is: "With what *zechus* did our forefathers merit their freedom from slavery and *yetzias Mitzrayim*?"

We know that *Bnei Yisrael* had become almost completely assimilated into Egyptian life. They had neglected the *bris milah* until shortly before their departure from Egypt, and had sunk deeply into the morass of Egyptian idolatry. Our *Chachamim* tell us that on the scale of the "forty-nine" possible levels of *tumah* (מ"ט שַׁעֲרֵי טֻמְאָה), *Bnei Yisrael* had sunk almost to the lowest one. Yechezkel HaNavi, in his lengthy chastisement (*Yechezkel* 20:8), decries the condition of our forefathers in Egypt: וְאֶת גִּלּוּלֵי מִצְרַיִם לֹא עָזָבוּ וָאֹמַר לִשְׁפֹּךְ חֲמָתִי עֲלֵיהֶם לְכַלּוֹת אַפִּי בָּהֶם בְּתוֹךְ אֶרֶץ מִצְרָיִם, *They did not forsake the idols of Egypt, so I had thought to pour out My wrath upon them, to spend My anger on them, in the midst of the land of Egypt.*

And our *Chachamim* tell us (see *Mechilta, Beshalach*), even at the moment of *krias Yam Suf,* the *sar shel yam,* the "master of the sea," the spiritual force which Hashem empowered over the sea, argued against saving *Bnei Yisrael,* saying that they were no better than the Egyptians, הַלָּלוּ עוֹבְדֵי עֲבוֹדָה זָרָה וְהַלָּלוּ עוֹבְדֵי עֲבוֹדָה זָרָה.

To be sure, they still kept their "old customs" of distinctive clothing, names, and language — and in this sense they were מְצֻיָּנִים שָׁם, "an ethnic minority" — but they were just as much Egyptian as the American Indians are Americans, notwithstanding the Indians' particular ethnicity.

So the "unasked" question remains: "With what *zechus* were our forefathers redeemed from Egypt?"

The answer to this question is that our forefathers were redeemed from Egypt in the merit of their emunah that HaKadosh Baruch Hu would redeem them. This is evident from the following.

The Torah tells us: וְאָכְלוּ אֶת הַבָּשָׂר בַּלַּיְלָה הַזֶּה צְלִי אֵשׁ וּמַצּוֹת עַל מְרֹרִים יֹאכְלֻהוּ (*Shemos* 12:8), which means that *Bnei Yisrael* ate the *korban Pesach* together with matzah and *maror* while they were yet in Mitzrayim. The obvious question here is: When our forefathers ate the first *korban Pesach* in Mitzrayim, during the night of the fifteenth of *Nissan,* together with *matzah* and *maror,* not a single *bechor* had yet died in Mitzrayim. The *korban Pesach* had to be eaten בְּחִפָּזוֹן, *quickly,* before *chatzos,* even though HaKadosh Baruch Hu had not yet "spared the Jewish houses," פָּסַח עַל בָּתֵּי בְּנֵי יִשְׂרָאֵל, during *makkas bechoros.* Also, the *neis* of the unleavened dough was yet to occur the next morning, hours later. Therefore, our forefathers ate the *korban pesach* and *matzah*, seemingly, in "commemoration" of something which was yet to happen!

And furthermore, astonishingly, while still in Mitzrayim they were commanded to eat the *maror* to remember their bitter lives: וַיְמָרְרוּ אֶת חַיֵּיהֶם בַּעֲבֹדָה קָשָׁה, *They embittered their lives with hard work* (Shemos 1:14). Does one have to eat *maror* while still in a concentration camp? At this point, they certainly did not need to refresh their bitter memories — they were still in Mitzrayim!

The answer to these questions is inherent in the father's answer, בַּעֲבוּר זֶה עָשָׂה ה' לִי בְּצֵאתִי מִמִּצְרָיִם, which must be given in the presence of *matzah* and *maror,* and, if possible, *korban pesach*. And the meaning is that when *HaKadosh Baruch Hu* commanded our forefathers to eat the *korban pesach* with *matzah* and *maror* while still in Mitzrayim, they did so with absolute *emunah* that the promise of *HaKadosh Baruch Hu* to redeem them would occur. They ate the *korban pesach* and *matzah* as if the events that these symbols were to commemorate had already occurred; and the *maror* as if their redemption had occurred so long ago that they had to be reminded of the bitterness that they had experienced. And it was in the merit of this *emunah* — בַּעֲבוּר זֶה — that Hashem acted on our behalf, עָשָׂה ה' לִי בְּצֵאתִי מִמִּצְרָיִם. I merited the redemption, because I kept the *mitzvos* of *pesach,* matzah, and *maror as I was* preparing to leave Mitzrayim. I kept these *mitzvos* before the events that they were to commemorate actually occurred. My *emunah* was so strong that I considered these events as if they had actually already occurred.

And this story has to be retold again every year, in the presence of *pesach*, matzah, and *maror,* on the night of the fifteenth of *Nissan,* בַּיּוֹם הַהוּא, to emphasize that we merited our redemption from Egypt because of our total *emunah* in *HaKadosh Baruch Hu* — that night in Egypt — that the *geulas Mitzrayim* would actually take place.

The power of emunah is such that it converts the future into the present.

We express this concept in our *tefillah*. The text of the *berachah* of *techiyas hameisim* is, וְנֶאֱמָן אַתָּה לְהַחֲיוֹת מֵתִים. At the end of time *techiyas hameisim* will occur, and we are so convinced that it will occur, that we end the *berachah,* מְחַיֵּה הַמֵּתִים, *You revive the dead,* in the present tense, as if we have already witnessed the *meisim* (corpses) rising from their graves.

Similarly, in רְאֵה בְעָנְיֵנוּ, we say וּגְאָלֵנוּ מְהֵרָה לְמַעַן שְׁמֶךָ כִּי גּוֹאֵל חָזָק אָתָּה; and although we are not yet redeemed, we end the *berachah* with בָּרוּךְ אַתָּה ה' גּוֹאֵל יִשְׂרָאֵל, in the present tense, as if the redemption had already occurred.

Also, הַמַּחֲזִיר שְׁכִינָתוֹ לְצִיּוֹן and בּוֹנֵה יְרוּשָׁלָיִם are in the present tense, as if Yerushalayim were already rebuilt, and the *Shechinah* were present there.

It is in this sense that בַּעֲבוּר זֶה עָשָׂה ה' לִי בְּצֵאתִי מִמִּצְרָיִם is the answer given on Seder night to the "unasked question" of the שֶׁאֵינוֹ יוֹדֵעַ לִשְׁאוֹל. However, it is one of the important basics of our faith in that it also serves to remind us that we merited our redermption only because of our *emunah*.

לֵאמֹר / Leimor

Following our outline, we have discussed the הִגַּדְתָּ לְבִנְךָ portion of the *Haggadah*, including the significance of telling the story especially on the day of the Exodus, בַּיּוֹם הַהוּא, and we have now reached the לֵאמֹר portion of the *Haggadah*. It is in this portion that we discuss, in detail, the events of *yetzias Mitzrayim*, in accordance with the *mitzvah*, לְסַפֵּר בִּיצִיאַת מִצְרַיִם, to tell all the details of *yetzias Mitzrayim*. This *mitzvah* is based on the previously quoted *pasuk*, וְהִגַּדְתָּ לְבִנְךָ בַּיּוֹם הַהוּא לֵאמֹר בַּעֲבוּר זֶה עָשָׂה ה' לִי בְּצֵאתִי מִמִּצְרַיִם, *And you shall tell your son on that day, saying, "It is because of this that Hashem acted on my behalf when I left Egypt"* (Shemos 13:8).

It is a long story, and our *Chachamim* tell us that one of the reasons that the matzah is called *lechem oni* is because שֶׁעוֹנִים עָלָיו דְּבָרִים הַרְבֵּה, *it is the subject of considerable discussion* (Pesachim 115). This means that in the presence of the matzah, but before we actually eat it, we have a lengthy discussion explaining its meaning, together with the other related topics regarding *yetzias Mitzrayim*. This discussion and explanation is done mainly in this portion of the *Haggadah*.

This לֵאמֹר portion of the *Haggadah* begins with מִתְּחִלָּה עוֹבְדֵי עֲבוֹדָה זָרָה הָיוּ אֲבוֹתֵינוּ and concludes with וּבְנֵה לָנוּ אֶת בֵּית הַבְּחִירָה לְכַפֵּר עַל כָּל עֲוֹנוֹתֵינוּ. The entire story is contained within this beginning and ending.

The Gemara states that when we tell the story of *yetzias Mitzrayim*, we are first to retrace our early, less than glorious, beginnings as idol worshipers, and later, as slaves in Egypt, מַתְחִיל בִּגְנוּת וּמְסַיֵּם בְּשֶׁבַח. We are to start with the lowly origins of our people, and finish with the praiseworthy (Pesachim 116a).

Today, the study of one's roots has become quite fashionable. One may discover that his ancestors came from Edelfingen, Pshemishel, Izmir, or wherever else one's investigations may lead. I once had a visitor who, after telling me of his own very important ancestral *yichus*, asked me about mine. My response was, "My *yichus* is that I come from very honest people, whose 'yes' meant 'yes,' and whose 'no' meant 'no'; and who always gave to the Torah, and never took from it."

However, the Jewish nation does not have a great *yichus*. The *Haggadah* reminds us that we originate from idol worshipers:

מִתְּחִלָּה עוֹבְדֵי עֲבוֹדָה זָרָה הָיוּ אֲבוֹתֵינוּ וְעַכְשָׁו קֵרְבָנוּ הַמָּקוֹם לַעֲבוֹדָתוֹ — At the beginning, our forefathers were idol worshipers. But, now, HaKadosh Baruch Hu has brought us close to His service.

Very significantly, the *baal Haggadah* uses the word וְעַכְשָׁו, meaning *now*, and not וְאָז, *and then* — thousands of years ago — *HaKadosh Baruch Hu brought us close to Him.* But, the telling use of the word וְעַבְשָׁו reflects the fact that it was not only *then* that קֵרְבָנוּ הַמָּקוֹם לַעֲבוֹדָתוֹ, but rather, וְעַבְשָׁו, *now, HaKadosh Baruch Hu is bringing us close to His service.* Serving *HaKadosh Baruch Hu* is an ongoing process. If we do not continually make an effort through *Torah* and *mitzvos* to stay within the confines of *Yiddishkeit,* and thereby remain close to *HaKadosh Baruch Hu,* we will still be the same *ovdei avodah zarah* — in whatever form it takes in each generation — as our ancestors were in the ancient *eiver hanahar.*

This same idea is expressed in the first *berachah* of the *Shemoneh Esrei.* Our *Chachamim* have instituted that we are to bow down twice in this *berachah* of מָגֵן אָבוֹת. When we begin, we bow when saying בָּרוּךְ אַתָּה ה' אֱלֹהֵינוּ וֵאלֹהֵי אֲבוֹתֵינוּ, and then we bow again, at the end, when saying בָּרוּךְ אַתָּה ה' מָגֵן אַבְרָהָם. These two acts of homage reflect two slightly different meanings.

The first bowing, at אֱלֹהֵינוּ וֵאלֹהֵי אֲבוֹתֵינוּ, expresses the thought that one source of strength for our recognition of *HaKadosh Baruch Hu* is based on the fact that our forefathers recognized *HaKadosh Baruch Hu* and accepted Him as their God, and this recognition and belief in Him was handed down to us by our parents, who received it from their parents, all the way back to *Matan Torah,* and further back to the original *Avos.*

However, the second bowing, at the end of the *berachah,* at מָגֵן אַבְרָהָם, expresses the thought that the strength of our *emunah* is based also on our own personal recognition and relationship with *HaKadosh Baruch Hu,* following the example of Avraham Avinu. Each individual is confronted by a world filled with *kefirah* and *avodah zarah,* and he must therefore work to create his own personal relationship with *HaKadosh Baruch Hu.* And when we say מֶלֶךְ עוֹזֵר וּמוֹשִׁיעַ וּמָגֵן, we ask *HaKadosh Baruch Hu* for His help and protection in our efforts to establish this personal relationship with Him. Therefore, by bowing at the end of the *berachah,* we express our thanks to *HaKadosh Baruch Hu* for allowing us to establish and to keep our own personal relationship with Him, just as Avraham Avinu did. While he was yet a child, Avraham Avinu already recognized the existence of *HaKadosh Baruch Hu* and consequently rebelled against the existing culture of idol worship in the world.

And *HaKadosh Baruch Hu* promised Avraham Avinu: אָנֹכִי מָגֵן לָךְ, *I will protect you* in your ongoing rebellion against *avodah zarah* (*Bereishis* 15:1). We, too, invoke this promise of protection in our efforts to maintain a strong relationship of *emunah* in *HaKadosh Baruch Hu* in a world filled with *kefirah* as we bow and say בָּרוּךְ אַתָּה ה' מָגֵן אַבְרָהָם.

Therefore, the *baal Haggadah* designates our relationship with *HaKadosh Baruch Hu* as an ongoing process: וְעַבְשָׁו קֵרְבָנוּ הַמָּקוֹם לַעֲבוֹדָתוֹ, *And now, HaKadosh Baruch Hu has brought us close to His service.* This process began with Avraham Avinu, and continues throughout the ages, and applies to each and every one of us. If one does not actively work on maintaining his relationship with *HaKadosh Baruch Hu,* through His Torah and *mitzvos,* it is very easy for him to slip back into his "roots," and become like the idol worshipers from whom we descended. He does not even have to change his personality, because that is his origin.

The source of the statement, מִתְּחִלָּה עוֹבְדֵי עֲבוֹדָה זָרָה הָיוּ אֲבוֹתֵינוּ וְגוֹ׳, that our forefathers were idol worshipers, is the farewell address that Yehoshua gave to the Jewish people in Shechem before his death (*Yehoshua* 24:2): וַיֹּאמֶר יְהוֹשֻׁעַ אֶל כָּל הָעָם כֹּה אָמַר ה׳ אֱלֹהֵי יִשְׂרָאֵל, בְּעֵבֶר הַנָּהָר יָשְׁבוּ אֲבוֹתֵיכֶם מֵעוֹלָם תֶּרַח אֲבִי אַבְרָהָם, וַאֲבִי נָחוֹר, וַיַּעַבְדוּ אֱלֹהִים אֲחֵרִים.

Speaking in the name of *HaKadosh Baruch Hu,* Yehoshua told them: "From time immemorial your forefathers lived across the (Euphratres) river, etc." עוֹלָם comes from נֶעְלָם, *hidden,* which means that this was in the hidden past for such a long time that no one remembers it. If it were not for the Torah, we would not know it.

Yehoshua tells *Bnei Yisrael* that we did not have a very noble beginning. Our forefather was Terach, and he and his sons Avraham and Nachor worshiped idols, just as all people in that part of the world did at that time. To put it into today's perspective, we come from countries like Iraq and Kuwait, and our distant cousins are people like Saddam Hussein, and his ilk. These are our *"landsleit."* If it would not have been for the grace of God, Who opened the eyes of Avraham Avinu to His existence, we would have remained just the same as any of the other nations that live in that part of the world, instead of a nation that produced Moshe Rabbeinu and Yeshayahu HaNavi and Eliyahu HaNavi, and the *Tannaim* and *Amoraim,* and so many *tzaddikim* and *kedoshim.*

The two sons of Terach were completely different. Nachor was a normal and regular person, who was typical of his times; there was even a town named for him, called עִיר נָחוֹר, *the city of Nachor* (*Bereishis* 24:10). The other son, Avraham, was a little "abnormal": He believed in an invisible God, and disdained idol worship. But in his early youth, he too worshiped idols, as did the rest of the world.

And Yehoshua continues to speak in the Name of *HaKadosh Baruch Hu*:

וָאֶקַּח אֶת אֲבִיכֶם אֶת אַבְרָהָם מֵעֵבֶר הַנָּהָר וָאוֹלֵךְ אוֹתוֹ בְּכָל אֶרֶץ כְּנָעַן וָאַרְבֶּה אֶת זַרְעוֹ — *And I took your father Avraham from across the (Euphrates) river and I caused him to walk through all the land of Canaan, and I gave him many children.* Avraham had eight children, but seven of these were "normal" ordinary citizens of the world. However, continues the speech, וָאֶתֵּן לוֹ אֶת יִצְחָק, *I gave him Yitzchak,* the only one of his children who was fit to be his son, a person who was worthy of being called the son of Avraham Avinu. And then:

וָאֶתֵּן לְיִצְחָק אֶת יַעֲקֹב וְאֶת עֵשָׂו — **To Yitzchak I gave Yaakov and Eisav.** Again, we have here two children. One, Eisav, was a "normal" person, who fit into the prevailing lifestyle and culture. The other was Yaakov, the אִישׁ תָּם יֹשֵׁב אֹהָלִים, *A wholesome man abiding in tents* (Bereishis 25:27), who was different. He was withdrawn and preferred to learn. And the history continues:

וָאֶתֵּן לְעֵשָׂו אֶת הַר שֵׂעִיר לָרֶשֶׁת אוֹתוֹ — **To Eisav I gave Mount Seir to inherit.** Being the "normal person" he was, Eisav went on to conquer Mount Seir and God gave it to him as an inheritance. And finally:

וְיַעֲקֹב וּבָנָיו יָרְדוּ מִצְרָיִם — **But Yaakov and his children went down to Egypt.** When Eisav was already well established and secure as a landowner, Yaakov and his children went down to Mitzrayim because of the famine in their land.

All of this is a description of the selection and refinement process of our early beginnings as a nation. From all of the people in *eiver hanahar,* there was one Avraham, who was selected by *HaKadosh Baruch Hu,* and from all of the children of Avraham, there was but one Yitzchak, and from the two sons of Yitzchak, there was only one Yaakov, who was fit to be the father of *Bnei Yisrael.*

However, notwithstanding all of this refinement, the coarseness of their origins had not yet fully been removed from them, and it was therefore necessary for their children to go through the further refinement of the כּוּר הַבַּרְזֶל, *the iron crucible,* of Mitzrayim, to make the Jewish character worthy of, finally, becoming the עַם נַחֲלָה, *a nation of heritage* of *HaKadosh Baruch Hu* (see *Devarim* 4:20).

The story of the development of the Jewish nation continues with:

בָּרוּךְ שׁוֹמֵר הַבְטָחָתוֹ לְיִשְׂרָאֵל, בָּרוּךְ הוּא — **Blessed is He Who keeps His pledge to Israel; Blessed is He!** In this section we acknowledge the fact that *HaKadosh Baruch Hu* has promised to preserve the Jewish people as a nation, beginning with the *bris bein habesarim,* in which He promised Avraham Avinu that after a period of four hundred years of being strangers in the land, enduring hardship and suffering, his descendants would emerge as a free and wealthy people. And this promise to preserve *Bnei Yisrael* as a nation, and eventually to redeem us, continues for all times, as is referred to in the Torah, and is repeated many times in the *Neviim.*

The first such promise was made to Avraham Avinu by *HaKadosh Baruch Hu* at the *bris bein habesarim,* and this was a reference to *yetzias Mitzrayim*: יָדֹעַ תֵּדַע כִּי גֵר יִהְיֶה זַרְעֲךָ בְּאֶרֶץ לֹא לָהֶם וַעֲבָדוּם וְעִנּוּ אֹתָם אַרְבַּע מֵאוֹת שָׁנָה. וְגַם אֶת הַגּוֹי אֲשֶׁר יַעֲבֹדוּ דָּן אָנֹכִי, וְאַחֲרֵי כֵן יֵצְאוּ בִּרְכֻשׁ גָּדוֹל, *Know with certainty that your* offspring shall be aliens in a land not their own — and they will serve them, and they will oppress them for four hundred years. But also the nation that they will serve, I shall judge, and afterwards they will leave with great wealth (Bereishis 15:13-14).

Avraham was told by HaKadosh Baruch Hu at that time that his descendants would endure four hundred years of various forms of hardships and suffering, and afterwards, their oppressors would be punished, and his descendants would be freed from their enslavement and leave the land of their bondage with great wealth.

בָּרוּךְ שׁוֹמֵר הַבְטָחָתוֹ לְיִשְׂרָאֵל refers to our complete history, including the here and now. We therefore say, בָּרוּךְ הוּא, which conveys the thought, *Blessed is He Who continues to keep His promise to Yisrael, for all time to come.* In this section, we express our *emunah* that HaKadosh Baruch Hu will continue to keep His promise, up to, and including, *bi'as HaMashiach.*

Now, we continue: שֶׁהַקָּדוֹשׁ בָּרוּךְ הוּא חִשַּׁב אֶת הַקֵּץ, HaKadosh Baruch Hu has His own way of calculating the קֵץ, the time of redemption. In Mitzrayim the קֵץ was shortened, as we will explain; and as far as *our* קֵץ is concerned, apparently, it was lengthened. However, like our forefathers in Mitzrayim, who had absolute *emunah* that their *geulah* would come — and, as we explained, this was how they merited their redemption — we, too, must have *emunah sheleimah* that our *geulah,* too, will come. If the Jewish nation today is worthy of *geulah,* it is only because of the power of our *emunah.* As to when this will occur — possibly today before nightfall, or two hundred years from now — we can only leave to HaKadosh Baruch Hu. Our duty, and the basis of our *zechus* for the *geulah,* is to have absolute *emunah sheleimah* that our *geulah* will come, אֲחַכֶּה לוֹ בְּכָל יוֹם שֶׁיָּבוֹא, be it sooner or later. It is this *emunah* which will make us worthy, once again, to become the *am segulah,* and to be redeemed by HaKadosh Baruch Hu.

There have been many attempts throughout the ages to calculate the time of the final *geulah* and *bi'as HaMashiach,* but all have proved to be wrong. In fact, the Gemara tells us תִּיפַּח עַצְמָן שֶׁל מְחַשְּׁבֵי קִצִּין, *This is a curse which means, approximately, may the bones of those who try to calculate when the End will come be destroyed* (Sanhedrin 97b), which strongly admonishes those who would attempt to calculate the קֵץ and *bi'as HaMashiach.* This is based there on כִּי עוֹד חָזוֹן לַמּוֹעֵד וְיָפֵחַ לַקֵּץ וְלֹא יְכַזֵּב, אִם יִתְמַהְמָהּ חַכֵּה לוֹ, כִּי בֹא יָבֹא לֹא יְאַחֵר, *For there is yet another vision about the appointed time; it will speak of the End and it will not deceive. Though it may tarry, await it, for it will surely come; it will not delay* (Chabakuk 2:3).

לַעֲשׂוֹת כְּמָה שֶׁאָמַר לְאַבְרָהָם אָבִינוּ בִּבְרִית בֵּין הַבְּתָרִים — **So that He would do as He promised Avraham Avinu at the *Bris Bein Hab'sarim.*** Here we thank HaKadosh Baruch Hu for decreasing the time till the קֵץ in Mitzrayim to bring the *geulah* earlier. This refers to the fact that the four hundred years of hardship and suffering which were decreed at the *Bris Bein Habesarim* were calculated from the birth of Yitzchak. In this way, the period of the actual suffering of *Bnei Yisrael* was reduced considerably from the four hundred years that were decreed (see *Rashi, Shemos* 12:40).

Interestingly, the *Seder Olam* (Ch. 1) tells us that the sequence of events in the Torah surrounding the entry of Avraham Avinu into Eretz Yisrael, and his experiences there, are not in chronological order. Actually, Avraham Avinu went to Eretz Yisrael twice. The first time was when *HaKadosh Baruch Hu* told him: לֶךְ לְךָ מֵאַרְצְךָ וּמִמּוֹלַדְתְּךָ וּמִבֵּית אָבִיךָ אֶל הָאָרֶץ אֲשֶׁר אַרְאֶךָּ, *Go for yourself from your land, from your birthplace, and from your father's house to the land that I will show you* (*Bereishis* 12:1).

On that occasion, he was told simply to leave his birthplace and father's home, and go to "the land that I will show you." He was not told where to go, and he left, accompanied only by his nephew Lot, and no one else. וַיֵּלֶךְ אַבְרָם כַּאֲשֶׁר דִּבֶּר אֵלָיו ה' וַיֵּלֶךְ אִתּוֹ לוֹט, *So Avram went as Hashem had spoken to him, and Lot went with him* (ibid. v. 4). And immediately thereafter, Avraham Avinu came to Eretz Yisrael.

And according to *Seder Olam,* while Avraham Avinu was in Eretz Yisrael that first time, he had the *nevuah* of the *Bris Bein Habesarim,* in which he was promised the land as an inheritance: וַיֹּאמֶר אֵלָיו אֲנִי ה' אֲשֶׁר הוֹצֵאתִיךָ מֵאוּר כַּשְׂדִּים לָתֶת לְךָ אֶת הָאָרֶץ הַזֹּאת לְרִשְׁתָּהּ, *He said to him, "I am Hashem Who brought you out of Ur-kasdim to give you this land to inherit it"* (ibid. 15:7). However, *HaKadosh Baruch Hu* told him then that his descendants would have to endure four hundred years of various forms of hardships and suffering before they would be redeemed and prepared to take possession of the land.

The *Seder Olam* says that after the *Bris Bein Habesarim,* Avraham went back to his homeland to convince his wife and his followers to return with him to Eretz Yisrael. It would be five years before Avraham returned to Eretz Yisrael with Sarah and his followers. And it was then that the Torah tells us: וְאַבְרָם בֶּן חָמֵשׁ שָׁנִים וְשִׁבְעִים שָׁנָה בְּצֵאתוֹ מֵחָרָן, *Avram was 75 years of age when he left Charan* (*Bereishis* 12:4). And 25 years later — which was 30 years after his first trip to Eretz Yisrael — his son Yitzchak, was born when Avraham was 100 years old.

[Ed. note: See *Tosafos, Berachos* 7b, for a detailed corroboration of this approach to the text. See also *Maayan Beis HaSho'evah, Lech Lecha* 15:1-2, for further elaboration on this.]

Based on all of this, we thank *HaKadosh Baruch Hu* here for calculating the four hundred years of the *Bris Bein Habesarim* so that these years did not have to consist only of וַעֲבָדוּם וְעִנּוּ אֹתָם, *And they will serve them and they will oppress them* (*Bereishis* 15:13), but also of גֵר יִהְיֶה זַרְעֲךָ בְּאֶרֶץ לֹא לָהֶם, *your offspring shall be aliens in a land not their own,* which began with the birth of

The Torah tells us: וּמוֹשַׁב בְּנֵי יִשְׂרָאֵל אֲשֶׁר יָשְׁבוּ בְּמִצְרַיִם שְׁלֹשִׁים שָׁנָה וְאַרְבַּע מֵאוֹת שָׁנָה, *The habitation of the Children of Israel during which they dwelled in Egypt was four hundred and thirty years* (*Shemos* 12:40). This, notwithstanding the fact that Avraham Avinu was told at the *Bris Bein Habesarim:* גֵּר יִהְיֶה זַרְעֲךָ בְּאֶרֶץ לֹא לָהֶם . . . אַרְבַּע מֵאוֹת שָׁנָה. The additional thirty years were not added to the four hundred, but rather, they began at the moment of the decree of the בְּרִית בֵּין הַבְּתָרִים, which was thirty years before the birth of Yitzchak, and the four hundred years began with the birth of Yitzchak. Our forefathers left Egypt on the fifteenth of Nissan, בְּעֶצֶם הַיּוֹם הַזֶּה, *On that very day* (*Shemos* 12:51), which was exactly four hundred thirty years after the *Bris Bein Habesarim,* which took place on the fifteenth of Nissan (see *Rashi* from *Mechilta* ibid.).

Continuing with the *Haggadah,* we now cover the matzah, because what we are about to say is not directly related to the story of *yetzias Mitzrayim.* We lift up our cup of wine as a sign of happiness, as we say:

וְהִיא שֶׁעָמְדָה לַאֲבוֹתֵינוּ וְלָנוּ — **It was that promise, which stood by our forefathers and us.** The promise to preserve *Bnei Yisrael* as a nation, and eventually to redeem us, is referred to in the Torah, and is repeated many times in the *Neviim,* and it continues for all times until *bi'as HaMashiach.*

שֶׁלֹּא אֶחָד בִּלְבַד עָמַד עָלֵינוּ לְכַלּוֹתֵנוּ. אֶלָּא שֶׁבְּכָל דּוֹר וָדוֹר עוֹמְדִים עָלֵינוּ לְכַלּוֹתֵנוּ וְהַקָּדוֹשׁ בָּרוּךְ הוּא מַצִּילֵנוּ מִיָּדָם — **For not only one has risen against us to annihilate us, but in every generation they rise against us to annihilate us. But *HaKadosh Baruch Hu,* rescues us from their hand.** Throughout the ages we have repeatedly been in danger of annihilation, but this promise that *HaKadosh Baruch Hu* would preserve us as a nation has prevailed each time our destruction was sought. The survival of the Jewish people in Mitzrayim, and our survival up to this very day — in spite of whatever may happen — is due only to the constant vigilance of *HaKadosh Baruch Hu,* Who will not allow us to cease to exist as His nation.

בְּכָל דּוֹר וָדוֹר עוֹמְדִים עָלֵינוּ לְכַלּוֹתֵנוּ — To support the statement that notwithstanding the fact that there were periods and places throughout our history when Jews lived a very tranquil life — the *baal Haggadah* is telling us that we can prove this.

צֵא וּלְמַד מַה בִּקֵּשׁ לָבָן הָאֲרַמִּי לַעֲשׂוֹת לְיַעֲקֹב אָבִינוּ — **Go and learn what Lavan the Aramean attempted to do to our father, Yaakov.** We can learn this from what Lavan HaArami wanted to do to our father Yaakov. This story is referred to in the opening phrase of the *parashah* that is to be recited aloud by every Jew who brings *bikkurim* to the *Beis HaMikdash.* And we now recite — and explain — the portions of this *parashah* that are relevant to the *Seder.* The *parashah* begins:

אֲרַמִּי אֹבֵד אָבִי — **"Arami,"** meaning Lavan HaArami, **is the destroyer of my father** (*Devarim* 26:5). We do not find anywhere that Lavan actually destroyed Yaakov. What we do know is that Lavan pursued Yaakov and his family — after they secretly left to return to Eretz Yisrael — ostensibly for the purpose of kissing his daughters and grandchildren good-bye (*Bereishis* 31:21-28). Nevertheless, by prescribing the use of the specific term אֲרַמִּי אֹבֵד אָבִי, *Arami is the destroyer of my father,* in retelling our history whenever we bring *bikkurim,* the Torah is telling us that the intention of Lavan at that time was to annihilate Yaakov, his own daughters, and all of his grandchildren. And it was only because of the intervention of *HaKadosh Baruch Hu,* Who warned him: הִשָּׁמֶר לְךָ פֶּן תְּדַבֵּר עִם יַעֲקֹב מִטּוֹב עַד רָע, *Beware lest you speak with Yaakov either good or bad* (ibid. v.24), that his murderous plan was not carried out.

This plan was even worse than that of Pharaoh, who wanted only to kill the Jewish firstborn, שֶׁפַּרְעֹה לֹא גָזַר אֶלָּא עַל הַזְּכָרִים. וְלָבָן בִּקֵּשׁ לַעֲקוֹר אֶת הַכֹּל, but Lavan wanted to "uproot everything."

This event is detailed here in the *Haggadah* as proof of the previous statement that בְּכָל דּוֹר וָדוֹר עוֹמְדִים עָלֵינוּ לְכַלּוֹתֵנוּ. While Lavan masqueraded as wanting only to give Yaakov a proper *send-off,* וָאֲשַׁלֵּחֲךָ בְּשִׂמְחָה וּבְשִׁרִים בְּתֹף וּבְכִנּוֹר, and to kiss his children good-bye, לְנַשֵּׁק לְבָנַי וְלִבְנֹתַי, the Torah tells us that his real intention was to destroy them all. We are told thereby that no matter how friendly and well we are treated in our life among the non-Jews we are to be wary and to make no mistake about the fact that "In every generation, there are people who want to destroy us." And it is only because הקב״ה מַצִּילֵנוּ מִיָּדָם that we do survive.

This was borne out when the highest military authorities in Washington were asked to bomb the railroad tracks leading to Auschwitz and other concentration camps, where thousands upon thousands of our brethren where brought to be murdered in the most brutal way during the Holocaust. A few bombs would have been enough to demolish those railroad tracks and save countless numbers of Jews. However, these pleas fell upon deaf ears, because בְּכָל דּוֹר וָדוֹר עוֹמְדִים עָלֵינוּ לְכַלּוֹתֵנוּ. The thinking was, "The less Jews in Europe, the better."

Why is Saddam Hussein still in power? Why was this virulent Jew-hater not removed in the days following the victory in the Gulf War? It was only because בְּכָל דּוֹר וָדוֹר עוֹמְדִים עָלֵינוּ לְכַלּוֹתֵנוּ. The thinking, there too, was, "If there are no Jews in the Middle East, we will have no problems."

Of course, this statement, בְּכָל דּוֹר וָדוֹר עוֹמְדִים עָלֵינוּ לְכַלּוֹתֵנוּ, does not apply to all people in all places, rather it means that in every generation there are certain people who would pursue the "Final Solution" and annihilate us all, ח״ו, if they had the opportunity to do so. Were it not for that fact that הקב״ה מַצִּילֵנוּ מִיָּדָם, *HaKadosh Baruch Hu rescues us from their evil intentions,* we could not exist.

Throughout our *galus,* we have existed through *nissim.* In spite of the animosity all around us, our nation continues to exist as "one sheep among seventy wolves." This thought also lies behind the words of מוֹדִים, in which we thank *HaKadosh Baruch Hu* for נִסֶּיךָ שֶׁבְּכָל יוֹם עִמָּנוּ. And, indeed, the Jewish nation says שֶׁהֶחֱיָנוּ every day for the fact that we are still existing: עַל שֶׁהֶחֱיִיתָנוּ וְקִיַּמְתָּנוּ, which is added in מוֹדִים דְּרַבָּנָן.

While there is so much to say, and explain, about each line in the *Haggadah,* the constraints of time make this impossible.

[Ed. note: For the Rav's remark at this point, see "Epilogue."]

I would therefore like to skip to the end of the לְאָמֹר portion of the *Haggadah,* in which we give eternal thanks to *HaKadosh Baruch Hu* for our survival by listing His many acts of goodness done on our behalf from *yetzias Mitzrayim* through the building of the *Beis HaMikdash.*

The heading of this list is כַּמָּה מַעֲלוֹת טוֹבוֹת לַמָּקוֹם עָלֵינוּ. This section consists of "levels of goodness," each one rising higher than the previous one. The first step is אִלּוּ הוֹצִיאָנוּ מִמִּצְרַיִם וְלֹא עָשָׂה בָּהֶם שְׁפָטִים דַּיֵּנוּ, **If He had taken us out of Egypt without punishing them, it would be enough.** This means that if *HaKadosh Baruch Hu* had merely redeemed us from Egyptian slavery, without punishing our oppressors, this, alone, would be reason enough for us to be eternally grateful to Him, and celebrate it each year with a *Seder.*

We then continue to list increasingly higher "levels of goodness," and some of these require special explanations. For instance:

אִלּוּ קֵרְבָנוּ לִפְנֵי הַר סִינַי וְלֹא נָתַן לָנוּ אֶת הַתּוֹרָה דַּיֵּנוּ — **If He had brought us before Mount Sinai, but not given us the Torah, it would be enough.** The obvious question is, of course, what benefit could we possibly have derived from standing at the foot of *Har Sinai* and just looking at it?

The answer is that while *Matan Torah* occurred on the sixth or seventh of Sivan (*Shabbos* 87b), *kabbalas haTorah* occurred the day before. This was the day when *Bnei Yisrael* prepared themselves to receive the Torah (see *Shemos* Ch. 24). On that day, *Moshe Rabbeinu* read the *sefer habris* to the people, and brought *korbanos* through which the Jewish nation entered into a *bris* with *HaKadosh Baruch Hu* to accept the Torah, which they willingly did, by saying *naaseh venishma* even before they knew what the Torah contained. On the following day, *HaKadosh Baruch Hu* revealed His Presence directly to our forefathers, when they heard the Heavenly voice speak the first two *dibros* (commandments).

We have no concept of the level of greatness of *Bnei Yisrael* while they stood at the foot of *Har Sinai* the day before *Matan Torah* when they were fully prepared to become an *am segulah* and מַמְלֶכֶת כֹּהֲנִים וְגוֹי קָדוֹשׁ, *a kingdom of priests and a holy people,* and to accept whatever *HaKadosh Baruch Hu* would ask of them, by saying *naaseh venishma,* even before they knew what these obligations would be.

This nation, which just seven weeks earlier left the morass of the idolatrous life in Egypt, where they had sunk down to the מ"ט שַׁעֲרֵי טֻמְאָה, the forty-ninth level of *tumah,* had now attained such a high spiritual level that each Jew was adorned with two invisible crowns by *malachim,* one for *naaseh* and one for *nishma* (see *Shabbos* 88a). So quickly had they risen that *HaKadosh Baruch Hu* describes their ascent as וָאֶשָּׂא אֶתְכֶם עַל כַּנְפֵי נְשָׁרִים וָאָבִא אֶתְכֶם אֵלָי, *and I have borne you on the wings of eagles and brought you to Me* (*Shemos* 19:4). And our *Chachamim* tell us that at that moment the power of the *malach hamaves* over them had been removed; they had reached the potential to return to the original state of immortality of Adam HaRishon before the sin (see *Avodah Zarah* 5a), which did not materialize because they committed the sin of the *eigel,* the golden calf.

And all of this great spiritual wealth was accumulated by our forefathers by entering into a *bris* with *HaKadosh Baruch Hu,* in which they bound themselves to accept whatever *HaKadosh Baruch Hu* would ask of them, even without knowing what this would entail. All of this is what is meant by *kabbalas haTorah,* and it was this that occurred on the fourth or fifth of Sivan, and it is this that is meant by קֵרְבָנוּ לִפְנֵי הַר סִינַי.

However, the actual *Matan Torah,* which occurred on the following day at *Har Sinai,* was something even greater. This consisted not only of the giving by *HaKadosh Baruch Hu* of the *Aseres HaDibros,* and all the rest of the 613 *mitzvos.* Bnei Yisrael had already received *mitzvos* earlier. For instance, they already had the seven Noahide laws; *milah;* the *korban pesach* with its sixty-two *mitzvos;* Shabbos; and the other *mitzvos* that were given at Marah (see *Shemos* 15:25). Therefore, *Matan Torah* was not merely the giving by *HaKadosh Baruch Hu* of more *mitzvos* to Bnei Yisrael, but rather, with *Matan Torah, HaKadosh Baruch Hu* infused the Jewish *neshamah* with a special *kedushah.* The Torah was put into our system as a gift by the *Nosein haTorah,* the Giver of the Torah, to elevate the *nishmas Yisrael,* the Jewish soul. With the revelation at *Har Sinai,* we had the unique experience of פָּנִים בְּפָנִים דִּבֶּר ה' עִמָּכֶם בָּהָר מִתּוֹךְ הָאֵשׁ (*Devarim* 5:4), and it was this revelation that infused a special *kedushah* into the Jewish personality. And all of this happened after *kabbalas haTorah.* We were given the "gift of Torah," after we had already agreed to abide by its *mitzvos.*

Based on the foregoing, the meaning of אִלּוּ קֵרְבָנוּ לִפְנֵי הַר סִינַי וְלֹא נָתַן לָנוּ אֶת הַתּוֹרָה דַּיֵּנוּ is that we would owe a lifetime of gratitude to *HaKadosh Baruch Hu,* with *mesiras nefesh* for Torah and *mitzvos,* just for giving our forefathers the opportunity to elevate themselves — and consequently, their progeny — through the covenant with *HaKadosh Baruch Hu* for the acceptance of His *mitzvos, kabbalas haTorah* — even without our having received the actual gift of *nesinas haTorah* on the following day.

And now we add:

אִלּוּ נָתַן לָנוּ אֶת הַתּוֹרָה וְלֹא הִכְנִיסָנוּ לְאֶרֶץ יִשְׂרָאֵל דַּיֵּנוּ — If He had given us the Torah, but not brought us into the Land of Israel, it would be enough.
Imagine, without Eretz Yisrael, we would have remained in the desert as a nation without a land, similar to Bedouins. Nevertheless the power and the *kedushah* of the Torah is so great that it would have lifted us up over all difficulties.

Every other nation in the world requires a land before it develops its laws and constitution. However, as far as *Bnei Yisrael* are concerned, we had our laws and constitution well before we took possession of Eretz Yisrael.

Our nationhood is not based on the land, but rather, our land is the place where we can best apply the Torah, and live our lives as an *am segulah*. We could not, for one moment, survive without Torah. However, unfortunately, we were forced to exist without a land for two thousand years.

Rav Samson R. Hirsch expresses this fundamental idea (in his commentary to *Devarim* 27:9-10): הַסְכֵּת וּשְׁמַע יִשְׂרָאֵל הַיּוֹם הַזֶּה נִהְיֵיתָ לְעָם לַה׳ אֱלֹהֶיךָ. וְשָׁמַעְתָּ בְּקוֹל ה׳ אֱלֹהֶיךָ וְעָשִׂיתָ אֶת מִצְוֹתָו וְאֶת חֻקָּיו אֲשֶׁר אָנֹכִי מְצַוְּךָ הַיּוֹם, *Pay attention and listen, Yisrael. Today you have become a people. You are to know, today, before you get the impending possession of the land, that the common obligation to and responsibility for the Torah is what makes you into a nation*. He continues: *You can lose the land, as indeed you may, but the Torah and your everlasting duty to it remains your permanent irrevocable bond which unites you as a nation*. Unlike the other nations, it is the Torah and not the land which unifies us as a people.

Similarly, the meaning of שֶׁלֹּא עָשָׂנוּ כְּגוֹיֵי הָאֲרָצוֹת in the *tefillah* of *Aleinu* is, "He did not *form* us into a nation, as other nations were formed." The origin of the formation of all other nations was based primarily on their possession of a land from which they could not be evicted. And their governmental systems were based either on the consent of the governed, as in democracies, or on the power of a king or ruler who forced his people to follow him. However, with the Jewish nation, our nationality, our unifying force, is only the Torah, and our land is the place where this law can best be upheld.

Rav Hirsch expounds on this idea in his commentary on *Sefiras HaOmer*, מֵהָחֵל חֶרְמֵשׁ בַּקָּמָה תָּחֵל לִסְפֹּר שִׁבְעָה שָׁבֻעוֹת (*Devarim* 16:9). Paraphrased, he explains this as: "After having attained independence in your own land, and you begin to put the sickle to the grain, you are not to think that now you have reached your goal. The opposite is true. 'Israel *begins* to count where other nations cease to count.' The day after the Jewish nation celebrates its freedom is when it begins counting the seven preparatory weeks for its renewed acceptance of the Torah, so that our freedom, our land, and our wealth can attain its highest value."

Similarly, the great wealth that the Jewish nation possessed when they left Egypt, וְאַחֲרֵי כֵן יֵצְאוּ בִּרְכֻשׁ גָּדוֹל (Bereishis 15:14), attained its highest value when it was put to use by our forefathers to build the *mishkan*.

אִלּוּ הִכְנִיסָנוּ לְאֶרֶץ יִשְׂרָאֵל וְלֹא בָנָה לָנוּ אֶת בֵּית הַבְּחִירָה דַּיֵּנוּ — **If He had brought us into the Land of Israel, but not built the Temple for us, it would be enough.** Now we go a step higher. The possession of the land, as the place for the practical application of the Torah, even without a *Beis HaMikdash*, would still have allowed us to live a full Torah life in the land. We would have had the *Mishkan*, which would have been the place of the *Shechinah*, and our *korbanos* could have been brought there. We would have been eternally grateful to *HaKadosh Baruch Hu* for this, on top of all of His previous gifts, even if He had not built the *Beis HaMikdash* for us.

But now that *HaKadosh Baruch Hu* did build for us the glorious and beautiful structure of the *Beis HaBechirah* in Yerushalayim to further enhance our *avodas Hashem*, how much greater is our debt of gratitude to *HaKadosh Baruch Hu*.

Since a large part of the לֵאמֹר portion of the *Haggadah* is based on the words of *mikra bikkurim*, which was recited when one brought his basket of first fruits to the *Beis HaMikdash*, we end this list of *maalos tovos* by thanking *HaKadosh Baruch Hu* for having given us the בֵּית הַמִּקְדָּשׁ שֶׁיִּבָּנֶה בִּמְהֵרָה בְיָמֵינוּ. The gift of the *Beis HaMikdash* follows the gift of the land, because it, the *Beis HaMikdash*, is Eretz Yisrael in its purest form.

This can be seen in the wording of *mikra bikkurim*, the declaration that a farmer is to make when he places his *bikkurim* basket, no matter how simple or how elaborate, in front of the *Mizbe'ach*: הִגַּדְתִּי הַיּוֹם לַה' אֱלֹהֶיךָ כִּי בָאתִי אֶל הָאָרֶץ אֲשֶׁר נִשְׁבַּע ה' לַאֲבֹתֵינוּ לָתֶת לָנוּ (Devarim 26:3). He tells the *Kohen*, "I have some good news for you: *Today, I have arrived in Eretz Yisrael!*" This, despite the fact that he and his ancestors were born in the land, and have lived in it for hundreds of years, and if he sells his land, it will revert to him — or his heirs — at *Yovel*. Nevertheless, when the farmer arrives with his basket of *bikkurim* and places it in front of the *Mizbe'ach* in the *azarah* of the *Beis HaMikdash*, he gratefully greets the *Kohen* and tells him, "Now I have arrived in Eretz Yisrael!" By prescribing this statement to be made by every person who brings the first fruits of his land to the *Beis HaMikdash*, the Torah conveys the idea that Eretz Yisrael in its purest form, at its core, is inside the *Beis HaMikdash*, the place of the *Shechinah*. One's own personal piece of Eretz Yisrael is only the peripheral part of the country.

עַל אַחַת כַּמָּה וְכַמָּה טוֹבָה כְפוּלָה וּמְכֻפֶּלֶת לַמָּקוֹם עָלֵינוּ — **Thus, how much more so should we be grateful to the Omnipresent for all the numerous favors He showered upon us.** In closing, we now say that if each of these fifteen "levels of goodness," starting from *yetzias Mitzrayim* through the building of the *Beis HaMikdash*, would have been enough reason for us to make a *Seder* and to be eternally grateful to *HaKadosh Baruch Hu*, how much greater is our debt of gratitude to Him for having done all of these things for us. However, now we add a new "level" of *tovah*, a fifteenth, that of:

לְכַפֵּר עַל כָּל עֲוֹנוֹתֵינוּ — **For the purpose of forgiving our sins.** I once heard a very profound explanation — which impressed me greatly — of the meaning of this ending of the מַעֲלוֹת טוֹבוֹת, from Dr. Yitzchok Breuer, whom I was privileged to have as my guest on *shevii shel Pesach* in Baltimore. [Ed. note: The year was 1940 — courtesy of Dr. Elliott Bondi.] It is especially relevant to repeat the source of this thought while discussing the *geulas Mitzrayim* in light of the *maamar Chazal*, כָּל הָאוֹמֵר דָּבָר בְּשֵׁם אוֹמְרוֹ מֵבִיא גְאֻלָּה לָעוֹלָם, *If one attributes something (of importance) to the one who said it, he is instrumental in bringing redemption into the world* (*Pirkei Avos* 6:6).

Dr. Breuer explained that לְכַפֵּר עַל כָּל עֲוֹנוֹתֵינוּ does not merely describe the purpose of the *Beis HaMikdash*, but it is actually the purpose and goal of all of the aforementioned fifteen מַעֲלוֹת טוֹבוֹת. The entire purpose and goal of *HaKadosh Baruch Hu*, in all of these acts of redemption and preservation of *Am Yisrael* — beginning with *yetzias Mitzrayim* and rising ever higher until its culmination with the *binyan Beis HaMikdash* and its *korbanos* which effect *kapparah* — was *to form a Jewish nation without sin; to bring the Jewish nation back to the level of Adam HaRishon in Gan Eden* (see *Ramban* on *Parashas Bechukosai* 26:6).

This is what *HaKadosh Baruch Hu* had in mind when He told us: וִהְיִיתֶם לִי סְגֻלָּה מִכָּל הָעַמִּים . . . וְאַתֶּם תִּהְיוּ לִי מַמְלֶכֶת כֹּהֲנִים וְגוֹי קָדוֹשׁ, *You will be a treasure to Me from among all the peoples . . . You will be to Me a kingdom of priests and a holy nation* (*Shemos* 19:5-6).

And the Jewish people is *mispallel* for the rebuilding of the *Beis HaMikdash*, שֶׁיִּבָּנֶה בֵּית הַמִּקְדָּשׁ בִּמְהֵרָה בְיָמֵינוּ, because only through the *Beis HaMikdash* with its *avodas hakorbanos* will we, who live with our *yetzer hara* and commit sins, have the possibility of effecting a complete *kapparah* for our *aveiros*.

With this, we conclude the לֵאמֹר portion of the *Haggadah*, which began with גְּנוּת, *our lowly origins* (*Pesachim* 116a), in which we described our beginnings as idol worshipers, as were the rest of the people in the world. But, through *nissim* and *niflaos*, *HaKadosh Baruch Hu* raised us up, step by step, to the highest possible level of *shevach*, that of *binyan Beis HaMikdash*, with which we were given the opportunity לְכַפֵּר עַל כָּל עֲוֹנוֹתֵינוּ.

רַבָּן גַּמְלִיאֵל הָיָה אוֹמֵר כָּל שֶׁלֹּא אָמַר שְׁלֹשָׁה דְבָרִים אֵלּוּ בַּפֶּסַח לֹא יָצָא יְדֵי חוֹבָתוֹ — Rabban Gamliel used to say, "Whoever has not explained the following three words on Pesach has not fulfilled his obligation." יָצָא יְדֵי חוֹבָתוֹ means, literally, he has not gone out of the hands of his indebtedness; he is still beholden to his obligation.

The phrase רַבָּן גַּמְלִיאֵל הָיָה אוֹמֵר, meaning *Rabban Gamliel used to say,* or *Rabban Gamliel would say* — contrasted with רַבָּן גַּמְלִיאֵל אוֹמֵר, *Rabban Gamliel says* (see *Berachos* 28b, second mishnah) which states a definitive Halachic ruling — indicates that this statement is similar to those found in *Pirkei Avos,* which consists of ethical teachings and statements of often-neglected ideal character traits as taught by the Torah, rather than definitive Halachic rulings.

Some examples of these are:

שִׁמְעוֹן הַצַּדִּיק הָיָה מִשְּׁיָרֵי כְּנֶסֶת הַגְּדוֹלָה, הוּא הָיָה אוֹמֵר עַל שְׁלֹשָׁה דְבָרִים הָעוֹלָם עוֹמֵד ... וגו׳ — *Shimon the Righteous was among the survivors of the Great Assembly. He would say, "The world exists because of three things,"* etc. (*Avos* 1:2);

אַנְטִיגְנוֹס אִישׁ סוֹכוֹ ... הוּא הָיָה אוֹמֵר אַל תִּהְיוּ כַּעֲבָדִים הַמְשַׁמְּשִׁין אֶת הָרַב עַל מְנָת לְקַבֵּל פְּרָס — *Antigenos of Socho ... He would say, "Be not like servants who serve their master for the purpose of receiving a reward,"* etc. (ibid. 1:3);

הִלֵּל ... הוּא הָיָה אוֹמֵר נְגִיד שְׁמָא אָבֵד שְׁמָא וגו׳ — *Hillel ... He would say, "He who seeks renown loses his reputation,"* etc. (ibid. 1:13).

Similarly, Rabban Gamliel's statement here, which is actually a Mishnah (*Pesachim* 116a), is to be understood in the sense of stating the ideal and proper way to complete the telling of the events of the Pesach — Exodus narrative. And since many people did not do so properly, he would make this statement often, hence: רַבָּן גַּמְלִיאֵל הָיָה אוֹמֵר, meaning, Rabban Gamliel would often stress this point.

Rabban Gamliel would stress that even after one has been sitting at the *Seder* table for several hours, has answered his children's questions, and has recounted all of the events of the Haggadah — our early history; which our forefathers experienced; our enslavement by the Egyptians; the miraculous

---

[Ed. Note. The explanations on the *Haggadah* by the Rav, beginning with Rabban Gamliel, were inadvertently omitted in the earlier editions of this *sefer*. Our earlier statement lamenting the fact that this *shiur* was never delivered was inaccurate. The error was brought to our attention by Mr. Howard Lorch, whose son, Yaakov, was a student at Yeshiva R.S.R.H and taped that *shiur* on Sunday, 3/28/1993 — ו׳ ניסן תשנ״ג. The following section, first published in the revised and expanded Second Edition of *Rav Schwab on Prayer* is an adaptation of that *shiur*. This was the Rav's third and final *shiur* on the *Haggadah* during the *Iyun Tefillah* series. I sincerely regret the oversight, and am thankful to Mr. Lorch for bringing it to my attention, and to Mr. Ben Ettlinger for providing me with the tape. MLS]

Eser Makkos, Ten Plagues, culminating with *makkas bechoros,* the death of the Egyptian firstborn sons; which led to the actual *yetzias Mitzrayim,* the Exodus from Egypt; and finally *kriyas Yam Suf,* the splitting of the *Suf Sea* — he has not comletely fulfilled the mitzvah of this night. Although by detailing all of the above events, one has fulfilled the *basic mitzvah* of *Sippur Yetzias Mitzrayim,* recounting the events of the Exodus from Egypt, nevertheless, he has not done so *fully and ideally* unless he also properly defines the three words which follow:

וְאֵלּוּ הֵן פֶּסַח מַצָּה וּמָרוֹר — **And these are: Pesach, Matzoh, and Maror.** Rabban Gamliel focuses our attention on the meaning of these *three words.*

Tosafos (*Pesachim* 116a s.v. "ואמרתם זבח פסח הוא") explains that since Rabban Gamliel, in this mishnah, bases his statement on *Shemos* 12:27 — וַאֲמַרְתֶּם זֶבַח פֶּסַח הוּא לַה' אֲשֶׁר פָּסַח עַל בָּתֵּי בְנֵי יִשְׂרָאֵל בְּמִצְרַיִם בְּנָגְפּוֹ אֶת מִצְרַיִם וְאֶת בָּתֵּינוּ הִצִּיל, *And you shall say, 'It is a pesach offering to God, Who passed over the houses of the Children of Israel in Egypt when He smote the Egyptians, but He saved our households'* — this means that one must "say," וַאֲמַרְתֶּם, and explain the meaning of the word *pesach* by declaring, "The *pesach* offering is so named because," etc. *Tosafos* continues to explain that since the *mitzvos* of *matzoh* and *maror* are likened to *korban pesach* (see *Pesachim* 120b), the requirement to talk about the meaning of these words applies to *matzoh* and *maror* as well. Rabban Gamliel teaches a new *halachah*: that one has not properly done his duty בְּפֶסַח, *at the Seder,* unless he has explained the meaning of, שְׁלֹשָׁה דְּבָרִים אֵלּוּ, **these three things:** Pesach, Matzoh, and Maror.

פֶּסַח

The first of the three words which must be properly defined is פֶּסַח, the *korban pesach,* or *pesach* offering. This, despite the fact that in the order of the *Seder,* the *matzah* and *maror* are eaten before the *korban pesach.* Today in the absence of the *Beis HaMikdash, the afikomen,* which is in commemoration of the *korban pesach,* serves in its place. Nevertheless, we begin with *pesach* because, as explained , the source for the *mitzvah* to define these three words is וַאֲמַרְתֶּם זֶבַח פֶּסַח הוּא לַה' וגו', *And you shall say, 'It is a pesach offering,'* etc. We therefore focus on *pesach* first.

פֶּסַח שֶׁהָיוּ אֲבוֹתֵינוּ אוֹכְלִים בִּזְמַן שֶׁבֵּית הַמִּקְדָּשׁ הָיָה קַיָּם עַל שׁוּם מָה — **Regarding the pesach offering which our forefathers would eat during the period when the Beis Hamikdash existed, why is it called "pesach"?** The question here is not why there is an obligation to eat the *korban pesach* — this question could just as well be asked concerning *Shabbos,* or *succah,* or any other *mitzvah,* and we do not find any obligation to ask such a question.

Furthermore, if that were its meaning, the question would be phrased as "לָמָה הָיוּ אֲבוֹתֵינוּ אוֹכְלִים פֶּסַח בִּזְמַן שֶׁבֵּית הַמִּקְדָּשׁ הָיָה קַיָּם", *Why did our forefathers eat the pesach offering when the Beis Hamikdash stood?*

Rather, Rabban Gamliel tells us here that we are obligated to explain why the *pesach* offering has the name "*pesach*": ?עַל שׁוּם מַה (שׁוּם in Aramaic is the same as the Hebrew שֵׁם). Rabban Gamliel sees the source of this obligation in the fact that the Torah itself instructs us to explain its meaning in answer to our children's question. And we are to answer them: "וַאֲמַרְתֶּם זֶבַח פֶּסַח הוּא לַה'", *You shall say, "It is a "pesach" offering to Hashem.* The Torah immediately explains that it is called פֶּסַח, *pesach,* because: "אֲשֶׁר פָּסַח עַל בָּתֵּי בְנֵי יִשְׂרָאֵל בְּמִצְרַיִם בְּנָגְפּוֹ אֶת מִצְרַיִם וְאֶת בָּתֵּינוּ הִצִּיל". This is usually translated: "*Because **He passed over** the houses of the Children of Israel when He smote the Egyptians, but He saved our households.* Based on this translation, the Yom Tov is called "Passover" in the vernacular.

However, this meaning of אֲשֶׁר פָּסַח is not quite accurate. Simply to "*pass over*" something would be better expressed as עָבַר. A more accurate definition of פָּסַח can be found in its relationship to פִּסֵּחַ, which means one who is lame, or has great difficulty walking, and can do so only slowly. [Due to his arthritic condition, which made his walking very slow and difficult, the Rav characterized himself as a פִּסֵּחַ.] Therefore, אֲשֶׁר פָּסַח עַל בָּתֵּי בְנֵי יִשְׂרָאֵל means, *He slowly, hesitatingly, passed over the households of the Jews.* This meaning of פָּסַח is also used by Rav Samson R. Hirsch (see *Shemos* 12:11) in his explanation there.

Targum Onkelos (ibid.) expands on this sense of the word in his rendering of our phrase as: דִּי חָס עַל בָּתֵּי בְנֵי יִשְׂרָאֵל, *That He mercifully protected the Houses occupied by the Jews.* Onkelos defines אֲשֶׁר פָּסַח to mean, *He slowly, protectively, walked,* which conveys the idea of a guard slowly pacing back and forth, עַל בָּתֵּי בְנֵי יִשְׂרָאֵל, *at,* or *near, the Jewish households,* to protect them.

Therefore, פֶּסַח, *pasach,* means that God mercifully lingered עַל בָּתֵּי בְנֵי יִשְׂרָאֵל, *at the houses whose occupants were Jewish,* and protectively passed over them as He was rapidly passing through Egypt and smiting the Egyptian firstborn.

The phrase אֲשֶׁר פָּסַח עַל בָּתֵּי בְנֵי יִשְׂרָאֵל, *He mercifully and protectively lingered at the houses whose occupants were Jewish,* gives us a picture of those "Jewish houses" at the Pesach celebration during that last night in Egypt. It does not say עַל דַּלְתֵי בְנֵי יִשְׂרָאֵל, *at the doors of the Jewish households,* but rather עַל בָּתֵּי בְנֵי יִשְׂרָאֵל, *at the Jewish households.* This indicates that the doors to these houses were open. Their occupants were full of *bitachon,* complete trust in God's protection. While they were complying with the *mitzvah* of *korban pesach,* they had absolutely no fear of the consequences of the Egyptians seeing them happily enjoying their *Pesach* meal of a roasted lamb or kid, its blood placed on the doorposts, in open defiance of the Egyptian idolatrous worship of these animals. (See *Shemos* 8:22.) This public display of *bitachon* is what designated these houses as בָּתֵּי בְּנֵי יִשְׂרָאֵל, truly *Jewish households*.

There is a *minhag* to open the house door before the saying of שְׁפֹךְ חֲמָתְךָ וגו', *Pour out Your wrath*. This commemorates the open doors of the Jewish houses in Egypt during the fullfilment of the *mitzvah* of *korban pesach*, evidence of our forefathers' absolute trust in *HaKadosh Baruch Hu* on this לֵיל שִׁמּוּרִים, *night of God's protection*.

Therefore, the Torah tells us to teach our children that the reason this offering has the special name *"pesach"* rather than *shelamim* or *todah*, the usual names for thanksgiving offerings, is אֲשֶׁר פָּסַח עַל בָּתֵּי בְּנֵי יִשְׂרָאֵל, in commemoration of this night in Egypt when God mercifully lingered at the Jewish households and protectively passed over them, during the מַכַּת בְּכוֹרוֹת, the smiting of the Egyptian firstborn.

There is no mention in the Torah of any specal protection of the Jews in connection with the other nine plagues, because these were directed only at the Egyptians. Why was God's special protection necessary at *makkas bechoros*, so that וְלֹא יִתֵּן הַמַּשְׁחִית לָבֹא אֶל בָּתֵּיכֶם לִנְגֹּף, *He (God) will not permit the destroyer to enter your homes to smite* (*Shemos* 12:23)? For what reason would the Jewish houses be affected? This protection was so significant that we celebrate it by bringing the *korban pesach,* and failure to do so is punishable by *kares,* the loss of one's spiritual reward in the World to Come. Further, the entire holiday is called *"Pesach"* because of this protection.

To understand the difference between *makkas bechoros* and the other nine plagues, let us remember the discussion in the *Haggadah* between Rabbi Eliezer and Rabbi Akiva: יְשַׁלַּח בָּם חֲרוֹן אַפּוֹ, עֶבְרָה, וָזַעַם, וְצָרָה מִשְׁלַחַת מַלְאֲכֵי רָעִים, *He sent upon them: His fierce anger, fury, wrath, and trouble, a band of emissaries of evil* (*Tehillim* 78:49). Rabbi Eliezer and Rabbi Akiva understand this *pasuk* as referring to four or five different ways that each of the *makkos* afflicted the Egyptians. In any catastrophe, different people suffer differently. For instance, in a terrorist bombing, some people are killed or wounded; some experience extreme fear; some suffer emotional or psychological trauma, etc. Similarly, during the plagues in Egypt different people suffered differently, which is what is meant by the four or five aspects of the plagues contained in the aforementioned *pasuk*.

The first nine of the plagues were sent by *HaKadosh Baruch Hu* through the means of מִשְׁלַחַת מַלְאֲכֵי רָעִים, *a band of emissaries of evil,* to punish the wicked Egyptians. This did not present any danger to the Jews, so they had no need of special protection from the effects of these plagues. However, with regard to the *makkas bechoros,* besides the aforementioned five aspects of the punishment, *HaKadosh Baruch Hu* Himself Personally meted out the punishment. We read in the *Haggadah,* based on *Shemos* 12:12: "וְעָבַרְתִּי בְאֶרֶץ מִצְרַיִם בַּלַּיְלָה הַזֶּה", *And I shall pass through the land of Egypt on this night,* which is explained there to mean: אֲנִי וְלֹא מַלְאָךְ, *I and not an angel;* וְהִכֵּתִי כָל בְּכוֹר בְּאֶרֶץ מִצְרַיִם, *and I shall smite all the firstborn in the land of Egypt,* which is explained there as אֲנִי וְלֹא שָׂרָף, *I and not a seraph angel;* וּבְכָל אֱלֹהֵי מִצְרַיִם אֶעֱשֶׂה שְׁפָטִים, *and upon all the gods of Egypt I will execute judgments,* which is explained as אֲנִי וְלֹא הַשָּׁלִיחַ, *I and not a messenger;* אֲנִי ה', *I Am Hashem,* which means אֲנִי הוּא וְלֹא אַחֵר, *It is I, and (there is) no other.*

So while all the *makkos* were effected by God's מִשְׁלַחַת מַלְאֲכֵי רָעִים, *a band of emissaries of evil, makkos bechoros* had the added aspect of being carried out by God Himself through His מִדַּת הַדִּין, *God's attribute of strict justice,* and this presented a danger to the Jews in Egypt. We know that the Jewish people in Egypt had become almost completely assimilated into Egyptian life. In fact our *chachamim* tell us that on the scale of the "forty-nine" possible levels of טוּמְאָה (מ"ט שַׁעֲרֵי טוּמְאָה), the Jewish people had sunk almost to the lowest one. Yechezkel HaNavi describes how the Jewish people had adopted almost all of the Egyptian culture, especially its idolatry (*Yechezkel* 20:5-10).

(In our time, we saw a similar situation with regard to the Jews under Soviet domination who, after only 70 years, became almost completely assimilated into the Russian culture. Those who were the exception and became religious Jews , or are attempting to do so, should be lifted up on a high pedestal — we should rise in their honor when they come into *shul* — because the Russians were so extremely effective at eradicating all vestiges of Judaism from the vast majority of Jews under their control.)

Therefore, during *makkas bechoros* our forefathers were not automatically immune to punishments decreed according to the standards of strict justice, the מִדַּת הַדִּין, which was being applied by God in personally meting out the punishment to the Egyptians, because the Jewish firstborn were not that different from the Egyptian firstborn. For this reason the Jewish firstborn were very much concerned that perhaps they, too, would somehow be affected by the *makkas bechoros,* obviously not with death, because that was decreed by God only for the Egyptians , but perhaps through illness or some other affliction. Based on this, we can understand why the Jewish households needed God's special protection at the moment of *makkas bechoros.*

Notwithstanding the מִדַּת הַדִּין by means of which *HaKadosh Baruch Hu* בִּכְבוֹדוֹ וּבְעַצְמוֹ, *Personally,* meted out strict justice to the Egyptian firstborn, the Jewish households were "protectively passed over" by Him as a special *neis,* miracle, in the merit of our forefathers' fulfillment of the *mitzvah* of *korban pesach,* eating it together with their families, with open doors in public defiance of the Egyptian idolatry with its ingrained reverence for the sheep. This public act of *bitachon,* trust in God, served as a כַּפָּרָה, an *atonement,* for their earlier shortcomings, and in this *zechus,* merit, they were protected from the מִדַּת הַדִּין. Therefore, the Torah tells us, וְלֹא יִתֵּן הַמַּשְׁחִית לָבֹא אֶל בָּתֵּיכֶם, *He (God) will not permit the destroyer to enter into your homes* לִנְגֹּף, *even if* only to smite the Jewish firstborn with some other sort of punishment, while He was meting out strict justice to the Egyptian firstborn (*Shemos* 12:23).

It is this public act of *bitachon,* trust in God, which caused *HaKadosh Baruch Hu* to protect our forefathers' households in Egypt and to "pass-over" them during that historic final night in Egypt. It is for this reason that the *korban* is *called pesach.*

The Origin of the Institution of בְּכוֹרָה, *Bechorah*

I would like to take this opportunity to explain the origin of the institution of בְּכוֹרָה, *bechorah,* or "primogeniture." *Adam HaRishon* was the quintessential *bechor,* by virtue of his having been the first human being to be created. Our *Chachamim* tell us that in his efforts to do *teshuvah,* to atone for the sin of the עֵץ הַדַּעַת, *the tree of knowledge* (see *Bereishis* 3:6), *Adam HaRishon* brought a *korban,* an animal, as a sacrificial offering to *Hashem.* By means of the animal *korban,* an individual symbolically offers all of his physical and mental capacities to *HaKadosh Baruch Hu,* and this is what *Adam HaRishon* wanted to express as part of his *teshuvah* efforts. (See *Avodah Zarah* 8a.)

Our *Chachamim* also tell us (ibid.) that the animal which *Adam HaRishon* chose for his *korban* was an ox, "*whose horns preceded its hooves,*" שׁוֹר שֶׁקַּרְנָיו קוֹדְמִין לְפַרְסוֹתָיו. Ordinarily, the horns of a calf develop only with its maturity, and its hooves precede them. However, explains *Rashi,* our *pasuk* is referring to the **very first ox created,** which arose from the earth, fully developed, in a standing position; thus "its horns preceded its hooves." The *Gemara* bases this on the *pasuk*: וְתִיטַב לַה׳ מִשּׁוֹר פָּר מַקְרִן מַפְרִיס, which, interpreted aggadically, refers to that first ox, which was created fully grown, complete with horns and hooves (*Tehillim* 69:32).

Therefore, the origin of the institution of *bechor* stems from the fact that *Adam HaRishon,* the quintessential *bechor,* chose the first ox ever created, the "*bechor*" of the bovine species, as the very first *korban* in history. From that time onward, mankind accepted the institution of *bechorah,* in which, automatically, every *bechor,* firstborn, was dedicated to *HaKadosh Baruch Hu,* to serve as a *kohen,* or ministrant, and that every firstborn animal was automatically dedicated as a *korban* to Him. The Torah tells us that קַיִן, *Kayin,* the *bechor* of *Adam HaRishon,* brought a *korban* to *Hashem* consisting of produce of the earth (*Bereishis* 4:3). The narrative continues there:

וְהֶבֶל הֵבִיא גַם הוּא ..., *and Hevel **also** brought . . . (a korban to Hashem)*. Rav Samson R. Hirsch explains that by using the word "also," the Torah stresses the fact that *Hevel* brought his *own* offering, notwithstanding the fact that he was not a *bechor*, because he saw that the *korban* of his brother, the *bechor*, was not accepted by *Hashem*.

This system, that every human *bechor* was automatically dedicated to *HaKadosh Baruch Hu* to serve as a *Kohen*, and that every firstborn animal was automatically dedicated as a *korban* to Him, continued for generations. *Korbanos* offerings to *HaKadosh Baruch Hu*, animal or otherwise, were a natural expression of pure human feelings and thoughts. (See Rav Samson R. Hirsch, ibid., for a broader explanation of *korbanos* as an expression of the thoughts which lie behind them.)

But during דּוֹר אֱנוֹשׁ, *the generation of Enosh*, the institution of *bechorah*, and with it *korbanos* — both having lost their underlying meaning — were adopted by those who practiced *avodah zarah*. Consequently, every *bechor* was automatically designated as the servant of the prevailing *avodah zarah*, and every firstborn animal was sacrificed to it. The Egyptians expanded on this practice and sanctified the firstborn male of both men and animals. [See *Rambam*, *Hilchos Avodah Zarah* 1:1 for an explanation of the origins of *avodah zarah*.]

This introduction gives us a clearer picture of the events described in the aforementioned quotation from the *Haggadah*, which is based on *Shemos* 12:12. The Torah tells us there: וְעָבַרְתִּי בְאֶרֶץ מִצְרַיִם בַּלַּיְלָה הַזֶּה, *And I shall pass through the land of Egypt on this night*, which is explained in the *Haggadah* to mean: "אֲנִי וְלֹא מַלְאָךְ, *I and not an angel*; וְהִכֵּיתִי כָל בְּכוֹר בְּאֶרֶץ מִצְרַיִם מֵאָדָם וְעַד בְּהֵמָה, *and I shall smite all the firstborn in the land of Egypt, animal or man*; which is explained there as אֲנִי וְלֹא שָׂרָף, *I and not a seraph angel*, וּבְכָל אֱלֹהֵי מִצְרַיִם אֶעֱשֶׂה שְׁפָטִים, *and upon all the gods of Egypt I will execute judgment*, which is explained as אֲנִי וְלֹא הַשָּׁלִיחַ, *I and not a messenger*. אֲנִי הוּא וְלֹא אַחֵר, *It is I, and (there is) no other*. That night in Egypt, when *HaKadosh Baruch Hu* made His Personal Presence known, גִּלּוּי שְׁכִינָה, and made it clear that אֲנִי ה', *I Am Hashem*, which means אֲנִי הוּא וְלֹא אַחֵר, *It is I, and (there is) no other*, every form of idol worship — its *bechorim*, ministrants, and symbols — automatically disintegrated. It is not to be presumed that the firstborn men and animals suffered great agonies during *makkas bechoros*, but rather, when God's Presence became manifestly clear, these symbols of idolatry suddenly ceased to exist; they simply died. Similarly, when the Torah tells us that during *makkas bechoros*, *HaKadosh Baruch Hu* said of the אֱלֹהֵי מִצְרַיִם, *the gods of Egypt*, אֶעֱשֶׂה שְׁפָטִים, *I will execute judgment*, this means that these icons, the objects of Egyptian idol worship, simply crumbled into heaps of rubble, in the face of אֲנִי הוּא וְלֹא אַחֵר, the Personal Revelation of *HaKadosh Baruch Hu*. (See Rashi, ibid.)

Our *Chachamim* tell us that during *makkas bechoros*, there were Egyptian houses in which many people died, not only the known "*bechor*." This was so because Egyptian wives were promiscuous and had relations with many different men, thus producing children who were the firstborn of several different men. Therefore, these heretofore unidentified *bechorim* in the house died together with the known *bechor* of the house. (See *Rashi, Shemos* 12:31,33, from *Mechilta*.) And since the husbands were not aware that there were really many other *bechorim* living in their houses — who were supposedly their children — they assumed that the deaths were random and, אָמְרוּ כֻּלָּנוּ מֵתִים (ibid. 12:33), *They said, "We are all dead"*; they thought they would all die by this plague.

However, the Jewish women were all צִדְקָנִיּוֹת, *righteous*, faithful to their husbands, and unsullied by Egyptian lechery. There was only one exception, that of *Shelomis bas Divri*, and she was only partially at fault. (See *Rashi* to *Shemos* 2:11, and *Vayikra* 24:11). The steadfast purity of the Jewish families throughout their stay in Egypt — notwithstanding the prevailing climate of moral depravity there — is attested to by the Torah when it accords the names of each of the Jewish families with the prefix ה and the suffix י, letters which combine to form the Name of Hashem, י-ה. (See *Rashi, Bamidbar* 26:5)

Therefore, on *Seder* night, we teach our children that we bring a *korban* which is called "*pesach*," because on this night God mercifully protected, and passed over our forefathers' houses and their *bechorim:* אֲשֶׁר פָּסַח עַל בָּתֵּי בְּנֵי יִשְׂרָאֵל, which families remained pure throughout the long Egyptian *galus*, בְּנָגְפּוֹ אֶת מִצְרַיִם, *while He was afflicting the Egyptian houses*, with their many *bechorim*, which was the result of their immoral life, וְאֶת בָּתֵּינוּ הִצִּיל, *and He saved our houses*, with their pure Jewish families, in which the known *bechor* was the only *bechor*.

We must also tell our children that when the first *korban pesach* was offered by our forefathers during that last night in Egypt, the miracle of *Pesach* had not yet occurred; no Egyptian *bechor* had yet died, and no Jewish *bechor* had yet to be spared. That first *korban pesach* was not yet commemorative of anything. Our forefathers fulfilled this *mitzvah* only because Hashem had ordered them to do so, כַּאֲשֶׁר צִוָּה ה׳ אֶת מֹשֶׁה וְאַהֲרֹן כֵּן עָשׂוּ, *As God had commanded Moshe and Aharon, so did they do* (*Shemos* 12:28).

מַצָּה

Rabban Gamliel's question now focuses on the matzoh:
מַצָּה זוּ שֶׁאָנוּ אוֹכְלִים עַל שׁוּם מָה — **This unleavened bread which we eat, why is it called matzoh?** Why not call it עוּגָה, *cake*, רָקִיק, *cracker*, or even לֶחֶם, *bread*? What significance does the name *matzoh* have?

The word מַצָּה is related to מָצָה, which means "to fight," as used in וְכִי יִנָּצוּ אֲנָשִׁים וגו', *And if people fight, etc.* (*Shemos* 21:22). The making of matzoh involves a fight against the fermentation process. As soon as flour and water are mixed, the natural fermentation process begins. And if the dough-mixture is left unattended for as little as 18 minutes it will ferment into leaven, or *chametz*. Therefore to make matzoh, unleavened bread, one must "fight" the fermentation process: the dough must be kneaded, worked, and baked before it has had time to ferment, and become *chametz*.

And Rabban Gamliel explains: עַל שׁוּם שֶׁלֹּא הִסְפִּיק בְּצֵקָם שֶׁל אֲבוֹתֵינוּ לְהַחֲמִיץ עַד שֶׁנִּגְלָה עֲלֵיהֶם מֶלֶךְ מַלְכֵי הַמְּלָכִים הַקָּדוֹשׁ בָּרוּךְ הוּא וּגְאָלָם, (*It is called matzoh*) *because the dough of our forefathers did not have time to become leavened before the King Who reigns over kings, HaKadosh Baruch Hu, revealed His presence to them and redeemed them.*

When our forefathers were told by Moshe that their redemption and exodus from Egypt was imminent: they were given the *mitzvah* of *korban pesach*, which included *matzoh and maror*, which were to be eaten in their houses on the night of the fifteenth of *Nissan*. And while they were told to eat it בְּחִפָּזוֹן, *in a hurried manner*, and to be fully dressed in their travel clothing in preparation for their departure, they were told not to leave their houses all that night, וְאַתֶּם לֹא תֵצְאוּ אִישׁ מִפֶּתַח בֵּיתוֹ עַד בֹּקֶר, *and none of you shall leave the doorway of his house until morning* (*Shemos* 12:22). They were told to ignore the predicted צְעָקָה גְדֹלָה בְּמִצְרָיִם, the great panicked outcry of the Egyptians which would begin at midnight when *makkas bechoros* would strike with its full fury, and to ignore Egyptian urgings that Bnei Yisrael leave their country immediately lest all Egyptians die, וַתֶּחֱזַק מִצְרַיִם עַל הָעָם לְמַהֵר לְשַׁלְּחָם מִן הָאָרֶץ כִּי אָמְרוּ כֻּלָּנוּ מֵתִים (ibid. v. 33). It was only at daybreak that they began to leave the country: בְּעֶצֶם הַיּוֹם הַזֶּה יָצְאוּ כָּל צִבְאוֹת ה' מֵאֶרֶץ מִצְרָיִם, *on the middle of this very day, the hosts of Hashem left the land of Egypt* (see Rashi from *Sifrei Devarim* 32:48).

The Torah tells us: כִּי גֹרְשׁוּ מִמִּצְרַיִם וְלֹא יָכְלוּ לְהִתְמַהְמֵהַּ וְגַם צֵדָה לֹא עָשׂוּ לָהֶם, *for they were driven from Egypt and they could not tarry, and they could not even prepare food for themselves* (*Shemos* 12:39). The seemingly redundant phrase כִּי גֹרְשׁוּ מִמִּצְרַיִם, וְלֹא יָכְלוּ לְהִתְמַהְמֵהַּ alludes to the fact that while they were not actually driven out physically by the Egyptians — they departed in an organized manner at daybreak as *HaKadosh Baruch Hu* had commanded — they *were* driven out by the need to immediately get out of the poisonous and polluted atmosphere of Egypt, in which they had sunk to the forty-ninth level of טוּמְאָה, *impurity*, for fear that they would sink to the fiftieth, at which point their *neshamos* would be so deeply stained that they could never rid themselves of טוּמְאַת מִצְרַיִם, Egyptian impurity.

Nevertheless, our forefathers had no idea that the actual *yetzias*

Mitzrayim, the Exodus from Egypt, would come from one moment to the next. They expected to have adequate time to at least prepare food for their trip. However, due to their unexpectedly hurried departure from Egypt, our forefathers did not have time to prepare food, or even to bake bread for their journey. All they could do was to quickly gather the leftover matzoh and *maror* from the *korban pesach,* and throw some flour and water together in their knapsacks, sling them over their shoulders, and hurry out of their houses to their rallying point, *Raameses,* and from there to their first destination, *Succos,* which was at the edge of the desert (see *Shemos* 12:29-39). This long trip, miraculously quick as it was (see *Rashi* ibid. v. 37), nevertheless, must have taken several hours in the heat of the day. And upon their arrival in Succos, they took out the dough-mixture from their knapsacks to bake bread, and instead of finding it fully fermented, they found that their dough-mixture, miraculously, *had not fermented,* כִּי לֹא חָמֵץ. Therefore, the bread which they baked resulted in עֻגֹת מַצּוֹת, *matzoh cakes* (ibid. v. 39).

The suspension of the natural fermentation process during the exodus of *Bnei Yisrael* from Egypt was a miraculous event, a *neis,* which occurred as the result of the Personal Presence of *HaKadosh Baruch Hu* when He redeemed our forefathers from Egypt. The natural process of fermentation involves time, but when *HaKadosh Baruch Hu* appears, all time is suspended, for He is לְמַעְלָה מִן הַזְּמַן, *above and beyond time.*

Rabban Gamliel tells us that the significance of the name *matzoh* for the special bread which we eat on this night is that we are to remember forever that the first food which our forefathers ate after their freedom from Egypt was unleavened bread, similar to that which they ate as slaves. As slaves, they were forced to eat matzoh, which they hurriedly slapped together and baked, in their constant fight against time to meet their daily quotas of work. As such, the matzoh was truly לַחְמָא עַנְיָא, *the bread of poverty and affliction.* And when *HaKadosh Baruch Hu* Personally redeemed them, there was also insufficient time for fermentation, because time itself had been suspended when God revealed His Presence at *yetzias Mitzrayim.* Therefore, the bread which they baked immediately upon their redemption was matzoh, *just as they had eaten when they were slaves.*

The lesson which our forefathers — and we — were taught by this was that their freedom from Egypt did not mean that they were free to live their lives as they wished, but rather, instead of being עֲבָדִים לְפַרְעֹה, *slaves of Pharaoh,* they were now *slaves of Hashem,* as the Torah tells us: כִּי לִי בְנֵי יִשְׂרָאֵל עֲבָדִים עֲבָדַי הֵם אֲשֶׁר הוֹצֵאתִי אֹתָם מֵאֶרֶץ מִצְרָיִם, *For Bnei Yisrael are servants to Me; they are My servants whom I have taken out from the land of Egypt* (*Vayikra* 25:55). They were taught that just as heretofore they were owned by an individual and were completely under his control, so too they were now owned and directly responsible only to the יְחִידוֹ שֶׁל עוֹלָם, *The One Unique One,* to

Whom they are עֲבָדִים, *servants,* and Whose will they must fulfill.

We confirm our status as servants of Hashem later in the *Seder* during *Hallel* in the words of David HaMelech: אֲנִי עַבְדְּךָ בֶּן אֲמָתֶךָ, *I am Your servant, the son of Your handmaid (Tehillim* 116:16). To emphasize this matzoh lesson of complete subservience to Hashem, we eat it for an entire week, or at least avoid *chametz,* leavened bread, which is symbolic of the opposite, that of complete independence from authority. So the unfermented matzoh which we eat on *Seder* night commemorates that great moment in our history when time stopped עַד שֶׁנִּגְלָה עֲלֵיהֶם מֶלֶךְ מַלְכֵי הַמְּלָכִים הַקָּדוֹשׁ בָּרוּךְ הוּא וּגְאָלָם, and *HaKadosh Baruch Hu* revealed Himself to them and Personally redeemed them from Egypt.

מָרוֹר

Rabban Gamliel's question now focuses on the *maror*:

מָרוֹר זֶה שֶׁאָנוּ אוֹכְלִים עַל שׁוּם מָה — **This maror which we eat, why is it called maror?**

The Torah tells us וּמַצּוֹת עַל מְרֹרִים יֹאכְלֻהוּ, to eat the *korban pesach* together with matzos and *"merorim" (Shemos* 12:8). The question is: Why does the Torah call the bitter herbs which we are to eat together with the *korban pesach* "*merorim*"?

In Hebrew, a bitter herb is called יֶרֶק מַר, and not מָרוֹר, which means to embitter something. The correct phrase would be וּמַצּוֹת עַל מָרִים יֹאכְלֻהוּ. The word מְרֹרִים does not mean *"bitter herbs,"* but rather, *"imposed bitterness."* And the commandment is, literally, to eat *"imposed bitterness,"* in the form of certain vegetables or herbs. So why does the Torah call these herbs מְרֹרִים? The answer given by Rabban Gamliel is that we eat these vegetables which are called *"maror,"* meaning *"imposed bitterness,"* עַל שׁוּם שֶׁמֵּרְרוּ הַמִּצְרִים אֶת חַיֵּי אֲבוֹתֵינוּ בְּמִצְרַיִם, because the Egyptians embittered the lives of our forefathers in Egypt.

The Gemara (*Pesachim* 39a) gives us a list of the herbs and vegetables which are suitable for the *mitzvah* of *maror*. On our *Seder* table we usually have two of these. One is תַּמְכָא, *horseradish,* which is extremely biting to the tongue, sharp, and full of acid. This form of *maror* is symbolic of the suffering and sharp pain which the Egyptians imposed on our forefathers. Egypt was one vast concentration camp in which the Egyptians mercilessly enslaved our forefathers and caused them enormous suffering.

The other type of *maror* which we usually have on our *Seder* table is חֲזֶרֶת, *lettuce,* which is sweet at first when it is crisp, but which, when it is repeatedly chewed, loses its sweetness; and which, when it is eventually swallowed, has absolutely no taste. This form of *maror* is symbolic of the tasteless, hopeless life which the Egyptians imposed on our forefathers. Generation after generation of people were born with nothing to look forward to in their lives except בְּחֹמֶר וּבִלְבֵנִים וּבְכָל עֲבֹדָה בַּשָּׂדֶה, *hard labor, with mortar and with bricks and with all manner of fieldwork* (Shemos 1:14). Their lives were lacking any sweetness. In Egypt the Jews were forced laborers, and while work in itself is not necessarily torturous when one becomes used to it — especially since we are told earlier in the *Hagaddah* that they were of sturdy stock, עָצוּם — nevertheless, this work is described in the Torah as אֵת כָּל עֲבֹדָתָם אֲשֶׁר עָבְדוּ בָהֶם בְּפָרֶךְ. The word פָּרֶךְ really means to break something into pieces. So this sentence, paraphrased, means the purpose of the Egyptians in imposing all of this hard labor on the Jews was to break their spirits; the goal of the Egyptians was the disintegration of the Jewish morale. Our forefathers were worked by the Egyptians just for the sake of work with no constructive purpose . This work was imposed on our forefathers only to break their spirits. (See *Vayikra* 25:43 and *Rashi* there for this meaning of בְּפָרֶךְ.)

These explanations of *maror* are very fitting as a reminder to us of the kinds of bitterness our forefathers experienced in Egypt. However, the commandment to eat *maror*, וּמַצּוֹת עַל מְרֹרִים יֹאכְלֻהוּ, was given to our forefathers as part of the *korban pesach* **while they were still in Egypt.** They surely did not have to be reminded of their own suffering; while one is still in the concentration camp, one does not need to be reminded of the Holocaust! In Egypt, our forefathers ate the *maror* only because it was God's *mitzvah* that they do so, כַּאֲשֶׁר צִוָּה ה' אֶת מֹשֶׁה וְאַהֲרֹן כֵּן עָשׂוּ, *As God had commanded Moshe and Aharon, so did they do* (Shemos 12:28).

Similarly, the purpose of our remembrance of the bitterness caused by the Egyptians to our forefathers is not to engender hate in our hearts against the Egyptians. On the contrary, the Torah tells us: לֹא תְתַעֵב מִצְרִי כִּי גֵר הָיִיתָ בְאַרְצוֹ, *Do not reject an Egyptian, for you were (for many years) a sojourner in his land* (Devarim 23:8-9). Rather, the purpose of remembering the bittterness of the Egyptian enslavement is *to accept it as the will of HaKadosh Baruch Hu*. The suffering of the Jewish people during the Egyptian exile was a purification process during which they were transformed from their origins as idol worshipers to become worthy of being עַם סְגוּלָה, *God's treasured nation*. We expressed this earlier in the *Haggadah*: מִתְּחִלָּה עוֹבְדֵי עֲבוֹדָה זָרָה הָיוּ אֲבוֹתֵינוּ, *At the beginning, our forefathers were idol worshipers*, וְעַכְשָׁיו קֵרְבָנוּ הַמָּקוֹם לַעֲבֹדָתוֹ, *But, now, God has brought us close to His service*. Eating of the *maror* is an expression of our acceptance of suffering, קַבָּלַת הַיִסּוּרִים, because it is the will of God. Of course, this is no excuse for the Egyptians — whose purpose was certainly not the fullfillment of God's will — and they were severely punished for their extreme cruelty to the Jewish nation.

When one fully accepts suffering as the will of *HaKadosh Baruch Hu,* there is a sweetness in it, This is reflected by dipping the *maror* in the sweet *charoses* which mitigates its bitterness. This thought is the extreme opposite of the purpose of the prevailing "Holocaust Remembrances," which is to keep the memory of our tormentors and our suffering alive in the eyes of the world in honor to those who suffered and died, and to prevent it from happening again. However, we eat the *maror* not simply to remember the bitterness, but rather, as our expression that we *accept our suffering* — whether caused by humans, disease, or other circumstances — as God's will; suffering purifies us. To be sure, we look to God to punish those who caused us so much grief and suffering, because no human being could exact enough punishment for this. But this is not why we remember the מְרוֹרִים, those who embittered our lives.

[Ed. note. See the Rav's essays on the concept of קַבָּלַת הַיִּסוּרִים, *acceptance of suffering,* on pp. 96-99; and on pp. 240-242.]

❧ בְּכָל דּוֹר וָדוֹר חַיָּב אָדָם לִרְאוֹת אֶת עַצְמוֹ כְּאִלּוּ הוּא יָצָא מִמִּצְרַיִם — **In every generation it is one's duty to regard himself as though he personally had gone out of Egypt.**

This is a continuation of the previously quoted mishnah (*Pesachim* 116b) in which Rabban Gamliel would always explain, הָיָה אוֹמֵר, that, ideally, one is to explain the reasons for the eating of פֶּסַח מַצָּה וּמָרוֹר. That, however, is לִפְנִים מִשּׁוּרַת הַדִּין, *doing more than one's basic obligation,* meaning one could fulfill the basic *mitzvos* of pesach, matzoh, and maror without explaining the detailed reasons for them. However, here, we have the definitive halachic statement that as a part of the yearly retelling of the narrative of *yetzias Mitzrayim,* חַיָּב אָדָם, a person is *obligated* to imagine that he himself was one of those who were redeemed from Egypt.

The simple meaning of this statement is that we are to imagine ourselves as formerly oppressed slaves, who were now redeemed and freed by Hashem's miraculous intervention. *Rambam* (*Hilchos Chametz U'Matzoh* 7:6) states: בְּכָל דּוֹר וָדוֹר חַיָּב אָדָם לְהַרְאוֹת אֶת עַצְמוֹ כְּאִלּוּ הוּא בְּעַצְמוֹ יָצָא עַתָּה מִשִּׁעְבּוּד מִצְרַיִם, *In every generation, a person is obligated to act as if he, himself, had just now left the servitude of Egypt.* It is for this reason that we set our *Seder* tables with our best settings, including gold and silver. This display of riches is commemorative of the כְּלֵי כֶסֶף וּכְלֵי זָהָב, the great wealth of gold and silver which the Egyptians gave to our forefathers when they left Egypt (*Shemos* 12:35-36). So when we look at our glittering *Seder* tables, we are to imagine that we have just now been enriched by the Egyptians immediately prior to our departure from Egypt.

However, the deeper meaning of this statement is that our forefathers who actually experienced *yetzias Mitzrayim,* and the *korban pesach* which immediately preceded it, did not yet experience the reason for eating *pesach, matzoh, and maror* during that last night in Egypt. No Egyptian firstborn had yet died, and no Jewish firstborn had yet been passed over, so the name

Pesach did not mean anything to them as yet. It did not yet commemorate anything. The miraculous suspension of the fermentation process which caused them to eat matzoh — instead of the usually leavened bread — as their first meal after the redemption had not yet occurred; and there was as yet no reason to eat *maror*: they did not have to be reminded of their bitterness while they were still in the land in which, until very recently, they had suffered so much bitterness. Our forefathers who ate the *korban pesach* — together with matzoh and *maror* on their last night in Egypt — did so not to commemorate anything, but only because Hashem had commanded them to do so: כַּאֲשֶׁר צִוָּה ה' אֶת מֹשֶׁה וְאַהֲרֹן כֵּן עָשׂוּ, As God had commanded Moshe and Aharon, so did they do (Shemos 12:28).

The Mishnah tells us here that בְּכָל דּוֹר וָדוֹר חַיָּב אָדָם לִרְאוֹת אֶת עַצְמוֹ כְּאִלּוּ הוּא יָצָא מִמִּצְרָיִם, each year, as we retell the *Pesach* narrative, and fulfill the *mitzvos* of *pesach, matzoh,* and *maror,* we are to do so with the same mindset as that of our forefathers who actually experienced the *korban pesach* in Egypt on this night. It is true that while we have just finished outlining the commemorative reasons for the names for these *mitzvos*, nevertheless, at their base, the reason we keep them is not simply to remember what happened to our forefathers in Egypt, but rather, we keep them for the same reason our forefathers kept them: because *HaKadosh Baruch Hu* commanded them to do so. All other reasons are secondary.

Similarly, the *minhag* to open our house door before the saying of שְׁפֹךְ חֲמָתְךָ וגו', which is commemorative of the open doors of the Jewish houses in Egypt during that last night in Egypt while their inhabitants were fullfilling the *mitzvah* of *korban pesach,* with absolute trust in *HaKadosh Baruch Hu,* in open defiance of the Egyptian idolatry, is in keeping with our obligation to imagine that we actually experienced *yetzias Mitzrayim* ourselves on this night.

At the end of the *Seder,* we say, חֲסַל סִדּוּר פֶּסַח כְּהִלְכָתוֹ בְּכָל מִשְׁפָּטוֹ וְחֻקָּתוֹ, The *Pesach Seder* has come to an end in accordance with its Halachah, in accordance with all of its laws and statutes. מִשְׁפָּט is a law for which we know the reasons, and חוּק is a law for which no reason is given. The *Seder* consists of מִשְׁפָּטִים and חוּקִים. Up to this point in the *Seder,* we have dealt with the מִשְׁפָּט aspect of *yetzias Mitzrayim*: we were explaining the reasons for the *mitzvos* of the night. However, at this point, we have come to the חוּקִים portion, in which we declare that we keep the *mitzvos* of the night — just as our forefathers in Egypt — for their primary reason, that *HaKadosh Baruch Hu* commanded us to do so. This is what is meant by כְּאִלּוּ הוּא יָצָא מִמִּצְרָיִם.

◆§ As — שֶׁנֶּאֱמַר וְהִגַּדְתָּ לְבִנְךָ בַּיּוֹם הַהוּא לֵאמֹר בַּעֲבוּר זֶה עָשָׂה ה' לִי בְּצֵאתִי מִמִּצְרָיִם the Torah says, You shall tell your son on that day, saying, "Because of this, God acted for me when I left Egypt" (Shemos 13:8). Paraphrased, this means that the miracles which Hashem performed for me when I went out of *Mitzrayim* were done בַּעֲבוּר זֶה, in the merit of these *mitzvos* of *pesach, matzoh,* and *maror,* which I did solely because God had commanded me to do them, without yet experiencing the reason for them.

❦ לֹא אֶת אֲבוֹתֵינוּ בִּלְבָד גָּאַל הַקָּדוֹשׁ בָּרוּךְ הוּא, אֶלָּא אַף אוֹתָנוּ גָּאַל עִמָּהֶם ❦ — **It was not only our forefathers whom HaKadosh Baruch Hu redeemed from slavery; we, too, were redeemed with them.**

❦ שֶׁנֶּאֱמַר וְאוֹתָנוּ הוֹצִיא מִשָּׁם ❦ — **As the Torah states, "And He brought us out of there"** (*Devarim* 6:23).

The quotation of this second *pasuk* adds a new thought. Not only are we to imagine that we experienced *yetzias Mitzrayim* on this night, but we are to know that, in a sense, *we really did experience it.* וְאוֹתָנוּ הוֹצִיא מִשָּׁם, *He took us out of there,* means that our *neshamos,* souls, were present at *yetzias Mitzrayim,* as well as at the climax of the redemption, that of *keriyas Yam Suf,* the splitting of the sea. Therefore, *HaKadosh Baruch Hu* actually redeemed each and every one of us together with our forefathers, אַף אוֹתָנוּ גָּאַל עִמָּהֶם.

The quotation continues:

❦ לְמַעַן הָבִיא אֹתָנוּ ❦ — **So that He might take *us* home.** Rav Samson R. Hirsch explains that the word הָבִיא is used here not in the simple sense of "bringing," but rather, in the same sense as it is used in *Tzephaniah* 3:20: בָּעֵת הַהִיא אָבִיא אֶתְכֶם, *At that time, I will bring you home.* However, "home" here refers to *Har Sinai,* where the Torah was given. This is a separate phrase, and it means *His purpose in redeeming us was to bring us home to Mount Sinai to receive the Torah, through which the Jewish nation became the* עַם סְגוּלָה, *God's treasured nation.*

And אֹתָנוּ, *us,* refers to each and every Jew who will ever exist, because every Jewish *neshamah* — even of future generations — was present at *Mattan Torah,* the giving of the Torah at Sinai. (See *Shevuos* 39a and *Maharsha*, ibid.)

And the *pasuk* ends:

❦ לָתֶת לָנוּ אֶת הָאָרֶץ אֲשֶׁר נִשְׁבַּע לַאֲבֹתֵנוּ ❦ — **To give us the land which He promised to our forefathers.** "*To give* us *the land*" means that every Jew has a share in Eretz Yisrael.

Our way of taking this *pasuk,* in which אֹתָנוּ literally means *us* — and is a reference to our *neshamos* which were present at *yetzias Mitzrayim* and at its ultimate purpose, that of *Mattan Torah* — is supported by the wording of the *pasuk,* הוֹצִיא ה' אֶת בְּנֵי יִשְׂרָאֵל מֵאֶרֶץ מִצְרַיִם עַל צִבְאֹתָם, *Hashem took Bnei Yisrael out of Egypt in their hosts* (*Shemos* 12:51). The word *hosts* here would be redundant if it were to refer only to בְּנֵי יִשְׂרָאֵל. We therefore believe that the word צִבְאֹתָם, *their hosts,* is an allusion to all the *neshamos* of כְּלַל יִשְׂרָאֵל, the entire Jewish nation, even of those who were yet unborn. These *neshamos* were also present in the redemption, and at its ultimate purpose, *Mattan Torah,* the giving of the Torah at Sinai, seven weeks later.

At this point in the *Seder,* before proceeding to the next paragraph in the *Haggadah* which begins with לְפִיכָךְ, we cover the matzos, because whenever we lift up the cup of wine, the bread must be covered. (See *Remah* 473:7, and *Mishnah Berurah* 78 ibid.)

לְפִיכָךְ אֲנַחְנוּ חַיָּבִים לְהוֹדוֹת לְהַלֵּל לְשַׁבֵּחַ לְפָאֵר לְרוֹמֵם לְהַדֵּר לְבָרֵךְ לְעַלֵּה וּלְקַלֵּס — Therefore — because we ourselves personally experienced *yetzias Mitzrayim,* as we have explained — it is our duty to thank, to praise, to laud, to elevate, to glorify, to bless, to exalt, to extol, and to acclaim.

[Ed. note: The Rav only loosely translated these words; his intention here was not to offer exact translations of each one of them. These Hebrew synonyms for the general idea of "praise" lose much of their exact meaning in English translation.]

We have here nine expressions of praise to *HaKadosh Baruch Hu,* and these will be complemented by a tenth, as we shall explain.

לְמִי שֶׁעָשָׂה לַאֲבוֹתֵינוּ וְלָנוּ אֶת כָּל הַנִּסִּים הָאֵלּוּ — To Him Who performed all these miracles for our forefathers and *for us.*

These miracles were experienced not only by our forefathers, *but we, ourselves,* also experienced them, as we have explained.

These miracles are now detailed:

הוֹצִיאָנוּ מֵעַבְדוּת לְחֵרוּת — He brought us forth from slavery to freedom. This means the actual *yetzias Mitzrayim.* We were there.

מִיָּגוֹן לְשִׂמְחָה — From grief to joy. This refers to *krias Yam Suf,* the splitting of the sea, We were there, too.

וּמֵאֵבֶל לְיוֹם טוֹב — From mourning to festivity. The simple meaning of this is that after *krias Yam Suf,* the Jewish nation, including the *neshamos* of those yet unborn, celebrated their final liberation from Egypt as a day of festivity.

However, the Vilna Gaon offers another, very beautiful explanation, as follows. After the חֵטְא הָעֵגֶל, *the sin of the golden calf,* for which the Jewish people were severely chastised and punished by *HaKadosh Baruch Hu,* the nation was grief stricken, וַיִּתְאַבָּלוּ (*Shemos* 33:3-4). But the result of their mourning and repentence, and the *tefillos* of Moshe Rabbeinu, was that on the following Yom Kippur, *HaKadosh Baruch Hu* gave Moshe the second *luchos,* stone tablets, containing the *Aseres Hidibros*, the Ten Commandments, which turned their mourning into a Yom Tov celebration.

Yom Kippur is the quintessential Yom Tov and cause for celebration, because it is the time of forgiveness of sin. The Mishnah tells us לֹא הָיוּ יָמִים טוֹבִים לְיִשְׂרָאֵל כַּחֲמִשָּׁה עָשָׂר בְּאָב וְכְיוֹם הַכִּפּוּרִים. Paraphrased, this means that formerly, the two most joyous holidays of the year in Israel were the fifteenth day of Av, and Yom Kippur. The Gemara explains that Yom Kippur was so joyous because it is the day of סְלִיחָה וּמְחִילָה, *forgiveness of sin,* יוֹם שֶׁנִּיתְּנוּ בּוֹ לוּחוֹת הָאַחֲרוֹנוֹת, *the day on which the second luchos were given* (*Taanis* 30b).

What follows now are glimpses into the future redemption of the Jewish people, for which we are already now offering our thanks to *HaKadosh Baruch Hu.*

וּמֵאֲפֵלָה לְאוֹר גָּדוֹל — **And from darkness to great light.** This refers to the deep darkness of the *galus,* exile, and its eventual enlightenment, with the coming of Mashiach, who will bring great light into the world.

וּמִשִּׁעְבּוּד לִגְאוּלָה — **And from bondage to redemption.** This is not the same as מֵעַבְדוּת לְחֵרוּת, *from slavery to freedom,* which was mentioned earlier. Rather, this refers to the eventual, ultimate גְּאוּלָה, *redemption,* לֶעָתִיד לָבוֹא, in the future world, which is after the coming of Mashiach, in which time the physical inclinations of our body will no longer be the master of our soul. This is known as בְּטוּל יֵצֶר הָרַע, *the disappearance of the desire to do evil.*

And at this future time of ultimate redemption, we, the Jewish nation, will offer a tenth form of praise to *HaKadosh Baruch Hu,* שִׁירָה חֲדָשָׁה, *a new song*:

וְנֹאמַר לְפָנָיו שִׁירָה חֲדָשָׁה, הַלְלוּיָהּ — **Let us, therefore, recite a new song before Him, Halleluyah.**

This tenth praise, שִׁירָה חֲדָשָׁה, *the new song,* is that which we will sing to *HaKadosh Baruch Hu* at that future time of our final redemption. This is based on the Gemara in *Arachin* 13b, which says:
כִּנּוֹר שֶׁל מִקְדָּשׁ שֶׁל שִׁבְעַת נִימִין הָיָה, וְשֶׁל יְמוֹת הַמָּשִׁיחַ שְׁמוֹנֶה, וְשֶׁל עוֹלָם הַבָּא עֶשֶׂר, *The harp used in the Beis HaMikdash had seven strings, and that which will be used at the time of Mashiach will have eight strings,* **but the one which will be used in the World to Come will have ten.** The Gemara there bases this on *Tehillim* 33:2-3: הוֹדוּ לַה׳ בְּכִנּוֹר בְּנֵבֶל עָשׂוֹר זַמְּרוּ לוֹ. שִׁירוּ לוֹ שִׁיר חָדָשׁ, *Give thanks to Hashem with the harp, with the ten-stringed lyre make music to Him. Sing to Him a new song.*

By listing these ten forms of praise, with the tenth one being שִׁירָה חֲדָשָׁה, *a new song,* the *baal HaHaggadah* is alluding to the שִׁיר חָדָשׁ which we will sing to *HaKadosh Baruch Hu,* accompanied by the *ten-stringed lyre,* to celebrate our final redemption and בְּטוּל יֵצֶר הָרַע, *the disappearance of the desire to do evil,* which will be the highlight of that final redemption. This is what is meant by מִשִּׁעְבּוּד לִגְאוּלָה, *from bondage to redemption.*

This שִׁירָה חֲדָשָׁה, *new song,* of praise to *HaKadosh Baruch Hu,* which will be sung after בִּיאַת הַמָּשִׁיחַ — in the world of *Olam Haba,* when man's יֵצֶר הָרַע, *evil inclination,* is eradicated — to celebrate our final redemption after thousands of years of *galus,* will not replace our daily remembrances of our redemption from Egypt, and our expressions of gratitude to *HaKadosh Baruch Hu* for it. This will never be forgotten, as the Torah tells us: לְמַעַן תִּזְכֹּר אֶת יוֹם צֵאתְךָ מֵאֶרֶץ מִצְרַיִם כֹּל יְמֵי חַיֶּיךָ, *so that you shall remember the day of your departure from Egypt all the days of your life* (*Devarim* 16:3).

Rather, our remembrances and expressions of gratitude to *HaKadosh Baruch Hu* for our redemption from Egypt will pale in comparison to the שִׁירָה חֲדָשָׁה, which will be sung to *Him* at our final redemption. This is expressed by the Gemara (*Berachos* 12b) as follows: לֹא שֶׁתֵּעָקֵר יְצִיאַת מִצְרַיִם מִמְּקוֹמָהּ אֶלָּא שֶׁתְּהֵא שִׁעְבּוּד מַלְכֻיוֹת עִיקָר וִיצִיאַת מִצְרַיִם טָפֵל לוֹ, *This does not mean that (the expressions of thanks to Hashem and remembrances of) the Exodus from Egypt will be eliminated, but rather, the (celebrations, songs, and expressions of thanks to HaKadosh Baruch Hu for) the submission of all governments and kingdoms to the Kingdom of Heaven will be primary, and the remembrances of the Exodus from Egypt will be secondary to it.*

This leads us directly to הַלֵּל, which represents the great celebration, שִׁירָה חֲדָשָׁה, *a new song,* which will be sung at יְמוֹת הַמָּשִׁיחַ, *the epoch of Mashiach,* because *Hallel* begins in the setting of this new world order:

◆ הַלְלוּיָהּ . . . יְהִי שֵׁם ה׳ מְבֹרָךְ מֵעַתָּה וְעַד עוֹלָם — **Halleluyah . . . Blessed is God's Name from now and forever;** מִמִּזְרַח שֶׁמֶשׁ עַד מְבוֹאוֹ מְהֻלָּל שֵׁם ה׳, which means that the entire world — from "from where the sun rises until it sets" — will recognize *HaKadosh Baruch Hu.* רָם עַל כָּל גּוֹיִם ה׳, עַל הַשָּׁמַיִם כְּבוֹדוֹ, *God is exalted above all nations, His glory is beyond Heaven.* The rest of this chapter, too, is obviously set in the epoch of Mashiach, during the time of שִׁעְבּוּד מַלְכֻיוֹת, *the submission of all governments and kingdoms to the Kingdom of Heaven.* This first chapter, then, is עִיקָר, *primary.*

It is only with the *second chapter,* בְּצֵאת יִשְׂרָאֵל מִמִּצְרַיִם וגו׳, *When Israel went forth from Egypt, etc.,* that we offer our praises to Hashem for our redemption from Egypt. This indicates that in the future world of *yemos HaMashiach,* that great שִׁירָה חֲדָשָׁה, *the "new" song of praise,* for our final redemption will be primary, עִיקָר, and יְצִיאַת מִצְרַיִם will be טָפֵל לוֹ, *secondary to it.*

After reciting the first two chapters of *Hallel,* we come to the *berachah* for our redemption:

◆ בָּרוּךְ אַתָּה ה׳ אֱלֹקֵינוּ מֶלֶךְ הָעוֹלָם, אֲשֶׁר גְּאָלָנוּ וְגָאַל אֶת אֲבוֹתֵינוּ מִמִּצְרַיִם — **Blessed are You, Hashem, our God, King of the universe, Who redeemed us and redeemed our forefathers from Egypt.**

This is a *berachah* for our גְּאוּלָה לֶעָתִיד לָבוֹא, *future redemption at the time of Mashiach,* and, secondarily, we include the redemption of our forefathers from Egypt in it. We are here thanking *HaKadosh Baruch Hu* already now in advance, for our final redemption at the time of Mashiach, although we are still in *galus.* This is a glimpse into the future world in which שִׁעְבּוּד מַלְכֻיוֹת עִיקָר וִיצִיאַת מִצְרַיִם טָפֵל לוֹ, as we have explained.

HAGGADAH SHEL PESACH 593

The *berachah* continues with the return to the present:

וְהִגִּיעָנוּ הַלַּיְלָה הַזֶּה לֶאֱכוֹל בּוֹ מַצָּה וּמָרוֹר — **And He enabled us to reach this night that we may eat on it matzoh and maror.**

Although we we are still in *galus,* we thank Hashem that He has enabled us, once again, to celebrate this *Seder* night, and to fulfill the *mitzvos* of matzoh and maror on it. Although we cannot now have a *korban pesach,* nevertheless, we are happy that, at least, we can fulfill the *mitzvos* of matzoh and maror while we are in *galus.*

כֵּן ה׳ אֱלֹקֵינוּ וֵאלֹקֵי אֲבוֹתֵינוּ יַגִּיעֵנוּ לְמוֹעֲדִים וְלִרְגָלִים אֲחֵרִים — **So Hashem, our God, and the God of our forefathers, enables us to reach other festivals and holidays.** This is a prayer that we may live to again experience another *Pesach.* As long as we are in *galus,* our Yomim Tovim are only called מוֹעֲדִים, but we add וְלִרְגָלִים, which refers to the time when we will again be able to celebrate the holidays as *shalosh regalim,* the three "foot" festivals, on which we make our pilgrimages to the *Beis HaMikdash* on the three *moadim,* with the coming of Mashiach.

הַבָּאִים לִקְרָאתֵנוּ לְשָׁלוֹם — **Which may come toward us in peace.** Although we know that the time before Mashiach will be a time of great wars and upheavals, we ask here that we may be protected from harm — as we were in *Mitzrayim* — when this occurs.

שְׂמֵחִים בְּבִנְיַן עִירֶךָ וְשָׂשִׂים בַּעֲבוֹדָתֶךָ וְנֹאכַל שָׁם מִן הַזְּבָחִים וּמִן הַפְּסָחִים אֲשֶׁר יַגִּיעַ דָּמָם עַל קִיר מִזְבַּחֲךָ לְרָצוֹן — **Gladdened in the building of Your city, and joyful at Your service. There we shall eat of the offerings and pesach korbanos, whose blood will reach the wall of Your Altar for gracious acceptance.**

The blood of the original *korban pesach* was placed on the doorposts of the Jewish houses in Egypt, but the permanent *mitzvah* of *korban pesach* requires that its blood be placed on the *Mizbe'ach,* Altar of the *Beis HaMikdash.* This expresses our yearning for celebrating our *pesach* in the *Beis HaMikdash,* rather than in our homes, as we now do.

וְנוֹדֶה לְךָ שִׁיר חָדָשׁ עַל גְּאֻלָּתֵנוּ וְעַל פְּדוּת נַפְשֵׁנוּ — **We shall then sing a new song of praise to You for our deliverance and for the redemption of our souls.**

גְּאֻלָּתֵנוּ refers to our physical deliverance; but פְּדוּת נַפְשֵׁנוּ refers to our ultimate redemption after the coming of Mashiach, when there will be בִּטּוּל יֵצֶר הָרַע, *the disappearance of the desire to do evil.* As long as we are possessed of the יֵצֶר הָרַע, our souls are enslaved by the unrelenting physical desires of our bodies which are often in conflict with the needs of our soul. So here we express a yearning to be free of that enslavement. This is what is meant by *"the redemption of our souls,"* which is the ultimate redemption.

בָּרוּךְ אַתָּה ה׳ גָּאַל יִשְׂרָאֵל — **Blessed are You, Hashem, Who has redeemed Yisrael.** We include in this the redemption from Egypt, *yetzias Mitzrayim*, as well as the future גְּאוּלָה, the final redemption of *Yisrael*, with the coming of Mashiach.

At this point in the *Seder*, we drink the second cup of wine, eat the matzoh and *maror*, and partake of our meal, שֻׁלְחָן עָרוּךְ. After we finish the meal, we eat the *afikoman*, recite *Birchas HaMazon*, and drink the third cup of wine. And after all of this, we return to finish *Hallel*! This is indeed very noteworthy. From this order, we see that the physical act of eating the entire festive Yom Tov meal on this *Seder* night — not only the matzoh and *maror* — with these thoughts in our mind *is also a part of Hallel.*

In closing, I would like to make a comment regarding the *mitzvah* of eating of the *afikoman* on *Seder* night. This *mitzvah m'deRabbanan*, rabbinic ordinance, which is in commemoration of the *korban pesach*, requires that at the very end of the meal, before *Birchas HaMazon*, we are to eat a piece of the *matzoh shemurah* having the volume of at least one כְּזַיִת, olive. [See *Orach Chaim* 486 and *Mishnah Berurah* §1 ועתה נחזור regarding the volume needed for "*kezayis.*"]

When we make the *berachah*, עַל אֲכִילַת מַצָּה, it refers to the *mitzvah* of *afikoman* as well. The *mitzvah* of *afikoman* was considered so precious by many *tzaddikim* that they kissed the matzoh before eating it, as one would kiss a *mezuzah* or *tefillin*. (See *Mishnah Berurah* 477 §5.)

While the *afikoman* is to be eaten עַל הַשֹּׂבַע, after a satisfying meal, as was the *korban pesach*, one cannot fulfill this *mitzvah* after one is completely and fully satiated. This would be called אֲכִילָה גַסָּה, gluttonous engorgement, which, halachically, is not considered eating at all. (See *Shabbos* 76a, and *Bava Kamma* 19b. Also see *Remah*, *Orach Chaim* 476:1, and *Mishnah Berurah*, §6.)

Therefore, to properly fulfill this *mitzvah*, one must still have some appetite left.

To avoid the problem of אֲכִילָה גַסָּה, and to fulfill the *mitzvah* of *afikoman* properly, I would like to share with you some advice which I have applied to myself over the years which works very well. After one has eaten the first two *kezeisim* of matzoh, and the one *kezayis* matzoh for *korech* (the matzoh and maror "sandwich"), do not eat any more matzoh during the entire meal.

This will ensure a good appetite for the proper fulfillment of the *mitzvah* of *afikoman* at the end of the meal. For me, this has been a tried and proven method, and I can fully recommend it to anyone who wants to fulfill the *mitzvah* of *afikoman* properly.

✻ ✻ ✻

When a person experiences the *Seder* with the thoughts which we have expressed, which bring one close to הקב״ה, he has come as close as he possibly can in this world to life after the גְאוּלָה. And every year, when we have this experience, we are *mispallel* that in this *zechus*:

לְשָׁנָה הַבָּאָה בִּירוּשָׁלָיִם

❧ ❧ ❧

Because of his ongoing health problems, this was the Rav's final *shiur* of the "עיון תפלה" series. The day was Sunday, 3/28/1993 — ו׳ ניסן תשנ״ג.

חֲבַל עַל דְּאָבְדִין וְלֹא מִשְׁתַּכְּחִין
זֵכֶר צַדִּיק לִבְרָכָה לְעוֹלָם הַבָּא

This volume is part of
THE ARTSCROLL SERIES®
an ongoing project of
translations, commentaries and expositions
on Scripture, Mishnah, Talmud, Halachah,
liturgy, history, the classic Rabbinic writings,
biographies and thought.

For a brochure of current publications
visit your local Hebrew bookseller
or contact the publisher:

Mesorah Publications, ltd
4401 Second Avenue
Brooklyn, New York 11232
(718) 921-9000
www.artscroll.com